KEY TO MAP PAGES

SCALE:

0 1 2 3 4 Miles

Greater London Boundary — · · — · ·

Nine Sheet, Master Map Areas ▬▬▬

NINE SHEET MASTER MAPS

These Nine Sheet Master Maps use the same grid references as the Master Atlas, thus enabling both Maps and Atlas to be used in conjunction.

Each Map is however complete in itself, and can be used independently.

Master Maps can be joined and mounted for wall use; prices on application.

KU-505-575

MASTER ATLAS OF GREATER LONDON

CONTENTS

REFERENCE

Motorway	M1	
Motorway *under construction*		
Dual Carriageway		
'A' Road	A40	
'A' Road *under construction*		
'B' Road	B106	
One Way Street	One-way traffic flow is indicated on 'A' roads by a heavy line on the drivers left.	traffic flow →
British Rail Line & Station		—■—
Underground Station		●
County Boundary		
District & Borough Boundaries		—·—·—
Postal District Boundary	By arrangement with the Post Office	E.C.1.
Fire Station		■
Hospital		Ⓗ
House Numbers *'A' & 'B' Roads only*		2 ... 45
Information Centre		🄸
Map Continuation		130
National Grid Reference		578
Place of Worship		✛
Police Station		▲
Post Office		★

The representation on the maps of a road, track or footpath is no evidence of the existence of a Right of Way.

Every possible care has been taken to ensure that the information given in this Atlas is accurate and whilst the publishers would be grateful to learn of any errors, they regret they can accept no responsibility for any expense of loss thereby caused.

The maps in this Atlas are based upon the Ordnance Survey 1:10,560 and 1:10,000 Maps with the sanction of The Controller of Her Majesty's Stationery Office. Crown Copyright Reserved.

No reproduction by any method whatsoever of any part of this publication is permitted without the prior consent of the copyright owners.

The grid on this map is the National Grid taken from the Ordnance Survey map with the permission of the Controller of Her Majesty's Stationery Office.

An A to Z publication   ISBN 0 85039 002 8   Edition 5B

SCALE

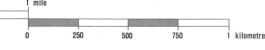

1:19,000   (Sectional Maps at approx. 3⅓ or 3.3347 inches to 1 mile)

© Copyright of the publishers

Geographers' A-Z Map Company Ltd.

Head Office : Vestry Road, Sevenoaks, Kent. TN14 5EP Telephone : 0732-451152
Showrooms : 44 Gray's Inn Road, London, WC1X 8LR   Telephone : 01-242 9246

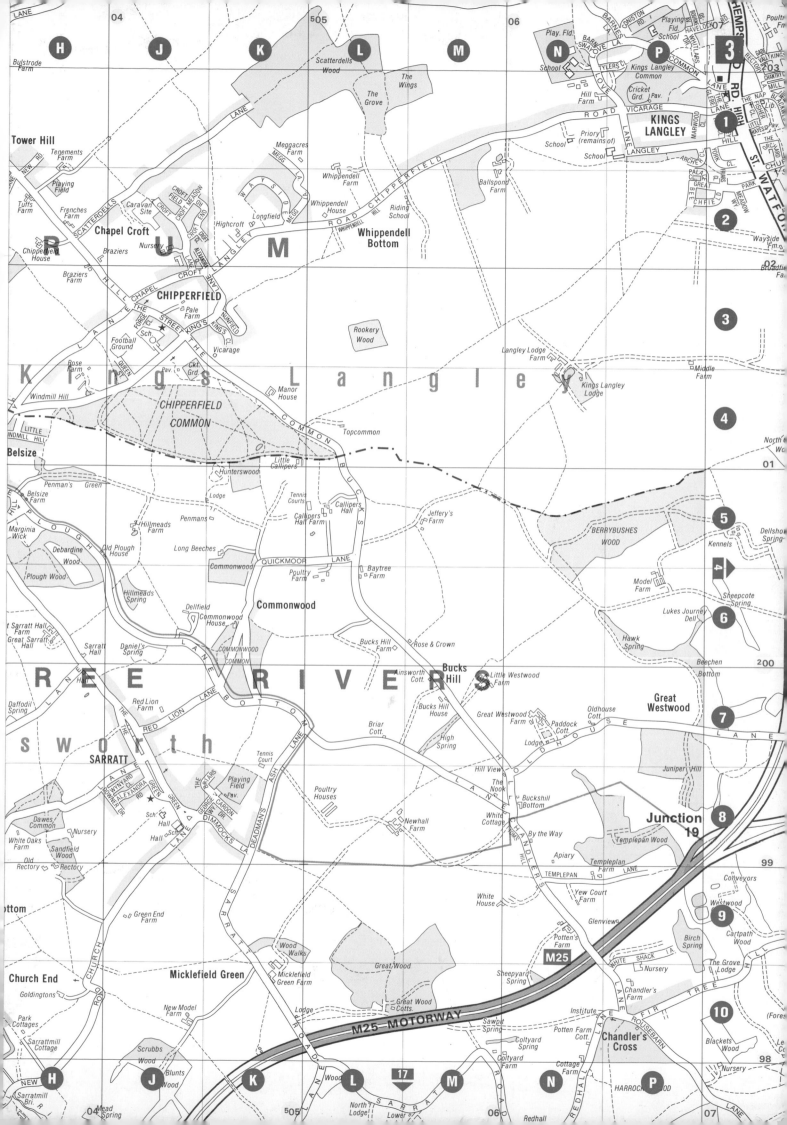

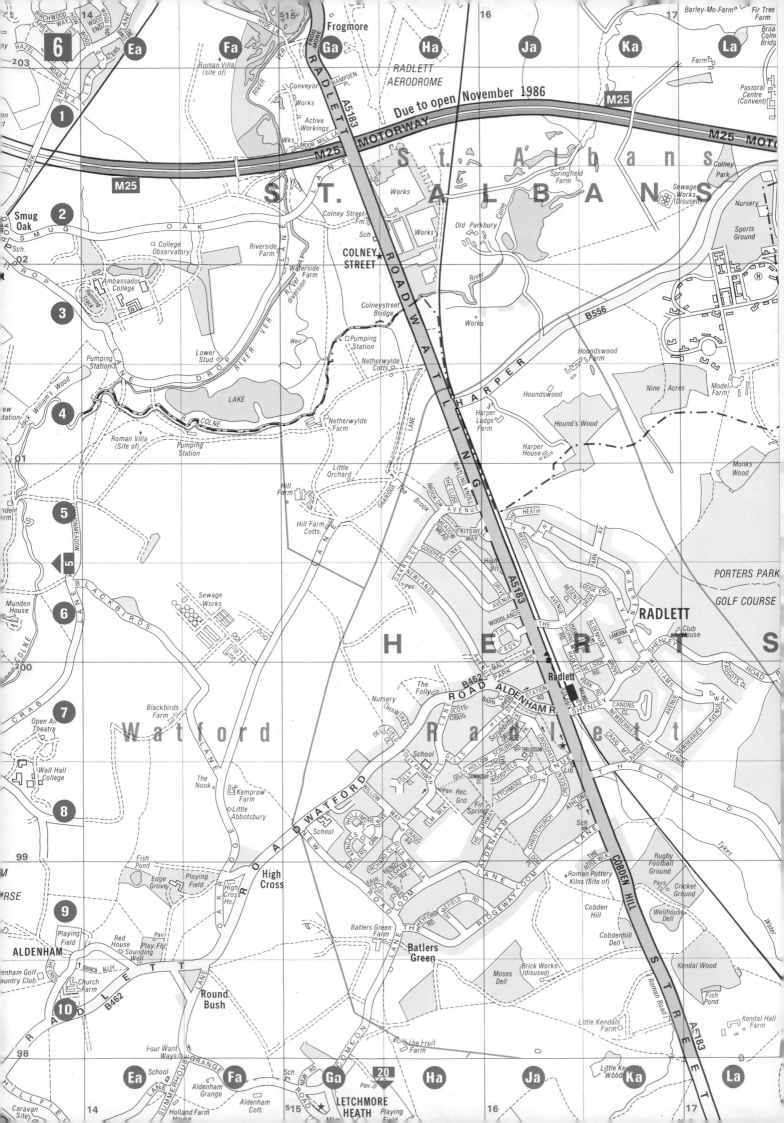

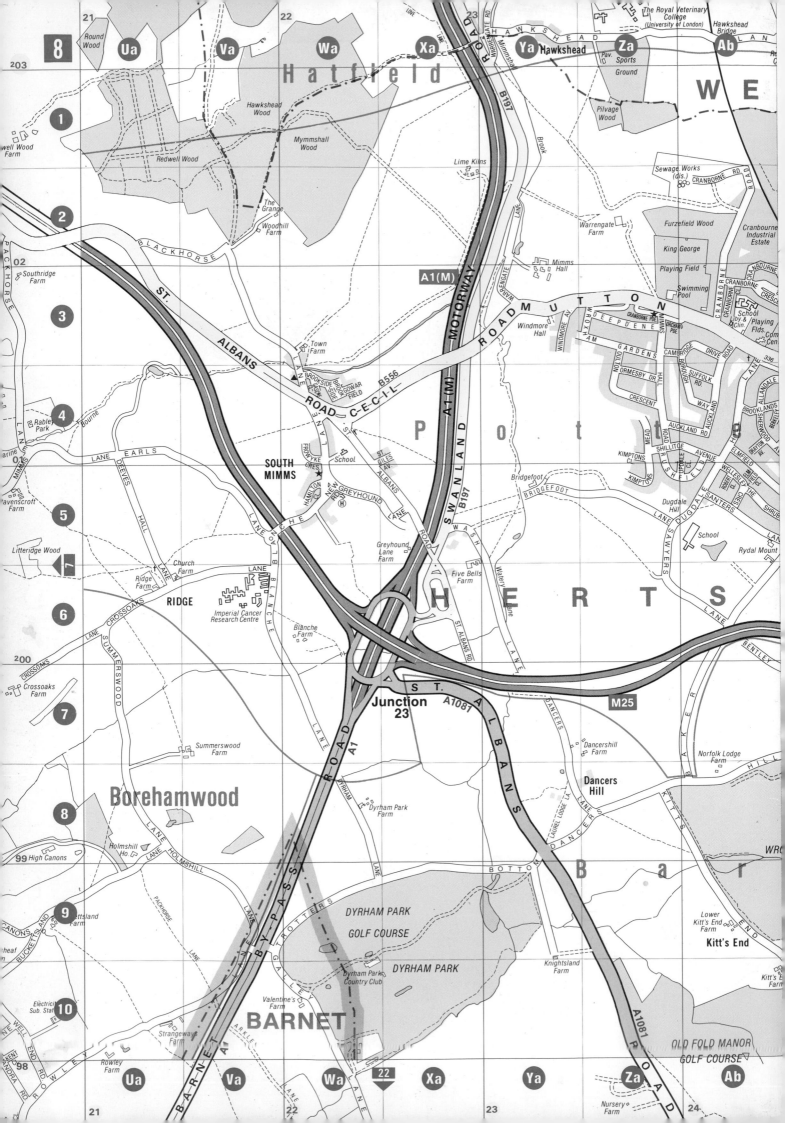

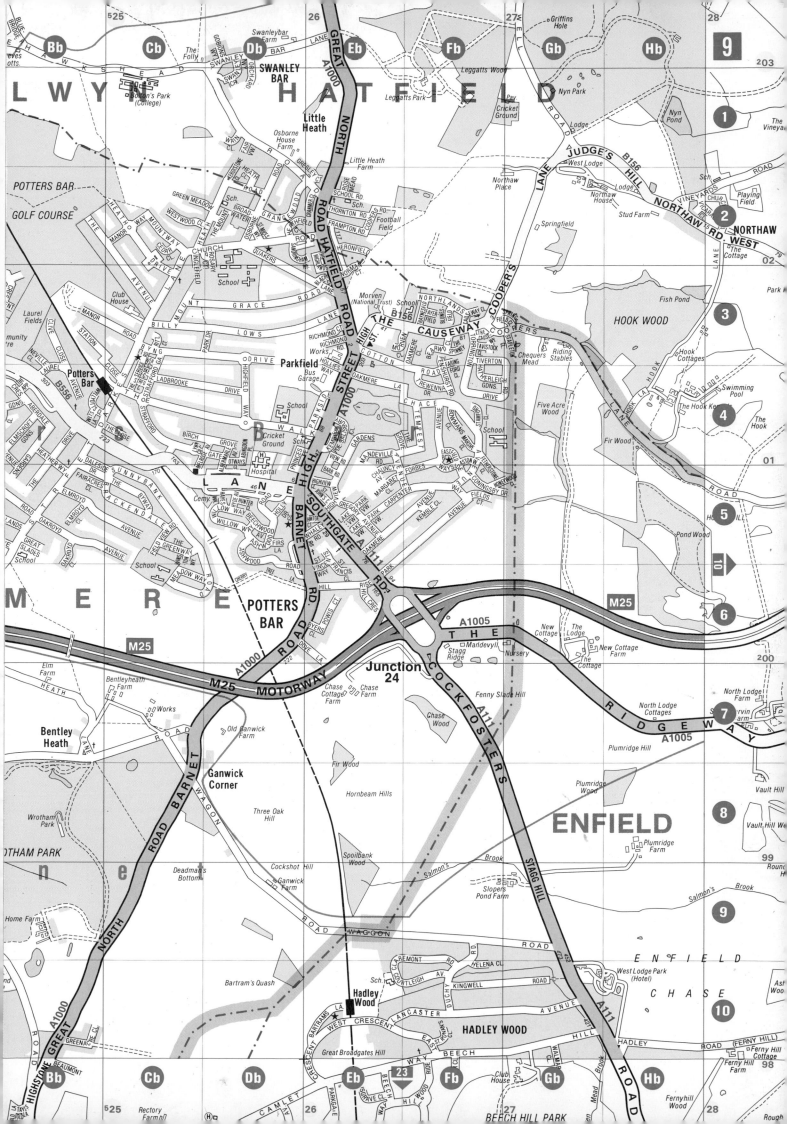

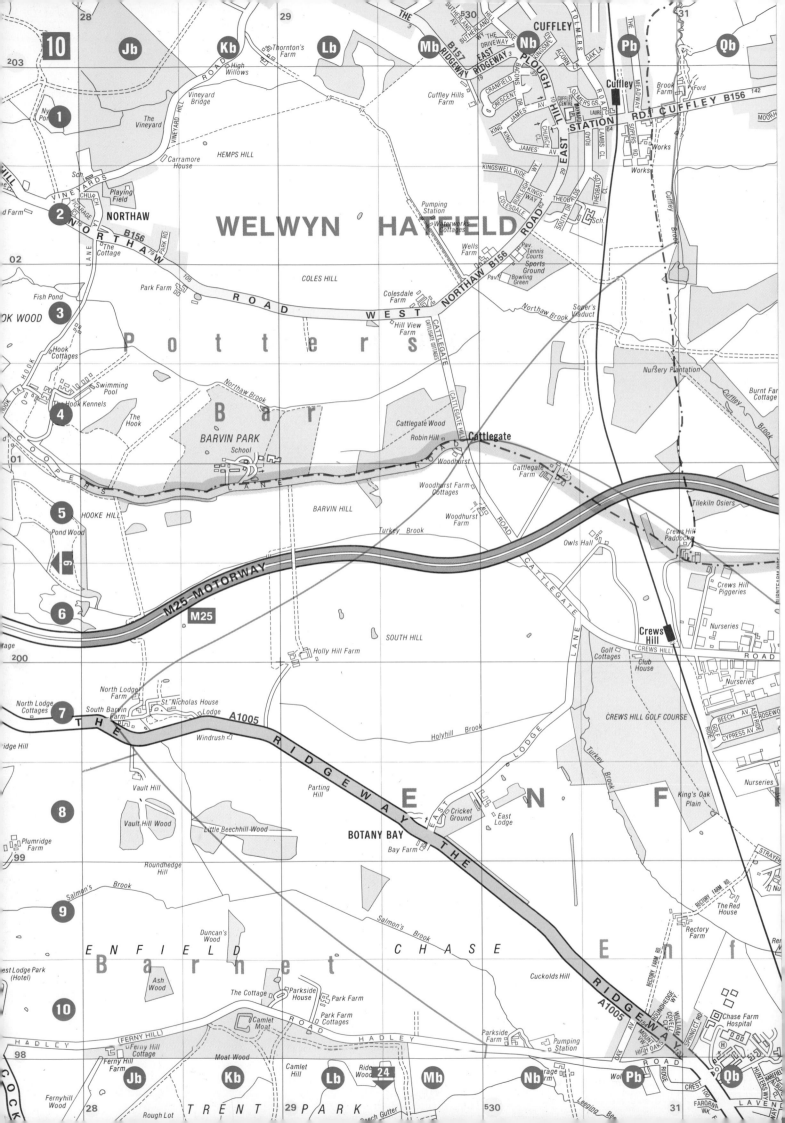

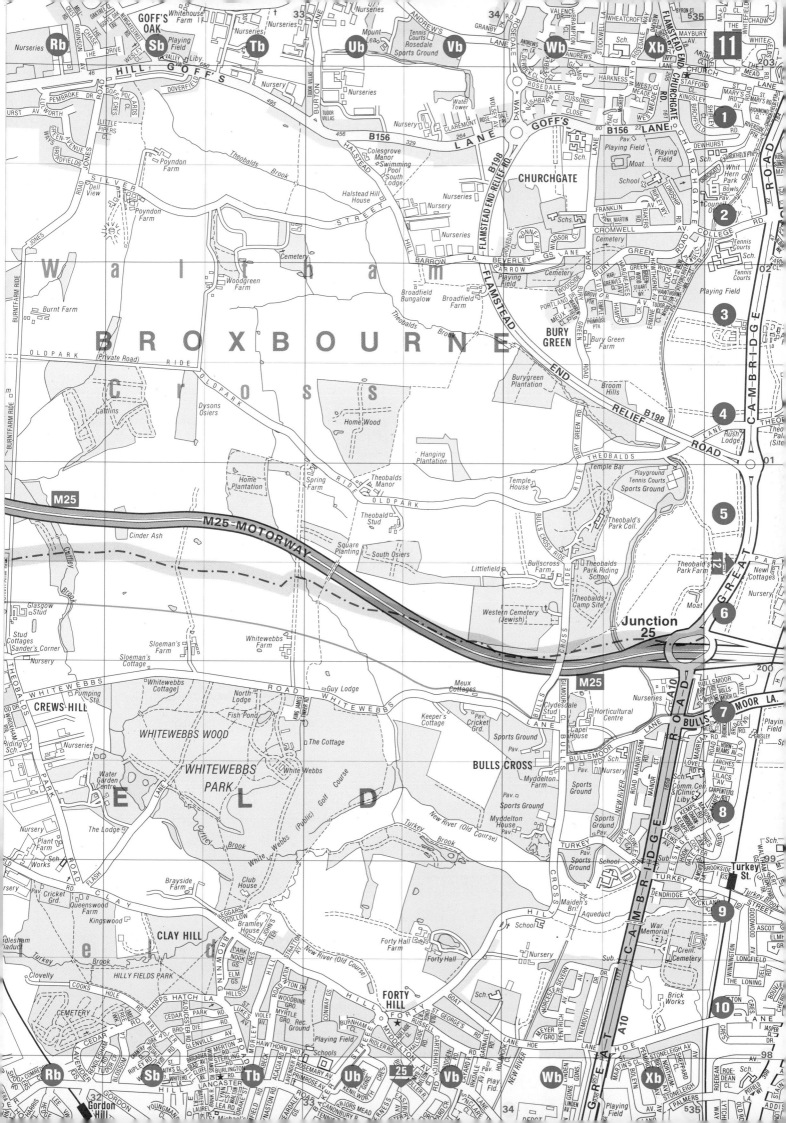

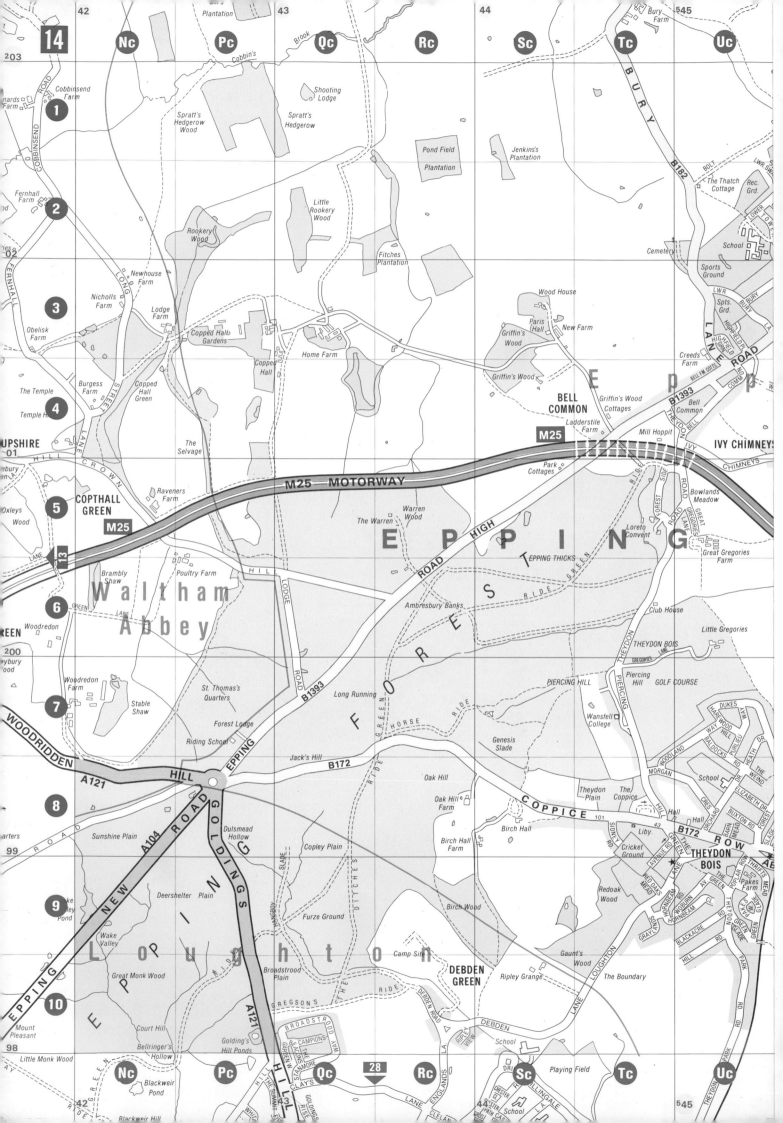

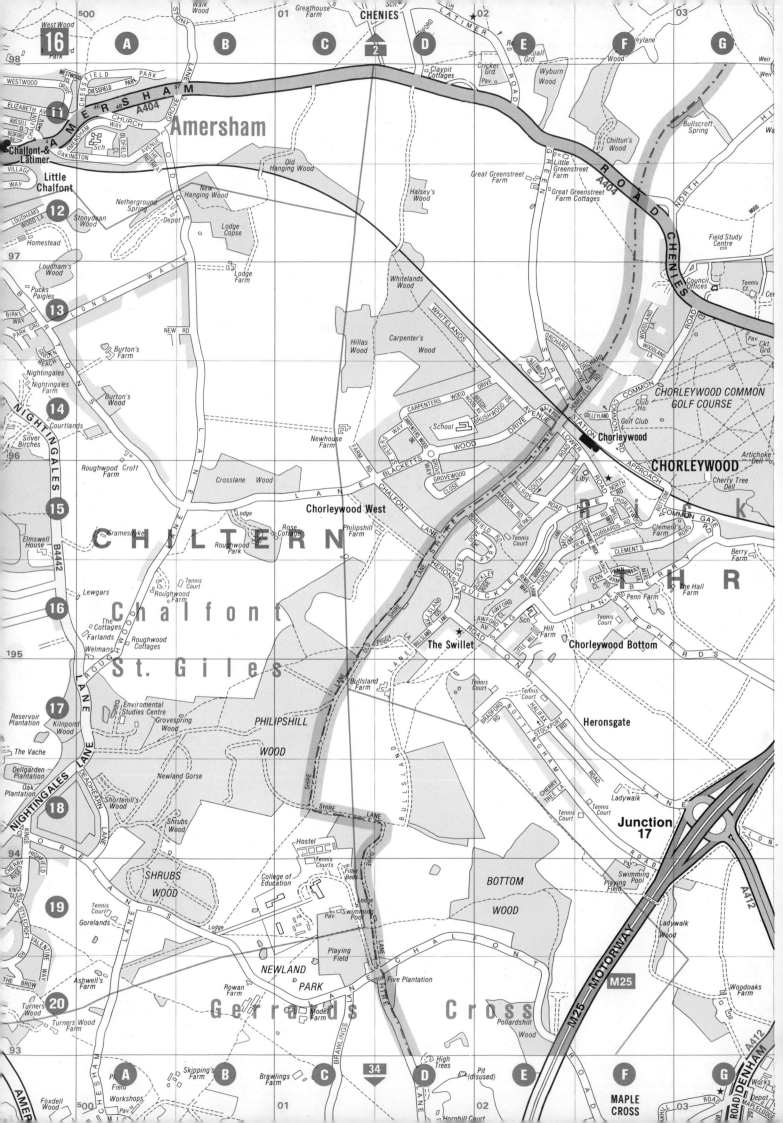

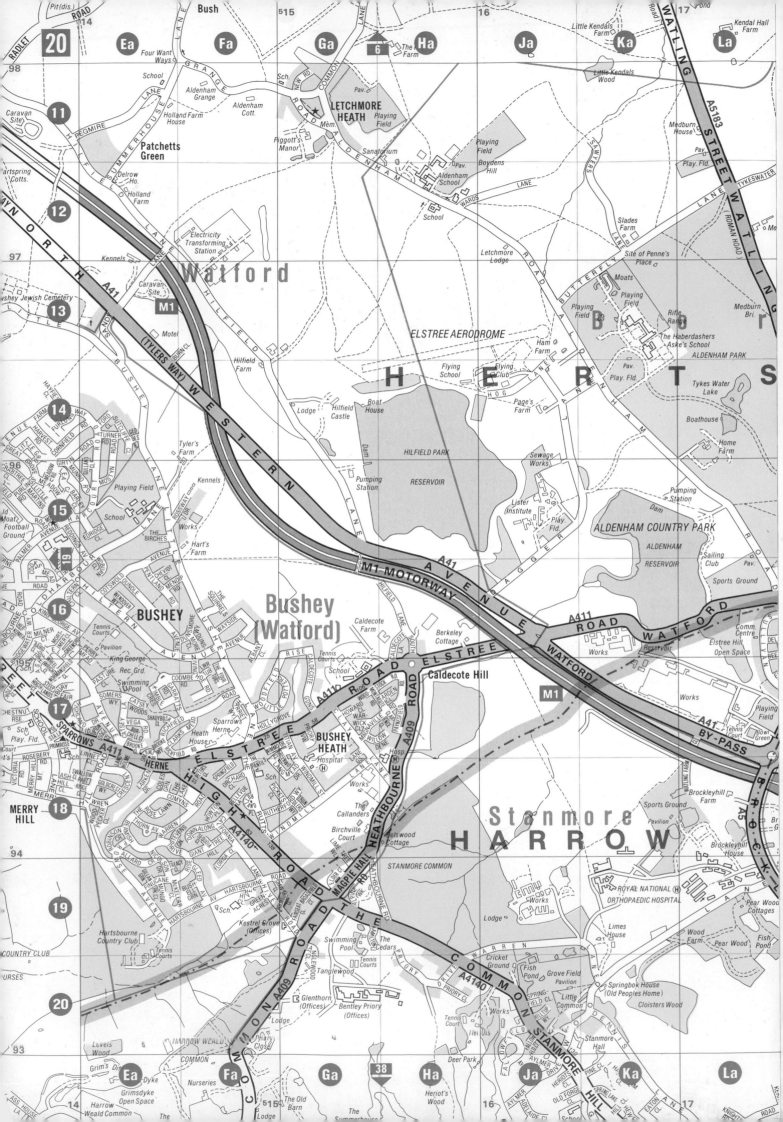

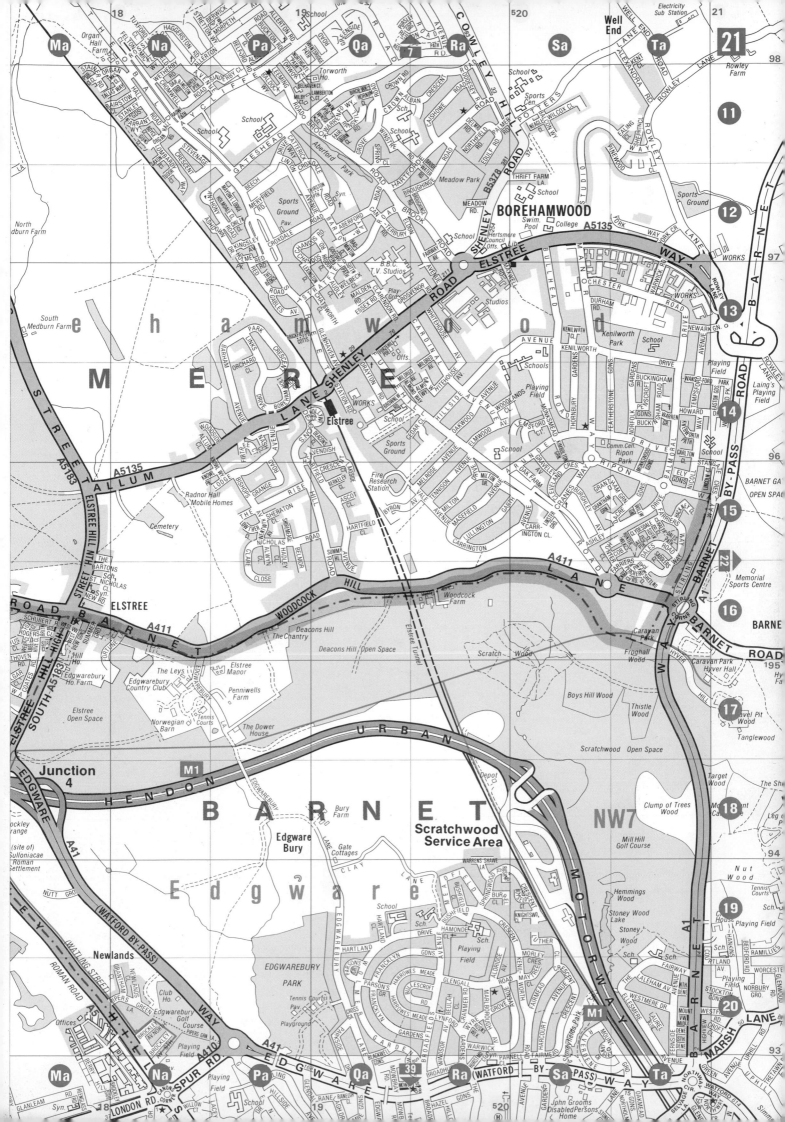

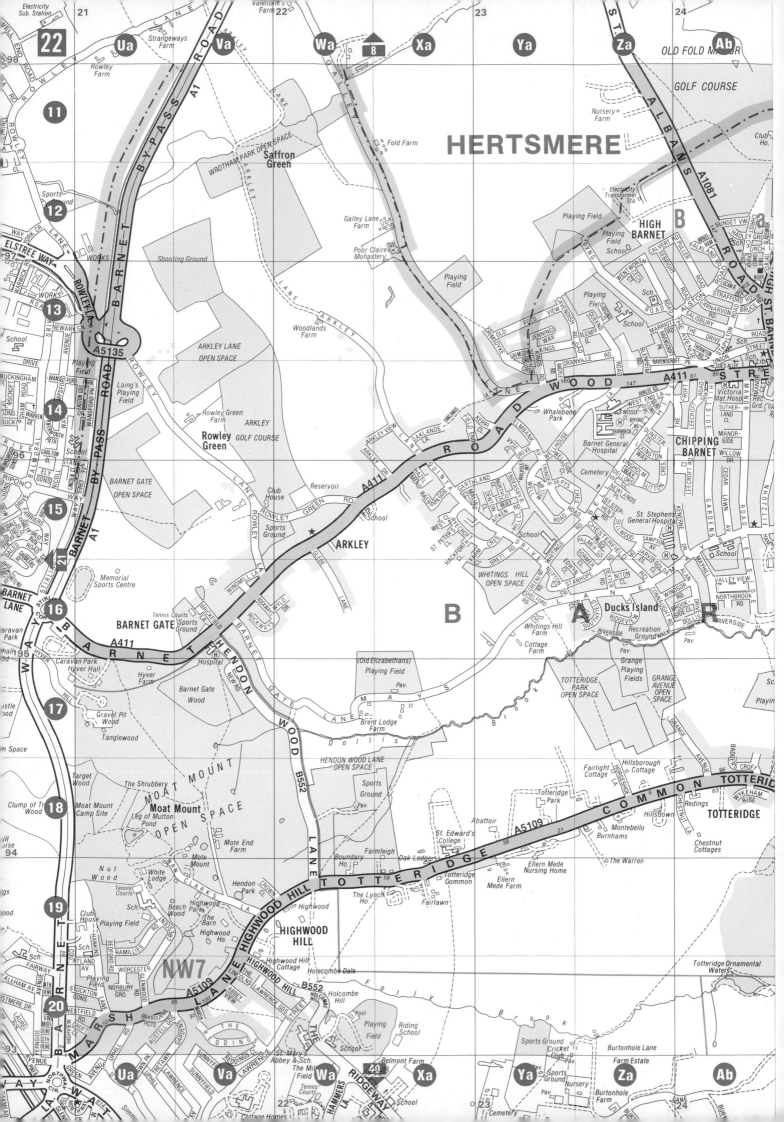

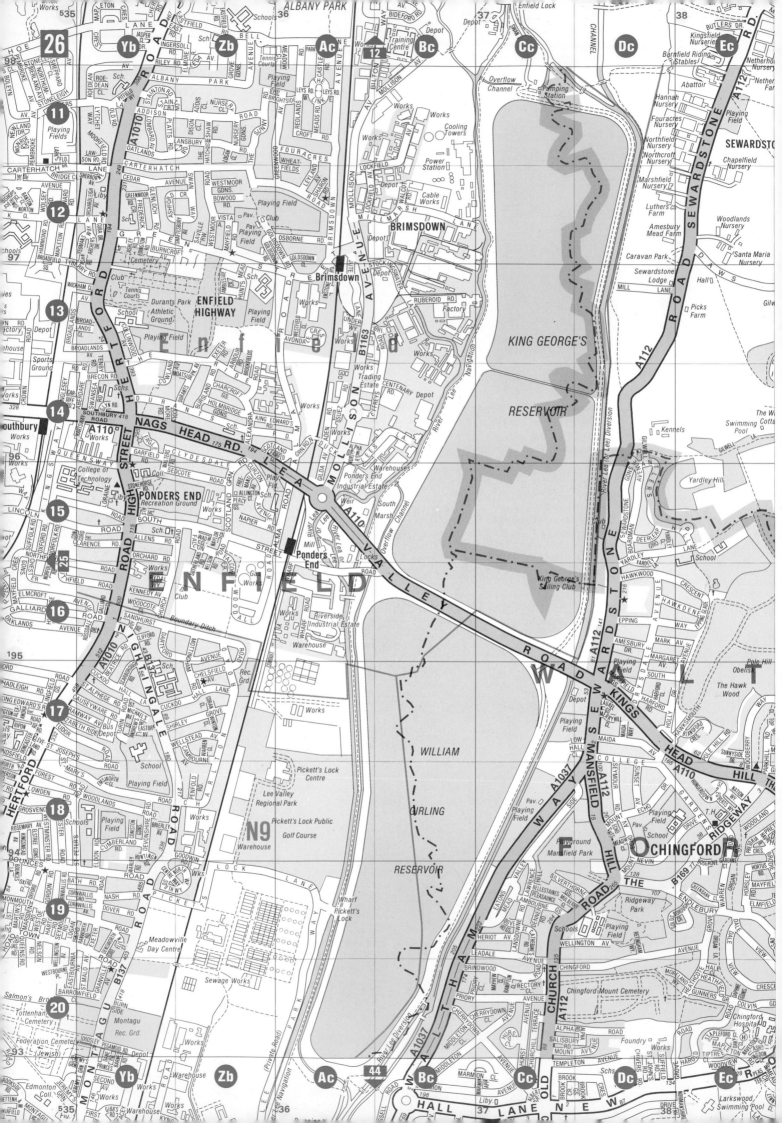

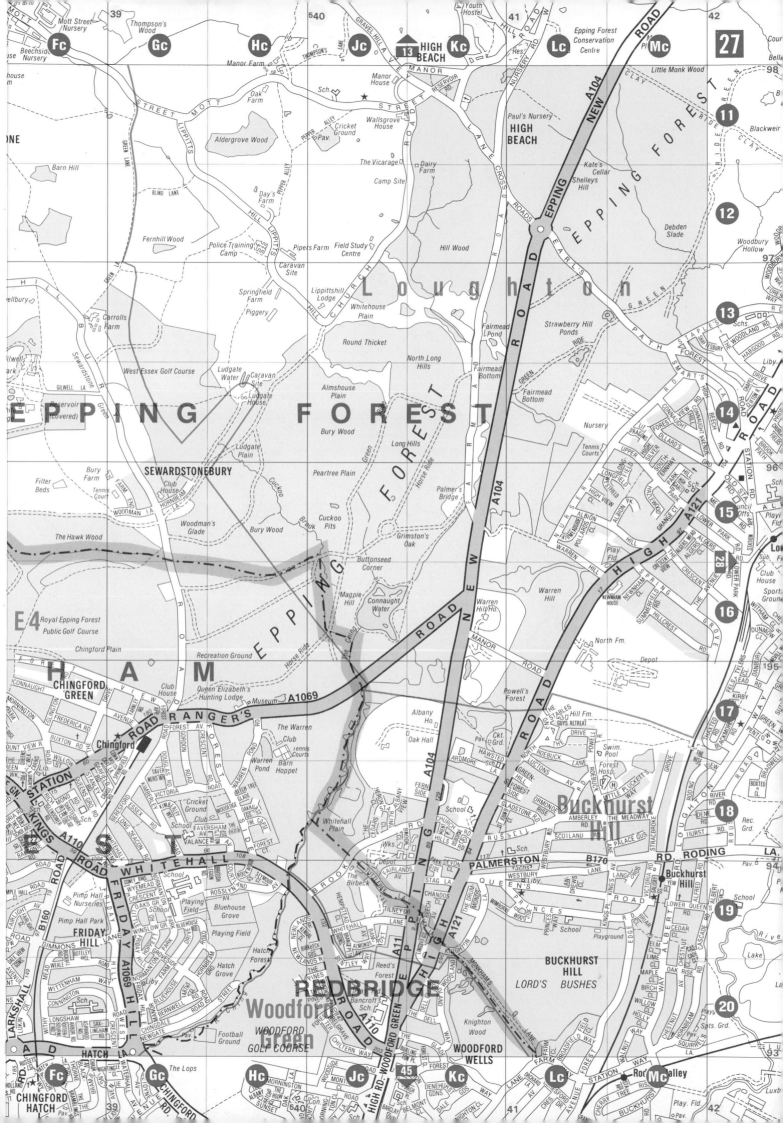

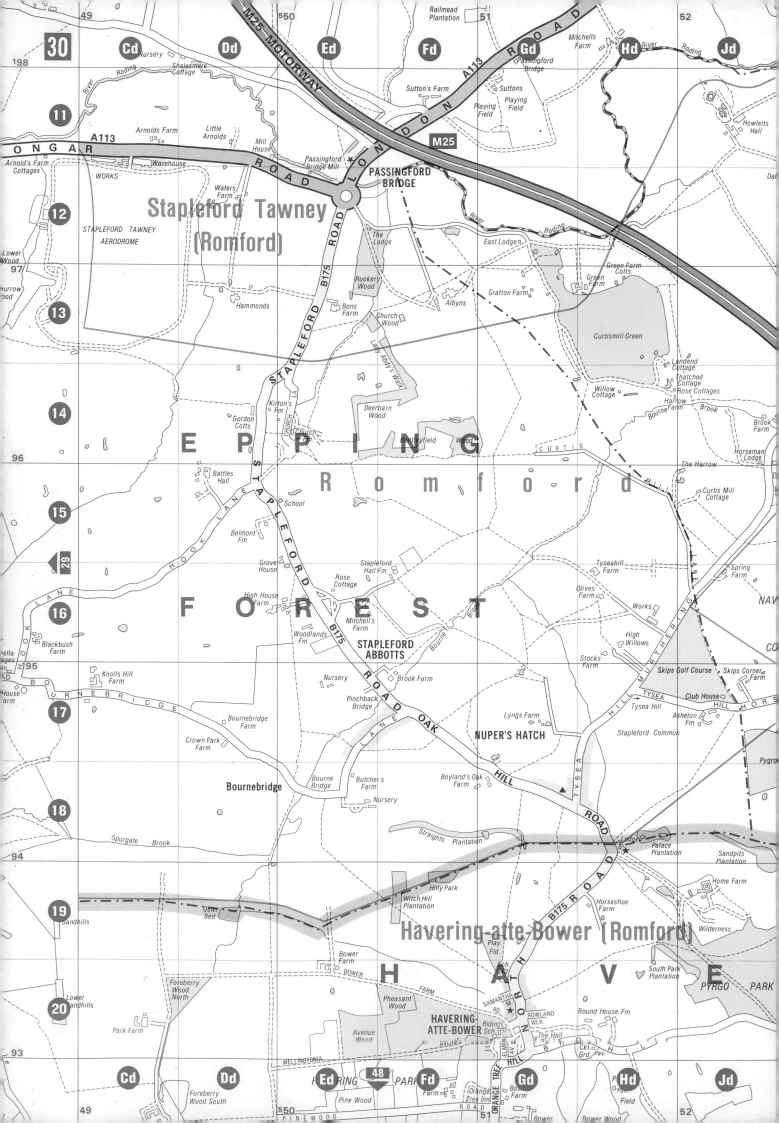

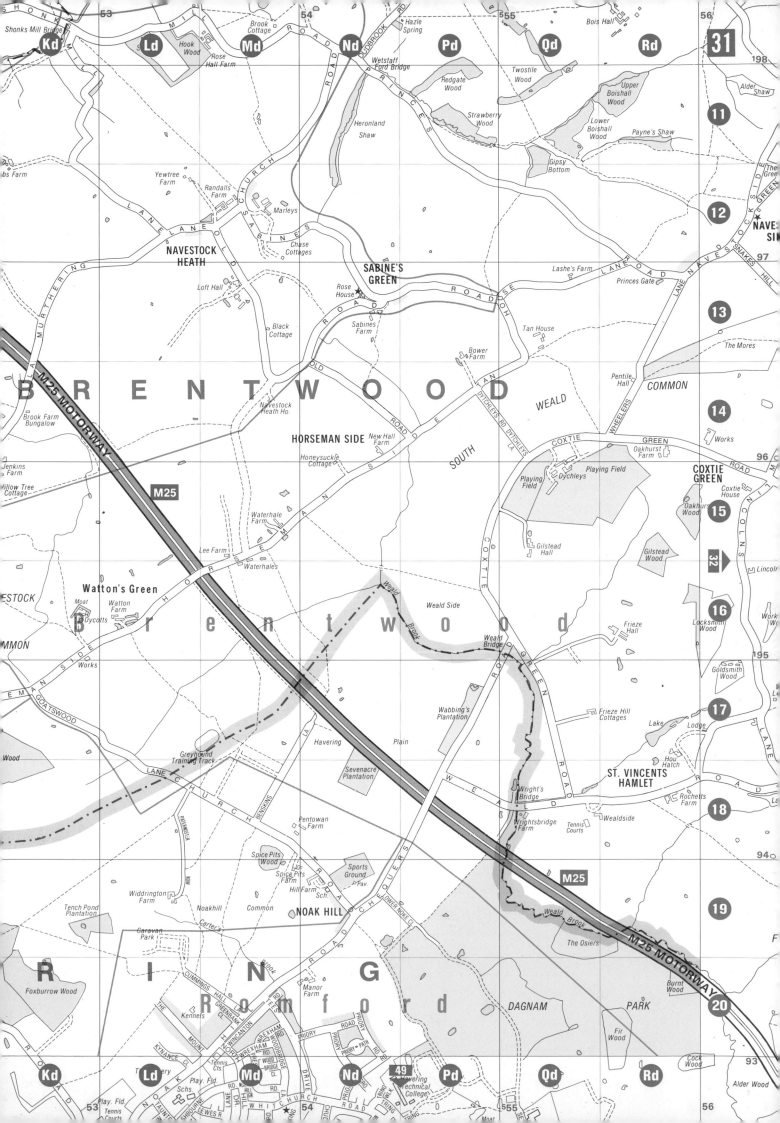

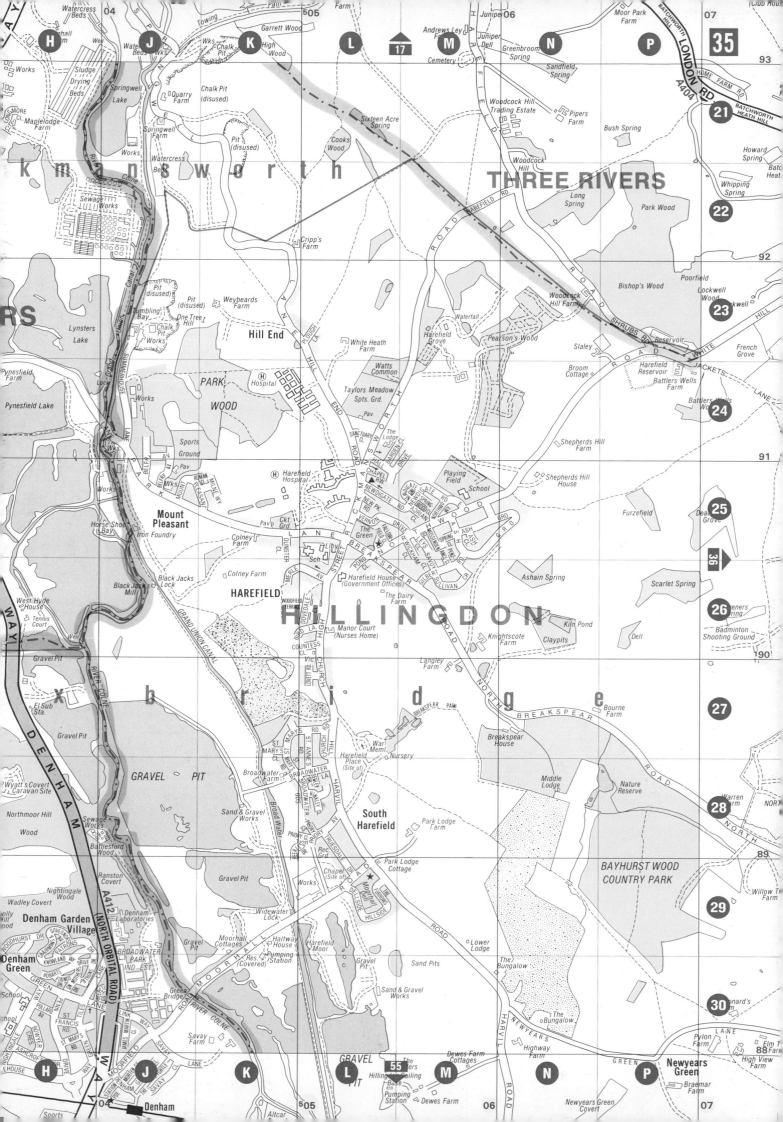

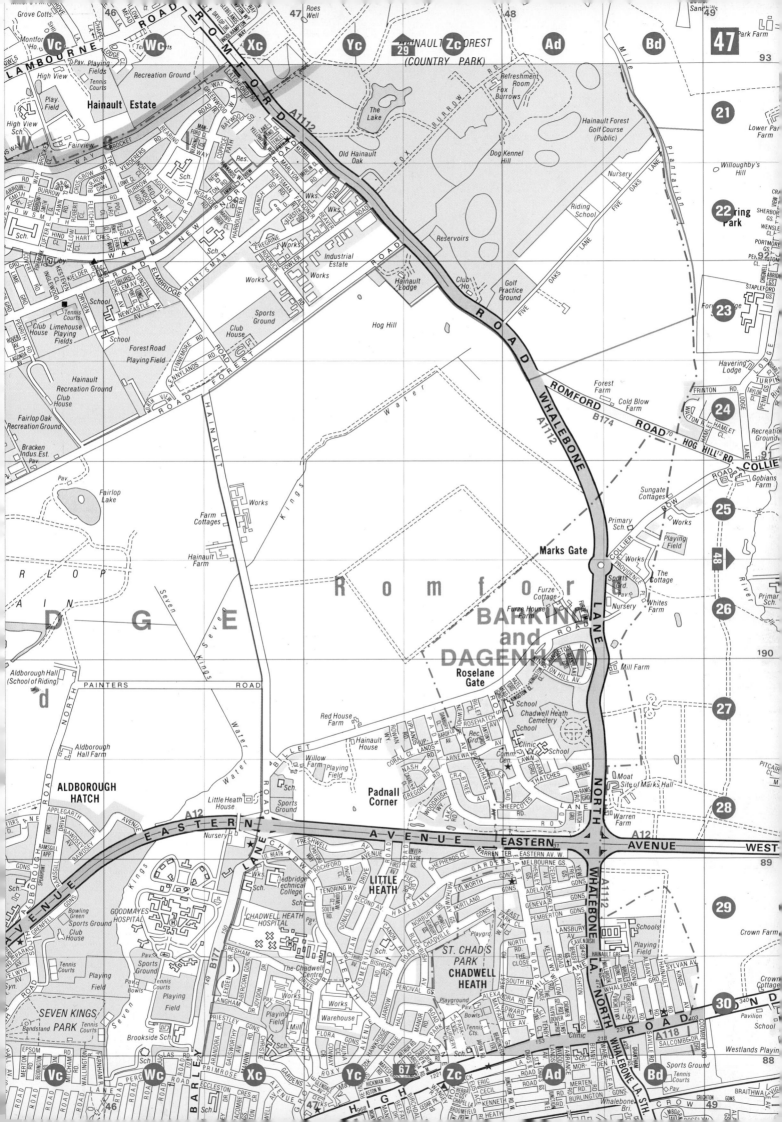

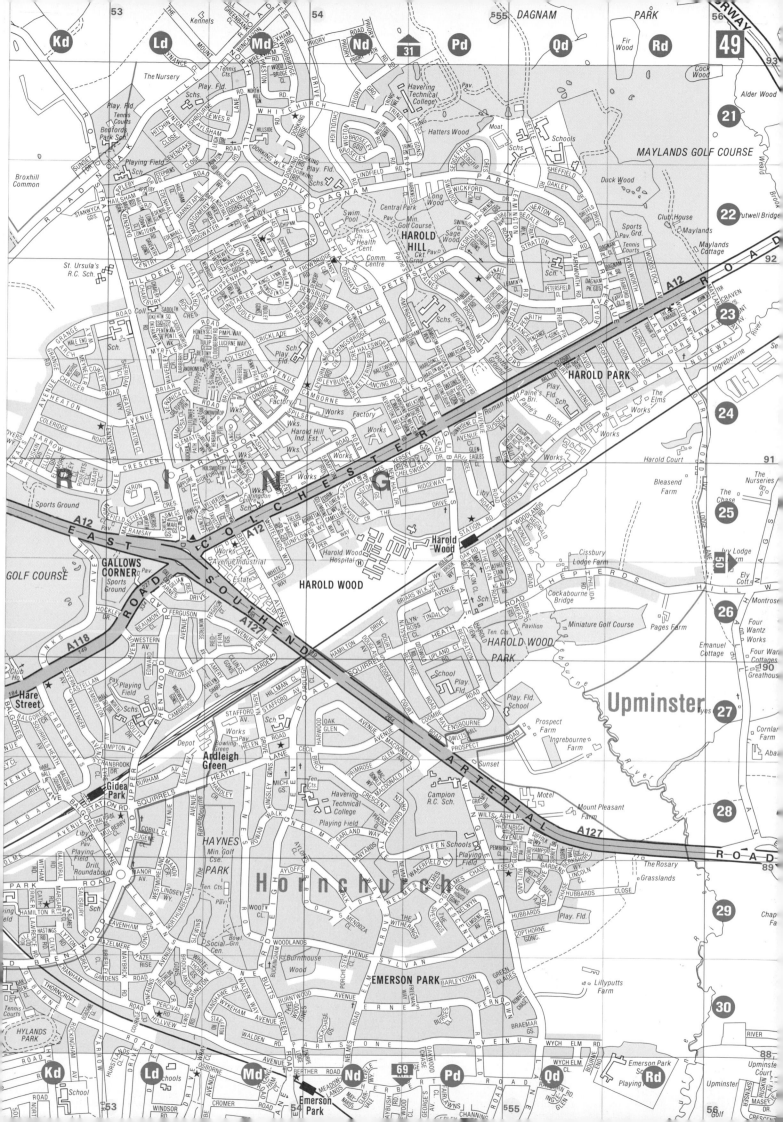

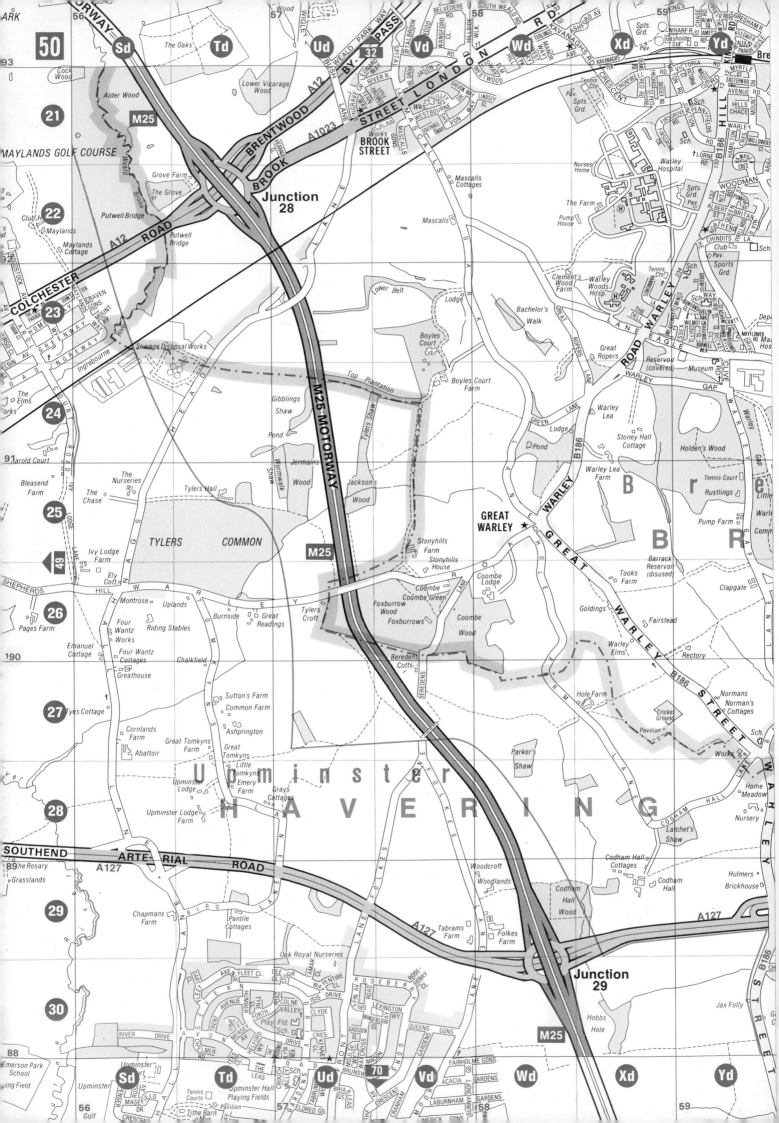

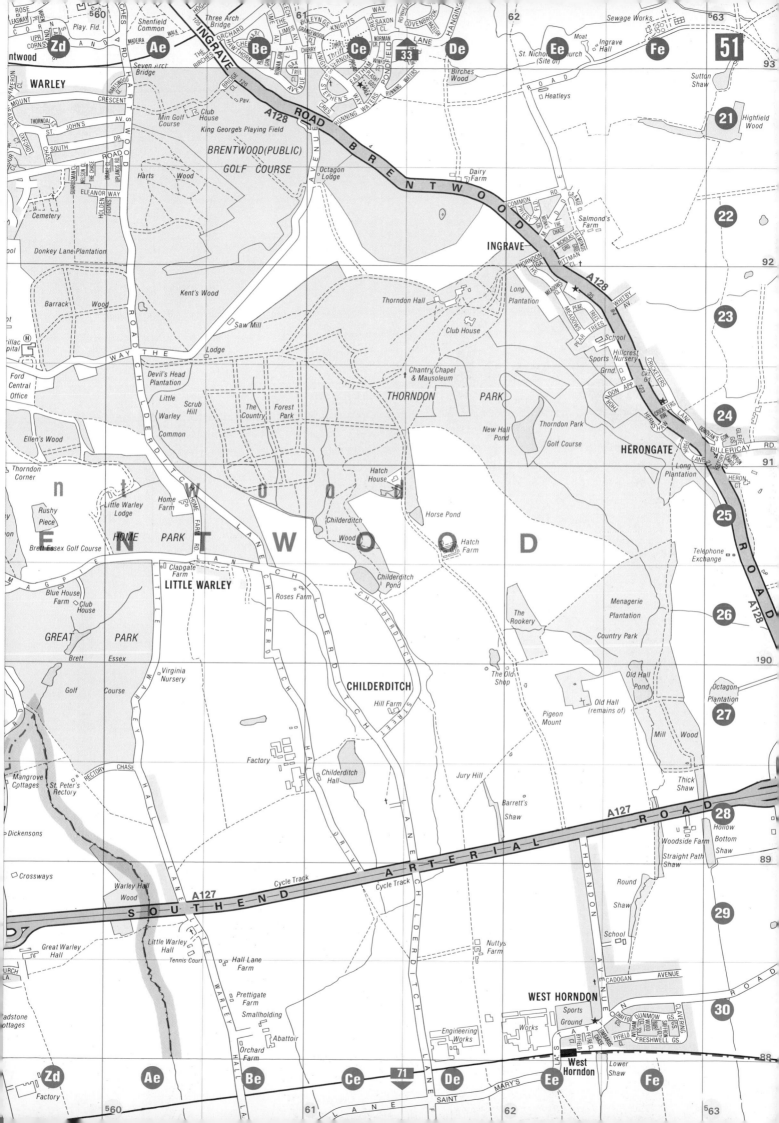

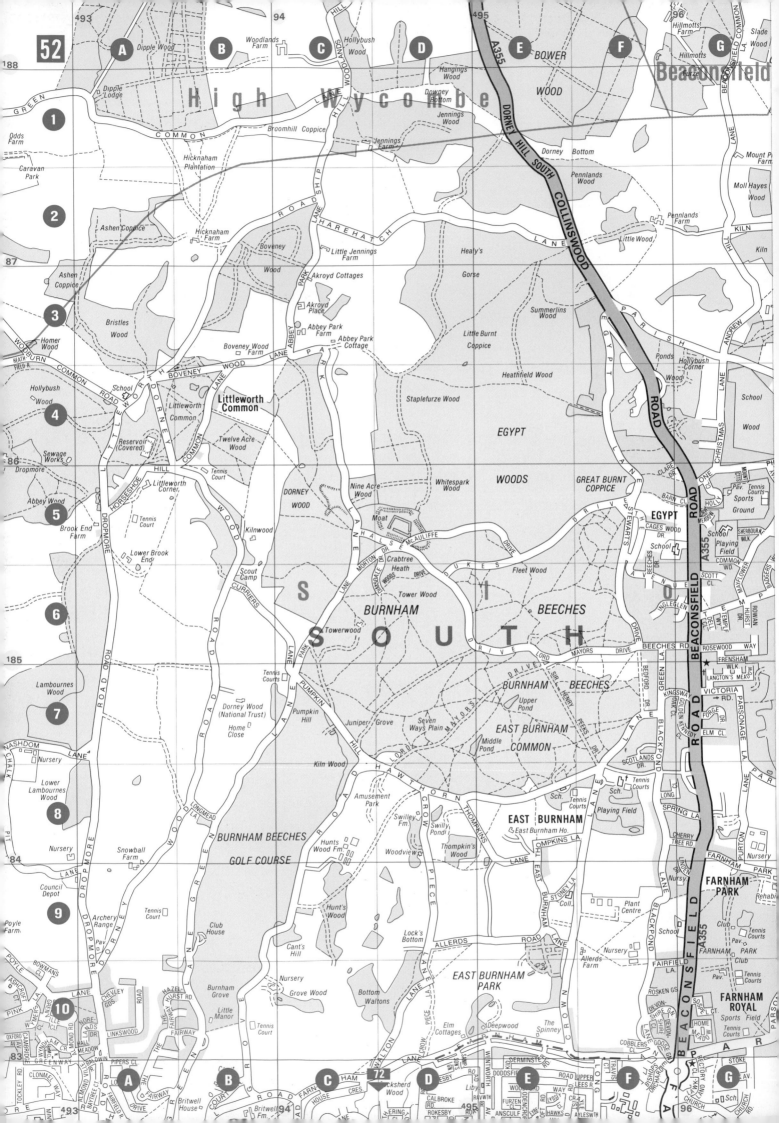

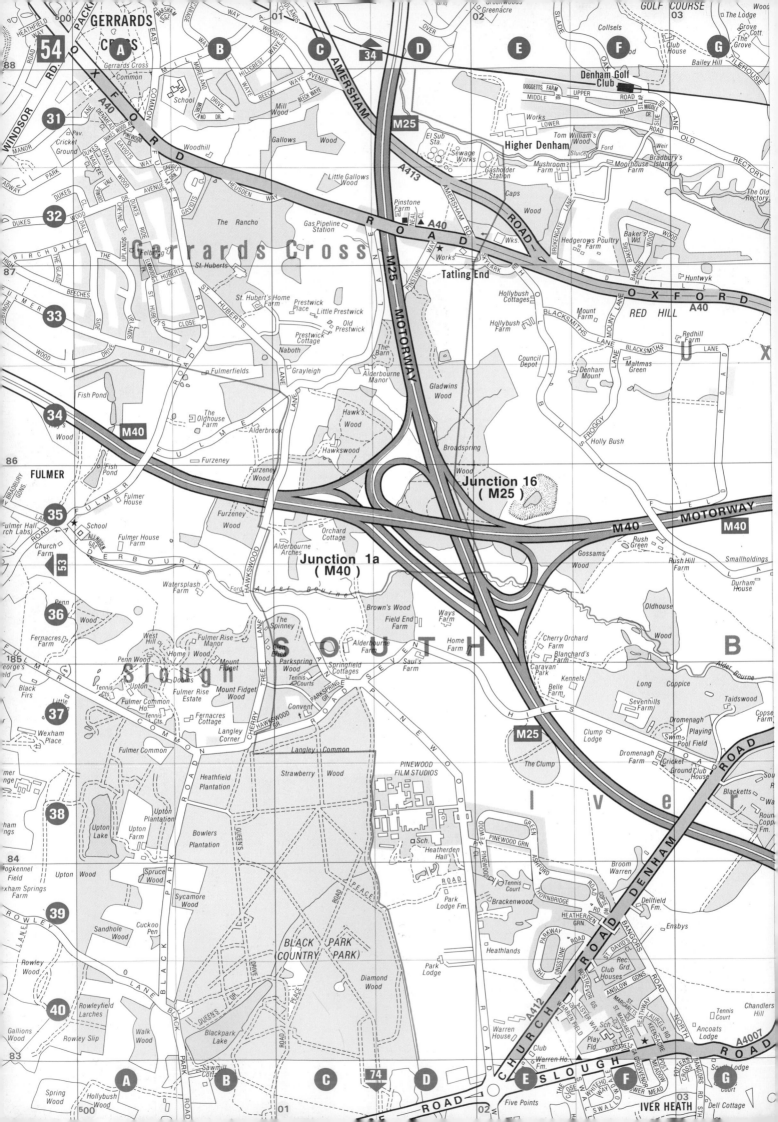

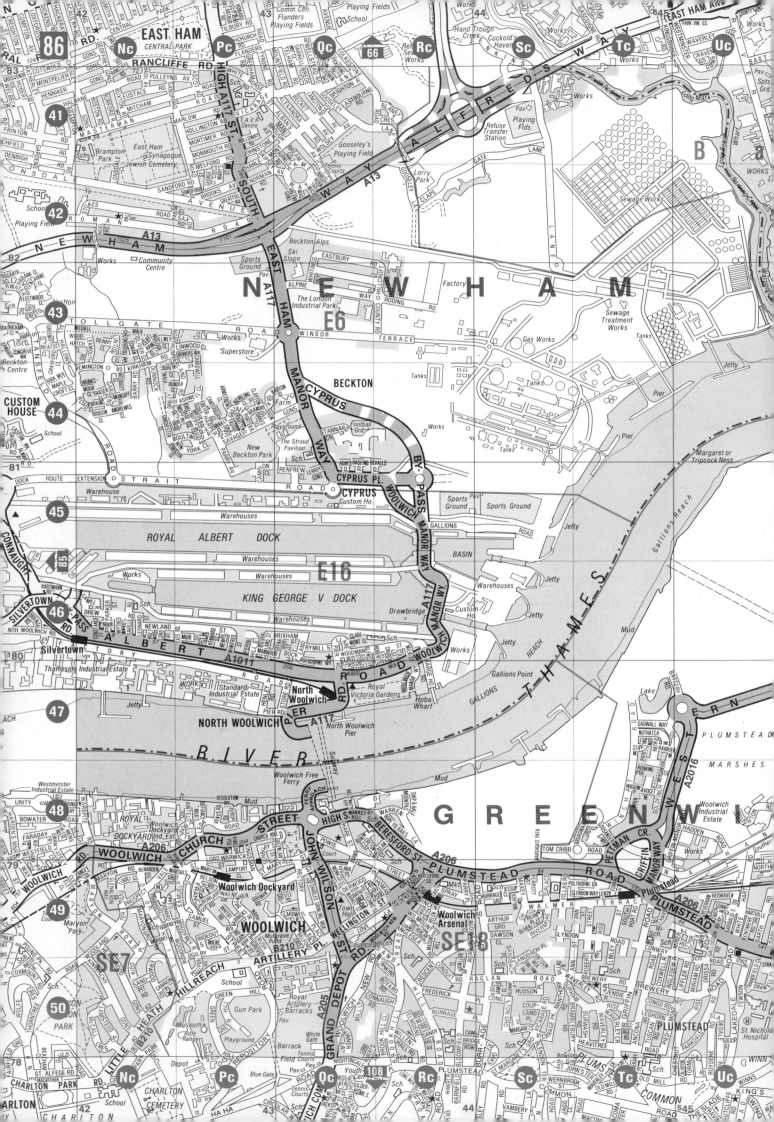

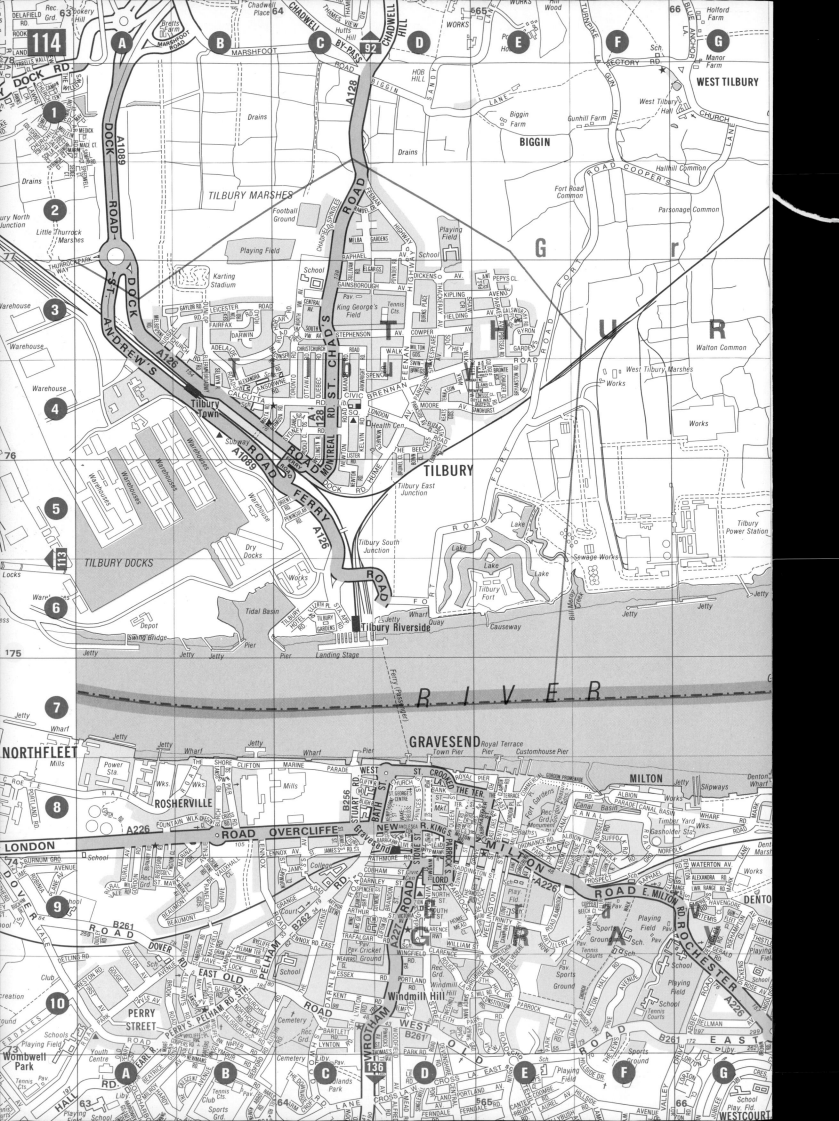

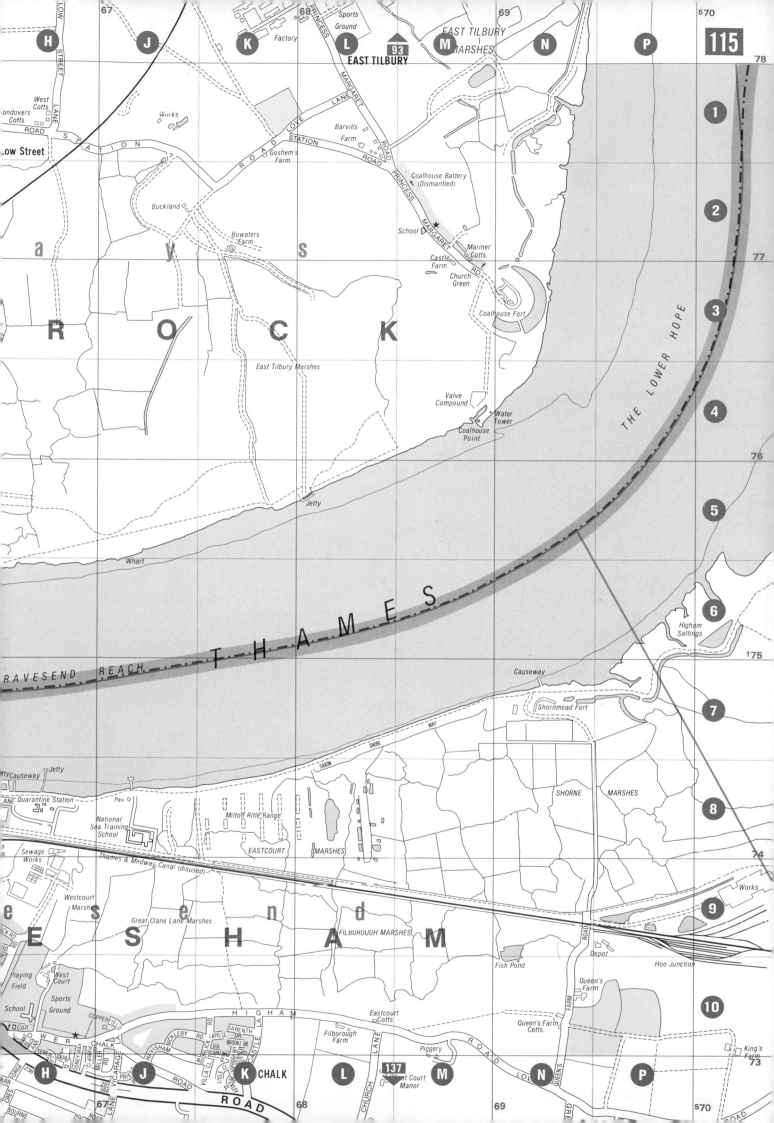

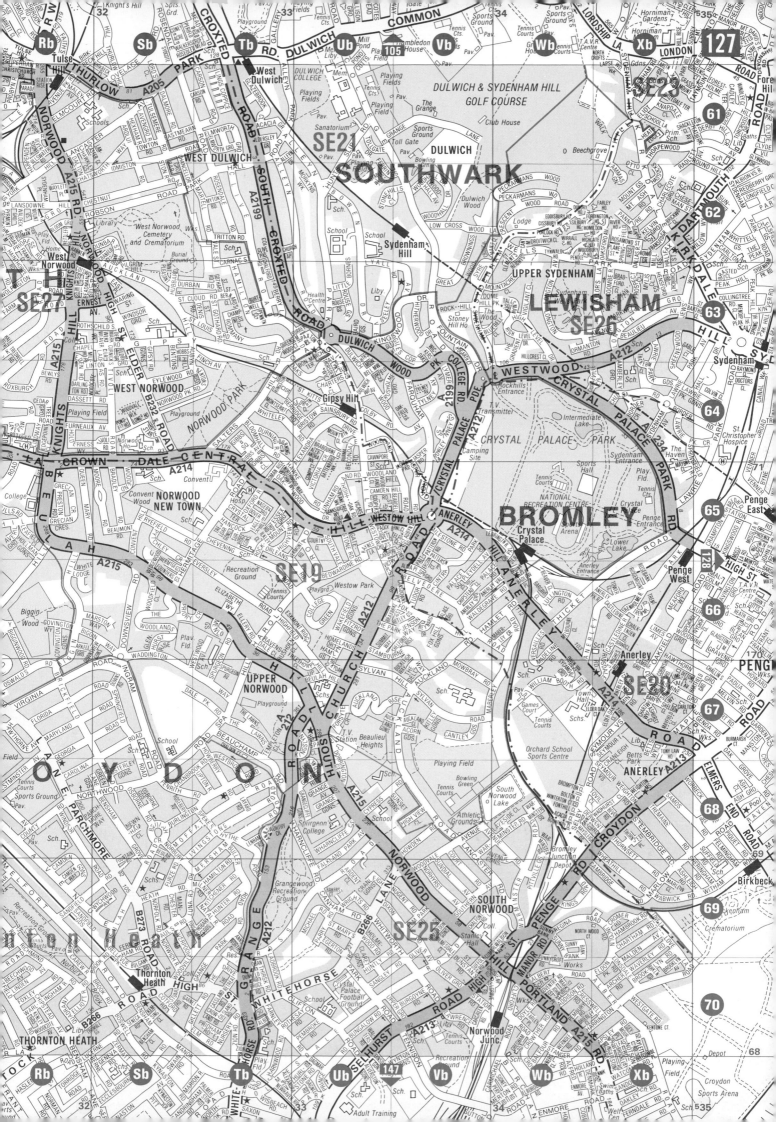

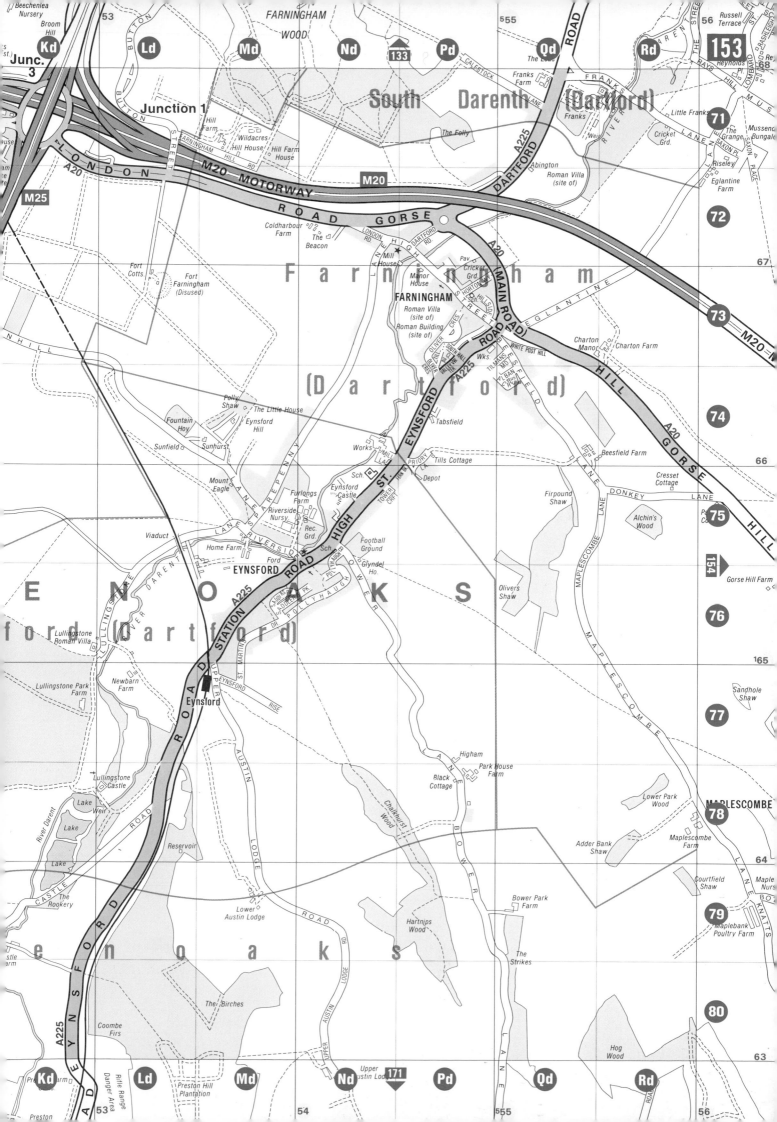

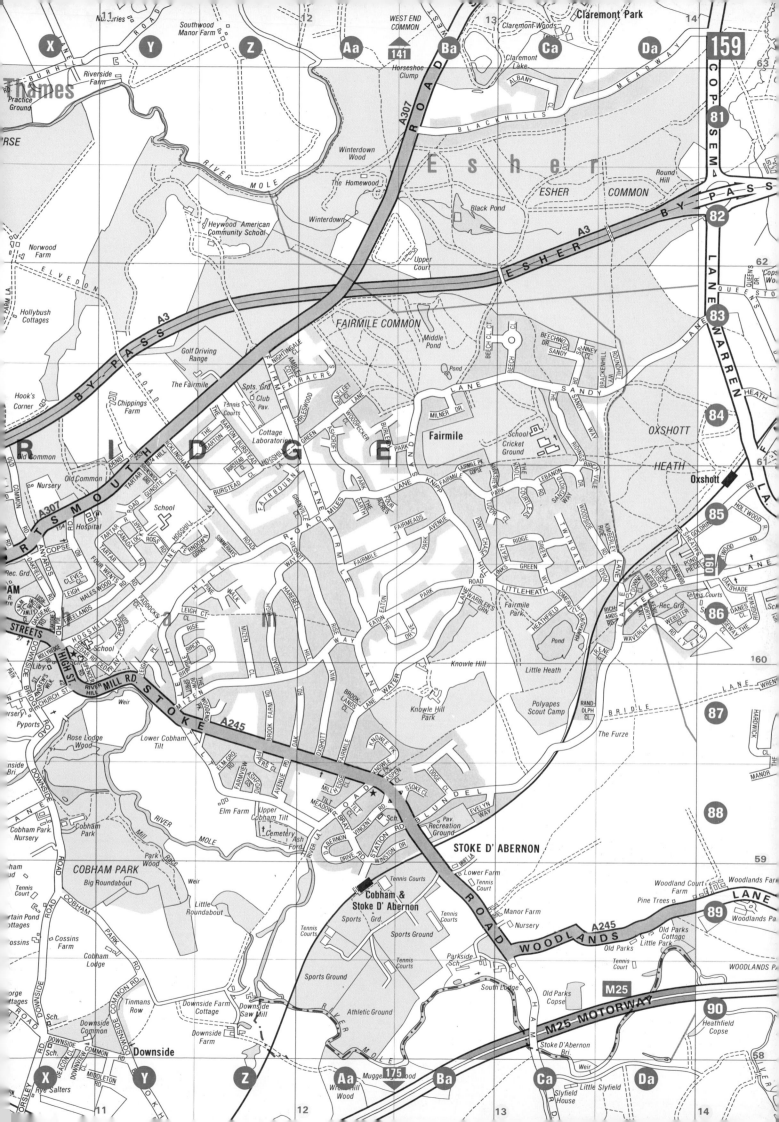

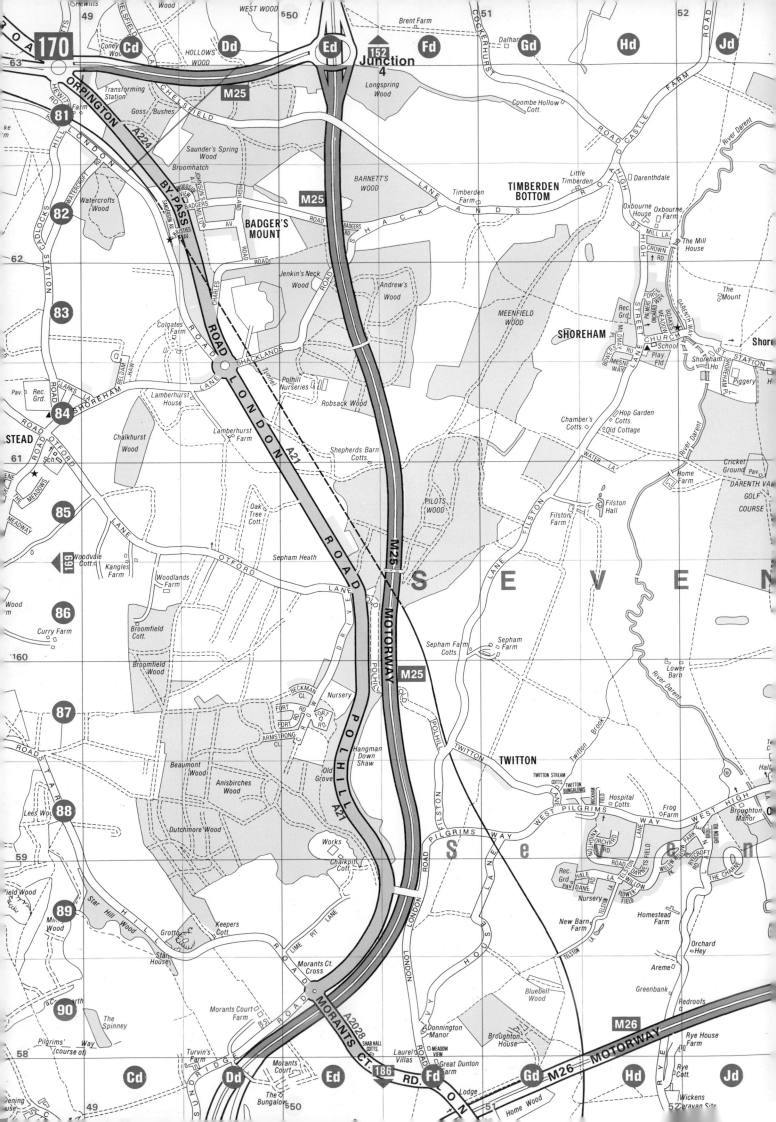

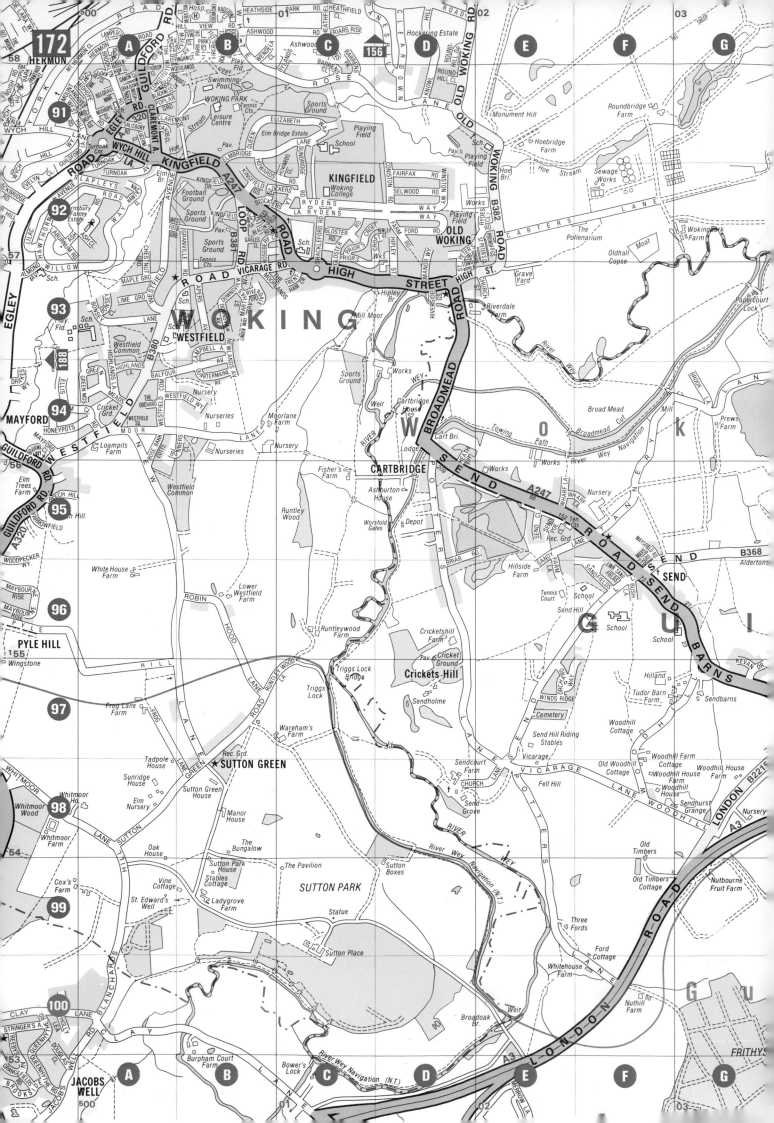

Large Scale Section

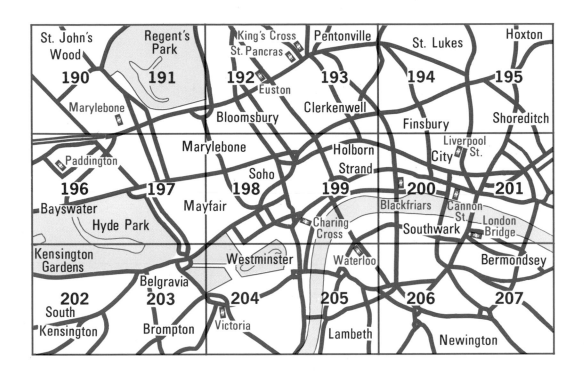

REFERENCE

Motorway	
'A' Road	A240
'B' Road	B463
Dual Carriageway	
House Numbers 'A' & 'B' Roads only	2 89
Buildings open to the Public	
District & Borough Boundary	— · — · —
Fire Station	■
Hospital	
Information Centre	🛈
Map Continuation	▲ 130
National Grid Reference	578
Places of Interest	
Police Station	▲
Postal Boundary	E.C.1.
Post Office	★
Railway Station Entrances	Underground ⊖ British Rail 🚄

Scale: 9 inches to 1 mile 1:7040

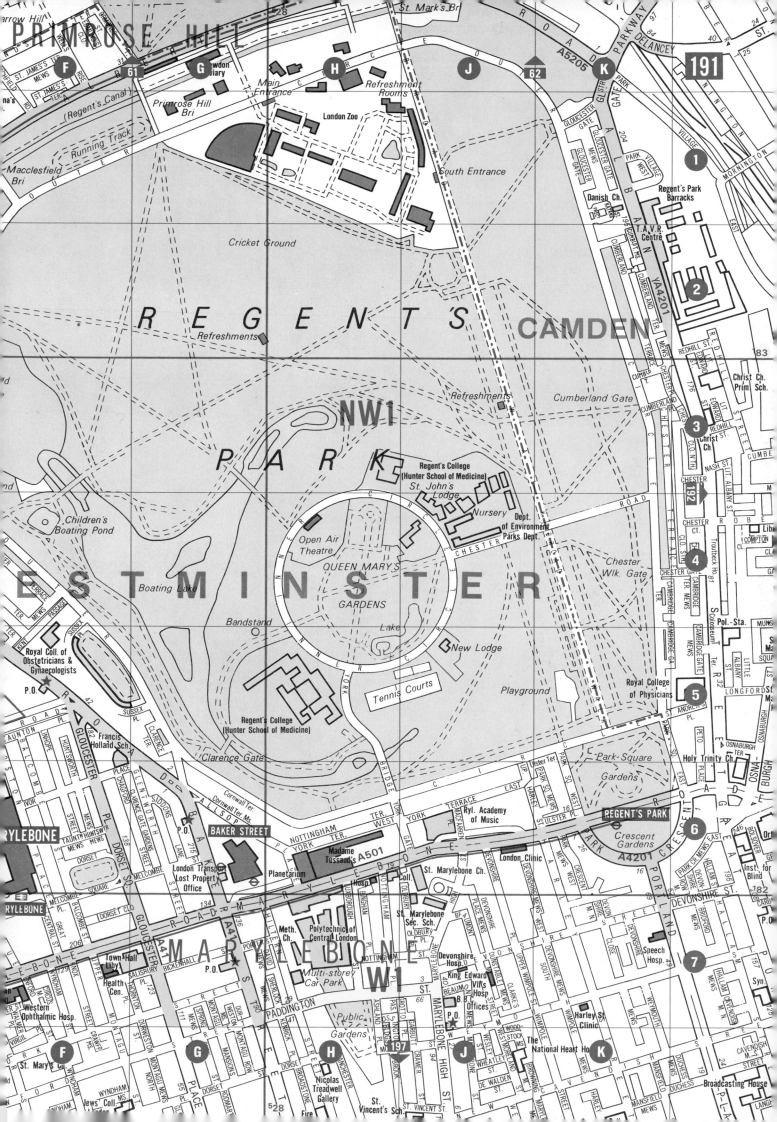

PRIMROSE HILL

St. Mark's Bri

F 61 **G** wdon riary **H** **J** 62 **K**

Main Entrance
Refreshment Rooms
Primrose Hill Bri
London Zoo

(Regent's Canal)
Running Track
Macclesfield Bri

South Entrance

Danish Ch.
Park Village West
Regent's Park Barracks
T.A.V.R. Centre

1

Cricket Ground

2

R E G E N T S CAMDEN

Refreshments

NW1

PARK

Refreshments

Cumberland Gate

Christ Ch. Prim Sch.

3

Christ Ch.

K
Regent's College
(Hunter School of Medicine)
St. John's Lodge
Nursery
Dept. of Environment
Parks Dept.

CHESTER
Chester Ct.

192

Children's Boating Pond

Open Air Theatre

Chester Wlk. Gate

4

QUEEN MARY'S GARDENS

ESTMINSTER

Boating Lake

Bandstand

Lake

New Lodge

5

Royal College of Physicians

Royal Coll. of Obstetricians & Gynaecologists

P.O.

Tennis Courts

Playground

Holy Trinity Ch.

Francis Holland Sch.

Clarence Gate

Regent's College
(Hunter School of Medicine)

Park Square Gardens

Cornwall Ter. Ms.

Ulster Ter.
Ryl. Academy of Music

REGENT'S PARK

6

P.O.
BAKER STREET

Madame Tussaud's A501

London Transport Lost Property Office
Planetarium

York Gate

Crescent Gardens

A4201

RYLEBONE

London Clinic

Inst. for Blind

St. Marylebone Ch.

Devonshire Hosp.

Speech Hosp.

7

RYLEBONE

St. Marylebone Sec. Sch.

Town Hall
Liby.
Health Cen.

MARYLEBONE
W1

Multi-storey Car Park

King Edward VII's Hosp.

Meth. Ch.
Polytechnic of Central London

Harley St. Clinic

Western Ophthalmic Hosp.

PADDINGTON

Public Gardens

P.O.
The National Heart Ho

Broadcasting House

F St. Mary's Ch. **G** **H** Nicolas Treadwell Gallery Fire **197** **J** **K**

St. Vincent's Sch.

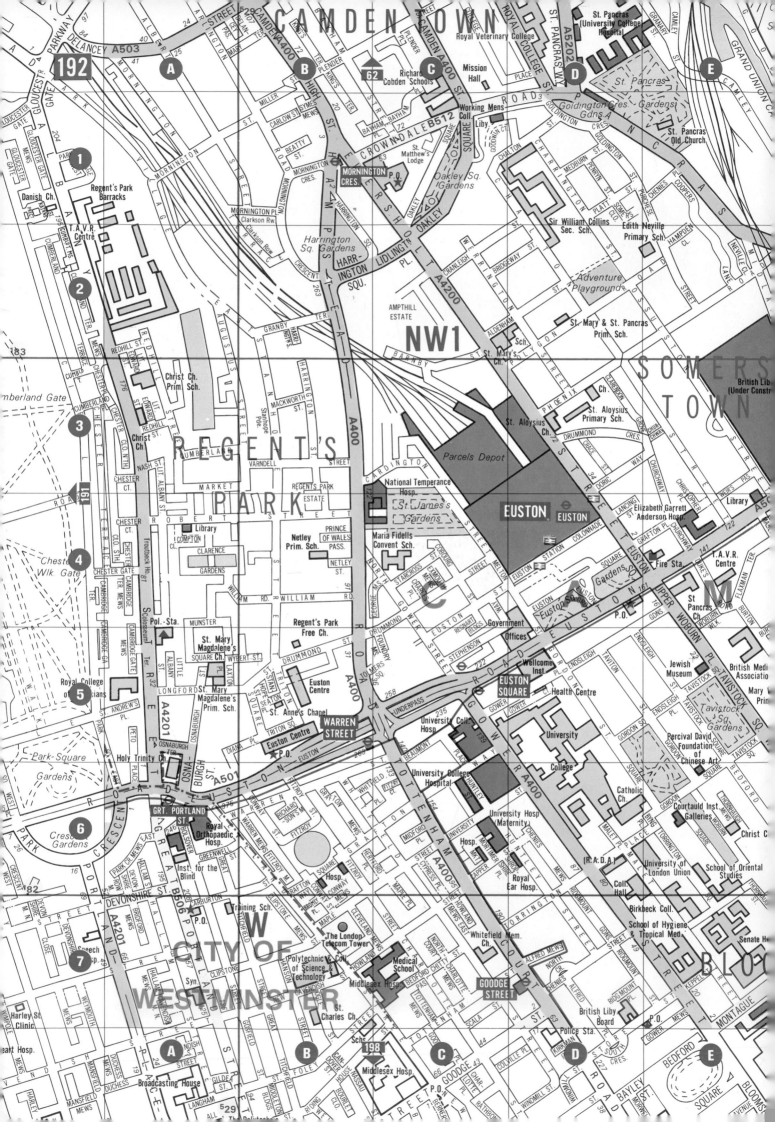

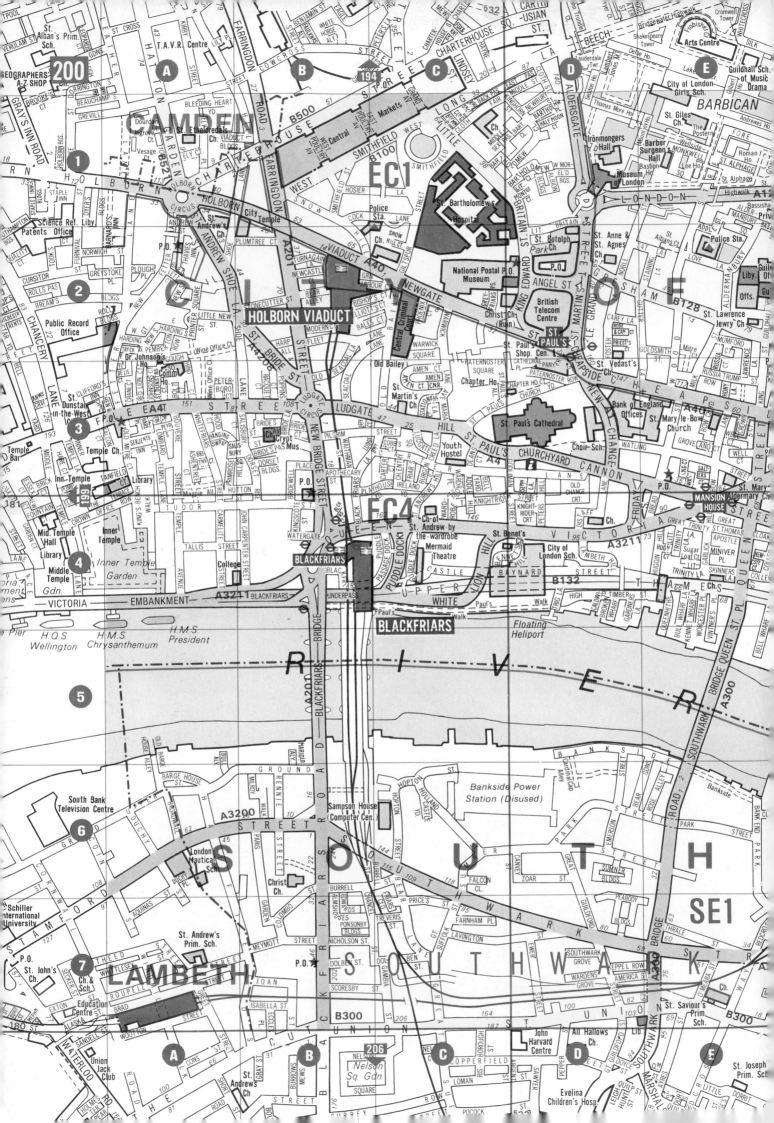

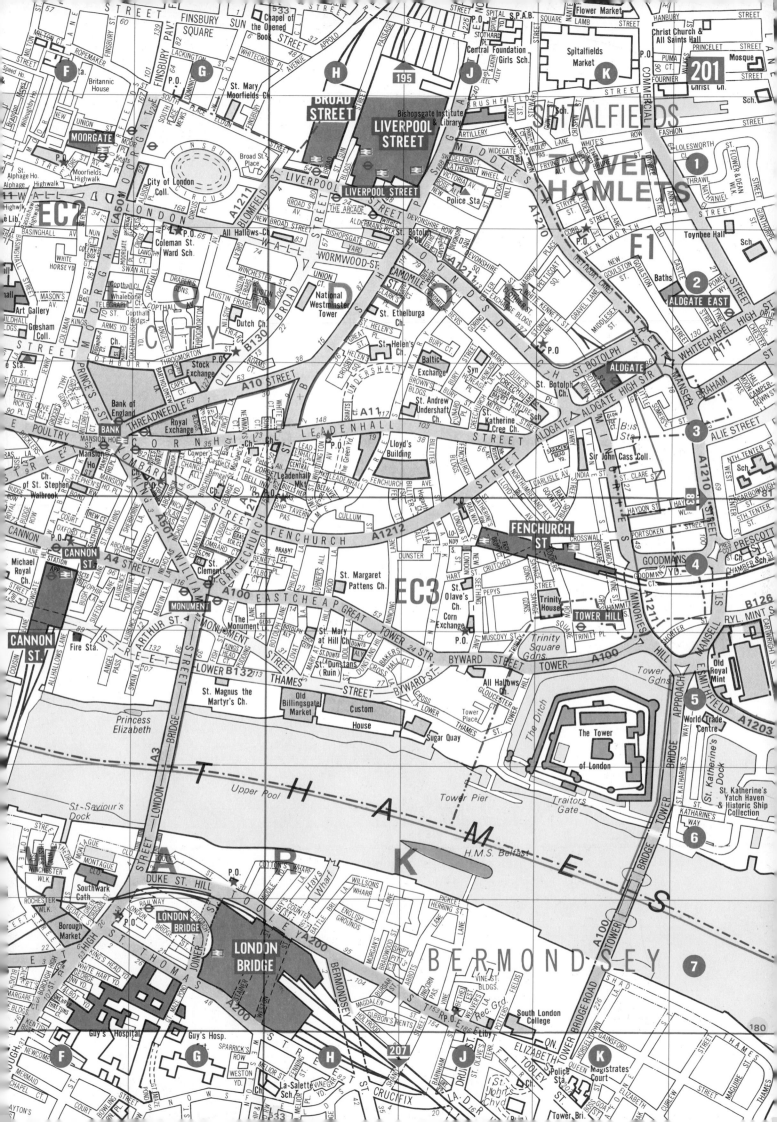

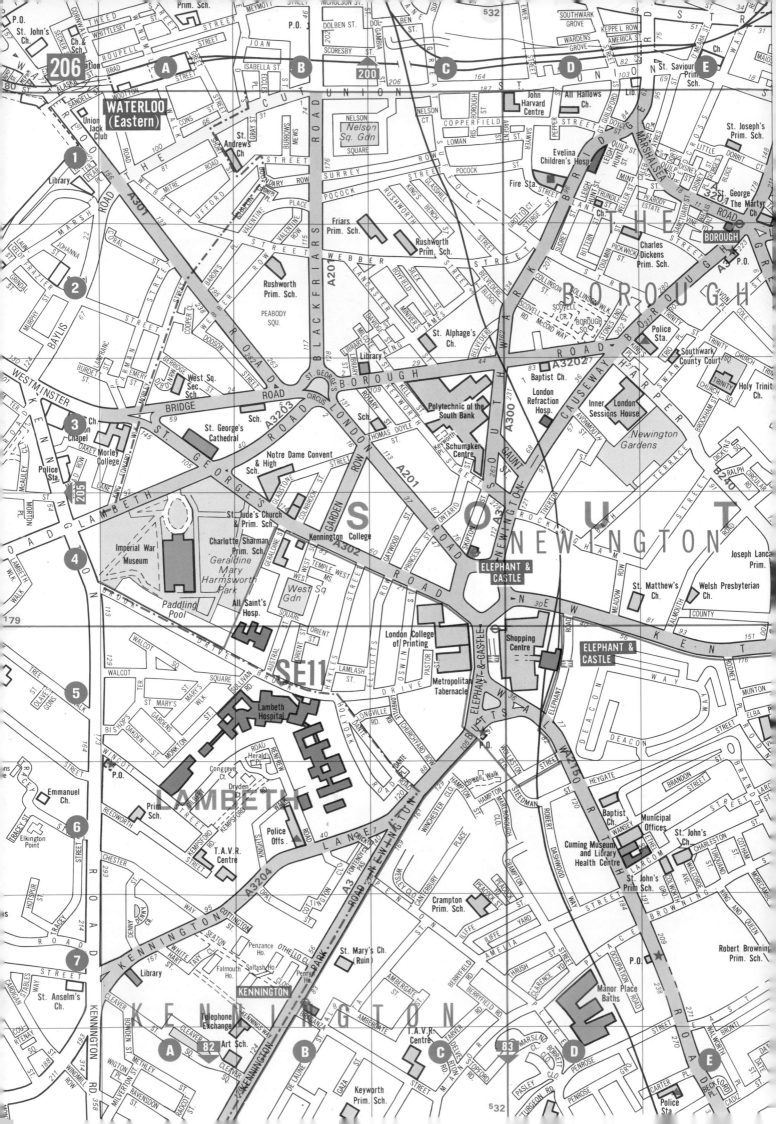

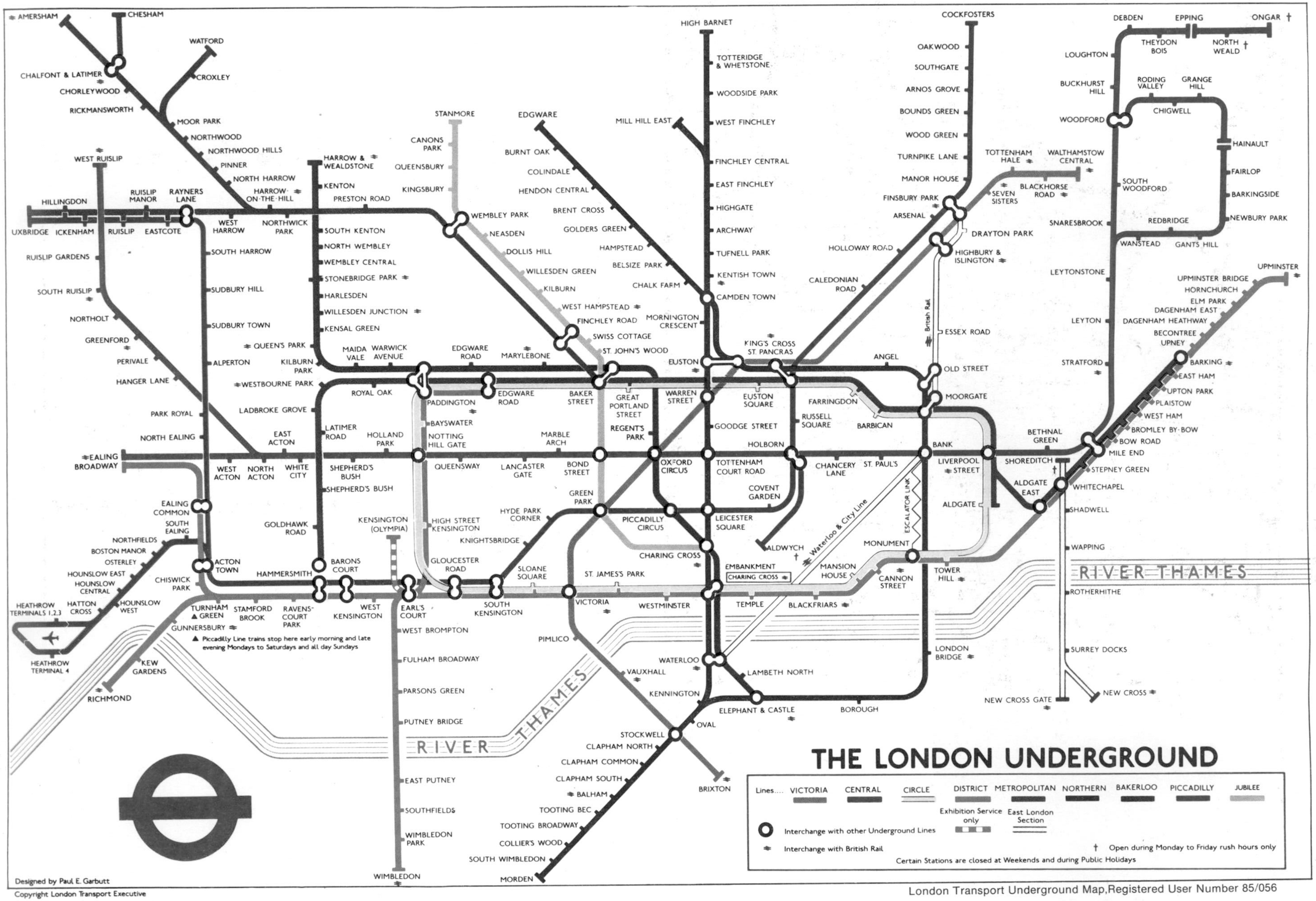

THE LONDON UNDERGROUND

RIVER THAMES

Lines.... VICTORIA CENTRAL CIRCLE DISTRICT METROPOLITAN NORTHERN BAKERLOO PICCADILLY JUBILEE

EAST LONDON
Section

Exhibition Service
only

○ Interchange with other Underground Lines

✠ Interchange with British Rail

✠ Open during Monday to Friday rush hours only

✠ Open during Monday to Friday rush hours only

✠ Certain Stations are closed at Weekends and during Public Holidays

ESCALATOR LINK

Waterloo & City Line

British Rail

RIVER THAMES

Designed by Paul E. Garbutt

Copyright London Transport Executive

London Transport Underground Map, Registered User Number 85/056

Road Maps

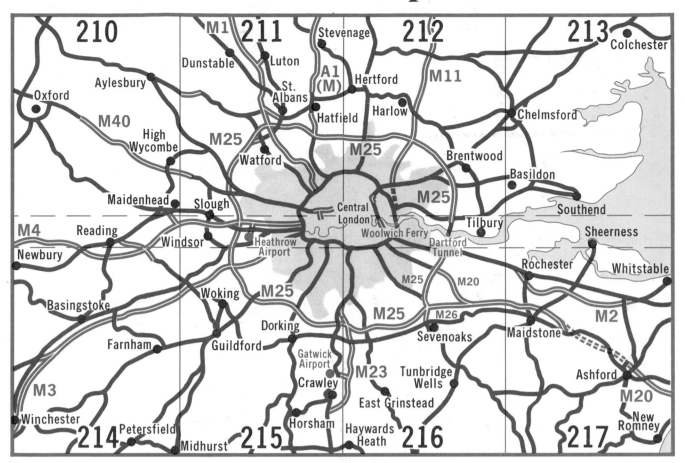

Reference and Tourist Information

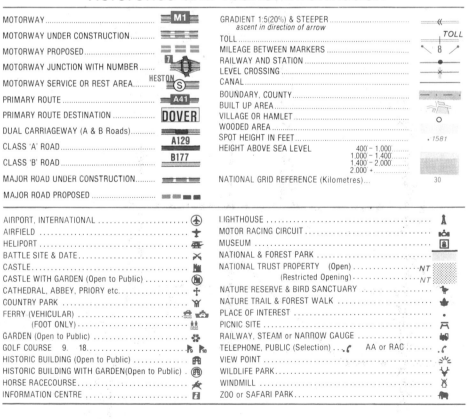

MOTORWAY	M1
MOTORWAY UNDER CONSTRUCTION	
MOTORWAY PROPOSED	
MOTORWAY JUNCTION WITH NUMBER	7
MOTORWAY SERVICE OR REST AREA	HESTON S
PRIMARY ROUTE	A41
PRIMARY ROUTE DESTINATION	DOVER
DUAL CARRIAGEWAY (A & B Roads)	
CLASS 'A' ROAD	A129
CLASS 'B' ROAD	B177
MAJOR ROAD UNDER CONSTRUCTION	
MAJOR ROAD PROPOSED	

GRADIENT 1:5(20%) & STEEPER	
ascent in direction of arrow	
TOLL	TOLL
MILEAGE BETWEEN MARKERS	8
RAILWAY AND STATION	
LEVEL CROSSING	
CANAL	
BOUNDARY, COUNTY	
BUILT UP AREA	
VILLAGE OR HAMLET	o
WOODED AREA	
SPOT HEIGHT IN FEET	•1581
HEIGHT ABOVE SEA LEVEL	400' – 1,000'
	1,000' – 1,400'
	1,400' – 2,000'
	2,000' +
NATIONAL GRID REFERENCE (Kilometres)	30

AIRPORT, INTERNATIONAL	✈
AIRFIELD	
HELIPORT	
BATTLE SITE & DATE	⚔
CASTLE	
CASTLE WITH GARDEN (Open to Public)	
CATHEDRAL, ABBEY, PRIORY etc.	✝
COUNTRY PARK	
FERRY (VEHICULAR)	
(FOOT ONLY)	
GARDEN (Open to Public)	
GOLF COURSE 9. 18	
HISTORIC BUILDING (Open to Public)	
HISTORIC BUILDING WITH GARDEN(Open to Public)	
HORSE RACECOURSE	
INFORMATION CENTRE	

LIGHTHOUSE	
MOTOR RACING CIRCUIT	
MUSEUM	
NATIONAL & FOREST PARK	
NATIONAL TRUST PROPERTY (Open)	NT
(Restricted Opening)	NT
NATURE RESERVE & BIRD SANCTUARY	
NATURE TRAIL & FOREST WALK	
PLACE OF INTEREST	
PICNIC SITE	
RAILWAY, STEAM or NARROW GAUGE	
TELEPHONE, PUBLIC (Selection) AA or RAC	
VIEW POINT	
WILDLIFE PARK	
WINDMILL	
ZOO or SAFARI PARK	

Scale:
3.156 miles to 1 inch
1:200,000

0 1 2 3 4 5   10 Miles

0 1 2 3 4 5   10   15 Kilometres

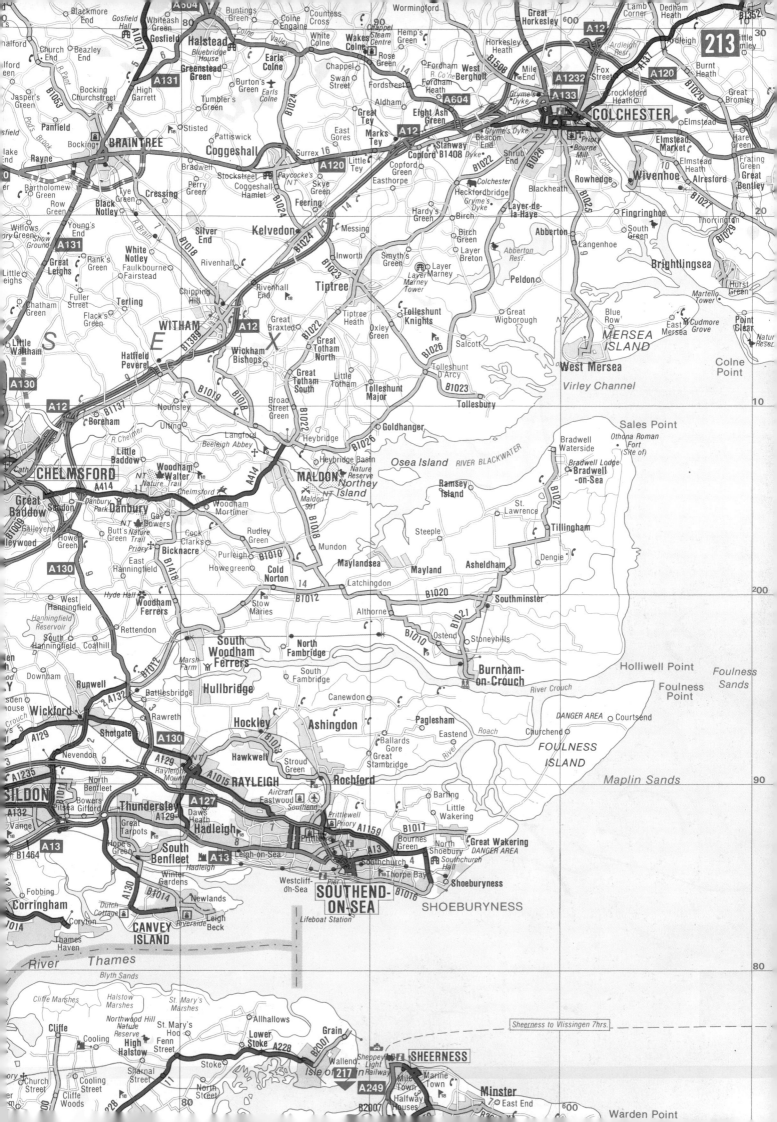

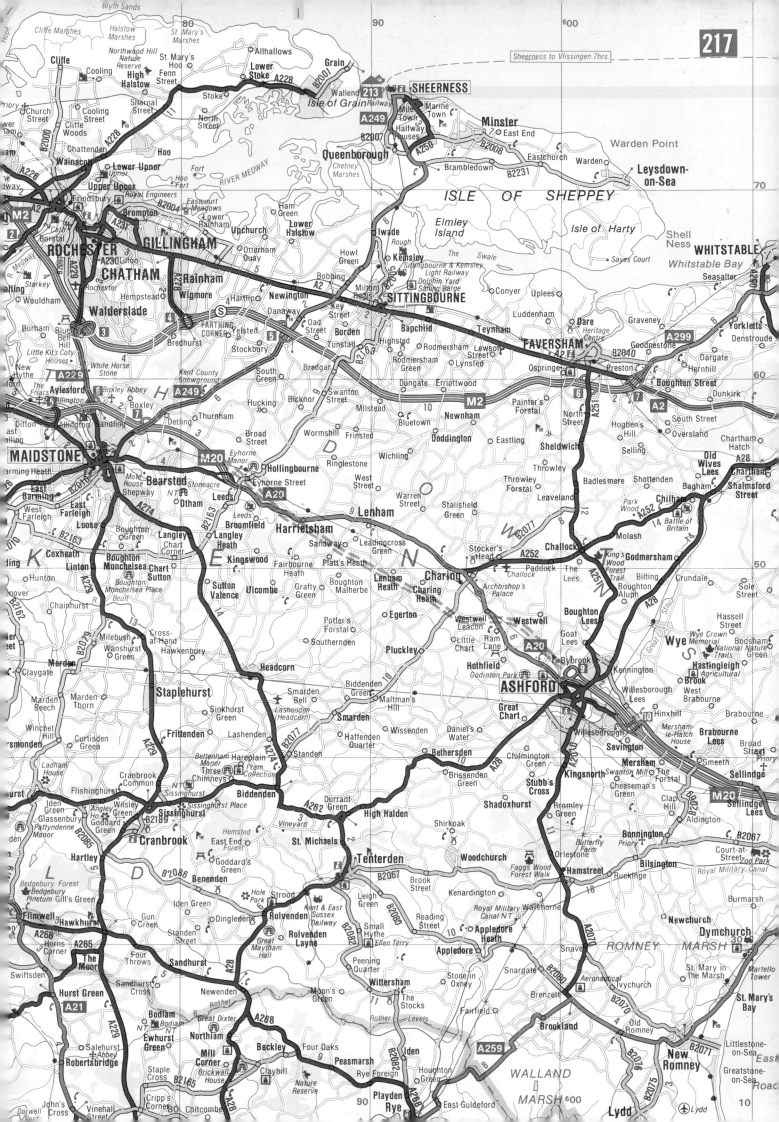

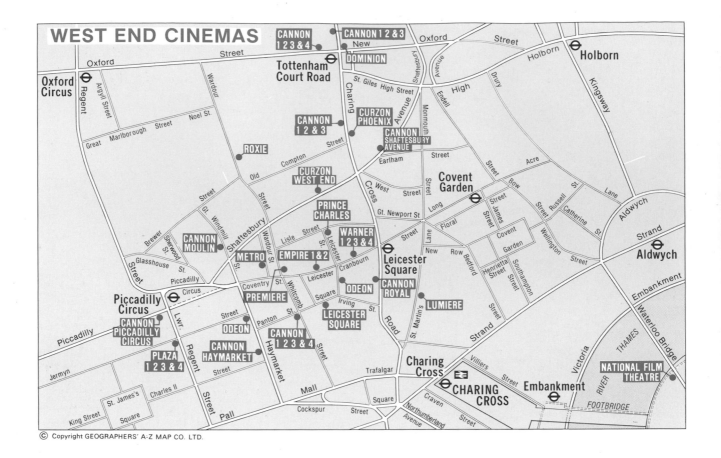

WEST END CINEMAS

Oxford Circus
Oxford Street
Argyll Street
Regent Street
Great Marlborough Street
Noel St.
Wardour Street

CANNON 1 2 3 & 4
CANNON 1 2 & 3
New
DOMINION
Oxford Street
Holborn
Holborn
Tottenham Court Road
St. Giles High Street
Charing
Shaftesbury Avenue
Endell
High
Drury
Kingsway

CURZON PHOENIX
CANNON 1 2 & 3
CANNON SHAFTESBURY AVENUE
ROXIE
Compton Street
Earlham
Monmouth
Covent Garden
Acre
Lane
Aldwych

CURZON WEST END
West Street
Cross
Street
Long
Bow
Russell Street
Strand

Brewer Street
Sherwood St.
Gt. Windmill St.
Shaftesbury
PRINCE CHARLES
Lisle Street
Leicester
WARNER 1 2 3 & 4
Gt. Newport St.
Floral
James Street
Covent Garden
Wellington
Catherine St.

CANNON MOULIN
METRO
EMPIRE 1 & 2
Cranbourn
Leicester Square
Leicester Square
New Row
Bedford
Henrietta Street
Southampton

Glasshouse St.
Piccadilly
Coventry St.
Whitcomb St.
Panton St.
ODEON
Irving St.
St. Martin's Lane
CANNON ROYAL
LUMIERE
Strand
Embankment

Piccadilly Circus
PREMIERE
Road
Charing Cross
THAMES
Waterloo Bridge

CANNON PICCADILLY CIRCUS
Lwr. Regent St.
ODEON
Haymarket
CANNON 1 2 3 & 4

Piccadilly
PLAZA 1 2 3 & 4
CANNON HAYMARKET
Trafalgar
Charing Cross
Victoria
Villiers Street
NATIONAL FILM THEATRE

Jermyn
King Street
St. James's Square
Charles II Street
Pall Mall
Cockspur Street
Square
CHARING CROSS
Craven Street
Northumberland Avenue
Embankment
RIVER
FOOTBRIDGE

© Copyright GEOGRAPHERS' A-Z MAP CO. LTD.

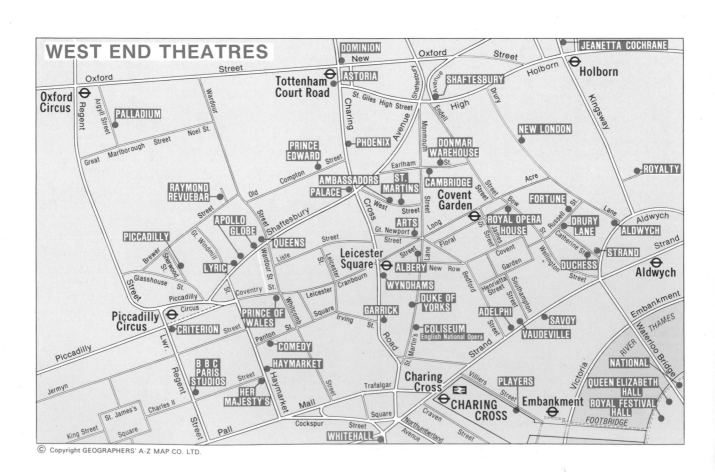

WEST END THEATRES

Oxford Circus
Oxford Street
Argyll Street
Regent Street
Great Marlborough Street
Noel St.
Wardour Street

DOMINION
New
ASTORIA
Oxford Street
JEANETTA COCHRANE
Holborn
Holborn
Tottenham Court Road
St. Giles High Street
Charing
Shaftesbury Avenue
SHAFTESBURY
Endell
High
Drury
Kingsway

PALLADIUM
PHOENIX
PRINCE EDWARD
DONMAR WAREHOUSE
NEW LONDON

Compton Street
Earlham St.
Monmouth
Covent Garden
Acre
Lane
ROYALTY
Aldwych

RAYMOND REVUEBAR
AMBASSADORS
ST. MARTINS
CAMBRIDGE
West Street
Cross
ROYAL OPERA HOUSE
FORTUNE
Russell Street
DRURY LANE
ALDWYCH
Strand

Brewer Street
Sherwood St.
Gt. Windmill St.
APOLLO
GLOBE
PALACE
ARTS
Gt. Newport St.
Long
Floral
James Street
Covent Garden
Wellington
Catherine St.
STRAND
Aldwych

PICCADILLY
LYRIC
QUEENS
Lisle Street
Leicester Square
Cranbourn
Leicester Square
ALBERY
New Row
Bedford
Henrietta Street
Southampton
DUCHESS

Glasshouse St.
Piccadilly
Coventry St.
PRINCE OF WALES
Whitcomb St.
Panton St.
WYNDHAMS
GARRICK
DUKE OF YORKS
Irving St.
St. Martin's Lane
ADELPHI
SAVOY
VAUDEVILLE
Embankment

Piccadilly Circus
CRITERION
COMEDY
COLISEUM
English National Opera
Road
Strand
THAMES
Waterloo Bridge

B B C PARIS STUDIOS
HAYMARKET
HER MAJESTY'S
Trafalgar
Charing Cross
CHARING CROSS
PLAYERS
Villiers Street
Victoria
Embankment
NATIONAL
QUEEN ELIZABETH HALL
ROYAL FESTIVAL HALL

Piccadilly
Jermyn
King Street
St. James's Square
Charles II Street
Regent Street
Lwr.
Pall
Cockspur Street
Square
Craven Street
Northumberland Avenue
WHITEHALL
FOOTBRIDGE

© Copyright GEOGRAPHERS' A-Z MAP CO. LTD.

INDEX TO STREETS

HOW TO USE THIS INDEX

1. Each street name is followed by its Postal District (or, if outside the London Postal District, by its Post Town), and then by its map reference; e.g. Abberton Wlk. Rain—39Hd **68** is in the Rainham Post Town and is found in square 39 Hd on page **68**. The page number being shown in bold type.

A strict alphabetical order is followed in which Av., Rd., St. etc. (though abbreviated) are read in full and as part of the street name; e.g. Abbeydale Rd. appears after Abbey Cres., but before Abbey Dri.

2. The streets in this index are cross referenced with those in the Nine Master Maps of London; e.g. Abbess Clo. SW2—60Rb **105** is in the South West 2 Postal District and appears in map square 60Rb of both map and atlas, which in the Master Atlas is on page **105**.
However, there are two exceptions as follows:-
★Abbott Rd. Sev—92Be. Streets preceded by this star appear on a Master Map but not in the Master Atlas.
Abbey Clo. Slou—5C **72** and *Abchurch Yd. EC4—(4F* **201**). Streets in italics appear in the Master Atlas but not on the Master Map.

3. Map references shown in brackets; e.g. Abbey Gdns. NW8—40Eb **61** (2A **190**) and *Abchurch Yd. EC4—(4F* **201**), refer to streets shown on the Super Scale Maps of Inner London, pages 190-207. In the first example Abbey Gdns. is shown as appearing in the Super Scale Map section as well as the standard Master Atlas section, whereas in the second example *Abchurch Yd.* is shown as appearing in the Super Scale Map section only.
4. With the now general usage of Postal Coding, it is not recommended that this index be used as a means of addressing mail.

GENERAL ABBREVIATIONS

All: Alley
App: Approach
Arc: Arcade
Av: Avenue
Bk: Back
Boulevd: Boulevard
Bri: Bridge
B'way: Broadway
Bldgs: Buildings
Chu: Church
Chyd: Churchyard
Circ: Circle
Cir: Circus
Clo: Close
Comn: Common
Cotts: Cottages
Ct: Court
Cres: Crescent
Dri: Drive
E: East
Embkmt: Embankment
Est: Estate
Gdns: Gardens
Ga: Gate
Gt: Great
Grn: Green
Gro: Grove
Ho: House
Junct: Junction
La: Lane
Lit: Little
Lwr: Lower
Mnr: Manor
Mans: Mansions
Mkt: Market
M: Mews
Mt: Mount
N: North
Pal: Palace
Pde: Parade
Pk: Park
Pas: Passage
Pl: Place
Rd: Road
S: South
Sq: Square
Sta: Station
St: Street
Ter: Terrace
Up: Upper
Vs: Villas
Wlk: Walk
W: West
Yd: Yard

POST TOWN and PLACE NAME ABBREVIATIONS

Abb L: Abbots Langley
Amer: Amersham
Asc: Ascot
Ashf: Ashford
Asht: Ashtead
Bans: Banstead
Bark: Barking
Barn: Barnet
Bea: Beaconsfield
Beck: Beckenham
Bedd: Beddington
Belv: Belvedere
Bex: Bexley
Bexh: Bexleyheath
Borwd: Borehamwood
Bren: Brentford
Brtwd: Brentwood
Brom: Bromley
Buck H: Buckhurst Hill
Bush: Bushey
Cars: Carshalton
Cat: Caterham
Chal: Chalfont St Giles
Cher: Chertsey
Che: Chesham
Chess: Chessington
Chig: Chigwell
Chst: Chislehurst
Chob: Chobham
Cob: Cobham
Coul: Coulsdon
Croy: Croydon
Dag: Dagenham
Dart: Dartford
Dor: Dorking
E Mol: East Molesey
Edgw: Edgware
Egh: Egham
Enf: Enfield
Epp: Epping
Eps: Epsom
Eri: Erith
Esh: Esher
Eyns: Eynsford
F'ham: Farningham
Felt: Feltham
Ger X: Gerrards Cross
God: Godstone
Grav: Gravesend
Grays: Grays
Gnfd: Greenford
Grnh: Greenhithe
Guild: Guildford
Hmptn: Hampton
Harr: Harrow
Hat: Hatfield
Hav: Havering atte Bower
Hay: Hayes
Hem: Hemel Hempstead
High W: High Wycombe
Horn: Hornchurch
Houn: Hounslow
Ilf: Ilford
Ing: Ingatestone
Iswth: Isleworth
Iver: Iver
Kenl: Kenley
Kes: Keston
K Lan: King's Langley
King: Kingston upon Thames
Lea: Leatherhead
Long: Longfield
Lou: Loughton
M'head: Maidenhead
Mitc: Mitcham
Mord: Morden
N Mald: New Malden
N'holt: Northolt
N'wd: Northwood
Ong: Ongar
Orp: Orpington
Oxt: Oxted
Pinn: Pinner
Pot B: Potters Bar
Purf: Purfleet
Purl: Purley
Rad: Radlett
Rain: Rainham
Rich: Richmond upon Thames
Rick: Rickmansworth
Roch: Rochester
Romf: Romford
Ruis: Ruislip
St Alb: Saint Albans
Sev: Sevenoaks
Shen: Shenley
Shep: Shepperton
Sidc: Sidcup
Slou: Slough
S'hall: Southall
S Croy: South Croydon
S Dar: South Darenth
S Ock: South Ockendon
Stai: Staines
Stanf: Stanford-le-Hope
Stan: Stanmore
Stap T: Stapleford Tawney
Sun: Sunbury on Thames
Surb: Surbiton
Sutt: Sutton
S at H: Sutton at Hone
Swan: Swanley
Tad: Tadworth
Tedd: Teddington
Th Dit: Thames Ditton
T Hth: Thornton Heath
Til: Tilbury
Upm: Upminster
Uxb: Uxbridge
Vir W: Virginia Water
Wall: Wallington
Wal A: Waltham Abbey
Wal X: Waltham Cross
W on T: Walton on Thames
Warl: Warlingham
Wat: Watford
Well: Welling
Wemb: Wembley
W Dray: West Drayton
West: Westerham
W Wick: West Wickham
Wey: Weybridge
Whyt: Whyteleafe
Wind: Windsor
Wok: Woking
Wfd G: Woodford Green
Wor Pk: Worcester Park
Wray: Wraysbury

INDEX TO STREETS

Abberton Wlk. Rain—39Hd 68
Abbess Clo. SW2—60Rb 105
Abbeville Rd. N8—28Mb 42
Abbeville Rd. SW4—58Lb 104
Abbey Av. Wemb—40Na 59
Abbey Clo. N'holt—41Ba 77
Abbey Clo. Pinn—27X 37
Abbey Clo. Slou—5C 72
Abbey Clo. Wok—88G 156
Abbey Ct. Wal A—6Dc 12
Abbey Cres. Belv—49Cd 88
Abbeydale Rd. Wemb—39Pa 59
Abbey Dri. Stai—70L 119
Abbey Est. NW8—39Db 61
Abbeyfield Clo. NW10—40Qa 59
Abbeyfield Rd. SE16—49Yb 84
(in two parts)
Abbey Gdns. NW8
—40Eb 61 (2A 190)
Abbey Gdns. W6—51Ab 102
Abbey Gdns. Cher—72J 139
Abbey Gdns. M. NW8
—40Eb 61 (2A 190)
Abbey Grn. Cher—72J 139
Abbey Gro. SE2—49Xc 87
Abbey Hill Rd. Sidc—61Yc 131
Abbey La. E15—40Ec 64
Abbey La. Beck—66Cc 128
Abbey Manufacturing Est. Wemb
—39Pa 59
Abbey Orchard St. SW1
—48Mb 82 (3D 204)
Abbey Pde. NW10—41Pa 79
Abbey Pk. Beck—66Cc 128
Abbey Pk. La. Slou—3C 52
Abbey Rd. E15—40Fc 65
Abbey Rd.—39Db 61
NW8 1-117 & 2-98
NW6 remainder
Abbey Rd. NW10—40Ra 59
Abbey Rd. SW19—66Eb 125
Abbey Rd. Bark—39Rc 66
Abbey Rd. Belv—49Zc 87
Abbey Rd. Bexh—56Ad 109
Abbey Rd. Cher—73K 139
Abbey Rd. Croy—76Rb 147
Abbey Rd. Enf—15Ub 25
Abbey Rd. Grav—10G 114
Abbey Rd. Grnh—57Yd 112
Abbey Rd. Ilf—29Tc 46
Abbey Rd. Shep—74Q 140
Abbey Rd. S Croy—82Zb 166
Abbey Rd. Vir W—10P 117
Abbey Rd. Wal X—6Ac 12
Abbey Rd. Wok—5F 188
Abbey St. E13—42Jc 85
Abbey St. SE1—48Vb 83 (3J 207)
Abbey Ter. NW10—40Pa 59
Abbey Ter. SE2—49Yc 87
Abbey View. NW7—20Va 22
Abbey View. Wal A—5Dc 12
Abbey Wlk. E Mol—69Da 121
Abbey Wood La. Rain—40Md 69
Abbey Wood Rd. SE2—49Xc 87
Abbot Clo. Stai—66M 119
Abbot Clo. Wey—82M 157
Abbotsbury Clo. E15—40Ec 64
Abbotsbury Clo. W14—47Bb 81
Abbotsbury Gdns. Pinn—30Y 37
Abbotsbury Rd. W14—47Ab 80
Abbotsbury Rd. Brom—75Hc 149
Abbotsbury Rd. Mord—71Db 145
Abbots Clo. Brtwd—18Ce 33
Abbots Clo. Orp—74Sc 150
Abbots Clo. Rain—40Ld 69
Abbots Clo. Ruis—34Z 57
Abbots Clo. Uxb—43M 75
Abbots Dri. Vir W—10M 117
Abbots Field. Grav—5E 136
Abbotsford Av. N15—28Sb 43
Abbotsford Clo. Wok—89C 156
Abbotsford Gdns. Wfd G—24Jc 45
Abbotsford Rd. Ilf—33Wc 67
Abbots Gdns. N2—28Fb 41
Abbot's Grn. Croy—79Zb 148
Abbotshall Av. N14—20Lb 24
Abbots Hall Chase. Stanf—1N 93
Abbotshall Rd. SE6—60Fc 107
Abbots La. SE1—46Ub 83 (7J 201)
Abbots La. Kenl—88Sb 165
Abbotsleigh Clo. Sutt—80Db 145
Abbotsleigh Rd. SW16—63Lb 126
Abbot's Mnr. Est. SW1
—50Kb 82 (7K 203)
Abbotsmede Clo. Twic—61Ha 122
Abbots Pk. SW2—60Qb 104
Abbot's Pl. NW6—39Db 61
Abbot's Rd. E6—39Mc 65
Abbots Rd. Abb L, Wat—3S 4
Abbots Rd. Edgw—24Sa 39
Abbots Ter. N8—30Nb 42
Abbot's Tilt. W on T—76Aa 141
Abbotstone Rd. SW15—55Ya 102
Abbot St. E8—37Vb 63
Abbots Wlk. Cat—94Xb 181
Abbots Wlk. Wind—4C 94
Abbots Way. Beck—71Ac 148
Abbotswell Rd. SE4—57Bc 106
Abbotswood Dri. Wey—82T 158
Abbotswood Gdns. Ilf—27Pc 46
Abbotswood Rd. SW16—62Mb 126
Abbott Av. SW20—67Za 124
Abbott Clo. Hmptn—65Aa 121
Abbott Clo. N'holt—37Ba 57
Abbott Rd. E14—44Ec 84
(in two parts)
★Abbott Rd. Sev—92Be
Abbotts Clo. N1—37Sb 63
Abbotts Clo. Romf—27Dd 48
Abbotts Clo. Swan—70Jd 132
Abbotts Cres. E4—21Fc 45
Abbotts Cres. Enf—12Rb 25
Abbott's Dri. Stanf—1M 93
Abbotts Dri. Wal A—5Jc 13
Abbotts Dri. Wemb—33Ka 58
Abbotts Pk. Rd. E10—31Ec 64
Abbotts Rd. Barn—14Db 23
Abbotts Rd. Mitc—70Lb 126
Abbotts Rd. S'hall—46Aa 77
Abbotts Rd. Sutt—77Ab 144
(in two parts)
Abbott's Wlk. Bexh—52Zc 109
Abbotts Way. Slou—6B 72
Abbs Cross. Horn—32Ld 69
Abbs Cross Gdns. Horn—32Ld 69
Abbs Cross La. Horn—34Ld 69
Abchurch La. EC4
—45Tb 83 (4G 201)
Abchurch Yd. EC4—(4F 201*)*
Abdale Rd. W12—46Xa 80
Abenburg Way. Brtwd—19De 33
Abenglen Industrial Est. Hay
—47T 76
Aberavon Rd. E3—41Ac 84
Abercairn Rd. SW16—66Lb 126
Aberconway Rd. Mord—70Db 125
Abercorn Clo. NW7—24Ab 40
Abercorn Clo. NW8
—41Eb 81 (2A 190)
Abercorn Clo. S Croy—84Zb 166
Abercorn Cres. Harr—32Da 57
Abercorn Gdns. Harr—31Ma 59
Abercorn Gdns. Romf—30Xc 47
Abercorn Gro. Ruis—28T 36
Abercorn Pl. NW8
—41Eb 81 (3A 190)
Abercorn Rd. NW7—24Ab 40
Abercorn Rd. Stan—24La 38
Abercorn Trading Est. Wemb
—40Ma 59
Abercorn Way. Wok—6D 188
Abercrombie St. SW11—54Gb 103
Aberdale Gdns. Pot B—4Bb 9
Aberdare Clo. W Wick—75Ec 148
Aberdare Gdns. NW6—38Db 61
Aberdare Gdns. NW7—24Za 40
Aberdare Rd. Enf—14Yb 26
Aberdeen Av. Slou—5E 72
Aberdeen La. N5—36Sb 63
Aberdeen Pde. N18—22Xb 43
Aberdeen Pk. N5—36Sb 63
Aberdeen Pl. NW8
—42Fb 81 (6B 190)
Aberdeen Rd. N5—35Sb 63
Aberdeen Rd. N18—22Xb 43
Aberdeen Rd. NW10—36Va 60
Aberdeen Rd. Croy—77Tb 147
Aberdeen Rd. Harr—26Ha 38
Aberdeen Ter. SE3—54Fc 107
Aberdour Rd. Ilf—34Xc 67
Aberdour St. SE1
—49Ub 83 (5H 207)
Aberfeldy St. E14—44Ec 84
(in two parts)
Aberford Gdns. SE18—53Nc 108
Aberford Rd. Borwd—12Qa 21
Aberfoyle Rd. SW16—66Mb 126
Abergeldie Rd. SE12—58Kc 107
Abernethy Rd. SE13—56Gc 107
Abersham Rd. E8—36Vb 63
Abery St. SE18—49Uc 86
Abingdon Clo. NW1—37Mb 62
Abingdon Clo. SW19—65Eb 125
Abingdon Clo. Uxb—39P 55
Abingdon Clo. Wok—6F 188
Abingdon Pl. Pot B—4Db 9
Abingdon Rd. N3—26Eb 41
Abingdon Rd. SW16—68Nb 126
Abingdon Rd. W8—48Cb 81
Abingdon St. SW1
—48Nb 82 (3F 205)
Abingdon Vs. W8—48Cb 81
Abinger Av. Sutt—82Za 162
Abinger Clo. Bark—35Wc 67
Abinger Clo. Brom—69Nc 130
Abinger Clo. Wall—78Nb 146
Abinger Gdns. Iswth—55Ga 100
Abinger Gro. SE8—51Bc 106
Abinger M. W9—42Cb 81
Abinger Rd. W4—48Ua 80
Ablett St. SE16—50Yb 84
Aboyne Dri. SW20—68Wa 124
Aboyne Rd. NW10—34Ua 60
Aboyne Rd. SW17—62Fb 125
Abridge Clo. Wal X—7Zb 12
Abridge Gdns. Romf—23Cd 48
Abridge Rd. Chig—16Tc 28
Abridge Rd. Epp & Romf—9Vc 15
Abridge Way. Bark—40Xc 67
Abyssinia Clo. SW11—56Gb 103
Acacia Av. N17—24Tb 43
Acacia Av. Bren—52Ka 100
Acacia Av. Hay—44V 76
Acacia Av. Horn—33Hd 68
Acacia Av. Rich—54Pa 101
Acacia Av. Ruis—32W 56
Acacia Av. Shep—71Q 140
Acacia Av. Wemb—36Na 59
Acacia Av. W Dray—45P 75
Acacia Av. Wok—8G 188
Acacia Av. Wray, Stai—56A 96
Acacia Clo. SE20—68Wb 127
Acacia Clo. Orp—71Tc 150
Acacia Clo. Stan—23Ga 38
Acacia Clo. Wey—82H 157
Acacia Dri. Bans—86Za 162
Acacia Dri. Sutt—74Cb 145
Acacia Dri. Upm—35Qd 69
Acacia Dri. Wey—82H 157
Acacia Gdns. NW8
—40Fb 61 (1C 190)
Acacia Gdns. Upm—31Vd 70
Acacia Gdns. W Wick—75Ec 148
Acacia Gro. SE21—61Tb 127
Acacia Gro. N Mald—69Ua 124
Acacia Pl. NW8—40Fb 61 (1C 190)
Acacia Rd. E11—33Gc 65
Acacia Rd. E17—30Ac 44
Acacia Rd. N22—25Qb 42
Acacia Rd. NW8—40Fb 61 (1C 190)
Acacia Rd. SW16—67Nb 126
Acacia Rd. W3—45Sa 79
Acacia Rd. Beck—69Bc 128
Acacia Rd. Dart—60Md 111
Acacia Rd. Enf—11Tb 25
Acacia Rd. Grnh—58Ud 112
Acacia Rd. Hmptn—65Ca 121
Acacia Rd. Mitc—68Jb 126
Acacia Rd. Stai—64K 119
Acacia Wlk. Swan—68Fd 132
Academy Bldgs. N1—(3H 195*)*
Academy Gdns. Croy—74Vb 147
Academy Gdns. N'holt—40Z 57
Academy Pl. SE18—53Pc 108
Academy Rd. SE18—53Pc 108
Acanthus Rd. SW11—55Jb 104
Accommodation La. W Dray
(in two parts) —53J 97
Accommodation Rd. NW11
—32Bb 61
Accommodation Rd. Cher
—77A 138
Accommodation Rd. Cher
—76A 138
Acer Av. Rain—41Md 89
Acer Rd. West—88Mc 167
Acers. St Alb—1Ea 6
Acfold Rd. SW6—53Db 103
Achilles Pl. Wok—5F 188
Achilles Rd. NW6—36Cb 61
Achilles St. SE14—52Bc 106
Achilles Way. W1
—46Jb 82 (7J 197)
Acklam Rd. W10—43Ab 80
Acklington Dri. NW9—25Ua 40
Ackmar Rd. SW6—53Cb 103
Ackroyd Dri. E3—43Bc 84
Ackroyd Rd. SE23—59Zb 106
Acland Cres. SE5—55Tb 105
Acland Rd. NW2—37Xa 60
Acme Rd. Wat—10W 4
Acol Cres. Ruis—36X 57
Acol Rd. NW6—38Db 61
Aconbury Rd. Dag—39Xc 67
Acorn Clo. E4—22Dc 44
Acorn Clo. Chst—64Sc 130
Acorn Clo. Enf—11Rb 25
Acorn Ct. Ilf—30Uc 46
Acorn Gdns. SE19—67Vb 127
Acorn Gdns. W3—43Ta 79
Acorn Gro. Ruis—35V 56
Acorn Industrial Est. Dart
—57Hd 110
Acorn La. Pot B—1Nb 10
Acorn Pde. SE15—52Xb 105
Acorn Pl. Wat—9W 4
Acorn Rd. Dart—57Hd 110
Acorns, The. Chig—21Uc 46
Acorn Wlk. SE16—46Ac 84
Acrefield Rd. Ger X—27A 34
Acre La. SW2—56Nb 104
Acre La. Cars & Wall—77Jb 146
Acre Pas. Wind—3H 95
Acre Rd. SW19—65Fb 125
Acre Rd. Dag—38Dd 68
Acre Rd. King—67Na 123
Acres Gdns. Tad—91Za 178
Acres, The. Stanf—1P 93
Acre Way. N'wd—25V 36
Acris St. SW18—57Eb 103
Acton Clo. Wal X—3Ac 12
Acton La. NW10—41Sa 79
Acton La.—47Sa to 49Sa 79
W4 1-287 & 2-280
W3 remainder
Acton M. E8—39Vb 63
Acton Pk. Industrial Est. W3
—47Ta 79
Acton St. WC1—41Pb 82 (4H 193)
Acuba Rd. SW18—61Db 125
Acworth Pl. Dart—58Ld 111
Ada Gdns. E14—44Fc 85
Ada Gdns. E15—39Hc 65
Adair Rd. W10—42Ab 80
Adam & Eve Ct. W1—(2C 198*)*
Adam & Eve M. W8—48Cb 81
Adam Ct. SW7—(5A 202*)*
Adams Clo. NW9—33Ra 59
Adams Ct. EC2—44Ub 83 (2G 201)
Adams Gdns. SE16—47Yb 84
Adamson Rd. E16—44Jc 85
Adamson Rd. NW3—38Fb 61
Adams Pl. N7—36Pb 62
Adamsrill Clo. Enf—16Tb 25
Adamsrill Rd. SE26—63Zb 128
Adams Rd. N17—26Tb 43
Adams Rd. Beck—71Ac 148
Adams Rd. Stanf—2N 93
Adam's Row. W1—45Jb 82 (5J 197)
Adams Sq. Bexh—55Ad 109
Adam St. WC2—45Nb 82 (5G 199)
Ada Pl. E2—39Wb 63
Adare Wlk. SW16—62Pb 126
Ada Rd. SE5—52Ub 105
Ada Rd. Wemb—34Ma 58
Ada St. E8—39Xb 63
Adcock Wlk. Orp—77Vc 151
Adderley Gdns. SE9—63Qc 130
Adderley Gro. SW11—57Jb 104
Adderley Rd. Harr—25Ha 38
Adderley St. E14—44Ec 84
Addington Clo. Wind—5E 94
Addington Dri. N12—23Fb 41
Addington Gro. SE26—63Ac 128
Addington Heights. Croy
—83Ec 166
Addington Rd. E3—41Cc 84
Addington Rd. E16—42Gc 85
Addington Rd. N4—30Qb 42
Addington Rd. Croy—74Qb 146
Addington Rd. S Croy—83Wb 165
Addington Rd. W Wick—77Ec 148
Addington Sq. SE5—51Tb 105
Addington St. SE1
—47Pb 82 (2J 205)
Addington Village Rd. Croy
—79Bc & 78Dc 148
Addis Clo. Enf—11Zb 26
Addiscombe Av. Croy—74Wb 147
Addiscombe Clo. Harr—29La 38
Addiscombe Ct. Rd. Croy
—74Ub 147
Addiscombe Gro. Croy—75Ub 147
Addiscombe Rd. Croy—75Ub 147
Addiscombe Rd. Wat—14X 19
Addison Av. N14—16Kb 24
Addison Av. W11—46Ab 80
Addison Av. Houn—53Ea 100
Addison Bri. Pl. W14—49Bb 81
Addison Clo. Cat—94Tb 181
Addison Clo. Iver—45G 74
Addison Clo. N'wd—25W 36
Addison Clo. Orp—72Sc 150
Addison Cres. W14—48Ab 80
Addison Gdns. W14—48Za 80
Addison Gdns. Surb—70Pa 123
Addison Gro. W4—48Ua 80
Addison Pl. SE25—70Wb 127
Addison Pl. W11—46Ab 80
Addison Pl. S'hall—45Ca 77
Addison Rd. E11—30Jc 45
Addison Rd. E17—29Dc 44
Addison Rd. SE25—70Wb 127
Addison Rd. W14—47Ab 80
Addison Rd. Brom—71Mc 149
Addison Rd. Cat—93Tb 181
Addison Rd. Enf—11Yb 26
Addison Rd. Ilf—25Sc 46

Addison Rd.—Allen Pl.

Addison Rd. Tedd—65Ka 122
Addison Rd. Wey—76K 139
Addisons Clo. Croy—75Bc 148
Addison Way. NW11—28Bb 41
Addison Way. Hay—44W 76
Addison Way. N'wd—25V 36
Addle Hill. EC4—44Rb 83 (3C 200)
Addlestone Moor. Wey—75L 139
Addlestone Pk. Wey—78K 139
Addlestone Rd. Wey—77N 139
Addle St. EC2—44Sb 83 (1E 200)
Adecroft Way. E Mol—69Ea 122
Adela Av. N Mald—71Xa 144
Adelaide Av. SE4—56Bc 106
Adelaide Clo. Enf—10Ub 11
Adelaide Clo. Slou—7E 72
Adelaide Clo. Stan—21Ja 38
Adelaide Cotts. W7—47Ha 78
Adelaide Ct. Beck—66Cc 128
Adelaide Gdns. Romf—29Ad 47
Adelaide Gro. W12—46Wa 80
Adelaide Pl. Wey—77T 140
Adelaide Rd. E10—34Ec 64
Adelaide Rd. NW3—38Fb 61
Adelaide Rd. W13—46Ja 78
Adelaide Rd. Ashf—64M 119
Adelaide Rd. Chst—64Rc 130
Adelaide Rd. Houn—53Aa 99
Adelaide Rd. Ilf—33Rc 66
Adelaide Rd. Rich—56Pa 101
Adelaide Rd. S'hall—49Aa 77
Adelaide Rd. Surb—71Na 143
Adelaide Rd. Tedd—65Ha 122
Adelaide Rd. Til—3B 114
Adelaide Rd. W on T—76W 140
Adelaide Sq. Wind—4H 95
Adelaide St. WC2
—45Nb 82 (5F 199)
Adelaide Ter. Bren—50Ma 79
Adelaide Wlk. SW9—56Qb 104
Adela St. W10—42Ab 80
Adelina Gro. E1—43Yb 84
Adeline Pl. WC1—43Mb 82 (1E 198)
Adelphi Cres. Hay—41V 76
Adelphi Cres. Horn—33Jd 68
Adelphi Gdns. Slou—7J 73
Adelphi Rd. Eps—85Ta 161
Adelphi Ter. WC2
—45Nb 82 (5G 199)
Adelphi Way. Hay—41V 76
Adeney Clo. W6—51Za 102
Aden Gro. N16—35Tb 63
Adenmore Rd. SE6—59Cc 106
Aden Rd. Enf—14Ac 26
Aden Rd. Ilf—31Sc 66
Aden Ter. N16—35Tb 63
Adhara Rd. N'wd—22V 36
Adie Rd. W6—48Ya 80
Adine Rd. E13—42Kc 85
Adler St. E1—44Wb 83
Adley St. E5—36Ac 64
Admaston Rd. SE18—52Sc 108
Admiral Hood Ho. Ger X—21A 34
Admirals Clo. E18—28Kc 45
Admiral Seymour Rd. SE9
—56Pc 108
Admirals Rd. Lea—100Ea 176
Admiral St. SE8—53Cc 106
Admirals Wlk. NW3—34Eb 61
Admirals Wlk. Coul—92Pb 180
Admiralty Rd. Tedd—65Ha 122
Adnams Wlk. Rain—37Jd 68
Adolf St. SE6—63Dc 128
Adolphus Rd. N4—32Rb 63
Adolphus St. SE8—52Bc 106
Adomar Rd. Dag—34Ad 67
Adpar St. W2—43Fb 81 (7B 190)
Adrian Av. NW2—32Xa 60
Adrian Clo. Uxb—25M 35
Adrian M. SW10—51Db 103
Adrian Rd. Abb L, Wat—3U 4
Adrienne Av. N'holt—41Ba 77
Ady's Rd. SE15—55Vb 105
Aerodrome Rd. NW9 & NW4
—27Va 40
Aerodrome Way. Houn—51Y 99
Aeroville. NW9—26Ua 40
Affleck St. N1—40Pb 62 (2J 193)
Afghan Rd. SW11—54Gb 103
Afton Dri. S Ock—44Xd 90
Agamemnon Rd. NW6—36Bb 61
Agar Clo. Surb—75Pa 143
Agar Gro. NW1—38Mb 62
Agar Gro. Est. NW1—38Mb 62
Agar Pl. NW1—38Lb 62
Agars Pl. Slou—1L 95
Agar St. WC2—45Nb 82 (5F 199)
Agate Rd. W6—48Ya 80
Agates La. Asht—90Ma 161
Agatha Clo. E1—46Xb 83
Agaton Rd. SE9—61Sc 130
Agave Rd. NW2—35Ya 60
Agdon St. EC1—42Rb 83 (5B 194)
Agincourt Rd. NW3—35Hb 61
Agister Rd. Chig—22Wc 47
Agnes Av. Ilf—35Qc 66
Agnes Clo. E6—45Qc 86
Agnes Gdns. Dag—35Zc 67
Agnes Rd. W3—46Va 80
Agnes St. E14—44Bc 84
Agnew Rd. SE23—59Zb 106
Agricola Pl. Enf—15Vb 25
Aidan Clo. Dag—35Ad 67
Aileen Wlk. E15—38Hc 65
Ailsa Av. Twic—57Ja 100
Ailsa Rd. Twic—57Ka 100
Ailsa St. E14—43Ec 84
Ainger Rd. NW3—38Hb 61
Ainsdale Cres. Pinn—27Ca 37
Ainsdale Rd. W5—42Ma 79
Ainsdale Rd. Wat—20Y 19
Ainsdale Way. Wok—6D 188
Ainsley Av. Romf—30Dd 48
Ainsley Clo. S Croy—86Xb 165
Ainsley St. E2—41Xb 83
Ainslie Wlk. SW12—59Kb 104
Ainslie Wood Cres. E4—22Dc 44
Ainslie Wood Gdns. E4—22Dc 44
Ainslie Wood Rd. E4—22Cc 44
Ainsty St. SE16—47Yb 84
Ainsworth Clo. NW2—34Wa 60
Ainsworth Rd. E9—38Yb 64
Ainsworth Rd. Croy—75Rb 147
Ainsworth Way. NW8—39Eb 61
Aintree Av. E6—39Nc 66
Aintree Clo. Grav—2D 136
Aintree Clo. Slou—53G 96
Aintree Clo. Uxb—44R 76
Aintree Cres. Ilf—26Sc 46
Aintree Gro. Upm—34Pd 69
Aintree Rd. Gnfd—40Ka 58
Aintree St. SW6—52Ab 102
Airdrie Clo. N1—38Pb 62
Airedale Av. W4—49Va 80
Airedale Av. S. W4—50Va 80
Airedale Clo. Dart—60Sd 112
Airedale Rd. SW12—59Hb 103
Airedale Rd. W5—48Ma 79
Aire Dri. S Ock—42Xd 90
Airfield Way. Horn—37Kd 69
Airlie Gdns. W8—46Cb 81
Airlie Gdns. Ilf—32Rc 66
Airlinks Industrial Est. Houn
—50Y 77
Airport Industrial Est. West
—87Mc 167
Airport Way. Stai—56J 97
Air St. W1—45Lb 82 (5C 198)
Airthrie Rd. Ilf—33Xc 67
Aisgill Av. W14—50Bb 81
Aisher Rd. SE28—45Yc 87
Aislibie Rd. SE12—56Gc 107
Aitken Clo. E8—39Wb 63
Aitken Rd. SE6—61Dc 128
Aitken Rd. Barn—15Ya 22
Ajax Av. NW9—27Ua 40
Ajax Av. Slou—5F 72
Ajax Rd. NW6—36Cb 61
Akehurst St. SW15—59Wa 102
Akenside Rd. NW3—36Fb 61
Akerman Rd. SW9—54Rb 105
Akerman Rd. Surb—72La 142
Akers La. Rick—16F 16
Alabama St. SE18—52Tc 108
Alacross Rd. W13—47La 78
Alamein Gdns. Dart—59Td 112
Alamein Rd. Swans—58Zd 113
Alanbrooke. Grav—9E 114
Alan Clo. Dart—56Ld 111
Alandale Dri. Pinn—25X 37
Alan Dri. Barn—16Ab 22
Alan Gdns. Romf—31Cd 68
Alan Rd. SW19—64Ab 124
Alanthus Clo. SE12—58Jc 107
Alan Way. Slou—44A 74
Alaska St. SE1—46Qb 82 (7K 199)
Alba Clo. Hay—42Z 77
Albacore Cres. SE13—58Dc 106
Alba Gdns. NW11—30Ab 40
Albain Cres. Ashf—61N 119
Alban Cres. Borwd—11Ra 21
Alban Cres. F'ham, Dart
—74Qd 153
Albans View. Wat—5X 5
Albany. W1—(5B 198)
Albany Clo. N15—28Rb 43
Albany Clo. SW14—56Ra 101
Albany Clo. Bex—59Yc 109
Albany Clo. Bush, Wat—16Fa 20
Albany Clo. Esh—81Ca 159
Albany Clo. Uxb—36Q 56
Albany Ct. Yd. W1—(5C 198)
Albany Cres. Edgw—24Qa 39
Albany Cres. Esh—79Ga 142
Albany M. King—65Ma 123
Albany Pde. Bren—51Na 101
Albany Pk. Av. Enf—11Yb 26
Albany Pk. Rd. King—65Ma 123
Albany Pk. Rd. Lea—91Ja 176
Albany Pas. Rich—57Na 101
Albany Pl. N7—35Qb 62
Albany Pl. Bren—51Na 101
Albany Pl. Egh—63D 118
Albany Rd. E10—31Cc 64
Albany Rd. E12—35Mc 65
Albany Rd. E17—30Ac 44
Albany Rd. N4—30Qb 42
Albany Rd. N18—22Xb 43
Albany Rd. SE5—51Tb 105 (7K 207)
Albany Rd. SW19—64Db 125
Albany Rd. W13—45Ka 78
Albany Rd. Belv—51Bd 109
Albany Rd. Bex—59Yc 109
Albany Rd. Bren—51Ma 101
Albany Rd. Brtwd—16Xd 32
Albany Rd. Chst—64Rc 130
Albany Rd. Enf—9Zb 12
Albany Rd. Horn—32Jd 68
Albany Rd. N Mald—70Ta 123
Albany Rd. Rich—57Pa 101
Albany Rd. Romf—30Bd 47
Albany Rd. W on T—77Z 141
Albany Rd. Wind—4H 95
Albany Rd. Wind—7L 95
(Old Windsor)
Albany St. NW1—40Kb 62 (1K 191)
Albany, The. Wfd G—21Hc 45
Albany View. Buck H—18Jc 27
Alba Pl. W11—44Bb 81
Albatross Gdns. S Croy—83Zb 166
Albatross St. SE18—52Uc 108
Albemarle App. Ilf—30Rc 46
Albemarle Av. Pot B—4Db 9
Albemarle Av. Twic—60Ba 99
Albemarle Clo. Grays—47Ce 91
Albemarle Gdns. Ilf—30Rc 46
Albemarle Gdns. N Mald
—70Ta 123
Albemarle Pk. Stan—22La 38
Albemarle Rd. Barn—17Gb 23
Albemarle Rd. Beck—67Dc 128
Albemarle St. W1—45Lb 82 (5A 198)
Albemarle Way. EC1
—42Rb 83 (6B 194)
Alberon Gdns. NW11—28Bb 41
Alberta Av. Sutt—78Ab 144
Alberta Rd. Enf—16Vb 25
Alberta Rd. Eri—53Ed 110
Alberta St. SE17—50Rb 83 (7B 206)
Albert Av. E4—21Cc 44
Albert Av. SW8—52Pb 104
Albert Av. Cher—69J 119
Albert Bri. SW3 & SW11—51Gb 103
Albert Bri. Rd. SW11—52Gb 103
Albert Carr Gdns. SW16
—64Nb 126
Albert Clo. N22—25Mb 42
Albert Clo. Slou—8K 73
Albert Ct. SW7—47Fb 81 (2B 202)
Albert Cres. E4—21Cc 44
Albert Dri. SW19—61Ab 124
Albert Dri. Wok—87E 156
Albert Embkmt. SE1
—50Nb 82 (7G 205)
(in two parts)
Albert Gdns. E1—44Zb 84
Albert Ga. SW1—47Hb 81 (1G 203)
Albert Gro. SW20—67Za 124
Albert Hall. Mans. SW7
—47Fb 81 (2B 202)
Albert M. W8—48Eb 81 (3A 202)
Albert Pl. N3—25Cb 41
Albert Pl. N17—27Vb 43
Albert Pl. W8—48Db 81
Albert Pl. Wind—10E 72
Albert Rd. E10—33Ec 64
Albert Rd. E16—46Nc 86
Albert Rd. E17—29Cc 44
Albert Rd. E18—27Kc 45
Albert Rd. N4—32Pb 62
Albert Rd. N15—30Ub 43
Albert Rd. N22—25Lb 42
Albert Rd. NW4—28Za 40
Albert Rd. NW6—40Bb 61
Albert Rd. NW7—22Va 40
Albert Rd. SE9—62Nc 130
Albert Rd. SE20—65Zb 128
Albert Rd. SE25—70Xb 127
Albert Rd. W5—42Ka 78
Albert Rd. Ashf—64P 119
Albert Rd. Asht—90Pa 161
Albert Rd. Barn—14Fb 23
Albert Rd. Belv—50Bd 87
Albert Rd. Bex—58Cd 110
Albert Rd. Brom—71Mc 149
Albert Rd. Buck H—19Mc 27
Albert Rd. Dag—32Cd 68
Albert Rd. Dart—62Ld 133
Albert Rd. Egh—5P 117
Albert Rd. Eps—85Va 162
Albert Rd. Hmptn—64Ea 122
Albert Rd. Harr—27Ea 38
Albert Rd. Hay—48U 76
Albert Rd. Houn—56Ca 99
Albert Rd. Ilf—34Sc 66
Albert Rd. King—68Pa 123
Albert Rd. Mitc—69Hb 125
Albert Rd. N Mald—70Va 124
Albert Rd. Orp—78Wc 151
(Chelsfield)
Albert Rd. Orp—72Xc 151
(St Mary Cray)
Albert Rd. Rich—57Na 101
Albert Rd. Romf—30Hd 48
Albert Rd. S'hall—48Z 77
Albert Rd. Sutt—78Fb 145
Albert Rd. Swans—58Be 113
Albert Rd. Tedd—65Ha 122
Albert Rd. Twic—60Ha 100
Albert Rd. Warl—89Bc 166
Albert Rd. W Dray—46N 75
Albert Rd. Wey—77M 139
Albert Rd. Wind—5H 95
Albert Rd. Est. Belv—50Bd 87
Albert Rd. N. Wat—13X 19
Albert Rd. S. Wat—13X 19
Albert Sq. E15—36Gc 65
Albert Sq. SW8—52Pb 104
Albert St. N12—22Eb 41
Albert St. NW1—39Kb 62 (1A 192)
Albert St. Brtwd—22Yd 50
Albert St. Slou—8K 73
(in two parts)
Albert St. Wat—14Y 19
Albert St. Wind—3F 94
Albert Studios. SW11—53Hb 103
Albert Ter. NW1—39Jb 62
Albert Ter. NW10—39Sa 59
Albert Ter. Buck H—19Nc 28
Albert Ter. M. NW1—39Jb 62
Albert Wlk. E16—47Qc 86
Albion Av. N10—25Jb 42
Albion Av. SW8—54Mb 104
Albion Bldgs. EC1
—43Sb 83 (1D 200)
Albion Clo. W2—45Gb 81 (4E 196)
Albion Clo. Romf—30Fd 48
Albion Clo. Slou—6L 73
Albion Dri. E8—38Vb 63
Albion Gdns. W6—49Xa 80
Albion Gro. N16—35Ub 63
Albion Hill. Lou—15Lc 27
Albion M. N1—38Qb 62
Albion M. NW6—38Bb 61
Albion M. W2—45Gb 81 (4E 196)
Albion Pde. Grav—8F 114
Albion Pk. Lou—15Mc 27
Albion Pl. EC1—43Tb 83 (7B 194)
Albion Pl. EC2—43Rb 83 (1G 201)
Albion Pl. SE25—69Wb 127
Albion Rd. E17—27Ec 44
Albion Rd. N16—35Tb 63
Albion Rd. N17—26Wb 43
Albion Rd. Bexh—56Cd 110
Albion Rd. Grav—9E 114
Albion Rd. Hay—44U 76
Albion Rd. Houn—56Ca 99
Albion Rd. King—67Sa 123
Albion Rd. Sutt—79Fb 145
Albion Rd. Twic—60Ga 100
Albion Sq. E8—38Vb 63
Albion St. SE16—47Yb 84
Albion St. W2—44Gb 81 (3E 196)
Albion St. Croy—74Rb 147
Albion Ter. E8—38Vb 63
Albion Ter. Grav—8E 114
Albion Vs. Rd. SE26—62Yb 128
Albion Way. SE13—56Ec 106
Albion Way. Wemb—34Qa 59
Albrighton Rd. SE5—55Ub 105
Albuhera Clo. Enf—11Qb 24
Albury Av. Bexh—54Ad 109
Albury Av. Iswth—52Ha 100
Albury Av. Sutt—81Ya 162
Albury Clo. Hmptn—65Da 121
Albury Dri. Pinn—25Y 37
Albury Gro. Rd. Wal X—2Zb 12
Albury Ride. Wal X—3Zb 12
Albury Rd. Chess—78Na 143
Albury Rd. Red—100Lb 180
Albury Rd. W on T—79U 140
Albury St. SE8—51Cc 106
Albury Wlk. Wal X—3Zb 12
Albyfield. Brom—69Pc 130
Albyn Rd. SE8—53Cc 106
Albyns Clo. Rain—38Jd 68
Alcester Cres. E5—33Xb 63
Alcester Rd. Wall—77Kb 146
Alcock Clo. Wall—80Mb 146
Alcock Rd. Houn—52Z 99
Alcocks Clo. Tad—92Ab 178
Alcocks La. Tad—93Ab 178
Alconbury Rd. E5—33Wb 63
Alcorn Clo. Sutt—75Cb 145
Alcott Clo. W7—43Ha 78
Aldam Pl. N16—33Vb 63
Aldborough Rd. Dag—37Ed 68
Aldborough Rd. Upm—33Pd 69
Aldborough Rd. N. Ilf—29Vc 47
Aldborough Rd. S. Ilf—32Uc 66
Aldborough Spur. Slou—4J 73
Aldbourne Rd. W12—46Va 80
Aldbourne Rd. Slou—3A 72
Aldbridge St. SE17
—50Ub 83 (7H 207)
Aldbury Av. Wemb—38Ra 59
Aldbury Clo. Wat—8Z 5
Aldbury M. N9—17Tb 25
Aldbury Rd. Rick—17H 17
Aldebert Ter. SW8—52Pb 104
Aldeburgh Clo. E5—33Xb 63
Aldeburgh Pl. Wfd G—21Jc 45
Aldeburgh St. SE10—50Jc 85
Alden Av. E3—41Hc 85
Aldenham Av. Rad—8Ja 6
Aldenham Dri. Uxb—42R 76
Aldenham Gro. Rad—6Ka 6
Aldenham Rd. Rad—7Ja 6
Aldenham Rd. Wat & Borwd
—11Ga 20
Aldenham Rd. Wat & Bush, Wat
Aldenham St. NW1
—40Mb 62 (2C 192)
Aldenholme. Wey—79U 140
Aldensley Rd. W6—48Xa 80
Alden View. Wind—3B 94
Alder Av. Upm—35Pd 69
Alderbourne La. Slou & Iver
—35A 54
Alderbrook Rd. SW12—58Kb 104
Alderbury Rd. SW13—51Wa 102
Alderbury Rd. Slou—47B 74
Alderbury Rd. W. Slou—47B 74
Alder Clo. SE15—51Vb 105
Alder Clo. Egh—64A 118
Aldercombe La. Cat—99Ub 181
Alder Croft. Coul—88Pb 164
Alder Gro. NW2—33Wa 60
Aldergrove Gdns. Houn—54Aa 99
Aldergrove Wlk. Horn—37Ld 69
Alderholt Way. SE15—52Ub 105
Alderman Av. Bark—41Wc 87
Aldermanbury. EC2
—44Sb 83 (2E 200)
Aldermanbury Sq. EC2
—43Sb 83 (1E 200)
Alderman Judge Mall. King
—68Na 123
Aldermans Hill. N13—21Nb 42
Alderman's Wlk. EC2
—43Ub 83 (1H 201)
Aldermary Rd. Brom—67Jc 129
Aldermaston St. W10—44Za 80
Alder M. N19—33Lb 62
Alderminster Rd. SE1—50Wb 83
Aldermour Rd. SE6—62Bc 128
Alderney Av. Houn—52Da 99
Alderney Gdns. N'holt—38Ba 57
Alderney Rd. E1—42Zb 84
Alderney Rd. Eri—52Jd 110
Alderney St. SW1
—50Kb 82 (7A 204)
Alder Rd. SW14—55Ta 101
Alder Rd. Sidc—62Vc 131
Alder Rd. Uxb—37L 55
Alders Av. Wfd G—23Gc 45
Aldersbrook Av. Enf—12Ub 25
Aldersbrook Dri. King—65Pa 123
Aldersbrook La. E12—34Pc 66
Aldersbrook Rd.—33Kc 65
E11 1-13
E12 remainder
Alders Clo. Edgw—22Sa 39
Aldersey Gdns. Bark—37Tc 66
Aldersford Clo. SE4—56Zb 106
Aldersgate St. EC1
—43Sb 83 (7D 194)
Aldersgrove. E Mol—71Fa 142
Aldersgrove. Wal A—6Gc 13
Aldersgrove Av. SE9—62Mc 129
Aldershot Rd. NW6—39Bb 61
Alderside Wlk. Egh—64A 118
Aldersmead Av. Croy—72Zb 148
Aldersmead Rd. Beck—66Ac 128
Alderson St. W10—42Ab 80
Alders Rd. Edgw—22Sa 39
Alderstead La. Red—96Mb 180
Alderstead La. Red—97Mb 180
Alders, The. N21—16Rb 25
Alders, The. Felt—63Aa 121
Alders, The. Houn—51Ba 99
Alders, The. W Wick—75Dc 148
Alderton Clo. Brtwd—15Xd 32
Alderton Clo. Lou—14Qc 28
Alderton Cres. NW4—29Xa 40
Alderton Hall La. Lou—14Qc 28
Alderton Hill. Lou—15Nc 28
Alderton Rise. Lou—14Qc 28
Alderton Rd. SE24—55Sb 105
Alderton Rd. Croy—73Vb 147
Alderton Way. NW4—29Xa 40
Alderton Way. Lou—15Pc 28
Alderville Rd. SW6—54Bb 103
Alder Way. Swan—68Fd 132
Alderwick Dri. Houn—55Fa 100
Alderwood Clo. Cat—97Ub 181
Alderwood Clo. Romf—13Xc 29
Alderwood Dri. Romf—13Xc 29
Alderwood Rd. SE9—58Tc 108
Aldford St. W1—46Jb 82 (6H 197)
Aldgate. EC3—44Vb 83 (3K 201)
Aldgate High St. EC3
—44Vb 83 (3K 201)
Aldin Av. N. Slou—7L 73
Aldin Av. S. Slou—7L 73
Aldine Pl. W12—47Ya 80
Aldine St. W12—47Ya 80
Aldingham Gdns. Horn—36Jd 68
Aldington Rd. SE18—48Mc 85
Aldis M. SW17—64Gb 125
Aldis St. SW17—64Gb 125
Aldred Rd. NW6—36Cb 61
Aldren Rd. SW17—62Eb 125
Aldrich Cres. Croy—81Ec 166
Aldriche Way. E4—23Ec 44
Aldrich Ter. SW18—61Eb 125
Aldridge Av. Edgw—20Ra 21
Aldridge Av. Enf—10Cc 12
Aldridge Av. Ruis—33Y 57
Aldridge Av. Stan—25Na 39
Aldridge Rise. N Mald—73Ua 144
Aldridge Rd. Slou—2E 72
Aldridge Rd. Vs. W11—43Bb 81
Aldridge Wlk. N14—17Nb 24
Aldrin Clo. Stanf—1N 93
Aldrington Rd. SW16—64Lb 126
Aldsworth Clo. W9—42Db 81
Aldwick Clo. SE9—62Tc 130
Aldwick Rd. Croy—76Pb 146
Aldworth Gro. SE13—58Ec 106
Aldworth Rd. E15—38Gc 65
Aldwych. WC2—44Pb 82 (4H 199)
Aldwych Av. Ilf—28Sc 46
Aldwych Clo. Horn—33Kd 69
Alers Rd. Bexh—57Zc 109
Alexander Av. NW10—38Xa 60
Alexander Clo. Brom—74Jc 149
Alexander Clo. Sidc—58Uc 108
Alexander Clo. Twic—61Ha 122
Alexander Godley Clo. Asht
—91Pa 177
Alexander La. Brtwd—15Ce 33
Alexander M. W2—44Db 81
Alexander Pl. SW7
—49Gb 81 (5D 202)
Alexander Rd. N19—34Nb 62
Alexander Rd. Bexh—54Zc 109
Alexander Rd. Chst—65Rc 130
Alexander Rd. Coul—87Kb 164
Alexander Rd. Egh—64E 118
Alexander Rd. Grnh—57Yd 112
Alexander Sq. SW3
—49Gb 81 (5D 202)
Alexander St. W2—44Db 81
Alexanders Wlk. Cat—98Vb 181
Alexandra Av. N22—25Mb 42
Alexandra Av. SW11—53Jb 104
Alexandra Av. W4—52Ta 101
Alexandra Av. Harr—32Ba 57
Alexandra Av. S'hall—45Ba 77
Alexandra Av. Sutt—76Cb 145
Alexandra Av. Warl—89Bc 166
Alexandra Clo. Ashf—66T 120
Alexandra Clo. Grays—7E 92
Alexandra Clo. Harr—34Ca 57
Alexandra Clo. K Lan—2J 3
Alexandra Clo. Stai—65M 119
Alexandra Clo. Swan—68Gd 132
Alexandra Clo. W on T—75W 140
Alexandra Cotts. SE14—53Bc 106
Alexandra Ct. N14—15Lb 24
Alexandra Cres. Brom—65Hc 129
Alexandra Dri. SE19—64Ub 127
Alexandra Dri. Surb—73Qa 143
Alexandra Gdns. N10—28Kb 42
Alexandra Gdns. W4—52Ua 102
Alexandra Gdns. Cars—81Jb 164
Alexandra Gdns. Houn—54Da 99
Alexandra Gro. N4—32Rb 63
Alexandra Gro. N12—22Db 41
Alexandra M. SW19—65Bb 125
Alexandra Pk. Rd.—26Kb 42
N10 1-121 & 2-126c
N22 remainder
Alexandra Pl. NW8—39Eb 61
Alexandra Pl. SE25—71Tb 147
Alexandra Pl. Croy—74Ub 147
Alexandra Rd. E6—41Qc 86
Alexandra Rd. E10—34Ec 64
Alexandra Rd. E17—31Bc 64
Alexandra Rd. E18—27Kc 45
Alexandra Rd. N8—27Qb 42
Alexandra Rd. N9—17Xb 25
Alexandra Rd. N10—25Kb 42
Alexandra Rd. N15—29Tb 43
Alexandra Rd. NW4—28Za 40
Alexandra Rd. NW8—39Eb 61
Alexandra Rd. SE26—65Zb 128
Alexandra Rd. SW14—55Ta 101
Alexandra Rd. SW19—65Bb 125
Alexandra Rd. W4—47Ta 79
Alexandra Rd. Ashf—66T 120
Alexandra Rd. Borwd—11Ta 21
Alexandra Rd. Bren—51Ma 101
Alexandra Rd. Brtwd—20Yd 32
Alexandra Rd. Croy—74Ub 147
Alexandra Rd. Egh—5N 117
Alexandra Rd. Enf—14Zb 26
Alexandra Rd. Eps—85Va 162
Alexandra Rd. Eri—51Hd 110
Alexandra Rd. Grav—9G 114
Alexandra Rd. Houn—54Da 99
Alexandra Rd. K Lan—1Q 4
Alexandra Rd. King—66Qa 123
Alexandra Rd. Mitc—66Gb 125
Alexandra Rd. Rain—39Hd 68
Alexandra Rd. Rich—54Pa 101
Alexandra Rd. Rick—8J 3
Alexandra Rd. Romf—30Hd 48
Alexandra Rd. Romf—30Zc 47
(Chadwell Heath)
Alexandra Rd. Slou—8H 73
Alexandra Rd. Th Dit—71Ha 142
Alexandra Rd. Til—4B 114
Alexandra Rd. Twic—58La 100
Alexandra Rd. Uxb—40M 55
Alexandra Rd. Warl—89Bc 166
Alexandra Rd. Wat—12W 18
Alexandra Rd. West—91Kc 183
Alexandra Rd. Wey—77M 139
Alexandra Rd. Wind—4H 95
Alexandra Sq. Mord—71Cb 145
Alexandra St. E16—43Jc 85
Alexandra St. SE14—52Ac 106
Alexandra Wlk. SE19—65Ub 127
Alexandra Way. Grays—9K 93
Alexandra Way. Wal X—6Bc 12
Alexandria Rd. W13—45Ka 78
Alexis St. SE16—49Wb 83
Alfan La. Dart—64Fd 132
Alfearn Rd. E5—35Yb 64
Alford Grn. Croy—79Fc 149
Alford Pl. N1—40Sb 63 (2E 194)
Alford Rd. SW8—53Mb 104
Alford Rd. Eri—50Ed 88
Alfoxton Av. N15—28Rb 43
Alfreda St. SW11—53Kb 104
Alfred Gdns. S'hall—45Aa 77
Alfred M. W1—43Mb 82 (7D 192)
Alfred Pl. WC1—43Mb 82 (7D 192)
Alfred Pl. Grav—10B 114
Alfred Rd. E15—36Hc 65
Alfred Rd. SE25—71Wb 147
Alfred Rd. W2—43Cb 81
Alfred Rd. W3—46Sa 79
Alfred Rd. Belv—50Bd 87
Alfred Rd. Brtwd—19Zd 33
Alfred Rd. Buck H—19Mc 27
Alfred Rd. Dart—63Pd 133
Alfred Rd. Felt—61Y 121
Alfred Rd. Grav—1D 136
Alfred Rd. King—69Pa 123
Alfred Rd. S Ock—46Sd 90
Alfred Rd. Sutt—78Eb 145
Alfred's Gdns. Bark—40Uc 66
Alfred St. E3—41Bc 84
Alfred St. E16—45Hc 85
Alfred St. Grays—51Ee 113
Alfreds Way. Bark—41Rc 86
Alfreton Clo. SW19—62Za 124
Alfriston. Surb—72Pa 143
Alfriston Av. Croy—73Nb 146
Alfriston Av. Harr—30Ca 37
Alfriston Clo. Surb—72Pa 143
Alfriston Rd. SW11—57Hb 103
Algar Clo. Iswth—55Ja 100
Algar Clo. Stan—22Ha 38
Algar Rd. Iswth—55Ja 100
Algarve Rd. SW18—60Db 103
Algernon Rd. NW4—30Wa 40
Algernon Rd. NW6—39Cb 61
Algernon Rd. SE13—56Dc 106
Algers Clo. Lou—15Mc 27
Algers Mead. Lou—15Mc 27
Algers Rd. Lou—15Nc 28
Algiers Rd. SE13—56Cc 106
Alibon Gdns. Dag—36Cd 68
Alibon Rd. Dag—36Cd 68
Alice Ruston Pl. Wok—7F 188
Alice St. SE1—48Ub 83 (4H 207)
Alica St. SE1
Alicia Av. Harr—28Ka 38
Alicia Clo. Harr—29La 38
Alicia Gdns. Harr—28Ka 38
Alie St. E1—44Vb 83 (3K 201)
Alington Cres. NW9—31Sa 59
Alington Gro. Wall—81Lb 164
Alison Clo. Croy—74Zb 148
Alison Clo. Wok—86A 156
Aliwal Rd. SW11—56Gb 103
Alkerden La. Grnh & Swans
—58Yd 112
Alkerden Rd. W4—50Ua 80
Alkham Rd. N16—33Vb 63
Allan Clo. N Mald—71Ta 143
Allandale Av. N3—27Ab 40
Allandale Cres. Pot B—4Ab 8
Allandale Pl. Orp—76Zc 151
Allandale Rd. Enf—8Zb 12
Allandale Rd. Horn—31Hd 68
Allan Way. W3—43Sa 79
Allard Clo. Orp—73Yc 151
Allard Cres. Bush, Wat—19Ea 20
Allardyce St. SW4—56Pb 104
Allbrook Clo. Tedd—64Ga 122
Allcroft Rd. NW5—36Jb 62
Allenby Av. S Croy—81Sb 165
Allenby Clo. Gnfd—41Ca 77
Allenby Cres. Grays—50Ee 91
Allenby Dri. Horn—32Nd 69
Allenby Rd. SE23—62Ac 128
Allenby Rd. S'hall—44Ca 77
Allenby Rd. West—89Nc 168
Allen Clo. Sun—67X 121
Allendale Av. S'hall—44Ca 77
Allendale Clo. SE5—53Tb 105
Allendale Clo. SE26—64Zb 128
Allendale Clo. Dart—60Td 112
Allendale Rd. Gnfd—37Ka 58
Allen Edwards Dri. SW8
—53Nb 104
Allen Pl. Twic—60Ja 100

Allen Rd.—Arcade, The

Allen Rd. E3—39Bc 64
Allen Rd. N16—35Ub 63
Allen Rd. Beck—68Zb 128
Allen Rd. Croy—74Qb 146
Allen Rd. Lea—98Da 175
Allen Rd. Rain—41Ld 89
Allen Rd. Sun—67X 121
Allensbury Pl. NW1—38Mb 62
Allens Rd. Enf—15Yb 26
Allen St. W8—48Cb 81
Allensway. Stanf—1P 93
Allenswood Rd. SE9—55Nc 108
Allerds Rd. Slou—9D 52
Allerford Ct. Harr—29Ea 38
Allerford Rd. SE6—62Dc 128
Allerton Clo. Borwd—10Pa 7
Allerton Rd. N16—33Sb 63
Allerton Rd. Borwd—10Na 7
Allerton Wlk. N7—33Pb 62
Allestree Rd. SW6—52Ab 102
Alleyn Cres. SE21—61Tb 127
Alleyndale Rd. Dag—33Yc 67
Alleyn Pk. SE21—61Tb 127
Alleyn Pk. S'hall—50Ca 77
Alleyn Rd. SE21—62Tb 127
Allfarthing La. SW18—58Db 103
Allgood Clo. Mord—72Za 144
Allgood St. E2—40Vb 63
Allhallows La. EC4
—45Tb 83 (5F 201)
All Hallows Rd. E6—43Mc 85
All Hallows Rd. N17—25Ub 43
Allhusen Gdns. Slou—35A 54
Alliance Rd. E13—43Lc 85
Alliance Rd. SE18—51Wc 109
Alliance Rd. W3—42Ra 79
Allingham Clo. W7—45Ha 78
Allingham St. N1
—40Sb 63 (1D 194)
Allington Av. N17—23Ub 43
Allington Clo. SW19—64Za 124
Allington Clo. Enf—15Zb 26
Allington Ct. Slou—5K 73
Allington Rd. NW4—30Xa 40
Allington Rd. W10—40Ab 60
Allington Rd. Harr—29Ea 38
Allington Rd. Orp—75Tc 150
Allington St. SW1
—48Kb 82 (4A 204)
Allison Clo. SE10—53Ec 106
Allison Clo. Wal A—4Jc 13
Allison Gro. SE21—60Ub 105
Allison Rd. N8—29Qb 42
Allison Rd. W3—44Sa 79
Allistonway. Stanf—1P 93
Allitsen Rd. NW8
—40Gb 61 (2D 190)
Allnuts Rd. Epp—5Wc 15
Allnutt Way. SW4—57Mb 104
Alloa Rd. SE8—50Ac 84
Alloa Rd. Ilf—33Wc 67
Allonby Gdns. Wemb—32La 58
Alloway Clo. Wok—6E 188
Alloway Rd. E3—41Ac 84
All Saints Clo. N9—19Wb 25
★All Saints Clo. Brtwd—8Xd
All Saints Clo. Chig—20Wc 29
All Saints Clo. Swans—57Be 113
All Saints Cres. Wat—5Z 5
All Saints Dri. SE3—54Gc 107
All Saints Dri. S Croy—84Vb 165
All Saints La. Rick—16Q 18
All Saints M. Harr—23Ga 38
All Saints Pas. SW18—57Cb 103
All Saint's Rd. SW19—66Eb 125
All Saints Rd. W3—48Sa 79
All Saints Rd. W11—43Bb 81
All Saints Rd. Grav—10B 114
All Saints Rd. Sutt—76Db 145
All Saints St. N1—40Pb 62 (1H 193)
Allsop Pl. NW1—42Hb 81 (6G 191)
All Souls Av. NW10—40Xa 60
All Soul's Pl. W1—43Kb 82 (1A 198)
Allum Clo. Borwd—14Na 21
Allum La. Borwd—15Na 21
Allum Way. N20—18Eb 23
Allwood Clo. SE26—63Ac 128
Allyn Clo. Stai—65H 119
Alma Av. E4—24Ec 44
Alma Av. Horn—35Nd 69
Almack Rd. E5—35Yb 64
Alma Clo. Wok—5B 188
Alma Ct. Borwd—10Pa 7
Alma Cres. Sutt—78Ab 144
Alma Gro. SE1—49Vb 83
Alma Pl. NW10—41Xa 80
Alma Pl. SE19—66Vb 127
Alma Pl. Sun—66W 120
Alma Pl. T Hth—71Qb 146
Alma Rd. N10—24Kb 42
Alma Rd. SW18—56Eb 103
Alma Rd. Cars.—78Gb 145
Alma Rd. Enf—15Ac 26
Alma Rd. Esh—74Ga 142
Alma Rd. Orp—75Zc 151
Alma Rd. Sidc—62Wc 131
Alma Rd. S'hall—45Aa 77
Alma Rd. Swans—57Be 113
Alma Rd. Wind—4G 94
Alma Rd. Wind—9D 72
(Eton Wick)
Alma Row. Harr—25Fa 38
Alma Sq. NW8—40Eb 61 (3A 190)
Alma St. E15—37Fc 65
Alma St. NW5—37Kb 62
Alma Ter. SW18—59Fb 103
Almeida St. N1—39Rb 63
Almeric Rd. SW11—56Hb 103
Almer Rd. SW20—66Wa 124
Almington St. N4—32Pb 62
Almners Rd. Cher—74C 138
Almond Av. W5—48Na 79
Almond Av. Cars—75Hb 145
Almond Av. Uxb—34R 56
Almond Av. W Dray—48Q 76
Almond Av. Wok—9G 188
Almond Clo. SE15—54Wb 105
Almond Clo. Brom—73Qc 150
Almond Clo. Egh—5M 117
Almond Clo. Grays—8C 92
Almond Clo. Hay—45U 76
Almond Clo. Ruis—34V 56
Almond Clo. Shep—68S 120
Almond Dri. Swan—68Fd 132
Almond Gro. Bren—52Ka 100
Almond Rd. N17—24Wb 43
Almond Rd. SE16—49Xb 83
Almond Rd. Dart—59Sd 112
Almond Rd. Eps—83Ta 161
Almond Rd. Slou—10A 52
Almonds Av. Buck H—19Jc 27
Almond Ville. Slou—1A 72
Almond Way. Borwd—14Ra 21
Almond Way. Brom—73Qc 150
Almond Way. Harr—26Ea 38
Almond Way. Mitc—71Mb 146
Almons Way. Slou—3M 73
Almorah Rd. N1—38Tb 63
Almorah Rd. Houn—53Z 99
Alms Heath. Wok—93R 174
Almshouse La. Chess—81Ma 161
Almshouse La. Enf—9Xb 11
Alnwick Av. E16—44Mc 85
Alnwick Gro. Mord—70Db 125
Alnwick Rd. E16—44Lc 85
Alnwick Rd. SE12—59Kc 107
Alperton La. Gnfd—41La 78
Alperton St. W10—42Bb 81
Alpha Clo. NW1—42Gb 81 (4E 190)
Alpha Gro. E14—47Cc 84
Alpha Pl. NW6—40Cb 61
Alpha Pl. SW3—51Gb 103
Alpha Rd. E4—20Cc 26
Alpha Rd. N18—23Wb 43
Alpha Rd. SE14—53Bc 106
Alpha Rd. Brtwd—16Fe 33
Alpha Rd. Croy—74Ub 147
Alpha Rd. Enf—14Ac 26
Alpha Rd. Surb—72Pa 143
Alpha Rd. Tedd—64Fa 122
Alpha Rd. Uxb—42R 76
Alpha Rd. Wok—88D 156
Alpha St. SE15—54Wb 105
Alpha St. Slou—8K 73
Alpha St. S. Slou—7K 73
Alpine Av. Surb—75Sa 143
Alpine Clo. Croy—76Ub 147
Alpine Copse. Brom—68Qc 130
Alpine Rd. SE16—49Yb 84
Alpine Rd. W on T—73W 140
Alpine Wlk. Stan—19Ga 20
Alpine Way. E6—43Qc 86
Alric Av. NW10—38Ta 59
Alric Av. N Mald—69Ua 124
Alroy Rd. N4—31Qb 62
Alsace Rd. SE17—50Ub 83 (7H 207)
Alscot Rd. SE1—48Vb 83 (5K 207)
Alscot Way. SE1
—49Vb 83 (5K 207)
Alsike Rd. SE2 & Eri—48Zc 87
Alsom Av. Wor Pk—77Wa 144
Alston Clo. Surb—73Ka 142
Alston Rd. N18—22Xb 43
Alston Rd. SW17—63Fb 125
Alston Rd. Barn—13Ab 22
Altair Clo. N17—23Vb 43
Altair Way. N'wd—21V 36
Altash Way. SE9—61Pc 130
Altenburg Av. W13—48Ka 78
Altenburg Gdns. SW11—56Hb 103
Alterton Clo. Wok—5D 188
Alt Gro. SW19—66Bb 125
Altham Rd. Pinn—24Aa 37
Althea St. SW6—54Db 103
Althorne Gdns. E18—28Hc 45
Althorne Way. Dag—33Cd 68
Althorpe M. SW11—53Fb 103
Althorpe Rd. Harr—29Ea 38
Althorp Rd. SW17—60Hb 103
Altmore Av. E6—38Pc 66
Alton Av. Stan—24Ha 38
Altona Way. Slou—4F 72
Alton Clo. Bex—60Ad 109
Alton Clo. Iswth—54Ha 100
Alton Gdns. Beck—66Cc 128
Alton Gdns. Twic—59Fa 100
Alton Rd. N17—27Tb 43
Alton Rd. SW15—60Wa 102
Alton Rd. Croy—76Qb 146
Alton Rd. Rich—56Na 101
Alton St. E14—44Dc 84
Altwood Clo. Slou—3C 72
Altyre Clo. Beck—71Bc 148
Altyre Rd. Croy—75Tb 147
Altyre Way. Beck—71Bc 148
Aluric Clo. Grays—9D 92
Alvanley Gdns. NW6—36Db 61
Alva Way. Wat—19Z 19
Alverstoke Rd. Romf—24Nd 49
Alverstone Av. SW19—61Cb 125
Alverstone Av. Barn—17Gb 23
Alverstone Gdns. SE9—60Sc 108
Alverstone Rd. E12—35Qc 66
Alverstone Rd. NW2—38Ya 60
Alverstone Rd. N Mald—70Va 124
Alverstone Rd. Wemb—32Pa 59
Alverston Gdns. SE25—71Ub 147
Alverton St. SE8—50Bc 84
Alveston Av. Harr—27Ka 38
Alvey St. SE17—50Ub 83 (7H 207)
Alvington Cres. E8—36Vb 63
Alvista Av. M'head—4A 72
Alway Av. Eps—78Ta 143
Alwen Gro. S Ock—44Xd 90
Alwold Cres. SE12—58Kc 107
Alwyn Av. W4—50Ta 79
Alwyn Clo. Borwd—15Pa 21
Alwyn Clo. Croy—80Dc 148
Alwyne Av. Brtwd—16Ce 33
Alwyne La. N1—38Rb 63
Alwyne Pl. N1—37Sb 63
Alwyne Rd. N1—38Sb 63
Alwyne Rd. SW19—65Bb 125
Alwyne Rd. W7—45Ga 78
Alwyne Sq. N1—37Sb 63
Alwyne Vs. N1—38Rb 63
Alwyn Gdns. W3—44Ra 79
Alwyns Clo. Cher—72J 139
Alyth Gdns. NW11—30Cb 41
Alywns La. Cher—72H 139
Amalgamated Rd. Bren—51Ka 100
Amanda Clo. Ilf—23Tc 46
Amanda Ct. Slou—8P 73
Amazon St. E1—44Wb 83
Ambassador Clo. Houn—54Aa 99
Ambassadors' Ct. SW1—(7C 198)
Amber Av. E17—25Ac 44
Ambercroft Way. Coul—91Rb 181
Amberden Av. N3—27Cb 41
Ambergate St. SE17
—50Rb 83 (7C 206)
Amberley Clo. Orp—78Vc 151
Amberley Clo. Pinn—27Ba 37
Amberley Clo. Wok—97H 173
Amberley Ct. Sidc—64Yc 131
Amberley Dri. Wey—83H 157
Amberley Gdns. Enf—17Ub 25
Amberley Gdns. Eps—77Va 144
Amberley Gro. SE26—64Xb 127
Amberley Gro. Croy—73Vb 147
Amberley Rd. E10—31Dc 64
Amberley Rd. N13—19Pb 24
Amberley Rd. SE2—51Zc 109
Amberley Rd. W9—43Cb 81
Amberley Rd. Buck H—18Lc 27
Amberley Rd. Enf—17Vb 25
Amberley Rd. Slou—3C 72
Amberley Way. Houn—57Y 99
Amberley Way. Mord—73Bb 145
Amberley Way. Romf—28Dd 48
Amber St. E15—37Fc 65
Amberwood Rise. N Mald
—72Ua 144
Amblecote. Cob—84Z 159
Amblecote Clo. SE12—62Kc 129
Amblecote Rd. SE12—62Kc 129
Ambler Rd. N4—34Rb 63
Ambleside. Brom—65Fc 129
Ambleside. Epp—3Wc 15
Ambleside Av. SW16—63Mb 126
Ambleside Av. Beck—71Ac 148
Ambleside Av. Horn—36Kd 69
Ambleside Av. W on T—74Y 141
Ambleside Clo. E9—36Yb 64
Ambleside Clo. E10—32Dc 64
Ambleside Cres. Enf—13Zb 26
Ambleside Gdns. SW16—64Mb 126
Ambleside Gdns. Ilf—29Nc 46
Ambleside Gdns. S Croy
—82Zb 166
Ambleside Gdns. Sutt—79Eb 145
Ambleside Gdns. Wemb—32Ma 59
Ambleside Rd. NW10—38Va 60
Ambleside Rd. Bexh—54Cd 110
Ambrey Way. Wall—81Mb 164
Ambrooke Rd. Belv—48Cd 88
Ambrosden Av. SW1
—48Lb 82 (4C 204)
Ambrose Av. NW11—30Bb 41
Ambrose Clo. Orp—76Vc 151
Ambrose St. SE16—49Xb 83
Ambrose Wlk. E3—40Cc 64
Amelia St. SE17—50Sb 83 (7C 206)
Amen Corner. EC4
—44Rb 83 (3C 200)
Amen Corner. SW17—65Hb 125
Amen Ct. EC4—44Rb 83 (3C 200)
Amerden Way. Slou—7E 72
America Sq. EC3
—45Vb 83 (4K 201)
America St. SE1—46Sb 83 (7D 200)
Ameriand Rd. SW18—58Bb 103
Amersham Av. N18—23Tb 43
Amersham Clo. Romf—23Pd 49
Amersham Dri. Romf—23Pd 49
Amersham Gro. SE14—52Bc 106
Amersham Rd. SE14—53Bc 106
Amersham Rd. Amer & Rick
—11A 16
Amersham Rd. Croy—72Sb 147
Amersham Rd. Ger X—21A 34
Amersham Rd. Ger X & Uxb
—31C 54
Amersham Rd. Harr—30Ga 38
Amersham Rd. Romf—23Pd 49
Amersham Vale. SE14—52Bc 106
Amersham Wlk. Romf—23Pd 49
Amersham Way. Amer—11A 16
Amery Gdns. NW10—39Xa 60
Amery Gdns. Romf—27Md 49
Amery Rd. Harr—33Ja 58
Amesbury. Wal A—4Jc 13
Amesbury Av. SW2—61Nb 126
Amesbury Clo. Epp—3Vc 15
Amesbury Clo. Wor Pk—74Ya 144
Amesbury Dri. E4—16Dc 26
Amesbury Rd. Brom—69Mc 129
Amesbury Rd. Dag—38Zc 67
Amesbury Rd. Epp—3Vc 15
Amesbury Rd. Felt—61Z 121
Ames Rd. Swans—58Ae 113
Amethyst Rd. E15—35Fc 65
Amey Dri. Lea—96Ea 176
Amhen Way. SE22—57Ub 105
Amherst Av. W13—44La 78
Amherst Clo. Orp—70Xc 131
Amherst Dri. Orp—70Vc 131
Amherst Hill. Sev—95Hd 186
Amherst Rd. W13—44La 78
Amherst Rd. Sev—94Kd 187
Amhurst Gdns. Iswth—54Ja 100
Amhurst Pk. N16—31Tb 63
Amhurst Pas. E8—36Wb 63
Amhurst Rd.—35Vb 63
E8 1-233 & 2-240
N16 remainder
Amhurst Ter. E8—35Wb 63
Amidas Gdns. Dag—35Xc 67
Amiel St. E1—42Yb 84
Amies St. SW11—55Hb 103
Amina Way. SE16—48Wb 83
Amis Av. Eps—79Ra 143
Amis Av. Wey—83J 157
Amis Rd. Wok—7B 188
Amity Gro. SW20—67Ya 124
Amity Rd. E15—38Hc 65
Amner Rd. SW11—58Jb 104
Amor Rd. W6—48Ya 80
Amos Est. SE16—46Zb 84
Amott Rd. SE15—55Wb 105
Amoy Pl. E14—45Cc 84
Ampleforth Rd. SE2—47Xc 87
Ampthill Est. NW1
—40Lb 62 (2C 192)
Ampton Pl. WC1—41Pb 82 (4H 193)
Ampton St. WC1—41Pb 82 (4H 193)
Amroth Clo. SE23—60Xb 105
Amwell Clo. Enf—15Tb 25
Amwell Ct. Wal A—5Hc 13
Amwell St. EC1—41Qb 82 (3K 193)
Amwell View. Ilf—22Xc 47
Amyand Cotts. Twic—58Ka 100
Amyand La. Twic—59Ka 100
Amyand Pk. Gdns. Twic
—59Ka 100
Amyand Pk. Rd. Twic—59Ja 100
Amy Rd. Oxt—100Gc 183
Amyruth Rd. SE4—57Cc 106
Anatola Rd. N19—33Lb 62
Ancaster Cres. N Mald—73Wa 144
Ancaster Rd. Beck—69Zb 128
Ancaster St. SE18—52Uc 108
Anchorage Clo. SW19—64Cb 125
Anchor & Hope La. SE7—48Kc 85
Anchor Bay Industrial Est. Eri
—51Jd 110
Anchor Ct. Enf—15Ub 25
Anchor Cres. Wok—5A 188
Anchor Dri. Rain—42Kd 89
Anchor Hill. Wok—5A 188
Anchor M. SW12—58Kb 104
Anchor St. SE16—49Xb 83
Anchor Yd. EC1—42Sb 83 (5E 194)
Ancill Clo. W6—51Za 102
Ancona Rd. NW10—40Wa 60
Ancona Rd. SE18—50Tc 86
Andalus Rd. SW9—55Nb 104
Ander Clo. Wemb—35Ma 59
Andermans. Wind—3B 94
Anderson Clo. Eps—83Ra 161
Anderson Dri. Ashf—63S 120
Anderson Pl. Houn—56Da 99
Anderson Rd. E9—37Zb 64
Anderson Rd. Shen, Rad—5Qa 7
Anderson Rd. Wey—76T 140
Anderson Rd. Wfd G—27Mc 45
Andersons. Stanf—1P 93
Anderson St. SW3
—50Hb 81 (7F 203)
Anderson Way. Belv—47Dd 88
Anderton Clo. SE5—55Tb 105
Andorra Ct. Brom—67Lc 129
Andover Clo. Eps—83Ta 161
Andover Clo. Gnfd—42Da 77
Andover Clo. Uxb—40K 55
Andover Ct. Wok—7G 188
Andover Pl. NW6—40Db 61
Andover Rd. N7—33Pb 62
Andover Rd. Orp—74Uc 150
Andover Rd. Twic—60Fa 100
Andreck Ct. Beck—68Ec 128
Andre St. E8—36Wb 63
Andrew Borde St. WC2
—44Mb 82 (2E 198)
Andrew Clo. Bex—57Fd 110
Andrew Clo. Ilf—23Tc 46
Andrewes Clo. E6—44Nc 86
Andrewes Ho. EC2—(1E 200)
Andrew Hill La. Slou—3G 52
Andrew Pl. SW8—52Mb 104
Andrews Clo. Buck H—19Lc 27
Andrew's Clo. Eps—86Va 162
Andrew's Clo. Orp—68Zc 131
Andrews Clo. Wor Pk—75Za 144
Andrews Crosse. WC2—(3K 199)
Andrew's La. Wal X—1Vb 11
(in two parts)
Andrew's Rd. E8—39Xb 63
Andrew St. E14—44Ec 84
Andrews Wlk. SE17—51Rb 105
Andromeda Ct. Romf—23Ld 49
Andwell Clo. SE2—47Xc 87
Anerley Gro. SE19—66Vb 127
Anerley Hill. SE19—65Vb 127
Anerley Pk. SE20—66Wb 127
Anerley Pk. Rd. SE20—66Xb 127
Anerley Rd.—66Wb 127
SE19 19-69 & 54-120
SE20 remainder
Anerley Sta. Rd. SE20—67Xb 127
Anerley St. SW11—54Hb 103
Anerley Vale. SE19—66Vb 127
Aneurin Bevan Ho. N11—24Mb 42
Anfield Clo. SW12—59Lb 104
Angas Ct. Wey—78S 140
Angel All. E1—44Wb 83
Angel Centre, The. N1 & EC1
—40Qb 62 (2A 194)
Angel Clo. N18—21Vb 43
Angel Ct. EC2—44Tb 83 (2G 201)
Angel Ct. SW1—46Lb 82 (7C 198)
Angelfield. Houn—56Da 99
Angel Hill. Sutt—76Db 145
Angel Hill Dri. Sutt—76Db 145
Angelica Gdns. Croy—74Zb 148
Angel La. E15—37Fc 65
Angel La. Hay—43T 76
Angell Pk. Gdns. SW9—55Qb 104
Angell Rd. SW9—55Qb 104
Angel M. N1—40Qb 62 (2A 194)
Angel Pas. EC4—45Tb 83 (5F 201)
Angel Pl. N18—22Vb 43
Angel Pl. SE1—47Tb 83 (1F 207)
Angel Rd. N18—22Wb 43
Angel Rd. Harr—30Ga 38
Angel Rd. Th Dit—73Ja 142
Angel St. EC1—44Sb 83 (2D 200)
Angel Wlk. W6—49Ya 80
Angel Way. Romf—29Gd 48
Angerstein La. SE3—53Hc 107
Angle Clo. Uxb—39Q 56
Angle Grn. Dag—32Yc 67
Angle Rd. Grays—51Zd 113
Anglers Clo. Rich—63La 122
Angler's La. NW5—37Kb 62
Anglesea Av. SE18—49Rc 86
Anglesea Pl. Grav—8D 114
Anglesea Rd. SE18—49Rc 86
Anglesea Rd. King—70Ma 123
Anglesea Rd. Orp—72Yc 151
Anglesea Shopping Centre. Grav
—8D 114
Anglesea St. E1—42Wb 83
Anglesey Clo. Ashf—62Q 120
Anglesey Ct. Rd. Cars—79Jb 146
Anglesey Dri. Rain—42Jd 88
Anglesey Gdns. Cars—79Jb 146
Anglesey Rd. Enf—14Xb 25
Anglesey Rd. Wat—22Y 37
Anglesmede Cres. Pinn—27Ca 37
Anglesmede Way. Pinn—27Ca 37
Angles Rd. SW16—63Nb 126
Anglo Rd. E3—40Bc 64
Angus Clo. Chess—78Qa 143
Angus Dri. Ruis—35Y 57
Angus Gdns. NW9—25Ta 39
Angus Rd. E13—41Lc 85
Angus St. SE14—52Ac 106
Anhalt Rd. SW11—52Gb 103
Ankerdine Cres. SE18—52Rc 108
Anlaby Rd. Tedd—64Ga 122
Anley Rd. W14—47Za 80
Anmersh Gro. Stan—25Ma 39
Annabel Clo. E14—44Dc 84
Anna Clo. E8—39Vb 63
Annalee Gdns. S Ock—43Xd 90
Annalee Rd. S Ock—43Xd 90
Annandale Gro. Uxb—34S 56
Annandale Rd. SE10—51Hc 107
Annandale Rd. W4—50Ua 80
Annandale Rd. Croy—75Wb 147
Annandale Rd. Sidc—59Uc 108
Annan Way. Romf—25Gd 48
Anne Boleyn's Wlk. King
—64Na 123
Anne Boleyn's Wlk. Sutt
—80Za 144
Anne of Cleves Rd. Dart
—57Md 111
Annesley Av. NW9—27Ta 39
Annesley Clo. NW10—34Ua 60
Annesley Dri. Croy—76Bc 148
Annesley Rd. SE3—53Kc 107
Annesley Wlk. N19—33Lb 62
Anne St. E13—42Jc 85
Anne's Wlk. Cat—92Ub 181
Annett Clo. Shep—70U 120
Annette Clo. Harr—26Ga 38
Annette Rd. N7—34Pb 62
Annett Rd. W on T—73W 140
Annett's Cres. N1—38Sb 63
★Annetts Hall. Sev—91Ce
Anne Way. E Mol—70Da 121
Anne Way. Ilf—23Sc 46
Annie Besant Clo. E3—39Bc 64
Annifer Way. S Ock—43Xd 90
Anning St. EC2—42Ub 83 (5J 195)
Annington Rd. N2—27Hb 41
Annis Rd. E9—37Ac 64
Ann La. SW10—51Fb 103
Ann's Clo. SW1—(2G 203)
Ann's Pl. E1—(1K 201)
Ann St. SE18—50Sc 86
(in two parts)
Annsworthy Av. T Hth—69Tb 127
Annsworthy Cres. SE25—68Tb 127
Ansculf Rd. Slou—1E 72
Ansdale Clo. Orp—74Tc 150
Ansdell Rd. SE15—54Yb 106
Ansdell St. W8—48Db 81
Ansdell Ter. W8—48Db 81
Ansell Gro. Cars—74Hb 145
Ansell Rd. SW17—62Gb 125
Anselm Clo. Croy—76Vb 147
Anselm Rd. SW6—51Cb 103
Anselm Rd. Pinn—24Ba 37
Ansford Rd. Brom—64Ec 128
Anslow Gdns. Iver—40F 54
Anslow Pl. Slou—3A 72
Anson Clo. Cat—92Tb 181
Anson Clo. Romf—26Dd 48
Anson Rd. N7—35Mb 62
Anson Rd. NW2—36Xa 60
Anson Ter. N'holt—37Da 57
Anson Wlk. N'wd—21S 36
Anstead Dri. Rain—40Jd 68
Anstey Rd. E16—43Kc 85
Anstey Rd. SE15—55Wb 105
Anstey Wlk. N15—28Rb 43
Anstice Clo. W4—52Ua 102
Anstridge Path. SE9—58Tc 108
Anstridge Rd. SE9—58Tc 108
Antelope Rd. SE18—48Pc 86
Anthony Clo. Sev—92Gd 188
Anthony Clo. Wat—18Y 19
Anthony La. Swan—67Jd 132
Anthony Rd. SE25—72Wb 147
Anthony Rd. Borwd—12Pa 21
Anthony Rd. Gnfd—41Ga 78
Anthony Rd. Well—53Wc 109
Anthony St. E1—44Xb 83
Anthony Way. Slou—5B 72
Anthus M. N'wd—24U 36
Antill Rd. E3—41Ac 84
Antill Rd. N15—28Wb 43
Antill Ter. E1—44Zb 84
Antlers Hill. E4—15Dc 26
Anton Cres. Sutt—76Cb 145
Antoneys Clo. Pinn—26Z 37
Anton Rd. S Ock—43Xd 90
Anton St. E8—36Wb 63
Antrim Gro. NW3—37Hb 61
Antrim Rd. NW3—37Hb 61
Antrobus Clo. Sutt—78Bb 145
Antrobus Rd. W4—49Sa 79
Anvil Ct. Slou—49C 74
Anvil La. Cob—86W 158
Anvil Rd. Sun—69W 120
Anworth Clo. Wfd G—23Kc 45
Anyards Rd. Cob—85X 159
Apeldoorn Dri. Wall—81Nb 164
Aperdele Rd. Lea—90Ja 160
Aperfield Rd. Eri—51Hd 110
Aperfield Rd. West—89Nc 168
Apers Av. Wok—93B 172
Apex Clo. Beck—67Dc 128
Apex Clo. Wey—76T 140
Aplin Way. Iswth—53Ga 100
Apollo Av. Brom—67Kc 129
Apollo Av. N'wd—22W 36
Apollo Clo. Horn—33Kd 69
Apollo Pl. SW10—52Fb 103
Apothecary St. EC4
—44Rb 83 (3B 200)
Appach Rd. SW2—58Qb 104
Appleby Clo. E4—23Ec 44
Appleby Clo. N15—29Tb 43
Appleby Clo. Twic—61Fa 122
Appleby Dri. Romf—22Ld 49
Appleby Grn. Romf—22Ld 49
Appleby Rd. E8—38Wb 63
Appleby Rd. E16—44Hc 85
Appleby St. E2—40Vb 63 (1K 195)
Applecroft. St Alb—1Da 5
Appledore Av. Bexh—53Ed 110
Appledore Av. Ruis—34Y 57
Appledore Clo. SW17—61Hb 125
Appledore Clo. Brom—71Jc 149
Appledore Clo. Edgw—25Qa 39
Appledore Clo. Romf—25Ld 49
Appledore Cres. Sidc—62Uc 130
Appleford Rd. W10—42Ab 80
Apple Garth. Bren—49Ma 79
Applegarth. Croy—80Dc 148
(in two parts)
Applegarth. Esh—78Ha 142
Applegarth Dri. Ilf—28Vc 47
Applegarth Rd. SE28—46Xc 87
Applegarth Rd. W14—48Za 80
Apple Ga. Brtwd—15Vd 32
Apple Gro. Chess—77Na 143
Apple Gro. Enf—13Ub 25
Apple Mkt. King—68Ma 123
Appleton Gdns. N Mald—72Wa 144
Appleton Rd. SE9—55Nc 108
Appleton Rd. Lou—13Rc 28
Appleton Way. Horn—33Md 69
Apple Tree Av. Uxb & W Dray
—43P 75
★Apple Tree Clo. Brtwd—10Zd
★Apple Tree Cres. Brtwd—10Yd
Apple Tree La. Slou—8N 73
Appletree Wlk. Wat—6X 5
Apple Tree Yd. SW1
—46Lb 82 (6C 198)
Applewood Clo. NW2—34Xa 60
Appleyard Ter. Enf—9Yb 12
Appold St. EC2—43Ub 83 (7H 195)
Appold St. Eri—51Hd 110
Approach Rd. E2—40Yb 64
Approach Rd. SW20—68Ya 124
Approach Rd. Ashf—65S 120
Approach Rd. Barn—14Fb 23
Approach Rd. E Mol—71Ca 141
Approach Rd. Purl—84Rb 165
Approach Rd. West—95Kc 183
Approach, The. NW4—29Za 40
Approach, The. W3—44Ta 79
Approach, The. Enf—12Xb 25
Approach, The. Lea—95Ba 175
Approach, The. Orp—75Vc 151
Approach, The. Pot B—4Bb 9
Approach, The. Upm—34Rd 69
Aprey Gdns. NW4—28Ya 40
April Clo. W7—45Ga 78
April Clo. Felt—62W 120
April Clo. Orp—78Vc 151
April Glen. SE23—62Zb 128
April St. E8—35Vb 63
Aprilwood Clo. Wey—83H 157
Apsledene. Grav—5F 136
Apsley Clo. Harr—29Ea 38
Apsley Rd. E17—29Bc 44
Apsley Rd. SE25—70Xb 127
Apsley Rd. N Mald—69Sa 123
Apsley Way. W1—47Jb 82 (1J 203)
Aquarius Way. N'wd—22W 36
Aquila Clo. Lea—93Na 177
Aquila Clo. N'wd—21W 36
Aquila St. NW8—40Fb 61 (1C 190)
Aquinas St. SE1—46Qb 82 (7A 200)
Arabella Dri. SW15—56Ua 102
Arabia Clo. E4—17Fc 27
Arabin Rd. SE4—56Bc 106
Araglen Av. S Ock—43Xd 90
Aragon Av. Eps—82Xa 162
Aragon Av. Th Dit—71Ha 142
Aragon Clo. Croy—82Gc 167
Aragon Dri. Ilf—24Sc 46
Aragon Dri. Ruis—32Z 57
Aragon Rd. King—64Na 123
Aragon Rd. Mord—72Za 144
Arandora Cres. Romf—30Xc 47
Aran Dri. Stan—21La 38
Arbery Rd. E3—41Ac 84
Arbor Clo. Beck—68Dc 128
Arborfield. Wok—88A 156
Arborfield Clo. Slou—8J 73
Arbor Rd. E4—20Fc 27
Arbour Clo. Brtwd—22Yd 50
Arbour Clo. Lea—95Ha 176
Arbour Rd. Enf—13Zb 26
Arbour Sq. E1—44Zb 84
Arbour Way. Horn—36Kd 69
Arbroath Grn. Wat—20X 19
Arbroath Rd. SE9—55Nc 108
Arbrook Clo. Orp—69Wc 131
Arbrook La. Esh—79Ea 142
Arbuthnot La. Bex—58Ad 109
Arbuthnot Rd. SE14—54Zb 106
Arbutus St. E8—39Vb 63
Arcade Pl. Romf—29Gd 48
Arcade, The. EC2—(1H 201)

Arcadia Av. N3—26Cb 41
Arcadian Av. Bex—58Ad 109
Arcadian Clo. Bex—58Ad 109
Arcadian Gdns. N22—24Pb 42
Arcadian Rd. Bex—58Ad 109
Arcadia Rd. Grav—7B 136
Arcadia St. E14—44Cc 84
Arcany Rd. S Ock—42Xd 90
Archbishop's Pl. SW2—59Pb 104
Archdale Rd. SE22—56Vb 105
Archel Rd. W14—51Bb 103
Archer Clo. K Lan—1P 3
Archer Rd. SE25—70Xb 127
Archer Rd. Orp—71Wc 151
Archers Dri. Enf—12Yb 26
Archer St. W1—45Mb 82 (4D 198)
Archer Way. Swan—68Hd 132
Archery Clo. W2—44Gb 81 (3E 196)
Archery Clo. Harr—27Ha 38
Archery Rd. SE9—57Pc 108
Arches, The. WC2—(6G 199)
Arches, The. Harr—33Da 57
Archibald M. W1—45Jb 82 (5K 197)
Archibald Rd. N7—35Mb 62
Archibald Rd. Romf—25Qd 49
Archibald St. E3—41Cc 84
Arch Rd. W on T—76Z 141
Arch Way. Romf—23Kd 49
Archway Clo. N19—33Lb 62
Archway Clo. SW19—62Db 125
Archway Mall. N19—33Lb 62
Archway Rd.—30Jb 42
N19 1-43 & 2-92
N6 remainder
Archway St. SW13—55Ua 102
Arcola St. E8—36Vb 63
Arctic St. NW5—36Kb 62
Arcus Rd. Brom—65Gc 129
Ardbeg Rd. SE24—57Tb 105
Arden Clo. Bush, Wat—17Ha 20
Arden Clo. Harr—34Fa 58
Arden Clo. Hem—1C 2
Arden Ct. Gdns. N2—30Fb 41
Arden Cres. Dag—38Yc 67
Arden Est. N1—40Ub 63 (2H 195)
Arden Mhor. Pinn—28X 37
Arden Rd. N3—27Bb 41
Arden Rd. W13—45La 78
Ardent Clo. SE25—69Ub 127
Ardesley Wood. Wey—77U 140
Ardfern Av. SW16—69Qb 126
Ardfillan Rd. SE6—60Fc 107
Ardgowan Rd. SE6—59Gc 107
Ardilaun Rd. N5—35Sb 63
Ardleigh Clo. Horn—27Md 49
Ardleigh Ct. Brtwd—17Be 33
Ardleigh Gdns. Brtwd—16Fe 33
Ardleigh Gdns. Sutt—73Cb 145
Ardleigh Grn. Rd. Horn—29Md 49
Ardleigh M. Ilf—34Rc 66
Ardleigh Rd. E17—25Bc 44
Ardleigh Rd. N1—37Ub 63
Ardleigh Ter. E17—25Bc 44
Ardley Clo. NW10—34Ua 60
Ardley Clo. SE6—62Ac 128
Ardley Clo. Ruis—31S 56
Ardlui Rd. SE27—61Sb 127
Ardmay Gdns. Surb—71Na 143
Ardmere Rd. SE13—58Fc 107
Ardmore La. Buck H—18Kc 27
Ardmore Rd. S Ock—42Xd 90
Ardoch Rd. SE6—61Fc 129
Ardrossan Gdns. Wor Pk —76Wa 144
Ardross Av. N'wd—22U 36
Ardshiel Clo. SW15—55Za 102
Ardwell Av. Ilf—29Sc 46
Ardwell Rd. SW2—61Nb 126
Ardwick Rd. NW2—35Cb 61
Argall Av. E10—31Zb 64
Argent St. SE1—(1D 206)
Argent St. Grays—51Ce 113
Argon M. SW6—52Cb 103
Argosy Gdns. Stai—65H 119
Argosy La. Stai—59M 97
Argus Clo. Romf—25Dd 48
Argus Way. W3—48Ra 79
Argus Way. N'holt—41Aa 77
Argyle Av. Houn—58Ca 99
Argyle Av. S'hall—46Da 77
Argyle Clo. W13—42Ja 78
Argyle Gdns. Upm—33Td 70
Argyle Pl. W6—49Xa 80
Argyle Rd. E1—42Zb 84
Argyle Rd. E15—35Gc 65
Argyle Rd. E16—44Lc 85
Argyle Rd. N12—22Db 41
Argyle Rd. N17—25Wb 43
Argyle Rd. N18—21Wb 43
Argyle Rd. Barn—14Ya 22
Argyle Rd. Grays—50Ce 91
Argyle Rd. Gnfd & W13—41Ha 78
Argyle Rd. Harr—30Da 37
Argyle Rd. Houn—57Da 99
Argyle Rd. Ilf—33Qc 66
Argyle Rd. Sev—97Kd 187
Argyle Rd. Tedd—64Ha 122
Argyle Sq. WC1—41Nb 82 (3G 193)
Argyle St. WC1—41Nb 82 (3F 193)
Argyle Wlk. WC1 —41Nb 82 (4F 193)
Argyll Av. Slou—5E 72
Argyll Gdns. Edgw—26Ra 39
Argyll Rd. SW9—55Pb 104
Argyll Rd. W8—47Cb 81
Argyll St. W1—44Lb 82 (3B 198)
Arica Rd. SE4—56Ac 106
Ariel Clo. Grav—3H 137
Ariel Rd. NW6—37Cb 61
Ariel Way. W12—46Ya 80
Arisdale Av. S Ock—43Xd 90
Aristotle Rd. SW4—55Mb 104
Arkell Gro. SE19—66Rb 127
Arkindale Rd. SE6—62Ec 128
Arkley Cres. E17—29Bc 44
Arkley Dri. Barn—14Wa 22
Arkley La. Barn—13Wa 22
Arkley Rd. E17—29Bc 44
Arkley View. Barn—14Xa 22
Arklow Rd. SE14—51Bc 106
Arkwright Rd. NW3—36Eb 61
Arkwright Rd. Slou—54G 96
Arkwright Rd. S Croy—82Vb 165
Arkwright Rd. Til—4C 114
Arlesey Clo. SW15—57Ab 102
Arlesford Rd. SW9—55Nb 104
Arlingford Rd. SW2—57Qb 104
Arlington. N12—20Cb 23
Arlington Av. N1 —39Sb 63 (1E 194)
Arlington Clo. Sidc—59Uc 108
Arlington Clo. Sutt—75Cb 145
Arlington Clo. Twic—58La 100
Arlington Ct. Hay—50U 76
Arlington Cres. Wal X—6Ac 12
Arlington Dri. Cars—75Hb 145
Arlington Dri. Ruis—30T 36
Arlington Gdns. W4—50Sa 79
Arlington Gdns. Ilf—32Qc 66
Arlington Gdns. Romf—25Nd 49
Arlington M. Twic—58La 100
Arlington Pas. Tedd—63Ha 122
Arlington Rd. N14—19Kb 24
Arlington Rd. NW1 —39Kb 62 (1A 192)
Arlington Rd. W13—44Ka 78
Arlington Rd. Ashf—64P 119
Arlington Rd. Rich—61Ma 123
Arlington Rd. Surb—72Ma 143
Arlington Rd. Tedd—63Ha 122
Arlington Rd. Twic—58La 100
Arlington Rd. Wfd G—24Kc 45
Arlington Sq. N1—39Sb 63 (1E 194)
Arlington St. SW1 —46Lb 82 (6B 198)
Arlington Way. EC1 —41Qb 82 (3A 194)
Arliss Way. N'holt—39Y 57
Arlow Rd. N21—18Qb 24
Armada Ct. SE8—51Cc 106
Armadale Clo. N17—28Xb 43
Armadale Rd. SW6—51Cb 103
Armadale Rd. Felt—57W 98
Armadale Rd. Wok—5D 188
Armagh Rd. E3—39Bc 64
Armand Clo. Wat—10V 4
Armfield Clo. E Mol—71Ba 141
Armfield Cres. Mitc—68Hb 125
Armfield Rd. Enf—11Tb 25
Arminger Rd. W12—46Xa 80
Armitage Clo. Rick—14M 17
Armitage Rd. NW11—32Ab 60
Armitage Rd. SE10—50Hc 85
Armour Clo. N7—37Pb 62
Armoury Dri. Grav—9E 114
Armoury Way. SW18—57Cb 103
Armstead Wlk. Dag—38Cd 68
Armstrong Av. Wfd G—23Gc 45
Armstrong Clo. E6—44Pc 86
Armstrong Clo. Pinn—30W 36
Armstrong Clo. Sev—87Dd 170
Armstrong Clo. Stanf—1N 93
Armstrong Cres. Barn—13Fb 23
Armstrong Rd. W3—46Va 80
Armstrong Rd. Egh—5N 117
Armstrong Rd. Felt—64Aa 121
Armstrong Way. S'hall—47Da 77
Armytage Rd. Houn—52Z 99
Arnal Cres. SW18—59Ab 102
Arndale Centre. SW18—58Db 103
Arndale Centre. Dart—59Nd 111
Arndale Wlk. SW18—57Db 103
Arndale Way. Egh—64C 118
Arne Gro. Orp—76Vc 151
Arne St. WC2—44Nb 82 (3G 199)
Arnett Clo. Rick—16J 17
Arnett Way. Rick—16J 17
Arne Wlk. SE3—56Hc 107
Arneways Av. Romf—27Zc 47
Arneway St. SW1 —48Mb 82 (4E 204)
Arnewood Clo. SW15—60Wa 102
Arnewood Clo. Lea—86Da 159
Arneys La. Mitc—72Jb 146
Arngask Rd. SE6—59Fc 107
Arnhem Av. S Ock—46Sd 90
Arnhem Dri. Croy—83Fc 167
Arnison Rd. E Mol—70Fa 122
Arnold Av. E. Enf—10Cc 12
Arnold Av. W. Enf—10Bc 12
Arnold Cir. E2—41Vb 83 (4K 195)
Arnold Clo. Harr—31Pa 59
Arnold Cres. Iswth—57Fa 100
Arnold Est. SE1—47Vb 83 (2K 207)
Arnold Gdns. N13—22Rb 43
Arnold Rd. E3—41Cc 84
Arnold Rd. N15—27Vb 43
Arnold Rd. SW17—66Hb 125
Arnold Rd. Dag—38Bd 67
Arnold Rd. Grav—1F 136
Arnold Rd. N'holt—37Aa 57
Arnold Rd. Stai—66L 119
Arnold Rd. Wok—87D 156
Arnolds Av. Brtwd—15Ee 33
Arnolds Clo. Brtwd—15Ee 33
Arnolds Farm La. Brtwd—13Fe 33
Arnold's La. S at H, Dart—65Qd 133
Arnos Gro. N14—21Mb 42
Arnos Rd. N11—21Lb 42
Arnott Clo. SE28—46Yc 87
Arnott Clo. W4—49Ta 79
Arnould Av. SE5—56Tb 105
Arnside Gdns. Wemb—32Ma 59
Arnside Rd. Bexh—53Cd 110
Arnside St. SE17—51Tb 105
Arnulf St. SE6—63Dc 128
Arnulls Rd. SW16—65Rb 127
Arodene Rd. SW2—58Pb 104
Arragon Gdns. SW16—66Nb 126
Arragon Gdns. W Wick—76Dc 148
Arragon Rd. Twic—59Ja 100
Arragon Way. E6—39Mc 65
Arran Clo. Eri—51Fd 110
Arran Clo. Wall—77Lb 146
Arran Dri. E12—33Mc 65
Arran M. W5—46Pa 79
Arran Rd. SE6—61Dc 128
Arran Wlk. N1—38Sb 63
Arran Way. Esh—75Da 141
Arras Av. Mord—71Eb 145
Arrol Rd. Beck—69Yb 128
Arrow Rd. E3—41Dc 84
Arrowscout Wlk. N'holt—41Aa 77
Arrowsmith Clo. Chig—22Vc 47
Arrowsmith Pl. Chig—22Vc 47
Arrowsmith Rd. Chig—22Vc 47
Arsenal Rd. SE9—54Pc 108
Artemis Clo. Grav—9G 114
Arterberry Rd. SW20—66Ya 124
Arterial Av. Rain—42Kd 89
Arterial Rd. North Stifford. Grays—47Zd 91
Arterial Rd. Purfleet, Purf—48Qd 89
Arterial Rd. West Thurrock. Grays—48Wd 90
Artesian Clo. Horn—30Hd 48
Artesian Rd. W2—44Cb 81
Arthingworth St. E15—39Gc 65
Arthurdon Rd. SE4—57Cc 106
Arthur Gro. SE18—49Sc 86
Arthur Rd. E6—40Pc 66
Arthur Rd. N7—35Pb 62
Arthur Rd. N9—19Vb 25
Arthur Rd. SW19—63Bb 125
Arthur Rd. King—66Qa 123
Arthur Rd. N Mald—71Xa 144
Arthur Rd. Romf—30Zc 47
Arthur Rd. Slou—7H 73
Arthur Rd. West—87Lc 167
Arthur Rd. Wind—3G 94
Arthur's Bri. Rd. Wok—5G 188
(in two parts)
Arthur St. EC4—45Tb 83 (4G 201)
Arthur St. Bush, Wat—14Z 19
Arthur St. Eri—52Hd 110
Arthur St. Grav—9C 114
Arthur St. Grays—51Ee 113
Arthur St. W. Grav—9C 114
Artichoke Hill. E1—45Xb 83
Artillery Clo. Ilf—30Sc 46
Artillery La. E1—43Ub 83 (1J 201)
Artillery Pas. E1—(1J 201)
Artillery Pl. SE18—49Qc 86
Artillery Pl. SW1—(4D 204)
Artillery Pl. Harr—24Ea 38
Artillery Row. SW1 —48Mb 82 (4D 204)
Artillery Row. Grav—9E 114
Artington Clo. Orp—77Sc 150
Arun. Grays—9L 93
Arun Ct. SE25—71Wb 147
Arundel Av. Eps—82Xa 162
Arundel Av. Mord—70Bb 125
Arundel Av. S Croy—82Wb 165
Arundel Bldgs. SE1—(4J 207)
Arundel Clo. E15—35Gc 65
Arundel Clo. SW11—57Gb 103
Arundel Clo. Bex—58Bd 109
Arundel Clo. Croy—76Rb 147
Arundel Clo. Hmptn—64Da 121
Arundel Clo. Wal X—1Yb 12
Arundel Ct. N12—23Gb 41
Arundel Ct. Brom—68Gc 129
Arundel Ct. Slou—9P 73
Arundel Dri. Borwd—14Sa 21
Arundel Dri. Harr—35Ba 57
Arundel Dri. Orp—78Xc 151
Arundel Dri. Wfd G—24Jc 45
Arundel Gdns. N21—18Qb 24
Arundel Gdns. W11—45Bb 81
Arundel Gdns. Edgw—24Ta 39
Arundel Gdns. Ilf—33Wc 67
Arundel Gro. N16—36Ub 63
Arundel Pl. N1—37Qb 62
Arundel Rd. Barn—13Gb 23
Arundel Rd. Croy—72Tb 147
Arundel Rd. Houn—55Y 99
Arundel Rd. King—68Ra 123
Arundel Rd. Romf—24Pd 49
Arundel Rd. Sutt—80Bb 145
Arundel Rd. Uxb—40K 55
Arundel Sq. N7—37Qb 62
Arundel St. WC2—45Pb 82 (4J 199)
Arundel Ter. SW13—51Xa 102
Arvon Rd. N5—36Qb 62
Ascalon St. SW8—52Lb 104
Ascension Rd. Romf—23Ed 48
Ascham Dri. E4—24Dc 44
Ascham End. E17—25Ac 44
Ascham St. NW5—36Lb 62
Aschurch Rd. Croy—73Vb 147
Ascot Clo. Borwd—15Qa 21
Ascot Clo. Ilf—23Uc 46
Ascot Clo. N'holt—36Ca 57
★Ascot Clo. Sev—92De
Ascot Gdns. Enf—9Yb 12
Ascot Gdns. Horn—35Nd 69
Ascot Gdns. S'hall—43Ba 77
Ascot Rd. E6—41Pc 86
Ascot Rd. N15—29Tb 43
Ascot Rd. N18—21Wb 43
Ascot Rd. SW17—65Jb 126
Ascot Rd. Felt—60Q 98
Ascot Rd. Grav—2D 136
Ascot Rd. Orp—70Vc 131
Ascot Rd. Wat—15U 18
Ascott Av. W5—47Na 79
Aseing Clo. E6—45Qc 86
Ashbeam Clo. Brtwd—23Yd 50
Ashbourne Av. E18—28Kc 45
Ashbourne Av. N20—19Hb 23
Ashbourne Av. NW11—29Bb 41
Ashbourne Av. Bexh—52Ad 109
Ashbourne Av. Harr—33Fa 58
Ashbourne Clo. N12—21Db 41
Ashbourne Clo. W5—43Qa 79
Ashbourne Clo. Coul—90Lb 164
Ashbourne Gro. NW7—22Ta 39
Ashbourne Gro. SE22—56Vb 105
Ashbourne Gro. W4—50Ua 80
Ashbourne Rise. Orp—77Uc 150
Ashbourne Rd. W5—42Pa 79
Ashbourne Rd. Mitc—66Jb 126
Ashbourne Rd. Romf—21Ld 49
Ashbourne Sq. N'wd—23U 36
Ashbourne Ter. SW19—66Cb 125
Ashbourne Way. NW11—28Bb 41
Ashbridge Rd. E11—31Hc 65
Ashbridge St. NW8 —42Gb 81 (6D 190)
Ashbrook Rd. N19—32Mb 62
Ashbrook Rd. Dag—34Dd 68
Ashbrook Rd. Wind—9M 95
Ashburn Gdns. SW7—49Eb 81
Ashburnham Av. Harr—30Ha 38
Ashburnham Clo. N2—27Fb 41
Ashburnham Clo. Wat—20W 18
Ashburnham Dri. Wat—20W 18
Ashburnham Gdns. Harr—30Ha 38
Ashburnham Gdns. Upm—32Rd 69
Ashburnham Gro. SE10—52Dc 106
Ashburnham Pl. SE10—52Dc 106
Ashburnham Retreat. SE10 —52Dc 106
Ashburnham Rd. NW10—41Ya 80
Ashburnham Rd. SW10—52Eb 103
Ashburnham Rd. Belv—49Ed 88
Ashburnham Rd. Rich—62Ka 122
Ashburn M. SW7 —49Eb 81 (5A 202)
Ashburn Pl. SW7 —49Eb 81 (5A 202)
Ashburton Av. Croy—74Xb 147
Ashburton Av. Ilf—36Uc 66
Ashburton Clo. Croy—74Wb 147
Ashburton Ct. Pinn—27Z 37
Ashburton Gdns. Croy—75Wb 147
Ashburton Gro. N7—35Qb 62
Ashburton Rd. E16—44Jc 85
Ashburton Rd. Croy—75Wb 147
Ashburton Rd. Ruis—33W 56
Ashburton Ter. E13—40Jc 65
Ashbury Dri. Uxb—34R 56
Ashbury Gdns. Romf—29Zc 47
Ashbury Rd. SW11—55Hb 103
Ashby Av. Chess—79Qa 143
Ashby Clo. Horn—32Qd 69
Ashby Gro. N1—38Sb 63
Ashby Rd. N15—29Wb 43
Ashby Rd. SE4—54Bc 106
Ashby Rd. Wat—10W 4
Ashby St. EC1—41Rb 83 (4C 194)
Ashby Wlk. Croy—72Sb 147
Ashby Way. W Dray—52Q 98
Ashchurch Ct. W12—48Wa 80
Ashchurch Gro. W12—48Wa 80
Ashchurch Pk. Vs. W12—48Wa 80
Ashchurch Ter. W12—48Wa 80
Ash Clo. SE20—68Yb 128
Ash Clo. Abb L, Wat—4T 4
Ash Clo. Brtwd—15Vd 32
Ash Clo. Cars—75Hb 145
Ash Clo. N Mald—68Ta 123
Ash Clo. Orp—71Tc 150
Ash Clo. Romf—24Dd 48
Ash Clo. Sidc—62Xc 131
Ash Clo. Slou—48D 74
Ash Clo. Stan—23Ja 38
Ash Clo. Swan—68Ed 132
Ash Clo. Uxb—25M 35
Ash Clo. Wok—92A 172
Ashcombe Av. Surb—73Ma 143
Ashcombe Gdns. Edgw—21Qa 39
Ashcombe Pk. NW2—34Ua 60
Ashcombe Rd. SW19—64Cb 125
Ashcombe Rd. Cars—79Jb 146
Ashcombe Rd. Red—99Lb 180
Ashcombe Sq. N Mald—69Sa 123
Ashcombe St. SW6—54Db 103
Ashcombe Ter. Tad—92Xa 178
Ash Ct. SW19—66Ab 124
Ash Ct. Eps—77Sa 143
Ash Croft. Pinn—23Ca 37
Ashcroft Av. Sidc—58Wc 109
Ashcroft Ct. Slou—10A 52
Ashcroft Cres. Sidc—58Wc 109
Ashcroft Dri. Uxb—31H 55
Ashcroft Pk. Cob—84Aa 159
Ashcroft Rise. Coul—88Nb 164
Ashcroft Rd. E3—41Ac 84
Ashcroft Rd. Chess—76Pa 143
Ashcroft Sq. W6—49Ya 80
Ashdale. Lea—98Ea 176
Ashdale Clo. Twic—59Ea 100
Ashdale Gro. Stan—23Ha 38
Ashdale Rd. SE12—60Kc 107
Ashdale Way. Twic—59Da 99
Ashdene. Pinn—27Y 37
Ashdene Clo. Ashf—66S 120
Ashdon Clo. Wfd G—23Kc 45
Ashdon Rd. NW10—39Va 60
Ashdon Rd. Bush, Wat—13Z 19
Ashdown Clo. Beck—68Dc 128
Ashdown Cres. NW5—36Jb 62
Ashdown Cres. Wal X—1Ac 12
Ashdown Dri. Borwd—12Pa 21
Ashdown Est. E11—35Fc 65
Ashdown Gdns. S Croy—87Xb 165
Ashdown Rd. Enf—12Yb 26
Ashdown Rd. Eps—85Wa 162
Ashdown Rd. King—68Na 123
Ashdown Rd. Uxb—40Q 56
Ashdown Wlk. Romf—25Dd 48
Ashdown Way. SW17—61Jb 126
Ashenden Rd. E5—36Ac 64
Ashenden Wlk. Slou—5H 53
Ashen Dri. Dart—58Jd 110
Ashen Gro. SW19—62Cb 125
Ashen Gro. Rd. Sev—82Rd 171
Ashentree Ct. EC4—(3A 200)
Ashen Vale. S Croy—81Zb 166
Ashfield Av. Bush, Wat—16Da 19
Ashfield Av. Felt—60X 99
Ashfield Clo. Rich—60Na 101
Ashfield La. Chst—65Sc 130
Ashfield Pde. N14—18Mb 24
Ashfield Rd. N4—30Sb 43
Ashfield Rd. N14—20Lb 24
Ashfield Rd. W3—46Va 80
Ashfields. Lou—12Pc 28
Ashfields. Wat—7V 4
Ashfield St. E1—43Xb 83
Ashford Av. N8—28Nb 42
Ashford Av. Ashf—65R 120
Ashford Av. Brtwd—20Xd 32
Ashford Av. Hay—44Z 77
Ashford Clo. E17—30Bc 44
Ashford Clo. Ashf—63N 119
Ashford Cres. Ashf—62N 119
Ashford Cres. Enf—12Yb 26
Ashford Gdns. Cob—88Z 159
Ashford Grn. Wat—23Z 37
Ashford Industrial Est. Ashf —63S 120
Ashford La. Wind—7A 72
Ashford Rd. E6—38Qc 66
Ashford Rd. E18—26Kc 45
Ashford Rd. NW2—35Za 60
Ashford Rd. Ashf—66S 120
Ashford Rd. Felt—63T 120
Ashford Rd. Iver—39E 54
Ashford Rd. Stai—67M 119
Ashford St. N1—41Ub 83 (3H 195)
Ash Grn. Lou—12Pc 28
Ash Grn. Uxb—37K 55
Ash Gro. E8—39Xb 63
Ash Gro. N13—20Sb 25
Ash Gro. NW2—35Za 60
Ash Gro. SE20—68Yb 128
Ash Gro. W5—47Na 79
Ash Gro. Enf—17Ub 25
Ash Gro. Felt—60U 98
Ash Gro. Hay—45T 76
Ash Gro. Houn—53Z 99
Ash Gro. Slou—8K 53
Ash Gro. S'hall—43Ca 77
Ash Gro. Stai—65L 119
Ash Gro. Uxb—25M 35
Ash Gro. Wemb—35Ja 58
Ash Gro. W Dray—45P 75
Ash Gro. W Wick—75Ec 148
Ashgrove Rd. Ashf—64S 120
Ashgrove Rd. Brom—65Fc 129
Ashgrove Rd. Ilf—32Vc 67
Ashgrove Rd. Sev—100Jd 186
Ash Hill Clo. Bush, Wat—18Da 19
Ash Hill Dri. Pinn—27Y 37
Ashingdon Clo. E4—20Ec 26
Ashington Rd. SW6—54Bb 103
Ashlake Rd. SW16—63Nb 126
Ashland Pl. W1—43Jb 82 (7H 191)
Ash La. Horn—28Qd 49
Ash La. Romf—23Jd 48
★Ash La. Sev—84Yd
Ash La. Wind—4B 94
Ashlar Pl. SE18—49Rc 86
Ashlea Rd. Ger X—26A 34
Ashleigh Av. Egh—66E 118
Ashleigh Gdns. Sutt—75Db 145
Ashleigh Gdns. Upm—34Td 70
Ashleigh Rd. SE20—69Xb 127
Ashleigh Rd. SW14—55Ua 102
Ashley Av. Eps—85Ta 161
Ashley Av. Ilf—26Rc 46
Ashley Av. Mord—71Cb 145
Ashley Centre. Eps—85Ta 161
Ashley Clo. NW4—26Ya 40
Ashley Clo. Lea—97Ba 175
Ashley Clo. Pinn—26X 37
Ashley Clo. Sev—96Kd 187
Ashley Clo. W on T—74V 140
Ashley Ct. Eps—85Ta 161
Ashley Cres. N22—26Qb 42
Ashley Cres. SW11—55Jb 104
Ashley Dri. Bans—86Cb 163
Ashley Dri. Borwd—15Sa 21
Ashley Dri. Twic—60Da 99
Ashley Dri. W on T—76W 140
Ashley Gdns. N13—21Sb 43
Ashley Gdns. Grays—46Fe 91
Ashley Gdns. Orp—78Uc 150
Ashley Gdns. Rich—61Ma 123
Ashley Gdns. Wemb—33Na 59
Ashley La. NW4—26Ya 40
Ashley La. Croy—77Rb 147
Ashley Pk. Av. W on T—75V 140
Ashley Pk. Cres. W on T—74W 140
Ashley Pk. Rd. W on T—75W 140
Ashley Pl. SW1—48Lb 82 (4B 204)
Ashley Rise. W on T—77V 140
Ashley Rd. E4—23Cc 44
Ashley Rd. E7—38Lc 65
Ashley Rd. N17—27Wb 43
Ashley Rd. N19—32Nb 62
Ashley Rd. SW19—65Db 125
Ashley Rd. Enf—12Yb 26
Ashley Rd. Eps—85Ta 161
Ashley Rd. Hmptn—67Ca 121
Ashley Rd. Rich—55Na 101
Ashley Rd. Sev—96Kd 187
Ashley Rd. Th Dit—72Ha 142
Ashley Rd. T Hth—70Pb 126
Ashley Rd. Uxb—40K 55
Ashley Rd. W on T—77V 140
Ashley Rd. Wok—6C 188
Ashleys. Rick—17H 17
Ashley Wlk. NW7—24Ya 40
Ashling Rd. Croy—74Wb 147
Ashlin Rd. E15—35Fc 65
Ashlone Rd. SW15—55Za 102
Ashlyn Clo. Bush, Wat—14Aa 19
Ashlyn Gro. Horn—27Md 49
Ashlyns Rd. Epp—2Vc 15
Ashlyns Way. Chess—79Ma 143
Ashmead. N14—15Lb 24
Ashmead Dri. Uxb—33J 55
Ashmead La. Uxb—33J 55
Ashmead Rd. SE8—54Cc 106
Ashmead Rd. Felt—60W 98
Ashmere Av. Beck—68Fc 129
Ashmere Clo. Sutt—78Za 144
Ashmere Gro. SW2—56Nb 104
Ash M. Eps—85Ua 162
Ashmill St. NW1—43Gb 81 (7D 190)
Ashmole Pl. SW8—51Pb 104
Ashmole St. SW8—51Pb 104
Ashmore Ct. Houn—51Ca 99
Ashmore Gro. Well—55Tc 108
Ashmore La. Kes—83Lc 167
Ashmore Rd. W9—41Bb 81
Ashmount Rd. N15—29Vb 43
Ashmount Rd. N19—31Lb 62
Ashmount Ter. W5—49Ma 79
Ashmour Gdns. Romf—26Fd 48
Ashneal Gdns. Harr—34Fa 58
Ashness Gdns. Gnfd—37Ka 58
Ashness Rd. SW11—57Hb 103
Ash Platt Rd. Sev—93Nd 187
Ash Platt, The. Sev—92Nd 187
Ash Ride. Enf—7Qb 10
Ashridge Clo. Harr—30La 38
Ashridge Cres. SE18—52Sc 108
Ashridge Dri. St Alb—2Aa 5
Ashridge Dri. Wat—22Y 37
Ashridge Gdns. N13—22Mb 42
Ashridge Gdns. Pinn—28Aa 37
Ashridge Way. Mord—70Bb 125
Ashridge Way. Sun—65W 120
Ash Rd. E15—36Gc 65
Ash Rd. Croy—75Cc 148
Ash Rd. Dart—60Md 111
Ash Rd. Dart—63Pd 133
(Hawley)
Ash Rd. Grav—3E 136
Ash Rd. Orp—80Vc 151
Ash Rd. Sev & Long, Dart —77Zd 155
Ash Rd. Shep—70Q 120
Ash Rd. Sutt—74Bb 145
Ash Rd. West—97Tc 184
Ash Rd. Wok—92A 172
Ash Rd. Wok—8G 188
Ash Row. Brom—73Qc 150
Ashtead Gap. Lea—88Ka 160
Ashtead Rd. E5—31Wb 63
Ashtead Woods Rd. Asht —89La 160
Ashton Clo. Sutt—77Cb 145
Ashton Clo. W on T—79X 141
Ashton Gdns. Houn—56Ba 99
Ashton Gdns. Romf—30Ad 47
Ashton Rd. E15—36Fc 65
Ashton Rd. Enf—8Ac 12
Ashton Rd. Romf—24Md 49
Ashton Rd. Wok—5C 188
Ashton St. E14—45Ec 84
Ashtree Av. Mitc—68Fb 125
Ash Tree Clo. Croy—72Ac 148
Ash Tree Clo. Sev—80Vd 154
Ash Tree Clo. Surb—75Na 143
Ashtree Dell. NW9—29Ta 39
Ash Tree Dri. Sev—80Vd 154
Ash Tree Rd. Wat—8X 5
Ash Tree Way. Croy—71Zb 148
Ashurst Clo. SE20—67Xb 127
Ashurst Clo. Dart—55Hd 110
Ashurst Clo. Kenl—87Tb 165
Ashurst Clo. N'wd—24U 36
Ashurst Dri. Ilf—30Rc 46
Ashurst Dri. Shep—71N 139
Ashurst Rd. N12—22Gb 41
Ashurst Rd. Barn—15Hb 23
Ashurst Rd. Tad—93Xa 178
Ashurst Wlk. Croy—75Xb 147
Ash Vale. Rick—22F 34
Ashvale Dri. Upm—33Ud 70
Ashvale Gdns. Romf—22Fd 48
Ashvale Gdns. Upm—33Ud 70
Ashvale Rd. SW17—64Hb 125
Ash View Clo. Ashf—64N 119
Ash View Gdns. Ashf—64N 119
Ashville Rd. E11—33Fc 65
Ashwater Rd. SE12—60Jc 107
Ashwell Clo. E6—44Pc 86
Ashwells Rd. Brtwd—13Td 32
Ashwindham Ct. Wok—6C 188
Ashwin St. E8—37Vb 63
Ashwood. Warl—92Yb 182
Ashwood Av. Rain—42Kd 89
Ashwood Av. Uxb—44Q 76
Ashwood Cres. Hay—49V 76
Ashwood Dri. Pot B—5Db 9
Ashwood Gdns. Croy—79Dc 148
Ashwood Pl. Dart—62Xd 134
Ashwood Rd. E4—20Fc 27
Ashwood Rd. Egh—5M 117
Ashwood Rd. Wok—90B 156
Ashworth Clo. SE5—54Tb 105
Ashworth Industrial Est. Croy —74Nb 146
Ashworth Rd. W9—41Db 81
Askern Clo. Bexh—56Zc 109
Aske St. N1—41Ub 83 (3H 195)
Askew Cres. W12—47Va 80
Askew Rd. W12—47Va 80
Askew Rd. N'wd—19T 18
Askham Rd. W12—46Wa 80
Askill Dri. SW15—57Ab 102
Askwith Rd. Rain—41Fd 88
Asland Rd. E15—39Gc 65
Aslett St. SW18—59Db 103
Asmara Rd. NW2—36Ab 60
Asmar Clo. Coul—87Nb 164
Asmuns Hill. NW11—29Cb 41
Asmuns Pl. NW11—29Bb 41
Aspdin Rd. Grav—62Fe 135
Aspen Clo. N19—33Lb 62
Aspen Clo. W5—47Pa 79
Aspen Clo. Cob—88Aa 159
Aspen Clo. Orp—78Wc 151
Aspen Clo. Slou—3F 72
Aspen Clo. Stai—62H 119
Aspen Clo. Swan—67Fd 132
Aspen Clo. W Dray—46P 75
Aspen Copse. Brom—68Pc 130
Aspen Dri. Wemb—34Ja 58
Aspen Gdns. W6—50Xa 80
Aspen Gdns. Mitc—71Jb 146
Aspen Grn. Eri—48Bd 87
Aspen Gro. Upm—35Qd 69
Aspen La. N'holt—41Aa 77
Aspenlea Rd. W6—51Za 102

Aspen Way—Baldwin St.

Aspen Way. Bans—86Za 162
Aspen Way. Enf—7Zb 12
Aspinall Rd. SE4—55Zb 106
Aspinden Rd. SE16—49Xb 83
Aspley Rd. SW18—57Db 103
Asplins Rd. N17—25Wb 43
Assam St. E1—44Wb 83
Assembly Pas. E1—43Yb 84
Assembly Wlk. Cars—73Gb 145
Assher Rd. W on T—76Aa 141
Ass Ho. La. Harr—21Da 37
Astall Clo. Harr—25Ga 38
Astbury Rd. SE15—53Yb 106
Astell St. SW3—50Gb 81 (7E 202)
Aste St. E14—47Ec 84
Astey's Row. N1—38Sb 63
Asthall Gdns. Ilf—28Sc 46
Astleham Rd. Shep—69N 119
Astle St. SW11—54Jb 104
Astley Av. NW2—36Ya 60
Aston Av. Harr—31La 58
Aston Clo. Sidc—62Wc 131
Aston Grn. Houn—54Y 99
Aston Mead. Wind—3C 94
Aston M. Romf—31Yc 67
Aston Rd. SW20—68Ya 124
Aston Rd. W5—44Ma 79
Aston Rd. Esh—78Ga 142
Astons Rd. N'wd—20S 18
Aston St. E14—43Ac 84
Astonville St. SW18—60Cb 103
Aston Way. Eps—87Va 162
Aston Way. Pot B—4Fb 9
Astor Av. Romf—30Ed 48
Astor Clo. King—65Ra 123
Astor Clo. Wey—77M 139
Astoria Wlk. SW9—55Qb 104
Astor Rd. Sev—79Ud 154
Astra Clo. Horn—37Kd 69
Astra Dri. Grav—4G 136
Astrop M. W6—48Ya 80
Astrop Ter. W6—47Ya 80
Astwood M. SW7—49Eb 81
Asylum Rd. SE15—52Xb 105
Atalanta St. SW6—52Za 102
Atbara Rd. Tedd—65Ka 122
Atcham Rd. Houn—56Ea 100
Atcost Rd. Bark—43Wc 87
Atheldene Rd. SW18—60Eb 103
Athelney St. SE6—62Cc 128
Athelstan Clo. Romf—26Pd 49
Athelstane Gro. E3—40Bc 64
Athelstane M. N4—32Qb 62
Athelstan Rd. King—70Pa 123
Athelstan Rd. Romf—26Pd 49
Athelstone Rd. Harr—26Fa 38
Athena Clo. Harr—33Fa 58
Athenaeum Pl. N10—27Kb 42
Athenaeum Rd. N20—18Eb 23
Athenlay Rd. SE15—57Zb 106
Atherden Rd. E5—35Yb 64
Atherfold Rd. SW9—55Nb 104
Athorley Way. Houn—59Ba 99
Atherstone M. SW7
—49Eb 81 (5A 202)
Atherton Clo. Stai—58M 97
Atherton Ct. Wind—2H 95
Atherton Dri. SW19—63Za 124
Atherton Heights. Wemb—37La 58
Atherton M. E7—37Hc 65
Atherton Pl. Harr—27Fa 38
Atherton Pl. S'hall—45Ca 77
Atherton Rd. E7—37Hc 65
Atherton Rd. SW13—52Wa 102
Atherton Rd. Ilf—26Nc 46
Atherton St. SW11—54Gb 103
Athill Ct. Sev—94Ld 187
Athlone. Esh—79Ga 142
Athlone Clo. E5—36Xb 63
Athlone Clo. Rad—8Ja 6
Athlone Rd. SW2—59Pb 104
Athlone Sq. Wind—3G 94
Athlone St. NW5—37Jb 62
Athlon Rd. Wemb—40Ma 59
Athol Clo. Pinn—25X 37
Athole Gdns. Enf—15Ub 25
Athol Gdns. Pinn—25X 37
Atholl Rd. Ilf—31Wc 67
Athol Rd. Eri—50Ed 88
Athol St. E14—44Ec 84
Athol Way. Uxb—41Q 76
Atkins Clo. Wok—6D 188
Atkinson Clo. Orp—78Wc 161
Atkinson Rd. E16—43Lc 85
Atkins Rd. E10—30Dc 44
Atkins Rd. SW12—59Lb 104
Atlantic Rd. SW9—56Qb 104
Atlas Gdns. SE7—49Lc 85
Atlas M. N7—37Pb 62
Atlas Rd. E13—40Jc 65
Atlas Rd. NW10—41Ua 80
Atlas Rd. Wemb—35Sa 59
Atley Rd. E3—39Cc 64
Atney Rd. SW15—56Ab 102
Atria Rd. N'wd—22W 36
Atterbury Rd. N4—30Rb 43
Atterbury St. SW1
—49Nb 82 (6F 205)
Attewood Av. NW10—34Ua 60
Attewood Rd. N'holt—37Aa 57
Attfield Clo. N20—19Fb 23
Attle Clo. Uxb—40Q 56
Attlee Clo. Hay—41X 77
Attlee Ct. Grays—48Ce 91
Attlee Dri. Dart—57Qd 111
Attlee Rd. SE28—45Xc 87
Attlee Rd. Hay—41W 76
Attneave St. WC1
—41Qb 82 (4K 193)
Attwell's Yd. Uxb—38M 55
Attwood Clo. S Croy—86Xb 165
Atwater Clo. SW2—60Qb 104
Atwell Rd. SE15—54Wb 105
Atwood. Lea—96Aa 175
Atwood Av. Rich—54Qa 101
Atwood Rd. W6—49Xa 80
Atwoods All. Rich—53Qa 101
Aubert Ct. N5—35Rb 63
Aubert Pk. N5—35Rb 63
Aubert Rd. N5—35Rb 63
Aubretia Clo. Romf—25Nd 49
Aubrey Pl. NW8—40Eb 61 (2A 190)
Aubrey Rd. E17—27Cc 44
Aubrey Rd. N8—29Nb 42
Aubrey Rd. W8—46Bb 81
Aubrey Wlk. W8—46Bb 81
Aubyn Hill. SE27—63Sb 127
Aubyn Sq. SW15—57Wa 102
Auckland Av. Rain—41Hd 88
Auckland Clo. SE19—67Vb 127
Auckland Clo. Enf—9Xb 11
Auckland Clo. Til—4C 114
Auckland Gdns. SE19—67Ub 127
Auckland Hill. SE27—63Sb 127
Auckland Rise. SE19—67Ub 127
Auckland Rd. E10—34Dc 64
Auckland Rd. SE19—67Vb 127
Auckland Rd. SW11—56Gb 103
Auckland Rd. Cat—94Ub 181
Auckland Rd. Ilf—32Rc 66
Auckland Rd. King—70Pa 123
Auckland Rd. Pot B—4Ab 8
Auckland St. SE11—50Pb 82
Auden Pl. NW1—39Jb 62
Audleigh Pl. Chig—23Qc 46
Audley Clo. SW11—55Jb 104
Audley Clo. Borwd—13Qa 21
Audley Clo. Wey—78K 139
Audley Ct. E18—28Hc 45
Audley Ct. Pinn—26Y 37
Audley Dri. Warl—87Yb 166
Audley Gdns. Ilf—33Vc 67
Audley Gdns. Lou—12Tc 28
Audley Gdns. Wal A—6Ec 12
Audley Pl. Sutt—80Db 145
Audley Rd. NW4—30Wa 40
Audley Rd. W5—43Pa 79
Audley Rd. Enf—12Rb 25
Audley Rd. Rich—57Pa 101
Audley Sq. W1—46Jb 82 (6J 197)
Audley Wlk. Orp—72Yc 151
Audrey Clo. Beck—72Dc 148
Audrey Gdns. Wemb—33Ka 58
Audrey Rd. Ilf—34Rc 66
Audrey St. E2—40Wb 63
Audric Clo. King—67Qa 123
Audwick Clo. Wal X—1Ac 12
Augurs La. E13—41Kc 85
Augusta Rd. Twic—61Ea 122
Augusta St. E14—44Dc 84
August End. Slou—44A 74
Augustine Clo. Slou—55G 96
Augustine Rd. W14—48Za 80
Augustine Rd. Grav—9E 114
Augustine Rd. Harr—25Ea 38
Augustine Rd. Orp—69Zc 131
Augustus Clo. Bren—52La 100
Augustus Rd. SW19—60Ab 102
Augustus St. NW1
—40Kb 62 (2A 192)
Aultone Way. Cars—76Hb 145
Aultone Way. Sutt—75Db 145
Aulton Pl. SE11—50Qb 82
Aurelia Gdns. Croy—71Pb 146
Aurelia Rd. Croy—72Nb 146
Auriel Av. Dag—37Fd 68
Auriga M. N1—36Tb 63
Auriol Clo. Wor Pk—76Ua 144
Auriol Dri. Gnfd—38Fa 58
Auriol Dri. Uxb—37Q 56
Auriol Pk. Rd. Wor.Pk—76Ua 144
Auriol Rd. W14—49Ab 80
Austell Gdns. NW7—20Ua 22
Austen Clo. SE28—46Xc 87
Austen Clo. Grnh—58Yd 112
Austen Clo. Til—4E 114
Austen Rd. Harr—33Da 57
Austenway. Ger X—27A 34
Austenwood Clo. Ger X—27A 34
Austenwood La. Ger X—26A 34
Austin Av. Brom—71Nc 150
Austin Clo. SE23—59Bc 106
Austin Clo. Coul—90Rb 165
Austin Clo. Lou—13Tc 28
Austin Clo. Twic—57La 100
Austin Ct. E6—39Lc 65
Austin Friars. EC2
—44Tb 83 (2G 201)
Austin Friars Pas. EC2—(2G 201)
Austin Friars Sq. EC2—(2G 201)
Austin Gdns. Dart—56Pd 111
Austin Rd. SW11—53Jb 104
Austin Rd. Grav—10B 114
Austin Rd. Hay—47V 76
Austin Rd. Orp—72Wc 151
Austin's La. Uxb—34S 56
Austin St. E2—41Vb 83 (4K 195)
Austin Waye. Uxb—39L 55
Austral Clo. Sidc—62Vc 131
Austral Dri. Horn—31Md 69
Australia Rd. W12—45Xa 80
Australia Rd. Slou—7M 73
Austral St. SE11—49Rb 83 (5B 206)
Austyn Gdns. Surb—74Ra 143
Autumn Clo. Enf—11Wb 25
Autumn Clo. Slou—6D 72
Autumn St. E3—39Cc 64
Avalon Clo. W13—43Ja 78
Avalon Clo. Enf—12Qb 24
Avalon Clo. Orp—76Zc 151
Avalon Rd. SW6—53Db 103
Avalon Rd. W13—42Ja 78
Avalon Rd. Orp—75Yc 151
Avard Gdns. Orp—77Sc 150
Avarn Rd. SW17—65Hb 125
Avebury. Slou—5E 72
Avebury Ct. N1—(1F 195)
Avebury Pk. Surb—73Ma 143
Avebury Rd. E11—32Fc 65
Avebury Rd. SW19—67Bb 125
Avebury Rd. Orp—76Tc 150
Avebury St. N1—39Tb 63
Aveley By-Pass. S Ock—45Sd 90
Aveley Clo. S Ock—46Td 90
Aveley Rd. Romf—28Gd 48
Aveley Rd. Upm—37Rd 69
Aveline St. SE11—50Qb 82 (7J 205)
Aveling Clo. Purl—85Pb 164
Aveling Pk. Rd. E17—26Cc 44
Avelon Rd. Rain—39Jd 68
Avelon Rd. Romf—23Fd 48
Ave Maria La. EC4
—44Rb 83 (3C 200)
Avenell Rd. N5—34Rb 63
Avening Rd. SW18—59Cb 103
Avening Ter. SW18—59Cb 103
Avenons Rd. E13—42Jc 85
Avenue App. K Lan—2Q 4
Avenue Clo. N14—16Lb 24
Avenue Clo. NW8
—39Gb 61 (1E 190)
Avenue Clo. Houn—53X 99
Avenue Clo. Romf—24Pd 49
Avenue Clo. Tad—94Xa 178
Avenue Clo. W Dray—48M 75
Avenue Cres. W3—47Ra 79
Avenue Cres. Houn—53X 99
Avenue Elmers. Surb—71Na 143
Avenue Gdns. SE25—68Wb 127
Avenue Gdns. SW14—55Ua 102
Avenue Gdns. W3—47Ra 79
Avenue Gdns. Houn—52X 99
Avenue Gdns. Tedd—66Ha 122
Avenue Industrial Est. Romf
—26Mb 42
Avenue M. N10—27Kb 42
Avenue Pk. Rd. SE27—61Rb 127
Avenue Rise. Bush, Wat—15Ca 19
Avenue Rd. E7—35Kc 65
Avenue Rd. N6—31Lb 62
Avenue Rd. N12—21Eb 41
Avenue Rd. N14—17Lb 24
Avenue Rd. N15—29Tb 43
Avenue Rd.—38Fb 61 (1E 190)
NW8 1-95 & 2-86
NW3 remainder
Avenue Rd. NW10—40Va 60
Avenue Rd.—67Yb 128
SE20 1-55 & 2-50
Beck remainder
Avenue Rd. SE25—68Wb 127
Avenue Rd. SW16—68Mb 126
Avenue Rd. SW20—68Xa 124
Avenue Rd. W3—47Ra 79
Avenue Rd. Bans—87Db 163
Avenue Rd. Belv—49Ed 88
Avenue Rd. Bexh—55Ad 109
Avenue Rd. Bren—50La 78
Avenue Rd. Brtwd—21Yd 50
Avenue Rd. Cat—94Ub 181
Avenue Rd. Cob—88Z 159
Avenue Rd. Epp—8Tc 14
Avenue Rd. Eps—86Ta 161
Avenue Rd. Eri—52Ed 110
Avenue Rd. Felt—62V 120
Avenue Rd. Hmptn—67Da 121
Avenue Rd. Iswth—53Ha 100
Avenue Rd. King—69Na 123
Avenue Rd. N Mald—70Ua 124
Avenue Rd. Pinn—27Aa 37
Avenue Rd. Romf—31Yc 67
(Chadwell Heath)
Avenue Rd. Romf—24Pd 49
(Harold Wood)
Avenue Rd. Sev—96Ld 187
Avenue Rd. S'hall—46Ba 77
Avenue Rd. Stai—64F 118
Avenue Rd. Sutt—82Cb 163
Avenue Rd. Tedd—66Ja 122
Avenue Rd. Wall—80Lb 146
Avenue Rd. West—92Nc 184
Avenue Rd. Wfd G—23Lc 45
Avenue S. Surb—73Qa 143
Avenue Ter. N Mald—69Sa 123
Avenue, The. E4—21Gc 45
Avenue, The. E11—29Kc 45
Avenue, The. N3—26Cb 41
Avenue, The. N8—27Qb 43
Avenue, The. N10—26Lb 42
Avenue, The. N11—22Kb 42
Avenue, The. N17—26Ub 43
Avenue, The. NW6—39Ab 60
Avenue, The. SE7—52Lc 107
Avenue, The. SE9—58Pc 108
Avenue, The. SE10—52Fc 107
Avenue, The. SW4—57Kb 104
Avenue, The. SW18 & SW11
—59Gb 103
Avenue, The. W4—48Ua 80
Avenue, The. W13—45Ka 78
Avenue, The. Barn—13Ab 22
Avenue, The. Beck—67Dc 128
Avenue, The. Bex—59Zc 109
Avenue, The. Brtwd—23Ae 51
Avenue, The. Brtwd—11Ud 32
(Doddinghurst)
Avenue, The. Brom—69Mc 129
Avenue, The. Bush, Wat—15Ba 19
Avenue, The. Cars—80Jb 146
Avenue, The. Coul—87Mb 164
Avenue, The. Croy—76Ub 147
Avenue, The. Egh—63D 118
Avenue, The. Eps & Sutt—80Za 144
Avenue, The. Esh—78Ga 142
Avenue, The. Grav—9C 114
Avenue, The. Grav—9L 137
(Cobham)
Avenue, The. Grnh—56Xd 112
Avenue, The. Hmptn—65Ba 121
Avenue, The. Harr—25Ha 38
Avenue, The. Horn—33Md 69
Avenue, The. Houn—57Da 99
Avenue, The. Houn—53W 98
(Cranford)
Avenue, The. Kes—76Mc 149
Avenue, The. Lea—84Ha 160
Avenue, The. Lou—16Nc 28
Avenue, The. N'wd—23S 36
Avenue, The. Orp—75Vc 151
Avenue, The. Orp—67Xc 131
(St Pauls Cray)
Avenue, The. Pinn—23Ba 37
(Hatch End)
Avenue, The. Pinn—31Ba 57
(Rayners Lane)
Avenue, The. Pot B—3Cb 9
Avenue, The. Rad—6Ka 6
Avenue, The. Rich—54Pa 101
Avenue, The. Romf—28Fd 48
★Avenue, The. Sev—91Ce
Avenue, The. Slou—3M 95
(Datchet)
Avenue, The. Slou—6F 52
(Farnham Common)
Avenue, The. Stai—67K 119
Avenue, The. Sun—69X 121
Avenue, The. Surb—73Qa 143
Avenue, The. Sutt—82Bb 163
Avenue, The. Tad—94Xa 178
Avenue, The. Twic—57Ka 100
Avenue, The. Uxb—42M 75
(Cowley)
Avenue, The. Uxb—34R 56
(Ickenham)
Avenue, The. Wat—12W 18
Avenue, The. Wemb—32Na 59
Avenue, The. West—95Qc 184
Avenue, The. W Wick—72Gc 149
Avenue, The. Wey—82J 157
Avenue, The. Whyt—91Wb 181
Avenue, The. Wind—7M 95
Avenue, The. Wor Pk—75Va 144
Avenue, The. Wray, Stai—56A 96
Averil Ct. M'head—4A 72
Averil Gro. SW16—65Rb 127
Averill St. W6—51Za 102
Avern Gdns. E Mol—70Da 121
Avern Rd. E Mol—70Da 121
Avery Farm Row. SW1
—49Kb 82 (6K 203)
Avery Gdns. Ilf—29Pc 46
Avery Hill Rd. SE9—58Tc 108
Avery Row. W1—45Kb 82 (4K 197)
Avey La. Wal A & Lou—8Fc 13
Aviary Clo. E16—43Hc 85
Aviary Rd. Wok—88J 157
Aviemore Clo. Beck—71Bc 148
Aviemore Way. Beck—71Ac 148
Avignon Rd. SE4—55Zb 106
Avington Gro. SE20—66Yb 128
Avington Way. SE15—52Vb 105
Avior Dri. N'wd—21V 36
Avis Sq. E1—44Zb 84
Avoca Rd. SW17—63Jb 126
Avocet M. SE28—48Tc 86
Avon Clo. Grav—1F 136
Avon Clo. Hay—42Y 77
Avon Clo. Slou—5C 72
Avon Clo. Sutt—77Eb 145
Avon Clo. Wat—6Y 5
Avon Clo. Wey—79J 139
Avon Clo. Wor Pk—75Wa 144
Avondale Av. N12—22Db 41
Avondale Av. NW2—34Ua 60
Avondale Av. Barn—18Hb 23
Avondale Av. Esh—76Ja 142
Avondale Av. Stai—66H 119
Avondale Av. Wor Pk—74Va 144
Avondale Clo. Lou—17Pc 28
Avondale Clo. W on T—78Y 141
Avondale Ct. E16—43Gc 85
Avondale Ct. E18—25Kc 45
Avondale Cres. Enf—13Ac 26
Avondale Cres. Ilf—29Mc 45
Avondale Dri. Hay—46W 76
Avondale Dri. Lou—17Pc 28
Avondale Gdns. Houn—57Ba 99
Avondale Pk. Gdns. W11—45Ab 80
Avondale Pk. Rd. W11—45Ab 80
Avondale Rise. SE15—55Vb 105
Avondale Rd. E16—43Gc 85
Avondale Rd. E17—31Cc 64
Avondale Rd. N3—25Eb 41
Avondale Rd. N13—19Qb 24
Avondale Rd. N15—29Rb 43
Avondale Rd. SE9—61Nc 130
Avondale Rd. SW14—55Ta 101
Avondale Rd. SW19—64Db 125
Avondale Rd. Ashf—62M 119
Avondale Rd. Brom—65Gc 129
Avondale Rd. Harr—27Ha 38
Avondale Rd. S Croy—79Sb 147
Avondale Rd. Well—54Yc 109
Avondale Sq. SE1—50Wb 83
Avon Grn. S Ock—44Xd 90
Avonley Rd. SE14—52Yb 106
Avonmead. Wok—6F 188
Avonmead M. Pinn—25Ba 37
Avonmore Rd. W14—49Bb 81
Avonmouth St. SE1
—48Sb 83 (3D 206)
Avon Path. S Croy—79Sb 147
Avon Pl. SE1—47Sb 83 (2E 206)
Avon Rd. E17—27Fc 45
Avon Rd. SE4—55Cc 106
Avon Rd. Gnfd—42Ca 77
Avon Rd. Sun—66V 120
Avon Rd. Upm—30Td 50
Avontar Rd. S Ock—42Xd 90
Avon Way. E18—27Jc 45
Avonwick Rd. Houn—54Da 99
Avril Way. E4—22Ec 44
Avro Way. Wall—80Nb 146
Awlfield Av. N17—25Tb 43
Awliscombe Rd. Well—54Vc 109
Axe St. Bark—39Sc 66
Axholme Av. Edgw—25Qa 39
Axminster Cres. Well—53Yc 109
Axminster Rd. N7—34Nb 62
Axtaine Rd. Orp—73Zc 151
Axwood. Eps—87Sa 161
Aybrook St. W1—43Jb 82 (1H 197)
Aycliffe Clo. Brom—70Pc 130
Aycliffe Rd. W12—46Wa 80
Aycliffe Rd. Borwd—11Na 21
Ayebridges Av. Egh—66E 118
Ayelands. Long, Dart—75Ae 155
Ayelands La. Long, Dart—76Ae 155
Aylands Rd. Enf—8Zb 12
Aylesbury Clo. E7—37Hc 65
Aylesbury Cres. Slou—4H 73
Aylesbury Rd. SE17
—50Tb 83 (7G 207)
Aylesbury Rd. Brom—69Jc 129
Aylesbury St. EC1
—42Rb 83 (6B 194)
Aylesbury St. NW10—34Ta 59
Aylesford Av. Beck—71Ac 148
Aylesford St. SW1
—50Mb 82 (7D 204)
Aylesham Rd. Orp—73Vc 151
Ayles Rd. Hay—41X 77
Aylestone Av. NW6—38Za 60
Aylesworth Av. Slou—1F 72
Aylesworth Spur. Wind—9M 95
Aylett Rd. SE25—70Xb 127
Aylett Rd. Iswth—54Ga 100
Aylett Rd. Upm—33Sd 70
Ayley Croft. Enf—15Wb 25
Aylmer Clo. Stan—21Ja 38
Aylmer Dri. Stan—21Ja 38
Aylmer Rd. E11—32Hc 65
Aylmer Rd. N2—29Gb 41
Aylmer Rd. W12—47Va 80
Aylmer Rd. Dag—34Ad 67
Ayloffe Rd. Dag—37Bd 67
Ayloffs Clo. Horn—28Md 49
Ayloffs Wlk. Horn—29Md 49
Aylsham Dri. Uxb—33S 56
Aylsham La. Romf—21Ld 49
Aylward Rd. SE23—61Zb 128
Aylward Rd. SW20—68Bb 125
Aylwards Rise. Stan—21Ja 38
Aylward St. E1—44Zb 84
Aylward St. E1
Aylwin Est. SE1—48Ub 83 (3J 207)
Aymer Clo. Stai—67G 118
Aymer Dri. Stai—67G 118
Aynhoe Rd. W14—49Za 80
Aynho St. Wat—15X 19
Aynscombe Angle. Orp—73Wc 151
Aynscombe Path. SW14
—54Sa 101
Ayot Path. Borwd—10Qa 7
Ayres Clo. E13—41Jc 85
Ayres Cres. NW10—38Ta 59
Ayres St. SE1—47Sb 83 (1E 206)
Ayr Grn. Romf—25Gd 48
Ayron Rd. S Ock—42Xd 90
Ayrsome Rd. N16—34Ub 63
Ayr Way. Romf—25Gd 48
Aysgarth Rd. SE21—59Ub 105
Aytoun Pl. SW9—54Pb 104
Aytoun Rd. SW9—54Pb 104
Azalea Clo. W7—46Ha 78
Azalea Ct. Wok—7G 188
Azalea Ct. Wfd G—24Gc 45
Azalea Dri. Swan—70Fd 132
Azalea Wlk. Pinn—29X 37
Azalea Way. Slou—44A 74
Azenby Rd. SE15—54Vb 105
Azof St. SE10—49Gc 85

Baalbec Rd. N5—36Rb 63
Babbacombe Clo. Chess
—78Ma 143
Babbacombe Gdns. Ilf—28Nc 46
Babbacombe Rd. Brom—67Jc 129
Baber Dri. Felt—58Y 99
Babington Rise. Wemb—37Ra 59
Babington Rd. NW4—28Xa 40
Babington Rd. SW16—64Mb 126
Babington Rd. Dag—36Yc 67
Babington Rd. Horn—32Kd 69
Babmaes St. SW1
—45Mb 82 (5D 198)
Babylon La. Tad—99Cb 179
Bacchus Wlk. N1—(2H 195)
Bachelors Acre. Wind—3H 95
Bachelors La. Wok—96Q 174
Bache's St. N1—41Tb 83 (4G 195)
Back All. EC3—(3J 201)
Bk. Church La. E1—44Wb 83
Back Grn. W on T—79Y 141
Back Hill. EC1—42Qb 82 (6A 194)
Backhouse Pl. SE17—(6J 207)
Back La. N8—29Nb 42
Back La. NW3—35Eb 61
Back La. Bex—59Cd 110
Back La. Bren—51Ma 101
★Back La. Brtwd—8Wd
Back La. Edgw—25Sa 39
Back La. Grays—48Xd 90
Back La. Red—100Fb 179
Back La. Rich—62La 122
(in two parts)
Back La. Rick—10D 2
Back La. Romf—31Zc 67
★Back La. Sev—96Yd
(Ightham Common)
Back La. Sev—96Qd 187
(Godden Green)
Back La. Sev—96Fd 186
(Whitley Row)
Back La. Sev—100Dd 186
(Whitley Row)
Back La. Wind—3H 95
Back Pas. EC1—(1C 200)
Back Rd. Sidc—63Wc 131
Back St. W3—46Ra 79
Bacon Gro. SE1—48Vb 83 (4K 207)
Bacon La. NW9—28Ra 39
Bacon La. Edgw—25Qa 39
Bacon Link. Romf—23Dd 48
Bacons Dri. Pot B—1Nb 10
Bacons La. N6—32Jb 62
Bacons Mead. Uxb—33J 55
Bacon St.—42Vb 83 (5K 195)
E1 1-21 & 2-22
E2 remainder
Bacton St. E2—41Yb 84
Badburgham Ct. Wal A—5Hc 13
Baddow Clo. Dag—39Cd 68
Baddows Clo. Wfd G—23Mc 45
Baden Clo. Stai—66K 119
Baden Pl. SE1—47Tb 83 (1F 207)
Baden Powell Clo. Surb—75Pa 143
Baden Powell Rd. Sev—94Gd 186
Baden Rd. N8—28Mb 42
Baden Rd. Ilf—36Rc 66
Bader Clo. Kenl—87Tb 165
Bader Wlk. Grav—2B 136
Bader Way. Rain—37Jd 68
Badger Clo. Felt—62X 121
Badger Clo. Houn—55Y 99
Badgersbridge Ride. Wind—9A 94
Badgers Clo. Enf—13Rb 25
Badgers Clo. Harr—30Fa 38
Badgers Clo. Hay—41U 76
Badgers Copse. Orp—75Vc 151
Badgers Copse. Wor Pk—75Va 144
Badgers Croft. N20—18Ab 22
Badgers Croft. SE9—62Qc 130
Badgers Hill. Vir W—10N 117
Badgers Hole. Croy—77Zb 148
Badgers La. Warl—92Yb 182
Badgers Mt. Grays—7B 92
Badgers Rd. Sev—82Dd 170
Badgers Wlk. N Mald—68Ua 124
Badgers Wlk. Whyt—90Vb 165
Badgers Wood. Cat—97Tb 181
Badgers Wood. Slou—6G 52
Badingham Dri. Lea—95Ga 176
Badlis Rd. E17—27Cc 44
Badlow Clo. Eri—52Gd 110
Badminton Clo. Borwd—12Qa 21
Badminton Clo. Harr—28Ga 38
Badminton Clo. N'holt—37Ca 57
Badminton Rd. SW12—58Jb 104
Badsworth Rd. SE5—53Sb 105
Baffins Pl. SE1—(2G 207)
Bagford St. N1—39Tb 63
Bagley Clo. W Dray—47N 75
Bagley's La. SW6—53Db 103
Bagleys Spring. Romf—28Ad 47
Bagot Clo. Asht—88Pa 161
Bagshot Ct. SE18—53Qc 108
Bagshot Rd. Egh—6N 117
Bagshot Rd. Enf—16Vb 25
Bagshot Rd. Wok—10A 188
Bagshot St. SE17
—50Ub 83 (7J 207)
Bahram Rd. Eps—82Ta 161
Baildon St. SE8—52Bc 106
Bailey Clo. Wind—4E 94
Bailey Pl. SE26—65Zb 128
Baillie Clo. Rain—42Kd 89
Baillies Wlk. W5—47Ma 79
Bainbridge Rd. Dag—35Bd 67
Bainbridge St. WC1
—44Mb 82 (2E 198)
Baird Av. S'hall—45Da 77
Baird Clo. NW9—30Sa 39
Baird Clo. Bush, Wat—16Da 19
Baird Gdns. SE21—63Ub 127
Baird Rd. Enf—14Xb 25
Baird St. EC1—42Sb 83 (5E 194)
Bairstow Clo. Borwd—11Na 21
Baizdon Rd. SE3—54Gc 107
Bakeham La. Egh—6P 117
Baker Boy La. Croy—85Ac 166
Bakerhill Clo. Grav—3B 136
Baker La. Mitc—68Jb 126
Baker Rd. NW10—39Ua 60
Baker Rd. SE18—52Nc 108
Bakers Av. E17—30Dc 44
Bakers Av. Sev—80Ud 154
Bakers Ct. SE25—69Ub 127
Bakers End. SW20—68Ab 124
Baker's Field. N7—35Mb 62
Bakers Hall Ct. EC3
—45Ub 83 (5H 201)
Bakers Hill. E5—32Yb 64
Bakers Hill. Barn—12Db 23
Bakers La. N6—30Hb 41
Bakers La. Epp—2Vc 15
★Bakers Meadow. Brtwd—9Yd
Baker's M. W1—44Jb 82 (2H 197)
Baker's Rents. E2
—41Vb 83 (4K 195)
Bakers Rd. Uxb—38M 55
Bakers Rd. Wal X—2Xb 11
Baker's Row. E15—40Gc 65
Baker's Row. EC1
—42Qb 82 (6K 193)
Baker St.—43Hb 81 (6G 191)
W1 1-133 & 2-136
NW1 remainder
Baker St. Enf—12Tb 25
Baker St. Grays—4A 92
Baker St. Pot B—7Ab 8
Baker St. Wey—77Q 140
Bakers Wood. Uxb—32F 54
Baker's Yd. Uxb—38M 55
Bakewell Way. N Mald—68Ua 124
Balaams La. N14—19Mb 24
Balaam St. E13—42Jc 85
Balaclava Rd. SE1
—49Vb 83 (6K 207)
Balaclava Rd. Surb—73La 142
Balben Path. E9—38Yb 64
Balcaskie Rd. SE9—57Pc 108
Balchen Rd. SE3—54Mc 107
Balchier Rd. SE22—58Xb 105
Balcombe St. NW1
—42Hb 81 (6F 191)
Balcon Way. Borwd—11Sa 21
Balcorne St. E9—38Yb 64
Balder Rise. SE12—61Kc 129
Balderton St. W1—44Jb 82 (3J 197)
Baldocks Rd. Epp—7Uc 14
Baldock St. E3—40Dc 64
Baldock Way. Borwd—11Pa 21
Baldry Gdns. SW16—65Nb 126
Baldwin Cres. SE5—53Sb 105
Baldwin Rd. Slou—1A 72
Baldwin's Gdns. EC1
—43Qb 82 (7K 193)
Baldwins Hill. Lou—12Pc 28
Baldwin's La. Rick—14Q 18
Baldwins Shore. Wind—1H 95
Baldwin St. EC1—41Tb 83 (4F 195)

Baldwin Ter.—Bath Rd.

Baldwin Ter. N1—40Sb 63 (1D 194)
Baldwyn Gdns. W3—45Ta 79
Baldwyn's Pk. Bex—61Fd 132
Baldwyn's Rd. Bex—61Fd 132
Bales Ct. EC4—(2B 200)
Bales Ter. N9—20Vb 25
Balfern Gro. W4—50Ua 80
Balfern St. SW11—54Gb 103
Balfe St. N1—40Nb 62 (1G 193)
Balfont Clo. S Croy—85Wb 165
Balfour App. Ilf—33Rc 66
Balfour Av. W7—46Ha 78
Balfour Av. Wok—94A 172
Balfour Gro. N20—20Hb 23
Balfour M. N9—20Wb 25
Balfour M. W1—46Jb 82 (6J 197)
Balfour of Burleigh Est. W10 —43Za 80
Balfour Pl. SW15—56Xa 102
Balfour Pl. W1—45Jb 82 (5J 197)
Balfour Rd. N5—35Sb 63
Balfour Rd. SE25—70Wb 127
Balfour Rd. SW19—66Db 125
Balfour Rd. W3—43Sa 79
Balfour Rd. W13—47Ja 78
Balfour Rd. Brom—71Mc 149
Balfour Rd. Cars—80Hb 145
Balfour Rd. Grays—49Ee 91
Balfour Rd. Harr—29Fa 38
Balfour Rd. Houn—55Da 99
Balfour Rd. Ilf—33Rc 66
Balfour Rd. S'hall—48Z 77
Balfour Rd. Wey—77Q 139
Balfour St. SE17—49Tb 83 (5F 207)
Balfour Ter. N3—26Db 41
Balgonie Rd. E4—18Fc 27
Balgores Cres. Romf—27Kd 49
Balgores La. Romf—27Kd 49
Balgores Sq. Romf—28Kd 49
Balgowan Clo. N Mald—70Ua 124
Balgowan Rd. Beck—69Ac 128
Balgowan St. SE18—49Vc 87
Balham Gro. SW12—59Jb 104
Balham High Rd.—62Jb 126
SW12 1-197 & 2-222
SW17 remainder
Balham Hill. SW12—59Kb 104
Balham New Rd. SW12—59Kb 104
Balham Pk. Rd. SW12—60Hb 103
Balham Rd. N9—19Wb 25
Balham Sta. Rd. SW12—60Kb 104
Ballamore Rd. Brom—62Jc 129
Ballance Rd. E9—37Zb 64
Ballands N., The. Lea—94Ga 176
Ballands S., The. Lea—95Ga 176
Ballantine St. SW18—56Eb 103
Ballantyne Dri. Tad—93Bb 179
Ballard Clo. King—66Ta 123
Ballard Grn. Wind—2C 94
Ballards Clo. Dag—39Dd 68
Ballards Farm Rd. S Croy & Croy—79Wb 147
Ballards Grn. Tad—91Ab 178
Ballards La.—25Cb 41
N3 1-265 & 2-240
N12 remainder
Ballards La. Oxt—100Lc 183
Ballards Rise. S Croy—79Wb 147
Ballards Rd. NW2—33Wa 60
Ballards Rd. Dag—39Dd 68
Ballards Way. S Croy & Croy —79Wb 147
Ballards Yd. Edgw—23Qa 39
Ballast Quay. SE10—50Fc 85
Ballater Clo. Wat—21Y 37
Ballater Rd. SW2—56Nb 104
Ballater Rd. S Croy—78Vb 147
Ball Ct. EC3—(3G 201)
Ballenger Ct. Wat—13X 19
Ballina St. SE23—59Zb 106
Ballingdon Rd. SW11—58Jb 104
Balliol Av. E4—21Gc 45
Balliol Rd. N17—25Ub 43
Balliol Rd. W10—44Ya 80
Balliol Rd. Well—54Xc 109
Balloch Rd. SE6—60Fc 107
Ballogie Av. NW10—35Ua 60
Ballow Clo. SE5—52Ub 105
Balls Pond Rd. N1—37Tb 63
Balmain Clo. W5—46Ma 79
Balmer Rd. E3—40Bc 64
Balmes Rd. N1—39Tb 63
Balmoral Av. Beck—70Ac 128
Balmoral Clo. SW15—58Za 102
Balmoral Clo. Slou—4C 72
Balmoral Ct. Wemb—34Pa 59
Balmoral Cres. E Mol—69Ca 121
Balmoral Dri. Borwd—15Ta 21
Balmoral Dri. Hay—42U 76
Balmoral Dri. S'hall—42Ba 77
Balmoral Dri. Wok—88E 156
Balmoral Gdns. W13—48Ja 78
Balmoral Gdns. Ilf—32Vc 67
Balmoral Gdns. Wind—5H 95
Balmoral Gro. N7—37Pb 62
Balmoral M. W12—48Va 80
Balmoral Rd. E7—35Lc 65
Balmoral Rd. E10—33Dc 64
Balmoral Rd. NW2—37Xa 60
Balmoral Rd. Brtwd—16Xd 32
Balmoral Rd. Enf—8Zb 12
Balmoral Rd. Harr—35Ca 57
Balmoral Rd. Horn—34Md 69
Balmoral Rd. King—70Pa 123
Balmoral Rd. Romf—29Kd 49
Balmoral Rd. S at H, Dart —66Rd 133
Balmoral Rd. Wat—10Y 5
Balmoral Rd. Wor Pk—75Xa 144
Balmoral Way. Sutt—82Cb 163
Balmore Cres. Barn—15Jb 24
Balmore St. N19—33Kb 62
Balmuir Gdns. SW15—56Ya 102
Balnacraig Av. NW10—35Ua 60
Balquhain Clo. Asht—89Ma 161
Baltic Clo. SW19—66Fb 125
Baltic St. EC1—42Sb 83 (6D 194)
Baltimore Pl. Well—54Vc 109
Balvernie Gro. SW18—59Bb 103
Bamborough Gdns. W12—47Ya 80
Bamford Av. Wemb—39Pa 59
Bamford Rd. Bark—37Sc 66
Bamford Rd. Brom—64Ec 128
Bamford Way. Romf—22Dd 48
Bampfylde Clo. Wall—76Lb 146
Bampton Rd. SE23—62Zb 128
Bampton Rd. Romf—25Nd 49
Bampton Way. Wok—6D 188
Banavie Gdns. Beck—67Ec 128
Banbury Av. Slou—3D 72
Banbury Ct. WC2—(4F 199)
Banbury Ct. Sutt—80Cb 145
Banbury Rd. E9—38Zb 64
Banbury St. SW11—54Gb 103
Banbury St. Wat—15W 18
Banchory Rd. SE3—52Kc 107
Banckside. Long, Dart—70Ae 135
Bancroft Av. N2—29Gb 41
Bancroft Av. Buck H—19Jc 27
Bancroft Clo. Ashf—64Q 120
Bancroft Ct. N'holt—39Y 57
Bancroft Gdns. Harr—25Ea 38
Bancroft Gdns. Orp—74Vc 151
Bancroft Rd. E1—41Zb 84
Bancroft Rd. Harr—26Ea 38
★Bancroft Rd. Sev—88Be
Band La. Egh—64B 118
Bandon Rise. Wall—78Mb 146
Bangalore St. SW15—55Za 102
Bangor Clo. N'holt—36Da 57
Bangors Clo. Iver—44G 74
Bangors Rd. N. Iver—39F 54
Bangors Rd. S. Iver—41G 74
Banim St. W6—49Xa 80
Banister Rd. W10—41Za 80
Bank Av. Mitc—68Fb 125
Bank Ct. Dart—58Nd 111
Bank End. SE1—46Sb 83 (6E 200)
Bankfoot Rd. Brom—63Gc 129
Bankhurst Rd. SE6—59Bc 106
Bank La. SW15—57Ua 102
Bank La. King—66Na 123
Bank Pl. Brtwd—19Yd 32
Banksian Wlk. Iswth—53Ga 100
Bankside. SE1—45Sb 83 (5D 200)
Bankside. Enf—11Rb 25
Bankside. Grav—58Ee 113
Bankside. S'hall—46Z 77
Bankside. S Croy—79Vb 147
Bankside. Wok—6E 188
(in two parts)
Bankside Av. N'holt—40W 56
Bankside Clo. Bex—63Fd 132
Bankside Clo. Cars—79Gb 145
Bankside Clo. West—90Lc 167
Bankside Dri. Th Dit—74Ka 142
Bankside Way. SE19—65Ub 127
Banks La. Bexh—56Bd 109
Banks La. Epp—4Ad 15
Bank's La. Lea—95W 174
Bank St. Grav—8D 114
Bank St. Sev—97Ld 187
Bank, The. N6—32Kb 62
Bankton Rd. SW2—56Qb 104
Bankwell Rd. SE13—56Gc 107
Bann Clo. S Ock—45Xd 90
Banner St. EC1—42Sb 83 (6E 194)
Banning St. SE10—50Gc 85
Bannister Clo. Gnfd—36Fa 58
Bannister Clo. Slou—47A 74
Bannister Rd. SW2—60Qb 104
Bannockburn Rd. SE18—49Uc 86
Banstead Gdns. N9—20Ub 25
Banstead Rd. Cars—81Fb 163
Banstead Rd. Cat—94Tb 181
Banstead Rd. Eps & Bans —83Ya 162
Banstead Rd. Purl—83Qb 164
Banstead Rd. S. Sutt—83Eb 163
Banstead Way. Wall—78Nb 146
Banstock Rd. Edgw—23Ra 39
Banton Clo. Enf—12Xb 25
Bantry St. SE5—52Tb 105
Banwell Rd. Bex—58Zc 109
Banyard Rd. SE16—48Xb 83
Banyards. Horn—28Nd 49
Bapchild Pl. Orp—70Yc 131
Baptist Gdns. NW5—37Jb 62
Barandon Wlk. W11—45Za 80
Barbara Clo. Shep—71R 140
Barbauld St. N16—34Ub 63
Barbel Clo. Wal X—6Cc 12
Barber Clo. N21—17Qb 24
Barberry Clo. Romf—24Ld 49
Barbers All. E13—41Kc 85
Barbers Rd. E15—40Dc 64
Barbican. EC2—43Sb 83 (1E 200)
Barbican Rd. Gnfd—44Da 77
Barb M. W6—48Ya 80
Barbon Clo. WC1 —43Pb 82 (7G 193)
Barbot Clo. N9—20Wb 25
Barchard St. SW18—57Db 103
Barchester Clo. W7—46Ha 78
Barchester Clo. Uxb—42L 75
Barchester Rd. Harr—26Fa 38
Barchester Rd. Slou—47B 74
Barchester St. E14—43Dc 84
Barclay Clo. SW6—52Cb 103
Barclay Clo. Lea—95Da 175
Barclay Oval. Wfd G—21Jc 45
Barclay Rd. E11—32Hc 65
Barclay Rd. E13—42Lc 85
Barclay Rd. E17—29Ec 44
Barclay Rd. N18—23Tb 43
Barclay Rd. SW6—52Cb 103
Barclay Rd. Croy—76Tb 147
Barcombe Av. SW2—61Nb 126
Barden Clo. Uxb—24L 35
Barden St. SE18—52Uc 108
Bardeswell Clo. Brtwd—19Yd 32
Bardfield Av. Romf—27Zc 47
Bardney Rd. Mord—70Db 125
Bardolph Av. Croy—81Bc 166
Bardolph Rd. N7—35Nb 62
Bardolph Rd. Rich—55Pa 101
Bardon Wlk. Wok—5E 188
Bard Rd. W10—45Za 80
Bardsey Pl. E1—42Yb 84
Bardsey Wlk. N1—37Sb 63
Bardsley Clo. Croy—76Vb 147
Bardsley La. SE10—51Ec 106
Barfett St. W10—42Bb 81
Barfield. S at H, Dart—67Rd 133
Barfield Av. N20—19Hb 23
Barfield Rd. E11—32Hc 65
Barfield Rd. Brom—69Qc 130
Barfields. Lou—14Qc 28
Barfields Gdns. Lou—14Qc 28
Barfields Path. Lou—14Qc 28
Barford Clo. NW4—26Wa 40
Barford St. N1—39Qb 62 (1A 194)
Barforth Rd. SE15—55Xb 105
Barfreston Way. SE20—67Xb 127
Bargate Clo. SE18—50Vc 87
Bargate Clo. N Mald—73Wa 144
Barge Ho. Rd. E16—47Rc 86
Barge Ho. St. SE1 —46Qb 82 (6A 200)
Bargery Rd. SE6—60Dc 106
Barge Wlk. E Mol & King 69Fa 122 to 69Ma 123
Barge Wlk. King—67Ma 123
Bargrove Clo. SE20—66Wb 127
Bargrove Cres. SE6—61Bc 128
Barham Av. Borwd—13Pa 21
Barham Clo. Brom—74Nc 150
Barham Clo. Chst—64Rc 130
Barham Clo. Romf 26Dd 48
Barham Clo. Wemb—37Ka 58
Barham Clo. Wey—77S 140
Barham Rd. SW20—66Wa 124
Barham Rd. Chst—64Rc 130
Barham Rd. Dart—59Qd 111
Barham Rd. S Croy—78Sb 147
Baring Clo. SE12—61Jc 129
Baring Rd. SE12—59Jc 107
Baring Rd. Barn—13Fb 23
Baring Rd. Croy—74Wb 147
Baring St. N1—39Tb 63
Barker Dri. NW1—38Lb 62
Barker Rd. Cher—73G 138
Barker St. SW10—51Eb 103
Barker Wlk. SW16—62Mb 126
Barkham Rd. N17—24Ub 43
Bark Hart Rd. Orp—74Xc 151
Barking Rd.—43Hc 85
E16 1-233 & 2-242
E13 remainder
Barkis Way. SE16—50Xb 83
Bark Pl. W2—45Db 81
Barkston Gdns. SW5—49Db 81
Barkston Path. Borwd—10Qa 7
Barkworth Rd. SE16—50Yb 84
Barlborough St. SE14—52Zb 106
Barlby Gdns. W10—42Za 80
Barlby Rd. W10—43Ya 80
Barlee Cres. Uxb—43L 75
Barle Gdns. S Ock—44Xd 90
Barley Clo. Bush, Wat—15Da 19
Barleycorn Way. E14—45Bc 84
Barleycorn Way. Horn—30Pd 49
★Barley Field. Brtwd—9Vd
Barley La. Ilf & Romf—31Wc 67
Barley Mow Clo. Wok—5A 188
Barley Mow La. Wok—4A 188
Barleymow Pas. EC1—(1C 200)
Barley Mow Pas. W4—50Ta 79
Barley Mow Rd. Egh—4N 117
Barleymow Way. Shep—70Q 120
Barlow Clo. Wall—79Nb 146
Barlow Pl. W1—(5A 198)
Barlow Rd. NW6—37Bb 61
Barlow Rd. W3—46Ra 79
Barlow Rd. Hmptn—66Ca 121
Barlow St. SE17—49Tb 83 (6G 207)
Barmeston Rd. SE6—61Dc 128
Barmor Clo. Harr—26Da 37
Barmouth Av. Gnfd—40Ha 58
Barmouth Rd. SW18—58Eb 103
Barmouth Rd. Croy—75Zb 148
Barnabas Rd. E9—36Zb 64
Barnaby Way. Chig—20Rc 28
Barnacre Clo. Uxb—44M 75
Barnard Clo. SE18—48Qc 86
Barnard Clo. Chst—67Tc 130
Barnard Clo. Sun—66X 121
Barnard Clo. Wall—80Mb 146
Barnard Ct. Wok—6B 188
Barnard Gdns. Hay—42X 77
Barnard Gdns. N Mald—70Wa 124
Barnard Gro. E15—38Hc 65
Barnard Hill. N10—25Kb 42
Barnard M. SW11—56Gb 103
Barnardo Dri. Ilf—28Sc 46
Barnardo St. E1—44Zb 84
Barnard Rd. SW11—56Gb 103
Barnard Rd. Enf—12Xb 25
Barnard Rd. Mitc—69Jb 126
Barnard Rd. Warl—91Dc 182
Barnard's Inn. EC1—(2A 200)
Barnards Pl. S Croy—81Rb 165
Barnby Rd. Wok—5A 188
Barnby Sq. E15—39Gc 65
Barnby St. E15—39Gc 65
Barnby St. NW1—40Lb 62 (2C 192)
Barn Clo. Ashf—64R 120
Barn Clo. N'holt—40Y 57
Barn Clo. Slou—5F 52
Barn Cres. Purl—85Tb 165
Barn Cres. Stan—23La 38
Barncroft Clo. Lou—15Qc 28
Barncroft Clo. Uxb—43R 76
Barncroft Rd. Lou—15Qc 28
Barnehurst Av. Eri & Bexh —53Ed 110
Barnehurst Clo. Eri—53Ed 110
Barnehurst Rd. Bexh—54Ed 110
Barn Elms Pk. SW15—55Ya 102
Barn End Dri. Dart—62Ld 133
Barn End La. Dart—64Ld 133
Barnes All. Hmptn—68Ea 122
Barnes Av. SW13—52Wa 102
Barnes Clo. E12—35Mc 65
Barnes Ct. E16—43Lc 85
Barnes Ct. Wfd G—22Mc 45
Barnes Cray Rd. Dart—56Jd 110
Barnes End. N Mald—71Wa 144
Barnes High St. SW13—54Wa 102
Barnes La. K Lan—1P 3
Barnes Pikle. W5—45Ma 79
Barnes Rd. N18—21Yb 44
Barnes Rd. Ilf—36Sc 66
Barnes St. E14—44Ac 84
Barnes Way. Iver—45H 75
Barnet By-Pass. NW7 & NW4 —23Va 40
Barnet By-Pass. Pot B & Hat—3Xa 8
Barnet By-Pass Rd. Borwd, Barn & Pot B—16Ta 21
Barn Clo. Rad—7Ja 6
Barnet Dri. Brom—75Nc 150
Barnet Ga. La. Barn—16Va 22
Barnet Gro. E2—41Wb 83
Barnet Hill. Barn—14Bb 23
Barnet La. N20 & Barn—18Bb 23
Barnet La. Borwd—16Na 21
Barnet Rd. Barn—16Ua 22
Barnet Rd. Pot B & Barn—5Db 9
Barnett Clo. Eri—54Hd 110
Barnett Clo. Lea—91Ka 176
Barnett's Shaw. Oxt—99Fc 183
Barnett St. E1—44Xb 83
Barnett Wood La. Lea & Asht —92Ka 176
Barnet Way. NW7—20Ta 21
Barnet Wood Rd. Brom—75Lc 149
Barney Clo. SE7—50Lc 85
Barnfield. Bans—86Db 163
Barnfield. Epp—1Wc 15
Barnfield. Iver—44G 74
Barnfield. N Mald—72Ua 144
Barnfield. Slou—6B 72
Barnfield Av. Croy—75Yb 148
Barnfield Av. King—63Ma 123
Barnfield Av. Mitc—69Kb 126
Barnfield Clo. Coul—91Sb 181
Barnfield Clo. Long, Dart —69Fe 135
Barnfield Clo. Swan—73Ed 152
Barnfield Cres. Sev—89Nd 171
Barnfield Gdns. King—63Na 123
Barnfield Rd. SE18—51Rc 108
(in two parts)
Barnfield Rd. W5—42La 78
Barnfield Rd. Belv—51Bd 109
Barnfield Rd. Edgw—25Sa 39
Barnfield Rd. Orp—69Zc 131
Barnfield Rd. Sev—95Gd 186
Barnfield Rd. S Croy—81Ub 165
Barnfield Rd. West—92Mc 183
Barnfield Wood Clo. Beck —72Fc 149
Barnfield Wood Rd. Beck —72Fc 149
Barnham Rd. Gnfd—41Ea 78
Barnham St. SE1 —47Ub 83 (1J 207)
Barnhill. Pinn—29Y 37
Barn Hill. Wemb—32Qa 59
Barnhill Av. Brom—71Hc 149
Barnhill La. Hay—41X 77
Barnhill Rd. Hay—42X 77
Barnhill Rd. Wemb—34Sa 59
Barnhurst Path. Wat—22Y 37
Barn Lea. Rick—18J 17
Barnlea Clo. Felt—61Aa 121
★Barn Mead. Brtwd—8Yd
Barn Mead. Epp—8Uc 14
Barnmead Gdns. Dag—36Bd 67
Barn Meadow La. Lea—96Ba 175
Barnmead Rd. Beck—67Zb 128
Barnmead Rd. Dag—36Bd 67
Barn Rise. Wemb—32Qa 59
Barnsbury Clo. N Mald—70Sa 123
Barnsbury Cres. Surb—74Sa 143
Barnsbury Farm Est. Wok—8G 188
Barnsbury Gro. N7—38Pb 62
Barnsbury La. Surb—75Ra 143
Barnsbury M. N1—38Qb 62
Barnsbury Pk. N1—38Qb 62
Barnsbury Rd. N1 —39Qb 62 (1K 193)
Barnsbury Sq. N1—38Qb 62
Barnsbury St. N1—38Qb 62
Barnsbury Ter. N1—38Pb 62
Barnscroft. SW20—69Xa 124
Barnsdale Cres. Orp—72Wc 151
Barnsdale Rd. W9—42Bb 81
Barnsfield Pl. Uxb—38L 55
Barnsley Rd. Romf—24Pd 49
Barnsley St. E1—42Xb 83
Barnstaple Path. Romf—22Md 49
Barnstaple Rd. Romf—22Ld 49
Barnstaple Rd. Ruis—34Y 57
Barn St. N16—33Ub 63
Barnsway. K Lan—1N 3
Barnway. Egh—4N 117
Barn Way. Wemb—32Qa 59
Barnwell Rd. SW2—57Qb 104
Barnwood Clo. W9—42Db 81
Barnwood Clo. Ruis—33T 56
Barnwood Ct. E16—46Kc 85
Barnyard, The. Tad—96Wa 178
Baron Clo. N1—40Qb 62 (1K 193)
Baroness Rd. E2—41Vb 83 (3K 195)
Baronet Gro. N17—25Wb 43
Baronet Rd. N17—25Wb 43
Baron Gdns. Ilf—27Sc 46
Baron Gro. Mitc—70Gb 125
Baron Rd. Dag—32Zc 67
Baronsclere Ct. N6—31Mb 62
Baron's Ct. Rd. W14—50Ab 80
Baronsfield Rd. Twic—58Ka 100
Barons Ga. Barn—16Gb 23
Baron's Hurst. Eps—88Sa 161
Barons Keep. W14—50Ab 80
Barons Mead. Harr—28Ga 38
Baronsmead Rd. SW13—53Wa 102
Baronsmede. W5—47Pa 79
Baronsmere Rd. N2—28Gb 41
Baron's Pl. SE1—47Qb 82 (2A 206)
Barons, The. Twic—58Ka 100
Baron St. N1—40Qb 62 (1K 193)
Baron's Wlk. Croy—72Ac 148
Barons Way. Egh—65F 118
Baron Wlk. E16—43Hc 85
Baron Wlk. Mitc—70Gb 125
Barque M. SE8—51Cc 106
Barrack Path. Wok—6C 188
Barrack Rd. Houn—56Z 99
Barrack Row. Grav—8D 114
Barracks, The. Wey—76K 139
Barra Hall Cir. Hay—45U 76
Barra Hall Rd. Hay—45U 76
Barratt Av. N22—26Pb 42
Barratt Industrial Pk. S'hall —46Ca 77
Barratt Way. Harr—27Fa 38
Barrenger Rd. N10—25Hb 41
Barrens Brae. Wok—90C 156
Barrens Clo. Wok—91C 172
Barrens Pk. Wok—90C 156
Barrets Grn. Rd. NW10—41Sa 79
Barrett Rd. E17—28Ec 44
Barrett Rd. Lea—96Fa 176
Barrett Rd. Lea—97Ea 176
Barrett's Gro. N16—36Ub 63
Barretts Rd. Sev—92Gd 186
Barrett St. W1—44Jb 82 (3J 197)
Barrhill Rd. SW2—61Nb 126
Barricane. Wok—7E 188
Barrie Clo. Coul—88Lb 164
Barriedale. SE14—54Ac 106
Barrier App. E16—46Lc 85
Barrier App. SE7—48Mc 85
Barringer Sq. SW17—63Jb 126
Barrington Clo. NW5—36Jb 62
Barrington Clo. Lou—13Sc 28
Barrington Ct. Brtwd—16Ee 33
Barrington Grn. Lou—14Sc 28
Barrington Rd. E12—37Qc 66
Barrington Rd. N8—29Mb 42
Barrington Rd. SW9—55Rb 105
Barrington Rd. Bexh—54Zc 109
Barrington Rd. Lou—14Sc 28
Barrington Rd. Purl—84Lb 164
Barrington Rd. Sutt—75Cb 145
Barrington Vs. SE18—53Qc 108
Barrosa Dri. Hmptn—67Ca 121
Barrow Av. Cars—80Hb 145
Barrow Clo. N21—20Rb 25
Barrowdene Clo. Pinn—26Aa 37
Barrowell Grn. N21—19Rb 25
Barrowfield Clo. N9—20Xb 25
Barrowfield La. N9—20Xb 25
Barrowgate Rd. W4—50Sa 79
Barrow Grn. Rd. Oxt—100Ec 182
Barrow Hedges Clo. Cars —80Gb 145
Barrow Hedges Way. Cars —80Gb 145
Barrow Hill. Wor Pk—75Ua 144
Barrow Hill Clo. Wor Pk—75Ua 144
Barrow Hill Rd. NW8 —40Gb 61 (2D 190)
Barrow La. Wal X—2Vb 11
(in two parts)
Barrow Point Av. Pinn—26Aa 37
Barrow Point La. Pinn—26Aa 37
Barrow Rd. SW16—65Mb 126
Barrow Rd. Croy—78Qb 146
Barrowsfield. S Croy—84Wb 165
Barr Rd. Grav—1H 137
Barr Rd. Pot B—5Eb 9
Barr's La. Wok—4A 188
Barrs Rd. NW10—38Ta 59
Barr's Rd. M'head—4A 72
Barry Av. N15—30Vb 43
Barry Av. Bexh—52Ad 109
Barry Av. Wind—2G 94
Barry Clo. Grays—8C 92
Barry Clo. Orp—76Uc 150
Barry Rd. E6—44Nc 86
Barry Rd. NW10—38Sa 59
Barry Rd. SE22—58Wb 105
Barset Rd. SE15—55Yb 106
Barson Clo. SE20—66Yb 128
Barstable Rd. Stanf—1M 93
Barston Rd. SE27—62Sb 127
Barstow Cres. SW2—60Pb 104
Bartelotts Rd. Slou—2C 72
Barter St. WC1—43Nb 82 (1G 199)
Bartholomew Clo. EC1 —43Sb 83 (1D 200)
Bartholomew Clo. SW18 —56Eb 103
Bartholomew Ct. Enf—9Ac 12
Bartholomew La. EC2 —44Tb 83 (3G 201)
Bartholomew Pl. EC1—(1D 200)
Bartholomew Rd. NW5—37Lb 62
Bartholomew Sq. EC1 —42Sb 83 (5E 194)
Bartholomew St. SE1 —48Tb 83 (4G 207)
Bartholomew Vs. NW5—37Lb 62
Bartholomew Way. Swan —69Gd 132
Barth Rd. SE18—49Uc 86
Bartle Av. E6—40Nc 66
Bartle Rd. W11—44Ab 80
Bartlett Ct. EC4—44Qb 82 (2A 200)
Bartlett Rd. Grav—10C 114
Bartlett Rd. West—98Sc 184
Bartlett St. S Croy—78Tb 147
Bartlow Gdns. Romf—25Fd 48
Barton Av. Romf—32Dd 68
Barton Clo. E6—44Pc 86
Barton Clo. E9—36Yb 64
Barton Clo. SE15—55Xb 105
Barton Clo. Bexh—57Ad 109
Barton Clo. Chig—19Sc 28
Barton Clo. Shep—72R 140
Barton Clo. Wey—79J 139
Barton Grn. N Mald—68Ta 123
Barton Meadows. Ilf—28Rc 46
Barton Rd. W14—50Ab 80
Barton Rd. Horn—32Jd 68
Barton Rd. Sidc—65Ad 131
Barton Rd. Slou—47B 74
Barton Rd. S at H, Dart—67Rd 133
Bartons, The. Borwd—16Ma 21
Barton St. SW1—48Nb 82 (3F 205)
Barton, The. Cob—84Z 159
Barton Way. Borwd—12Qa 21
Barton Way. Rick—15R 18
Bartram Clo. Uxb—42R 76
Bartram Rd. SE4—57Ac 106
Bartrams La. Barn—10Eb 9
Barwell Trading Est. Chess —80Ma 143
Barwick Rd. E7—35Kc 65
Barwood Av. W Wick—74Dc 148
Baryta Clo. Stanf—2L 93
Basden Gro. Felt—61Ca 121
Basedale Rd. Dag—38Xc 67
Basford Way. Wind—5B 94
Bashley Rd. NW10—42Ta 79
Basil Av. E6—41Nc 86
Basildene Rd. Houn—55Z 99
Basildon Av. Ilf—25Qc 46
Basildon Clo. Sutt—81Db 163
Basildon Rd. SE2—50Wc 87
Basil Gdns. Croy—74Zb 148
Basilon Rd. Bexh—54Ad 109
Basil St. SW3—48Hb 81 (3F 203)
Basing Clo. Th Dit—73Ha 142
Basing Ct. SE15—53Vb 105
Basingdon Way. SE5—56Tb 105
Basing Dri. Bex—58Bd 109
Basingfield Rd. Th Dit—73Ha 142
Basinghall Av. EC2 —44Tb 83 (2F 201)
Basinghall Gdns. Sutt—81Db 163
Basinghall St. EC2 —44Tb 83 (2F 201)
Basing Hill. NW11—32Bb 61
Basing Hill. Wemb—33Pa 59
Basing Ho. Yd. E2 —41Ub 83 (3J 195)
Basing Pl. E2—41Ub 83 (3J 195)
Basing Rd. Bans—86Bb 163
Basing Rd. Rick—18H 17
Basing St. W11—44Bb 81
Basing Way. N3—27Cb 41
Basing Way. Th Dit—73Ha 142
Basire St. N1—39Sb 63
Baskerville Rd. SW18—59Gb 103
Basket Gdns. SE9—57Nc 108
Baslow Clo. Harr—25Fa 38
Basnett Rd. SW11—55Jb 104
Bassano St. SE22—57Vb 105
Bassant Rd. SE18—51Vc 109
Bassein Pk. Rd. W12—47Va 80
Basset Clo. Wey—82L 157
Bassett Clo. Sutt—81Db 163
Bassett Gdns. Iswth—52Ea 100
Bassett Rd. W10—44Za 80
Bassett Rd. Uxb—38L 55
Bassett Rd. Wok—88E 156
Bassett's Clo. Orp—77Rc 150
Bassett St. NW5—37Jb 62
Bassett's Way. Orp—77Rc 150
Bassett Way. Gnfd—44Da 77
Bassett Way. Slou—2D 72
Bassingham Rd. SW18—59Eb 103
Bassingham Rd. Wemb—37Ma 59
Bassishaw Highwalk. EC2 —(1F 201)
Basswood Clo. SE15—55Xb 105
Bastable Av. Bark—40Vc 67
★Basted La. Sev—95Ce
Bastion Rd. SE2—50Wc 87
Baston Mnr. Rd. Brom—77Kc 149
Baston Rd. Brom—75Kc 149
Bastwick St. EC1 —42Sb 83 (5D 194)
Basuto Rd. SW6—53Cb 103
Bata Av. Grays—10K 93
Batavia Clo. Sun—67X 121
Batavia M. SE14—52Ac 106
Batavia Rd. SE14—52Ac 106
Batavia Rd. Sun—67X 121
Batchelor St. N1—39Qb 62 (1A 194)
Batchwood Grn. Orp—69Wc 131
Batchworth Heath Hill. Rick —21Q 36
Batchworth Hill. Rick—19N & 20P 17
Batchworth La. N'wd—22S 36
Bateman Clo. Bark—37Sc 66
Bateman Rd. E4—23Cc 44
Bateman Rd. Rick—16Q 18
Bateman's Bldgs. W1—(3D 198)
Bateman's Row. EC2 —42Ub 83 (5J 195)
Bateman St. W1 —44Mb 82 (3D 198)
Bates Cres. Croy—78Qb 146
★Bates Hill. Sev—94Yd
Bateson St. SE18—49Uc 86
Bateson Way. Wok—86E 156
Bates Rd. Romf—24Qd 49
Bate St. E14—45Bc 84
Bates Wlk. Wey—79L 139
Bath Clo. SE15—53Yb 106
Bath Ct. EC1—(6K 193)
Bath Ct. Clo. EC1—(4H 195)
Bathgate Rd. SW19—62Za 124
Bath Gro. E2—40Wb 63
Bath Ho. Rd. Croy—74Nb 146
Bathhurst Rd. Ilf—32Rc 66
Bath Pl. EC1—41Ub 83 (4H 195)
Bath Pl. Barn—13Bb 23
Bath Rd. E7—37Mc 65
Bath Rd. N9—19Yb 26
Bath Rd. W4—49Ua 80
Bath Rd. Dart—59Kd 111
Bath Rd. M'head—4A 72
Bath Rd. Mitc—69Fb 125
Bath Rd. Romf—30Ad 47

Bath Rd.—53G 96 to 55Ca 99
Slou—53G 96
W Dray—53J 97
Hay—53R 98
Houn—53W 98
Bath Rd. Slou—51D 96
(Colnbrook)
Baths Rd. Brom—70Mc 129
Bath St. EC1—41Sb 83 (4E 194)
Bath St. Grav—8D 114
Bath Ter. SE1—48Sb 83 (4D 206)
Bathurst Av. SW19—67Db 125
Bathurst Clo. Iver—47H 75
Bathurst Gdns. NW10—40Xa 60
Bathurst M. W2—45Fb 81 (4C 196)
Bathurst St. W2—45Fb 81 (4C 196)
Bathurst Wlk. Iver—47G 74
Bathway. SE18—49Qc 86
Batley Pl. N16—34Vb 63
Batley Rd. N16—34Vb 63
Batley Rd. Enf—11Sb 25
Batman Clo. W12—46Xa 80
Batoum Gdns. W6—48Ya 80
Batson St. W12—47Wa 80
Batsworth Rd. Mitc—69Fb 125
Batten Av. Wok—7B 188
Battenberg Wlk. SE19—65Ub 127
Batten Clo. E6—44Pc 86
Batten St. SW11—55Gb 103
Battersby Rd. SE6—61Fc 129
Battersea Bri. SW3 & SW11
—52Fb 103
Battersea Bri. Rd. SW11
—52Gb 103
Battersea Chu. Rd. SW11
—53Fb 103
Battersea High St. SW11
—53Fb 103
Battersea Pk. Rd.—54Gb 103
SW8 1-179 & 2-18
SW11 remainder
Battersea Rise. SW11—57Gb 103
Battery Rd. SE28—47Tc 86
Battishill St. N1—38Rb 63
Battle Bri. La. SE1
—46Ub 83 (7H 201)
Battle Bri. Rd. NW1
—40Nb 62 (2F 193)
Battle Clo. SW19—65Eb 125
Battledean Rd. N5—36Rb 63
★Battlefields Rd. Sev—88Be
Battle Rd. Belv & Eri—49Ed 88
Battlers Grn. Dri. Rad—8Ga 6
Battle St. Grav—9H 137
Battle Wood. Sev—100Ld 187
Batt's Rd. Grav—10J 137
Batty St. E1—44Wb 83
Baudwin Rd. SE6—61Gc 129
Baugh Rd. Sidc—64Yc 131
Baulk, The. SW18—59Cb 103
Bavant Rd. SW16—68Nb 126
Bavaria Rd. N19—33Nb 62
Bavent Rd. SE5—54Sb 105
Bawdale Rd. SE22—57Vb 106
Bawdsey Av. Ilf—28Vc 47
Bawtree Clo. Sutt—82Eb 163
Bawtree Rd. SE14—52Ac 106
Bawtree Rd. Uxb—37M 55
Bawtry Rd. N20—20Hb 23
Baxendale. N20—19Eb 23
Baxendale St. E2—41Wb 83
Baxter Clo. Uxb—41R 76
Baxter Rd. E16—44Lc 85
Baxter Rd. N1—37Tb 63
Baxter Rd. N17—27Wb 43
Baxter Rd. N18—21Xb 43
Baxter Rd. Ilf—36Rc 66
Bayards. Warl—90Yb 166
Bayfield Rd. SE9—56Mc 107
Bayford Rd. NW10—41Za 80
Bayford St. E8—38Xb 63
Bayham Pl. NW1
—40Lb 62 (1C 192)
Bayham Rd. W4—48Ta 79
Bayham Rd. W13—45Ka 78
Bayham Rd. Mord—70Db 125
Bayham Rd. Sev—95Ld 187
Bayham St. NW1
—39Lb 62 (1B 192)
Bayhurst Dri. N'wd—23V 36
Bayleys Mead. Brtwd—19Ee 33
Bayley St. WC1—43Mb 82 (1D 198)
Bayley Wlk. SE2—50Ad 87
Baylin Rd. SW18—58Db 103
Baylis Pde. Slou—4J 73
Baylis Rd. SE1—47Qb 82 (2K 205)
Baylis Rd. Slou—5H 73
Bayliss Av. SE28—45Zc 87
Bayly Rd. Dart—58Qd 111
Bay Mnr. La. Grays—51Vd 112
Bayne Clo. E6—44Pc 86
Baynes Clo. Enf—11Wb 25
Baynes M. NW3—37Fb 61
Baynes St. NW1—38Lb 62
Bayonne Rd. SW6—51Ab 102
Bayston Rd. N16—34Vb 63
Bayswater Rd. W2
—45Db 81 (5A 196)
Baythorne St. E3—43Bc 84
Baythorne St. E3
Baytree Ct. Slou—1A 72
Baytree Rd. SW2—56Pb 104
Bay Tree Wlk. Wat—10V 4
Baywood Sq. Chig—21Xc 47
Bazalgette Clo. N Mald—71Ta 143
Bazalgette Gdns. N Mald
—71Ta 143
Bazely St. E14—45Ec 84
Bazes Shaw. Long, Dart—75Be 155
(in two parts)
Bazile Rd. N21—16Qb 24
Beacham Clo. SE7—51Mc 107
Beachborough Rd. Brom
—63Ec 128
Beachcroft Rd. E11—34Gc 65
Beachcroft Way. N19—32Mb 62
Beach Gro. Felt—61Ca 121
Beachy Rd. E3—38Cc 64
Beacon Clo. Bans—88Za 162
Beacon Clo. Uxb—36M 55
Beacon Dri. Dart—62Xd 134
Beaconfield Av. Epp—1Vc 15
Beaconfield Rd. Epp—1Vc 15
Beaconfield Way. Epp—1Vc 15
Beacon Gro. Cars—77Jb 146
Beacon Hill. N7—36Nb 62
★Beacon Hill. Brtwd—9Sd
Beacon Hill. Purf—50Rd 89
Beacon Hill. Wok—7F 188
★Beacon Hill Rd. Brtwd—9Rd
Beacon Rise. Sev—98Jd 186
Beacon Rd. SE13—58Fc 107
Beacon Rd. Eri—52Kd 111
Beacon Rd. Houn—58Q 98
Beaconsfield. Sev—98Jd 186
Beaconsfield Clo. N11—22Jb 42
Beaconsfield Clo. SE3—51Jc 107
Beaconsfield Clo. W4—50Sa 79
Beaconsfield Comn. La. Bea
—1G 52
Beaconsfield Pl. Eps—84Ua 162
Beaconsfield Rd. E10—34Ec 64
Beaconsfield Rd. E16—42Hc 85
Beaconsfield Rd. E17—30Bc 44
Beaconsfield Rd. N9—20Wb 25
Beaconsfield Rd. N11—20Jb 24
Beaconsfield Rd. N15—28Ub 43
Beaconsfield Rd. NW10—37Va 60
Beaconsfield Rd. SE3—52Hc 107
Beaconsfield Rd. SE9—61Nc 130
Beaconsfield Rd. SE17—50Ub 83
Beaconsfield Rd. W4—48Ta 79
Beaconsfield Rd. W5—47Ma 79
Beaconsfield Rd. Bex—61Gd 132
Beaconsfield Rd. Brom—69Mc 129
Beaconsfield Rd. Croy—72Tb 147
Beaconsfield Rd. Enf—9Zb 12
Beaconsfield Rd. Eps—91Ta 177
Beaconsfield Rd. Esh—80Ga 142
Beaconsfield Rd. Hay—46Y 77
Beaconsfield Rd. N Mald
—68Ta 123
Beaconsfield Rd. Slou—10G 52
Beaconsfield Rd. S'hall—46Z 77
Beaconsfield Rd. Surb—73Pa 143
Beaconsfield Rd. Til—3C 114
Beaconsfield Rd. Twic—58Ka 100
Beaconsfield Rd. Wok—92B 172
Beaconsfield Ter. Romf—30Zc 47
Beaconsfield Ter. Rd. W14
—48Ab 80
Beaconsfield Wlk. SW6—53Cb 103
Beacons, The. Lou—10Qc 14
Beacontree Rd. E11—31Hc 65
Beacon Way. Bans—88Za 162
Beacon Way. Rick—17J 17
Beadlow Clo. Cars—72Fb 145
Beadman St. SE27—63Rb 127
Beadnell Rd. SE23—60Zb 106
Beadon Rd. W6—49Ya 80
Beadon Rd. Brom—70Jc 129
Beads Hall La. Brtwd—14Xd 32
Beaford Gro. SW20—69Ab 124
Beagle Clo. Felt—63X 121
Beagle Clo. Rad—9Ha 6
Beagles Clo. Orp—75Zc 151
Beak St. W1—45Lb 82 (4C 198)
Beal Clo. Well—53Wc 109
Beale Clo. N13—22Rb 43
Beale Pl. E3—40Bc 64
Beale Rd. E3—39Bc 64
Beales La. Wey—76R 140
Beales Rd. Lea—99Da 175
Beal Rd. Ilf—33Qc 66
Beam Av. Dag—39Dd 68
Beaminster Gdns. Ilf—27Rc 46
Beamish Dri. Bush, Wat—18Ea 20
Beamish Ga. NW1—38Mb 62
Beamish Rd. N9—18Wb 25
Beamish Rd. Orp—73Yc 151
Beamway. Dag—38Fd 68
Beanacre Clo. E9—37Bc 64
Bean La. Dart—61Xd 134
Bean Rd. Bexh—56Zc 109
Bean Rd. Grnh—60Wd 112
Beanshaw. SE9—63Qc 130
Beansland Gro. Romf—27Ad 47
Bear All. EC4—44Rb 83 (2B 200)
Beardell St. SE19—65Vb 127
Beardow Gro. N14—16Lb 24
Beard Rd. King—64Pa 123
Beardsfield. E13—40Jc 65
Beard's Hill. Hmptn—67Ca 121
Beard's Hill Clo. Hmptn—67Ca 121
Beardsley Way. W3—47Ta 79
Beard's Rd. Ashf—65U 120
Bearfield Rd. King—66Na 123
Bear Gdns. SE1—46Sb 83 (6D 200)
Bearing Clo. Chig—21Wc 47
Bearing Way. Chig—21Wc 47
Bear La. SE1—46Rb 83 (6C 200)
Bear Rd. Felt—63Z 121
Bears Den. Tad—94Bb 179
Bearstead Rise. SE4—57Bc 106
Bearsted Ter. Beck—67Cc 128
Bear St. WC2—45Mb 82 (4E 198)
Bearwood Clo. Pot B—3Fb 9
Bearwood Clo. Wey—79J 139
Beasley's Ait La. Sun—72V 140
Beatrice Av. SW16—68Pb 126
Beatrice Av. Wemb—36Na 59
Beatrice Clo. E13—42Jc 85
Beatrice Clo. Pinn—29W 36
Beatrice Gdns. Grav—1A 136
Beatrice Rd. E17—29Cc 44
Beatrice Rd. N4—31Qb 62
Beatrice Rd. N9—17Yb 26
Beatrice Rd. SE1—49Wb 83
Beatrice Rd. Oxt—100Gc 183
Beatrice Rd. Rich—57Pa 101
Beatrice Rd. S'hall—46Ba 77
Beatson Wlk. SE16—46Ac 84
Beattie Clo. Lea—96Ba 175
Beattock Rise. N10—28Kb 42
Beatty Rd. N16—35Ub 63
Beatty Rd. Stan—23La 38
Beatty St. NW1—40Lb 62 (1B 192)
Beattyville Gdns. Ilf—28Qc 46
Beauchamp Gdns. Rick—18J 17
Beauchamp Pl. SW3
—48Gb 81 (3E 202)
Beauchamp Rd. E7—38Kc 65
Beauchamp Rd. SE19—67Tb 127
Beauchamp Rd. SW11—56Gb 103
Beauchamp Rd. E Mol—71Da 141
Beauchamp Rd. Sutt—77Cb 145
Beauchamp Rd. Twic—59Ja 100
Beauchamp St. EC1
—43Qb 82 (1K 199)
Beauchamp Ter. SW15—55Xa 102
Beauclare Clo. Lea—93Ma 177
Beauclerc Ct. Sun—68Y 121
Beauclerc Rd. W6—48Ya 80
Beauclerk Clo. Felt—60X 99
Beaudesert M. W Dray—48N 75
Beaufort Av. Harr—28Ja 38
Beaufort Clo. SW15—59Xa 102
Beaufort Clo. W5—43Pa 79
Beaufort Clo. Romf—28Ed 48
Beaufort Clo. Wok—88E 156
Beaufort Ct. Rich—63La 122
Beaufort Dri. NW11—28Cb 41
Beaufort Gdns. NW4—30Ya 40
Beaufort Gdns. SW3
—48Gb 81 (3E 202)
Beaufort Gdns. SW16—66Pb 126
Beaufort Gdns. Houn—53Aa 99
Beaufort Gdns. Ilf—32Qc 66
Beaufort Rd. W5—43Pa 79
Beaufort Rd. King—70Na 123
Beaufort Rd. Rich—63La 122
Beaufort Rd. Ruis—33T 56
Beaufort Rd. Twic—59La 100
Beaufort Rd. Wok—88E 156
Beauforts. Egh—4N 117
Beaufort St. SW3—51Fb 103
Beaufort Way. Eps—80Wa 144
Beaufoy Rd. N17—24Ub 43
Beaufoy Wlk. SE11
—49Pb 82 (6J 205)
Beaulieu Av. SE26—63Xb 127
Beaulieu Clo. NW9—28Ua 40
Beaulieu Clo. SE5—55Tb 105
Beaulieu Clo. Mitc—67Jb 126
Beaulieu Clo. Slou—3M 95
Beaulieu Clo. Twic—58Ma 101
Beaulieu Clo. Wat—18Y 19
Beaulieu Dri. Pinn—30Z 37
Beaulieu Gdns. N21—17Sb 25
Beauly Way. Romf—25Gd 48
Beaumanor Gdns. SE9—63Qc 130
Beaumaris Ct. Slou—3F 72
Beaumaris Dri. Wfd G—24Mc 45
Beaumont Av. W14—50Bb 81
Beaumont Av. Harr—30Da 37
Beaumont Av. Rich—55Pa 101
Beaumont Av. Wemb—36La 58
Beaumont Clo. King—66Qa 123
Beaumont Clo. Romf—26Ld 49
Beaumont Cres. W14—50Bb 81
Beaumont Cres. Rain—37Jd 68
Beaumont Dri. Ashf—64T 120
Beaumont Dri. Grav—9B 114
Beaumont Gdns. NW3—33Cb 61
Beaumont Gro. E1—42Zb 84
Beaumont M. W1
—43Jb 82 (7J 191)
Beaumont Pl. W1
—42Lb 82 (5C 192)
Beaumont Pl. Barn—11Bb 23
Beaumont Rise. N19—32Mb 62
Beaumont Rd. E10—31Dc 64
(in two parts)
Beaumont Rd. E13—41Kc 85
Beaumont Rd. SE19—65Sb 127
Beaumont Rd. SW19—59Ab 102
Beaumont Rd. W4—48Sa 79
Beaumont Rd. Orp—72Tc 150
Beaumont Rd. Purl—85Qb 164
Beaumont Rd. Slou—2H 73
Beaumont Rd. Wind—4G 94
Beaumont Sq. E1—43Zb 84
Beaumont St. W1
—43Jb 82 (7J 191)
Beaumont Wlk. NW3—38Hb 61
Beauvais Ter. N'holt—41Z 77
Beauval Rd. SE22—58Vb 105
Beaverbank Rd. SE9—60Tc 108
Beaver Clo. SE20—66Wb 127
Beaver Clo. Hmptn—67Da 121
Beavercote Wlk. Belv—50Bd 87
Beaver Rd. Ilf—22Yc 47
Beavers Cres. Houn—56Y 99
Beavers La. Houn—55Y 99
Beaverwood Rd. Chst—64Uc 130
Beavor La. W6—49Wa 80
(in two parts)
Bebbington Rd. SE18—49Uc 86
Bebletts Clo. Orp—78Vc 151
Beccles Dri. Bark—37Uc 66
Beccles St. E14—45Bc 84
Bec Clo. Ruis—34Z 57
Beckenham Gdns. N9—20Ub 25
Beckenham Gro. Brom—68Fc 129
Beckenham Hill Est. Beck
—64Dc 128
Beckenham Hill Rd.—65Dc 128
SE6 1-95 & 2-62
Beck remainder
Beckenham La. Brom—68Gc 129
Beckenham Pl. Pk. Beck
—66Dc 128
Beckenham Rd. Beck—67Zb 128
Beckenham Rd. W Wick—73Ec 148
Beckenshaw Gdns. Bans
—87Gb 163
Becket Av. E6—41Qc 86
Becket Clo. SE25—72Wb 147
Becket Clo. Brtwd—23Yd 50
Becket Fold. Harr—29Ha 38
Becket Rd. N18—21Yb 44
Becket St. SE1—48Tb 83 (3F 207)
Beckett Av. Kenl—87Rb 165
Beckett Clo. NW10—37Ua 60
Beckett Clo. SW16—61Mb 126
Becketts Clo. Orp—76Vc 151
Becketts Pl. Tedd—67Ma 123
Beckett Wlk. Beck—65Ac 128
Beckford Pl. SE17
—50Sb 83 (7E 206)
Beckford Rd. Croy—72Vb 147
Beck La. Beck—69Zb 128
Beckley Clo. Grav—1K 137
Becklow Rd. W12—47Wa 80
Beckman Clo. Sev—87Ed 170
Beck River Pk. Beck—67Cc 128
Beck Rd. E8—39Xb 63
Becks Rd. Sidc—62Wc 131
Beckton Rd. E16—43Hc 85
Beckway. Beck—69Bc 128
Beckway Rd. SW16—68Mb 126
Beckway St. SE17
—49Ub 83 (6H 207)
(in two parts)
Beckwith Rd. SE24—57Tb 105
Beclands Rd. SW17—65Jb 126
Becmead Av. SW16—63Mb 126
Becmead Av. Harr—29Ka 38
Becondale Rd. SE19—64Ub 127
Becontree Av. E17—25Fc 45
Becontree Av. Dag—35Xc 67
Bective Pl. SW15—56Bb 103
Bective Rd. E7—35Jc 65
Bective Rd. SW15—56Bb 103
Becton Pl. Eri—53Dd 110
Bedale Rd. Enf—10Sb 11
Bedale Rd. Romf—22Qd 49
Bedale St. SE1—46Tb 83 (7F 201)
Bedale Wlk. Dart—60Rd 111
Beddington Farm Rd. Croy
—73Nb 146
Beddington Gdns. Cars—79Jb 146
Beddington Gdns. Wall—79Kb 146
Beddington Grn. Orp—67Vc 131
Beddington Gro. Wall—78Mb 146
Beddington La. Croy—72Lb 146
Beddington Path. Orp—67Vc 131
Beddington Rd. Ilf—31Vc 67
Beddington Rd. Orp—67Uc 130
Beddlestead La. Warl—90Hc 167
Bede Clo. Pinn—25Z 37
Bedens Rd. Sidc—65Ad 131
Bede Rd. Romf—30Yc 47
Bedfont Clo. Felt—58S 98
Bedfont Clo. Mitc—68Jb 126
Bedfont Ct. Stai—55J 97
Bedfont La. Felt—59V 98
Bedfont Rd. Felt—60S 98
Bedfont Rd. Stai—58N 97
Bedford Av. WC1
—43Mb 82 (1E 198)
Bedford Av. Amer—11A 16
Bedford Av. Barn—15Bb 23
Bedford Av. Hay—45X 77
Bedford Av. Slou—4D 72
Bedfordbury. WC2
—45Nb 82 (5F 199)
Bedford Clo. N10—24Jb 42
Bedford Clo. Rick—10D 2
Bedford Ct. WC2—45Nb 82 (5F 199)
Bedford Cres. Enf—7Ac 12
Bedford Dri. Slou—7F 52
Bedford Gdns. W8—46Cb 81
Bedford Gdns. Horn—33Ld 69
Bedford Hill—60Kb 104
SW12 1-203 & 2-210
SW16 remainder
Bedford Pk. Croy—74Sb 147
Bedford Pk. Corner. W4—49Ua 80
Bedford Pas. W1—43Lb 82 (7C 192)
Bedford Pl. WC1—43Nb 82 (7F 193)
Bedford Pl. Croy—74Tb 147
Bedford Rd. E6—39Qc 66
Bedford Rd. E17—26Cc 44
Bedford Rd. E18—26Jc 45
Bedford Rd. N2—27Gb 41
Bedford Rd. N8—30Mb 42
Bedford Rd. N9—17Xb 25
Bedford Rd. N15—28Ub 43
Bedford Rd. N22—26Nb 42
Bedford Rd. NW7—19Ua 22
Bedford Rd. SW4—56Nb 104
Bedford Rd. W4—48Ta 79
Bedford Rd. W13—45Ka 78
Bedford Rd. Dart—59Qd 111
Bedford Rd. Grav—1B 136
Bedford Rd. Grays—50De 91
Bedford Rd. Harr—30Ea 38
Bedford Rd. Ilf—34Rc 66
Bedford Rd. N'wd—21S 36
Bedford Rd. Orp—75Xc 151
Bedford Rd. Ruis—35V 56
Bedford Rd. Sidc—62Uc 130
Bedford Rd. Twic—62Fa 122
Bedford Rd. Wor Pk—75Ya 144
Bedford Row. WC1
—43Pb 82 (7J 193)
Bedford Sq. WC1
—43Mb 82 (1E 198)
Bedford St. WC2—45Nb 82 (4F 199)
Bedford St. Wat—11X 19
Bedford Way. WC1
—42Mb 82 (6E 192)
Bedgebury Gdns. SW19—61Ab 124
Bedgebury Rd. SE9—56Mc 107
Bedivere Rd. Brom—62Jc 129
Bedlow Way. Croy—77Pb 146
Bedmond Rd. Abb L, Wat—1V 4
Bedonwell Rd.—51Ad 109
SE2 365-397 & 402-434
Belv & Bexh remainder
Bedser Dri. Gnfd—36Fa 58
Bedster Gdns. E Mol—68Da 121
Bedwardine Rd. SE19—66Ub 127
Bedwell Gdns. Hay—50U 76
(in two parts)
Bedwell Rd. N17—25Ub 43
Bedwell Rd. Belv—50Cd 88
Bedwin Way. SE16—50Xb 83
Beeby Rd. E16—43Kc 85
Beech Av. N20—18Gb 23
Beech Av. W3—46Ua 80
Beech Av. Bren—52Ka 100
Beech Av. Brtwd—20Be 33
Beech Av. Buck H—19Kc 27
Beech Av. Enf—7Qb 10
Beech Av. Lea—100Z 175
Beech Av. Rad—5Ja 6
Beech Av. Ruis—32X 57
Beech Av. Sidc—59Wc 109
Beech Av. S Croy—83Tb 165
Beech Av. Swan—70Hd 132
Beech Av. Upm—34Rd 69
Beech Av. West—91Mc 183
Beech Clo. N9—16Xb 25
Beech Clo. SW15—59Wa 102
Beech Clo. SW19—65Ya 124
Beech Clo. Ashf—64T 120
Beech Clo. Cars—75Hb 145
Beech Clo. Cob—83Ca 159
Beech Clo. Horn—34Kd 69
Beech Clo. Lea—100Z 175
Beech Clo. Sun—68Z 121
Beech Clo. W on T—77Y 141
Beech Clo. W Dray—48Q 76
Beech Clo. Wey—84N 157
Beech Clo. Ct. Cob—83Ba 159
Beech Copse. Brom—68Pc 130
Beech Copse. S Croy—78Ub 147
Beech Ct. E17—27Fc 45
Beech Ct. Surb—73Ma 143
Beechcroft. Asht—91Pa 177
Beechcroft. Chst—66Qc 130
Beechcroft. Stanf—9J 93
Beechcroft Av. NW11—31Bb 61
Beechcroft Av. Bexh—53Fd 110
Beechcroft Av. Harr—31Ca 57
Beechcroft Av. Kenl—87Tb 165
Beechcroft Av. N Mald—68Sa 123
Beechcroft Av. Rick—16S 18
Beechcroft Av. S'hall—46Ba 77
Beechcroft Clo. Houn—52Aa 99
Beechcroft Clo. Orp—77Tc 150
Beech Croft Ct. N5—35Rb 63
Beechcroft Gdns. Wemb—34Pa 59
Beechcroft Manor. Wey—76T 140
Beechcroft Rd. E18—26Kc 45
Beechcroft Rd. SW14—55Sa 101
Beechcroft Rd. SW17—61Gb 125
Beechcroft Rd. Bush, Wat
—15Aa 19
Beechcroft Rd. Chess—76Pa 143
Beechcroft Rd. Orp—77Tc 150
Beechdale. N21—19Pb 24
Beechdale Rd. SW2—58Pb 104
Beech Dell. Orp—77Pc 150
Beechdene. Tad—94Xa 178
Beech Dri. N2—26Hb 41
Beech Dri. Borwd—12Pa 21
Beech Dri. Tad—94Bb 179
Beech Dri. Wok—96J 173
Beechen Cliff Way. Iswth
—54Ha 100
Beechen Gro. Pinn—27Ba 37
Beechen Gro. Wat—13X 19
Beechen La. Tad—97Bb 179
Beechenlea La. Swan—70Jd 132
Beechen Pl. SE23—61Zb 128
Beeches Av. Cars—80Gb 145
Beeches Clo. Tad—95Cb 179
Beeches Dri. Slou—6F 52
Beeches Rd. SW17—62Gb 125
Beeches Rd. Slou—6F 52
Beeches Rd. Sutt—74Ab 144
Beeches, The. Bans—88Db 163
Beeches, The. Croy—78Tb 147
Beeches, The. Grav—10F 136
Beeches, The. Lea—96Ga 176
Beeches, The. Til—4D 114
Beeches Wlk. Cars—81Fb 163
Beeches Wood. Tad—94Cb 179
Beech Farm Rd. Warl—92Ec 182
Beechfield. Bans—85Db 163
Beechfield. K Lan—2P 3
Beechfield Gdns. Romf—31Ed 68
Beechfield Rd. N4—30Sb 43
Beechfield Rd. SE6—60Bc 106
Beechfield Rd. Brom—68Lc 129
Beechfield Rd. Eri—52Gd 110
Beechfield Wlk. Wal A—7Fc 13
Beech Gdns. W5—47Na 79
Beech Gdns. Dag—38Ed 68
Beech Gdns. Wok—87A 156
Beech Gro. Cat—98Ub 181
Beech Gro. Eps—89Xa 162
Beech Gro. Ilf—23Uc 46
Beech Gro. Mitc—71Mb 146
Beech Gro. N Mald—69Ta 123
Beech Gro. S Ock—47Sd 90
Beech Gro. Wey—77K 139
Beech Hall Cres. E4—24Fc 45
Beech Hall Rd. E4—24Ec 44
Beech Hill. Barn—10Fb 9
Beech Hill. Wok—95A 172
Beech Hill Av. Barn—11Eb 23
Beech Hill Gdns. Wal A—9Kc 13
Beech Ho. Rd. Croy—76Tb 147
Beechhill Rd. SE9—57Qc 108
★Beechin Wood Rd. Sev—94Ee
Beechlands Clo. Long, Dart
—71Ce 155
Beech La. Buck H—19Kc 27
Beech Lawns. N12—22Fb 41
Beechmont Av. Vir W—71A 138
Beechmont Clo. Brom—64Gc 129
Beechmore Gdns. Sutt—75Za 144
Beechmore Rd. SW11—53Hb 103
Beechmount Av. W7—43Fa 78
Beecholme. Bans—86Ab 162
Beecholme Av. Mitc—67Kb 126
Beechpark Way. Wat—9U 4
Beech Pl. Epp—3Vc 15
Beech Rd. N11—23Nb 42
Beech Rd. SW16—69Pb 126
Beech Rd. Dart—60Md 111
Beech Rd. Eps—87Va 162
Beech Rd. Felt—59U 98
Beech Rd. Orp—80Wc 151
Beech Rd. Red—98Lb 180
Beech Rd. Sev—97Kd 187
Beech Rd. Slou—47A 74
Beech Rd. Wat—9W 4
Beech Rd. West—91Kc 183
Beech Rd. Wey—77T 140
Beechrow. King—63Na 123
Beech St. EC2—43Sb 83 (7D 194)
Beech St. Romf—28Ed 48
Beechtree Av. Egh—5M 117
Beechtree Clo. Stan—22La 38
Beech Tree Glade. E4—18Hc 27
Beech Tree La. Stai—68K 119
Beechvale Clo. N12—22Gb 41
Beech Wlk. NW7—23Ua 40
Beech Wlk. Dart—56Jd 110
Beech Wlk. Eps—83Wa 162
Beech Way. NW10—38Ta 59
Beechway. Bex—58Zc 109
Beech Way. Eps—87Va 162
Beech Way. S Croy—85Zb 166
Beech Way. Twic—62Ca 121
Beech Waye. Ger X—31C 54
Beechwood Av. N3—27Bb 41
Beechwood Av. Coul—87Kb 164
Beechwood Av. Gnfd—41Da 77
Beechwood Av. Harr—34Da 57
Beechwood Av. Hay—45T 76
Beechwood Av. Orp—79Uc 150
Beechwood Av. Pot B—5Db 9
Beechwood Av. Rich—53Qa 101
Beechwood Av. Rick—14E 16
Beechwood Av. Ruis—33V 56
Beechwood Av. Stai—65K 119
Beechwood Av. Sun—66W 120
Beechwood Av. Tad—93Cb 179
Beechwood Av. T Hth—70Rb 127
Beechwood Av. Uxb—44Q 76
Beechwood Av. Wey—77U 140
Beechwood Circ. Harr—34Ea 58
Beech Wood Clo. NW7—22Ua 40
Beechwood Clo. Surb—73Ma 143
Beechwood Clo. Wey—77U 140
Beechwood Clo. Wok—5B 188
Beechwood Ct. Sun—66W 120
Beechwood Cres. Bexh—55Ad 109
Beechwood Dri. Cob—83Ca 159
Beechwood Dri. Kes—77Mc 149
Beechwood Dri. Wfd G—22Hc 45
Beechwood Gdns. NW10—41Pa 79
Beechwood Gdns. Cat—94Wb 181
Beechwood Gdns. Harr—34Da 57
Beechwood Gdns. Ilf—29Pc 46
Beechwood Gdns. Rain—43Kd 89
Beechwood Gdns. Slou—7J 73
Beechwood La. Warl—91Zb 182
Beechwood Mnr. Wey—77U 140
Beechwood Pk. E18—27Jc 45
Beechwood Rise. Wat—8X 5
Beechwood Rd. E8—37Vb 63
Beechwood Rd. N8—27Mb 42
Beechwood Rd. Cat—94Wb 181
Beechwood Rd. Slou—3H 73
Beechwood Rd. S Croy—81Ub 165
Beechwood Rd. Wok—5B 188
Beechworth Clo. NW3—33Db 61
Beechy Lees Rd. Sev—88Nd 171
Beecot La. W on T—75Y 141
Beecroft Rd. SE4—57Ac 106
★Beehive Chase. Brtwd—7Zd
Beehive Clo. Borwd—16Ma 21
Beehive La. Ilf—29Pc 46
Beehive Pl. EC3—(3H 201)
Beehive Pl. SW9—55Qb 104
Beehive Rd. Stai—64H 119
Beeken Dene. Orp—77Sc 150
Beeleigh Rd. Mord—70Db 125
Beesfield La. F'ham, Dart
—73Qd 153
Beeston Clo. Wat—21Z 37
Beeston Ct. E8—36Wb 63
Beeston Pl. SW1—48Kb 82 (4A 204)
Beeston Rd. Barn—16Fb 23
Beeston Way. Felt—58Y 99
Beethoven Rd. Borwd—16Ma 21
Beethoven St. W10—41Ab 80
Beeton Clo. Pinn—24Ca 37
Begbie Rd. SE3—53Lc 107
★Beggar Hill. Ing—4Fe
Beggars Hill. Eps—80Va 144
Beggars Hollow. Enf—9Tb 11
Beggars La. West—96Uc 184
Beggars La. West—97Vc 185
Begonia Pl. Hmptn—65Ca 121
Begonia Wlk. W12—44Va 80
Beira St. SW12—59Kb 104
Bekesbourne St. E14—44Ac 84
Belasis Av. SW2—61Nb 126
Belcroft Clo. Brom—66Hc 129
Beldam Haw. Sev—84Cd 170
Beldham Gdns. E Mol—69Da 121
Belfairs Dri. Romf—31Yc 67
Belfairs Gdns. Wat—22Z 37
Belfast Av. Slou—4G 72
Belfast Gdns. SE3—51Hc 107
Belfast Rd. N16—33Vb 63
Belfast Rd. SE25—70Xb 127
Belfield Rd. Eps—81Ta 161
Belfont Wlk. N7—35Nb 62
Belford Gro. SE18—49Qc 86
Belford Rd. Borwd—10Pa 7
Belfort Rd. SE15—54Yb 106
Belfry Av. Uxb—25J 35
Belfry La. Rick—18L 17
Belgrade Rd. N16—35Ub 63
Belgrade Rd. Hmptn—67Da 121
Belgrave Av. Romf—27Ld 49
Belgrave Av. Wat—15V 18
Belgrave Clo. N14—15Lb 24
Belgrave Clo. W3—47Ra 79
Belgrave Clo. Orp—70Yc 131
Belgrave Clo. W on T—77X 141
Belgrave Cres. Sun—67X 121
Belgrave Gdns. N14—14Mb 24

Belgrave Gdns.—Bexhill Rd.

Belgrave Gdns. NW8—39Db 61
Belgrave Gdns. Stan—22La 38
Belgrave Mnr. Wok—91A 172
Belgrave M. Uxb—42M 75
Belgrave M. N. SW1
—47Jb 82 (2H 203)
Belgrave M. S. SW1
—48Jb 82 (3J 203)
Belgrave M. W. SW1
—48Jb 82 (3H 203)
Belgrave Pl. SW1
—48Jb 82 (3J 203)
Belgrave Pl. Slou—7M 73
Belgrave Rd. E10—32Ec 64
Belgrave Rd. E11—33Jc 65
Belgrave Rd. E13—42Lc 85
Belgrave Rd. E17—29Cc 44
Belgrave Rd. SE25—70Vb 127
Belgrave Rd. SW1
—49Kb 82 (6A 204)
Belgrave Rd. SW13—52Va 102
Belgrave Rd. Houn—55Ba 99
Belgrave Rd. Ilf—32Pc 66
Belgrave Rd. Mitc—69Fb 125
Belgrave Rd. Slou—5J 73
Belgrave Rd. Sun—67X 121
Belgrave Sq. SW1
—48Jb 82 (3H 203)
Belgrave St. E1—44Zb 84
Belgrave Ter. Wfd G—20Jc 27
Belgrave Wlk. Mitc—69Fb 125
Belgrave Yd. SW1—(4K 203)
Belgravia Gdns. Brom—65Gc 129
Belgravia M. King—70Ma 123
Belgrove St. WC1
—41Nb 82 (3G 193)
Belham Wlk. SE5—53Tb 105
Belhaven Ct. Borwd—11Pa 21
Belinda Rd. SW9—55Rb 105
Belitha Vs. N1—38Pb 62
Bellamy Clo. W14—50Bb 81
Bellamy Clo. Uxb—34Q 56
Bellamy Clo. Wat—11W 18
Bellamy Dri. Stan—25Ka 38
Bellamy Rd. E4—23Dc 44
Bellamy Rd. Enf—12Tb 25
Bellamy Rd. Wal X—1Ac 12
Bellamy St. SW12—59Kb 104
Bell Av. Romf—25Kd 49
Bell Av. W Dray—48P 75
Bell Clo. Grnh—57Vd 112
Bell Clo. Pinn—27Y 37
Bell Clo. Ruis—34V 55
Bell Clo. Slou—3M 73
Bellclose Rd. W Dray—47N 75
Bell Comn. Epp—4Uc 14
Bell Corner. Upm—33Sd 70
Bell Cres. Coul—93Kb 180
Bell Dri. SW18—59Ab 102
Bellefield Rd. Orp—71Xc 151
Bellefields Rd. SW9—55Pb 104
Bellegrove Clo. Well—54Vc 109
Bellegrove Rd. Well—54Uc 108
Bellenden Rd. SE15—54Vb 105
Bellestaines Pleasaunce. E4
—19Cc 26
Belleville Rd. SW11—57Gb 103
Belle Vue. Gnfd—39Fa 58
Belle Vue Clo. Stai—67J 119
Bellevue La. Bush, Wat—18Fa 20
Bellevue Pk. T Hth—69Sb 127
Bellevue Pl. E1—42Yb 84
Belle Vue Rd. E17—26Fc 45
Bellevue Rd. N11—21Jb 42
Belle Vue Rd. NW4—28Ya 40
Bellevue Rd. SW13—54Wa 102
Bellevue Rd. SW17—60Gb 103
Bellevue Rd. W13—42Ka 78
Bellevue Rd. Bexh—57Bd 109
Bellevue Rd. Horn—32Pd 69
Bellevue Rd. King—69Na 123
Belle Vue Rd. Orp—82Qc 168
Bellevue Rd. Romf—23Ed 48
Bellew St. SW17—62Eb 125
Bell Farm Av. Dag—34Ed 68
Bell Farm Cotts. Epp—4Uc 14
Bellfield. Croy—81Ac 166
Bellfield Av. Harr—23Fa 38
Bellflower Path. Romf—24Ld 49
Bell Gdns. Orp—71Yc 151
Bellgate M. NW5—35Kb 62
Bell Grn. SE26—63Bc 128
Bell Grn. La. SE26—64Bc 128
Bell Hill. Croy—75Sb 147
Bellhouse La. Brtwd—15Ud 32
Bell Ho. Rd. Romf—32Ed 68
Bellingham Grn. SE6—62Cc 128
Bellingham Rd. SE6—62Dc 128
Bell Inn Yd. EC3—44Tb 83 (3G 201)
Bell Junct. Houn—55Da 99
Bell La. E1—43Vb 83 (1K 201)
Bell La. E16—46Jc 85
Bell La. NW4—28Ya 40
Bell La. Enf—10Zb 12
Bell La. Lea—95Fa 176
Bell La. St Alb—1Na 7
Bell La. Twic—60Ja 100
Bell La. Wind—9D 72
Bell La. Clo. Lea—95Fa 176
Bellman Av. Grav—10G 114
Bell Meadow. SE19—64Ub 127
Bellmount Wood Av. Wat—11U 18
Bellot St. SE10—50Gc 85
Bell Pde. Wind—4D 94
Bellring Clo. Belv—51Cd 110
Bell Rd. E Mol—71Fa 142
Bell Rd. Enf—11Tb 25
Bell Rd. Houn—55Da 99
Bells All. SW6—54Cb 103
Bells Hill. Barn—15Za 22
Bells Hill. Slou—9L 53
Bells Hill Grn. Slou—8L 53
Bells La. Slou—55D 96
Bell St. NW1—43Gb 81 (7D 190)
Bellswood La. Iver—43D 74
Bell Trees Gro. SW16—64Pb 126
Bell View. Wind—5D 94
Bell View Clo. Wind—4D 94
Bellvue Pl. Slou—8K 73
Bell Water Ga. SE18—48Qc 86
Bellweir Clo. Stai—61D 118
Bell Wharf La. EC4
—45Sb 83 (5E 200)
Bellwood Rd. SE15—56Zb 106
Bell Yd. EC4—(3C 200)
Bell Yd. WC2—44Qb 82 (3K 199)
Belmarsh Rd. Wey—77K 139
Belmont. Slou—3E 72
Belmont Av. N9—18Wb 25
Belmont Av. N13—22Pb 42
Belmont Av. N17—27Sb 43
Belmont Av. Barn—15Hb 23
Belmont Av. N Mald—71Wa 144
Belmont Av. S'hall—48Aa 77
Belmont Av. Upm—33Pd 69
Belmont Av. Well—55Uc 108
Belmont Av. Wemb—39Pa 59
Belmont Circ. Harr—25Ka 38
Belmont Clo. N20—18Db 23
Belmont Clo. SW4—55Lb 104
Belmont Clo. Barn—14Hb 23
Belmont Clo. Uxb—37M 55
Belmont Clo. Wfd G—21Kc 45
Belmont Gro. SE13—55Fc 107
Belmont Hill. SE13—55Fc 107
Belmont La. Chst—64Sc 130
Belmont La. Stan—24La 38
Belmont Pk. SE13—56Fc 107
Belmont Pk. Clo. SE13—56Gc 107
Belmont Pk. Rd. E10—30Dc 44
Belmont Rise. Sutt—80Bb 145
Belmont Rd.—28Sb 43
N15 1-47 & 2-46
N17 remainder
Belmont Rd. SE25—71Xb 147
Belmont Rd. SW4—55Lb 104
Belmont Rd. W4—49Ta 79
Belmont Rd. Beck—68Bc 128
Belmont Rd. Bush, Wat—15Aa 19
Belmont Rd. Chst—64Rc 130
Belmont Rd. Eri—52Cd 110
Belmont Rd. Grays—51Be 113
Belmont Rd. Harr—27Ha 38
Belmont Rd. Horn—34Md 69
Belmont Rd. Ilf—34Sc 66
Belmont Rd. Lea—94Ja 176
Belmont Rd. Sev—96Kd 187
Belmont Rd. Sutt—82Cb 163
Belmont Rd. Twic—61Fa 122
Belmont Rd. Uxb—38M 55
Belmont Rd. Wall—78Kb 146
Belmont St. NW1—38Jb 62
Belmor. Borwd—15Pa 21
Belmore Av. Hay—44W 76
Belmore Av. Wok—88F 156
Belmore La. N7—36Mb 62
Belmore St. SW8—53Mb 104
Belsham St. E9—37Yb 64
Belsize Av. N13—23Pb 42
Belsize Av. NW3—37Fb 61
Belsize Av. W13—48Ka 78
Belsize Ct. NW3—36Fb 61
Belsize Cres. NW3—36Fb 61
Belsize Gdns. Sutt—77Db 145
Belsize Gro. NW3—37Gb 61
Belsize La. NW3—37Fb 61
Belsize M. NW3—37Fb 61
Belsize Pk. NW3—37Fb 61
Belsize Pk. M. NW3—37Fb 61
Belsize Pl. NW3—36Fb 61
Belsize Rd. NW6—39Db 61
Belsize Rd. Harr—24Fa 38
Belsize Sq. NW3—37Fb 61
Belsize Ter. NW3—37Fb 61
Belson Rd. SE18—49Pc 86
Beltana Dri. Grav—3G 136
Beltane Dri. SW19—62Za 124
Belthorn Cres. SW12—59Lb 104
Beltinge Rd. Romf—27Pd 49
Belton Rd. E7—38Kc 65
Belton Rd. E11—35Gc 65
Belton Rd. N17—27Ub 43
Belton Rd. NW2—37Wa 60
Belton Rd. Sidc—63Wc 131
Belton Way. E3—43Cc 84
Beltran Rd. SW6—54Db 103
Beltwood Rd. Belv—49Ed 88
Belvedere Av. SW19—64Ab 124
Belvedere Av. Ilf—26Rc 46
Belvedere Bldgs. SE1
—47Rb 83 (2C 206)
Belvedere Clo. Esh—78Da 141
Belvedere Clo. Grav—10E 114
Belvedere Clo. Tedd—64Ga 122
Belvedere Clo. Wey—78Q 140
Belvedere Dri. SW19—64Ab 124
Belvedere Gdns. E Mol—71Ba 141
Belvedere Gro. SW19—64Ab 124
Belvedere Mans. Slou—7H 73
Belvedere Pl. SE1
—47Rb 83 (2C 206)
Belvedere Rd. E10—32Ac 64
Belvedere Rd. SE1
—47Pb 82 (1J 205)
Belvedere Rd. SE2—46Yc 87
Belvedere Rd. W7—48Ha 78
Belvedere Rd. Bexh—55Bd 109
Belvedere Rd. Brtwd—20Vd 32
Belvedere Rd. Brom—66Vb 127
Belvedere Rd. West—90Pc 168
Belvedere Sq. SW19—64Ab 124
Belvedere Strand. NW9—26Va 40
Belvedere Way. Harr—30Na 39
Belvoir Clo. SE9—62Nc 130
Belvoir Rd. SE22—59Wb 105
Belvue Clo. N'holt—38Ca 57
Belvue Rd. N'holt—38Ca 57
Bembridge Clo. NW6—38Ab 60
Bembridge Gdns. Ruis—33T 56
Bemerton St. N1—39Pb 62
Bemish Rd. SW15—55Za 102
Bempton Dri. Ruis—33X 57
Bemsted Rd. E17—27Bc 44
Benares Rd. SE18—49Vc 87
Benbow Rd. W6—48Xa 80
Benbow St. SE8—51Cc 106
Benbow Waye. Uxb—43L 75
Benbury Clo. Brom—64Ec 128
Bence, The. Egh—69D 118
Bench Field. S Croy—78Vb 147
Bench, The. Rich—62La 122
Bencombe Rd. Purl—86Qb 164
Bencroft Rd. SW16—66Lb 126
Bencurtis Pk. W Wick—76Fc 149
Bendall M. NW1—(7E 190)
Bendemeer Rd. SW15—55Za 102
Bendish Rd. E6—38Nc 66
Bendmore Av. SE2—50Wc 87
Bendon Valley. SW18—59Db 103
Bendysh Rd. Bush, Wat—13Aa 19
Benedict Clo. Orp—76Uc 150
Benedict Dri. Felt—59T 98
Benedict Rd. SW9—55Pb 104
Benedict Rd. Mitc—69Fb 125
Benedict Way. N2—27Eb 41
Benenden Grn. Brom—71Jc 149
Benen-Stock Rd. Stai—57J 97
Benets Rd. Horn—32Qd 69
Benett Gdns. SW16—68Nb 126
Benfleet Clo. Cob—84Aa 159
Benfleet Clo. Sutt—76Eb 145
Bengal Ct. EC3—(3G 201)
Bengal Rd. Ilf—34Rc 66
Bengarth Dri. Harr—26Fa 38
Bengarth Rd. N'holt—39Aa 57
Bengeworth Rd. SE5—55Sb 105
Bengeworth Rd. Harr—34Ja 58
Ben Hale Clo. Stan—22Ka 38
Benham Clo. SW11—55Fb 103
Benham Clo. Coul—90Rb 165
Benham Gdns. Houn—57Ca 99
Benham Rd. W7—43Ga 78
Benhill Av. Sutt—77Db 145
(in two parts)
Benhill Rd. SE5—52Tb 105
Benhill Rd. Sutt—76Eb 145
Benhill Wood Rd. Sutt—76Eb 145
Benhilton Gdns. Sutt—76Db 145
Benhurst Av. Horn—34Kd 69
Benhurst Clo. S Croy—82Zb 166
Benhurst Ct. SW16—64Qb 126
Benhurst Gdns. S Croy—82Yb 166
Benin St. SE13—59Fc 107
Benjafield Clo. N18—21Xb 43
Benjamin Clo. E8—39Wb 63
Benjamin Clo. Horn—30Jd 48
Benjamin St. EC1
—43Rb 83 (7B 194)
Ben Jonson Ho. EC2—(7E 194)
Ben Jonson Rd. E1—43Ac 84
Benledi St. E14—44Fc 85
Bennerley Rd. SW11—57Gb 103
Bennets Copse. Chst—65Nc 130
Bennet's Hill. EC4
—45Sb 83 (4C 200)
Bennet St. SW1—46Lb 82 (6B 198)
Bennett Clo. Cob—85W 158
Bennett Clo. King—67La 122
Bennett Clo. N'wd—24V 36
Bennett Clo. Well—54Wc 109
Bennett Gro. SE13—53Dc 106
Bennett Ho. Grav—2B 136
Bennett Pk. SE3—55Hc 107
Bennett Rd. E13—42Lc 85
Bennett Rd. Romf—31Ad 67
Bennetts Av. Croy—75Ac 148
Bennetts Av. Gnfd—39Ga 58
★Bennetts Av. Sev—83Yd
Bennett's Castle La. Dag—33Yc 67
Bennetts Clo. N17—23Wb 43
Bennetts Clo. Slou—6E 72
Bennett St. W4—51Ua 102
Bennetts Way. Croy—75Ac 148
Bennett's Yd. SW1
—48Mb 82 (4E 204)
Bennett's Yd. Uxb—38L 55
Bennett Way. Dart—63Td 134
Bennett Way. Guild—100J 173
Benning Clo. Wind—5B 94
Benningholme Rd. Edgw—23Ua 40
Bennington Rd. N17—25Ub 43
Bennington Rd. Wfd G—24Gc 45
Bennions Clo. Horn—37Md 69
Benn's All. Hmptn—68Da 121
Benn St. E9—37Ac 64
Benns Wlk. Rich—56Na 101
Benrek Clo. Ilf—24Sc 46
Bensbury Clo. SW15—59Xa 102
Bensham Clo. T Hth—70Sb 127
Bensham Gro. T Hth—68Sb 127
Bensham La. Croy & T Hth
—73Rb 147
Bensham Mnr. Rd. T Hth
—70Sb 127
Benskin Rd. Wat—15W 18
Benskins La. Hav, Romf & Brtwd
—18Md 31
Bensley Clo. N11—22Hb 41
Ben Smith Way. SE16—48Wb 83
Benson Av. E6—40Mc 65
Benson Clo. Houn—56Ca 99
Benson Clo. Slou—6L 73
Benson Clo. Uxb—43N 75
Benson Rd. SE23—60Yb 106
Benson Rd. Croy—76Qb 146
Benson Rd. Grays—51Ee 113
Bentfield Gdns. SE9—62Mc 129
Benthal Rd. N16—34Wb 63
Bentham Av. Wok—87E 156
Bentham Rd. E9—37Zb 64
Bentham Rd. SE28—46Xc 87
Bentham Wlk. NW10—36Sa 59
Ben Tillet Clo. Bark—38Wc 67
Bentinck M. W1—44Jb 82 (2J 197)
Bentinck Rd. W Dray—46M 75
Bentinck St. W1—44Jb 82 (2J 197)
Bentley Clo. Long, Dart—69Ee 135
Bentley Dri. Ilf—30Sc 46
Bentley Heath La. Barn—6Ab 8
Bentley Rd. N1—37Ub 63
Bentley Rd. Slou—6E 72
Bentley's Meadow. Sev—92Pd 187
Bentley St. Grav—8E 114
Bentley Way. Stan—22Ja 38
Bentley Way. Wfd G—20Jc 27
Benton Rd. Ilf—32Tc 66
Benton Rd. Wat—22Z 37
Bentons La. SE27—63Sb 127
Bentons Rise. SE27—64Tb 127
Bentry Clo. Dag—33Ad 67
Bentry Rd. Dag—33Ad 67
Bentworth Rd. W12—44Xa 80
Benwell Rd. N7—36Qb 62
Benworth St. E3—41Bc 84
Berberis Wlk. W Dray—49N 75
Berber Rd. SW11—57Hb 103
Berceau Wlk. Wat—11U 18
Bercta Rd. SE9—61Sc 130
Beredens La. Brtwd—27Vd 50
Berens Rd. NW10—41Za 80
Berens Rd. Orp—71Zc 151
Berens Way. Chst—70Vc 131
Beresford Av. N20—19Hb 23
Beresford Av. W7—43Fa 78
Beresford Av. Slou—5N 73
Beresford Av. Surb—74Ra 143
Beresford Av. Twic—58La 100
Beresford Av. Wemb—39Pa 59
Beresford Dri. Brom—69Nc 130
Beresford Dri. Wfd G—21Lc 45
Beresford Gdns. Enf—14Ub 25
Beresford Gdns. Houn—57Ba 99
Beresford Gdns. Romf—29Ad 47
Beresford Rd. E4—18Gc 27
Beresford Rd. E17—25Dc 44
Beresford Rd. N2—27Gb 41
Beresford Rd. N5—36Tb 63
Beresford Rd. N8—29Qb 42
Beresford Rd. Grav—9A 114
Beresford Rd. Harr—29Fa 38
Beresford Rd. King—67Pa 123
Beresford Rd. N Mald—70Sa 123
Beresford Rd. Rick—18H 17
Beresford Rd. S'hall—46Z 77
Beresford Rd. Sutt—80Bb 145
Beresford Sq. SE18—49Rc 86
Beresford St. SE18—48Rc 86
Beresford Ter. N5—36Sb 63
Berestede Rd. W6—50Va 80
Bere St. E1—45Zb 84
Berger Clo. Orp—72Tc 150
Berger Rd. E9—37Zb 64
Bergholt Av. Ilf—29Nc 46
Bergholt Cres. N16—31Ub 63
Bergholt M. NW1—38Lb 62
Berkeley Av. Bexh—53Zc 109
Berkeley Av. Gnfd—37Ga 58
Berkeley Av. Houn—54W 98
Berkeley Av. Ilf—26Qc 46
Berkeley Av. Romf—24Ed 48
Berkeley Clo. Borwd—15Qa 21
Berkeley Clo. Orp—73Uc 150
Berkeley Clo. Pot B—4Ab 8
Berkeley Clo. Ruis—34W 56
Berkeley Clo. Upm—33Rd 69
Berkeley Ct. N14—16Lb 24
Berkeley Ct. Surb—73Ma 143
Berkeley Ct. Swan—69Gd 132
Berkeley Ct. Wey—75T 140
Berkeley Cres. Barn—15Fb 23
Berkeley Cres. Dart—60Pd 111
Berkeley Dri. E Mol—69Ba 121
Berkeley Dri. Horn—32Qd 69
Berkeley Dri. Wind—10A 94
Berkeley Gdns. N21—17Tb 25
Berkeley Gdns. W8—46Cb 81
Berkeley Gdns. Esh—80Ja 142
Berkeley Gdns. W on T—73V 140
Berkeley M. W1—44Hb 81 (3G 197)
Berkeley M. Slou—4B 72
Berkeley Pl. SW19—65Za 124
Berkeley Rd. E12—36Nc 66
Berkeley Rd. N8—29Mb 42
Berkeley Rd. N15—30Tb 43
Berkeley Rd. NW9—28Qa 39
Berkeley Rd. SW13—53Wa 102
Berkeley Rd. Bren—51Ja 100
Berkeley Rd. Uxb—38S 56
Berkeley Sq. W1
—45Kb 82 (5A 198)
Berkeley St. W1—46Kb 82 (5A 198)
Berkeley Waye. Houn—51Z 99
Berkhampstead Rd. Belv
—50Cd 88
Berkhamsted Av. Wemb—37Pa 59
Berkley Av. Wal X—6Zb 12
Berkley Clo. Stai—61F 118
Berkley Gdns. Wey—86H 157
Berkley Gro. NW1—38Jb 62
Berkley Rd. NW1—38Hb 61
Berkley Rd. Grav—8D 114
Berks Hill. Rick—15E 16
Berkshire Av. Slou—4F 72
Berkshire Clo. Cat—94Tb 181
Berkshire Gdns. N13—23Qb 42
Berkshire Gdns. N18—22Xb 43
Berkshire Rd. E9—37Bc 64
Berkshire Way. Horn—29Qd 49
Berkshire Way. Mitc—70Nb 126
Berley Cres. Grav—8E 114
Bermans Clo. Brtwd—19De 33
Bermans Way. NW10—35Ua 60
Bermondsey Sq. SE1
—48Ub 83 (3J 207)
Bermondsey St. SE1
—47Ub 83 (1H 207)
Bermondsey Wall E. SE16
—47Xb 83
Bermondsey Wall W. SE16
—47Wb 83
Bermuda Rd. Til—4C 114
Bernal Clo. SE28—45Zc 87
Bernard Av. W13—48Ka 78
Bernard Cassidy St. E16—43Hc 85
Bernard Gdns. SW19—64Bb 125
Bernard Rd. N15—29Vb 43
Bernard Rd. Romf—31Ed 68
Bernard Rd. Wall—77Kb 146
Bernard St. WC1—42Nb 82 (6F 193)
Bernard St. Grav—8D 114
Bernays Clo. Stan—23La 38
Bernay's Gro. SW9—56Pb 104
Bernel Dri. Croy—76Bc 148
Berne Rd. T Hth—71Sb 147
Berners Clo. Slou—5C 72
Berners M. W1—43Lb 82 (1C 198)
Berners Pl. W1—44Lb 82 (2C 198)
Berners Rd. N1—39Rb 63 (1B 194)
Berners Rd. N22—26Qb 42
Berners St. W1—43Lb 82 (1C 198)
Berney Rd. Croy—73Tb 147
Bernville Way. Harr—29Pa 39
Bernwell Rd. E4—20Gc 27
Berridge Grn. Edgw—24Qa 39
Berridge Rd. SE19—64Tb 127
Berriman Rd. N7—34Pb 62
Berriton Rd. Harr—32Ba 57
Berry Av. Wat—8X 5
Berry Clo. N21—18Rb 25
Berry Clo. NW10—38Ua 60
Berry Clo. Rick—17K 17
Berrydale Rd. Hay—42Aa 77
Berryfield. Slou—4N 73
Berryfield Clo. E17—28Dc 44
Berryfield Clo. Brom—68Nc 130
Berryfield Rd. SE17
—50Rb 83 (7C 206)
Berry Gro. La. Wat—10Aa 5
(in two parts)
Berryhill. SE9—56Rc 108
Berry Hill. Stan—21Ma 39
Berryhill Gdns. SE9—56Rc 108
Berrylands. SW20—69Ya 124
Berrylands. Long, Dart—72Ce 155
Berrylands. Orp—76Yc 151
Berrylands. Surb—72Pa 143
Berry La. SE21—63Tb 127
Berry La. Rick—16F 16
Berry La. Wok—10B 188
Berryman Clo. Dag—34Yc 67
Berryman's La. SE26—63Zb 128
Berry Meade. Asht—89Pa 161
Berrymead Gdns. W3—47Sa 79
Berrymede Rd. W4—48Ta 79
Berry Pl. EC1—41Rb 83 (4C 194)
Berryscroft Rd. Stai—66L 119
Berry's Grn. Rd. West—88Rc 168
Berry's Hill. West—87Rc 168
Berry's La. Wey—83M 157
Berry St. EC1—42Rb 83 (5C 194)
Berry Wlk. Asht—91Pa 177
Berry Way. W5—48Na 79
Berry Way. Rick—17K 17
Bertal Rd. SW17—63Fb 125
Berther Rd. Horn—31Nd 69
Berthon St. SE8—52Cc 106
Bertie Rd. NW10—37Wa 60
Bertie Rd. SE26—65Zb 128
Bertram Cotts. SW19—66Cb 125
Bertram Rd. NW4—30Wa 40
Bertram Rd. Enf—14Wb 25
Bertram Rd. King—66Qa 123
Bertram St. N19—33Kb 62
Bertram Way. Enf—14Vb 25
Bertrand St. SE13—55Dc 106
Bertrand Way. SE28—45Yc 87
Bert Rd. T Hth—71Sb 147
Berwick Av. Hay—44Z 77
Berwick Av. Slou—5F 72
Berwick Clo. Stan—23Ha 38
Berwick Clo. Wal X—6Cc 12
Berwick Cres. Sidc—59Uc 108
★Berwick La. Ong—5Gd
Berwick Pond Clo. Rain
—40Md 69
Berwick Pond Rd. Rain & Upm
—40Nd 69
Berwick Rd. E16—44Kc 85
Berwick Rd. N22—25Rb 43
Berwick Rd. Borwd—10Pa 7
Berwick Rd. Rain—40Md 69
Berwick Rd. Well—53Xc 109
Berwick St. W1—44Lb 82 (2C 198)
Berwick Way. Orp—74Wc 151
Berwyn Av. Houn—53Da 99
Berwyn Rd. SE24—60Rb 105
Berwyn Rd. Rich—56Ra 101
Beryl Rd. W6—50Za 80
Berystede. King—66Ra 123
Besant Rd. NW2—35Ab 60
Besant Wlk. N7—33Pb 62
Besant Way. NW10—36Sa 59
Besley St. SW16—65Lb 126
Bessborough Gdns. SW1
—50Mb 82 (7E 204)
Bessborough Pl. SW1
—50Mb 82 (7D 204)
Bessborough Rd. SW15
—60Wa 102
Bessborough Rd. Harr—31Fa 58
Bessborough St. SW1
—50Mb 82 (7D 204)
Bessels Grn. Rd. Sev—96Fd 186
Bessels Way. Sev—96Ed 186
Bessemer Rd. SE5—54Sb 105
Bessingby Rd. Ruis—33X 57
Besson Rd. SE14—53Zb 106
Bessy St. E2—41Yb 84
Bestobell Rd. Slou—4G 72
Bestwood St. SE8—49Zb 84
Beswick M. NW6—36Db 61
Betam Rd. Hay—47T 76
Beta Rd. Wok—88D 156
Betchworth Clo. Sutt—78Fb 145
Betchworth Rd. Ilf—33Uc 66
Betchworth Way. Croy—81Ec 166
Betenson Av. Sev—94Hd 186
Betham Rd. Gnfd—42Fa 78
Bethany Waye. Felt—59U 98
Bethecar Rd. Harr—29Ga 38
Bethel Av. Ilf—31Qc 66
Bethel Est. SE1—(7J 201)
Bethell Av. E16—42Hc 85
Bethel Rd. Sev—95Ld 187
Bethel Rd. Well—55Yc 109
Bethersden Clo. Beck—66Bc 128
Bethnal Grn. Rd.—42Vb 83 (5K 195)
E1 1-99 & 2-94
E2 remainder
Bethune Av. N11—21Hb 41
Bethune Clo. N16—32Ub 63
Bethune Rd. N16—31Tb 63
Bethune Rd. NW10—42Ta 79
Bethwin Rd. SE5—52Rb 105
Betjeman Clo. Pinn—28Ca 37
Betley Ct. W on T—76X 141
Betony Clo. Croy—74Zb 148
Betony Rd. Romf—23Md 49
Betoyne Av. E4—21Gc 45
Betsham Rd. Eri—52Hd 110
Betsham Rd. Grav—64Zd 135
Betsham Rd. Swans—59Ae 113
Betstyle Cir. N11—21Kb 42
Betstyle Rd. N11—21Kb 42
Betterton Dri. Sidc—61Ad 131
Betterton Rd. Rain—41Gd 88
Betterton St. WC2
—44Nb 82 (3G 199)
Bettles Clo. Uxb—40L 55
Bettons Pk. E15—39Gc 65
Bettridge Rd. SW6—54Bb 103
Betts Clo. Beck—68Ac 128
Betts Rd. E16—45Kc 85
Betts St. E1—45Xb 83
Betts Way. SE20—67Xb 127
Betts Way. Surb—74Ka 142
Betula Clo. Kenl—87Tb 165
Betula Wlk. Rain—41Md 89
Between Streets. Cob—86W 158
Beulah Av. T Hth—68Sb 127
Beulah Clo. Edgw—20Ra 21
Beulah Cres. T Hth—68Sb 127
Beulah Gro. Croy—72Sb 147
Beulah Hill. SE19—65Rb 127
Beulah Rd. E17—29Dc 44
Beulah Rd. SW19—66Bb 125
Beulah Rd. Epp—1Wc 15
Beulah Rd. Horn—34Ld 69
Beulah Rd. Sutt—77Cb 145
Beulah Rd. T Hth—69Sb 127
Beulah Wlk. Cat—92Ac 182
Beult Rd. Dart—56Jd 110
Bevan Av. Bark—38Wc 67
Bevan Ct. Croy—78Qb 146
Bevan Pl. Swan—70Hd 132
Bevan Rd. SE2—50Xc 87
Bevan Rd. Barn—14Hb 23
Bevan St. N1—39Sb 63 (1E 194)
Bevan Way. Horn—35Pd 69
Bevenden St. N1—41Tb 83 (3G 195)
Beveridge Rd. NW10—38Ua 60
Beverley Av. SW20—67Va 124
Beverley Av. Houn—56Ba 99
Beverley Av. Sidc—59Vc 109
Beverley Clo. N21—18Sb 25
Beverley Clo. SW11—56Fb 103
Beverley Clo. SW13—54Wa 102
Beverley Clo. Chess—77La 142
Beverley Clo. Enf—14Ub 25
Beverley Clo. Eps—83Ya 162
Beverley Clo. Horn—31Pd 69
Beverley Clo. Wey—78M 139
(Addlestone)
Beverley Clo. Wey—75U 140
(Oatlands Park)
Beverley Ct. SE4—55Bc 106
Beverley Ct. W4—50Sa 79
Beverley Ct. Slou—7M 73
Beverley Cres. Wfd G—25Kc 45
Beverley Dri. Edgw—27Qa 39
Beverley Gdns. NW11—31Ab 60
Beverley Gdns. SW13—55Va 102
Beverley Gdns. Horn—31Pd 69
Beverley Gdns. Stan—25Ja 38
Beverley Gdns. Wal X—2Wb 11
Beverley Gdns. Wemb—32Pa 59
Beverley Gdns. Wor Pk—74Wa 144
Beverley La. SW15—62Va 124
Beverley La. King—66Ua 124
Beverley Path. SW13—54Va 102
Beverley Rd. E4—23Fc 45
Beverley Rd. E6—41Mc 85
Beverley Rd. SE20—68Xb 127
Beverley Rd. SW13—55Va 102
Beverley Rd. W4—50Va 80
Beverley Rd. Bexh—54Ed 110
Beverley Rd. Brom—75Nc 150
Beverley Rd. Dag—35Ad 67
Beverley Rd. King—67La 122
Beverley Rd. Mitc—70Mb 126
Beverley Rd. N Mald—70Wa 124
Beverley Rd. Ruis—33X 57
Beverley Rd. S'hall—49Aa 77
Beverley Rd. Sun—67V 120
Beverley Rd. Whyt—89Ub 165
Beverley Rd. Wor Pk—75Ya 144
Beverley Way. King & SW20
—67Va 124
Beversbrook Rd. N19—34Mb 62
Beverstone Rd. SW2—57Pb 104
Beverstone Rd. T Hth—70Qb 126
Bevill Allen Clo. SW17—64Hb 125
Bevin Clo. SE16—46Ac 84
Bevington Rd. W10—43Ab 80
Bevington Rd. Beck—68Dc 128
Bevington St. SE16—47Wb 83
Bevin Rd. Hay—41W 76
Bevin Wlk. Stanf—1M 93
Bevin Way. WC1
—40Qb 62 (3K 193)
Bevis Clo. Dart—59Sd 112
Bevis Marks. EC3
—44Ub 83 (2J 201)
Bewcastle Gdns. Enf—14Nb 24
Bewdley St. N1—38Qb 62
Bewick St. SW8—54Kb 104
Bewley Clo. Wal X—3Zb 12
Bewley St. E1—45Yb 84
Bewlys Rd. SE27—64Rb 127
Bexhill Clo. Felt—61Aa 121
Bexhill Rd. N11—22Mb 42
Bexhill Rd. SE4—58Bc 106
Bexhill Rd. SW14—55Sa 101

Bexhill Wlk.—Bloomsbury Sq.

Bexhill Wlk. E15—39Gc 65
Bexley Clo. Dart—57Gd 110
Bexley Gdns. N9—20Tb 25
Bexley High St. Bex—59Cd 110
Bexley La. Dart—57Gd 110
Bexley La. Sidc—63Yc 131
Bexley Rd. SE9—57Rc 108
Bexley Rd. Eri—52Ed 110
Bexley St. Wind—3G 94
Beynon Rd. Cars—78Hb 145
Bianca Rd. SE15—51Wb 105
Bibsworth Rd. N3—26Bb 41
Bibury Clo. SE15—51Ub 105
Bicester Rd. Rich—55Qa 101
Bickenhall St. W1 —43Hb 81 (7G 191)
Bickersteth Rd. SW17—65Hb 125
Bickerton Rd. N19—33Lb 62
Bickley Cres. Brom—70Nc 130
Bickley Pk. Rd. Brom—69Nc 130
Bickley Rd. E10—31Dc 64
Bickley Rd. Brom—68Mc 129
Bickley St. SW17—64Gb 125
Bicknell Rd. SE5—55Sb 105
Bicknoller Clo. Sutt—82Db 163
Bicknoller Rd. Enf—11Vb 25
Bicknor Rd. Orp—73Vc 151
Bidborough Clo. Brom—71Hc 149
Bidborough St. WC1 —41Nb 82 (4F 193)
Biddenden Way. SE9—63Qc 130
Biddenden Way. Grav—6A 136
Biddenham Turn. Wat—7Y 5
Bidder St. E16—43Gc 85
(in two parts)
Biddestone Rd. N7—35Pb 62
Biddulph Rd. W9—41Db 81
Biddulph Rd. S Croy—81Sb 165
Bideford Av. Gnfd—40Ka 58
Bideford Clo. Edgw—25Qa 39
Bideford Clo. Felt—62Ba 121
Bideford Clo. Romf—25Ld 49
Bideford Gdns. Enf—17Ub 25
Bideford Rd. Brom—62Hc 129
Bideford Rd. Enf—10Bc 12
Bideford Rd. Ruis—34X 57
Bideford Rd. Well—52Xc 109
Bidhams Cres. Tad—93Ya 178
Bidwell Gdns. N11—24Lb 42
Bidwell.St. SE15—53Xb 105
Bigbury Clo. N17—24Ub 43
Biggerstaff Rd. E15—39Ec 64
Biggerstaff St. N4—33Qb 62
Biggin Av. Mitc—67Hb 125
Biggin Hill. SE19—66Rb 127
Biggin La. Grays—1D 114
Biggin Way. SE19—66Rb 127
Bigginwood Rd. SW16—66Rb 127
Biggs Row. SW15—55Za 102
Big Hill. E5—32Xb 63
Bigland Est. E1—44Xb 83
Bigland St. E1—44Xb 83
Bignell Rd. SE18—50Rc 86
Bignold Rd. E7—35Jc 65
Bigwood Rd. NW11—29Db 41
Billericay Rd. Brtwd—24Fe 51
Billet Clo. Horn—32Md 69
Billet Clo. Romf—27Zc 47
Billet Hill. Sev—77Yd 154
Billet La. Horn—32Md 69
Billet La. Iver & Slou—41D 74
Billet La. Stanf—2M 93
Billet Rd. E17—25Zb 44
Billet Rd. Romf—27Xc 47
Billet Rd. Stai—62J 119
Billingford Clo. SE4—56Zb 106
Billing Pl. SW10—52Db 103
Billing Rd. SW10—52Db 103
Billing St. SW10—52Db 103
Billington Rd. SE14—52Zb 106
Billison St. E14—49Ec 84
Billiter Sq. EC3—(3J 201)
Billiter St. EC3—44Ub 83 (3J 201)
Billockby Clo. Chess—79Pa 143
Billy Lows La. Pot B—3Cb 9
Bilsby Gro. SE9—63Mc 129
Bilton Clo. Slou—54G 96
Bilton Rd. Eri—52Jd 110
Bilton Rd. Gnfd—39Ja 58
Bilton Way. Enf—11Ac 26
Bilton Way. Hay—47X 77
Bina Gdns. SW5—49Eb 81 (6A 202)
Bincote Rd. Enf—13Pb 24
Binden Rd. W12—48Va 80
Bindon Grn. Mord—70Db 125
Binfield Rd. SW4—53Nb 104
Binfield Rd. S Croy—79Vb 147
Binfield Rd. Wey—84N 157
Bingfield St. N1—39Nb 62
(in two parts)
Bingham Clo. S Ock—44Yd 90
Bingham Dri. Stai—66M 119
Bingham Dri. Wok—6C 188
Bingham Pl. W1—43Jb 82 (7H 191)
Bingham Rd. Croy—74Wb 147
Bingham St. N1—37Tb 63
Bingley Rd. E16—44Lc 85
Bingley Rd. Gnfd—42Ea 78
Bingley Rd. Sun—66W 120
Binney St. W1—44Jb 82 (3J 197)
Binns Rd. W4—50Ua 80
Binsey Wlk. SE2—47Yc 87
Binyon Cres. Stan—22Ha 38
Birbetts Rd. SE9—61Pc 130
Birchanger Rd. SE25—71Wb 147
Birch Av. N13—20Sb 25
Birch Av. Cat—96Tb 181
Birch Av. W Dray—44P 75
Birch Clo. E16—43Gc 85
Birch Clo. N19—33Lb 62
Birch Clo. SE15—54Wb 105
Birch Clo. Bren—52Ka 100
Birch Clo. Buck H—20Mc 27
Birch Clo. Long, Dart—68Ee 135
Birch Clo. Romf—27Dd 48
Birch Clo. Shep—68U 120
Birch Clo. Tedd—64Ja 122
Birch Clo. Wey—81M 157
Birch Clo. Wok—7F 188
Birch Clo. Wok—97H 173
(Send)
Birch Copse. St Alb—2Aa 5
Birch Ct. N'wd—23S 36
Birch Cres. Horn—28Nd 49
Birch Cres. Uxb—39P 55
Birchdale. Ger X—2P 53
Birchdale Clo. Wey—83L 157
Birchdale Gdns. Romf—31Zc 67
Birchdale Rd. E7—36Lc 65
Birch Dri. Rick—22F 34
Birchen Clo. NW9—33Ta 59
Birchen Gro. NW9—33Ta 59
Birches Clo. Eps—87Ua 162
Birches Clo. Pinn—29Aa 37
Birches, The. N21—16Pb 24
Birches, The. SE7—51Kc 107
Birches, The. Brtwd—20Ae 33
Birches, The. Bush, Wat—15Ea 20
Birches, The. Lea—98U 174
Birches, The. Orp—77Qc 150
Birches, The. Wok—90B 156
Birchfield Clo. Coul—88Pb 164
Birchfield Clo. Wey—77K 139
Birchfield Gro. Eps—82Ya 162
Birchfield Rd. Wal X—1Xb 11
Birchfields. E14—45Cc 84
Birch Gdns. Dag—34Ed 68
Birch Grn. NW9—24Ua 40
Birch Grn. Stai—63J 119
Birch Gro. SE12—59Hc 107
Birch Gro. W3—46Qa 79
Birch Gro. Cob—86Y 159
Birch Gro. Pot B—4Cb 9
Birch Gro. Shep—68U 120
Birch Gro. Slou—3F 72
Birch Gro. Tad—96Ab 178
Birch Gro. Well—56Wc 109
Birch Gro. Wind—3B 94
Birch Gro. Wok—87F 156
Birch Hill. Croy—78Zb 148
Birchin Cross Rd. Sev—87Nd 171
Birchington Clo. Bexh—53Dd 110
Birchington Clo. Orp—74Yc 151
Birchington Rd. N8—30Mb 42
Birchington Rd. NW6—39Cb 61
Birchington Rd. Surb—73Pa 143
Birchington Rd. Wind—4E 94
Birchin La. EC3—44Tb 83 (3G 201)
Birchlands Av. SW12—59Hb 103
Birch La. Hem—5D 2
Birch La. Purl—83Nb 164
Birchmead. Orp—75Qc 150
Birchmead. Wat—10V 4
Birchmead Av. Pinn—28Y 37
Birchmere Row. SE3—54Hc 107
Birchmore Wlk. N5—34Sb 63
(in two parts)
Birch Pk. Harr—24Ea 38
Birch Pl. Grnh—58Ud 112
Birch Rd. Felt—64Z 121
Birch Rd. Romf—27Dd 48
Birch Row. Brom—73Qc 150
Birch Tree Av. W Wick—78Hc 149
Birch Tree Wlk. Wat—9V 4
Birch Tree Way. Croy—75Xb 147
Birch Vale. Cob—85Ca 159
Birchview. Epp—1Xc 15
Birch Wlk. Borwd—11Qa 21
Birch Wlk. Eri—51Ed 110
Birch Wlk. Mitc—67Kb 126
Birchway. Hay—46W 76
Birchway. Sev—80Vd 154
Birch Way. Warl—90Ac 166
Birchwood. Wal A—6Gc 13
Birchwood Av. N10—27Jb 42
Birchwood Av. Beck—70Bc 128
Birchwood Av. Sidc—62Xc 131
Birchwood Av. Wall—76Jb 146
Birchwood Clo. Brtwd—23Yd 50
Birchwood Ct. N13—22Rb 43
Birchwood Ct. Edgw—26Sa 39
Birchwood Dri. NW3—34Db 61
Birchwood Dri. Dart—63Gd 132
Birchwood Dri. Wey—84J 157
Birchwood Gro. Hmptn—65Ca 121
Birchwood La. Cat—97Rb 181
Birchwood La. Esh & Lea —81Fa 160
Birchwood Pk. Av. Swan —69Gd 132
Birchwood Rd. SW17—64Kb 126
Birchwood Rd. Orp—70Tc 130
Birchwood Rd. Swan & Dart —67Ed 132
Birchwood Rd. Wey—84J 157
Birchwood Way. St Alb—1Da 5
Birdbrook Clo. Dag—38Ed 68
Birdbrook Rd. SE3—55Lc 107
Birdcage Wlk. SW1 —47Lb 82 (2B 204)
Birdham Clo. Brom—71Nc 150
Birdhouse La. Orp—87Qc 168
Birdhurst Av. S Croy—77Tb 147
Birdhurst Gdns. S Croy—77Tb 147
Birdhurst Rise. S Croy—78Ub 147
Birdhurst Rd. SW18—57Eb 103
Birdhurst Rd. SW19—65Gb 125
Birdhurst Rd. S Croy—78Ub 147
Bird-in-Bush Rd. SE15—52Wb 105
Bird in Hand La. Brom—68Mc 129
Bird-in-Hand Pas. SE23—61Yb 128
Bird La. Brtwd—27Yd 50
Bird La. Upm—29Td 50
Bird La. Uxb—26L 35
Birdlip Clo. SE15—51Ub 105
Birds Farm Av. Romf—25Dd 48
Birds Hill Dri. Lea—85Fa 160
Birds Hill Rise. Lea—85Fa 160
Birds Hill Rd. Lea—84Fa 160
Bird St. W1—44Jb 82 (3J 197)
Birdswood Dri. Wok—8B 188
Bird Wlk. Twic—60Ba 99
Birdwood Clo. S Croy—83Zb 166
Birdwood Clo. Tedd—63Ga 122
Birkbeck Av. W3—45Sa 79
Birkbeck Av. Gnfd—39Ea 58
Birkbeck Gdns. Wfd G—19Jc 27
Birkbeck Gro. W3—47Ta 79
Birkbeck Hill. SE21—60Rb 105
Birkbeck Pl. SE21—61Sb 127
Birkbeck Rd. E8—36Vb 63
Birkbeck Rd. N8—28Nb 42
Birkbeck Rd. N12—22Eb 41
Birkbeck Rd. N17—25Vb 43
Birkbeck Rd. NW7—22Va 40
Birkbeck Rd. SW19—64Db 125
Birkbeck Rd. W3—46Ta 79
Birkbeck Rd. W5—49La 78
Birkbeck Rd. Beck—68Yb 128
Birkbeck Rd. Brtwd—16Fe 33
Birkbeck Rd. Enf—11Tb 25
Birkbeck Rd. Ilf—29Tc 46
Birkbeck Rd. Romf—32Fd 68
Birkbeck Rd. Sidc—62Wc 131
Birkbeck St. E2—41Xb 83
Birkbeck Way. Gnfd—39Fa 58
Birkdale Av. Pinn—27Ca 37
Birkdale Av. Romf—24Qd 49
Birkdale Clo. Orp—73Tc 150
Birkdale Gdns. Wat—20Z 19
Birkdale Rd. SE2—49Wc 87
Birkdale Rd. W5—42Na 79
Birkenhead Av. King—68Pa 123
Birkenhead St. WC1 —41Nb 82 (3G 193)
Birken M. N'wd—22R 36
Birkett Way. Chal—13A 16
Birkhall Rd. SE6—60Fc 107
Birkwood Clo. SW12—59Mb 104
Birley Rd. N20—19Eb 23
Birley Rd. Slou—4H 73
Birley St. SW11—54Jb 104
Birling Rd. Eri—52Fd 110
Birnam Rd. N4—33Pb 62
Birnbeck Ct. NW11—29Bb 41
Birnbeck Ct. Barn—14Za 22
Birnham Clo. Wok—96J 173
Birse Cres. NW10—34Ua 60
Birstall Grn. Wat—21Z 37
Birstall Rd. N15—29Ub 43
Birtley Path. Borwd—11Na 21
Birtrick Dri. Grav—10B 136
Biscay Rd. W6—50Za 80
Biscoe Clo. Houn—51Ca 99
Biscoe Way. SE13—55Fc 107
Bisenden Rd. Croy—75Ub 147
Bisham Clo. Cars—74Hb 145
Bisham Ct. Slou—7K 73
Bisham Gdns. N6—32Jb 62
Bishop Butt Clo. Orp—76Vc 151
Bishop Craven Clo. Enf—11Rb 25
Bishop Duppas Pk. Shep—73U 140
Bishop Ken Rd. Harr—26Ha 38
Bishop King's Rd. W14—49Ab 80
Bishop Rd. N14—17Kb 24
Bishop's Av. E13—39Kc 65
Bishop's Av. SW6—54Za 102
Bishops Av. Borwd—15Pa 21
Bishops Av. Brom—68Lc 129
Bishops Av. N'wd—21U 36
Bishops Av. Romf—30Yc 47
Bishops Av., The. N2—30Fb 41
Bishop's Bri. Rd. W2 —44Db 81 (2A 196)
Bishops Clo. E17—28Dc 44
Bishop's Clo. SE9—61Sc 130
Bishops Clo. Barn—16Za 22
Bishop's Clo. Coul—90Qb 164
Bishops Clo. Enf—12Xb 25
Bishops Clo. Rich—62Ma 123
Bishops Clo. Sutt—76Cb 145
Bishops Clo. Uxb—40Q 56
Bishop's Ct. EC4—(2B 200)
Bishop's Ct. WC2—(2K 199)
Bishops Ct. Rich—55Na 101
Bishops Farm Clo. Wind—4A 94
Bishopsford Rd. Mord—73Eb 145
Bishopsgate. EC2 —44Ub 83 (2H 201)
Bishopsgate Chu. Yd. EC2 —44Ub 83 (2H 201)
Bishopsgate Rd. Egh—2L 117
Bishops Gro. N2—30Gb 41
Bishop's Gro. Hmptn—63Ba 121
Bishop's Hall. King—68Ma 123
Bishop's Hall Rd. Brtwd—16Xd 32
Bishopsmead Clo. Lea—100U 174
Bishopsmead Dri. Lea—100V 174
Bishopsmead Pde. Lea—100U 174
Bishops Orchard. Slou—1F 72
Bishop's Pk. Rd. SW6—54Za 102
Bishops Pk. Rd. SW16—67Nb 126
Bishops Rd. N6—30Jb 42
Bishop's Rd. SW6—53Bb 103
Bishop's Rd. SW11—52Gb 103
Bishop's Rd. W7—47Ga 78
Bishop's Rd. Croy—73Rb 147
Bishop's Rd. Hay—44S 76
Bishops Rd. Slou—7L 73
Bishops Rd. Stanf—1P 93
Bishop's Rd. Bri. W2—(1A 196)
Bishop's Ter. SE11 —49Qb 82 (5A 206)
Bishopsthorpe Rd. SE26 —63Zb 128
Bishop St. N1—39Sb 63
Bishops Wlk. Chst—67Sc 130
Bishops Wlk. Croy—78Zb 148
Bishops Wlk. Pinn—27Aa 37
Bishop's Way. E2—40Xb 63
Bishops Way. NW10—38Ua 60
Bishops Way. Egh—65F 118
Bishops Wood. Wok—5C 188
Bishopswood Rd. N6—31Hb 61
Biskra Flats. Wat—11W 18
Bisley Clo. Wal X—5Zb 12
Bisley Clo. Wor Pk—74Ya 144
Bispham Rd. NW10—41Pa 79
Bisson Rd. E15—40Ec 64
Bisterne Av. E17—27Fc 45
Bittacy Clo. NW7—23Za 40
Bittacy Hill. NW7—23Za 40
Bittacy Pk. Av. NW7—22Za 40
Bittacy Rise. NW7—23Ya 40
Bittacy Rd. NW7—23Za 40
Bittams La. Cher—77F 138
Bitterne Dri. Wok—5C 188
Bittern Pl. N22—26Pb 42
Bittern St. SE1—47Sb 83 (2D 206)
Bittoms, The. King—69Ma 123
Bixley Clo. S'hall—49Ba 77
Blackacre Rd. Epp—9Uc 14
Blackall St. EC2—42Ub 83 (5H 195)
Blackberry Clo. Shep—70U 120
Blackberry Farm Clo. Houn —52Aa 99
Blackbird Hill. NW9—33Sa 59
Blackbirds La. Wat—6Ea 6
Blackborne Rd. Dag—37Cd 68
Black Boy La. N15—29Sb 43
Black Boy Wood. St Alb—2Ca 5
Blackbridge Rd. Wok—8G 188
Blackbrook La. Brom—71Qc 150
Blackburne's M. W1 —45Jb 82 (4H 197)
Blackburn Rd. NW6—37Db 61
Blackburn, The. Lea—96Ba 175
Blackbury Clo. Pot B—3Eb 9
Blackbush Av. Romf—29Zc 47
Blackbush Clo. Sutt—80Db 145
Black Bush La. Stanf—1F 92
Black Ditch Rd. Wal A—8Ec 12
Blackdown Av. Wok—87G 156
Blackdown Clo. Wok—88F 156
Blackett St. SW15—55Za 102
Blacketts Wood Dri. Rick—15D 16
Blackfen Rd. Sidc—57Uc 108
Blackford Clo. S Croy—81Rb 165
Blackford Rd. Wat—22Z 37
Blackford's Path. SW15 —59Wa 102
Blackfriars Bri. SE1 & EC4 —45Rb 83 (5B 200)
Black Friars Ct. EC4—(4B 200)
Black Friars La. EC4 —44Rb 83 (4B 200)
Blackfriars Pas. EC4 —45Rb 83 (4B 200)
Blackfriars Rd. SE1 —47Rb 83 (2B 206)
Blackfriars Underpass. EC4 —(4B 200)
Black Gates. Pinn—27Ba 37
Blackhall La. Sev—95Nd 187
Blackheath Av. SE10—52Fc 107
Blackheath Gro. SE3—54Hc 107
Blackheath Hill. SE10—53Ec 106
Blackheath Pk. SE3—55Hc 107
Blackheath Rise. SE13—54Ec 106
Blackheath Rd. SE10—53Dc 106
Blackheath Vale. SE3—54Gc 107
Blackheath Village. SE3 —55Hc 107
Blackhills. Esh—81Ba 159
Black Horse Clo. Wind—4B 94
Black Horse Ct. SE1—(3G 207)
Blackhorse La. E17—26Zb 44
Black Horse La. Croy—73Wb 147
Blackhorse La. Pot B—4Wa 8
Blackhorse La. Pot B—2Ua 8
Blackhorse La. Tad—100Db 179
Blackhorse Rd. E17—28Zb 44
Blackhorse Rd. SE8—51Ac 106
Blackhorse Rd. Sidc—63Wc 131
Blackhorse Rd. Wok—8A 188
Black Lake Clo. Egh—67C 118
Blacklands Dri. Hay—42S 76
Blacklands Rd. SE6—63Ec 128
Blacklands Ter. SW3 —49Hb 81 (6G 203)
Blackley Clo. Wat—9V 4
Black Lion Hill. Shen, Rad—4Na 7
Black Lion La. W6—49Wa 80
Blackman's La. Warl—86Hc 167
Blackmore Av. S'hall—46Fa 78
Blackmore Ct. Wal A—5Jc 13
Blackmore Cres. Wok—87E 156
★Blackmore Rd. Brtwd & Ing —10Ud
Blackmore Rd. Buck H—17Nc 28
★Blackmore Rd. Ing—5Be
Blackmore's Gro. Tedd—65Ja 122
Blackmore Way. Uxb—37M 55
Blackness La. Kes—81Mc 167
Blackness La. Wok—91A 172
Blacknest Rd. Asc & Vir W—9H 117
Black Pk. Rd. Slou—40A 54
Black Path. E10—31Zb 64
Blackpond La. Slou—7F 52
Blackpool Gdns. Hay—42U 76
Blackpool Rd. SE15—54Xb 105
Black Prince Clo. Wey—86P 157
Black Prince Rd. SE1 & SE11 —49Pb 82 (6H 205)
Black Rod Clo. Hay—48V 76
Blackshaw Pl. N1—38Ub 63
Blackshaw Rd. SW17—63Eb 125
Blackshots La. Grays—45Ee 91
Blacksmith Row. Slou—49C 74
Blacksmith's Clo. Asht—91Pa 177
Blacksmiths Hill. S Croy —85Xb 165
Blacksmiths La. Cher—73J 139
Blacksmith's La. Orp—71Yc 151
Blacksmiths La. Rain—39Hd 68
Blacksmiths La. Stai—69L 119
Blacksmiths La. Uxb—33E 54
★Blacksole Cotts. Sev—87Be
★Blacksole La. Sev—88Be
★Blacksole Rd. Sev—88Be
Blacks Rd. W6—49Ya 80
Blackstock Rd.—33Rb 63
N4 3-175 & 2-156a
N5 remainder
Blackstone Rd. NW2—36Ya 60
Black Swan All. EC2—(1F 201)
Black Swan Yd. SE1 —47Ub 83 (1H 207)
Blackthorn Av. W Dray—49Q 76
Blackthorn Clo. Wat—4X 5
Blackthorn Ct. Houn—52Aa 99
Blackthorne Av. Croy—74Yb 148
Blackthorne Dri. E4—21Fc 45
Blackthorne Rd. Lea—98Ea 176
Blackthorne Rd. Slou—55G 96
Blackthorn Gro. Bexh—55Ad 109
Blackthorn Rd. Grays—46De 91
Blackthorn Rd. West—88Mc 167
Blackthorn St. E3—42Cc 84
Blacktree M. SW9—55Qb 104
Blackwall La. SE10—50Gc 85
Blackwall Tunnel—46Fc 85
Blackwall Tunnel App. E14 —45Ec 84
Blackwall Tunnel Northern App. E3 & E14—40Dc 64
Blackwall Tunnel Southern App. SE10—48Gc 85
Blackwall Way. E14—45Ec 84
Blackwater Rd. Sutt—77Db 145
Blackwater St. SE22—57Vb 105
Blackwell Clo. E5—35Zb 64
Blackwell Clo. Harr—24Fa 38
Blackwell Dri. Wat—16Y 19
Blackwell Gdns. Edgw—21Qa 39
Blackwell Rd. K Lan—1Q 4
Blackwood Clo. Wey—84L 157
Blackwood St. SE17 —50Tb 83 (7F 207)
Bladen Clo. Wey—79U 140
Blades Clo. Lea—92Ma 177
Bladindon Dri. Bex—59Yc 109
Bladon Gdns. Harr—30Da 37
Blagdens Clo. N14—19Mb 24
Blagdens La. N14—19Mb 24
Blagdon Rd. SE13—58Dc 106
Blagdon Rd. N Mald—70Va 124
Blagdon Wlk. Tedd—65La 122
Blagrove Rd. W10—43Ab 80
Blair Av. NW9—31Ua 60
Blair Av. Esh—75Ea 142
Blair Clo. N1—37Sb 63
Blair Clo. Sidc—57Uc 108
Blairderry Rd. SW2—61Nb 126
Blair Dri. Sev—95Kd 187
Blairhead Dri. Wat—20X 19
Blair Rd. Slou—6J 73
Blair St. E14—44Ec 84
Blake Av. Bark—39Uc 66
Blake Clo. Rain—39Hd 68
Blake Clo. Well—53Uc 108
Blakeden Dri. Esh—79Ha 142
Blake Gdns. SW6—53Db 103
Blake Gdns. Dart—56Pd 111
Blake Hall Cres. E11—32Jc 65
Blake Hall Rd. E11—31Jc 65
Blakehall Rd. Cars—79Hb 145
Blakeley Cotts. SE10—47Fc 85
Blakemore Rd. SW16—62Nb 126
Blakemore Rd. T Hth—71Pb 146
Blakeney Av. Beck—67Bc 128
Blakeney Clo. E8—36Wb 63
Blakeney Clo. N20—18Eb 23
Blakeney Clo. Eps—83Ta 161
Blakeney Rd. Beck—66Bc 128
Blakenham Rd. SW17—63Hb 125
Blake Rd. E16—42Hc 85
Blake Rd. N11—24Lb 42
Blake Rd. Croy—75Ub 147
Blake Rd. Mitc—69Gb 125
Blaker Rd. E15—39Ec 64
Blakes Av. N Mald—71Va 144
Blakes Grn. W Wick—74Ec 148
Blakes La. N Mald—71Va 144
Blakesley Av. W5—44La 78
Blakesley Wlk. SW20—68Bb 125
Blakes Rd. SE15—52Ub 105
Blakes Ter. N Mald—71Wa 144
Blakesware Gdns. N9—17Tb 25
Blake Way. Til—4E 114
Blakewood Clo. Felt—63Y 121
Blanchard Clo. SE9—62Nc 130
Blanchards Hill. Guild—100A 172
Blanchard Way. E8—37Wb 63
Blanch Clo. SE15—52Yb 106
Blanchedowne. SE5—56Tb 105
Blanche La. Pot B—6Va 8
Blanche St. E16—42Hc 85
Blanchland Rd. Mord—71Db 145
Blanchman's Rd. Warl—90Ac 166
Blandfield Rd. SW12—59Jb 104
Blandford Av. Beck—68Ac 128
Blandford Av. Twic—60Da 99
Blandford Clo. N2—28Eb 41
Blandford Clo. Croy—76Nb 146
Blandford Clo. Romf—28Cd 48
Blandford Clo. Slou—8P 73
Blandford Clo. Wok—89D 156
Blandford Ct. Slou—8P 73
Blandford Cres. E4—17Ec 26
Blandford Rd. W4—48Ua 80
Blandford Rd. W5—47Ma 79
Blandford Rd. Beck—68Zb 128
Blandford Rd. S'hall—49Ca 77
Blandford Rd. Tedd—64Fa 122
Blandford Rd. N. Slou—8P 73
Blandford Rd. S. Slou—8P 73
Blandford Sq. NW1 —42Gb 81 (6E 190)
Blandford St. W1 —43Jb 82 (1H 197)
Blandford Waye. Hay—44Y 77
Bland St. SE9—56Mc 107
Blaney Cres. E6—41Rc 86
Blanmerle Rd. SE9—60Rc 108
Blann Clo. SE9—58Mc 107
Blantyre St. SW10—52Fb 103
Blashford St. SE13—59Fc 107
Blawith Rd. Harr—28Ga 38
Blaydon Clo. N17—24Xb 43
Blaydon Clo. Ruis—31U 56
Blaydon Wlk. N17—24Xb 43
Blay's Clo. Egh—5N 117
Blay's La. Egh—6M 117
Bleak Hill La. SE18—51Vc 109
Blean Gro. SE20—66Yb 128
Bleasdale Av. Gnfd—40La 58
Blechynden St. W10—45Za 80
Bleddyn Clo. Sidc—58Yc 109
Bledlow Clo. SE28—45Yc 87
Bledlow Rise. Gnfd—40Ea 58
Bleeding Heart Yd. EC1—(1A 200)
Blegborough Rd. SW16—65Lb 126
Blencarn Clo. Wok—4C 188
Blendon Dri. Bex—58Zc 109
Blendon Path. Brom—67Hc 129
Blendon Rd. Bex—58Zc 109
Blendon Ter. SE18—50Sc 86
Blendworth Way. SE15—52Ub 105
Blenheim Av. Ilf—30Qc 46
Blenheim Clo. N21—18Sb 25
Blenheim Clo. SW20—69Ya 124
Blenheim Clo. Dart—58Ld 111
Blenheim Clo. Gnfd—40Fa 58
Blenheim Clo. Romf—28Ed 48
Blenheim Clo. Upm—32Ud 70
Blenheim Clo. Wall—80Lb 146
Blenheim Clo. Wat—17Y 19
Blenheim Clo. Wey—85H 157
Blenheim Ct. N19—33Nb 62
Blenheim Ct. Horn—36Ld 69
Blenheim Ct. Sidc—62Tc 130
Blenheim Cres. W11—45Ab 80
Blenheim Cres. Ruis—33T 56
Blenheim Cres. S Croy—80Sb 147
Blenheim Dri. Well—53Vc 109
Blenheim Gdns. NW2—37Ya 60
Blenheim Gdns. SW2—58Pb 104
Blenheim Gdns. King—66Ra 123
Blenheim Gdns. S Croy—84Wb 165
Blenheim Gdns. S Ock—46Rd 89
Blenheim Gdns. Wall—80Lb 146
Blenheim Gdns. Wemb—34Na 59
Blenheim Gdns. Wok—7E 188
Blenheim Pk. Rd. S Croy —81Sb 165
Blenheim Pas. NW8 —40Eb 61 (1A 190)
Blenheim Rise. N15—28Vb 43
Blenheim Rd. E6—41Mc 85
Blenheim Rd. E15—35Gc 65
Blenheim Rd. E17—27Zb 44
Blenheim Rd. NW8 —40Eb 61 (1A 190)
Blenheim Rd. SE15—54Wb 105
Blenheim Rd. SE20—66Yb 128
Blenheim Rd. SW20—69Ya 124
Blenheim Rd. W4—48Ua 80
Blenheim Rd. Barn—13Za 22
Blenheim Rd. Brtwd—16Wd 32
Blenheim Rd. Brom—70Nc 130
Blenheim Rd. Dart—58Ld 111
Blenheim Rd. Eps—83Ta 161
Blenheim Rd. Harr—30Da 37
Blenheim Rd. N'holt—37Da 57
Blenheim Rd. Orp—75Yc 151
Blenheim Rd. Sidc—60Yc 109
Blenheim Rd. Slou—9P 73
Blenheim Rd. Sutt—76Db 145
Blenheim Shopping Centre. SE20 —66Yb 128
Blenheim St. W1—44Kb 82 (3K 197)
Blenheim Ter. NW8 —40Eb 61 (1A 190)
Blenkarne Rd. SW11—58Hb 103
Bleriot Rd. Houn—52Y 99
Blessbury Rd. Edgw—25Sa 39
Blessington Clo. SE13—55Fc 107
Blessington Rd. SE13—56Fc 107
Bletchingley Clo. Red—100Lb 180
Bletchingley Rd. Red—100Lb 180
Bletchley St. N1—40Sb 63 (2E 194)
Bletchmore Clo. Hay—50T 76
Bletsoe Wlk. N1—40Sb 63 (1E 194)
Bligh Rd. Grav—8C 114
Bligh's Rd. Sev—97Ld 187
Blincoe Clo. SW19—61Za 124
Blinco La. Slou—44A 74
Blind La. Bans—87Gb 163
Blind La. Lou—12Gc 27
Blind La. Wal A—5Lc 13
Blindman's La. Wal X—2Zb 12
Bliss Cres. SE13—54Dc 106
Blissett St. SE10—53Ec 106
Blithbury Rd. Dag—37Xc 67
Blithdale Rd. SE2—49Wc 87
Blithfield St. W8—48Db 81
Blockhouse Rd. Grays—51Ee 113
Blockley Rd. Wemb—33Ka 58
Bloemfontein Av. W12—46Xa 80
Bloemfontein Rd. W12—45Xa 80
Blomfield Rd. W9 —43Db 81 (7A 190)
Blomfield St. EC2 —43Tb 83 (1G 201)
Blomfield Vs. W2—43Db 81
Blomville Rd. Dag—34Bd 67
Blondel St. SW11—54Jb 104
Blondin Av. W5—49La 78
Blondin St. E3—40Cc 64
Bloomburg St. SW1 —49Mb 82 (6C 204)
Bloomfield Cres. Ilf—30Rc 46
Bloomfield Pl. W1—(4A 198)
Bloomfield Rd. N6—30Jb 42
Bloomfield Rd. SE18—50Rc 86
Bloomfield Rd. Brom—71Mc 149
Bloomfield Rd. King—69Na 123
Bloomfield Ter. SW1 —50Jb 82 (7J 203)
Bloomfield Ter. West—97Uc 184
Bloom Gro. SE27—62Rb 127
Bloomhall Rd. SE19—64Tb 127
Bloom Pk. Rd. SW6—52Bb 103
Bloomsbury Clo. W5—45Pa 79
Bloomsbury Clo. Eps—82Ta 161
Bloomsbury Ct. WC1—(1G 199)
Bloomsbury Ct. Pinn—27Ba 37
Bloomsbury Pl. WC1 —43Nb 82 (7G 193)
Bloomsbury Sq. WC1 —43Nb 82 (1G 199)

Bloomsbury St.—Braddyll St.

Bloomsbury St. WC1
—43Mb 82 (1E 198)
Bloomsbury Way.WC1
—43Nb 82 (1G 199)
Blore Clo. SW8—53Mb 104
Blossom Clo. W5—47Na 79
Blossom Clo. S Croy—78Vb 147
Blossom La. Enf—11Sb 25
Blossom St. E1—42Ub 83 (6K 195)
Blossom Way. Uxb—38P 55
Blossom Way. W Dray—49Q 76
Blossom Waye. Houn—51Aa 99
Blount St. E14—44Ac 84
Bloxhall Rd. E10—32Bc 64
Bloxham Cres. Hmptn—66Ba 121
Bloxham Gdns. SE9—57Nc 108
Bloxworth Clo. Wall—76Lb 146
Blucher Rd. SE5—52Sb 105
Blue Anchor La. SE16—49Wb 83
Blue Anchor La. Grays—10G 92
Blue Anchor Yd. E1—45Wb 83
Blue Ball La. Egh—64B 118
Blue Ball Yd. SW1
—46Lb 82 (7B 198)
Blue Barn La. Wey—83Q 158
Bluebell Clo. SE26—63Vb 127
Bluebell Clo. Orp—75Sc 150
Bluebell Ct. Wok—7G 188
Blueberry Gdns. Coul—88Pb 164
Blueberry La. Sev—88Yc 169
Bluebridge Rd. Hat—1Bb 9
Bluefield Clo. Hmptn—64Ca 121
Bluehouse La. Oxt—100Gc 183
Bluehouse Rd. E4—20Gc 27
Blumfield Cres. Slou—3B 72
Blundel La. Cob 88Ba 159
Blundell Rd. Edgw—25Ta 39
Blundell St. N7—38Nb 62
Blunesfield. Pot B—3Fb 9
Blunt Rd. Croy—78Tb 147
Blunts Av. W Dray—52Q 98
Blunts Rd. SE9—57Qc 108
Blurton Rd. E5—35Yb 64
Blythe Clo. SE6—59Bc 106
Blythe Clo. Iver—44H 75
Blythe Hill. SE6—59Bc 106
Blythe Hill. Orp—67Vc 131
Blythe Hill La. SE6—59Bc 106
Blythe Rd. W14—48Za 80
Blythe St. E2—41Xb 83
Blythe Vale. SE6—60Bc 106
Blyth Rd. E17—31Bc 64
Blyth Rd. SE28—45Yc 87
Blyth Rd. Brom—67Hc 129
Blyth Rd. Hay—47U 76
Blythswood Rd. Ilf—32Wc 67
Blyth Wlk. Upm—30Ud 50
Blythwood Rd. N4—31Nb 62
Blythwood Rd. Pinn—25Z 37
Boade's M. NW3—35Fb 61
Boadicea St. N1—39Pb 62 (1H 193)
Boakes Meadow. Sev—83Hd 170
Boar Clo. Chig—22Wc 47
Boardman Av. E4—15Dc 26
Board School Rd. Wok—88B 156
Boarer's Manorway. Belv
—48Ad 87
Boarlands Clo. Slou—5D 72
Boarlands Path. Slou—5D 72
Boars Head Yd. Bren—52Ma 101
Boathouse Wlk. SE15—52Wb 105
Bobbin Clo. SW4—55Lb 104
Bob Marley Way. SE24—56Qb 104
Bobs La. Romf—24Jd 48
Bocketts La. Lea—96Ha 176
Bockhampton Rd. King—66Pa 123
Bocking St. E8—39Xb 63
Boddicott Clo. SW19—61Ab 124
Bodell Clo. Grays—48De 91
Bodiam Clo. Enf—12Ub 25
Bodiam Rd. SW16—66Mb 126
Bodle Av. Swans—59Ae 113
Bodley Clo. N Mald—71Ua 144
Bodley Mnr. Way. SW2—59Qb 104
Bodley Rd. N Mald—72Ta 143
Bodmin Av. Slou—3E 72
Bodmin Clo. Harr—34Ba 57
Bodmin Gro. Mord—71Db 145
Bodmin St. SW18—60Cb 103
Bodnant Gdns. SW20—69Wa 124
Bodney Rd. E8—36Xb 63
Boeing Way. S'hall—48X 77
Boevey Path. Belv—50Bd 87
Bogey La. Orp—80Qc 150
Bognor Gdns. Wat—22Y 37
Bognor Rd. Well—53Zc 109
Bohemia Pl. E8—37Yb 64
Bohun Gro. Barn—16Gb 23
Boileau Rd. SW13—52Wa 102
Boileau Rd. W5—44Pa 79
Bois Hall Rd. Wey—78M 139
Bolden St. SE8—54Dc 106
Boldero Pl. NW8—42Gb 81 (6D 190)
Bolderwood Way. W Wick
—75Dc 148
Boldmore Rd. Pinn—31Y 57
Boleyn Av. Enf—11Xb 25
Boleyn Av. Eps—82Xa 162
Boleyn Clo. Stai—64G 118
Boleyn Dri. E Mol—69Ba 121
Boleyn Dri. Ruis—33Z 57
Boleyn Gdns. Brtwd—20Ce 33
Boleyn Gdns. Dag—38Ed 68
Boleyn Gdns. W Wick—75Dc 148
Boleyn Gro. W Wick—75Ec 148
Boleyn Rd. E6—40Mc 65
Boleyn Rd. E7—38Jc 65
Boleyn Rd. N16—36Ub 63
Boleyn Rd. Sev—89Nd 171
Boleyn Wlk. Lea—92Ha 176
Boleyn Way. Barn—13Eb 23
Boleyn Way. Ilf—23Sc 46
Bolina Rd. SE16—50Yb 84
Bolingbroke Gro. SW11—57Gb 103
Bolingbroke Rd. W14—48Za 80
Bolingbroke Wlk. SW11
—53Gb 103
Bolingbroke Way. Hay—46T 76
Bollo Bri. Rd. W3—48Ra 79
Bollo La.—47Ra 79
W4 1-95 & 2-100
W3 remainder
Bolney Ga. SW7—47Gb 81 (2D 202)
Bolney St. SW8—52Pb 104
Bolney Way. Felt—62Aa 121
Bolsover Gro. Red—100Nb 180
Bolsover St. W1—42Kb 82 (6A 192)
Bolstead Rd. Mitc—67Kb 126
Bolt Cellar La. Epp—2Uc 14
Bolt Ct. EC4—44Qb 82 (3A 200)
Bolters La. Bans—86Bb 163
Boltmore Clo. NW4—27Za 40
Bolton Av. Wind—5H 95
Bolton Clo. SE20—68Wb 127
Bolton Clo. Chess—79Ma 143
Bolton Cres. SE5—52Rb 105
Bolton Cres. Wind—5G 94
Bolton Gdns. NW10—40Za 60
Bolton Gdns. SW5—50Db 81
Bolton Gdns. Brom—65Hc 129
Bolton Gdns. Tedd—65Ja 122
Bolton Gdns. M. SW10—50Eb 81
Bolton Rd. E15—37Hc 65
Bolton Rd. N18—22Vb 43
Bolton Rd. NW8—39Db 61
Bolton Rd. NW10—39Ua 60
Bolton Rd. W4—52Sa 101
Bolton Rd. Chess—79Ma 143
Bolton Rd. Harr—28Ea 38
Bolton Rd. Wind—5G 94
Boltons Clo. Wok—88J 157
Bolton's La. Hay—52S 98
Boltons La. Wok—88J 157
Boltons, The. SW10
—50Eb 81 (7A 202)
Boltons, The. Wemb—35Ha 58
Bolton St. W1—46Kb 82 (6A 198)
Bombay St. SE16—49Xb 83
Bombers La. West—91Tc 184
Bomer Clo. W Dray—52Q 98
Bomore Rd. W11—45Ab 80
Bonar Pl. Chst—66Nc 130
Bonar Rd. SE15—52Wb 105
Bonaventure Ct. Grav—3H 137
Bonchester Clo. Chst—66Qc 130
Bonchurch Clo. Sutt—80Db 145
Bonchurch Rd. W10—43Ab 80
Bonchurch Rd. W13—46Ka 78
Bond Clo. Sev—87Zc 169
Bond Ct. EC4—45Tb 83 (3F 201)
Bondfield Rd. Hay—41W 76
Bondfield Wlk. Dart—55Pd 111
Bond Gdns. Wall—77Lb 146
Bond Rd. Mitc—68Gb 125
Bond Rd. Surb—75Pa 143
Bond Rd. Warl—90Ac 166
Bond St. E15—36Gc 65
Bond St. (New) W1
—44Kb 82 (4A 198)
Bond St. (Old) W1
Bond St. W5—45Ma 79
Bond St. Egh—4M 117
Bond St. Grays—51Ee 113
Bond St. Sev—87Ad 169
Bond Way. SW8—51Nb 104
Boneta Rd. SE18—48Pc 86
Bonfield Rd. SE13—56Ec 106
Bonham Gdns. Dag—33Zc 67
Bonham Rd. SW2—57Pb 104
Bonham Rd. Dag—33Zc 67
Bonheur Rd. W4—47Ta 79
Bonhill St. EC2—42Tb 83 (6G 195)
Boniface Gdns. Harr—24Da 37
Boniface Rd. Uxb—34R 56
Boniface Wlk. Harr—24Da 37
Bonington Rd. Horn—36Md 69
Bon Marche Ter. SE27—63Ub 127
Bonner Hill Rd. King—68Pa 123
Bonner Rd. E2—40Yb 64
Bonners Clo. Wok—94B 172
Bonnersfield Clo. Harr—30Ha 38
Bonnersfield La. Harr—30Ha 38
Bonner St. E2—40Yb 64
Bonneville Gdns. SW4—58Lb 104
Bonney Gro. Wal X—2Wb 11
Bonney Way. Swan—68Gd 132
Bonningtons. Brtwd—20De 33
Bonnington Sq. SW8—51Pb 104
Bonny St. NW1—38Lb 62
Bonser Rd. Twic—61Ha 122
Bonsey Clo. Wok—93A 172
Bonsey La. Wok—93A 172
Bonseys La. Chob—81B 156
Bonsey's Yd. Uxb—38M 55
Bonsor Dri. Tad—94Ab 178
Bonsor St. SE5—52Ub 105
Bonville Rd. Brom—64Hc 129
Booker Clo. E14—43Bc 84
Booker Rd. N18—22Wb 43
Bookham Ct. Lea—95Ba 175
Bookham Industrial Pk. Lea
—95Ba 175
Bookham Rd. Cob—91Y 175
Boones Rd. SE13—56Gc 107
Boone St. SE13—56Gc 107
Boord St. SE10—48Gc 85
Boothby Rd. N19—33Mb 62
Booth Clo. SE28—46Xc 87
Booth Dri. Stai—65M 119
Booth Rd. NW9—26Ta 39
Booth Rd. Croy—75Rb 147
Booth's Pl. W1—43Lb 82 (1C 198)
Boot St. N1—41Ub 83 (4H 195)
Bordars Rd. W7—43Ga 78
Bordars Wlk. W7—43Ga 78
Borden Av. Enf—16Tb 25
Border Cres. SE26—64Xb 127
Border Gdns. Croy—77Dc 148
Bordergate. Mitc—67Hb 125
Border Rd. SE26—64Xb 127
Borderside. Slou—4L 73
Border's La. Lou—14Qc 28
Bordesley Rd. Mord—70Db 125
Bordon Wlk. SW15—59Wa 102
Boreas Wlk. N1—(2C 194)
Boreham Av. E16—44Jc 85
Boreham Clo. E11—32Ec 64
Boreham Holt. Borwd—14Pa 21
Boreham Rd. N22—26Sb 43
Borgard Rd. SE18—49Pc 86
Borkwood Pk. Orp—77Vc 151
Borkwood Way. Orp—77Uc 150
Borland Rd. SE15—56Yb 106
Borland Rd. Tedd—66Ka 122
Borneo St. SW15—55Ya 102
★Borough Grn. Rd. Sev—93Zd
(Ightham)
★Borough Grn. Rd. sev—90Ce
(Wrotham)
Borough High St. SE1
—47Sb 83 (2E 206)
Borough Hill. Croy—76Rb 147
Borough Rd. SE1
—48Rb 83 (3C 206)
Borough Rd. Iswth—53Ga 100
Borough Rd. King—67Qa 123
Borough Rd. Mitc—68Gb 125
Borough Rd. West—93Mc 183
Borough Sq. SE1—(2D 206)
Borough Way. Pot B—4Ab 8
Borrett Clo. SE17
—50Sb 83 (7D 206)
Borrodaile Rd. SW18—58Db 103
Borrowdale Av. Harr—26Ja 38
Borrowdale Clo. Ilf—28Nc 46
Borrowdale Clo. S Croy—85Vb 165
Borrowdale Dri. S Croy—84Vb 165
Borthwick M. E15—35Gc 65
Borthwick Rd. E15 35Gc 65
Borthwick Rd. NW9—30Va 40
Borthwick St. SE8—50Cc 84
Borwick Av. E17—27Bc 44
Bosanquet Clo. Uxb—42M 75
Bosbury Rd. SE6—62Ec 128
Boscastle Rd. NW5—34Kb 62
Boscobel Pl. SW1
—49Jb 82 (5J 203)
Boscobel St. NW8
—42Fb 81 (6C 190)
Bosco Clo. Orp—77Vc 151
Boscombe Av. E10—31Fc 65
Boscombe Av. Grays—49Fe 91
Boscombe Av. Horn—31Md 69
Boscombe Clo. E5—36Ac 64
Boscombe Clo. Egh—67E 118
Boscombe Gdns. SW16—65Nb 126
Boscombe Rd. SW17—65Jb 126
Boscombe Rd. SW19—67Db 125
Boscombe Rd. W12—47Wa 80
Boscombe Rd. Wor Pk—74Ya 144
Bosgrove. E4—19Ec 26
Boss St. SE1—47Vb 83 (1K 207)
Bostall Hill. SE2—50Wc 87
Bostall Hill Rd. SE2 51Yc 109
Bostall La. SE2—50Xc 87
Bostall Mnr. Way. SE2—49Xc 87
Bostall Pk. Av. Bexh—52Ad 109
Bostall Rd. Orp—66Xc 131
Bostal Row. Bexh—55Bd 109
Boston Gdns. W4—51Ua 102
Boston Gdns. W7—49Ja 78
Boston Gdns. Bren—49Ja 78
Boston Gro. Ruis—30S 36
Boston Gro. Slou—4G 72
Boston Mnr. Rd. Bren—49Ka 78
Boston Pk. Rd. Bren—50La 78
Boston Pl. NW1—42Hb 81 (6F 191)
Boston Rd. E6—41Nc 86
Boston Rd. E17—30Cc 44
Boston Rd. W7—47Ha 78
Boston Rd. Croy—72Pb 146
Boston Rd. Edgw—24Sa 39
Boston St. E2—40Wb 63
Bostonthorpe Rd. W7—47Ga 78
Boston Vale. W7—49Ja 78
Bosville Av. Sev—95Jd 186
Bosville Dri. Sev—95Jd 186
Bosville Rd. Sev—95Jd 186
Boswell Clo. Orp—72Yc 151
Boswell Ct. WC1
—43Nb 82 (7G 193)
Boswell Path. Hay—49V 76
Boswell Rd. T Hth—70Sb 127
Boswell St. WC1
—43Nb 82 (7G 193)
Bosworth Clo. E17—25Bc 44
Bosworth Cres. Romf—23Ld 49
Bosworth Rd. N11—23Mb 42
Bosworth Rd. W10—42Ab 80
Bosworth Rd. Barn—13Cb 23
Bosworth Rd. Dag—34Cd 68
Botany Bay La. Chst—68Sc 130
Botany Rd. Grav—56Ce 113
Boteley Clo. E4—19Fc 27
Botha Rd. E13—43Kc 85
Bothwell Clo. E16—43Hc 85
Bothwell Rd. Croy—82Ec 166
Bothwell St. W6—51Za 102
Botolph All. EC3—(4H 201)
Botolph La. EC3—45Ub 83 (5H 201)
Botsford Rd. SW20—68Ab 124
Botsom Hill. Sev—80Td 154
Botsom La. Sev—79Sd 154
Bottle Cotts. Sev—94Jd 186
Bottom La. Rick & K Lan—7K 3
Bott Rd. Dart—63Pd 133
Botts M. W2—44Cb 81
Botwell Comn. Rd. Hay—45T 76
Botwell Cres. Hay—44U 76
Botwell La. Hay—45U 76
Boucher Clo. Tedd—64Ha 122
Boucher Dri. Grav—2B 136
Bouchier Wlk. Rain—37Jd 68
Boughton Av. Brom—73Hc 149
Boughton Hall Av. Wok—96H 173
Boughton Rd. SE28—48Uc 86
Boulcott St. E1—44Zb 84
Boulevard, The. Pinn—28Ca 37
Boulmer Rd. Uxb—41L 75
Boulogne Rd. Croy—72Sb 147
Boulter Gdns. Horn—36Jd 68
Boulters Clo. Slou—7E 72
Boulton Rd. Dag—34Bd 67
Boultwood Rd. E6—44Pc 86
Bounces La. N9—19Xb 25
Bounces Rd. N9—19Xb 25
Boundaries Rd. SW12—61Hb 125
Boundaries Rd. Felt—60Y 99
Boundary Av. E17—31Bc 64
Boundary Clo. SE20—68Wb 127
Boundary Clo. Ilf—35Uc 66
Boundary Clo. King—69Ra 123
Boundary Clo. S'hall—50Ca 77
Boundary Dri. Brtwd—17Fe 33
Boundary La. E13—42Mc 85
Boundary La. SE17—51Sb 105
Boundary Pas. E2
—42Vb 83 (5K 195)
Boundary Rd. E13—40Lc 65
Boundary Rd. E17—31Bc 64
Boundary Rd. N9—16Yb 26
Boundary Rd. N22—27Rb 43
Boundary Rd. NW8—39Eb 61
Boundary Rd. SW19—65Fb 125
Boundary Rd. Ashf—64L 119
Boundary Rd. Bark—40Sc 66
(in two parts)
Boundary Rd. Pinn—31Z 57
Boundary Rd. Romf—30Jd 48
Boundary Rd. Sidc—57Uc 108
Boundary Rd. Upm—34Qd 69
Boundary Rd. Wall—79Kb 146
Boundary Rd. Wok—88C 156
Boundary Rd. S. Wall & Cars
—81Jb 164
Boundary Row. SE1
—47Rb 83 (1B 206)
Boundary St. E2—41Vb 83 (4K 195)
(in two parts)
Boundary St. Eri—52Hd 110
Boundary Way. Croy—78Cc 148
Boundary Way. Wat—4X 5
Boundary Yd. Wok—88C 156
Boundfield Rd. SE6—62Gc 129
Bounds Grn. Industrial Est.
N11—23Lb 42
Bounds Grn. Rd.—23Lb 42
N22 1-107
N11 remainder
Bourchier St. W1
—45Mb 82 (4D 198)
Bourdon Pl. W1—(4A 198)
Bourdon Rd. SE20—68Yb 128
Bourdon St. W1—45Kb 82 (5K 197)
Bourke Clo. NW10—37Ua 60
Bourke Clo. SW4—58Nb 104
Bourke Hill. Coul—90Hb 163
Bourlet Clo. W1—(1B 198)
Bourn Av. Uxb—42Q 76
Bournbrook Rd. SE3—55Mc 107
Bourne Av. N14—19Nb 24
Bourne Av. N15—28Tb 43
Bourne Av. Barn—15Fb 23
Bourne Av. Hay—48S 76
Bourne Av. Ruis—36Y 57
Bourne Av. Wind—5G 94
Bournebridge Clo. Brtwd—17Fe 33
Bournebridge La. Romf—17Bd 29
Bourne Clo. Wey—85K 157
Bourne Ct. Ruis—36X 57
Bourne End. Horn—31Qd 69
Bourne End Rd. N'wd—21U 36
Bournefield Rd. Whyt—90Wb 165
Bourne Gdns. E4—21Dc 44
Bournehall Av. Bush, Wat
—15Ca 19
Bournehall La. Bush, Wat
—16Ca 19
Bournehall Rd. Bush, Wat
—16Ca 19
Bourne Hill. N13—19Pb 24
Bourne Industrial Pk. Dart
—57Gd 110
Bourne La. Cat—93Tb 181
Bourne Mead. Bex—57Fd 110
Bournemead Av. N'holt—40W 56
Bournemead Clo. N'holt—41W 76
Bourne Meadow. Egh—70D 118
Bournemead Way. N'holt—40X 57
Bournemouth Rd. SE15
—54Wb 105
Bournemouth Rd. SW19
—67Cb 125
Bourne Pk. Clo. Kenl—88Ub 165
Bourne Pl. W4—50Ta 79
Bourne Rd. E7—34Hc 65
Bourne Rd. N8—30Nb 42
Bourne Rd. Bex—59Dd 110
Bourne Rd. Brom—70Mc 129
Bourne Rd. Bush, Wat—15Ca 19
Bourne Rd. Grav—1H 137
Bourne Rd. Slou—7H 73
Bourne Rd. Vir W—71A 138
Bourneside. Wey—75L 139
Bourneside Rd. Wey—77M 139
Bourne St. SW1—49Jb 82 (6H 203)
Bourne St. Croy—75Rb 147
Bourne Ter. W2—43Db 81
Bourne, The. N14—19Nb 24
Bourne Vale. Brom—74Hc 149
Bournevale Rd. SW16—63Nb 126
Bourne View. Gnfd—36Ha 58
Bourne View. Kenl—87Tb 165
Bourneville Rd. SE6—59Cc 106
Bourne Way. Brom—75Hc 149
Bourne Way. Eps—77Sa 143
Bourne Way. Sutt—78Bb 145
Bourne Way. Swan—69Ed 132
Bourne Way. Wey—78L 139
Bourne Way. Wok—10G 188
Bournewood Rd. SE18—52Wc 109
Bournewood Rd. Orp—73Yc 151
Bournwell Clo. Barn—13Hb 23
Bousefield Rd. SE14—54Zb 106
Bousley Rise. Cher—79F 138
Boutflower Rd. SW11—56Gb 103
Bouverie Gdns. Harr—30Ma 39
Bouverie M. N16—33Ub 63
Bouverie Pl. W2—44Fb 81 (2C 196)
Bouverie Rd. N16—33Ub 63
Bouverie Rd. Coul—90Jb 164
Bouverie Rd. Harr—30Ea 38
Bouverie St. EC4
—44Qb 82 (3A 200)
Bouverie Way. Slou—5A 74
Bouvier Rd. Enf—10Yb 12
Bovay Pl. N7—35Pb 62
Bovay St. N7—35Pb 62
Boveney Clo. Slou—7E 72
Boveney New Rd. Wind—9C 72
Boveney Rd. SE23—59Zb 106
Boveney Rd. Wind—9A 72
Boveney Wood La. Slou—4B 52
Bovey Way. S Ock—43Xd 90
Bovill Rd. SE23—59Zb 106
Bovingdon Av. Wemb—37Qa 59
Bovingdon Clo. N19—33Lb 62
Bovingdon Cres. Wat—6Z 5
Bovingdon Grn. La. Hem—1B 2
Bovingdon La. NW9—25Ua 40
Bovingdon Rd. SW6—53Db 103
Bow Arrow La. Dart—58Qd 111
Bowater Clo. NW9—29Ta 39
Bowater Clo. SW2—58Nb 104
Bowater Pl. SE3—52Kc 107
Bowater Rd. SE18—48Mc 85
Bow Bri. Est. E3—41Dc 84
Bow Chyd. EC4—(3E 200)
Bow Comn. La. E3—42Ac 84
Bowden Dri. Horn—32Nd 69
Bowden Rd. Asc—10A 116
Bowden St. SE11
—50Qb 82 (7A 206)
Bowditch. SE8—50Bc 84
Bowdon Rd. E17—31Cc 64
Bowen Dri. SE21—62Ub 127
Bowen Rd. Harr—31Ea 58
Bowen St. E14—44Dc 84
Bowens Wood. Croy—81Bc 166
Bower Av. SE10—53Gc 107
Bower Clo. N'holt—40Y 57
Bower Clo. Romf—24Fd 48
Bower Ct. Epp—4Wc 15
Bower Ct. Wok—88D 156
Bowerdean St. SW6—53Db 103
Bower Farm Rd. Hav, Romf
—20Ed 30
Bower Hill. Epp—4Wc 15
Bower Hill. Epp—3Wc 15
Bower La. Eyns, Dart & Sev
—76Nd 153
Bowerman Av. SE14—51Ac 106
Bowerman Rd. Grays—9C 92
Bower Rd. Swan—66Jd 132
Bowers Av. Grav—3B 136
Bowers Rd. Sev—83Hd 170
Bower St. E1—44Zb 84
Bowers Wlk. E6—43Pc 86
Bower Ter. Epp—4Wc 15
Bower Vale. Epp—4Wc 15
Bower Way. Slou—5C 72
Bowes Clo. Sidc—58Xc 109
Bowesdon La. Grav—6P 137
Bowes-Lyon Clo. Wind—3G 94
Bowes Rd.—22Lb 42
N13 1-153 & 2-138
N11 remainder
Bowes Rd. W3—45Ua 80
Bowes Rd. Dag—35Yc 67
Bowes Rd. Stai—65G 118
Bowes Rd. W on T—75X 141
Bowes Wood. Long, Dart
—76Ce 155
Bowfell Rd. W6—51Ya 102
Bowford Av. Bexh—53Ad 109
Bowhay. Brtwd—19De 33
Bowie Clo. SW4—59Mb 104
Bowland Rd. SW4—56Mb 104
Bowland Rd. Wfd G—22Lc 45
Bowland Yd. SW1—(2G 203)
Bow La. EC4—44Sb 83 (3E 200)
Bow La. N12—24Eb 41
Bow La. Mord—72Ab 144
Bowl Ct. EC2—42Ub 83 (6J 195)
Bowles Grn. Enf—8Xb 11
Bowles Rd. SE1—51Wb 105
Bowley La. SE19—64Vb 127
Bowley St. E14—45Bc 84
Bowling Grn. Clo. SW15—59Xa 102
Bowling Grn. La. EC1
—42Qb 82 (5A 194)
Bowling Grn. Pl. SE1
—47Tb 83 (1F 207)
Bowling Grn. Row. SE18—48Nc 86
Bowling Grn. St. SE11—51Qb 104
Bowling Grn. Wlk. N1
—41Ub 83 (3H 195)
Bowls Clo. Stan—22Ka 38
Bowls, The. Chig—21Uc 46
Bowman Av. E16—45Hc 85
Bowmans Clo. W13—46Ka 78
Bowmans Clo. Pot B—4Fb 9
Bowmans Clo. Slou—10A 52
Bowmans Grn. Wat—8Aa 5
Bowmans Lea. SE23—59Yb 106
Bowmans Meadwow. Wall
—76Kb 146
Bowman's Pl. N7—34Nb 62
Bowman's Rd. Dart—59Hd 110
Bowmead. SE9—61Pc 130
Bowmore Wlk. NW1—38Mb 62
Bown Clo. Til—5D 114
Bowness Cres. SW15—64Ua 124
Bowness Dri. Houn—56Aa 99
Bowness Rd. SE6—59Dc 106
Bowness Rd. Bexh—54Dd 110
Bowness Way. Horn—36Jd 68
Bowood Rd. SW11—57Jb 104
Bowood Rd. Enf—12Zb 26
Bowring Grn. Wat—22Y 37
Bow Rd. E3—41Bc 84
Bowrons Av. Wemb—38Ma 59
Bowry Dri. Wray, Stai—58B 96
Bowsprit, The. Cob—87Y 159
Bow St. E15—36Gc 65
Bow St. WC2—44Nb 82 (3G 199)
Bowyer Cres. Uxb—30H 35
Bowyer Dri. Slou—5C 72
Bowyer Pl. SE5—52Sb 105
Bowyers Clo. Asht—90Pa 161
Bowyer St. SE5—52Sb 105
Boxall Rd. SE21—58Ub 105
Boxford Clo. S Croy—84Zb 166
Boxgrove Rd. SE2—48Yc 87
Boxhill Rd. Tad—100Ta 177
Box La. Bark—40Xc 67
Boxley Rd. Mord—70Eb 125
Boxley St. E16—46Kc 85
Boxmoor Rd. Harr—28Ka 38
Boxmoor Rd. Romf—22Ed 48
Boxoll Rd. Dag—35Bd 67
Box Ridge Av. Purl—84Pb 164
Boxted Clo. Buck H—18Nc 28
Boxtree La. Harr—25Ea 38
Boxtree Rd. Harr—24Fa 38
Box Tree Wlk. Orp—74Zc 151
Boxwood Way. Warl—89Zb 166
Boxworth Gro. N1—39Pb 62
Boyard Rd. SE18—50Rc 86
Boyce Clo. Borwd—11Na 21
Boyce Rd. Stanf—1L 93
Boyce St. SE1—(7K 199)
Boyce Way. E13—42Jc 85
Boycroft Av. NW9—30Sa 39
Boyd Av. S'hall—46Ba 77
Boyd Clo. King—66Qa 123
Boydel Ct. NW8—38Fb 61
Boyd Rd. SW19—65Fb 125
Boyd St. E1—44Wb 83
Boyfield St. SE1—47Rb 83 (2C 206)
Boyland Rd. Brom—64Hc 129
Boyle Av. Stan—23Ja 38
Boyle Clo. W4—52Ta 101
Boyle Farm Rd. Th Dit—72Ja 142
Boyle St. W1—45Lb 82 (4B 198)
Boyne Av. NW4—28Za 40
Boyne Rd. SE13—55Ec 106
Boyne Rd. Dag—34Cd 68
Boyne Ter. M. W11—46Bb 81
Boyseland Ct. Edgw—19Sa 21
Boyson Rd. SE17—51Sb 105
Boythorn Rd. SE16—50Xb 83
Boythorn Way. SE16—50Xb 83
Boyton Clo. E1—42Yb 84
Boyton Clo. N8—27Nb 42
Boyton Rd. N8—27Nb 42
Brabant Ct. EC3—(4H 201)
Brabant Rd. N22—26Pb 42
Brabazon Av. Wall—80Nb 146
Brabazon Rd. Houn—52Y 99
Brabazon Rd. N'holt—40Ca 57
Brabazon St. E14—43Dc 84
Brabourne Clo. SE19—64Ub 127
Brabourne Cres. Bexh—51Bd 109
Brabourne Heights. NW7
—20Ua 22
Brabourne Rise. Beck—71Ec 148
Brabourn Gro. SE15—54Yb 106
Bracewell Av. Gnfd—37Ja 58
Bracewell Rd. W10—43Ya 80
Bracewood Gdns. Croy—76Vb 147
Bracey St. N4—33Nb 62
Bracken Av. SW12—59Jb 104
Bracken Av. Croy—76Dc 148
Brackenbridge Dri. Ruis—34Z 57
Brackenbury Gdns. W6—48Xa 80
Brackenbury Rd. N2—27Eb 41
Brackenbury Rd. W6—48Xa 80
Bracken Clo. Slou—5H 53
Bracken Clo. Twic—59Ca 99
Bracken Clo. Wok—90B 156
Brackendale. N21—19Pb 24
Brackendale. Pot B—5Cb 9
Brackendale Clo. Houn—53Da 99
Brackendale Gdns. Upm—35Sd 70
Brackendene. Dart—63Gd 132
Bracken Dene. St Alb—2Ba 5
Brackendene Clo. Wok—87C 156
Bracken Dri. Chig—23Rc 46
Bracken End. Iswth—57Fa 100
Brackenfield Clo. E5—34Xb 63
Brackenforde. Slou—7N 73
Bracken Gdns. SW13—54Wa 102
Brackenhill. Cob—84Da 159
Bracken Hill Clo. Brom—67Hc 129
Bracken Hill La. Brom—67Hc 129
Bracken Industrial Est. Ilf
—24Vc 47
Bracken M. Romf—30Dd 48
Bracken Path. Eps—85Ra 161
Brackens. Beck—66Cc 128
Brackens, The. Enf—17Ub 25
Brackens, The. Orp—78Wc 151
Brackenwood. Sun—67W 120
Brackenwood Rd. Wok—7A 188
Brackley. Wey—78T 140
Brackley Clo. Wall—80Nb 146
Brackley Rd. W4—50Ua 80
Brackley Rd. Beck—66Bc 128
Brackley Sq. Wfd G—24Mc 45
Brackley St. EC1
—42Sb 83 (6E 194)
Brackley Ter. W4—50Ua 80
Bracklyn St. N1—40Tb 63 (1F 195)
Bracknell Clo. N22—25Qb 42
Bracknell Gdns. NW3—35Db 61
Bracknell Way. NW3—35Db 61
Bracondale. Esh—78Ea 142
Bracondale Av. Grav—7B 136
Bracondale Rd. SE2—49Wc 87
Bradbery. Rick—22F 34
Bradbourne Pk. Rd. Sev—95Jd 186
Bradbourne Rd. Bex—59Cd 110
Bradbourne Rd. Grays—51De 113
Bradbourne Rd. Sev—94Kd 187
Bradbourne St. SW6—54Cb 103
Bradbourne Vale Rd. Sev
—94Hd 186
Bradbury Gdns. Slou—5P 53
Bradbury St. N16—36Ub 63
Braddon Rd. Rich—55Pa 101
Braddyll St. SE10—50Gc 85

Bradenham Av.—Brighton Rd.

Bradenham Av. Well—56Wc 109
Bradenham Rd. Harr—28Ka 38
Bradenham Rd. Hay—41U 76
Bradenhurst Clo. Cat—97Vb 181
Braden St. W9—42Db 81
Bradfield Clo. Wok—90A 156
Bradfield Dri. Bark—36Wc 67
Bradfield Rd. E16—47Jc 85
Bradfield Rd. Ruis—36Aa 57
Bradford Clo. SE26—63Xb 127
Bradford Clo. Brom—74Pc 150
Bradford Dri. Eps—79Va 144
Bradford Rd. W3—47Ua 80
Bradford Rd. Ilf—32Tc 66
Bradford Rd. Rick—17E 16
Bradford Rd. Slou—4E 72
Bradgate Rd. SE6—58Dc 106
Brading Cres. E11—33Kc 65
Brading Rd. SW2—59Pb 104
Brading Rd. Croy—72Pb 146
Bradiston Rd. W9—41Bb 81
Bradleigh Av. Grays—50Ee 91
Bradley Clo. N7—37Nb 62
Bradley Gdns. W13—44Ka 78
Bradley Rd. N22—26Pb 42
Bradley Rd. SE19—65Sb 127
Bradley Rd. Enf—10Ac 12
Bradley Rd. Slou—5J 73
Bradley's Clo. N1
—40Qb 62 (1A 194)
Bradmead. SW8—52Kb 104
Bradmore Pk. Rd. W6—49Xa 80
Bradmore Way. Coul—89Nb 164
Bradshaw Clo. Wind—3C 94
Bradshawe Rd. Grays—46Ce 91
Bradshawe Waye. Uxb—43P 75
Bradshaw Rd. Wat—11Y 19
Bradstock Rd. E9—37Zb 64
Bradstock Rd. Eps—78Wa 144
Brad St. SE1—46Qb 82 (7A 200)
Bradwell Av. Dag—33Cd 68
Bradwell Clo. E18—28Hc 45
Bradwell Clo. Horn—37Kd 69
Bradwell M. N18—21Wb 43
Bradwell Rd. Buck H—18Nc 28
Brady Av. Lou—12Sc 28
Brady St. E1—42Xb 83
Braemar Av. N22—25Nb 42
Braemar Av. NW10—34Ta 59
Braemar Av. SW19—61Cb 125
Braemar Av. Bexh—56Ed 110
Braemar Av. S Croy—82Sb 165
Braemar Av. T Hth—69Rb 127
Braemar Av. Wemb—38Ma 59
Braemar Gdns. NW9—25Ta 39
Braemar Gdns. Horn—30Qd 49
Braemar Gdns. Sidc—62Tc 130
Braemar Gdns. W Wick—74Ec 148
Braemar Rd. E13—42Hc 85
Braemar Rd. N15—29Ub 43
Braemar Rd. Bren—51Ma 101
Braemar Rd. Wor Pk—76Xa 144
Braeside. Beck—64Cc 128
Braeside. Wey—83K 157
Braeside Av. SW19—67Ab 124
Braeside Av. Sev—96Hd 186
Braeside Clo. Pinn—24Ca 37
Braeside Clo. Sev—95Hd 186
Braeside Cres. Bexh—56Ed 110
Braeside Rd. SW16—66Lb 126
Braes St. N1—38Rb 63
Braesyde Clo. Belv—49Bd 87
Brafferton Rd. Croy—77Sb 147
Braganza St. SE17
—50Rb 83 (7B 206)
Bragmans La. Rick—6E 2
Braham St. E1—44Vb 83 (3K 201)
Braid Av. W3—44Ua 80
Braid Clo. Felt—61Ba 121
Braidwood Rd. SE6—60Fc 107
Braidwood St. SE1
—46Ub 83 (7H 201)
Brailsford Rd. SW2—58Qb 104
Brainton Av. Felt—59X 99
Braintree Av. Ilf—28Nc 46
Braintree Rd. Dag—34Cd 68
Braintree Rd. Ruis—35X 57
Braintree St. E2—41Yb 84
Braithwaite Av. Romf—31Cd 68
Braithwaite Gdns. Stan—25La 38
Brakefield Rd. Grav—65De 135
Bramah Grn. SW9—53Qb 104
Bramalea Clo. N6—30Jb 42
Bramall Clo. E15—36Hc 65
Bramber Ct. Slou—6E 72
Bramber Rd. N12—22Gb 41
Bramber Rd. W14—51Bb 103
Bramble Av. Dart—62Yd 134
Bramble Banks. Cars—81Jb 164
Bramblebury Rd. SE18—50Sc 86
Bramble Clo. Croy—77Cc 148
Bramble Clo. Shep—69T 120
Bramble Clo. Stan—24Ma 39
Bramble Clo. Uxb—44P 75
Bramble Clo. Wat—6W 4
Bramble Croft. Eri—49Ed 88
Brambledene Clo. Wok—6F 188
Brambledown. Long, Dart
—70Be 135
Bramble Down. Stai—67K 119
Brambledown Clo. Brom
—71Gc 149
Brambledown Rd. Cars & Wall
—80Jb 146
Brambledown Rd. S Croy
—80Ub 147
Bramble Field Clo. Long, Dart
—69Ae 135
Bramble Gdns. SW16—69Pb 126
Bramble Gdns. W12—45Va 80
Bramble La. Sev—100Kd 187
Bramble La. Upm—39Sd 70
Bramble Rise. Cob—87Y 159
Brambles Clo. Bren—52Ka 100
Brambles Clo. Cat—94Ub 181
Brambles Farm Dri. Uxb—41Q 76
Brambles, The. Chig—22Sc 46
Brambles, The. W Dray—49N 75
Bramble Wlk. Eps—86Ra 161
Bramble Way. Wok—96H 173
Bramblewood Clo. Cars
—74Gb 145
Bramblings, The. E4—21Fc 45
Bramcote Av. Mitc—70Hb 125
Bramcote Gro. SE16—50Yb 84
Bramcote Rd. SW15—56Xa 102
Bramdean Cres. SE12—60Jc 107
Bramdean Gdns. SE12—60Jc 107
Bramerton Rd. Beck—69Bc 128
Bramerton St. SW3—51Gb 103
Bramfield Rd. SW11—58Gb 103
Bramford Rd. SW18—56Eb 103
Bramham Gdns. SW5—50Db 81
Bramham Gdns. Chess—77Ma 143
Bramhope La. SE7—51Kc 107
Bramlands Clo. SW11—55Gb 103
Bramleas. Wat—14V 18
Bramley Av. Coul—87Lb 164
Bramley Clo. E17—26Ac 44
Bramley Clo. N14—15Kb 24
Bramley Clo. Cher—74K 139
Bramley Clo. Grav—6B 136
Bramley Clo. Hay—45W 76
Bramley Clo. Orp—74Rc 150
Bramley Clo. S Croy—78Sb 147
Bramley Clo. Stai—65L 119
Bramley Clo. Swan—70Gd 132
Bramley Clo. Twic—58Ea 100
Bramley Ct. Well—53Xc 109
Bramley Cres. Ilf—30Qc 46
Bramley Gdns. Wat—22Y 37
Bramley Hill. S Croy—78Rb 147
Bramley Pde. N14—14Mb 24
Bramley Pl. Dart—56Jd 110
Bramley Rd. N14—15Kb 24
Bramley Rd. W5—48La 78
Bramley Rd. W10—45Za 80
Bramley Rd. Sutt—78Fb 145
Bramley Rd. Sutt—81Za 162
(East Ewell)
Bramleys. Stanf—1M 93
Bramley Shaw. Wal A—5Hc 13
Bramley St. W10—44Za 80
Bramley Way. Asht—89Pa 161
Bramley Way. W Wick—75Dc 148
Brammas Clo. Slou—8G 72
Brampton Clo. E5—33Xb 63
Brampton Clo. Wal X—1Wb 11
Brampton Gdns. N15—29Sb 43
Brampton Gdns. W on T—78Y 141
Brampton Gro. NW4—28Xa 40
Brampton Gro. Harr—28Ja 38
Brampton Gro. Wemb—32Qa 59
Brampton La. NW4—28Ya 40
Brampton Pk. Rd. N8—27Qb 42
Brampton Rd. E6—41Mc 85
Brampton Rd. N15—29Sb 43
Brampton Rd. NW9—28Qa 39
Brampton Rd. Bexh & SE2
—55Zc 109
Brampton Rd. Croy—72Vb 147
Brampton Rd. Uxb—40R 56
Brampton Rd. Wat—20W 18
Bramshaw Gdns. Wat—22Z 37
Bramshaw Rise. N Mald
—72Ua 144
Bramshaw Rd. E9—37Zb 64
Bramshill Clo. Chig—22Uc 46
Bramshill Gdns. NW5—34Kb 62
Bramshill Rd. NW10—40Ua 60
Bramshot Av. SE7—51Jc 107
Bramshot Way. Wat—19W 18
Bramston Rd. NW10—40Wa 60
Bramwell Clo. Sun—68Z 121
Brancaster La. Purl—83Sb 165
Brancaster Rd. E12—35Pc 66
Brancaster Rd. SW16—62Nb 126
Brancaster Rd. Ilf—30Uc 46
Brancepeth Gdns. Buck H
—19Jc 27
Branch Hill. NW3—34Eb 61
Branch Hill Ho. NW3—34Db 61
Branch Pl. N1—39Tb 63
Branch Rd. E14—45Ac 84
Branch Rd. Ilf—22Xc 47
Brancker Clo. Wall—80Nb 146
Brancker Rd. Harr—27Ma 39
Brandbury Clo. S'hall—49Ca 77
Brandlehow Rd. SW15—56Bb 103
Brandon Est. SE17—51Rb 105
Brandon M. EC2—(1F 201)
Brandon Rd. E17—28Ec 44
Brandon Rd. N7—38Nb 62
Brandon Rd. Dart—59Qd 111
Brandon Rd. S'hall—50Ba 77
Brandon Rd. Sutt—77Db 145
Brandon St. SE17
—49Sb 83 (6E 206)
(in two parts)
Brandon St. Grav—9D 114
Brandram Rd. SE13—55Gc 107
Brandreth Rd. E6—44Pc 86
Brandreth Rd. SW17—61Kb 126
Brandries, The. Wall—76Mb 146
Brands Hatch Rd. Long, Dart
—76Wd 154
Brands Rd. Slou—51D 96
Brand St. SE10—52Ec 106
Brandville Gdns. Ilf—28Rc 46
Brandville Rd. W Dray—47N 75
Brandy Way. Sutt—80Cb 145
Branfill Rd. Upm—33Rd 69
Brangbourne Rd. Brom—64Ec 128
Brangton Rd. SE11
—50Pb 82 (7J 205)
Brangwyn Cres. SW19—68Eb 125
Branksea St. SW6—52Ab 102
Branksome Av. N18—22Vb 43
Branksome Clo. W on T—75Z 141
Branksome Rd. SW2—57Nb 104
Branksome Rd. SW19—67Cb 125
Branksome Way. Harr—30Pa 39
Branksome Way. N Mald
—67Sa 123
Bransby Rd. Chess—79Na 143
Branscombe Gdns. N21—17Qb 24
Branscombe St. SE13—55Dc 106
Bransdale Clo. NW6—39Cb 61
Bransell Clo. Swan—72Ed 152
Bransgrove Rd. Edgw—25Pa 39
Branston Cres. Orp—74Tc 150
Branstone Rd. Rich—53Pa 101
Branton Rd. Grnh—58Vd 112
Brants Wlk. W7—42Ga 78
Brantwood Av. Eri—52Ed 110
Brantwood Av. Iswth—56Ja 100
Brantwood Clo. E17—27Ec 44
Brantwood Clo. Wey—85J 157
Brantwood Dri. Wey—85H 157
Brantwood Gdns. Enf—14Nb 24
Brantwood Gdns. Ilf—28Nc 46
Brantwood Gdns. Wey—85H 157
Brantwood Rd. N17—23Wb 43
Brantwood Rd. SE24—57Sb 105
Brantwood Rd. Bexh—54Dd 110
Brantwood Rd. S Croy—81Sb 165
Brantwood Way. Orp—69Yc 131
Brasher Clo. Gnfd—36Fa 58
Brassey Rd. NW6—37Bb 61
Brassey Sq. SW11—55Jb 104
Brassie Av. W3—44Ua 80
Brasted Clo. SE26—63Yb 128
Brasted Clo. Bexh—57Zc 109
Brasted Clo. Orp—75Wc 151
Brasted Hill. Sev & West
—92Wc 185
Brasted Hill Rd. West—93Xc 185
Brasted La. Sev—91Wc 185
Brasted Rd. Eri—52Gd 110
Brathway Rd. SW18—59Cb 103
Bratley St. E1—42Wb 83
Bratten Ct. Croy—72Tb 147
Braund Av. Gnfd—42Da 77
Braundton Av. Sidc—60Vc 109
Bravington Clo. Shep—71P 139
Bravington Pl. W9—42Bb 81
Bravington Rd. W9—41Bb 81
Brawlings La. Ger X—21C 34
Braxfield Rd. SE4—56Ac 106
Braxted Pk. SW16—65Pb 126
Brayards Rd. SE15—54Xb 105
Braybourne Clo. Uxb—37L 55
Braybourne Dri. Iswth—52Ha 100
Braybrooke Gdns. SE19
—66Ub 127
Braybrook St. W12—43Va 80
Brayburne Av. SW4—54Lb 104
Braycourt Av. W on T—73X 141
Braydon Rd. N16—32Wb 63
Bray Dri. E16—45Hc 85
Brayfield Ter. N1—38Qb 62
Brayford Sq. E1—44Yb 84
Bray Gdns. Wok—88G 156
Bray Pas. E16—45Jc 85
Bray Pl. SW3—49Hb 81 (6F 203)
Bray Rd. NW7—23Za 40
Bray Rd. Cob—88Aa 159
Brayton Gdns. Enf—14Mb 24
Braywood Av. Egh—65B 118
Braywood Rd. SE9—56Tc 108
Breach La. Dag—41Cd 88
Bread St. EC4—44Sb 83 (4E 200)
Breakfield. Coul—88Nb 164
Break Neck Hill. Grnh—57Xd 112
Breakspeare Clo. Wat—10X 5
Breakspeare Rd. Abb L, Wat—3U 4
Breakspear Path. Uxb—27M 35
Breakspear Rd. Ruis—30R 36
Breakspear Rd. N. Uxb—25L 35
Breakspear Rd. S. Uxb—34P 55
Breakspears Dri. Orp—67Wc 131
Breakspears Rd. SE4—56Bc 106
Bream Gdns. E6—41Qc 86
Breamore Clo. SW15—60Wa 102
Breamore Rd. Ilf—33Vc 67
Bream's Bldgs. EC4
—44Qb 82 (2K 199)
Bream St. E3—38Cc 64
Breamwater Gdns. Rich
—62Ka 122
Brearley Clo. Uxb—37N 55
Breasley Clo. SW15—56Xa 102
Brechin Pl. SW7—49Eb 81 (7A 202)
Brecknock Rd.—35Lb 62
N7 1-113 & 2-142
N19 remainder
Brecon Clo. Mitc—69Nb 126
Brecon Ct. Slou—7G 72
Brecon Rd. W6—51Ab 102
Brecon Rd. Enf—14Yb 26
Brede Clo. E6—41Qc 86
Bredgar Rd. N19—33Lb 62
Bredhurst Clo. SE20—65Yb 128
Bredon Rd. SE5—55Sb 105
Bredon Rd. Croy—73Vb 147
Bredune. Kenl—87Tb 165
Breech La. Tad—96Wa 178
Breer St. SW6—55Db 103
Breezer's Hill. E1—45Wb 83
Brember Rd. Harr—33Ea 58
Bremer Rd. Stai—62J 119
Bremner Clo. Swan—70Jd 132
Bremner Rd. SW7
—48Eb 81 (3A 202)
Brenchley Av. Grav—4D 136
Brenchley Clo. Brom—72Hc 149
Brenchley Clo. Chst—67Qc 130
Brenchley Gdns. SE23—58Yb 106
Brenchley Rd. Orp—68Vc 131
Brendans Clo. Horn—32Nd 69
Brenda Rd. SW17—61Hb 125
Brenda Ter. Swans—59Ae 113
Brende Gdns. E Mol—70Da 121
Brendon Av. NW10—36Ua 60
Brendon Clo. Eri—53Gd 110
Brendon Clo. Esh—79Ea 142
Brendon Dri. Esh—79Ea 142
Brendon Gdns. Harr—35Da 57
Brendon Gdns. Ilf—29Uc 46
Brendon Rd. SE9—61Tc 130
Brendon Rd. Dag—32Cd 68
Brendon St. W1—44Gb 81 (2E 196)
Brendon Way. Enf—17Ub 25
Brenley Clo. Mitc—69Jb 126
Brenley Gdns. SE9—56Mc 107
Brennan Rd. Til—4D 114
Brent Clo. Bex—60Ad 109
Brent Clo. Dart—58Rd 111
Brentcot Clo. W13—42Ka 78
Brent Cres. NW10—40Pa 59
Brent Cross Fly-Over. NW2
—31Za 60
Brent Cross Shopping Centre.
NW4—31Ya 60
Brentfield. NW10—38Ra 59
Brentfield Clo. NW10—37Ta 59
Brentfield Gdns. NW2—31Za 60
Brentfield Rd. NW10—37Ta 59
Brentfield Rd. Dart—58Qd 111
Brentford Clo. Hay—42Z 77
Brent Grn. NW4—29Za 40
Brent Grn. Wlk. Wemb—34Sa 59
Brentham Way. W5—42Ma 79
Brenthouse Rd. E9—37Yb 64
Brenthurst Rd. NW10—37Va 60
Brentlands Dri. Dart—60Qd 111
Brent La. Dart—59Pd 111
Brent Lea. Bren—52La 100
Brentmead Clo. W7—45Ga 78
Brentmead Gdns. NW10—40Pa 59
Brentmead Pl. NW11—30Za 40
Brenton St. E14—44Ac 84
Brent Pk. Rd. NW4—31Xa 60
(in two parts)
Brent Pl. Barn—15Bb 23
Brent Rd. E16—44Jc 85
Brent Rd. SE18—52Rc 108
Brent Rd. Bren—51La 100
Brent Rd. S'hall—48Y 77
Brent Rd. S Croy—81Xb 165
Brent Side. Bren—51La 100
Brentside Clo. W13—42Ja 78
Brent St. NW4—28Ya 40
Brent Ter. NW2—32Ya 60
Brent, The. Dart—59Rd 111
Brent Trading Centre. NW10
—36Ua 60
Brentvale Av. S'hall—46Fa 78
Brentvale Av. Wemb—39Pa 59
Brent View Rd. NW9—31Wa 60
Brent Way. N3—23Cb 41
Brent Way. Bren—52Ma 101
Brent Way. Dart—58Rd 111
Brent Way. Wemb—37Ra 59
Brentwick Gdns. Bren—49Na 79
Brentwood By-Pass. Brtwd
—21Ud 50
Brentwood Clo. SE9—60Sc 108
Brentwood Ct. Wey—77K 139
Brentwood Pl. Brtwd—18Zd 33
Brentwood Rd. Brtwd—21Ce 51
Brentwood Rd. Grays—9D 92
Brentwood Rd. Romf—30Hd 48
Brereton Rd. N17—24Vb 43
Bressenden Pl. SW1
—48Lb 82 (3A 204)
Bressey Gro. E18—26Hc 45
Bretlands Rd. Cher—75G 138
Breton Ho. EC1—(7E 194)
Brett Clo. N16—33Ub 63
Brett Clo. N'holt—41Z 77
Brett Cres. NW10—39Ta 59
Brettell St. SE17—50Tb 83 (7G 207)
Brettenham Av. E17—25Cc 44
Brettenham Rd. E17—26Cc 44
Brettenham Rd. N18—21Wb 43
Brett Gdns. Dag—38Ad 67
Brettgrave. Eps—82Sa 161
Brett Ho. Clo. SW15—59Za 102
Brett Pl. Wat—9W 4
Brett Rd. E8—36Xb 63
Brett Rd. Barn—15Ya 22
Brewer's Field. Dart—63Ld 133
Brewer's Grn. SW1—(3C 204)
Brewers La. Rich—57Ma 101
Brewers Rd. Grav—7L 137
Brewer St. W1—45Lb 82 (4C 198)
Brewery La. Sev—97Kd 187
Brewery La. Twic—59Ha 100
Brewery La. Wey—85N 157
Brewery Rd. N7—38Nb 62
Brewery Rd. SE18—50Tc 86
Brewery Rd. Brom—74Nc 150
Brewery Rd. Wok—89A 156
Brewery Rd. Wok—5G 188
Brewhouse La. E1—46Xb 83
Brewhouse Rd. SE18—49Pc 86
Brewhouse St. SW15—55Ab 102
Brewhouse Wlk. SE16—46Ac 84
Brewhouse Yd. EC1
—42Rb 83 (5B 194)
Brewood Rd. Dag—37Xc 67
Brewster Gdns. W10—43Ya 80
Brewster Rd. E10—32Dc 64
Brian Av. S Croy—84Ub 165
Brian Clo. Horn—35Kd 69
Briane Rd. Eps—82Ta 161
Brian Rd. Romf—29Yc 47
Briants Clo. Pinn—26Ba 37
Briant St. SE14—53Zb 106
Briar Av. SW16—66Pb 126
Briarbank Rd. W13—44Ja 78
Briar Banks. Cars—81Jb 164
Briar Clo. N2—27Db 41
Briar Clo. N13—20Sb 25
Briar Clo. Buck H—19Mc 27
Briar Clo. Hmptn—64Ba 121
Briar Clo. Iswth—57Ha 100
Briar Clo. M'head—4A 72
Briar Clo. Wal X—1Yb 12
Briar Clo. Wey—83L 157
Briar Ct. Sutt—77Ya 144
Briar Cres. N'holt—37Da 57
Briardale Gdns. NW3—34Cb 61
Briarfield Av. N3—26Db 41
Briar Gdns. Brom—74Hc 149
Briar Gro. S Croy—85Wb 165
Briar Hill. Purl—83Nb 164
Briar La. Cars—81Jb 164
Briar La. Croy—77Dc 148
Briarleas Gdns. Upm—31Ud 70
Briar Rd. NW2—35Ya 60
Briar Rd. SW16—69Nb 126
Briar Rd. Bex—62Fd 132
Briar Rd. Harr—29La 38
Briar Rd. Romf—24Ld 49
Briar Rd. Shep—71P 139
Briar Rd. Twic—60Ga 100
Briar Rd. Wat—6W 4
Briar Rd. Wok—95D 172
Briars Clo. N17—24Xb 43
Briars Ct. Lea—86Fa 160
Briars, The. Brtwd—11Ud 32
Briars, The. Rick—8K 3
Briars, The. Slou—50B 74
Briars, The. Wal X—3Ac 12
Briars Wlk. Romf—26Pd 49
Briars Way. Long, Dart—71Ce 155
Briarswood Way. Orp—78Vc 151
Briar Wlk. SW15—56Xa 102
Briar Wlk. W10—42Ab 80
Briar Wlk. Edgw—25Sa 39
Briar Way. Slou—3F 72
Briar Way. W Dray—47Q 76
★Briarwood. Brtwd—9Vd
Briar Wood Clo. NW9—30Sa 39
Briarwood Dri. N'wd—26W 36
Briarwood Rd. SW4—57Mb 104
Briarwood Rd. Eps—79Wa 144
Briarwood Rd. Wok—7A 188
Briary Clo. NW3—38Gb 61
Briary Ct. Sidc—64Xc 131
Briary Gdns. Brom—64Kc 129
Briary La. N9—20Vb 25
Briavels Ct. Eps—87Ua 162
Brick Ct. EC4—44Qb 82 (3K 199)
Brickenden Ct. Wal A—5Hc 13
Brickett Clo. Ruis—29S 36
Brick Farm Clo. Rich—53Ra 101
Brickfield Clo. Bren—52La 100
Brickfield Cotts. SE18—51Vc 109
★Brickfield Cotts. Sev—91Td
Brickfield La. Barn—16Va 22
Brickfield La. Hay—51T 98
Brickfield Rd. E3—42Dc 84
Brickfield Rd. SW19—63Db 125
Brickfield Rd. Epp—1Zc 15
Brickfield Rd. T Hth—67Rb 127
Brickfields Cotts. Borwd—13Pa 21
Brick La.—42Vb 83 (5K 195)
E1 1-165 & 2-226
E2 remainder
Brick La. Enf—12Xb 25
Brick La. Stan—24Ma 39
Brick St. W1—46Kb 82 (7K 197)
Brickwall La. Ruis—32U 56
Brickwood Clo. SE26—62Xb 127
Brickwood Rd. Croy—75Ub 147
Brickworks Cotts. Sev—92Md 187
Bride Ct. EC4—(3B 200)
Bride La. EC4—44Rb 83 (3B 200)
Bride St. N7—37Pb 62
Bridewell Pl. EC4
—44Rb 83 (3B 200)
Bridford M. W1—43Kb 82 (7A 192)
Bridge App. NW1—38Jb 62
Bridge Av. W6—49Ya 80
Bridge Av. W7—43Fa 78
Bridge Av. Upm—34Qd 69
Bridge Clo. Brtwd—21Be 51
Bridge Clo. Enf—12Xb 25
Bridge Clo. Romf—30Gd 48
Bridge Clo. Slou—5D 72
Bridge Clo. Wey—84P 157
Bridge Clo. Wok—5F 188
Bridge End. E17—25Ec 44
Bridgefield Clo. Bans—87Ya 162
Bridgefield Rd. Sutt—79Cb 145
Bridge Foot. SE1
—50Nb 82 (7G 205)
Bridge Foot. Sun—67V 120
Bridgefoot La. Pot B—5Ya 8
Bridgeford St. SW18—62Eb 125
Bridge Gdns. Ashf—66S 120
Bridge Gdns. E Mol—70Fa 122
Bridge Ga. N21—17Sb 25
Bridgeham Clo. Wey—78Q 140
Bridge Hill. Epp—5Vc 15
Bridgeland Rd. E16—44Jc 85
Bridge La. NW11—29Ab 40
Bridge La. SW11—53Gb 103
Bridge La. Vir W—71A 138
Bridgeman Dri. Wind—4E 94
Bridgeman Rd. N1—38Pb 62
Bridgeman Rd. Tedd—65Ja 122
Bridgeman St. NW8
—40Gb 61 (2D 190)
Bridgend Rd. SW18—56Eb 103
Bridgend Rd. Enf—7Yb 12
Bridgenhall Rd. Enf—11Vb 25
Bridgen Rd. Bex—59Ad 109
Bridge Pl. SW1—49Kb 82 (5A 204)
Bridge Pl. Croy—74Tb 147
Bridge Pl. Wat—15Z 19
Bridger Clo. Wat—5Z 5
Bridge Rd. E6—38Pc 66
Bridge Rd. E15—39Fc 65
Bridge Rd. E17—31Bc 64
Bridge Rd. N9—20Wb 25
Bridge Rd. N22—25Nb 42
Bridge Rd. NW10—37Ua 60
Bridge Rd. Beck—66Bc 128
Bridge Rd. Bexh—54Ad 109
Bridge Rd. Cher—73K 139
Bridge Rd. Chess—78Na 143
Bridge Rd. E Mol—70Fa 122
Bridge Rd. Eps—84Va 162
Bridge Rd. Eri—53Hd 110
Bridge Rd. Grays—51De 113
Bridge Rd. Houn & Iswth
—55Fa 100
Bridge Rd. K Lan—5S 4
Bridge Rd. Orp—72Xc 151
Bridge Rd. Rain—42Jd 88
Bridge Rd. S'hall—47Ba 77
Bridge Rd. Sutt—79Db 145
Bridge Rd. Twic—58Ka 100
Bridge Rd. Uxb—40L 55
Bridge Rd. Wall—78Lb 146
Bridge Rd. Wemb—34Qa 59
Bridge Rd. Wey—77P 139
Bridge Row. Croy—74Tb 147
Bridges Ct. SW11—55Fb 103
Bridges La. Croy—77Nb 146
Bridges M. SW19—65Db 125
Bridges Pl. SW6—53Bb 103
Bridges Rd. SW19—65Db 125
Bridges Rd. Dart—57Rd 111
Bridges Rd. Stan—22Ha 38
Bridge St. SW1—47Nb 82 (2F 205)
Bridge St. W4—49Ta 79
Bridge St. Lea—94Ja 176
Bridge St. Pinn—27Aa 37
Bridge St. Rich—57Ma 101
Bridge St. Slou—52F 96
Bridge St. Stai—63G 118
Bridge St. W on T—74U 140
Bridge Ter. E15—38Fc 65
Bridge, The. Harr—28Ha 38
Bridge View. W6—50Ya 80
Bridgeview Ct. Ilf—23Uc 46
Bridgewater Clo. Chst—69Uc 130
Bridgewater Gdns. Edgw—26Pa 39
Bridgewater Highwalk. EC2
—(7D 194)
Bridgewater Rd. Ruis—35W 56
Bridgewater Rd. Wemb—37La 58
Bridgewater Rd. Wey—79T 140
Bridgewater Sq. EC2
—43Sb 83 (7D 194)
Bridgewater St. EC2
—43Sb 83 (7D 194)
Bridgewater Ter. Wind—3H 95
Bridgewater Way. Bush, Wat
—16Da 19
Bridge Way. N11—20Lb 24
Bridge Way. NW11—29Bb 41
Bridgeway. Bark—38Vc 67
Bridge Way. Coul—91Gb 179
Bridge Way. Twic—59Ea 100
Bridge Way. Uxb—36R 56
Bridge Way. Wemb—38Pa 59
Bridgeway St. NW1
—40Mb 62 (2C 192)
Bridge Wharf. Cher—73L 139
Bridgewood Clo. SE20—66Xb 127
Bridgewood Rd. SW16—66Mb 126
Bridgewood Rd. Wor Pk—77Wa 144
Bridgman Rd. W4—48Sa 79
Bridgwater Clo. Romf—22Md 49
Bridgwater Rd. E15—39Ec 64
Bridgwater Rd. Romf—22Ld 49
Bridgwater Wlk. Romf—22Md 49
Bridle Clo. Enf—9Bc 12
Bridle Clo. Eps—78Ta 143
Bridle Clo. King—70Ma 123
Bridle Clo. Sun—69W 120
Bridle End. Eps—86Va 162
Bridle La. W1—45Lb 82 (4C 198)
Bridle La. Cob & Lea—87Da 159
Bridle La. Rick—13L 17
Bridle Path. Croy—76Nb 146
Bridle Path. Wat—12X 19
Bridle Path, The. Wfd G—24Gc 45
Bridlepath Way. Felt—59U 98
Bridle Rd. Croy—76Cc 148
(in two parts)
Bridle Rd. Eps—85Va 162
Bridle Rd. Esh—79Ka 142
Bridle Rd. Pinn—30Y 37
Bridle Rd. S Croy—81Wb 165
Bridle Rd., The. Purl—82Nb 164
Bridle Way. Croy—76Cc 148
(in two parts)
Bridle Way. Orp—77Sc 150
Bridle Way, The. Croy—82Bc 166
Bridle Way, The. Wall—78Lb 146
Bridlington Clo. West—91Kc 183
Bridlington Rd. N9—17Xb 25
Bridlington Rd. Wat—20Z 19
Bridport Av. Romf—30Dd 48
Bridport Pl. N1—39Tb 63 (1G 195)
(in two parts)
Bridport Rd. N18—22Ub 43
Bridport Rd. Gnfd—39Da 57
Bridport Rd. T Hth—69Qb 126
Bridport Ter. SW8—53Mb 104
Bridstow Pl. W2—44Cb 81
Brief St. SE5—53Rb 105
Brier Lea. Tad—98Bb 179
Brierley. Croy—79Dc 148
(in two parts)
Brierley Av. N9—18Yb 26
Brierley Clo. SE25—70Wb 127
Brierley Clo. Horn—30Ld 49
Brierley Rd. E11—35Fc 65
Brierley Rd. SW12—61Lb 126
Brierly Gdns. E2—41Yb 84
Brigade Clo. Harr—33Fa 58
Brigade St. SE3—54Hc 107
Brigadier Av. Enf—11Sb 25
Brigadier Hill. Enf—10Sb 11
Briggeford Clo. E5—33Wb 63
Brightfield Rd. SE13—57Gc 107
Brightling Rd. SE4—58Bc 106
Brightlingsea Pl. E14—45Bc 84
Brightman Rd. SW18—60Fb 103
Brighton Bldgs. SE1—(4H 207)
Brighton Clo. Uxb—38R 56
Brighton Clo. Wey—78L 139
Brighton Dri. N'holt—37Ca 57
Brighton Gro. SE14—53Ac 106
Brighton Rd. E6—41Qc 86
Brighton Rd. E17—29Bc 44
Brighton Rd. N2—26Eb 41
Brighton Rd. N16—35Ub 63
Brighton Rd. Red, Coul, Purl,
& S Croy—95Kb 180
Brighton Rd. Surb—72La 142
Brighton Rd. Tad—98Bb 179
Brighton Rd. Tad, Bans & Sutt
—93Ab 178

Brighton Rd. Wat—10W 4
Brighton Rd. Wey—78L 139
Brighton Ter. SW9—56Pb 104
Brights Av. Rain—42Kd 89
Brightside Av. Stai—66L 119
Brightside Rd. SE13—58Fc 107
Brightside, The. Enf—11Ac 26
Bright St. E14—44Dc 84
Brightwell Cres. SW17—64Hb 125
Brightwell Rd. Wat—15W 18
Brig M. SE8—51Cc 106
Brigstock Rd. Belv—49Dd 88
Brigstock Rd. Coul—88Kb 164
Brigstock Rd. T Hth—71Qb 146
Brim Hill. N2—28Eb 41
Brimsdown Av. Enf—12Ac 26
Brimstone Clo. Orp—80Yc 151
Brindles Clo. Brtwd—19Ee 33
Brindles, The. Bans—89Bb 163
Brindley St. SE14—53Bc 106
Brindley Way. S'hall—45Da 77
Brindwood Rd. E4—20Cc 26
Brinkburn Clo. SE2—49Wc 87
Brinkburn Clo. Edgw—27Ra 39
Brinkburn Gdns. Edgw—27Qa 39
Brinkley Rd. Wor Pk—75Xa 144
Brinklow Cres. SE18—52Rc 108
Brinkworth Rd. Ilf—27Nc 46
Brinkworth Way. E9—37Bc 64
Brinley Clo. Wal X—3Zb 12
Brinsdale Rd. NW4—27Za 40
Brinsley Rd. Harr—26Fa 38
Brinsley St. E1—44Xb 83
Brinsmead Rd. Romf—26Qd 49
Brinsworth Clo. Twic—61Fa 122
Brion Pl. E14—43Ec 84
Brisbane Av. SW19—67Db 125
Brisbane Rd. E10—33Dc 64
Brisbane Rd. W13—47Ja 78
Brisbane Rd. Ilf—31Rc 66
Brisbane St. SE5—52Tb 105
Briscoe Clo. E11—34Hc 65
Briscoe Rd. SW19—65Fb 125
Briscoe Rd. Rain—40Ld 69
Briset Rd. SE9—55Mc 107
Briset St. EC1—43Rb 83 (7B 194)
Briset Way. N7—33Pb 62
Bristol Clo. Stai—58N 97
Bristol Gdns. SW15—59Ya 102
Bristol Gdns. W9—42Db 81
Bristol M. W9—42Db 81
Bristol Pk. Rd. E17—28Ac 44
Bristol Rd. E7—37Lc 65
Bristol Rd. Grav—2F 136
Bristol Rd. Gnfd—39Da 57
Bristol Rd. Mord—71Eb 145
Briston Gro. N8—30Nb 42
Bristow Rd. SE19—64Ub 127
Bristow Rd. Bexh—53Ad 109
Bristow Rd. Croy—77Nb 146
Bristow Rd. Houn—55Ea 100
Britannia Clo. SW4—56Mb 104
Britannia Clo. N'holt—41Z 77
Britannia Dri. Grav—4H 137
Britannia La. Twic—59Ea 100
Britannia Rd. N12—20Eb 23
Britannia Rd. SW6—52Db 103
Britannia Rd. Brtwd—22Yd 50
Britannia Rd. Ilf—34Rc 66
Britannia Rd. Surb—73Pa 143
Britannia Rd. Wal X—6Bc 12
Britannia Row. N1—39Rb 63
Britannia St. WC1
—41Pb 82 (3H 193)
Britannia Wlk. N1
—41Tb 83 (3F 195)
(in two parts)
Britannia Way. NW10—42Ra 79
Britannia Way. Stai—59M 97
British Gro. W4—50Va 80
British Gro. Pas. W6—50Va 80
British Gro. S. W6—50Va 80
British Legion Rd. E4—19Hc 27
British St. E3—41Bc 84
Briton Clo. S Croy—83Ub 165
Briton Cres. S Croy—83Ub 165
Briton Hill Rd. S Croy—82Ub 165
Brittain Rd. Dag—34Ad 67
Brittain Rd. W on T—78Z 141
Brittains La. Sev—96Hd 186
Britten Clo. NW11—32Db 61
Britten Clo. Borwd—16Ma 21
Brittenden Clo. Orp—79Vc 151
Britten Dri. S'hall—44Ca 77
Britten's Ct. E1—45Wb 83
Britten St. SW3—50Gb 81 (7D 202)
Britton's Ct. EC4—(3A 200)
Britton St. EC1—42Rb 83 (6B 194)
Britwell Rd. Slou—1B 72
Brixham Cres. Ruis—32W 56
Brixham Gdns. Ilf—36Uc 66
Brixham Rd. Well—53Zc 109
Brixham St. E16—46Qc 86
Brixton Est. Edgw—26Ra 39
Brixton Hill. SW2—59Nb 104
Brixton Hill Pl. SW2—59Nb 104
Brixton Rd. SW9—55Qb 104
Brixton Rd. Wat—11X 19
Brixton Sta. Rd. SW9—55Qb 104
Brixton Water La. SW2—57Pb 104
Broad Acre. St Alb—2Aa 5
Broadacre. Stai—64J 119
Broadacre Clo. Uxb—34R 56
Broadbent Clo. N6—32Kb 62
Broadbent St. W1
—45Kb 82 (4K 197)
Broadbridge Clo. SE3—52Jc 107
Broadbury Ct. N18—23Xb 43
Broad Clo. W on T—76Aa 141
Broadcoombe. S Croy—80Zb 148
Broad Ct. WC2—44Nb 82 (3G 199)
Broadcroft Av. Stan—26Ma 39
Broadcroft Rd. Orp—73Tc 150
Broad Ditch Rd. Grav—66Ee 135
Broadfield Clo. NW2—34Ya 60
Broadfield Clo. Romf—29Hd 48
Broadfield Clo. Tad—92Ya 178

Broadfield Ct. Bush, Wat—19Ga 20
Broadfield La. NW1—38Mb 62
Broadfield Rd. SE6—59Gc 107
Broadfields. E Mol—72Ga 142
Broadfields. Harr—26Da 37
Broadfields. Wal X—1Rb 11
Broadfields Av. N21—17Qb 24
Broadfields Av. Edgw—21Ra 39
Broadfields La. Wat—18X 19
Broadfield Sq. Enf—12Xb 25
Broadfield Way. Buck H—20Lc 27
Broadford La. Chob—1B 188
Broadgate. Wal A—5Hc 13
Broadgates Av. Barn—11Db 23
Broadgates Rd. SW18—60Fb 103
Broad Grn. Av. Croy—73Rb 147
Broadhead Strand. NW9—26Va 40
Broadheath Dri. Chst—64Pc 130
Broad High Way. Cob—86Z 159
Broadhinton Rd. SW4—55Kb 104
Broadhope Rd. Stanf—3L 93
Broadhurst. Asht—88Na 161
Broadhurst Av. Edgw—21Ra 39
Broadhurst Av. Ilf—35Vc 67
Broadhurst Clo. NW6—37Eb 61
Broadhurst Clo. Rich—57Pa 101
Broadhurst Gdns. NW6—37Db 61
Broadhurst Gdns. chig—21Sc 46
Broadhurst Gdns. Ruis—33Y 57
Broadhurst Wlk. Rain—37Jd 68
Broadlands Av. SW16—61Nb 126
Broadlands Av. Enf—13Xb 25
Broadlands Av. Shep—72S 140
Broadlands Clo. N6—31Jb 62
Broadlands Clo. SW16—61Nb 126
Broadlands Clo. Enf—13Yb 26
Broadlands Clo. Wal X—6Zb 12
Broadlands Dri. Warl—91Yb 182
Broadlands Rd. N6—31Hb 61
Broadlands Rd. Brom—63Kc 129
Broadlands, The. Felt—62Ca 121
Broadlands Way. N Mald
—72Va 144
Broad La. N8—29Pb 42
Broad La. N15—28Vb 43
Broad La. Dart—63Jd 132
Broad La. Hmptn—66Ba 121
Broad Lawn. SE9—61Qc 130
Broad Lawns Ct. Harr—25Ha 38
Broadley St. NW8
—43Fb 81 (7C 190)
Broadley Ter. NW1
—42Gb 81 (6E 190)
Broadmark Rd. Slou—5M 73
Broadmead. SE6—62Cc 128
Broadmead. Asht—89Pa 161
Broadmead Av. N Mald
—73Wa 144
Broadmead Clo. Hmptn—65Ca 121
Broadmead Clo. Pinn—24Aa 37
★Broad Meadow. Brtwd—10Vd
Broadmead Rd. Hay & N'holt
—42Aa 77
Broadmead Rd. Wok—94D 172
Broadmead Rd. Wfd G—23Jc 45
Broad Oak. Slou—2G 72
Broad Oak. Wfd G—22Kc 45
Broadoak Av. Enf—7Zb 12
Broadoak Ct. Slou—2G 72
Broadoak Rd. Eri—52Fd 110
Broadoaks. Epp—3Vc 15
Broadoaks. Surb—75Ra 143
Broadoaks Cres. Wey—85K 157
Broadoaks Way. Brom—71Hc 149
Broad Platts. Slou—8P 73
Broad Rd. Swans—58Ae 113
Broad Sanctuary. SW1
—47Mb 82 (2E 204)
Broadstone Pl. W1
—43Jb 82 (1H 197)
Broadstone Rd. Horn—33Jd 68
Broad St. Dag—38Cd 68
Broad St. Tedd—65Ha 122
Broad St. Av. EC2
—43Ub 83 (1H 201)
Broad St. Bldgs. EC2—(1H 201)
Broad St. Pl. EC2—(1G 201)
Broadstrood. Lou—10Qc 14
Broad View. NW9—30Qa 39
Broadview Av. Grays—47Fe 91
Broadview Rd. SW16—66Mb 126
Broadwalk. E18—27Hc 45
Broad Wlk. N21—19Pb 24
Broad Wlk. NW1—40Jb 62 (1J 191)
Broad Wlk. SE3—54Lc 107
Broad Wlk. Cat—94Vb 181
Broad Wlk. Coul—95Jb 180
Broad Wlk. Eps—91Za 178
Broadwalk. Harr—29Ca 37
Broad Wlk. Houn—53Z 99
Broad Wlk. Orp—76Zc 151
Broad Wlk. Rich—52Pa 101
Broad Wlk. Sev—100Nd 187
Broad Wlk. La. NW11—31Bb 61
Broad Wlk., The. W8
—46Db 81 (2A 202)
Broad Wlk., The. Brtwd—20Ce 33
Broad Wlk., The. E Mol—70Ha 122
Broadwalk, The. N'wd—26S 36
Broadwall. SE1—46Qb 82 (6A 200)
Broadwater. Pot B—2Db 9
Broadwater Clo. W on T—78W 140
Broadwater Clo. Wok—84F 156
Broadwater Clo. Wray, Stai
—59B 96
Broadwater Gdns Orp—77Rc 150
Broadwater Gdns. Uxb—28L 35
Broadwater La. Uxb—28L 35
Broadwater Pk. Industrial Est.
Uxb—30J 35
Broadwater Rd. N17—26Ub 43
Broadwater Rd. SE28—48Tc 86
Broadwater Rd. SW17—63Gb 125
Broadwater Rd. N. W on T
—78V 140
Broadwater Rd. S. W on T
—78V 140

Broadway. E13—40Kc 65
Broadway. E15—38Fc 65
Broadway. SW1
—48Mb 82 (3D 204)
Broadway. W7 & W13—46Ha 78
Broadway. Bark—39Sc 66
Broadway. Bexh—56Ad 109
Broadway. Eps—78Wa 144
Broadway. Grays—51Ee 113
Broadway. Gnfd—42Ea 78
Broadway. Rain—42Jd 88
Broadway. Romf—26Jd 48
Broadway. Surb—74Ra 143
Broadway. Swan—72Ed 152
Broadway. Til—4B 114
Broadway. Wind—10A 94
Broadway. Wok—89B 156
Broadway. Wok—6A 188
(Knaphill)
Broadway Av. Croy—71Tb 147
Broadway Av. Twic—58Ka 100
Broadway Clo. S Croy—86Xb 165
Broadway Clo. Wfd G—23Kc 45
Broadway Ct. SW19—65Cb 125
Broadway Ct. Beck—69Ec 128
Broadway Gdns. Mitc—70Gb 125
Broadway Mkt. E8—39Xb 63
Broadway M. N13—22Pb 42
Broadway M. N21—18Rb 25
Broadway Pde. Harr—29Da 37
Broadway Pl. SW19—65Bb 125
Broadway Shopping Centre. Bexh
—56Cd 110
Broadway, The. E4—23Fc 45
Broadway, The. N8—30Nb 42
Broadway, The. N9—20Wb 25
Broadway, The. N22—26Qb 42
Broadway, The. NW7—22Ua 40
Broadway, The. SW19—66Cb 125
Broadway, The. W5—45Ma 79
Broadway, The. Croy—77Nb 146
Broadway, The. Dag—33Cd 68
Broadway, The. Esh—74Ga 142
Broadway, The. Harr—26Ga 38
Broadway, The. Horn—35Kd 69
Broadway, The. Lou—14Sc 28
Broadway, The. Pinn—24Ba 37
Broadway, The. S'hall—46Aa 77
Broadway, The. Stai—68L 119
Broadway, The. Stan—22La 38
Broadway, The. Sutt—79Ab 144
Broadway, The. Wat—13Y 19
Broadway, The. Wemb—34Na 59
Broadway, The. Wey—82J 157
Broadway, The. Wfd G—23Kc 45
Broadwick St. W1
—45Lb 82 (4C 198)
Broadwood Av. Ruis—30U 36
Broad Yd. EC1—42Rb 83 (6B 194)
Brocas Clo. NW3—38Gb 61
Brocas St. Wind—2H 95
Brockdish Av. Bark—36Vc 67
Brockenhurst. E Mol—72Ba 141
Brockenhurst Av. Wor Pk
—74Ua 144
Brockenhurst Clo. Wok—86B 156
Brockenhurst Dri. Stanf—3L 93
Brockenhurst Gdns. NW7
—23Ua 40
Brockenhurst Gdns. Ilf—36Sc 66
Brockenhurst Rd. Croy—73Xb 147
Brockenhurst Way. SW16
—68Mb 126
Brocket Clo. Chig—21Vc 47
Brockett Rd. Grays—8C 92
Brocket Way. Chig—22Uc 46
Brock Grn. S Ock—44Xd 90
Brockham Clo. SW19—64Bb 125
Brockham Cres. Croy—80Fc 149
Brockham Dri. SW2—59Pb 104
Brockham Dri. Ilf—29Sc 46
Brockham St. SE1
—48Sb 83 (3E 206)
Brockhurst Clo. Stan—23Ha 38
Brockill Cres. SE4—56Ac 106
Brocklebank Rd. SW18—59Eb 103
Brocklehurst St. SE14—52Zb 106
Brocklesbury Clo. Wat—13Z 19
Brocklesby Rd. SE25—70Xb 127
Brockley Av. N. Stan—20Na 21
Brockley Av. S. Stan—20Na 21
Brockley Clo. Stan—21Na 39
Brockley Combe. Wey—77T 140
Brockley Cres. Romf—24Ed 48
Brockley Cross. SE4—55Ac 106
Brockley Footpath. SE4
—57Ac 106
Brockley Footpath. SE15
—56Yb 106
Brockley Gdns. SE4—54Bc 106
Brockley Gro. SE4—57Bc 106
Brockley Gro. Brtwd—18Ce 33
Brockley Hall Rd. SE4—57Ac 106
Brockley Hill. Stan—18La 20
Brockley Pk. SE23—59Ac 106
Brockley Rise. SE23—60Ac 106
Brockley Rd. SE4—57Ac 106
Brockleyside. Stan—21Na 39
Brockley View. SE23—59Ac 106
Brockley Way. SE4—57Ac 106
Brockman Rise. Brom—63Fc 129
Brock Pl. E3—42Dc 84
Brock Rd. E13—43Kc 85
Brocks Dri. Sutt—76Ab 144
Brockshot Clo. Bren—50Ma 79
Brocksparkwood. Brtwd—20De 33
Brock St. SE15—55Yb 106
★Brockway. Sev—92Ce
Brock Way. Vir W—10N 117
Brockwell Clo. Orp—71Vc 151
Brockwell Pk. Gdns. SE24
—59Rb 105
Brockworth Clo. SE15—51Ub 105
Broderick Gro. SE2—49Xc 87
Brodewater Rd. Borwd—12Ra 21
Brodia Rd. N16—34Ub 63
Brodie Rd. E4—18Ec 26

Brodie Rd. Enf—10Sb 11
Brodlove La. E1—45Zb 84
Brodrick Gro. Lea—98Ca 175
Brodrick Rd. SW17—61Gb 125
Brograve Gdns. Beck—68Dc 128
Brograve Rd. N17—27Wb 43
Broke Farm Dri. Orp—81Yc 169
Broken Furlong. Wind—10F 72
Brokengate La. Uxb—32E 54
Broken Wharf. EC4
—45Sb 83 (4D 200)
Brokesley St. E3—41Bc 84
Broke Wlk. E8—39Wb 63
Bromar Rd. SE5—55Ub 105
Bromborough Grn. Wat—22Y 37
Bromefield. Stan—25La 38
Bromefield Ct. Wal A—5Jc 13
Bromells Rd. SW4—56Lb 104
Brome Rd. SE9—55Pc 108
Bromet Clo. Wat—10V 4
Bromfelde Rd. SW4—55Mb 104
Bromfelde Wlk. SW4—54Nb 104
Bromfield St. N1
—40Qb 62 (1A 194)
Bromhall Rd. Dag—37Xc 67
Bromhedge. SE9—62Pc 130
Bromholm Rd. SE2—48Xc 87
Bromley Av. Brom—66Gc 129
Bromley Comn. Brom—70Lc 129
Bromley Cres. Brom—69Hc 129
Bromley Cres. Ruis—35V 56
Bromley Gdns. Brom—69Hc 129
Bromley Gro. Brom—68Fc 129
Bromley Hall Rd. E14—43Ec 84
Bromley High St. E3—41Dc 84
Bromley Hill. Brom—65Gc 129
Bromley La. Chst—66Sc 130
Bromley Pl. W1—43Lb 82 (7B 192)
Bromley Rd. E10—30Dc 44
Bromley Rd. E17—27Cc 44
Bromley Rd. N17—25Wb 43
Bromley Rd. N18—20Tb 25
Bromley Rd.—60Dc 106
SE6 1-427 & 2-394
Brom remainder
Bromley Rd. Beck—67Dc 128
Bromley Rd. Beck & Brom
—68Dc 128
Bromley Rd. Chst—67Rc 130
Bromley St. E1—44Zb 84
Brompton Arc. SW3—(2G 203)
Brompton Clo. SE20—68Wb 127
Brompton Clo. Houn—57Ba 99
Brompton Dri. Eri—52Kd 111
Brompton Gro. N2—28Gb 41
Brompton Pl. SW3
—48Hb 81 (3E 202)
Brompton Rd. SW3 & SW1
—49Gb 81 (5D 202)
Brompton Sq. SW3
—48Gb 81 (3D 202)
Brompton Ter. SE18—53Qc 108
Bromwich Av. N6—33Jb 62
Bromyard Av. W3—45Ua 80
Bromycroft Rd. Slou—1E 72
Brondesbury M. NW6—38Cb 61
Brondesbury Pk.—38Ya 60
NW6 1-97 & 2-64
NW2 remainder
Brondesbury Rd. NW6—40Bb 61
Brondesbury Vs. NW6—40Bb 61
Bronsart Rd. SW6—52Ab 102
Bronsdon Way. Uxb—33H 55
Bronson Rd. SW20—68Za 124
Bronte Clo. Ilf—28Qc 46
Bronte Clo. Til—4E 114
Bronte Gro. Dart—56Pd 111
Bronti Clo. SE17—50Sb 83 (7E 206)
Bronze St. SE8—52Cc 106
Brook Av. Dag—38Dd 68
Brook Av. Edgw—22Ra 39
Brook Av. Wemb—34Qa 59
Brookbank Av. W7—42Fa 78
Brookbank Rd. SE13—55Cc 106
Brook Clo. NW7—24Ab 40
Brook Clo. SW20—69Xa 124
Brook Clo. Buck H—18Jc 27
Brook Clo. Romf—25Hd 48
Brook Clo. Ruis—31U 56
Brook Clo. Stai—59P 97
Brook Cres. E4—21Cc 44
Brook Cres. N9—21Xb 43
Brook Cres. Slou—4C 72
Brookdale. N11—21Lb 42
Brookdale Av. Upm—34Qd 69
Brookdale Clo. Upm—34Rd 69
Brookdale Rd. E17—27Cc 44
Brookdale Rd. SE6—59Dc 106
Brookdale Rd. Bex—58Ad 109
Brookdene Av. Wat—17X 19
Brookdene Dri. N'wd—24V 36
Brookdene Rd. SE18—49Vc 87
Brook Dri. SE11—48Qb 82 (4A 206)
Brook Dri. Harr—28Ea 38
Brook Dri. Rad—5Ha 6
Brook Dri. Ruis—31U 56
Brook Dri. Sun—65U 120
Brooke Av. Harr—34Ea 58
Brooke Clo. Bush, Wat—17Ea 20
Brooke Dri. Grav—10K 115
Brookehowse Rd. SE6—61Cc 128
Brookend Rd. Sidc—60Uc 108
Brooke Rd. E17—28Ec 44
Brooke Rd.—34Vb 63
N16 1-147 & 6-160
E5 remainder
Brooke Rd. N18—20Ub 25
Brooke Rd. Grays—50Ce 91
Brooker Rd. Wal A—6Ec 12
Brookers Clo. Asht—89Ma 161
Brooke's Ct. EC1
—43Qb 82 (7K 193)
Brooke's Mkt. EC1—(7K 193)
Brooke St. EC1—43Qb 82 (1K 199)
Brooke Way. Bush, Wat—17Ea 20
Brook Farm Rd. Cob—87Z 159
Brookfield. N6—34Jb 62

Brookfield. Sev—89Nd 171
Brookfield. Wok—4E 188
Brookfield Av. E17—28Ec 44
Brookfield Av. NW7—23Xa 40
Brookfield Av. W5—42Ma 79
Brookfield Av. Sutt—76Gb 145
Brookfield Clo. NW7—23Xa 40
Brookfield Clo. Brtwd—16Fe 33
Brookfield Ct. Gnfd—41Ea 78
Brookfield Cres. NW7—23Xa 40
Brookfield Cres. Harr—29Na 39
Brookfield Gdns. Esh—79Ha 142
Brookfield Pk. NW5—34Kb 62
Brookfield Path. Wfd G—23Gc 45
Brookfield Rd. E9—37Ac 64
Brookfield Rd. N9—20Wb 25
Brookfield Rd. W4—47Ta 79
Brookfields. Enf—14Zb 26
Brookfields Av. Mitc—71Gb 145
Brook Gdns. E4—21Dc 44
Brook Gdns. SW13—55Va 102
Brook Gdns. King—67Sa 123
Brook Ga. W1—45Hb 81 (5G 197)
Brook Grn. W6—48Za 80
Brook Hill Clo. SE18—50Rc 86
Brookhill Clo. Barn—15Gb 23
Brookhill Rd. SE18—50Rc 86
Brookhill Rd. Barn—15Gb 23
Brook Ho. Gdns. E4—21Gc 45
Brookhurst Rd. Wey—79K 139
Brooking Rd. E7—36Jc 65
Brookland Clo. NW11—28Db 41
Brookland Garth. NW11—28Db 41
Brookland Hill. NW11—28Db 41
Brookland Rise. NW11—28Cb 41
Brooklands App. Romf—28Fd 48
Brooklands Av. SW19—61Db 125
Brooklands Av. Sidc—61Tc 130
Brooklands Clo. Cob—87Aa 159
Brooklands Clo. Romf—28Fd 48
Brooklands Clo. Sun—67U 120
Brooklands Dri. Gnfd—39La 58
Brooklands Gdns. Horn—30Ld 49
Brooklands Gdns. Pot B—4Ab 8
Brooklands La. Romf—28Fd 48
Brooklands La. Wey—79P 139
Brooklands Pk. SE3—55Jc 107
Brooklands Rd. Romf—28Fd 48
Brooklands Rd. Th Dit—74Ha 142
Brooklands Rd. Wey—83Q 158
Brooklands St. SW8—53Mb 104
Brook La. SE3—54Kc 107
Brook La. Bex—58Zc 109
★Brook La. Brtwd—9Yd
Brook La. Brom—65Jc 129
Brook La. Wok—94G 172
Brook La. N. Bren—50Ma 79
(in two parts)
Brooklea Clo. NW9—25Ua 40
Brooklyn Av. SE25—70Xb 127
Brooklyn Av. Lou—14Nc 28
Brooklyn Clo. Wok—91A 172
Brooklyn Gro. SE25—70Xb 127
Brooklyn Rd. SE25—70Xb 127
Brooklyn Rd. Brom—71Mc 149
Brooklyn Rd. Wok—90A 156
Brooklyn Way. W Dray—48M 75
Brookmans Av. Grays—46Fe 91
Brookmans Clo. Upm—31Ud 70
Brook Mead. Eps—79Ua 144
Brookmead Av. Brom—71Pc 150
Brookmead Clo. Orp—73Xc 151
Brookmead Industrial Est. Croy
—72Lb 146
Brook Meadow. N12—20Db 23
Brookmead Rd. Croy—72Lb 146
Brookmead Way. Orp—72Xc 151
Brook M. N. W2—45Eb 81 (4A 196)
Brookmill Rd. SE8—53Cc 106
Brook Pde. Chig—20Rc 28
Brook Path. Lou—14Nc 28
Brook Path. Slou—5D 72
Brook Pl. Barn—15Cb 23
Brook Rise. Chig—20Qc 28
Brook Rd. N8—28Nb 42
Brook Rd. N22—26Pb 42
Brook Rd. NW2—33Va 60
Brook Rd. Borwd—11Qa 21
Brook Rd. Brtwd—20Vd 32
Brook Rd. Buck H—19Jc 27
Brook Rd. Epp—5Wc 15
Brook Rd. Grav—10A 114
Brook Rd. Ilf—30Uc 46
Brook Rd. Lou—15Nc 28
Brook Rd. Red—100Lb 180
Brook Rd. Romf—26Hd 48
Brook Rd. Surb—75Na 143
Brook Rd. Swan—69Fd 132
Brook Rd. T Hth—70Sb 127
Brook Rd. Twic—58Ja 100
Brook Rd. Wal X—6Bc 12
Brook Rd. S. Bren—51Ma 101
Brooks Av. E6—42Pc 86
Brooksbank St. E9—37Yb 64
Brooksby M. N1—38Qb 62
Brooksby St. N1—38Qb 62
Brooksby's Wlk. E9—36Zb 64
Brooks Clo. SE9—61Qc 130
Brooks Clo. Wey—82Q 158
Brookscroft. Croy—82Bc 166
Brookscroft Rd. E17—25Dc 44
Brookshill. Harr—22Fa 38
Brookshill Av. Harr—22Fa 38
Brookshill Dri. Harr—22Fa 38
Brookside. N21—16Pb 24
Brookside. Barn—16Gb 23
Brookside. Cars—78Jb 146
Brookside. Cher—73G 138
Brookside. Guild—100A 172
Brookside. Horn—29Nd 49
Brookside. Ilf—23Sc 46
Brookside. Orp—73Vc 151
Brookside. Pot B—4Wa 8
Brookside. Slou—52E 96
Brookside. Uxb—38P 55
Brookside. Wal A—4Gc 13
Brookside. Wat—17X 19

Brookside Av. Ashf—64L 119
Brookside Av. Wray, Stai—55A 96
Brookside Clo. Barn—16Ab 22
Brookside Clo. Harr—29Ma 39
(Kenton)
Brookside Clo. Harr—35Aa 57
(South Harrow)
Brookside Cres. Wor Pk
—74Wa 144
Brookside Gdns. Enf—9Yb 12
Brookside Rd. N9—21Xb 43
Brookside Rd. N19—33Lb 62
Brookside Rd. NW11—30Ab 40
Brookside Rd. Grav—6B 136
Brookside Rd. Hay—45Y 77
Brookside S. Barn—17Jb 24
Brookside Wlk. N3—27Ab 40
Brookside Wlk. N12—23Cb 41
Brookside Wlk. NW11—28Bb 41
Brookside Way. Croy—72Zb 148
Brooks La. W4—51Qa 101
Brook's M. W1—45Kb 82 (4K 197)
Brooks Rd. E13—39Jc 65
Brooks Rd. W4—50Qa 79
Brook St. N17—26Vb 43
Brook St. W1—45Kb 82 (4K 197)
Brook St. W2—45Fb 81 (4C 196)
Brook St. Belv & Eri—50Dd 88
Brook St. Brtwd—22Td 50
Brook St. King—68Na 123
Brook St. Wind—4H 95
Brooksville Av. NW6—39Ab 60
Brooks Way. Orp—68Yc 131
Brookvale. Eri—53Dd 110
Brookview Ct. Enf—15Ub 25
Brookview Rd. SW16—64Lb 126
Brookville Rd. SW6—52Bb 103
Brook Wlk. N2—25Fb 41
Brook Wlk. Edgw—23Ta 39
Brookway. SE3—55Jc 107
Brook Way. Chig—20Qc 28
Brookway. Lea—90Ja 160
Brookway. Rain—43Kd 89
Brookwood Av. SW13—54Va 102
Brookwood Clo. Houn—54Da 99
Brookwood Lye Rd. Wok—8A 188
Brookwood Rd. SW18—60Bb 103
Broom Av. Orp—68Xc 131
Broom Clo. Brom—72Nc 150
Broom Clo. Esh—78Da 141
Broom Clo. Tedd—66Ma 123
Broomcroft Av. N'holt—41Y 77
Broomcroft Clo. Wok—88F 156
Broomcroft Dri. Wok—87F 156
Broome Clo. Eps—98Sa 177
Broome Pl. S Ock—46Td 90
Broome Rd. Hmptn—66Ba 121
Broome Way. SE5—52Tb 105
Broomfield. E17—31Bc 64
Broomfield. Grav—63Ae 135
Broomfield. Sun—67W 120
Broomfield Av. N13—22Pb 42
Broomfield Av. Lou—16Pc 28
Broomfield Ct. Wey—79R 140
Broomfield La. N13—21Nb 42
Broomfield Pl. W13—46Ka 78
Broomfield Ride. Lea—84Fa 160
Broomfield Rise. Abb L, Wat—4T 4
Broomfield Rd. N13—22Nb 42
Broomfield Rd. W13—46Ka 78
Broomfield Rd. Beck—69Bc 128
Broomfield Rd. Bexh—57Cd 110
Broomfield Rd. Rich—53Pa 101
Broomfield Rd. Romf—31Zc 67
Broomfield Rd. Sev—94Hd 186
Broomfield Rd. Surb—74Pa 143
Broomfield Rd. Swans—57Ae 113
Broomfield Rd. Tedd—65La 122
Broomfield Rd. Wey—83K 157
Broomfield St. E14—43Dc 84
Broom Gdns. Croy—76Cc 148
Broom Gro. Wat—10W 4
Broomgrove Gdns. Edgw
—25Qa 39
Broomgrove Rd. SW9—54Pb 104
Broom Hall. Lea—86Fa 160
Broomhall End. Wok—88A 156
Broom Hall La. Wok—88A 156
Broomhall Rd. S Croy—81Tb 165
Broomhall Rd. Wok—88A 156
Broom Hill. Slou—8L 53
Broomhill Rise. Bexh—57Cd 110
Broomhill Rd. SW18—57Cb 103
Broomhill Rd. Dart—58Kd 111
Broomhill Rd. Ilf—33Wc 67
Broomhill Rd. Orp—73Wc 151
Broomhill Rd. Wfd G—23Jc 45
(in two parts)
Broomhill Wlk. Wfd G—24Hc 45
Broomhouse La. SW6—54Cb 103
Broomhouse Rd. SW6—54Cb 103
Broomlands La. Oxt—98Mc 183
Broomloan La. Sutt—75Cb 145
Broom Lock. Tedd—65La 122
Broom Mead. Bexh—57Cd 110
Broom Pk. Tedd—66Ma 123
Broom Rd. Croy—76Cc 148
Broom Rd. Tedd—64Ka 122
Broomsleigh St. NW6—36Bb 61
Broomstick Hall Rd. Wal A
—5Gc 13
Broom Water. Tedd—65La 122
Broom Water W. Tedd—64La 122
Broom Way. Wey—77U 140
Broomwood Gdns. Brtwd
—16Wd 32
Broomwood Rd. SW11—58Hb 103
Broomwood Rd. Orp—68Yc 131
Broseley Gdns. Romf—21Nd 49
Broseley Gro. SE26—64Ac 128
Broseley Rd. Romf—21Nd 49
Brougham Rd. E8—39Wb 63
Brougham Rd. W3—44Sa 79
Brough Clo. SW8—52Nb 104
Broughinge Rd. Borwd—12Ra 21
Broughton Av. N3—27Ab 40
Broughton Av. Rich—62Ka 122

Broughton Dri.—Burtons Ct.

Broughton Dri. SW9—56Rb 105
Broughton Gdns. N6—30Lb 42
Broughton Rd. SW6—54Db 103
Broughton Rd. W13—45Ka 78
Broughton Rd. Orp—75Tc 150
Broughton Rd. Sev—88Jd 170
Broughton Rd. T Hth—72Qb 146
Broughton St. SW8—54Kb 104
Brouncker Rd. W3—47Sa 79
Brow Clo. Orp—73Zc 151
Brow Cres. Orp—74Yc 151
Browells La. Felt—61X 121
Brown Clo. Wall—80Nb 146
Browne Clo. Romf—22Dd 48
Brownfield St. E14—44Ec 84
Browngraves Rd. Hay—52S 98
Brown Hart Gdns. W1 —45Jb 82 (4J 197)
Brownhill Rd. SE6—59Dc 106
Browning Av. W7—44Ha 78
Browning Av. Sutt—77Gb 145
Browning Av. Wor Pk—74Xa 144
Browning Clo. W9 —42Eb 81 (6A 190)
Browning Clo. Hmptn—63Ba 121
Browning Clo. Well—53Uc 108
Browning M. W1—43Jb 82 (1J 197)
Browning Rd. E11—31Hc 65
Browning Rd. E12—36Pc 66
Browning Rd. Dart—56Pd 111
Browning Rd. Enf—10Tb 11
Browning Rd. Lea—97Fa 176
Browning St. SE17 —50Sb 83 (7E 206)
Browning Wlk. Til—4E 114
Browning Way. Houn—53Z 99
Brownlea Gdns. Ilf—33Wc 67
Brownlow M. WC1 —42Pb 82 (6J 193)
Brownlow Rd. E8—39Wb 63
Brownlow Rd. N3—24Db 41
Brownlow Rd. N11—23Nb 42
Brownlow Rd. NW10—38Ua 60
Brownlow Rd. W13—46Ja 78
Brownlow Rd. Borwd—14Qa 21
Brownlow Rd. Croy—77Ub 147
Brownlow St. WC1 —43Pb 82 (1J 199)
Brownrigg Rd. Ashf—63Q 120
Brown Rd. Grav—10G 114
Brown's Arc. W1—(5C 198)
Brown's Bldgs. EC3 —44Ub 83 (3J 201)
Brown's Ct. W2—44Gb 81 (2E 196)
Browns La. Lea—99Z 175
Brownspring Dri. SE9—63Rc 130
Browns Rd. E17—27Cc 44
Brown's Rd. Surb—73Pa 143
Brown St. W1—44Hb 81 (2F 197)
Brownswell Rd. N2—26Fb 41
Brownswood Rd. N4—33Rb 63
Brow, The. Chal—20A 16
Brow, The. Wat—5X 5
Broxash Rd. SW11—58Jb 104
Broxbourne Av. E18—28Kc 45
Broxbourne Rd. E7—34Jc 65
Broxbourne Rd. Orp—74Vc 151
Broxburn Dri. S Ock—45Xd 90
Broxhill Rd. Hav, Romf—20Hd 30
Broxholm Rd. SE27—62Qb 126
Brox La. Cher & Wey—80E 138
Brox Rd. Cher—81E 156
Broxted Rd. SE6—61Bc 128
Broxwood Way. NW8 —39Gb 61 (1E 190)
Bruce Av. Horn—33Ld 69
Bruce Av. Shep—72S 140
Bruce Castle Rd. N17—25Vb 43
Bruce Clo. Well—53Xc 109
Bruce Clo. Wey—85N 157
Bruce Dri. S Croy—81Zb 166
Bruce Gdns. N20—20Hb 23
Bruce Gro. N17—26Vb 43
Bruce Gro. Orp—74Wc 151
Bruce Gro. Wat—10Y 5
Bruce Hall M. SW17—63Jb 126
Bruce Rd. E3—41Dc 84
Bruce Rd. NW10—38Ta 59
Bruce Rd. SE25—70Tb 127
Bruce Rd. Barn—13Ab 22
Bruce Rd. Harr—26Ga 38
Bruce Rd. Mitc—66Jb 126
Bruce Wlk. Wind—4B 94
Bruce Way. Wal X—5Zb 12
Bruckner St. W10—41Ab 81
Brudenell. Wind—6D 94
Brudenell Rd. SW17—62Hb 125
Bruffs Meadow. N'holt—37Aa 57
Brumana Clo. Wey—79R 140
Brumfield Rd. Eps—78Sa 143
Brummel Clo. Bexh—55Ed 110
Brumwill Rd. W5—40Na 59
Brunel Clo. SE19—65Vb 127
Brunel Clo. Houn—52X 99
Brunel Clo. N'holt—41Ba 77
Brunel Clo. Til—5D 114
Brunel Est. W2—43Cb 81
Brunel Pl. S'hall—44Da 77
Brunel Rd. SE16—47Yb 84
Brunel Rd. W3—43Ua 80
Brunel Rd. Wfd G—22Pc 46
Brunel St. E16—44Hc 85
Brunel Wlk. N15—28Ub 43
Brunel Wlk. Twic—59Ca 99
Brunel Way. Slou—6K 73
Brune St. E1—43Vb 83 (1K 201)
Brunner Clo. NW11—29Eb 41
Brunner Rd. E17—29Ac 44
Brunner Rd. W5—42Ma 79
Brunswick Av. N11—20Jb 24
Brunswick Av. Upm—31Ud 70
Brunswick Centre. WC1 —42Nb 82 (5F 193)
Brunswick Clo. Bexh—56Zc 109
Brunswick Clo. Pinn—30Aa 37
Brunswick Clo. Th Dit—74Ha 142
Brunswick Clo. W on T—75Y 141
Brunswick Clo. Est. EC1—(4B 194)
Brunswick Ct. SE1 —47Ub 83 (2J 207)
Brunswick Cres. N11—20Jb 24
Brunswick Gdns. W5—42Na 79
Brunswick Gdns. W8—46Cb 81
Brunswick Gdns. Ilf—24Sc 46
Brunswick Gro. N11—20Jb 24
Brunswick Gro. Cob—85Y 159
Brunswick M. W1 —44Hb 81 (2G 197)
Brunswick Pk. SE5—53Ub 105
Brunswick Pk. Gdns. N11—19Jb 24
Brunswick Pk. Rd. N11—19Jb 24
Brunswick Pl. N1 —41Tb 83 (4G 195)
Brunswick Pl. SE19—66Wb 127
Brunswick Rd. E10—32Ec 64
Brunswick Rd. E14—44Ec 84
Brunswick Rd. N15—29Ub 43
(in two parts)
Brunswick Rd. W5—42Ma 79
Brunswick Rd. Bexh—56Zc 109
Brunswick Rd. King—67Qa 123
Brunswick Rd. Sutt—77Db 145
Brunswick Sq. N17—23Vb 43
Brunswick Sq. WC1 —42Nb 82 (5G 193)
Brunswick St. E17—29Ec 44
Brunswick Vs. SE5—53Ub 105
Brunswick Wlk. Grav—9F 114
Brunswick Way. N11—21Kb 42
Brunton Pl. E14—44Ac 84
Brushfield St. E1 —43Ub 83 (7J 195)
Brushwood Dri. Rick—14E 16
Brussels Rd. SW11—56Fb 103
Bruton Clo. Chst—66Pc 130
Bruton La. W1—45Kb 82 (5A 198)
Bruton Pl. W1—45Kb 82 (5A 198)
Bruton Rd. Mord—70Eb 125
Bruton St. W1—45Kb 82 (5A 198)
Bruton Way. W13—43Ja 78
Bryan Av. NW10—38Xa 60
Bryan Clo. Sun—66W 120
Bryan Rd. SE16—47Bc 84
Bryanston Av. Twic—60Da 99
Bryanston Clo. S'hall—49Ba 77
Bryanstone Rd. N8—30Mb 42
Bryanston M. E. W1 —43Hb 81 (1F 197)
Bryanston M. W. W1 —44Hb 81 (1F 197)
Bryanston Pl. W1 —43Hb 81 (1F 197)
Bryanston Rd. Til—4E 114
Bryanston Sq. W1 —44Hb 81 (2F 197)
Bryanston St. W1 —44Hb 81 (3G 197)
Bryant Av. Romf—25Md 49
Bryant Av. Slou—3H 73
Bryant Clo. Barn—15Bb 23
Bryant Ct. E2—(1K 195)
Bryant Rd. N'holt—41Y 77
Bryant St. E15—38Fc 65
Bryantwood Rd. N7—36Qb 62
Brycedale Cres. N14—20Mb 24
Bryce Rd. Dag—35Yc 67
Bryden Clo. SE26—64Ac 128
Brydges Pl. WC2 —45Nb 82 (5F 199)
Brydges Rd. E15—36Fc 65
Brydon Wlk. N1—39Nb 62
Bryer Ct. EC2—(7D 194)
Bryer Pl. Wind—5B 94
Bryett Rd. N7—34Nb 62
Brynford Clo. Wok—87A 156
Brynmaer Rd. SW11—53Hb 103
Brynmawr Rd. Enf—14Vb 25
Bryony Clo. Uxb—43P 75
Bryony Rd. W12—45Wa 80
Bubblestone Rd. Sev—88Kd 171
Buccleuch Rd. Slou—2L 95
Buchanan Clo. S Ock—46Sd 90
Buchanan Gdns. NW10—40Xa 60
Buchan Clo. Uxb—42L 75
Buchan Rd. SE15—55Yb 106
Bucharest Rd. SW18—59Eb 103
Buckbean Path. Romf—24Ld 49
Buckden Clo. SE12—58Jc 107
Buckettsland La. Borwd—10Ta 7
Buckfast Rd. Mord—70Db 125
Buckfast St. E2—41Wb 83
Buckham Thorns Rd. West —98Sc 184
Buck Hill Wlk. W2 —45Fb 81 (5C 196)
Buckhold Rd. SW18—58Cb 103
Buckhurst Av. Cars—74Gb 145
Buckhurst Av. Sev—97Ld 187
Buckhurst La. Asc—9D 116
Buckhurst La. Sev—97Ld 187
Buckhurst Rd. Asc—8D 116
Buckhurst Rd. West—92Rc 184
Buckhurst St. E1—42Xb 83
Buckhurst Way. Buck H—21Mc 45
Buckingham Arc. WC2—(5G 199)
Buckingham Av. N20—17Eb 23
Buckingham Av. E Mol—68Da 121
Buckingham Av. Felt—58X 99
Buckingham Av. Gnfd—39Ja 58
Buckingham Av. Slou—4D 72
Buckingham Av. T Hth—67Qb 126
Buckingham Av. Well—56Uc 108
Buckingham Av. E. Slou—4G 72
Buckingham Clo. W5—43La 78
Buckingham Clo. Enf—12Ub 25
Buckingham Clo. Hmptn —64Ba 121
Buckingham Clo. Horn—30Md 49
Buckingham Clo. Orp—73Uc 150
Buckingham Ct. NW4—27Wa 40
Buckingham Ct. Sutt—81Cb 163
Buckingham Gdns. E Mol —68Da 121
Buckingham Gdns. Edgw—24Na 39
Buckingham Gdns. Slou—7K 73
Buckingham Gdns. T Hth —68Qb 126
Buckingham Ga. SW1 —47Lb 82 (3B 204)
Buckingham Gro. Uxb—40Q 56
Buckingham Hill Rd. Stanf—6H 93
Buckingham La. SE23—59Ac 106
Buckingham M. NW10—40Va 60
Buckingham M. SW1—(3B 204)
Buckingham Pal. Rd. SW1 —49Kb 82 (6K 203)
Buckingham Pde. Stan—22La 38
Buckingham Pl. SW1 —48Lb 82 (3B 204)
Buckingham Rd. E10—34Dc 64
Buckingham Rd. E11—29Lc 45
Buckingham Rd. E15—36Hc 65
Buckingham Rd. E18—25Hc 45
Buckingham Rd. N1—37Ub 63
Buckingham Rd. N22—25Nb 42
Buckingham Rd. NW10—40Va 60
Buckingham Rd. Borwd—14Ta 21
Buckingham Rd. Edgw—24Pa 39
Buckingham Rd. Grav—59Fe 113
Buckingham Rd. Hmptn —64Ba 121
Buckingham Rd. Harr—29Fa 38
Buckingham Rd. Ilf—33Tc 66
Buckingham Rd. King—70Pa 123
Buckingham Rd. Mitc—71Nb 146
Buckingham Rd. Rich—61Ma 123
Buckingham Rd. Wat—9Y 5
Buckingham St. WC2 —45Nb 82 (5G 199)
Buckingham Way. Wall—81Lb 164
Buckland Av. Slou—8M 73
Buckland Cres. NW3—37Fb 61
Buckland Cres. Wind—3D 94
Buckland Rise. Pinn—25Y 37
Buckland Rd. E10—33Ec 64
Buckland Rd. Chess—78Pa 143
Buckland Rd. Orp—77Uc 150
Buckland Rd. Sutt—82Ya 162
Buckland Rd. Tad—100Bb 179
Bucklands Rd. Tedd—65La 122
Buckland St. N1—40Tb 63 (2G 195)
Buckland Wlk. W3—47Sa 79
Buckland Wlk. Mord—70Eb 125
Buckland Way. Wor Pk—74Ya 144
Buck La. NW9—29Ta 39
Buckleigh Av. SW20—69Bb 125
Buckleigh Rd. SW16—65Mb 126
Buckleigh Way. SE19—67Vb 127
Buckler Gdns. SE9—62Pc 130
Bucklers All. SW6—51Bb 103
Bucklersbury. EC4 —44Tb 83 (3F 201)
Buckler's Way. Cars—76Hb 145
Buckles La. S Ock—43Yd 90
Buckles Way. Bans—88Ab 162
Buckley Clo. Dart—54Hd 110
Buckley Rd. NW6—38Bb 61
Buckley St. SE1—(7K 199)
Buckmaster Rd. SW11—57Gb 103
Bucknalls Clo. Wat—4Aa 5
Bucknalls Dri. St Alb—3Ba 5
Bucknalls La. Wat—4Z 5
Bucknall St. WC2 —44Nb 82 (2E 198)
Buckner Rd. SW2—56Pb 104
Bucknills Clo. Eps—86Sa 161
Buckrell Rd. E4—19Fc 27
Buck's Av. Wat—17Aa 19
Bucks Clo. Wey—86K 157
Bucks Cross Rd. Grav—2B 136
Bucks Cross Rd. Orp—78Ad 151
Bucks Hill. K Lan—5L 3
Buckstone Clo. SE23—58Yb 106
Buckstone Rd. N18—22Wb 43
Buck St. NW1—38Kb 62
Buckters Rents. SE16—46Ac 84
Buckthorne Rd. SE4—57Ac 106
Buckton Rd. Borwd—10Pa 7
Buck Wlk. E17—28Fc 45
Buddings Circ. Wemb—34Sa 59
Budd's All. Twic—57La 100
Budebury Rd. Stai—64J 119
Budge Row. EC4—45Tb 83 (3F 201)
Budgin's Hill. Orp—84Yc 169
Budleigh Cres. Well—53Yc 109
Budoch Ct. Ilf—33Wc 67
Budoch Dri. Ilf—33Wc 67
Buer Rd. SW6—54Ab 102
Buff Av. Bans—86Db 163
Bug Hill. Cat & Warl—92Zb 182
Bugsby's Way. SE10 & SE7 —49Hc 85
Bulbeggars La. Wok—4E 188
Bulganak Rd. T Hth—70Sb 127
Bulinga St. SW1—49Nb 82 (6F 205)
Bulkeley Av. Wind—5F 94
Bulkeley Clo. Egh—4N 117
Bullace La. Dart—58Nd 111
(in two parts)
Bull All. SE1—45Qb 82 (5A 200)
Bull All. Well—55Xc 109
Bullard's Pl. E2—41Zb 84
Bullbanks Rd. Belv—49Ed 88
Bullen St. SW11—54Gb 103
Buller Clo. SE15—52Wb 105
Buller Rd. N17—26Wb 43
Buller Rd. N22—26Qb 42
Buller Rd. NW10—41Za 80
Buller Rd. Bark—38Uc 66
Buller Rd. T Hth—68Tb 127
Bullers Clo. Sidc—64Ad 131
Bullers Wood Dri. Chst—66Pc 130
Bullescroft Rd. Edgw—20Ra 21
Bullfinch Clo. Sev—94Fd 186
Bullfinch Dene. Sev—94Fd 186
Bullfinch La. Sev—94Gd 186
Bullfinch Rd. S Croy—82Zb 166
Bullhead Rd. Borwd—13Sa 21
Bull Hill. Lea—93Ja 176
Bull Inn Ct. WC2—(5G 199)
Bullivant St. E14—45Ec 84
Bull La. N18—22Ub 43
Bull La. Chst—66Tc 130
Bull La. Dag—34Dd 68
Bull La. Ger X—27A 34
★Bull La. Sev—88Ce
Bull Rd. E15—40Hc 65
Bull's All. SW14—54Ta 101
Bulls Bri. Industrial Est. S'hall —49X 77
Bullsbridge Rd. S'hall—49Y 77
Bullsbrook Rd. Hay—46Y 77
Bull's Cross. Enf—7Wb 11
Bulls Cross Ride. Wal X—7Wb 11
Bull's Gdns. SW3 —49Gb 81 (5E 202)
Bull's Head Pas. EC3—(3H 201)
Bullsland Gdns. Rick—16D 16
Bullsland La. Rick & Ger X—16D 16
Bullsmoor Clo. Wal X—7Yb 12
Bullsmoor Gdns. Wal X—7Xb 11
Bullsmoor La. Enf—7Wb 11
Bullsmoor Ride. Wal X—7Yb 12
Bullsmoor Way. Wal X—7Yb 12
Bullwell Cres. Wal X—1Ac 12
Bull Wharf La. EC4 —45Sb 83 (4E 200)
Bull Yd. SE15—53Wb 105
Bulmer Gdns. Harr—31Ma 59
Bulmer M. W11—46Cb 81
Bulmer Wlk. Rain—40Ld 69
Bulstrode Av. Houn—54Ba 99
Bulstrode Gdns. Houn—55Ca 99
Bulstrode La. K Lan—1G 2
Bulstrode Pl. W1—43Jb 82 (1J 197)
Bulstrode Rd. Houn—55Ca 99
Bulstrode St. W1—44Jb 82 (2J 197)
Bulstrode Way. Ger X—29A 34
Bulwer Ct. Rd. E11—32Fc 65
Bulwer Gdns. Barn—14Eb 23
Bulwer Rd. E11—32Fc 65
Bulwer Rd. N18—21Ub 43
Bulwer Rd. Barn—14Db 23
Bulwer St. W12—46Ya 80
Bunby Rd. Slou—8K 53
Bunces Clo. Wind—10F 72
Bunce's La. Wfd G—24Hc 45
Bundy's Way. Stai—65H 119
Bungalow Rd. SE25—70Ub 127
Bungalow Rd. Wok—96S 174
Bungalows, The. SW16—66Kb 126
Bungalows, The. Ilf—25Uc 46
Bunhill Row. EC1 —42Tb 83 (5F 195)
Bunhouse Pl. SW1 —50Jb 82 (7J 203)
★Bunish La. Sev—93Ee
Bunkers Hill. NW11—31Eb 61
Bunkers Hill. Belv—49Cd 88
Bunker's Hill. Sev—79De 155
Bunkers Hill. Sidc—62Bd 131
Bunns La. NW7—23Ua 40
Bunsen St. E3—40Ac 64
Bunten Meade. Slou—6F 72
Buntingbridge Rd. Ilf—29Tc 46
Bunting Clo. Mitc—71Hb 145
Bunton St. SE18—48Qc 86
Bunyan Ct. EC2—(7D 194)
Bunyan Rd. E17—27Ac 44
Bunyans Clo. Brtwd—23Yd 50
Bunyan's La. Wok—2A 188
Bunyard Dri. Wok—86E 156
Burbage Clo. SE1 —48Tb 83 (4F 207)
Burbage Clo. Wal X—3Bc 12
Burbage Rd.—58Sb 105
SE24 1-105 & 2-118
SE21 remainder
Burberry Clo. N Mald—68Ua 124
Burbridge Rd. Shep—70Q 120
Burbridge Way. N17—26Wb 43
Burcham St. E14—44Ec 84
Burcharbro Rd. SE2—51Zc 109
Burchell Ct. Bush, Wat—17Ea 20
Burchell Rd. E10—32Dc 64
Burchell Rd. SE15—53Xb 105
Burchetts Way. Shep—72R 140
Burchett Way. Romf—30Bd 47
Burch Rd. Grav—8B 114
Burchwall Clo. Romf—24Ed 48
Burcote. Wey—79T 140
Burcote Rd. SW18—59Fb 103
Burcott Gdns. Wey—79L 139
Burcott Rd. Purl—86Qb 164
Burden Clo. Bren—50La 78
Burdenshott Av. Rich—56Ra 101
Burden Way. E11—33Kc 65
Burder Clo. N1—37Ub 63
Burder Rd. N1—37Ub 63
Burdett Av. SW20—67Wa 124
Burdett Av. Grav—3N 137
Burdett Clo. Sidc—64Ad 131
Burdett M. W2—44Db 81
Burdett Rd.—42Ac 84
E3 1-207 & 2-230
E14 remainder
Burdett Rd. Croy—72Tb 147
Burdett Rd. Rich—54Pa 101
Burdett St. SE1—48Qb 82 (3K 205)
Burdock Clo. Croy—74Zb 148
Burdon La. Sutt—81Bb 163
Bure. Grays—8L 93
Burfield Clo. SW17—63Fb 125
Burfield Rd. Rick—15E 16
Burfield Rd. Wind—9L 95
Burford Clo. Dag—34Yc 67
Burford Clo. Ilf—29Sc 46
Burford Clo. Uxb—35N 55
Burford Gdns. N13—20Pb 24
Burford Gdns. Slou—3A 72
Burford La. Eps—83Ya 162
Burford Rd. E6—41Nc 86
Burford Rd. E15—39Fc 65
Burford Rd. SE6—61Bc 128
Burford Rd. Bren—50Na 79
Burford Rd. Brom—70Nc 130
Burford Rd. N Mald—73Wa 144
Burford Rd. Sutt—75Cb 145
Burford Way. Croy—79Ec 148
Burgate Clo. Dart—55Hd 110
Burges Clo. Horn—30Pd 49
Burges Rd. E6—38Nc 66
Burgess Av. NW9—30Ta 39
Burgess Av. Stanf—2N 93
Burgess Clo. Felt—63Aa 121
Burgess Hill. NW2—35Cb 61
Burgess Rd. E15—35Gc 65
Burgess Rd. Sutt—77Db 145
Burgess St. E14—43Cc 84
Burgett Rd. Slou—8F 72
Burghfield. Eps—87Va 162
Burghfield Rd. Grav—6B 136
Burgh Heath Rd. Eps—86Va 162
Burghill Rd. SE26—63Ac 128
Burghley Av. Borwd—15Sa 21
Burghley Av. N Mald—67Ta 123
Burghley Pl. Mitc—71Hb 145
Burghley Rd. E11—32Gc 65
Burghley Rd. N8—27Qb 42
Burghley Rd. NW5—35Kb 62
Burghley Rd. SW19—63Ab 124
Burgh Mt. Bans—87Bb 163
Burgh St. N1—40Rb 63 (1C 194)
Burgh Wood. Bans—87Ab 162
Burgon St. EC4—(3C 200)
Burgos Gro. SE10—53Dc 106
Burgoyne Rd. N4—30Rb 43
Burgoyne Rd. SE25—70Vb 127
Burgoyne Rd. SW9—55Pb 104
Burgoyne Rd. Sun—65V 120
Burgundy St. SE1 —50Vb 83 (7K 207)
Burham Clo. SE20—66Yb 128
Burhill Gro. Pinn—26Aa 37
Burhill Rd. W on T—80X 141
Burke Clo. SW15—56Ua 102
Burke St. E16—43Hc 85
Burland Rd. SW11—57Hb 103
Burland Rd. Brtwd—18Zd 33
Burland Rd. Romf—23Ed 48
Burlea Clo. W on T—78X 141
Burleigh Av. Sidc—57Vc 109
Burleigh Av. Wall—76Jb 146
Burleigh Clo. Wey—78K 139
Burleigh Gdns. N14—18Lb 24
Burleigh Gdns. Ashf—64S 120
Burleigh Pk. Cob—84Ba 159
Burleigh Rd. Enf—14Ub 25
Burleigh Rd. Sutt—74Ab 144
Burleigh Rd. Uxb—39R 56
Burleigh Rd. Wal X—4Ac 12
Burleigh Rd. Wey—78K 139
Burleigh St. WC2 —45Pb 82 (4H 199)
Burleigh Way. Enf—13Tb 25
Burleigh Way. Pot B—2Nb 10
Burley Clo. E4—22Cc 44
Burley Clo. SW16—68Mb 126
Burley Rd. E16—44Lc 85
Burlings La. Sev—89Vc 169
Burlington Arc. W1 —45Lb 82 (5B 198)
Burlington Av. Rich—53Qa 101
Burlington Av. Romf—30Dd 48
Burlington Av. Slou—7J 73
Burlington Clo. E6—44Nc 86
Burlington Clo. W9—42Cb 81
Burlington Clo. Felt—59T 98
Burlington Clo. Orp—75Rc 150
Burlington Gdns. W1 —45Lb 82 (5B 198)
Burlington Gdns. W3—46Sa 79
Burlington Gdns. W4—50Sa 79
Burlington Gdns. Romf—31Ad 67
Burlington La. W4—52Ta 101
Burlington M. W3—46Sa 79
Burlington Pl. SW6—54Ab 102
Burlington Pl. Wfd G—20Kc 27
Burlington Rise. Barn—18Gb 23
Burlington Rd. N10—27Jb 42
Burlington Rd. N17—25Wb 43
Burlington Rd. SW6—54Ab 102
Burlington Rd. W4—50Sa 79
Burlington Rd. Enf—11Tb 25
Burlington Rd. Iswth—53Fa 100
Burlington Rd. N Mald—70Va 124
Burlington Rd. Slou—7J 73
Burlington Rd. Slou—2A 72
(Burnham)
Burlington Rd. T Hth—68Sb 127
Burma M. N16—35Tb 63
Burma Rd. N16—35Tb 63
Burmarsh Ct. SE20—67Yb 128
Burma Ter. SE19—64Ub 127
Burmester Rd. SW17—62Eb 125
Burnaby Cres. W4—51Sa 101
Burnaby Gdns. W4—51Ra 101
Burnaby Rd. Grav—9A 114
Burnaby St. SW10—52Eb 103
Burnbrae Clo. N12—23Db 41
Burnbury Rd. SW12—60Lb 104
Burn Clo. Wat—13Fa 20
Burn Clo. Wey—77M 139
Burncroft Av. Enf—12Yb 26
Burnell Av. Rich—64La 122
Burnell Av. Well—54Wc 109
Burnell Gdns. Stan—26Ma 39
Burnell Rd. Sutt—77Db 145
Burnell Wlk. Brtwd—23Yd 50
Burnels Av. E6—41Qc 86
Burness Clo. N7—37Pb 62
Burness Clo. Uxb—40M 55
Burnet Gro. Eps—85Sa 161
Burnett Clo. E9—36Yb 64
Burnett Rd. Eri—51Md 111
Burnetts Rd. Wind—3C 94
Burney Av. Surb—71Pa 143
Burney Clo. Lea—97Ea 176
Burney Dri. Lou—12Rc 28
Burney St. SE10—52Ec 106
Burnfoot Av. SW6—53Ab 102
Burnham Av. Uxb—35S 56
Burnham Clo. Enf—10Ub 11
Burnham Clo. Wind—4B 94
Burnham Clo. Wok—6A 188
Burnham Cres. E11—28Lc 45
Burnham Cres. Dart—56Ld 111
Burnham Dri. Wor Pk—75Za 144
Burnham Gdns. Hay—48T 76
Burnham Gdns. Houn—53X 99
Burnham La. Slou—3B 72
Burnham Rd. E4—22Bc 44
Burnham Rd. Dag—38Xc 67
Burnham Rd. Dart—56Ld 111
Burnham Rd. Mord—70Db 125
Burnham Rd. Romf—27Fd 48
Burnham Rd. Sidc—61Ad 131
Burnham Rd. Wok—6A 188
Burnhams Rd. Lea—96Aa 175
Burnham St. E2—41Yb 84
Burnham St. King—67Qa 123
Burnham Ter. Dart—57Md 111
Burnham Way. W13—49Ka 78
Burnhill Rd. Beck—68Cc 128
Burnley Clo. Wat—22Y 37
Burnley Rd. NW10—36Va 60
Burnley Rd. SW9—54Pb 104
Burnsall St. SW3 —50Gb 81 (7E 202)
Burns Av. Felt—58W 98
Burns Av. Sidc—58Xc 109
Burns Av. S'hall—45Ca 77
Burns Clo. Eri—53Hd 110
Burns Clo. Hay—43V 76
Burns Clo. Lea—87Fa 160
Burns Clo. Well—53Vc 109
Burn Side. N9—20Yb 26
Burnside. Asht—90Pa 161
Burnside Clo. Barn—13Cb 23
Burnside Clo. Twic—58Ja 100
Burnside Cres. Wemb—39Ma 59
Burnside Rd. Dag—33Yc 67
Burns Pl. Til—3D 114
Burns Rd. NW10—39Va 60
Burns Rd. SW11—54Hb 103
Burns Rd. W13—47Ka 78
Burns Rd. Wemb—40Na 59
Burns Way. Brtwd—16Fe 33
Burns Way. Houn—54Z 99
Burnt Ash Hill. SE12—58Hc 107
Burnt Ash La. Brom—65Jc 129
Burnt Ash Rd. SE12—57Hc 107
Burnt Comn. Clo. Wok—97H 173
Burnt Comn. La. Wok—97J 173
Burntfarm Ride. Enf & Wal X —6Qb 10
Burntfarm Ride. Wal X—3Rb 11
Burnthouse La. Dart—63Nd 133
Burnthwaite Rd. SW6—52Bb 103
Burnt Oak B'way. Edgw—24Ra 39
Burnt Oak Fields. Edgw—25Sa 39
Burnt Oak La. Sidc—58Wc 109
Burntwood Av. Horn—30Md 49
Burntwood Clo. SW18—60Gb 103
Burntwood Clo. Brtwd—30Fe 51
Burntwood Clo. Cat—93Wb 181
Burntwood Grange Rd. SW18 —60Gb 103
Burntwood La. SW17—62Eb 125
Burntwood La. Cat—94Ub 181
Burntwood Rd. Sev—100Kd 187
Burn Wlk. Slou—1A 72
Burnway. Horn—31Nd 69
Buross St. E1—44Xb 83
Burrage Gro. SE18—49Sc 86
Burrage Pl. SE18—50Rc 86
Burrage Rd. SE18—50Sc 86
Burrard Rd. E16—44Kc 85
Burrard Rd. NW6—35Cb 61
Burr Clo. E1—46Wb 83
Burr Clo. Bexh—55Bd 109
Burrel Clo. Edgw—19Ra 21
Burrell Clo. Croy—72Ac 148
Burrell Row. Beck—68Cc 128
Burrell St. SE1—46Rb 83 (6B 200)
Burrfield Dri. Orp—71Zc 151
Burritt Rd. King—68Qa 123
Burroughs Gdns. NW4—28Xa 40
Burroughs, The. NW4—28Xa 40
Burroway Rd. Slou—48D 74
Burrow Clo. Chig—22Vc 47
Burrow Grn. Chig—22Vc 47
Burrow Rd. Chig—22Vc 47
Burrows Clo. Lea—96Ba 175
Burrows Hill Clo. Stai—55L 97
Burrows Hill La. Stai—56L 97
Burrows M. SE1—47Rb 83 (1B 206)
Burrows Rd. NW10—41Ya 80
Burrow Wlk. SE21—59Sb 105
Burr Rd. SW18—60Cb 103
Bursar St. SE1—(7H 201)
Bursdon Clo. Sidc—61Vc 131
Burses Way. Brtwd—17De 33
Bursland Rd. Enf—14Zb 26
Burslem Av. Ilf—23Wc 47
Burslem St. E1—44Wb 83
Burstead Clo. Cob—84Z 159
Burstock Rd. SW15—56Ab 102
Burston Rd. SW15—57Za 102
Burstow Rd. SW20—67Ab 124
Burtenshaw Rd. Th Dit—72Ja 142
Burtley Clo. N4—32Sb 63
Burton Av. Wat—14W 18
Burton Clo. NW7—21Za 40
Burton Clo. Chess—80Ma 143
Burton Gdns. Houn—53Ba 99
Burton Gro. SE17 —50Tb 83 (7F 207)
Burtonhole La. NW7—22Ya 40
Burtonhole La. Farm Est. NW7 —21Za 40
Burton La. SW9—54Qb 104
Burton La. Wal X—1Ub 11
Burton M. SW1—49Jb 82 (6J 203)
Burton Pl. WC1—42Mb 82 (4E 192)
Burton Rd. E18—27Kc 45
Burton Rd. NW6—38Bb 61
Burton Rd. SW9—54Qb 104 & 54Rb 105
Burton Rd. King—66Na 123
Burton Rd. Lou—14Sc 28
Burtons Ct. E15—38Fc 65

Burtons La.—Campion Ter.

Burtons La. Chal—13A 16
Burtons La. Chal & Rick—14A 16
Burton's Rd. Hmptn—63Da 121
Burton St. WC1—42Mb 82 (4E 192)
Burton Way. Wind—5C 94
Burt Rd. E16—46Lc 85
Burtwell La. SE27—63Tb 127
Burwash Rd. SE18—50Tc 86
Burwell Av. Gnfd—37Ga 58
Burwell Clo. E1—44Xb 83
Burwell Rd. E10—32Ac 64
Burwell Wlk. E3—42Cc 84
Burwood Av. Brom—75Kc 149
Burwood Av. Kenl—86Rb 165
Burwood Av. Pinn—29Y 37
Burwood Clo. Surb—74Qa 143
Burwood Clo. W on T—79Y 141
Burwood Gdns. Rain—41Hd 88
Burwood Pk. Rd. W on T—77X 141
Burwood Pl. W2—44Gb 81 (2E 196)
Burwood Rd. W on T—80U 140
Bury Av. Hay—40U 56
Bury Av. Ruis—30S 36
Bury Clo. Wok—4G 188
Bury Ct. EC3—44Ub 83 (2J 201)
Bury Grn. Rd. Wal X—4Wb 11
Bury Grn. Rd. Wal X—3Wb 11
Bury Gro. Mord—71Db 145
Bury Hall Vs. N9—17Vb 25
Bury La. Epp—1Tc 14
Bury La. Rick—18M 17
Bury La. Wok—4F 188
Bury Meadows. Rick—18M 17
Bury Pl. WC1—43Nb 82 (1F 199)
Bury Rd. E4—13Fc 27
Bury Rd. N22—27Qb 42
Bury Rd. Dag—36Dd 68
Bury Rd. Epp—3Uc 14
Bury St. EC3—44Ub 83 (3J 201)
Bury St. N9—17Vb 25
Bury St. SW1—46Lb 82 (6B 198)
Bury St. Ruis—29S 36
Bury St. W. N9—17Tb 25
Bury Wlk. SW3—49Gb 81 (6D 202)
Busby M. NW5—37Mb 62
Busby Pl. NW5—37Mb 62
Busby St. E2—42Vb 83
Bushbarns. Wal X—1Wb 11
Bushberry Rd. E9—37Ac 64
Bush Clo. Ilf—29Tc 46
Bush Clo. Wey—78L 139
Bush Cotts. SW18—57Cb 103
Bushell Clo. SW2—61Pb 126
Bushell Grn. Bush, Wat—19Fa 20
Bushell St. E1—46Wb 83
Bushell Way. Chst—64Qc 130
Bush Elms Rd. Horn—31Jd 68
Bushetts Gro. Red—100Kb 180
Bushey Av. E18—27Hc 45
Bushey Av. Orp—73Tc 150
Bushey Clo. Uxb—33Q 56
Bushey Clo. Whyt—88Vb 165
Bushey Ct. SW20—68Xa 124
Bushey Down. SW12—61Kb 126
Bushey Gro. Rd. Bush, Wat—14Z 19
Bushey Hall Dri. Bush, Wat
—14Aa 19
Bushey Hall Rd. Bush, Wat—14Z 19
Bushey Hill Rd. SE5—53Ub 105
Bushey La. Sutt—77Cb 145
Bushey Mill Cres. Wat—9Y 5
Bushey Mill La. Wat & Bush, Wat
—9Y 5
Bushey Rd. E13—40Lc 65
Bushey Rd. N15—30Ub 43
Bushey Rd. SW20—69Xa 124
Bushey Rd. Croy—75Cc 148
Bushey Rd. Sutt—77Cb 145
Bushey Rd. Uxb—33Q 56
Bushey Shaw. Asht—89La 160
Bushey View Wlk. Wat—12Z 19
Bushey Way. Beck—72Fc 149
Bush Fair Ct. N14—16Kb 24
Bushfield Clo. Edgw—19Ra 21
Bushfield Cres. Edgw—19Ra 21
Bushfields. Lou—15Qc 28
Bushfield Wlk. Swans—58Ae 113
Bush Gro. NW9—31Sa 59
Bush Gro. Stan—24Ma 39
Bushgrove Rd. Dag—35Zc 67
Bush Hill. N21—17Sb 25
Bush Hill Pde. Enf—17Tb 25
Bush Hill Rd. N21—16Tb 25
Bush Hill Rd. Harr—30Pa 39
Bush Industrial Est. N19—34Mb 62
Bush La. EC4—45Tb 83 (4F 201)
Bush La. Wok—96F 172
Bushmoor Cres. SE18—52Rc 108
Bushnell Rd. SW17—62Kb 126
Bushrise. Wat—8X 5
Bush Rd. E8—39Xb 63
Bush Rd. E11—31Hc 65
Bush Rd. SE8—49Zb 84
Bush Rd. Buck H—21Mc 45
Bush Rd. Rich—51Pa 101
Bush Rd. Shep—71P 139
Bushway. Dag—35Zc 67
Bushwood. E11—32Hc 65
Bushwood Rd. Rich—51Qa 101
Bushy Lees. Sidc—58Vc 109
Bushy Pk. Gdns. Tedd—64Fa 122
Bushy Pk. Rd. Tedd—66Ka 122
Bushy Rd. Hay—49U 76
Bushy Rd. Lea—94Da 175
Bushy Rd. Tedd—65Ha 122
Butcher Row—45Zb 84
E1 4-12
E14 remainder
Butchers Hill. Grav—4N 137
Butchers Rd. E16—44Jc 85
Butcher Wlk. Swans—59Ae 113
Bute Av. Rich—61Na 123
Bute Gdns. W6—49Za 80
Bute Gdns. Wall—78Lb 146
Bute Gdns. W. Wall—78Lb 146
Bute Rd. Croy—74Qb 146
Bute Rd. Ilf—29Rc 46
Bute Rd. Wall—77Lb 146
Bute St. SW7—49Fb 81 (5B 202)
Bute Wlk. N1—37Tb 63
Butler Av. Harr—31Fa 58
Butler Pl. SW1—(3D 204)
Butler Rd. NW10—38Ua 60
Butler Rd. Dag—35Xc 67
Butler Rd. Harr—31Ea 58
Butlers Clo. Wind—4B 94
Butlers Dene Rd. Cat—92Bc 182
Butlers Dri. E4—10Ec 12
Butler's Pl. Long, Dart—76Ae 155
Butler St. E2—41Yb 84
Butler St. Uxb—42R 76
Butler Wlk. Grays—49Fe 91
Buttercross La. Epp—2Wc 15
Buttercup Clo. Romf—25Md 49
Butterfields. E17—29Ec 44
Butterfield Sq. E6—44Pc 86
Butterfly La. SE9—58Rc 108
Butterfly La. Borwd—13Ka 20
Butterfly Wlk. Warl—92Yb 182
Butter Hill. Wall—76Jb 146
Buttermere Av. Slou—3A 72
Buttermere Clo. Mord—72Za 144
Buttermere Dri. SW15—57Ab 102
Buttermere Gdns. Purl—85Tb 165
Buttermere Rd. Orp—70Zc 131
Buttermere Wlk. E8—37Vb 63
Butterwick. W6—49Za 80
Butterwick. Wat—8Aa 5
Buttesland St. N1
—41Tb 83 (3G 195)
Buttfield Clo. Dag—37Dd 68
Buttlehide. Rick—22F 34
Buttmarsh Clo. SE18—50Rc 86
Button St. Swan—68Ld 133
Buttsbury Rd. Ilf—36Sc 66
Butts Cotts. Felt—62Aa 121
Butts Cres. Felt—62Ca 121
Butts Grn. Rd. Horn—30Md 49
Butts La. Stanf—2K 93
Buttsmead. N'wd—24S 36
Butts Rd. Brom—64Gc 129
Butts Rd. Stanf—2L 93
Butts Rd. Wok—89A 156
Butts, The. Bren—51Ma 101
Butts, The. Sev—89Kd 171
Butts, The. Sun—69Y 121
Buxted Clo. E8—38Vb 63
Buxted Rd. N12—22Gb 41
Buxton Av. Cat—93Ub 181
Buxton Clo. Wfd G—23Mc 45
Buxton Ct. N1—(3E 194)
Buxton Cres. Sutt—77Ab 144
Buxton Dri. E11—28Gc 45
Buxton Dri. N Mald—68Ta 123
Buxton Gdns. W3—45Ra 79
Buxton La. Cat—92Ub 181
Buxton Path. Wat—20Y 19
Buxton Rd. E4—17Fc 27
Buxton Rd. E6—41Nc 86
Buxton Rd. E15—36Gc 65
Buxton Rd. E17—28Ac 44
Buxton Rd. N19—32Mb 62
Buxton Rd. NW2—37Xa 60
Buxton Rd. SW14—55Ua 102
Buxton Rd. Ashf—64M 119
Buxton Rd. Epp—8Uc 14
Buxton Rd. Eri—52Fd 110
Buxton Rd. Grays—7A 92
Buxton Rd. Ilf—30Uc 46
Buxton Rd. T Hth—71Rb 147
Buxton Rd. Wal A—5Jc 13
Buxton St. E1—42Vb 83
Buzzard Creek Indusrial Est.
Bark—43Wc 87
Byam St. SW6—54Eb 103
Byards Croft. SW16—67Mb 126
Byatt Wlk. Hmptn—65Aa 121
Bycliffe Ter. Grav—9B 114
Bycroft Rd. S'hall—42Ca 77
Bycroft St. SE20—66Zb 128
Bycullah Av. Enf—13Rb 25
Bycullah Rd. Enf—12Rb 25
Byegrove Rd. SW19—65Fb 125
Byers Clo. Pot B—6Eb 9
Bye, The. W3—44Ua 80
Bye Ways. Twic—62Da 121
Byeways, The. Surb—71Qa 143
Byeway, The. SW14—55Sa 101
Byeway, The. Eps—77Va 144
Bye Way, The. Harr—25Ha 38
Byeway, The. Rick—19N 17
Byfeld Gdns. SW13—53Wa 102
Byfield Ct. Brtwd—30Ee 51
Byfield Pas. Iswth—55Ja 100
Byfield Rd. Iswth—55Ja 100
Byfleet Corner. Wey—85J 157
Byfleet Rd. Wey—80M 139
Byfleet Rd. Wey & Cob—84Q 158
Byford Clo. E15—38Gc 65
Byford Ho. Barn—14Za 22
Bygrove. Croy—80Dc 148
Bygrove St. E14—44Dc 84
Byland Clo. N21—17Pb 24
Bylands. Wok—90C 156
Bylands Clo. SE2—48Xc 87
Byne Rd. SE26—65Yb 128
Byne Rd. Cars—75Gb 145
Bynes Rd. S Croy—80Tb 147
Byng Dri. Pot B—3Cb 9
Byng Pl. WC1—42Mb 82 (6E 192)
Byng Rd. Barn—12Za 22
Byng St. E14—47Cc 84
Bynon Av. Bexh—55Bd 109
By-Pass Rd. Stanf—1J 93
Byrd Way. Stanf—1L 93
Byrne Rd. SW12—60Kb 104
Byron Av. E12—37Nc 66
Byron Av. E18—27Hc 45
Byron Av. NW9—28Ra 39
Byron Av. Borwd—15Qa 21
Byron Av. Coul—87Nb 164
Byron Av. Houn—54W 98
Byron Av. N Mald—71Wa 144
Byron Av. Sutt—77Fb 145
Byron Av. Wat—11Z 19
Byron Av. E. Sutt—77Fb 145
Byron Clo. E8—39Wb 63
Byron Clo. N2—30Fb 41
Byron Clo. SE28—46Yc 87
Byron Clo. Hmptn—63Ba 121
Byron Clo. W on T—74Aa 141
Byron Ct. Enf—12Rb 25
Byron Ct. Wal X—1Xb 11
Byron Ct. Wok—5B 188
Byron Gdns. Sutt—77Fb 145
Byron Gdns. Til—3E 114
Byron Hill Rd. Harr—32Fa 58
Byron Mans. Upm—34Sd 70
Byron Pl. Lea—94Ka 176
Byron Rd. E10—32Dc 64
Byron Rd. E17—27Cc 44
Byron Rd. NW2—33Xa 60
Byron Rd. NW7—22Wa 40
Byron Rd. W5—46Pa 79
Byron Rd. Brtwd—17Fe 33
Byron Rd. Dart—56Rd 111
Byron Rd. Harr—30Ga 38
(Greenhill)
Byron Rd. Harr—26Ha 38
(Wealdstone)
Byron Rd. S Croy—82Xb 165
Byron Rd. Wemb—33La 58
Byron Rd. Wey—77N 139
Byron St. E14—44Ec 84
Byron Way. Hay—42V 76
Byron Way. N'holt—41Aa 77
Byron Way. Romf—25Ld 49
Byron Way. W Dray—49P 75
Bysouth Clo. Ilf—25Rc 46
By the Wood. Wat—19Z 19
Bythorn St. SW9—55Pb 104
Byton Rd. SW17—65Hb 125
Byttom Hill. Dor—98La 176
Byward Av. Felt—58Y 99
Byward St. EC3—45Ub 83 (5J 201)
Bywater St. SW3
—50Hb 81 (7F 203)
Byway, The. E11—29Lc 45
Byways, The. Asht—90Ma 161
Byway, The. Pot B—5Cb 9
Byway, The. Sutt—81Fb 163
Bywell Pl. W1—(1B 198)
Bywood Av. Croy—72Yb 148
Bywood Clo. Kenl—87Rb 165
Byworth Wlk. N19—32Nb 62
Cabbell Pl. Wey—77L 139
Cabbell St. NW1—43Gb 81 (1D 196)
Cabborns Cres. Stanf—3M 93
Cabinet Way. E4—22Bc 44
Cable St. E1—45Wb 83
Cabot Way. E6—39Mc 65
Cabrera Av. Vir W—71A 138
Cabul Rd. SW11—54Gb 103
Cacket's La. Sev—87Tc 168
Cacketts Cotts. West—98Yc 185
Cactus Wlk. W12—44Va 80
Cadbury Clo. Iswth—53Ja 100
Cadbury Clo. Sun—66U 120
Cadbury Rd. Sun—66U 120
Cadbury Wlk. SE16
—49Vb 83 (5K 207)
Cadbury Way. SE16—49Wb 83
Caddington Clo. Barn—15Gb 23
Caddington Rd. NW2—34Ab 60
Caddis Clo. Stan—24Ha 38
Cade La. Sev—100Ld 187
Cadell Clo. E2—40Vb 63 (2K 195)
Cade Rd. SE10—53Fc 107
Cader Rd. SW18—58Eb 103
Cadet Pl. SE10—50Gc 85
Cadiz Rd. Dag—38Ed 68
Cadiz St. SE17—50Sb 83 (7E 206)
Cadley Ter. SE23—61Yb 128
Cadlocks Hill. Sev—82Bd 169
Cadmer Clo. N Mald—70Ua 124
Cadmore Ct. Wal X—1Zb 12
Cadmore La. Wal X—1Zb 12
Cadogan Av. Brtwd—30Fe 51
Cadogan Av. Dart—59Td 112
Cadogan Clo. E9—38Bc 64
Cadogan Clo. Beck—67Fc 129
Cadogan Clo. Harr—35Da 57
Cadogan Clo. Tedd—64Ga 122
Cadogan Ct. Sutt—79Db 145
Cadogan Gdns. E18—27Kc 45
Cadogan Gdns. N3—25Db 41
Cadogan Gdns. N21—15Qb 24
Cadogan Gdns. SW3
—49Hb 81 (5G 203)
Cadogan Ga. SW1
—49Hb 81 (5G 203)
Cadogan La. SW1
—48Jb 82 (4H 203)
Cadogan Pl. SW1
—48Hb 81 (3G 203)
Cadogan Rd. Surb—71Ma 143
Cadogan Sq. SW1
—48Hb 81 (4F 203)
Cadogan St. SW3
—49Hb 81 (6F 203)
Cadogan Ter. E9—37Bc 64
Cadoxton Av. N15—30Vb 43
Cadwallon Rd. SE9—61Rc 130
Caedmon Rd. N7—35Pb 62
Caenshill Rd. Wey—80Q 140
Caenswood Hill. Wey—82Q 158
Caenwood Clo. Wey—79Q 140
Caen Wood Rd. Asht—90La 160
Caerleon Clo. Sidc—64Yc 131
Caerleon Ter. SE2—49Xc 87
Caernarvon Clo. Horn—32Qd 69
Caernarvon Clo. Mitc—69Nb 126
Caernarvon Dri. Ilf—25Qc 46
Caesars Wlk. Mitc—71Hb 145
Caesars Way. Shep—72T 140
Cage Pond Rd. Shen, Rad—5Pa 7
Cages Wood Dri. Slou—5F 52
Cahill St. EC1—42Sb 83 (6F 195)
Cahir St. E14—49Dc 84
Caillard Rd. Wey—83N 157
Cain's La. Felt—57U 98
Caird St. W10—41Ab 80
Cairn Av. W5—46Ma 79
Cairndale Clo. Brom—66Hc 129
Cairnfield Av. NW2—34Ua 60
Cairngorm Pl. Slou—2H 73
Cairns Av. Wfd G—23Pc 46
Cairns Clo. Dart—57Md 111
Cairns Rd. SW11—57Gb 103
Cairn Way. Stan—23Ha 38
Cairo New Rd. Croy—75Rb 147
Cairo Rd. E17—28Cc 44
Caishowe Rd. Borwd—11Ra 21
Caistor M. SW12—59Kb 104
Caistor Pk. Rd. E15—39Hc 65
Caistor Rd. SW12—59Kb 104
Caithness Gdns. Sidc—58Vc 109
Caithness Rd. W14—48Za 80
Caithness Rd. Mitc—66Kb 126
Calabria Rd. N5—37Rb 63
Calais Ga. SE5—53Rb 105
Calais St. SE5—53Rb 105
Calbourne Av. Horn—36Kd 69
Calbourne Rd. SW12—59Hb 103
Calbroke Rd. Slou—2D 72
Calcott Clo. Brtwd—18Xd 32
Calcott Wlk. SE9—63Nc 130
Calcutta Rd. Til—4B 114
Caldbeck. Wal A—6Fc 13
Caldbeck Av. Wor Pk—74Xa 144
Caldecote Gdns. Bush, Wat
—17Ga 20
Caldecote La. Bush, Wat—16Ha 20
Caldecot Rd. SE5—54Sb 105
Caldecott Way. E5—34Zb 64
Calder. Grays—9L 93
Calder Av. Gnfd—40Ha 58
Calder Clo. Enf—13Ub 25
Calder Ct. Slou—50B 74
Calder Gdns. Edgw—27Qa 39
Calderon Pl. W10—43Ya 80
Calderon Rd. E11—35Ec 64
Calder Rd. Mord—71Eb 145
Caldervale Rd. SW4—57Mb 104
Calderwood St. SE18—49Qc 86
Caldew St. SE5—51Tb 105
Caldwell Rd. Stanf—2K 93
Caldwell Rd. Wat—21Z 37
Caldwell St. SW9—52Pb 104
Caldwell Yd. EC4
—45Sb 83 (4D 200)
Caldy Rd. Belv—48Dd 88
Caldy Wlk. N1—37Sb 63
Caleb St. SE1—47Sb 83 (1E 206)
Caledonian Rd.—40Nb 62 (2G 193)
N1 1-351 & 2-400
N7 remainder
Caledonia Rd. Stai—60N 97
Caledonia St. N1
—40Nb 62 (2G 193)
Caledon Rd. E6—39Pc 66
Caledon Rd. Wall—77Jb 146
Cale St. SW3—50Gb 81 (7D 202)
Caletock Way. SE10—50Hc 85
Calfstock La. S Dar, Dart
—71Pd 153
California La. Bush, Wat—18Fa 20
California Rd. N Mald—69Sa 123
Caling Croft. Long, Dart—74Be 155
(in two parts)
Caliph Clo. Grav—2H 137
Callaghan Clo. SE13—56Gc 107
Callander Rd. SE6—61Dc 128
Callan Gro. S Ock—45Xd 90
Callard Av. N13—21Rb 43
Callcott Rd. NW6—38Bb 61
Callcott St. W8—46Cb 81
Calley Down Cres. Croy—82Fc 167
Callingham Clo. E14—43Bc 84
Callis Farm Clo. Stai—58N 97
Callis Rd. E17—30Bc 44
Callow Field. Purl—85Qb 164
Callow Hill. Vir W—9N 117
Callow St. SW3—51Fb 103
Calluna Ct. Wok—90B 156
Calmington Rd. SE5—51Ub 105
Calmont Rd. Brom—65Fc 129
Calmore Clo. Horn—36Ld 69
Calne Av. Ilf—25Rc 46
Calonne Rd. SW19—63Za 124
Calshot Rd. Houn—54Q 98
(in two parts)
Calshot St. N1—40Pb 62 (1H 193)
Calshot Way. Enf—13Rb 25
Calthorpe Gdns. Edgw—22Na 39
Calthorpe Gdns. Sutt—76Eb 145
Calthorpe St. WC1
—42Pb 82 (5J 193)
Calton Av. SE21—58Ub 105
Calton Rd. Barn—16Eb 23
Calverley Clo. Beck—65Dc 128
Calverley Cres. Dag—33Cd 68
Calverley Gdns. Harr—31Ma 59
Calverley Gro. N19—32Mb 62
Calverley Rd. Eps—79Wa 144
Calvert Av. E2—41Vb 83 (4J 195)
Calvert Clo. Belv—49Cd 88
Calvert Clo. Sidc—65Ad 131
Calverton Rd. E6—39Qc 66
Calvert Rd. SE10—50Hc 85
Calvert Rd. Barn—12Za 22
Calvert Rd. Lea—100X 175
Calvert's Bldgs. SE1—(7F 201)
Calvert St. NW1—39Jb 62
Calvin Clo. Orp—69Zc 131
Calvin St. E1—42Vb 83 (6K 195)
Calydon Rd. SE7—50Kc 85
Camac Rd. Twic—60Fa 100
Cambalt Rd. SW15—57Za 102
Camberley Av. SW20—68Xa 124
Camberley Av. Enf—14Ub 25
Camberley Rd. Houn—55Q 98
Camberl Way. SE3—56Kc 107
Camberwell Chu. St. SE5
—53Tb 105
Camberwell Glebe. SE5—53Ub 105
Camberwell Grn. SE5—53Tb 105
Camberwell Gro. SE5—53Tb 105
Camberwell New Rd. SE5
—52Qb 104
Camberwell Pas. SE5—53Sb 105
Camberwell Rd. SE5—51Sb 105
Camberwell Sta. Rd. SE5
—53Sb 105
Cambeys Rd. Dag—36Dd 68
Camborne Av. W13—47Ka 78
Camborne Av. Romf—24Nd 49
Camborne M. W11—44Ab 80
Camborne Rd. SW18—59Cb 103
Camborne Rd. Croy—73Wb 147
Camborne Rd. Houn—55Q 98
Camborne Rd. Mord—71Za 144
Camborne Rd. Sidc—62Yc 131
Camborne Rd. Sutt—80Db 145
Camborne Rd. Well—54Vc 109
Camborne Way. Houn—53Ca 99
Camborne Way. Romf—24Nd 49
Cambourne Av. N9—17Zb 26
Cambourne Wlk. Rich—58Ma 101
Cambray Rd. SW12—60Lb 104
Cambray Rd. Orp—73Vc 151
Cambria Clo. Houn—56Ca 99
Cambria Clo. Sidc—60Tc 108
Cambria Ct. Slou—7N 73
Cambria Cres. Grav—3G 136
Cambria Gdns. Stai—59N 97
Cambrian Av. Ilf—29Uc 46
Cambrian Clo. SE27—62Rb 127
Cambrian Clo. Grav—9C 114
Cambrian Rd. E10—32Cc 64
Cambrian Rd. Rich—58Pa 101
Cambria Rd. SE5—55Sb 105
Cambria St. SW6—52Db 103
Cambridge Av. NW6—40Cb 61
Cambridge Av. Gnfd—36Ha 58
Cambridge Av. N Mald—68Ua 124
Cambridge Av. Romf—27Ld 49
Cambridge Av. Slou—4E 72
Cambridge Av. Slou—10A 52
(Burnham)
Cambridge Av. Well—56Vc 109
Cambridge Barracks Rd. SE18
—49Pc 86
Cambridge Cir. WC2
—44Mb 82 (3E 198)
Cambridge Clo. SW20—67Xa 124
Cambridge Clo. Houn—56Aa 99
Cambridge Clo. Wal X—1Yb 12
Cambridge Clo. W Dray—51M 97
Cambridge Clo. Wok—6C 188
Cambridge Cotts. Rich—51Qa 101
Cambridge Cres. E2—40Xb 63
Cambridge Cres. Tedd—64Ja 122
Cambridge Dri. SE12—57Jc 107
Cambridge Dri. Pot B—3Za 8
Cambridge Dri. Ruis—33Y 57
Cambridge Gdns. N17—24Tb 43
Cambridge Gdns. N21—17Tb 25
Cambridge Gdns. NW6—40Cb 61
Cambridge Gdns. W10—44Za 80
Cambridge Gdns. Enf—12Wb 25
Cambridge Gdns. Grays—9C 92
Cambridge Gdns. King—68Qa 123
Cambridge Ga. NW1
—42Kb 82 (5K 191)
Cambridge Ga. M. NW1
—42Kb 82 (5A 192)
Cambridge Grn. SE9—60Rc 108
Cambridge Gro. SE20—67Xb 127
Cambridge Gro. W6—49Xa 80
Cambridge Gro. Rd. King
(in two parts) —69Qa 123
Cambridge Heath Rd.—42Xb 83
E1 1-183 & 2-154a
E2 remainder
Cambridge Lodge Vs. E8—39Xb 63
Cambridge Pde. Enf—11Wb 25
Cambridge Pk. E11—31Jc 65
Cambridge Pk. Twic—58La 100
Cambridge Pl. NW6—41Cb 81
Cambridge Pl. W8—47Db 81
Cambridge Rd. E4—18Fc 27
Cambridge Rd. E11—30Hc 45
Cambridge Rd. NW6—41Cb 81
(in two parts)
Cambridge Rd. SE20—69Xb 127
Cambridge Rd. SW11—53Hb 103
Cambridge Rd. SW13—54Va 102
Cambridge Rd. SW20—67Wa 124
Cambridge Rd. W7—47Ha 78
Cambridge Rd. Ashf—66S 120
Cambridge Rd. Bark—38Sc 66
Cambridge Rd. Brom—66Jc 129
Cambridge Rd. Cars—79Gb 145
Cambridge Rd. Hmptn—66Ba 121
Cambridge Rd. Harr—29Ca 37
Cambridge Rd. Houn—56Aa 99
Cambridge Rd. Ilf—32Uc 66
Cambridge Rd. King—68Pa 123
Cambridge Rd. Mitc—69Lb 126
Cambridge Rd. N Mald—70Ua 124
Cambridge Rd. Rich—52Qa 101
Cambridge Rd. Sidc—63Uc 130
Cambridge Rd. S'hall—46Ba 77
Cambridge Rd. Tedd—63Ja 122
Cambridge Rd. Twic—58Ma 101
Cambridge Rd. Uxb—37M 55
Cambridge Rd. W on T—72X 141
Cambridge Rd. Wat—14Y 19
Cambridge Rd. N. W4—50Ra 79
Cambridge Rd. S. W4—50Ra 79
Cambridge Row. SE18—50Rc 86
Cambridge Sq. W2
—44Gb 81 (2D 196)
Cambridge St. SW1
—49Kb 82 (7A 204)
Cambridge Ter. N9—17Vb 25
Cambridge Ter. NW1
—41Kb 82 (4K 191)
Cambridge Ter. M. NW1
—41Kb 82 (4A 192)
Cambus Rd. E16—43Jc 85
Camdale Rd. SE18—52Vc 109
Camden Av. Felt—60Y 99
Camden Av. Hay—45Z 77
Camden Clo. Chst—67Sc 130
Camden Clo. Grays—9D 92
Camden Gdns. NW1—38Kb 62
Camden Gdns. Sutt—78Db 145
Camden Gdns. T Hth—69Rb 127
Camden Gro. Chst—65Rc 130
Camden High St. NW1
—39Kb 62 (1B 192)
Camden Hill Rd. SE19—65Ub 127
Camdenhurst St. E14—44Ac 84
Camden La. N7—36Mb 62
Camden Lock Pl. NW1—38Kb 62
Camden M. NW1—37Mb 62
Camden Pk. Rd. NW1—37Mb 62
Camden Pk. Rd. Chst—66Pc 130
Camden Pas. N1—39Rb 63 (1B 194)
Camden Rd. E11—30Kc 45
Camden Rd. E17—30Bc 44
Camden Rd.—38Lb 62
NW1 1-227 & 2a-282
N7 remainder
Camden Rd. Bex—60Bd 109
Camden Rd. Cars—77Hb 145
Camden Rd. Sev—94Kd 187
Camden Rd. Sutt—78Db 145
Camden Row. SE3—54Gc 107
Camden Row. Pinn—27Y 37
Camden Sq. NW1—37Mb 62
Camden Sq. SE15—53Vb 105
Camden St. NW1
—38Lb 62 (1C 192)
Camden Ter. NW1—37Mb 62
Camden Ter. Sev—93Pd 187
Camden Wlk. N1
—39Rb 63 (1B 194)
Camden Way. Chst—66Qc 130
Camden Way. T Hth—69Rb 127
Camelford Ct. W11—44Ab 80
Camelford Wlk. W11—44Ab 80
Camellia Clo. Romf—25Nd 49
Camellia Pl. Twic—59Da 99
Camellia St. SW8—52Nb 104
Camelot Clo. SW19—63Cb 125
Camelot Clo. West—88Lc 167
Camel Rd. E16—46Nc 86
Camera Pl. SW10—51Fb 103
Cameron Clo. N18—21Xb 43
Cameron Clo. N20—19Fb 23
Cameron Clo. Bex—62Gd 132
Cameron Clo. Brtwd—21Zd 51
Cameron Dri. Wal X—6Zb 12
Cameron Pl. E1—44Xb 83
Cameron Rd. SE6—61Bc 128
Cameron Rd. Brom—71Jc 149
Cameron Rd. Croy—72Rb 147
Cameron Rd. Ilf—32Uc 66
Cameron Ter. SE12—62Kc 129
Camerton Clo. E8—37Vb 63
Cam Grn. S Ock—44Xd 90
Camilla Clo. Lea—97Da 175
Camilla Rd. SE16—49Xb 83
Camlan Rd. Brom—63Hc 129
Camlet St. E2—42Vb 83 (5K 195)
Camlet Way. Barn—12Cb 23
Camley St. NW1
—38Mb 62 (1E 192)
Camm Av. Wind—5C 94
Camm Gdns. King—68Pa 123
Camm Gdns. Th Dit—73Ha 142
Camomile Av. Mitc—67Hb 125
Camomile St. EC3
—44Ub 83 (2J 201)
Campana Rd. SW6—53Cb 103
Campbell Av. Ilf—28Sc 46
Campbell Av. Wok—93B 172
Campbell Clo. SE18—53Qc 108
Campbell Clo. Romf—23Gd 48
Campbell Clo. Ruis—30W 36
Campbell Clo. Twic—61Fa 122
Campbell Croft. Edgw—22Qa 39
Campbell Rd. E3—41Cc 84
Campbell Rd. E6—39Nc 66
Campbell Rd. E15—35Hc 65
Campbell Rd. E17—28Bc 44
Campbell Rd. N17—25Vb 43
Campbell Rd. W7—45Ga 78
Campbell Rd. Cat—93Tb 181
Campbell Rd. Croy—72Rb 147
Campbell Rd. E Mol—69Ga 122
Campbell Rd. Grav—10B 114
Campbell Rd. Twic—61Fa 122
Campbell Rd. Wey—80Q 140
Campdale Rd. N7—34Mb 62
Campden Clo. SW19—61Ab 124
Campden Cres. Dag—35Xc 67
Campden Cres. Wemb—34Ka 58
Campden Gro. W8—47Cb 81
Campden Hill. W8—47Cb 81
Campden Hill Gdns. W8—46Cb 81
Campden Hill Pl. W11—46Bb 81
Campden Hill Rd. W8—46Cb 81
Campden Hill Sq. W8—46Bb 81
Campden Rd. S Croy—78Ub 147
Campden Rd. Uxb—34P 55
Campden St. W8—46Cb 81
Camp End Rd. Cob & Wey
—84S 158
Camperdown St. E1
—44Vb 83 (3K 201)
Campfield Rd. SE9—59Mc 107
Camphill Ct. Wey—84J 157
Camphill Industrial Site. Wey
—83K 157
Camphill Rd. Wey—84J 157
Campion Clo. E6—45Pc 86
Campion Clo. Croy—77Ub 147
Campion Clo. Uxb—43P 75
Campion Ct. Grays—51Fe 113
Campion Cres. SE26—63Ac 128
Campion Pl. SE28—46Xc 87
Campion Rd. SW15—57Ya 102
Campion Rd. Iswth—53Ha 100
Campions. Lou—10Qc 14
Campions Clo. Borwd—9Ra 7
Campion Ter. NW2—34Za 60

Cample La.—Catford Hill

Cample La. S Ock—45Wd 90
Camplin Rd. Harr—29Na 39
Camplin St. SE14—52Zb 106
Camp Rd. SW19—64Ya 124
(in two parts)
Camp Rd. Cat—93Ac 182
Camp Rd. Ger X—1N 53
Campsbourne Rd. N8—27Nb 42
(in two parts)
Campsbourne, The. N8—28Nb 42
Campsey Gdns. Dag—38Xc 67
Campsey Rd. Dag—38Xc 67
Campsfield Rd. N8—27Nb 42
Campshill Pl. SE13—57Ec 106
Campshill Rd. SE13—57Ec 106
Campus Rd. E17—30Bc 44
Camp View. SW19—64Xa 124
Cam Rd. E15—39Fc 65
Camrose Av. Edgw—26Pa 39
Camrose Av. Eri—51Dd 110
Camrose Av. Felt—63Y 121
Camrose Clo. Mord—70Cb 125
Camrose St. SE2—50Wc 87
Canada Av. N18—23Sb 43
Canada Cres. W3—43Sa 79
Canada Farm Rd. S Dar, Dart & Long, Dart—70Wd 134
Canada Rd. SE16—47Zb 84
Canada Rd. W3—43Sa 79
Canada Rd. Cob—85Y 159
Canada Rd. Slou—7M 73
Canada Rd. Wey—83M 157
Canada Way. W12—45Xa 80
Canadian Av. SE6—60Dc 106
Canadian Memorial Av. Asc —8K 117
Canal Basin. Grav—8F 114
Canal Clo. E1—42Ac 84
Canal Gro. SE15—51Wb 105
Canal Head. SE15—53Wb 105
Canal Industrial Est. Slou—47C 74
Canal Rd. E3—42Ac 84
Canal Rd. Grav—8E 114
Canal St. SE5—51Tb 105
Canal Wlk. N1—39Tb 63
Canal Wlk. SE26—64Yb 128
Canal Wharf. Slou—47C 74
Canary Wharf. E14—46Cc 84
Canberra Clo. Dag—39Fd 68
Canberra Clo. Horn—36Ld 69
Canberra Cres. Dag—38Fd 68
Canberra Dri. N'holt—41Y 77
Canberra Rd. E6—39Pc 66
Canberra Rd. SE7—51Lc 107
Canberra Rd. Bexh—51Zc 109
Canberra Rd. Houn—55Q 98
Canberra Sq. Til—4C 114
Canbury Av. King—67Pa 123
Canbury M. SE26—62Wb 127
Canbury Pk. Rd. King—67Na 123
Canbury Pas. King—67Na 123
Canbury Path. Orp—70Wc 131
Canbury Pl. King—67Na 123
Cancell Rd. SW9—53Qb 104
Candahar Rd. SW11—54Gb 103
Cander Way. S Ock—45Xd 90
Candler St. N15—30Tb 43
Candover Clo. W Dray—52M 97
Candover Rd. Horn—32Kd 69
Candover St. W1 —43Lb 82 (1B 198)
Candy Croft. Lea—98Da 175
Candy St. E3—39Bc 64
Cane Clo. Wall—80Nb 146
Caneland Ct. Wal A—6Hc 13
Canewden Clo. Wok—91A 172
Canfield Dri. Ruis—36X 57
Canfield Gdns. NW6—38Db 61
Canfield Pl. NW6—37Eb 61
Canfield Rd. Rain—39Hd 68
Canfield Rd. Wfd G—24Nc 46
Canford Av. N'holt—39Ba 57
Canford Clo. Enf—12Qb 24
Canford Dri. Wey—75K 139
Canford Gdns. N Mald—72Ua 144
Canford Rd. SW11—57Jb 104
Canham Rd. SE25—69Ub 127
Canham Rd. W3—47Ua 80
Can Hatch. Tad—90Ab 162
Canmore Gdns. SW16—66Lb 126
Cann Hall Rd. E11—35Gc 65
Canning Cres. N22—25Pb 42
Canning Cross. SE5—54Ub 105
Canning Pas. W8—48Eb 81
Canning Pl. W8—48Eb 81 (3A 202)
Canning Pl. M. W8—(3A 202)
Canning Rd. E15—40Fc 65
Canning Rd. E17—28Ac 44
Canning Rd. N5—34Rb 63
Canning Rd. Croy—75Vb 147
Canning Rd. Harr—27Ha 38
Cannington Rd. Dag—37Yc 67
Cannizaro Rd. SW19—64Ya 124
Cannonbury Av. Pinn—30Z 37
Cannon Clo. SW20—69Ya 124
Cannon Clo. Hmptn—65Da 121
Cannon Clo. Stanf—1P 93
Cannon Dri. E14—46Cc 84
Cannon Gro. Lea—94Ga 176
Cannon Hill. N14—20Nb 24
Cannon Hill. NW6—36Cb 61
Cannon Hill La. SW20 —71Za 144
Cannon Hill M. N14—20Nb 24
Cannon La. NW3—34Fb 61
Cannon La. Pinn—29Aa 37
Cannon Pl. NW3—34Fb 61
Cannon Pl. SE7—50Nc 86
Cannon Rd. N14—20Nb 24
Cannon Rd. Bexh—53Ad 109
Cannon Rd. Wat—15Y 19
Cannon Row. SW1 —47Nb 82 (1F 205)
Cannonside. Lea—94Ga 176
★Cannons Mead. Brtwd—5Wd
Cannon St. EC4—44Sb 83 (3D 200)
Cannon St. Rd. E1—44Xb 83
Cannon Trading Est. Wemb —35Ra 59
Cannon Wlk. Grav—9E 114
Cannon Way. E Mol—70Ca 121
Cannon Way. Lea—93Ga 176
Canon Av. Romf—29Yc 47
Canon Beck Rd. SE16—47Yb 84
Canonbie Rd. SE23—59Yb 106
Canonbury Gro. N1—38Sb 63
Canonbury La. N1—38Rb 63
Canonbury Pk. N. N1—37Sb 63
Canonbury Pk. S. N1—37Sb 63
Canonbury Pl. N1—37Rb 63
Canonbury Rd. N1—37Rb 63
Canonbury Rd. Enf—11Ub 25
Canonbury Sq. N1—38Rb 63
Canonbury St. N1—38Sb 63
Canonbury Vs. N1—38Rb 63
Canon Murnane Rd. SE1—(4K 207)
Canon Rd. Brom—69Lc 129
Canon's Clo. N2—31Fb 61
Canons Clo. Edgw—23Pa 39
Canons Clo. Rad—7Ka 6
Canons Corner. Edgw—21Na 39
Canons Dri. Edgw—23Na 39
Canons Hill. Coul—90Qb 164
Canons La. Tad—90Ab 162
Canonsleigh Rd. Dag—38Xc 67
Canons Pk. Stan—23Ma 39
Canon St. N1—39Sb 63
Canon's Wlk. Croy—76Zb 148
Canopus Way. N'wd—21W 36
Canopus Way. Stai—59N 97
Canrobert St. E2—40Xb 63
Cantelowes Rd. NW1—37Mb 62
Canterbury Av. Ilf—31Nc 66
Canterbury Av. Sidc—61Yc 131
Canterbury Av. Slou—2G 72
Canterbury Av. Upm—32Vd 70
Canterbury Clo. E6—44Pc 86
Canterbury Clo. Beck—67Dc 128
Canterbury Clo. Chig—20Xc 29
Canterbury Clo. Dart—59Qd 111
Canterbury Clo. Gnfd—43Da 77
Canterbury Cres. SW9—55Qb 104
Canterbury Gro. SE27—63Qb 126
Canterbury Pde. S Ock—41Yd 90
Canterbury Pl. SE17 —49Rb 83 (6C 206)
Canterbury Rd. E10—31Ec 64
Canterbury Rd. NW6—40Cb 61
Canterbury Rd. Borwd—12Qa 21
Canterbury Rd. Croy—73Pb 146
Canterbury Rd. Felt—61Aa 121
Canterbury Rd. Grav—1E 136
Canterbury Rd. Harr—29Da 37
Canterbury Rd. Mord—73Db 145
Canterbury Rd. Wat—12X 19
Canterbury Ter. NW6—40Cb 61
Canterbury Way. Brtwd—23Yd 50
Canterbury Way. Grays —52Ud 112
Canterbury Way. Rick—13S 18
Cantley Gdns. SE19—67Vb 127
Cantley Gdns. Ilf—30Sc 46
Cantley Rd. W7—48Ja 78
Canton St. E14—44Cc 84
Cantrell Rd. E3—42Bc 84
Cantwell Rd. SE18—52Rc 108
Canvey St. SE1—46Sb 83 (6D 200)
Cape Clo. Bark—38Rc 66
Capelands. Long, Dart—75Ce 155
Capel Av. Wall—78Pb 146
Capel Clo. N20—20Eb 23
Capel Clo. Brom—74Nc 150
Capel Clo. Stanf—1N 93
Capel Ct. EC2—(3G 201)
Capel Gdns. Ilf—35Vc 67
Capel Gdns. Pinn—28Ba 37
Capella Rd. N'wd—21V 36
Capell Av. Rick—15E 16
Capell Rd. Rick—15F 16
Capell Way. Rick—15F 16
Capel Pl. Dart—63Ld 133
Capel Rd.—35Kc 65
E7 1-165
E12 remainder
Capel Rd. Barn—16Gb 23
Capel Rd. Enf—8Xb 11
Capel Rd. Wat—16Aa 19
Capelvere Wlk. Wat—11U 18
Capener's Clo. SW1—(2H 203)
Capern Rd. SW18—60Eb 103
Cape Rd. N17—27Wb 43
Capital Interchange Way. Bren —50Qa 79
Capitol Industrial Est. NW9 —27Sa 39
Capitol Way. NW9—27Sa 39
Capland St. NW8 —42Fb 81 (5C 190)
Caple Rd. NW10—40Va 60
Capon Clo. Brtwd—18Xd 32
Capper St. WC1—42Lb 82 (6C 192)
Caprea Clo. Hay—43Z 77
Capri Rd. Croy—74Vb 147
Capstan Ride. Enf—12Qb 24
Capstan Sq. E14—47Ec 84
Capstan Way. SE16—46Ac 84
Capstone Rd. Brom—63Hc 129
Capthorne Av. Harr—32Aa 57
Capuchin Clo. Stan—23Ka 38
Capworth St. E10—32Cc 64
Caractacus Cottage View. Wat —17W 18
Caractacus Grn. Wat—16V 18
Caradoc Clo. W2—44Cb 81
Caradoc St. SE10—50Gc 85
Caradon Clo. Wok—6E 188
Caradon Way. N15—28Tb 43
Caravan La. Rick—17N 17
Caravel M. SE8—51Cc 106
Carberry Rd. SE19—65Ub 127
Carbery Av. W3—47Pa 79
Carbery La. Asc—9A 116
Carbis Clo. E4—18Fc 27
Carbis Rd. E14—44Bc 84
Carbuncle Pas. Way. N17 —26Wb 43
Carburton St. W1 —43Kb 82 (7A 192)
Carbury Clo. Horn—37Md 69
Cardale St. E14—48Ec 84
Carden Rd. SE15—55Xb 105
Cardiff Rd. W7—48Ja 78
Cardiff Rd. Enf—14Xb 25
Cardiff Rd. Wat—15X 19
Cardiff St. SE18—52Uc 108
Cardigan Clo. Wok—6C 188
Cardigan Gdns. Ilf—33Wc 67
Cardigan Rd. E3—40Bc 64
Cardigan Rd. SW13—54Wa 102
Cardigan Rd. SW19—65Eb 125
Cardigan Rd. Rich—58Na 101
Cardigan St. SE11 —50Qb 82 (7K 205)
Cardinal Av. Borwd—13Ra 21
Cardinal Av. King—64Na 123
Cardinal Av. Mord—72Ab 144
Cardinal Cap All. SE1 —46Sb 83 (6D 200)
Cardinal Clo. Chst—67Uc 130
Cardinal Clo. Mord—72Ab 144
Cardinal Clo. Wor Pk—77Wa 144
Cardinal Cres. N Mald—68Sa 123
Cardinal Dri. Ilf—23Sc 46
Cardinal Dri. W on T—74Z 141
Cardinal Pl. SW15—56Za 102
Cardinal Rd. Felt—60X 99
Cardinal Rd. Ruis—32Z 57
Cardinals Wlk. Hmptn—66Ea 122
Cardinals Wlk. M'head—4A 72
Cardinals Wlk. Sun—65U 120
Cardinals Way. N19—32Mb 62
Cardinal Way. Rain—40Md 69
Cardine M. SE15—52Xb 105
Cardington Rd. Houn—55R 98
Cardington Sq. Houn—56Z 99
Cardington St. NW1 —41Lb 82 (3C 192)
Cardozo Rd. N7—36Nb 62
Cardrew Av. N12—22Fb 41
Cardrew Clo. N12—22Gb 41
Cardross St. W6—48Xa 80
Cardwell Cres. Asc—10A 116
Cardwell Rd. N7—35Nb 62
Cardwell Rd. SE18—49Qc 86
Carew Clo. N7—33Pb 62
Carew Clo. Coul—91Rb 181
Carew Rd. N17—26Wb 43
Carew Rd. W13—47La 78
Carew Rd. Ashf—65S 120
Carew Rd. Mitc—68Jb 126
Carew Rd. N'wd—23U 36
Carew Rd. T Hth—70Rb 127
Carew Rd. Wall—79Lb 146
Carew St. SE5—54Sb 105
Carey Clo. Wind—5F 94
Carey Ct. Bexh—57Dd 110
Carey Gdns. SW8—53Lb 104
Carey La. EC2—44Sb 83 (2D 200)
Carey Pl. SW1—(6D 204)
Carey Pl. Wat—14Y 19
Carey Rd. Dag—35Ad 67
Carey St. WC2—44Pb 82 (3J 199)
Carfax Pl. SW4—56Mb 104
Carfax Rd. Hay—50V 76
Carfax Rd. Horn—35Hd 68
Carfree Clo. N1—38Qb 62
Carganey Wlk. SE28—45Yc 87
Cargill Rd. SW18—60Eb 103
Cargreen Rd. SE25—70Vb 127
Carholme Rd. SE23—60Bc 106
Carillon Ct. W5—45Ma 79
Carisbrook Clo. Stan—26Ma 39
Carisbrooke Av. Bex—60Zc 109
Carisbrooke Av. Wat—11Z 19
Carisbrooke Clo. Enf—11Vb 25
Carisbrooke Clo. Horn—32Qd 69
Carisbrooke Ct. Slou—5K 73
Carisbrooke Gdns. SE15 —52Vb 105
Carisbrooke Rd. E17—28Ac 44
Carisbrooke Rd. Brtwd—16Xd 32
Carisbrooke Rd. Brom—70Lc 129
Carisbrooke Rd. Mitc—70Nb 126
Carker's La. NW5—36Kb 62
Carleton Av. Wall—81Mb 164
Carleton Gdns. N19—36Lb 62
Carleton Pl. S Dar, Dart—70Sd 134
Carleton Rd. N7—36Mb 62
(in two parts)
Carleton Rd. Dart—59Qd 111
Carlile Clo. E3—40Bc 64
Carlingford Gdns. Mitc—66Jb 126
Carlingford Rd. N15—27Rb 43
Carlingford Rd. NW3—35Fb 61
Carlingford Rd. Mord—72Za 144
Carlisle Av. EC3—44Vb 83 (3K 201)
Carlisle Av. W3—44Ua 80
Carlisle Clo. King—67Qa 123
Carlisle Gdns. Harr—31Ma 59
Carlisle Gdns. Ilf—30Nc 46
Carlisle La. SE1—48Pb 82 (3J 205)
Carlisle M. NW8—43Fb 81 (7C 190)
Carlisle M. King—67Qa 123
Carlisle Pl. N11—21Kb 42
Carlisle Pl. SW1—48Lb 82 (4B 204)
Carlisle Rd. E10—32Cc 64
Carlisle Rd. N4—31Qb 62
Carlisle Rd. NW6—39Ab 60
Carlisle Rd. NW9—27Sa 39
Carlisle Rd. Dart—58Qd 111
Carlisle Rd. Hmptn—66Da 121
Carlisle Rd. Romf—29Jd 48
Carlisle Rd. Slou—5H 73
Carlisle Rd. Sutt—79Bb 145
Carlisle St. W1—44Mb 82 (3D 198)
Carlisle Wlk. E8—37Vb 63
Carlos Pl. W1—45Jb 82 (5J 197)
Carlow St. NW1—40Lb 62 (1B 192)
Carlton Av. N14—15Mb 24
Carlton Av. Felt—58Y 99
Carlton Av. Harr—29Ka 38
Carlton Av. Hay—49U 76
Carlton Av. S Croy—80Ub 147
Carlton Av. E. Wemb—33Ma 59
Carlton Av. W. Wemb—33Ka 58
Carlton Clo. NW3—33Cb 61
Carlton Clo. Borwd—14Ta 21
Carlton Clo. Chess—79Ma 143
Carlton Clo. Edgw—22Qa 39
Carlton Clo. Esh—75Fa 142
Carlton Clo. N'holt—36Ea 58
Carlton Clo. Upm—33Rd 69
Carlton Clo. Wok—86B 156
Carlton Ct. SE20—67Xb 127
Carlton Ct. Ilf—27Tc 46
Carlton Cres. Sutt—77Ab 144
Carlton Dri. SW15—57Ab 102
Carlton Dri. Ilf—27Tc 46
Carlton Gdns. SW1 —46Mb 82 (7D 198)
Carlton Gdns. W5—44La 78
Carlton Grn. SW9—53Rb 105
Carlton Gro. SE15—53Xb 105
Carlton Hill. NW8 —40Db 61 (1A 190)
Carlton Ho. Ter. SW1 —46Mb 82 (7D 198)
Carlton Pde. Orp—73Xc 151
Carlton Pk. Av. SW20—68Za 124
Carlton Rd. E11—32Hc 65
Carlton Rd. E12—35Mc 65
Carlton Rd. E17—25Ac 44
Carlton Rd. N4—31Qb 62
Carlton Rd. N11—22Jb 42
Carlton Rd. N15—27Vb 43
Carlton Rd. SW14—56Sa 101
Carlton Rd. W4—47Ta 79
Carlton Rd. W5—45La 78
Carlton Rd. Eri—51Dd 110
Carlton Rd. Grays—7B 92
Carlton Rd. Grnh—58Ud 112
Carlton Rd. N Mald—68Ua 124
Carlton Rd. Romf—29Jd 48
Carlton Rd. Sidc—64Vc 131
Carlton Rd. Slou—5M 73
Carlton Rd. S Croy—80Tb 147
Carlton Rd. Sun—66V 120
Carlton Rd. W on T—73X 141
Carlton Rd. Well—55Xc 109
Carlton Rd. Wok—86C 156
Carlton Sq. E1—42Zb 84
(in two parts)
Carlton St. SW1—45Mb 82 (5D 198)
Carlton Ter. E11—29Kc 45
Carlton Ter. N18—20Tb 25
Carlton Ter. SE26—62Yb 128
Carlton Vale. NW6—40Bb 61
Carlwell St. SW17—64Gb 125
Carlyle Av. Brom—69Mc 129
Carlyle Av. S'hall—45Ba 77
Carlyle Clo. N2—30Eb 41
Carlyle Clo. NW10—39Ta 59
Carlyle Clo. E Mol—68Da 121
Carlyle Gdns. S'hall—45Ba 77
Carlyle Rd. E12—35Nc 66
Carlyle Rd. SE28—45Xc 87
Carlyle Rd. W5—49La 78
Carlyle Rd. Croy—75Wb 147
Carlyle Rd. Stai—66J 119
Carlyle Sq. SW3—50Fb 81
Carlyon Av. Harr—35Ba 57
Carlyon Clo. Wemb—39Na 59
Carlyon Rd. Hay—43Y 77
Carlyon Rd. Wemb—40Na 59
Carmalt Gdns. SW15—56Ya 102
Carmalt Gdns. W on T—78Y 141
Carmarthen Rd. Slou—5J 73
Carmelite Clo. Harr—25Ea 38
Carmelite Rd. Harr—25Ea 38
Carmelite St. EC4 —45Qb 82 (4A 200)
Carmelite Wlk. Harr—25Ea 38
Carmelite Way. Harr—26Ea 38
Carmelite Way. Long, Dart —71Be 155
Carmen St. E14—44Dc 84
Carmichael Clo. SW11—55Fb 103
Carmichael Clo. Ruis—35W 56
Carmichael Rd. SE25—71Wb 147
Carminia Rd. SW17—61Kb 126
Carnaby St. W1—44Lb 82 (3B 198)
Carnach Grn. S Ock—45Xd 90
Carnac St. SE27—63Tb 127
Carnanton Rd. E17—25Fc 45
Carnarvon Av. Enf—13Vb 25
Carnarvon Dri. Hay—48S 76
Carnarvon Rd. E10—29Ec 44
Carnarvon Rd. E15—37Hc 65
Carnarvon Rd. E18—25Hc 45
Carnarvon Rd. Barn—13Ab 22
Carnation St. SE2—50Xc 87
Carnecke Gdns. SE9—57Nc 108
Carnegie Clo. Surb—75Pa 143
Carnegie Pl. SW19—62Za 124
Carnegie St. N1—39Pb 62 (1J 193)
Carnforth Clo. Eps—79Ra 143
Carnforth Gdns. Horn—36Jd 68
Carnforth Rd. SW16—66Mb 126
Carnie Hall. SW17—62Kb 125
Carnoustie Dri. N1—38Pb 62
Carnwath Rd. SW6—55Cb 103
Carolina Rd. T Hth—68Rb 127
Caroline Clo. N10—26Kb 42
Caroline Clo. Croy—77Ub 147
Caroline Clo. Iswth—52Ga 100
Caroline Clo. W Dray—47M 75
Caroline Ct. Ashf—65R 120
Caroline Ct. Stan—23Ja 38
Caroline Gdns. E2 —41Ub 83 (3J 195)
Caroline Pl. SW11—54Jb 104
Caroline Pl. Wat—16Aa 19
Caroline Pl. M. W2—45Db 81
Caroline Rd. SW19—66Bb 125
Caroline St. E1—44Zb 84
Caroline Ter. SW1 —49Jb 82 (6H 203)
Caroline Wlk. W6—51Ab 102
Carol St. NW1—39Lb 62
Carolyn Clo. Wok—7C 188
Carolyn Dri. Orp—76Wc 151
Caroon Dri. Rick—8K 3
Carpenders Av. Wat—20Aa 19
Carpenter Gdns. N21—19Rb 25
Carpenters Path. Brtwd—15Fe 33
Carpenters Pl. SW4—56Mb 104
Carpenter's Rd. E15—37Cc 64
Carpenters Rd. Enf—8Yb 12
Carpenter St. W1 —45Kb 82 (5K 197)
Carpenters Wood Dri. Rick —14D 16
Carpenter Way. Pot B—5Eb 9
Carrara Wlk. SW9—56Qb 104
Carriage Dri. E. SW11—52Jb 104
Carriage Dri. N. SW11—52Hb 103
Carriage Dri. S. SW11—53Hb 103
Carriage Dri. W. SW11—52Hb 103
Carrick Dri. Sev—95Kd 187
Carrick Gdns. N17—24Ub 43
Carrick Ga. Esh—76Fa 142
Carrick M. SE8—51Cc 106
Carrington Av. Borwd—15Ra 21
Carrington Av. Houn—57Da 99
Carrington Clo. Borwd—15Sa 21
Carrington Clo. Croy—73Ac 148
Carrington Rd. Dart—58Qd 111
Carrington Rd. Rich—56Qa 101
Carrington Rd. Slou—5J 73
Carrington St. W1 —46Kb 82 (7K 197)
Carrol Clo. NW5—35Kb 62
Carroll Clo. E15—36Hc 65
Carroll Hill. Lou—13Pc 28
Carroun Rd. SW8—52Pb 104
Carroway La. Gnfd—41Fa 78
Carrow Clo. E14—44Dc 84
Carrow Rd. Dag—38Xc 67
Carrow Rd. W on T—76Z 141
Carr Rd. E17—26Cc 44
Carr Rd. N'holt—37Ca 57
Carrs La. N21—15Sb 25
Carr St. E14—43Ac 84
(in two parts)
Carshalton Gro. Sutt—78Fb 145
Carshalton Pk. Rd. Cars —79Hb 145
Carshalton Pl. Cars—78Jb 146
Carshalton Rd. Bans—86Hb 163
Carshalton Rd. Mitc—71Jb 146
Carshalton Rd. Sutt & Cars —78Eb 145
Carsington Gdns. Dart—61Md 133
Carslake Rd. SW15—58Ya 102
Carson Rd. E16—42Jc 85
Carson Rd. SE21—61Tb 127
Carson Rd. Barn—14Hb 23
Carstairs Rd. SE6—62Ec 128
Carston Clo. SE12—57Hc 107
Carswell Clo. Brtwd—16Fe 33
Carswell Clo. Ilf—28Mc 45
Carswell Rd. SE6—59Ec 106
Carter Clo. Romf—24Dd 48
Carter Clo. Wall—80Mb 146
Carter Clo. Wind—4E 94
Carter Ct. EC4—(3C 200)
Carter Dri. Romf—24Dd 48
Carteret St. SW1 —47Mb 82 (2D 204)
Carteret Way. SE8—49Ac 84
Carterhatch La. Enf—11Vb 25
Carterhatch Rd. Enf—12Yb 26
Carter La. EC4—44Rb 83 (3C 200)
Carter Pl. SE17—50Sb 83 (7E 206)
Carter Rd. E13—39Kc 65
Carter Rd. SW19—65Fb 125
Carters Clo. Wor Pk—74Za 144
Cartersfield Rd. Wal A—6Ec 12
Carter's Hill. Sev—100Rd 186
Carters Hill Clo. SE9—60Lc 107
Carters La. SE23—61Ac 128
Carters La. Wok—92E 172
Carters Rd. Eps—87Va 162
Carters Row. Grav—1B 136
Carter St. SE17—51Sb 105
Carter's Yd. SW18—57Cb 103
Carthew Rd. W6—48Xa 80
Carthew Vs. W6—48Xa 80
Carthouse La. Wok—2B 188
Carthusian St. EC1 —43Sb 83 (7D 194)
Carting La. WC2—45Pb 82 (5G 199)
Cart La. E4—18Gc 27
Cartmel Clo. N17—24Xb 43
Cartmell Gdns..Mord—71Eb 145
Cartmel Rd. Bexh—53Cd 110
Cart Path. Wat—5Y 5
Cartwright Gdns. WC1 —41Nb 82 (4F 193)
Cartwright Rd. Dag—38Bd 67
Cartwright St. E1 —45Vb 83 (4K 201)
Carver Rd. SE24—58Sb 105
Carville Cres. Bren—49Na 79
Cary Rd. E11—35Gc 65
Carysfort Rd. N8—29Mb 42
Carysfort Rd. N16 34Tb 63
Cascade Av. N10—28Lb 42
Cascade Clo. Buck H—19Mc 27
Cascade Clo. Orp—69Yc 131
Cascade Rd. Buck H—19Mc 27
Cascades Way. Croy—82Bc 166
Caselden Clo. Wey—78L 139
Casella Rd. SE14—52Zb 106
Casewick Rd. SE27—64Qb 126
Casimir Rd. E5—34Xb 63
Casino Av. SE24—57Tb 105
Caspian St. SE5—52Tb 105
Caspian Wlk. E16—44Mc 85
Casselden Rd. NW10—38Ta 59
Cassidy Rd. SW6—52Cb 103
(in two parts)
Cassilda Rd. SE2—49Wc 87
Cassilis Rd. Twic—58Ka 100
Cassiobridge Rd. Wat—14U 18
Cassiobury Av. Felt—59V 98
Cassiobury Dri. Wat—11U 18
Cassiobury Pk. Av. Wat—13U 18
Cassiobury Rd. E17—29Ac 44
Cassio Rd. Wat—13X 19
Cassland Rd. E9—38Zb 64
Cassland Rd. T Hth—70Tb 127
Casslee Rd. SE6—59Bc 106
Casson St. E1—43Wb 83
Casstine Clo. Swan—66Hd 132
Castalia Sq. E14—47Ec 84
Castano Ct. Abb L, Wat—3U 4
Castellain Rd. W9—42Db 81
Castellan Av. Romf—27Kd 49
Castellane Clo. Stan—24Ha 38
Castello Av. SW15—57Ya 102
Castell Rd. Lou—11Sc 28
Castelnau. SW13—53Wa 102
Castelnau Gdns. SW13—51Xa 102
Castelnau Pl. SW13—51Xa 102
Castelnau Row. SW13—51Xa 102
Casterbridge Rd. SE3—55Jc 107
Castile Rd. SE18—49Qc 86
Castile Way. Eps—81Wa 162
Castillon Rd. SE6—61Gc 129
Castlands Rd. SE6—61Bc 128
Castle Av. E4—22Fc 45
Castle Av. Eps—81Wa 162
Castle Av. Rain—38Gd 68
Castle Av. Slou—1L 95
Castle Av. W Dray—45N 75
Castlebar Ct. W5—43La 78
Castlebar Hill. W5—43La 78
Castlebar M. W5—43La 78
Castlebar Pk. W5—43Ka 78
Castlebar Rd. W5—44La 78
Castle Baynard St. EC4 —45Rb 83 (4C 200)
Castle Clo. E9—36Ac 64
Castle Clo. SW19—62Za 124
Castle Clo. Brom—69Gc 129
Castle Clo. Bush, Wat—16Da 19
Castle Clo. Sun—66U 120
Castlecombe Dri. SW19—59Za 102
Castlecombe Rd. SE9—63Nc 130
Castle Ct. EC3—(3G 201)
Castledine Rd. SE20—66Xb 127
Castle Dri. Ilf—30Nc 46
Castle Dri. Sev—89Nd 171
Castle Farm Rd. Sev—81Hd 170
Castlefields. Grav—7B 136
Castleford Av. SE9—60Rc 108
Castlegate. Rich—55Pa 101
Castle Grn. Wey—76U 140
Castle Gro. Rd. Chob—1A 188
Castlehaven Rd. NW1—38Kb 62
Castle Hill. Long, Dart—71Zd 155
Castle Hill. Wind—3H 95
Castle Hill Av. Croy—81Dc 166
Castle Hill Rd. Egh—2N 117
Castle La. SW1—48Lb 82 (3B 204)
Castle La. Grav—1K 137
Castleleigh Ct. Enf—15Tb 25
Castlemaine Av. Eps—81Xa 162
Castlemaine Av. S Croy —78Vb 147
Castle M. NW1—37Kb 62
Castle Pde. Eps—80Wa 144
Castle Pl. W4—49Ua 80
Castlereagh St. W1 —44Hb 81 (2F 197)
Castle Rd. N12—22Eb 41
Castle Rd. NW1—37Kb 62
Castle Rd. Coul—92Qb 179
Castle Rd. Dag—39Xc 67
Castle Rd. Enf—11Ac 26
Castle Rd. Eps—87Ra 161
Castle Rd. Grays—51Be 113
Castle Rd. Iswth—54Ha 100
Castle Rd. N'holt—37Da 57
Castle Rd. Sev & Eyns, Dart —79Kd 153
Castle Rd. S'hall—48Ba 77
Castle Rd. Swans—58Be 113
Castle Rd. Wey—76U 140
Castle Rd. Wok—86B 156
Castle St. E6—40Mc 65
Castle St. Grnh—57Wd 112
Castle St. King—68Na 123
Castle St. Slou—8K 73
Castle St. Swans—58Be 113
Castleton Av. Bexh—53Fd 110
Castleton Av. Wemb—35Na 59
Castleton Clo. Bans—87Cb 163
Castleton Dri. Bans—86Cb 163
Castleton Gdns. Wemb—34Na 59
Castleton Rd. E17—26Fc 45
Castleton Rd. SE9—63Mc 129
Castleton Rd. Ilf—32Wc 67
Castleton Rd. Mitc—70Mb 126
Castleton Rd. Ruis—32Z 57
Castletown Rd. W14—50Ab 80
Castle View. Eps—86Ra 161
Castleview Gdns. Ilf—30Nc 46
Castleview Rd. Slou—9N 73
Castle View Rd. Wey—77R 140
Castle Wlk. Sun—69Y 121
Castle Way. SW19—62Za 124
Castle Way. Felt—63Y 121
Castlewood Dri. SE9—54Pc 108
Castlewood Rd.—31Wb 63
N16 1-121 & 2-102
N15 remainder
Castlewood Rd. Barn—13Fb 23
Castle Yd. N6—31Jb 62
Castle Yd. SE1—46Rb 83 (6C 200)
Castle Yd. Rich—57Ma 101
Caterham Av. Ilf—26Pc 46
Caterham By-Pass. Cat—93Xb 181
Caterham Clo. Cat—92Ub 181
Caterham Ct. Wal A—6Hc 13
Caterham Dri. Coul—90Rb 165
Caterham Rd. SE13—55Fc 107
Catesby St. SE17 —49Tb 83 (6G 207)
Catford B'way. SE6—59Dc 106
Catford Hill. SE6—60Bc 106

Catford Rd.—Charcroft Gdns.

Catford Rd. SE6—59Cc **106**
Cathall Rd. E11—33Fc **65**
Cathay St. SE16—47Xb **83**
Cathcart Dri. Orp—75Uc **150**
Cathcart Hill. N19—34Lb **62**
Cathcart Rd. SW10—51Db **103**
Cathcart St. NW5—37Kb **62**
Cathedral Piazza. SW1 —48Lb **82** (4B **204**)
*Cathedral Pl. EC4—(2D **200**)*
Cathedral St. SE1 —46Tb **83** (6F **201**)
Catherall Rd. N5—34Sb **63**
Catherine Clo. Brtwd—15Wd **32**
Catherine Clo. Wey—86N **157**
Catherine Ct. N14—15Lb **24**
Catherine Dri. Sun—65V **120**
Catherine Gdns. Houn—56Fa **100**
Catherine Gro. SE10—53Dc **106**
Catherine Pl. SW1 —48Lb **82** (3B **204**)
Catherine Rd. Enf—9Ac **12**
Catherine Rd. Romf—29Kd **49**
Catherine Rd. Surb—71Ma **143**
Catherines Clo. W Dray—47M **75**
Catherine St. WC2 —45Pb **82** (4H **199**)
Catherine Wheel All. E1 —43Ub **83** (1J **201**)
*Catherine Wheel Yd. SW1 —(7B **198**)*
Catherine Wheel Yd. Bren —52Ma **101**
Cat Hill. Barn—15Gb **23**
Cathles Rd. SW12—58Kb **104**
Cathnor Hall Ct. W12—47Xa **80**
Cathnor Rd. W12—47Xa **80**
Catisfield Rd. Enf—9Ac **12**
Catlin Cres. Shep—71T **140**
Catling Clo. SE23—62Yb **128**
Catlins La. Pinn—27X **37**
Catlin St. SE16—50Wb **83**
Cator Clo. Croy—83Gc **167**
Cator Cres. Croy—83Gc **167**
Cator La. Beck—67Bc **128**
Cato Rd. SW4—56Mb **104**
Cator Rd. SE26—65Zb **128**
Cator Rd. Cars—78Hb **145**
Cator St. SE15—51Vb **105** (in two parts)
Cato's Hill. Esh—77Da **141**
Cato St. W1—44Gb **81** (1E **196**)
Catsey La. Bush, Wat—17Ea **20**
Catsey Woods. Bush, Wat —17Ea **20**
Catterick Way. Borwd—11Pa **21**
Cattistock Rd. SE9—64Nc **130**
*Cattlegate Cotts. Pot B—3Mb **10***
Cattlegate Hill. Pot B—4Mb **10**
*Cattlegate Rd. Pot B—3Mb **10***
Cattlegate Rd. Pot B & Enf —4Mb **10**
Catton St. WC1—43Pb **82** (1H **199**)
Caudwell Ter. SW18—58Fb **103**
Caulfield Rd. E6—38Pc **66**
Caulfield Rd. SE15—54Xb **105**
*Causeway Clo. Pot B—3Fb **9***
*Causeway Ct. Wok—6C **188***
Causeway, The. N2—28Gb **41**
Causeway, The. SW18—56Db **103**
Causeway, The. SW19—64Ya **124**
Causeway, The. Cars—75Jb **146**
Causeway, The. Chess—77Na **143**
Causeway, The. Esh—80Ha **142**
Causeway, The. Felt & Houn —55X **99**
*Causeway, The. Pot B—3Fb **9***
Causeway, The. Stai—63F **118**
Causeway, The. Sutt—81Eb **163**
Causeway, The. Tedd—65Ha **122**
Causeyware Rd. N9—17Yb **26**
Causton Rd. N6—31Kb **62**
Causton St. SW1 —49Mb **82** (6E **204**)
Cautley Av. SW4—57Lb **104**
Cavalier Clo. Romf—28Zc **47**
Cavalier Ct. Surb—72Pa **143**
Cavalier Gdns. Hay—44T **76**
Cavalry Cres. Houn—56Z **99**
*Cavalry Cres. Wind—5G **94***
Cavaye Pl. SW10—50Eb **81**
Cavell Cres. Dart—56Qd **111**
Cavell Dri. Enf—12Qb **24**
Cavell Rd. N17—24Tb **43**
Cavell St. E1—43Xb **83**
Cavendish Av. N3—26Cb **41**
Cavendish Av. NW8 —40Fb **61** (2C **190**)
Cavendish Av. W13—43Ja **78**
Cavendish Av. Eri—51Ed **110**
Cavendish Av. Harr—35Fa **58**
Cavendish Av. Horn—37Kd **69**
Cavendish Av. N Mald—70Xa **124**
Cavendish Av. Ruis—36X **57**
Cavendish Av. Sev—94Jd **186**
Cavendish Av. Sidc—59Wc **109**
Cavendish Av. Well—55Vc **109**
Cavendish Av. Wfd G—24Kc **45**
Cavendish Clo. N18—22Xb **43**
Cavendish Clo. NW6—37Bb **61**
Cavendish Clo. NW8 —41Fb **81** (3C **190**)
Cavendish Clo. Hay—43U **76**
Cavendish Clo. Sun—65V **120**
*Cavendish Ct. EC3—(2J **201**)*
Cavendish Cres. Borwd—14Qa **21**
Cavendish Cres. Horn—37Kd **69**
Cavendish Dri. E11—32Fc **65**
Cavendish Dri. Edgw—23Pa **39**
Cavendish Dri. Esh—78Ga **142**
Cavendish Gdns. Bark—36Uc **66**
Cavendish Gdns. Ilf—32Qc **66**
Cavendish Gdns. Romf—29Ad **47**
Cavendish M. N. W1 —43Kb **82** (7A **192**)
Cavendish M. S. W1 —43Kb **82** (1A **198**)
Cavendish Pl. W1 —44Kb **82** (2A **198**)
Cavendish Rd. E4—23Ec **44**
Cavendish Rd. N4—30Rb **43**
Cavendish Rd. N18—22Xb **43**
Cavendish Rd. NW6—38Ab **60**
Cavendish Rd. SW12—58Lb **104**
Cavendish Rd. SW19—66Fb **125**
Cavendish Rd. W4—53Sa **101**
Cavendish Rd. Barn—13Ya **22**
Cavendish Rd. Croy—74Rb **147**
Cavendish Rd. N Mald—70Va **124**
Cavendish Rd. Sun—65V **120**
Cavendish Rd. Sutt—80Eb **145**
Cavendish Rd. Wey—81R **158**
*Cavendish Rd. Wok—7G **188***
Cavendish Sq. W1 —44Kb **82** (2A **198**)
Cavendish St. N1 —40Tb **63** (2F **195**)
Cavendish Ter. Felt—61W **120**
Cavendish Way. W Wick —74Dc **148**
Cavenham Clo. Wok—91A **172**
Cavenham Gdns. Horn—29Ld **49**
Cavenham Gdns. Ilf—34Tc **66**
Caverleigh Way. Wor Pk —74Wa **144**
Cave Rd. E13—41Kc **85**
Cave Rd. Rich—63La **122**
Caversham Av. N13—20Qb **24**
Caversham Av. Sutt—75Ab **144**
Caversham Ct. N11—19Jb **24**
Caversham Rd. N15—28Sb **43**
Caversham Rd. NW5—37Lb **62**
Caversham Rd. King—68Pa **123**
Caversham St. SW3—51Hb **103**
Caverswall St. W12—44Ya **80**
Caveside Clo. Chst—67Qc **130**
*Cawcott Dri. Wind—3C **94***
Cawdor Av. S Ock—45Xd **90**
Cawdor Cres. W7—49Ja **78**
Cawnpore St. SE19—64Ub **127**
Cawsey Way. Wok—89A **156**
Caxton Av. Wey—79J **139**
Caxton Clo. Long, Dart—70Be **135**
Caxton Dri. Uxb—40M **55**
Caxton Gro. E3—41Cc **84**
Caxton Rd. N22—26Pb **42**
Caxton Rd. SW19—64Eb **125**
Caxton Rd. W12—47Za **80**
Caxton Rd. S'hall—48Z **77**
Caxton St. SW1—48Mb **82** (3C **204**)
Caxton St. N. E16—44Hc **85**
Caxton St. S. E16—45Hc **85**
Caxton Way. Wat—16T **18**
Caygill Clo. Brom—70Hc **129**
Cayley Clo. Wall—80Nb **146**
*Cayton Pl. EC1—(4F **195**)*
Cayton Rd. Gnfd—40Ga **58**
Cayton St. EC1—41Tb **83** (4F **195**)
Cazenove Rd. E17—25Cc **44**
Cazenove Rd. N16—33Vb **63**
Cearns Ho. E6—39Mc **65**
Cearn Way. Coul—87Pb **164**
Cecil Av. Bark—38Tc **66**
Cecil Av. Enf—14Vb **25**
Cecil Av. Horn—27Nd **49**
Cecil Av. Wemb—36Pa **59**
Cecil Clo. Ashf—66S **120**
Cecil Clo. Chess—77Ma **143**
Cecil Ct. WC2—45Nb **82** (4F **199**)
Cecil Ct. Barn—13Za **22**
Cecile Pk. N8—30Nb **42**
Cecilia Clo. N2—27Eb **41**
Cecilia Rd. E8—36Vb **63**
Cecil Pk. Pinn—28Aa **37**
Cecil Pl. Mitc—71Hb **145**
Cecil Rd. E11—34Hc **65**
Cecil Rd. E13—39Jc **65**
Cecil Rd. E17—25Cc **44**
Cecil Rd. N10—26Kb **42**
Cecil Rd. N14—18Lb **24**
Cecil Rd. NW9—27Ua **40**
Cecil Rd. NW10—39Ua **60**
Cecil Rd. SW19—66Db **125**
Cecil Rd. W3—43Sa **79**
Cecil Rd. Ashf—66S **120**
Cecil Rd. Croy—72Pb **146**
Cecil Rd. Enf—14Sb **25**
*Cecil Rd. Grav—10B **114***
Cecil Rd. Harr—27Fa **38**
Cecil Rd. Houn—54Ea **100**
Cecil Rd. Ilf—35Rc **66**
Cecil Rd. Iver—44G **74**
Cecil Rd. Pot B—4Wa **8**
Cecil Rd. Romf—31Zc **67**
Cecil Rd. Sutt—79Bb **145**
Cecil Rd. Wal X—4Ac **12**
Cecil St. Wat—10X **5**
Cecil Way. Brom—74Jc **149**
*Cecil Way. Slou—2D **72***
Cedar Av. Barn—17Gb **23**
Cedar Av. Cob—87Y **159**
Cedar Av. Enf—12Yb **26**
*Cedar Av. Grav—3E **136***
Cedar Av. Hay—44W **76**
Cedar Av. Romf—29Ad **47**
Cedar Av. Ruis—36Y **57**
Cedar Av. Sidc—59Wc **109**
Cedar Av. Twic—58Da **99**
Cedar Av. Upm—35Qd **69**
Cedar Av. Wal X—5Zb **12**
Cedar Av. W Dray—45P **75**
Cedar Clo. SW15—63Ta **123**
Cedar Clo. Borwd—14Ra **21**
Cedar Clo. Brtwd—17Fe **33**
Cedar Clo. Brom—68Pc **130** (Bickley)
Cedar Clo. Brom—76Nc **150** (Keston Mark)
Cedar Clo. Buck H—19Mc **27**
Cedar Clo. E Mol—70Ga **122**
Cedar Clo. Eps—86Va **162**
Cedar Clo. Esh—79Ba **141**
*Cedar Clo. Pot B—2Cb **9***
Cedar Clo. Romf—28Ed **48**
Cedar Clo. Stai—69L **119**
Cedar Clo. Swan—68Ed **132**
Cedar Clo. Warl—91Ac **182**
Cedar Ct. E11—38Sb **63**
Cedar Ct. N11—22Lb **42**
Cedar Ct. SW19—62Za **124**
Cedar Ct. Egh—63C **118**
Cedar Cres. Brom—76Nc **150**
Cedarcroft Rd. Chess—77Pa **143**
Cedar Dri. N2—28Gb **41**
*Cedar Dri. Asc—10H **117***
Cedar Dri. Lea—95Ga **176**
Cedar Dri. Pinn—23Ca **37**
Cedar Dri. S at H, Dart—68Rd **133**
Cedar Gdns. Sutt—79Eb **145**
Cedar Gdns. Upm—34Sd **70**
Cedar Grange. Enf—15Ub **25**
Cedar Gro. W5—48Na **79**
Cedar Gro. Bex—58Zc **109**
Cedar Gro. S'hall—43Ca **77**
Cedar Gro. Wey—77S **140**
Cedar Heights. Rich—60Na **101**
Cedar Hill. Eps—88Sa **161**
Cedarhurst Dri. SE9—57Lc **107**
Cedar Lawn Av. Barn—15Ab **22**
Cedar Mt. SE9—60Mc **107**
Cedarne Rd. SW6—52Db **103**
Cedar Pk. Gdns. Romf—31Zc **67**
Cedar Pk. Rd. Enf—10Sb **11**
Cedar Rise. N14—17Jb **24**
Cedar Rd. N17—25Vb **43**
Cedar Rd. NW2—35Ya **60**
Cedar Rd. Brtwd—16Fe **33**
Cedar Rd. Brom—68Lc **129**
Cedar Rd. Cob—86X **159**
Cedar Rd. Croy—75Ub **147**
Cedar Rd. Dart—60Md **111**
Cedar Rd. E Mol—70Ga **122**
Cedar Rd. Enf—10Rb **11**
Cedar Rd. Eri—53Jd **110**
Cedar Rd. Felt—60T **98**
*Cedar Rd. Grays—8C **92***
Cedar Rd. Horn—34Ld **69**
Cedar Rd. Houn—54Y **99**
Cedar Rd. Romf—28Ed **48**
Cedar Rd. Sutt—79Eb **145**
Cedar Rd. Tedd—64Ja **122**
Cedar Rd. Wat—16Y **19**
Cedar Rd. Wey—77Q **140**
*Cedar Rd. Wok—8E **188***
Cedars. Bans—86Hb **163**
*Cedars. Stanf—1N **93***
Cedars Av. E17—29Cc **44**
Cedars Av. Mitc—70Jb **126**
Cedars Av. Rick—18L **17**
Cedars Clo. NW4—27Za **40**
Cedars Clo. Ger X—22A **34**
Cedars Ct. N9—19Ub **25**
Cedars Dri. Uxb—40P **55**
Cedars M. SW4—56Kb **104**
Cedars Rd. E15—37Gc **65**
Cedars Rd. N9—19Wb **25**
Cedars Rd. N21—19Rb **25**
Cedars Rd. SW4—55Kb **104**
Cedars Rd. SW13—54Wa **102**
Cedars Rd. W4—51Sa **101**
Cedars Rd. Beck—68Ac **128**
Cedars Rd. Croy—76Nb **146**
Cedars Rd. King—67La **122**
Cedars Rd. Mord—70Cb **125**
Cedars, The. Buck H—18Jc **27**
Cedars, The. Tedd—65Ha **122**
Cedars, The. Wey—84P **157**
Cedar Ter. Rich—56Pa **101**
Cedar Ter. Rd. Sev—95Ld **187**
Cedar Tree Gro. SE27—64Rb **127**
Cedarville Gdns. SW16—65Pb **126**
Cedar Vista. Rich—54Na **101** (in two parts)
Cedar Wlk. Kenl—88Sb **165**
Cedar Wlk. Tad—92Ab **178**
Cedar Wlk. Wal A—6Fc **13**
Cedar Way. NW1—38Mb **62**
Cedar Way. Slou—50A **74**
Cedar Way. Sun—66U **120**
Cedra Ct. N16—32Wb **63**
Cedric Av. Romf—27Gd **48**
Cedric Rd. SE9—62Sc **130**
Celandine Clo. E3—43Cc **84**
Celandine Clo. S Ock—42Yd **90**
Celandine Dri. SE28—46Xc **87**
Celandine Rd. W on T—77Aa **141**
Celandine Way. E15—41Gc **85**
Celia Cres. Ashf—65M **119**
Celia Rd. N19—35Lb **62**
*Cell Farm Av. Wind—7M **95***
Celtic Av. Brom—69Gc **129**
Celtic Rd. Wey—86N **157**
Celtic St. E14—43Dc **84**
Cement Block Cotts. Grays —51Ee **113**
Cemetery La. SE7—51Nc **108**
Cemetery La. Shep—73R **140**
Cemetery Rd. E7—35Hc **65**
Cemetery Rd. N17—24Ub **43**
Cemetery Rd. SE2—52Xc **109**
Cenacle Clo. NW3—34Cb **61**
Centaur St. SE1—48Pb **82** (3J **205**)
Centaury Ct. Grays—51Fe **113**
Centenary Rd. Enf—14Bc **26**
Central Av. E11—33Fc **65**
Central Av. N2—26Fb **41**
Central Av. N9—20Ub **25**
Central Av. SW11—52Hb **103**
Central Av. E Mol—70Ba **121**
Central Av. Enf—12Xb **25**
*Central Av. Grav—1D **136***
Central Av. Hay—46V **76**
Central Av. Houn—56Ea **100**
Central Av. Pinn—30Ba **37**
Central Av. S Ock—47Sd **90**
*Central Av. Til—3C **114***
Central Av. Wall—78Nb **146**
Central Av. Wal X—5Ac **12**
Central Av. Well—54Vc **109**
Central Cir. NW4—29Xa **40**
Central Dri. Horn—34Nd **69**
*Central Dri. Slou—5D **72***
Central Hill. SE19—64Tb **127**
*Central Mkt. EC3—(3H **201**)*
Central Pde. Croy—82Ec **166**
Central Pde. Gnfd—41Ja **78**
Central Pk. Av. Dag—34Dd **68**
Central Pk. Est. Houn—57Z **99**
Central Pk. Rd. E6—40Mc **65**
Central Rd. Dart—57Nd **111**
Central Rd. Mord—72Cb **145**
*Central Rd. Stanf—2M **93***
Central Rd. Wemb—36Ka **58**
Central Rd. Wor Pk—74Wa **144**
Central School Path. SW14 —55Sa **101**
Central Sq. NW11—30Db **41**
Central Sq. Wemb—37Na **59**
Central St. EC1—41Sb **83** (3D **194**)
Central Way. SE28—46Wc **87**
Central Way. Cars—80Gb **145**
Central Way. Felt—57W **98**
*Central Way. Oxt—99Fc **183***
Centre Av. W3—46Ta **79**
Centre Av. Epp—4Vc **15**
Centre Clo. Epp—4Vc **15**
Centre Comn. Rd. Chst—66Sc **130**
*Centre Ct. W2—(5A **196**)*
Centre Dri. Epp—4Vc **15**
Centre Grn. Epp—4Vc **15**
Centre Rd. E11 & E7—33Jc **65**
Centre Rd. Dag—40Dd **68**
Centre Rd. Long, Dart—76Ae **155**
Centre St. E2—40Xb **63**
Centre, The. Felt—61W **120**
Centre, The. W on T—74V **140**
Centre Way. E17—24Ec **44**
Centre Way. N9—19Yb **26**
Centre Way. Ilf—33Sc **66**
Centre Way. Wal A—7Ec **12**
Centric Clo. NW1—39Kb **62**
Centurion Clo. N7—38Pb **62**
Centurion Way. Purf—49Pd **89**
Centuryan Pl. Dart—56Kd **111**
Century Rd. E17—27Ac **44**
Century Rd. Stai—64E **118**
Cephas Av. E1—42Yb **84**
Cephas St. E1—42Yb **84**
Ceres Rd. SE18—49Vc **87**
Cerise Rd. SE15—54Wb **105**
Cerne Clo. Hay—45Y **77**
*Cerne Rd. Grav—3G **136***
Cerne Rd. Mord—72Eb **145**
Cerotus Pl. Cher—73H **139**
Cervantes Ct. N'wd—24V **36**
*Cervia Way. Grav—2H **137***
Ceylon Rd. W14—48Za **80**
Chace Av. Pot B—4Fb **9**
Chadacre Av. Ilf—27Pc **46**
Chadacre Rd. Eps—79Xa **144**
Chadbourn St. E14—43Dc **84**
Chadd Dri. Brom—69Nc **130**
*Chadfields. Til—2C **114***
Chad Grn. E13—39Jc **65**
Chad St. E3—40Bc **64**
Chadville Gdns. Romf—29Zc **47**
Chadway. Dag—32Yc **67**
Chadwell Av. Romf—31Xc **67**
*Chadwell Av. Wal X—1Yb **12***
*Chadwell By-Pass. Grays—9B **92***
Chadwell Heath La. Romf —28Xc **47**
*Chadwell Hill. Grays—10D **92***
Chadwell Rd. Grays—49Ee **91**
Chadwell St. EC1 —41Qb **82** (3A **194**)
Chadwick Av. E4—21Fc **45**
*Chadwick Clo. Grav—1A **136***
Chadwick Clo. Tedd—65Ja **122**
Chadwick Rd. E11—31Gc **65**
Chadwick Rd. NW10—39Va **60**
Chadwick Rd. SE15—54Vb **105**
Chadwick Rd. Ilf—34Rc **66**
Chadwick St. SW1 —48Mb **82** (4D **204**)
Chadwick Way. SE28—45Zc **87**
Chadwin Rd. E13—43Kc **85**
Chaffers Mead. Asht—88Pa **161**
Chaffinch Av. Croy—72Zb **148**
Chaffinch Clo. Croy—72Zb **148**
*Chaffinch Gdns. Grav—1A **136***
Chaffinch La. Wat—17V **18**
Chaffinch Rd. Beck—67Ac **128**
Chafford Gdns. Brtwd—30Fe **51**
Chafford Wlk. Rain—40Ld **69**
Chafford Way. Grays—46De **91**
Chafford Way. Romf—28Yc **47**
Chagford St. NW1 —42Hb **81** (6F **191**)
Chailey Av. Enf—12Vb **25**
Chailey Pl. W on T—77Aa **141**
Chailey St. E5—34Yb **64**
Chairmans Av. Uxb—29H **35**
Chalbury Wlk. N1 —40Pb **62** (1K **193**)
Chalcombe Rd. SE2—48Xc **87**
Chalcot Clo. Sutt—80Cb **145**
Chalcot Cres. NW1—39Hb **61**
Chalcot Gdns. NW3—37Hb **61**
Chalcot Rd. NW1—38Jb **62**
Chalcot Sq. NW1—38Jb **62**
Chalcott Gdns. Surb—74La **142**
Chalcroft Rd. SE13—57Gc **107**
Chaldon Comn. Rd. Cat—96Sb **181**
Chaldon Ct. SE19—67Tb **127**
Chaldon Rd. SW6—52Ab **102**
Chaldon Rd. Cat—95Tb **181**
Chaldon Way. Coul—89Nb **164**
Chale Rd. SW2—58Nb **104**
Chalet Clo. Bex—63Fd **132**
Chale Wlk. Sutt—81Db **163**
*Chalfont Av. Amer—11A **16***
Chalfont Av. Wemb—37Ra **59**
Chalfont Ct. NW9—27Va **40**
Chalfont Grn. N9—20Ub **25**
Chalfont La. Ger X & Rick—23E **34**
Chalfont La. Rick—15D **16**
Chalfont Rd. N9—20Ub **25**
Chalfont Rd. SE25—69Vb **127**
Chalfont Rd. Ger X & Rick—19D **16**
Chalfont Rd. Hay—47W **76**
Chalfont Saint Peter By-Pass. Ger X—25A **34**
Chalfont Wlk. Pinn—26Y **37**
Chalfont Way. W13—48Ka **78**
Chalford Clo. E Mol—70Ca **121**
Chalforde Gdns. Romf—28Kd **49**
Chalford Rd. SE21—63Tb **127**
Chalford Wlk. Wfd G—25Mc **45**
Chalgrove Av. Mord—71Cb **145**
Chalgrove Cres. Ilf—26Nc **46**
Chalgrove Gdns. N3—27Ab **40**
Chalgrove Rd. E9—37Yb **64**
Chalgrove Rd. N17—25Xb **43**
Chalgrove Rd. Sutt—80Fb **145**
Chalice Clo. Wall—79Mb **146**
Chalkenden Clo. SE20—66Xb **127**
Chalk Farm Rd. NW1—38Jb **62**
Chalk Hill. Wat—16Aa **19**
Chalkhill Rd. W6—49Za **80**
Chalkhill Rd. Wemb—34Ra **59**
Chalklands. Wemb—34Sa **59**
Chalk La. Asht—91Pa **177**
Chalk La. Barn—13Hb **23**
Chalk La. Eps—87Ta **161**
Chalk Paddock. Eps—87Ta **161**
Chalk Pit Av. Orp—69Yc **131**
*Chalkpit La. Lea—100Ba **175***
*Chalkpit La. Oxt—98Ec **182***
*Chalk Pit La. Slou—8A **52***
Chalk Pit Rd. Bans—89Cb **163**
Chalk Pit Rd. Eps—91Sa **177**
*Chalkpit Wood. Oxt—99Fc **183***
Chalk Rd. E13—43Kc **85**
*Chalk Rd. Grav—10J **115***
Chalkwell Pk. Av. Enf—14Ub **25**
*Chalky Bank. Grav—3C **136***
Chalky La. Chess—82Ma **161**
Challacombe Clo. Brtwd—18De **33**
*Challenge Clo. Grav—3H **137***
Challenge Rd. Ashf—62T **120**
Challice Way. SW2—60Pb **104**
Challin St. SE20—67Yb **128**
Challis Rd. Bren—50Ma **79**
Challock Clo. West—88Lc **167**
Challoner Clo. N2—26Fb **41**
Challoner Cres. W14—50Bb **81**
Challoners Clo. E Mol—70Fa **122**
Challoner St. W14—50Bb **81**
Chalmers Rd. Ashf—64R **120**
Chalmers Rd. Bans—87Fb **163**
Chalmers Rd. E. Ashf—64R **120**
Chalmers Way. Felt—57Y **99**
Chalsey Rd. SE4—56Bc **106**
Chalton Dri. N2—30Fb **41**
Chalton St. NW1 —40Mb **62** (1D **192**)
*Chalvey Gdns. Slou—7J **73***
*Chalvey Gro. Slou—8F **72***
*Chalvey Pk. Slou—7J **73***
*Chalvey Rd. E. Slou—7J **73***
*Chalvey Rd. W. Slou—7H **73***
Chamberlain Cotts. SE5 —53Tb **105**
Chamberlain Cres. W Wick —74Dc **148**
Chamberlain La. Pinn—28W **36**
Chamberlain Rd. N2—26Eb **41**
Chamberlain Rd. N9—20Wb **25**
Chamberlain Rd. W13—47Ja **78**
Chamberlain St. NW1—38Hb **61**
Chamberlain Wlk. Felt—63Aa **121**
Chamberlain Way. Pinn—27X **37**
Chamberlain Way. Surb —73Na **143**
Chamberlayne Rd. NW10 —39Ya **60**
Chambers Gdns. N2—25Fb **41**
Chambers Rd. N7—35Nb **62**
Chambers St. SE16—47Wb **83**
Chamber St. E1—45Vb **83** (4K **201**)
Chambord St. E2 —41Vb **83** (4K **195**)
Champion Gro. SE5—55Tb **105**
Champion Hill. SE5—55Tb **105**
Champion Pk. SE5—54Tb **105**
Champion Rd. SE26—63Ac **128**
Champion Rd. Upm—33Rd **69**
Champness Clo. SE27—63Tb **127**
Champneys Clo. Sutt—80Bb **145**
Chancel Industrial Est. NW10 —37Va **60**
Chancellor Gro. SE21—62Sb **127**
Chancellor's Rd. W6—50Ya **80**
Chancellor's St. W6—50Ya **80**
Chancellor Way. Sev—94Jd **186**
Chancelot Rd. SE2—49Xc **87**
Chancel St. SE1—46Rb **83** (7B **200**)
Chancery La. WC2 —44Qb **82** (1J **199**)
Chancery La. Beck—68Dc **128**
Chance St. E2 & E1 —42Vb **83** (5K **195**)
Chanctonbury Clo. SE9—62Rc **130**
Chanctonbury Gdns. Sutt —80Db **145**
Chanctonbury Way. N12—21Bb **41**
Chandler Av. E16—43Jc **85**
Chandler Clo. Hmptn—67Ca **121**
Chandler Rd. Lou—11Rc **28**
Chandler's La. Rick—8N **3**
Chandler St. E1—46Xb **83**
Chandlers Way. SW2—59Qb **104**
Chandlers Way. Romf—29Gd **48**
Chandos Av. E17—26Cc **44**
Chandos Av. N14—20Lb **24**
Chandos Av. N20—18Eb **23**
Chandos Av. W5—49La **78**
Chandos Clo. Buck H—19Kc **27**
Chandos Cres. Edgw—24Pa **39**
*Chandos Mall. Slou—7K **73***
Chandos Pl. WC2 —45Nb **82** (5F **199**)
Chandos Rd. E15—36Fc **65**
Chandos Rd. N2—26Fb **41**
Chandos Rd. N17—26Ub **43**
Chandos Rd. NW2—36Ya **60**
Chandos Rd. NW10—42Ua **80**
Chandos Rd. Borwd—12Pa **21**
Chandos Rd. Harr—29Ea **38**
Chandos Rd. Pinn—31Z **57**
Chandos Rd. Stai—64F **118**
Chandos St. W1—43Kb **82** (1A **198**)
Chandos Way. NW11—32Db **61**
Change All. EC3—44Tb **83** (3G **201**)
Chanlock Path. S Ock—45Xd **90**
Channel Clo. Houn—53Ca **99**
Channelsea Rd. E15—39Fc **65**
Channing Clo. Horn—31Pd **69**
Chanton Dri. Sutt—82Ya **162**
Chantrey Rd. SW9—55Pb **104**
Chantreywood. Brtwd—20Ce **33**
Chantry Av. Long, Dart—72Ae **155**
Chantry Clo. Asht—91La **176**
Chantry Clo. Enf—10Sb **11**
Chantry Clo. Harr—29Pa **39**
*Chantry Clo. K Lan—1Q **4***
Chantry Clo. Sidc—64Ad **131**
Chantry Clo. W Dray—45M **75**
*Chantry Clo. Wind—3E **94***
*Chantry Cres. Stanf—2L **93***
Chantry Hurst. Eps—87Ta **161**
Chantry La. Brom—71Mc **149**
Chantry Pl. Harr—25Da **37**
Chantry Rd. Cher—73L **139**
Chantry Rd. Chess—78Pa **143**
Chantry Rd. Harr—25Da **37**
Chantry St. N1—39Rb **63** (1C **194**)
Chantry, The. Uxb—41P **75**
Chantry Way. Rain—40Fd **68**
Chant Sq. E15—38Fc **65**
Chant St. E15—38Fc **65**
Chapel Av. Wey—77K **139**
Chapel Clo. Dart—57Gd **110**
Chapel Clo. Grays—51Xd **112**
Chapel Clo. Wat—6V **4**
Chapel Ct. N2—27Gb **41**
Chapel Ct. SE1—47Tb **83** (1F **207**)
*Chapel Croft. K Lan—3J **3***
Chapel Farm Rd. SE9—62Pc **130**
Chapel Gro. Eps—91Ya **178**
Chapel Gro. Wey—77K **139**
Chapel High. Brtwd—19Yd **32**
Chapel Hill. Dart—57Gd **110**
*Chapel Hill. Lea—99Z **175***
Chapel Ho. St. E14—50Dc **84**
Chapel La. Chig—20Vc **29**
Chapel La. Houn—55Ca **99**
*Chapel La. Lea—100Ea **176***
Chapel La. Pinn—27Z **37**
Chapel La. Romf—31Zc **67**
*Chapel La. Slou—8M **53***
Chapel La. Uxb—44Q **76**
Chapel Link. Ilf—34Qc **66**
Chapel Mkt. N1—40Qb **62** (1K **193**)
Chapel Pk. Rd. Wey—77K **139**
Chapel Pl. N1—40Qb **62** (1A **194**)
Chapel Pl. N17—24Vb **43**
Chapel Pl. W1—44Kb **82** (3K **197**)
Chapel Pl. Wok—89B **156**
Chapel Rd. SE27—63Rb **127**
Chapel Rd. W13—46Ka **78**
Chapel Rd. Bexh—56Cd **110**
*Chapel Rd. Epp—2Vc **15***
Chapel Rd. Houn—55Da **99**
★Chapel Rd. Sev—93Yd
Chapel Rd. Tad—95Ya **178**
Chapel Rd. Twic—59Ka **100**
Chapel Rd. Warl—90Zb **166**
Chapel Row. Uxb—25L **35**
Chapel Side. W2—45Db **81**
Chapel St. E15—38Fc **65**
Chapel St. NW1—43Gb **81** (1D **196**)
Chapel St. SW1—48Jb **82** (3J **203**)
Chapel St. Enf—13Tb **25**
*Chapel St. Slou—7K **73***
Chapel St. Uxb—39L **55**
Chapel Ter. Lou—14Nc **28**
Chapel View. S Croy—79Yb **148**
Chapel Wlk. NW4—28Xa **40** (in two parts)
Chapel Wlk. Croy—75Sb **147**
Chapel Way. N7—34Pb **62**
Chapel Way. Brom—68Jc **129**
Chapel Way. Eps—91Ya **178**
Chapel Wood. Long, Dart (in two parts) —74Ae **155**
Chapel Wood Rd. Long, Dart —76Ae **155**
Chaplaincy Gdns. Horn—32Nd **69**
Chaplin Clo. SE1 —47Rb **83** (1B **206**)
Chaplin Cres. Sun—65U **120**
Chaplin Rd. E15—40Hc **65**
Chaplin Rd. N17—27Vb **43**
Chaplin Rd. NW2—37Wa **60**
Chaplin Rd. Dag—38Ad **67**
Chaplin Rd. Wemb—37La **58**
Chapman Clo. W Dray—48P **75**
Chapman Cres. Harr—30Na **39**
Chapman Rd. E9—37Bc **64**
Chapman Rd. Belv—50Dd **88**
Chapman Rd. Croy—74Qb **146**
*Chapman's Hill. Grav—79Fe **155***
Chapman's La. SE2 & Belv —49Zc **87**
Chapman's La. Orp—68Zc **131**
Chapmans Rd. Sev—96Ad **185**
Chapman St. E1—45Xb **83**
Chapmans Yd. Wat—14Z **19**
*Chapone Pl. W1—(3D **198**)*
Chapter Clo. Uxb—38P **55**
*Chapter Ho. Ct. EC4—(3D **200**)*
*Chapter M. Wind—2H **95***
Chapter Rd. NW2—36Wa **60**
Chapter Rd. SE17—50Rb **83**
Chapter St. SW1 —49Mb **82** (6D **204**)
Chapter Ter. SE17—51Rb **105**
Chapter Way. Hmptn—63Ca **121**
Chara Pl. W4—51Ta **101**
Charcroft Gdns. Enf—14Zb **26**

Chardin Rd.—Chestnut Av.

Chardin Rd. W4—49Ua 80
Chardmore Rd. N16—32Wb 63
Chard Rd. Houn—54R 98
Chardwell Clo. E6—44Pc 86
Charecroft Way. W12—47Za 80
Charford Rd. E16—43Jc 85
Chargate Clo. W on T—79V 140
Chargeable La. E13—42Hc 85
Chargeable St. E16—42Hc 85
Charing Clo. Orp—77Vc 151
Charing Cross. SW1—(6F 199)
Charing Cross Rd. WC2
—44Mb 82 (2E 198)
Charing Cross Shopping Concourse. WC2—(5F 199)
Chariots Pl. Wind—3H 95
Charlbert St. NW8
—40Gb 61 (1D 190)
Charlbury Av. Stan—22Ma 39
Charlbury Clo. Romf—23Ld 49
Charlbury Cres. Romf—23Ld 49
Charlbury Gdns. Ilf—33Vc 67
Charlbury Gro. W5—44La 78
Charlbury Rd. Uxb—34P 55
Charldane Rd. SE9—62Rc 130
Charlecote Gro. SE26—62Xb 127
Charlecote Rd. Dag—34Ad 67
Charlemont Rd. E6—41Pc 86
Charles Av. Ilf—34Rc 66
Charles Clo. Sidc—63Xc 131
Charles Ct. Eri—51Gd 110
Charles Cres. Harr—31Fa 58
(in two parts)
Charlesfield. SE9—62Lc 129
Charles Gdns. Slou—4M 73
Charles Grinling Wlk. SE18
—49Qc 86
Charles La. NW8
—40Gb 61 (1D 190)
Charles Pl. NW1—41Lb 82 (4C 192)
Charles Rd. E7—38Lc 65
Charles Rd. SW19—67Cb 125
Charles Rd. W13—44Ja 78
Charles Rd. Dag—37Fd 68
Charles Rd. Romf—30Zc 47
Charles Rd. Sev—83Dd 170
Charles Rd. Stai—65M 119
Charles II St. SW1
—46Mb 82 (6D 198)
Charles Sq. N1—41Tb 83 (4G 195)
Charles St. E16—46Lc 85
Charles St. SW13—54Ua 102
Charles St. W1—46Kb 82 (6K 197)
Charles St. Cher—74H 139
Charles St. Enf—15Vb 25
Charles St. Epp—4Wc 15
Charles St. Grays—51De 113
Charles St. Grnh—57Vd 112
Charles St. Houn—54Ba 99
Charles St. Uxb—42R 76
Charles St. Wind—3G 94
Charles St. Trading Est. E16
—46Lc 85
Charleston St. SE17
—49Sb 83 (6E 206)
Charles Utton Ct. E8—35Wb 63
Charleville Cir. SE26—64Wb 127
Charleville Rd. W14—50Ab 80
Charlieville Rd. Eri—52Ed 110
Charlmont Rd. SW17—65Gb 125
Charlock Way. Wat—16V 18
Charlotte Despard Av. SW11
—53Jb 104
Charlotte Gdns. Romf—23Dd 48
Charlotte M. W1—43Lb 82 (7C 192)
Charlotte Pl. W1—43Lb 82 (1C 198)
Charlotte Pl. Grays—51Xd 112
Charlotte Rd. EC2
—41Ub 83 (4H 195)
Charlotte Rd. SW13—53Va 102
Charlotte Rd. Dag—37Dd 68
Charlotte Rd. Wall—79Lb 146
Charlotte Row. SW4—55Lb 104
Charlotte Sq. Rich—58Pa 101
Charlotte St. W1—43Lb 82 (7C 192)
Charlotte Ter. N1
—39Pb 62 (1J 193)
Charlton. Wind—4A 94
Charlton Av. W on T—77X 141
Charlton Chu. La. SE7—50Lc 85
Charlton Clo. Uxb—33R 56
Charlton Cres. Bark—40Vc 67
Charlton Dene. SE7—52Lc 107
Charlton Dri. West—89Mc 167
Charlton Gdns. Coul—90Lb 164
Charlton Kings. Wey—76U 140
Charlton King's Rd. NW5
—36Mb 62
Charlton La. SE7—49Mc 85
Charlton La. Shep—69S 120
Charlton Pk. La. SE7—52Mc 107
Charlton Pk. Rd. SE7—51Mc 107
Charlton Pl. N1—40Rb 63 (1B 194)
Charlton Rd. N9—18Zb 26
Charlton Rd. NW10—39Ua 60
Charlton Rd.—52Jc 107
SE3 1-121 & 2-78
SE7 remainder
Charlton Rd. Harr—28Ma 39
Charlton Rd. Shep—69S 120
Charlton Rd. Wemb—32Pa 59
Charlton Sq. Wind—4A 94
Charlton St. Grays—51Zd 113
Charlton Way. SE3—53Gc 107
Charlwood. Croy—81Bc 166
Charlwood Clo. Harr—23Ga 38
Charlwood Dri. Lea—87Fa 160
Charlwood Pl. SW1
—49Lb 82 (6C 204)
Charlwood Rd. SW15—56Za 102
Charlwood St. SW1
—50Lb 82 (7B 204)
Charlwood Ter. SW15—56Za 102
Charmian Av. Stan—27Ma 39
Charminster Av. SW19—68Cb 125
Charminster Ct. Surb—73Ma 143
Charminster Rd. SE9—63Mc 129
Charminster Rd. Wor Pk
—74Za 144
Charmouth Rd. Well—53Yc 109
Charmwood La. Orp—82Xc 169
Charne, The. Sev—89Jd 170
Charnock. Swan—70Gd 132
Charnock Rd. E5—34Xb 63
Charnwood Av. SW19—68Cb 125
Charnwood Clo. N Mald
—70Ua 124
Charnwood Dri. E18—27Kc 45
Charnwood Pl. N20—20Eb 23
Charnwood Rd. SE25—71Tb 147
Charnwood Rd. Enf—8Xb 11
Charnwood Rd. Uxb—40Q 56
Charnwood St. E5—33Xb 63
Charrington Rd. Croy—75Sb 147
Charrington St. NW1
—40Mb 62 (1D 192)
Charsley Rd. SE6—61Dc 128
Charta Rd. Egh—65E 118
Chart Clo. Brom—67Gc 129
Chart Clo. Croy—72Yb 148
Charter Av. Ilf—32Tc 66
Charter Clo. Slou—8K 73
Charter Ct. New Mald—69Ua 124
Charter Cres. Houn—56Aa 99
Charter Dri. Bex—59Ad 109
Charterhouse Av. Wemb—36La 58
Charterhouse Bldgs. EC1
—42Sb 83 (6D 194)
Charterhouse M. EC1
—43Rb 83 (7C 194)
Charterhouse Rd. Orp—76Wc 151
Charterhouse Sq. EC1
—43Rb 83 (7C 194)
Charterhouse St. EC1
—43Rb 83 (1A 200)
Charteris Rd. N4—32Qb 62
Charteris Rd. NW6—39Bb 61
Charteris Rd. Wfd G—24Kc 45
Charter Pl. Wat—13Y 19
Charter Rd. King—69Ra 123
Charter Rd. Slou—5C 72
Charter Rd., The. Wfd G
—23Gc 45
Charters Clo. SE19—64Ub 127
Charter Sq. King—68Ra 123
Charter Way. N3—28Bb 41
Charter Way. N14—16Mb 24
Chartfield Av. SW15—57Xa 102
Chartfield Sq. SW15—57Za 102
Chartham Gro. SE27—62Rb 127
Chartham Rd. SE25—69Xb 127
Chart La. West—96Yc 185
Chart La. West—100Xc 185
Chartley Av. NW2—34Ua 60
Chartley Av. Stan—23Ha 38
Charton Clo. Belv—51Cd 110
Chart St. N1—41Tb 83 (3G 195)
Chartway. Sev—96Ld 187
Chart Way. Sev—90Rd 171
(Kemsing)
Chartwell Clo. SE9—61Tc 130
Chartwell Clo. Wal A—5Hc 13
Chartwell Pl. Eps—86Ua 162
Chartwell Pl. Sutt—76Bb 145
Chartwell Rd. N'wd—23V 36
Chartwell Way. SE20—67Xb 127
Charville La. Hay—41S 76
Charville La. W. Uxb—41R 76
Charwood. SW16—63Qb 126
Chase Ct. Gdns. Enf—13Sb 25
Chase Cross Rd. Romf—24Ed 48
Chase End. Eps—84Ta 161
Chasefield Rd. SW17—63Hb 125
Chase Gdns. E4—21Cc 44
Chase Gdns. Twic—59Fa 100
Chase Grn. Enf—13Sb 25
Chase Grn. Av. Enf—12Rb 25
Chase Hill. Enf—13Sb 25
Chase Ho. Gdns. Horn—29Pd 49
Chase La. Chig—20Wc 29
Chase La. Ilf—29Tc 46
(in two parts)
Chaseley St. E14—44Ac 84
Chasemore Gdns. Croy—78Qb 146
Chase Ridings. Enf—12Qb 24
Chase Rd. N14—15Lb 24
Chase Rd. W3—43Ta 79
Chase Rd. Brtwd—20Yd 32
Chase Rd. Eps—84Ta 161
Chase Side. N14—16Jb 24
Chase Side. Enf—13Sb 25
Chaseside Av. SW20—68Ab 124
Chase Side Av. Enf—12Sb 25
Chaseside Clo. Romf—23Gd 48
Chase Side Cres. Enf—11Sb 25
Chaseside Gdns. Cher—73K 139
Chase Side Pl. Enf—13Sb 25
Chase, The. E12—35Mc 65
Chase, The. SW4—56Kb 104
Chase, The. SW16—66Qb 126
Chase, The. SW20—67Ab 124
Chase, The. Asht—90La 160
Chase, The. Bexh—55Dd 110
Chase, The. Brtwd—21Xd 50
(Cromwell Rd.)
Chase, The. Brtwd—22Ee 51
(Ingrave)
Chase, The. Brtwd—20Zd 33
(Seven Arches Rd.)
Chase, The. Brtwd—22Zd 51
(Warley)
Chase, The. Brom—69Kc 129
Chase, The. Chig—21Sc 46
Chase, The. Coul—86Mb 164
Chase, The. Edgw—25Ra 39
Chase, The. Grays—51Zd 113
Chase, The. Lea—98V 174
(East Horsley)
Chase, The. Lea—87Ea 160
(Oxshott)
Chase, The. Pinn—28Ba 37
Chase, The. Pinn—30Y 37
(Eastcote)
Chase, The. Romf—27Gd 48
Chase, The. Romf—30Ad 47
(Chadwell Heath)
Chase, The. Romf—34Gd 68
(Rush Green)
Chase, The. Sev—88Nd 171
Chase, The. Stan—23Ja 38
Chase, The. Sun—67X 121
Chase, The. Tad—93Eb 179
Chase, The. Upm—34Ud 70
Chase, The. Uxb—36R 56
Chase, The. Wall—78Pb 146
Chase, The. Wal X—1Rb 11
Chase, The. Wat—14U 18
Chaseville Pde. N21—15Pb 24
Chaseville Pk. Rd. N21—15Nb 24
Chase Way. N14—19Kb 24
Chasewood Av. Enf—12Rb 25
Chastilian Rd. Dart—59Hd 110
Chaston St. NW5—36Jb 62
Chatfield. Slou—3E 72
Chatfield Rd. SW11—55Eb 103
Chatfield Rd. Croy—74Rb 147
Chatham Av. Brom—73Hc 149
Chatham Clo. NW11—29Cb 41
Chatham Clo. Sutt—73Bb 145
★Chatham Grn. La. Sev—82Zd
Chatham Hill Rd. Sev—93Ld 187
Chatham Pl. E9—37Yb 64
Chatham Rd. E17—27Ac 44
Chatham Rd. E18—26Hc 45
Chatham Rd. SW11—57Hb 103
Chatham Rd. King—68Qa 123
Chatham Rd. Orp—78Sc 150
Chatham St. SE17
—49Tb 83 (5F 207)
Chatsfield. Eps—82Wa 162
Chatsfield Pl. W5—44Na 79
Chatsworth Av. NW4—26Ya 40
Chatsworth Av. SW20—67Ab 124
Chatsworth Av. Brom—63Kc 129
Chatsworth Av. Sidc—60Wc 109
Chatsworth Av. Wemb—36Pa 59
Chatsworth Clo. NW4—26Ya 40
Chatsworth Clo. Borwd—13Qa 21
Chatsworth Cres. Houn—56Fa 100
Chatsworth Dri. Enf—17Wb 25
Chatsworth Gdns. W3—46Ra 79
Chatsworth Gdns. Harr—32Da 57
Chatsworth Gdns. N Mald
—71Va 144
Chatsworth Pl. Tedd—63Ja 122
Chatsworth Rise. W5—42Pa 79
Chatsworth Rd. E5—34Yb 64
Chatsworth Rd. E15—36Hc 65
Chatsworth Rd. NW2—37Za 60
Chatsworth Rd. W4—51Sa 101
Chatsworth Rd. W5—42Pa 79
Chatsworth Rd. Croy—77Tb 147
Chatsworth Rd. Dart—56Ld 111
Chatsworth Rd. Hay—42X 77
Chatsworth Rd. Sutt—78Za 144
Chatsworth Way. SE27—62Rb 127
Chatteris Av. Romf—23Ld 49
Chattern Hill. Ashf—63R 120
Chattern Rd. Ashf—63S 120
Chatterton Rd. N4—34Rb 63
Chatterton Rd. Brom—70Mc 129
Chatto Rd. SW11—57Hb 103
Chaucer Av. Hay—43W 76
Chaucer Av. Houn—54X 99
Chaucer Av. Rich—55Qa 101
Chaucer Av. Wey—80Q 140
Chaucer Clo. N11—22Lb 42
Chaucer Clo. Til—4E 114
Chaucer Gdns. Sutt—76Cb 145
Chaucer Grn. Croy—73Yb 148
Chaucer Rd. E7—37Jc 65
Chaucer Rd. E11—30Jc 45
Chaucer Rd. E17—26Ec 44
Chaucer Rd. SE24—57Qb 104
Chaucer Rd. W3—46Sa 79
Chaucer Rd. Ashf—63N 119
Chaucer Rd. Grav—62Fe 135
Chaucer Rd. Romf—24Kd 49
Chaucer Rd. Sidc—60Yc 109
Chaucer Rd. Sutt—77Cb 145
Chaucer Rd. Well—53Uc 108
Chaucer Way. Dart—56Qd 111
Chaucer Way. Wey—79J 139
Chauncey Clo. N9—20Wb 25
Chauncy Av. Pot B—5Eb 9
Chaundrye Clo. SE9—58Pc 108
Chave Rd. Dart—62Nd 133
Chaworth Rd. Cher—79E 138
Cheam Clo. Tad—93Xa 178
Cheam Comn. Rd. Wor Pk
—75Xa 144
Cheam Pk. Way. Sutt—79Ab 144
Cheam Rd. Eps & Sutt—82Wa 162
Cheam Rd. Sutt—79Bb 145
Cheam St. SE15—55Yb 106
Cheapside. EC2—44Sb 83 (3E 200)
Cheapside. N13—21Sb 43
Cheapside. Wok—2G 188
Cheapside La. Uxb—33H 55
Cheapside Rd. Asc—9A 116
Cheddar Rd. Houn—54Q 98
Chedder Waye. Hay—44X 77
Cheddington Rd. N18—21Ub 43
Chedworth Clo. E16—44Hc 85
Cheelson Rd. S Ock—40Yd 70
Cheeseman Clo. Hmptn—65Aa 121
Cheeseman's Ter. W14—50Bb 81
Chelford Rd. Brom—64Fc 129
Chelmer Cres. Bark—40Xc 67
Chelmer Dri. Brtwd—16Fe 33
Chelmer Rd. E9—36Zb 64
Chelmer Rd. Upm—30Td 50
Chelmsford Av. Romf—24Fd 48
Chelmsford Clo. E6—44Pc 86
Chelmsford Clo. W6—51Za 102
Chelmsford Dri. Upm—34Pd 69
Chelmsford Gdns. Ilf—31Nc 66
Chelmsford Rd. E11—32Fc 65
Chelmsford Rd. E17—30Cc 44
Chelmsford Rd. E18—25Hc 45
Chelmsford Rd. N14—17Lb 24
Chelmsford Rd. Brtwd—16Be 33
Chelmsford Rd. Brtwd—13Ee 33
(Mountnessing)
Chelmsford Sq. NW10—39Ya 60
Chelsea Bri. SW1 & SW8
—51Kb 104
Chelsea Bri. Rd. SW1
—50Jb 82 (7H 203)
Chelsea Clo. NW10—39Ta 59
Chelsea Clo. Edgw—26Qa 39
Chelsea Clo. Hmptn—64Ea 122
Chelsea Embkmt. SW3—51Gb 103
Chelsea Mnr. Gdns. SW3—50Gb 81
Chelsea Mnr. St. SW3
—50Gb 81 (7E 202)
Chelsea Pk. Gdns. SW3—51Fb 103
Chelsea Sq. SW3
—50Fb 81 (7C 202)
Chelsfield Av. N9—17Zb 26
Chelsfield Gdns. SE26—62Yb 128
Chelsfield Hill. Orp—81Yc 169
Chelsfield La. Orp—73Zc 151
Chelsfield La. Orp & Sev
—80Cd 152
Chelsfield Rd. Orp—72Yc 151
Chelsham Clo. Warl—90Ac 166
Chelsham Comn. Rd. Warl
—88Cc 166
Chelsham Ct. Rd. Warl—90Fc 167
Chelsham Rd. SW4—55Mb 104
Chelsham Rd. S Croy—79Tb 147
Chelsham Rd. Warl—90Bc 166
Chelston App. Ruis—33W 56
Chelston Rd. Ruis—32W 56
Chelsworth Clo. Romf—25Pd 49
Chelsworth Dri. SE18—51Tc 108
Chelsworth Dri. Romf—25Pd 49
Cheltenham Av. Twic—59Ja 100
Cheltenham Clo. N'holt—37Da 57
Cheltenham Gdns. E6—40Nc 66
Cheltenham Gdns. Lou—16Nc 28
Cheltenham Pl. W3—46Ra 79
Cheltenham Pl. Harr—28Na 39
Cheltenham Rd. E10—30Ec 44
Cheltenham Rd. SE15—56Yb 106
Cheltenham Rd. Orp—76Wc 151
Cheltenham Ter. SW3
—50Hb 81 (7G 203)
Cheltenham Vs. Stai—58H 97
Chelverton Rd. SW15—56Za 102
Chelwood Clo. Eps—84Va 162
Chelwood Clo. N'wd—24S 36
Chelwood Gdns. Rich—54Qa 101
Chelwood Gdns. Pas. Rich
—54Qa 101
Chelwood Wlk. SE4—56Ac 106
Chenappa Clo. E13—41Jc 85
Chenduit Way. Stan—22Ha 38
Cheney Rd. N1—40Nb 62 (2F 193)
Cheney Row. E17—25Bc 44
Cheneys Rd. E11—34Gc 65
Cheney St. Pinn—29Y 37
Chenies M. WC1
—42Mb 82 (6D 192)
Chenies Pl. NW1
—40Mb 62 (1E 192)
Chenies Rd. Rick—12F 16
Chenies St. WC1
—43Mb 82 (7D 192)
Chenies, The. Dart—63Gd 132
Chenies, The. Orp—72Uc 150
Cheniston Clo. Wey—85J 157
Cheniston Gdns. W8—48Db 81
Chepstow Av. Horn—34Nd 69
Chepstow Clo. SW15—58Ab 102
Chepstow Cres. W11—45Cb 81
Chepstow Cres. Ilf—30Uc 46
Chepstow Gdns. S'hall—44Ba 77
Chepstow Pl. W2—45Cb 81
Chepstow Rise. Croy—76Ub 147
Chepstow Rd. W2—44Cb 81
Chepstow Rd. W7—48Ja 78
Chepstow Rd. Croy—76Ub 147
Chepstow Vs. W11—45Bb 81
Chepstow Way. SE15—53Vb 105
Chequers Clo. Grav—8A 136
Chequers Clo. Orp—70Vc 131
Chequers Clo. Tad—97Wa 178
Chequers La. Dag—42Bd 87
Chequers La. Tad—96Wa 178
Chequers La. Tad—97Wa 178
Chequers La. Wat—2Y 5
Chequers Orchard. Iver—44H 75
Chequers Rd. Lou—15Qc 28
Chequers Rd. Romf & Brtwd
—19Nd 31
Chequers Sq. Uxb—38L 55
Chequer St. EC1—42Sb 83 (6E 194)
Chequers Wlk. Wal A—5Hc 13
Chequers Way. N13—22Rb 43
Chequer Tree Clo. Wok—4B 188
Cherbury St. N1—40Tb 63 (2G 195)
Cherimoya Gdns. E Mol—69Da 121
Cherington Rd. W7—46Ha 78
Cheriton Av. Brom—71Hc 149
Cheriton Av. Ilf—26Qc 46
Cheriton Clo. W5—43La 78
Cheriton Ct. SE12—59Jc 107
Cheriton Ct. W on T—74Y 141
Cheriton Dri. SE18—52Tc 108
Cheriton Sq. SW17—61Jb 126
Cherkley Hill. Lea—98La 176
Cherries, The. Slou—4M 73
Cherry Av. Brtwd—20Be 33
Cherry Av. Slou—7P 73
Cherry Av. S'hall—46Z 77
Cherry Av. Swan—70Fd 132
Cherry Clo. W5—48Ma 79
Cherry Clo. Bans—86Za 162
Cherry Clo. Cars—75Hb 145
Cherry Clo. Mord—70Ab 124
Cherry Clo. Ruis—34V 56
Cherrycot Hill. Orp—77Tc 150
Cherrycot Rise. Orp—77Sc 150
Cherry Cres. Bren—52Ka 100
Cherry Croft Gdns. Pinn—24Ba 37
Cherrydale. Wat—14V 18
Cherrydown. Grays—46Fe 91
Cherrydown Av. E4—20Bc 26
Cherrydown Clo. E4—20Cc 26
Cherrydown Rd. Sidc—61Zc 131
Cherrydown Wlk. Romf—26Dd 48
Cherry Gdns. Dag—36Bd 67
Cherry Garden St. SE16—47Xb 83
Cherry Garth. Bren—50Ma 79
Cherry Gro. Hay—46X 77
Cherry Gro. Uxb—43S 76
Cherry Hill. Barn—16Db 23
Cherry Hill. Rick—13K 17
Cherry Hill Gdns. Croy—77Pb 146
Cherry La. W Dray—49P 75
Cherry Laurel Wlk. SW2
—58Pb 104
Cherry Orchard. SE7—51Lc 107
Cherry Orchard. Asht—90Ra 161
Cherry Orchard. Slou—8M 53
Cherry Orchard. Stai—64J 119
Cherry Orchard. W Dray—47N 75
Cherry Orchard Clo. Orp
—71Yc 151
Cherry Orchard Gdns. E Mol
—69Ba 121
Cherry Orchard Rd. Brom
—75Nc 150
Cherry Orchard Rd. Croy
—75Tb 147
Cherry Orchard Rd. E Mol
—69Ca 121
Cherry Rise. Chal—19A 16
Cherry Rd. Enf—10Yb 12
Cherry St. Romf—29Fd 48
Cherry St. Wok—90A 156
Cherry Tree Av. Stai—65K 119
Cherry Tree Av. W Dray—44P 75
Cherry Tree Clo. Grays—51Fe 113
Cherry Tree Clo. Rain—40Jd 68
Cherry Tree Ct. Coul—90Pb 164
Cherrytree Dri. SW16—62Nb 126
Cherry Tree Grn. S Croy—86Xb 165
Cherry Tree Gro. Sev—82Rd 171
Cherry Tree Hill. N2—29Gb 41
Cherrytree La. Ger X—26A 34
Cherrytree La. Iver—39J 55
Cherry Tree La. Pot B—6Db 9
Cherry Tree La. Rain—41Gd 88
Cherry Tree La. Rick—18E 16
Cherry Tree La. Slou—37B 54
Cherry Tree Rise. Buck H—21Lc 45
Cherry Tree Rd. N2—28Hb 41
Cherry Tree Rd. Slou—7G 52
Cherry Tree Rd. Wat—8X 5
Cherry Trees. Long, Dart
—72Be 155
Cherry Tree Wlk. EC1
—42Sb 83 (6E 194)
Cherry Tree Wlk. Beck—70Bc 128
Cherry Tree Wlk. West—89Lc 167
Cherry Tree Wlk. W Wick
—77Hc 149
Cherrytree Way. Stan—23Ka 38
Cherry Wlk. Brom—74Jc 149
Cherry Wlk. Grays—8C 92
Cherry Wlk. Rain—40Jd 68
Cherry Wlk. Rick—12L 17
Cherry Way. Eps—79Ta 143
Cherry Way. Shep—70T 120
Cherrywood Av. Egh—6M 117
Cherrywood Clo. King—66Qa 123
Cherrywood Dri. SW15—57Za 102
Cherrywood Dri. Grav—3A 136
Cherrywood La. Mord—70Ab 124
Cherry Wood Way. W5—43Qa 79
Cherston Gdns. Lou—14Qc 28
Cherston Rd. Lou—14Qc 28
Chertsey Bri. Rd. Shep—73M 139
Chertsey Clo. Kenl—87Rb 165
Chertsey Cres. Croy—82Ec 166
Chertsey Dri. Sutt—75Ab 144
Chertsey La. Stai & Cher—64G 118
Chertsey Rd. E11—33Fc 65
Chertsey Rd. Ashf & Sun—65T 120
Chertsey Rd. Chob—82A 156
Chertsey Rd. Felt—64U 120
Chertsey Rd. Ilf—35Tc 66
Chertsey Rd. Shep—73N 139
Chertsey Rd. Twic—61Da 121
Chertsey Rd. Wey—76K 139
(Addlestone)
Chertsey Rd. Wey—75K 139
(Addlestonemoor)
Chertsey Rd. Wey—83M 157
(Byfleet)
Chertsey Rd. Wok—88B 156
(in two parts)
Chertsey St. SW17—64Jb 126
Chervil M. SE28—46Xc 87
Cherwell Clo. Slou—51D 96
Cherwell Ct. Eps—77Sa 143
Cherwell Gro. S Ock—45Xd 90
Cherwell Way. Ruis—30S 36
Cheryls Clo. SW6—53Db 103
Cheseman St. SE26—62Xb 127
Chesfield Rd. King—66Na 123
Chesham Av. Orp—72Rc 150
Chesham Clo. SW1—(4H 203)
Chesham Clo. Romf—28Fd 48
Chesham Clo. Sutt—82Ab 162
Chesham Ct. N'wd—23V 36
Chesham Cres. SE20—67Yb 128
Chesham La. Ger X & Chal—21A 34
Chesham M. SW1—(3H 203)
Chesham Pl. SW1
—48Jb 82 (4H 203)
Chesham Rd. SE20—68Yb 128
Chesham Rd. SW19—65Fb 125
Chesham Rd. Hem—1B 2
Chesham Rd. King—68Qa 123
Chesham St. NW10—34Ta 59
Chesham St. SW1
—48Jb 82 (4H 20)
Chesham Ter. W13—47Ka 78
Chesham Way. Wat—16U 18
Cheshire Clo. Horn—29Qd 49
Cheshire Clo. Mitc—69Nb 126
Cheshire Gdns. Chess—79Ma 143
Cheshire Rd. N22—24Pb 42
Cheshire St. E2—42Wb 83
Chesholm Rd. N16—34Ub 63
Cheshunt Rd. E7—37Kc 65
Cheshunt Rd. Belv—50Cd 88
Chesilton Rd. SW6—53Bb 103
Chesil Way. Hay—41V 76
Chesley Gdns. E6—40Mc 65
Chesney Cres. Croy—80Ec 148
Chesney St. SW11—53Jb 104
Chesnut Gro. N17—27Vb 43
Chesnut Rd. N17—27Vb 43
Chess Clo. Rick—14M 17
Chessfield Pk. Amer—11A 16
Chess Hill. Rick—14M 17
Chessholme Rd. Ashf—65S 120
Chessington Av. N3—27Ab 40
Chessington Av. Bexh—52Ad 109
Chessington Clo. N16—36Ub 63
Chessington Clo. Eps—79Sa 143
Chessington Ct. Pinn—28Ba 37
Chessington Hall Gdns. Chess
—79Ma 143
Chessington Hill Pk. Chess
—78Qa 143
Chessington Pde. Chess
—79Ma 143
Chessington Rd. Eps—79Qa 143
Chessington Way. W Wick
—75Dc 148
Chess La. Rick—14M 17
Chesson Rd. W14—51Bb 103
Chess Vale Rise. Rick—16P 17
Chess Way. Rick—13J 17
Chesswood Way. Pinn—26Z 37
Chester Av. Rich—58Pa 101
Chester Av. Twic—60Ba 99
Chester Av. Upm—33Ud 70
Chester Clo. SW1
—47Kb 82 (3K 203)
Chester Clo. SW15—55Xa 102
Chester Clo. Ashf—64T 120
Chester Clo. Lou—11Sc 28
Chester Clo. Sutt—75Cb 145
Chester Clo. Uxb—44R 76
Chester Clo. N. NW1
—41Kb 82 (3A 192)
Chester Clo. S. NW1
—41Kb 82 (4A 192)
Chester Cotts. SW1—(6H 203)
Chester Ct. NW1—41Kb 82 (3A 192)
Chester Dri. Harr—30Ba 37
Chesterfield Clo. Orp—70Ad 131
Chesterfield Dri. Esh—75Ja 142
Chesterfield Dri. Sev—93Fd 186
Chesterfield Gdns. N4—29Rb 43
Chesterfield Gdns. W1
—46Kb 82 (6K 197)
Chesterfield Gro. SE22—57Vb 105
Chesterfield Hill. W1
—46Kb 82 (6K 197)
Chesterfield Rd. E10—30Ec 44
Chesterfield Rd. N3—23Cb 41
Chesterfield Rd. W4—51Sa 101
Chesterfield Rd. Ashf—63N 119
Chesterfield Rd. Barn—15Za 22
Chesterfield Rd. Enf—9Ac 12
Chesterfield Rd. Eps—80Ta 143
Chesterfield St. W1
—46Kb 82 (6K 197)
Chesterfield Wlk. SE10—53Fc 107
Chesterfield Way. SE15—52Yb 106
Chesterfield Way. Hay—47W 76
Chesterford Gdns. NW3—35Db 61
Chesterford Rd. E12—36Pc 66
Chester Gdns. Enf—16Xb 25
Chester Gdns. Mord—72Eb 145
Chester Ga. NW1
—41Kb 82 (4A 192)
Chester Grn. Lou—11Sc 28
Chester M. SW1—48Kb 82 (3K 203)
Chester Path. Lou—11Sc 28
Chester Pl. NW1—41Kb 82 (3K 192)
Chester Rd. E7—38Mc 65
Chester Rd. E11—30Kc 45
Chester Rd. E16—42Gc 85
Chester Rd. E17—29Zb 44
Chester Rd. N9—18Xb 25
Chester Rd. N17—27Ub 43
Chester Rd. N19—33Kb 62
Chester Rd. NW1—41Jb 82 (4J 191)
Chester Rd. SW19—65Ya 124
Chester Rd. Borwd—13Sa 21
Chester Rd. Chig—20Qc 28
Chester Rd. Houn—55X 99
Chester Rd. Houn—55Q 98
(Heathrow)
Chester Rd. Ilf—32Vc 67
Chester Rd. Lou—12Rc 28
Chester Rd. N'wd—24U 36
Chester Rd. Sidc—57Uc 108
Chester Rd. Slou—4H 73
Chester Rd. Wat—15W 18
Chester Row. SW1
—49Jb 82 (6H 203)
Chester Sq. SW1—49Jb 82 (5J 203)
Chester Sq. M. SW1—(4K 203)
Chesters, The. N Mald—67Ua 124
Chester St. E2—42Wb 83
Chester St. SW1—48Jb 82 (3J 203)
Chester Ter. NW1
—41Kb 82 (3K 191)
Chesterton Clo. SW18—57Cb 103
Chesterton Clo. Gnfd—40Da 57
Chesterton Dri. Red—100Nb 180
Chesterton Rd. E13—41Jc 85
Chesterton Rd. W10—43Za 80
Chesterton Ter. E13—41Jc 85
Chesterton Ter. King—68Qa 123
Chesterton Way. Til—4E 114
Chester Way. SE11
—49Qb 82 (6A 206)
Chesthunte Rd. N17—25Sb 43
Chestnut All. SW6—51Bb 103
Chestnut Av. E7—35Kc 65
Chestnut Av. N8—29Nb 42

Chestnut Av.—Church Rd.

Chestnut Av. SW14—55Ta 101
Chestnut Av. Bren—49Ma 79
Chestnut Av. Buck H—20Mc 27
Chestnut Av. Edgw—23Na 39
Chestnut Av. Eps—77Ua 144
Chestnut Av. Esh—73Fa 142
Chestnut Av. Grays—47De 91
Chestnut Av. Hmptn—66Ca 121
Chestnut Av. Horn—33Hd 68
Chestnut Av. N'wd—26V 36
Chestnut Av. Rick—15J 17
Chestnut Av. Slou—47A 74
Chestnut Av. Tedd—68Ha 122
Chestnut Av. Vir W—10K 117
Chestnut Av. W on T—81U 158
Chestnut Av. Wemb—36Ka 58
Chestnut Av. W Dray—45P 75
Chestnut Av. West—94Mc 183
Chestnut Av. W Wick—78Gc 149
Chestnut Av. Wey—80S 140
Chestnut Av. N. E17—28Ec 44
Chestnut Av. S. E17—29Ec 44
Chestnut Clo. N14—15Mb 24
Chestnut Clo. N16—33Tb 63
Chestnut Clo. Ashf—63R 120
Chestnut Clo. Buck H—19Mc 27
Chestnut Clo. Cars—74Hb 145
Chestnut Clo. Egh—5N 117
Chestnut Clo. Ger X—25B 34
Chestnut Clo. Grav—8B 114
Chestnut Clo. Hay—45U 76
Chestnut Clo. Horn—35Ld 69
Chestnut Clo. Orp—78Wc 151
Chestnut Clo. Sun—65V 120
Chestnut Clo. Tad—95Cb 179
Chestnut Clo. W. Dray—52R 98
Chestnut Clo. Wey—78M 139
Chestnut Clo. Wok—97H 173
Chestnut Ct. SW6—51Bb 103
Chestnut Dri. E11—30Jc 45
Chestnut Dri. Bexh—55Zc 109
Chestnut Dri. Egh—5P 117
Chestnut Dri. Harr—24Ha 38
Chestnut Dri. Pinn—30Z 37
Chestnut Dri. Wind—6D 94
Chestnut Glen. Horn—33Jd 68
Chestnut Gro. SW12—59Jb 104
Chestnut Gro. W5—48Ma 79
Chestnut Gro. Barn—15Hb 23
Chestnut Gro. Brtwd—19Yd 32
Chestnut Gro. Dart—64Fd 132
Chestnut Gro. Ilf—23Uc 46
Chestnut Gro. Iswth—56Ja 100
Chestnut Gro. Mitc—71Mb 146
Chestnut Gro. N Mald—69Ta 123
Chestnut Gro. S Croy—80Xb 147
Chestnut Gro. Stai—65L 119
Chestnut Gro. Wemb—36Ka 58
Chestnut Gro. Wok—92A 172
Chestnut La. N20—18Ab 22
Chestnut La. Wey—78R 140
Chestnut Mnr. Clo. Stai—64K 119
Chestnut Rise. SE18—51Tc 108
Chestnut Rise. Bush, Wat—17Da 19
Chestnut Rd. SE27—62Sb 127
Chestnut Rd. SW20—68Za 124
Chestnut Rd. Ashf—63R 120
Chestnut Rd. Dart—60Md 111
Chestnut Rd. Enf—8Ac 12
Chestnut Rd. King—66Na 123
Chestnut Rd. Twic—61Ga 122
Chestnuts. Brtwd—17De 33
Chestnuts, The. Romf—13Xc 29
Chestnuts, The. W on T—75W 140
Chestnut Wlk. Ger X—24A 34
Chestnut Wlk. Sev—100Pd 187
Chestnut Wlk. Shep—70U 120
Chestnut Wlk. W on T—81U 158
Chestnut Wlk. Wat—9W 4
Chestnut Wlk. Wfd G—22Jc 45
Chestnut Way. Felt—62X 121
Cheston Av. Croy—75Ac 148
Chestwood Gro. Uxb—38P 55
Chesworth Clo. Eri—54Gd 110
Chettle Clo. SE1—(3F 207)
Chetwode Dri. Eps—90Za 162
Chetwode Rd. SW17—62Jb 126
Chetwode Rd. Tad—91Ya 178
Chetwood Wlk. E6—43Nc 86
Chetwynd Av. Barn—18Hb 23
Chetwynd Dri. Uxb—40P 55
Chetwynd Rd. NW5—35Kb 62
Cheval Pl. SW7—48Gb 81 (3E 202)
Cheval St. E14—48Cc 84
Cheveley Clo. Romf—25Nd 49
Chevely Clo. Epp—1Zc 15
Chevening La. Sev—88Ad 169
Chevening Rd. NW6—40Za 60
Chevening Rd. SE10—50Hc 85
Chevening Rd. SE19—65Tb 127
Chevening Rd. Sev—91Bd 185
(Chevening)
Chevening Rd. Sev—95Ad 185
(Sundridge)
Chevenings, The. Sidc—62Yc 131
Cheverton Rd. N19—32Mb 62
Chevet St. E9—36Ac 64
Chevington Way. Horn—35Md 69
Cheviot Clo. Bans—87Db 163
Cheviot Clo. Bexh—54Gd 110
Cheviot Clo. Bush, Wat—16Ea 20
Cheviot Clo. Enf—12Tb 25
Cheviot Clo. Hay—52T 98
Cheviot Clo. Sutt—81Fb 163
Cheviot Gdns. NW2—33Za 60
Cheviot Ga. NW2—33Ab 60
Cheviot Rd. SE27—64Qb 126
Cheviot Rd. Horn—31Jd 68
Cheviot Rd. Slou—50C 74
Cheviot Way. Gnfd—40Ka 58
Cheviot Way. Ilf—28Uc 46
Chevley Gdns. Slou—10A 52
Chewton Rd. E17—28Ac 44
Cheyham Gdns. Sutt—82Za 162
Cheyham Way. Sutt—82Ab 162
Cheyne Av. E18—27Hc 45
Cheyne Av. Twic—60Ba 99
Cheyne Clo. Brom—76Nc 150
Cheyne Clo. Ger X—32A 54
Cheyne Ct. SW3—51Hb 103
Cheyne Ct. Bans—87Db 163
Cheyne Gdns. SW3—51Gb 103
Cheyne Hill. Surb—70Pa 123
Cheyne M. SW3—51Gb 103
Cheyne Path. W7—44Ha 78
Cheyne Rd. Ashf—65T 120
Cheyne Row. SW3—51Gb 103
Cheyne Wlk. N21—15Rb 25
Cheyne Wlk. NW4—30Ya 40
Cheyne Wlk.—52Fb 103
SW3 1-90
SW10 remainder
Cheyne Wlk. Croy—75Wb 147
Cheyneys Av. Edgw—23Ma 39
Chichele Gdns. Croy—77Ub 147
Chichele Rd. NW2—36Za 60
Chichele Rd. Oxt—100Gc 183
Chicheley Gdns. Harr—24Ea 38
Chicheley Rd. Harr—24Ea 38
Chicheley St. SE1
—47Pb 82 (1J 205)
Chichester Av. Ruis—33T 56
Chichester Bldgs. SE1—(4H 207)
Chichester Clo. E6—44Nc 86
Chichester Clo. SE3—53Lc 107
Chichester Clo. S Ock—46Td 90
Chichester Ct. Eps—81Va 162
Chichester Ct. Slou—7M 73
Chichester Ct. Stan—27Na 39
Chichester Dri. Purl—84Pb 164
Chichester Dri. Sev—97Hd 186
Chichester Gdns. Ilf—31Pc 66
Chichester Rents. WC2—(2K 199)
Chichester Rise. Grav—3F 136
Chichester Rd. E11—34Gc 65
Chichester Rd. N9—18Wb 25
Chichester Rd. NW6—40Cb 61
Chichester Rd. W02—43Db 81
Chichester Rd. Croy—76Ub 147
Chichester Rd. Grnh—58Vd 112
Chichester St. SW1
—50Lb 82 (7C 204)
Chichester Way. Felt—59Y 99
Chichester Way. Wat—5Aa 5
Chicksand St. E1—43Wb 83
Chiddingfold. N12—20Cb 23
Chiddingstone Av. Bexh
—52Bd 109
Chiddingstone St. SW6—54Cb 103
Chieftan Dri. Purf—49Qd 89
Chieveley Rd. Bexh—56Dd 110
Chignell Pl. W13—46Ja 78
Chigwell Hill. E1—45Xb 83
Chigwell Hurst Ct. Pinn—27Z 37
Chigwell La. Lou & Chig—15Sc 28
Chigwell Pk. Chig—21Rc 46
Chigwell Pk. Dri. Chig—21Qc 46
Chigwell Rise. Chig—19Qc 28
Chigwell Rd.—27Kc 45 to 22Pc46
E18 1-179 & 2-234
Wfd G remainder
Chigwell View. Romf—23Cd 48
Chilbrook Rd. Cob—90W 158
Chilcott Rd. Wat—8U 4
Childebert Rd. SW17—61Kb 126
Childerditch Hall Dri. Brtwd
—26Be 51
Childerditch La. Brtwd—24Ae 51
to 31De 71
Childerditch St. Brtwd—26Ce 51
Childeric Rd. SE14—52Ac 106
Childerley St. SW6—53Ab 102
Childers St. SE8—51Ac 106
Childsbridge La. Sev—90Nd 171
Childsbridge Way. Sev—92Pd 187
Childs Clo. Horn—30Ld 49
Childs Cres. Swans—58Fd 113
Childs Hall Clo. Lea—97Ba 175
Childs Hall Rd. Lea—97Ba 175
Child's La. SE19—65Ub 127
Child's Pl. SW5—49Cb 81
Child's St. SW5—49Cb 81
Childs Way. NW11—29Bb 41
Chilham Clo. Gnfd—40Ja 58
Chilham Rd. SE9—63Nc 130
Chilham Way. Brom—73Jc 149
Chillot Clo. E14—44Dc 84
Chillerton Rd. SW17—64Kb 126
Chillingworth Gdns. Twic
—61Ha 122
Chillingworth Rd. N7—36Qb 62
Chilmans Dri. Lea—97Da 175
Chilmark Gdns. N Mald
—72Wa 144
Chilmark Gdns. Red—100Nb 180
Chilmark Rd. SW16—67Mb 126
Chilsey Grn. Rd. Cher—72G 138
Chiltern Av. Bush, Wat—16Ea 20
Chiltern Av. Twic—60Ca 99
Chiltern Clo. Bexh—53Gd 110
Chiltern Clo. Borwd—12Pa 21
Chiltern Clo. Bush, Wat—16Da 19
Chiltern Clo. Croy—76Ub 147
Chiltern Clo. Uxb—33Q 56
Chiltern Clo. Wok—10F 188
Chiltern Dene. Enf—14Pb 24
Chiltern Dri. Rick—17H 17
Chiltern Dri. Surb—72Ra 143
Chiltern Gdns. NW2—34Za 60
Chiltern Gdns. Brom—70Hc 129
Chiltern Gdns. Horn—34Ld 69
Chiltern Hill. Ger X—25A 34
Chiltern Rd. E3—42Cc 84
Chiltern Rd. Grav—2A 136
Chiltern Rd. Ilf—29Uc 46
Chiltern Rd. Pinn—29Y 37
Chiltern Rd. Slou—3A 72
Chiltern Rd. Sutt—82Db 163
Chiltern St. W1—43Jb 82 (7H 191)
Chiltern View Rd. Uxb—40L 55
Chiltern Way. Wfd G—20Jc 27
Chilthorne Clo. SE6—59Bc 106
Chilton Av. W5—49Ma 79
Chilton Ct. M'head—4A 72
Chilton Ct. W on T—77W 140
Chilton Gro. SE8—49Ac 84
Chilton Rd. Edgw—23Qa 39
Chilton Rd. Grays—8C 92
Chilton Rd. Rich—55Qa 101
Chiltons Clo. Bans—87Db 163
Chiltons, The. E18—26Jc 45
Chilton St. E2—42Vb 83
Chilvers St. SE10—50Hc 85
Chilwell Gdns. Wat—21Y 37
Chilwick Rd. Slou—2D 72
Chilworth Ct. SW19—60Za 102
Chilworth Gdns. Sutt—76Eb 145
Chilworth M. W2
—44Fb 81 (3B 196)
Chilworth St. W2
—44Eb 81 (3A 196)
Chimes Av. N13—22Qb 42
China La. Upm—34Fe 71
Chinbrook Cres. SE12—62Kc 129
Chinbrook Rd. SE12—62Kc 129
Chinchilla Dri. Houn—54Y 99
Chindits La. Brtwd—22Yd 50
Chine, The. N10—28Lb 42
Chine, The. N21—16Rb 25
Chine, The. Wemb—36La 58
Chingdale Rd. E4—20Gc 27
Chingford Av. E4—20Cc 26
Chingford La. Wfd G—21Gc 45
Chingford Mt. Rd. E4—21Cc 44
Chingford Rd.—23Cc 44
E17 1-425 & 2-290
E4 remainder
Chingley Clo. Brom—65Gc 129
Chinnor Cres. Gnfd—40Da 57
Chipka St. E14—47Ec 84
(in two parts)
Chipley St. SE14—51Ac 106
Chippendale All. Uxb—38M 55
Chippendale St. E5—34Zb 64
Chippendale Waye. Uxb—38M 55
Chippenham Av. Wemb—36Ra 59
Chippenham Clo. Pinn—28V 36
Chippenham Clo. Romf—22Md 49
Chippenham Gdns. NW6—41Cb 81
Chippenham Gdns. Romf
—22Md 49
Chippenham M. W9—42Cb 81
Chippenham Rd. W9—42Cb 81
Chippenham Rd. Romf—23Md 49
Chippenham Wlk. Romf—23Md 49
Chipperfield Clo. Upm—32Ud 70
Chipperfield Rd. Hem—1E 2
Chipperfield Rd. K Lan—2L 3
Chipperfield Rd. Orp—67Wc 131
(in two parts)
Chipstead Av. T Hth—70Rb 127
Chipstead Clo. SE19—66Vb 127
Chipstead Clo. Coul—88Jb 164
Chipstead Ct. Wok—5B 188
Chipstead Gdns. NW2—33Xa 60
Chipstead La. Sev—94Fd 186
Chipstead La. Tad—97Bb 179
Chipstead La. Tad & Coul
—96Cb 179
Chipstead Pk. Sev—94Fd 186
Chipstead Pk. Clo. Sev—94Ed 186
Chipstead Pl. Gdns. Sev—94Ed 186
Chipstead Rd. Bans—89Bb 163
Chipstead Rd. Eri—52Gd 110
Chipstead Rd. Houn—55Q 98
Chipstead Sq. Sev—94Ed 186
Chipstead Sta. Pde. Coul
—90Hb 163
Chipstead St. SW6—54Cb 103
Chipstead Valley Rd. Coul
—88Jb 164
Chipstead Way. Bans—88Hb 163
Chip St. SW4—56Mb 104
Chirton Wlk. Wok—6D 188
Chisenhale Rd. E3—40Ac 64
Chisholm Rd. Croy—75Ub 147
Chisholm Rd. Rich—58Pa 101
Chislehurst Av. N12—24Eb 41
Chislehurst Rd. Brom & Chst
—68Mc 129
Chislehurst Rd. Orp—70Uc 130
Chislehurst Rd. Rich—57Na 101
Chislehurst Rd. Sidc—64Wc 131
Chislet Clo. Beck—66Cc 128
Chisley Rd. N15—30Ub 43
Chiswell Sq. SE3—54Kc 107
Chiswell St. EC1—43Tb 83 (7F 195)
Chiswick Bri. SW14 & W4
—54Sa 101
Chiswick Clo. Croy—76Pb 146
Chiswick Comn. Rd. W4—49Ta 79
Chiswick Ct. Pinn—27Ba 37
Chiswick High Rd. W4—50Qa 79
to 49Va 80
Chiswick La. N. W4—50Ua 80
Chiswick La. S. W4—51Va 102
Chiswick Mall. W4 & W6
—51Va 102
Chiswick Quay. W4—53Sa 101
Chiswick Rd. N9—19Wb 25
Chiswick Rd. W4—49Sa 79
Chiswick Sq. W4—51Ua 102
Chiswick Staithe. W4—53Ra 101
Chiswick Village. W4—51Ra 101
Chiswick Wlk. W4—51Ua 102
Chitterfield Ga. W Dray—52Q 98
Chitty's La. Dag—33Zc 67
Chitty St. W1—43Lb 82 (7C 192)
Chivalry Rd. SW11—57Gb 103
Chive Clo. Croy—74Zb 148
Chivers Rd. E4—21Dc 44
★Chivers Rd. Brtwd—8Vd
Choats Mnr. Way. Dag—40Bd 67
Choats Rd. Dag—41Ad 87
Chobham Clo. Cher—79D 138
Chobham Gdns. SW19—61Za 124
Chobham Rd. E15—36Fc 65
Chobham Rd. Cher—80C 138
Chobham Rd. Chob & Wok
—86A 156
Chobham Rd. Chob & Wok—2F 188
Chobham Rd. Wok—88A 156
(in two parts)
Chobham Rd. Wok—4A 188
(Knaphill)
Choir Grn. Wok—5B 188
Cholmeley Cres. N6—31Kb 62
Cholmeley Pk. N6—32Kb 62
Cholmley Gdns. NW6—36Cb 61
Cholmley Rd. Th Dit—72Ka 142
Cholmondeley Av. NW10
—40Wa 60
Cholmondeley Wlk. Rich
—57La 100
Choppin's Ct. E1—46Xb 83
Chorleywood Bottom. Rick
—15F 16
Chorleywood Clo. Rick—17M 17
Chorleywood Cres. Orp—68Vc 131
Chorleywood Rd. Rick—14J 17
Choumert Gro. SE15—54Wb 105
Choumert Rd. SE15—55Vb 105
Choumert Sq. SE15—54Wb 105
Chrislaine Clo. Stai—58M 97
Chrisp St. E14—44Dc 84
Christchurch Av. N12—23Eb 41
Christchurch Av. NW6—39Za 60
Christchurch Av. Eri—51Gd 110
Christchurch Av. Harr—28Ha 38
Christchurch Av. Rain—41Hd 88
Christchurch Av. Tedd—64Ja 122
Christchurch Av. Wemb—37Na 59
Christchurch Clo. SW19—66Fb 125
Christchurch Cres. Rad—8Ja 6
Christchurch Gdns. Eps—83Ra 161
Christchurch Gdns. Harr—28Ja 38
Christchurch Grn. Wemb—37Na 59
Christchurch Hill. NW3—34Fb 61
Christchurch La. Barn—12Ab 22
Christchurch Mt. Eps—84Ra 161
Christchurch Pk. Sutt—80Eb 145
Christchurch Pas. NW3—34Eb 61
Christchurch Pas. Barn—12Ab 22
Christchurch Path. Hay—48S 76
Christchurch Pl. SW8—54Mb 104
Christchurch Pl. Eps—83Ra 161
Christchurch Rd. N8—30Nb 42
Christchurch Rd. SW2—60Pb 104
Christ Chu. Rd. SW14—57Ra 101
Christchurch Rd. SW19—67Fb 125
Christ Chu. Rd. Beck—68Cc 128
Christchurch Rd. Dart—58Ld 111
Christ Chu. Rd. Eps—84Na 161
Christchurch Rd. Grav—9E 114
Christchurch Rd. Houn—54Q 98
Christchurch Rd. Ilf—32Rc 66
Christchurch Rd. Purl—83Rb 165
Christchurch Rd. Sidc—63Vc 131
Christchurch Rd. Surb—72Pa 143
Christchurch Rd. Til—3C 114
Christchurch Rd. Vir W—70A 118
Christchurch Rd. Vir W—9L 117
Christchurch St. SW3—51Hb 103
Christchurch Way. SE10—50Gc 85
Christian Fields. SW16—66Qb 126
Christian Fields Av. Grav—3E 136
Christian Sq. Wind—3G 94
Christian St. E1—44Wb 83
Christie Ct. N19—33Nb 62
Christie Gdns. Romf—30Xc 47
Christie Rd. E9—37Ac 64
Christies Av. Sev—82Cd 170
Christina St. EC2
—42Ub 83 (5H 195)
Christmas La. Slou—4G 52
Christopher Av. W7—48Ja 78
Christopher Clo. Sidc—58Vc 109
Christopher Ct. Tad—95Ya 178
Christopher Gdns. Dag—36Zc 67
Christopher Pl. NW1
—41Mb 82 (3E 192)
Christopher Rd. S'hall—49X 77
Christopher St. EC2
—42Tb 83 (6G 195)
Christopher Way. Horn—35Md 69
Christy Rd. West—87Lc 167
Chryssell Rd. SW9—52Qb 104
Chrystie La. Lea—98Da 175
Chubworthy St. SE14—51Ac 106
Chucks La. Tad—96Xa 178
Chudleigh Cres. Ilf—35Uc 66
Chudleigh Gdns. Sutt—76Eb 145
Chudleigh Rd. NW6—38Za 60
Chudleigh Rd. SE4—57Bc 106
Chudleigh Rd. Romf—21Nd 49
Chudleigh Rd. Twic—58Ga 100
Chudleigh St. E1—44Zb 84
Chudleigh Way. Ruis—32W 56
Chulsa Rd. SE26—64Xb 127
Chumleigh St. SE5—51Ub 105
Chumleigh Wlk. Surb—70Pa 123
Church All. Croy—74Qb 146
Church All. Wat—10Ea 6
Church App. SE21—62Tb 127
Church App. Egh—69E 118
Church App. Sev—87Sc 168
Church App. Stai—58M 97
Church Av. E4—23Fc 45
Church Av. NW1—37Kb 62
Church Av. SW14—55Ta 101
Church Av. Beck—67Cc 128
Church Av. N'holt—38Ba 57
Church Av. Pinn—30Aa 37
Church Av. Ruis—32T 56
Church Av. Sidc—64Wc 131
Church Av. S'hall—48Aa 77
Churchbury Clo. Enf—12Ub 25
Churchbury La. Enf—13Tb 25
Churchbury Rd. SE9—59Mc 107
Churchbury Rd. Enf—12Ub 25
Church Cloisters. EC3—(5H 201)
Church Clo. N20—20Gb 23
★Church Clo. Brtwd—9Td
(Kelvedon Hatch)
Church Clo. Brtwd—11Fe 33
(Mountnessing)
Church Clo. Edgw—22Sa 39
Church Clo. Hay—43T 76
Church Clo. Lea—96Fa 176
Church Clo. Lou—12Pc 28
Church Clo. N'wd—24V 36
Church Clo. Pot B—1Nb 10
Church Clo. Tad—99Bb 179
Church Clo. Uxb—40K 55
Church Clo. W Dray—48N 75
Church Clo. Wey—77K 139
Church Clo. Wind—1H 95
Church Clo. Wok—88A 156
Church Ct. Rich—57Ma 101
Church Cres. E9—38Zb 64
Church Cres. N3—25Bb 41
Church Cres. N10—28Kb 42
Church Cres. N20—20Gb 23
Church Cres. Brtwd—11Fe 33
Church Cres. S Ock—41Yd 90
Churchcroft Clo. SW12—59Jb 104
Churchdown. Brom—63Gc 129
Church Dri. NW9—32Ta 59
Church Dri. Harr—30Ca 37
Church Dri. W Wick—76Gc 149
Church Elm La. Dag—37Cd 68
Church End. E17—28Dc 44
Church End. NW4—27Xa 40
Church Entry. EC4—(3C 200)
Church Farm Clo. Swan—72Ed 152
Church Farm La. Sutt—79Ab 144
Church Field. Sev—94Hd 186
Churchfield Av. N12—23Fb 41
Churchfield Clo. Harr—28Ea 38
Churchfield Clo. Hay—45V 76
Church Field Path. Wal X—1Yb 12
(in two parts)
Churchfield Rd. W3—46Sa 79
Churchfield Rd. W7—47Ga 78
Churchfield Rd. W13—46Ka 78
Churchfield Rd. Ger X—25A 34
Churchfield Rd. W on T—74W 140
Churchfield Rd. Well—55Wc 109
Churchfield Rd. Wey—77Q 140
Churchfields. E18—25Jc 45
Churchfields. SE10—51Ec 106
Churchfields. E Mol—69Ca 121
Churchfields. Lou—14Nc 28
Churchfields Av. Felt—62Ba 121
Churchfields Av. Wey—77R 140
Churchfields Rd. Beck—68Zb 128
Church Gdns. W5—47Ma 79
Church Gdns. Lea—92Ka 176
Church Gdns. Wemb—35Ja 58
Church Ga. SW6—55Ab 102
Churchgate. Wal X—1Xb 11
Churchgate Rd. Wal X—1Xb 11
Church Grn. Hay—44V 76
Church Grn. W on T—79Y 141
Church Gro. SE13—57Dc 106
Church Gro. Amer—11A 16
Church Gro. King—67La 122
Church Gro. Slou—3N 73
Church Hill. E17—28Cc 44
Church Hill. N21—17Pb 24
Church Hill. SE18—48Pc 86
Church Hill. SW19—64Bb 125
Church Hill. Cars—78Hb 145
Church Hill. Cat—96Vb 181
Church Hill. Dart—61Md 133
Church Hill. Dart—56Gd 110
(Crayford)
Church Hill. Epp—1Wc 15
Church Hill. Grnh—57Ud 112
Church Hill. Harr—32Ga 58
Church Hill. Lou—13Pc 28
Church Hill. Orp—73Wc 151
Church Hill. Purl—82Nb 164
Church Hill. Red—98Kb 180
Church Hill. Sev—87Sc 168
Church Hill. Stanf—2L 93
Church Hill. Uxb—27L 35
Church Hill. West—94Mc 183
Church Hill. Wok—4G 188
Church Hill. Wok—89H 157
(Pyrford)
Church Hill Rd. E17—28Dc 44
Church Hill Rd. Barn—16Gb 23
Church Hill Rd. Surb—71Na 143
Church Hill Rd. Sutt—76Za 144
Church Hill Wood. Orp—71Vc 151
Church Hyde. SE18—51Uc 108
Churchill Av. Harr—30Ka 38
Churchill Av. Uxb—41R 76
Churchill Clo. Lea—95Ga 176
Churchill Clo. Uxb—41R 76
Churchill Clo. Warl—89Yb 166
Churchill Ct. W5—42Pa 79
Churchill Dri. Wey—77S 140
Churchill Gdns. SW1—50Lb 82
Churchill Gdns. Est. SW1—50Lb 82
Churchill Gdns. Rd. SW1—50Kb 82
Churchill Pl. Harr—28Ga 38
Churchill Rd. E16—44Lc 85
Churchill Rd. NW2—37Xa 60
Churchill Rd. NW5—35Kb 62
Churchill Rd. Edgw—23Pa 39
Churchill Rd. Grav—10B 114
Churchill Rd. Grays—51Fe 113
Churchill Rd. Slou—49B 74
Churchill Rd. S Croy—80Sb 147
Churchill Rd. S Dar, Dart
—70Sd 134
Churchill Ter. E4—20Cc 26
Churchill Wlk. E9—36Yb 64
Churchill Way. Sun—65W 120
Church La. E11—32Gc 65
Church La. E17—28Dc 44
Church La. N2—27Fb 41
Church La. N8—28Pb 42
Church La. N9—19Wb 25
Church La. N17—25Ub 43
Church La. NW9—30Sa 39
Church La. SW17—64Hb 125
Church La. SW19—67Cb 125
Church La. W13—47La 78
Church La. Asc—10F 116
(Sunningdale)
Church La. Asc—10B 116
(Sunninghill)
★Church La. Brtwd—10Wd
(Doddinghurst)
Church La. Brtwd—30Zd 51
(Great Warley)
Church La. Brom—74Nc 150
Church La. Cat—96Qb 180
Church La. Chess—79Pa 143
Church La. Chst—67Sc 130
Church La. Coul—94Jb 180
Church La. Dag—38Ed 68
Church La. Enf—13Tb 25
Church La. Eps—89Za 162
(Great Burgh)
Church La. Eps—96Sa 177
(Headley)
Church La. Ger X—25A 34
Church La. Grav—1L 137
Church La. Harr—25Ha 38
Church La. K Lan—1Q 4
Church La. Lou—13Pc 28
Church La. Oxt—100Gc 183
Church La. Pinn—27Aa 37
Church La. Pot B—2Jb 10
Church La. Purl—50Qd 89
Church La. Rain—44Md 89
Church La. Rick—18J 17
Church La. Rick—10H 3
(Sarratt)
Church La. Romf—28Gd 48
Church La. Romf—12Ad 29
(Abridge)
Church La. Romf—14Ed 30
(Stapleford Abbotts)
Church La. Sev—89Rd 171
Church La. Slou—2M 73
Church La. Slou—2K 73
(Stoke Poges)
Church La. Tedd—64Ha 122
Church La. Th Dit—72Ha 142
Church La. Twic—60Ja 100
Church La. Upm—36Xd 70
Church La. Uxb—40K 55
Church La. Wall—76Mb 146
Church La. Wal X—1Yb 12
Church La. Warl—89Zb 166
Church La. Warl—88Dc 166
(Chelsham)
Church La. West—94Mc 183
Church La. Wind—3H 95
Church La. Wok—98D 172
Church La. Av. Coul—94Kb 180
Church La. Dri. Coul—94Kb 180
Churchley Rd. SE26—63Xb 127
Church Manorway. SE2—49Wc 87
Church Manorway. Eri—48Fd 88
Churchmead Clo. Barn—16Gb 23
Church Meadow. Surb—75La 142
Churchmore Rd. SW16—67Lb 126
Church Mt. N2—29Fb 41
Church Pde. Ashf—63P 119
Church Pas. Barn—14Ab 22
Church Pas. Surb—71Na 143
Church Pas. Twic—60Ka 100
Church Path. E11—29Jc 45
Church Path. E17—28Dc 44
Church Path. N5—36Rb 63
Church Path. N12—21Eb 41
Church Path. N17—25Ub 43
Church Path. NW10—38Ua 60
Church Path. SW14—55Ta 101
(in two parts)
Church Path. SW19—68Bb 125
Church Path. W4—48Sa 79
Church Path. W7—46Ga 78
Church Path. Asc—8C 116
Church Path. Cob—86X 159
Church Path. Coul—90Qb 164
Church Path. Croy—75Sb 147
Church Path. Grav—58Ee 113
Church Path. Grays—51Be 113
Church Path. Grnh—57Vd 112
Church Path. Mitc—69Gb 125
(in two parts)
Church Path. Romf—29Gd 48
Church Path. S'hall—46Ca 77
Church Path. S'hall—48Ba 77
(in three parts)
Church Path. Wok—89B 156
Church Pl. SW1—45Lb 82 (5C 198)
Church Pl. W5—47Ma 79
Church Pl. Mitc—69Gb 125
Church Rise. SE23—61Zb 128
Church Rise. Chess—79Pa 143
Church Rd. E10—32Cc 64
Church Rd. E12—36Nc 66
Church Rd. E17—26Ac 44
Church Rd. N6—30Jb 42
Church Rd. N17—25Ub 43
Church Rd. NW4—28Xa 40
Church Rd. NW10—38Ua 60
Church Rd. SE19—67Ub 127
Church Rd. SW13—54Va 102
Church Rd. SW19—64Ab 124
Church Rd.—67Fb 125
SW19 311-413 & 338-406
Mitc remainder
Church Rd. W3—46Sa 79
Church Rd. W7—45Fa 78
Church Rd. Ashf—62P 119
Church Rd. Asht—90Ma 161
Church Rd. Bark—37Sc 66
Church Rd. Bexh—54Bd 109
★Church Rd. Brtwd—9Sd
Church Rd. Brom—68Jc 129
Church Rd. Brom—69Gc 129
(Shortlands)
Church Rd. Buck H—18Kc 27
Church Rd. Cat—95Vb 181
Church Rd. Cat—94Ac 182
(Woldingham)
Church Rd. Croy—76Sb 147
(in two parts)
Church Rd. E Mol—70Fa 122
Church Rd. Egh—64C 118
Church Rd. Enf—16Yb 26
Church Rd. Eps—85Ua 162

Church Rd. Eps—80Ta 143
(West Ewell)
Church Rd. Eri—50Fd 88
Church Rd. Esh—79Ha 142
Church Rd. Felt—64Z 121
Church Rd. Grav—8E 136
(in two parts)
Church Rd. Grays—1G 114
Church Rd. Grnh—57Vd 112
Church Rd. Hav, Romf—18Ld 31
Church Rd. Hay—46V 76
Church Rd. Houn—50X 77
(Cranford)
Church Rd. Houn—52Ca 99
(Heston)
Church Rd. Ilf—30Uc 46
Church Rd. Iswth—52Ga 100
Church Rd. Iver—40E 54
Church Rd. Kenl—87Tb 165
Church Rd. Kes—80Mc 149
Church Rd. King—68Pa 123
Church Rd. Lea—94Ka 176
Church Rd. Lea—95Ba 175
(Great Bookham)
Church Rd. Long, Dart—71Be 155
Church Rd. Lou—13Jc 27
Church Rd. N'holt—40Z 57
Church Rd. N'wd—24V 36
★Church Rd. Ong—5Ld
Church Rd. Orp—80Yc 151
(Chelsfield)
Church Rd. Orp—78Sc 150
(Farnborough)
Church Rd. Pot B—2Db 9
Church Rd. Purl—82Nb 164
Church Rd. Rich—56Na 101
Church Rd. Rich—63Na 123
(Ham)
Church Rd. Romf—25Qd 49
(Harold Wood)
Church Rd. Romf—12Md 31
(Navestock)
Church Rd. Sev—83Ad 169
(Halstead)
Church Rd. Sev—93Pd 187
(Seal)
★Church Rd. Sev—95Ud
(Seal Chart)
Church Rd. Sev—96Ad 185
(Sundridge)—96Ad 185
Church Rd. Sev—99Ad 185
(Sundridge)
Church Rd. Sev—80Ud 154
(West Kingsdown)
Church Rd. Shep—73R 140
Church Rd. Sidc—63Wc 131
Church Rd. Slou—1G 72
Church Rd. S'hall—48Ba 77
Church Rd. Stan—22Ka 38
Church Rd. Surb—74La 142
Church Rd. Sutt—79Ab 144
Church Rd. S at H. Dart—66Nd 133
Church Rd. Swan—73Fd 152
(Crockenhill)
Church Rd. Swan—67Md 133
(Swanley Village)
Church Rd. Swans—58Be 113
Church Rd. Tedd—63Ga 122
Church Rd. Til—3B 114
Church Rd. Uxb—42M 75
Church Rd. Uxb—27L 35
(Harefield)
Church Rd. Wall—76Mb 146
Church Rd. Warl—89Zb 166
Church Rd. Wat—11W 18
Church Rd. Well—54Xc 109
Church Rd. W Dray—48M 75
Church Rd. West—96Xc 185
Church Rd. West—89Mc 167
(Biggin Hill)
Church Rd. Wey—78J 139
(Addlestone)
Church Rd. Wey—86N 157
(Byfleet)
Church Rd. Whyt—90Vb 165
Church Rd. Wind—7L 95
Church Rd. Wok—7D 188
Church Rd. Wok—87A 156
(Horsell)
Church Rd. Wor Pk—74Ua 144
Church Row. NW3—35Eb 61
Church Row. Chst—67Sc 130
Church Side. Eps—85Ra 161
Churchside Clo. West—89Lc 167
Church Sq. E9—39Yb 64
Church Sq. Shep—73R 140
Church St. E15—39Gc 65
Church St. E16—46Rc 86
Church St. N9—17Tb 25
Church St.—43Fb 81 (7C 190)
NW8 1-127 & 2-142
W2 remainder
Church St. W4—51Va 102
Church St. Cob—87X 159
Church St. Croy—75Sb 147
Church St. Dag—37Dd 68
Church St. Enf—13Sb 25
Church St. Eps—85Ua 162
Church St. Eps—81Wa 162
(Ewell)
Church St. Esh—77Da 141
Church St. Grav—8D 114
Church St. Grav—64Ce 135
(Southfleet)
Church St. Grays—51Ee 113
Church St. Hmptn—67Ea 122
Church St. Iswth—55Ka 100
Church St. King—68Ma 123
Church St. Lea—94Ka 176
Church St. Lea—99Z 175
(Effingham)
Church St. Rick—18N 17
Church St. Sev—93Qd 187
(Seal)
Church St. Sev—83Hd 170
(Shoreham)
Church St. Slou—7K 73
Church St. Slou—2A 72
(Burnham)
Church St. Slou—7G 72
(Chalvey)
Church St. Stai—63F 118
Church St. Sun—69X 121
Church St. Sutt—78Db 145
Church St. Twic—60Ja 100
Church St. Wal A—5Ec 12
Church St. W on T—74W 140
Church St. Wat—14Y 19
Church St. Wey—77Q 140
Church St. Wind—3H 95
Church St. Wok—89A 156
Church St. Wok—93E 172
(Old Woking)
Church St. E. Wok—89B 156
Church St. N. E15—39Gc 65
Church St. Pas. E15—39Gc 65
Church Stretton Rd. Houn
—57Ea 100
Church Ter. NW4—27Xa 40
Church Ter. SE13—55Gc 107
Church Ter. Rich—57Ma 101
Church Ter. Wind—4C 94
Church Trading Est. Eri—52Jd 110
Church Vale. N2—27Hb 41
Church Vale. SE23—61Zb 128
Church View. S Ock—47Sd 90
Church View. Upm—33Rd 69
Churchview Rd. Twic—60Fa 100
Church Wlk. N6—34Jb 62
Church Wlk. N16—35Tb 63
Church Wlk. NW2—34Bb 61
Church Wlk. NW4—27Ya 40
Church Wlk. NW9—33Ta 59
Church Wlk. SW13—53Wa 102
Church Wlk. SW15—57Xa 102
Church Wlk. SW16—68Lb 126
Church Wlk. SW20—69Ya 124
Church Wlk. Bren—51La 100
Church Wlk. Cat—96Wb 181
Church Wlk. Cher—72J 139
Church Wlk. Dart—62Md 133
Church Wlk. Grav—10F 114
(in two parts)
Church Wlk. Hay—44U 76
Church Wlk. Rich—57Ma 101
Church Wlk. Slou—2A 72
Church Wlk. Th Dit—72Ha 142
Church Wlk. W on T—74W 140
Church Wlk. Wey—76Q 140
Church Way. N20—20Gb 23
Churchway. NW1
—41Mb 82 (3E 192)
Church Way. Barn—14Hb 23
Church Way. Edgw—23Qa 39
Church Way. S Croy—82Vb 165
Churchwell Path. E9—36Yb 64
Churchyard Row. SE11
—49Rb 83 (5C 206)
Churston Av. E13—39Kc 65
Churston Dri. Mord—71Za 144
Churston Gdns. N11—23Lb 42
Churton Pl. SW1—49Lb 82 (6C 204)
Churton St. SW1—49Lb 82 (6C 204)
Chusan Pl. E14—44Bc 84
Chuters Gro. Eps—84Va 162
Chyngton Clo. Sidc—62Vc 131
Cibber Rd. SE23—61Zb 128
Cicada Rd. SW18—58Eb 103
Cicely Rd. SE15—53Wb 105
Cimba Wood. Grav—3G 136
Cinderford Way. Brom—63Gc 129
Cinder Path. Wok—7F 188
Cinema Pde. W5—42Pa 79
Cinnamon St. E1—46Xb 83
Cintra Pk. SE19—66Vb 127
Cippenham Clo. Slou—5D 72
Cippenham La. Slou—5D 72
Circle Gdns. SW19—68Cb 125
Circle Gdns. Wey—85P 157
Circle Rd. W on T—81U 158
Circle, The. NW2—34Ua 60
Circle, The. NW7—23Ta 39
Circle, The. Til—3C 114
Circuits, The. Pinn—28Y 37
Circular Rd. N17—27Vb 43
Circular Rd. SE1—48Sb 83 (3E 206)
Circular Way. SE18—51Pc 108
Circus M. W1—(7F 191)
Circus Pl. EC2—43Tb 83 (1G 201)
Circus Rd. NW8 41Fb 81 (3B 190)
Circus St. SE10—52Ec 106
Cirencester St. W2—43Db 81
Cirrus Cres. Grav—4G 136
Cissbury Ho. SE26—62Wb 127
Cissbury Ring N. N12—22Bb 41
Cissbury Ring S. N12—22Bb 41
Cissbury Rd. N15—29Tb 43
Citizen Rd. N7—35Qb 62
City Garden Row. N1
—40Rb 63 (2C 194)
City Rd. EC1—40Rb 63 (2B 194)
Civic Sq. Til—4C 114
Civic Way. Ilf—28Sc 46
Clabon M. SW1—48Hb 81 (4F 203)
Clacket La. West—96Nc 184
Clacket La. West—98Pc 184
Clack La. Ruis—32S 56
Clack St. SE16—47Yb 84
Clacton Rd. E6—41Mc 85
Clacton Rd. E17—30Ac 44
Clacton Rd. N17—26Vb 43
Claigmar Gdns. N3—25Db 41
Claire Ct. N12—21Eb 41
Claire Ct. Pinn—24Ba 37
Clairvale. Horn—31Nd 69
Clairvale Rd. Houn—53Aa 99
Clairview Rd. SW16—64Kb 126
Clairville Gdns. W7—46Ga 78
Clammas Waye. Uxb—43L 75
Clamp Hill. Stan—21Fa 38
Clancarty Rd. SW6—54Cb 103
Clandon Av. Egh—66E 118
Clandon Clo. W3—47Ra 79
Clandon Clo. Eps—79Va 144
Clandon Gdns. N3—27Cb 41
Clandon Rd. Ilf—33Uc 66
Clandon Rd. Wok & Guild
—97H 173
Clandon St. SE8—54Cc 106
Clanfield Way. SE15—52Vb 105
Clanricarde Gdns. W2—45Cb 81
Clapgate Rd. Bush, Wat—16Da 19
Clapham Comn. N. Side. SW4
—56Jb 104
Clapham Comn. S. Side. SW4
—58Kb 104
Clapham Comn. W. Side. SW4
(in three parts) —56Hb 103
Clapham Cres. SW4—56Mb 104
Clapham High St. SW4—56Mb 104
Clapham Junct. App. SW11
—56Gb 103
Clapham Mnr. St. SW4—55Lb 104
Clapham Pk. Rd. SW4—56Mb 104
Clapham Rd. SW9—55Nb 104
Clap La. Dag—33Dd 68
Claps Ga. La. Bark—42Rc 86
Clapton Comn. E5—31Vb 63
Clapton Comn. N16—32Wb 63
Clapton Pk. Est. E5—35Zb 64
Clapton Pas. E5—36Yb 64
Clapton Sq. E5—36Yb 64
Clapton Ter. N16—32Wb 63
Clapton Way. E5—35Wb 63
Clara Pl. SE18—49Qc 86
Clare Clo. N2—27Eb 41
Clare Clo. Borwd—16Pa 21
Clare Clo. Wey—85J 157
Clare Corner. SE9—59Rc 108
Clare Ct. Cat—95Cc 182
Clare Ct. Enf—7Ac 12
Clare Cres. Lea—91Ja 176
Claredale St. E2—40Wb 63
Clare Dri. Slou—5F 52
Clare Gdns. E7—35Jc 65
Clare Gdns. W11—44Ab 80
Clare Gdns. Bark—37Vc 67
Clare Gdns. Stan—22La 38
Clare Hill. Esh—79Da 141
Clare La. N1—38Sb 63
Clare Lawn Av. SW14—57Ta 101
Clare Mkt. WC2—44Pb 82 (3J 199)
Claremont. St Alb—3Ca 5
Claremont. Shep—72R 140
Claremont. Wal X—1Vb 11
Claremont Av. Esh—79Ba 141
Claremont Av. Harr—29Na 39
Claremont Av. N Mald—71Xa 144
Claremont Av. Sun—67X 121
Claremont Av. W on T—77Z 141
Claremont Av. Wok—91A 172
Claremont Clo. E16—46Qc 86
Claremont Clo. N1
—40Qb 62 (2A 194)
Claremont Clo. Grays—48Ee 91
Claremont Clo. Orp—77Qc 150
Claremont Clo. S Croy—87Xb 165
Claremont Clo. W on T—78Z 141
Claremont Cres. Dart—56Gd 110
Claremont Cres. Rick—15S 18
Claremont Dri. Esh—79Da 141
Claremont Dri. Wok—91A 172
Claremont End. Esh—79Da 141
Claremont Gdns. Ilf—33Uc 66
Claremont Gdns. Surb—71Na 143
Claremont Gdns. Upm—32Td 70
Claremont Gro. W4—52Ua 102
Claremont Gro. Wfd G—23Lc 45
Claremont La. Esh—78Da 141
Claremont Pk. N3—25Ab 40
Claremont Pk. Rd. Esh—79Da 141
Claremont Rd. E7—36Kc 65
Claremont Rd. E11—34Fc 65
Claremont Rd. E17—26Ac 44
Claremont Rd. N6—31Lb 62
Claremont Rd. NW2—32Za 60
Claremont Rd. W9—40Bb 61
Claremont Rd. W13—43Ja 78
Claremont Rd. Barn—9Fb 9
Claremont Rd. Brom—70Nc 130
Claremont Rd. Croy—74Wb 147
Claremont Rd. Esh—80Ga 142
Claremont Rd. Harr—26Ga 38
Claremont Rd. Horn—30Jd 48
Claremont Rd. Stai—64F 118
Claremont Rd. Surb—71Na 143
Claremont Rd. Swan—66Gd 132
Claremont Rd. Tedd—64Ha 122
Claremont Rd. Twic—58La 100
Claremont Rd. Wey—84J 157
Claremont Rd. Wind—4G 94
Claremont Sq. N1
—40Qb 62 (2K 193)
Claremont St. E16—46Qc 86
Claremont St. N18—23Wb 43
Claremont St. SE10—51Dc 106
Claremont Way. NW2—32Ya 60
Claremount Gdns. Eps—89Za 162
Clarence Av. SW4—59Mb 104
Clarence Av. Brom—70Nc 130
Clarence Av. Ilf—30Qc 46
Clarence Av. N Mald—68Sa 123
Clarence Av. Upm—33Qd 69
Clarence Clo. Bush, Wat—17Ha 20
Clarence Clo. W on T—77X 141
Clarence Cres. SW4—58Mb 104
Clarence Cres. Sidc—62Xc 131
Clarence Cres. Wind—3G 94
Clarence Dri. Egh—3N 117
Clarence Gdns. NW1
—41Kb 82 (4A 192)
Clarence Ga. Gdns. NW1—(6G 191)
Clarence La. SW15—58Ua 102
Clarence M. E5—36Xb 63
Clarence Pas. NW1
—40Nb 62 (2F 193)
Clarence Pl. E5—36Xb 63
Clarence Pl. Grav—9D 114
Clarence Rd. E5—35Xb 63
Clarence Rd. E12—36Mc 65
Clarence Rd. E16—42Gc 85
Clarence Rd. E17—26Zb 44
Clarence Rd. N15—29Sb 43
Clarence Rd. N22—24Nb 42
Clarence Rd. NW6—38Bb 61
Clarence Rd. SE9—61Nc 130
Clarence Rd. SW19—65Db 125
Clarence Rd. W4—50Qa 79
Clarence Rd. Bexh—56Ad 109
Clarence Rd. Brtwd—16Xd 32
Clarence Rd. Brom—69Mc 129
Clarence Rd. Croy—73Tb 147
Clarence Rd. Enf—15Yb 26
Clarence Rd. Grays—50De 91
Clarence Rd. Rich—53Pa 101
Clarence Rd. Sidc—62Xc 131
Clarence Rd. Sutt—78Db 145
Clarence Rd. Tedd—65Ha 122
Clarence Rd. Wall—78Kb 146
Clarence Rd. W on T—77X 141
Clarence Rd. West—90Pc 168
Clarence Rd. Wind—3E 94
(in two parts)
Clarence Row. Grav—9D 114
Clarence St. Egh—65B 118
Clarence St. King—68Ma 123
Clarence St. S'hall—48Z 77
Clarence St. Stai—63G 118
Clarence Ter. NW1
—42Hb 81 (5G 191)
Clarence Ter. Houn—56Da 99
Clarence Wlk. SW4—54Nb 104
Clarence Way. NW1—38Kb 62
Clarence Yd. SE17—(7D 206)
Clarendon Av. SE5—52Sb 105
Clarendon Clo. W2
—45Gb 81 (4D 196)
Clarendon Clo. Orp—69Wc 131
Clarendon Ct. Slou—5M 73
Clarendon Cres. Twic—62Fa 122
Clarendon Cross. W11—45Ab 80
Clarendon Dri. SW15—56Ya 102
Clarendon Gdns. NW4—27Xa 40
Clarendon Gdns. W9
—42Eb 81 (6A 190)
Clarendon Gdns. Dart—59Td 112
Clarendon Gdns. Ilf—31Pc 66
Clarendon Gdns. Wemb—34Ma 59
Clarendon Grn. Orp—70Wc 131
Clarendon Gro. NW1
—41Mb 82 (3D 192)
Clarendon Gro. Mitc—69Hb 125
Clarendon Gro. Orp—70Wc 131
Clarendon M. W2
—45Gb 81 (4D 196)
Clarendon Pde. Wal X—1Zb 12
Clarendon Path. Orp—69Wc 131
(in two parts)
Clarendon Pl. W2
—45Gb 81 (4D 196)
Clarendon Rise. SE13—56Ec 106
Clarendon Rd. E11—32Fc 65
Clarendon Rd. E17—30Dc 44
Clarendon Rd. E18—27Jc 45
Clarendon Rd. N8—27Pb 42
Clarendon Rd. N15—28Sb 43
Clarendon Rd. N18—23Wb 43
Clarendon Rd. N22—26Pb 42
Clarendon Rd. SW19—66Gb 125
Clarendon Rd. W5—42Na 79
Clarendon Rd. W11—45Ab 80
Clarendon Rd. Ashf—63P 119
Clarendon Rd. Borwd—13Qa 21
Clarendon Rd. Croy—75Rb 147
Clarendon Rd. Grav—8E 114
Clarendon Rd. Harr—30Ga 38
Clarendon Rd. Hay—47V 76
Clarendon Rd. Sev—96Jd 186
Clarendon Rd. Wall—79Lb 146
Clarendon Rd. Wal X—1Zb 12
Clarendon Rd. Wat—12X 19
Clarendon St. SW1
—50Kb 82 (7A 204)
Clarendon Ter. W9
—42Eb 81 (5A 190)
Clarendon Wlk. W11—44Ab 80
Clarendon Way. N21—16Sb 25
Clarendon Way. Chst & Orp
—69Vc 131
Clarens St. SE6—61Bc 128
Clare Rd. E11—30Fc 45
Clare Rd. NW10—38Wa 60
Clare Rd. SE14—54Bc 106
Clare Rd. Gnfd—37Fa 58
Clare Rd. Houn—55Ba 99
Clare Rd. M'head—4A 72
Clare Rd. Stai—60M 97
Clare St. E2—40Xb 63
Claret Gdns. SE25—69Ub 127
Clareville Gro. SW7
—49Eb 81 (6A 202)
Clareville Rd. Cat—96Wb 181
Clareville Rd. Orp—75Sc 150
Clareville St. SW7
—49Eb 81 (6A 202)
Clare Way. Bexh—53Ad 109
Clare Way. Sev—100Ld 187
Clare Wood. Lea—90Ka 160
Clarewood Wlk. SW9—56Qb 104
Clarges M. W1—46Kb 82 (6K 197)
Clarges St. W1—46Kb 82 (6A 198)
Claribel Rd. SW9—54Rb 105
Clarice Way. Wall—81Nb 164
Claridge Rd. Dag—32Zc 67
Clarissa Rd. Romf—31Zc 67
Clarissa St. E8—39Vb 63
Clarkbourne Dri. Grays—51Fe 113
Clark Clo. Eri—53Jd 110
Clarke Path. N16—32Wb 63
Clarkes Av. Wor Pk—74Za 144
Clarke's Grn. Rd. Sev—86Qd 171
Clarke's M. W1—(7J 191)
Clarke Way. Wat—7W 4
Clarkfield. Rick—18K 17
Clarks La. Sev—84Bd 169
Clarks La. Warl & West—95Jc 183
Clarks Mead. Bush, Wat—17Ea 20
Clarkson Rd. E16—44Hc 85
Clarkson Row. NW1—(1B 192)
Clarksons, The. Bark—40Sc 66
Clarkson St. E2—41Xb 83
Clark's Pl. EC2—44Ub 83 (2H 201)
Clarks Rd. Ilf—33Tc 66
Clark St. E1—43Yb 84
Clark Way. Houn—52Z 99
Claston Clo. Dart—56Gd 110
Claude Rd. E10—32Ec 64
Claude Rd. E13—39Kc 65
Claude Rd. SE15—55Xb 105
Claude St. E14—49Cc 84
Claudian Way. Grays—8D 92
Claudia Pl. SW19—60Ab 102
Claughton Rd. E13—40Lc 65
Claughton Way. Brtwd—16Fe 33
Clausen Way. Gnfd—40Ja 58
Clauson Av. N'holt—36Da 57
Clavell St. SE10—51Ec 106
Claverdale Rd. SW2—59Pb 104
Claverhambury Rd. Wal A
—1Hc 13
Clavering Av. SW13—51Xa 102
Clavering Clo. Twic—63Ja 122
Clavering Gdns. Brtwd—30Fe 51
Clavering Rd. E12—33Mc 65
Claverley Gro. N3—25Db 41
Claverley Vs. N3—25Db 41
Claverton Clo. Hem—1C 2
Claverton St. SW1
—50Lb 82 (7C 204)
Clave St. E1—46Yb 84
Claxton Gro. W6—50Za 80
Clay Av. Mitc—68Kb 126
Claybridge Rd. SE12—63Lc 129
Claybrook Rd. W6—51Za 102
Clayburn Gdns. S Ock—45Xd 90
Claybury. Bush, Wat—17Da 19
Claybury B'way. Ilf—27Nc 46
Claybury Rd. Wfd G—24Nc 46
Claydon End. Ger X—27A 34
Claydon.La. Ger X—27A 34
Claydon Rd. Wok—4D 188
Clay Farm Rd. SE9—61Sc 130
Claygate Clo. Horn—35Jd 68
Claygate Cres. Croy—79Ec 148
Claygate La. Esh & Th Dit
—76Ja 142
Claygate La. Wal A—2Gc 13
Claygate Lodge Clo. Esh
—80Ga 142
Claygate Rd. W13—48Ka 78
Clayhall Av. Ilf—26Nc 46
Clayhall La. Wind—7K 95
Clay Hill. Enf—9Sb 11
Clayhill. Surb—71Qa 143
Clayhill Cres. SE9—63Mc 129
Claylands Pl. SW8—52Qb 104
Claylands Rd. SW8—51Pb 104
Clay La. Bush, Wat—17Ga 20
Clay La. Edgw—19Qa 21
Clay La. Eps—96Ra 177
Clay La. Guild—100A 172
Clay La. Stai—59P 97
Claymore Clo. Mord—73Cb 145
Claypit Hill. Wal A—8Lc 13
Claypole Rd. E15—40Ec 64
Clayponds Av. W5 & Bren
—49Na 79
Clayponds Gdns. W5—49Ma 79
Clayponds La. Bren—50Na 79
Clay Ride. Lou—11Mc 27
Clayside. Chig—22Sc 46
Clays La. E15—36Dc 64
Clay's La. Lou—11Qc 28
Clays La. Clo. E15—36Dc 64
Clay St. W1—43Hb 81 (1G 197)
Clayton Av. Upm—36Rd 69
Clayton Av. Wemb—38Na 59
Clayton Clo. E6—44Pc 86
Clayton Cres. Bren—50Ma 79
Clayton Croft Rd. Dart—61Jd 132
Clayton Field. NW9—24Ua 40
Clayton Rd. SE15—53Wb 105
Clayton Rd. Chess—77La 142
Clayton Rd. Eps—85Ua 162
Clayton Rd. Hay—47U 76
Clayton Rd. Iswth—55Ga 100
Clayton Rd. Romf—32Ed 68
Clayton St. SE11—51Qb 104
Clayton Ter. Hay—43Aa 77
Clayton Way. Uxb—42M 75
Clay Tye Rd. Upm—33Yd 70
Claywood Clo. Orp—73Uc 150
Clayworth Clo. Sidc—58Xc 109
Cleall Av. Wal A—6Ec 12
Cleanthus Clo. SE18—53Rc 108
Cleanthus Rd. SE18—53Rc 108
Clearbrook Way. E1—44Yb 84
Cleardown. Wok—90D 156
Clearwell Dri. W9—42Db 81
Cleave Av. Hay—49U 76
Cleave Av. Orp—79Uc 150
Cleaveland Rd. Surb—71Ma 143
Cleave Prior. Coul—91Gb 179
Cleaverholme Clo. Croy
—72Xb 147
Cleaver Sq. SE11
—50Qb 82 (7A 206)
Cleaver St. SE11
—50Qb 82 (7A 206)
Cleeve Hill. SE23—60Xb 105
Cleeve Rd. Lea—92Ha 176
Clegg St. E1—46Xb 83
Clegg St. E13—40Jc 65
Cleland Path. Lou—11Rc 28
Cleland Rd. Ger X—26A 34
Clematis Clo. Romf—24Ld 49
Clematis St. W12—45Wa 80
Clem Attlee Ct. SW6—51Bb 103
Clemence St. E14—43Bc 84
Clement Clo. NW10—38Ya 60
Clement Clo. W4—49Ta 79
Clement Clo. Purl—88Rb 165
Clement Gdns. Hay—49U 76
Clementhorpe Rd. Dag—37Yc 67
Clementina Rd. E10—32Bc 64
Clementine Clo. W13—47Ka 78
Clement Rd. SW19—64Ab 124
Clement Rd. Beck—68Zb 128
Clement's Av. E16—45Jc 85
Clement's Av. Grays—51Xd 112
Clements Clo. Slou—7M 73
Clements Ct. Houn—56Z 99
Clement's Inn. WC2
—44Pb 82 (3J 199)
Clement's Inn Pas. WC2—(3J 199)
Clement's La. EC4
—45Tb 83 (4G 201)
Clements La. Ilf—34Rc 66
Clements Mead. Lea—91Ja 176
Clements Pl. Bren—50Ma 79
Clements Rd. E6—38Pc 66
Clement's Rd. SE16—48Wb 83
Clements Rd. Ilf—34Rc 66
Clements Rd. Lea—91Ja 176
Clement's Rd. Rick—15F 16
Clements Rd. W on T—75Y 141
Clement St. Swan & S at H,
Dart—65Md 133
Clement Way. Upm—34Pd 69
Clenches Farm La. Sev—98Jd 186
Clenches Farm Rd. Sev—98Jd 186
Clendon Way. SE18—49Tc 86
Clennam St. SE1—47Sb 83 (1E 206)
Clensham La. Sutt—75Cb 145
Clenston M. W1—44Hb 81 (2F 197)
Clephane Rd. N1—37Sb 63
Clere Pl. EC2—42Tb 83 (5G 195)
Clere St. EC2—42Tb 83 (5G 195)
Clerkenwell Clo. EC1
—42Qb 82 (5A 194)
Clerkenwell Grn. EC1
—42Rb 83 (6B 194)
Clerkenwell Rd. EC1
—42Qb 82 (6K 193)
Clerks Piece. Lou—13Pc 28
Clermont Rd. E9—39Yb 64
Clevedon. Wey—78T 140
Clevedon Clo. N16—34Vb 63
Clevedon Gdns. Hay—48T 76
Clevedon Gdns. Houn—53X 99
Clevedon Rd. SE20—67Zb 128
Clevedon Rd. King—68Qa 123
Clevedon Rd. Twic—58Ma 101
Clevehurst Clo. Slou—7L 53
Cleveland Av. SW20—68Bb 125
Cleveland Av. W4—49Va 80
Cleveland Av. Hmptn—66Ba 121
Cleveland Clo. W on T—76X 141
Cleveland Cres. Borwd—15Sa 21
Cleveland Dri. Stai—68K 119
Cleveland Gdns. N4—29Sb 43
Cleveland Gdns. NW2—33Za 60
Cleveland Gdns. SW13—54Va 102
Cleveland Gdns. W2
—44Eb 81 (3A 196)
Cleveland Gdns. Wor Pk
—75Ua 144
Cleveland Gro. E1—42Yb 84
Cleveland M. W1
—43Lb 82 (7B 192)
Cleveland Pk. Av. E17—28Cc 44
Cleveland Pk. Cres. E17—28Cc 44
Cleveland Pl. SW1
—46Lb 82 (6C 198)
Cleveland Rise. Mord—73Za 144
Cleveland Rd. E18—27Jc 45
Cleveland Rd. N1—38Tb 63
Cleveland Rd. N9—17Xb 25
Cleveland Rd. SW13—54Va 102
Cleveland Rd. W4—48Sa 79
Cleveland Rd. W13—43Ja 78
Cleveland Rd. Ilf—34Rc 66
Cleveland Rd. Iswth—56Ja 100
Cleveland Rd. N Mald—70Ua 124
Cleveland Rd. Uxb—42M 75
Cleveland Rd. Well—54Vc 109
Cleveland Rd. Wor Pk—75Ua 144
Cleveland Row. SW1
—46Lb 82 (7B 198)
Cleveland Sq. W2
—44Eb 81 (3A 196)
Cleveland St. W1
—42Kb 82 (6A 192)
Cleveland Ter. W2
—44Eb 81 (2A 196)
Cleveland Way. E1—42Yb 84
Cleveley Clo. SE7—49Mc 85
Cleveley Cres. W5—40Na 59
Cleveleys Rd. E5—34Xb 63
Cleverley Est. W12—46Wa 80
Cleve Rd. NW6—38Db 61
Cleve Rd. Sidc—62Zc 131
Cleves Av. Eps—81Xa 162
Cleves Clo. Cob—86X 159
Cleves Cres. Croy—83Ec 166
Cleves Rd. E6—39Mc 65
Cleves Rd. Rich—62La 122
Cleves Rd. Sev—89Nd 171
Cleves Wlk. Ilf—24Sc 46
Cleves Way. Hmptn—66Ba 121
Cleves Way. Ruis—32Z 57
Cleves Wood. Wey—77U 140
Clewer Av. Wind—4E 94
Clewer Ct. Rd. Wind—2F 94
Clewer Cres. Harr—25Fa 38
Clewer Fields. Wind—3G 94
Clewer Hill Rd. Wind—4C 94
Clewer New Town. Wind—4E 94
Clewer Pk. Wind—2F 94
Clichy Est. E1—43Yb 84
Clifden Rd. E5—36Yb 64
Clifden Rd. Bren—51Ma 101
Clifden Rd. Twic—60Ha 100
Cliff End. Purl—84Rb 165
Cliffe Rd. S Croy—78Tb 147
Clifford Av. SW14—55Ra 101
Clifford Av. Chst—65Pc 130
Clifford Av. Ilf—26Rc 46
Clifford Av. Wall—77Lb 146
Clifford Clo. N'holt—39Aa 57
Clifford Dri. SW9—56Rb 105

Clifford Gdns.—Colonel's Wlk., The

Clifford Gdns. NW10—40Ya 60
Clifford Gro. Ashf—63Q 120
Clifford Rd. E16—42Hc 85
Clifford Rd. E17—26Ec 44
Clifford Rd. N9—16Yb 26
Clifford Rd. SE25—70Wb 127
Clifford Rd. Barn—13Db 23
Clifford Rd. Houn—55Z 99
Clifford Rd. Rich—61Ma 123
Clifford Rd. Wemb—38Ma 59
Clifford's Inn. EC4—(3K 199)
Clifford St. W1—45Lb 82 (5B 198)
Clifford St. Wat—14Y 19
Clifford Way. NW10—35Va 60
Cliff Pl. S Ock—41Zd 91
Cliff Rd. NW1—37Mb 62
Cliff St. E16—43Hc 85
Cliff Ter. SE8—54Cc 106
Cliffview Rd. SE13—55Cc 106
Cliff Vs. NW1—37Mb 62
Cliff Wlk. E16—43Hc 85
Clifton Av. E17—27Zb 44
Clifton Av. N3—25Bb 41
Clifton Av. W12—46Va 80
Clifton Av. Felt—62Y 121
Clifton Av. Stan—26Ka 38
Clifton Av. Sutt—83Db 163
Clifton Av. Wemb—37Pa 59
Clifton Clo. Cat—95Tb 181
Clifton Clo. Orp—78Sc 150
Clifton Clo. Wal X—1Ac 12
Clifton Clo. Wey—75K 139
Clifton Ct. W9—(5B 190)
Clifton Cres. SE15—52Yb 106
(in two parts)
Clifton Est. SE15—53Xb 105
Clifton Gdns. N15—30Vb 43
Clifton Gdns. NW11—30Bb 41
Clifton Gdns. W4—49Ta 79
Clifton Gdns. W9
—42Eb 81 (6A 190)
Clifton Gdns. Enf—14Nb 24
Clifton Gdns. Uxb—40R 56
Clifton Gro. E8—37Wb 63
Clifton Gro. Grav—9D 114
Clifton Hill. NW8—40Db 61
Clifton Marine Pde. Grav—8B 114
Clifton Pk. Av. SW20—68Ya 124
Clifton Pl. W2—44Fb 81 (3C 196)
Clifton Pl. Bans—87Cb 163
Clifton Rise. SE14—52Ac 106
Clifton Rise. Wind—3B 94
Clifton Rd. E7—37Mc 65
Clifton Rd. E16—43Gc 85
Clifton Rd. N3—25Eb 41
Clifton Rd. N8—30Mb 42
Clifton Rd. N22—25Lb 42
Clifton Rd. NW10—40Wa 60
Clifton Rd. SE25—70Ub 127
Clifton Rd. SW19—65Za 124
Clifton Rd. W9—42Eb 81 (5A 190)
Clifton Rd. Coul—87Kb 164
Clifton Rd. Grav—8C 114
Clifton Rd. Gnfd—42Ea 78
Clifton Rd. Harr—28Pa 39
Clifton Rd. Horn—30Jd 48
Clifton Rd. Ilf—30Tc 46
Clifton Rd. Iswth—54Ga 100
Clifton Rd. King—66Pa 123
Clifton Rd. Lou—14Nc 28
Clifton Rd. Sidc—63Uc 130
Clifton Rd. Slou—7M 73
Clifton Rd. S'hall—49Aa 77
Clifton Rd. Tedd—63Ga 122
Clifton Rd. Wall—78Kb 146
Clifton Rd. Wat—15X 19
Clifton Rd. Well—55Yc 109
Clifton St. EC2—43Ub 83 (7H 195)
Clifton Ter. N4—33Qb 62
Clifton Vs. W9—43Eb 81
Clifton Way. SE15—52Yb 106
Clifton Way. Brtwd—18Fe 33
Clifton Way. Wemb—39Na 59
Clifton Way. Wok—5C 188
Climb, The. Rick—16K 17
Clinch Ct. E16—43Jc 85
Cline Rd. N11—23Lb 42
Clinger Ct. N1—39Ub 63 (1H 195)
Clink St. SE1—46Tb 83 (6E 200)
Clinton Av. E Mol—70Ea 122
Clinton Av. Well—56Wc 109
Clinton Clo. Wok—6A 188
Clinton Cres. Ilf—23Uc 46
Clinton Rd. E3—41Ac 84
Clinton Rd. E7—35Jc 65
Clinton Rd. N15—28Tb 43
Clinton Rd. Lea—95La 176
Clipper Cres. Grav—3H 137
Clipper Way. SE13—56Ec 106
Clippesby Clo. Chess—79Pa 143
Clipstone M. W1—43Lb 82 (7B 192)
Clipstone Rd. Houn—55Ca 99
Clipstone St. W1
—43Lb 82 (7A 192)
Clissold Clo. N2—27Hb 41
Clissold Ct. N4—33Sb 63
Clissold Cres. N16—34Tb 63
Clissold Rd. N16—34Tb 63
Clitheroe Av. Harr—32Ca 57
Clitheroe Gdns. Wat—20Z 19
Clitheroe Rd. SW9—54Nb 104
Clitheroe Rd. Romf—22Ed 48
Clitherow Av. W7—48Ja 78
Clitherow Pas. Bren—50La 78
Clitherow Rd. Bren—50Ka 78
Clitterhouse Cres. NW2—32Ya 60
Clitterhouse Rd. NW2—32Ya 60
Clive Av. N18—23Wb 43
Clive Av. Dart—58Hd 110
Clive Clo. Pot B—3Bb 9
Clive Ct. W9—(5A 190)
Clive Ct. Slou—7H 73
Cliveden Clo. N12—21Eb 41
Cliveden Clo. Brtwd—17Be 33
Cliveden Pl. SW1
—49Jb 82 (5H 203)
Cliveden Pl. Shep—72S 140
Cliveden Rd. SW19—67Bb 125
Clivedon Ct. W13—43Ka 78
Clivedon Rd. E4—22Gc 45
Clive Pas. SE21—62Tb 127
Clive Rd. SE21—62Tb 127
Clive Rd. SW19—65Gb 125
Clive Rd. Belv—49Cd 88
Clive Rd. Brtwd—24Yd 50
Clive Rd. Enf—14Wb 25
Clive Rd. Esh—77Da 141
Clive Rd. Felt—58W 98
Clive Rd. Grav—8D 114
Clive Rd. Romf—29Kd 49
Clive Rd. Twic—63Ha 122
Clivesdale Dri. Hay—46X 77
Clive Way. Enf—14Wb 25
Clive Way. Wat—11Y 19
Cloak La. EC4—45Sb 83 (4E 200)
Clockhouse Av. Bark—39Sc 66
Clockhouse Clo. SW19—61Ya 124
Clock Ho. Clo. Wey—84P 157
Clockhouse Industrial Est.
Felt—60R 98
Clockhouse La. Ashf & Felt
—63Q 120
Clockhouse La. Grays—47Ae 91
(in two parts)
Clockhouse La. Romf—24Dd 48
Clock Ho. La. Sev—95Jd 186
Clockhouse La. E. Egh—66D 118
Clockhouse La. W. Egh—66C 118
Clock Ho. Mead. Lea—86Da 159
Clockhouse Pde. N13—22Qb 42
Clock Ho. Rd. Beck—69Ac 128
Clock Pde. Enf—15Tb 25
Clock Tower M. N1
—39Sb 63 (1E 194)
Clock Tower Pl. N7—37Nb 62
Clock Tower Rd. Iswth—55Ha 100
Clodhouse Hill. Wok—10A 188
Cloister Gdns. Croy—72Xb 147
Cloister Gdns. Edgw—22Sa 39
Cloister Rd. NW2—34Bb 61
Cloister Rd. W3—43Sa 79
Cloisters. Stanf—1N 93
Cloisters Av. Brom—71Pc 150
Cloisters, The. E1—(7K 195)
Cloisters, The. SW9—53Qb 104
Cloisters, The. Rick—17N 17
Clonard Way. Pinn—23Ca 37
Clonbrook Rd. N16—35Ub 63
Cloncurry St. SW6—54Za 102
Clonmel Clo. Harr—33Fa 58
Clonmell Rd. N17—27Tb 43
Clonmel Rd. SW6—53Bb 103
Clonmel Rd. Tedd—63Fa 122
Clonmel Way. Slou—1A 72
Clonmore St. SW18—60Bb 103
Cloonmore Av. Orp—77Vc 151
Clorane Gdns. NW3—34Cb 61
Closemead Clo. N'wd—23S 36
Close, The. E4—24Ec 44
Close, The. N14—19Mb 24
Close, The. N20—19Bb 23
Close, The. Barn—16Hb 23
Close, The. Beck—70Ac 128
Close, The. Bex—58Cd 110
Close, The. Brtwd—20Zd 33
Close, The. Bush, Wat—16Ca 19
Close, The. Cars—81Gb 163
Close, The. Dart—62Md 133
Close, The. Grays—47Ee 91
Close, The. Harr—26Ea 38
Close, The. Iswth—54Fa 100
Close, The. Iver—41E 74
Close, The. Long, Dart—68De 135
Close, The. Mitc—70Hb 125
Close, The. N Mald—68Sa 123
Close, The. Orp—72Uc 150
Close, The. Pinn—31Y 57
(Eastcote)
Close, The. Pinn—31Ba 57
(Rayners Lane)
Close, The. Pot B—4Cb 9
Close, The. Purl—82Rb 165
(Pampisford Rd.)
Close, The. Purl—82Pb 164
(Russell Hill)
Close, The. Rad—5Ha 6
Close, The. Rich—55Ra 101
Close, The. Rick—18K 17
Close, The. Romf—30Ad 47
Close, The. Sev—96Gd 186
★Close, The. Sev—91Ce
(Borough Green)
Close, The. Sidc—63Xc 131
Close, The. Slou—5B 72
Close, The. Sutt—73Bb 145
Close, The. Uxb—38N 55
Close, The. Uxb—39Q 56
(Hillingdon)
Close, The. Vir W—10P 117
Close, The. Wemb—34Sa 59
(Barnhill Rd.)
Close, The. Wemb—37Na 59
(Lyon Pk. Av.)
Close, The. Wey—85J 157
Cloth Ct. EC1—(1C 200)
Cloth Fair. EC1—43Rb 83 (1C 200)
Clothier St. E1—44Ub 83 (2J 201)
Cloth St. EC1—43Sb 83 (7D 194)
Cloudberry Rd. Romf—23Md 49
Cloudesdale Rd. SW17—61Kb 126
Cloudesley Pl. N1—39Qb 62 (1A 194)
Cloudesley Rd. N1
—39Qb 62 (1K 193)
Cloudesley Rd. Bexh—53Bd 109
Cloudesley Rd. Eri—53Hd 110
Cloudesley Sq. N1—39Qb 62
Cloudesley St. N1
—39Qb 62 (1A 194)
Clouston Clo. Wall—78Nb 146
Clova Rd. E7—37Hc 65
Clovelly Av. NW9—28Va 40
Clovelly Av. Uxb—35S 56
Clovelly Av. Warl—91Xb 181
Clovelly Clo. Uxb—35S 56
Clovelly Ct. Horn—33Qd 69
Clovelly Gdns. Enf—17Ub 25
Clovelly Gdns. Romf—25Dd 48
Clovelly Rd. N8—28Mb 42
Clovelly Rd. W4—47Ta 79
Clovelly Rd. W13—47La 78
Clovelly Rd. Bexh—51Ad 109
Clovelly Rd. Houn—54Ca 99
Clovelly Way. E1—44Yb 84
Clovelly Way. Harr—33Ba 57
Clovelly Way. Orp—72Vc 151
Clover Clo. E11—33Fc 65
Clover Ct. Grays—51Fe 113
Clover Ct. Wok—7G 188
Cloverdale Gdns. Sidc—58Vc 109
Clover Hill. Coul—93Kb 180
Clover Leas. Epp—1Vc 15
Clove St. E13—42Jc 85
Clowders Rd. SE6—62Bc 128
Cloysters Grn. E1—46Wb 83
Cloyster Wood. Edgw—24Ma 39
Club Gdns. Rd. Brom—73Jc 149
Club Row—42Vb 83 (5K 195)
E1 1-11 & 2-10
E2 remainder
Clumps, The. Ashf—63T 120
Clump, The. Rick—15K 17
Clunas Gdns. Romf—27Md 49
Clunbury Av. S'hall—50Ba 77
Clunbury St. N1—40Tb 63 (2G 195)
Cluny M. SW5—49Cb 81
Cluny Pl. SE1—48Ub 83 (3H 207)
Clutton St. E14—43Dc 84
Clydach Rd. Enf—14Vb 25
Clyde. Grays—9L 93
Clyde Av. S Croy—87Xb 165
Clyde Cir. N15—28Ub 43
Clyde Cres. Upm—30Ud 50
Clyde Pl. E10—31Dc 64
Clyde Rd. N15—28Ub 43
Clyde Rd. N22—25Mb 42
Clyde Rd. Croy—75Vb 147
Clyde Rd. Stai—60M 97
Clyde Rd. Sutt—78Cb 145
Clyde Rd. Wall—79Lb 146
Clydesdale. Enf—14Zb 26
Clydesdale Av. Stan—27Ma 39
Clydesdale Clo. Borwd—15Ta 21
Clydesdale Ct. N20—18Fb 23
Clydesdale Gdns. Rich—56Ra 101
Clydesdale Rd. W11—44Bb 81
Clydesdale Rd. Horn—31Hd 68
Clyde St. SE8—51Bc 106
Clyde Ter. SE23—61Yb 128
Clyde Vale. SE23—61Yb 128
Clyde Way. Romf—24Gd 48
Clydon Clo. Eri—51Gd 110
Clyfford Rd. Ruis—35V 56
Clymping Dene. Felt—59X 99
Clyston Rd. Wat—16V 18
Clyston St. SW8—54Lb 104
Clyve Way. Stai—67G 118
Coach & Horses Yd. W1
—45Lb 82 (4B 198)
Coach Ho. La. N5—35Rb 63
Coach Ho. La. SW19—63Za 124
Coach Rd. Cher—79E 138
Coach Rd. Grav—8A 114
★Coach Rd. Sev—96Wd
Coaldale Wlk. SE21—59Sb 105
Coalecroft Rd. SW15—56Ya 102
Coaley Row. Dag—40Bd 67
Coal Rd. Grays—9H 93
Coal Wharf Rd. W12—47Za 80
Coates Dell. Wat—5Aa 5
Coates Hill Rd. Brom—68Qc 130
Coates Rd. Borwd—17Ma 21
Coate St. E2—40Wb 63
Coates Wlk. Bren—50Na 79
Coates Way. Wat—5Z 5
Cobb Clo. Slou—3P 95
Cobbett Rd. SE9—55Nc 108
Cobbett Rd. Twic—60Ca 99
Cobbetts Av. Ilf—29Mc 45
Cobbetts Clo. Wok—5E 188
Cobbetts Hill. Wey—79R 140
Cobbett St. SW8—52Pb 104
Cobb Grn. Wat—4X 5
Cobbinsend Rd. Wal A—1Mc 13
Cobbins, The. Wal A—5Gc 13
Cobblers Clo. Slou—10F 52
Cobbler's Wlk. Hmptn & Tedd
—66Ea 122
Cobbles, The. Brtwd—19Ae 33
Cobbles, The. Upm—31Vd 70
Cobbold Est. NW10—37Va 60
Cobbold Rd. E11—34Hc 65
Cobbold Rd. NW10—37Va 60
Cobbold Rd. W12—47Ua 80
Cobb's Ct. EC4—(3C 200)
Cobb's Rd. Houn—56Ba 99
Cobb St. E1—43Vb 83 (1K 201)
Cob Clo. Borwd—15Ta 21
Cobden Clo. Uxb—39L 55
Cobden Hill. Rad—9Ka 6
Cobden Rd. E11—34Gc 65
Cobden Rd. SE25—71Wb 147
Cobden Rd. Orp—77Tc 150
Cobden Rd. Sev—95Ld 187
Cob Dri. Grav—4N 137
Cobham. Grays—47De 91
Cobham Av. N Mald—71Wa 144
Cobhambury Rd. Grav—10J 137
Cobham Clo. SW11—58Gb 103
Cobham Clo. Brom—73Nc 150
Cobham Clo. Wall—79Nb 146
Cobham Pk. Rd. Cob—89X 159
Cobham Rd. E17—25Ec 44
Cobham Rd. N22—27Rb 43
Cobham Rd. Cob & Lea—90Ca 159
Cobham Rd. Houn—52Y 99
Cobham Rd. Ilf—33Uc 66
Cobham Rd. King—68Qa 123
Cobham St. Grav—9D 114
Cobham Way. Lea—98U 174
Cobill Clo. Horn—28Ld 49
Cobland Rd. SE12—63Lc 129
Coborn Rd. E3—41Bc 84
Coborn St. E3—41Bc 84
Cobourg Rd. SE5
—51Vb 105 (7K 207)
Cobourg St. NW1
—41Lb 82 (4C 192)
Cobsdene. Grav—5F 136
Cobs Way. Wey—82L 157
Coburg Cres. SW2—60Pb 104
Coburg Rd. N22—27Pb 42
Cochrane Clo. NW8—(2C 190)
Cochrane M. NW8
—40Fb 61 (2C 190)
Cochrane Rd. SW19—66Bb 125
Cochrane St. NW8
—40Fb 61 (2C 190)
Cockayne Way. SE8—49Ac 84
Cockerhurst Rd. Sev—79Fd 152
Cocker Rd. Enf—8Xb 11
Cockett Rd. Slou—48A 74
Cockfosters Pde. Barn—14Jb 24
Cockfosters Rd. Barn—13Hb 23
Cockfosters Rd. Pot B & Barn
—7Fb 9
Cock Hill. E1—43Ub 83 (1J 201)
Cock La. EC1—43Rb 83 (1B 200)
Cock La. Lea—94Ea 176
Cockmannings La. Orp—74Zc 151
Cockmannings Rd. Orp—73Zc 151
Cockpit Steps. SW1—(2E 204)
Cockpit Yd. WC1—43Pb 82 (7J 193)
Cocks Cres. N Mald—70Va 124
Cocksett Av. Orp—79Uc 150
Cockspur Ct. SW1
—46Mb 82 (6E 198)
Cockspur St. SW1
—46Mb 82 (6E 198)
Cocksure La. Sidc—62Cd 132
Code St. E1—42Vb 83
Codham Hall La. Brtwd—28Xd 50
Codicote Dri. Wat—6Z 5
Codmore Wood Rd. Che—5A 2
Codrington Ct. Wok—6C 188
Codrington Cres. Grav—4E 136
Codrington Gdns. Grav—4F 136
Codrington Hill. SE23—59Ac 106
Codrington M. W11—44Ab 80
Cody Clo. Harr—27Ma 39
Cody Clo. Wall—80Mb 146
Cody Rd. E16—42Gc 85
Coe's All. Barn—14Ab 22
Cofers Circ. Wemb—34Ra 59
Coftards. Slou—4N 73
Cogan Av. E17—25Ac 44
Coin St. SE1—46Qb 82 (6K 199)
Coity Rd. NW5—37Jb 62
Cokers La. SE21—60Tb 105
Coke St. E1—44Wb 83
Colbeck M. SW7—49Db 81
Colbeck Rd. Harr—31Ea 58
Colberg Pl. N16—31Vb 63
Colborne Way. Wor Pk—76Ya 144
Colbrook Av. Hay—48T 76
Colbrook Clo. Hay—48T 76
Colburn Av. Cat—96Vb 181
Colburn Av. Pinn—23Aa 37
Colburn Way. Sutt—76Fb 145
Colby Rd. SE19—64Ub 127
Colby Rd. W on T—74W 140
Colchester Av. E12—34Pc 66
Colchester Dri. Pinn—29Z 37
Colchester Rd. E10—31Ec 64
Colchester Rd. E17—30Cc 44
Colchester Rd. Edgw—24Sa 39
Colchester Rd. N'wd—26W 36
Colchester Rd. Romf & Brtwd
—25Md 49
Colchester St. E1—44Vb 83
Colcokes Rd. Bans—88Cb 163
Cold Arbor Rd. Sev—96Fd 186
Coldbath Sq. EC1
—42Qb 82 (5K 193)
Coldbath St. SE13—53Dc 106
Cold Blow Cres. Bex—60Fd 110
Coldblow La. SE14—52Zb 106
Cold Blows. Mitc—69Hb 125
Coldershaw Rd. W13—46Ja 78
Coldfall Av. N10—26Jb 42
Coldham Gro. Enf—9Ac 12
Coldharbour. E14—46Ec 84
Coldharbour Clo. Egh—69E 118
Coldharbour La.—56Qb 104
SE5 1-199 & 2-200
SW9 remainder
Coldharbour La. Bush, Wat
—16Da 19
Coldharbour La. Egh—69E 118
Coldharbour La. Hay—46W 76
Coldharbour La. Purl—82Qb 164
Coldharbour La. Wok—87H 157
Coldharbour Rd. Croy—78Qb 146
Coldharbour Rd. Grav—1A 136
Coldharbour Rd. Wey & Wok
—86H 157
Coldharbour Way. Croy
—78Qb 146
Coldstream Gdns. SW18
—58Bb 103
Colebeck M. N1—37Rb 63
Colebert Av. E1—42Yb 84
Colebrook. Cher—79F 138
Colebrook Clo. SW15—59Za 102
Colebrooke Av. W13—44Ka 78
Colebrooke Dri. E11—31Lc 65
Colebrooke Pl. N1—(1C 194)
Colebrooke Rise. Brom—68Gc 129
Colebrooke Rd. SW16—67Nb 126
Colebrooke Row. N1
—40Rb 63 (2B 194)
Colebrook Gdns. Lou—12Rc 28
Colebrook La. Lou—12Rc 28
Colebrook Path. Lou—12Rc 28
Colebrook Way. N11—22Kb 42
Coleby Path. SE5—52Tb 105
Cole Clo. SE28—46Xc 87
Coledale Dri. Stan—25La 38
Coleford Rd. SW18—57Eb 103
Cole Gdns. Houn—52W 98
Colegrave Rd. E15—36Fc 65
Colegrove Rd. SE15—51Vb 105
Coleherne Ct. SW5—50Db 81
Coleherne M. SW10—50Db 81
Coleherne Rd. SW10—50Db 81
Colehill Gdns. SW6—53Ab 102
Colehill La. SW6—53Ab 102
Coleman Fields. N1—39Sb 63
Coleman Rd. SE5—52Ub 105
Coleman Rd. Belv—49Cd 88
Coleman Rd. Dag—37Ad 67
Colemans Heath. SE9—62Rc 130
Coleman St. EC2—44Tb 83 (2F 201)
Coleman St. Bldgs. EC2—(2F 201)
Colenorton Cres. Wind—9C 72
Colenso Rd. E5—35Yb 64
Colenso Rd. Ilf—32Uc 66
Cole Pk. Gdns. Twic—57Ja 100
Cole Pk. Rd. Twic—58Ja 100
Colepits Wood Rd. SE9—57Tc 108
Coleraine Rd. N8—27Qb 42
Coleraine Rd. SE3—51Hc 107
Coleridge Av. E12—37Nc 66
Coleridge Av. Sutt—77Gb 145
Coleridge Clo. SW8—54Kb 104
Coleridge Cres. Slou—53G 96
Coleridge Gdns. NW6—38Eb 61
Coleridge La. N8—30Nb 42
Coleridge Rd. E17—28Bc 44
Coleridge Rd. N4—33Qb 62
Coleridge Rd. N8—30Mb 42
Coleridge Rd. N12—22Eb 41
Coleridge Rd. Ashf—63N 119
Coleridge Rd. Croy—73Yb 148
Coleridge Rd. Dart—56Rd 111
Coleridge Rd. Romf—24Kd 49
Coleridge Rd. Til—4E 114
Coleridge Wlk. NW11—28Cb 41
Coleridge Wlk. Brtwd—17Ee 33
Coleridge Way. Hay—44W 76
Coleridge Way. Orp—72Wc 151
Coleridge Way. W Dray—49P 75
Cole Rd. Twic—58Ja 100
Cole Rd. Wat—11X 19
Colesburg Rd. Beck—69Bc 128
Coles Cres. Harr—33Da 57
Colescroft Hill. Purl—87Qb 164
Colesdale. Pot B—2Nb 10
Coles Grn. Bush, Wat—18Ea 20
Coles Grn. Lou—11Qc 28
Coles Grn. Rd. NW2—32Wa 60
Coleshill Rd. Tedd—65Ga 122
Coles La. West—95Yc 185
Colestown St. SW11—54Gb 103
Cole St. SE1—47Sb 83 (2E 206)
Colet Gdns. W14—49Za 80
Colet Rd. Brtwd—15Ee 33
Colets Orchard. Sev—88Kd 171
Coley Av. Wok—90C 156
Coley St. WC1—42Pb 82 (6J 193)
Colfe Rd. SE23—60Ac 106
Colham Av. W Dray—46N 75
Colham Grn. Rd. Uxb—43Q 76
Colham Mill Rd. W Dray—47M 75
Colham Rd. Uxb—42P 75
Colina M. N15—28Rb 43
Colina Rd. N15—29Rb 43
Colin Clo. NW9—28Ua 40
Colin Clo. Croy—76Bc 148
Colin Clo. Dart—58Rd 111
Colin Clo. W Wick—76Hc 149
Colin Cres. NW9—28Va 40
Colindale Av. NW9—27Ta 39
Colindeep Gdns. NW4—28Wa 40
Colindeep La.—27Ua 40
NW4 2-28
NW9 remainder
Colin Dri. NW9—29Va 40
Colinette Rd. SW15—56Ya 102
Colin Gdns. NW9—28Va 40
Colin Pk. Rd. NW9—28Ua 40
Colin Rd. NW10—37Wa 60
Colin Rd. Cat—95Wb 181
Colinton Rd. Ilf—33Xc 67
Colin Way. Slou—8F 72
Collamore Av. SW18—60Gb 103
Collapit Clo. Harr—30Da 37
Collard Av. Lou—12Sc 28
Collard Grn. Lou—12Sc 28
College App. SE10—51Ec 106
College Av. Egh—65D 118
College Av. Eps—86Va 162
College Av. Grays—49De 91
College Av. Harr—25Ga 38
College Av. Slou—8J 73
College Clo. E5—36Yb 64
College Clo. N18—22Vb 43
College Clo. Harr—24Ga 38
College Clo. Twic—60Fa 100
College Clo. Wey—76M 139
College Ct. Wal X—2Yb 12
College Cres. NW3—37Fb 61
College Cres. Wind—4F 94
College Cross. N1—38Qb 62
College Dri. Ruis—31W 56
College Gdns. E4—17Dc 26
College Gdns. N18—22Wb 43
College Gdns. SE21—60Ub 105
College Gdns. SW17—61Gb 125
College Gdns. Ilf—29Nc 46
College Gdns. N Mald—71Va 144
College Gdns. Rd. Enf—11Tb 25
College Grn. SE19—66Ub 127
College Gro. NW1—39Mb 62
College Hill. EC4—45Sb 83 (4E 200)
College Hill Rd. Harr—24Ga 38
College La. NW5—35Kb 62
College La. Wok—7F 188
College M. SW1—(3F 205)
College Pk. Clo. SE13—56Fc 107
College Pk. Rd. N17—23Vb 43
College Pl. E17—28Gc 45
College Pl. NW1—39Lb 62 (1C 192)
College Rd. E17—29Ec 44
College Rd. N17—23Vb 43
College Rd. N21—19Qb 24
College Rd. NW10—40Ya 60
College Rd.—59Ub 105
SE21 1-111 & 2-120
SE19 remainder
College Rd. SW19—65Fb 125
College Rd. W13—44Ka 78
College Rd. Abb L, Wat—3V 4
College Rd. Brom—67Jc 129
College Rd. Croy—75Tb 147
College Rd. Eps—86Va 162
College Rd. Grav—57De 113
College Rd. Grays—49Ee 91
College Rd. Harr—30Ga 38
College Rd. Harr—25Ga 38
(Harrow Weald)
College Rd. Iswth—53Ha 100
College Rd. Slou—6D 72
College Rd. Swan—67Gd 132
College Rd. Wal X—2Yb 12
College Rd. Wemb—32Ma 59
College Rd. Wok—88D 156
College Row. E9—36Zb 64
College Slip. Brom—67Jc 129
College St. EC4—45Sb 83 (4E 200)
College Ter. E3—41Bc 84
College Ter. N3—26Bb 41
College View. SE9—60Mc 107
College Wlk. King—69Na 123
Collent St. E9—37Yb 64
Coller Cres. Dart—64Ud 134
Colless Rd. N15—29Vb 43
Collet Rd. Sev—89Nd 171
Collett Rd. SE16—48Xb 83
Collett Way. S'hall—47Da 77
Colley Hill La. Slou—4K 53
Colleyland. Rick—14F 16
Collier Clo. Eps—79Qa 143
Collier Dri. Edgw—26Qa 39
Collier Row La. Romf—25Dd 48
Collier Row Rd. Romf—25Bd 47
Colliers. Cat—97Wb 181
Colliers Clo. Wok—5E 188
Colliers Shaw. Kes—78Mc 149
Collier St. N1—40Pb 62 (2H 193)
Colliers Water La. T Hth
—71Qb 146
Collindale Av. Eri—51Dd 110
Collindale Av. Sidc—60Wc 109
Collingbourne Rd. W12—46Xa 80
Collingham Gdns. SW5—49Db 81
Collingham Pl. SW5—49Db 81
Collingham Rd. SW5—49Db 81
Collington Clo. Grav—9A 114
Collingtree Rd. SE26—63Yb 128
Collingwood Av. N10—27Jb 42
Collingwood Av. Surb—74Sa 143
Collingwood Clo. SE20—67Xb 127
Collingwood Clo. Twic—59Ca 99
Collingwood Pl. W on T—76W 140
Collingwood Rd. E17—30Cc 44
Collingwood Rd. N15—28Ub 43
Collingwood Rd. Mitc—69Gb 125
Collingwood Rd. Sutt—76Cb 145
Collingwood Rd. Uxb—42R 76
Collingwood St. E1—42Xb 83
Collins Av. Stan—26Na 39
Collins Clo. Stanf—1N 93
Collins Ct. E8—37Wb 63
Collins Dri. Ruis—33Y 57
Collinson St. SE1
—47Sb 83 (2D 206)
Collinson Wlk. SE1
—47Sb 83 (2D 206)
Collins Path. Hmptn—65Ba 121
Collins Rd. N5—35Sb 63
Collins St. SE3—54Gc 107
Collinswood Rd. Slou—2E 52
Collin's Yd. N1—39Rb 63
Collinwood Av. Enf—13Yb 26
Collinwood Gdns. Ilf—29Pc 46
Collis All. Twic—60Ga 100
Colls Rd. SE15—53Yb 106
Collum Grn. Rd. Slou—4H 53
Collyer Av. Croy—77Nb 146
Collyer Pl. SE15—53Vb 105
Collyer Rd. Croy—77Nb 146
Colman Clo. Eps—89Ya 162
Colman Rd. E16—43Lc 85
Colmar Clo. E1—42Zb 84
Colmer Pl. Harr—24Fa 38
Colmer Rd. SW16—67Nb 126
Colmore Rd. Enf—14Yb 26
Colnbrook By-Pass. Slou &
W Dray—51E 96 to 52M 97
Colnbrook Ct. Slou—53H 97
Colnbrook St. SE1
—48Rb 83 (4B 206)
Colndale Rd. Slou—54G 96
Colne. Grays—8L 93
Colne Av. Rick—19J 17
Colne Av. Wat—16X 19
Colne Av. W Dray—47L 75
Colnebridge Clo. Stai—64G 118
Colne Ct. Eps—77Sa 143
Colnedale Rd. Uxb—36M 55
Colne Dri. Romf—23Pd 49
Colne Dri. W on T—76Z 141
Colne Mead. Rick—19J 17
Colne Orchard. Iver—44H 75
Colne Rd. E5—35Ac 64
Colne Rd. N21—17Tb 25
Colne Rd. Twic—60Ga 100
Colne St. E13—41Jc 85
Colne Valley. Upm—30Ud 50
Colne Way. Stai—61D 118
Colne Way. Wat—9Z 5
Colney Hatch La.—23Hb 41
N10 1-187 & 2-270
N11 remainder
Colney Rd. Dart—58Pd 111
Cologne Rd. SW11—56Fb 103
Colombo Rd. Ilf—31Sc 66
Colombo St. SE1
—46Rb 83 (7B 200)
Colomb St. SE10—50Gc 85
Colonel's La. Cher—72J 139
Colonel's Wlk., The. Enf—13Rb 25

Colonial Av.—Corkran Rd.

Colonial Av. Twic—58Ea 100
Colonial Dri. W4—49Sa 79
Colonial Rd. Felt—59U 98
Colonial Rd. Slou—7L 73
Colonial Way. Wat—11Y 19
Colonnade. WC1
—42Nb 82 (6G 193)
Colonnade, The. SE8—49Bc 84
Colosseum Ter. NW1—(5A 192)
Colour Ct. SW1—(7C 198)
Colpse Bank. Sev—92Pd 187
Colson Gdns. Lou—14Rc 28
Colson Path. Lou—14Qc 28
Colson Rd. Croy—75Ub 147
Colson Rd. Lou—14Rc 28
Colson Way. SW16—63Lb 126
Colsterworth Rd. N15—28Vb 43
(in two parts)
Colston Av. Cars—77Gb 145
Colston Pas. SW18—59Cb 103
Colston Rd. E7—37Mc 65
Colston Rd. SW14—56Sa 101
Coltishall Rd. Horn—37Ld 69
Coltness Cres. SE2—50Xc 87
Colton Gdns. N17—27Sb 43
Colton Rd. Harr—29Ga 38
Coltsfoot Ct. Grays—51Fe 113
Coltsfoot Path. Romf—24Ld 49
Coltstead. Long, Dart—75Ae 155
Columbia Av. Edgw—25Ra 39
Columbia Av. Wor Pk—73Va 144
Columbia Rd. E2—41Vb 83 (3K 195)
Columbia Rd. E13—42Hc 85
Columbia Sq. SW14—56Sa 101
Columbine Av. S Croy—80Rb 147
Columbine Way. SE13—54Ec 106
Columbine Way. Romf—25Nd 49
Colva Wlk. N19—33Kb 62
Colvestone Cres. E8—36Vb 63
Colview Ct. SE9—60Mc 107
Colville Gdns. W11—44Bb 81
Colville Houses. W11—44Bb 81
Colville M. W11—44Bb 81
Colville Pl. W1—43Mb 82 (1C 198)
Colville Rd. E11—34Ec 64
Colville Rd. E17—26Ac 44
Colville Rd. N9—18Xb 26
Colville Rd. W3—48Ra 79
Colville Rd. W11—44Bb 81
Colville Sq. W11—44Bb 81
Colville Sq. M. W11—44Bb 81
Colville Ter. W11—44Bb 81
Colvin Clo. SE26—64Yb 128
Colvin Gdns. E4—20Ec 26
Colvin Gdns. E11—28Kc 45
Colvin Gdns. Ilf—25Sc 46
Colvin Gdns. Wal X—7Zb 12
Colvin Rd. E6—38Nc 66
Colvin Rd. T Hth—71Qb 146
Colwell Rd. SE22—57Vb 105
Colwick Clo. N6—31Mb 62
Colwith Rd. W6—51Ya 102
Colwood Gdns. SW19—66Fb 125
Colworth Gro. SE17
—49Sb 83 (6E 206)
Colworth Rd. E11—30Gc 45
Colworth Rd. Croy—74Wb 147
Colwyn Av. Gnfd—40Ha 58
Colwyn Cres. Houn—53Ea 100
Colwyn Rd. NW2—34Xa 60
Colyer Clo. N1—40Pb 62 (1J 193)
Colyer Clo. SE9—61Rc 130
Colyer Rd. Grav—61Ee 135
Colyers Clo. Eri—53Fd 110
Colyers La. Eri—53Ed 110
Colyers Wlk. Eri—53Gd 110
Colyton Clo. Well—53Zc 109
Colyton Clo. Wemb—37La 58
Colyton Clo. Wok—6F 188
Colyton Rd. SE22—57Xb 105
Colyton Way. N18—22Wb 43
Combe Av. SE3—52Hc 107
Combedale Rd. SE10—50Jc 85
Combe Lodge. SE7—51Lc 107
Combemartin Rd. SW18
—59Ab 102
Combe M. SE3—52Hc 107
Comber Clo. NW2—33Xa 60
Comber Gro. SE5—52Sb 105
Combermere Clo. Wind—4F 94
Combermere Rd. SW9—55Pb 104
Combermere Rd. Mord—72Db 145
Combe Rd. Wat—16V 18
Comberton Rd. E5—33Xb 63
Combeside. SE18—52Vc 109
Combwell Cres. SE2—48Wc 87
Comely Bank Rd. E17—29Ec 44
Comeragh Clo. Wok—8D 188
Comeragh M. W14—50Ab 80
Comeragh Rd. W14—50Ab 80
Comerford Rd. SE4—56Ac 106
Comet Clo. Purf—49Qd 89
Comet Clo. Wat—6V 4
Comet Pl. SE8—52Cc 106
Comet Rd. Stai—59M 97
Comet St. SE8—52Cc 106
Comfrey Ct. Grays—51Fe 113
Commerce Rd. N22—25Pb 42
Commerce Rd. Bren—52La 100
Commerce Way. Croy—75Pb 146
Commercial Dock Pas. SE16
—48Bc 84
Commercial Pl. Grav—8E 114
Commercial Rd.—44Wb 83
E1 1-601a & 2-554
E14 remainder
Commercial Rd. N18—23Ub 43
Commercial Rd. Stai—65J 119
Commercial St. E1
—43Vb 83 (6K 195)
Commercial Way. NW10—40Ra 59
Commercial Way. SE15—52Vb 105
Commercial Way. Wok—89B 156
Commerell St. SE10—50Gc 85
Commodore St. E1—42Ac 84
Common Clo. Wok—2G 188
Commondale. SW15—55Ya 102
Commonfield La. SW17—64Gb 125
Commonfield Rd. Bans—86Cb 163
Common Ga. Rd. Rick—15G 16
Common La. Dart—61Jd 132
Common La. Esh—81Ja 160
Common La. K Lan—1P 3
Common La. Slou—4B 52
Common La. Wat & Rad—11Ga 20
Common La. Wey—81L 157
Common La. Wind—10G 72
Commonmeadow La. Wat—5Da 5
Common Rd. SW13—55Xa 102
Common Rd. Brtwd—22Ee 51
Common Rd. Esh—79Ja 142
Common Rd. Lea—93Aa 175
Common Rd. Rick—14F 16
★Common Rd. Sev—95Xd
Common Rd. Slou—49C 74
Common Rd. Stan—21Fa 38
Common Rd. Wind—9A 72
(Dorney)
Common Rd. Wind—9E 72
(Eton Wick)
Commonside. Kes—77Lc 149
Commonside. Lea—94Ca 175
(in two parts)
Commonside E. Mitc—69Jb 126
Commonside W. Mitc—69Hb 125
Common, The. W5—46Na 79
Common, The. K Lan—4K 3
Common, The. Rich—62Ma 123
Common, The. S'hall—49Z 77
Common, The. Stan—20Ha 20
Commonwealth Av. W12—45Xa 80
Commonwealth Av. Hay—44T 76
Commonwealth Rd. N17—24Wb 43
Commonwealth Rd. Cat
—95Wb 181
Commonwealth Way. SE2
—50Xc 87
Common Wood. Slou—5G 52
Community Clo. Uxb—34S 56
Community Rd. E15—36Fc 65
Community Rd. Gnfd—39Ea 58
Como Rd. SE23—61Ac 128
Como St. Romf—29Fd 48
Compass Hill. Rich—58Ma 101
Compayne Gdns. NW6—38Db 61
★Comp La. Sev—93Ee
Comport Clo. Croy—84Gc 167
Comport Grn. Croy—84Gc 167
Compton Av. E6—40Mc 65
Compton Av. N1—37Rb 63
Compton Av. N6—31Gb 61
Compton Av. Brtwd—18Ee 33
Compton Av. Romf—27Ld 49
Compton Clo. NW1—(4A 192)
Compton Clo. W13—44Ja 78
Compton Clo. Esh—79Fa 142
Compton Ct. SE19—65Ub 127
Compton Ct. Slou—4C 72
Compton Cres. N17—24Sb 43
Compton Cres. W4—51Sa 101
Compton Cres. Chess—79Na 143
Compton Cres. N'holt—39Z 57
Compton Pas. EC1
—42Rb 83 (5C 194)
Compton Pl. WC1
—42Nb 82 (5F 193)
Compton Pl. Eri—51Hd 110
Compton Pl. Wat—20Aa 19
Compton Rise. Pinn—29Aa 37
Compton Rd. N1—37Rb 63
Compton Rd. N21—18Rb 25
Compton Rd. NW10—41Za 80
Compton Rd. SW19—65Bb 125
Compton Rd. Croy—74Xb 147
Compton Rd. Hay—45U 76
Compton St. EC1
—42Rb 83 (5B 194)
Compton Ter. N1—37Rb 63
Comreddy Clo. Enf—11Rb 25
Comus Pl. SE17—49Ub 83 (6H 207)
Comyne Rd. Wat—8V 4
Comyn Rd. SW11—56Gb 103
Comyns Clo. E16—43Hc 85
Comyns Rd. Dag—38Cd 68
Comyns, The. Bush, Wat—18Ea 20
Conaways Clo. Eps—82Wa 162
Concanon Rd. SW2—56Pb 104
Concert Hall App. SE1
—46Pb 82 (7J 199)
Concord Clo. N'holt—41Aa 77
Concorde Clo. Houn—54Da 99
Concorde Clo. Uxb—40N 55
Concorde Way. Slou—7G 72
Concord Rd. W3—42Ra 79
Concord Rd. Enf—15Yb 26
Concourse, The. NW9—25Va 40
Condell Rd. SW8—53Lb 104
Conder St. E14—44Ac 84
Conderton Rd. SE5—55Sb 105
Condor Rd. Stai—69L 119
Condor Wlk. Rain—38Kd 69
Condover Cres. SE18—52Rc 108
Conduit Ct. WC2—(4F 199)
Conduit La. N18—21Tb 43
Conduit La. Enf—16Zb 26
Conduit La. Slou—51A 96
Conduit La. S Croy & Croy
—78Wb 147
Conduit M. W2—44Fb 81 (3B 196)
Conduit Pl. W2—44Fb 81 (3B 196)
Conduit Rd. SE18—50Rc 86
Conduit St. W1—45Kb 82 (4A 198)
Conduit, The. Red—100Tb 181
Conduit Way. NW10—38Sa 59
Conegar Ct. Slou—6J 73
Conewood St. N5—34Rb 63
Coney Acre. SE21—60Sb 105
Coney Burrows. E4—19Gc 27
Coneybury Clo. Warl—91Xb 181
Coney Gro. Uxb—41Q 76
Coney Hill Rd. W Wick—75Gc 149
Coney Way. SW8—51Pb 104
Conference Rd. SE2—49Yc 87
Congleton Gro. SE18—50Sc 86
Congo Rd. SE18—50Tc 86
Congress Rd. SE2—49Yc 87
Congreve Ct. SE11
—49Qb 82 (6A 206)
Congreve Rd. SE9—55Pc 108
Congreve St. SE17
—49Ub 83 (5H 207)
Congreve Wlk. E16—43Mc 85
Conical Corner. Enf—12Sb 25
Conifer Av. Long, Dart—72Ae 155
Conifer Av. Romf—22Dd 48
Conifer Clo. Orp—77Tc 150
Conifer Gdns. SW16—62Pb 126
Conifer Gdns. Enf—16Ub 25
Conifer Gdns. Sutt—75Db 145
Conifer La. Egh—64E 118
Conifer Rd. Swan—67Ed 132
Conifers. Wey—77U 140
Conifers Clo. Tedd—66Ka 122
Conifer Way. Hay—45W 76
Coniger Rd. SW6—54Cb 103
Coningesby Dri. Wat—11U 18
Coningham M. W12—46Wa 80
Coningham Rd. W12—47Xa 80
Coningsby Cotts. W5—47Ma 79
Coningsby Ct. Rad—8Ha 6
Coningsby Dri. Pot B—5Fb 9
Coningsby Gdns. E4—23Dc 44
Coningsby Rd. N4—31Rb 63
Coningsby Rd. W5—47Ma 79
Coningsby Rd. S Croy—81Sb 165
Conington Rd. SE13—54Ec 106
Conisbee Ct. N14—15Lb 24
Conisborough Cres. SE6
—62Ec 128
Coniscliffe Rd. N13—20Sb 25
Conista Ct. Wok—4C 188
Coniston Av. Bark—38Uc 66
Coniston Av. Gnfd—41Ka 78
Coniston Av. Upm—35Sd 70
Coniston Av. Well—55Uc 108
Coniston Clo. N20—20Eb 23
Coniston Clo. SW20—72Za 144
Coniston Clo. W4—52Sa 101
Coniston Clo. Bark—38Uc 66
Coniston Clo. Bexh—53Ed 110
Coniston Clo. Dart—60Kd 111
Coniston Clo. Eri—52Gd 110
Coniston Cres. Slou—3A 72
Conistone Way. N7—38Nb 62
Coniston Gdns. N9—18Yb 26
Coniston Gdns. NW9—29Ta 39
Coniston Gdns. Ilf—28Nc 46
Coniston Gdns. Pinn—28W 36
Coniston Gdns. Sutt—79Fb 145
Coniston Gdns. Wemb—32La 58
Coniston Rd. N10—26Kb 42
Coniston Rd. N17—23Wb 43
Coniston Rd. Bexh—53Ed 110
Coniston Rd. Brom—65Gc 129
Coniston Rd. Coul—88Lb 164
Coniston Rd. Croy—73Wb 147
Coniston Rd. K Lan—1P 3
Coniston Rd. Twic—58Da 99
Coniston Rd. Wok—92D 172
Coniston Wlk. E9—36Yb 64
Coniston Way. Chess—76Na 143
Coniston Way. Horn—36Jd 68
Conlan St. W10—42Ab 80
Conley Rd. NW10—37Ua 60
Conley St. SE10—50Gc 85
Connaught Av. E4—17Fc 27
Connaught Av. SW14—56Sa 101
Connaught Av. Ashf—63N 119
Connaught Av. Barn—18Hb 23
Connaught Av. Enf—12Ub 25
Connaught Av. Grays—47De 91
Connaught Av. Houn—56Aa 99
Connaught Av. Lou—14Mc 27
Connaught Clo. E10—33Ac 64
Connaught Clo. W2—(3E 196)
Connaught Clo. Enf—12Ub 25
Connaught Clo. Sutt—75Fb 145
Connaught Clo. Uxb—42S 76
Connaught Dri. NW11—28Cb 41
Connaught Gdns. N10—29Kb 42
Connaught Gdns. N13—21Rb 43
Connaught Hill. Lou—14Mc 27
Connaught La. Ilf—33Sc 66
Connaught M. W2—(3F 197)
Connaught Pl. W2
—45Hb 81 (3F 197)
Connaught Rd. E4—17Gc 27
Connaught Rd. E11—32Fc 65
Connaught Rd. E16—45Lc 85
Connaught Rd. E17—29Cc 44
Connaught Rd. N4—31Qb 62
Connaught Rd. NW10—39Ua 60
Connaught Rd. SE18—50Rc 86
Connaught Rd. W13—45Ka 78
Connaught Rd. Barn—16Za 22
Connaught Rd. Harr—25Ha 38
Connaught Rd. Horn—34Md 69
Connaught Rd. Ilf—33Tc 66
Connaught Rd. N Mald—70Ua 124
Connaught Rd. Rich—57Pa 101
Connaught Rd. Slou—7M 73
Connaught Rd. Sutt—75Fb 145
Connaught Rd. Tedd—64Fa 122
Connaught Sq. W2
—44Hb 81 (3F 197)
Connaught St. W2
—44Gb 81 (3E 196)
Connaught Way. N13—21Rb 43
Connell Cres. W5—42Pa 79
Connemara Clo. Borwd—16Ta 21
Connicut La. Lea—100Da 175
Connington Cres. E4—20Fc 27
Connop Rd. Enf—10Zb 12
Connor Rd. Dag—35Bd 67
Connor St. E9—39Zb 64
Conolly Rd. W7—46Ga 78
Conquest Rd. Wey—78J 139
Conrad Dri. Wor Pk—74Ya 144
Conrad Rd. Stanf—1N 93
Consfield Av. N Mald—71Wa 144
Consort M. Iswth—57Fa 100
Consort Rd. SE15—53Xb 105
Cons St. SE1—47Qb 82 (1A 206)
Constable Clo. NW11—30Db 41
Constable Clo. Hay—40S 56
Constable Cres. N15—29Wb 43
Constable Gdns. Edgw—25Qa 39
Constable Gdns. Iswth—57Fa 100
Constable Rd. Grav—2A 136
Constable Wlk. SE21—62Ub 127
Constance Cres. Brom—73Hc 149
Constance Rd. Croy—73Rb 147
Constance Rd. Enf—16Ub 25
Constance Rd. Sutt—77Eb 145
Constance Rd. Twic—59Da 99
Constance St. E16—46Nc 86
Constantine Rd. NW3—35Hb 61
Constitution Hill. SW1
—47Kb 82 (1K 203)
Constitution Hill. Grav—10E 114
Constitution Hill. Wok—91A 172
Constitution Rise. SE18—53Qc 108
Content St. SE17—49Tb 83 (6F 207)
Contessa Clo. Orp—78Uc 150
Control Tower Rd. Houn—55Q 98
Convair Wlk. N'holt—41Z 77
Convent Gdns. W5—49La 78
Convent Gdns. W11—44Ab 80
Convent Hill. SE19—65Sb 127
Convent La. Cob—83U 158
Convent Rd. Ashf—64R 120
Convent Rd. Wind—4E 94
Convent Way. S'hall—49Y 77
Conway Clo. Rain—38Jd 68
Conway Clo. Stan—23Ja 38
Conway Cres. Gnfd—40Ga 58
Conway Cres. Romf—30Yc 47
Conway Dri. Ashf—65S 120
Conway Dri. Hay—48S 76
Conway Dri. Sutt—80Db 145
Conway Gdns. Enf—10Ub 11
Conway Gdns. Mitc—70Nb 126
Conway Gdns. Wemb—31La 58
Conway Gro. W3—43Ta 79
Conway M. W1—(6B 192)
Conway Rd. N14—20Nb 24
Conway Rd. N15—29Rb 43
Conway Rd. NW2—33Ya 60
Conway Rd. SE18—49Tc 86
Conway Rd. SW20—67Ya 124
Conway Rd. Felt—64Z 121
Conway Rd. Houn—59Ba 99
Conway Rd. Houn—55R 98
(Heathrow Airport)
Conway Rd. M'head—4A 72
Conway's Rd. Grays—1C 92
Conway St. W1—42Lb 82 (6B 192)
(in two parts)
Conway Wlk. Hmptn—65Ba 121
Conybeare. NW3—39Gb 61
Conybury Clo. Wal A—4Jc 13
★Conyerd Rd. Sev—93Be
Conyers Clo. W on T—78Z 141
Conyers Clo. Wfd G—23Gc 45
Conyer's Rd. SW16—64Mb 126
Conyer St. E3—40Ac 64
Conyers Way. Lou—13Rc 28
Cooden Clo. Brom—66Kc 129
Cookes Clo. E11—33Hc 65
Cookes La. Sutt—79Ab 144
Cookham Hill. Orp—76Dd 152
Cookham Rd. Sidc, Orp & Swan
—67Cd 132
Cookhill Rd. SE2—48Xc 87
Cooks Hole Rd. Enf—10Rb 11
Cooks Mead. Bush, Wat—16Da 19
Cook's Rd. E15—40Dc 64
Cook's Rd. SE17—51Rb 105
Coolfin Rd. E16—44Jc 85
Coolgardie Av. E4—22Fc 45
Coolgardie Av. Chig—20Qc 28
Coolgardie Rd. Ashf—64S 120
Coolhurst Rd. N8—30Mb 42
Cooling Way. Wemb—35Ma 59
Cool Oak La. NW9—32Ua 60
Coomassie Rd. W9—42Bb 81
Coombe Av. Croy—77Ub 147
Coombe Av. Sev—92Kd 187
Coombe Bank. King—67Ua 124
Coombe Clo. Edgw—26Pa 39
Coombe Clo. Houn—56Ca 99
Coombe Corner. N21—18Rb 25
Coombe Cres. Hmptn—66Ba 121
Coombe Dri. Ruis—32X 57
Coombe Dri. Wey—79H 139
Coombe End. King—66Ta 123
Coombefield Clo. N Mald
—71Ua 144
Coombe Gdns. SW20—68Wa 124
Coombe Gdns. N Mald—70Ua 124
Coombe Hill Glade. King
—66Ua 124
Coombe Hill Rd. King—66Ua 124
Coombe Hill Rd. Rick—17J 17
Coombe Ho. E4—23Cc 44
Coombe Ho. Chase. N Mald
—67Ta 123
Coombehurst Clo. Barn—12Hb 23
Coombelands La. Wey—79J 139
Coombe La. SW20—67Wa 124
Coombe La. Asc—10A 116
Coombe La. Croy—78Xb 147
Coombe La. W. King—67Ra 123
Coombe Lea. Brom—69Nc 130
Coombe Neville. King—66Ta 123
Coombe Pk. King—65Sa 123
Coombe Ridings. King—64Sa 123
Coombe Rise. Brtwd—18Be 33
Coombe Rise. King—67Sa 123
Coombe Rise. Stanf—1N 93
Coombe Rd. N22—26Qb 42
Coombe Rd. NW10—34Ta 59
Coombe Rd. SE26—63Xb 127
Coombe Rd. W4—50Ua 80
Coombe Rd. W13—48Ka 78
Coombe Rd. Bush, Wat—17Fa 20
Coombe Rd. Croy—77Tb 147
Coombe Rd. Grav—1E 136
Coombe Rd. Hmptn—65Ba 121
Coombe Rd. King—67Qa 123
Coombe Rd. N Mald—68Ua 124
Coombe Rd. Romf—27Pd 49
Coombe Rd. Sev—87Ld 171
Coomber Way. Croy—73Mb 146
Coombes Rd. Dag—39Bd 67
Coombe Vale. Ger X—32A 54
Coombe Wlk. Sutt—76Db 145
Coombe Way. Wey—84P 157
Coombe Wood Dri. Romf—30Bd 47
Coombe Wood Hill. Purl
—85Sb 165
Coombewood Rd. King—64Sa 123
Coombfield Dri. Dart—63Td 134
Coombs St. N1—40Rb 63 (2C 194)
Coomer Pl. SW6—51Bb 103
Cooms Wlk. Edgw—25Sa 39
Cooperage Clo. N17—23Vb 43
Cooper Av. E17—25Ac 44
Cooper Clo. SE1—47Qb 82 (2A 206)
Cooper Cres. Cars—76Hb 145
Cooper Mead Clo. NW2—34Ya 60
Cooper Rd. NW4—30Za 40
Cooper Rd. NW10—36Wa 60
Cooper Rd. Croy—77Rb 147
Coopersale Clo. Wfd G—24Lc 45
Coopersale Comn. Epp—1Zc 15
Coopersale La. Epp—9Wc 15
Coopersale Rd. E9—36Zb 64
Coopers Clo. Chig—19Xc 29
Coopers Clo. Stai—64G 118
Coopers Hill. Egh—3N 117
Cooper's Hill La. Egh—63A 118
Coopers Hill La. Egh—2N 117
Coopers La. E10—32Dc 64
Coopers La. NW1
—40Mb 62 (1E 192)
Cooper's La. SE12—61Kc 129
Cooper's La. Grays—2F 114
Coopers La. Pot B—3Fb 9
Coopers La. Rd. Pot B—4Gb 9
Coopers La. Rd. Pot B—3Gb 9
Cooper's Rd. SE1
—50Vb 83 (7K 207)
Coopers Rd. Grav—10B 114
Coopers Rd. Pot B—2Eb 9
Coopers Rd. S Dar, Dart—67Td 134
Cooper's Row. EC3
—45Vb 83 (4K 201)
Coopers Row. Iver—42E 74
Cooper St. E16—43Hc 85
Coopers Wlk. Wal X—1Zb 12
Cooper's Yd. SE19—65Ub 127
Coote Gdns. Dag—34Bd 67
Coote Rd. Bexh—53Bd 109
Coote Rd. Dag—34Bd 67
Copeland Rd. E17—30Dc 44
Copeland Rd. SE15—54Wb 105
Copeman Rd. Brtwd—17Fe 33
Copenhagen Pl. E14—44Bc 84
Copenhagen St. N1
—39Nb 62 (1K 193)
Copenhagen Way. W on T
—76X 141
Copen Rd. Dag—31Bd 67
Cope Pl. W8—48Cb 81
Copers Cope Rd. Beck—66Bc 128
Copesfield. E Mol—69Ca 121
Cope St. SE16—49Zb 84
Copford Clo. Wfd G—23Nc 46
Copinger Wlk. Edgw—25Ra 39
Copland Av. Wemb—36Ma 59
Copland Clo. Wemb—36La 58
Copland Rd. Stanf—2M 93
Copland Rd. Wemb—37Na 59
Copleigh Dri. Tad—92Ab 178
Copleston Pas. SE15—54Ub 105
Copleston Rd. SE15—55Vb 105
Copley Clo. SE17—51Sb 105
Copley Clo. W7—42Ha 78
Copley Clo. Wok—7B 188
Copley Dene. Brom—67Mc 129
Copley Pk. SW16—65Pb 126
Copley Rd. Stan—22La 38
Copley Way. Tad—92Za 178
Copmans Wick. Rick—15F 16
Copner Way. SE15—52Vb 105
Coppelia Rd. SE3—56Hc 107
Copperas St. SE8—51Dc 106
Copperbeech Clo. NW3—36Fb 61
Copper Beech Clo. Grav—9F 114
Copper Beech Clo. Ilf—25Rc 46
Copper Beech Clo. Orp—71Yc 151
Copper Beech Clo. Wind—3B 94
Copper Beech Clo. Wok—9E 188
Copper Beech Ct. Lou—11Qc 28
Copper Beeches Ct. Iswth
—53Fa 100
Copper Beech Rd. S Ock—41Yd 90
Copperdale Rd. Hay—47W 76
Copperfield. Chig—22Tc 46
Copperfield Av. Uxb—43Q 76
Copperfield Clo. Grav—10J 115
Copperfield Clo. S Croy—83Sb 165
Copperfield Ct. Lea—93Ja 176
Copperfield Gdns. Brtwd—18Xd 32
Copperfield M. N18—22Ub 43
Copperfield Rise. Wey—78H 139
Copperfield Rd. E3—43Ac 84
Copperfields. Sev—89Pd 171
Copperfields Clo. Sev—89Pd 171
Copperfields Ct. W3—47Qa 79
Copperfields Orchard. Sev
—89Pd 171
Copperfield St. SE1
—47Rb 83 (1C 206)
Copperfields Way. Romf
—25Md 49
Copper Field Way. Chst—65Sc 130
Copperfield Way. Pinn—28Ba 37
Coppermill La. E17—29Zb 44
Copper Mill La. SW17—63Eb 125
Coppermill La. Rick & Uxb
—24G 34
Coppermill Rd. Wray, Stai—58D 96
Copper Ridge. Ger X—22B 34
Coppetts Clo. N12—24Gb 41
Coppetts Rd. N10—24Hb 41
Coppice Clo. SW20—69Ya 124
Coppice Clo. Ruis—30T 36
Coppice Dri. SW15—58Xa 102
Coppice Dri. Wray, Stai—9P 95
Coppice End. Wok—88G 156
Coppice Path. Chig—21Xc 47
Coppice Row. Epp—8Sc 14
★Coppice, The. Brtwd—8Ud
Coppice, The. Enf—14Rb 25
Coppice, The. Wat—16Y 19
Coppice, The. W Dray—44N 75
Coppice Wlk. N20—20Cb 23
Coppice Way. E18—28Hc 45
Coppies Gro. N11—21Kb 42
Copping Clo. Croy—77Ub 147
Coppins La. Iver—43H 75
Coppins, The. Croy—79Dc 148
Coppins, The. Harr—23Ga 38
Coppock Clo. SW11—54Gb 103
Copse Av. W Wick—76Dc 148
Copse Clo. N'wd—26S 36
Copse Clo. W Dray—48M 75
Copse Edge Av. Eps—85Va 162
Copse Glade. Surb—73Ma 143
Copse Hill. SW20—67Wa 124
Copse Hill. Purl—85Nb 164
Copse Hill. Sutt—80Db 145
Copsem Dri. Esh—79Da 141
Copsem La. Esh & Lea—79Ea 142
Copse Rd. Cob—85X 159
Copse Rd. Wok—6C 188
Copse Side. Long, Dart—69Ae 135
Copse, The. E4—18Hc 27
Copse, The. Lea—95Da 175
Copse, The. Wat—4Aa 5
Copse View. S Croy—81Zb 166
Copse Wood. Iver—39F 54
Copsewood Rd. Wat—11X 19
Copse Wood Way. N'wd—25R 36
Coptfold Rd. Brtwd—19Zd 33
Copthall Av. EC2—44Tb 83 (2G 201)
(in two parts)
Copthall Bldgs. EC2—(2G 201)
Copthall Clo. EC2
—44Tb 83 (2F 201)
Copthall Clo. Ger X—24B 34
Copthall Corner. Ger X—24A 34
Copthall Dri. NW7—24Wa 40
Copthall Gdns. NW7—24Wa 40
Copthall Gdns. Twic—60Ha 100
Copthall La. Ger X—24A 34
Copt Hall La. Grav—10D 136
★Copt Hall Rd. Sev—95Xd
Copthall Rd. E. Uxb—33Q 56
Copthall Rd. W. Uxb—33Q 56
Copthall Way. Wey—82H 157
Copt Hill La. Tad—92Ab 178
Copthorne Av. SW12—59Mb 104
Copthorne Av. Brom—75Pc 150
Copthorne Av. Ilf—23Rc 46
Copthorne Chase. Ashf—63P 119
Copthorne Clo. Rick—15P 17
Copthorne Clo. Shep—72S 140
Copthorne Gdns. Horn—29Qd 49
Copthorne M. Hay—49U 76
Copthorne Rise. S Croy—85Tb 165
Copthorne Rd. Lea—92Ka 176
Copthorne Rd. Rick—16P 17
Coptic St. WC1—43Nb 82 (1F 199)
Copwood Clo. N12—21Gb 41
Coral Clo. Romf—28Yc 47
Coralline Wlk. SE2—47Yc 87
Coral St. SE1—47Qb 82 (2A 206)
Coram Grn. Brtwd—16Fe 33
Coram St. WC1—42Nb 82 (6F 193)
Coran Clo. N9—17Zb 26
Corban Rd. Houn—55Ca 99
Corbar Clo. Barn—11Fb 23
Corbet Clo. Wall—74Jb 146
Corbet Ct. EC3—44Tb 83 (3G 201)
Corbet Pl. E1—43Vb 83 (7K 195)
Corbet Rd. Eps—82Ua 162
Corbets Av. Upm—36Rd 69
Corbets Tey Rd. Upm—35Rd 69
Corbett Gro. N22—24Nb 42
Corbett Rd. E11—30Lc 45
Corbett Rd. E17—27Fc 44
Corbett's La. SE16—49Yb 84
Corbett's Pas. SE16—49Yb 84
Corbiere Ct. SW19—65Za 124
Corbins La. Harr—34Da 57
Corbridge Cres. E2—40Xb 63
Corby Cres. Enf—14Nb 24
Corby Dri. Egh—5N 117
Corbylands Rd. Sidc—60Uc 108
Corbyn St. N4—32Nb 62
Corby Rd. NW10—40Ta 59
Corby Way. E3—42Cc 84
Corcorans. Brtwd—16Xd 32
Cordelia Gdns. Stai—59N 97
Cordelia Rd. Stai—59N 97
Cordelia St. E14—44Dc 84
Cordingley Rd. Ruis—33T 56
Cording St. E14—43Dc 84
Cordons Clo. Ger X—25A 34
Cordova Rd. E3—41Ac 84
Cordrey Gdns. Coul—87Nb 164
(in two parts)
Cord Way. E14—48Cc 84
Cordwell Rd. SE13—57Gc 107
Corelli Rd. SE3—54Nc 108
Corfe Av. Harr—35Ca 57
Corfe Clo. Asht—90La 160
Corfe Gdns. Slou—5E 72
Corfield St. E2—41Xb 63
Corfton Rd. W5—44Na 79
Corinium Clo. Wemb—35Pa 59
Corinne Rd. N19—35Lb 62
Corinthian Manorway. Eri
—49Fd 88
Corinthian Rd. Eri—49Fd 88
Corinthian Way. Stai—59M 97
Corkers Path. Ilf—33Sc 66
Corker Wlk. N7—33Pb 62
Corkran Rd. Surb—73Ma 143

Corkscrew Hill. W Wick—75Ec 148
Cork St. W1—45Lb 82 (5B 198)
Cork St. M. W1—(5B 198)
Corlett St. NW1—43Gb 81 (7D 190)
Cormont Rd. SE5—53Rb 105
Cormorant Wlk. Rain—37Kd 69
Cornbury Rd. Edgw—24Ma 39
Cornel Gdns. Swan—68Fd 132
Cornelia Pl. Eri—51Gd 110
Cornelia St. N7—37Pb 62
Cornell Clo. Sidc—65Ad 131
Cornell Way. Romf—22Dd 48
Corner Grn. SE3—54Jc 107
Corner Ho. St. WC2—(6F 199)
Corner Mead. NW9—24Va 40
Cornerside. Ashf—66S 120
Corney Rd. W4—51Ua 102
Cornfield Clo. Uxb—40M 55
Cornfield Rd. Bush, Wat—14Da 19
Cornflower La. Croy—74Zb 148
Cornflower Ter. SE22—58Xb 105
Cornflower Way. Romf—25Nd 49
Cornford Clo. Brom—71Jc 149
Cornford Gro. SW12—61Kb 126
Cornhill. EC3—44Tb 83 (3G 201)
Cornish Gro. SE20—67Xb 127
Cornmill. Wal A—5Dc 12
Corn Mill Dri. Orp—73Wc 151
Cornmill La. SE13—55Ec 106
Cornshaw Rd. Dag—32Zc 67
Cornsland. Brtwd—20Zd 33
Cornthwaite Rd. E5—34Yb 64
Cornwall Av. E2—41Yb 84
Cornwall Av. N3—24Cb 41
Cornwall Av. N22—25Nb 42
Cornwall Av. Esh—80Ha 142
Cornwall Av. Grav—2E 136
Cornwall Av. Slou—2G 72
Cornwall Av. S'hall—43Ba 77
Cornwall Av. Well—55Uc 108
Cornwall Av. Wey—86P 157
Cornwall Clo. Bark—37Vc 67
Cornwall Clo. Horn—28Qd 49
Cornwall Clo. Wal X—5Ac 12
Cornwall Clo. Wind—10C 72
Cornwall Cres. W11—44Ab 80
Cornwall Cres. Stanf—1N 93
Cornwall Dri. Orp—66Yc 131
Cornwall Gdns. NW10—37Xa 60
Cornwall Gdns. SW7
—48Db 81 (4A 202)
Cornwall Gdns. Wlk. SW7
—48Db 81
Cornwall Gro. W4—50Ua 80
Cornwallis Av. N9—19Yb 26
Cornwallis Av. SE9—62Tc 130
Cornwallis Gro. N9—19Yb 26
Cornwallis Rd. E17—28Zb 44
Cornwallis Rd. N9—19Xb 25
Cornwallis Rd. N19—33Nb 62
Cornwallis Rd. Dag—35Zc 67
Cornwallis Wlk. SE9—55Pc 108
Cornwall M. S. SW7
—48Eb 81 (4A 202)
Cornwall M. W. SW7—48Db 81
Cornwall Rd. N4—31Qb 62
Cornwall Rd. N15—29Tb 43
Cornwall Rd. N18—22Wb 43
Cornwall Rd. SE1
—46Qb 82 (6K 199)
Cornwall Rd. Brtwd—15Xd 32
Cornwall Rd. Croy—75Rb 147
Cornwall Rd. Harr—30Ea 38
Cornwall Rd. Pinn—24Ba 37
Cornwall Rd. Ruis—33V 56
Cornwall Rd. Sutt—80Bb 145
Cornwall Rd. Twic—60Ja 100
Cornwall Rd. Uxb—37M 55
Cornwall Rd. Wind—8L 95
Cornwall St. E1—45Xb 83
Cornwall Ter. NW1
—42Hb 81 (6G 191)
Cornwall Ter. M. NW1—(6G 191)
Cornwall Way. Stai—65G 118
Cornwood Clo. N2—28Fb 41
Cornwood Dri. E1—44Yb 84
Cornworthy Rd. Dag—36Yc 67
Corona Rd. SE12—59Jc 107
Coronation Av. Grays—9K 93
Coronation Av. Slou—44A 74
Coronation Av. Wind—4L 95
Coronation Clo. Bex—58Zc 109
Coronation Clo. Ilf—28Sc 46
Coronation Dri. Horn—36Kd 69
Coronation Hill. Epp—1Vc 15
Coronation Rd. E13—41Lc 85
Coronation Rd. NW10—41Pa 79
Coronation Rd. Hay—49V 76
Coronation Wlk. Twic—60Ca 99
Coronet St. N1—41Ub 83 (4H 195)
Corporation Av. Houn—56Aa 99
Corporation Row. EC1
—42Qb 82 (5A 194)
Corporation St. E15—40Gc 65
Corporation St. N7—36Nb 62
Corrance Rd. SW2—56Nb 104
Corran Way. S Ock—45Xd 90
Corri Av. N14—21Mb 42
Corricum. E11—31Gc 65
Corrie Rd. Wey—77M 139
Corrie Rd. Wok—92D 172
Corrigan Av. Coul—87Jb 164
Corringham Rd. NW11—31Cb 61
Corringham Rd. Stanf—2M 93
Corringham Rd. Wemb—33Qa 59
Corringway. NW11—31Db 61
Corringway. W5—42Qa 79
Corsair Clo. Stai—59M 97
Corsair Rd. Stai—59N 97
Corscombe Clo. King—64Sa 123
Corsehill St. SW16—65Lb 126
Corsham St. N1—41Tb 83 (4G 195)
Corsica St. N5—37Rb 63
Corsley Way. E9—37Bc 64
Cortayne Rd. SW6—54Bb 103
Cortis Rd. SW15—58Xa 102
Cortis Ter. SW15—58Xa 102

Corunna Rd. SW8—53Lb 104
Corunna Ter. SW8—53Lb 104
Corve La. S Ock—45Xd 90
Corvette Sq. SE10—51Fc 107
Corwell Gdns. Uxb—44S 76
Corwell La. Uxb—44S 76
Cory Dri. Brtwd—17De 33
Coryton Path. W9—42Bb 81
Cosbycote Av. SE24—57Sb 105
Cosdach Av. Wall—80Mb 146
Cosedge Cres. Croy—78Qb 146
Cosgrove Clo. Hay—42Aa 77
Cosmo Pl. WC1—43Nb 82 (7G 193)
Cosmur Clo. W12—48Va 80
Cossall Wlk. SE15—54Xb 105
Cosser St. SE1—48Qb 82 (3K 205)
Costa St. SE15—54Wb 105
Costead Mnr. Rd. Brtwd—18Xd 32
Costells Meadow. West—98Tc 184
Costons Av. Gnfd—41Fa 78
Costons La. Gnfd—41Fa 78
Cosway St. NW1
—43Gb 81 (7E 190)
Cotall St. E14—43Cc 84
Coteford Clo. Lou—12Rc 28
Coteford Clo. Pinn—29W 36
Coteford St. SW17—63Hb 125
Cotelands. Croy—76Ub 147
Cotesbach Rd. E5—34Yb 64
Cotesmore Gdns. Dag—35Yc 67
Cotford Rd. T Hth—70Sb 127
Cotham St. SE17
—49Sb 83 (6E 206)
Cotheritone. Eps—82Ta 161
Cotherstone Rd. SW2—60Pb 104
Cotleigh Av. Bex—61Zc 131
Cotleigh Rd. NW6—38Cb 61
Cotleigh Rd. Romf—30Fd 48
Cotman Clo. NW11—30Eb 41
Cotman Clo. SW15—58Za 102
Cotmandene Cres. Orp—68Xc 131
Cotman Gdns. Edgw—26Qa 39
Cotman's Ash La. Sev—86Rd 171
★Cotman's Ash La. Sev—87Td
Cotmans Clo. Hay—46W 76
Coton Rd. Well—55Wc 109
Cotsford Av. N Mald—71Sa 143
Cotswold Av. Bush, Wat—16Ea 20
Cotswold Clo. Bexh—54Gd 110
Cotswold Clo. King—65Sa 123
Cotswold Clo. Slou—8G 72
Cotswold Clo. Stai—64J 119
Cotswold Clo. Uxb—39L 55
Cotswold Ct. N11—21Jb 42
Cotswold Gdns. E6—41Mc 85
Cotswold Gdns. NW2—33Za 60
Cotswold Gdns. Brtwd—17Fe 33
Cotswold Gdns. Ilf—31Tc 66
Cotswold Ga. NW2—32Ab 60
Cotswold Grn. Enf—14Pb 24
Cotswold Rise. Orp—72Vc 151
Cotswold Rd. Grav—2A 136
Cotswold Rd. Hmptn—65Ca 121
Cotswold Rd. Romf—26Pd 49
Cotswold Rd. Sutt—82Db 163
Cotswold St. SE27—63Rb 127
Cotswold Way. Enf—13Pb 24
Cottage Av. Brom—74Nc 150
Cottage Clo. Cher—79E 138
Cottage Clo. Ruis—32T 56
Cottage Farm Way. Egh—69E 118
Cottage Field Clo. Sidc—60Yc 109
Cottage Grn. SE5—52Tb 105
Cottage Gro. SW9—55Nb 104
Cottage Gro. Surb—72Ma 143
Cottage Pk. Rd. Slou—3H 53
Cottage Pl. SW3—48Gb 81 (3D 202)
Cottage Rd. Eps—80Ta 143
Cottage St. E14—45Dc 84
Cottage Wlk. SE15—53Vb 105
Cottage Wlk. SW1
—48Hb 81 (3G 203)
Cottenham Dri. SW20—66Xa 124
Cottenham Pk. Rd. SW20
(in two parts) —67Wa 124
Cottenham Pl. SW20—66Xa 124
Cottenham Rd. E17—28Bc 44
Cotterill Rd. Surb—75Na 143
Cottesbrook Clo. Slou—53F 96
Cottesbrook St. SE14—52Ac 106
Cottesmore Av. Ilf—26Qc 46
Cottesmore Gdns. W8—48Db 81
Cottimore Av. W on T—74X 141
Cottimore Cres. W on T—73X 141
Cottimore La. W on T—73X 141
Cottimore Ter. W on T—73X 141
Cottingham Chase. Ruis—34W 56
Cottingham Rd. SE20—66Zb 128
Cottingham Rd. SW8—52Pb 104
Cottington Clo. SE11
—50Rb 83 (7B 206)
Cottington Rd. Felt—63Z 121
Cottington St. SE11
—50Rb 83 (7B 206)
Cotton Av. W3—44Ta 79
Cottongrass Clo. Croy—74Zb 148
Cotton Hill. Brom—63Ec 128
Cotton La. Dart & Grnh—57Sd 112
Cotton Rd. Pot B—4Fb 9
Cotton Rd. Pot B—3Eb 9
Cottons App. Romf—29Fd 48
Cottons Ct. Romf—29Fd 48
Cotton's Gdns. E2
—41Ub 83 (3J 195)
Cotton St. E14—45Ec 84
Cotton's Wharf. SE1—(6H 201)
Couchmore Av. Esh—75Ga 142
Couchmore Av. Ilf—26Pc 46
Coulgate St. SE4—55Ac 106
Coulsdon Ct. Rd. Coul—88Pb 164
Coulsdon La. Coul—91Jb 180
Coulsdon Pl. Cat—94Tb 181
Coulsdon Rise. Coul—89Nb 164
Coulsdon Rd. Coul & Cat
—87Pb 164
Coulson St. SW3
—50Hb 81 (7F 203)

Coulston Rd. SW18—59Cb 103
Coulter Clo. Hay—42Aa 77
Coulter Rd. W6—48Xa 80
Coulton Av. Grav—10A 114
Council Av. Grav—58Ee 113
Councillor St. SE5—52Sb 105
Counter Ct. SE1—(7F 201)
Counter St. SE1—(7H 201)
Countess Clo. Uxb—26L 35
Countess Rd. NW5—36Lb 62
Countisbury Av. Enf—17Vb 25
Countisbury Gdns. Wey—78K 139
Country Way. Felt—65X 121
County Gdns. Bark—40Uc 66
County Ga. SE9—62Sc 130
County Ga. Barn—16Db 23
County Gro. SE5—53Sb 105
County Rd. E6—43Rc 86
County Rd. T Hth—68Rb 127
County St. SE1—48Sb 83 (4E 206)
Coupland Pl. SE18—50Sc 86
Courage Clo. Horn—30Ld 49
Courage Wlk. Brtwd—16Fe 33
Courcy Rd. N8—27Qb 42
Courland Gro. SW8—53Mb 104
Courland Rd. Wey—76K 139
Courland St. SW8—54Mb 104
Course, The. SE9—62Qc 130
Courtauld Rd. N19—32Nb 62
Court Av. Belv—50Bd 87
Court Av. Coul—90Qb 164
Court Av. Romf—24Qd 49
Court Bushes Rd. Whyt
—91Wb 181
Court Clo. Harr—27Na 39
Court Clo. Twic—62Da 121
Court Clo. Wall—80Mb 146
Court Clo. Av. Twic—62Da 121
Court Cres. Chess—79Ma 143
Court Cres. Slou—4H 73
Court Cres. Swan—70Gd 132
Court Downs Rd. Beck—68Dc 128
Court Dri. Croy—77Pb 146
Court Dri. Stan—21Na 39
Court Dri. Sutt—77Gb 145
Court Dri. Uxb—39P 55
Courtenay Av. N6—31Gb 61
Courtenay Av. Harr—24Ea 38
Courtenay Gdns. Harr—26Ea 38
Courtenay Gdns. Upm—32Sd 70
Courtenay Pl. E17—29Ac 44
Courtenay Rd. E11—34Hc 65
Courtenay Rd. E17—28Zb 44
Courtenay Rd. SE20—65Zb 128
Courtenay Rd. Wok—88C 156
Courtenay Rd. Wor Pk—76Ya 144
Courtenay Sq. SE11
—50Qb 82 (7K 205)
Courtenay St. SE11
—50Qb 82 (7K 205)
Court Farm Av. Eps—78Ta 143
Court Farm La. N'holt—38Ca 57
Court Farm Rd. SE9—61Mc 129
Court Farm Rd. N'holt—38Ca 57
Court Farm Rd. Warl—90Wb 165
Courtfield Av. Harr—29Ha 38
Courtfield Cres. Harr—29Ha 38
Courtfield Gdns. SW5—49Db 81
Courtfield Gdns. W13—44Ja 78
Courtfield Gdns. Ruis—33V 56
Courtfield Gdns. Uxb—34J 55
Courtfield M. SW7—49Eb 81
Courtfield Rise. W Wick—76Fc 149
Courtfield Rd. SW7
—49Eb 81 (5A 202)
Courtfield Rd. Ashf—65R 120
Court Gdns. Romf—23Qd 49
Court Grn. Heights. Wok—8F 188
Court Haw. Bans—87Gb 163
Court Hill. Coul—90Gb 163
Court Hill. S Croy—84Ub 165
Courthill Rd. SE13—56Ec 106
Courthope Rd. NW3—35Hb 61
Courthope Rd. SW19—64Ab 124
Courthope Rd. Gnfd—40Fa 58
Courthope Vs. SW19—66Ab 124
Court Ho. Gdns. N3—23Cb 41
Courthouse Rd. N12—23Db 41
Courtland Av. E4—19Hc 27
Courtland Av. NW7—20Ua 22
Courtland Av. SW16—66Pb 126
Courtland Av. Ilf—33Pc 66
Courtland Dri. Chig—20Rc 28
Courtland Rd. E6—39Nc 66
Courtlands. Rich—57Qa 101
Courtlands Av. SE12—57Kc 107
Courtlands Av. Brom—74Hc 149
Courtlands Av. Esh—79Ba 141
Courtlands Av. Hmptn—65Ba 121
Courtlands Av. Rich—54Ra 101
Courtlands Av. Slou—9P 73
Courtlands Clo. Ruis—31V 56
Courtlands Clo. S Croy—82Vb 165
Courtlands Cres. Bans—88Cb 163
Courtlands Dri. Eps—79Ua 144
Courtlands Dri. Wat—9U 4
Courtlands Rd. Surb—73Qa 143
Court La. SE21—58Ub 105
Court La. Eps—85Sa 161
Court La. Iver—46J 75
(in two parts)
Court La. Slou—1B 72
Court La. Wind—8A 72
Court La. Gdns. SE21—59Ub 105
Courtleas. Cob—85Ca 159
Courtleet Dri. Eri—53Dd 110
Courtleigh Av. Barn—10Fb 9
Courtleigh Gdns. NW11—28Ab 40
Court Lodge. Grav—5N 137
Courtman Rd. N17—24Sb 43
Court Mead. N'holt—41Ba 77
Courtmead Clo. SE24—58Sb 105
Courtnell St. W2—44Cb 81
Courtney Clo. SE19—65Ub 127
Courtney Cres. Cars—80Hb 145
Courtney Pl. Croy—76Qb 146
Courtney Rd. N7—36Qb 62

Courtney Rd. SW19—66Gb 125
Courtney Rd. Croy—76Qb 146
Courtney Rd. Grays—7E 92
Courtney Rd. Houn—55Q 98
Courtrai Rd. SE23—58Ac 106
Court Rd. SE9—58Pc 108
Court Rd. SE25—68Vb 127
Court Rd. Bans—88Cb 163
Court Rd. Cat—95Tb 181
Court Rd. Dart—64Ud 134
Court Rd. Orp—73Xc 151
Court Rd. S'hall—50Ba 77
Court Rd. Uxb—36R 56
Courtside. N8—30Mb 42
Court St. E1—43Xb 83
Court St. Brom—68Jc 129
Court, The. Ruis—35Aa 57
Court, The. Warl—90Ac 166
Court Way. NW9—28Ua 40
Court Way. W3—43Sa 79
Court Way. Ilf—27Sc 46
Court Way. Romf—26Nd 49
Court Way. Twic—59Ha 100
Court Way. Wfd G—22Lc 45
Courtway, The. Wat—19Aa 19
Courtwood Dri. Sev—96Jd 186
Court Wood La. Croy—83Bc 166
Court Yd. SE9—58Pc 108
Courtyard, The. N1—38Pb 62
Courtyard, The. NW1—38Jb 62
Cousin La. EC4—45Tb 83 (5F 201)
Couthurst Rd. SE3—52Kc 107
Coutts Av. Chess—78Na 143
Coutts Av. Grav—3N 137
Coval Gdns. SW14—56Ra 101
Coval La. SW14—56Ra 101
Coval Pas. SW14—56Sa 101
Coval Rd. SW14—56Sa 101
Coveham Cres. Cob—85W 158
Covenbrook. Brtwd—20De 33
Covent Garden. WC2
—45Nb 82 (4G 199)
Coventry Clo. E6—44Pc 86
Coventry Clo. NW6—40Cb 61
Coventry Rd. E1 & E2—42Xb 83
Coventry Rd. SE25—70Wb 127
Coventry Rd. Ilf—33Rc 66
Coventry St. W1
—45Mb 82 (5D 198)
Coverack Clo. N14—16Lb 24
Coverack Clo. Croy—73Ac 148
Coverdale Clo. Stan—22Ka 38
Coverdale Gdns. Croy—76Vb 147
Coverdale Rd. NW2—38Za 60
Coverdale Rd. W12—47Xa 80
Coverdales, The. Bark—40Tc 66
Coverdale Way. Slou—2C 72
Coverley Clo. E1—43Wb 83
Coverley Clo. Brtwd—23Yd 50
Coverton Rd. SW17—64Gb 125
Covert Rd. Ilf—23Vc 47
Coverts Rd. Esh—80Ha 142
Coverts, The. Brtwd—18Ce 33
Covert, The. N'wd—25S 36
Covert, The. Orp—72Uc 150
Covert Way. Barn—12Eb 23
Covington Gdns. SW16—66Rb 127
Covington Way. SW16—65Pb 126
(in two parts)
Cowan Clo. E6—43Nc 86
Cowan St. SE5—51Ub 105
Cowbridge La. Bark—38Rc 66
Cowbridge Rd. Harr—28Pa 39
Cowcross St. EC1
—43Rb 83 (7B 194)
Cowdenbeath Path. N1—39Pb 62
Cowden Rd. Orp—73Vc 151
Cowden St. SE6—63Cc 128
Cowdray Rd. Uxb—39S 56
Cowdray Way. Horn—35Jd 68
Cowdrey Clo. Enf—12Ub 25
Cowdrey Ct. Dart—59Kd 111
Cowdrey Rd. SW19—64Eb 125
Cowdry Rd. E9—37Ac 64
Cowen Av. Harr—33Fa 58
Cowgate Rd. Gnfd—41Fa 78
Cowick Rd. SW17—63Hb 125
Cowings Mead. N'holt—37Aa 57
Cowland Av. Enf—14Yb 26
Cow La. Gnfd—40Fa 58
Cow La. Wat—8Y 5
Cowleaze Rd. King—67Na 123
Cowley Av. Cher—73H 139
Cowley Clo. S Croy—82Yb 166
Cowley Cres. Uxb—43L 75
Cowley Cres. W on T—77Y 141
Cowley Hill. Borwd—9Ra 7
Cowley La. E11—34Gc 65
Cowley La. Cher—73H 139
Cowley Mill Rd. Uxb—40K 55
Cowley Pl. NW4—29Ya 40
Cowley Rd. E11—29Kc 45
Cowley Rd. SW9—53Qb 104
Cowley Rd. SW14—55Ua 102
Cowley Rd. W3—46Va 80
Cowley Rd. Ilf—31Pc 66
Cowley Rd. Romf—24Kd 49
Cowley Rd. Uxb—40L 55
Cowley St. SW1—48Nb 82 (4F 205)
Cowling Clo. W11—46Ab 80
Coworth Rd. Asc—10E 116
Cowper Av. E6—38Nc 66
Cowper Av. Sutt—77Fb 145
Cowper Av. Til—3D 114
Cowper Clo. Brom—70Mc 129
Cowper Clo. Cher—72H 139
Cowper Clo. Well—57Wc 109
Cowper Ct. Wat—9W 4
Cowper Gdns. N14—16Kb 24
Cowper Gdns. Wall—79Lb 146
Cowper Rd. N14—18Kb 24
Cowper Rd. N16—36Ub 63
Cowper Rd. N18—22Wb 43
Cowper Rd. SW19—65Eb 125
Cowper Rd. W3—46Ta 79
Cowper Rd. W7—45Ha 78
Cowper Rd. Belv—49Cd 88
Cowper Rd. Brom—70Mc 129

Cowper Rd. King—64Pa 123
Cowper Rd. Rain—42Jd 88
Cowper Rd. Slou—2E 72
Cowper's Ct. EC3—(3G 201)
Cowper St. EC2—42Tb 83 (5G 195)
Cowper Ter. W10—43Za 80
Cowslip La. Dor—100Ja 176
Cowslip La. Wok—3E 188
Cowslip Rd. E18—26Kc 45
Cowthorpe Rd. SW8—53Mb 104
Coxdean. Eps—91Ya 178
Cox La. Chess—77Pa 143
Cox La. Eps—78Ra 143
Coxley Rise. Purl—85Sb 165
Coxmount Rd. SE7—50Mc 85
Coxson Pl. SE1—47Vb 83 (2K 207)
Cox's Wlk. SE21 & SE26
—60Wb 105
Coxtie Grn. Rd. Brtwd—15Pd &
14Qd 31
Coxwald Path. Chess—80Na 143
Coxwell Rd. SE18—50Tc 86
Crabbs Croft Clo. Orp—78Sc 150
Crab Hill. Beck—66Fc 129
Crab La. Wat—7Da 5
Crabtree Av. Romf—28Zc 47
Crabtree Av. Wemb—40Pa 59
Crabtree Clo. Bush, Wat—15Da 19
Crabtree Clo. Lea—98Ea 176
Crabtree Dri. Lea—96La 176
Crabtree La. SW6—52Ya 102
Crabtree La. Lea—98Ea 176
Crabtree Manorway. Belv
—48Ed 88
Crabtree Rd. Egh—68E 118
Crabwood. Oxt—100Gc 183
Crace St. NW1—41Mb 82 (3D 192)
Craddock Rd. Enf—13Vb 25
Craddocks Av. Asht—89Na 161
Craddocks Pde. Asht—89Na 161
Craddock St. NW5—37Jb 62
Cradley Rd. SE9—60Tc 108
Cragg Av. Rad—8Ha 6
Craigdale Rd. Horn—30Hd 48
Craig Dri. Uxb—44R 76
Craigen Av. Croy—74Xb 147
Craigerne Rd. SE3—52Kc 107
Craig Gdns. E18—26Hc 45
Craigholm. SE18—54Qc 108
Craig Mt. Rad—7Ka 6
Craigmuir Pk. Wemb—39Pa 59
Craignair Rd. SW2—59Qb 104
Craignish Av. SW16—68Pb 126
Craig Pk. Rd. N18—22Xb 43
Craig Rd. Rich—63La 122
Craig's Ct. SW1—46Nb 82 (6F 199)
Craigton Rd. SE9—56Pc 108
Craigweil Clo. Stan—22Ma 39
Craigweil Dri. Stan—22Ma 39
Craigwell Av. Felt—62W 120
Craigwell Av. Rad—7Ka 6
Crail Row. SE17—49Tb 83 (6G 207)
Cramer St. W1—43Jb 82 (1J 197)
Crammavill St. Grays—46Ce 91
Crammerville Wlk. Rain—42Kd 89
Cramond Clo. W6—51Ab 102
Crampshaw La. Asht—91Pa 177
Crampton Rd. SE20—65Yb 128
Cramptons Rd. Sev—92Kd 187
Crampton St. SE17
—49Sb 83 (6D 206)
Cranberry Clo. N'holt—40Z 57
Cranberry St. E1—42Wb 83
Cranborne Av. S'hall—49Ca 77
Cranborne Av. Surb—76Qa 143
Cranborne Clo. Pot B—3Ab 8
Cranborne Cres. Pot B—3Ab 8
Cranborne Gdns. Upm—33Rd 69
Cranborne Pde. Pot B—3Za 8
Cranborne Rd. N10—26Kb 42
Cranborne Rd. Bark—39Tc 66
Cranborne Rd. Pot B—3Ab 8
Cranborne Rd. Wal X—4Zb 12
Cranborne Waye. Hay—44X 77
Cranbourn All. WC2—(4E 198)
Cranbourne Av. E11—28Kc 45
Cranbourne Av. Wind—4D 94
Cranbourne Clo. SW16—69Nb 126
Cranbourne Clo. Slou—6G 72
Cranbourne Dri. Pinn—29Z 37
Cranbourne Gdns. NW11—29Ab 40
Cranbourne Gdns. Ilf—27Sc 46
Cranbourne Rd. E12—36Nc 66
Cranbourne Rd. E15—35Ec 64
Cranbourne Rd. N'wd—27V 36
Cranbourne Rd. Slou—6G 72
Cranbourn Pas. SE16—47Xb 83
Cranbourn St. WC2
—45Mb 82 (4E 198)
Cranbrook Clo. Brom—72Jc 149
Cranbrook Dri. Esh—74Ea 142
Cranbrook Dri. Romf—28Ld 49
Cranbrook Dri. Twic—60Da 99
Cranbrook Est. E2—40Zb 64
Cranbrook M. E17—29Bc 44
Cranbrook Pk. N22—25Qb 42
Cranbrook Rise. Ilf—30Pc 46
Cranbrook Rd. SE3—55Mc 107
Cranbrook Rd. SE8—53Cc 106
Cranbrook Rd. SW19—66Ab 124
Cranbrook Rd. W4—50Ua 80
Cranbrook Rd. Barn—16Fb 23
Cranbrook Rd. Bexh—53Bd 109
Cranbrook Rd. Houn—56Ba 99
Cranbrook Rd. Ilf—31Qc 66
Cranbrook Rd. T Hth—68Sb 127
Cranbrook St. E2—40Zb 64
Cranbury Rd. SW6—54Db 103
Crane Av. W3—45Sa 79
Crane Av. Iswth—57Ja 100
Cranebrook. Twic—61Ea 122
Crane Clo. Dag—37Cd 68
Crane Ct. EC4—44Qb 82 (3A 200)
Crane Ct. Eps—77Sa 143
Cranefield Dri. Wat—4Aa 5
Craneford Clo. Twic—59Ha 100
Craneford Way. Twic—59Ga 100

Crane Gdns. Hay—49V 76
Crane Gro. N7—37Qb 62
Cranell Grn. S Ock—46Xd 90
Crane Lodge Rd. Houn—51X 99
Cranemead. SE16—49Zb 84
Crane Pk. Rd. Twic—61Da 121
Crane Rd. Twic—60Ga 100
Cranes Dri. Surb—70Na 123
Cranes Pk. Surb—70Na 123
Cranes Pk. Av. Surb—70Na 123
Cranes Pk. Cres. Surb—70Pa 123
Crane St. SE10—50Fc 85
Craneswater. Hay—52V 98
Craneswater Pk. S'hall—50Ba 77
Cranes Way. Borwd—15Sa 21
Crane Way. Twic—59Ea 100
Cranfield Clo. SE27—62Sb 127
Cranfield Ct. Wok—6D 188
Cranfield Cres. Pot B—1Nb 10
Cranfield Dri. NW9—24Ua 40
Cranfield Rd. SE4—55Bc 106
Cranfield Rd. E. Cars—81Jb 164
Cranfield Rd. W. Cars—81Jb 164
Cranford Av. N13—22Nb 42
Cranford Av. Stai—59N 97
Cranford Clo. SW20—66Xa 124
Cranford Clo. Stai—59N 97
Cranford Dri. Hay—49V 76
Cranford La. Hay—51T 98
Cranford La. Houn—55V 98
(Hatton)
Cranford La. Houn—52X 99
(Heston)
Cranford Pk. Rd. Hay—49V 76
Cranford Rd. Dart—60Nd 111
Cranford St. E1—45Zb 84
Cranford Way. N8—28Pb 42
Cranham Gdns. Upm—32Ud 70
Cranham Rd. Horn—30Kd 49
Cranhurst Rd. NW2—36Ya 60
Cranleigh Clo. SE20—68Xb 127
Cranleigh Clo. Bex—58Dd 110
Cranleigh Clo. Orp—76Wc 151
Cranleigh Clo. S Croy—84Wb 165
Cranleigh Dri. Swan—70Gd 132
Cranleigh Gdns. N21—15Qb 24
Cranleigh Gdns. SE25—69Ub 127
Cranleigh Gdns. Bark—38Tc 66
Cranleigh Gdns. Harr—29Na 39
Cranleigh Gdns. King—65Pa 123
Cranleigh Gdns. Lou—16Pc 28
Cranleigh Gdns. S'hall—44Ba 77
Cranleigh Gdns. S Croy
Cranleigh Gdns. Sutt—75Db 145
Cranleigh Rd. N15—29Sb 43
Cranleigh Rd. SW19—69Cb 125
Cranleigh Rd. Esh—74Ea 142
Cranleigh Rd. Felt—63V 120
Cranleigh St. NW1
—40Lb 62 (2C 192)
Cranley Dene Ct. N10—28Kb 42
Cranley Dri. Ilf—31Sc 66
Cranley Dri. Ruis—33V 56
Cranley Gdns. N10—28Kb 42
Cranley Gdns. N13—20Pb 24
Cranley Gdns. SW7
—50Eb 81 (7A 202)
Cranley Gdns. Wall—80Lb 146
Cranley M. SW7—50Eb 81 (7A 202)
Cranley Pl. SW7—49Fb 81 (6B 202)
Cranley Rd. E13—43Kc 85
Cranley Rd. Ilf—30Sc 46
Cranley Rd. W on T—78V 140
Cranmer Av. W13—48Ka 78
Cranmer Clo. Mord—72Za 144
Cranmer Clo. Pot B—2Eb 9
Cranmer Clo. Ruis—32Z 57
Cranmer Clo. Stan—24La 38
Cranmer Clo. Warl—89Ac 166
Cranmer Clo. Wey—80Q 140
Cranmer Ct. SW3
—49Gb 81 (6E 202)
Cranmer Ct. SW4—55Mb 104
Cranmer Farm Clo. Mitc
—70Hb 125
Cranmer Gdns. Dag—35Ed 68
Cranmer Gdns. Warl—89Ac 166
Cranmer Rd. E7—35Kc 65
Cranmer Rd. SW9—52Qb 104
Cranmer Rd. Croy—76Rb 147
Cranmer Rd. Edgw—20Ra 21
Cranmer Rd. Hmptn—64Da 121
Cranmer Rd. Hay—44T 76
Cranmer Rd. King—64Na 123
Cranmer Rd. Mitc—70Hb 125
Cranmer Rd. Sev—95Gd 186
Cranmer Ter. SW17—64Fb 125
Cranmore Av. Iswth—52Ea 100
Cranmore La. Lea—100R 174
(in two parts)
Cranmore Rd. Brom—62Hc 129
Cranmore Rd. Chst—64Pc 130
Cranmore Way. N10—28Lb 42
Cranston Clo. Houn—54Aa 99
Cranston Clo. Uxb—33T 56
Cranston Est. N1
—40Tb 63 (2G 195)
Cranston Gdns. E4—23Dc 44
Cranston Pk. Av. Upm—35Sd 70
Cranston Rd. SE23—60Ac 106
Cranswick Rd. SE16—50Xb 83
Crantock Rd. SE6—61Dc 128
Cranwell Clo. E3—42Dc 84
Cranwell Gro. Shep—70P 119
Cranwell Rd. Houn—54R 98
Cranwich Av. N21—17Tb 25
Cranwich Rd. N16—31Tb 63
Cranwood St. EC1
—41Tb 83 (4G 195)
Cranworth Cres. E4—18Fc 27
Cranworth Gdns. SW9—53Qb 104
Craster Rd. SW2—59Pb 104
Crathie Rd. SE12—58Kc 107
Crathorn St. SE13—55Ec 106
Craven Av. W5—45La 78
Craven Av. Felt—61W 120
Craven Av. S'hall—43Ba 77

Craven Clo. Hay—44W 76
Craven Gdns. SW19—64Db 125
Craven Gdns. Bark—40Uc 66
Craven Gdns. Ilf—26Tc 46
Craven Gdns. Romf—23Sd 50
(Harold Wood)
Craven Gdns. Romf—22Cd 48
(Havering Park)
Craven Hill. W2—45Eb 81 (4A 196)
Craven Hill Gdns. W2
—45Eb 81 (4A 196)
Craven Hill M. W2
—45Eb 81 (4A 196)
Craven M. SW11—55Jb 104
Craven Pk. NW10—39Ta 59
Craven Pk. M. NW10—39Ua 60
Craven Pk. Rd. N15—30Vb 43
Craven Pk. Rd. NW10—39Ua 60
Craven Pas. WC2—(6F 199)
Craven Rd. NW10—39Ta 59
Craven Rd. W2—44Fb 81 (4A 196)
Craven Rd. W5—45La 78
Craven Rd. Croy—74Xb 147
Craven Rd. King—67Pa 123
Craven Rd. Orp—76Zc 151
Craven St. WC2—46Nb 82 (6F 199)
Craven Ter. W2—45Eb 81 (4A 196)
Craven Wlk. N16—31Wb 63
Crawford Av. Grays—46De 91
Crawford Av. Wemb—36Ma 59
Crawford Clo. Iswth—54Ga 100
Crawford Gdns. N13—20Rb 25
Crawford Gdns. N'holt—41Ba 77
Crawford M. W1—43Hb 81 (1F 197)
Crawford Pas. EC1
—42Qb 82 (6A 194)
Crawford Pl. W1—44Gb 81 (2E 196)
Crawford Rd. SE5—53Sb 105
Crawford St. W1
—43Hb 81 (1F 197)
Crawley Rd. E10—32Dc 64
Crawley Rd. N22—26Sb 43
Crawley Rd. Enf—17Ub 25
Crawshay Clo. Sev—95Jd 186
Crawshay Ct. SW9—53Qb 104
Crawthew Gro. SE22—56Vb 105
Cray Av. Orp—72Xc 151
Craybrooke Rd. Sidc—63Xc 131
Crayburne. Grav—64Be 135
Craybury End. SE9—61Sc 130
Cray Clo. Dart—56Jd 110
Craydene Rd. Eri—53Hd 110
Crayford Av. Asht—88Na 161
Crayford High St. Dart—57Gd 110
Crayford Rd. N7—35Nb 62
Crayford Rd. Dart—57Hd 110
Crayford Way. Dart—57Hd 110
Crayke Hill. Chess—80Na 143
Craylands. Orp—69Yc 131
Craylands La. Swans—57Zd 113
Craylands Sq. Swans—57Zd 113
Crayle St. Slou—1E 72
Craymill Sq. Dart—54Hd 110
Crayonne Clo. Sun—67U 120
Cray Rd. Belv—51Cd 110
Cray Rd. Sidc—65Yc 131
Cray Rd. Swan—72Ed 152
Crayside Industrial Est. Dart
—56Kd 111
Cray Valley Rd. Orp—71Wc 151
Crealock Gro. Wfd G—22Hc 45
Crealock St. SW18—58Db 103
Creasy St. SE1—48Ub 83 (4H 207)
Crebor St. SE22—58Wb 105
Credenhall Dri. Brom—74Pc 150
Credenhill St. SW16—65Lb 126
Credenhill Way. SE15—52Xb 105
Crediton Hill. NW6—36Db 61
Crediton Rd. E16—44Jc 85
Crediton Rd. NW10—39Za 60
Crediton Way. Esh—78Ja 142
Credon Rd. E13—40Lc 65
Credon Rd. SE16—50Xb 83
Credo Way. Grays—51Xd 112
Creechurch La. EC3
—44Ub 83 (3J 201)
Creechurch Pl. EC3—(3J 201)
Creed La. EC4—44Rb 83 (3C 200)
Creek Rd.—51Cc 106
SE8 1-201 & 2-194
SE10 remainder
Creek Rd. Bark—41Vc 87
Creek Rd. E Mol—70Ga 122
Creekside. SE8—52Dc 106
Creekside. Rain—42Hd 88
Creek, The. Grav—57De 113
Creek, The. Sun—71W 140
Creeland Gro. SE6—60Bc 106
Cree Way. Romf—24Gd 48
Crefeld Clo. W6—51Ab 102
Creffield Rd.—45Pa 79
W5 1-51 & 2-56
W3 remainder
Creighton Av. E6—40Mc 65
Creighton Av.—27Gb 41
N10 1-79 & 2-78
N2 remainder
Creighton Rd. N17—24Ub 43
Creighton Rd. NW6—40Za 60
Creighton Rd. W5—48Ma 79
Cremer St. E2—40Vb 63 (2K 195)
Cremorne Gdns. Eps—82Ta 161
Cremorne Rd. SW10—52Fb 103
Cremorne Rd. Grav—9B 114
Crescent. EC3—(4K 201)
Crescent Av. Grays—50Fe 91
Crescent Av. Horn—33Hd 68
Crescent Ct. Surb—71Ma 143
Crescent Dri. Brtwd—18Ae 33
Crescent Dri. Orp—72Rc 150
Crescent E. Barn—10Eb 9
Crescent Gdns. SW19—62Cb 125
Crescent Gdns. Ruis—31X 57
Crescent Gdns. Swan—68Ed 132
Crescent Gro. SW4—56Lb 104
Crescent Gro. Mitc—71Gb 145
Crescent La. SW4—56Lb 104

Crescent Pl. SW3
—49Gb 81 (5E 202)
Crescent Rise. N22—25Mb 42
Crescent Rise. Barn—15Gb 23
Crescent Rd. E4—17Gc 27
Crescent Rd. E6—39Lc 65
Crescent Rd. E10—33Dc 64
Crescent Rd. E13—39Jc 65
Crescent Rd. E18—25Lc 45
Crescent Rd. N3—25Bb 41
Crescent Rd. N8—30Mb 42
Crescent Rd. N9—18Wb 25
Crescent Rd. N11—21Hb 41
Crescent Rd. N15—27Rb 43
Crescent Rd. N22—25Mb 42
Crescent Rd. SE18—50Rc 86
Crescent Rd. SW20—67Za 124
Crescent Rd. Barn—14Fb 23
Crescent Rd. Beck—68Dc 128
Crescent Rd. Brtwd—21Xd 50
Crescent Rd. Brom—66Jc 129
Crescent Rd. Cat—96Wb 181
Crescent Rd. Dag—34Dd 67
Crescent Rd. Enf—14Rb 25
Crescent Rd. Eri—51Hd 110
Crescent Rd. King—66Qa 123
Crescent Rd. Sev—92Gd 186
Crescent Rd. Shep—71S 140
Crescent Rd. Sidc—62Vc 131
Crescent Rd. S Ock—47Sd 90
Crescent Row. EC1
—42Sb 83 (6D 194)
Crescent St. N1—38Pb 62
Crescent, The. E17—29Ac 44
Crescent, The. N11—21Jb 42
Crescent, The. NW2—34Xa 60
Crescent, The. SW13—54Wa 102
Crescent, The. SW19—62Cb 125
Crescent, The. W3—44Ua 80
Crescent, The. Abb L. Wat—2V 4
Crescent, The. Ashf—64P 119
Crescent, The. Barn—12Db 23
Crescent, The. Beck—67Cc 128
Crescent, The. Bex—59Yc 109
Crescent, The. Cat—95Cc 182
Crescent, The. Croy—72Tb 147
Crescent, The. E Mol—70Ca 121
Crescent, The. Egh—65B 118
Crescent, The. Epp—4Vc 15
Crescent, The. Eps—86Qa 161
(in two parts)
Crescent, The. Grav—1B 136
Crescent, The. Grnh—57Yd 112
Crescent, The. Harr—32Ea 58
Crescent, The. Hay—52T 98
Crescent, The. Ilf—30Qc 46
Crescent, The. Lea—94Ka 176
Crescent, The. Lou—16Nc 28
Crescent, The. N Mald—68Ta 123
Crescent, The. Rick—16R 18
Crescent, The. St Alb—2Ca 5
Crescent, The. Sev—93Md 187
★Crescent, The. Sev—91Ce
(Borough Green)
Crescent, The. Shep—73V 140
Crescent, The. Sidc—63Vc 131
Crescent, The. Slou—7J 73
Crescent, The. S'hall—47Ba 77
Crescent, The. Surb—71Na 143
Crescent, The. Sutt—78Fb 145
Crescent, The. Sutt—83Cb 163
(Belmont)
Crescent, The. Upm—31Vd 70
Crescent, The. Wat—14Y 19
Crescent, The. Wat—10Da 5
(Aldenham)
Crescent, The. Wemb—33Ka 58
Crescent, The. W Wick—72Gc 149
Crescent, The. Wey—76Q 140
Crescent View. Lou—16Mc 27
Crescent Wlk. S Ock—47Sd 90
Crescent Way. N12—23Gb 41
Crescent Way. SE4—55Cc 106
Crescent Way. SW16—66Pb 126
Crescent Way. Orp—78Uc 150
Crescent Way. S Ock—46Td 90
Crescent W. Barn—10Eb 9
Crescent Wood Rd. SE26—62Wb 127
Cresford Rd. SW6—53Db 103
Crespigny Rd. NW4—30Xa 40
Cressage Clo. S'hall—42Ca 77
Cressal Clo. Lea—92Ka 176
Cressal Mead. Lea—92Ka 176
Cresset Rd. E9—37Yb 64
Cresset St. SW4—55Mb 104
Cressfield Clo. NW5—36Jb 62
Cressida Rd. N19—32Lb 62
Cressingham Gdns. Est. SW2
—59Qb 104
Cressingham Gro. Sutt—77Eb 145
Cressingham Rd. SE13—55Ec 106
Cressingham Rd. Edgw—23Ta 39
Cress Rd. Slou—7F 72
Cresswell Gdns. SW5
—50Eb 81 (7A 202)
Cresswell Pk. SE3—55Hc 107
Cresswell Pl. SW10
—50Eb 81 (7A 202)
Cresswell Rd. SE25—70Wb 127
Cresswell Rd. Felt—62Aa 121
Cresswell Rd. Twic—58Ma 101
Cresswell Way. N21—17Qb 24
Cressy Ct. E1—43Yb 84
Cressy Pl. E1—43Yb 84
Cressy Rd. NW3—36Hb 61
Cresta Dri. Wey—82H 157
Crestbrook Av. N13—20Rb 25
Crest Dri. Enf—10Yb 12
Crestfield St. WC1
—41Nb 82 (3G 193)
Crest Gdns. Ruis—34Y 57
Cresthill Av. Grays—49Ee 91
Creston Av. Wok—5B 188
Creston Way. Wor Pk—74Za 144
Crest Rd. NW2—33Wa 60
Crest Rd. Brom—73Hc 149
Crest Rd. S Croy—80Xb 147

Crest, The. N13—21Qb 42
Crest, The. NW4—29Ya 40
Crest, The. Surb—71Qa 143
Crest View. Pinn—28Z 37
Crest View Dri. Orp—71Rc 150
Crestway. SW15—58Wa 102
Creswick Rd. W3—45Ra 79
Creswick Wlk. E3—41Cc 84
Creswick Wlk. NW11—28Bb 41
Crete Hall Rd. Grav—58Fe 113
Creton St. SE18—48Qc 86
Crewdson Rd. SW9—52Qb 104
Crewe Pl. NW10—41Va 80
Crewe's Av. Warl—88Yb 166
Crewe's Clo. Warl—89Yb 166
Crewe's Farm La. Warl—89Zb 166
Crewe's La. Warl—88Yb 166
Crews Hill. Enf—6Pb 10
Crews St. E14—49Cc 84
Crewys Rd. NW2—33Bb 61
Crewys Rd. SE15—54Xb 105
Crichton Av. Wall—78Mb 146
Crichton Gdns. Romf—31Bd 67
Crichton Rd. Cars—80Hb 145
Cricketers Arms Rd. Enf—12Sb 25
Cricketers Clo. Chess—77Ma 143
Cricketer's Ct. SE11—(6B 206)
Cricketers La. Brtwd—24Fe 51
Cricketers Row. Brtwd—24Fe 51
Cricketfield Rd. E5—35Xb 63
Cricket Field Rd. Uxb—39M 55
Cricketfield Rd. W Dray—49L 75
Cricket Grn. Mitc—70Hb 125
Cricket Ground Rd. Chst
—67Rc 130
Cricket Way. Wey—75U 140
Cricklade Av. SW2—61Nb 126
Cricklade Av. Romf—23Md 49
Cricklewood B'way. NW2
—34Za 60
Cricklewood La. NW2—35Za 60
Cricklewood Trading Est. NW2
—34Ab 60
Cridland St. E15—39Hc 65
Crieff Ct. Tedd—66La 122
Crieff Rd. SW18—58Eb 103
Criffel Av. SW2—61Mb 126
Crimp Hill. Wind & Egh—9K 95
Crimscott St. SE1
—48Ub 83 (4J 207)
Crimsworth Rd. SW8—52Mb 104
Crinan St. N1—40Nb 62 (1G 193)
Cringle St. SW8—52Lb 104
Cripplegate St. EC2
—43Sb 83 (7E 194)
Cripps Grn. Hay—42X 77
Crispen Rd. Felt—63Aa 121
Crispian Clo. NW10—35Ua 60
Crispin Clo. Asht—89Pa 161
Crispin Clo. Croy—75Nb 146
Crispin Cres. Croy—76Mb 146
Crispin Rd. Edgw—23Sa 39
Crispin St. E1—43Vb 83 (1K 201)
Crispin Way. Slou—5H 53
Crisp Rd. W6—50Ya 80
Cristowe Rd. SW6—54Bb 103
Criterion M. N19—33Mb 62
Crockenhall Way. Grav—6A 136
Crockenhill La. Swan & Eyns,
Dart—73Jd 152
Crockenhill Rd. Orp & Swan
—71Zc 151
Crockerton Rd. SW17—61Hb 125
Crockford Clo. Wey—77L 139
Crockford Pk. Rd. Wey—78L 139
Crockham Way. SE9—63Qc 130
Crocus Clo. Croy—74Zb 148
Crocus Field. Barn—16Bb 23
Crocus Wlk. W12—44Va 80
Croft Av. W Wick—74Ec 148
Croft Clo. NW7—20Ua 22
Croft Clo. Belv—50Bd 87
Croft Clo. Chst—64Pc 130
Croft Clo. Hay—52S 98
Croft Clo. K Lan—2J 3
Croft Clo. Uxb—38Q 56
Croftdown Rd. NW5—34Jb 62
Croft End Rd. K Lan—2J 3
Crofters Clo. Iswth—57Fa 100
Crofters Mead. Croy—81Bc 166
Crofters Rd. N'wd—21U 36
Crofters Way. NW1—39Mb 62
Croft Field. K Lan—2J 3
Croft Gdns. W7—47Ja 78
Croft Gdns. Ruis—32V 56
Crofthill Rd. Slou—2F 72
Croft La. K Lan—2J 3
Croftleigh Av. Purl—88Rb 165
Croft Lodge Clo. Wfd G—23Kc 45
Croft Meadow. K Lan—2J 3
Crofton Av. Bex—59Zc 109
Crofton Av. Orp—75Sc 150
Crofton Av. W on T—76Y 141
Crofton Clo. Cher—80E 138
Crofton La. Orp—74Tc 150
Crofton Pk. Rd. SE4—58Bc 106
Crofton Rd. E13—42Kc 85
Crofton Rd. SE5—53Ub 105
Crofton Rd. Grays—7A 92
Crofton Rd. Orp—76Qc 150
Crofton Ter. E5—36Ac 64
Crofton Ter. Rich—56Pa 101
Crofton Way. Barn—16Db 23
Crofton Way. Enf—12Qb 24
Croft Rd. SW16—67Qb 126
Croft Rd. SW19—66Eb 125
Croft Rd. Brom—65Jc 129
Croft Rd. Cat—94Cc 182
Croft Rd. Enf—11Ac 26
Croft Rd. Ger X—26A 34
Croft Rd. Sutt—78Gb 145
Croft Rd. West—98Rc 184
Crofts Rd. Harr—30Ja 38
Crofts St. E1—45Wb 83
Crofts, The. Shep—70U 120
Croft St. SE8—49Ac 84
Croft, The. NW10—40Va 60

Croft, The. W5—43Na 79
Croft, The. Barn—14Ab 22
Croft, The. Houn—52Aa 99
Croft, The. Lou—12Qc 28
Croft, The. Pinn—31Ba 57
Croft, The. Ruis—35Y 57
Croft, The. Swan—69Ed 132
Croft, The. Wemb—36La 58
Croftway. NW3—35Cb 61
Croftway. Rich—62Ka 122
Croft Way. Sev—97Hd 186
Croft Way. Sidc—62Uc 130
Crogsland Rd. NW1—38Jb 62
Croham Clo. S Croy—79Ub 147
Croham Mnr. Rd. S Croy
—80Ub 147
Croham Mt. S Croy—80Ub 147
Croham Pk. Av. S Croy—78Vb 147
Croham Rd. S Croy—78Tb 147
Croham Valley Rd. S Croy
—79Wb 147
Croindene Rd. SW16—67Nb 126
Cromar Ct. Wok—4F 188
Cromartie Rd. N19—31Mb 62
Crombie Clo. Ilf—29Pc 46
Crombie Rd. Sidc—60Tc 108
Cromer Clo. Uxb—44S 76
Cromer Pl. Orp—74Tc 150
Cromer Rd. E10—31Fc 65
Cromer Rd. N17—26Wb 43
Cromer Rd. SE25—69Xb 127
Cromer Rd. SW17—65Jb 126
Cromer Rd. Barn—14Eb 23
Cromer Rd. Horn—31Md 69
Cromer Rd. Houn—54Q 98
Cromer Rd. Romf—30Ed 48
Cromer Rd. Romf—30Ad 47
(Chadwell Heath)
Cromer Rd. Wat—10Y 5
Cromer Rd. Wfd G—21Jc 45
Cromer Rd. W. Houn—55Q 98
Cromer St. WC1—41Nb 82 (4F 193)
Cromer Ter. E8—36Wb 63
Cromer Vs. Rd. SW18—58Bb 103
Cromford Clo. Orp—76Uc 150
Cromford Path. E5—35Zb 64
Cromford Rd. SW18—57Cb 103
Cromford Way. N Mald—67Ta 123
Cromlix Clo. Chst—68Rc 130
Crompton St. W2
—42Fb 81 (6B 190)
Cromwell Av. N6—32Kb 62
Cromwell Av. Brom—70Kc 129
Cromwell Av. N Mald—71Va 144
Cromwell Av. Wal X—2Xb 11
Cromwell Clo. N2—28Fb 41
Cromwell Clo. Brom—70Kc 129
Cromwell Clo. W on T—74X 141
Cromwell Cres. SW5—49Cb 81
Cromwell Dri. Slou—4J 73
Cromwell Gdns. SW7
—48Fb 81 (4C 202)
Cromwell Gro. W6—48Ya 80
Cromwell Gro. Cat—93Sb 181
Cromwell La. W6—50Xa 80
Cromwell M. SW7
—49Fb 81 (5C 202)
Cromwell Pl. N6—32Kb 62
Cromwell Pl. SW7
—49Fb 81 (5C 202)
Cromwell Pl. SW14—55Sa 101
Cromwell Rd. E7—38Lc 65
Cromwell Rd. E17—29Ec 44
Cromwell Rd. N3—25Eb 41
Cromwell Rd. N10—24Jb 42
(in two parts)
Cromwell Rd.—49Db 81 (5A 202)
SW7 1-147 & 2-156
SW5 remainder
Cromwell Rd. SW9—53Rb 105
Cromwell Rd. SW19—64Cb 125
Cromwell Rd. Beck—68Ac 128
Cromwell Rd. Borwd—11Na 21
Cromwell Rd. Brtwd—21Xd 50
Cromwell Rd. Cat—93Sb 181
Cromwell Rd. Croy—73Tb 147
Cromwell Rd. Felt—60X 99
Cromwell Rd. Grays—49Ce 91
Cromwell Rd. Hay—44T 76
Cromwell Rd. Houn—56Ca 99
Cromwell Rd. King—67Na 123
Cromwell Rd. Tedd—65Ja 122
Cromwell Rd. W on T—74X 141
Cromwell Rd. Wemb—40Na 59
Cromwell Rd. Wor Pk—76Ta 143
Cromwells Mere. Romf—23Fd 48
Cromwell St. Houn—56Ca 99
Cromwell Tower. EC2—(7E 194)
Crondace Rd. SW6—53Cb 103
Crondall St. N1—40Ub 63 (2H 195)
Crooked Billet. SW19—65Ya 124
Crooked Billet Yd. E2
—41Ub 83 (3J 195)
Crooked La. Grav—8D 114
Crooked Mile. Wal A—4Ec 12
Crooked Mile. Wal A—2Ec 12
Crooked Usage. N3—27Ab 40
Crooke Rd. SE8—50Ac 84
Crookham Rd. SW6—53Bb 103
Crook Log. Bexh—55Zc 109
Crookston Rd. SE9—55Qc 108
Croombs Rd. E16—43Lc 85
Croom's Hill. SE10—52Ec 106
Croom's Hill Gro. SE10—52Ec 106
Cropath Rd. Dag—35Cd 68
Cropley St. N1—40Tb 63 (1F 195)
Cropthorne Ct. W9—(4A 190)
Crosby Clo. Brtwd—11Fe 33
Crosby Clo. Felt—62Aa 121
Crosby Ct. SE1—(1F 207)
Crosby Ct. Chig—20Wc 29
Crosby Rd. E7—37Jc 65
Crosby Rd. Dag—40Dd 68
Crosby Row. SE1
—47Tb 83 (2F 207)
Crosby Sq. EC3—44Ub 83 (2H 201)
Crosby Wlk. E8—37Vb 63

Crosby Wlk. SW2—59Qb 104
Crosier Rd. Uxb—35S 56
Crosier Way. Ruis—34U 56
Crossacres. Wok—87G 156
Cross Av. SE10—51Gc 107
Crossbow Rd. Chig—22Vc 47
Crossbrook Rd. SE3—55Nc 108
Crossbrook St. Wal X—4Zb 12
Crossbrook St. Wal X—3Zb 12
Cross Deep. Twic—61Ha 122
Cross Deep Gdns. Twic—61Ha 122
Crossfield Pl. Wey—80R 140
Crossfield Rd. N17—27Sb 43
Crossfield Rd. NW3—37Fb 61
Crossfields. Lou—15Rc 28
Crossfield St. SE8—52Cc 106
Crossford St. SW9—54Pb 104
Cross Ga. Edgw—20Qa 21
Crossgate. Gnfd—37Ka 58
Crossharbour. E14—48Dc 84
Crossing Rd. Epp—4Wc 15
Cross Keys Clo. W1
—43Jb 82 (1J 197)
Cross Keys Cotts. Sev—99Jd 186
Cross Keys Ct. EC2
—44Tb 83 (2G 201)
Cross Lances Rd. Houn—56Da 99
Crossland Rd. T Hth—72Rb 147
Crosslands. Cher—77G 138
Crosslands Av. W5—46Pa 79
Crosslands Av. S'hall—50Ba 77
Crosslands Rd. Eps—79Ta 143
Cross La. EC3—45Ub 83 (5H 201)
Cross La. N8—27Pb 42
(in two parts)
Cross La. Bex—59Bd 109
Cross La. Cher—79E 138
Cross La. E. Grav—1D 136
Cross Lanes. Ger X—22A 34
Cross Lanes Clo. Ger X—22B 34
Cross La. W. Grav—1D 136
Crosslet St. SE17
—49Tb 83 (5G 207)
Crossley Clo. West—87Mc 167
Crossley St. N7—37Qb 62
Crossmead. SE9—60Pc 108
Crossmead. Wat—16X 19
Crossmead Av. Gnfd—41Ca 77
Crossness Footpath. Eri—47Bd 87
Crossness Rd. Bark—41Vc 87
Cross Oak. Wind—4E 94
Crossoaks La. Borwd & Pot B
—7Ta 7
Crosspath, The. Rad—7Ja 6
Cross Rd. E4—18Gc 27
Cross Rd. N8—27Nb 42
Cross Rd. N11—22Kb 42
Cross Rd. N22—24Qb 42
Cross Rd. SE5—54Ub 105
Cross Rd. SW19—66Cb 125
Cross Rd. Brom—75Nc 150
Cross Rd. Croy—74Tb 147
Cross Rd. Dart—58Ld 111
Cross Rd. Dart—63Pd 133
(Hawley)
Cross Rd. Enf—14Ub 25
Cross Rd. Felt—63Aa 121
Cross Rd. Grav—8B 114
Cross Rd. Harr—28Fa 38
(Headstone)
Cross Rd. Harr—34Da 57
(South Harrow)
Cross Rd. King—66Pa 123
Cross Rd. Orp—71Xc 151
Cross Rd. Purl—85Rb 165
Cross Rd. Romf—27Cd 48
Cross Rd. Romf—31Yc 67
(Chadwell Heath)
Cross Rd. Sidc—63Xc 131
Cross Rd. Stan—26Ja 38
Cross Rd. Sutt—78Fb 145
Cross Rd. Sutt—82Cb 163
(Belmont)
Cross Rd. Tad—94Ya 178
Cross Rd. Wal X—5Ac 12
Cross Rd. Wat—16Aa 19
Cross Rd. Wey—76T 140
Cross Rd. Wfd G—23Pc 46
Cross Roads. Lou—12Kc 27
Crossroads, The. Lea—100Z 175
Cross St. N1—39Rb 63
Cross St. N18—22Wb 43
Cross St. SW13—54Ua 102
Cross St. Eri—51Gd 110
Cross St. Hmptn—64Ea 122
Cross St. Uxb—38L 55
Cross St. Wat—13Y 19
Crossthwaite Av. SE5—56Tb 105
Crosswall. EC3—45Vb 83 (4K 201)
Crossway. N12—23Fb 41
Crossway. N16—36Ub 63
Crossway. NW9—28Va 40
Cross Way. SE28—45Yc 87
Crossway. SW20—70Ya 124
Crossway. W13—42Ja 78
Crossway. Dag—34Yc 67
Crossway. Enf—17Ub 25
Crossway. Hay—46W 76
Crossway. Orp—70Uc 130
Cross Way. Pinn—26Z 37
Crossway. Ruis—35Y 57
Crossway. W on T—75X 141
Cross Way. Wfd G—21Lc 45
Crossways. N21—16Sb 25
Crossways. Brtwd—16Ce 33
Crossways. Egh—65F 118
Crossways. Lea—99Z 175
Crossways. Romf—27Kd 49
Crossways. S Croy—80Ac 148
Crossways. Sun—66V 120
Crossways. Sutt—81Fb 163
Crossways. West—92Lc 183
Crossways La. Red—100Eb 179
Crossways Rd. Beck—70Cc 128
Crossways Rd. Mitc—69Kb 126
Crossways, The. Coul—91Qb 180
Crossways, The. Houn—52Ba 99

Crossways, The. Surb—74Ra 143
Crossways, The. Wemb—33Qa 59
Crossway, The. N22—24Rb 43
Crossway, The. SE9—61Mc 129
Cross Way, The. Harr—26Ga 38
Crossway, The. Uxb—40P 55
Crosswell Clo. Shep—68S 120
Crosthwaite Way. Slou—3B 72
Croston Rd. E8—39Wb 63
Crouch Av. Bark—40Xc 67
Crouch Clo. Beck—65Cc 128
Crouch Croft. SE9—62Qc 130
Crouch End Hill. N8—31Mb 62
Crouch Hall Rd. N8—30Mb 42
Crouch Hill—30Nb 42
N4 1-75 & 2-58
N8 remainder
★Crouch La. Sev—93Ce
Crouchman's Clo. SE26—62Vb 127
Crouch Oak La. Wey—77L 139
Crouch Rd. NW10—38Ta 59
Crouch Rd. Grays—10C 92
Crouch Valley. Upm—31Ud 70
Crowborough Clo. Warl
—90Ac 166
Crowborough Dri. Warl—90Ac 166
Crowborough Path. Wat—21Z 37
Crowborough Rd. SW17
—65Jb 126
Crowden Way. SE28—45Yc 87
Crowder St. E1—45Xb 83
Crow Dri. Sev—87Ed 170
Crow Grn. La. Brtwd—15Wd 32
Crow Grn. Rd. Brtwd—15Vd 32
★Crow Hill. Sev—92Ce
★Crow Hill Rd. Sev—92Ce
Crowhurst Clo. SW9—54Qb 104
★Crowhurst La. Sev—96Ae
★Crowhurst Rd. Sev—93Be
Crowhurst Way. Orp—71Yc 151
Crowland Av. Hay—49U 76
Crowland Gdns. N14—17Nb 24
Crowland Rd. N15—29Vb 43
Crowland Rd. T Hth—70Tb 127
Crowlands Av. Romf—30Dd 48
Crowland Ter. N1—38Tb 63
Crowland Wlk. Mord—72Eb 145
Crow La. Romf—31Bd 67
Crowley Cres. Croy—78Qb 146
Crowlin Wlk. N1—37Tb 63
Crown Arc. King—68Ma 123
Crown Ash Hill. West—86Kc 167
Crown Ash La. Warl & West
—88Jc 167
Crown Clo. E3—39Cc 64
Crown Clo. NW6—37Db 61
Crown Clo. NW7—19Va 22
Crown Clo. Hay—47V 76
Crown Clo. Orp—78Wc 151
Crown Clo. W on T—73Y 141
Crown Ct. EC2—(3E 200)
Crown Ct. SE12—58Kc 107
Crown Ct. WC2—44Nb 82 (3G 199)
Crown Dale. SE19—65Rb 127
Crowndale Rd. NW1
—40Lb 62 (1C 192)
Crownfield Av. Ilf—30Uc 46
Crownfield Rd. E15—35Fc 65
Crownfields. Sev—97Kd 187
Crown Grn. Grav—4N 137
Crown Hill. Croy—75Sb 147
Crown Hill. Wal A & Epp—5Nc 14
Crown Hill Rd. NW10—39Va 60
Crownhill Rd. Wfd G—24Nc 46
Crownhurst La. Sev—80Wd 154
★Crownhurst La. Sev—81Wd
Crown La. N14—18Lb 24
Crown La. SW16—64Qb 126
Crown La. Brom—71Mc 149
Crown La. Chst—67Sc 130
Crown La. Grav—3N 137
Crown La. Mord—70Cb 125
Crown La. Slou—10E 52
Crown La. Vir W—72A 138
Crown La. Gdns. SW16—64Qb 126
Crown La. Spur. Brom—72Mc 149
Crown Meadow. Slou—52E 96
Crownmead Way. Romf—28Dd 48
Crown Office Row. EC4
—45Qb 82 (4K 199)
Crown Pas. SW1—46Lb 82 (7C 198)
Crown Pas. Wat—14Y 19
Crown Pl. NW5—37Kb 62
Crown Rise. Wat—6Y 5
Crown Rd. N10—24Jb 42
Crown Rd. Borwd—11Qa 21
★Crown Rd. Brtwd—9Sd
(Beacon Hill)
Crown Rd. Brtwd—11Td 32
(Navestock Side)
Crown Rd. Enf—14Xb 25
Crown Rd. Grays—51Ce 113
Crown Rd. Ilf—28Tc 46
Crown Rd. Mord—70Db 125
Crown Rd. N Mald—67Sa 123
Crown Rd. Orp—78Wc 151
Crown Rd. Sev—82Hd 170
Crown Rd. Sutt—77Db 145
Crown Rd. Twic—58Ka 100
Crownstone Rd. SW2—57Qb 104
Crown St. SE5—52Sb 105
Crown St. W3—46Ra 79
Crown St. Brtwd—19Yd 32
Crown St. Dag—37Ed 68
(in two parts)
Crown St. Egh—63C 118
Crown St. Harr—32Fa 58
Crown Ter. Rich—56Pa 101
Crowntree Clo. Iswth—51Ha 100
Crown Wlk. Uxb—38L 55
Crown Wlk. Wemb—34Pa 59
Crown Way. W Dray—46P 75
Crown Woods La. SE18—54Rc 108
Crown Woods Way. SE9
—57Tc 108
Crow Piece La. Slou—8D 52
Crowshott Av. Stan—26La 38

Devonshire Rd. SE9—61Nc 130
Devonshire Rd. SE23—60Yb 106
Devonshire Rd. SW19—66Gb 125
Devonshire Rd. W4—50Ua 80
Devonshire Rd. W5—48La 78
Devonshire Rd. Bexh—56Ad 109
Devonshire Rd. Croy—73Tb 147
Devonshire Rd. Felt—62Aa 121
Devonshire Rd. Grav—1D 136
Devonshire Rd. Harr—30Fa 38
Devonshire Rd. Horn—33Ld 69
Devonshire Rd. Ilf—31Uc 66
Devonshire Rd. Orp—73Wc 151
Devonshire Rd. Pinn—31Y 57
  (Eastcote)
Devonshire Rd. Pinn—25Ba 37
  (Hatch End)
Devonshire Rd. S'hall—43Ca 77
Devonshire Rd. Sutt—80Eb 145
Devonshire Rd. Wall—77Jb 146
Devonshire Rd. Wey—77Q 140
Devonshire Row. EC2
    —43Ub 83 (1J 201)
Devonshire Row M. W1—(6A 192)
Devonshire Sq. EC2
    —44Ub 83 (2J 201)
Devonshire Sq. Brom—70Kc 129
Devonshire St. W1
    —43Jb 82 (7J 191)
Devonshire St. W4—50Ua 80
Devonshire Ter. W2
    —44Eb 81 (3A 196)
Devonshire Way. Croy—75Ab 148
Devonshire Way. Hay—44X 77
Devons Rd. E3—43Cc 84
Devon St. SE15—51Xb 105
Devon Way. Chess—78La 142
Devon Way. Eps—78Ra 143
Devon Way. Uxb—40P 55
Devon Waye. Houn—52Ba 99
De Walden St. W1
    —43Jb 82 (1J 197)
Dewar St. SE15—55Wb 105
Dewey Path. Horn—37Ld 69
Dewey Rd. N1—40Qb 62 (1K 193)
  (in two parts)
Dewey Rd. Dag—37Dd 68
Dewey St. SW17—64Hb 125
Dewgrass Gro. Wal X—7Yb 12
Dewhurst Rd. W14—48Za 80
Dewhurst Rd. Wal X—1Yb 12
Dewlands Av. Dart—59Rd 111
Dewsberry St. E14—43Ec 84
Dewsbury Clo. Pinn—30Aa 37
Dewsbury Clo. Romf—23Md 49
Dewsbury Ct. SW4—49Sa 79
Dewsbury Gdns. Romf—23Md 49
Dewsbury Gdns. Wor Pk
    —76Wa 144
Dewsbury Rd. NW10—36Wa 60
Dewsbury Rd. Romf—23Nd 49
Dewsbury Ter. NW1—39Kb 62
Dexter Clo. Grays—48Ce 91
Dexter Rd. Barn—16Za 22
Deyncourt Gdns. E11—28Lc 45
Deyncourt Gdns. Upm—33Sd 70
Deyncourt Rd. N17—25Sb 43
D'Eynsford Rd. SE5—53Tb 105
Diadem Ct. W1—(3D 198)
Diamedes Av. Stai—59M 97
Diameter Rd. Orp—72Sc 150
Diamond Rd. Ruis—35Z 57
Diamond Rd. Slou—7L 73
Diamond Rd. Wel—10W 4
Diamond St. SE15—52Ub 105
Diamond Ter. SE10—53Ec 106
Diana Clo. E18—25Kc 45
Diana Clo. Slou—44A 74
Diana Ct. Eri—51Gd 110
Diana Gdns. Surb—75Pa 143
Diana Ho. SW13—53Va 102
Diana Pl. NW1—42Kb 82 (5A 192)
Diana Rd. E17—27Bc 44
Diana Way. Ilf—34Rc 66
Dianthus Clo. SE2—50Xc 87
Dianthus Clo. Cher—73G 138
Dianthus Ct. Wok—7G 188
Diban Av. Horn—35Kd 69
Dibden La. Sev—98Gd 186
Dibden St. N1—39Sb 63
Dibdin Clo. Sutt—76Cb 145
Dibdin Rd. Sutt—76Cb 145
Dibdin Row. SE1
    —48Qb 82 (3A 206)
Diceland Rd. Bans—88Bb 163
Dicey Av. NW2—35Ya 60
Dickens Av. N3—25Eb 41
Dickens Av. Uxb—44R 76
Dickens Clo. Harr—33Da 57
Dickens Clo. Hay—49U 76
Dickens Clo. Long, Dart—71Be 155
Dickens Clo. Rich—61Na 123
Dickens Dri. Chst—65Sc 130
Dickens Dri. Wey—79H 139
Dickens La. N18—22Ub 43
Dickenson Rd. N8—31Nb 62
Dickensons La. SE25—72Wb 147
Dickensons Pl. SE25—72Wb 147
Dickenson St. NW5—37Kb 62
Dickens Rise. Chig—20Rc 28
Dickens Rd. E6—40Mc 65
Dickens Rd. Grav—10G 114
Dickens Sq. SE1—48Sb 83 (3E 206)
Dickens St. SW8—54Kb 104
Dickerage La. N Mald—69Sa 123
Dickerage Rd. King—69Sa 123
Dickinson Sq. Rick—16Q 18
Dickinson Rd. Rick—16Q 18
Dickson Fold. Pinn—28Z 37
Dickson Rd. SE9—55Nc 108
Dick Turpin Way. Felt—56V 98
Didsbury Clo. E6—39Pc 66
Digby Cres. N4—33Sb 63
Digby Gdns. Dag—39Cd 68
Digby Pl. Croy—76Vb 147

Digby Rd. E9—37Zb 64
Digby Rd. Bark—38Vc 67
Digby St. E2—41Yb 84
Digby Wlk. Horn—37Ld 69
Digby Wlk. Wey—84P 157
Digdens Rise. Eps—87Sa 161
Dighton Rd. SW18—57Eb 103
Dignum St. N1—40Qb 62 (1K 193)
Digswell St. N7—37Qb 62
Dilhorne Clo. SE12—62Kc 129
Dilke St. SW3—51Hb 103
Dillon Pl. N7—34Pb 62
Dillwyn Clo. SE26—63Ac 128
Dilston Clo. N'holt—41Y 77
Dilston Gdns. SW15—60Xa 102
Dilton Gdns. SW15—60Xa 102
Dimes Pl. W6—49Xa 80
Dimmock Dri. Gnfd—36Fa 58
Dimmocks La. Rick—8K 3
Dimond Clo. E7—35Jc 65
Dimsdale Dri. NW9—32Sa 59
Dimsdale Dri. Enf—16Wb 25
Dimsdale Dri. Slou—6D 52
Dimsdale Wlk. E13—40Jc 65
Dingle Gdns. E14—45Cc 84
Dingle Rd. Ashf—64R 120
Dingle, The. Uxb—41R 76
Dingley La. SW16—61Mb 126
Dingley Pl. EC1—41Sb 83 (4E 194)
Dingley Rd. EC1—41Sb 83 (4D 194)
Dingwall Av. Croy—75Sb 147
Dingwall Gdns. NW11—30Cb 41
Dingwall Rd. SW18—59Eb 103
Dingwall Rd. Cars—81Hb 163
Dingwall Rd. Croy—75Tb 147
Dinmont Est. E2—40Wb 63
Dinmont St. E2—40Wb 63
Dinsdale Clo. Wok—90C 156
Dinsdale Gdns. SE25—71Ub 147
Dinsdale Gdns. Barn—15Db 23
Dinsdale Rd. SE3—51Hc 107
Dinsmore Rd. SW12—59Kb 104
Dinton Rd. King—66Pa 123
Diploma Av. N2—28Gb 41
Dippers Gdns. SE9—89Pd 171
Dirdene Clo. Eps—84Va 162
Dirdene Gdns. Eps—84Va 162
Dirdene Gro. Eps—84Ua 162
Dirleton Rd. E15—39Hc 65
Dirtham La. Lea—100X 175
  (in two parts)
Disbrowe Rd. W6—51Ab 102
Dishforth La. NW9—25Ua 40
Disney Pl. SE1—47Sb 83 (1E 206)
Disney St. SE1—47Sb 83 (1E 206)
Dison Clo. Enf—11Zb 26
Disraeli Clo. SE28—46Yc 87
Disraeli Clo. W4—49Ta 79
Disraeli Rd. E7—37Jc 65
Disraeli Rd. NW10—40Ta 59
Disraeli Rd. SW15—56Ab 102
Disraeli Rd. W5—46Ma 79
Diss St. E2—41Vb 83 (3K 195)
Distaff La. EC4—45Sb 83 (4D 200)
Distillery La. W6—50Ya 80
Distillery Rd. W6—50Ya 80
Distillery Wlk. Bren—51Na 101
District Rd. Wemb—36Ka 58
Ditch All. SE10—53Dc 106
Ditchburn St. E14—45Ec 84
Ditches La. Coul & Cat—93Nb 180
Ditches Ride, The. Lou & Epp
    —9Qc 14
Dittisham Rd. SE9—63Nc 130
Ditton Clo. Th Dit—73Ja 142
Ditton Grange Clo. Surb
    —74Ma 143
Ditton Grange Dri. Surb
    —74Ma 143
Ditton Hill. Surb—74La 142
Ditton Hill Rd. Surb—74La 142
Ditton Lawn. Th Dit—74Aa 142
Ditton Pk. Rd. Slou—51A 96
Ditton Pl. SE20—67Xb 127
Ditton Reach. Th Dit—72Ka 142
Ditton Rd. Bexh—57Ad 109
Ditton Rd. Slou—50B 74
Ditton Rd. Slou—3P 95
  (Datchet)
Ditton Rd. S'hall—50Ba 77
Ditton Rd. Surb—76Ma 143
Divis Way. SW15—58Xa 102
Dixon Clo. E6—44Pc 86
Dixon Pl. W Wick—74Dc 148
Dixon Rd. SE14—53Ac 106
Dixon Rd. SE25—69Ub 127
Dixon's All. SE16—47Xb 83
Dobbin Clo. Harr—26Ja 38
Dobell Rd. SE9—57Pc 108
Dobree Av. NW10—38Xa 60
Dobson Clo. NW6—38Fb 61
Dobson Rd. Grav—4G 136
Dockett Eddy La. Shep—74P 139
Dockhead. SE1—47Vb 83 (2K 207)
Dockland St. E16—46Qc 86
Dockley Rd. SE16—48Wb 83
Dock Rd. E16—45Hc 85
Dock Rd. Bren—52Ma 101
Dock Rd. Grays—51Fe 113
Dock Rd. Grays & Til—1A 114
Dock St. E1—45Wb 83
Dockwell Clo. Felt—56W 98
Doctor Johnson Av. SW17
    —62Kb 126
Doctors Clo. SE26—64Yb 128
Doctors La. Cat—95Qb 180
Docwra's Bldgs. N1—37Ub 63
Dodbrooke Rd. SE27—62Qb 126
Doddinghurst Rd. Brtwd—16Yd 32
★Doddinghurst Rd. Brtwd—9Yd
Doddington Gro. SE17—51Rb 105
Doddington Pl. SE17—51Rb 105
Dodd's Cres. Wey—86K 157
Dodd's La. Wok—86K 157
Dodsley Pl. N9—20Yb 26

Dodson St. SE1—47Qb 82 (2A 206)
Dod St. E14—44Cc 84
Doel Clo. SW19—66Eb 125
Doggett Rd. SE6—59Cc 106
Doggetts Courts. Barn—15Gb 23
Doggetts Farm Rd. Uxb—31E 54
Doghurst Av. Hay—52R 98
Doghurst Dri. W Dray—52R 98
Doghurst La. Coul—92Hb 179
Dog Kennel Hill. SE5—55Ub 105
Dog Kennel La. Rick—14H 17
Dog La. NW10—35Ua 60
Doherty Rd. E13—42Jc 85
Dolben St. SE1—46Rb 83 (7C 200)
  (in two parts)
Dolby Rd. SW6—54Bb 103
Dole St. NW7—24Ya 40
Dolland St. SE11—50Pb 82 (7J 205)
Dollis Av. N3—25Bb 41
Dollis Brook Wlk. Barn—16Ab 22
Dollis Cres. Ruis—32Y 57
Dollis Hill Av. NW2—34Xa 60
Dollis Hill La. NW2—35Va 60
Dollis Pk. N3—25Bb 41
Dollis Rd. N3—25Bb 41
  N3 1-89 & 2-66
  NW7 remainder
Dollis Valley Way. Barn—16Bb 23
Dolman Rd. W4—49Ta 79
Dolman St. SW4—56Pb 104
Dolphin App. Romf—28Hd 48
Dolphin Clo. Surb—71Ma 143
Dolphin Ct. Slou—7M 73
Dolphin Ct. Stai—62J 119
Dolphin La. E14—45Dc 84
Dolphin Rd. Slou—7M 73
Dolphin Rd. N'holt—40Ba 57
Dolphin Rd. Sun—67U 120
Dolphin Rd. N. Sun—67U 120
Dolphin Rd. S. Sun—67U 120
Dolphin Rd. W. Sun—67U 120
Dolphin Sq. SW1—50Lb 82
Dombey St. WC1
    —43Pb 82 (7H 193)
Dome Hill. Cat—99Ub 181
Dome Hill Pk. SE26—63Vb 127
Dome Hill Peak. Cat—98Ub 181
Domett Clo. SE5—56Tb 105
Domingo St. EC1
    —42Sb 83 (6D 194)
Dominion Dri. Romf—23Dd 48
Dominion Rd. Croy—73Vb 147
Dominion Rd. S'hall—48Aa 77
Dominion St. EC2
    —43Tb 83 (7G 195)
Dominion Way. Rain—41Jd 88
Domitian Pl. Enf—15Vb 25
Domonic Dri. SE9—63Rc 130
Domville Rd. N20—19Fb 23
Domville Gro. SE5
    —50Vb 83 (7K 207)
Donald Dri. Romf—29Yc 47
Donald Rd. E13—39Kc 65
Donald Rd. Croy—73Pb 146
Donaldson Rd. NW6—39Bb 61
Donaldson Rd. SE18—53Qc 108
Doncaster Dri. N'holt—36Ba 57
Doncaster Gdns. N4—30Sb 43
Doncaster Gdns. N'holt—36Ba 57
Doncaster Grn. Wat—22Y 37
Doncaster Rd. N9—17Xb 25
Doncaster Way. Upm—34Pd 69
Doneraile St. SW6—54Za 102
Dongola Rd. E13—41Kc 85
Dongola Rd. N17—27Ub 43
Dongola Rd. W. E13—41Kc 85
Donington Av. Ilf—29Sc 46
Donkey La. Enf—12Wb 25
Donkey La. F'ham, Dart—75Rd 153
Donkey La. W Dray—49L 75
Donne Ct. SE24—58Sb 105
Donnefield Av. Edgw—24Na 39
Donne Gdns. Wok—87G 156
Donnelly Rd. SW16—61Mb 126
Donne Pl. SW3—49Gb 81 (5E 202)
Donne Pl. Mitc—70Kb 126
Donne Rd. Dag—33Yc 67
Donnington Rd. NW10—38Xa 60
Donnington Rd. Harr—29La 38
Donnington Rd. Sev—92Fd 186
Donnington Rd. Wor Pk
    —75Wa 144
Donnybrook Rd. SW16—66Lb 126
Donovan Av. N10—26Lb 42
Donovan Clo. Eps—82Ta 161
Donovan's Garden. Brtwd
    —24Fe 51
Don Phelan Clo. SE5—53Tb 105
Dorado Gdns. Orp—76Zc 151
Doon St. SE1—46Qb 82 (7K 199)
Doral Way. Cars—78Hb 145
Doran Gro. SE18—52Uc 108
Doran Wlk. E15—38Ec 64
Dora Rd. SW19—64Cb 125
Dora St. E14—44Bc 84
Dorchester Av. N13—21Sb 43
Dorchester Av. Bex—60Zc 109
Dorchester Av. Harr—30Ea 38
Dorchester Clo. Dart—60Pd 111
Dorchester Clo. Felt—58U 98
Dorchester Clo. Orp—66Xc 131
Dorchester Ct. N14—17Kb 24
Dorchester Dri. SE24—57Sb 105
Dorchester Gdns. E4—21Cc 44
Dorchester Gdns. NW11—28Cb 41
Dorchester Gro. W4—50Ua 80
Dorchester M. N Mald—70Ta 123
Dorchester Rd. Mord—73Db 145
Dorchester Rd. N'holt—36Ca 57
Dorchester Rd. Wey—76R 140

Dorchester Way. Harr—30Pa 39
Dorchester Waye. Hay—44X 77
Dorcis Av. Bexh—54Ad 109
Dordrecht Rd. W3—47Ua 80
Dore Av. E12—36Qc 66
Doreen Av. NW9—32Ta 59
Dore Gdns. Mord—73Db 145
Dorell Clo. S'hall—43Ba 77
Doria Dri. Grav—2H 137
Dorian Rd. Horn—32Jd 68
Doria Rd. SW6—54Bb 103
Doric Dri. Tad—92Bb 179
Doric Way. NW1
    —41Mb 82 (3D 192)
Dorien Rd. SW20—68Za 124
Dorincourt. Wok—87G 156
Dorinda St. N7—37Qb 62
Doris Av. Eri—53Ed 110
Doris Emmerton Ct. SW11
    —56Eb 103
Doris Rd. E7—38Jc 65
Doris Rd. Ashf—65T 120
Dorking Clo. SE8—51Bc 106
Dorking Clo. Wor Pk—75Za 144
Dorking Rise. Romf—21Md 49
Dorking Rd. Eps—87Ra 161
Dorking Rd. Lea—95Ka 176
Dorking Rd. Lea—98Da 175
  (Great Bookham)
Dorking Rd. Romf—22Md 49
Dorking Rd. Tad—96Ya 178
Dorking Rd. Tad—100Ua 178
Dorking Wlk. Romf—21Md 49
Dorkins Way. Upm—31Ud 70
Dorlcote Rd. SW18—59Gb 103
Dorling Dri. Eps—84Va 162
Dorly Clo. Shep—71U 140
Dorman Pl. N9—19Wb 25
Dormans Clo. N'wd—24T 36
Dorman Wlk. NW10—36Ta 59
Dorman Way. NW8—39Fb 61
Dormay St. SW18—57Db 103
Dormer Clo. E15—37Hc 65
Dormer Clo. Barn—15Za 22
Dormer's Av. S'hall—44Ca 77
Dormers Rise. S'hall—44Da 77
Dormer's Wells La. S'hall
    —44Ca 77
Dormywood. Ruis—29V 36
Dornberg Clo. SE3—52Jc 107
Dorncliffe Rd. SW6—54Ab 102
Dornels. Slou—4N 73
Dorney Gro. Wey—75R 140
Dorney Hill S. High W & Slou
    —1E 52
Dorney Rise. Orp—70Vc 131
Dorney Wood Rd. Slou—9A 52
Dornfell St. NW6—36Bb 61
Dornford Gdns. Coul—91Sb 181
Dornton Rd. SW12—61Kb 126
Dornton Rd. S Croy—78Tb 147
Dorothy Av. Wemb—38Na 59
Dorothy Evans Clo. Bexh
    —56Dd 110
Dorothy Gdns. Dag—35Xc 67
Dorothy Rd. SW11—55Hb 103
Dorrell Pl. SW9—56Qb 104
Dorrien Wlk. SW16—61Mb 126
Dorrington Ct. SE25—68Ub 127
Dorrington Gdns. Horn—32Md 69
Dorrington St. EC1
    —43Qb 82 (7K 193)
Dorrit St. SE1—(1E 206)
Dorrit Way. Chst—65Sc 130
Dorrofield Clo. Rick—15S 18
Dorryn Ct. SE26—64Zb 128
Dors Clo. NW9—32Ta 59
Dover Clo. NW2—33Za 60
Dover Rd. Slou—4D 72
Dover Rd. E. Grav—9A 114
Doversmead. Wok—4B 188
Dover St. W1—45Kb 82 (5A 198)
Dover Way. Rick—14S 18
Dover Yd. W1—(6B 198)
Doves Clo. Brom—75Nc 150
Doveton Rd. S Croy—78Tb 147
Doveton St. E1—42Yb 84
Dove Wlk. Rain—37Kd 69
Dowanhill Rd. SE6—60Fc 107
Dowdeswell Clo. SW15—56Ua 102
Dowding Pl. Stan—23Ja 38
Dowding Rd. West—87Mc 167
Dowding Wlk. Grav—2A 136
Dower Pk. Wind—6C 94
Dowgate Hill. EC4
    —45Tb 83 (4F 201)
Dowin St. E Mol—71Ca 141
Dowland Clo. Stanf—1L 93
Dowland St. W10—41Ab 80
Dowlans Clo. Lea—99Ca 175
Dowlans Rd. Lea—99Da 175
Dowlas St. SE5—52Ub 105
Dowlerville Rd. Orp—79Vc 151
Dowman Clo. SW19—66Db 125
Downage. NW4—27Ya 40
Downage, The. Grav—1C 136
Downalong. Bush, Wat—18Fa 20
Downbank Av. Bexh—53Fd 110
Down Barns Rd. Ruis—34Z 57
Down Clo. N'holt—40X 57
Downderry Rd. Brom—62Fc 129
Downe Av. Sev—83Tc 168
Downe Clo. Well—52Yc 109
Downe End. SE18—52Rc 108
Downe Rd. Kes—81Nc 168
Downe Rd. Mitc—68Hb 125
Downe Rd. Sev—86Sc 168
Downer Rd. Rick—8J 3
Downers Cotts. SW4—56Lb 104
Downes Clo. Twic—58Ka 100
Downes Ct. N21—18Qb 24
Downes Pl. SE15—51Wb 105
Downe Ter. Rich—58Na 101
Downfield. Wor Pk—74Va 144
Downfield Clo. W9—42Db 81

Downfield Rd. Wal X—3Ac 12
Down Hall Rd. King—67Ma 123
Downham Clo. Romf—24Cd 48
Downham Rd. N1—38Tb 63
Downham Way. Brom—64Fc 129
Downhills Av. N17—27Tb 43
Downhills Pk. Rd. N17—27Sb 43
Downhills Way. N17—27Sb 43
Downhurst Av. NW7—22Ta 39
Downing Clo. Harr—27Ea 38
Downing Dri. Gnfd—39Ga 58
Downing Path. Slou—2C 72
Downing Rd. Dag—38Bd 67
Downing St. SW1
    —47Nb 82 (1F 205)
Downings Wood. Rick—22F 34
Downland Clo. N20—18Eb 23
Downland Clo. Coul—86Kb 164
Downland Gdns. Eps—90Xa 162
Downlands. Wal A—6Hc 13
Downlands Rd. Purl—85Nb 164
Downland Way. Eps—90Xa 162
Downley Clo. SE9—61Pc 130
Downman Rd. SE9—55Nc 108
Down Pl. W6—49Xa 80
Down Rd. Tedd—65Ka 122
Downs Av. Chst—64Pc 130
Downs Av. Dart—59Qd 111
Downs Av. Eps—86Ua 162
Downs Av. Pinn—30Ba 37
Downsbridge Rd. Beck—67Fc 129
Downs Ct. Rd. Purl—84Rb 165
Downsell Rd. E15—35Fc 65
Downsfield Rd. E17—30Ac 44
Downshall Av. Ilf—30Uc 46
Downs Hill. Beck—66Fc 129
Downs Hill. Grav—66Ee 135
Downs Hill Rd. Eps—86Ua 162
Downshire Hill. NW3—35Fb 61
Downs Ho. Rd. Eps—90Ua 162
Downside. Eps—86Ua 162
Downside. Twic—62Ha 122
Downside Bri. Rd. Cob—87X 159
Downside Clo. SW19—65Eb 125
Downside Comn. Rd. Cob
    —90X 159
Downside Cres. NW3—36Gb 61
Downside Cres. W13—42Ja 78
Downside Rd. Cob—88X 159
Downside Rd. Sutt—79Fb 145
Downside Wlk. N'holt—41Ba 77
Downsland Dri. Brtwd—20Yd 32
Downs La. E5—35Xb 63
Downs La. Lea—95Ka 176
Downs Pk. Rd.—36Vb 63
  E8 1-73 & 2-90
  E5 remainder
Downs Rd. E5—35Wb 63
Downs Rd. Beck—68Dc 128
Downs Rd. Coul—90Mb 164
Downs Rd. Dor—100La 176
Downs Rd. Enf—14Ub 25
Downs Rd. Eps—87Ua 162
Downs Rd. Grav—63Fe 135
Downs Rd. Grav—6A 136
Downs Rd. Purl—83Rb 165
Downs Rd. Slou—47A 74
Downs Rd. Slou—7P 73
Downs Rd. Sutt—82Db 163
Downs Rd. T Hth—67Sb 127
Downs Side. Sutt—83Bb 163
Downs, The. SW20—66Za 124
Downs, The. Lea—91La 176
Down St. W1—46Kb 82 (7K 197)
Down St. M. W1—46Kb 82 (7K 197)
Downs Valley. Long, Dart
    —70Ae 135
Downs View. Iswth—53Ha 100
Downs View. Tad—93Xa 178
Downsview Av. Wok—93B 172
Downs View Clo. Orp—82Yc 169
Downsview Clo. Swan—69Hd 132
Downsview Gdns. SE19—66Rb 127
Downsview Rd. SE19—66Sb 127
Downs View Rd. Lea—99Ea 176
Downsview Rd. Sev—97Hd 186
Downs Way. Eps—88Va 162
Downs Way. Lea—98Ea 176
Downsway. Orp—78Uc 150
Downs Way. Oxt—99Gc 183
Downsway. S Croy—83Ub 165
Downs Way. Tad—93Xa 178
Downsway. Whyt—88Vb 165
Downs Way. Clo. Tad—93Wa 178
Downsway, The. Sutt—81Eb 163
Downs Wood. Eps—89Xa 162
Downton Av. SW2—61Nb 126
Downtown Rd. SE16—47Ac 84
Downview Clo. Cob—91X 175
Down Way. N'holt—40X 57
Dowrey St. N1—39Qb 62
Dowsett Rd. N17—26Vb 43
Dowson Clo. SE5—56Tb 105
Doyce St. SE1—47Sb 83 (1D 206)
Doyle Gdns. NW10—39Wa 60
Doyle Rd. SE25—70Wb 127
Doyle Way. Til—4E 114
D'Oyley St. SW1—49Jb 82 (5H 203)
Doynton St. N19—33Kb 62
Draco St. SE17—51Sb 105
Dragmire La. Mitc—69Fb 125
Dragon La. Wey—83Q 158
Dragon Rd. SE15—51Ub 105
Dragon Yd. WC1—(2G 199)
Dragoon Rd. SE8—50Bc 84
Dragor Rd. NW10—42Sa 79
Drake Av. Slou—9P 73
Drake Clo. Brtwd—22Ae 51
Drakefell Rd.—54Zb 106
  SE14 1-87 & 2-134
  SE4 remainder
Drakefield Rd. SW17—62Jb 126
Drakeley Ct. N5—35Rb 63
Drake Rd. SE4—55Cc 106
Drake Rd. Chess—78Qa 143
Drake Rd. Croy—73Pb 146
Drake Rd. Harr—33Ba 57

Drake Rd.—East Av.

Drake Rd. Mitc—72Jb 146
Drakes Av. Stai—64H 119
Drake's Clo. Esh—77Ca 141
Drakes Dri. N'wd—25R 36
Drake St. WC1—43Pb 82 (1H 199)
Drake St. Enf—11Tb 25
Drakes Wlk. E6—40Pc 66
Drakes Way. Wok—10G 188
Drakewood Rd. SW16—66Mb 126
Draper Clo. Belv—49Bd 87
Draper Ct. Brom—70Nc 130
Draper's Gdns. EC2 —44Tb 83 (2G 201)
Drapers Rd. E15—35Fc 65
Drapers Rd. N17—27Vb 43
Drapers Rd. Enf—12Rb 25
Drappers Way. SE16—49Wb 83
Drawdock Rd. SE10—47Fc 85
Drawell Clo. SE18—50Uc 86
Drax Av. SW20—66Wa 124
Draxmont App. SW19—65Ab 124
Draycot Rd. E11—30Kc 45
Draycot Rd. Surb—74Qa 143
Draycott Av. SW3 —49Gb 81 (5E 202)
Draycott Av. Harr—30Ka 38
Draycott Clo. Harr—30Ka 38
Draycott Pl. SW3 —49Hb 81 (6F 203)
Draycott Ter. SW3 —49Hb 81 (6G 203)
Drayford Clo. W9—42Bb 81
Dray Gdns. SW2—57Pb 104
Drayson M. W8—47Cb 81
Drayton Av. W13—45Ja 78
Drayton Av. Lou—17Pc 28
Drayton Av. Orp—74Rc 150
Drayton Av. Pot B—4Ab 8
Drayton Bri. Rd. W7 & W13 —45Ha 78
Drayton Clo. Lea—96Ga 176
Drayton Gdns. N21—17Rb 25
Drayton Gdns. SW10 —50Eb 81 (7A 202)
Drayton Gdns. W13—45Ja 78
Drayton Gdns. W Dray—47N 75
Drayton Grn. W13—45Ja 78
Drayton Grn. Rd. W13—45Ka 78
Drayton Gro. W13—45Ja 78
Drayton Pk. N5—35Qb 62
Drayton Rd. E11—32Fc 65
Drayton Rd. N17—26Ub 43
Drayton Rd. NW10—39Va 60
Drayton Rd. W13—45Ka 78
Drayton Rd. Borwd—14Qa 21
Drayton Rd. Croy—75Rb 147
Drayton Waye. Harr—30Ka 38
Dreadnought St. SE10—48Gc 85
Drenon Sq. Hay—45V 76
Dresden Clo. NW6—37Db 61
Dresden M. NW6—37Db 61
Dresden Rd. N19—32Mb 62
Dresden Way. Wey—78S 140
Dressington Av. SE4—58Cc 106
Drew Av. NW7—23Za 40
Drew Gdns. Gnfd—37Ha 58
Drewitts Ct. W on T—74V 140
Drew Meadow. Slou—5G 52
Drew Rd. E16—46Nc 86
Drewstead Rd. SW16—61Mb 126
Drey, The. Ger X—22A 34
Driffield Rd. E3—40Ac 64
Drift La. Cob—88Ba 159
Drift Rd. Lea—96U 174
Drift, The. Kes—76Mc 149
Drift Way. Slou—53E 96
Driftway, The. Bans—87Ya 162
Driftway, The. Mitc—67Jb 126
Driftway, The (Worple Rd.) Lea —95La 176
Driftwood Dri. Kenl—89Sb 165
Drill Hall Rd. Cher—73J 139
Drinkwater Rd. Harr—33Da 57
Drive Mead. Coul—86Nb 164
Drive Rd. Coul—92Mb 180
Drive Spur. Tad—93Db 179
Drive, The. E4—17Fc 27
Drive, The. E17—27Dc 44
Drive, The. E18—27Jc 45
Drive, The. N3—24Cb 41
Drive, The. N7—37Pb 62
Drive, The. N11—23Mb 42
Drive, The. NW11—31Ab 60
Drive, The. SW16—69Pb 126
Drive, The. SW20—66Ya 124
Drive, The. W3—44Sa 79
Drive, The. Ashf—66T 120
Drive, The. Bans—88Bb 163
Drive, The. Bark—38Vc 67
Drive, The. Barn—13Ab 22 (High Barnet)
Drive, The. Barn—16Eb 23 (New Barnet)
Drive, The. Beck—68Cc 128
Drive, The. Bex—59Zc 109
Drive, The. Brtwd—22Yd 50
Drive, The. Buck H—17Lc 27
Drive, The. Chst—69Vc 131
Drive, The. Cob—86Ba 159
Drive, The. Coul—86Nb 164
Drive, The. Edgw—22Qa 39
Drive, The. Enf—11Tb 25
Drive, The. Eps—79Va 144
Drive, The. Eri—51Dd 110
Drive, The. Esh—74Ea 142
Drive, The. Felt—59Y 99
Drive, The. Ger X—24A 34
Drive, The. Grav—3G 136
Drive, The. Harr—31Ca 57
Drive, The. Houn & Iswth —54Fa 100
Drive, The. Ilf—31Pc 66
Drive, The. King—66Sa 123
Drive, The. Lea—94Ga 176
Drive, The. Lea & Eps—95Pa 177
Drive, The. Long, Dart—69De 135
Drive, The. Lou—14Nc 28
Drive, The. Mord—71Fb 145
Drive, The. N'wd—25U 36
Drive, The. Orp—75Vc 151
Drive, The. Pot B—4Bb 9
Drive, The. Purf—51Sd 112
Drive, The. Rad—6Ka 6
Drive, The. Rick—15K 17
Drive, The. Romf—24Fd 48 (Collier Row)
Drive, The. Romf—25Pd 49 (Harold Wood)
Drive, The. Sev—96Kd 187
Drive, The. Sidc—63Xc 131
Drive, The. Slou—47A 74
Drive, The. Slou—3M 95 (Datchet)
Drive, The. Surb—73Na 143
Drive, The. Sutt—83Cb 163
Drive, The. T Hth—70Tb 127
Drive, The. Uxb—34N 55
Drive, The. Vir W—71B 138
Drive, The. Wall—81Mb 164
Drive, The. Wal X—1Sb 11
Drive, The. Wat—9T 4
Drive, The. Wemb—33Sa 59
Drive, The. W Wick—73Fc 149
Drive, The. Wok—8F 188
Drive, The. Wray. Stai—7P 95
Driveway, The. Pot B—1Nb 10
Droitwich Clo. SE26—62Wb 127
Dromey Gdns. Harr—24Ha 38
Dromore Rd. SW15—58Ab 102
Dronfield Gdns. Dag—36Yc 67
Droop St. W10—41Ab 80
Drop La. St Alb—4Ea 6
Drop La. St Alb—3Da 5
Dropmore Rd. Slou—9A 52
Drovers Rd. S Croy—78Tb 147
Droveway. Lou—12Rc 28
Drove Way, The. Grav—6A 136
Druce Rd. SE21—58Ub 105
Drudgeon Way. Grav—62Xd 134
Druids Clo. Asht—92Pa 177
Druid St. SE1—47Ub 83 (1J 207)
Druids Way. Brom—70Fc 129
Drumaline Ridge. Wor Pk—75Ua 144
Drummond Av. Romf—28Fd 48
Drummond Cres. NW1 —41Mb 82 (3D 192)
Drummond Dri. Stan—24Ha 38
Drummond Gdns. Eps—83Ra 161
Drummond Ga. SW1 —50Mb 82 (7E 204)
Drummond Ho. N2—26Eb 41
Drummond Pl. Shopping Centre. Croy—75Sb 147
Drummond Rd. E11—30Lc 45
Drummond Rd. SE16—48Xb 83
Drummond Rd. Croy—75Sb 147
Drummond Rd. Romf—28Fd 48
Drummonds, The. Buck H—19Kc 27
Drummonds, The. Epp—2Wc 15
Drummond St. NW1 —42Lb 82 (5B 192)
Drum St. E1—44Vb 83 (2K 201)
Drury La. WC2—44Nb 82 (2G 199)
Drury Rd. Harr—31Ea 58
Drury Way. NW10—36Ta 59
Dryad St. SW15—55Za 102
Dryburgh Gdns. NW9—27Qa 39
Dryburgh Rd. SW15—55Xa 102
Dryden Av. W7—44Ha 78
Dryden Clo. Ilf—23Vc 47
Dryden Ct. SE11—49Rb 83 (6B 206)
Dryden Rd. SW19—65Eb 125
Dryden Rd. Enf—16Ub 25
Dryden Rd. Harr—25Ha 38
Dryden Rd. Well—53Vc 109
Dryden St. WC2—44Nb 82 (3G 199)
Dryden Way. Orp—74Wc 151
Dryfield Clo. NW10—37Sa 59
Dryfield Rd. Edgw—23Sa 39
Dryfield Wlk. SE8—51Cc 106
Dryhill La. Sev—95Dd 186
Dryhill Rd. Belv—51Bd 109
Dryland Av. Orp—77Vc 151
★Dryland Rd. Sev—93Be
Drylands Rd. N8—30Nb 42
Drynham Pk. W on T—76U 140
Drysdale Av. E4—17Dc 26
Drysdale Clo. N'wd—24U 36
Drysdale Pl. N1—41Ub 83 (3J 195)
Drysdale St. N1—41Ub 83 (3J 195)
Du Burstow Ter. W7—47Ga 78
Ducal St. E2—41Vb 83 (4K 195)
Du Cane Ct. SW12—60Jb 104
Du Cane Rd. W12—44Va 80
Duchess M. W1—43Kb 82 (1A 198)
Duchess of Bedford's Wlk. W8 —47Cb 81
Duchess St. W1—43Kb 82 (1A 198)
Duchess' Wlk. Sev—97Nd 187
Duchy Pl. SE1—46Qb 82 (6A 200)
Duchy Rd. Barn—10Fb 9
Duchy St. SE1—46Qb 82 (6A 200)
Ducie St. SW4—56Pb 104
Duckett Rd. N4—30Rb 43
Ducketts Rd. Dart—57Hd 110
Duckett St. E1—42Zb 84
Ducking Stool Ct. Romf—28Gd 48
Duck La. W1—(3D 198)
Duck Lees La. Enf—14Ac 26
Duck's Hill Rd. N'wd & Ruis —25R 36
Ducks Wlk. Twic—57La 100
Du Cros Dri. Stan—23Ma 39
Du Cros Rd. W3—46Ua 80
Dudbrook Rd. Brtwd—11Nd 31 (in two parts)
★Dudbrook Rd. Brtwd—10Rd
Dudden Hill La. NW10—35Va 60
Duddington Clo. SE9—63Mc 129
Dudley Av. Harr—27La 38
Dudley Av. Wal X—4Zb 12
Dudley Clo. Wey—76L 139
Dudley Clo. Slou—8L 73
Dudley Dri. Mord—74Ab 144
Dudley Dri. Ruis—36X 57
Dudley Gdns. W13—47Ka 78
Dudley Gdns. Harr—32Fa 58
Dudley Gdns. Romf—23Md 49
Dudley Gro. Eps—86Sa 161
Dudley Rd. E17—26Cc 44
Dudley Rd. N3—26Db 41
Dudley Rd. NW6—40Ab 60
Dudley Rd. SW19—65Cb 125
Dudley Rd. Ashf—64P 119
Dudley Rd. Felt—60S 98
Dudley Rd. Grav—9A 114
Dudley Rd. Harr—33Ea 58
Dudley Rd. Ilf—35Rc 66
Dudley Rd. King—69Pa 123
Dudley Rd. Rich—54Pa 101
Dudley Rd. Romf—23Md 49
Dudley Rd. S'hall—47Z 77
Dudley Rd. W on T—72W 140
Dudley St. W2—43Fb 81 (1B 196)
Dudlington Rd. E5—33Yb 64
Dudmaston M. SW3—(7C 202)
Dudsbury Rd. Dart—58Kd 111
Dudsbury Rd. Sidc—65Xc 131
Dudset La. Houn—53W 98
Dufferin Av. EC1—(6F 195)
Dufferin St. EC1—42Sb 83 (6E 194)
Duffield Clo. Harr—29Ha 38
Duffield La. Slou—7K 53
Duffield Pk. Slou—1L 73
Duffield Rd. Tad—96Xa 178
Duffins Orchard. Cher—80E 138
Duff St. E14—44Dc 84
Dufour's Pl. W1—44Lb 82 (3C 198)
Dugdale Hill La. Pot B—5Ab 8
Dugdales. Rick—14Q 18
Duke Gdns. Ilf—28Tc 46
Duke Humphrey Rd. SE3 —53Gc 107
Duke of Cambridge Clo. Twic —58Fa 100
Duke of Edinburgh Rd. Sutt —75Fb 145
Duke of Wellington Pl. SW1 —47Jb 82 (2J 203)
Duke of York St. SW1 —46Lb 82 (6C 198)
Duke Rd. W4—50Ta 79
Duke Rd. Ilf—28Tc 46
Dukes Av. N3—25Db 41
Duke's Av. N10—27Kb 42
Duke's Av. W4—50Ta 79
Dukes Av. Edgw—23Pa 39
Dukes Av. Epp—7Uc 14
Dukes Av. Grays—47Ce 91
Dukes Av. Harr—30Ba 37 (North Harrow)
Dukes Av. Harr—28Ga 38 (Wealdstone)
Dukes Av. Houn—56Aa 99
Dukes Av. N Mald—69Va 124
Dukes Av. N'holt—38Aa 57
Dukes Av. Rich & King—63La 122
Dukes Clo. Ashf—63S 120
Dukes Clo. Ger X—32A 54
Dukes Clo. Ger X—2P 53
Dukes Clo. Hmptn—64Ba 121
Dukes Ct. E6—39Qc 66
Dukes Dri. Slou—6D 52
Dukes Head Pas. Hmptn —66Ea 122
Dukes Hill. Cat—92Ac 182
Dukes Kiln Dri. Ger X—2N 53
Dukes La. W8—47Db 81
Dukes La. Asc & Wind—6E 116
Dukes La. Ger X—31A 54
Dukes M. N10—27Kb 42
Duke's M. W1—(2J 197)
Dukes Orchard. Bex—60Ed 110
Duke's Pl. EC3—44Ub 83 (3J 201)
Dukes Pl. Brtwd—18Yd 32
Dukes Ride. Ger X—32A 54
Dukes Rd. E6—39Qc 66
Dukes Rd. W3—42Qa 79
Duke's Rd. WC1—41Mb 82 (4E 192)
Dukes Rd. W on T—78Z 141
Dukesthorpe Rd. SE26—63Zb 128
Duke St. W1—44Jb 82 (2J 197)
Duke St. Rich—57Ma 101
Duke St. Sutt—77Fb 145
Duke St. Wat—13Y 19
Duke St. Wind—2G 94
Duke St. Wok—89B 156
Duke St. Hill. SE1 —46Tb 83 (6G 201)
Duke St. Saint James's. SW1 —46Lb 82 (6C 198)
Dukes Valley. Ger X—3M 53
Dukes Way. Brom—69Hc 129
Dukes Way. W Wick—76Gc 149
Dukes Wood Av. Ger X—31A 54
Dukes Wood Dri. Ger X—32A 54
Dukes Wood Dri. Ger X—2N 53
Duke's Yd. W1—45Jb 82 (4J 197)
Dulas St. N4—32Pb 62
Dulford St. W11—45Ab 80
Dulka Rd. SW11—57Hb 103
Dulverton Rd. SE9—61Tc 130
Dulverton Rd. Romf—23Md 49
Dulverton Rd. Ruis—32W 56
Dulverton Rd. S Croy—82Wb 166
Dulwich Comn. SE21—60Ub 105
Dulwich Rd. SE24—57Qb 104
Dulwich Village. SE21—58Ub 105
Dulwich Way. Rick—15Q 18
Dulwich Wood Av. SE19 —63Ub 127
Dulwich Wood Pk. SE19 —63Ub 127
Dumbarton Av. Wal X—6Zb 12
Dumbarton Rd. SW2—58Nb 104
Dumbleton Clo. King—67Ra 123
Dumbreck Rd. SE9—56Pc 108
Dumfries Clo. Wat—20V 18
Dumont Rd. N16—34Ub 63
Dunally Pk. Shep—73T 140
Dunbar Av. SW16—68Qb 126
Dunbar Av. Beck—70Ac 128
Dunbar Av. Dag—34Cd 68
Dunbar Clo. Hay—44X 77
Dunbar Ct. W on T—74Y 141
Dunbar Gdns. Dag—36Dd 68
Dunbar Rd. E7—37Jc 65
Dunbar Rd. N22—25Qb 42
Dunbar Rd. N Mald—70Sa 123
Dunbar St. SE27—62Sb 127
Dunblane Rd. SE9—54Nc 108
Dunboe Pl. Shep—73S 140
Dunboyne Rd. NW3—36Hb 61
Dunbridge St. E2—42Wb 83
Duncan Clo. Barn—14Eb 23
Duncan Gro. W3—44Ua 80
Duncannon Cres. Wind—5B 94
Duncannon St. WC2 —45Nb 82 (5F 199)
Duncan Rd. E8—39Xb 63
Duncan Rd. Rich—56Na 101
Duncan Rd. Tad—91Ab 178
Duncan St. N1—40Rb 63 (1B 194)
Duncans Yd. West—98Tc 184
Duncan Ter. N1—40Rb 63 (2B 194)
Duncan Way. Bush, Wat—12Ba 19
Dunch St. E1—44Xb 83
Duncombe Hill. SE23—59Ac 106
Duncombe Rd. N19—32Mb 62
Duncrievie Rd. SE13—58Fc 107
Duncroft. SE18—52Uc 108
Duncroft. Wind—5D 94
Dundalk Rd. SE4—55Ac 106
Dundas Rd. SE15—54Yb 106
Dundee Rd. E13—40Kc 65
Dundee Rd. SE25—71Xb 147
Dundee Rd. Slou—4D 72
Dundee St. E1—46Xb 83
Dundela Gdns. Wor Pk—77Xa 144
Dundonald Clo. E6—44Nc 86
Dundonald Rd. NW10—39Za 60
Dundonald Rd. SW19—66Ab 124
Dundrey Cres. Red—100Nb 180
Dundry Ho. SE26—62Wb 127
Dundus Gdns. E Mol—69Da 121
Dunedin Dri. Cat—97Ub 181
Dunedin Rd. E10—34Dc 64
Dunedin Rd. Ilf—32Sc 66
Dunedin Rd. Rain—41Hd 88
Dunedin Way. Hay—42Y 77
Dunelm St. E1—44Zb 84
Dunfield Gdns. SE6—64Dc 128
Dunfield Rd. SE6—64Dc 128 (in two parts)
Dunford Rd. N7—35Pb 62
Dungarvan Av. SW15—56Wa 102
Dunheved Clo. T Hth—72Qb 146
Dunheved Rd. N. T Hth—72Qb 146
Dunheved Rd. S. T Hth—72Qb 146
Dunheved Rd. W. T Hth—72Qb 146
Dunholme Grn. N9—20Vb 25
Dunholme La. N9—20Vb 25
Dunholme Rd. N9—20Vb 25
Dunkeld Rd. SE25—70Tb 127
Dunkeld Rd. Dag—33Xc 67
Dunkellin Gro. S Ock—44Wd 90
Dunkellin Way. S Ock—44Wd 90
Dunkery Rd. SE9—63Mc 129
Dunkin Rd. Dart—56Qd 111
Dunkirk Clo. Grav—4E 136
Dunlace Rd. E5—35Yb 64
Dunleary Clo. Houn—59Ba 99
Dunlem Gro. SE27—62Sb 127
Dunley Dri. Croy—80Dc 148
Dunloe Av. N17—27Tb 43
Dunloe St. E2—40Vb 63 (2K 195)
Dunlop Pl. SE16—48Vb 83
Dunlop Rd. Til—3B 114
Dunmail Dri. Purl—86Ub 165
Dunmore Rd. NW6—39Ab 60
Dunmore Rd. SW20—67Ya 124
Dunmow Clo. Felt—63Aa 121
Dunmow Clo. Lou—16Nc 28
Dunmow Dri. Rain—39Hd 68
Dunmow Gdns. Brtwd—30Fe 51
Dunmow Rd. E15—35Fc 65
Dunnets. Wok—5B 188
Dunnimans Rd. Bans—86Bb 163
Dunning Clo. S Ock—44Wd 90
Dunningford Clo. Horn—36Hd 68
Dunnings La. Brtwd & Upm —33De 71
Dunn Mead. NW7—24Va 40
Dunnock Rd. E6—44Nc 86
Dunnow Clo. Romf—29Yc 47
Dunn's Pas. WC1—(2G 199)
Dunn St. E8—36Vb 63
Dunny La. K Lan—4Q 3
Dunollie Rd. NW5—36Lb 62
Dunoon Rd. SE23—59Yb 106
Dunraven Dri. Enf—12Qb 24
Dunraven Rd. W12—46Wa 80
Dunraven St. W1 —45Hb 81 (4G 197)
Dunsany Rd. W14—48Za 80
Dunsbury Clo. Sutt—81Db 163
Dunsfold Rise. Coul—85Mb 164
Dunsfold Way. Croy—80Dc 148
Dunsmore Clo. Bush, Wat—16Fa 20
Dunsmore Clo. Hay—42Aa 77
Dunsmore Rd. W on T—72X 141
Dunsmore Way. Bush, Wat —16Fa 20
Dunsmure Rd. N16—32Ub 63
Dunspring La. Ilf—26Rc 46
Dunstable Clo. Romf—23Md 49
Dunstable M. W1—43Jb 82 (7J 191)
Dunstable Rd. E Mol—70Ba 121
Dunstable Rd. Rich—56Na 101
Dunstable Rd. Romf—23Md 49
Dunstable Rd. Stanf—1M 93
Dunstall Rd. SW20—65Xa 124
Dunstall Way. E Mol—69Da 121
Dunstall Welling Est. Well —54Xc 109
Dunstan Clo. N2—27Eb 41
Dunstan Rd. NW11—32Bb 61
Dunstan Rd. Coul—89Mb 164
Dunstan's Gro. SE22—58Xb 105
Dunstan's Rd. SE22—59Wb 105
Dunster Av. Mord—74Za 144
Dunster Clo. Barn—14Za 22
Dunster Clo. Romf—26Ed 48
Dunster Clo. Uxb—25K 35
Dunster Ct. EC3—45Ub 83 (4J 201)
Dunster Cres. Upm—33Rd 69
Dunster Dri. NW9—32Sa 59
Dunster Gdns. NW6—38Bb 61
Dunster Gdns. Slou—5E 72
Dunsterville Way. SE1 —47Tb 83 (2G 207)
Dunster Way. Ruis—34Aa 57
Dunston Rd. E8—39Vb 63
Dunston Rd. SW11—55Jb 104
Dunston St. E8—39Vb 63
Dunton Clo. Surb—74Na 143
Dunton Rd. E10—31Dc 64
Dunton Rd. SE1—49Vb 83 (7K 207)
Dunton Rd. SW19—65Fb 125
Dunton Rd. Romf—28Gd 48
Duntshill Rd. SW18—60Db 103
Dunvegan Clo. E Mol—70Ca 121
Dunvegan Rd. SE9—56Pc 108
Dunwich Rd. Bexh—53Bd 109
Dunworth M. W11—44Bb 81
Duplex Ride. SW1 —47Hb 81 (2G 203)
Dupont Rd. SW20—68Za 124
Dupont St. E14—43Ac 84
Duppas Av. Croy—77Rb 147
Duppas Clo. Shep—71T 140
Duppas Hill La. Croy—77Rb 147
Duppas Hill Rd. Croy—77Qb 146
Duppas Hill Ter. Croy—76Rb 147
Duppas Rd. Croy—76Qb 146
Dupree Rd. SE7—50Kc 85
Dura Den Clo. Beck—66Dc 128
Durand Clo. Cars—74Hb 145
Durand Gdns. SW9—53Pb 104
Durands Wlk. SE16—47Ac 84
Durand Way. NW10—38Sa 59
Durant Rd. Swan—65Jd 132
Durants Pk. Av. Enf—14Zb 26
Durants Rd. Enf—14Yb 26
Durant St. E2—41Wb 83
Durban Gdns. Dag—38Ed 68
Durban Rd. E15—41Gc 85
Durban Rd. E17—25Bc 44
Durban Rd. N17—23Ub 43
Durban Rd. SE27—63Sb 127
Durban Rd. Beck—68Bc 128
Durban Rd. Ilf—32Uc 66
Durban Rd. E. Wat—14W 18
Durban Rd. W. Wat—14W 18
Durbin Rd. Chess—77Na 143
Durdans Rd. S'hall—44Ba 77
Durell Gdns. Dag—36Zc 67
Durell Rd. Dag—36Zc 67
Durford Cres. SW15—60Xa 102
Durham Av. Brom—70Hc 129
Durham Av. Houn—50Ba 77
Durham Av. Romf—28Ld 49
Durham Av. Slou—4E 72
Durham Av. Wfd G—22Mc 45
Durham Clo. SW20—68Xa 124
Durham Hill. Brom—63Hc 129
Durham Ho. St. WC2—(5G 199)
Durham Pl. SW3—(7F 203)
Durham Rise. SE18—50Sc 86
Durham Rd. E12—35Mc 65
Durham Rd. E16—42Gc 85
Durham Rd. N2—27Gb 41
Durham Rd. N7—33Pb 62
Durham Rd. N9—19Wb 25
Durham Rd. SW20—67Xa 124
Durham Rd. W5—48Ma 79
Durham Rd. Borwd—13Sa 21
Durham Rd. Brom—69Hc 129
Durham Rd. Dag—36Ed 68
Durham Rd. Felt—59Y 99
Durham Rd. Harr—29Da 37
Durham Rd. Sidc—64Xc 131
Durham Row. E1—43Zb 84
Durham St. SE11—51Pb 104
Durham Ter. W2—44Db 81
Durham Wharf. Bren—52La 100
Durleston Pk. Dri. Lea—96Ea 176
Durleston Pk. Dri. Lea—97Ea 176
Durley Av. Pinn—31Aa 57
Durley Rd. N16—31Ub 63
Durlston Rd. E5—33Wb 63
Durlston Rd. King—65Na 123
Durndale La. Grav—3A 136 (in two parts)
Durnell Way. Lou—13Qc 28
Durnford St. N15—29Ub 43
Durnford St. SE10—51Ec 106
Durninge Wlk. Grays—45De 91
Durning Rd. SE19—64Tb 127
Durnsford Av. SW19—61Cb 125
Durnsford Rd. N11—25Mb 42
Durnsford Rd. SW19—61Cb 125
Durrants Clo. Rain—40Ld 69
Durrants Dri. Rick—13S 18
Durrant Way. Orp—78Tc 150
Durrant Way. Swans—59Ae 113
Durrell Rd. SW6—53Bb 103
Durrell Way. Shep—72T 140
Durrington Av. SW20—66Ya 124
Durrington Pk. Rd. SW20 —67Ya 124
Durrington Rd. E5—35Ac 64
Dursley Clo. SE3—54Lc 107
Dursley Gdns. SE3—53Mc 107
Dursley Rd. SE3—54Lc 107
Durward St. E1—43Xb 83 (in two parts)
Durweston M. W1—(7G 191)
Durweston St. W1 —43Hb 81 (1G 197)
Dury Falls Clo. Horn—32Pd 69
Dury Rd. Barn—11Bb 23
Dutch Elm Av. Wind—2K 95
Dutch Yd. SW18—57Cb 103
Duthie St. E14—45Ec 84
Dutton St. SE10—53Ec 106
Dutton Way. Iver—44G 74
Duxford Clo. Horn—37Ld 69
Dye Ho. La. E3—39Cc 64
Dyer's Bldgs. EC1 —43Qb 82 (1K 199)
Dyers Hall Rd. E11—33Gc 65
Dyers La. SW15—55Xa 102
Dyers Way. Romf—24Kd 49
Dyke Dri. Orp—73Yc 151
Dykes Path. Wok—87E 156
Dykewood Clo. Bex—62Fd 132
Dylan Rd. Belv—48Cd 88
Dylways. SE5—56Tb 105
Dymchurch Clo. Ilf—26Qc 46
Dymchurch Clo. Orp—77Uc 150
Dymes Path. SW19—61Za 124
Dymock St. SW6—55Db 103
Dymoke Rd. Horn—31Hd 68
Dyneley Rd. SE12—62Lc 129
Dyne Rd. NW6—38Ab 60
Dynes Rd. Sev—89Md 171
Dynes, The. Sev—89Md 171
Dynevor Rd. N16—34Ub 63
Dynevor Rd. Rich—57Na 101
Dynham Rd. NW6—38Cb 61
Dyott St. WC1—44Mb 82 (2E 198)
Dyrham La. Barn—8Wa 8
Dysart Av. King—64La 122
Dysart St. EC2—42Ub 83 (6H 195)
Dyson Clo. Wind—5F 94
Dyson Rd. E11—30Gc 45
Dyson Rd. E15—37Hc 65
Dysons Clo. Wal X—5Zb 12
Dysons Rd. N18—22Xb 43
Dytchleys La. Brtwd—14Qd 31
Dytchleys Rd. Brtwd—14Pd 31

Eade Rd. N4—31Sb 63
Eagle Av. Romf—30Ad 47
Eagle Clo. Enf—14Yb 26
Eagle Clo. Rain—37Kd 69
Eagle Ct. EC1—43Rb 83 (7B 194)
Eagle Hill. SE19—65Tb 127
Eagle La. E11—28Jc 45
★Eagle La. Brtwd—9Ud
Eagle Pl. SW1—(5C 198)
Eagle Rd. Wemb—38Ma 59
Eagles Dri. West—90Mc 167
Eaglesfield Rd. SE18—53Rc 108
Eagle St. WC1—43Pb 82 (1H 199)
Eagle Ter. Wfd G—24Kc 45
Eagle Way. Brtwd—23Xd 50
Eagle Wharf Rd. N1 —40Sb 63 (1E 194)
Eagons Clo. N2—27Fb 41
Ealdham Sq. SE9—56Lc 107
Ealing B'way Centre. W5 —45Ma 79
Ealing Clo. Borwd—11Ta 21
Ealing Grn. W5—46Ma 79
Ealing Pk. Gdns. W5—49La 78
Ealing Rd. Bren—50Ma 79
Ealing Rd. N'holt—39Ca 57
Ealing Rd. Wemb—37Na 59
Ealing Village. W5—44Na 79
Eamont St. NW8—40Gb 61 (1D 190)
Eardemont Clo. Dart—56Hd 110
Eardley Cres. SW5—50Cb 81
Eardley Rd. SW16—64Lb 126
Eardley Rd. Belv—50Cd 88
Eardley Rd. Sev—96Kd 187
Earl Cotts. SE1—50Vb 83 (7K 207)
Earldom Rd. SW15—56Ya 102
Earle Gdns. King—66Na 123
Earleswood. Cob—84Aa 159
Earlham Gro. E7—36Hc 65
Earlham Gro. N22—24Pb 42
Earlham St. WC2 —44Nb 82 (3F 199)
Earl Rise. SE18—49Tc 86
Earl Rd. SE1—50Vb 83 (7K 207)
Earl Rd. SW14—56Sa 101
Earl Rd. Grav—1A 136
Earls Ct. Gdns. SW5—49Db 81
Earls Ct. Rd. W8—48Cb 81
W8 1-109 & 4-138
SW5 remainder
Earls Ct. Sq. SW5—50Db 81
Earls Cres. Harr—28Ga 38
Earlsferry Way. N1—38Pb 62
Earlsfield Rd. SW18—60Eb 103
Earlshall Rd. SE9—56Pc 108
Earls La. Pot B—4Ua 8
Earlsmead. Harr—35Ba 57
Earlsmead Rd. N15—29Vb 43
Earlsmead Rd. NW10—41Ya 80
Earl's Path. Lou—12Lc 27
Earls Ter. W8—48Bb 81
Earlsthorpe M. SW12—58Jb 104
Earlsthorpe Rd. SE26—63Zb 128
Earlstoke St. EC1 —41Rb 83 (3B 194)
Earlston Gro. E9—39Xb 63
Earl St. EC2—43Tb 83 (7H 195)
Earl St. Wat—13Y 19
Earls Wlk. W8—48Cb 81
Earl's Wlk. Dag—35Xc 67
Earlswood Av. T Hth—71Qb 146
Earlswood Clo. SE10—50Gc 85
Earlswood Gdns. Ilf—27Qc 46
Earlswood St. SE10—50Gc 85
Early M. NW1—39Kb 62
Earnshaw St. WC2 —44Mb 82 (2E 198)
Earsby St. W14—49Ab 80
Easby Cres. Mord—72Db 145
Easebourne Rd. Dag—36Yc 67
Easedale Dri. Horn—36Jd 68
Easington Way. S Ock—43Wd 90
Easley's M. W1—(2J 197)
E. Acton La. W3—46Ua 80
E. Arbour St. E1—44Zb 84
East Av. E12—38Nc 66
East Av. E17—28Dc 44
East Av. Hay—46V 76

East Av.—Elf Row

East Av. S'hall—45Ba 77
East Av. Wall—78Pb 146
East Av. W on T—82V 158
East Bank. N16—31Ub 63
Eastbank Rd. Hmptn—64Ea 122
E. Barnet Rd. Barn—14Fb 23
Eastbourne Av. W3—44Ta 79
Eastbourne Bldgs. SE1—(4H 207)
Eastbourne Gdns. SW14 —55Sa 101
Eastbourne M. W2 —44Eb 81 (2A 196)
Eastbourne Rd. E6—41Qc 86
Eastbourne Rd. E15—39Gc 65
Eastbourne Rd. N15—30Ub 43
Eastbourne Rd. SW17—65Jb 126
Eastbourne Rd. W4—51Sa 101
Eastbourne Rd. Bren—50Ma 79
Eastbourne Rd. Felt—61Z 121
Eastbourne Rd. Slou—4E 72
Eastbourne Ter. W2 —44Eb 81 (2A 196)
Eastbournia Av. N9—20Xb 25
East Bri. Slou—6M 73
Eastbrook Av. N9—17Yb 26
Eastbrook Av. Dag—35Ed 68
E. Brook Clo. Wok—88C 156
Eastbrook Dri. Romf—34Gd 68
Eastbrook Rd. SE3—53Kc 107
Eastbrook Rd. Wal A—5Gc 13
E. Burnham La. Slou—9E 52
Eastbury Av. Bark—39Uc 66
Eastbury Av. Enf—11Vb 25
Eastbury Av. N'wd—22V 36
Eastbury Ct. Bark—39Uc 66
Eastbury Gro. W4—50Ua 80
Eastbury Rd. E6—42Qc 86
Eastbury Rd. King—66Na 123
Eastbury Rd. N'wd—23U 36
Eastbury Rd. Orp—72Tc 150
Eastbury Rd. Romf—30Fd 48
Eastbury Rd. Wat—17X 19
Eastbury Sq. Bark—39Vc 67
Eastbury Ter. E1—42Zb 84
Eastcastle St. W1 —44Lb 82 (2B 198)
Eastcheap. EC3—45Ub 83 (4H 201)
E. Churchfield Rd. W3—46Ta 79
Eastchurch Rd. Houn—55U 98
East Clo. W5—42Qa 79
East Clo. Barn—14Jb 24
East Clo. Gnfd—40Ea 58
East Clo. Rain—42Kd 89
East Clo. Wok—89E 156
Eastcombe Av. SE7—51Kc 107
East Comn. Ger X—30A 34
Eastcote. Orp—74Vc 151
Eastcote Av. E Mol—71Ba 141
Eastcote Av. Gnfd—36Ja 58
Eastcote Av. Harr—33Da 57
Eastcote High Rd. Pinn—30W 36
Eastcote La. Harr—35Ba 57
Eastcote La. N'holt—36Ba 57
Eastcote La. N. N'holt—37Ca 57
Eastcote Rd. Harr—34Ea 58
Eastcote Rd. Pinn—29Z 37
Eastcote Rd. Ruis—31U 56
Eastcote Rd. Well—54Tc 108
Eastcote St. SW9—54Pb 104
Eastcote View. Pinn—28Y 37
East Ct. Wemb—33La 58
East Cres. N11—21Hb 41
East Cres. Enf—15Vb 25
East Cres. Wind—3D 94
E. Crescent Rd. Grav—8E 114
Eastcroft. Slou—2F 72
Eastcroft Rd. Eps—80Ua 144
Eastdean Av. Eps—85Ra 161
E. Dene Dri. Romf—22Md 49
Eastdown Pk. SE13—56Fc 107
East Dri. Cars—81Gb 163
East Dri. N'wd—19U 18
East Dri. Orp—72Xc 151
East Dri. Slou—1J 73
East Dri. Wat—8X 5
E. Dulwich Gro. SE22—57Ub 105
E. Dulwich Rd. SE22—56Vb 105
(in two parts)
East End Rd.—26Cb 41
N3 1-55 & 2-120
N2 remainder
E. End Way. Pinn—27Aa 37
E. Entrance. Dag—40Dd 68
Eastern Av.—30Kc 45 to 28Zc 47
E11 61-75 & 48-120
Ilf & Romf remainder
Eastern Av. Cher—69K 119
Eastern Av. Pinn—31Z 57
Eastern Av. S Ock—47Sd 90
Eastern Av. Wal X—5Ac 12
Eastern Av. E. Romf—27Fd 48
Eastern Av. W. Romf—28Ad 47
Eastern Industrial Est. Eri —47Cd 88
Eastern Perimeter Rd. Houn —54V 98
Eastern Rd. E13—40Kc 65
Eastern Rd. E17—29Ec 44
Eastern Rd. N2—28Hb 41
Eastern Rd. N22—25Nb 42
Eastern Rd. SE4—56Cc 106
Eastern Rd. Grays—49Fe 91
Eastern Rd. Romf—29Gd 48
Eastern View. West—89Lc 167
Easternville Gdns. Ilf—30Sc 46
Eastern Way. SE28—47Wc 87
Eastern Way. Grays—50Ce 91
E. Ferry Rd. E14—49Dc 84
Eastfield Av. Wat—11Z 19
Eastfield Gdns. Dag—35Cd 68
Eastfield Pde. Pot B—4Fb 9
Eastfield Rd. E17—28Cc 44
Eastfield Rd. N8—27Nb 42
Eastfield Rd. Bexh—55Ed 110
Eastfield Rd. Brtwd—19Zd 33
Eastfield Rd. Dag—35Bd 67
Eastfield Rd. Enf—10Zb 12
Eastfield Rd. Wal X—4Bc 12
Eastfields. Pinn—29Y 37
Eastfields Rd. W3—43Sa 79
Eastfields Rd. Mitc—68Jb 126
East Gdns. SW17—65Gb 125
Eastgate. Bans—86Bb 163
Eastglade. N'wd—22V 36
Eastglade. Pinn—27Ba 37
E. Hall La. Rain—44Md 89
E. Hall Rd. Orp—73Ad 151
East Ham and Barking By-Pass. Bark—40Uc 66
Eastham Cres. Brtwd—21Ce 51
East Ham Mnr. Way. E6—43Qc 86
E. Harding St. EC4 —44Qb 82 (2A 200)
E. Heath Rd. NW3—34Eb 61
East Hill. SW18—57Db 103
East Hill. Dart—59Nd 111
East Hill. S Croy—82Ub 165
East Hill. S Dar, Dart—67Sd 134
East Hill. Wemb—33Qa 59
East Hill. West—90Kc 167
East Hill. Wok—88E 156
E. Hill Dri. Dart—59Pd 111
E. Hill Rd. Sev—84Rd 171
Eastholm. NW11—28Db 41
East Holme. Eri—53Fd 110
East Holme. Hay—46W 76
E. India Dock Rd. E14—44Cc 84
E. India Dock Wall Rd. E14 —45Fc 85
E. Kent Av. Grav—58Ee 113
Eastlake Rd. SE5—54Sb 105
Eastlands Clo. Oxt—99Fc 183
Eastlands Cres. SE21—58Vb 105
Eastlands Way. Oxt—99Fc 183
East La. SE16—47Wb 83
East La. Abb L, Wat—1W 4
(in two parts)
East La. King—69Ma 123
East La. Lea—98S 174
East La. Wemb—34Ka 58
Eastlea Av. Wat—9Aa 5
Eastleigh Av. Harr—33Da 57
Eastleigh Clo. NW2—34Ua 60
Eastleigh Clo. Sutt—80Db 145
Eastleigh Wlk. SW15—59Wa 102
E. Lodge La. Enf—8Mb 10
East Mall. Stai—63H 119
Eastman Rd. W3—47Ta 79
East Mead. Ruis—34Z 57
Eastmead. Wok—5E 188
Eastmead Av. Gnfd—41Da 77
Eastmead Clo. Brom—68Nc 130
Eastmearn Rd. SE21—61Sb 127
E. Milton Rd. Grav—9F 114
Eastmont Rd. Esh—75Ha 142
Eastmoor Pl. SE7—48Mc 85
Eastmoor St. SE7—48Mc 85
Eastney Rd. Croy—74Rb 147
Eastney St. SE10—50Fc 85
Eastnor Rd. SE9—60Sc 108
Easton Gdns. Borwd—14Ua 22
Easton St. WC1—42Qb 82 (5K 193)
E. Park Clo. Romf—29Ad 47
East Pas. EC1—(7D 194)
East Pier. E1—46Wb 83
East Pl. SE27—63Sb 127
E. Poultry Av. EC1 —43Rb 83 (1B 200)
East Ramp. Houn—53R 98
E. Ridgeway. Pot B—1Nb 10
East Rd. E15—39Jc 65
East Rd. N1—41Tb 83 (4G 195)
East Rd. SW19—65Eb 125
East Rd. Barn—18Jb 24
East Rd. Edgw—25Ra 39
East Rd. Enf—10Yb 12
East Rd. Felt—59T 98
East Rd. King—67Na 123
East Rd. Purf—51Rd 111
East Rd. Romf—29Ad 47
(Chadwell Heath)
East Rd. Romf—31Fd 68
(Rush Green)
East Rd. Well—54Xc 109
East Rd. W Dray—49P 75
East Rd. Wey—80T 140
E. Rochester Way. Sidc & Bex —57Uc 108
East Row. E11—30Jc 45
East Row. W10—42Ab 80
Eastry Av. Brom—72Hc 149
Eastry Rd. Eri—52Dd 110
E. Sheen Av. SW14—57Ta 101
Eastside. Wey—75L 139
Eastside Rd. NW11—28Bb 41
E. Smithfield. E1—45Vb 83 (5K 201)
East St. SE17—50Sb 83 (7E 206)
East St. Bark—39Sc 66
East St. Bexh—56Cd 110
East St. Bren—52La 100
East St. Brom—68Jc 129
East St. Cher—73J 139
East St. Eps—85Ua 162
East St. Grays—51Ee 113
East St. Grays—51Ae 113
(South Stifford)
East St. Lea—97Da 175
E. Surrey Gro. SE15—52Vb 105
E. Tenter St. E1—44Vb 83
East Ter. Grav—8E 114
E. Thurrock Rd. Grays—51Ee 113
E. Tilbury Rd. Stanf—7J 93
East Towers. Pinn—29Z 37
East View. E4—22Ec 44
East View. Barn—12Bb 23
Eastview Av. SE18—52Uc 108
Eastville Av. NW11—30Bb 41
East Wlk. Barn—17Jb 24
East Wlk. Hay—46W 76
Eastway. E9—37Bc 64
East Way. E11—29Kc 45
East Way. Brom—73Jc 149
East Way. Croy—75Ac 148
Eastway. Eps—83Ta 161
East Way. Hay—46W 76
Eastway. Mord—71Za 144
East Way. Ruis—32W 56
Eastway. Wall—77Lb 146
Eastway Commercial Centre. E15 —36Cc 64
Eastwell Clo. Beck—66Ac 128
Eastwick Cres. Rick—19H 17
Eastwick Dri. Lea—95Ca 175
Eastwick Pk. Av. Lea—96Da 175
Eastwick Rd. Lea—97Da 175
Eastwick Rd. W on T—79X 141
Eastwood Clo. E18—26Jc 45
Eastwood Dri. Rain—44Kd 89
Eastwood Rd. E18—26Jc 45
Eastwood Rd. N10—26Jb 42
Eastwood Rd. Ilf—31Wc 67
E. Woodside. Bex—60Ad 109
Eastwood St. SW16—65Lb 126
Eastworth Rd. Cher—74J 139
Eatington Rd. E10—29Fc 45
Eaton Clo. SW1—49Jb 82 (6H 203)
Eaton Clo. Stan—21Ka 38
Eaton Dri. SW9—56Rb 105
Eaton Dri. King—66Qa 123
Eaton Dri. Romf—24Dd 48
Eaton Gdns. Dag—38Ad 67
Eaton Ga. SW1—49Jb 82 (5H 203)
Eaton Ga. N'wd—23S 36
Eaton La. SW1—48Kb 82 (4A 204)
Eaton M. N. SW1—48Jb 82 (4J 203)
Eaton M. S. SW1—48Kb 82 (4K 203)
Eaton M. W. SW1 —49Jb 82 (5J 203)
Eaton Pk. Cob—86Aa 159
Eaton Pk. Rd. N13—19Qb 24
Eaton Pk. Rd. Cob—86Aa 159
Eaton Pl. SW1—48Jb 82 (4H 203)
Eaton Rise. E11—29Lc 45
Eaton Rise. W5—43Ma 79
Eaton Rd. NW4—29Ya 40
Eaton Rd. Enf—14Ub 25
Eaton Rd. Houn—56Fa 100
Eaton Rd. Sidc—61Zc 131
Eaton Rd. Sutt—79Fb 145
Eaton Row. SW1 —48Kb 82 (4K 203)
Eatons Mead. E4—19Cc 26
Eaton Sq. SW1—49Jb 82 (4J 203)
Eaton Ter. SW1—49Jb 82 (5H 203)
Eaton Ter. M. SW1—(5H 203)
Eatonville Rd. SW17—61Hb 125
Eatonville Vs. SW17—61Hb 125
Ebbas Way. Eps—87Ra 161
Ebbisham Dri. SW8—51Pb 104
Ebbisham La. Tad—93Va 178
Ebbisham Rd. Eps—86Ra 161
Ebbisham Rd. Wor Pk—75Ya 144
Ebbsfleet Rd. NW2—36Ab 60
Ebbsfleet Wlk. Grav—58De 113
Ebdon Way. SE3—55Kc 107
Ebenezer St. N1—41Tb 83 (3F 195)
Ebenezer Wlk. SW16—67Lb 126
Ebley Clo. SE15—51Vb 105
Ebner St. SW18—57Db 103
Ebor St. E1—42Vb 83 (5K 195)
Ebrington Rd. Harr—30Ma 39
Ebsworth St. SE23—59Zb 106
Eburne Rd. N7—34Nb 62
Ebury App. Rick—18M 17
Ebury Bri. SW1—50Kb 82 (7K 203)
Ebury Bri. Rd. SW1 —50Jb 82 (7J 203)
Ebury Bri. Est. SW1—(7K 203)
Ebury Clo. Kes—76Nc 150
Ebury Clo. N'wd—22S 36
Ebury M. SW1—49Kb 82 (5J 203)
Ebury M. E. SW1—48Kb 82 (5K 203)
Ebury Rd. Rick—18M 17
Ebury Rd. Wat—13Y 19
Ebury Sq. SW1—49Kb 82 (6J 203)
Ebury St. SW1—49Jb 82 (6J 203)
Ecclesbourne Clo. N13—22Qb 42
Ecclesbourne Gdns. N13—22Qb 42
Ecclesbourne Rd. N1—38Sb 63
Ecclesbourne Rd. T Hth—71Sb 147
Eccles Pl. SE1—(7B 200)
Eccles Rd. SW11—56Hb 103
Eccleston Bri. SW1 —49Kb 82 (5A 204)
Eccleston Clo. Barn—14Hb 23
Eccleston Clo. Orp—74Tc 150
Eccleston Cres. Romf—31Xc 67
Ecclestone Ct. Wemb—36Na 59
Ecclestone M. Wemb—36Na 59
Ecclestone Pl. Wemb—36Pa 59
Eccleston Rd. W13—46Ja 78
Eccleston M. SW1 —48Jb 82 (4J 203)
Eccleston Pl. SW1 —49Kb 82 (5K 203)
Eccleston Sq. SW1 —49Kb 82 (6A 204)
Eccleston Sq. M. SW1 —49Lb 82 (6B 204)
Eccleston St. SW1 —48Kb 82 (4K 203)
Echelforde Dri. Ashf—63Q 120
Echo Heights. E4—18Dc 26
Echo Sq. Grav—1E 136
Eckersley St. E1—42Vb 83
Eckford St. N1—40Qb 62 (1K 193)
Eckstein Rd. SW11—56Gb 103
Eclipse Rd. E13—43Kc 85
Ecton Rd. Wey—77K 139
Ector Rd. SE6—61Gc 129
Edam Ct. Sidc—62Wc 131
Edbrooke Rd. W9—42Cb 81
Eddington St. N4—32Qb 62
Eddisbury Ho. SE26—62Wb 127
Eddiscombe Rd. SW6—54Bb 103
Eddy Clo. Romf—30Dd 48
Eddystone Rd. SE4—57Ac 106
Eddystone Wlk. Stai—59N 97
Ede Clo. Houn—55Ba 99
Edenbridge Clo. Orp—70Zc 131
Edenbridge Rd. E9—38Zb 64
Edenbridge Rd. Enf—16Ub 25
Eden Clo. Bex—63Fd 132
Eden Clo. Slou—50C 74
Eden Clo. Wemb—39Ma 59
Eden Clo. Wey—82K 157
Edencourt Rd. SW16—65Kb 126
Edendale Rd. Bexh—53Fd 110
Edenfield Gdns. Wor Pk—76Va 144
Eden Grn. S Ock—43Xd 90
Eden Gro. E17—29Dc 44
Eden Gro. N7—36Pb 62
Eden Gro. Rd. Wey—85N 157
Edenhall Clo. Romf—22Ld 49
Edenhall Glen. Romf—22Ld 49
Edenhall Rd. Romf—22Ld 49
Edenham Way. W10—42Bb 81
Edenhurst. Sev—97Jd 186
Edenhurst Av. SW6—55Bb 103
Eden Pk. Av. Beck—70Bc 128
Eden Rd. E17—29Dc 44
Eden Rd. SE27—64Rb 127
Eden Rd. Beck—70Ac 128
Eden Rd. Bex—63Ed 132
Eden Rd. Croy—77Tb 147
Edenside Rd. Lea—96Ba 175
Edensor Gdns. W4—52Ua 102
Edensor Rd. W4—52Ua 102
Eden St. King—68Ma 123
Edenvale Rd. Mitc—66Jb 126
Edenvale St. SW6—54Eb 103
Eden Wlk. King—68Na 123
Eden Way. Beck—71Bc 148
Eden Way. Warl—90Ac 166
Ederline Av. SW16—69Pb 126
Edgar Clo. Swan—69Hd 132
Edgar Ho. E11—31Jc 65
Edgarley Ter. SW6—53Ab 102
Edgar Rd. E3—41Dc 84
Edgar Rd. Houn—59Ba 99
Edgar Rd. Romf—31Zc 67
Edgar Rd. Sev—89Nd 171
Edgar Rd. S Croy—81Tb 165
Edgar Rd. W Dray—46N 75
Edgar Rd. West—93Mc 183
Edgbaston Rd. Wat—20X 19
Edgeborough Way. Brom —67Mc 129
Edgebury. Chst—63Rc 130
Edgebury Wlk. Chst—63Sc 130
Edge Clo. Wey—80Q 140
Edgecombe Rd. E11—32Hc 65
Edgecoombe. S Croy—80Yb 148
Edgecoombe Clo. King—66Ta 123
Edgecot Gro. N15—29Ub 43
Edgefield Av. Bark—38Vc 67
Edgefield Clo. Dart—60Rd 111
Edge Hill. SE18—51Rc 108
Edge Hill. SW19—66Za 124
Edgehill Av. N3—28Cb 41
Edgehill Gdns. Dag—35Cd 68
Edgehill Gdns. Grav—7B 136
Edgehill Rd. W13—43La 78
Edgehill Rd. Chst—63Sc 130
Edgehill Rd. Mitc—67Kb 126
Edgehill Rd. Purl—82Qb 164
Edgeley. Lea—96Aa 175
Edgeley La. SW4—55Mb 104
Edgeley Rd. SW4—55Mb 104
Edgell Clo. Vir W—69B 118
Edgell Rd. Stai—64H 119
Edgel St. SW18—56Db 103
Edgepoint Clo. SE27—64Rb 127
Edge St. W8—46Cb 81
Edgewood Dri. Orp—78Wc 151
Edgewood Grn. Croy—74Zb 148
Edgeworth Av. NW4—29Wa 40
Edgeworth Clo. NW4—29Wa 40
Edgeworth Clo. Whyt—90Wb 165
Edgeworth Cres. NW4—29Wa 40
Edgeworth Rd. SE9—56Lc 107
Edgeworth Rd. Barn—14Gb 23
Edgington Rd. SW16—65Mb 126
Edgwarebury Gdns. Edgw —22Qa 39
Edgwarebury La. Borwd—17Na 21
Edgwarebury La. Edgw—19Qa 21
Edgware Rd. NW2—32Xa 60
Edgware Rd. NW9—26Sa 39
Edgware Rd. W2—42Fb 81 (6B 190)
Edgware Way. Edgw—18Ma 21
Edinburgh Av. Rick—16J 17
Edinburgh Av. Slou—3E 72
Edinburgh Clo. Uxb—35R 56
Edinburgh Cres. Wal X—5Ac 12
Edinburgh Dri. Stai—65M 119
Edinburgh Dri. Uxb—35R 56
Edinburgh Gdns. Wind—4H 95
Edinburgh Ga. SW1 —47Hb 81 (2F 203)
Edinburgh M. Til—4D 114
Edinburgh Rd. E13—40Kc 65
Edinburgh Rd. E17—29Cc 44
Edinburgh Rd. N18—22Wb 43
Edinburgh Rd. W7—47Ha 78
Edinburgh Rd. Sutt—75Fb 145
Edington Rd. SE2—48Xc 87
Edington Rd. Enf—12Yb 26
Edison Av. Horn—32Hd 68
Edison Clo. Horn—32Hd 68
Edison Dri. S'hall—44Da 77
Edison Gro. SE18—52Vc 109
Edison Rd. N8—30Mb 42
Edison Rd. Brom—68Jc 129
Edison Rd. Well—53Vc 109
Edis St. NW1—39Jb 62
Edith Gdns. Surb—73Ra 143
Edith Gro. SW10—51Eb 103
Edithna St. SW9—55Nb 104
Edith Rd. E6—38Mc 65
Edith Rd. E15—36Fc 65
Edith Rd. N11—24Mb 42
Edith Rd. SE25—71Tb 147
Edith Rd. SW19—65Db 125
Edith Rd. W14—49Ab 80
Edith Rd. Orp—78Wc 151
Edith Rd. Romf—31Zc 67
Edith Row. SW6—53Db 103
Edith Ter. SW10—52Eb 103
Edith Vs. W14—49Bb 81
Edith Yd. SW10—52Eb 103
Ediva Rd. Grav—10C 136
Edmanson's Clo. N17—25Vb 43
Edmund Clo. Grav—10C 136
Edmund Rd. Mitc—69Gb 125
Edmund Rd. Orp—72Yc 151
Edmund Rd. Rain—40Gd 68
Edmund Rd. Well—55Wc 109
Edmunds Av. Orp—69Zc 131
Edmunds Clo. Hay—43Y 77
Edmund St. SE5—52Tb 105
Edmunds Wlk. N2—28Gb 41
Edmunds Way. Slou—4M 73
Edna Rd. SW20—68Za 124
Edna St. SW11—53Gb 103
Edrick Rd. Edgw—23Sa 39
Edrick Wlk. Edgw—23Sa 39
Edric Rd. SE14—52Zb 106
Edridge Clo. Bush, Wat—15Ea 20
Edridge Clo. Horn—36Md 69
Edridge Rd. Croy—76Sb 147
Edulf Rd. Borwd—11Ra 21
Edward Av. E4—23Dc 44
Edward Av. Mord—71Fb 145
Edward Clo. N9—17Vb 25
Edward Clo. Hmptn—64Ea 122
Edward Clo. N'holt—40Y 57
Edward Clo. Romf—27Ld 49
Edward Ct. E16—43Jc 85
Edward Ct. Wal A—5Hc 13
Edwardes Sq. W8—48Bb 81
Edward Gro. Barn—15Fb 23
Edward M. W1—44Jb 82 (3H 197)
Edward Pl. SE8—51Bc 106
Edward Rd. E17—28Zb 44
Edward Rd. SE20—65Zb 128
Edward Rd. Barn—15Fb 23
Edward Rd. Belv—49Cd 88
Edward Rd. Brom—66Kc 129
Edward Rd. Chst—64Rc 130
Edward Rd. Coul—87Mb 164
Edward Rd. Croy—73Ub 147
Edward Rd. Felt—57Y 98
Edward Rd. Hmptn—64Ea 122
Edward Rd. Harr—27Ea 38
Edward Rd. N'holt—40Y 57
Edward Rd. Romf—30Ad 47
Edward Rd. West—90Nc 168
Edwards Almshouses. SE1 —(7B 200)
Edward's Av. Ruis—37X 57
Edwards Clo. Brtwd—16Fe 33
Edwards Clo. Wor Pk—75Za 144
Edward's Cotts. N1—37Rb 63
Edwards Ct. Slou—7J 73
Edward II Av. Wey—86P 157
Edwards Gdns. Swan—70Fd 132
Edward's La. N16—33Tb 63
Edward Sq. N1—39Pb 62 (1H 193)
Edward St. E16—42Jc 85
Edward St.—52Ac 106
SE8 1-95 & 2-86
SE14 remainder
Edwards Way. Brtwd—16Fe 33
Edward Temme Av. E15—38Hc 65
Edward Way. Ashf—61P 119
Edwick Ct. Wal X—1Zb 12
Edwina Gdns. Ilf—29Nc 46
Edwin Av. E6—41Qc 86
Edwin Clo. Bexh—51Bd 109
Edwin Clo. Rain—41Hd 88
Edwin Pl. Croy—74Tb 147
Edwin Rd. Dart—62Kd 133
Edwin Rd. Edgw—23Ta 39
Edwin Rd. Lea—97S 174
Edwin Rd. Twic—60Ga 100
Edwin's Mead. E9—35Ac 64
Edwin St. E1—42Yb 84
Edwin St. E16—43Jc 85
Edwin St. Grav—9D 114
Edwin Ware Ct. Pinn—26Y 37
Edwyn Clo. Barn—16Ya 22
Effie Pl. SW6—52Cb 103
Effie Rd. SW6—52Cb 103
Effingham Clo. Sutt—80Db 145
Effingham Comn. Rd. Lea —95W 174
Effingham Ct. Wok—90B 156
Effingham Rd. N8—29Qb 42
Effingham Rd. SE12—57Gc 107
Effingham Rd. Croy—73Pb 146
Effingham Rd. Surb—73Ka 142
Effort St. SW17—64Gb 125
Effra Pde. SW2—57Qb 104
Effra Rd. SW2—57Qb 104
Effra Rd. SW19—65Db 125
Egan Way. SE16—50Xb 83
Egan Way. Hay—45U 76
Egbert St. NW1—39Jb 62
Egerton Av. Swan—66Hd 132
Egerton Clo. Dart—60Kd 111
Egerton Clo. Pinn—28W 36
Egerton Cres. SW3 —49Gb 81 (5E 202)
Egerton Dri. SE10—53Dc 106
Egerton Gdns. NW4—28Xa 40
Egerton Gdns. NW10—39Ya 60
Egerton Gdns. SW3 —48Gb 81 (4D 202)
Egerton Gdns. W13—44Ka 78
Egerton Gdns. Ilf—34Vc 67
Egerton Gdns. M. SW3 —48Gb 81 (4E 202)
Egerton Pl. SW3—48Gb 81 (4E 202)
Egerton Pl. Wey—79S 140
Egerton Rd. N16—31Vb 63
Egerton Rd. SE25—69Ub 127
Egerton Rd. N Mald—70Va 124
Egerton Rd. Slou—2C 72
Egerton Rd. Twic—59Ga 100
Egerton Rd. Wemb—38Pa 59
Egerton Rd. Wey—79S 140
Egerton Ter. SW3 —48Gb 81 (4E 202)
Egg Hall. Epp—1Wc 15
Egham By-Pass. Egh—64B 118
Egham Clo. SW19—61Ab 124
Egham Clo. Sutt—75Ab 144
Egham Cres. Sutt—76Za 144
Egham Hill. Egh—65A 118
Egham Hill. Egh—5P 117
Egham Rd. E13—43Kc 85
Eglantine La. F'ham & S Dar, Dart—73Qd 153
Eglantine Rd. SW18—57Eb 103
Egleston Rd. Mord—72Db 145
Egley Dri. Wok—10G 188
Egley Rd. Wok—91A 172
Egley Rd. Wok—10G 188
Eglington Rd. E4—17Fc 27
Eglington Rd. Swans—58Be 113
Eglinton Hill. SE18—51Rc 108
Eglinton Rd. SE18—51Qc 108
Eglise Rd. Warl—89Ac 166
Egliston M. SW15—55Ya 102
Egliston Rd. SW15—55Ya 102
Egmont Av. Surb—74Pa 143
Egmont Pk. Rd. Tad—97Wa 178
Egmont Rd. N Mald—70Va 124
Egmont Rd. Surb—74Pa 143
Egmont Rd. Sutt—80Eb 145
Egmont Rd. W on T—73X 141
Egmont St. SE14—52Zb 106
Egmont Way. Tad—91Ab 178
Egremont Gdns. Slou—6E 72
Egremont Rd. SE27—62Qb 126
Egypt La. Slou—3F 52
Eight Acres. Slou—2A 72
Eighteenth Rd. Mitc—70Nb 126
Eighth Av. E12—35Pc 66
Eighth Av. Hay—46W 76
Eighth Av. Wey—75L 139
Eileen Rd. SE25—71Tb 147
Eisenhower Dri. E6—43Nc 86
Elaine Gro. NW5—36Jb 62
Elam Clo. SE5—54Rb 105
Elam St. SE5—54Rb 105
Eland Pl. Croy—76Rb 147
Eland Rd. SW11—55Hb 103
Eland Rd. Croy—76Rb 147
Elan Rd. S Ock—43Wd 90
Elba Pl. SE17—49Sb 83 (5E 206)
Elberon Av. Croy—72Lb 146
Elbe St. SW6—54Eb 103
Elborough Rd. SE25—71Wb 147
Elborough St. SW18—60Cb 103
Elbow Meadow. Slou—53H 97
Elbury Dri. E16—44Jc 85
Elcho St. SW11—52Gb 103
Elcot Av. SE15—52Xb 105
Elder Av. N8—29Nb 42
Elderbek Clo. Wal X—1Wb 11
Elderberry Gro. SE27—63Sb 127
Elderberry Rd. W5—47Na 79
Elder Ct. Bush, Wat—19Ga 20
Elderfield Rd. E5—35Yb 64
Elderfield Rd. Slou—7K 53
Elderfield Wlk. E11—29Kc 45
Elder Oak Clo. SE20—67Xb 127
Elder Oak Ct. SE20—67Xb 127
Elder Rd. SE27—64Sb 127
Elderslie Clo. Beck—72Dc 148
Elderslie Rd. SE9—57Qc 108
Elder St. E1—42Vb 83 (6K 195)
Elderton Rd. SE26—63Ac 128
Eldertree Pl. Mitc—67Lb 126
Eldertree Way. Mitc—67Lb 126
Elder Way. Rain—41Md 89
Elderwood Pl. SE27—64Sb 127
Eldon Av. Borwd—12Qa 21
Eldon Av. Croy—75Yb 148
Eldon Av. Houn—52Ca 99
Eldon Gro. NW3—36Fb 61
Eldon Pk. SE25—70Xb 127
Eldon Rd. E17—28Bc 44
Eldon Rd. N9—18Yb 26
Eldon Rd. N22—25Rb 43
Eldon Rd. W8—48Db 81
Eldon Rd. Cat—93Tb 181
Eldon St. EC2—43Tb 83 (1G 201)
Eldonwall Trading Est. NW2 —32Wa 60
Eldon Way. NW10—41Ra 79
Eldred Dri. Orp—75Yc 151
Eldred Gdns. Upm—31Ud 70
Eldred Rd. Bark—39Uc 66
Eldridge Clo. Felt—60W 98
Eleanor Av. Eps—82Ta 161
Eleanor Cres. NW7—22Za 40
Eleanor Cross Rd. Wal X—6Ac 12
Eleanor Gdns. Barn—15Za 22
Eleanor Gdns. Dag—34Bd 67
Eleanor Gro. SW13—55Ua 102
Eleanor Gro. Uxb—34R 56
Eleanor Rd. E8—37Xb 63
Eleanor Rd. E15—37Hc 65
Eleanor Rd. N11—23Nb 42
Eleanor Rd. Wal X—5Ac 12
Eleanor St. E3—41Cc 84
Eleanor Wlk. SE18—49Nc 86
Eleanor Way. Brtwd—22Zd 51
Electric Av. SW9—56Qb 104
Electric La. SW9—56Qb 104
Electric Pde. Surb—72Ma 143
Elephant & Castle. SE1 —49Rb 83 (5C 206)
Elephant La. SE16—47Yb 84
Elephant Rd. SE17 —49Sb 83 (5D 206)
Elers Rd. W13—47La 78
Elers Rd. Hay—49T 76
Eleven Acre Rise. Lou—13Pc 28
Eley Rd. N18—21Yb 44
Eley's Est. N18—22Zb 44
Elfindale Rd. SE24—57Sb 105
Elfin Gro. Tedd—64Ha 122
Elford Clo. SE3—56Lc 107
Elfort Rd. N5—35Qb 62
Elfrida Cres. SE6—63Cc 128
Elfrida Rd. Wat—15Y 19
Elf Row. E1—45Yb 84

Elfwine Rd.—Engadine St.

Elfwine Rd. W7—43Ga 78
Elgal Clo. Orp—78Rc 150
Elgar Av. SW16—69Nb 126
Elgar Av. W5—47Na 79
Elgar Av. Surb—74Qa 143
Elgar Clo. SE8—52Cc 106
Elgar Clo. Borwd—17Ma 21
Elgar Clo. Uxb—33Q 56
Elgar Gdns. Til—3C 114
Elgar St. SE16—48Ac 84
Elgin Av. W9—42Cb 81
Elgin Av. Ashf—65S 120
Elgin Av. Harr—26Ka 38
Elgin Av. Romf—23Rd 49
Elgin Ct. W9—42Db 81
Elgin Cres. W11—45Ab 80
Elgin Cres. Cat—94Wb 181
Elgin Cres. Houn—54U 98
Elgin Dri. N'wd—24U 36
Elgin Est. W9—42Cb 81
Elgin M. W11—44Ab 80
Elgin M. N. W9—41Db 81
Elgin M. S. W9—41Db 81
Elgin Rd. N22—26Lb 42
Elgin Rd. Croy—75Vb 147
Elgin Rd. Ilf—32Uc 66
Elgin Rd. Sutt—76Eb 145
Elgin Rd. Wall—79Lb 146
Elgin Rd. Wal X—2Yb 12
Elgin Rd. Wey—78Q 140
Elgood Av. N'wd—23W 36
Elgood Clo. W11—45Ab 80
Elham Clo. Brom—66Mc 129
Elia M. N1—40Rb 63 (2B 194)
Elias Pl. SW8—51Qb 104
Elia St. N1—40Rb 63 (2B 194)
Elibank Rd. SE9—56Pc 108
Elim Est. SE1—48Ub 83 (3G 207)
Elim St. SE1—(3G 207)
(in two parts)
Elim Way. E13—41Hc 85
Eliot Bank. SE23—61Xb 127
Eliot Cotts. SE3—54Gc 107
Eliot Dri. Harr—33Da 57
Eliot Hill. SE13—54Ec 106
Eliot Ho. Rich—58Pa 101
Eliot Pk. SE13—54Ec 106
Eliot Pl. SE3—54Gc 107
Eliot Rd. Dag—35Zc 67
Eliot Rd. Dart—57Rd 111
Eliot Sq. NW3—38Gb 61
Eliot Vale. SE3—54Fc 107
Elizabethan Clo. Stai—59M 97
Elizabethan Way. Stai—59M 97
Elizabeth Av. N1—38Tb 63
Elizabeth Av. Amer—11A 16
Elizabeth Av. Enf—13Rb 25
Elizabeth Av. Ilf—33Tc 66
Elizabeth Av. Stai—65L 119
Elizabeth Bri. SW1
—49Kb 82 (6K 203)
Elizabeth Clo. E14—44Dc 84
Elizabeth Clo. W9
—42Eb 81 (6A 190)
Elizabeth Clo. Barn—13Za 22
Elizabeth Clo. Romf—25Dd 48
Elizabeth Clo. Til—4D 114
Elizabeth Clyde Clo. N15—28Ub 43
Elizabeth Cotts. Rich—53Pa 101
Elizabeth Ct. SW1—(4E 204)
Elizabeth Ct. Grav—8C 114
Elizabeth Ct. Slou—7L 73
Elizabeth Ct. Wat—10V 4
Elizabeth Dri. Epp—8Uc 14
Elizabeth Gdns. W3—46Va 80
Elizabeth Gdns. Asc—10A 116
Elizabeth Gdns. Stan—23La 38
Elizabeth Gdns. Sun—69Y 121
Elizabeth M. NW3—37Hb 61
Elizabeth Pl. N15—28Tb 43
Elizabeth Ride. N9—17Xb 25
Elizabeth Rd. E6—39Mc 65
Elizabeth Rd. N15—29Ub 43
Elizabeth Rd. Brtwd—16Xd 32
Elizabeth St. SW1
—49Jb 82 (5J 203)
Elizabeth St. Grnh—57Ud 112
Elizabeth Ter. SE9—58Pc 108
Elizabeth Way. SE19—66Tb 127
Elizabeth Way. Felt—63Y 121
Elizabeth Way. Orp—71Yc 151
Elizabeth Way. Slou—9K 53
Elkington Point. SE11—(6K 205)
Elkington Rd. E13—42Kc 85
Elkins Rd. Slou—3J 53
Elkins, The. Romf—26Gd 48
Elkstone Rd. W10—43Bb 81
Ellaline Rd. W6—51Za 102
Ellanby Cres. N18—22Xb 43
Elland Rd. SE15—56Yb 106
Elland Rd. W on T—75Z 141
Ella Rd. N8—31Nb 62
Ellement Clo. Pinn—29Z 37
Ellenborough Pl. SW15—56Wa 102
Ellenborough Rd. N22—25Sb 43
Ellenborough Rd. Sidc—64Zc 131
Ellenbridge Way. S Croy
—81Ub 165
Ellen Clo. Brom—69Mc 129
Ellen Ct. N9—19Yb 26
Ellen St. E1—44Wb 83
Elleray Rd. Tedd—65Ha 122
Ellerby St. SW6—53Za 102
Ellerdale Clo. NW3—35Eb 61
Ellerdale Rd. NW3—36Eb 61
Ellerdale St. SE13—56Dc 106
Ellerdine Rd. Houn—56Fa 100
Ellerker Gdns. Rich—58Na 101
Ellerman Av. Twic—60Ba 99
Ellerman Rd. Til—4B 114
Ellerslie. Grav—9F 114
Ellerslie Gdns. NW10—39Wa 60
Ellerslie Rd. W12—46Xa 80
Ellerslie Sq. Industrial Est.
SW2—57Nb 104
Ellerton Gdns. Dag—38Yc 67
Ellerton Rd. SW13—53Wa 102
Ellerton Rd. SW18—60Fb 103
Ellerton Rd. SW20—66Wa 124
Ellerton Rd. Dag—38Yc 67
Ellerton Rd. Surb—75Pa 143
Ellery Rd. SE19—66Tb 127
Ellery St. SE15—54Xb 105
Ellesborough Clo. Wat—22Y 37
Ellesmere Av. NW7—20Ta 21
Ellesmere Av. Beck—68Dc 128
Ellesmere Clo. E11—29Hc 45
Ellesmere Clo. Ruis—31S 56
Ellesmere Dri. S Croy—86Xb 165
Ellesmere Gdns. Ilf—30Nc 46
Ellesmere Gro. Barn—15Bb 23
Ellesmere Rd. E3—40Ac 64
Ellesmere Rd. NW10—36Wa 60
Ellesmere Rd. W4—51Ta 101
Ellesmere Rd. Gnfd—42Ea 78
Ellesmere Rd. Twic—58La 100
Ellesmere Rd. Wey—80U 140
Ellesmere St. E14—44Dc 84
Elleswood Ct. Surb—73Ma 143
Ellice Rd. Oxt—100Hc 183
Elliman Av. Slou—5J 73
Elliman Sq. Slou—7K 73
Ellingfort Rd. E8—38Xb 63
Ellingham Rd. E15—35Fc 65
Ellingham Rd. W12—47Wa 80
Ellingham Rd. Chess—79Ma 143
Ellington Rd. N10—28Kb 42
Ellington Rd. Felt—63V 120
Ellington Rd. Houn—54Da 99
Ellington St. N7—37Qb 62
Elliot Clo. E15—38Gc 65
Elliot Gdns. Shep—70Q 120
Elliot Rd. NW4—30Xa 40
Elliot Rd. Brom—70Mc 129
Elliott Clo. Wemb—34Qa 59
Elliott Gdns. Romf—25Kd 49
Elliott Rd. SW9—52Rb 105
Elliott Rd. W4—49Ua 80
Elliott Rd. Stan—23Ja 38
Elliott Rd. T Hth—70Rb 127
Elliott's Ct. EC4—(2B 200)
Elliotts La. West—96Yc 185
Elliotts Row. SE11
—49Rb 83 (5C 206)
Elliott St. Grav—9F 114
Ellis Av. Ger X—25B 34
Ellis Av. Rain—43Jd 88
Ellis Av. Slou—7J 73
Ellis Clo. SE9—61Sc 130
Ellis Clo. Coul—92Pb 180
Elliscombe Rd. SE7—51Lc 107
Ellis Ct. W7—43Ha 78
Ellis Farm Clo. Wok—94A 172
Ellis Farm Clo. Wok—10G 188
Ellisfield Dri. SW15—59Wa 102
Ellis M. SE7—51Lc 107
Ellison Clo. Wind—5D 94
Ellison Gdns. S'hall—49Ba 77
Ellison Rd. SW13—54Va 102
Ellison Rd. SW16—66Mb 126
Ellison Rd. Sidc—60Tc 108
Ellis Rd. Coul—92Pb 180
Ellis Rd. Mitc—72Hb 145
Ellis St. SW1—49Jb 82 (5G 203)
Ellmore Clo. Romf—25Kd 49
Ellora Rd. SW16—64Mb 126
Ellsworth St. E2—41Xb 83
Ellwood Gdns. Wat—6Y 5
Elmar Grn. Slou—1E 72
Elmar Rd. N15—28Tb 43
Elm Av. W5—46Na 79
Elm Av. Ruis—32W 56
Elm Av. Upm—34Rd 69
Elm Av. Wat—17Aa 19
Elm Bank. N14—17Nb 24
Elmbank Av. Barn—14Ya 22
Elmbank Av. Egh—5M 117
Elm Bank Gdns. SW13—54Ua 102
Elmbank Way. W7—43Fa 78
Elmbidge La. Wok—91B 172
Elmbourne Dri. Belv—49Dd 88
Elmbourne Rd. SW17—62Kb 126
Elmbridge Av. Surb—71Ra 143
Elmbridge Clo. Ruis—30W 36
Elmbridge Dri. Ruis—29V 36
Elmbridge Rd. Ilf—23Wc 47
Elmbridge Wlk. E8—38Wb 63
Elmbrook Gdns. SE9—56Nc 108
Elmbrook Rd. Sutt—77Bb 145
Elm Clo. E11—30Kc 45
Elm Clo. N19—33Lb 62
Elm Clo. NW4—29Za 40
Elm Clo. SW20—70Ya 124
Elm Clo. Buck H—19Mc 27
Elm Clo. Cars—74Hb 145
Elm Clo. Dart—60Ld 111
Elm Clo. Harr—30Da 37
Elm Clo. Hay—44W 76
Elm Clo. Lea—94Ka 176
Elm Clo. Romf—25Dd 48
Elm Clo. Slou—7G 52
Elm Clo. S Croy—79Ub 147
Elm Clo. Surb—73Sa 143
Elm Clo. Twic—61Da 121
Elm Clo. Wal A—6Fc 13
Elm Clo. Warl—89Zb 166
Elm Clo. Wok—3G 188
Elm Clo. Wok—96J 173
(Send Marsh)
Elmcote Way. Rick—16P 17
Elm Ct. EC4—(4K 199)
Elm Ct. Wat—13X 19
Elm Ct. Wok—5A 188
Elmcourt Rd. SE27—61Rb 127
Elm Cres. W5—46Na 79
Elm Cres. King—67Na 123
Elm Croft. Slou—3N 95
Elmcroft Av. E11—29Kc 45
Elmcroft Av. N9—16Xb 25
Elmcroft Av. NW11—31Bb 61
Elmcroft Av. Sidc—58Wc 109
Elmcroft Clo. E11—28Kc 45
Elmcroft Clo. W5—44Ma 79
Elmcroft Clo. Chess—76Na 143
Elmcroft Clo. Felt—58V 98
Elmcroft Cres. NW11—31Ab 60
Elmcroft Cres. Harr—27Ca 37
Elmcroft Dri. Ashf—64Q 120
Elmcroft Dri. Chess—76Na 143
Elmcroft Gdns. NW9—29Qa 39
Elmcroft Rd. Orp—73Wc 151
Elmcroft St. E5—35Yb 64
Elmdale Rd. N13—22Pb 42
Elmdene. Surb—74Sa 143
Elmdene Av. Horn—29Pd 49
Elmdene Clo. Beck—72Bc 148
Elmdene Rd. SE18—50Rc 86
Elmdon Rd. Houn—54Aa 99
Elmdon Rd. Houn—55V 98
(Hatton)
Elm Dri. Harr—30Da 37
Elm Dri. Lea—95Ka 176
Elm Dri. Sun—68Y 121
Elm Dri. Swan—68Fd 132
Elm Dri. Wal X—1Ac 12
Elm Dri. Wind—10A 94
Elmer Av. Hav, Romf—20Gd 30
Elmer Clo. Enf—13Pb 24
Elmer Clo. Rain—38Jd 68
Elmer Cotts. Lea—95Ja 176
(in two parts)
Elmer Gdns. Edgw—24Ra 39
Elmer Gdns. Iswth—55Fa 100
Elmer Gdns. Rain—38Jd 68
Elmer Rd. SE6—59Ec 106
Elmers Dri. Tedd—65Ka 122
Elmers End Rd.—68Yb 128
SE20 1-81 & 2-82
Beck remainder
Elmerside Rd. Beck—70Ac 128
Elmers Rd. SE25—73Wb 147
Elmfield. Lea—95Ca 175
Elmfield Av. N8—29Nb 42
Elmfield Av. Mitc—67Jb 126
Elmfield Av. Tedd—64Ha 122
Elmfield Clo. Grav—10D 114
Elmfield Clo. Pot B—5Ab 8
Elmfield Pk. Brom—69Jc 129
Elmfield Rd. E4—19Ec 26
Elmfield Rd. E17—30Zb 44
Elmfield Rd. N2—27Fb 41
Elmfield Rd. SW17—61Jb 126
Elmfield Rd. Brom—69Jc 129
Elmfield Rd. Pot B—4Ab 8
Elmfield Rd. S'hall—48Aa 77
Elmfield Way. S Croy—81Vb 165
Elm Friars Wlk. NW1—38Mb 62
Elm Gdns. N2—27Eb 41
Elm Gdns. Enf—10Tb 11
Elm Gdns. Eps—91Ya 178
Elm Gdns. Esh—79Ha 142
Elm Gdns. Mitc—70Mb 126
Elmgate Av. Felt—62Y 121
Elmgate Gdns. Edgw—22Sa 39
Elm Grn. W3—44Ua 80
Elm Gro. N8—30Nb 42
Elm Gro. NW2—35Za 60
Elm Gro. SE15—54Vb 105
Elm Gro. SW19—66Ab 124
Elm Gro. Cat—94Ub 181
Elm Gro. Eps—86Sa 161
Elm Gro. Eri—52Fd 110
Elm Gro. Harr—31Ca 57
Elm Gro. Horn—30Nd 49
Elm Gro. King—67Na 123
Elm Gro. Orp—74Vc 151
Elm Gro. Sutt—77Db 145
Elm Gro. Wat—9W 4
Elm Gro. W Dray—45P 75
Elm Gro. Wfd G—22Hc 45
Elmgrove Clo. Wok—7A 188
Elmgrove Cres. Harr—29Ja 38
Elmgrove Gdns. Harr—29Ja 38
Elm Gro. Pde. Wall—76Jb 146
Elm Gro. Rd. SW13—54Wa 102
Elm Gro. Rd. W5—47Na 79
Elm Gro. Rd. Cob—88Z 159
Elmgrove Rd. Croy—73Xb 147
Elmgrove Rd. Harr—29Ha 38
Elmgrove Rd. Wey—76Q 140
Elmhall Gdns. E11—30Kc 45
Elmhurst. Belv—51Ad 109
Elmhurst Av. N2—27Fb 41
Elmhurst Av. Mitc—66Kb 126
Elmhurst Dri. E18—26Jc 45
Elmhurst Dri. Horn—32Ld 69
Elmhurst Rd. E7—38Kc 65
Elmhurst Rd. N17—26Vb 43
Elmhurst Rd. SE9—61Nc 130
Elmhurst Rd. Enf—9Yb 12
Elmhurst Rd. Slou—48C 74
Elmhurst St. SW4—55Mb 104
Elmhurst Way. Lou—17Pc 28
Elmington Clo. Bex—58Dd 110
Elmington Rd. SE5—52Tb 105
Elmira St. SE13—55Dc 106
Elm La. SE6—61Bc 128
Elm La. Wok—91Q 174
Elm Lawn Clo. Uxb—38N 55
Elmlea Dri. Hay—43U 76
Elmlee Clo. Chst—65Pc 130
Elmley Clo. E6—43Nc 86
Elmley St. SE18—49Tc 86
Elm M. Rich—58Pa 101
Elmore Rd. E11—34Ec 64
Elmore Rd. Coul—93Hb 179
Elmore Rd. Enf—10Zb 12
Elmores. Lou—13Qc 28
Elmore St. N1—38Tb 63
Elm Pk. SW2—58Pb 104
Elm Pk. Stan—22Ka 38
Elm Pk. Av. N15—29Vb 43
Elm Pk. Av. Horn—35Jd 68
Elm Pk. Gdns. NW4—29Za 40
Elm Pk. Gdns. SW10
—50Fb 81 (7B 202)
Elm Pk. Gdns. S Croy—82Yb 166
Elm Pk. La. SW3—50Fb 81
Elm Pk. Rd. E10—32Ac 64
Elm Pk. Rd. N3—24Bb 41
Elm Pk. Rd. N21—17Sb 25
Elm Pk. Rd. SE25—69Vb 127
Elm Pk. Rd. SW3—51Fb 103
Elm Pk. Rd. Pinn—26Y 37
Elm Pas. Barn—14Bb 23
Elm Pl. SW7—50Fb 81 (7B 202)
Elm Rd. E7—37Hc 65
Elm Rd. E11—33Fc 65
Elm Rd. E17—29Ec 44
Elm Rd. SW14—55Sa 101
Elm Rd. Barn—14Bb 23
Elm Rd. Beck—68Bc 128
Elm Rd. Chess—77Na 143
Elm Rd. Dart—60Md 111
Elm Rd. Eps—79Va 144
Elm Rd. Eri—53Jd 110
Elm Rd. Esh—79Ha 142
Elm Rd. Felt—60T 98
Elm Rd. Grav—2E 136
Elm Rd. Grays—51Ee 113
Elm Rd. Grnh—58Ud 112
Elm Rd. Houn—54Aa 99
Elm Rd. King—67Pa 123
Elm Rd. Lea—94Ka 176
Elm Rd. N Mald—69Ta 123
Elm Rd. Orp—80Wc 151
Elm Rd. Purl—85Rb 165
Elm Rd. Romf—26Dd 48
Elm Rd. Sidc—63Wc 131
Elm Rd. S Ock—46Td 90
Elm Rd. T Hth—70Tb 127
Elm Rd. Wall—74Jb 146
Elm Rd. Warl—89Zb 166
Elm Rd. Wemb—36Na 59
Elm Rd. West—97Uc 184
Elm Rd. Wind—5F 94
Elm Rd. Wok—87B 156
(Horsell)
Elm Rd. Wok—6G 188
(Mount Hermon)
Elm Rd. W. Sutt—73Bb 145
Elm Row. NW3—33Eb 61
Elmroyd Av. Pot B—5Bb 9
Elmroyd Clo. Pot B—5Bb 9
Elms Av. N10—27Kb 42
Elms Av. NW4—29Za 40
Elmscott Gdns. N21—16Sb 25
Elmscott Rd. Brom—64Hc 129
Elms Ct. Wemb—35Ja 58
Elms Cres. SW4—58Lb 104
Elmscroft Gdns. Pot B—4Bb 9
Elmsdale Rd. E17—28Bc 44
Elms Farm Rd. Horn—36Ld 69
Elms Gdns. Dag—35Bd 67
Elms Gdns. Wemb—35Ja 58
Elmshaw Rd. SW15—57Wa 102
Elmshorn. Eps—88Ya 162
Elmshott La. Slou—5C 72
Elmshurst Cres. N2—28Fb 41
Elmside. Croy—79Dc 148
Elmside Rd. Wemb—34Qa 59
Elms La. Wemb—34Ja 58
Elmsleigh Av. Harr—28Ka 38
Elmsleigh Rd. Stai—64H 119
Elmsleigh Rd. Twic—61Fa 122
Elmsleigh Shopping Centre.
Stai—63H 119
Elmslie Clo. Eps—86Ta 161
Elmslie Clo. Wfd G—23Pc 46
Elms M. W2—45Fb 81 (4B 196)
Elms Pk. Av. Wemb—35Ja 58
Elms Rd. SW4—57Lb 104
Elms Rd. Ger X—24A 34
Elms Rd. Harr—24Ga 38
Elmstead Av. Chst—64Pc 130
Elmstead Av. Wemb—32Na 59
Elmstead Clo. N20—19Cb 23
Elmstead Clo. Eps—78Ua 144
Elmstead Clo. Sev—94Gd 186
Elmstead Gdns. Wor Pk
—76Wa 144
Elmstead Glade. Chst—65Pc 130
Elmstead La. Chst—66Nc 130
Elmstead Rd. Eri—53Gd 110
Elmstead Rd. Ilf—33Uc 66
Elmstead Rd. Wey—85J 157
Elmsted Cres. Well—51Yc 109
Elms, The. SW13—55Va 102
Elmstone Rd. SW6—53Cb 103
Elm St. WC1—42Pb 82 (6J 193)
Elmsway. Ashf—64Q 120
Elmsworth Av. Houn—54Da 99
Elm Ter. NW2—34Cb 61
Elm Ter. NW3—35Gb 61
Elm Ter. SE9—58Qc 108
Elm Ter. Grays—51Xd 112
Elm Ter. Harr—25Fa 38
Elm Ter. Stan—22La 38
Elmton Way. E5—34Wb 63
★Elmtree Av. Brtwd—9Vd
Elm Tree Av. Esh—73Fa 142
Elm Tree Clo. NW8
—41Fb 81 (3B 190)
Elm Tree Clo. Ashf—64R 120
Elm Tree Clo. Cher—75G 138
Elm Tree Clo. N'holt—40Ba 57
Elm Tree Clo. Wey—85N 157
Elm Tree Rd. NW8
—41Fb 81 (3B 190)
Elmtree Rd. Tedd—63Ga 122
Elm Wlk. NW3—33Cb 61
Elm Wlk. SW20—70Ya 124
Elm Wlk. Orp—76Pc 150
Elm Wlk. Rad—8Ha 6
Elm Wlk. Romf—27Jd 48
Elm Way. N11—23Jb 42
Elm Way. NW10—35Ua 60
Elm Way. Brtwd—21Wd 50
Elm Way. Eps—78Ta 143
Elmway. Grays—46Ee 91
Elm Way. Rick—18K 17
Elm Way. Wor Pk—76Ya 144
Elmwood Av. N13—22Nb 42
Elmwood Av. Borwd—14Ra 21
Elmwood Av. Felt—61W 120
Elmwood Av. Harr—29Ja 38
Elmwood Clo. Asht—89Ma 161
Elmwood Clo. Wall—75Kb 146
Elmwood Ct. Wemb—34Ja 58
Elmwood Cres. NW9—28Sa 39
Elmwood Dri. Bex—59Ad 109
Elmwood Dri. Eps—79Wa 144
Elmwood Gdns. W7—44Ga 78
Elmwood Pk. Ger X—32A 54
Elmwood Rd. SE24—57Tb 105
Elmwood Rd. W4—51Sa 101
Elmwood Rd. Croy—73Rb 147
Elmwood Rd. Mitc—69Hb 125
Elmwood Rd. Slou—5M 73
Elmwood Rd. Wok—7A 188
Elmworth Gro. SE21—61Tb 127
Elnathan M. W9—42Db 81
Elphinstone Rd. E17—26Bc 44
Elphinstone St. N5—35Rb 63
Elrick Clo. Eri—51Gd 110
Elrington Rd. E8—37Wb 63
Elruge Clo. W Dray—48M 75
Elsa Rd. Well—54Xc 109
Elsa St. E1—43Ac 84
Elsdale St. E9—37Yb 64
Elsden M. E2—40Yb 64
Elsden Rd. N17—25Vb 43
Elsdon Rd. Wok—6D 188
Elsenham Rd. E12—36Qc 66
Elsenham St. SW18—60Bb 103
Elsham Rd. E11—35Gc 65
Elsham Rd. W14—47Ab 80
Elsiedene Rd. N21—17Sb 25
Elsiemaud Rd. SE4—57Bc 106
Elsie Rd. SE22—56Vb 105
Elsinge Rd. Enf—8Xb 11
Elsinore Av. Stai—59N 97
Elsinore Rd. SE23—60Ac 106
Elsley Rd. SW11—55Hb 103
Elspeth Rd. SW11—56Hb 103
Elspeth Rd. Wemb—36Na 59
Elsrick Av. Mord—71Cb 145
Elstan Way. Croy—73Ac 148
Elsted St. SE17—49Tb 83 (6G 207)
Elstow Clo. SE9—57Qc 108
(in two parts)
Elstow Clo. Ruis—31Z 57
Elstow Gdns. Dag—39Ad 67
Elstow Rd. Dag—39Ad 67
Elstree Gdns. N9—18Xb 25
Elstree Gdns. Belv—49Ad 87
Elstree Gdns. Ilf—36Sc 66
Elstree Hill. Brom—66Gc 129
Elstree Hill N. Borwd—15Ma 21
Elstree Hill S. Borwd—17Ma 21
Elstree Rd. Bush, Wat & Borwd
—17Fa 20
Elstree Way. Borwd—12Ra 21
Elswick Rd. SE13—54Dc 106
Elswick St. SW6—54Eb 103
Elsworthy. Th Dit—72Ga 142
Elsworthy Rise. NW3—38Gb 61
Elsworthy Rd. NW3—39Gb 61
Elsworthy Ter. NW3—38Gb 61
Elsynge Rd. SW18—57Fb 103
Eltham Grn. SE9—57Mc 107
Eltham Grn. Rd. SE9—56Lc 107
Eltham High St. SE9—58Pc 108
Eltham Hill. SE9—57Mc 107
Eltham Pal. Rd. SE9—58Lc 107
Eltham Pk. Gdns. SE9—56Qc 108
Eltham Rd.—57Jc 107
SE12 1-101 & 2-120
SE9 remainder
Elthiron Rd. SW6—53Cb 103
Elthorne Av. W7—47Ha 78
Elthorne Ct. Felt—60Y 99
Elthorne Pk. Rd. W7—47Ja 78
Elthorne Rd. N19—33Mb 62
Elthorne Rd. NW9—31Ta 59
Elthorne Rd. Uxb—40M 55
Elthorne Way. NW9—30Ta 39
Elthruda Rd. SE13—58Fc 107
Eltisley Rd. Ilf—35Rc 66
Elton Av. Barn—15Bb 23
Elton Av. Gnfd—37Ha 58
Elton Av. Wemb—36Ka 58
Elton Clo. Tedd—66La 122
Elton Pl. N16—36Ub 63
Elton Rd. King—67Pa 123
Elton Rd. Purl—84Lb 164
Elton Way. Wat—12Da 19
Eltringham St. SW18—56Eb 103
Elvaston M. SW7
—48Eb 81 (4A 202)
Elvaston Pl. SW7
—48Eb 81 (4A 202)
Elveden Clo. Wok—89K 157
Elveden Pl. NW10—40Qa 59
Elveden Rd. NW10—40Qa 59
Elvedon Rd. Cob—83X 159
Elvendon Rd. N13—23Nb 42
Elver Gdns. E2—41Wb 83
Elverson Rd. SE8—54Dc 106
Elverton St. SW1
—49Mb 82 (5D 204)
Elvet Av. Romf—28Ld 49
Elvington Grn. Brom—71Hc 149
Elvington La. NW9—25Ua 40
Elvino Rd. SE26—64Ac 128
Elvis Rd. NW2—37Ya 60
Elwick Rd. S Ock—44Yd 90
Elwill Way. Beck—70Ec 128
Elwill Way. Grav—7B 136
Elwin St. E2—41Wb 83
Elwood St. N5—34Rb 63
Elwyn Gdns. SE12—59Jc 107
Ely Av. Slou—3G 72
Ely Clo. Eri—54Hd 110
Ely Clo. N Mald—68Va 124
Ely Ct. EC1—(1A 200)
Ely Gdns. Borwd—15Ta 21
Ely Gdns. Dag—34Ed 68
Ely Gdns. Ilf—31Nc 66
Elyne Rd. N4—30Qb 42
Ely Pl. EC1—43Qb 82 (1A 200)
Ely Pl. Wfd G—23Qc 46
Ely Rd. E10—31Ec 64
Ely Rd. Croy—71Tb 147
Ely Rd. Houn—55Y 99
Ely Rd. Houn—54V 98
(Hatton)
Elysian Rd. Orp—72Vc 151
Elysium St. SW6—54Bb 103
Elystan Clo. Wall—81Lb 164
Elystan Pl. SW3—50Hb 81 (7E 202)
Elystan St. SW3—49Gb 81 (6D 202)
Elystan Wlk. N1—39Qb 62 (1K 193)
Emanuel Av. W3—44Sa 79
Embankment. SW15—54Za 102
Embankment Gdns. SW3
—51Hb 103
Embankment Pl. WC2
—46Nb 82 (6G 199)
Embankment, The. Twic—60Ja 100
Embankment, The. Wray, Stai
—9N 95
Embassy Ct. Sidc—62Xc 131
Embassy Ct. Well—55Xc 109
Emba St. SE16—47Wb 83
Ember Clo. Orp—73Sc 150
Ember Clo. Wey—78M 139
Embercourt Rd. Th Dit—72Ga 142
Ember Farm Av. E Mol—72Fa 142
Ember Farm Way. E Mol
—72Fa 142
Ember Gdns. Th Dit—73Ga 142
Ember La. Esh & E Mol—73Fa 142
Ember Rd. Slou—48D 74
Embleton Rd. SE13—56Dc 106
Embleton Rd. Wat—20W 18
Embleton Wlk. Hmptn—64Ba 121
Embry Clo. Stan—21Ja 38
Embry Dri. Stan—23Ja 38
Embry Way. Stan—21Ja 38
Emden St. SW6—53Db 103
Emerald Ct. Slou—7J 73
Emerald Gdns. Dag—32Cd 68
Emerald St. WC1
—43Pb 82 (7H 193)
Emerson Dri. Horn—31Md 69
Emerson Gdns. Harr—30Pa 39
Emerson Pk. Romf—29Gd 48
Emerson Rd. Ilf—31Qc 66
Emerson St. SE1
—46Sb 83 (6D 200)
Emerton Rd. Lea—93Ea 176
Emery Hill St. SW1
—48Lb 82 (4C 204)
Emery St. SE1—48Qb 82 (3A 206)
Emes Rd. Eri—52Ed 110
Emily Pl. N7—35Qb 62
Emlyn Gdns. W12—47Ua 80
Emlyn La. Lea—94Ja 176
Emlyn Rd. W12—47Ua 80
Emmanuel Rd. SW12—60Lb 104
Emmanuel Rd. N'wd—24V 36
Emma Rd. E13—40Hc 65
Emma St. E2—40Xb 63
Emmaus Way. Chig—22Qc 46
Emmetts Clo. Wok—5G 188
Emmett St. E14—45Bc 84
Emmott Av. Ilf—29Sc 46
Emmott Clo. E1—42Ac 84
Emmott Clo. NW11—30Eb 41
Emms Pas. King—68Ma 123
Emperor's Ga. SW7—48Eb 81
Empire Av. N18—22Sb 43
Empire Pde. N18—23Tb 43
Empire Rd. Gnfd—39Ka 58
Empire Way. Wemb—35Pa 59
Empire Wharf Rd. E14—49Fc 85
Empire Yd. N7—34Nb 62
Empress Av. E4—24Dc 44
Empress Av. E12—33Lc 65
Empress Av. Ilf—33Pc 66
Empress Av. Wfd G—24Hc 45
Empress Dri. Chst—65Rc 130
Empress Pl. SW6—50Cb 81
Empress Rd. Grav—9G 114
Empress St. SE17—51Sb 105
Empson St. E3—42Dc 84
Emsworth Clo. N9—18Yb 26
Emsworth Rd. Ilf—26Rc 46
Emsworth St. SW2—61Pb 126
Emu Rd. SW8—54Kb 104
Ena Rd. SW16—69Nb 126
Enborne Grn. S Ock—43Wd 90
Enbrook St. W10—41Ab 80
Endale Clo. Cars—75Hb 145
Endeavour Way. SW19—63Db 125
Endeavour Way. Bark—40Wc 67
Endeavour Way. Croy—73Nb 146
Endell St. WC2—44Nb 82 (2F 199)
Enderby St. SE10—50Gc 85
Enderley Clo. Harr—26Ga 38
Enderley Rd. Harr—25Ga 38
Endersby Rd. Barn—15Ya 22
Endersleigh Gdns. NW4—28Wa 40
Endlebury Rd. E4—19Ec 26
Endlesham Rd. SW12—59Jb 104
Endsleigh Clo. S Croy—82Yb 166
Endsleigh Gdns. WC1
—42Mb 82 (5D 192)
Endsleigh Gdns. Ilf—33Pc 66
Endsleigh Gdns. Surb—72La 142
Endsleigh Gdns. W on T—78Y 141
Endsleigh Pl. WC1
—42Mb 82 (5E 192)
Endsleigh Rd. W13—45Ja 78
Endsleigh Rd. S'hall—49Aa 77
Endsleigh St. WC1
—42Mb 82 (5D 192)
End Way. Surb—73Qa 143
Endwell Rd. SE4—54Ac 106
Endymion Rd. N4—31Qb 62
Endymion Rd. SW2—58Pb 104
Enfield Clo. Uxb—40M 55
Enfield Rd. N1—38Ub 63
Enfield Rd. W3—47Ra 79
Enfield Rd. Bren—50Ma 79
Enfield Rd. Enf—14Mb 24
Enfield Rd. Houn—54U 98
Enfield Rd. E. Bren—50Ma 79
Enford St. W1—43Hb 81 (7F 191)
Engadine Clo. Croy—76Vb 147
Engadine St. SW18—60Cb 103

Engate St. SE13—56Ec 106
Engayne Gdns. Upm—32Rd 69
Engel Pk. NW7—23Ya 40
Engine Ct. SW1—(7C 198)
Engineer Clo. SE18—51Qc 108
Engineers Dri. Bush, Wat—14Ca 19
Engineers Way. Wemb—35Qa 59
England's La. NW3—37Hb 61
Englands La. Lou—12Qc 28
Englefield Clo. Croy—72Sb 147
Englefield Clo. Enf—12Qb 24
Englefield Clo. Orp—70Vc 131
Englefield Cres. Orp—70Vc 131
Englefield Path. Orp—70Wc 131
Englefield Rd. N1—38Tb 63
Englefield Rd. Wok—5A 188
Englehart Dri. Felt—58V 98
Engleheart Rd. SE6—59Dc 106
Englehurst. Egh—5N 117
Englewood Rd. SW12—58Kb 104
Engliff La. Wok—88J 157
English Gdns. Stai—7P 95
English Grounds. SE1 —46Ub 83 (7H 201)
English St. E3—42Bc 84
Enid St. SE16—48Vb 83 (3K 207)
Enkel St. N7—34Pb 62
Enmore Av. SE25—71Wb 147
Enmore Gdns. SW14—57Ta 101
Enmore Rd. SE25—71Wb 147
Enmore Rd. SW15—56Ya 102
Enmore Rd. S'hall—42Ca 77
Ennerdale Av. Horn—36Jd 68
Ennerdale Av. Stan—27La 38
Ennerdale Cres. Slou—3A 72
Ennerdale Dri. NW9—29Ua 40
Ennerdale Gdns. Wemb—32La 58
Ennerdale Rd. Bexh—53Cd 110
Ennerdale Rd. Rich—54Pa 101
Ennersdale Rd. SE13—57Fc 107
Ennismore Av. W4—49Va 80
Ennismore Av. Gnfd—37Ga 58
Ennismore Gdns. SW7 —47Gb 81 (3D 202)
Ennismore Gdns. Th Dit—72Ga 142
Ennismore Gdns. M. SW7 —48Gb 81 (3D 202)
Ennismore M. SW7 —48Gb 81 (3D 202)
Ennismore St. SW7 —48Gb 81 (3D 202)
Ennis Rd. N4—32Qb 62
Ennis Rd. SE18—51Sc 108
Ensign Clo. Stai—60M 97
Ensign Dri. N13—20Sb 25
Ensign St. E1—45Wb 83
Ensign Way. Stai—60M 97
Enslin Rd. SE9—59Qc 108
Ensor M. SW7—50Fb 81 (7B 202)
Enstone Rd. Enf—13Ac 26
Enstone Rd. Uxb—34P 55
Enterprise Business Pk. E14 —47Dc 84
Enterprise Way. SW18—56Cb 103
Enterprise Way. Tedd—65Ha 122
Epirus M. SW6—52Cb 103
Epirus Rd. SW6—52Bb 103
Epping Clo. Romf—27Dd 48
Epping Glade. E4—16Ec 26
Epping New Rd. Buck H & Lou —19Kc 27
Epping Pl. N1—37Qb 62
Epping Rd. Epp—1Yc 15
Epping Rd. Epp—7Pc 14
(Epping Forest)
Epping Way. E4—16Dc 26
Epple Rd. SW6—53Bb 103
Epsom Clo. Bexh—55Dd 110
Epsom Clo. N'holt—36Ba 57
Epsom Gap. Lea—87Ka 160
Epsom La. N. Eps & Tad—91Xa 178
Epsom La. S. Tad—93Ya 178
Epsom Rd. E10—30Ec 44
Epsom Rd. Asht—90Pa 161
Epsom Rd. Croy—77Qb 146
Epsom Rd. Eps—83Va 162
Epsom Rd. Ilf—30Vc 47
Epsom Rd. Lea—93Ka 176
Epsom Rd. Sutt & Mord—73Bb 145
Epsom Sq. Houn—54V 98
Epsom Way. Horn—35Pd 69
Epstein Rd. SE28—46Wc 87
Epworth Rd. Iswth—52Ka 100
Epworth St. EC2—42Tb 83 (6G 195)
Erasmus St. SW1 —49Mb 82 (6E 204)
Erby Rd. Grays—50De 91
Erconwald St. W12—44Va 80
Eresby Dri. Beck—74Cc 148
Eresby Pl. NW6—38Cb 61
Erica Clo. Slou—5C 72
Erica Ct. Swan—70Gd 132
Erica Ct. Wok—7G 188
Erica Gdns. Croy—76Dc 148
Erica St. W12—45Wa 80
Eric Clo. E7—35Jc 65
Ericcson Clo. SW18—57Cb 103
Eric Rd. E7—35Jc 65
Eric Rd. NW10—37Va 60
Eric Rd. Romf—31Zc 67
Eric St. E3—42Bc 84
Eridge Rd. W4—48Ta 79
Erin Clo. Brom—66Gc 129
Erindale. SE18—51Tc 108
Erindale Ter. SE18—51Tc 108
Eriswell Cres. W on T—79U 140
Eriswell Rd. W on T—78V 140
Erith Cres. Romf—25Ed 48
Erith High St. Eri—50Gd 88
Erith Rd. Belv & Eri—50Dd 88
Erith Rd. Bexh & Eri—56Dd 110
Erkenwald Clo. Cher—72G 138
Erlanger Rd. SE14—53Zb 106
Erlesmere Gdns. W13—48Ja 78
Ermine Clo. Houn—54Y 99
Ermine Clo. Wal X—3Xb 11
Ermine Rd. N15—30Vb 43
Ermine Rd. SE13—56Dc 106
Ermine Side. Enf—15Wb 25
Ermington Rd. SE9—61Sc 130
Ermyn Clo. Lea—93Ma 177
Ermyn Way. Lea—93Ma 177
Ernald Av. E6—40Nc 66
Ernan Clo. S Ock—43Wd 90
Ernan Rd. S Ock—43Wd 90
Erncroft Way. Twic—58Ha 100
Ernest Av. SE27—63Rb 127
Ernest Clo. Beck—71Cc 148
Ernest Gdns. W4—51Ra 101
Ernest Gro. Beck—71Bc 148
Ernest Rd. Horn—30Nd 49
Ernest Rd. King—68Ra 123
Ernest Sq. King—68Ra 123
Ernest St. E1—42Zb 84
Ernle Rd. SW20—66Xa 124
Ernshaw Pl. SW15—57Ab 102
Erpingham Rd. SW15—55Ya 102
Erridge Rd. SW19—68Cb 125
Erriff Dri. S Ock—43Wd 90
Errington Rd. W9—42Bb 81
Errol Gdns. Hay—42X 77
Errol Gdns. N Mald—70Wa 124
Erroll Rd. Romf—28Hd 48
Errol St. EC1—42Sb 83 (6E 194)
Erskine Clo. Sutt—76Gb 145
Erskine Cres. N17—28Xb 43
Erskine Hill. NW11—28Cb 41
Erskine Rd. E17—28Bc 44
Erskine Rd. NW3—38Hb 61
Erskine Rd. Sutt—77Fb 145
Erwood Rd. SE7—50Nc 86
Esam Way. SW16—64Qb 126
Escott Gdns. SE9—63Nc 130
Escot Way. Barn—15Ya 22
Escreet Gro. SE18—49Qc 86
Esdaile Gdns. Upm—31Td 70
Esher Av. Romf—30Ed 48
Esher Av. Sutt—76Za 144
Esher Av. W on T—73W 140
Esher By-Pass. Cob, Esh, Lea & Chess—85V 158 to 76La 143
Esher Clo. Bex—60Ad 109
Esher Clo. Esh—78Da 141
Esher Cres. Houn—54V 98
Esher Gdns. SW19—61Za 124
Esher Grn. Esh—77Da 141
Esher M. Mitc—69Jb 126
Esher Pk. Av. Esh—77Ea 142
Esher Pl. Av. Esh—77Da 141
Esher Rd. E Mol—72Fa 142
Esher Rd. Ilf—34Uc 66
Esher Rd. W on T & Esh—78Z 141
Eskdale Av. N'holt—39Ba 57
Eskdale Clo. Wemb—33Ma 59
Eskdale Gdns. Purl—86Tb 165
Eskdale Rd. Bexh—54Cd 110
Eskdale Rd. Dart—60Sd 112
Eskdale Rd. Uxb—40K 55
Eskley Gdns. S Ock—43Xd 90
Eskmont Ridge. SE19—66Ub 127
Esk Rd. E13—42Kc 85
Esk Way. Romf—24Gd 48
Esmar Cres. NW9—31Wa 60
Esmeralda Rd. SE1—49Wb 83
Esmond Clo. Rain—38Kd 69
Esmond Rd. NW6—39Bb 61
Esmond Rd. W4—49Ta 79
Esmond St. SW15—56Ab 102
Esparto St. SW18—59Db 103
Essendene Clo. Cat—95Ub 181
Essendene Rd. Cat—95Ub 181
Essenden Rd. Belv—50Cd 88
Essenden Rd. S Croy—80Ub 147
Essendine Rd. W9—41Cb 81
Essex Av. Iswth—55Ga 100
Essex Av. Slou—3G 72
Essex Clo. E17—28Ac 44
Essex Clo. Mord—73Za 144
Essex Clo. Romf—28Dd 48
Essex Clo. Ruis—32Z 57
Essex Clo. Wey—77L 139
Essex Ct. EC4—(3K 199)
Essex Ct. SW13—54Va 102
Essex Gdns. N4—30Rb 43
Essex Gdns. Horn—29Qd 49
Essex Gdns. Stanf—7J 93
Essex Gro. SE19—65Tb 127
Essex La. K Lan & Abb L, Wat—5T 4
Essex Pk. N3—23Db 41
Essex Pk. M. W3—46Ua 80
Essex Pl. W4—49Sa 79
Essex Pl. Sq. W4—49Ta 79
Essex Rd. E4—18Gc 27
Essex Rd. E10—30Ec 44
Essex Rd. E12—36Nc 66
Essex Rd. E17—30Ac 44
Essex Rd. E18—26Kc 45
Essex Rd. N1—39Rb 63
Essex Rd. NW10—38Ua 60
Essex Rd. W3—45Sa 79
Essex Rd. W4—49Ta 79
Essex Rd. Bark—38Tc 66
Essex Rd. Borwd—13Qa 21
Essex Rd. Dag—36Ed 68
Essex Rd. Dart—58Md 111
Essex Rd. Enf—14Tb 25
Essex Rd. Grav—10C 114
Essex Rd. Grays—51Wd 112
Essex Rd. Long, Dart—68Zd 135
Essex Rd. Romf—28Dd 48
Essex Rd. Romf—31Yc 67
(Chadwell Heath)
Essex Rd. Wat—12X 19
Essex Rd. S. E11—31Fc 65
Essex St. E7—36Jc 65
Essex St. WC2—45Qb 82 (3K 199)
Essex Vs. W8—47Cb 81
Essex Way. Brtwd—23Yd 50
Essex Wharf. E5—33Zb 64
Essian St. E1—43Ac 84
Essoldo Way. Edgw—27Pa 39
Estate Way. E10—32Cc 64
Estcourt Rd. SE25—72Xb 147
Estcourt Rd. SW6—52Bb 103
Estcourt Rd. Wat—13Y 19
Estella Av. N Mald—70Xa 124
Estelle Rd. NW3—35Hb 61
Esterbrooke St. SW1 —49Mb 82 (6D 204)
Este Rd. SW11—55Gb 103
Esther Clo. N21—17Qb 24
Esther Rd. E11—31Gc 65
Estreham Rd. SW16—65Mb 126
Estridge Clo. Houn—56Ca 99
Eswyn Rd. SW17—63Hb 125
Etchingham Pk. Rd. N3—24Db 41
Etchingham Rd. E15—35Ec 64
Eternit Wlk. SW6—53Za 102
Etfield Gro. Sidc—64Xc 131
Ethelbert Clo. Brom—69Jc 129
Ethelbert Gdns. Ilf—29Pc 46
Ethelbert Rd. SW20—67Za 124
Ethelbert Rd. Brom—69Jc 129
Ethelbert Rd. Dart—63Nd 133
Ethelbert Rd. Eri—52Ed 110
Ethelbert Rd. Orp—69Zc 131
Ethelbert St. SW12—60Kb 104
Ethelburga Rd. Romf—25Pd 49
Ethelburga St. SW11—53Gb 103
Ethelden Av. N10—28Lb 42
Ethelden Rd. W12—46Xa 80
Ethel Rd. E16—44Kc 85
Ethel Rd. Ashf—64N 119
Ethel St. SE17—49Sb 83 (6E 206)
Ethel Ter. Orp—81Yc 169
Etheridge Rd. NW4—31Ya 60
Etheridge Rd. Lou—12Rc 28
Etherley Rd. N15—29Sb 43
Etherow St. SE22—59Wb 105
Etherstone Grn. SW16—63Qb 126
Etherstone Rd. SW16—63Qb 126
Ethnard Rd. SE15—51Xb 105
Ethorpe Clo. Ger X—29A 34
Ethronvi Rd. Bexh—55Ad 109
Etloe Rd. E10—33Cc 64
Eton Av. N12—24Eb 41
Eton Av. NW3—38Fb 61
Eton Av. Barn—16Gb 23
Eton Av. Houn—51Ba 99
Eton Av. N Mald—71Ta 143
Eton Av. Wemb—35Ka 58
Eton Clo. Slou—1L 95
Eton Clo. Wemb—35La 58
Eton College Rd. NW3—37Hb 61
Eton Ct. Wind—2H 95
Eton Garages. NW3—37Gb 61
Eton Gro. NW9—27Qa 39
Eton Gro. SE13—55Gc 107
Eton Pl. NW3—38Jb 62
Eton Rd. NW3—38Hb 61
Eton Rd. Hay—52V 98
Eton Rd. Ilf—35Sc 66
Eton Rd. Orp—77Xc 151
Eton Rd. Slou—10K 73
Eton Sq. Wind—2H 95
Eton St. Rich—57Na 101
Eton Vs. NW3—37Hb 61
Eton Wick Rd. Wind—9C 72
Etta St. SE8—51Ac 106
Etton Clo. Horn—33Nb 62
Ettrick St. E14—44Ec 84
(in two parts)
Etwell Pl. Surb—72Pa 143
Eugene Clo. Romf—28Ld 49
Eugenia Rd. SE16—49Yb 84
Eureka Rd. King—68Qa 123
Europa Pl. EC1—41Sb 83 (4D 194)
Europa Trading Est. Eri—50Fd 88
Europe Rd. SE18—48Pc 86
Eustace Rd. E6—41Nc 86
Eustace Rd. SW6—52Cb 103
Eustace Rd. Romf—31Zc 67
Euston Av. Wat—15V 18
Euston Rd. NW1 —41Mb 82 (6A 192)
Euston Rd. Croy—74Qb 146
Euston Sq. NW1 —41Mb 82 (4D 192)
Euston Sta. Colonnade. NW1 —41Mb 82 (4D 192)
Euston St. NW1—41Lb 82 (4C 192)
Euston Underpass. NW1—(5B 192)
Evandale Rd. SW9—54Qb 104
Evangelist Rd. NW5—35Kb 62
Evans Av. Wat—7V 4
Evans Clo. E8—37Vb 63
Evans Clo. Rick—15Q 18
Evansdale. Rain—41Hd 88
Evans Gro. Felt—61Ca 121
Evans Rd. SE6—61Gc 129
Evanston Av. E4—24Ec 44
Evanston Gdns. Ilf—30Nc 46
Eva Rd. Romf—31Yc 67
Evelina Rd. SE15—55Yb 106
Evelina Rd. SE20—66Yb 128
Eveline Rd. Mitc—67Hb 125
Evelyn Av. NW9—28Ta 39
Evelyn Av. Ruis—31U 56
Evelyn Clo. Twic—59Da 99
Evelyn Clo. Wok—8G 188
Evelyn Ct. E8—35Wb 63
Evelyn Cres. Sun—67V 120
Evelyn Dri. Pinn—24Z 37
Evelyn Gdns. SW7 —50Fb 81 (7B 202)
Evelyn Gdns. Rich—56Na 101
Evelyn Gro. W5—46Pa 79
Evelyn Gro. S'hall—44Ba 77
Evelyn Rd. E16—46Kc 85
Evelyn Rd. E17—28Ec 44
Evelyn Rd. SW19—65Db 125
Evelyn Rd. W4—48Ta 79
Evelyn Rd. Barn—14Hb 23
Evelyn Rd. Rich—55Na 101
Evelyn Rd. Rich—62La 122
(Ham)
Evelyn Rd. Sev—88Ld 171
Evelyns Clo. Uxb—44Q 76
Evelyn Sharp Clo. Romf—27Md 49
Evelyn St. SE8—50Ac 84
Evelyn Ter. Rich—55Na 101
Evelyn Wlk. N1—40Tb 63 (2F 195)
Evelyn Wlk. Brtwd—22Yd 50
Evelyn Way. Cob—88Ba 159
Evelyn Way. Sun—67V 120
Evelyn Way. Wall—77Mb 146
Evelyn Yd. W1—44Mb 82 (2D 198)
Evening Hill. Beck—66Ec 128
Evenwood Clo. SW15—57Ab 102
Everard Av. Brom—74Jc 149
Everard Av. Slou—7J 73
Everard La. Cat—94Xb 181
Everard Way. Wemb—34Na 59
Everdon Rd. SW13—51Wa 102
Everest Clo. Grav—2A 136
Everest Ct. Wok—4B 188
Everest Pl. E14—43Ec 84
Everest Pl. Swan—70Fd 132
Everest Rd. SE9—57Pc 108
Everest Rd. Stai—59M 97
Everett Clo. Pinn—27V 36
Everett Wlk. Belv—50Bd 87
Everglade. West—90Mc 167
Everglade Strand. NW9—25Va 40
Evergreen Oak Av. Wind—5L 95
Evergreen Way. Hay—45V 76
Evering Rd.—34Vb 63
N16 1-183 & 2-158
E5 remainder
Everington Rd. N10—26Hb 41
Everington St. W6—51Za 102
Everitt Rd. NW10—41Ta 79
Everlands Clo. Wok—90A 156
Everleigh St. N4—32Pb 62
Eve Rd. E11—35Gc 65
Eve Rd. E15—40Gc 65
Eve Rd. N17—27Ub 43
Eve Rd. Iswth—56Ja 100
Eve Rd. Wok—87D 156
Eversfield Gdns. NW7—23Ua 40
Eversfield Rd. Rich—54Pa 101
Eversholt St. NW1 —40Lb 62 (1B 192)
Evershot Rd. N4—32Pb 62
Eversleigh Gdns. Upm—32Td 70
Eversleigh Rd. E6—39Mc 65
Eversleigh Rd. N3—24Bb 41
Eversleigh Rd. SW11—55Hb 103
Eversleigh Rd. Barn—15Eb 23
Eversley Av. Bexh—54Fd 110
Eversley Av. Wemb—33Qa 59
Eversley Clo. N21—16Pb 24
Eversley Cres. N21—16Qb 24
Eversley Cres. Iswth—53Fa 100
Eversley Cres. Ruis—33U 56
Eversley Cross. Bexh—54Gd 110
Eversley Mt. N21—16Pb 24
Eversley Pk. SW19—64Xa 124
Eversley Pk. Rd. N21—16Pb 24
Eversley Rd. SE7—51Kc 107
Eversley Rd. SE19—66Tb 127
Eversley Rd. Surb—70Pa 123
Eversley Way. Croy—76Cc 148
Everthorpe Rd. SE15—55Vb 105
Everton Dri. Stan—27Na 39
Everton Rd. Croy—74Wb 147
Evesham Av. E17—26Cc 44
Evesham Clo. Gnfd—40Da 57
Evesham Clo. Sutt—80Cb 145
Evesham Grn. Mord—72Db 145
Evesham Rd. E15—38Hc 65
Evesham Rd. N11—22Lb 42
Evesham Rd. W11—45Za 80
Evesham Rd. Grav—1F 136
Evesham Rd. Mord—72Db 145
Evesham Wlk. SE5—54Tb 105
Evesham Wlk. SW9—54Qb 104
Evesham Way. SW11—55Jb 104
Evesham Way. Ilf—27Qc 46
Evreham Rd. Iver—44G 74
Evry Rd. Sidc—65Yc 131
Ewald Rd. SW6—54Bb 103
Ewanrigg Ter. Wfd G—22Lc 45
Ewart Gro. N22—25Qb 42
Ewart Rd. SE23—59Zb 106
Ewe Clo. N7—37Nb 62
Ewell By-Pass. Eps—82Wa 162
Ewell Ct. Av. Eps—78Ua 144
Ewell Downs Rd. Eps—83Wa 162
Ewell Ho. Gro. Eps—82Va 162
Ewellhurst Rd. Ilf—26Nc 46
Ewell Pk. Way. Eps—79Wa 144
Ewell Rd. Surb—73Ka 142
Ewell Rd. Surb—72Na 143
(Long Ditton)
Ewell Rd. Sutt—80Za 144
Ewelme Rd. SE23—60Yb 106
Ewen Cres. SW2—60Qb 104
Ewer St. SE1—46Sb 83 (7D 200)
Ewhurst Av. S Croy—81Vb 165
Ewhurst Clo. Sutt—81Ya 162
Ewhurst Rd. SE4—58Bc 106
Exbury Rd. SE6—61Cc 128
Excel Ct. WC2—(5E 198)
Excelsior Clo. King—68Qa 123
Excelsior Gdns. SE13—54Ec 106
Exchange Bldgs. E1 —44Ub 83 (2J 201)
Exchange Ct. WC2 —45Nb 82 (5G 199)
Exchange Rd. Asc—10A 116
Exchange Rd. Wat—14X 19
Exchange St. Romf—29Gd 48
★Exedown Rd. Sev—86Xd
Exeford Av. Ashf—63Q 120
Exeter Clo. E6—44Pc 86
Exeter Gdns. Ilf—32Nc 66
Exeter Rd. E16—43Jc 85
Exeter Rd. E17—29Cc 44
Exeter Rd. N9—19Yb 26
Exeter Rd. N14—18Kb 24
Exeter Rd. NW2—36Ab 60
Exeter Rd. SE15—53Vb 105
Exeter Rd. Croy—73Ub 147
Exeter Rd. Dag—37Dd 68
Exeter Rd. Enf—13Zb 26
Exeter Rd. Felt—62Ba 121
Exeter Rd. Grav—2F 136
Exeter Rd. Harr—33Aa 57
Exeter Rd. Well—54Vc 109
Exeter St. WC2—45Nb 82 (4G 199)
Exeter Way. SE14—52Bc 106
Exford Gdns. SE12—60Kc 107
Exford Rd. SE12—61Kc 129
Exhibition Clo. W12—45Ya 80
Exhibition Rd. SW7 —47Fb 81 (2C 202)
Exmoor St. W10—43Za 80
Exmouth Mkt. EC1 —42Qb 82 (5K 193)
Exmouth M. NW1 —41Lb 82 (4C 192)
Exmouth Pl. E8—38Xb 63
Exmouth Rd. E17—29Bc 44
Exmouth Rd. Brom—69Kc 129
Exmouth Rd. Grays—51De 113
Exmouth Rd. Hay—41U 76
Exmouth Rd. Ruis—34Y 57
Exmouth Rd. Well—53Yc 109
Exmouth St. E1—44Yb 84
Exning Rd. E16—42Hc 85
Exon St. SE17—50Ub 83 (6H 207)
Explorer Av. Stai—60N 97
Exton Cres. NW10—38Sa 59
Exton Gdns. Dag—36Yc 67
Exton St. SE1—46Qb 82 (7K 199)
Eyebright Clo. Croy—74Zb 148
Eyhurst Av. Horn—34Jd 68
Eyhurst Clo. NW2—33Xa 60
Eyhurst Clo. Tad—95Bb 179
Eyhurst Spur. Tad—96Bb 179
Eylewood Rd. SE27—64Sb 127
Eynella Rd. SE22—59Vb 105
Eynham Rd. W12—44Ya 80
Eynsford Clo. Orp—73Sc 150
Eynsford Cres. Sidc—60Yc 109
Eynsford Rise. Eyns, Dart —77Md 153
Eynsford Rd. F'ham, Dart —74Pd 153
Eynsford Rd. Grnh—57Yd 112
Eynsford Rd. Ilf—33Uc 66
Eynsford Rd. Sev & Eyns, Dart —80Kd 153
Eynsford Rd. Swan—72Fd 152
Eynsham Dri. SE2—49Wc 87
Eynswood Dri. Sidc—64Xc 131
Eyot Gdns. W6—50Va 80
Eyot Grn. W4—50Va 80
Eyre Clo. Romf—28Ld 49
Eyre Ct. NW8—40Fb 61 (1B 190)
Eyre Grn. Slou—1E 72
Eyre St. Hill. EC1 —42Qb 82 (6K 193)
Eythorne Rd. SW9—53Qb 104
Ezra Rd. SE5—53Tb 105
Ezra St. E2—41Vb 83

Faber Gdns. NW4—29Wa 40
Fabian Rd. SW6—52Bb 103
Fabian St. E6—42Pc 86
Fackenden La. Sev—85Kd 171
Factory La. N17—26Vb 43
Factory La. Croy—74Qb 146
Factory Path. Stai—63G 118
Factory Pl. E14—50Dc 84
Factory Rd. E16—46Nc 86
Factory Rd. Grav—58Ee 113
Factory Sq. SW16—65Nb 126
Factory Yd. W7—46Ga 78
Faesten Way. Dart—62Gd 132
Faggots Clo. Rad—7La 6
Fagg's Rd. Felt—56V 98
Fagus Av. Rain—41Md 89
Fairacre. N Mald—69Ua 124
Fairacres. SW15—56Wa 102
Fair Acres. Brom—71Jc 149
Fairacres. Cob—84Aa 159
Fairacres. Croy—81Bc 166
Fairacres. Ruis—31V 56
Fairacres. Wind—4B 94
Fairacres Clo. Pot B—5Bb 9
Fairbairn Grn. SW9—53Rb 105
Fairbank Av. Orp—75Rc 150
Fairbank Est. N1—40Tb 63 (3F 195)
Fairbanks Rd. N17—27Wb 43
Fairbourne. Cob—85Z 159
Fairbourne Clo. Wok—6D 188
Fairbourne Rd. N17—27Ub 43
Fairbridge Rd. N19—33Mb 62
Fairbrook Clo. N13—22Qb 42
Fairbrook Rd. N13—23Qb 42
Fairburn Clo. Borwd—11Qa 21
Fairby La. Long, Dart—72Ae 155
Fairby Rd. SE12—57Kc 107
Fairchildes Av. Croy—84Fc 167
Fairchildes Rd. Warl—86Fc 167
Fairchild Pl. EC2—(6J 195)
Fairchild St. EC2 —42Ub 83 (6J 195)
Fair Clo. Bush, Wat—17Da 19
Fairclough St. E1—44Wb 83
Faircroft. Slou—2F 72
Faircross Av. Bark—37Sc 66
Faircross Av. Romf—24Fd 48
Fairdale Gdns. SW15—56Xa 102
Fairdale Gdns. Hay—47W 76
Fairdene Rd. Coul—90Mb 164
Fairey Av. Hay—48V 76
Fairfax Av. Eps—81Xa 162
Fairfax Clo. W on T—74X 141
Fairfax Gdns. SE3—53Lc 107
Fairfax Pl. NW6—38Eb 61
Fairfax Rd. N8—28Qb 42
Fairfax Rd. NW6—38Eb 61
Fairfax Rd. W4—48Ua 80
Fairfax Rd. Grays—50De 91
Fairfax Rd. Tedd—65Ja 122
Fairfax Rd. Til—3B 114
Fairfax Rd. Wok—92D 172
Fairfield App. Wray, Stai—8P 95
Fairfield Av. NW4—30Xa 40
Fairfield Av. Edgw—23Ra 39
Fairfield Av. Grays—45Ee 91
Fairfield Av. Ruis—31S 56
Fairfield Av. Slou—2N 95
Fairfield Av. Stai—63H 119
Fairfield Av. Twic—60Da 99
Fairfield Av. Upm—34Sd 70
Fairfield Av. Wat—20Y 19
Fairfield Clo. N12—21Eb 41
Fairfield Clo. Enf—14Ac 26
Fairfield Clo. Horn—33Jd 68
Fairfield Clo. N'wd—23S 36
Fairfield Clo. Rad—9Ga 6
Fairfield Clo. Sidc—58Vc 109
Fairfield Clo. Slou—2P 95
Fairfield Cotts. Lea—97Da 175
Fairfield Ct. NW10—39Wa 60
Fairfield Cres. Edgw—23Ra 39
Fairfield Dri. SW18—57Db 103
Fairfield Dri. Gnfd—39La 58
Fairfield Dri. Harr—27Ea 38
Fairfield E. King—68Na 123
Fairfield Gdns. N8—29Nb 42
Fairfield Gro. SE7—51Mc 107
Fairfield La. Slou—10F 52
Fairfield N. King—68Na 123
Fairfield Path. Croy—76Ub 147
Fairfield Pl. King—69Na 123
Fairfield Rd. E3—40Cc 64
Fairfield Rd. E17—26Ac 44
Fairfield Rd. N8—29Nb 42
Fairfield Rd. N18—21Wb 43
Fairfield Rd. W7—48Ja 78
Fairfield Rd. Beck—68Cc 128
Fairfield Rd. Bexh—54Bd 109
Fairfield Rd. Brtwd—20Yd 32
Fairfield Rd. Brom—66Jc 129
Fairfield Rd. Croy—76Tb 147
Fairfield Rd. Epp—1Xc 15
Fairfield Rd. Ilf—37Rc 66
Fairfield Rd. King—68Na 123
Fairfield Rd. Lea—93Ka 176
Fairfield Rd. Orp—72Tc 150
★Fairfield Rd. Sev—91Be
Fairfield Rd. Slou—1A 72
Fairfield Rd. S'hall—44Ba 77
Fairfield Rd. Uxb—37M 55
Fairfield Rd. W Dray—45N 75
Fairfield Rd. Wfd G—23Jc 45
Fairfield Rd. Wray, Stai—8P 95
Fairfields Clo. NW9—29Sa 39
Fairfields Cres. NW9—29Sa 39
Fairfield S. King—68Na 123
Fairfields Rd. Houn—55Ea 100
Fairfield St. SW18—57Db 103
Fairfield Wlk. Wal X—1Ac 12
Fairfield Way. Barn—15Cb 23
Fairfield Way. Coul—86Mb 164
Fairfield Way. Eps—78Ua 144
Fairfield W. King—68Na 123
Fairfolds. Wat—7Aa 5
Fairfoot Rd. E3—42Cc 84
Fairford Av. Bexh—53Fd 110
Fairford Av. Croy—71Zb 148
Fairford Clo. Croy—71Ac 148
Fairford Clo. Romf—23Rd 49
Fairford Clo. Wey—86H 157
Fairford Gdns. Wor Pk—76Va 144
Fairford Way. Romf—23Rd 49
Fairgreen. Barn—13Hb 23
Fairgreen E. Barn—13Hb 23
Fairgreen Rd. T Hth—71Rb 147
Fairham Av. S Ock—45Wd 90
Fairhaven Av. Croy—72Zb 148
Fairhaven Cres. Wat—20W 18
Fairhazel Gdns. NW6—37Db 61
Fairholme Av. Romf—29Jd 48
Fairholme Clo. N3—28Ab 40
Fairholme Cres. Asht—89La 160
Fairholme Cres. Hay—42V 76
Fairholme Est. Felt—59T 98
Fairholme Gdns. N3—27Ab 40
Fairholme Gdns. Upm—31Vd 70
Fairholme Rd. W14—50Ab 80
Fairholme Rd. Ashf—64P 119
Fairholme Rd. Croy—73Qb 146
Fairholme Rd. Harr—29Ha 38
Fairholme Rd. Ilf—30Qc 46
Fairholme Rd. Sutt—79Bb 145
Fairholt Rd. N16—32Tb 63
Fairholt St. SW7—(3E 202)
Fairkytes Av. Horn—32Md 69
Fairland Rd. E15—38Hc 65
Fairlands Av. Buck H—19Jc 27
Fairlands Av. Sutt—75Cb 145
Fairlands Av. T Hth—70Pb 126
Fairlands Ct. SE9—58Qc 108
Fair La. Coul—97Eb 179
Fairlawn. SE7—51Lc 107
Fairlawn. Lea—96Ba 175
Fairlawn Av. N2—28Gb 41
Fairlawn Av. W4—49Sa 79
Fairlawn Av. Bexh—54Zc 109
Fairlawn Clo. N14—16Lb 24
Fair Lawn Clo. Esh—79Ha 142
Fairlawn Clo. Felt—63Ba 121
Fairlawn Clo. King—65Sa 123
Fairlawn Dri. Wfd G—24Jc 45
Fairlawn Gdns. S'hall—45Ba 77
Fairlawn Gro. W4—49Sa 79
Fairlawn Gro. Bans—85Fb 163
Fairlawn Pk. SE26—64Ac 128
Fairlawn Rd. SW19—66Bb 125
Fairlawn Rd. Sutt—83Eb 163
Fairlawns. Epp—1Xc 15
Fairlawns. Pinn—26Z 37
Fairlawns. Sun—69V 120
Fairlawns. Twic—58La 100
Fairlawns. Wat—10V 4
Fairlawns. Wey—83H 157
Fairlawns Clo. Horn—31Pd 69
Fairlawns Clo. Stai—65K 119
Fairlea Pl. W5—42La 78
Fairley Way. Wal X—1Xb 11
Fairlie Gdns. SE23—59Yb 106
Fairlie Rd. Slou—4E 72
Fairlight Av. E4—19Fc 27
Fairlight Av. NW10—40Ua 60
Fairlight Av. Wind—4H 95

Fairlight Av.—Ferrings

Fairlight Av. Wfd G—23Jc 45
Fairlight Clo. E4—19Fc 27
Fairlight Clo. Wor Pk—77Ya 144
Fairlight Cross. Long, Dart
—69Ee 135
Fairlight Rd. SW17—63Fb 125
Fairline Ct. Beck—68Ec 128
Fairlop Clo. Horn—37Kd 69
Fairlop Gdns. Ilf—24Sc 46
Fairlop Rd. E11—31Fc 65
Fairlop Rd. Ilf—26Sc 46
Fairmark Dri. Uxb—37Q 56
Fairmead. Brom—70Pc 130
Fairmead. Surb—74Ra 143
Fairmead. Wok—6F 188
Fairmead Clo. Brom—70Pc 130
Fairmead Clo. Houn—52Z 99
Fairmead Clo. N Mald—69Ta 123
Fairmead Cres. Edgw—20Sa 21
Fairmead Gdns. Ilf—29Nc 46
Fairmead Rd. N19—34Nb 62
Fairmead Rd. Croy—73Pb 146
Fairmead Rd. Lou—14Kc 27
Fairmeads. Cob—85Ba 159
Fairmeadside. Lou—15Lc 27
Fairmile Av. SW16—64Mb 126
Fairmile Av. Cob—85Aa 159
Fairmile La. Cob—84Z 159
Fairmile Pk. Copse. Cob—85Ba 159
Fairmile Pk. Rd. Cob—85Ba 159
Fairmount Rd. SW2—58Pb 104
Fairoak Clo. Kenl—87Rb 165
Fairoak Clo. Lea—84Fa 160
Fairoak Clo. Orp—73Rc 150
Fairoak Dri. SE9—57Tc 108
Fairoak Gdns. Romf—26Gd 48
Fairoak La. Lea & Chess
—84Ea 160
Fairseat Clo. Bush, Wat—19Ga 20
Fairseat La. Sev—80Ce 155
(Fairseat)
*Fairseat La. Sev—87De
(Wrotham)
Fairs Rd. Lea—91Ja 176
Fair St. SE1—47Ub 83 (1J 207)
Fair St. Houn—55Ea 100
Fairthorn Rd. SE7—50Jc 85
Fairtrough Rd. Orp—84Xc 169
Fairview. Eps—83Ya 162
Fairview. Eri—52Hd 110
Fair View. Pot B—1Db 9
Fairview Av. Brtwd—17Fe 33
Fairview Av. Rain—40Md 69
Fairview Av. Stanf—2L 93
Fairview Av. Wemb—37Ma 59
Fairview Av. Wok—90B 156
Fairview Clo. E17—25Ac 44
Fairview Clo. Chig—21Uc 46
Fairview Clo. Wok—90B 156
Fairview Ct. Ashf—64Q 120
Fairview Cres. Harr—32Ca 57
Fairview Dri. Chig—21Uc 46
Fairview Dri. Orp—77Tc 150
Fairview Dri. Shep—71P 139
Fairview Dri. Wat—8U 4
Fairview Gdns. Wfd G—25Kc 45
Fairview Pl. SW2—59Pb 104
Fairview Rd. N15—30Vb 43
Fairview Rd. SW16—67Pb 126
Fairview Rd. Chig—21Uc 46
Fairview Rd. Enf—11Qb 24
Fairview Rd. Eps—83Va 162
Fairview Rd. Grav—66Fe 135
Fairview Rd. Grav—6A 136
Fairview Rd. Slou—2D 72
Fairview Rd. Sutt—78Gb 145
Fairview Way. Edgw—21Qa 39
Fairwater Av. Well—56Wc 109
Fairway. SW20—69Ya 124
Fairway. Bexh—57Ad 109
Fairway. Cars—83Eb 163
Fairway. Cher—74K 139
Fairway. Grays—46De 91
Fairway. Orp—71Tc 150
Fair Way. Wfd G—22Lc 45
Fairway Av. NW9—27Ra 39
Fairway Av. Borwd—12Ra 21
Fairway Av. W Dray—46L 75
Fairway Clo. NW11—31Eb 61
Fairway Clo. Croy—71Ac 148
Fairway Clo. Eps—77Sa 143
Fairway Clo. Houn—57Y 99
Fairway Clo. W Dray—46M 75
Fairway Clo. Wok—7E 188
Fairway Dri. Dart—59Rd 111
Fairway Dri. Gnfd—38Ea 58
Fairway End. Wey—84Q 158
Fairway Gdns. Ilf—36Sc 66
Fairways. Ashf—65R 120
Fairways. Kenl—89Sb 165
Fairways. Stan—26Na 39
Fairways. Tedd—66Ma 123
Fairways. Wal A—6Gc 13
Fairway, The. N13—20Tb 25
Fairway, The. N14—16Lb 24
Fairway, The. NW7—20Ta 21
Fairway, The. W3—44Ua 80
Fairway, The. Abb L, Wat—4T 4
Fairway, The. Barn—16Db 23
Fairway, The. Brom—71Pc 150
Fairway, The. E Mol—69Da 121
Fairway, The. Grav—1D 136
Fairway, The. Lea—90Ja 160
Fairway, The. N Mald—67Ta 123
Fairway, The. N'holt—37Ea 58
Fairway, The. N'wd—21U 36
Fairway, The. Ruis—35Y 57
Fairway, The. Slou—10A 52
Fairway, The. Upm—31Td 70
Fairway, The. Uxb—40P 55
Fairway, The. Wemb—33Ka 58
Fairway, The. Wey—83Q 158
Fairweather Clo. N15—28Ub 43
Fairweather Rd. N16—30Wb 43
Fairwell La. Lea—100R 174
Fairwyn Rd. SE26—63Ac 128
Falaise. Egh—64A 118
Falcon Av. Brom—70Nc 130
Falconberg Ct. W1—(2E 198)
Falconberg M. W1—(2D 198)
Falcon Clo. SE1—46Rb 83 (6C 200)
Falcon Clo. N'wd—24U 36
Falcon Ct. EC4—44Qb 82 (3A 200)
Falcon Cres. Enf—16Zb 26
Falcon Dri. Stai—58M 97
Falconer Rd. Bush, Wat—16Ba 19
Falconer Rd. Ilf—22Xc 47
Falconer Wlk. N7—33Pb 62
Falcon Gro. SW11—55Gb 103
Falcon La. SW11—55Hb 103
Falcon Rd. SW11—54Gb 103
Falcon Rd. Enf—15Zb 26
Falcon Rd. Hmptn—66Ba 121
Falcon St. E13—42Jc 85
Falcon Ter. SW11—55Gb 103
Falcon Way. Felt—57X 99
Falcon Way. Harr—29Na 39
Falcon Way. Rain—38Jd 68
Falcon Way. Shep—68U 120
Falcon Way. Wat—6Aa 5
Falconwood Av. Well—54Tc 108
Falconwood Pde. Well—56Vc 109
Falconwood Rd. Croy—81Bc 166
Falcourt Clo. Sutt—78Db 145
Falkirk Clo. Horn—32Qd 69
Falkirk Gdns. Wat—22Z 37
Falkirk St. N1—40Ub 63 (2J 195)
Falkland Av. N3—24Cb 41
Falkland Av. N11—21Kb 42
Falkland Pk. Av. SE25—68Ub 127
Falkland Rd. N8—28Qb 42
Falkland Rd. NW5—36Lb 62
Falkland Rd. Barn—12Ab 22
Fallaize Av. Ilf—35Rc 66
Falling La. W Dray—45N 75
Falloden Way. NW11—28Cb 41
Fallow Clo. Chig—22Vc 47
Fallow Ct. Av. N12—23Eb 41
Fallowfield. Stan—20Ja 20
Fallowfield Clo. Uxb—25L 35
Fallowfield Ct. Stan—20Ja 20
Fallsbrook Rd. SW16—66Lb 126
Falmer Rd. E17—27Dc 44
Falmer Rd. N15—29Tb 43
Falmer Rd. Enf—14Ub 25
Falmouth Av. E4—22Fc 45
Falmouth Clo. N22—24Pb 42
Falmouth Clo. SE12—57Hc 107
Falmouth Gdns. Ilf—28Mc 45
Falmouth Ho. SE11—(7A 206)
Falmouth Rd. SE1
—48Sb 83 (4E 206)
Falmouth Rd. Slou—4E 72
Falmouth Rd. W on T—77Y 141
Falmouth St. E15—36Fc 65
Falstone. Wok—6E 188
Fambridge Rd. SE26—63Bc 128
Fambridge Rd. Dag—32Cd 68
Famet Av. Purl—85Sb 165
Famet Clo. Purl—85Sb 165
Famet Gdns. Kenl—85Sb 165
Famet Wlk. Purl—85Sb 165
Fane St. W14—51Bb 103
Fann St. EC1—42Sb 83 (6D 194)
Fanshawe Av. Bark—37Sc 66
Fanshawe Cres. Dag—36Bd 67
Fanshawe Cres. Horn—30Md 49
Fanshawe Rd. Grays—8C 92
Fanshawe Rd. Rich—63La 122
Fanshaw St. N1—41Ub 83 (3H 195)
Fanthorpe St. SW15—55Ya 102
Faraday Av. Sidc—61Wc 131
Faraday Clo. N7—37Pb 62
Faraday Clo. Slou—3F 72
Faraday Clo. Wat—16T 18
Faraday Rd. E15—37Hc 65
Faraday Rd. SW19—65Db 125
Faraday Rd. W3—45Sa 79
Faraday Rd. W10—43Ab 80
Faraday Rd. E Mol—70Ca 121
Faraday Rd. Slou—3F 72
Faraday Rd. S'hall—45Da 77
Faraday Rd. Well—55Wc 109
Faraday Way. SE18—48Mc 85
Faraday Way. Orp—70Xc 131
Fareham Rd. Felt—59Y 99
Fareham St. W1—44Mb 82 (2D 198)
Farewell Pl. Mitc—67Gb 125
Faringdon Av. Brom—73Qc 150
Faringdon Av. Romf—24Md 49
Faringford Clo. Pot B—3Fb 9
Faringford Rd. E15—38Gc 65
Farington Acres. Wey—76T 140
Faris Barn Dri. Wey—84H 157
Faris La. Wey—83H 157
Farjeon Rd. SE3—53Mc 107
Farleigh Av. Brom—73Hc 149
Farleigh Ct. Rd. Warl—86Bc 166
Farleigh Dean Cres. Croy
—83Dc 166
Farleigh Pl. N16—35Vb 63
Farleigh Rd. N16—35Vb 63
Farleigh Rd. Warl—89Ac 166
Farleigh Rd. Wey—83J 157
Farleton Clo. Wey—79T 140
Farleycroft. West—98Sc 184
Farley Dri. Ilf—32Uc 66
Farley Ho. SE26—62Xb 127
Farley La. West—99Rc 184
Farley Pl. SE25—70Wb 127
Farley Rd. SE6—59Dc 106
Farley Rd. S Croy—80Xb 147
Farleys Clo. Lea—98S 174
Farlington Pl. SW15—59Xa 102
Farlow Clo. Grav—2B 136
Farlow Rd. SW15—55Za 102
Farlton Rd. SW18—60Db 103
Farman Way. Wall—80Mb 146
Farm Av. NW2—34Ab 60
Farm Av. SW16—63Nb 126
Farm Av. Harr—30Ca 37
Farm Av. Swan—69Ed 132
Farm Av. Wemb—37La 58
Farm Clo. Asc—10A 116
Farm Clo. Barn—15Ya 22
Farm Clo. Brtwd—17Ee 33
Farm Clo. Buck H—20Lc 27
Farm Clo. Cher—72D 138
Farm Clo. Dag—38Ed 68
Farm Clo. Lea—96Fa 176
Farm Clo. Lea—100V 174
(East Horsley)
Farm Clo. Shep—73Q 140
Farm Clo. S'hall—45Da 77
Farm Clo. Stai—64G 118
Farm Clo. Sutt—80Fb 145
Farm Clo. Uxb—33R 56
Farm Clo. Wall—82Lb 164
Farm Clo. Wal X—2Yb 12
Farm Clo. W Wick—76Hc 149
Farm Clo. Wey—84N 157
Farmcote Rd. SE12—60Jc 107
Farm Cres. Slou—3M 73
Farm Croft. Grav—1C 136
Farmdale Rd. SE10—50Jc 85
Farmdale Rd. Cars—80Gb 145
Farm Dri. Croy—75Bc 148
Farm Dri. Purl—83Mb 164
Farm End. E4—15Gc 27
Farm End. N'wd—25R 36
Farmer Rd. E10—32Dc 64
Farmers Clo. Wat—5X 5
Farmers Ct. Wal A—5Jc 13
Farmer's Rd. SE5—52Rb 105
Farmers Rd. Stai—64G 118
Farmer St. W8—46Cb 81
Farm Field. Wat—10U 4
Farmfield Rd. Brom—64Gc 129
Farm Fields. S Croy—83Ub 165
Farm Hill Rd. Wal A—5Fc 13
Farm Holt. Long, Dart—74Be 155
(in two parts)
Farm Ho. Clo. Wok—87F 156
Farmhouse Rd. SW16—66Lb 126
Farmilo Rd. E17—31Bc 64
Farmington Av. Sutt—76Fb 145
Farmlands. Enf—11Qb 24
Farmlands. Pinn—28W 36
Farmlands, The. N'holt—37Ca 57
Farmland Wlk. Chst—64Rc 130
Farm La. N14—16Jb 24
Farm La. SW6—52Cb 103
Farm La. Asht & Eps—89Qa 161
Farm La. Croy—75Bc 148
Farm La. Lea—100V 174
Farm La. Purl—82Lb 164
Farm La. Rick—13L 17
Farm La. Slou—5H 73
Farm La. Wok—96E 172
Farmleigh Gro. W on T—78V 140
Farmleigh Rd. N14—17Lb 24
Farm Pl. W8—46Cb 81
Farm Pl. Dart—56Jd 110
Farm Rd. N21—18Sb 25
Farm Rd. Edgw—23Ra 39
Farm Rd. Esh—74Da 141
Farm Rd. Grays—9L 93
(East Tilbury)
Farm Rd. Grays—7B 92
(Orsett)
Farm Rd. Houn—60Aa 99
Farm Rd. Mord—71Db 145
Farm Rd. N'wd—22S 36
Farm Rd. Rain—41Ld 89
Farm Rd. Rick—14C 16
Farm Rd. Sev—92Ld 187
Farm Rd. Stai—65K 119
Farm Rd. Sutt—80Fb 145
Farm Rd. Warl—91Ac 182
Farm Rd. Wok—92D 172
Farmstead Rd. SE6—63Dc 128
Farmstead Rd. Harr—25Fa 38
Farm St. W1—45Kb 82 (5K 197)
Farm Vale. Bex—58Dd 110
Farmview. Cob—88Z 159
Farm Wlk. NW11—29Bb 41
Farm Way. Buck H—21Lc 45
Farm Way. Bush, Wat—14Da 19
Farmway. Dag—34Yc 67
Farm Way. Horn—35Ld 69
Farm Way. N'wd—21U 36
Farm Way. Stai—58H 97
Farm Way. Wor Pk—76Ya 144
Farm Yd. Wind—2H 95
Farnaby Dri. Sev—98Jd 186
Farnaby Rd. SE9—56Lc 107
Farnaby Rd. Brom—66Fc 129
Farnaby Way. Stanf—1L 93
Farnan Av. E17—26Cc 44
Farnan Rd. SW16—64Nb 126
Farnborough Av. E17—27Ac 44
Farnborough Av. S Croy
—80Zb 148
Farnborough Clo. Wemb—34Ra 59
Farnborough Comn. Orp
—76Pc 150
Farnborough Cres. S Croy
—81Ac 166
Farnborough Hill. Orp—78Tc 150
(in two parts)
Farnborough Way. SE15
—52Vb 105
Farnborough Way. Orp—77Sc 150
Farnburn Av. Slou—3F 72
Farncombe St. SE16—47Wb 83
Farndale Av. N13—20Rb 25
Farndale Cres. Gnfd—41Ea 78
Farnell M. SW5—50Db 81
Farnell Rd. Iswth—55Fa 100
Farnell Rd. Stai—62J 119
Farnes Dri. Romf—26Ld 49
Farnham Clo. N20—17Eb 23
Farnham Clo. Hem—1C 2
Farnham Gdns. SW20—68Xa 124
Farnham La. Slou—1C 72
Farnham Pk. La. Slou—9G 52
Farnham Pl. SE1
—46Rb 83 (7C 200)
Farnham Rd. Ilf—31Vc 67
Farnham Rd. Romf—22Md 49
Farnham Rd. Slou—1F 72
Farnham Rd. Well—54Yc 109
Farnham Royal. SE11—50Pb 82
Farningham Cres. Cat—95Wb 181
Farningham Hill Rd. F'ham,
Dart—71Ld 153
Farningham Rd. N17—24Wb 43
Farningham Rd. Cat—95Wb 181
Farnley. Wok—5C 188
Farnley Rd. E4—17Gc 27
Farnley Rd. SE25—70Tb 127
Farnol Rd. Dart—57Qd 111
Faro Clo. Brom—68Qc 130
Faroe Rd. W14—48Za 80
Farorna Wlk. Enf—11Qb 24
Farquhar Rd. SE19—64Vb 127
Farquhar Rd. SW19—62Cb 125
Farquharson Rd. Croy—74Sb 147
Farraline Rd. Wat—14X 19
Farrance Rd. Romf—31Ad 67
Farrance St. E14—44Cc 84
Farrant Av. N22—26Qb 42
Farrant Clo. Orp—80Wc 151
Farrant Way. Borwd—11Na 21
Farr Av. Bark—40Wc 67
Farren Rd. SE23—61Ac 128
Farrer M. N8—28Lb 42
Farrer Rd. N8—28Lb 42
Farrer Rd. Harr—29Na 39
Farrier Clo. Sun—69W 120
Farrier Rd. N'holt—40Ca 57
Farriers Clo. Grav—10H 115
Farrier St. NW1—38Kb 62
Farriers Way. Borwd—15Ta 21
Farringdon La. EC1
—42Qb 82 (6A 194)
Farringdon Rd. EC1
—42Qb 82 (5K 193)
Farringdon St. EC4
—43Rb 83 (1B 200)
Farrington Av. Orp—69Xc 131
Farrins Rents. SE16—46Ac 84
Farrow Gdns. Grays—46De 91
Farrow Pl. SE16—48Ac 84
Farr Rd. Enf—11Tb 25
Farthing All. SE1—47Wb 83
Farthing Barn La. Orp—81Qc 168
Farthing Clo. Dart—56Pd 111
Farthing Clo. Pinn—30X 37
Farthing Fields. E1—46Xb 83
Farthing Grn. La. Slou—10L 53
Farthings. Wok—4B 188
Farthings Clo. E4—20Gc 27
Farthings, The. King—67Qa 123
Farthing St. Orp—80Pc 150
Farwell Rd. Sidc—63Xc 131
Farwig La. Brom—67Hc 129
Fashion St. E1—43Vb 83 (1K 201)
Fashoda Rd. Brom—70Mc 129
Fassett Rd. E8—37Wb 63
Fassett Rd. King—70Na 123
Fassett Sq. E8—37Wb 63
Fassnidge View. Uxb—38L 55
Fauconberg Rd. W4—51Sa 101
Faulkner's All. EC1
—43Rb 83 (7B 194)
Faulkners Rd. W on T—78Y 141
Faulkner St. SE14—53Yb 106
Fauna Clo. Romf—30Yc 47
Faunce St. SE17—50Rb 83
Favart Rd. SW6—53Cb 103
Faversham Av. E4—18Gc 27
Faversham Av. Enf—16Tb 25
Faversham Clo. Chig—19Xc 29
Faversham Rd. SE6—60Bc 106
Faversham Rd. Beck—68Bc 128
Faversham Rd. Mord—72Db 145
Fawcett Clo. SW11—54Fb 103
Fawcett Est. E5—32Wb 63
Fawcett Rd. NW10—38Va 60
Fawcett Rd. Croy—76Sb 147
Fawcett Rd. Wind—3F 94
Fawcett St. SW10—51Eb 103
Fawcus Clo. Esh—79Ga 142
Fawe Pk. Rd. SW15—56Bb 103
Fawe St. E14—43Dc 84
Fawkham Av. Long, Dart
—69Ee 135
Fawkham Grn. Rd. Long, Dart
—76Xd 154
Fawkham Rd. Long, Dart
—70Zd 135
*Fawkham Rd. Sev—81Wd
Fawkham Rd. Sev & Long, Dart
—80Wd 154
Fawley Rd. N17—28Wb 43
Fawley Rd. NW6—36Db 61
Fawnbrake Av. SE24—57Sb 105
Fawn Rd. E13—40Lc 65
Fawn Rd. Chig—22Vc 47
Fawns Mnr. Rd. Felt—60T 98
Fawood Av. NW10—38Ta 59
Fawsley Clo. Slou—52G 96
Fawters Clo. Brtwd—16Fe 33
Fayerfield. Pot B—3Fb 9
Faygate Cres. Bexh—57Cd 110
Faygate Rd. SW2—61Pb 126
Fay Grn. Abb L, Wat—5T 4
Fayland Av. SW16—64Lb 126
Faymore Gdns. S Ock—44Wd 90
Fearn Clo. Lea—100U 174
Fearney Mead. Rick—18J 17
Fearnley Cres. Hmptn—65Ba 121
Fearnley St. Wat—14X 19
Fearon St. SE10—50Jc 85
Featherbed La. Croy & Warl
—81Bc 166
Featherbed La. Romf—17Ad 29
Feathers La. Wray, Stai—61C 118
Feathers Pl. SE10—51Fc 107
Featherstone Av. SE23
—61Xb 127
Featherstone Gdns. Borwd
—14Sa 21
Featherstone Industrial Est.
S'hall—48Aa 77
Featherstone Rd. NW7—23Xa 40
Featherstone Rd. S'hall—48Aa 77
Featherstone St. EC1
—42Tb 83 (5F 195)
Featherstone Ter. S'hall—48Aa 77
Featley Rd. SW9—55Rb 105
Federal Rd. Gnfd—39La 58
Federal Way. Wat—11Y 19
Federation Rd. SE2—49Xc 87
Fee Farm Rd. Esh—80Ha 142
Feenan Highway. Til—4D 114
Felbridge Av. Stan—25Ja 38
Felbridge Clo. SW16—63Qb 126
Felbridge Clo. Sutt—81Db 163
Felbrigge Rd. Ilf—33Vc 67
Felday Rd. SE13—58Dc 106
Felden Clo. Wat—6Z 5
Felden St. SW6—53Bb 103
Feldman Clo. N16—32Wb 63
Feldon Clo. Pinn—24Aa 37
Felgate M. W6—49Xa 80
Felhampton Rd. SE9—62Rc 130
Felhurst Cres. Dag—35Dd 68
Felicia Way. Grays—9D 92
Felix Av. N8—30Nb 42
Felix Dri. Guild—100J 173
Felix La. Shep—72U 140
Felix Rd. W13—45Ja 78
Felix Rd. W on T—72W 140
Felixstowe Rd. N9—21Wb 43
Felixstowe Rd. N17—27Vb 43
Felixstowe Rd. NW10—41Xa 80
Felixstowe Rd. SE2—48Xc 87
Felix St. E2—40Xb 63
Fellbrigg Rd. SE22—57Vb 105
Fellbrigg St. E1—42Xb 83
Fellbrook. Rich—62Ka 122
Fellcott Clo. W on T—76Y 141
Fellcott Rd. W on T—76Y 141
Fellowes Clo. Hay—42Z 77
Fellowes Rd. Cars—76Gb 145
Fellows Ct. E2—(2K 195)
Fellows Rd. NW3—38Fb 61
Fell Rd. Croy—76Sb 147
Felltram Way. SE7—50Jc 85
Fell Wlk. Edgw—25Sa 39
Felmersham Clo. SW4—56Nb 104
Felmingham Rd. SE20—68Yb 128
Felnex Trading Est. NW10
—40Ta 59
Felsberg Rd. SW2—59Nb 104
Fels Clo. Dag—34Dd 68
Fels Farm Av. Dag—34Ed 68
Felsham Rd. SW15—55Ya 102
Felspar Clo. SE18—50Vc 87
Felstead Av. Ilf—25Qc 46
Felstead Gdns. E14—50Ec 84
Felstead Rd. E11—31Jc 65
Felstead Rd. Eps—83Ta 161
Felstead Rd. Lou—17Nc 28
Felstead Rd. Orp—75Wc 151
Felstead Rd. Romf—24Ed 48
Felstead Rd. Wal X—4Ac 12
Felstead St. E9—37Bc 64
Felsted Rd. E16—44Mc 85
Feltham Av. E Mol—70Ga 122
Felthambrook Way. Felt—62X 121
Felthamhill Rd. Ashf—64R 120
Felthamhill Rd. Felt—63W 120
Feltham Rd. Ashf—63R 120
Feltham Rd. Mitc—68Jb 126
Felton Clo. Borwd—10Na 7
Felton Clo. Orp—72Rc 150
Felton Gdns. Bark—39Uc 66
Felton Lea. Sidc—64Vc 131
Felton Rd. W13—47La 78
Felton Rd. Bark—40Uc 66
Felton St. N1—39Tb 63
Fencepiece Rd. Chig & Ilf—22Sc 46
Fenchurch Av. EC3
—44Ub 83 (3H 201)
Fenchurch Bldgs. EC3
—44Ub 83 (3J 201)
Fenchurch St. EC3
—45Ub 83 (4H 201)
Fen Clo. Brtwd—14De 33
Fen Ct. EC3—44Ub 83 (3H 201)
Fendall Rd. Eps—78Sa 143
Fendall St. SE1—48Ub 83 (4J 207)
Fendt Clo. E16—44Hc 85
Fendyke Rd. Belv—49Zc 87
Fenelon Pl. W14—49Bb 81
Fen Gro. Sidc—57Vc 109
Fenham Rd. SE15—52Wb 105
Fen La. Brtwd—31De 71
Fen La. Grays—2A 92
Fen La. Upm—37Yd 70
Fenman Ct. N17—25Xb 43
Fenn Clo. Brom—65Jc 129
Fennel Clo. Croy—74Zb 148
Fennells Mead. Eps—81Va 162
Fennell St. SE18—51Qc 108
Fenner Sq. SW11—55Fb 103
Fenning St. SE1—47Ub 83 (1H 207)
Fenn St. E9—36Yb 64
Fenns Way. Wok—87A 156
*Fen Pond Rd. Sev—89Yd
Fenstanton Av. N12—23Fb 41
Fen St. E16—45Hc 85
Fens Way. Swan—65Jd 132
Fentiman Rd. SW8—51Nb 104
Fentiman Way. Horn—32Nd 69
Fenton Av. Stai—64L 119
Fenton Clo. E8—37Vb 63
Fenton Clo. SW9—54Pb 104
Fenton Clo. Chst—64Pc 130
Fenton Rd. N17—24Sb 43
Fentons Av. E13—41Kc 85
Fenton St. E1—44Xb 83
Fenton St. SE10—50Gc 85
Fenwick Clo. SE18—51Qc 108
Fenwick Clo. Wok—6E 188
Fenwick Gro. SE15—55Wb 105
Fenwick Path. Borwd—10Pa 7
Fenwick Pl. SW9—55Nb 104
Fenwick Rd. SE15—55Wb 105
Ferdinand Pl. NW1—38Jb 62
Ferdinand St. NW1—38Jb 62
Ferguson Av. Grav—3E 136
Ferguson Av. Romf—26Ld 49
Ferguson Av. Surb—71Pa 143
Ferguson Ct. Romf—26Md 49
Fergus Rd. N5—36Rb 63
Ferme Pk. Rd.—29Nb 42
N4 1-53 & 2-66a
N8 remainder
Fermor Rd. SE23—60Ac 106
Fermoy Rd. W9—42Bb 81
Fermoy Rd. Gnfd—42Da 77
Fern Av. Mitc—70Mb 126
Fern Bank. Eyns, Dart—75Pd 153
Fernbank. Ilf—35Ld 69
Fernbank Av. W on T—73Aa 141
Fernbank Av. Wemb—35Ha 58
Fernbank Rd. Wey—78J 139
Fernbrook Av. Sidc—57Uc 108
Fernbrook Dri. Harr—31Da 57
Fernbrook Rd. SE13—58Gc 107
Ferncliff Rd. E8—36Wb 63
Fern Clo. Warl—90Ac 166
Ferncroft Av. N12—23Hb 41
Ferncroft Av. NW3—34Cb 61
Ferncroft Av. Ruis—33Y 57
Ferndale. Brom—68Lc 129
Ferndale Av. E17—29Fc 45
Ferndale Av. Cher—76G 138
Ferndale Av. Houn—55Aa 99
Ferndale Cres. Uxb—41L 75
Ferndale Rd. E7—38Kc 65
Ferndale Rd. E11—33Gc 65
Ferndale Rd. N15—30Vb 43
Ferndale Rd. SE25—71Xb 147
Ferndale Rd.—56Nb 104
SW4 1-169 & 2-172
SW9 remainder
Ferndale Rd. Ashf—64M 119
Ferndale Rd. Bans—88Bb 163
Ferndale Rd. Enf—9Ac 12
Ferndale Rd. Grav—1D 136
Ferndale Rd. Romf—26Ed 48
Ferndale Rd. Wok—88B 156
Ferndale Ter. Harr—28Ha 38
Ferndale Way. Orp—78Tc 150
Ferndell Av. Bex—62Fd 132
Fern Dene. W13—43Ka 78
Ferndene. Long, Dart—69Fe 135
Ferndene Rd. SE24—56Sb 105
Fernden Way. Romf—30Dd 48
Ferndown. Horn—30Pd 49
Ferndown. N'wd—26W 36
Ferndown Av. Orp—74Tc 150
Ferndown Clo. Pinn—24Aa 37
Ferndown Clo. Sutt—79Fb 145
Ferndown Gdns. Cob—85Y 159
Ferndown Rd. SE9—59Mc 107
Ferndown Rd. Wat—21Y 37
Fern Dri. M'head—4A 72
Fernery, The. Stai—64G 118
Fernes Clo. Uxb—44L 75
Ferney Rd. Barn—17Jb 24
Ferney Rd. Wey—84M 157
Fern Gro. Felt—59X 99
Fernhall Dri. Ilf—29Mc 45
Fernhall La. Wal A—4Mc 13
Fernhall La. Wal A—3Mc 13
Fernham Rd. T Hth—69Sb 127
Fernhead Rd. W9—41Bb 81
Fernheath Way. Dart—64Fd 132
Fern Hill. Lea—86Fa 160
Fernhill Clo. Wok—8F 188
Fernhill Ct. E17—26Fc 45
Fernhill Gdns. King—64Ma 123
Fernhill La. Wok—8F 188
Fernhill Pk. Wok—8F 188
Fernhills. Abb L, Wat—5T 4
Fernhill St. E16—46Pc 86
Fernholme Rd. SE15—57Zb 106
Fernhurst Gdns. Edgw—23Qa 39
Fernhurst Rd. SW6—53Ab 102
Fernhurst Rd. Ashf—63S 120
Fernhurst Rd. Croy—74Xb 147
Fernie Clo. Chig—22Wc 47
Fernie Way. Chig—22Wc 47
Fernlands Clo. Cher—76G 138
Fern La. Houn—50Ba 77
Fernlea. Lea—96Da 175
Fernlea Rd. SW12—60Kb 104
Fernlea Rd. Mitc—68Jb 126
Fernleigh Clo. Croy—77Qb 146
Fernleigh Ct. Harr—26Da 37
Fernleigh Ct. Wemb—33Na 59
Fernleigh Rd. N21—19Qb 24
Fernsbury St. WC1
—41Qb 82 (4K 193)
Ferns Clo. Enf—8Ac 12
Ferns Clo. S Croy—82Xb 165
Fernshaw Rd. SW10—51Eb 103
Fernside. NW11—33Cb 61
Fern Side. Buck H—18Kc 27
Fernside Av. NW7—20Ta 21
Fernside Av. Felt—63X 121
Fernside Rd. SW12—60Hb 103
Ferns Rd. E15—37Hc 65
Fern St. E3—42Cc 84
Fernthorpe Rd. SW16—65Lb 126
Ferntower Rd. N5—36Tb 63
Fern Towers. Cat—97Wb 181
Fern Way. Wat—7X 5
Fernways. Ilf—35Rc 66
Fernwood. Croy—81Ac 166
Fernwood Av. SW16—63Mb 126
Fernwood Av. Wemb—37La 58
Fernwood Clo. Brom—68Lc 129
Fernwood Cres. N20—20Hb 23
Ferny Hill. Barn—10Jb 10
Ferranti Clo. SE18—49Mc 85
Ferraro Clo. Houn—51Ca 99
Ferrers Av. Wall—77Mb 146
Ferrers Av. W Dray—47M 75
Ferrers Rd. SW16—64Mb 126
Ferrestone Rd. N8—28Pb 42
Ferriby Clo. N1—38Qb 62
Ferrier St. SW18—56Db 103
Ferriers Way. Eps—91Za 178
Ferring Clo. Harr—32Ea 58
Ferrings. SE21—62Ub 127

Ferris Av. Croy—76Bc 148
Ferris Rd. SE22—56Wb 105
Ferron Rd. E5—34Xb 63
Ferro Rd. Rain—42Jd 88
Ferry App. SE18—48Qc 86
Ferry Av. Stai—66G 118
Ferryhills Clo. Wat—20Z 19
Ferry La. N17—28Wb 43
Ferry La. SW13—51Va 102
Ferry La. Bren—51Na 101
Ferry La. Cher—71K 139
Ferry La. Rain—44Gd 88
Ferry La. Rich—51Pa 101
Ferry La. Shep—74Q 140
Ferry La. Stai—69L 119
Ferry La. Wray, Stai—61D 118
Ferrymead Av. Gnfd—41Ca 77
Ferrymead Dri. Gnfd—40Ca 57
Ferrymead Gdns. Gnfd—40Da 57
Ferrymoor. Rich—62Ka 122
Ferry Rd. SW13—52Wa 102
Ferry Rd. E Mol—69Ca 121
Ferry Rd. Tedd—64Ka 122
Ferry Rd. Th Dit—72Ka 142
Ferry Rd. Til—5C 114
Ferry Rd. Twic—60Ka 100
Ferry Sq. Bren—52Na 101
Ferry Sq. Shep—73R 140
Ferry St. E14—50Ec 84
Feryby Rd. Grays—8D 92
Festing Rd. SW15—55Za 102
Festival Av. Long, Dart—69Fe 135
Festival Clo. Bex—60Zc 109
Festival Clo. Eri—52Hd 110
Festival Clo. Uxb—39R 56
Festival Wlk. Cars—78Hb 145
Fetcham Comn. La. Lea—93Da 175
Fetcham Pk. Dri. Lea—95Ga 176
Fetherstone Clo. Pot B—4Fb 9
Fetherston Rd. Stanf—2M 93
Fetter La. EC4—44Qb 82 (3A 200)
Ffinch St. SE8—52Cc 106
Fiddicroft Av. Bans—86Db 163
Fidler Pl. Bush, Wat—16Da 19
Field Clo. E4—23Dc 44
Field Clo. Brom—68Lc 129
Field Clo. Buck H—20Lc 27
Field Clo. Chess—78La 142
Field Clo. E Mol—71Da 141
Field Clo. Hay—52S 98
Field Clo. Houn—53X 99
Field Clo. Romf—13Xc 29
Field Clo. Ruis—32S 56
Field Clo. S Croy—86Xb 165
Field Clo. Uxb—33R 56
Fieldcommon La. W on T —74Aa 141
Field Ct. WC1—43Pb 82 (1J 199)
Field Ct. Oxt—99Gc 183
Field End. Barn—14Xa 22
Field End. Coul—86Mb 164
Field End. N'holt—37Aa 57
Field End. Ruis—37Y 57
Field End. Twic—63Ha 122
Field End Clo. Wat—17Aa 19
Fieldend Rd. SW16—67Lb 126
Field End Rd. Pinn & Ruis—29X 37
Fieldfare Rd. SE28—45Yc 87
Fieldgate La. Mitc—68Gb 125
Fieldgate St. E1—43Wb 83
Fieldhouse Rd. SW12—60Lb 104
Fieldhurst. Slou—50B 74
Fieldhurst Clo. Wey—78K 139
Fielding Av. Til—3D 114
Fielding Av. Twic—62Ea 122
Fielding Rd. W4—48Ta 79
Fielding Rd. W14—48Za 80
Fieldings Rd. Wal X—1Bc 12
Fieldings, The. SE23—60Yb 106
Fielding St. SE17—51Sb 105
Fielding Way. Brtwd—16Ee 33
Field La. Bren—52La 100
Field La. Tedd—64Ja 122
Field Mead. NW9 & NW7—24Ua 40
Field Pl. N Mald—72Va 144
Field Rd. E7—35Jc 65
Field Rd. N17—27Tb 43
Field Rd. SE28—45Yc 87
Field Rd. W6—50Ab 80
Field Rd. Felt—58X 99
Field Rd. S Ock—46Sd 90
Field Rd. Uxb—35G 54
Field Rd. Wat—16Aa 19
Fields Ct. Pot B—5Fb 9
Fieldsend Rd. Sutt—78Ab 144
Fieldside Rd. Brom—64Fc 129
Fields Pk. Cres. Romf—29Zc 47
Fields, The. Slou—7H 73
Field St. WC1—41Pb 82 (3H 193)
Fieldview. SW18—60Fb 103
Field View. Egh—64E 118
Field View. Felt—63T 120
Field View Rise. St Alb—1Aa 5
Field View Rd. Pot B—5Cb 9
Field Way. NW10—38Sa 59
Field Way. Croy—80Dc 148
Fieldway. Dag—35Yc 67
Field Way. Ger X—24A 34
Fieldway. Grays—46Ce 91
Field Way. Gnfd—39Da 57
Field Way. Orp—72Tc 150
Field Way. Rick—18K 17
Field Way. Ruis—32S 56
Field Way. Wok—97H 173
Fieldway Cres. N5—36Qb 62
Field Waye. Uxb—42M 75
Fiennes Clo. Dag—32Yc 67
Fifehead Clo. Ashf—65P 119
Fife Rd. E16—43Jc 85
Fife Rd. N22—24Rb 43
Fife Rd. SW14—57Sa 101
Fife Rd. King—68Na 123
Fife Ter. N1—40Pb 62 (1J 193)
Fife Way. Lea—97Ca 175
Fifield Path. SE23—62Zb 128
Fifth Av. E12—35Pc 66
Fifth Av W10—41Ab 80
Fifth Av. Grays—51Wd 112
Fifth Av. Hay—46V 76
Fifth Av. Wat—7Z 5
Fifth Av. Wey—75L 139
Fifth Cross Rd. Twic—61Fa 122
Fifth Way. Wemb—35Ra 59
Figges Rd. Mitc—66Jb 126
Filborough Way. Grav—1K 137
Filby Rd. Chess—79Pa 143
Filey Av. N16—32Wb 63
Filey Clo. Sutt—80Eb 145
Filey Clo. West—91Kc 183
Filey Waye. Ruis—33W 56
Fillebrook Av. Enf—12Ub 25
Fillebrook Rd. E11—32Gc 65
Filmer La. Sev—93Nd 187
Filmer Rd. SW6—53Bb 103
Filmer Rd. Wind—4B 94
Filston La. Sev—88Fd 170
Filston Rd. Eri—50Ed 88
Finborough Rd. SW10—51Db 103
Finborough Rd. SW17—65Hb 125
Finchale Rd. SE2—48Wc 87
Fincham Clo. Uxb—34S 56
Finch Av. SE27—63Tb 127
Finch Clo. NW10—37Ta 59
Finch Clo. Wok—5A 188
Finchdean Way. SE15—52Ub 105
Finch Dri. Felt—59Z 99
Finchingfield Av. Wfd G—24Lc 45
Finch La. EC3—44Tb 83 (3G 201)
Finch La. Bush, Wat—14Ca 19
Finchley Clo. Dart—58Qd 111
Finchley Ct. N3—23Db 41
Finchley La. NW4—28Ya 40
Finchley Pk. N12—21Eb 41
Finchley Pl. NW8 —40Fb 61 (1B 190)
Finchley Rd.—28Bb 41 to 39Fb 61 (1B 190)
NW8 1-97 & 2-82
NW3 99-617 & 84-378
NW2 619-707 & 380-450
NW11 remainder
Finchley Rd. Grays—51De 113
Finchley Way. N3—24Cb 41
Finch's Ct. E14—45Dc 84
Finck St. SE1—47Pb 82 (2J 205)
Finden Rd. E7—36Lc 65
Findhorn Av. Hay—43X 77
Findhorn St. E14—44Ec 84
Findon Clo. SW18—58Cb 103
Findon Clo. Harr—34Da 57
Findon Gdns. Rain—43Kd 89
Findon Rd. N9—18Xb 25
Findon Rd. W12—47Wa 80
Fine Bush La. Ruis—30R 36
Fingal St. SE10—50Hc 85
Finland Rd. SE4—55Ac 106
Finlans Clo. Uxb—38P 55
Finlay Gdns. Wey—77L 139
Finlays Clo. Chess—78Qa 143
Finlay St. SW6—53Za 102
Finleigh Ct. Slou—6J 73
Finnart Clo. Wey—77S 140
Finnemore Rd. Ilf—23Wc 47
Finnis St. E2—42Xb 83
Finnymore Rd. Dag—38Ad 67
Finsbury Av. EC2 —43Tb 83 (1G 201)
Finsbury Cir. EC2 —43Tb 83 (1G 201)
Finsbury Mkt. EC2 —42Ub 83 (6H 195)
(in two parts)
Finsbury Pk. Av. N4—30Rb 43
Finsbury Pk. Rd. N4—33Rb 63
Finsbury Pavement. EC2 —43Tb 83 (7G 195)
Finsbury Rd. N22—24Pb 42
Finsbury Sq. EC2 —43Tb 83 (7G 195)
Finsbury St. EC2—43Tb 83 (7F 195)
Finsen Rd. SE5—55Sb 105
Finstock Rd. W10—44Za 80
Finucane Dri. Orp—73Yc 151
Finucane Gdns. Rain—37Jd 68
Finucane Rise. Bush, Wat—19Ea 20
Fiona Clo. Lea—96Ca 175
Firbank Clo. E16—43Mc 85
Firbank Clo. Enf—14Sb 25
Firbank Dri. Wat—17Aa 19
Firbank Dri. Wok—7E 188
Firbank La. Wok—7E 188
Firbank Pl. Egh—5M 117
Firbank Rd. SE15—54Xb 105
Firbank Rd. Romf—22Dd 48
Fir Clo. W on T—73W 140
Fircroft Clo. Slou—7L 53
Fircroft Clo. Wok—90B 156
Fircroft Ct. Wok—90B 156
Fircroft Gdns. Harr—34Ga 58
Fircroft Rd. SW17—61Hb 125
Fircroft Rd. Chess—77Pa 143
Fir Dene. Orp—76Qc 150
Firdene. Surb—74Sa 143
Fire Bell All. Surb—72Na 143
Firecrest Clo. Long, Dart —69De 135
Firecrest Dri. NW3—34Db 61
Firefly Clo. Wall—80Nb 146
Fire Sta. All. Barn—12Ab 22
Firfield Rd. Wey—77J 139
Firfields. Wey—79R 140
Fir Grange Av. Wey—78R 140
Fir Gro. N Mald—72Va 144
Fir Gro. Wok—7D 188
Firham Pk. Av. Romf—24Qd 49
Firhill Rd. SE6—63Cc 128
Firlands. Wey—79U 140
Firmingers Rd. Orp—78Dd 152
Firmin Rd. Dart—57Ld 111
Fir Rd. Felt—64Z 121
Fir Rd. Sutt—74Bb 145
Firs Av. N10—27Jb 42
Firs Av. N11—23Jb 42
Firs Av. SW14—56Sa 101
Firs Av. Wind—5D 94
Firsby Av. Croy—74Zb 148
Firsby Rd. N16—32Wb 63
Firs Clo. N10—28Jb 42
Firs Clo. SE23—59Ac 106
Firs Clo. Esh—80Ga 142
Firs Clo. Mitc—67Kb 126
Firs Croft. N13—20Sb 25
Firs Dene Clo. Cher—79F 138
Firs Dri. Houn—52X 99
Firs Dri. Lou—11Qc 28
Firsgrove Cres. Brtwd—21Xd 50
Firsgrove Rd. Brtwd—21Xd 50
Firs La.—20Sb 25
N21 1-253 & 2-144
N13 remainder
Firs La. Pot B—5Db 9
Firs Pk. Av. N21—18Tb 25
Firs Pk. Gdns. N21—18Tb 25
Firs Rd. Kenl—87Rb 165
First Av. E12—35Nc 66
First Av. E13—41Jc 85
First Av. E17—29Cc 44
First Av. N18—21Yb 44
First Av. NW4—28Ya 40
First Av. SW14—55Ua 102
First Av. W3—46Va 80
First Av. W10—42Bb 81
★First Av. Brtwd—6Yd
First Av. Cher—74L 139
First Av. Dag—40Dd 68
First Av. E Mol—70Ba 121
First Av. Enf—15Vb 25
First Av. Eps—81Ua 162
First Av. Grav—10A 114
First Av. Grays—51Wd 112
First Av. Hay—46V 76
First Av. Romf—29Yc 47
First Av. Stanf—1M 93
First Av. W on T—72X 141
First Av. Wat—7Y 5
First Av. Well—52Yc 109
First Av. Wemb—33Ma 59
First Clo. E Mol—69Ea 122
First Cres. Slou—3G 72
First Cross Rd. Twic—61Ga 122
Firs, The. N20—18Fb 23
Firs, The. W5—43Ma 79
Firs, The. Bex—60Fd 110
Firs, The. Grays—46Ee 91
First Slip. Lea—90Ja 160
First St. SW3—49Gb 81 (5E 202)
Firstway. SW20—68Ya 124
First Way. Wemb—35Ra 59
Firs Wlk. N'wd—23T 36
Firs Wlk. Wfd G—22Jc 45
Firswood Av. Eps—78Va 144
Firth Gdns. SW6—53Ab 102
Firtree Av. Mitc—68Jb 126
Fir Tree Av. Slou—2K 73
Fir Tree Av. W Dray—48Q 76
Fir Tree Clo. Eps—87Ya 162
(Nork)
Firtree Clo. Eps—77Va 144
(Stoneleigh)
Fir Tree Clo. Esh—78Ea 142
Fir Tree Clo. Lea—95La 176
Firtree Clo. Orp—78Vc 151
Fir Tree Clo. Romf—27Fd 48
Fir Tree Ct. Borwd—14Pa 21
Firtree Gdns. Croy—77Cc 148
Fir Tree Gro. Cars—80Hb 145
Fir Tree Hill. Rick—10P 3
Fir Tree Pl. Ashf—64Q 120
Fir Tree Rd. Eps & Bans—88Xa 162
Fir Tree Rd. Houn—56Aa 99
Fir Tree Rd. Lea—95La 176
Fir Trees. Epp—1Xc 15
Fir Trees Clo. SE16—46Ac 84
Fir Tree Wlk. Dag—34Ed 68
Fir Tree Wlk. Enf—13Tb 25
Fir Wlk. Sutt—79Ya 144
Firwood Clo. Wok—7B 188
Fisher Clo. Croy—74Vb 147
Fisher Clo. Gnfd—41Ca 77
Fisher Clo. K Lan—1Q 4
Fisher Clo. W on T—77X 141
Fisherman Clo. Rich—63La 122
Fisherman's Pl. W4—51Va 102
Fishermens Hill. Grav—57De 113
Fisher Rd. Harr—26Ha 38
Fishers Clo. Wal X—6Cc 12
Fishers Ct. SE14—53Zb 106
Fishers Dene. Esh—80Ja 142
Fishers La. W4—49Ta 79
Fisher St. E16—43Jc 85
Fisher St. WC1—43Pb 82 (1H 199)
Fishers Way. Belv—46Ed 88
Fisherton St. NW8 —42Fb 81 (6B 190)
Fishponds Rd. SW17—63Gb 125
Fishponds Rd. Kes—78Mc 149
Fish St. Hill. EC3—45Tb 83 (5G 201)
Fitzalan Rd. N3—27Ab 40
Fitzalan Rd. Esh—80Ga 142
Fitzalan St. SE11 —49Qb 82 (5J 205)
Fitzgeorge Av. W14—49Ab 80
Fitzgeorge Av. N Mald—67Ta 123
Fitzgerald Av. SW14—55Ua 102
Fitzgerald Rd. E11—29Jc 45
Fitzgerald Rd. SW14—55Ta 101
Fitzgerald Rd. Th Dit—72Ja 142
Fitzhardinge St. W1 —44Jb 82 (2H 197)
Fitzherbert Ho. Rich—58Pa 101
Fitzhugh Gro. SW18—58Fb 103
Fitzilian Av. Romf—25Pd 49
Fitzjames Av. W14—49Ab 80
Fitzjames Av. Croy—75Wb 147
Fitzjohn Av. Barn—15Ab 22
Fitzjohn's Av. NW3—35Eb 61
Fitzmaurice Pl. W1 —46Kb 82 (6A 198)
Fitzneal St. W12—44Va 80
Fitzroy Clo. N6—32Hb 61
Fitzroy Ct. W1—(6C 192)
Fitzroy Gdns. SE19—66Ub 127
Fitzroy M. W1—(6B 192)
Fitzroy Pk. N6—32Hb 61
Fitzroy Rd. NW1—39Jb 62
Fitzroy Sq. W1—42Lb 82 (6B 192)
Fitzroy St. W1—42Lb 82 (6B 192)
(in two parts)
Fitzstephen Rd. Dag—36Xc 67
Fitzwarren Gdns. N19—32Lb 62
Fitzwilliam Av. Rich—54Pa 101
Fitzwilliam Ho. Rich—56Ma 101
Fitzwilliam Rd. SW4—55Lb 104
Fitz Wygram Clo. Hmptn—64Ea 122
Five Acre. NW9—26Va 40
Five Acres Av. St Alb—1Ba 5
Fiveash Rd. Grav—9B 114
Five Elms Rd. Brom—76Lc 149
Five Elms Rd. Dag—34Bd 67
Five Oaks. Wey—79H 139
Five Oaks Clo. Wok—7B 188
Five Oaks La. Chig—23Ad 47
Fiveways Rd. SW9—54Qb 104
Five Wents. Swan—68Jd 132
Fladbury Rd. N15—30Tb 43
Fladgate Rd. E11—30Gc 45
Flag Clo. Croy—74Zb 148
Flagstaff Rd. Wal A—5Dc 12
Flag Wlk. Pinn—30W 36
Flambard Rd. Harr—30Ja 38
Flamborough Clo. West—91Kc 183
Flamborough Rd. Ruis—34W 56
Flamborough St. E14—44Ac 84
Flamingo Wlk. Rain—38Jd 68
Flamstead End Relief Rd. Wal X —4Wb 11
Flamstead End Relief Rd. Wal X —3Vb 11
Flamstead End Rd. Wal X—1Xb 11
Flamstead Gdns. Dag—38Yc 67
Flamstead Rd. Dag—38Yc 67
Flamsted Av. Wemb—37Qa 59
Flamsteed Rd. SE7—50Nc 86
Flanchford Rd. W12—48Va 80
Flanders Cres. SW17—66Hb 125
Flanders Rd. E6—40Pc 66
Flanders Rd. W4—49Ua 80
Flanders Way. E9—37Zb 64
Flank St. E1—45Wb 83
Flash La. Enf—9Rb 11
Flask Wlk. NW3—35Eb 61
Flaunden Bottom. Che & Hem —8A 2
Flaunden Hill. Hem—5B 2
Flaunden La. Hem—4D 2
Flaunden La. Hem—3D 2
Flaunden La. Rick—5E 2
Flaxey Rd. Mord—73Db 145
Flaxman Ct. W1—(3D 198)
Flaxman Rd. SE5—54Rb 105
Flaxman Ter. WC1 —41Mb 82 (4E 192)
Flaxton Rd. SE18—52Uc 108
Flecker Clo. Stan—22Ha 38
Fleece Rd. Surb—74Ka 142
Fleece Wlk. N7—37Nb 62
Fleeming Clo. E17—26Bc 44
Fleeming Rd. E17—26Bc 44
Fleet Av. Dart—60Sd 112
Fleet Av. Upm—30Td 50
Fleet Clo. E Mol—71Ba 141
Fleet Clo. Ruis—30S 36
Fleet Clo. Upm—30Td 50
Fleetdale Pde. Dart—60Sd 112
Fleethall Gro. Grays—46Ce 91
Fleet La. EC4—44Rb 83 (2B 200)
Fleet La. E Mol—72Ba 141
Fleet Rd. NW3—36Gb 61
Fleet Rd. Dart—60Sd 112
Fleet Rd. Grav—62Ee 135
Fleetside. E Mol—71Ba 141
Fleet Sq. WC1—41Pb 82 (4J 193)
Fleet St. EC4—44Qb 82 (3K 199)
Fleet St. Hill. E1—42Wb 83
Fleetway. Egh—69E 118
Fleetwood Clo. E16—43Mc 85
Fleetwood Clo. Chess—80Ma 143
Fleetwood Clo. Tad—92Za 178
Fleetwood Ct. Wey—85J 157
Fleetwood Rd. NW10—36Wa 60
Fleetwood Rd. King—69Ra 123
Fleetwood Rd. Slou—6K 73
Fleetwood Sq. King—69Ra 123
Fleetwood St. N16—33Ub 63
Fleetwood Way. Wat—21Y 37
Fleming Ct. W2—(7B 190)
Fleming Ct. Croy—78Qb 146
Fleming Gdns. Til—3E 114
Fleming Mead. Mitc—66Hb 125
Fleming Rd. SE17—51Rb 105
Fleming Rd. S'hall—44Da 77
Flemings. Brtwd—23Yd 50
Fleming Way. SE28—45Zc 87
Fleming Way. Iswth—55Ha 100
Flemish Fields. Cher—73J 139
Flempton Rd. E10—32Ac 64
Fletcher Clo. Cher—79G 138
Fletcher La. E10—31Ec 64
Fletcher Path. SE8—52Cc 106
Fletcher Rd. W4—48Sa 79
Fletcher Rd. Cher—79F 138
Fletcher Rd. Chig—22Vc 47
Fletchers Clo. Brom—70Kc 129
Fletcher St. E1—45Wb 83
Fletching Rd. E5—34Yb 64
Fletching Rd. SE7—51Mc 107
Fletton Rd. N11—24Nb 42
Fleur de Lis Ct. EC4—(3A 200)
Fleur de Lis St. E1 —42Ub 83 (6K 195)
Fleur Gates. SW19—59Za 102
Flexmere Gdns. N17—25Ub 43
Flexmere Rd. N17—25Tb 43
Flight App. NW9—26Va 40
Flimwell Clo. Brom—64Gc 129
Flint Clo. Lea—98Ea 176
Flintlock Clo. Stai—56J 97
Flintmill Cres. SE3—54Nc 108
Flinton St. SE17—50Ub 83 (7J 207)
Flint St. SE17—49Tb 83 (6G 207)
Flint St. Grays—51Xd 112
Flitcroft St. WC2 —44Mb 82 (3E 198)
Flockton St. SE16—47Wb 83
Flodden Rd. SE5—53Sb 105
Flood St. SW3—50Gb 81 (7E 202)
Flood Wlk. SW3—51Gb 103
Flora Clo. E14—44Dc 84
Flora Gdns. W6—49Xa 80
Flora Gdns. Romf—30Yc 47
Floral Ct. Asht—90La 160
Floral St. WC2—45Nb 82 (4F 199)
Flora St. Belv—50Bd 87
Florence Av. Enf—13Sb 25
Florence Av. Mord—71Eb 145
Florence Av. Wey—83J 157
Florence Clo. Grays—51Ae 113
Florence Clo. Horn—33Nd 69
Florence Clo. W on T—73X 141
Florence Clo. Wat—7W 4
Florence Cotts. SE14—53Bc 106
Florence Ct. W9—(4A 190)
Florence Dri. Enf—13Sb 25
Florence Gdns. W4—51Sa 101
Florence Gdns. Stai—66K 119
Florence Rd. E6—39Lc 65
Florence Rd. E13—40Jc 65
Florence Rd. N4—31Pb 62
Florence Rd. SE2—49Yc 87
Florence Rd. SE14—53Bc 106
Florence Rd. SW19—65Db 125
Florence Rd. W4—48Ta 79
Florence Rd. W5—45Na 79
Florence Rd. Beck—68Ac 128
Florence Rd. Brom—67Jc 129
Florence Rd. Felt—60X 99
Florence Rd. King—66Pa 123
Florence Rd. S'hall—49Z 77
Florence Rd. S Croy—81Tb 165
Florence Rd. W on T—73X 141
Florence St. E16—42Hc 85
Florence St. N1—38Rb 63
Florence St. NW4—28Ya 40
Florence Ter. SE14—53Bc 106
Florence Ter. SW15—62Ua 124
Florfield Rd. E8—37Xb 63
Florian Av. Sutt—77Fb 145
Florian Rd. SW15—56Ab 102
Florida Clo. Bush, Wat—19Fa 20
Florida Rd. T Hth—67Rb 127
Florida St. E2—41Wb 83
Floriston Av. Uxb—38S 56
Floriston Clo. Stan—25Ka 38
Floriston Gdns. Stan—25Ka 38
Floss St. SW15—54Ya 102
Flower & Dean Wlk. E1 —43Vb 83 (1K 201)
Flower Cres. Cher—79D 138
Flowerfield. Sev—89Hd 170
Flowerhill Way. Grav—6A 136
Flower Ho. Clo. SE6—64Ec 128
Flower Ho. Est. SE6—63Ec 128
Flower La. NW7—22Va 40
Flower La. God—100Ac 182
Flowersmead. SW17—61Jb 126
Flower Wlk., The. SW7 —47Eb 81 (2A 202)
Floyd Rd. SE7—50Lc 85
Floyd's La. Wok—88J 157
Fludyer St. SE13—56Gc 107
Flyers Way, The. West—98Tc 184
Folair Way. SE16—50Xb 83
Foley Rd. Esh—80Ga 142
Foley Rd. West—90Mc 167
Foley St. W1—43Lb 82 (1B 198)
Folgate St. E1—43Ub 83 (7J 195)
Foliot St. W12—44Va 80
Folkes La. Upm—28Vd 50
Folkestone Rd. E6—40Qc 66
Folkestone Rd. E17—28Dc 44
Folkestone Rd. N18—21Wb 43
Folkingham La. NW9—25Ta 39
Folkington Corner. N12 —22Bb 41
Follet Dri. Abb L, Wat—3V 4
Follett Clo. Wind—8M 95
Follett St. E14—44Ec 84
Follingham Ct. N1—(3J 195)
Folly Clo. Rad—8Ha 6
Follyfield Rd. Bans—86Cb 163
Folly La. E17—24Bc 44
Folly M. W11—44Bb 81
Folly Pathway. Rad—7Ha 6
Folly Wall. E14—47Ec 84
Fontaine Rd. SW16—66Pb 126
Fontarabia Rd. SW11—56Jb 104
Fontayne Av. Chig—21Sc 46
Fontayne Av. Rain—38Gd 68
Fontayne Av. Romf—26Gd 48
Fontenoy Pas. SE11—(6B 206)
Fontenoy Rd. SW12—61Kb 126
Fonteyne Gdns. Wfd G—26Mc 45
Fonthill Clo. SE20—68Wb 127
Fonthill M. N4—33Qb 62
Fonthill Rd. N4—32Pb 62
Font Hills. N2—26Eb 41
Fontley Way. SW15—59Wa 102
Fontmell Clo. Ashf—64Q 120
Fontmell Pk. Ashf—64P 119
Fontwell Clo. Harr—24Ga 38
Fontwell Clo. N'holt—37Ca 57
Fontwell Dri. Brom—71Qc 150
Football La. Harr—32Ha 58
Footbury Hill Rd. Orp—73Wc 151
Footpath, The. SW15—57Wa 102
Foots Cray High St. Sidc —65Yc 131
Foots Cray La. Sidc—60Yc 109
Footscray Rd. SE9—58Qc 108
Forbes Av. Pot B—5Fb 9
Forbes St. E1—44Wb 83
Forburg Rd. N16—32Wb 63
Force Grn. La. West—96Tc 184
Fordbridge Clo. Cher—74K 139
Fordbridge Rd. Ashf—65N 119
Fordbridge Rd. Shep & Sun —72U 140
Ford Clo. Ashf—65N 119
Ford Clo. Bush, Wat—14Ea 20
Ford Clo. Harr—31Fa 58
Ford Clo. Rain—38Hd 68
Ford Clo. Shep—70Q 120
Ford Clo. T Hth—71Rb 147
Fordcroft Rd. Orp—71Xc 151
Forde Av. Brom—69Lc 129
Fordel Rd. SE6—60Fc 107
Ford End. Wfd G—23Kc 45
Fordham Clo. Barn—13Gb 23
Fordham Clo. W Dray—44P 75
Fordham Rd. Barn—13Fb 23
Fordham St. E1—44Wb 83
Fordhook Av. W5—45Pa 79
Fordingley Rd. W9—41Bb 81
Fordington Ho. SE26—62Xb 127
Fordington Rd. N6—29Hb 41
Ford La. Iver—44J 75
Ford La. Rain—38Hd 68
Fordmill Rd. SE6—61Cc 128
Ford Rd. E3—40Bc 64
Ford Rd. Ashf—63P 119
Ford Rd. Cher—74K 139
Ford Rd. Dag—38Bd 67
Ford Rd. Grav—57De 113
Ford Rd. Wok—92D 172
Fords Gro. N21—18Sb 25
Fords Pk. Rd. E16—44Jc 85
Ford Sq. E1—43Xb 83
Ford St. E3—39Ac 64
(in two parts)
Ford St. E16—44Hc 85
Fordwater Rd. Cher—74K 139
Fordwater Trading Est. Cher —74L 139
Fordwich Clo. Orp—73Vc 151
Fordwych Rd. NW2—36Ab 60
Fordyce Rd. SE13—58Ec 106
Fordyke Rd. Dag—33Bd 67
Foreign St. SE5—54Rb 105
Foreland Ct. NW4—25Za 40
Foreland St. SE18—49Tc 86
Foreman Ct. W6—49Ya 80
Foremark Clo. Ilf—22Vc 47
Foreshore. SE8—49Bc 84
Forest App. E4—17Gc 27
Forest App. Wfd G—24Jc 45
Forest Av. E4—17Gc 27
Forest Av. Chig—22Qc 46
Forest Clo. E11—29Jc 45
Forest Clo. Chst—67Qc 130
Forest Clo. Lea—97V 174
Forest Clo. Wal A—9Kc 13
Forest Clo. Wok—87F 156
Forest Clo. Wfd G—20Kc 27
Forest Ct. E4—18Hc 27
Forest Ct. E11—28Gc 45
Forest Cres. Asht—88Qa 161
Forestdale. N14—21Mb 42
Forestdale Centre, The. Croy —80Bc 148
Forest Dri. E12—34Mc 65
Forest Dri. Epp—8Uc 14
Forest Dri. Kes—77Nc 150
Forest Dri. Sun—66V 120
Forest Dri. Tad—93Cb 179
Forest Dri. Wfd G—24Fc 45
Forest Dri. E. E11—31Fc 65
Forest Dri. W. E11—31Ec 64
Forest Edge. Buck H—21Lc 45
Forester Rd. SE15—55Xb 105
Foresters Clo. Wall—80Mb 146
Foresters Clo. Wok—6C 188
Foresters Cres. Bexh—56Dd 110
Foresters Dri. E17—28Fc 45
Foresters Dri. Wall—80Mb 146
Forest Gdns. N17—26Vb 43
Forest Ga. NW9—29Ua 40
Forest Glade. E4—22Gc 45
Forest Glade. E11—30Gc 45
Forest Gro. E8—38Vb 63
Forest Hill Rd.—58Xb 105
SE22 3-41 & 2-128
SE23 remainder
Forestholme Clo. SE23—61Yb 128
Forest Industrial Pk. Ilf—25Uc 46
Forest La.—36Gc 65
E15 1-91
E7 remainder
Forest La. Chig—22Qc 46
Forest La. Lea—96V 174
Forest Mt. Rd. Wfd G—24Fc 45
Fore St. EC2—43Sb 83 (1E 200)
Fore St. Pinn—28V 36
Fore St. Av. EC2—43Tb 83 (1F 201)
Forest Ridge. Beck—69Cc 128
Forest Ridge. Kes—77Nc 150
Forest Rise. E17—28Fc 45
(in three parts)
Forest Rd. E7—35Jc 65
Forest Rd. E8—37Vb 63
Forest Rd. E11—31Fc 65
Forest Rd. E17—28Yb 44
Forest Rd. N9—18Xb 25
Forest Rd. Enf—8Ac 12
Forest Rd. Eri—53Jd 110
Forest Rd. Felt—61Y 121
Forest Rd. Ilf—26Tc 46
Forest Rd. Lea—96W 174
Forest Rd. Lea—98V 174
Forest Rd. Lou—13Mc 27
Forest Rd. Rich—52Qa 101
Forest Rd. Romf—27Dd 48
Forest Rd. Sutt—74Cb 145
Forest Rd. Wal X—1Zb 12
Forest Rd. Wat—5X 5
Forest Rd. Wind—4C 94
Forest Rd. Wok—87F 156
Forest Rd. Wfd G—20Jc 27
Forest Side. E4—17Hc 27
Forest Side. E7—35Kc 65
Forest Side. Buck H—18Lc 27
Forest Side. Epp—5Tc 14
Forest Side. Wal A—8Lc 13

Goodley Stock—Gt. Ormond St.

Goodley Stock. West—100Rc 184
Goodman Cres. SW2—61Mb 126
Goodman Pk. Slou—6N 73
Goodman Pl. Stai—63H 119
Goodman Rd. E10—31Ec 64
Goodman's Ct. E1
—45Vb 83 (4K 201)
Goodman's Stile. E1—44Wb 83
Goodman's Yd. E1
—45Vb 83 (4K 201)
Goodmayes Av. Ilf—32Wc 67
Goodmayes La. Ilf—34Wc 67
Goodmayes Rd. Ilf—32Wc 67
Goodmead Rd. Orp—73Wc 151
Goodrich Clo. Wat—7W 4
Goodrich Rd. SE22—58Vb 105
Goodson Rd. NW10—38Ua 60
Goods Way. NW1
—39Mb 62 (1F 193)
Goodway Gdns. E14—44Fc 85
Goodwin Ct. NW1—(1C 192)
Goodwin Ct. SW19—66Gb 125
Goodwin Dri. Sidc—62Zc 131
Goodwin Gdns. Croy—79Rb 147
Goodwin Rd. N9—18Zb 26
Goodwin Rd. W12—47Wa 80
Goodwin Rd. Croy—78Rb 147
Goodwin Rd. Slou—1D 72
Goodwins Ct. WC2—(4F 199)
Goodwin St. N4—33Qb 62
Goodwood Av. Enf—9Yb 12
Goodwood Av. Horn—35Nd 69
Goodwood Av. Wat—7U 4
Goodwood Clo. Mord—70Cb 125
Goodwood Cres. Grav—5E 136
Goodwood Dri. N'holt—37Ca 57
Goodwood Pde. Beck—70Ac 128
Goodwood Path. Borwd—12Qa 21
Goodwood Rd. SE14—52Ac 106
★Goodworth. Sev—88Be
Goodwyn Av. NW7—22Ua 40
Goodwyns Vale. N10—25Kb 42
Goodyear Pl. SE5—51Sb 105
Goodyear Ter. Grays—51Wd 112
Goodyers Av. Rad—5Ha 6
Goodyers Gdns. NW4—29Za 40
Goosander Way. SE28—48Tc 86
Gooseacre La. Harr—29Ma 39
Goose Grn. Cob—91X 175
Goose Grn. Slou—10F 52
Goose Grn. Clo. Orp—68Wc 131
Goose La. Wok—10E 188
Gooseley La. E6—41Qc 86
(in two parts)
Goose Sq. E6—44Pc 86
Gooshays Dri. Romf—22Nd 49
Gooshays Gdns. Romf—23Nd 49
Gophir La. EC4—45Tb 83 (4F 201)
Gopsall St. N1—39Tb 63 (1G 195)
Goral Mead. Rick—18M 17
Gordon Av. E4—23Gc 45
Gordon Av. SW14—56Ua 102
Gordon Av. Horn—33Hd 68
Gordon Av. S Croy—82Sb 165
Gordon Av. Stan—24Ha 38
Gordon Av. Twic—57Ja 100
Gordonbrock Rd. SE4—57Cc 106
Gordon Clo. E17—30Cc 44
Gordon Clo. N19—33Lb 62
Gordon Clo. Cher—76G 138
Gordon Clo. Stai—65K 119
Gordon Ct. W12—44Ya 80
Gordon Cres. Croy—74Vb 147
Gordon Cres. Hay—49W 76
Gordondale Rd. SW19—61Cb 125
Gordon Dri. Cher—76G 138
Gordon Gdns. Edgw—26Ra 39
Gordon Gro. SE5—54Rb 105
Gordon Hill. Enf—11Sb 25
Gordon Ho. Rd. NW5—35Jb 62
Gordon Pl. W8—47Cb 81
Gordon Pl. Grav—8E 114
Gordon Prom. Grav—8E 114
Gordon Rd. E4—17Gc 27
Gordon Rd. E11—30Jc 45
Gordon Rd. E15—35Ec 64
Gordon Rd. E18—25Kc 45
Gordon Rd. N3—24Bb 41
Gordon Rd. N9—19Xb 25
Gordon Rd. N11—24Mb 42
Gordon Rd. SE15—54Xb 105
Gordon Rd. W4—51Ra 101
Gordon Rd.—45Ka 78
W5 1-95 & 2-84
W13 remainder
Gordon Rd. Ashf—62N 119
Gordon Rd. Bark—39Uc 66
Gordon Rd. Beck—69Bc 128
Gordon Rd. Belv—49Ed 88
Gordon Rd. Brtwd—18Ce 33
Gordon Rd. Cars—79Hb 145
Gordon Rd. Cat—93Tb 181
Gordon Rd. Dart—59Md 111
Gordon Rd. Enf—11Sb 25
Gordon Rd. Esh—80Ga 142
Gordon Rd. Grav—9A 114
Gordon Rd. Grays—7A 92
Gordon Rd. Harr—27Ga 38
Gordon Rd. Houn—56Ea 100
Gordon Rd. Ilf—34Tc 66
Gordon Rd. King—67Pa 123
Gordon Rd. Rich—54Pa 101
Gordon Rd. Romf—30Bd 47
Gordon Rd. Sev—97Kd 187
Gordon Rd. Shep—72T 140
Gordon Rd. Sidc—57Uc 108
Gordon Rd. S'hall—49Aa 77
Gordon Rd. Stai—63E 118
Gordon Rd. Stanf—1H 93
Gordon Rd. Surb—73Pa 143
Gordon Rd. Wal A—6Cc 12
Gordon Rd. W Dray
—45N 75
Gordon Rd. Wind—4D 94
Gordon Sq. WC1
—42Mb 82 (5D 192)
Gordon St. E13—41Jc 85
Gordon St. WC1—42Mb 82 (5D 192)
Gordons Way. Oxt—100Hc 183
Gordon Way. Barn—14Bb 23
Gore Ct. NW9—29Qa 39
Gorefield Pl. NW6—40Cb 61
Gorelands La. Chal—18A 16
Gorelands La. Chal & Ger X
—19A 16
Gore Rd. E9—39Yb 64
Gore Rd. SW20—68Ya 124
Gore Rd. Dart—61Sd 134
Gore Rd. Slou—1A 72
Goresbrook Rd. Dag—39Xc 67
Gore St. SW7—48Eb 81 (3A 202)
Gorham Pl. W11—45Ab 80
Goring Clo. Romf—25Ed 48
Goring Gdns. Dag—35Yc 67
Goring Rd. N11—23Nb 42
Goring Rd. Dag—37Fd 68
Goring Rd. Stai—64F 118
Goring Sq. Stai—63G 118
Goring St. EC3—(2J 210)
Goring Way. Gnfd—40Ea 58
Gorle Clo. Wat—7W 4
Gorleston Rd. N15—29Tb 43
Gorleston St. W14—49Ab 80
Gorman Rd. SE18—49Pc 86
Gorringe Av. S Dar, Dart—68Td 134
Gorringe Pk. Av. Mitc—66Jb 126
Gorse Hill. F'ham, Dart—72Pd 153
Gorse Hill La. Vir W—70A 118
Gorse Hill La. Vir W—10P 117
Gorse Hill Rd. Vir W—10P 117
Gorselands Clo. Wey—83L 157
Gorse Rise. SW17—64Jb 126
Gorse Rd. Croy—77Cc 148
Gorse Rd. Orp—75Cd 152
Gorse Wlk. W Dray—44N 75
Gorse Way. Long, Dart—71Be 155
Gorseway. Romf—32Gd 68
Gorsewood Rd. Long, Dart
—71Be 155
(in two parts)
Gorsewood Rd. Wok—7A 188
Gorst Rd. NW10—42Sa 79
Gorst Rd. SW11—58Hb 103
Gorsuch Pl. E2—41Vb 83 (3K 195)
Gorsuch St. E2—41Vb 83 (3K 195)
Gosberton Rd. SW12—60Jb 104
Gosbury Hill. Chess—77Na 143
Gosfield Rd. Dag—33Cd 68
Gosfield Rd. Eps—84Ta 161
Gosfield St. W1—43Lb 82 (1B 198)
Gosford Gdns. Ilf—29Pc 46
Gosforth La. Wat—20W 18
Gosforth Path. Wat—20W 18
Goshawk Gdns. Hay—41U 76
Goslar Way. Wind—4F 94
Goslett Yd. WC2—44Mb 82 (2E 198)
Gosling Clo. Gnfd—41Ca 77
Gosling Grn. Slou—48A 74
Gosling Rd. Slou—48A 74
Gosling Way. SW9—53Qb 104
Gosmore Farm Clo. Cher—73H 139
Gospatrick Rd. N17—24Sb 43
Gospel Oak Est. NW5—36Hb 61
Gosport Dri. Horn—37Ld 69
Gosport Rd. E17—29Bc 44
Gosport Wlk. N17—28Xb 43
Gosport Way. SE15—52Vb 105
Gossage Rd. SE18—50Tc 86
Gossage Rd. Uxb—38P 55
Gossamers, The. Wat—7Aa 5
Gosset St. E2—41Vb 83 (3K 195)
Goss Hill. Swan—65Ld 133
Gosshill Rd. Chst—68Qc 130
Gosterwood St. SE8—51Ac 106
Gostling Rd. Twic—60Ca 99
Goston Gdns. T Hth—69Qb 126
Goswell Hill. Wind—3H 95
Goswell Pl. EC1—(4C 194)
Goswell Rd. EC1—41Rb 83 (2B 194)
Goswell Rd. Wind—3H 95
Gothic Clo. Dart—62Md 133
Gothic Ct. Hay—51T 98
Gothic Rd. Twic—61Fa 122
Goudhurst Rd. Brom—64Gc 129
Gouge Av. Grav—10A 114
Gough Rd. E15—35Hc 65
Gough Rd. Enf—12Xb 25
Gough Sq. EC4—44Qb 82 (2A 200)
Gough St. WC1—42Pb 82 (5J 193)
Gough Wlk. E14—44Cc 84
Gould Rd. Felt—59U 98
Gould Rd. Twic—60Ga 100
Gould's Grn. Uxb—45R 76
Gould Ter. E8—36Xb 63
Goulston St. E1—44Vb 83 (2K 201)
Goulton Rd. E5—35Xb 63
Gourley Pl. N15—29Ub 43
Gourley St. N15—29Ub 43
Gourney Gro. Grays—45De 91
Gourock Rd. SE9—57Qc 108
Govan St. E2—39Wb 63
Government Row. Enf—10Cc 12
Governors Av. Uxb—29H 35
Govett Av. Shep—71S 140
Govier Clo. E15—38Gc 65
Gowan Av. SW6—53Ab 102
Gowan Rd. NW10—37Xa 60
Gowar Field. Pot B—4Wa 8
Gower Ct. WC1—42Mb 82 (5D 192)
Gower M. WC1—43Mb 82 (7E 192)
Gower Pl. WC1—42Mb 82 (5C 192)
Gower Rd. E7—37Jc 65
Gower Rd. Iswth—51Ha 100
Gower Rd. Wey—79T 140
Gowers La. Grays—7B 92
Gower St. WC1—42Lb 82 (5C 192)
Gowers Wlk. E1—44Wb 83
Gower, The. Egh—69D 118
Gowland Pl. Beck—68Bc 128
Gowlett Rd. SE15—55Wb 105
Gowrie Rd. SW11—55Jb 104
Graburn Way. E Mol—69Fa 122
Grace Av. Bexh—54Bd 109
Gracechurch Ct. EC3—(4G 201)
Gracechurch St. EC3
—45Tb 83 (4G 201)
Grace Clo. SE9—62Mc 129
Gracedale Rd. SW16—64Kb 126
Gracefield Gdns. SW16—62Nb 126
Grace Path. SE26—63Yb 128
Grace Rd. Croy—72Sb 147
Grace's All. E1—45Wb 83
Grace's M. SE5—54Ub 105
Grace's Rd. SE5—54Ub 105
Grace St. E3—41Dc 84
Gradient, The. SE26—63Wb 127
Graeme Rd. Enf—12Tb 25
Graemesdyke Av. SW14
—56Ra 101
Grafton Clo. W13—44Ja 78
Grafton Clo. Houn—60Aa 99
Grafton Clo. Slou—44A 74
Grafton Clo. Wey—85H 157
Grafton Clo. Wor Pk—76Ua 144
Grafton Cres. NW1—37Kb 62
Grafton Gdns. N4—30Sb 43
Grafton Gdns. Dag—33Ad 67
Grafton M. W1—42Lb 82 (6B 192)
Grafton Pk. Rd. Wor Pk—76Ua 144
Grafton Pl. NW1—41Mb 82 (4E 192)
Grafton Rd. NW5—36Jb 62
Grafton Rd. W3—45Sa 79
Grafton Rd. Croy—74Qb 146
Grafton Rd. Dag—33Ad 67
Grafton Rd. Enf—13Pb 24
Grafton Rd. Harr—29Ea 38
Grafton Rd. N Mald—69Ua 124
Grafton Rd. Wor Pk—76Ta 143
Grafton Sq. SW4—55Lb 104
Graftons, The. NW2—34Cb 61
Grafton St. W1—45Kb 82 (5A 198)
Grafton Ter. NW5—36Hb 61
Grafton Way. W1
—42Lb 82 (6B 192)
Grafton Yd. NW5—37Kb 62
Graham Av. W13—47Ka 78
Graham Av. Mitc—67Jb 126
Graham Clo. Brtwd—15Ee 33
Graham Clo. Croy—75Cc 148
Grahame Pk. Way. NW9 & NW7
—26Va 40
Graham Gdns. Surb—74Na 143
Graham Rd. E8—37Wb 63
Graham Rd. E13—42Jc 85
Graham Rd. N15—27Rb 43
Graham Rd. NW4—30Xa 40
Graham Rd. SW19—66Bb 125
Graham Rd. W4—48Ta 79
Graham Rd. Bexh—56Bd 109
Graham Rd. Hmptn—63Ca 121
Graham Rd. Harr—27Ga 38
Graham Rd. Mitc—67Jb 126
Graham Rd. Purl—85Qb 164
Graham St. N1—40Rb 63 (2C 194)
Graham Ter. SW1
—49Jb 82 (6H 203)
Grainger Clo. N'holt—37Ea 58
Grainger Rd. N22—25Sb 43
Grainger Rd. Iswth—54Ha 100
Grainges Yd. Uxb—38L 55
Gramer Clo. E11—33Fc 65
Grampian Clo. Hay—52T 98
Grampian Clo. Orp—72Vc 151
Grampian Gdns. NW2—32Ab 60
Grampian Way. Slou—50C 74
Granada St. SW17—64Hb 125
Granard Av. SW15—57Xa 102
Granard Rd. SW12—59Hb 103
★Granary Meadow. Brtwd—8Ae
Granary St. NW1—39Mb 62
Granby Bldgs. SE11—(6H 205)
Granby Pk. Rd. Wal X—1Vb 11
Granby Rd. SE9—54Pc 108
Granby Rd. Grav—58Ee 113
Granby St. E2—42Vb 83
Granby Ter. NW1
—40Lb 62 (2B 192)
Grand Av. EC1—43Rb 83 (7C 194)
Grand Av. N10—28Jb 42
Grand Av. Surb—71Ra 143
Grand Av. Wemb—36Qa 59
Grand Av. E. Wemb—36Ra 59
Grand Depot Rd. SE18—50Qc 86
Grand Dri. SW20—68Ya 124
Granden Rd. SW16—68Nb 126
Grandfield Av. Wat—11W 18
(in two parts)
Grandison Rd. SW11—57Hb 103
Grandison Rd. Wor Pk—75Ya 144
Grand Pde. N4—29Rb 43
Grand Pde. M. SW15—57Ab 102
Grand Stand Rd. Eps—89Va 162
Grand Union Industrial Est.
NW10—40Ra 59
Grand View Av. West—88Lc 167
Grand Wlk. E1—42Ac 84
Granfield St. SW11—53Fb 103
Grange Av. N12—22Eb 41
Grange Av. N20—17Ab 22
Grange Av. SE25—68Ub 127
Grange Av. Barn—18Gb 23
Grange Av. Stan—26Ka 38
Grange Av. Twic—61Ga 122
Grange Av. Wfd G—24Jc 45
Grangecliffe Gdns. SE25
—68Ub 127
Grange Clo. Brtwd—22Ee 51
Grange Clo. E Mol—70Da 121
Grange Clo. Edgw—22Sa 39
Grange Clo. Ger X—25A 34
Grange Clo. Hay—43U 76
Grange Clo. Houn—51Ba 99
Grange Clo. Lea—92Ma 177
Grange Clo. Red—100Kb 180
Grange Clo. Sidc—62Wc 131
Grange Clo. West—98Sc 184
Grange Clo. Wfd G—24Jc 45
Grange Clo. Wray, Stai—58A 96
Grange Ct. WC2—44Pb 82 (3J 199)
Grange Ct. Lou—15Mc 27
Grange Ct. N'holt—40Y 57
Grange Ct. Red—100Kb 180
Grange Ct. Wal A—6Ec 12
Grange Ct. W on T—75W 140
Grangecourt Rd. N16—32Ub 63
Grange Cres. SE28—44Yc 87
Grange Cres. Chig—22Tc 46
Grangedale Clo. N'wd—24U 36
Grange Dri. Chst—65Nc 130
Grange Dri. Orp—81Yc 169
Grange Dri. Red—100Kb 180
Grange Dri. Wok—87A 156
Grange Farm Clo. Harr—33Ea 58
Grange Field. Ger X—25A 34
Grangefields Rd. Guild—100A 172
Grange Gdns. N14—18Mb 24
Grange Gdns. NW3—34Db 61
Grange Gdns. SE25—68Ub 127
Grange Gdns. Bans—85Db 163
Grange Gdns. Pinn—27Aa 37
Grange Gdns. Slou—6H 53
Grange Gro. N1—37Sb 63
Grange Hill. SE25—68Ub 127
Grange Hill. Edgw—22Sa 39
Grangehill Rd. SE9—56Pc 108
Grange La. SE21—61Vb 127
Grange La. Long, Dart—73Ce 155
Grange Mans. Eps—80Va 144
Grange Meadow. Bans—85Db 163
Grangemill Rd. SE6—62Cc 128
Grangemill Way. SE6—61Cc 128
Grange Mt. Lea—92Ma 177
Grange Pde. Hay—43U 76
Grange Pk. W5—46Na 79
Grange Pk. Wok—87A 156
Grange Pk. Av. N21—16Sb 25
Grange Pk. Rd. E10—32Dc 64
Grange Pk. Rd. T Hth—70Tb 127
Grange Pl. NW6—38Cb 61
Grange Pl. Stai—68L 119
Grange Rd. E10—32Cc 64
Grange Rd. E13—41Hc 85
Grange Rd. E17—29Ac 44
Grange Rd. N6—30Jb 42
Grange Rd.—23Wb 43
N17 1-51 & 2-10a
N18 remainder
Grange Rd. NW10—37Xa 60
Grange Rd. SE1—48Ub 83 (4J 207)
Grange Rd.—69Tb 127
SE25 31-313 & 216-248
SE19 315-361 & 250-352
T Hth remainder
Grange Rd. SW13—53Wa 102
Grange Rd. W4—50Ra 79
Grange Rd. W5—46Ma 79
Grange Rd. Borwd—15Pa 21
Grange Rd. Cat—97Wb 181
Grange Rd. Chess—77Na 143
Grange Rd. E Mol—70Da 121
Grange Rd. Edgw—23Ta 39
Grange Rd. Egh—64B 118
Grange Rd. Ger X—25A 34
Grange Rd. Grav—9C 114
Grange Rd. Grays—51De 113
Grange Rd. Harr—29Ja 38
Grange Rd. Harr—33Fa 58
(Roxeth)
Grange Rd. Hay—44U 76
Grange Rd. Ilf—35Rc 66
Grange Rd. King—69Na 123
Grange Rd. Lea—92Ma 177
Grange Rd. Orp—76Sc 150
Grange Rd. Romf—23Kd 49
Grange Rd. Sev—99Jd 186
Grange Rd. Sev
Grange Rd. S'hall—47Aa 77
Grange Rd. S Croy—82Sb 165
Grange Rd. S Ock—46Sd 90
Grange Rd. Sutt—80Cb 145
Grange Rd. W on T—77Aa 141
Grange Rd. Wat—11Fa 20
Grange Rd. Wey—82J 157
Grange Rd. Wok—86A 156
Granger Way. Romf—30Jd 48
Grange St. N1—39Tb 63 (1G 195)
Grange, The. SE1—48Vb 83 (4K 207)
Grange, The. SW19—65Za 124
Grange, The. Croy—75Bc 148
Grange, The. S Dar, Dart—67Td 134
Grange, The. Wemb—38Qa 59
Grange, The. Wor Pk—77Ta 143
Grange Vale. Sutt—80Db 145
Grangeview Rd. N20—18Eb 23
Grange Wlk. SE1
—48Ub 83 (3J 207)
Grange Way. N12—21Db 41
Grange Way. NW6—38Cb 61
Grange Way. Eri—52Kd 111
Grange Way. Iver—44H 75
Grange Way. Long, Dart—72Be 155
Grange Way. Wfd G—21Lc 45
Grangeway Gdns. Ilf—29Nc 46
Grangeways Clo. Grav—3B 136
Grangeway, The. N21—16Rb 25
Grangewood. Bex—60Bd 109
Grangewood. Pot B—2Db 9
Grangewood. Slou—3N 73
Grangewood Av. Grays—8A 92
Grangewood Av. Rain—42Ld 89
Grangewood Clo. Brtwd—20Ce 33
Grange Wood Clo. Pinn—29W 36
Grange Wood Dri. Sun—66V 120
Grange Wood La. Beck—65Bc 128
Grangewood St. E6—39Mc 65
Grange Yd. SE1—48Vb 83 (4K 207)
Granham Gdns. N9—19Vb 25
Granite St. SE18—50Vc 87
Granleigh Rd. E11—33Gc 65
Gransden Av. E8—38Xb 63
Gransden Rd. W12—47Va 80
Grant Av. Slou—4J 73
Grantbridge St. N1
—40Rb 63 (1C 194)
Grant Clo. N14—17Lb 24
Grant Clo. Shep—72R 140
Grantham Clo. Edgw—20Na 21
Grantham Gdns. Romf—31Bd 67
Grantham Grn. Borwd—15Sa 21
Grantham Pl. W1
—46Kb 82 (7K 197)
Grantham Rd. E12—35Qc 66
Grantham Rd. SW9—54Nb 104
Grantham Rd. W4—52Ua 102
Grantham Way. Grays—46Ce 91
Grantley Rd. Houn—54Y 99
Grantley St. E1—41Zb 84
Grantock Rd. E17—25Fc 45
Granton Av. Upm—33Pd 69
Granton Rd. SW16—67Lb 126
Granton Rd. Ilf—32Wc 67
Granton Rd. Sidc—65Yc 131
Grant Pl. Croy—74Vb 147
Grant Rd. SW11—56Fb 103
Grant Rd. Croy—74Vb 147
Grant Rd. Harr—27Ga 38
Grants Clo. NW7—24Ya 40
Grant St. E13—41Jc 85
Grant St. N1—40Qb 62 (1K 193)
Grantully Rd. W9—41Db 81
Granville Av. N9—20Yb 26
Granville Av. Felt—61W 120
Granville Av. Houn—57Ca 99
Granville Clo. Croy—75Ub 147
Granville Clo. Wey—79S 140
Granville Clo. Wey—85P 157
(Byfleet)
Granville Gdns. SW16—66Pb 126
Granville Gdns. W5—46Pa 79
Granville Gro. SE13—55Ec 106
Granville M. Sidc—63Wc 131
Granville Pk. SE13—55Ec 106
Granville Pl. N12—24Eb 41
Granville Pl. W1—44Jb 82 (3H 197)
Granville Rd. E17—30Dc 44
Granville Rd. E18—26Kc 45
Granville Rd. N4—30Pb 42
Granville Rd. N12—24Eb 41
Granville Rd. N13—23Pb 42
Granville Rd. N22—25Rb 43
Granville Rd. NW2—33Bb 61
Granville Rd. NW6—40Cb 61
(in two parts)
Granville Rd. SW18—59Bb 103
Granville Rd. SW19—66Cb 125
Granville Rd. Barn—13Za 22
Granville Rd. Epp—1Xc 15
Granville Rd. Grav—9B 114
Granville Rd. Hay—49W 76
Granville Rd. Ilf—32Rc 66
Granville Rd. Oxt—100Hc 183
Granville Rd. Sev—96Jd 186
Granville Rd. Sidc—63Wc 131
Granville Rd. Slou—3H 73
Granville Rd. Uxb—37R 56
Granville Rd. Wat—14Y 19
Granville Rd. Well—55Yc 109
Granville Rd. West—98Sc 184
Granville Rd. Wey—80S 140
Granville Rd. Wok—92B 172
Granville Sq. WC1
—41Pb 82 (4J 193)
Granville St. WC1
—41Pb 82 (4J 193)
Grape St. WC2—44Nb 82 (2F 199)
Grasdene Rd. SE18—52Wc 109
Grasmere Av. SW15—63Ta 123
Grasmere Av. SW19—69Cb 125
Grasmere Av. W3—45Ta 79
Grasmere Av. Houn—58Da 99
Grasmere Av. Orp—76Rc 150
Grasmere Av. Ruis—31S 56
Grasmere Av. Slou—5L 73
Grasmere Av. Wemb—31La 58
Grasmere Clo. Lou—12Pc 28
Grasmere Gdns. Harr—26Ja 38
Grasmere Gdns. Ilf—29Pc 46
Grasmere Gdns. Orp—76Rc 150
Grasmere Pde. Slou—5M 73
Grasmere Rd. E13—40Jc 65
Grasmere Rd. N10—25Kb 42
Grasmere Rd. N17—23Wb 43
Grasmere Rd. SE25—71Xb 147
Grasmere Rd. SW16—64Pb 126
Grasmere Rd. Bexh—54Ed 110
Grasmere Rd. Brom—67Hc 129
Grasmere Rd. Horn—28Pd 49
Grasmere Rd. Orp—76Rc 150
Grasmere Rd. Purl—83Rb 165
Grasmere Way. Wey—84P 157
Grassingham End. Ger X—24A 34
Grassingham Rd. Ger X—24A 34
Grassington Clo. St Alb—2Ca 5
Grassington Rd. Sidc—63Wc 131
Grassmount. SE23—61Xb 127
Grassmount. Purl—82Lb 164
Grass Pk. N3—25Bb 41
Grass Rd. Long, Dart—71Ee 155
Grass Way. Wall—77Lb 146
Grassy La. Sev—98Kd 187
Grasvenor Av. Barn—15Cb 23
Grateley Way. SE15—52Vb 105
Gratton Dri. Wind—6C 94
Gratton Rd. W14—48Ab 80
Gratton Ter. NW2—34Za 60
Gravel Clo. Chig—19Wc 29
Graveley Av. Borwd—15Sa 21
Gravel Hill. N3—26Bb 41
Gravel Hill. Bexh—57Dd 110
Gravel Hill. Croy—79Zb 148
Gravel Hill. Ger X—25A 34
Gravel Hill. Lea—93Ka 176
Gravel Hill. Lou—10Jc 13
Gravel Hill. Uxb—36M 55
Gravel Hill Clo. Bexh—57Dd 110
Gravel La. E1—44Vb 83 (2K 201)
Gravel La. Chig—15Vc 29
Gravelly Hill. Cat—100Vb 181
Gravel Pit La. SE9—57Rc 108
Gravel Pits. Brom—69Jc 129
Gravel Rd. Brom—75Nc 150
Gravel Rd. Twic—60Ga 100
Gravelwood Clo. Chst—62Sc 130
Graveney Gro. SE20—66Yb 128
Graveney Rd. SW17—63Gb 125
Gravesend Rd. W12—45Wa 80
Gravesend Rd. Grav & Roch
—2M 137
★Gravesend Rd. Sev—87De
Gray Av. Dag—32Bd 67
Grayford Clo. E6—43Mc 85
Gray Gdns. Rain—37Jd 68
Grayham Cres. N Mald—70Ta 123
Grayham Rd. N Mald—70Ta 123
Grayland Clo. Brom—67Mc 129
Graylands. Epp—9Tc 14
Graylands. Wok—88A 156
Graylands Clo. Wok—88A 156
Grayling Rd. N16—33Tb 63
Grayling Sq. E2—41Wb 83
Graylings, The. Abb L, Wat—5T 4
Grayscroft Rd. SW16—66Mb 126
Gray's End Clo. Grays—48Ce 91
Grays Farm Rd. Orp—67Xc 131
Grayshott Rd. SW11—55Jb 104
Gray's Inn Ct. WC1
—43Pb 82 (1J 199)
Gray's Inn Rd. WC1
—41Pb 82 (3G 193)
Gray's Inn Sq. WC1
—43Pb 82 (7K 193)
Grays La. Ashf—63R 120
Gray's La. Asht & Eps—91Pa 177
Gray's Pk. Rd. Slou—10L 53
Grays Pl. Slou—6K 73
Gray's Rd. Slou—6K 73
Gray's Rd. Uxb—39N 55
Grays Rd. West & Sev—93Rc 184
Gray St. SE1—47Rb 83 (1B 206)
Grays Wlk. Brtwd—17Fe 33
Grayswood Gdns. SW20
—68Xa 124
Gray's Yd. W1—(2J 197)
Graywood Ct. N12—24Eb 41
Grazebrook Rd. N16—33Tb 63
Grazeley Clo. Bexh—57Ed 110
Grazeley Ct. SE19—64Ub 127
Gt. Bell All. EC2—44Tb 83 (2F 201)
Gt. Benty. W Dray—49N 75
Gt. Brownings. SE21—63Vb 127
Gt. Bushey Dri. N20—18Db 23
Gt. Cambridge Rd.—24Tb 43 to 1Yb 12
N17—24Tb 43
N18—23Tb 43
N9—20Tb 25
Enf—17Vb 25
Wal X—7Xb 11
Gt. Cambridge Rd. Wal X—3Yb 12
Gt. Castle St. W1—44Lb 82 (2B 198)
Gt. Central Av. Ruis—36Y 57
Gt. Central St. NW1
—43Hb 81 (7F 191)
Gt. Central Way. NW10—35Sa 59
Gt. Chapel St. W1
—44Mb 82 (2D 198)
Gt. Chertsey Rd. W4—53Ta 101
& 51Va 102
Gt. Chertsey Rd. Felt & Twic
—62Ba 121
Gt. Church La. W6—49Za 80
Gt. College St. SW1
—48Nb 82 (3F 205)
Gt. Cross Av. SE10—52Gc 107
Gt. Cullings. Romf—33Gd 68
Gt. Cumberland M. W1
—44Hb 81 (3F 197)
Gt. Cumberland Pl. W1
—44Hb 81 (3G 197)
Gt. Dover St. SE1
—48Tb 83 (2E 206)
Greatdown Rd. W7—43Ha 78
Gt. Eastern Rd. E15—38Fc 65
Gt. Eastern Rd. Brtwd—21Yd 50
Gt. Eastern St. EC2
—42Ub 83 (4H 195)
Gt. Ellshams. Bans—88Cb 163
Gt. Elms Rd. Brom—70Lc 129
Great Field. NW9—25Ua 40
Greatfield Av. E6—42Pc 86
Greatfield Clo. N19—35Lb 62
Gt. Field Clo. SE4—56Cc 106
Greatfields Dri. Uxb—43Q 76
Greatfields Rd. Bark—39Tc 66
★Gt. Fox Meadow. Brtwd—10Vd
Great Gdns. Rd. Horn—30Kd 49
Gt. George St. SW1
—47Mb 82 (2E 204)
Gt. Gregories La. Epp—5Uc 14
Great Gro. Bush, Wat—14Da 19
Gt. Guildford St. SE1
—46Sb 83 (6D 200)
Greatham Rd. Bush, Wat—13Z 19
Greatham Wlk. SW15—60Wa 102
Gt. Harry Dri. SE9—62Qc 130
Greathurst End. Lea—96Ba 175
Gt. James St. WC1
—43Pb 82 (7H 193)
Gt. Marlborough St. W1
—44Lb 82 (3B 198)
Gt. Maze Pond. SE1
—47Tb 83 (7G 201)
(in two parts)
Gt. Nelmes Chase. Horn—29Pd 49
Greatness La. Sev—93Ld 187
Greatness Rd. Sev—93Ld 187
Gt. Newport St. WC2
—45Nb 82 (4F 199)
Gt. New St. EC4—44Qb 82 (2A 200)
Gt. North Rd.—29Gb 41
N6 2-66
N2 remainder
Gt. North Rd. Barn—15Cb 23
(High Barnet)
Gt. North Rd. Barn—12Bb 23
(New Barnet)
Gt. North Rd. Pot B—1Eb 9
Gt. North Way. NW4—26Xa 40
Gt. Oaks. Brtwd—16De 33
Gt. Oaks. Chig—21Sc 46
Greatorex St. E1—43Wb 83
Gt. Ormond St. WC1
—43Nb 82 (7G 193)

Gt. Owl Rd. Chig—20Qc 28
Great Pk. K Lan—2Q 4
Gt. Percy St. WC1—41Pb 82 (3J 193)
Gt. Peter St. SW1—48Mb 82 (4D 204)
Gt. Portland St. W1—42Kb 82 (6A 192)
Gt. Pulteney St. W1—45Lb 82 (4C 198)
Gt. Queen St. WC2—44Nb 82 (3G 199)
Gt. Queen St. Dart—58Pd 111
Gt. Ropers La. Brtwd—23Wd 50
Gt. Russell St. WC1—44Mb 82 (2E 198)
Gt. Saint Helen's. EC3—44Ub 83 (2H 201)
Gt. Saint Thomas Apostle. EC4—45Sb 83 (4E 200)
Gt. Scotland Yd. SW1—46Nb 82 (6F 199)
Gt. Slades. Pot B—5Bb 9
Gt. Smith St. SW1—48Mb 82 (3E 204)
Gt. South West Rd. Felt & Houn—59S 98
Gt. Spilmans. SE22—57Ub 105
Gt. Strand. NW9—25Va 40
Gt. Suffolk St. SE1—46Rb 83 (7C 200)
Gt. Sutton St. EC1—42Rb 83 (6C 194)
Gt. Swan All. EC2—44Tb 83 (2F 201)
Gt. Tattenhams. Eps—90Xa 162
Gt. Thrift. Orp—70Sc 130
Gt. Titchfield St. W1—43Lb 82 (7B 192)
Gt. Tower St. EC3—45Ub 83 (4H 201)
Gt. Trinity La. EC4—45Sb 83 (4E 200)
Gt. Turnstile. WC1—43Pb 82 (1J 199)
Gt. Warley St. Brtwd—25Wd 50
Gt. Western Industrial Pk. S'hall—47Da 77
Gt. Western Rd.—43Bb 81
W9 1-59 & 2-56
W11 remainder
Gt. West Rd. W4 & W6—50Va 80
Gt. West Rd. Houn, Iswth & Bren—54Z 99
Gt. West Rd. Trading Est. Bren—52Ka 100
Gt. Winchester St. EC2—44Tb 83 (2G 201)
Gt. Windmill St. W1—45Mb 82 (4D 198)
Greatwood. Chst—66Qc 130
Greatwood Clo. Cher—81E 156
Gt. Woodcote Dri. Purl—82Mb 164
Gt. Woodcote Pk. Purl—82Mb 164
Great Yd. SE1—(1J 207)
Greaves Pl. SW17—63Gb 125
Grecian Cres. SE19—65Rb 127
Greding Wlk. Brtwd—19De 33
Greek Ct. W1—44Mb 82 (3E 198)
Greek St. W1—44Mb 82 (3E 198)
Greenacre. Egh—5N 117
Greenacre. Wind—4C 94
Greenacre. Wok—4B 188
Greenacre Clo. Barn—10Bb 9
Greenacre Clo. Swan—70Gd 132
Greenacres. SE9—58Qc 108
Greenacres. Bush, Wat—19Fa 20
Green Acres. Croy—76Vb 147
Greenacres. Epp—1Vc 15
Greenacres. Lea—96Da 175
Greenacres. Oxt—99Gc 183
Greenacres Av. Uxb—34P 55
Greenacres Clo. Rain—41Nd 89
Greenacres Dri. Stan—24Ka 38
Greenacre Wlk. N14—20Mb 24
Greenall Clo. Wal X—2Ac 12
Green Arbour Ct. EC1—(2B 200)
Green Av. NW7—21Ta 39
Green Av. W13—48Ka 78
Greenaway Gdns. NW3—35Db 61
Green Bank. N12—21Db 41
Greenbank Av. Wemb—36Ja 58
Greenbank Clo. E4—19Ec 26
Greenbank Clo. Romf—20Md 31
Greenbank Cres. NW4—28Ab 40
Greenbank Rd. Wat—8T 4
Greenbanks. Dart—61Nd 133
Green Banks. Upm—33Ud 70
Greenbay Rd. SE7—52Mc 107
Greenberry St. NW8—40Gb 61 (2D 190)
Greenbrook Av. Barn—11Eb 23
Greenbury Clo. Rick—14E 16
Green Clo. NW9—30Sa 39
Green Clo. NW11—31Eb 61
Green Clo. Brom—69Gc 129
Green Clo. Cars—75Hb 145
Green Clo. Felt—64Aa 121
Green Clo. Wal X—3Ac 12
Greencoat Pl. SW1—49Lb 82 (5C 204)
Greencoat Row. SW1—48Lb 82 (4C 204)
Green Comn. La. High W—1A 52
Greencourt Av. Croy—75Xb 147
Greencourt Av. Edgw—25Ra 39
Greencourt Gdns. Croy—75Xb 147
Greencourt Rd. Orp—71Uc 150
Green Ct. Rd. Swan—71Fd 152
Greencroft. Edgw—22Sa 39
Greencroft Av. Ruis—33Y 57
Greencroft Clo. E6—43Mc 85
Greencroft Gdns. NW6—38Db 61
Greencroft Gdns. Enf—13Ub 25
Greencroft Rd. Houn—53Ba 99
Green Curve. Bans—86Bb 163
Green Dale. SE22 & SE5—57Ub 105
Green Dale Clo. SE22—57Ub 105
Greendale Wlk. Grav—3A 136
Green Dragon Ct. SE1—(7F 201)
Green Dragon La. N21—16Qb 24
Green Dragon La. Bren—50Na 79
Green Dragon Yd. E1—43Wb 83
Green Dri. Slou—49A 74
(in two parts)
Green Dri. S'hall—46Ca 77
Green Dri. Wok—95H 173
Greene Fielde End. Stai—66M 119
Green End. N21—19Rb 25
Green End. Chess—77Na 143
Greenend Rd. W4—47Ua 80
Green Farm Clo. Orp—78Vc 151
Green Farm La. Grav—1N 137
Greenfell St. SE10—48Gc 85
Greenfern Av. Slou—4A 72
Greenfield Av. Surb—73Ra 143
Greenfield Av. Wat—19Z 19
Greenfield End. Ger X—24B 34
Greenfield Gdns. NW2—33Ab 60
Greenfield Gdns. Dag—39Zc 67
Greenfield Gdns. Orp—73Tc 150
Greenfield Link. Coul—87Nb 164
Greenfield Pas. Barn—13Ab 22
Greenfield Rd. E1—44Wb 83
Greenfield Rd. N15—29Ub 43
Greenfield Rd. Dag—39Yc 67
Greenfield Rd. Dart—64Fd 132
Greenfields. Lou—14Qc 28
Greenfields. S'hall—44Ca 77
Greenfields Clo. Brtwd—23Yd 50
Greenfields Clo. Lou—14Qc 28
Greenfield St. Wal A—6Ec 12
Greenfield Way. Harr—27Da 37
Greenfinches. Long, Dart—69De 135
Greenford Av. W7—42Ga 78
Greenford Av. S'hall—45Ba 77
Greenford Gdns. Gnfd—41Da 77
Greenford Grn. Gnfd—37Ga 58
Greenford Industrial Est. N'holt—38Da 57
Greenford Rd. S'hall, Gnfd & Harr—45Ea 78
Greenford Rd. Sutt—77Db 145
Green Gdns. Orp—78Sc 150
Greengate. Gnfd—37Ka 58
Greengate St. E13—40Kc 65
Green Glade. Epp—9Uc 14
Green Glades. Horn—30Qd 49
Greenhalgh Wlk. N2—28Eb 41
Greenham Rd. N10—26Jb 42
Greenham Wlk. Wok—6F 188
Greenhayes Av. Bans—86Cb 163
Greenhayes Gdns. Bans—87Cb 163
Greenhays Pl. Wok—90B 156
Greenheys Clo. N'wd—25U 36
Greenheys Dri. E18—27Hc 45
Green Hill. NW3—35Fb 61
Green Hill. SE18—50Pc 86
Greenhill. Buck H—18Lc 27
Green Hill. Orp—84Pc 168
Greenhill. Sutt—75Eb 145
Greenhill. Wemb—33Ra 59
Greenhill Av. Cat—93Xb 181
Greenhill Cres. Wat—16U 18
Greenhill Gdns. N'holt—40Ba 57
Greenhill Gro. E12—35Nc 66
Green Hill La. Warl—89Ac 166
Greenhill Pk. NW10—39Ua 60
Greenhill Pk. Barn—15Db 23
Greenhill Rd. NW10—39Ua 60
Greenhill Rd. Grav—1B 136
Greenhill Rd. Harr—30Ga 38
Greenhill Rd. Sev—87Ld 171
Greenhills Clo. Rick—15K 17
Greenhill's Rents. EC1—43Rb 83 (7B 194)
Greenhills Ter. N1—37Tb 63
Greenhill Ter. N'holt—40Ba 57
Greenhill Way. Harr—30Ga 38
Greenhill Way. Wemb—33Ra 59
Greenhithe Clo. Sidc—59Uc 108
Greenholm Rd. SE9—57Rc 108
Green Hundred Rd. SE15—51Wb 105
Greenhurst Rd. SE27—64Qb 126
Greening St. SE2—49Yc 87
Greenland Cres. S'hall—48Y 77
Greenland Pl. NW1—39Kb 62
Greenland Rd. NW1—39Kb 62
Greenland Rd. Barn—16Ya 22
★Greenlands. Sev—92Ee
Greenlands Rd. Sev—91Rd 187
Greenlands Rd. Stai—63J 119
Greenlands Rd. Wey—76R 140
Greenland St. NW1—39Kb 62
Green La. E4—11Gc 27
Green La. NW4—28Za 40
Green La. SE9 & Chst—60Rc 108
Green La. SE20—66Zb 128
Green La. SW16 & T Hth—66Pb 126
Green La. W7—47Ga 78
Green La. Asc—7C 116
Green La. Asht—89La 160
Green La. Brtwd—18Wd 32
Green La. Brtwd—24Wd 50
(Great Warley)
Green La. Brtwd—12Sd 32
(Navestock Side)
Green La. Brtwd—15Yd 32
(Pilgrims Hatch)
Green La. Cat—94Sb 181
Green La. Cher—75G 138
Green La. Chess—81Na 161
Green La. Chig—18Sc 28
Green La. Cob—84Aa 159
Green La. E Mol—71Da 141
Green La. Edgw—21Pa 39
Green La. Egh—64D 118
Green La. Felt—64Aa 121
Green La. Grav—5M 137
Green La. Grays—43Ee 91
Green La. Guild—99J 173
Green La. Harr—34Ga 58
Green La. Houn—55X 99
Green La. Ilf & Dag—37Tc 66
Green La. Lea—93Ma 177
Green La. Mord—72Cb 145
Green La. N Mald—71Sa 143
Green La. N'wd—23T 36
Green La. Purl—83Lb 164
Green La. Red—100Ub 181
Green La. Rick—15P 17
Green La. Shep—72S 140
Green La. Slou—3M 95
Green La. Slou—1A 72
(Burnham)
Green La. Slou—7F 52
(Farnham Common)
Green La. Stai—67G 118
Green La. Stan—21Ka 38
Green La. Sun—66V 120
Green La. Tad & Coul—98Bb 179
Green La. Uxb—43S 76
Green La. Wal A—6Lc 13
Green La. W on T—79X 141
Green La. Warl—88Ac 166
Green La. Wat—17Y 19
Green La. Wey—84P 157
Green La. Wind—4E 94
Green La. Wok—9E 188
(Mayford)
Green La. Wok—96R 174
(Ockham)
Green La. Wor Pk & Mord—74Wa 144
Green La. Av. W on T—78Y 141
Green La. Clo. Cher—75G 138
Green La. Clo. Wey—84P 157
Green La. Gdns. T Hth—68Sb 127
Green Lanes—23Pb 42
N13 1-615 & 2-604
N21 remainder
Green Lanes—28Rb 43
N16 1-203 & 2-162
N4 205-531 & 182-430
N8 remainder
Green Lanes. Eps—81Ua 162
Green La. W. Lea—97Q 174
Greenlaw Gdns. N Mald—73Va 144
Green Lawns. Ruis—32Y 57
Greenlaw St. SE18—48Qc 86
Greenleafe Dri. Ilf—27Rc 46
Greenleaf Rd. E6—39Lc 65
Greenleaf Rd. E17—27Bc 44
Greenlea Park Industrial Est. SW19—67Fb 125
Green Leas. Sun—66V 120
Greenleas. Wal A—6Gc 13
Greenleaves Ct. Ashf—65R 120
Green Man Gdns. W13—45Ja 78
Green Man La. W13—46Ja 78
Green Man La. Felt—56W 98
Green Mnr. Way. Grav—56Be 113
Green Man Pas. W13—46Ka 78
Greenman St. N1—39Sb 63
Green Meadow. Pot B—2Cb 9
Green Meads. Wok—94A 172
Green Moor Link. N21—17Rb 25
Greenmoor Rd. Enf—12Yb 26
Greenoak Rise. West—90Lc 167
Greenoak Way. SW19—63Za 124
Greenock Rd. SW16—67Mb 126
Greenock Rd. W3—48Ra 79
Greenock Rd. Slou—4E 72
Greenock Way. Romf—24Gd 48
Greeno Cres. Shep—71Q 140
Green Pk. Stai—62G 118
Greenpark Ct. Gnfd—38La 58
Green Pl. Dart—57Gd 110
Green Pond Rd. E17—27Ac 44
Green Ride. Epp—7Rc 14
Green Ride. Lou—14Lc 27
Green Rd. N14—16Kb 24
Green Rd. N20—20Eb 23
Green Rd. Vir W & Egh—71B 138
Greens Clo., The. Lou—12Qc 28
Green's Ct. W1—(4D 198)
Green's End. SE18—49Rc 86
Greenshaw. Brtwd—18Wd 32
Greenshield Industrial Est. E16—47Kc 85
Greenside. Bex—60Ad 110
Greenside. Borwd—10Qa 7
Greenside. Dag—32Yc 67
Greenside. Slou—3E 72
Greenside. Swan—68Fd 132
Greenside Rd. W12—48Wa 80
Greenside Rd. Croy—73Qb 146
Greenside Wlk. West—90Kc 167
Greenslade Av. Asht—91Ra 177
Greenstead Av. Wfd G—23Lc 45
Greenstead Clo. Wfd G—23Lc 45
Greenstead Gdns. SW15—57Xa 102
Greenstead Gdns. Wfd G—23Lc 45
Greensted Rd. Lou—17Nc 28
Greenstone M. E11—30Jc 45
Green St.—37Kc 65
E7 1-283 & 2-304
E13 remainder
Green St. W1—45Jb 82 (4G 197)
Green St. Enf—12Yb 26
★Green St. Ing—5Ee
Green St. Rick—12E 16
Green St. Shen, Rad—7Qa 7
Green St. Sun—67W 120
Green Street Grn. Rd. Dart & Long, Dart—60Rd 111
Greensward. Bush, Wat—16Da 19
Green, The. E4—18Fc 27
Green, The. E11—30Kc 45
Green, The. E15—37Hc 65
Green, The. N9—19Wb 25
Green, The. N14—20Mb 24
Green, The. N21—18Qb 24
Green, The. W3—44Ua 80
Green, The. W5—45Ma 79
Green, The. Bexh—53Cd 110
Green, The. Brom—62Jc 129
(Grove Park)
Green, The. Brom—73Jc 149
(Hayes)
Green, The. Cars—77Jb 146
Green, The. Cat—95Cc 182
Green, The. Croy—81Bc 166
Green, The. Epp—8Uc 14
(in two parts)
Green, The. Eps—84Wa 162
Green, The. Esh—79Ha 142
Green, The. Felt—61Y 121
Green, The. Grays—3C 92
Green, The. Houn—51Ca 99
Green, The. Lea—96Fa 176
Green, The. Mord—70Ab 124
Green, The. N Mald—69Sa 123
Green, The. Orp—78Rc 150
(Farnborough)
Green, The. Orp—66Xc 131
(St Paul's Cray)
Green, The. Rain—45Nd 89
Green, The. Rich—57Ma 101
Green, The. Rick—15P 17
(Croxley Green)
Green, The. Rick—8J 3
(Sarratt)
Green, The. Sev—94Md 187
Green, The. Shep—70U 120
Green, The. Sidc—63Wc 131
Green, The. Slou—8H 73
Green, The. Slou—3A 72
(Burnham)
Green, The. Slou—2M 95
(Datchet)
Green, The. S'hall—47Ba 77
Green, The. Sutt—76Db 145
Green, The. Tad—91Ab 178
Green, The. Twic—61Ga 122
Green, The. Wal A—6Ec 12
Green, The. Wal X—1Yb 12
Green, The. W on T—82U 158
Green, The. Warl—90Zb 166
Green, The. Well—56Uc 108
Green, The. Wemb—33Ja 58
Green, The. W Dray—48M 75
Green, The. West—98Tc 184
Green, The. Wfd G—22Jc 45
Green, The. Wray, Stai—58A 96
Green Tiles La. Uxb—30H 35
Green Vale. W5—44Pa 79
Green Vale. Bexh—57Zc 109
Greenvale Rd. SE9—56Pc 108
Greenvale Rd. Wok—6A 188
Green Verges. Stan—24Ma 39
Green View. Chess—80Pa 143
Greenview Av. Beck—72Ac 148
Greenview Av. Croy—72Ac 148
Green View Clo. Hem—1C 2
Greenview Ct. Ashf—63P 119
Green Wlk. NW4—29Za 40
Green Wlk. SE1—48Ub 83 (4H 207)
Green Wlk. Dart—57Hd 110
Green Wlk. Hmptn—65Ba 121
Green Wlk. Lou—17Nc 28
Green Wlk. Ruis—32V 56
Green Wlk. S'hall—50Ca 77
Green Wlk. Wfd G—23Nc 46
Green Wlk., The. E4—18Fc 27
Greenway. N14—19Nb 24
Greenway. N20—19Cb 23
Green Way. SE9—57Mc 107
Greenway. SW20—70Ya 124
Greenway. Brtwd—17Ce 33
Green Way. Brom—72Nc 150
Greenway. Chst—64Qc 130
Greenway. Dag—32Yc 67
Greenway. Harr—29Na 39
Greenway. Hay—42X 77
Greenway. Lea—95Da 175
Green Way. Long, Dart—71Ae 155
Greenway. Pinn—26X 37
Greenway. Romf—23Rd 49
Greenway. Slou—1A 72
Green Way. Sun—70W 120
Green Way. Wall—77Lb 146
Greenway. West—92Lc 183
Green Way. Wfd G—22Lc 45
Greenway Av. E17—28Fc 45
Greenway Clo. N4—33Sb 63
Greenway Clo. N20—19Cb 23
Greenway Clo. NW9—26Ta 39
Greenway Clo. Wey—85J 157
Greenway Dri. Stai—67M 119
Greenway Gdns. NW9—26Ta 39
Greenway Gdns. Croy—76Bc 148
Greenway Gdns. Gnfd—41Ca 77
Green Way Gdns. Harr—26Ga 38
Greenways. Abb L, Wat—4U 4
Greenways. Beck—68Cc 128
Greenways. Egh—64A 118
Greenways. Esh—77Ga 142
Greenways. Long, Dart—69Fe 135
Greenways. Tad—97Xa 178
Greenways. Wal X—1Rb 11
Greenways Clo. N11—23Jb 42
Greenway, The. NW9—26Ta 39
Greenway, The. Enf—7Zb 12
Greenway, The. Eps—87Qa 161
Greenway, The. Ger X—27A 34
Green Way, The. Harr—25Ga 38
Greenway, The. Houn—56Ba 99
Greenway, The. Orp—72Xc 151
Greenway, The. Pinn—30Ba 37
Greenway, The. Pot B—5Cb 9
Greenway, The. Rick—17J 17
Greenway, The. Slou—6B 72
Greenway, The. Uxb—40M 55
Greenway, The. Uxb—33S 56
(West Ruislip)
Greenwell St. W1—42Kb 82 (6A 192)
Greenwich Chu. St. SE10—51Ec 106
Greenwich High Rd. SE10—52Dc 106
Greenwich Pk. St. SE10—51Fc 107
Greenwich S. St. SE10—53Dc 106
Greenwood Av. Dag—35Dd 68
Greenwood Av. Enf—11Ac 26
Greenwood Av. Wal X—3Xb 11
Greenwood Clo. Bush, Wat—17Ga 20
Greenwood Clo. Mord—70Ab 124
Greenwood Clo. Orp—72Uc 150
Greenwood Clo. Sidc—61Wc 131
Greenwood Clo. Th Dit—74Ja 142
Greenwood Clo. Wal X—3Xb 11
Greenwood Clo. Wey—83H 157
Greenwood Ct. SW1—(7C 204)
Greenwood Dri. E4—22Fc 45
Greenwood Dri. Wat—6X 5
Greenwood Gdns. N13—20Rb 25
Greenwood Gdns. Cat—97Wb 181
Greenwood Gdns. Ilf—24Sc 46
Greenwood Ho. N22—25Qb 42
Greenwood La. Hmptn—64Da 121
Greenwood Pk. King—66Ua 124
Greenwood Path. E13—40Jc 65
Greenwood Pl. NW5—36Kb 62
Greenwood Rd. E8—37Wb 63
Greenwood Rd. E13—40Hc 65
Greenwood Rd. Bex—63Fd 132
Greenwood Rd. Chig—21Xc 47
Greenwood Rd. Croy—73Rb 147
Greenwood Rd. Iswth—55Ha 100
Greenwood Rd. Mitc—69Mb 126
Greenwood Rd. Th Dit—75Ja 142
Greenwood Rd. Wok—8B 188
Greenwood Ter. NW10—40Ta 59
Greenwood Way. Sev—97Hd 186
Green Wrythe Cres. Cars—74Gb 145
Green Wrythe La. Cars—72Fb 145
Greenyard. Wal A—5Ec 12
Green Yd., The. EC3—(3H 201)
Greer Rd. Harr—25Ea 38
Greet St. SE1—46Qb 82 (7A 200)
Gregories La. Epp—7Tc 14
Gregory Av. Pot B—5Eb 9
Gregory Cres. SE9—59Mc 107
Gregory M. SE3—52Jc 107
Gregory Pl. W8—47Db 81
Gregory Rd. Romf—28Zc 47
Gregory Rd. Slou—3H 53
Gregory Rd. S'hall—48Ca 77
Gregson's Ride. Lou—10Qc 14
Greig Clo. N8—29Nb 42
Greig Ter. SE17—51Rb 105
Grenaby Av. Croy—73Tb 147
Grenaby Rd. Croy—73Tb 147
Grenada Rd. SE7—52Lc 107
Grenade St. E14—45Bc 84
Grenadier St. E16—46Qc 86
Grena Gdns. Rich—56Pa 101
Grena Rd. Rich—56Pa 101
Grendon Gdns. Wemb—33Qa 59
Grendon St. NW8—42Gb 81 (5D 190)
Grenfell Av. Horn—32Hd 68
Grenfell Gdns. Harr—31Na 59
Grenfell Gdns. Ilf—29Vc 47
Grenfell Rd. W11—45Za 80
Grenfell Rd. Mitc—65Hb 125
Grenfell Tower. W11—45Za 80
Grenfell Wlk. W11—45Za 80
Grennell Clo. Sutt—75Fb 145
Grennell Rd. Sutt—75Eb 145
Grenoble Gdns. N13—23Qb 42
Grenside Rd. Wey—76R 140
Grenville Clo. Cob—85Aa 159
Grenville Clo. Slou—10A 52
Grenville Clo. Surb—74Sa 143
Grenville Clo. Wal X—4Zb 12
Grenville Gdns. Wfd G—24Lc 45
Grenville M. SW7—(6A 202)
Grenville M. Hmptn—64Da 121
Grenville Pl. NW7—22Ta 39
Grenville Pl. SW7—48Eb 81 (4A 202)
Grenville Rd. N19—32Nb 62
Grenville Rd. Croy—81Ec 166
Grenville St. WC1—42Nb 82 (6G 193)
Gresham Av. N20—21Hb 41
Gresham Av. Long, Dart—71Be 155
Gresham Av. Warl—90Ac 166
Gresham Clo. Bex—58Bd 109
Gresham Clo. Enf—13Sb 25
Gresham Dri. Romf—29Xc 47
Gresham Gdns. NW11—32Ab 60
Gresham Rd. E6—40Pc 66
Gresham Rd. E16—44Kc 85
Gresham Rd. NW10—36Ta 59
Gresham Rd. SE25—70Wb 127
Gresham Rd. SW19—55Qb 104
Gresham Rd. Beck—68Ac 128
Gresham Rd. Brtwd—20Yd 32
Gresham Rd. Edgw—23Pa 39
Gresham Rd. Hmptn—65Ca 121
Gresham Rd. Houn—53Ea 100
Gresham Rd. Oxt—100Hc 183
Gresham Rd. Slou—4E 72
Gresham Rd. Stai—64H 119
Gresham Rd. Uxb—40Q 56
Gresham St. EC2—44Sb 83 (2D 200)
Gresham Way. SW19—62Db 125
Gresley Clo. N15—28Tb 43
Gresley Ct. Enf—7Yb 12
Gresley Ct. Pot B—2Eb 9
Gresley Rd. N19—32Lb 62
Gressenhall Rd. SW18—58Bb 103
Gresse St. W1—44Mb 82 (1D 198)
Gresswell Clo. Sidc—62Wc 131
Greswell St. SW6—53Za 102
Greta Bank. Lea—98S 174
Gretton Rd. N17—24Vb 43
Greville Av. S Croy—82Zb 166
Greville Clo. Asht—91Na 177
Greville Clo. Twic—59Ka 100
Greville Ct. Lea—97Da 175
Greville Pk. Av. Asht—90Na 161
Greville Pk. Rd. Asht—90Na 161
Greville Pl. NW6—40Db 61
Greville Rd. E17—28Ec 44
Greville Rd. NW6—39Db 61
Greville Rd. Rich—58Pa 101
Greville St. EC1—43Qb 82 (1K 199)
Greycaine Rd. Wat—9Z 5
Greycaine Trading Est. Wat—9Z 5
Grey Clo. NW11—30Eb 41
Greycoat Pl. SW1—48Mb 82 (4D 204)
Greycoat St. SW1—48Mb 82 (4D 204)
Greycot Rd. Beck—64Cc 128
Grey Eagle St. E1—42Vb 83 (6K 195)
Greyfell Clo. Stan—22La 38
Greyfields Clo. Purl—85Rb 165
Greyfriars Clo. Wok—96J 173
Greyfriars Pas. EC1—44Rb 83 (2C 200)
Greyhound Ct. WC2—45Pb 82 (4J 199)
Greyhound Hill. NW4—27Xa 40
Greyhound La. SW16—65Mb 126
Greyhound La. Grays—7C 92
Greyhound La. Pot B—5Wa 8
Greyhound Rd. N17—27Ub 43
Greyhound Rd. NW10—41Xa 80
Greyhound Rd.—51Za 102
W6 1-183 & 2-136
W14 remainder
Greyhound Rd. Sutt—78Eb 145
Greyhound Ter. SW16—67Lb 126
Greys Pk. Clo. Kes—78Mc 149
Greystead Rd. SE23—59Yb 106
Greystoke Av. Pinn—27Ca 37
Greystoke Gdns. W5—42Na 79
Greystoke Gdns. Enf—14Mb 24
Greystoke Pk. Ter. W5—41Ma 79
Greystoke Pl. EC4—44Qb 82 (2K 199)
Greystoke Rd. Slou—3D 72
Greystone Clo. S Croy—83Yb 166
Greystone Gdns. Harr—30La 38
Greystone Gdns. Ilf—26Sc 46
Greystone Pk. Sev—97Ad 185
Greystones Clo. Sev—89Nd 171
Greyswood St. SW16—65Kb 126
Greythorne Rd. Wok—6D 188
Grey Towers Av. Horn—32Md 69
Grey Towers Gdns. Horn—31Ld 69
Grice Av. West—85Kc 167
Gridiron Pl. Upm—33Rd 69
Grierson Rd. SE23—58Zb 106
Grieves Rd. Grav—2B 136
Griffin Av. Upm—30Ud 50
Griffin Clo. NW10—36Xa 60
Griffin Clo. Slou—7G 72
Griffin Mnr. Way. SE28—49Tc 86
Griffin Rd. N17—26Ub 43
Griffin Rd. SE18—50Tc 86
Griffins, The. Grays—47De 91
Griffin Way. Lea—98Ca 175
Griffin Way. Sun—68W 120
Griffiths Clo. Wor Pk—75Xa 144
Griffiths Rd. SW19—66Cb 125
Griggs App. Rd. Ilf—33Sc 66
Grigg's Pl. SE1—(3J 207)
Griggs Rd. E10—30Ec 44
Grimsby St. E2—42Vb 83
Grimsdyke Cres. Barn—13Ya 22
Grimsdyke Rd. Pinn—24Aa 37
Grimsell Path. SE5—52Rb 105
Grimstone Clo. Romf—23Dd 48
Grimston Rd. SW6—54Bb 103
Grimwade Av. Croy—76Wb 147
Grimwade Cres. SE15—55Yb 106
Grimwood Rd. Twic—59Ha 100
Grindal St. SE1—47Qb 82 (2K 205)
Grinling Pl. SE8—51Cc 106
Grinstead Rd. SE8—50Ac 84
Grisedale Clo. Purl—86Ub 165
Grisedale Gdns. Purl—86Ub 165
Grittleton Av. Wemb—37Ra 59
Grittleton Rd. W9—42Cb 81
Grizedale Ter. SE23—61Xb 127
Grobars Av. Wok—3F 188
Grocer's Hall Ct. EC2—44Tb 83 (3F 201)
Grocer's Hall Gdns. EC2—(3F 201)
Grogan Clo. Hmptn—65Ba 121
Groombridge Clo. W on T—78X 141
Groombridge Clo. Well—57Wc 109
Groombridge Rd. E9—38Zb 64
Groom Cres. SW18—59Fb 103
Groomfield Clo. SW17—63Jb 126
Groom Pl. SW1—48Jb 82 (3J 203)
Grosmont Rd. SE18—51Vc 109
Grosse Way. SW15—58Xa 102
Grosvenor Av. N5—36Sb 63
Grosvenor Av. SW14—55Ua 102
Grosvenor Av. Cars—79Jb 146
Grosvenor Av. Harr—30Da 37
Grosvenor Av. Hay—40V 56
Grosvenor Av. Rich—57Na 101
Grosvenor Clo. Iver—41F 74
Grosvenor Clo. Lou—11Rc 28
Grosvenor Cotts. SW1—49Jb 82 (5H 203)
Grosvenor Ct. N14—17Lb 24
Grosvenor Ct. Slou—4J 73
Grosvenor Cres. N14—15Mb 24
Grosvenor Cres. NW9—28Qa 39
Grosvenor Cres. SW1—47Jb 82 (2J 20)
Grosvenor Cres. Dart—57Md 111
Grosvenor Cres. Uxb—38R 56
Grosvenor Cres. M. SW1—47Jb 82 (2H 203)
Grosvenor Dri. Horn—32Ld 69
Grosvenor Dri. Lou—12Rc 28
Grosvenor Est. SW1—49Mb 82 (5E 204)
Grosvenor Gdns. E6—41Mc 85
Grosvenor Gdns. N10—27Lb 42
Grosvenor Gdns. NW2—37Ya 60
Grosvenor Gdns. NW11—30Bb 41
Grosvenor Gdns. SW1—48Kb 82 (3K 203)
Grosvenor Gdns. SW14—55Ua 102

Grosvenor Gdns.—Hameway

Grosvenor Gdns. King—65Ma 123
Grosvenor Gdns. Upm—32Td 70
Grosvenor Gdns. Wall—80Lb 146
Grosvenor Gdns. Wfd G—23Jc 45
Grosvenor Gdns. M. E. SW1 —(3A 204)
Grosvenor Gdns. M. N. SW1 —(4K 203)
Grosvenor Gdns. M. S. SW1 —(4A 204)
Grosvenor Ga. W1 —45Jb 82 (5H 197)
Grosvenor Hill. SW19—65Ab 124
Grosvenor Hill. W1 —45Kb 82 (4K 197)
Grosvenor Pk. SE5—52Sb 105
Grosvenor Pk. Rd. E17—29Dc 44
Grosvenor Path. Lou—11Sc 28
Grosvenor Pl. SW1 —47Kb 82 (2J 203)
Grosvenor Pl. Houn—55Ea 100
Grosvenor Rise. E. E17—29Dc 44
Grosvenor Rd. E6—39Mc 65
Grosvenor Rd. E7—37Kc 65
Grosvenor Rd. E10—32Ec 64
Grosvenor Rd. E11—29Kc 45
Grosvenor Rd. N3—24Bb 41
Grosvenor Rd. N9—18Xb 25
Grosvenor Rd. N10—25Kb 42
Grosvenor Rd. SE25—70Wb 127
Grosvenor Rd. SW1 —51Kb 104 (7E 204)
Grosvenor Rd. W4—50Ra 79
Grosvenor Rd. W7—46Ja 78
Grosvenor Rd. Belv—51Cd 110
Grosvenor Rd. Bexh—57Zc 109
Grosvenor Rd. Borwd—13Qa 21
Grosvenor Rd. Bren—51Ma 101
Grosvenor Rd. Chob—1A 188
Grosvenor Rd. Dag—32Bd 67
Grosvenor Rd. Eps—91Ta 177
Grosvenor Rd. Grays—4F 92
Grosvenor Rd. Houn—55Ba 99
Grosvenor Rd. Ilf—34Sc 66
Grosvenor Rd. N'wd—22V 36
Grosvenor Rd. Orp—72Uc 150
Grosvenor Rd. Rich—57Na 101
Grosvenor Rd. Romf—31Fd 68
Grosvenor Rd. S'hall—48Ba 77
Grosvenor Rd. Stai—66J 119
Grosvenor Rd. Twic—60Ja 100
Grosvenor Rd. Wall—79Kb 146
Grosvenor Rd. Wat—13Y 19
Grosvenor Rd. W Wick—75Dc 148
Grosvenor Sq. W1 —45Jb 82 (4J 197)
Grosvenor Sq. Long. Dart —69Ae 135
Grosvenor St. W1 —45Kb 82 (4K 197)
Grosvenor Ter. SE5—51Sb 105
Grosvenor Vale. Ruis—33V 56
Grosvenor Wharf Rd. E14 —49Fc 85
Grote's Bldgs. SE3—54Gc 107
Grote's Pl. SE3—54Gc 107
Groton Rd. SW18—61Db 125
Grotto Ct. SE1—47Sb 83 (1D 206)
Grotto Pas. W1—43Jb 82 (7J 191)
Grotto Rd. Twic—61Ha 122
Grotto Rd. Wey—76R 140
Grove Av. N3—24Cb 41
Grove Av. N10—26Lb 42
Grove Av. W7—44Ga 78
Grove Av. Eps—85Ua 162
Grove Av. Pinn—28Aa 37
Grove Av. Sutt—79Cb 145
Grove Av. Twic—60Ha 100
Grovebury Clo. Eri—51Fd 110
Grovebury Ct. Bexh—57Dd 110
Grovebury Rd. SE2—47Xc 87
Grove Clo. SE23—60Ac 106
Grove Clo. Brom—75Jc 149
Grove Clo. Felt—63Aa 121
Grove Clo. King—70Pa 123
Grove Clo. Slou—8L 73
Grove Clo. Uxb—36Q 56
Grove Clo. Wind—9M 95
Grove Ct. E Mol—71Fa 142
Grove Ct. Wal A—6Dc 12
Grove Cres. E18—26Hc 45
Grove Cres. NW9—28Sa 39
Grove Cres. SE5—54Ub 105
Grove Cres. Felt—63Aa 121
Grove Cres. King—69Na 123
Grove Cres. Rick—14Q 18
Grove Cres. W on T—73X 141
Grove Cres. Rd. E15—37Fc 65
Grovedale Clo. Wal X—2Wb 11
Grovedale Rd. N19—33Mb 62
Grove End. E18—26Hc 45
Grove End La. Esh—74Fa 142
Grove End Rd. NW8 —41Fb 81 (3B 190)
Grove Farm Industrial Est. Mitc—71Hb 145
Grove Farm Pk. N'wd—22T 36
Grove Footpath. Surb—70Na 123
Grove Gdns. E15—37Gc 65
Grove Gdns. NW4—29Wa 40
Grove Gdns. NW8 —41Gb 81 (4E 190)
Grove Gdns. Dag—34Ed 68
Grove Gdns. Enf—11Zb 26
Grove Gdns. Tedd—63Ja 122
Grove Grn. N'wd—22T 36
Grove Grn. Rd. E11—34Ec 64
Grove Hall Ct. NW8 —41Eb 81 (3A 190)
Grove Hall Rd. Bush, Wat—14Aa 19
Grove Heath N. Wok—94K 173
Grove Heath Rd. Wok—95K 173
Grove Hill. E18—26Hc 45
Grove Hill. Harr—31Ga 58
Grove Hill Rd. SE5—55Ub 105
Grove Hill Rd. Harr—31Ha 58
Grove Ho. Bush, Wat—16Ba 19
Grove Ho. Rd. N8—28Nb 42
Groveland Av. SW16—66Pb 126
Groveland Ct. EC4—(3E 200)
Groveland Rd. Beck—69Bc 128
Grovelands. E Mol—70Ca 121
Grovelands Clo. SE5—54Ub 105
Grovelands Rd. N13—21Pb 42
Grovelands Rd. N15—30Wb 43
Grovelands Rd. Orp—66Wc 131
Grovelands Rd. Purl—84Pb 164
Grovelands Way. Grays—50Be 91
Groveland Way. N Mald —71Sa 143
Grove La. SE5—53Tb 105
Grove La. Chig—20Vc 29
Grove La. Coul—86Kb 164
Grove La. Epp—2Wc 15
Grove La. King—70Na 123
Grove La. Uxb—42P 75
Grove La. M. SE5—54Ub 105
Groveley Rd. Sun & Felt—64V 120
Grove Mkt. Pl. SE9—58Pc 108
Grove M. W6—48Ya 80
Grove Mill La. Rick & Wat—9R 4
Grove Pde. Slou—7L 73
Grove Pk. E11—29Kc 45
Grove Pk. NW9—28Sa 39
Grove Pk. SE5—54Ub 105
Grove Pk. Av. E4—24Dc 44
Grove Pk. Bri. W4—52Sa 101
Grove Pk. Gdns. W4—52Ra 101
Grove Pk. M. W4—52Sa 101
Grove Pk. Rd. N15—28Ub 43
Grove Pk. Rd. SE9—62Lc 129
Grove Pk. Rd. W4—52Ra 101
Grove Pk. Rd. Rain—39Jd 68
Grove Pk. Ter. W4—52Ra 101
Grove Pas. E2—40Xb 63
Grove Path. Wal X—3Wb 11
Grove Pl. NW3—34Fb 61
Grove Pl. W3—46Sa 79
Grove Pl. Bark—39Sc 66
Grove Pl. Wey—78S 140
Grove Rd. E3—39Zb 64
Grove Rd. E4—21Ec 44
Grove Rd. E11—31Hc 65
Grove Rd. E17—30Dc 44
Grove Rd. E18—26Hc 45
Grove Rd. N11—22Kb 42
Grove Rd. N12—22Fb 41
Grove Rd. N15—29Ub 43
Grove Rd. NW2—37Ya 60
Grove Rd. SW13—54Va 102
Grove Rd. SW19—66Eb 125
Grove Rd. W3—46Sa 79
Grove Rd. W5—45Ma 79
Grove Rd. Asht—90Pa 161
Grove Rd. Barn—13Gb 23
Grove Rd. Belv—51Bd 109
Grove Rd. Bexh—56Ed 110
Grove Rd. Borwd—11Qa 21
Grove Rd. Bren—50La 78
Grove Rd. Cher—72H 139
Grove Rd. E Mol—70Fa 122
Grove Rd. Edgw—23Qa 39
Grove Rd. Eps—85Ua 162
Grove Rd. Grav—57De 113
Grove Rd. Grays—51Ee 113
Grove Rd. Houn—56Ca 99
Grove Rd. Iswth—53Ga 100
Grove Rd. Mitc—69Jb 126
Grove Rd. N'wd—22T 36
Grove Rd. Pinn—29Ba 37
Grove Rd. Rich—58Pa 101
Grove Rd. Rick—19J 17
Grove Rd. Romf—31Xc 67
Grove Rd. Sev—93Ld 187
Grove Rd. Sev—94Qd 187 (Seal)
Grove Rd. Shep—72S 140
Grove Rd. Slou—10B 52
Grove Rd. Stanf—3M 93
Grove Rd. Surb—71Ma 143
Grove Rd. Sutt—79Cb 145
Grove Rd. T Hth—70Qb 126
Grove Rd. Twic—62Fa 122
Grove Rd. Uxb—38M 55
Grove Rd. West—92Lc 183
Grove Rd. Wind—4G 94
Grove Rd. Wok—88B 156
Grove Rd. W. Enf—9Yb 12
Grover Rd. Wat—17Z 19
Groveside. Lea—99Ca 175
Groveside Clo. Lea—99Ca 175
Groveside Rd. E4—19Gc 27
Grovestile Waye. Felt—59T 98
Grove St. N18—23Vb 43
Grove St. SE8—49Bc 84
Grove Ter. NW5—34Kb 62
Grove Ter. Tedd—63Ja 122
Grove, The. E15—37Gc 65
Grove, The. N3—25Cb 41
Grove, The. N4—31Pb 62
Grove, The. N6—32Jb 62
Grove, The. N8—29Mb 42
Grove, The. N13—21Qb 42
Grove, The. NW9—29Ta 39
Grove, The. NW11—31Ab 60
Grove, The. W5—45Na 79
Grove, The. Bexh—56Zc 109
Grove, The. Brtwd—21Vd 50
Grove, The. Cat—93Sb 181
Grove, The. Che—8A 2
Grove, The. Coul—86Mb 164
Grove, The. Edgw—21Ra 39
Grove, The. Egh—64C 118
Grove, The. Enf—12Qb 24
Grove, The. Eps—85Ua 162
Grove, The. Eps—82Va 162 (Ewell)
Grove, The. Grav—9D 114
Grove, The. Gnfd—44Ea 78
Grove, The. Iswth—53Ga 100
Grove, The. Pot B—4Eb 9
Grove, The. Rad—6Ja 6
★Grove, The. Sev—82Vd
Grove, The. Sidc—63Ad 131
Grove, The. Slou—8L 73
Grove, The. Swan—69Hd 132
Grove, The. Swans—57Be 113
Grove, The. Tedd—63Ja 122
Grove, The. Twic—58La 100
Grove, The. Upm—36Rd 69
Grove, The. Uxb—36Q 56
Grove, The. W on T—73X 141
Grove, The. West—90Nc 168
Grove, The. W Wick—75Ec 148
Grove, The. Wey—78K 139
Grove, The. Wok—88B 156
Grove Vale. SE22—56Vb 105
Grove Vale. Chst—65Qc 130
Grove Vs. E14—45Dc 84
Groveway. SW9—53Pb 104
Groveway. Dag—35Zc 67
Grove Way. Esh—74Ea 142
Grove Way. Rick—15D 16
Groveway. Wemb—36Sa 59
Grove Waye. Uxb—38M 55
Grovewood. Rich—53Qa 101
Grovewood Clo. Rick—15D 16
Grove Wood Hill. Coul—86Lb 164
Grub St. Oxt—100Lc 183
Grummant Rd. SE15—53Vb 105
Grundy St. E14—44Dc 84
Gruneisen Rd. N3—24Db 41
Guardsman Clo. Brtwd—22Zd 51
Guards Rd. Wind—4A 94
Guards Wlk. Wind—4A 94
Gubbins La. Romf—24Pd 49
Gubyon Av. SE24—57Rb 105
Guerin Sq. E3—41Bc 84
Guernsey Clo. Houn—52Ca 99
Guernsey Farm Dri. Wok—3G 188
Guernsey Gro. SE21—59Sb 105
Guernsey Ho. N1—37Sb 63
Guernsey Rd. E11—32Fc 65
Guest St. EC1—(6E 194)
Guibal Rd. SE12—59Kc 107
Guildersfield Rd. SW16—66Nb 126
Guildford Av. Felt—61V 120
Guildford Gdns. Romf—23Nd 49
Guildford Gro. SE10—53Dc 106
Guildford La. Wok—91A 172
Guildford La. Wok—7G 188
Guildford Lodge Dri. Lea —100V 174
Guildford Rd. E6—44Pc 86
Guildford Rd. E17—25Ec 44
Guildford Rd. SW8—53Nb 104
Guildford Rd. Cher—78E 138
Guildford Rd. Chob—1A 188
Guildford Rd. Croy—72Tb 147
Guildford Rd. Ilf—33Uc 66
Guildford Rd. Lea—96Ga 176
Guildford Rd. Lea—100Y 175 (Effingham)
Guildford Rd. Romf—23Nd 49
Guildford Rd. Wok—91A 172
Guildford Rd. Wok—10G 188
Guildford Rd. Wok & Cher —83D 156
Guildford St. Cher—73J 139
Guildford St. Stai—65J 119
Guildford Way. Wall—78Nb 146
Guildhall Bldgs. EC2—(2F 201)
Guildhall Yd. EC2 —44Sb 83 (2E 200)
Guildhouse St. SW1 —49Lb 82 (5B 204)
Guildown Av. N12—21Db 41
Guild Rd. SE7—50Mc 85
Guild Rd. Eri—52Hd 110
Guildsway. E17—25Bc 44
Guileshill La. Wok—94P 173
Guilford Av. Surb—71Pa 143
Guilford Pl. WC1—42Pb 82 (6H 193)
Guilford St. WC1 —42Nb 82 (6G 193)
Guillemot Pl. N22—26Pb 42
Guilsborough Clo. NW10—38Ua 60
Guiness Ct. Wok—6C 188
Guiness Trust Est. N16—32Ub 63
Guinness Clo. E9—38Ac 64
Guinness Clo. Hay—48T 76
Guinness Ct. NW8 —39Gb 61 (1E 190)
Guinness Sq. SE1 —49Ub 83 (5H 207)
Guion Rd. SW6—54Bb 103
Gulland Clo. Bush, Wat—15Ea 20
Gull Clo. Wall—80Nb 146
Gullet Wood Rd. Wat—7W 4
Gulliver Clo. N'holt—39Ba 57
Gulliver Rd. Sidc—61Tc 130
Gulliver St. SE16—48Bc 84
Gull Wlk. Rain—38Kd 69
Gumleigh Rd. W5—49La 78
Gumley Gdns. Iswth—55Ja 100
Gumley Rd. Grays—51Zd 113
Gumping Rd. Orp—75Sc 150
Gundulph Rd. Brom—69Lc 129
Gunfleet Clo. Grav—9G 114
Gun Hill. Grays—1F 114
Gunmaker's La. E3—39Ac 64
Gunner La. SE18—50Qc 86
Gunnersbury Av.—46Pa 79
W5 1-119 & 2-114
W3 127-143 & 144-248
W4 remainder
Gunnersbury Clo. W4—50Ra 79
Gunnersbury Cres. W3—47Qa 79
Gunnersbury Dri. W5—47Pa 79
Gunnersbury Gdns. W3—47Qa 79
Gunnersbury La. W3—47Qa 79
Gunnersbury M. W4—50Ra 79
Gunners Gro. E4—20Ec 26
Gunners Rd. SW18—61Fb 125
Gunning St. SE18—49Uc 86
Gunn Rd. Swans—58Ae 113
Gunsite La. Cob—85Y 159
Gunstor Rd. N16—35Ub 63
Gun St. E1—43Vb 83 (1K 201)
Gunter Gro. SW10—51Eb 103
Gunter Gro. Edgw—25Ta 39
Gunterstone Rd. W14—49Ab 80
Gunthorpe St. E1 —43Vb 83 (1K 201)
Gunton Rd. E5—33Xb 63
Gunton Rd. SW17—65Jb 126
Gurdon Rd. SE7—50Jc 85
Gurnard Clo. W Dray—45M 75
Gurnell Gro. W13—42Ha 78
Gurney Clo. E15—36Gc 65
Gurney Clo. Bark—37Rc 66
Gurney Cres. Croy—74Pb 146
Gurney Dri. N2—28Eb 41
Gurney Rd. E15—36Gc 65
Gurney Rd. Cars—77Jb 146
Gurney Rd. N'holt—41X 77
Guthrie St. SW3—50Fb 81 (7D 202)
Gutter La. EC2—44Sb 83 (2D 200)
Guyatt Gdns. Mitc—68Jb 126
Guy Rd. Wall—76Mb 146
Guyscliff Rd. SE13—57Ec 106
Guysfield Clo. Rain—39Jd 68
Guysfield Dri. Rain—39Jd 68
Guys Retreat. Buck H—17Lc 27
Guy St. SE1—47Tb 83 (1G 207)
Gwalior Rd. SW15—56Za 102
Gwendolen Av. SW15—56Za 102
Gwendolen Clo. SW15—57Za 102
Gwendoline Av. E13—39Kc 65
Gwendwr Rd. W14—50Ab 80
Gwent Clo. Wat—6Z 5
Gwillim Clo. Sidc—57Wc 109
Gwydor Rd. Beck—69Zb 128
Gwydyr Rd. Brom—69Hc 129
Gwyn Clo. SW6—52Eb 103
Gwynne Av. Croy—73Zb 148
Gwynne Clo. Wind—3C 94
Gwynne Pk. Av. Wfd G—23Pc 46
Gwynne Pl. WC1—41Pb 82 (4J 193)
Gwynne Rd. SW11—54Fb 103
Gwynn Rd. Grav—61Ee 135
Gyfford Wlk. Wal X—3Xb 11
Gylcote Clo. SE5—56Tb 105
Gyles Pk. Stan—25La 38
Gyllyngdune Gdns. Ilf—34Vc 67
Gypsy La. K Lan—7T 4
Gypsy La. Slou—5J 53
Haarlem Rd. W14—48Za 80
Haberdasher Pl. N1 —41Tb 83 (3H 195)
Haberdasher St. N1 —41Tb 83 (3G 195)
Haberton Rd. N19—32Lb 62
Habgood Rd. Lou—13Nc 28
Haccombe Rd. SW19—65Eb 125
Hackbridge Grn. Wall—75Jb 146
Hackbridge Pk. Gdns. Cars —75Hb 145
Hackbridge Rd. Wall—75Jb 146
Hacketts La. Wok—86H 157
Hackford Rd. SW9—53Pb 104
Hackforth Clo. Barn—15Xa 22
Hackington Cres. Beck—65Cc 128
Hackney Clo. Borwd—15Ta 21
Hackney Gro. E8—37Xb 63
Hackney Rd. E2—41Vb 83 (4K 195)
Hacton Dri. Horn—35Md 69
Hacton La. Horn & Upm—33Pd 69
Hadden Rd. SE28—48Uc 86
Hadden Way. Gnfd—37Fa 58
Haddington Rd. Brom—62Fc 129
Haddon Clo. Borwd—13Qa 21
Haddon Clo. Enf—16Wb 25
Haddon Clo. N Mald—71Va 144
Haddon Clo. Wey—76U 140
Haddon Gro. Sidc—59Wc 109
Haddon Rd. Orp—71Yc 151
Haddon Rd. Rick—15E 16
Haddon Rd. Sutt—77Db 145
Haddo St. SE10—51Ec 106
Hadfield Rd. Stai—58M 97
Hadfield Rd. Stanf—2M 93
Hadleigh Clo. E1—42Yb 84
Hadleigh Rd. N9—17Xb 25
Hadleigh St. E2—41Yb 84
Hadleigh Wlk. E6—44Nc 86
Hadley Clo. N21—16Qb 24
Hadley Clo. Borwd—15Pa 21
Hadley Comn. Barn—12Cb 23
Hadley Ct. N16—32Wb 63
Hadley Gdns. W4—50Ta 79
Hadley Gdns. S'hall—50Ba 77
Hadley Grn. Rd. Barn—12Bb 23
Hadley Grn. W. Barn—12Bb 23
Hadley Gro. Barn—12Ab 22
Hadley Highstone. Barn—11Bb 23
Hadley Ridge. Barn—13Bb 23
Hadley Rd. Barn—13Db 23
Hadley Rd. Barn & Enf—10Hb 9
Hadley Rd. Belv—49Bd 87
Hadley Rd. Mitc—70Mb 126
Hadley St. NW1—37Kb 62
Hadley Way. N21—16Qb 24
Hadley Wood Rise. Kenl —87Rb 165
Hadlow Ct. Slou—6G 72
Hadlow Pl. SE19—66Wb 127
Hadlow Rd. Sidc—63Wc 131
Hadlow Rd. Well—52Yc 109
Hadlow Way. Grav—6A 136
Hadrian Clo. Stai—59N 97
Hadrian Clo. Wall—80Nb 146
Hadrians Ride. Enf—15Vb 25
Hadrian St. SE10—50Gc 85
Hadrian Way. Stai—59M 97 (in two parts)
Hadyn Pk. Rd. W12—47Wa 80
Hafer Rd. SW11—56Hb 103
Hafton Rd. SE6—60Gc 107
Hagden La. Wat—15V 18
Haggard Rd. Twic—59Ka 100
Haggerston Rd. E8—38Vb 63
Haggerston Rd. Borwd—10Na 7
Hague St. E2—41Wb 83
Ha Ha Rd. SE18—51Pc 108
Haig Rd. Stan—22La 38
Haig Rd. Uxb—43R 76
Haig Rd. West—89Nc 168
Haig Rd. E. E13—41Lc 85
Haig Rd. W. E13—41Lc 85
Haigville Gdns. Ilf—28Rc 46
Hailes Clo. SW19—65Eb 125
Haileybury Av. Enf—16Vb 25
Haileybury Rd. Orp—77Wc 151
Hailey Rd. Eri—47Cd 88
Hailsham Av. SW2—61Pb 126
Hailsham Clo. Romf—22Ld 49
Hailsham Clo. Surb—73Ma 143
Hailsham Gdns. Romf—22Ld 49
Hailsham Rd. SW17—65Jb 126
Hailsham Rd. Romf—22Ld 49
Hailsham Ter. N18—21Tb 43
Haimo Rd. SE9—57Mc 107
Hainault Gore. Romf—29Ad 47
Hainault Gro. Chig—21Sc 46
Hainault Rd. E11—32Ec 64
Hainault Rd. Chig—20Rc 28
Hainault Rd. Romf—26Ed 48
Hainault Rd. Romf—30Bd 47 (Chadwell Heath)
Hainault Rd. Romf—24Xc 47 (Little Heath)
Hainault St. SE9—60Rc 108
Hainault St. Ilf—33Sc 66
Haines Ct. Wey—78T 140
Haines St. SW8—52Lb 104
Haines Wlk. Mord—73Db 145
Haines Way. Wat—6W 4
Hainthorpe Rd. SE27—62Rb 127
Hainton Path. E1—44Xb 83
Halberd M. E5—33Xb 63
Halbutt Gdns. Dag—34Bd 67
Halbutt St. Dag—35Bd 67
Halcomb St. N1—39Ub 63
Halcot Av. Bexh—57Dd 110
Halcrow St. E1—43Xb 83
Halcyon Way. Horn—32Pd 69
Haldane Clo. N10—24Kb 42
Haldane Pl. SW18—60Db 103
Haldane Rd. E6—41Mc 85
Haldane Rd. SE28—45Zc 87
Haldane Rd. SW6—52Bb 103
Haldane Rd. S'hall—44Ea 78
Haldan Rd. E4—23Ec 44
Haldon Clo. Chig—22Uc 46
Haldon Rd. SW18—58Bb 103
Hale Clo. E4—20Ec 26
Hale Clo. Edgw—22Sa 39
Hale Clo. Orp—77Sc 150
Hale Dri. NW7—23Sa 39
Hale End. Romf—23Kd 49
Hale End Clo. Ruis—30W 36
Hale End Rd.—23Fc 45
E17 1-197 & 2-148
E4 433-509 & 350-428
Wfd G remainder
Halefield Rd. N17—25Xb 43
Hale Gdns. N17—27Wb 43
Hale Gdns. W3—46Qa 79
Hale Gro. Gdns. NW7—22Ua 40
Hale La. Edgw & NW7—22Ra 39
Hale La. Sev—89Hd 170
Hale Path. SE27—63Rb 127
Hale Pit Rd. Lea—98Ea 176
Hale Rd. E6—42Nc 86
Hale Rd. N17—27Wb 43
Halesowen Rd. Mord—73Db 145
Hales St. SE8—52Cc 106
Hale St. E14—45Dc 84
Hale St. Stai—63G 118
Hales Wood. Cob—86Y 159
Halesworth Clo. E5—33Yb 64
Halesworth Clo. Romf—24Nd 49
Halesworth Rd. SE13—55Dc 106
Halesworth Rd. Romf—23Nd 49
Hale, The. E4—24Fc 45
Hale, The. N17—27Wb 43
Hale Wlk. W7—43Ga 78
Haley Rd. NW4—30Ya 40
Half Acre. Bren—51Ma 101
Half Acre Hill. Ger X—25B 34
Halfacre Rd. W7—46Ga 78
Halfhides. Wal A—5Fc 13
Half Moon Ct. EC1—(1D 200)
Half Moon Cres. N1 —40Pb 62 (1J 193)
Half Moon La. SE24—58Sb 105
Half Moon Pas. E1 —44Vb 83 (3K 201) (in two parts)
Half Moon St. W1 —46Kb 82 (6A 198)
Halford Rd. E10—29Fc 45
Halford Rd. SW6—51Cb 103
Halford Rd. Rich—57Na 101
Halford Rd. Uxb—36Q 56
Halfpence La. Grav—9K 137
Halfway Grn. W on T—76X 141
Halfway St. Sidc—59Tc 108
Haliburton Rd. Twic—57Ja 100
Halidon Clo. E9—36Yb 64
Halidon Rise. Romf—23Rd 49
Halifax Rd. Enf—12Sb 25
Halifax Rd. Gnfd—39Da 57
Halifax Rd. Rick—17E 16
Halifax St. SE26—62Xb 127
Haling Down Pas. Purl & S Croy —82Rb 165
Haling Gro. S Croy—80Sb 147
Haling Pk. Gdns. S Croy—79Rb 147
Haling Pk. Rd. S Croy—78Rb 147
Haling Rd. S Croy—79Tb 147
Halings La. Uxb—28F 34
Halkin Arc. SW1—48Jb 82 (3G 203)
Halkingcroft. Slou—7N 73
Halkin M. SW1—48Jb 82 (3H 203)
Halkin Pl. SW1—48Jb 82 (3H 203)
Halkin St. SW1—47Jb 82 (2J 203)
★Hallam Clo. Brtwd—8Xd
Hallam Clo. Chst—64Pc 130
Hallam Gdns. Pinn—24Aa 37
Hallam M. W1—43Kb 82 (7A 192)
Hallam Rd. N15—28Rb 43
Hallam St. W1—43Kb 82 (7A 192)
Halland Way. N'wd—23T 36 (in two parts)
Hall Av. S Ock—46Sd 90
Hall Clo. W5—43Na 79
Hall Clo. Rick—18J 17
Hall Ct. Slou—2M 95
Hall Ct. Tedd—64Ha 122
Hall Cres. S Ock—47Sd 90
Hall Dri. SE26—64Yb 128
Hall Dri. W7—44Ga 78
Hall Dri. Uxb—25L 35
Halley Pl. E14—43Ac 84
Halley Rd.—37Lc 65
E7 1-207 & 2-188
E12 remainder
Halley St. E14—43Ac 84
Halley's Wlk. Wey—80L 139
Hall Farm Clo. Stan—21Ka 38
Hall Farm Dri. Twic—59Fa 100
Hallfield Est. W2 —44Eb 81 (2A 196)
Hallford Way. Dart—58Ld 111
Hall Gdns. E4—21Bc 44
Hall Ga. NW8—41Fb 81 (3B 190)
Hall Grn. La. Brtwd—17Ee 33
Hall Hill. Sev—95Rd 187
Halliford Clo. Shep—70T 120
Halliford Rd. Shep & Sun—71U 140
Halliford St. N1—38Sb 63
Hallington Clo. Wok—5E 188
Halliwell Rd. SW2—58Pb 104
Halliwick Rd. N10—25Jb 42
Hall La. E4—22Ac 44
Hall La. NW4—25Wa 40
Hall La. Brtwd—16Be 33
Hall La. Hay—52T 98
Hall La. Upm—26Sd 50 to 32Sd 70
Hall Meadow. Slou—10A 52
Hallmead Rd. Sutt—76Db 145
Hallowell Av. Croy—77Nb 146
Hallowell Clo. Mitc—69Jb 126
Hallowell Rd. N'wd—24U 36
Hallowes Cres. Wat—20W 18
Hall Pk. Rd. Upm—36Sd 70
Hall Pl. W2—42Fb 81 (6B 190)
Hall Pl. Wok—88C 156
Hall Pl. Cres. Bex—57Ed 110
Hall Pl. Dri. Wey—78U 140
Hall Rd. E6—39Pc 66
Hall Rd. E15—35Fc 65
Hall Rd. NW8—41Eb 81 (4A 190)
Hall Rd. Dart—56Pd 111
Hall Rd. Grav—62Ee 135
Hall Rd. Iswth—57Fa 100
Hall Rd. Romf—30Yc 47 (Chadwell Heath)
Hall Rd. Romf—27Kd 49 (Gidea Park)
Hall Rd. S Ock—47Sd 90
Hall Rd. Wall—81Kb 164
Halls Farm Clo. Wok—5A 188
Hallside Rd. Enf—10Vb 11
Hall St. EC1—41Rb 83 (3C 194)
Hall St. N12—22Eb 41
Hallsville Rd. E16—44Hc 85
Hallswelle Rd. NW11—29Bb 41
Hall Ter. Romf—24Qd 49
Hall Ter. S Ock—47Td 90
Hall, The. SE3—55Jc 107
Hall View. SE9—61Mc 129
Hall Way. Purl—85Rb 165
Hallwood Cres. Brtwd—17Ae 33
Halons Rd. SE9—59Qc 108
Halpin Pl. SE17—49Tb 83 (6G 207)
Halsbrook Rd. SE3—55Mc 107
Halsbury Clo. Stan—21Ka 38
Halsbury Rd. W12—46Xa 80
Halsbury Rd. E. Harr—35Ea 58
Halsbury Rd. W. N'holt—35Da 57
Halse Dri. Slou—5D 52
Halsend. Hay—46X 77
Halsey Pl. Wat—10X 5
Halsey Rd. Wat—13X 19
Halsey St. SW3—49Hb 81 (5F 203)
Halsham Cres. Bark—36Vc 67
Halstead Gdns. N21—18Tb 25
Halstead Hill. Wal X—1Ub 11
Halstead La. Sev—87Ad 169
Halstead Rd. E11—29Jc 45
Halstead Rd. N21—18Tb 25
Halstead Rd. Enf—14Ub 25
Halstead Rd. Eri—53Gd 110
Halston Clo. SW11—58Hb 103
Halstow Rd. NW10—41Za 80
Halstow Rd. SE10—50Jc 85
Halsway. Hay—46W 76
Halt Dri. Grays—9J 93
Halter Clo. Borwd—15Ta 21
Halton Rd. N1—38Rb 63
Halton Rd. Grays—8E 92
Halt Robin La. Belv—49Dd 88
Halt Robin Rd. Belv—49Cd 88
Hambalt Rd. SW4—57Lb 104
Hamble Clo. Ruis—33U 56
Hamble Clo. Wok—5D 188
Hambledon Clo. Uxb—42R 76
Hambledon Gdns. SE25—69Vb 127
Hambledon Hill. Eps—88Sa 161
Hambledon Rd. SW18—59Bb 103
Hambledon Vale. Eps—88Sa 161
Hambledown Rd. Sidc—59Tc 108
Hamble La. S Ock—43Vd 90
Hamble St. SW6—55Db 103
Hamble Wlk. Wok—6D 188
Hambridge Way. SW2—59Qb 104
Hambro Av. Brom—74Jc 149
Hambrook Rd. SE25—69Xb 127
Hambro Rd. SW16—65Mb 126
Hambro Rd. Brtwd—19Zd 33
Hambrough Rd. S'hall—46Aa 77
Ham Clo. Rich—62La 122 (in two parts)
Hamden Cres. Dag—34Dd 68
Hamelin St. E14—44Ec 84
Hamerton Rd. Grav—57De 113
Hameway. E6—42Qc 86

Ham Farm Rd.—Hartland Rd.

Ham Farm Rd. Rich—63Ma 123
Hamfield Clo. Oxt—99Ec 182
Hamfrith Rd. E15—37Hc 65
Ham Ga. Av. Rich—62Ma 123
Hamilton Av. N9—17Wb 25
Hamilton Av. Cob—85W 158
Hamilton Av. Ilf—28Rc 46
Hamilton Av. Romf—26Fd 48
Hamilton Av. Surb—75Qa 143
Hamilton Av. Sutt—75Ab 144
Hamilton Av. Wok—88G 156
Hamilton Bldgs. EC2—(6J 195)
Hamilton Clo. N17—27Vb 43
Hamilton Clo. NW8 —41Fb 81 (4B 190)
Hamilton Clo. SE16—47Ac 84
Hamilton Clo. Barn—14Gb 23
Hamilton Clo. Cher—74H 139
Hamilton Clo. Eps—84Sa 161
Hamilton Clo. Felt—64V 120
Hamilton Clo. Pot B—5Wa 8
Hamilton Clo. St Alb—3Ca 5
Hamilton Clo. Stan—19Ga 20
Hamilton Cres. N13—21Qb 42
Hamilton Cres. Brtwd—21Yd 50
Hamilton Cres. Harr—34Ba 57
Hamilton Cres. Houn—57Da 99
Hamilton Dri. Romf—26Nd 49
Hamilton Gdns. NW8 —41Eb 81 (3A 190)
Hamilton La. N5—35Rb 63
Hamilton M. W1—(7K 197)
Hamilton Pk. N5—35Rb 63
Hamilton Pk. W. N5—35Rb 63
Hamilton Pl. W1—46Jb 82 (7J 197)
Hamilton Pl. Sun—66X 121
Hamilton Rd. E15—41Gc 85
Hamilton Rd. E17—26Ac 44
Hamilton Rd. N2—27Eb 41
Hamilton Rd. N9—17Wb 25
Hamilton Rd. NW10—36Wa 60
Hamilton Rd. NW11—31Za 60
Hamilton Rd. SE27—63Tb 127
Hamilton Rd. SW19—66Db 125
Hamilton Rd. W4—47Ua 80
Hamilton Rd. W5—45Na 79
Hamilton Rd. Barn—14Gb 23
Hamilton Rd. Bexh—54Ad 109
Hamilton Rd. Bren—51Ma 101
Hamilton Rd. Felt—63V 120
Hamilton Rd. Harr—29Ga 38
Hamilton Rd. Hay—45X 77
Hamilton Rd. Ilf—35Rc 66
Hamilton Rd. K Lan—5S 4
Hamilton Rd. Romf—29Kd 49
Hamilton Rd. Sidc—63Wc 131
Hamilton Rd. Slou—4E 72
Hamilton Rd. S'hall—46Ba 77
Hamilton Rd. T Hth—69Tb 127
Hamilton Rd. Twic—60Ga 100
Hamilton Rd. Uxb—42M 75
Hamilton Rd. Wat—20X 19
Hamilton Sq. SE1—(1G 207)
Hamilton St. SE8—51Cc 106
Hamilton St. Wat—15Y 19
Hamilton Ter. NW8 —40Eb 61 (3A 190)
Hamilton Way. N3—23Cb 41
Hamilton Way. Wall—81Mb 164
Ham La. Egh—3M 117
Ham La. Wind—7N 95
Hamlet Clo. Romf—24Cd 48
Hamlet Gdns. W6—49Wa 80
Hamlet Rd. SE19—66Vb 127
Hamlet Rd. Romf—24Cd 48
Hamlets Way. E3—42Bc 84
Hamlet, The. SE5—55Tb 105
Hamlin Cres. Pinn—29Y 37
Hamlin Rd. Sev—93Gd 186
Hamlyn Gdns. SE19—66Ub 127
Hamm Ct. Est. Wey—75P 139
Hammelton Grn. SW9—53Rb 105
Hammelton Rd. Brom—67Hc 129
Hammers La. NW7—22Wa 40
Hammersley Av. E16—44Hc 85
Hammersmith Bri. SW13 & W6 —51Xa 102
Hammersmith Bri. Rd. W6 —50Ya 80
Hammersmith B'way. W6 —49Ya 80
Hammersmith Flyover. W6 —50Ya 80
Hammersmith Gro. W6—48Ya 80
Hammersmith Rd.—49Za 80
W14 1-155 & 2-92
W6 remainder
Hammersmith Ter. W6—50Wa 80
Hammett St. EC3 —45Vb 83 (4K 201)
Hamm Moor Est. Wey—77N 139
Hamm Moor La. Wey—78N 139
Hammond Av. Mitc—68Kb 126
Hammond Clo. Barn—15Ab 22
Hammond Clo. Gnfd—36Fa 58
Hammond Clo. Hmptn—67Ca 121
Hammond Clo. Wok—3F 188
Hammond Rd. Enf—12Xb 25
Hammond Rd. S'hall—48Aa 77
Hammond Rd. Wok—3F 188
Hammonds La. Brtwd—23Xd 50
Hammond St. NW5—37Lb 62
Hamonde Clo. Edgw—19Ra 21
Hamond Sq. N1—(1H 195)
Ham Pk. Rd.—38Hc 65
E15 1-111 & 2-66
E7 remainder
Hampden Av. Beck—68Ac 128
Hampden Clo. NW1 —40Mb 62 (2E 192)
Hampden Clo. Slou—1L 73
Hampden Cres. Brtwd—21Yd 50
Hampden Cres. Wal X—3Xb 11
Hampden Gurney St. W1 —44Hb 81 (3F 197)
Hampden Ho. SW9—54Qb 104
Hampden La. N17—25Wb 43
Hampden Pl. St Alb—1Ga 6
Hampden Rd. N8—28Qb 42
Hampden Rd. N10—24Jb 42
Hampden Rd. N17—25Wb 43
Hampden Rd. N19—33Mb 62
Hampden Rd. Beck—68Ac 128
Hampden Rd. Ger X—25A 34
Hampden Rd. Grays—50De 91
Hampden Rd. Harr—25Ea 38
Hampden Rd. King—69Qa 123
Hampden Rd. Romf—24Dd 48
Hampden Rd. Slou—48B 74
Hampden Sq. N14—18Kb 24
Hampden Way. N14—18Kb 24
Hampden Way. Wat—8U 4
Hampermill La. Wat—19V 18
Hampshire Av. Slou—3G 72
Hampshire Clo. N18—22Xb 43
Hampshire Gdns. Stanf—7J 93
Hampshire Ho. Ger X—22A 34
Hampshire Rd. N22—24Pb 42
Hampshire Rd. Horn—28Qd 49
Hampshire St. NW5—37Mb 62
Hampson Way. SW8—53Pb 104
Hampstead Clo. SE28—46Xc 87
Hampstead Gdns. NW11—30Cb 41
Hampstead Grn. NW3—36Gb 61
Hampstead Gro. NW3—34Eb 61
Hampstead High St. NW3 —35Eb 61
Hampstead Hill Gdns. NW3 —35Fb 61
Hampstead La.—32Fb 61
NW3 50-56
N6 remainder
Hampstead Rd. NW1 —40Lb 62 (1B 192)
Hampstead Sq. NW3—34Eb 61
Hampstead Way. NW11—29Bb 41
Hampton Clo. NW6—41Cb 81
Hampton Clo. SW20—66Ya 124
Hampton Ct. N1—37Rb 63
Hampton Ct. Av. E Mol—72Fa 142
Hampton Ct. Bri. E Mol—70Ga 122
Hampton Ct. Pde. E Mol—70Ga 122
Hampton Ct. Rd. Hmptn, E Mol & King—68Ea 122
Hampton Ct. Way. Th Dit & E Mol—74Ga 142
Hampton Cres. Grav—1G 136
Hampton Farm Industrial Est. Felt—62Aa 121
Hampton Gro. Eps—83Va 162
Hampton La. Felt—63Aa 121
Hampton Mead. Lou—13Rc 28
Hampton Rise. Harr—30Na 39
Hampton Rd. E4—22Bc 44
Hampton Rd. E7—36Kc 65
Hampton Rd. E11—32Fc 65
Hampton Rd. Croy—72Sb 147
Hampton Rd. Ilf—35Sc 66
Hampton Rd. Tedd—64Fa 122
Hampton Rd. Twic—62Fa 122
Hampton Rd. Wor Pk—75Xa 144
Hampton Rd. E. Felt—63Ba 121
Hampton Rd. W. Felt—62Aa 121
Hampton St. SE17 & SE1 —49Sb 83 (6C 206)
Ham Ridings. Rich—64Pa 123
Hamsey Grn. Gdns. Warl —88Xb 165
Hamsey Way. S Croy—87Xb 165
Hamshades Clo. Sidc—62Vc 131
Ham St. Rich—60Ka 100
Ham, The. Bren—52La 100
Ham View. Croy—72Ac 148
Ham Yd. W1—45Mb 82 (4D 198)
Hanah Ct. SW19—66Za 124
Hanameel St. E16—46Kc 85
Hanbury Clo. Wal X—1Ac 12
Hanbury Dri. West—85Kc 167
Hanbury Path. Wok—86F 156
Hanbury Rd. N17—26Xb 43
Hanbury Rd. W3—47Ra 79
Hanbury St. E1—43Vb 83 (7K 195)
Hanbury Wlk. Bex—62Gd 132
Hancock Rd. E3—41Ec 84
Hancock Rd. SE19—65Tb 127
Handa Wlk. N1—37Tb 63
Hand Ct. WC1—43Pb 82 (1J 199)
Handcroft Rd. Croy—73Rb 147
Handel Clo. Edgw—23Pa 39
Handel Cres. Til—2C 114
Handel St. WC1—42Nb 82 (5F 193)
Handel Way. Edgw—24Qa 39
Handen Rd. SE12—57Gc 107
Handforth Rd. SW9—52Qb 104
Handforth Way. Ilf—34Rc 66
Handley Rd. E9—39Yb 64
Handside Clo. Wor Pk—74Za 144
Hands Wlk. E16—44Jc 85
Handsworth Av. E4—23Fc 45
Handsworth Clo. Wat—20W 18
Handsworth Rd. N17—27Tb 43
Handtrough Way. Bark—40Rc 66
Hanford Clo. SE4—56Zb 106
Hanford Clo. SW18—60Cb 103
Hanford Rd. S Ock—46Sd 90
Hanford Row. SW19—65Ya 124
Hangar Ruding. Wat—20Ba 19
Hangboy Slade. Lou—9Qc 14
Hanger Grn. W5—42Qa 79
Hanger Hill. Wey—79R 140
Hanger La. W5—40Na 59
Hanger Vale La. W5—44Pa 79
Hanger View Way. W3—44Qa 79
Hanging Hill La. Brtwd—20De 33
Hanging Sword All. EC4—(3A 200)
Hangrove Hill. Orp—85Rc 168
Hankey Pl. SE1—47Tb 83 (2G 207)
Hankins La. NW7—19Ua 22
Hanley Clo. Wind—3B 94
Hanley Rd. N4—32Nb 62
Hanmer Wlk. N7—33Pb 62
Hannah Mary Way. SE1—49Wb 83
Hannards Way. Ilf—22Xc 47
Hannay Wlk. SW16—61Mb 126
Hannell Rd. SW6—52Ab 102
Hannen Rd. SE27—62Rb 127
Hannibal Gdns. Stai—59N 97
Hannibal Rd. E1—43Yb 84
Hannibal Rd. Stai—59M 97
Hannibal Way. Croy—78Pb 146
Hannington Rd. SW4—55Kb 104
Hanover Av. Felt—60W 98
Hanover Circ. Hay—44S 76
Hanover Clo. Red—100Lb 180
Hanover Clo. Rich—52Qa 101
Hanover Clo. Slou—8L 73
Hanover Clo. Sutt—77Ab 144
Hanover Ct. NW9—27Ua 40
Hanover Est. N22—27Pb 42
Hanover Gdns. SE11—51Qb 104
Hanover Gdns. Ilf—24Sc 46
Hanover Ga. NW1 —41Gb 81 (4E 190)
Hanover Mead. NW11—29Ab 40
Hanover Pk. SE15—53Wb 105
Hanover Pl. WC2 —44Nb 82 (3G 199)
Hanover Pl. Egh—5M 117
Hanover Rd. N15—28Vb 43
Hanover Rd. NW10—38Ya 60
Hanover Rd. SW19—66Eb 125
Hanover Sq. W1—44Kb 82 (3A 198)
Hanover St. W1—44Kb 82 (3A 198)
Hanover St. Croy—76Rb 147
Hanover Ter. NW1 —41Hb 81 (4F 191)
Hanover Ter. Iswth—53Ja 100
Hanover Ter. M. NW1 —41Hb 81 (4F 191)
Hanover Wlk. Wey—76U 140
Hanover Way. Bexh—55Zc 109
Hanover Way. Wind—4D 94
Hanover W. Industrial Est. NW10—41Ta 79
Hanover Yd. N1—(1C 194)
Hansard M. W14—47Za 80
Hansart Way. Enf—12Qb 24
Hans Cres. SW1—48Hb 81 (3F 203)
Hanselin Clo. Stan—22Ha 38
Hanshawe Dri. Edgw—25Ta 39
Hansler Gro. E Mol—70Fa 122
Hansler Rd. SE22—57Vb 105
Hansol Rd. Bexh—57Ad 109
Hanson Clo. SW12—59Kb 104
Hanson Clo. Lou—12Sc 28
Hanson Dri. Lou—12Sc 28
Hanson Gdns. S'hall—47Aa 77
Hanson Grn. Lou—12Sc 28
Hanson St. W1—43Lb 82 (7B 192)
Hans Pl. SW1—48Hb 81 (3G 203)
Hans Rd. SW3—48Hb 81 (3F 203)
Hans St. SW1—49Hb 81 (4G 203)
Hanway Pl. W1—44Mb 82 (2D 198)
Hanway Rd. W7—44Fa 78
Hanway St. W1—44Mb 82 (2D 198)
Hanworth La. Cher—74H 139
Hanworth Rd. Felt—60X 99
Hanworth Rd. Hmptn—63Ba 121
Hanworth Rd. Houn—60Ba 99
Hanworth Rd. Sun—66W 120
(in two parts)
Hanworth Ter. Houn—56Da 99
Hanworth Trading Est. Cher —74H 139
Hanworth Trading Est. Felt
Hapgood Clo. Gnfd—36Fa 58
Harad's Pl. E1—45Wb 83
Harben Rd. NW6—38Eb 61
Harberson Rd. E15—39Hc 65
Harberson Rd. SW12—60Kb 104
Harbet Rd. E4—22Zb 44
Harbet Rd. W2—43Fb 81 (1C 196)
Harbex Clo. Bex—59Dd 110
Harbinger Rd. E14—49Dc 84
Harbledown Pl. Orp—70Yc 131
Harbledown Rd. SW6—53Cb 103
Harbledown Rd. S Croy —83Wb 165
Harbord Clo. SE5—54Tb 105
Harbord St. SW6—53Za 102
Harborne Clo. Wat—22Y 37
Harborough Av. Sidc—59Vc 109
Harborough Clo. Slou—6B 72
Harborough Rd. SW16—63Pb 126
Harbourer Clo. Ilf—22Xc 47
Harbourer Rd. Ilf—22Xc 47
Harbourfield Rd. Bans—87Db 163
Harbour Rd. SE5—55Sb 105
Harbridge Av. SW15—59Wa 102
Harbury Rd. Cars—81Gb 163
Harbut Rd. SW11—56Fb 103
Harcombe Rd. N16—34Ub 63
Harcourt Av. E12—35Pc 66
Harcourt Av. Edgw—20Sa 21
Harcourt Av. Sidc—58Yc 109
Harcourt Av. Wall—77Kb 146
Harcourt Clo. Egh—65E 118
Harcourt Clo. Iswth—55Ja 100
Harcourt Field. Wall—77Kb 146
Harcourt Rd. E15—40Hc 65
Harcourt Rd. N22—25Mb 42
Harcourt Rd. SE4—55Bc 106
Harcourt Rd. SW19—66Cb 125
Harcourt Rd. Bexh—56Ad 109
Harcourt Rd. Bush, Wat—15Ea 20
Harcourt Rd. T Hth—72Pb 146
Harcourt Rd. Wall—77Kb 146
Harcourt Rd. Wind—3C 94
Harcourt St. W1—43Gb 81 (1E 196)
Harcourt Ter. SW10—50Db 81
Hardcourts Clo. W Wick —76Dc 148
Hardel Rise. SW2—60Rb 105
Hardel Wlk. SW2—59Qb 104
Harden Rd. Grav—2B 136
Harden's Mnr. Way. SE7—48Mc 85
Harden St. SE18—49Nc 85
Harders Rd. SE15—53Xb 105
(in two parts)
Harders Rd. M. SE15—53Xb 105
Hardess St. SE24—55Sb 105
Hardie Clo. NW10—36Ta 59
Hardie Rd. Dag—34Ed 68
Hardie Rd. Stanf—1M 93
Harding Clo. SE17—51Sb 105
Harding Clo. Wat—5Y 5
Hardinge Clo. Uxb—43R 76
Hardinge Rd. N18—23Ub 43
Hardinge Rd. NW10—39Xa 60
Hardinge St. E1—44Yb 84
(in two parts)
Harding Rd. Bexh—54Bd 109
Harding Rd. Eps—91Ua 178
Harding Rd. Grays—8C 92
Hardings Clo. Iver—41E 74
Hardings La. SE20—65Zb 128
Hardings Row. Iver—41E 74
Hardley Cres. Horn—28Md 49
Hardman Rd. SE7—50Kc 85
Hardman Rd. King—68Na 123
Hardwick Clo. Lea—87Ea 160
Hardwick Clo. Stan—22La 38
Hardwick Ct. Eri—51Fd 110
Hardwicke Av. Houn—53Ca 99
Hardwicke Rd. N13—23Nb 42
Hardwicke Rd. W4—49Ta 79
Hardwicke Rd. Rich—63La 122
Hardwicke St. Bark—39Sc 66
Hardwick Grn. W13—43Ka 78
Hardwick La. Cher—73E 138
Hardwick St. EC1 —41Qb 82 (4A 194)
Hardwicks Way. SW18—57Cb 103
Hardwidge St. SE1 —47Ub 83 (1H 207)
Hardy Av. Grav—1A 136
Hardy Av. Ruis—36X 57
Hardy Clo. Pinn—31Z 57
Hardy Clo. Slou—6E 72
Hardy Gro. Dart—56Qd 111
Hardy Rd. SE3—51Hc 107
Hardy Rd. SW19—66Db 125
Hardy Way. Enf—11Qb 24
Hare & Billet Rd. SE3—53Fc 107
Harebell Hill. Cob—86Z 159
Harebell Way. Romf—24Md 49
Harebreaks, The. Wat—9W 4
Hare Ct. EC4—44Qb 82 (3K 199)
Harecourt Rd. N1—37Sb 63
Hare Cres. Wat—4W 4
Harecroft. Lea—96Da 175
Haredale Rd. SE24—56Sb 105
Haredon Clo. SE23—59Zb 106
Harefield. Esh—76Ga 142
Harefield Av. Sutt—81Ab 162
Harefield Clo. Enf—11Qb 24
Harefield Grn. NW7—23Ya 40
Harefield Rd. N8—29Mb 42
Harefield Rd. SE4—55Bc 106
Harefield Rd. SW16—66Pb 126
Harefield Rd. Rick—20M 17
Harefield Rd. Sidc—62Zc 131
Harefield Rd. Uxb—37L 55
Hare Hall La. Romf—28Kd 49
Harehatch La. Slou—2C 52
Hare Hill. Wey—79G 138
Harehill Clo. Wok—87J 157
Harelands Clo. Wok—5F 188
Harelands La. Wok—5F 188
(in two parts)
Hare La. Esh—79Fa 142
Hare Marsh. E2—42Wb 83
Hare Pl. EC4—(3A 200)
Hare Row. E2—40Xb 63
Hares Bank. Croy—82Fc 167
Haresfield Rd. Dag—37Dd 68
Harestone Dri. Cat—97Vb 181
Harestone Hill. Cat—96Wb 181
Harestone Hill. Cat—98Vb 181
Harestone La. Cat—97Ub 181
Harestone Valley Rd. Cat —96Vb 181
Harestone Valley Rd. Cat —98Vb 181
Hare St. SE18—48Qc 86
Hare Wlk. N1—40Ub 63 (2J 195)
Harewood. Rick—14K 17
(in two parts)
Harewood Av. NW1 —42Gb 81 (6E 190)
Harewood Av. N'holt—38Ba 57
Harewood Clo. N'holt—38Ba 57
Harewood Dri. Ilf—26Pc 46
Harewood Gdns. S Croy —87Xb 165
Harewood Hill. Epp—7Uc 14
Harewood Pl. W1 —44Kb 82 (3A 198)
Harewood Pl. Slou—8L 73
Harewood Rd. SW19—65Gb 125
Harewood Rd. Brtwd—16Xd 32
Harewood Rd. Iswth—52Ha 100
Harewood Rd. S Croy—79Ub 147
Harewood Rd. Wat—20X 19
Harewood Row. NW1 —43Gb 81 (7E 190)
Harewood Ter. S'hall—49Ba 77
Harfield Gdns. SE5—55Ub 105
Harfield Rd. Sun—68Z 121
Harford Clo. E4—17Dc 26
Harford Dri. Wat—10U 4
Harford Rd. E4—17Dc 26
Harford St. E1—42Ac 84
Harford Wlk. N2—28Fb 41
Hargood Clo. Harr—30Na 39
Hargood Rd. SE3—53Lc 107
Hargrave Pk. N19—33Lb 62
Hargrave Pl. N7—36Mb 62
Hargravé Rd. N19—33Lb 62
Hargreaves Av. Wal X—3Xb 11
Hargreaves Clo. Wal X—3Xb 11
Hargwyne St. SW9—55Pb 104
Haringey Pk. N8—30Nb 42
Haringey Rd. N8—28Nb 42
Harington Ter. N18—20Tb 25
Harkett Clo. Harr—26Ha 38
Harkness. Wal X—1Xb 11
Harkness Clo. Eps—88Ya 162
Harkness Clo. Romf—22Pd 49
Harland Av. Croy—76Wb 147
Harland Av. Sidc—62Tc 130
Harland Rd. SE12—60Jc 107
Harlech Gdns. Houn—51Y 99
Harlech Rd. N14—20Nb 24
Harlequin Av. Bren—51Ja 100
Harlequin Av. Tedd—66Ka 122
Harlescott Rd. SE15—56Zb 106
Harlesden Clo. Romf—24Pd 49
Harlesden Gdns. NW10—39Va 60
Harlesden La. NW10—39Wa 60
Harlesden Rd. NW10—39Wa 60
Harlesden Rd. Romf—23Pd 49
Harlesden Wlk. Romf—24Pd 49
Harleston Clo. E5—33Yb 64
Harley Clo. Wemb—37Ma 59
Harley Ct. E11—31Jc 65
Harley Cres. Harr—28Fa 38
Harleyford. Brom—67Lc 129
Harleyford Rd. SE11—51Pb 104
Harleyford St. SE11—51Qb 104
Harley Gdns. SW10 —50Eb 81 (7A 202)
Harley Gdns. Orp—77Uc 150
Harley Gro. E3—41Bc 84
Harley Pl. W1—43Kb 82 (1K 197)
Harley Rd. NW3—38Fb 61
Harley Rd. NW10—40Ua 60
Harley Rd. Harr—28Fa 38
Harley St. W1—43Kb 82 (6K 191)
Harlington Clo. Hay—52S 98
Harlington Rd. Bexh—55Ad 109
Harlington Rd. Uxb—41Q 76
Harlington Rd. E. Felt—59X 99
Harlington Rd. W. Felt—58X 99
Harlowe Clo. E8—39Wb 63
Harlow Gdns. Romf—23Ed 48
Harlow Rd. N13—20Tb 25
Harlow Rd. Rain—39Hd 68
Harlton Ct. Wal A—6Hc 13
Harlyn Dri. Pinn—27X 37
Harman Av. Grav—4D 136
Harman Av. Wfd G—23Hc 45
Harman Clo. E4—21Fc 45
Harman Clo. NW2—34Ab 60
Harman Dri. NW2—34Ab 60
Harman Dri. Sidc—58Vc 109
Harman Rd. Enf—15Vb 25
Harmer Rd. Swans—58Be 113
Harmer St. Grav—8E 114
Harmondsworth La. W Dray —51N 97
Harmondsworth Rd. W Dray —50N 75
Harmony Clo. NW11—29Ab 40
Harmony Clo. Wall—81Nb 164
Harmony Lodge. S'hall—48Ca 77
Harmood Pl. NW1—38Kb 62
Harmood St. NW1—37Kb 62
Harmsworth St. SE17—51Rb 105
Harmsworth Way. N20—18Bb 23
Harness Rd. SE28—47Wc 87
Harold Av. Belv—50Bd 87
Harold Av. Hay—48Y 76
Harold Ct. Rd. Romf—23Rd 49
Harold Cres. Wal A—4Ec 12
Harold Est. SE1—48Ub 83 (4J 207)
Harold Hill Industrial Est. Romf—24Md 49
Harold Pl. SE11—50Qb 82
Harold Rd. E4—20Ec 26
Harold Rd. E11—32Gc 65
Harold Rd. E13—39Kc 65
Harold Rd. N8—29Pb 42
Harold Rd. N15—29Vb 43
Harold Rd. NW10—41Ta 79
Harold Rd. SE19—66Tb 127
Harold Rd. Dart—63Pd 133
Harold Rd. Sutt—77Fb 145
Harold Rd. Wfd G—25Jc 45
Haroldstone Rd. E17—29Ac 44
Harold View. Romf—26Pd 49
Harold Wilson Ho. SE28—46Xc 87
Harp All. EC4—44Rb 83 (2B 200)
Harpenden Rd. E12—33Lc 65
Harpenden Rd. SE27—61Rb 127
Harper La. Rad—4Ha 6
Harper La. Rad & Shen, Rad —3Ja 6
Harper Rd. E6—44Pc 86
Harper Rd. SE1—48Sb 83 (3E 206)
★Harpers La. Brtwd—9Zd
Harpley Sq. E1—42Zb 84
Harpour Rd. Bark—37Sc 66
Harp Rd. W7—42Ha 78
Harpsden St. SW11—53Jb 104
Harps Oak La. Red—97Hb 179
Harpur M. WC1—43Pb 82 (7H 193)
Harpur St. WC1—43Pb 82 (7H 193)
Harraden Rd. SE3—53Lc 107
Harrap St. E14—45Fc 85
Harrier Clo. Rain—37Kd 69
Harrier M. SE28—47Tc 86
Harriers Clo. W5—45Na 79
Harriescourt. Wal A—4Jc 13
Harries Rd. Hay—42Y 77
Harriet Clo. E8—39Wb 63
Harriet Gdns. Croy—75Wb 147
Harriet St. SW1—47Hb 81 (2G 203)
Harriet Wlk. SW1 —47Hb 81 (2G 203)
Harriet Way. Bush, Wat—17Fa 20
Harringay Gdns. N8—28Rb 43
Harringay Pas. N8 & N4—28Qb 42
Harringay Rd. N15—28Rb 43
Harrington Clo. Croy—75Nb 146
Harrington Clo. Wind—6D 94
Harrington Gdns. SW7 —49Eb 81 (6A 202)
Harrington Hill. E5—32Yb 64
Harrington Rd. E11—32Gc 65
Harrington Rd. SE25—70Xb 127
Harrington Rd. SW7 —49Fb 81 (5B 202)
Harrington Sq. NW1 —40Lb 62 (2B 192)
Harrington St. NW1 —41Lb 82 (3B 192)
Harrington Way. SE18—48Mc 85
Harriott Clo. SE10—49Hc 85
Harriotts La. Asht—91La 176
Harris Clo. Enf—11Rb 25
Harris Clo. Grav—2B 136
Harris Clo. Houn—53Ca 99
Harris La. Shen, Rad—6Qa 7
Harrison Clo. Brtwd—15Fe 33
Harrison Clo. N'wd—23S 36
Harrison Ct. Shep—71R 140
Harrison Rd. Dag—37Dd 68
★Harrison Rd. Sev—92Be
Harrisons Rise. Croy—76Rb 147
Harrison St. WC1 —41Nb 82 (4G 193)
Harrison Wlk. Wal X—2Zb 12
Harrison Way. Slou—6B 72
Harris Rd. Bexh—53Bd 109
Harris Rd. Dag—36Bd 67
Harris Rd. Wat—7W 4
Harris St. E17—31Bc 64
Harris St. SE5—52Tb 105
Harris Way. Sun—67U 120
Harrogate Ct. Slou—50C 74
Harrogate Rd. Wat—20Y 19
Harrold Rd. Dag—36Xc 67
Harrow Av. Enf—16Vb 25
Harroway Rd. SW11—54Fb 103
Harrow Bottom Rd. Vir W —72B 138
Harrowby Gdns. Grav—1A 136
Harrowby St. W1 —44Gb 81 (2E 196)
Harrow Clo. Chess—80Ma 143
Harrow Clo. Wey—75K 139
Harrow Cres. Romf—24Kd 49
Harrowdene Clo. Wemb—35Ma 59
Harrowdene Gdns. Tedd —66Ja 122
Harrowdene Rd. Wemb—34Ma 59
Harrow Dri. N9—18Vb 25
Harrow Dri. Horn—30Kd 49
Harrowes Meade. Edgw—20Qa 21
Harrow Fields Gdns. Harr —34Ga 58
Harrow Gdns. Warl—88Bc 166
Harrowgate Rd. E9—38Ac 64
Harrow Grn. E11—34Gc 65
Harrow La. E14—45Ec 84
Harrow Mnr. Way. SE2—47Yc 87
Harrow Pk. Harr—33Ga 58
Harrow Pl. E1—44Vb 83 (2J 201)
Harrow Rd. E6—39Nc 66
Harrow Rd. E11—34Gc 65
Harrow Rd.—41Xa 80
W2 1-281 & 2-322
W9 283-421a & 324-570
W10 421-625 & 572-742
NW10 remainder
Harrow Rd. Bark—39Uc 66
Harrow Rd. Cars—79Gb 145
Harrow Rd. Felt—61Q 120
Harrow Rd. Ilf—35Sc 66
Harrow Rd. Sev—87Ad 169
Harrow Rd. Slou—48B 74
Harrow Rd. Warl—87Bc 166
Harrow Rd. Wemb—35Ha 58 to 38Ra 59
Harrow Rd. Wemb—36Qa 59
(Tokyngton)
Harrow Rd. Bri. W2—43Eb 81
Harrow St. NW1—43Gb 81 (7D 190)
Harrow View. Harr—26Ea 38
Harrow View. Hay—44W 76
Harrow View. Uxb—41S 76
Harrow View Rd. W5—42Ka 78
Harrow Way. Shep—68S 120
Harrow Way. Wat—20Aa 19
Harrow Weald Pk. Harr—23Fa 38
Hart Cres. Chig—22Vc 47
Hart Dyke Cres. Swan—69Fd 132
Hart Dyke Rd. Orp—74Yc 151
Hart Dyke Rd. Swan—69Fd 132
Harte Rd. Houn—54Ba 99
Hartfield Av. Borwd—15Qa 21
Hartfield Av. N'holt—40X 57
Hartfield Clo. Borwd—15Qa 21
Hartfield Cres. SW19—66Bb 125
Hartfield Cres. W Wick—76Jc 149
Hartfield Gro. SE20—67Xb 127
Hartfield Pl. Grav—59Fe 113
Hartfield Rd. SW19—66Bb 125
Hartfield Rd. Chess—78Ma 143
Hartfield Rd. W Wick—77Jc 149
Hartfield Ter. E3—40Cc 64
Hartford Av. Harr—27Ja 38
Hartforde Rd. Borwd—12Qa 21
Hartford Rd. Bex—58Cd 110
Hartford Rd. Eps—79Ra 143
Hart Gro. W5—46Qa 79
Hart Gro. S'hall—43Ca 77
Hartham Clo. N7—36Nb 62
Hartham Clo. Iswth—53Ja 100
Hartham Rd. N7—36Nb 62
Hartham Rd. N17—26Vb 43
Hartham Rd. Iswth—53Ha 100
Hartin Clo. Uxb—40N 55
Harting Rd. SE9—62Nc 130
Hartington Clo. Harr—35Ga 58
Hartington Rd. E16—44Kc 85
Hartington Rd. E17—30Ac 44
Hartington Rd. SW8—53Nb 104
Hartington Rd. W4—52Ra 101
Hartington Rd. W13—45Ka 78
Hartington Rd. S'hall—48Aa 77
Hartington Rd. Twic—59Ka 100
Hartismere Rd. SW6—52Bb 103
Hartlake Rd. E9—37Zb 64
Hartland Clo. Edgw—19Qa 21
Hartland Clo. Wey—82L 157
Hartland Dri. Edgw—19Qa 21
Hartland Dri. Ruis—34X 57
Hartland Rd. E15—38Hc 65
Hartland Rd. N11—22Hb 41
Hartland Rd. NW1—38Kb 62

Hartland Rd. NW6—40Bb **61**
Hartland Rd. Epp—3Wc **15**
Hartland Rd. Hmptn—63Da **121**
Hartland Rd. Horn—33Jd **68**
Hartland Rd. Iswth—55Ja **100**
Hartland Rd. Mord—73Cb **145**
Hartland Rd. Wal X—2Zb **12**
Hartland Rd. Wey—80J **139**
Hartland Way. Croy—76Ac **148**
Hartland Way. Mord—73Bb **145**
Hartley Av. E6—39Nc **66**
Hartley Av. NW7—22Va **40**
Hartley Bottom Rd. Long, Dart —75De **155**
Hartley Bottom Rd. Sev & Long, Dart—78Ce **155**
Hartley Clo. NW7—22Va **40**
Hartley Clo. Brom—68Pc **130**
Hartley Clo. Slou—9N **53**
Hartley Down. Purl—87Pb **164**
Hartley Farm Est. Purl—87Pb **164**
Hartley Grange. Long, Dart —72Be **155**
Hartley Hill. Long, Dart—74Ce **155**
Hartley Hill. Purl—87Pb **164**
Hartley Old Rd. Purl—87Pb **164**
Hartley Rd. E11—32Hc **65**
Hartley Rd. Croy—73Sb **147**
Hartley Rd. Long, Dart—68Ae **135**
Hartley Rd. Well—52Yc **109**
Hartley Rd. West—97Tc **184**
Hartley St. E2—41Yb **84**
Hartley Way. Purl—87Pb **164**
Hartmann Rd. E16—46Mc **85**
Hartnoll St. N7—36Pb **62**
Harton Clo. Brom—67Mc **129**
Harton Rd. N9—19Xb **25**
Harton St. SE8—53Cc **106**
Hart Rd. Wey—85N **157**
Hartsbourne Av. Bush, Wat —19Ea **20**
Hartsbourne Rd. Bush, Wat —19Fa **20**
Harts Clo. Bush, Wat—12Ca **19**
Harts Croft. Croy—81Ac **166**
Hart Shaw. Long, Dart—68De **135**
Hartshill Clo. Uxb—37R **56**
Hartshill Rd. Grav—1B **136**
Hartshill Wlk. Wok—4E **188**
Hartshorn All. EC3—(3J **201***)*
Hartshorn Gdns. E6—42Qc **86**
Hartsland Rd. Sev—95Ld **187**
Hart's La. SE14—53Ac **106**
Harts La. Bark—37Rc **66**
Hartslock Dri. SE2—47Zc **87**
Hartsmead Rd. SE9—61Pc **130**
Hartspring La. Bush, Wat & Wat —12Ca **19**
Hart St. EC3—45Ub **83** (4J **201**)
Hart St. Brtwd—19Yd **32**
Hartsway. Enf—14Yb **26**
Hartswood Clo. Brtwd—21Ae **51**
Hartswood Rd. W12—47Va **80**
Hartswood Rd. Brtwd—21Ae **51**
Hartville Rd. SE18—49Uc **86**
Hartwell Dri. E4—23Ec **44**
Hartwell St. E8—37Vb **63**
Harty Clo. Grays—46De **91**
Harvard Hill. W4—51Ra **101**
Harvard La. W4—50Sa **79**
Harvard Rd. SE13—57Ec **106**
Harvard Rd. W4—50Ra **79**
Harvard Rd. Iswth—53Ga **100**
Harvard Wlk. Horn—35Jd **68**
Harvel Cres. SE2—50Zc **87**
Harvest Bank Rd. W Wick —76Hc **149**
Harvest End. Wat—8Z **5**
Harvester Rd. Eps—82Ta **161**
Harvesters Clo. Iswth—57Fa **100**
Harvest Rd. Bush, Wat—14Da **19**
Harvest Rd. Egh—4P **117**
Harvest Rd. Felt—63W **120**
Harvest Way. Swan—73Fd **152**
Harvey. Grays—47De **91**
Harveyfields. Wal A—6Ec **12**
Harvey Gdns. E11—32Hc **65**
Harvey Gdns. SE7—49Mc **85**
Harvey Gdns. Lou—13Rc **28**
Harvey Rd. E11—32Hc **65**
Harvey Rd. N8—29Pb **42**
Harvey Rd. SE5—53Tb **105**
Harvey Rd. Houn—59Ba **99**
Harvey Rd. Ilf—36Rc **66**
Harvey Rd. N'holt—38Y **57**
Harvey Rd. Rick—16Q **18**
Harvey Rd. Slou—48D **74**
Harvey Rd. Uxb—40Q **56**
Harvey Rd. W on T—73W **140**
Harvey's Bldgs. WC2 —45Nb **82** (5G **199**)
Harveys La. Romf—33Fd **68**
Harvey St. N1—39Tb **63**
Harvill Rd. Sidc—64Ad **131**
Harvil Rd. Uxb—28L **35**
Harvington Wlk. E8—38Wb **63**
Harvist Est. N7—35Qb **62**
Harvist Rd. NW6—40Za **60**
Harwater Dri. Lou—12Pc **28**
Harwell Clo. Ruis—32T **56**
Harwell Pas. N2—28Hb **41**
Harwich Rd. Slou—4E **72**
Harwood Av. Brom—68Kc **129**
Harwood Av. Horn—27Nd **49**
Harwood Av. Mitc—69Gb **125**
Harwood Gdns. Wind—9M **95**
Harwood Hall La. Upm—37Rd **69**
Harwood Rd. SW6—52Cb **103**
Harwoods Rd. Wat—14W **18**
Harwoods Yd. N21—17Qb **24**
Harwood Ter. SW6—53Db **103**
Haselbury Rd.—21Ub **43**
N9 176-306 & 163-279
N18 remainder
Haselrigge Rd. SW4—56Mb **104**
Haseltine Rd. SE26—63Bc **128**
Haselwood Dri. Enf—14Rb **25**
Haskard Rd. Dag—35Zc **67**
Hasker St. SW3—49Gb **81** (5E **202**)
Haskins. Stanf—1P **93**
Haslam Av. Sutt—74Ab **144**
Haslam Clo. N1—38Qb **62**
Haslam Clo. Uxb—33S **56**
Haslemere Av. NW4—30Za **40**
Haslemere Av. SW18—61Db **125**
Haslemere Av.—48Ja **78**
W13 1-69 & 2-84
W7 remainder
Haslemere Av. Barn—18Hb **23**
Haslemere Av. Houn—54Y **99**
Haslemere Av. Mitc—68Fb **125**
Haslemere Clo. Hmptn—64Ba **121**
Haslemere Clo. Wall—78Nb **146**
Haslemere Gdns. N3—27Bb **41**
Haslemere Rd. N8—31Nb **62**
Haslemere Rd. N21—19Rb **25**
Haslemere Rd. Bexh—54Bd **109**
Haslemere Rd. Ilf—33Vc **67**
Haslemere Rd. T Hth—71Rb **147**
Haslemere Rd. Wind—3E **94**
Hasler Clo. SE28—45Xc **87**
Haslett Rd. Shep—68U **120**
Hasluck Gdns. Barn—16Db **23**
Hassard St. E2—40Vb **63** (3K **195**)
Hassenbrook Rd. Stanf—1M **93**
Hassendean Rd. SE3—52Kc **107**
Hassett Rd. E9—37Zb **64**
Hassocks Clo. SE26—62Xb **127**
Hassocks Rd. SW16—67Mb **126**
Hassock Wood. Kes—77Mc **149**
Hassop Rd. NW2—35Za **60**
Hassop Wlk. SE9—63Nc **130**
Hasted Rd. SE7—50Mc **85**
Hastings Av. Ilf—28Sc **46**
Hastings Bldgs. SE1—(4H **207***)*
Hastings Clo. SE15—52Wb **105**
Hastings Clo. Barn—14Eb **23**
Hastings Rd. N11—22Mb **42**
Hastings Rd. N17—27Tb **43**
Hastings Rd. W13—45Ka **78**
Hastings Rd. Brom—74Nc **150**
Hastings Rd. Croy—74Vb **147**
Hastings Rd. Romf—29Kd **49**
Hastings St. WC1 —41Nb **82** (4F **193**)
Hastings Way. Bush, Wat —14Aa **19**
Hastings Way. Rick—14S **18**
Hastingwood Ct. E17—29Dc **44**
Hastoe Clo. Hay—42Aa **78**
Hatcham Pk. M. SE14—53Zb **106**
Hatcham Pk. Rd. SE14—53Zb **106**
Hatcham Rd. SE15—51Yb **106**
Hatchard Rd. N19—33Mb **62**
Hatch Clo. Wey—76K **139**
Hatch Croft. NW4—27Xa **40**
Hatchet La. Wind—2A **116**
Hatchett Rd. Felt—60S **98**
Hatch Gdns. Tad—92Za **178**
Hatchgate Gdns. Slou—1B **72**
Hatch Gro. Romf—28Ad **47**
Hatch La. E4—21Fc **45**
Hatch La. Coul—87Jb **164**
Hatch La. W Dray—52M **97**
Hatch La. Wind—5E **94**
Hatch La. Wok—92R **174**
(Bridge End)
Hatch La. Wok—90R **158**
(Elm Corner)
Hatch Rd. SW16—68Nb **126**
Hatch Rd. Brtwd—15Wd **32**
Hatch Side. Chig—22Qc **46**
Hatch, The. Enf—11Zb **26**
Hatch, The. Wind—2A **94**
Hatchwood Clo. Wfd G—21Hc **45**
Hatcliffe Clo. SE3—55Hc **107**
Hatfeild Clo. Mitc—70Fb **125**
Hatfeild Mead. Mord—71Cb **145**
Hatfield Clo. SE14—52Zb **106**
Hatfield Clo. Brtwd—17Fe **33**
Hatfield Clo. Horn—36Md **69**
Hatfield Clo. Ilf—27Rc **46**
Hatfield Rd. E15—36Gc **65**
Hatfield Rd. W4—47Ta **79**
Hatfield Rd. W13—46Ja **78**
Hatfield Rd. Asht—91Pa **177**
Hatfield Rd. Dag—37Ad **67**
Hatfield Rd. Pot B—2Eb **9**
Hatfield Rd. Slou—7L **73**
Hatfield Rd. Wat—11X **19**
Hatfields. SE1—46Qb **82** (6A **200**)
Hatfields Rd. Lou—13Rc **28**
Hathaway Clo. Ruis—35V **56**
Hathaway Clo. Stan—22Ja **38**
Hathaway Cres. E12—37Pc **66**
Hathaway Gdns. W13—43Ja **78**
Hathaway Gdns. Romf—29Zc **47**
Hathaway Rd. Croy—73Rb **147**
Hathaway Rd. Grays—49De **91**
Hatherleigh Clo. Chess—78Ma **143**
Hatherleigh Clo. Mord—70Cb **125**
Hatherleigh Gdns. Pot B—4Fb **9**
Hatherleigh Rd. Ruis—33W **56**
Hatherleigh Way. Romf—25Md **49**
Hatherley Cres. Sidc—61Wc **131**
Hatherley Gdns. E6—41Mc **85**
Hatherley Gdns. N8—30Nb **42**
Hatherley Gro. W2—44Db **81**
Hatherley Rd. E17—28Bc **44**
Hatherley Rd. Rich—53Pa **101**
Hatherley Rd. Sidc—63Wc **131**
Hatherley St. SW1 —49Lb **82** (6C **204**)
Hathern Gdns. SE9—63Qc **130**
Hatherop Rd. Hmptn—66Ba **121**
Hatherwood. Lea—93Ma **177**
Hathway St. SE15—54Zb **106**
Hatley Av. Ilf—28Sc **46**
Hatley Clo. N11—22Hb **41**
Hatley Rd. N4—33Pb **62**
Hatteraick St. SE16—47Yb **84**
Hattersfield Clo. Belv—49Bd **87**
Hatton Av. Slou—2H **73**
Hatton Clo. SE18—52Tc **108**
Hatton Clo. Grav—1A **136**
Hatton Garden. EC1 —43Qb **82** (7A **194**)
Hatton Gdns. Mitc—71Hb **145**
Hatton Grn. Felt—56W **98**
Hatton Gro. W Dray—47M **75**
Hatton Pl. EC1—43Qb **82** (7A **194**)
Hatton Rd. Croy—74Qb **146**
Hatton Rd. Felt—59S **98**
Hatton Rd. Wal X—1Zb **12**
Hatton Rd. S. Felt—56V **98**
Hatton Row. NW8—(6C **190***)*
Hatton St. NW8—42Fb **81** (6C **190**)
Hatton Wall. EC1 —43Qb **82** (7A **194**)
Haunch of Venison Yd. W1 —44Kb **82** (3K **197**)
Havana Clo. Romf—29Gd **48**
Havana Rd. SW19—61Cb **125**
Havannah St. E14—47Cc **84**
Havant Rd. E17—27Ec **44**
Havant Way. SE15—52Vb **105**
Havelock Pl. Harr—30Ga **38**
Havelock Rd. N17—26Wb **43**
Havelock Rd. SW19—64Eb **125**
Havelock Rd. Belv—49Bd **87**
Havelock Rd. Brom—70Lc **129**
Havelock Rd. Croy—75Vb **147**
Havelock Rd. Dart—59Kd **111**
Havelock Rd. Grav—10B **114**
Havelock Rd. Harr—27Ga **38**
Havelock Rd. K Lan—1P **3**
Havelock Rd. S'hall—48Aa **77**
Havelock St. N1—39Nb **62**
Havelock St. Ilf—33Rc **66**
Havelock Ter. SW8—53Kb **104**
Havelock Wlk. SE23—60Yb **106**
Haven Clo. SW19—62Za **124**
Haven Clo. Grav—7B **136**
Haven Clo. Hay—42U **76**
Haven Clo. Swan—68Hd **132**
Haven Ct. Beck—68Ec **128**
Havengore Av. Grav—9G **114**
Haven Grn. W5—44Ma **79**
Haven Hill. Sev—79Ce **155**
Havenhurst Rise. Enf—12Qb **24**
Haven La. W5—44Na **79**
Haven Pl. W5—45Ma **79**
Haven Pl. Grays—47Ee **91**
Haven Rd. Ashf—63R **120**
Haven St. NW1—38Kb **62**
Haven Ter. W5—45Ma **79**
Haven, The. Rich—55Qa **101**
Havenwood. Wemb—34Ra **59**
Havenwood Clo. Brtwd—23Yd **50**
Haverfield Gdns. Rich—52Qa **101**
Haverfield Rd. E3—41Ac **84**
Haverford Way. Edgw—25Pa **39**
Haverhill Rd. E4—18Ec **26**
Haverhill Rd. SW12—60Lb **104**
Havering Dri. Romf—28Gd **48**
Havering Gdns. Romf—29Zc **47**
Havering Rd. Romf—26Fd **48**
Havering St. E1—44Zb **84**
Havering Way. Bark—41Xc **87**
Havers Av. W on T—78Z **141**
Haversham Clo. Twic—58Ma **101**
Haverstock Ct. Orp—68Wc **131**
Haverstock Hill. NW3—36Gb **61**
Haverstock Rd. NW5—36Jb **62**
Haverstock St. N1 —40Rb **63** (2C **194**)
Haverthwaite Rd. Orp—76Tc **150**
Havil St. SE5—52Ub **105**
Havisham Rd. Grav—10J **115**
Hawarden Gro. SE21—59Sb **105**
Hawarden Hill. NW2—34Wa **60**
Hawarden Rd. E17—28Zb **44**
Hawarden Rd. Cat—93Sb **181**
Hawbridge Rd. E11—32Fc **65**
Hawes Clo. N'wd—24V **36**
Hawes La. E4—10Ec **12**
Hawes La. W Wick—74Ec **148**
Hawes Rd. N18—23Xb **43**
Hawes Rd. Brom—67Kc **129**
Hawes Rd. Tad—92Za **178**
Hawes St. N1—38Rb **63**
Hawfield Bank. Orp—76Zc **151**
Hawgood St. E3—43Cc **84**
Hawkdene. E4—16Ec **26**
Hawke Pk. Rd. N22—27Rb **43**
Hawke Pl. SE16—47Zb **84**
Hawker Clo. Wall—80Nb **146**
Hawker Ct. Slou—48C **74**
Hawke Rd. SE19—65Ub **127**
Hawkesbury Rd. SW15—57Xa **102**
Hawkes Clo. Grays—51De **113**
Hawkesfield Rd. SE23—61Ac **128**
Hawkesley Clo. Twic—63Ja **122**
Hawkesmead Clo. Enf—8Zb **12**
Hawkes Rd. Felt—61X **120**
Hawkes Rd. Mitc—67Hb **125**
Hawkesworth Clo. N'wd—24U **36**
Hawkewood Rd. Sun—69W **120**
Hawkhirst Rd. Kenl—87Tb **165**
Hawkhurst. Cob—86Ca **159**
Hawkhurst Gdns. Chess —77Na **143**
Hawkhurst Gdns. Romf—22Fd **48**
Hawkhurst Rd. SW16—67Mb **126**
Hawkhurst Rd. Whyt—89Ub **165**
Hawkhurst Way. N Mald —71Ta **143**
Hawkhurst Way. W Wick —75Dc **148**
Hawkinge Wlk. Orp—69Xc **131**
Hawkinge Way. Horn—37Ld **69**
Hawkins Av. Grav—3E **136**
Hawkins Clo. Harr—31Fa **58**
Hawkins Rd. Tedd—65Ka **122**
Hawkley Gdns. SE27—61Rb **127**
Hawkridge Clo. Romf—30Yc **47**
Hawksbrook La. Beck—72Dc **148**
Hawkshaw Clo. SW2—60Nb **104**
Hawkshead Clo. Brom—66Gc **129**
Hawkshead La. Hat—1Ya **8**
Hawkshead Rd. NW10—38Va **60**
Hawkshead Rd. W4—47Ua **80**
Hawkshead Rd. Pot B—1Bb **9**
Hawkshill Clo. Esh—79Ca **141**
Hawks Hill Clo. Lea—95Ha **176**
Hawkshill Rd. Slou—1E **72**
Hawkshill Way. Esh—79Ba **141**
Hawkslade Rd. SE15—57Zb **106**
Hawksley Rd. N16—34Ub **63**
Hawks M. SE10—52Ec **106**
Hawksmoor. Shen, Rad—5Qa **7**
Hawksmoor Clo. E6—44Nc **86**
Hawksmoor Grn. Brtwd—15Fe **33**
Hawksmoor St. W6—51Za **102**
Hawksmouth. E4—17Ec **26**
Hawks Rd. King—68Pa **123**
Hawkstone Rd. SE16—49Yb **84**
Hawksview. Cob—85Ba **159**
Hawks Way. Stai—62H **119**
Hawkswell Clo. Wok—5C **188**
Hawkswell Wlk. Wok—5C **188**
Hawkswood Gro. Slou—37B **54**
Hawkswood La. Slou & Ger X —36B **54**
Hawkwood Cres. E4—16Dc **26**
Hawkwood Dell. Lea—98Ca **175**
Hawkwood La. Chst—67Sc **130**
Hawkwood Mt. E5—32Xb **63**
Hawkwood Rise. Lea—98Ca **175**
Hawlands Dri. Pinn—31Aa **57**
Hawley Clo. Hmptn—65Ba **121**
Hawley Cres. NW1—38Kb **62**
Hawley M. NW1—38Kb **62**
Hawley Rd. NW1—38Kb **62**
Hawley Rd. Dart—61Nd **133**
Hawley St. NW1—38Kb **62**
Hawley Way. Ashf—64R **120**
Haws La. Stai—58J **97**
Hawstead La. Orp—78Bd **151**
Hawstead Rd. SE6—58Dc **106**
Hawsted. Buck H—17Kc **27**
Hawsworth Clo. E13—40Hc **65**
Hawthorn Av. N13—22Nb **42**
Hawthorn Av. Brtwd—20Be **33**
Hawthorn Av. Cars—80Jb **146**
Hawthorn Av. Rain—42Kd **89**
Hawthorn Av. Rich—54Na **101**
Hawthorn Av. West—87Mc **167**
Hawthorn Clo. N1—37Ub **63**
Hawthorn Clo. Hmptn—64Ca **121**
Hawthorn Clo. Orp—72Tc **150**
Hawthorn Clo. Wat—10V **4**
Hawthorn Clo. Wok—92A **172**
Hawthorndene Clo. Brom —75Hc **149**
Hawthorndene Rd. Brom —75Hc **149**
Hawthorn Dri. Harr—30Ca **37**
Hawthorn Dri. Uxb—37L **55**
Hawthorn Dri. W Wick—77Gc **149**
Hawthorne Av. Harr—30Ja **38**
Hawthorne Av. Mitc—68Fb **125**
Hawthorne Av. Ruis—30X **37**
Hawthorne Av. T Hth—67Rb **127**
Hawthorne Av. Wal X—3Xb **11**
Hawthorne Clo. SE15—54Yb **106**
Hawthorne Clo. Brom—69Pc **130**
Hawthorne Clo. S Croy—83Yb **166**
Hawthorne Clo. Sutt—75Eb **145**
Hawthorne Clo. Wal X—3Xb **11**
Hawthorne Cres. Slou—4J **73**
Hawthorne Farm Av. N'holt —39Aa **57**
Hawthorne Gro. NW9—31Sa **59**
Hawthorne Pl. Eps—84Ua **162**
Hawthorne Rd. E17—27Cc **44**
Hawthorne Rd. NW10—38Wa **60**
Hawthorne Rd. Brom—69Pc **130**
Hawthorne Rd. Rad—6Ja **6**
Hawthorn Gdns. W5—48Ma **79**
Hawthorn Gro. SE20—67Xb **127**
Hawthorn Gro. Enf—10Tb **11**
Hawthorn Hatch. Bren—52Ka **100**
Hawthorn La. Sev—94Hd **188**
Hawthorn La. Slou—8D **52**
Hawthorn M. NW7—25Ab **40**
Hawthorn Pl. Hay—45V **76**
Hawthorn Rd. N8—27Mb **42**
Hawthorn Rd. N18—22Vb **43**
Hawthorn Rd. Bexh—56Bd **109**
Hawthorn Rd. Bren—52Ka **100**
Hawthorn Rd. Buck H—21Mc **45**
Hawthorn Rd. Dart—61Md **133**
Hawthorn Rd. Stai—63E **118**
Hawthorn Rd. Sutt—79Gb **145**
Hawthorn Rd. Wall—80Kb **146**
Hawthorn Rd. Wok—92A **172**
Hawthorn Rd. Wok—8G **188**
Hawthorn Rd. Wok—96J **173**
(Send Marsh)
Hawthorns. Long, Dart—70Be **135**
Hawthorns. Wfd G—20Jc **27**
Hawthorns, The. Lou—14Qc **28**
Hawthorns, The. Rick—22F **34**
Hawthorn Wlk. W10—42Ab **80**
Hawthorn Way. N9—19Vb **25**
Hawthorn Way. Shep—70T **120**
Hawthorn Way. Wey—82L **157**
Hawtrees. Rad—7Ha **6**
Hawtrey Av. N'holt—40Z **57**
Hawtrey Clo. Slou—7M **73**
Hawtrey Dri. Ruis—31W **56**
Hawtrey Rd. NW3—38Gb **61**
Hawtrey Rd. Wind—4G **94**
Haxted Rd. Brom—67Kc **129**
Hayburn Way. Horn—32Hd **68**
Hay Clo. E15—38Gc **65**
Haycroft Clo. Coul—90Rb **165**
Haycroft Gdns. NW10—39Wa **60**
Haycroft Rd. SW2—57Nb **104**
Haycroft Rd. Surb—75Na **143**
Hay Currie St. E14—44Dc **84**
Hayday Rd. E16—43Jc **85**
Hayden Ct. Wey—83K **157**
Haydens Clo. Orp—72Yc **151**
Hayden's Pl. W11—44Bb **81**
Hayden Way. Romf—26Ed **48**
Haydn Av. Purl—86Qb **164**
Haydn's M. W3—44Sa **79**
Haydock Av. N'holt—37Ca **57**
Haydock Clo. Horn—35Pd **69**
Haydock Grn. N'holt—37Ca **57**
Haydon Clo. NW9—28Sa **39**
Haydon Dri. Pinn—28W **36**
Haydon Pk. Rd. SW19—64Cb **125**
Haydon Rd. Dag—33Yc **67**
Haydon Rd. Wat—16Aa **19**
Haydons Rd. SW19—64Db **125**
Haydon St. EC3—45Vb **83** (4K **201**)
Haydon Wlk. E1—44Vb **83** (3K **201**)
Hayes Barton. Wok—88F **156**
Hayes Chase. W Wick—72Fc **149**
Hayes Clo. Brom—75Jc **149**
Hayes Cres. NW11—29Bb **41**
Hayes Cres. Sutt—77Za **144**
Hayes Dri. Rain—38Kd **69**
Hayes End Clo. Hay—43T **76**
Hayes End Dri. Hay—42T **76**
Hayes End Rd. Hay—42T **76**
Hayesford Pk. Dri. Brom —71Hc **149**
Hayes Garden. Brom—74Jc **149**
Hayes Hill. Brom—74Gc **149**
Hayes Hill Rd. Brom—74Hc **149**
Hayes La. Beck—69Ec **128**
Hayes La. Brom—71Jc **149**
Hayes La. Kenl & Cat—88Rb **165**
Hayes Mead. Brom—74Gc **149**
Hayes Pl. NW1—42Gb **81** (6E **190**)
Hayes Rd. Brom—70Jc **129**
Hayes Rd. Grnh—59Ud **112**
Hayes Rd. S'hall—49X **77**
Hayes St. Brom—74Kc **149**
Hayes, The. Eps—91Ua **178**
Hayes Wlk. Pot B—5Db **9**
Hayes Way. Beck—70Ec **128**
Hayes Wood Av. Brom—74Kc **149**
Hayfield Clo. Bush, Wat—14Da **19**
Hayfield Pas. E1—42Yb **84**
Hayfield Rd. Orp—71Wc **151**
Haygarth Pl. SW19—64Za **124**
Haygreen Clo. King—65Ra **123**
★Hay Grn. La. Brtwd & Ing—7Zd
Hay Hill. W1—45Kb **82** (5A **198**)
Hayland Clo. NW9—28Ta **39**
Hay La. NW9—28Sa **39**
Hay La. Slou—5P **53**
Hayle. Grays—8L **93**
Hayles St. SE11—49Rb **83** (5B **206**)
Haylett Gdns. King—70Ma **123**
Hayling Av. Felt—62W **120**
Hayling Clo. N16—36Ub **63**
Hayling Rd. Wat—20W **18**
Hayman Cres. Hay—40T **56**
Hayman St. N1—38Rb **63**
Haymarket. SW1 —45Mb **82** (5D **198**)
Haymarket Arc. SW1—(5D **198***)*
Haymeads Dri. Esh—79Ea **142**
Haymer Gdns. Wor Pk—76Wa **144**
Haymerle Rd. SE15—51Wb **105**
Haymill Rd. Slou—2B **72**
Hayne Rd. Beck—68Bc **128**
Haynes Clo. N17—24Xb **43**
Haynes Clo. SE3—55Gc **107**
Haynes Clo. Slou—50B **74**
Haynes La. SE19—65Ub **127**
Haynes Rd. Grav—2B **136**
Haynes Rd. Horn—28Md **49**
Haynes Rd. Wemb—38Na **59**
Hayne St. EC1—43Rb **83** (7C **194**)
Haynt Wlk. SW20—69Ab **124**
Hayse Hill. Wind—3B **94**
Hay's La. SE1—46Ub **83** (7H **201**)
Haysleigh Gdns. SE20—68Wb **127**
Hay's M. W1—46Kb **82** (6K **197**)
Haysoms Clo. Romf—28Gd **48**
Haystall Clo. Hay—40U **56**
Hay St. E2—39Wb **63**
Hays Wlk. Sutt—82Za **162**
Hayter Rd. SW2—57Nb **104**
Hayton Clo. E8—37Vb **63**
Hayward Clo. SW19—67Db **125**
Hayward Clo. Bex—57Fd **110**
Hayward Gdns. SW15—58Ya **102**
Hayward Rd. N20—19Eb **23**
Haywards Mead. Wind—10D **72**
Hayward's Pl. EC1 —42Rb **83** (5B **194**)
Haywood Clo. Pinn—26Z **37**
Haywood Ct. Wal A—6Hc **13**
Haywood Pk. Rick—15H **17**
Haywood Rise. Orp—78Uc **150**
Haywood Rd. Brom—70Mc **129**
Hazel Av. W Dray—48Q **76**
Hazel Bank. Surb—74Sa **143**
Hazelbank Rd. SE6—61Fc **129**
Hazelbank Rd. Cher—73L **139**
Hazelbourne Rd. SW12—58Kb **104**
Hazelbrouck Gdns. Ilf—24Tc **46**
Hazelbury Av. Abb L, Wat—4S **4**
Hazelbury Grn. N9—20Ub **25**
Hazelbury La. N9—20Ub **25**
Hazel Clo. N13—20Tb **25**
Hazel Clo. N19—33Lb **62**
Hazel Clo. SE15—54Wb **105**
Hazel Clo. Bren—52Ka **100**
Hazel Clo. Egh—5M **117**
Hazel Clo. Horn—34Kd **69**
Hazel Clo. Mitc—70Mb **126**
Hazel Clo. Twic—59Ea **100**
Hazel Croft. Pinn—23Da **37**
Hazeldean Ct. Kenl—87Tb **165**
★Hazelden Clo. Sev—81Wd
Hazel Dene. Wey—78L **139**
Hazeldene Dri. Pinn—27Y **37**
Hazeldene Gdns. Uxb—39S **56**
Hazeldene Rd. NW10—38Ta **59**
Hazeldene Rd. Ilf—33Xc **67**
Hazeldene Rd. Well—54Yc **109**
Hazeldon Rd. SE4—57Ac **106**
Hazel Dri. Eri—53Kd **111**
Hazel Dri. Wok—97H **173**
Hazeleigh. Brtwd—20De **33**
Hazeleigh Gdns. Wfd G—22Nc **46**
Hazel End. Swan—71Gd **152**
Hazel Gdns. Edgw—21Ra **39**
Hazel Gdns. Grays—8A **92**
Hazelgreen Clo. N21—18Rb **25**
Hazel Gro. SE26—63Zb **128**
Hazel Gro. Enf—16Wb **25**
Hazel Gro. Orp—75Rc **150**
Hazel Gro. Romf—27Ad **47**
Hazel Gro. Stai—65K **119**
Hazel Gro. Wemb—39Na **59**
Hazelhurst. Beck—67Fc **129**
Hazelhurst Rd. SW17—63Fb **125**
Hazelhurst Rd. Slou—10A **52**
Hazel La. Rich—61Na **123**
Hazell Cres. Romf—25Dd **48**
Hazell Way. Slou—8K **53**
Hazel Mead. Barn—15Xa **22**
Hazel Mead. Eps—82Wa **162**
Hazelmere Clo. Felt—58U **98**
Hazelmere Clo. Lea—91Ka **176**
Hazelmere Clo. N'holt—40Ba **57**
Hazelmere Dri. N'holt—40Ba **57**
Hazelmere Gdns. Horn—29Ld **49**
Hazelmere Rd. NW6—39Cb **61**
Hazelmere Rd. SE5—53Rb **105**
Hazelmere Rd. N'holt—40Ba **57**
Hazelmere Rd. Orp—70Sc **130**
Hazelmere Wlk. N'holt—40Ba **57**
Hazelmere Way. Brom—72Jc **149**
Hazel Pde. Lea—94Ea **176**
Hazel Rise. Horn—30Ld **49**
Hazel Rd. NW10—41Ya **80**
Hazel Rd. Dart—61Md **133**
Hazel Rd. Eri—53Jd **110**
Hazel Rd. St Alb—1Da **5**
Hazel Rd. Wey—86J **157**
Hazeltree La. N'holt—41Aa **77**
Hazel Tree Rd. Wat—8X **5**
Hazelville Rd. N19—31Mb **62**
Hazel Wlk. Brom—72Qc **150**
Hazel Way. E4—23Bc **44**
Hazel Way. SE1—49Vb **83** (5K **207**)
Hazel Way. Lea—94Ea **176**
Hazelwood. Stanf—9J **93**
Hazelwood Av. Mord—70Db **125**
Hazelwood Clo. W5—47Na **79**
Hazel Wood Ct. NW10—34Ua **60**
Hazelwood Ct. Surb—72Na **143**
Hazelwood Cres. N13—21Qb **42**
Hazelwood Dri. Pinn—26X **37**
Hazelwood Gdns. Brtwd —16Wd **32**
Hazelwood Gro. S Croy—85Xb **165**
Hazelwood La. N13—21Qb **42**
Hazelwood La. Coul—91Gb **179**
Hazelwood La. K Lan & Abb L, Wat—4T **4**
Hazelwood Rd. E17—29Ac **44**
Hazelwood Rd. Enf—16Vb **25**
Hazelwood Rd. Rick—16S **18**
Hazelwood Rd. Sev—84Tc **168**
Hazelwood Rd. Wok—6B **188**
Hazlebury Rd. SW6—54Db **103**
Hazledean Rd. Croy—75Tb **147**
Hazledene. Wal X—4Ac **12**
Hazledene Rd. W4—51Sa **101**
Hazlemere Gdns. Wor Pk —74Wa **144**
Hazlemere Rd. Slou—6M **73**
Hazlewell Rd. SW15—57Ya **102**
Hazlewood. Lou—15Mc **27**
Hazlewood Cres. W10—42Ab **80**
Hazlitt Rd. W14—48Ab **80**
Hazon Way. Eps—84Ta **161**
Heacham Av. Uxb—33S **56**
Headcorn Rd. N17—24Vb **43**
Headcorn Rd. Brom—64Hc **129**
Headcorn Rd. T Hth—70Pb **126**
Headfort Pl. SW1 —47Jb **82** (2J **203**)
Headington Rd. SW18—61Eb **125**
Headlam Rd. SW4—59Mb **104**
Headlam St. E1—42Xb **83**
Headley App. Ilf—29Rc **46**
Headley Av. Wall—78Pb **146**
Headley Chase. Brtwd—21Zd **51**
Headley Clo. Eps—79Qa **143**
Headley Comn. Rd. Eps & Tad —99Ta **177**
Headley Dri. Croy—80Dc **148**
Headley Dri. Eps—91Ya **178**
Headley Dri. Ilf—30Rc **46**
Headley Gro. Tad—92Ya **178**
Headley Rd. Dor—100La **176**
Headley Rd. Eps—90Ra **161**
Headley Rd. Lea & Eps—94La **176**
Headley St. SE15—54Xb **105**
Head's M. W11—44Cb **81**
Headstone Dri. Harr—27Fa **38**
Headstone Gdns. Harr—28Ea **38**
Headstone La. Harr—28Da **37**
Headstone Rd. Harr—30Ga **38**
Head St. E1—44Zb **84**
(in two parts)
Headway Clo. Rich—63La **122**
Headway, The. Eps—81Va **162**
Heald St. SE14—53Cc **106**
Healey Rd. Wat—16V **18**
Healey St. NW1—37Kb **62**
Healy Dri. Orp—77Vc **151**
Heards La. Brtwd—13Be **33**
Hearne Rd. W4—51Qa **101**
Hearn Rise. N'holt—39Z **57**
Hearn Rd. Romf—30Hd **48**
Hearn's Clo. Orp—70Yc **131**
Hearn's Rise. Orp—70Zc **131**
Hearn's Rd. Orp—70Yc **131**
Hearn St. EC2—42Ub **83** (6J **195**)
Hearnville Rd. SW12—60Jb **104**
Hearsall Av. Stanf—1N **93**
Heatham Pk. Twic—59Ha **100**
Heath Av. Bexh—51Zc **109**
Heathbourne Rd. Bush, Wat & Stan—18Ga **20**
Heath Brow. NW3—34Eb **61**
Heath Clo. NW11—31Db **61**
Heath Clo. W5—42Pa **79**
Heath Clo. Bans—86Db **163**
Heath Clo. Hay—52T **98**

Heath Clo.—Hide Pl.

Heath Clo. Orp—73Yc 151
Heath Clo. Pot B—2Db 9
Heath Clo. Romf—27Jd 48
Heath Clo. Stai—58L 97
Heath Clo. Vir W—10P 117
Heathclose Av. Dart—59Kd 111
Heathclose Rd. Dart—60Jd 110
Heathcote Av. Ilf—26Pc 46
Heathcote Gro. E4—20Ec 26
Heathcote Rd. Eps—86Ta 161
Heathcote Rd. Twic—58Ka 100
Heathcote St. WC1
—42Pb 82 (5H 193)
Heathcote Way. W Dray—4M 75
Heathcroft. NW11—32Db 61
Heathcroft. W5—42Pa 79
Heathcroft Av. Sun—66V 120
Heathdale Av. Houn—55Aa 99
Heathdene Dri. Belv—49Dd 88
Heathdene Rd. SW16—66Pb 126
Heathdene Rd. Wall—80Kb 146
Heathdown Rd. Wok—87F 156
Heath Dri. NW3—35Db 61
Heath Dri. SW20—70Ya 124
Heath Dri. Epp—7Uc 14
Heath Dri. Pot B—2Cb 9
Heath Dri. Romf—25Jd 48
Heath Dri. Sutt—81Eb 163
Heath Dri. Tad—97Wa 178
Heath Dri. Wok—94D 172
Heathedge. SE26—61Xb 127
Heathend Rd. Bex—60Gd 110
Heather Av. Romf—26Fd 48
Heatherbank. SE9—54Pc 108
Heatherbank. Chst—68Qc 130
Heather Clo. SW8—55Kb 104
Heather Clo. Brtwd—15Xd 32
Heather Clo. Hmptn—67Ba 121
Heather Clo. Iswth—57Fa 100
Heather Clo. Romf—25Fd 48
Heather Clo. Tad—94Ab 178
Heather Clo. Uxb—43P 75
Heather Clo. Wey—82K 157
Heather Clo. Wok—3F 188
Heatherdale Clo. King—65Qa 123
Heatherdene. Lea—97T 174
Heatherdene Clo. Mitc—70Gb 125
Heatherden Grn. Iver—39F 54
Heather Dri. Dart—59Jd 110
Heather Dri. Romf—26Gd 48
Heather End. Swan—70Fd 132
Heather Gdns. NW11—30Ab 40
Heather Gdns. Romf—26Fd 48
Heather Gdns. Sutt—79Cb 145
Heather Glen. Romf—26Fd 48
Heatherlands. Sun—65W 120
Heather La. W Dray—44N 75
Heatherley Dri. Ilf—27Nc 46
Heather Pk. Dri. Wemb—38Qa 59
Heather Pl. Esh—77Da 141
Heather Rise. Bush, Wat—12Ba 19
Heather Rd. NW2—33Va 60
Heather Rd. SE12—60Jc 107
Heatherset Gdns. SW16—66Pb 126
Heatherside Gdns. Slou—4H 53
Heatherside Rd. Eps—80Ta 143
Heatherside Rd. Sidc—62Yc 131
Heatherton Ter. N3—26Db 41
Heathervale Rd. Wey—82K 157
Heather Wlk. W10—42Ab 80
Heather Wlk. Edgw—22Ra 39
Heather Wlk. W on T—82U 158
Heather Way. Pot B—4Bb 9
Heather Way. Romf—25Fd 48
Heather Way. S Croy—81Zb 166
Heather Way. Stan—23Ha 38
Heatherwood Clo. E12—33Lc 65
Heath Farm Ct. Wat—9T 4
Heathfield. E4—20Ec 26
Heathfield. Chst—65Sc 130
Heathfield. Cob—86Ca 159
Heathfield Av. SW18—59Fb 103
Heathfield Av. Asc—10C 116
Heathfield Clo. E16—43Mc 85
Heathfield Clo. Kes—78Lc 149
Heathfield Clo. Pot B—2Db 9
Heathfield Clo. Wok—90C 156
Heathfield Ct. SE20—66Yb 128
Heathfield Ct. W4—50Ta 79
Heathfield Gdns. NW11—30Za 40
Heathfield Gdns. SW18—58Fb 103
Heathfield Gdns. W4—50Sa 79
Heathfield La. Chst—65Sc 130
Heathfield N. Twic—59Ha 100
Heathfield Pk. NW2—37Ya 60
Heathfield Rise. Ruis—31S 56
Heathfield Rd. SW18—58Fb 103
Heathfield Rd. W3—47Ra 79
Heathfield Rd. Bexh—56Bd 109
Heathfield Rd. Brom—66Hc 129
Heathfield Rd. Bush, Wat—14Aa 19
Heathfield Rd. Croy—77Tb 147
Heathfield Rd. Kes—78Lc 149
Heathfield Rd. Sev—94Hd 186
Heathfield Rd. Slou—3A 52
Heathfield Rd. W on T—77Aa 141
Heathfield Rd. Wok—90C 156
Heathfield S. Twic—59Ha 100
Heathfield Sq. SW18—59Fb 103
Heathfield Ter. SE18—51Uc 108
Heathfield Ter. W4—50Sa 79
Heathfield Vale. S Croy—81Zb 166
Heathfield Way. Ger X—1P 53
Heath Gdns. Twic—60Ha 100
Heathgate. NW11—30Db 41
Heath Gro. SE20—66Yb 128
Heath Gro. Sun—66V 120
Heath Ho. Rd. Wok—10A 188
Heath Hurst Rd. NW3—35Gb 61
Heathland Rd. N16—32Ub 63
Heathlands Clo. Sun—68W 120
Heathlands Clo. Twic—60Ha 100
Heathlands Clo. Wok—86A 156
Heathlands Rise. Dart—58Kd 111
Heath La. SE3—54Fc 107
Heath La. (Lower). Dart—60Ld 111
Heath La. (Upper). Dart—61Jd 132
Heathlee Rd. SE3—56Hc 107
Heathley End. Chst—65Sc 130
Heathmans Rd. SW6—53Bb 103
Heath Mead. SW19—62Za 124
Heath Pk. Ct. Romf—29Jd 48
Heath Pk. Rd. Romf—29Jd 48
Heath Ridge Grn. Cob—85Ca 159
Heath Rise. SW15—58Za 102
Heath Rise. Brom—72Hc 149
Heath Rise. Vir W—10P 117
Heath Rise. Wok—95K 173
Heath Rd. SW8—54Kb 104
Heath Rd. Bex—60Ed 110
Heath Rd. Cat—96Tb 181
Heath Rd. Dart—58Hd 110
Heath Rd. Grays—6B 92
Heath Rd. Harr—31Ea 58
Heath Rd. Houn—56Da 99
Heath Rd. Lea—84Ea 160
Heath Rd. Pot B—2Cb 9
Heath Rd. Romf—31Zc 67
Heath Rd. T Hth—69Sb 127
Heath Rd. Twic—60Ha 100
Heath Rd. Uxb—42S 76
Heath Rd. Wat—17Z 19
Heath Rd. Wey—77Q 140
Heath Rd. Wok—87B 156
Heathrow Clo. W Dray—53K 97
Heath Side. NW3—35Fb 61
Heathside. Esh—76Ga 142
Heathside. Houn—59Ba 99
Heathside. Orp—73Sc 150
Heathside. Wey—78R 140
Heathside Av. Bexh—54Ad 109
Heathside Clo. Esh—76Ga 142
Heathside Clo. N'wd—22T 36
Heathside Cres. Wok—89B 156
Heathside Gdns. Wok—89C 156
Heathside Pk. Rd. Wok—90B 156
Heathside Rd. N'wd—21T 36
Heathside Rd. Wok—90B 156
Heathstan Rd. W12—44Wa 80
Heath St. NW3—34Eb 61
Heath St. Dart—59Md 111
Heath, The. W7—46Ga 78
Heath, The. Cat—96Tb 181
Heath, The. Rad—5Ja 6
Heathurst Rd. S Croy—81Tb 165
Heath View. N2—28Eb 41
Heath View. Lea—97V 174
Heathview Av. Dart—58Gd 110
Heath View Clo. N2—28Eb 41
Heathview Cres. Dart—60Kd 111
Heathview Gdns. SW15—59Ya 102
Heath View Gdns. Grays—48Ee 91
Heath View Rd. Grays—47Ee 91
Heathview Rd. T Hth—70Qb 126
Heath Vs. SE18—50Xc 87
Heathville Rd. N19—31Nb 62
Heathwall St. SW11—55Hb 103
Heathway. SE3—52Jc 107
Heathway. Cat—97Sb 181
Heathway. Croy—76Bc 148
Heathway. Dag—34Bd 67
Heath Way. Eri—53Ed 110
Heathway. Iver—40F 54
Heathway. Lea—96V 174
Heath Way. Wfd G—22Lc 45
Heathwood Gdns. SE7—50Nc 86
Heathwood Gdns. Swan
—68Ed 132
Heathwood Wlk. Bex—60Gd 110
Heaton Av. Romf—24Kd 49
Heaton Clo. Romf—24Ld 49
Heaton Ct. Wal X—1Zb 12
Heaton Grange Rd. Romf—26Hd 48
Heaton Pl. E15—36Fc 65
Heaton Rd. SE15—54Xb 105
Heaton Rd. Mitc—66Jb 126
Heaton Way. Romf—24Ld 49
Heaverham Rd. Sev—89Rd 171
Heaver Rd. SW11—55Fb 103
Heavitree Rd. SE18—50Tc 86
Hebdon Rd. SW17—62Gb 125
Heber Rd. NW2—36Za 60
Heber Rd. SE22—58Vb 105
Hebert Gdns. NW10—40Xa 60
Hebron Rd. W6—48Ya 80
Hecham Clo. E17—26Ac 44
Heckfield Pl. SW6—52Cb 103
Heckford St. E1—45Zb 84
Hector St. SE18—49Uc 86
Heddon Clo. Iswth—56Ja 100
Heddon Ct. Av. Barn—15Hb 23
Heddon Rd. Barn—15Hb 23
Heddon St. W1—45Lb 82 (4B 198)
Hedge Hill. Enf—11Rb 25
Hedge La. N13—20Rb 25
Hedgemans Rd. Dag—38Zc 67
Hedgemans Way. Dag—37Ad 67
Hedge Pl. Rd. Grnh—58Vd 112
Hedgerley Gdns. Gnfd—40Ea 58
Hedgerley Hill. Slou—3H 53
Hedgerley La. Slou & Ger X—1J 53
Hedgerow. Ger X—23A 34
Hedgers Gro. E9—37Ac 64
Hedgeside Rd. N'wd—22S 36
Hedgewood Gdns. Ilf—29Qc 46
Hedgley. Ilf—28Pc 46
Hedgley St. SE12—57Hc 107
Hedingham Clo. N1—38Sb 63
Hedingham Rd. Dag—36Xc 67
Hedingham Rd. Horn—32Qd 69
Hedley Av. Grays—52Yd 112
Hedley Rd. Twic—59Ca 99
Hedley Row. N5—36Tb 63
Hedworth Av. Wal X—5Zb 12
Heenan Clo. Bark—37Sc 66
Heene Rd. Enf—11Tb 25
Heideck Gdns. Brtwd—19De 33
Heigham Rd. E6—38Nc 66
Heighton Gdns. Croy—78Rb 147
Heights Clo. SW20—66Xa 124
Heights Clo. Bans—88Ab 162
Heights, The. SE7—50Lc 85
Heights, The. Beck—66Ec 128
Heights, The. Lou—12Pc 28
Heights, The. N'holt—36Ca 57
Helby Rd. SW4—58Mb 104
Heldar Ct. SE1—47Tb 83 (2G 207)
Helder Gro. SE12—59Hc 107
Helder St. S Croy—79Tb 147
Heldman Clo. Iswth—56Fa 100
Helena Clo. Barn—10Fb 9
Helena Clo. Wall—80Pb 146
Helena Ct. W5—43Ma 79
Helena Rd. E13—40Hc 65
Helena Rd. E17—29Cc 44
Helena Rd. NW10—36Xa 60
Helena Rd. W5—43Ma 79
Helena Rd. Wind—4H 95
Helen Av. Felt—59X 99
Helen Clo. N2—27Eb 41
Helen Clo. Dart—59Kd 111
Helen Clo. E Mol—70Da 121
Helen Rd. Horn—27Md 49
Helenslea Av. NW11—32Cb 61
Helen's Pl. E2—41Yb 84
Helen St. SE18—49Rc 86
Helford Clo. Ruis—33U 56
Helford Ct. S Ock—45Xd 90
Helford Wlk. Wok—6D 188
Helford Way. Upm—30Td 50
Helgiford Gdns. Sun—66U 120
Helix Gdns. SW2—58Pb 104
Helix Rd. SW2—58Pb 104
Hellings St. E1—46Wb 83
Helme Clo. SW19—64Bb 125
Helmet Row. EC1
—42Sb 83 (5E 194)
Helmsdale. Wok—6E 188
Helmsdale Clo. Hay—42Aa 77
Helmsdale Clo. Romf—24Gd 48
Helmsdale Rd. SW16—67Mb 126
Helmsdale Rd. Romf—24Gd 48
Helmsley Pl. E8—38Xb 63
Helmsley St. E8—38Xb 63
Helston Clo. Pinn—24Ba 37
Helston Pl. Abb L, Wat—4V 4
Helvetia St. SE6—61Bc 128
Hemans St. SW8—52Mb 104
Hemans St. Est. SW8—52Mb 104
Hemberton Rd. SW9—55Nb 104
Hemery Rd. Gnfd—36Fa 58
Hemingford Rd. N1—39Pb 62
Hemingford Rd. Sutt—77Ya 144
Hemingford Rd. Wat—8U 4
Heming Rd. Edgw—24Ra 39
Hemington Av. N11—22Hb 41
Hemlock Rd. W12—45Va 80
Hemmen La. Hay—44W 76
Hemming Clo. Hmptn—67Ca 121
Hemming St. E1—42Wb 83
Hemming Way. Wat—7W 4
Hemnall St. Epp—3Vc 15
Hempshaw Av. Bans—88Hb 163
Hempson Av. Slou—8N 73
Hempstead Clo. Buck H—19Jc 27
Hempstead Rd. E17—26Fc 45
Hempstead Rd. K Lan—1Q 4
Hempstead Rd. Wat—8T 4
Hemp Walk. SE17
—49Tb 83 (5G 207)
Hemsby Rd. Chess—79Pa 143
Hemstal Rd. NW6—38Cb 61
Hemsted Rd. Eri—52Gd 110
Hemswell Dri. NW9—25Ua 40
Hemsworth Ct. N1
—40Ub 63 (1H 195)
Hemsworth St. N1
—40Ub 63 (1H 195)
Hemus Pl. SW3—50Gb 81 (7E 202)
Hemwood Rd. Wind—5B 94
Hen & Chickens Ct. EC4
—44Qb 82 (3A 200)
Henbane Path. Romf—24Md 49
Henbury Way. Wat—20Z 19
Henchman St. W12—44Va 80
Hencroft St. Slou—8K 73
Hendale Av. NW4—27Xa 40
Henderson Clo. Wemb—37Sa 59
Henderson Dri. NW8
—42Fb 81 (5B 190)
Henderson Dri. Dart—56Pd 111
Henderson Rd. E7—37Lc 65
Henderson Rd. N9—18Xb 25
Henderson Rd. SW18—59Gb 103
Henderson Rd. Croy—72Tb 147
Henderson Rd. Hay—41W 76
Henderson Rd. West—84Lc 167
Hendham Rd. SW17—61Gb 125
Hendon Av. N3—25Ab 40
Hendon Gdns. Romf—23Ed 48
Hendon La. N3—27Ab 40
Hendon Pk. Row. NW11—30Bb 41
Hendon Rd. N9—19Wb 25
Hendon Way.—30Xa 40
NW2 17-223 & 38-176
NW4 remainder
Hendon Way. Stai—58M 97
Hendon Wood La. NW7—16Va 22
Hendren Clo. Gnfd—36Fa 58
Hendre Rd. SE1—49Ub 83 (6J 207)
Hendrick Av. SW12—59Hb 103
Heneage Cres. Croy—82Ec 166
Heneage La. EC3
—44Ub 83 (3J 201)
Heneage Pl. EC3—44Ub 83 (3J 201)
Heneage St. E1—43Vb 83
Henfield Clo. N19—32Lb 62
Henfield Clo. Bex—58Cd 110
Henfield Rd. SW19—67Bb 125
Hengelo Gdns. Mitc—70Fb 125
Hengist Rd. SE12—59Kc 107
Hengist Rd. Eri—52Dd 110
Hengist Way. Brom—70Gc 129
Hengrave Rd. SE23—59Yb 106
Hengrove Ct. Bex—60Ad 109
Hengrove Cres. Ashf—62M 119
Henhurst Rd. Grav—8G 136
Henley Av. Sutt—76Ab 144
Henley Clo. Gnfd—40Ea 58
Henley Clo. Iswth—53Ha 100
Henley Ct. N14—17Lb 24
Henley Ct. Wok—92D 172
Henley Dri. King—66Va 124
Henley Gdns. Pinn—27X 37
Henley Gdns. Romf—29Ad 47
Henley Rd. E16—47Pc 86
Henley Rd. N18—21Ub 43
Henley Rd. NW10—39Ya 60
Henley Rd. Ilf—35Sc 66
Henley Rd. Slou—4C 72
Henley St. SW11—54Jb 104
Henley Way. Felt—64Z 121
Hennel Clo. SE23—62Yb 128
Henniker Gdns. E6—41Mc 85
Henniker M. SW3—51Fb 103
Henniker Rd. E15—36Fc 65
Henningham Rd. N17—25Tb 43
Henning St. SW11—53Gb 103
Henrietta M. WC1
—42Nb 82 (5G 193)
Henrietta Pl. W1—44Kb 82 (3K 197)
Henrietta St. E15—36Ec 64
Henrietta St. WC2
—45Nb 82 (4G 199)
Henriques St. E1—44Wb 83
Henry Cooper Way. SE9
—63Mc 129
Henry Darlot Dri. NW7—22Za 40
Henry Dickens Ct. W11—45Za 80
Henry Jackson Rd. SW15
—55Za 102
Henry Rd. E6—40Nc 66
Henry Rd. N4—32Sb 63
Henry Rd. Barn—15Fb 23
Henry Rd. Slou—7H 73
Henrys Av. Wfd G—22Hc 45
Henryson Rd. SE4—57Cc 106
★Henry's Ter. Brtwd—6Xd
Henry St. Brom—67Kc 129
Henry St. Grays—51Ee 113
Henry's Wlk. Ilf—24Tc 46
Hensford Gdns. SE26—63Xb 127
Henshall St. N1—37Tb 63
Henshawe Rd. Dag—34Zc 67
Henshaw St. SE17
—49Tb 83 (5F 207)
Henslowe Rd. SE22—57Wb 105
Henslow Way. Wok—86F 156
Henson Av. NW2—36Ya 60
Henson Clo. Orp—75Rc 150
Henson Path. Harr—27Ma 39
Henson Pl. N'holt—39Y 57
Henstridge Pl. NW8
—39Gb 61 (1D 190)
Hensworth Rd. Ashf—64M 119
Henty Clo. SW11—52Gb 103
Henty Wlk. SW15—57Xa 102
Henville Rd. Brom—67Kc 129
Henwick Rd. SE9—55Nc 108
Henwood Rd. SE16—48Yb 84
Hepburn Gdns. Brom—74Hc 149
Hepburn M. SW11—57Hb 103
Hepple Clo. Iswth—54Ka 100
Hepplestone Clo. SW15—58Xa 102
Hepscott Rd. E9—38Cc 64
Hepworth Gdns. Bark—36Wc 67
Hepworth Rd. SW16—66Nb 126
Hepworth Way. W on T—74V 140
Heracles Clo. Wall—80Nb 146
Herald's Pl. SE11
—49Rb 83 (5B 206)
Herald St. E2—42Xb 83
Herbal Hill. EC1—42Qb 82 (6A 194)
Herbal Pl. EC1—(6A 194)
Herbert Cres. SW1
—48Hb 81 (3G 203)
Herbert Cres. Wok—6B 188
Herbert Gdns. W4—51Ra 101
Herbert Gdns. Romf—31Zc 67
Herbert Pl. SE18—51Rc 108
Herbert Rd. E12—35Nc 66
Herbert Rd. E17—31Bc 64
Herbert Rd. N11—24Nb 42
Herbert Rd. N15—29Vb 43
Herbert Rd. NW9—30Wa 40
Herbert Rd. SE18—52Qc 108
Herbert Rd. SW19—66Bb 125
Herbert Rd. Bexh—54Ad 109
Herbert Rd. Brom—71Nc 150
Herbert Rd. Horn—31Nd 69
Herbert Rd. Ilf—33Uc 66
Herbert Rd. King—69Pa 123
Herbert Rd. S'hall—46Ba 77
Herbert Rd. Swan—65Kd 133
Herbert Rd. Swans—58Be 113
Herbert St. E13—40Jc 65
Herbert St. NW5—37Jb 62
Herbert Ter. SE18—52Rc 108
Herbrand St. WC1
—42Nb 82 (5F 193)
Hercies Rd. Uxb—38P 55
Hercules Pl. N7—34Nb 62
Hercules Rd. SE1
—48Pb 82 (4J 205)
Hercules St. N7—34Nb 62
Hereford Av. Barn—18Hb 23
Hereford Clo. Eps—85Ta 161
Hereford Clo. Stai—67K 119
Hereford Gdns. Ilf—31Nc 66
Hereford Gdns. Pinn—29Aa 37
Hereford Gdns. Twic—60Ea 100
Hereford M. W2—44Cb 81
Hereford Rd. E11—29Kc 45
Hereford Rd. W2—44Cb 81
Hereford Rd. W3—45Ra 79
Hereford Rd. W5—48La 78
Hereford Rd. Felt—60Y 99
Hereford Sq. SW7
—49Eb 81 (6A 202)
Hereford St. E2—42Wb 83
Hereford Way. Chess—78La 142
Herent Dri. Ilf—27Pc 46
Hereward Av. Purl—83Qb 164
Hereward Clo. Wal A—4Fc 13
Hereward Gdns. N13—22Qb 42
Hereward Rd. SW17—63Hb 125
Herga Ct. Harr—34Ga 58
Herga Ct. Wat—12W 18
Herga Hyll. Grays—3C 92
Herga Rd. Harr—28Ha 38
Herington Gro. Brtwd—17Ce 33
Heriot Av. E4—19Cc 26
Heriot Rd. NW4—29Ya 40
Heriot Rd. Cher—73J 139
Heriots Clo. Stan—21Ja 38
Heritage Clo. Uxb—42L 75
Herkomer Clo. Bush, Wat—16Da 19
Herkomer Rd. Bush, Wat—15Ca 19
Herlwyn Av. Ruis—34U 56
Herlwyn Gdns. SW17—63Hb 125
Hermes St. N1—40Qb 62 (2K 193)
Hermes Wlk. N'holt—40Ca 57
Hermes Way. Wall—80Mb 146
Herm Ho. N1—37Sb 63
Hermiston Av. N8—29Nb 42
Hermitage Clo. E18—28Hc 45
Hermitage Clo. Enf—12Rb 25
Hermitage Clo. Esh—79Ja 142
Hermitage Clo. Shep—70Q 120
Hermitage Clo. Slou—8N 73
Hermitage Ct. E18—28Jc 45
Hermitage Ct. NW2—34Cb 61
Hermitage Ct. Pot B—5Eb 9
Hermitage Gdns. NW2—34Cb 61
Hermitage Gdns. SE19—66Sb 127
Hermitage Grn. SW16—67Nb 126
Hermitage Hill. Kes—78Lc 149
Hermitage La. N18—22Tb 43
Hermitage La. NW2—34Cb 61
Hermitage La. SE25 & Croy
—72Wb 147
Hermitage La. SW16—66Pb 126
Hermitage La. Wind—6E 94
Hermitage Path. SW16—67Nb 126
Hermitage Rd.—31Sb 63
N4 1-293 & 2-308
N15 remainder
Hermitage Rd. SE19—66Sb 127
Hermitage Rd. Kenl—88Sb 165
Hermitage Rd. Wok—7A 188
Hermitage St. W2
—43Fb 81 (1B 196)
Hermitage, The. SE23—60Yb 106
Hermitage, The. SW13—53Va 102
Hermitage, The. Felt—62V 120
Hermitage, The. Rich—57Na 101
Hermitage, The. Uxb—38N 55
Hermitage Wlk. E18—28Hc 45
Hermitage Wall. E1—46Wb 83
(in two parts)
Hermitage Way. Stan—25Ja 38
Hermitage Woods Cres. Wok
—8B 188
Hermitage Woods Est. Wok
—7B 188
Hermit Pl. NW6—39Db 61
Hermit Rd. E16—43Hc 85
Hermit St. EC1—41Rb 83 (3B 194)
Hermon Gro. Hay—46W 76
Hermon Hill.—29Jc 45
E11 1-47 & 2-88
E18 remainder
Herndon Rd. SW18—57Eb 103
Herne Clo. NW10—36Ta 59
Herne Hill. SE24—57Sb 105
Herne Hill Rd. SE24—55Sb 105
Herne M. N18—21Wb 43
Herne Pl. SE24—57Rb 105
Herne Rd. Bush, Wat—16Da 19
Herne Rd. Surb—75Ma 143
Hernshaw. Brtwd—24Fe 51
Heron Chase. Brtwd—24Fe 51
Heron Clo. E17—26Bc 44
Heron Clo. NW10—37Ua 60
Heron Clo. Buck H—18Jc 27
Heron Clo. Rick—19M 17
Heron Clo. Uxb—37M 55
Heron Ct. Brtwd—25Fe 51
Heron Ct. Brom—70Lc 129
Heron Ct. Rich—57Ma 101
Heron Cres. Sidc—62Uc 130
Herondale. S Croy—81Zb 166
Heron Dale. Wey—78M 139
Herondale Av. SW18—60Fb 103
Heronfield. Pot B—2Eb 9
Heron Flight Av. Rain—38Kd 69
Herongate Clo. Enf—12Vb 25
Herongate Rd. E12—33Lc 65
Herongate Rd. Swan—65Gd 132
Heron Hill. Belv—50Bd 87
Heron Industrial Est. E15—40Dc 64
Heron M. Ilf—33Rc 66
Heron Rd. SE24—56Sb 105
Heron Rd. Croy—75Ub 147
Heron Rd. Twic—56Ja 100
Heronry, The. W on T—79W 140
Herons Croft. Wey—79T 140
Heronsforde. W13—44La 78
Herons Ga. Edgw—22Qa 39
Heronsgate Rd. Rick—16D 16
Heronslea. Wat—8Y 5
Heronslea Dri. Stan—22Na 39
Herons Rise. Barn—14Gb 23
Herons, The. E11—30Hc 45
Heron St. SE17—51Rb 105
Heronswood. Wal A—6Gc 13
Heronway. Brtwd—18De 33
Heron Way. Upm—32Ud 70
Heron Way. Wfd G—21Lc 45
Heron Wharf. E14—46Cc 84
Herrick Rd. N5—34Sb 63
Herrick St. SW1—49Mb 82 (6E 204)
Herries St. W10—41Ab 80
Herringham Rd. SE7—48Lc 85
Herrings La. Cher—72J 139
Herring St. SE5—51Ub 105
Hersant Clo. NW10—39Wa 60
Herschell Rd. SE23—59Ac 106
Herschel Pk. Dri. Slou—7K 73
Herschel St. Slou—7K 73
Hersham By-Pass. W on T
—78X 141
Hersham Centre, The. W on T
—78Z 141
Hersham Clo. SW15—59Wa 102
Hersham Rd. W on T—75W 140
Hersham Trading Est. W on T
—75Aa 141
Hertford Av. SW14—56Ua 102
Hertford Clo. Barn—13Fb 23
Hertford Pl. W1—42Lb 82 (6B 192)
Hertford Rd. N1—38Ub 63
(in two parts)
Hertford Rd. N2—27Gb 41
Hertford Rd. N9, Enf & Wal X
—19Xb 25
Hertford Rd. Bark—38Qc 66
Hertford Rd. Barn—13Eb 23
Hertford Rd. Enf—13Yb 26
Hertford Rd. Ilf—30Uc 46
Hertford St. W1—46Kb 82 (7K 197)
Hertford Wlk. Belv—50Cd 88
Hertford Way. Mitc—70Nb 126
Hertslet Rd. N7—34Pb 62
Hervey Clo. N3—25Cb 41
Hervey Pk. Rd. E17—28Ac 44
Hervey Rd. SE3—53Kc 107
Hervey Way. N3—25Cb 41
Hesa Rd. Hay—44W 76
Hesiers Hill. Warl—89Gc 167
Hesiers Rd. Warl—88Gc 167
Hesketh Av. Dart—60Rd 111
Hesketh Pl. W11—45Ab 80
Hesketh Rd. E7—34Jc 65
Heslop Rd. SW12—60Hb 103
Hesper M. SW5—49Db 81
Hesperus Cres. E14—49Dc 84
Hessel Rd. W13—47Ja 78
Hessel St. E1—44Xb 83
Hesselyn Dri. Rain—38Kd 69
Hessle Gro. Eps—83Va 162
Hestercombe Av. SW6—53Ab 102
Hester Rd. N18—22Wb 43
Hester Rd. SW11—52Gb 103
Heston Av. Houn—51Aa 99
Heston Grange La. Houn—51Ba 99
Heston Industrial Est. Houn
—51Y 99
Heston Industrial Mall. Houn
—52Ba 99
Heston Rd. Houn—52Ca 99
Heston St. SE14—53Cc 106
Heswall Grn. Wat—20W 18
Hether Gro. Est. SE13—57Ec 106
Hetherington Clo. Slou—1D 72
Hetherington Rd. SW4—56Nb 104
Hetherington Rd. Shep—68S 120
Hetherington Way. Uxb—35N 55
Hetley Gdns. SE19—66Vb 127
Hetley Rd. W12—46Xa 80
Heusden Way. Ger X—32B 54
Hevelius Clo. SE10—50Hc 85
Hever Av. Sev—80Ud 154
Hever Ct. Rd. Grav—5E 136
Hever Croft. SE9—63Qc 130
Hever Gdns. Brom—68Qc 130
Heverham Rd. SE18—49Uc 86
Hever Rd. Sev—79Ud 154
Heversham Rd. Bexh—54Cd 110
Hever Wood Rd. Sev—80Ud 154
Hewens Rd. Uxb—42S 76
Hewer St. W10—43Za 80
Hewers Way. Tad—92Ya 178
Hewett Clo. Stan—21Ka 38
Hewett Rd. Dag—36Zc 67
Hewett St. EC2—42Ub 83 (6J 195)
Hewish Rd. N18—21Ub 43
Hewitt Av. N22—26Rb 43
Hewitt Pl. Swan—70Fd 132
Hewitt Rd. N8—29Qb 42
Hewitts Rd. Orp—80Bd 151
(in two parts)
Hewlett Rd. E3—40Ac 64
Hexagon, The. N6—32Hb 61
Hexal Rd. SE6—62Gc 129
Hexfam Gdns. Iswth—52Ja 100
Hexham Rd. SE27—61Sb 127
Hexham Rd. Barn—14Db 23
Hexham Rd. Mord—74Db 145
Hextalls La. Red—100Tb 181
Heybourne Rd. N17—24Xb 43
Heybridge Av. SW16—66Nb 126
Heybridge Dri. Ilf—27Tc 46
Heybridge Way. E10—32Bc 64
Heyford Av. SW8—52Nb 104
Heyford Av. SW20—69Bb 125
Heyford Rd. Mitc—68Gb 125
Heyford Rd. Rad—9Ha 6
Heygate St. SE17
—49Sb 83 (6D 206)
Heylyn Sq. E3—41Bc 84
Heymede. Lea—95La 176
Heynes Rd. Dag—35Yc 67
Heysham Dri. Wat—22Y 37
Heysham Rd. N15—30Tb 43
Heythorp Clo. Wok—5C 188
Heythorp St. SW18—60Bb 103
Heywood Av. NW9—25Ua 40
Heywood Ct. Stan—22La 38
Heyworth Rd. E5—35Xb 63
Heyworth Rd. E15—35Hc 65
Hibbert Av. Wat—10Z 5
Hibbert Rd. E17—31Bc 64
Hibbert Rd. Harr—26Ha 38
Hibbert's All. Wind—3H 95
Hibbert St. SW11—55Fb 103
Hibernia Dri. Grav—2H 137
Hibernia Gdns. Houn—56Ca 99
Hibernia Rd. Houn—56Ca 99
Hichisson Rd. SE15—57Yb 106
Hickin Clo. SE7—49Mc 85
Hickin St. E14—48Ec 84
Hickling Rd. Ilf—36Rc 66
Hickman Av. E4—23Ec 44
Hickman Clo. E16—43Mc 85
Hickman Rd. Romf—31Yc 67
Hickmore Wlk. SW4—55Mb 104
Hicks Av. Gnfd—41Fa 78
Hicks Clo. SW11—55Gb 103
Hicks St. SE8—50Ac 84
Hidcote Gdns. SW20—69Xa 124
Hide Pl. SW1—49Mb 82 (6D 204)

Hide Rd. Harr—28Ea 38
Hides St. N7—37Pb 62
High Acres. Abb L, Wat—4T 4
Higham Hill Rd. E17—25Ac 44
Higham Path. E17—27Ac 44
Higham Pl. E17—27Ac 44
Higham Rd. N17—27Tb 43
Higham Rd. Wfd G—23Jc 45
Highams Hill. Warl—84Jc 167
Higham Sta. Av. E4—23Dc 44
Higham St. E17—27Ac 44
High Ash Clo. Stanf—9J 93
Highbanks Clo. Well—52Xc 109
Highbanks Rd. Pinn—23Da 37
Highbarn Rd. Lea—100Z 175
Highbarrow Rd. Croy—74Wb 147
High Beech. S Croy—80Ub 147
High Beeches. Bans—86Za 162
High Beeches. Ger X—33A 54
High Beeches. Ger X—2P 53
High Beeches. Orp—79Wc 151
High Beeches. Sidc—64Ad 131
High Beech Rd. Lou—14Nc 28
High Bri. SE10—50Fc 85
Highbridge Rd. Bark—39Rc 66
Highbridge St. Wal A—5Dc 12
(in two parts)
Highbrook Rd. SE3—55Mc 107
High Broom Cres. W Wick —73Dc 148
Highbury Av. T Hth—68Qb 126
Highbury Clo. N Mald—70Sa 123
Highbury Clo. W Wick—75Dc 148
Highbury Cres. N5—36Rb 63
Highbury Gdns. Ilf—33Uc 66
Highbury Grange. N5—35Sb 63
Highbury Gro. N5—36Rb 63
Highbury Hill. N5—35Rb 63
Highbury M. N7—37Qb 62
Highbury New Pk. N5—36Sb 63
Highbury Pk. N5—35Rb 63
Highbury Pk. M. N5—35Sb 63
Highbury Pl. N5—37Rb 63
Highbury Quadrant. N5—34Sb 63
Highbury Rd. SW19—64Ab 124
Highbury Sta. Rd. N1—37Qb 62
Highbury Ter. N5—36Rb 63
Highbury Ter. M. N5—36Rb 63
High Canons. Borwd—9Sa 7
Highclere. Asc—10B 116
Highclere Clo. Kenl—87Sb 165
Highclere Ct. Wok—5A 188
Highclere Gdns. Wok—5A 188
Highclere Rd. N Mald—69Ta 123
Highclere Rd. Wok—5A 188
Highclere St. SE26—63Ac 128
Highcliffe Dri. SW15—58Va 102
Highcliffe Gdns. Ilf—29Nc 46
High Clo. Rick—15L 17
Highcombe. SE7—51Kc 107
Highcombe Clo. SE9—60Nc 108
Highcotts La. Guild—98H 173
Highcotts La. Wok—97H 173
Highcroft. NW9—29Ua 40
Highcroft Av. Wemb—39Qa 59
Highcroft Gdns. NW11—30Bb 41
Highcroft Rd. N19—31Nb 62
High Cross Rd. N17—27Wb 43
Highcross Rd. Grav—64Zd 135
Highcross Way. SW15—60Wa 102
Highdaun Dri. SW16—70Pb 126
Highdown. Wor Pk—75Va 144
Highdown Rd. SW15—58Xa 102
High Dri. Cat—94Cc 182
High Dri. Lea—86Fa 160
High Dri. N Mald—67Sa 123
High Elms. Chig—21Uc 46
High Elms. Upm—32Ud 70
High Elms. Wfd G—22Jc 45
High Elms Clo. N'wd—23T 36
High Elms La. Wat—4Z 5
High Elms La. Wat—3X 5
High Elms Rd. Orp—83Qc 168
Higher Dri. Bans—84Za 162
Higher Dri. Lea—99U 174
Higher Dri. Purl—86Qb 164
Higher Grn. Eps—85Wa 162
Highfield. Bans—89Gb 163
Highfield. Chal—18A 16
Highfield. Felt—60W 98
Highfield Av. NW9—29Sa 39
Highfield Av. NW11—31Za 60
Highfield Av. Eri—51Dd 110
Highfield Av. Gnfd—36Ga 58
Highfield Av. Orp—78Vc 151
Highfield Av. Pinn—29Ba 37
Highfield Av. Wemb—34Pa 59
Highfield Clo. NW9—29Sa 39
Highfield Clo. Egh—5N 117
Highfield Clo. N'wd—25U 36
Highfield Clo. Romf—23Ed 48
Highfield Clo. Surb—74La 142
Highfield Clo. Wey—85J 157
Highfield Ct. N14—16Lb 24
Highfield Cres. Horn—33Pd 69
Highfield Cres. N'wd—25U 36
Highfield Dri. Brom—70Gc 129
Highfield Dri. Eps—79Va 144
Highfield Dri. Uxb—34N 55
Highfield Dri. W Wick—75Dc 148
Highfield Gdns. NW11—30Ab 40
Highfield Gdns. Grays—47Fe 91
Highfield Grn. Epp—3Uc 14
Highfield Hill. SE19—66Tb 127
Highfield Link. Romf—23Ed 48
Highfield Pl. Epp—3Uc 14
Highfield Rd. N21—19Rb 25
Highfield Rd. NW11—30Ab 40
Highfield Rd. W3—43Ra 79
Highfield Rd. Bexh—57Bd 109
Highfield Rd. Brom—70Pc 130
Highfield Rd. Bush, Wat—15Aa 19
Highfield Rd. Cat—94Wb 181
Highfield Rd. Cher—74J 139
Highfield Rd. Chst—69Vc 131
Highfield Rd. Dart—59Md 111
Highfield Rd. Felt—61W 120
Highfield Rd. Horn—33Pd 69
Highfield Rd. Iswth—53Ha 100
Highfield Rd. N'wd—25U 36
Highfield Rd. Purl—82Pb 164
Highfield Rd. Romf—24Ed 48
Highfield Rd. Sev—88Nd 171
Highfield Rd. Sun—71V 140
Highfield Rd. Surb—73Sa 143
Highfield Rd. Sutt—78Gb 145
Highfield Rd. W on T—74W 140
Highfield Rd. West—89Lc 167
Highfield Rd. Wey—85J 157
Highfield Rd. Wind—5D 94
Highfield Rd. Wfd G—24Nc 46
Highfield Rd. N. Dart—58Md 111
Highfields. Asht—91Ma 177
Highfields. Lea—96Fa 176
Highfields. Lea—100V 174
(East Horsley)
Highfield Way. Horn—33Pd 69
Highfield Way. Pot B—4Db 9
Highfield Way. Rick—16J 17
High Firs. Swan—70Gd 132
High Foleys. Esh—80Ka 142
High Gables. Lou—15Mc 27
High Garth. Esh—79Ea 142
Highgate Av. N6—31Kb 62
Highgate Clo. N6—31Jb 62
Highgate High St. N6—32Jb 62
Highgate Hill. N19—32Kb 62
Highgate Ho. SE26—62Wb 127
Highgate Rd. NW5—34Jb 62
Highgate W. Hill. N6—33Jb 62
High Gro. SE18—52Tc 108
Highgrove Clo. Chst—67Nc 130
Highgrove Ct. Beck—66Cc 128
Highgrove Ct. Wal X—6Zb 12
Highgrove Rd. Dag—36Yc 67
Highgrove Way. Ruis—31W 56
High Hill Est. E5—32Xb 63
High Hill Ferry. E5—32Xb 63
High Hill Rd. Warl—87Ec 166
High Holborn. WC1 —44Nb 82 (2F 199)
High Ho. La. Grays—8F 92
Highland Av. W7—44Ga 78
Highland Av. Brtwd—18Yd 32
Highland Av. Dag—34Ed 68
Highland Av. Lou—16Nc 28
Highland Cotts. Wall—77Kb 146
Highland Ct. E18—25Kc 45
Highland Croft. Beck—65Dc 128
Highland Dri. Bush, Wat—17Ea 20
Highland Pk. Felt—63V 120
Highland Rd. SE19—65Ub 127
Highland Rd. Bexh—57Cd 110
Highland Rd. Brom—67Hc 129
Highland Rd. N'wd—26V 36
Highland Rd. Purl—86Qb 164
Highland Rd. Sev—82Dd 170
Highlands. Wat—18Y 19
Highlands Av. W3—45Sa 79
Highlands Av. Lea—94La 176
Highlands Clo. Ger X—24B 34
Highlands Clo. Houn—53Da 99
Highlands Clo. Lea—94Ka 176
Highlands End. Ger X—24B 34
Highlands Gdns. Ilf—32Pc 66
Highlands Heath. SW15 —59Ya 102
Highlands Hill. Swan—67Jd 133
Highlands La. Ger X—24B 34
Highlands La. Wok—94A 172
Highlands Pk. Lea—95Ma 177
Highlands Pk. Sev—93Nd 187
Highlands Rd. Barn—15Cb 23
Highlands Rd. Lea—94Ka 176
Highlands Rd. Orp—73Xc 151
Highlands, The. Edgw—26Ra 39
Highlands, The. Lea—97U 174
Highlands, The. Pot B—2Eb 9
Highlands, The. Rick—17K 17
High La. W7—44Fa 78
High La. Warl & Cat—90Bc 166
Highlea Clo. NW9—24Ua 40
High Level Dri. SE26—63Wb 127
Highlever Rd. W10—43Ya 80
Highmead. SE18—52Vc 109
High Mead. Chig—19Sc 28
High Mead. Harr—29Ga 38
High Mead. W Wick—75Fc 149
Highmead Cres. Wemb—38Pa 59
High Meadow Clo. Pinn—28Y 37
High Meadow Cres. NW9—29Ta 39
High Meadows. Chig—22Tc 46
Highmore Rd. SE3—52Gc 107
High Mt. NW4—30Wa 40
High Oaks. Enf—10Pb 10
High Pk. Av. Lea—98V 174
High Pk. Av. Rich—53Qa 101
High Pk. Rd. Rich—53Qa 101
High Path. SW19—67Db 125
High Pine Clo. Wey—78S 140
High Point. SE9—62Rc 130
High Point. Wey—78Q 140
Highridge Clo. Eps—86Ua 162
High Rd. Buck H & Lou—19Kc 27
High Rd. Bushey Heath, Bush, Wat—18Fa 20
High Rd. Byfleet, Wey—84N 157
High Rd. Chig—22Qc 46
High Rd. Coul—96Gb 179
High Rd. Cowley, Uxb—43L 75
High Rd. Dart—62Ld 133
High Rd. E. Finchley, N2—25Fb 41
High Rd. Epp—5Sc 14
High Rd. Harr—24Ga 38
High Rd. Ilf & Romf—33Sc 66
High Rd. Leavesden Green, Wat —7V 4
High Rd. Leyton—30Dc 44
E15 1-185 & 2-164
E10 remainder
High Rd. Leytonstone, E11 —35Gc 65
High Rd. Mugswell, Red & Coul —99Eb 179
High Rd. New Southgate, N11 —22Kb 42
High Rd. N. Finchley, N12—21Eb 41
High Rd. North Stifford, Grays —46Zd 91
High Rd. Orsett, Grays—4A 92
High Rd. South Woodford, E18 —25Jc 45
High Rd. Stanf—2P 93
High Rd. Tottenham—28Vb 43
N15 1-363 & 2-344
N17 remainder
High Rd. Uxb—34S 56
High Rd. Wemb—36Ma 59
High Rd. Whetstone, N20—17Eb 23
High Rd. Willesden, NW10 —37Va 60
High Rd. Wood End Green, Hay —43U 76
High Rd. Wfd G—23Hc 45
High Rd. Wood Green, N22 —25Pb 42
Highshore Rd. SE15—54Vb 105
High Silver. Lou—14Mc 27
Highstead Cres. Eri—53Gd 110
Highstone Av. E11—30Jc 45
High St. Abb L, Wat—3U 4
High St. Acton, W3—46Ra 79
High St. Addlestone, Wey—77K 139
High St. Aveley, S Ock—46Sd 90
High St. Bans—87Cb 163
High St. Barkingside, Ilf—27Sc 46
High St. Barn—13Ab 22
High St. Bean, Dart—62Xd 134
High St. Beck—68Cc 128
★High St. Borough Green, Sev —92Be
High St. Brasted, West—96Xc 185
High St. Bren—52La 100
High St. Brtwd—19Yd 32
High St. Brom—68Jc 129
High St. Burnham, Slou—1A 72
High St. Bush, Wat—16Ca 19
High St. Cars—77Jb 146
High St. Cat—95Ub 181
High St. Chalfont Saint Peter, Ger X—25A 34
High St. Chalvey, Slou—8G 72
High St. Cheam, Sutt—79Ab 144
High St. Cheshunt, Wal X—1Zb 12
High St. Chipstead, Sev—94Ed 186
High St. Chst—65Rc 130
High St. Claygate, Esh—79Ha 142
High St. Cob—87X 159
High St. Colliers Wood. SW19 —66Fb 125
High St. Colnbrook, Slou—52E 96
High St. Cowley, Uxb—42L 75
High St. Cranford, Houn—53W 98
High St. Croy—76Sb 147
High St. Dart—58Nd 111
High St. Datchet, Slou—3M 95
High St. Downe, Orp—83Qc 168
High St. Ealing, W5—45Ma 79
High St. East Ham, E6—40Pc 66
High St. E Mol—70Ca 121
High St. Edgw—23Qa 39
High St. Egh—64B 118
High St. Elstree, Borwd—16Ma 21
High St. Epp—3Vc 15
High St. Eps—85Ta 161
High St. Esh—77Da 141
High St. Eton, Wind—1H 95
High St. Ewell, Eps—81Va 162
High St. Eyns, Dart—75Nd 153
High St. Farnborough, Orp —78Rc 150
High St. F'ham, Dart—72Pd 153
High St. Felt—62V 120
High St. Grav—8D 114
High St. Grays—51Ce 113
(in two parts)
High St. Great Bookham, Lea —97Da 175
High St. Grnh—56Xd 112
High St. Green Street Green, Orp—80Vc 151
High St. Hmptn—67Ea 122
High St. Hampton Hill, Hmptn —65Ea 122
High St. Hampton Wick, King —67La 122
High St. Harefield, Uxb—26L 35
High St. Harlesden, NW10 —40Va 60
High St. Harrow on the Hill, Harr—32Ga 58
High St. Hay—51T 98
High St. Horn—32Md 69
High St. Hornsey, N8—28Nb 42
High St. Horsell, Wok—3E 188
High St. Houn—55Da 99
High St. Iver—44G 74
High St. Kemsing, Sev—89Rd 171
High St. K Lan—1Q 4
High St. King—69Ma 123
High St. Knaphill, Wok—5A 188
High St. Langley, Slou—50B 74
High St. Lea—94Ka 176
High St. Limpsfield, Oxt —100Jc 183
High St. Merstham, Red —100Kb 180
High St. Mill Hill, NW7—22Xa 40
High St. N Mald—70Ua 124
High St. Northfleet, Grav —58De 113
High St. N'wd—25V 36
High St. Old Woking, Wok —93C 172
High St. Orp—72Yc 151
High St. Otford, Sev—88Jd 170
High St. Oxshott, Lea—85Fa 160
High St. Penge, SE20—65Yb 128
High St. Pinn—27Aa 37
High St. Plaistow, E13—40Jc 65
High St. Ponders End, Enf—15Yb 26
High St. Pot B—5Db 9
High St. Pot B—5Db 9
High St. Purf—50Qd 89
High St. Purl—83Qb 164
High St. Rick—18M 17
High St. Ripley, Wok—93L 173
High St. Romf—29Gd 48
High St. Ruis—31U 56
High St. Saint Mary Cray, Orp —72Yc 151
High St. Seal. Sev—93Pd 187
High St. Sev—96Ld 187
High St. Sev—97Ld 187
High St. Shep—72R 140
High St. Shoreham, Sev—82Hd 170
High St. Slou—7K 73
(in two parts)
High St. S'hall—46Ba 77
High St. Southgate, N14—18Mb 24
High St. South Norwood, SE25 —70Vb 127
High St. Stai—63H 119
High St. Stanf—2L 93
High St. Stanwell, Stai—58M 97
High St. Stratford, E15—40Ec 64
High St. Sunningdale, Asc—10E 116
High St. Sunninghill, Asc—10B 116
High St. Sutt—77Db 145
(in four parts)
High St. Swan—70Hd 132
High St. Swans—57Be 113
High St. Tad—95Ya 178
High St. Tedd—64Ha 122
High St. Th Dit—72Ja 142
High St. T Hth—70Sb 127
High St. Uxb—38L 55
(in three parts)
High St. Wal X—5Ac 12
(in two parts)
High St. Walthamstow, E17 —29Ac 44
High St. W on T—74W 140
High St. Wanstead, E11—29Jc 45
High St. Wat—14X 19
High St. Wealdstone, Harr —26Ga 38
High St. Wembley Park, Wemb —35Pa 59
High St. W Dray—51M 97
High St. West—99Sc 184
High St. W Wick—74Dc 148
High St. Wey—77Q 140
High St. Whitton, Twic—59Ea 100
High St. Wimbledon. SW19 —64Za 124
High St. Wind—3H 95
High St. Wok—89B 156
High St. Woolwich, SE18—48Qc 86
High St. Wray, Stai—58B 96
★High St. Wrotham, Sev—88Ce
High St. Yiewsley, W Dray—45M 75
High St. M. SW19—64Ab 124
High St. N.—36Nc 66
E6 1-239 & 2-226
E12 remainder
High St. S. E6—40Pc 66
High St. W. Slou—7J 73
High Timber St. EC4 —45Sb 83 (4D 200)
High Tor Clo. Brom—66Kc 129
High Tree Clo. Wey—78J 139
High Trees. SW2—60Qb 104
High Trees. Barn—15Gb 23
High Trees. Croy—74Ac 148
High Trees Clo. Cat—94Vb 181
Highview. NW7—20Ta 21
Highview. Pinn—27Y 37
High View. Rick—14J 17
High View. Sutt—83Bb 163
High View. Wat—16V 18
Highview Av. Edgw—21Sa 39
Highview Av. Grays—50Ee 91
Highview Av. Wall—78Pb 146
High View Clo. SE19—68Vb 127
High View Clo. Lou—15Lc 27
Highview Clo. Pot B—5Eb 9
Highview Cres. Brtwd—16Ee 33
Highview Gdns. N3—27Ab 40
Highview Gdns. N11—22Lb 42
Highview Gdns. Edgw—21Sa 39
Highview Gdns. Pot B—5Eb 9
Highview Gdns. Upm—33Rd 69
High View Rd. E18—26Hc 45
Highview Rd. SE19—65Tb 127
Highview Rd. W13—44Ja 78
High View Rd. Orp—82Qc 168
High View Rd. Sidc—63Xc 131
Highway, The—45Zb 84
E1 1-485 & 2-388
E14 remainder
Highway, The. Orp—77Yc 151
Highway, The. Stan—24Ja 38
Highway, The. Sutt—81Eb 163
Highwold. Coul—90Jb 164
Highwood. Brom—69Fc 129
Highwood Av. N12—21Eb 41
Highwood Av. Bush, Wat—11Ba 19
Highwood Clo. Brtwd—17Xd 32
Highwood Clo. Kenl—89Sb 165
Highwood Clo. Orp—75Sc 150
Highwood Dri. Orp—75Sc 150
Highwood Gdns. Ilf—29Pc 46
Highwood Gro. NW7—22Ta 39
Highwood Hill. NW7—19Va 22
Highwood La. Lou—15Qc 28
Highwood Rd. N19—34Nb 62
Highwoods. Lea—93La 176
High Worple. Harr—31Aa 57
Highworth Rd. N11—23Mb 42
Hilary Av. Mitc—69Jb 126
Hilary Clo. E11—29Jc 45
Hilary Clo. SW6—52Db 103
Hilary Clo. Bexh—53Ed 110
Hilary Clo. Horn—36Md 69
Hilary Rd. W12—45Va 80
Hilbert Rd. Sutt—76Za 144
Hilborough Clo. SW19—66Eb 125
Hilborough Way. Orp—78Tc 150
Hilda Ct. Surb—73Ma 143
Hilda May Av. Swan—68Gd 132
Hilda Rd. E6—38Mc 65
Hilda Rd. E16—42Gc 85
(in two parts)
Hilda Ter. SW9—56Qb 104
Hilda Vale Clo. Orp—77Rc 150
Hilda Vale Rd. Orp—77Rc 150
Hildenborough Gdns. Brom —65Gc 129
Hilden Dri. Eri—52Kd 111
Hildenlea Pl. Brom—68Gc 129
Hildenley Clo. Red—100Mb 180
Hilders, The. Asht—89Ra 161
Hilditch Ho. Rich—58Pa 101
Hildreth St. SW12—60Kb 104
Hildyard Rd. SW6—51Cb 103
Hiley Rd. NW10—41Ya 80
Hilfield La. Wat—11Da 19
Hilfield La. S. Bush, Wat—16Ha 20
Hilgrove Rd. NW6—38Eb 61
Hiliary Gdns. Stan—26La 38
Hiljon Cres. Ger X—25A 34
Hillars Heath Rd. Coul—87Nb 164
Hillary Av. Grav—2A 136
Hillary Cres. W on T—74Y 141
Hillary Rise. Barn—14Cb 23
Hillary Rd. Slou—47A 74
Hillary Rd. S'hall—48Ca 77
Hill Barn. S Croy—83Ub 165
Hillbeck Clo. SE15—52Yb 106
Hillbeck Way. Gnfd—39Fa 58
Hillborne Clo. Hay—50W 76
Hillborough Av. Sev—94Md 187
Hillbrook Gdns. Wey—80Q 140
Hillbrook Rd. SW17—62Hb 125
Hill Brow. Brom—67Mc 129
Hill Brow. Dart—58Hd 110
Hillbrow. N Mald—69Ua 124
Hill Brow Clo. Bex—63Fd 132
Hillbrow Rd. Brom—65Gc 129
Hillbrow Rd. Esh—77Ea 142
Hillbury Av. Harr—29Ka 38
Hillbury Clo. Warl—90Yb 166
Hillbury Rd. SW17—62Kb 126
Hillbury Rd. Warl—89Wb 165
Hill Clo. NW2—34Ya 60
Hill Clo. NW11—30Cb 41
Hill Clo. Barn—15Ya 22
Hill Clo. Chst—64Rc 130
Hill Clo. Grav—6A 136
Hill Clo. Harr—34Ga 58
Hill Clo. Purl—85Sb 165
Hill Clo. Stan—21Ka 38
Hill Clo. Wok—4G 188
Hillcote Av. SW16—66Qb 126
Hill Ct. Romf—28Hd 48
Hillcourt Av. N12—23Db 41
Hillcourt Est. N16—32Tb 63
Hillcourt Rd. SE22—58Xb 105
Hill Cres. N20—19Db 23
Hill Cres. Bex—60Ed 110
Hill Cres. Harr—29Ja 38
Hill Cres. Horn—30Ld 49
Hill Cres. Pot B—6Eb 9
Hill Cres. Surb—71Pa 143
Hill Cres. Wor Pk—75Ya 144
Hillcrest. N6—31Jb 62
Hillcrest. N21—17Qb 24
Hill Crest. Sev—94Jd 186
Hillcrest. Sidc—59Wc 109
Hillcrest. Wey—77R 140
Hillcrest Av. NW11—29Bb 41
Hillcrest Av. Cher—76G 138
Hillcrest Av. Edgw—21Ra 39
Hillcrest Av. Grays—51Wd 112
Hillcrest Av. Pinn—28Z 37
Hillcrest Clo. SE26—63Wb 127
Hillcrest Clo. Beck—72Bc 148
Hillcrest Clo. Eps—87Va 162
Hillcrest Dri. Grnh—57Wd 112
Hillcrest Gdns. N3—28Ab 40
Hill Crest Gdns. NW2—34Wa 60
Hillcrest Gdns. Esh—76Ha 142
Hillcrest Pde. Coul—86Kb 164
Hillcrest Rd. E17—26Fc 45
Hillcrest Rd. E18—26Jc 45
Hillcrest Rd. W3—46Ra 79
Hillcrest Rd. W5—43Na 79
Hillcrest Rd. Brom—64Jc 129
Hillcrest Rd. Dart—59Hd 110
Hillcrest Rd. Horn—31Jd 68
Hillcrest Rd. Lou—16Mc 27
Hillcrest Rd. Orp—75Wc 151
Hillcrest Rd. Purl—82Pb 164
Hillcrest Rd. Shen, Rad—5Qa 7
Hill Crest Rd. West—88Mc 167
Hillcrest Rd. Whyt—89Vb 165
Hillcrest Way. Beck—72Bc 148
Hillcrest Way. Epp—3Wc 15
Hillcrest Waye. Ger X—30B 34
Hillcroft. Lou—12Qc 28
Hillcroft Av. Pinn—30Ba 37
Hillcroft Av. Purl—85Lb 164
Hillcroft Cres. W5—44Na 79
Hillcroft Cres. Ruis—34Z 57
Hillcroft Cres. Wat—18X 19
Hillcroft Cres. Wemb—35Pa 59
Hillcroft Rd. E6—43Rc 86
Hillcroome Rd. Sutt—79Fb 145
Hillcross Av. Mord—72Za 144
Hilldale Rd. Sutt—77Bb 145
Hilldene Av. Romf—23Ld 49
Hilldene Clo. Romf—22Md 49
Hilldown Rd. SW16—66Nb 126
Hilldown Rd. Brom—74Hc 149
Hill Dri. NW9—32Sa 59
Hilldrop Cres. N7—36Mb 62
Hilldrop La. N7—36Mb 62
Hilldrop Rd. N7—36Mb 62
Hilldrop Rd. Brom—65Jc 129
Hillend. SE18—53Qc 108
Hill End. Orp—75Vc 151
Hill End Rd. Uxb—24L 35
Hillersdon. Slou—3M 73
Hillersdon Av. SW13—54Wa 102
Hillersdon Av. Edgw—22Pa 39
Hillery Clo. SE17 —49Tb 83 (6G 207)
Hilley Field La. Lea—94Ea 176
Hill Farm Av. Wat—5W 4
Hill Farm Clo. Wat—5W 4
Hill Farm Rd. W10—43Ya 80
Hill Farm Rd. Ger X—24A 34
Hill Farm Rd. Uxb—35T 56
Hillfield Av. N8—29Nb 42
Hillfield Av. NW9—29Ua 40
Hillfield Av. Mord—72Gb 145
Hillfield Av. Wemb—38Na 59
Hillfield Clo. Harr—28Ea 38
Hillfield Ct. NW3—36Gb 61
Hillfield Ct. Esh—78Da 141
Hillfield Pk. N10—28Kb 42
Hillfield Pk. N21—19Qb 24
Hillfield Pk. M. N10—28Kb 42
Hillfield Rd. NW6—36Bb 61
Hillfield Rd. Ger X—24A 34
Hillfield Rd. Hmptn—66Ba 121
Hillfield Rd. Sev—92Gd 186
Hillfield Sq. Ger X—24A 34
Hillfoot Av. Romf—25Ed 48
Hillfoot Rd. Romf—25Ed 48
Hillgate Pl. W8—46Cb 81
Hillgate St. W8—46Cb 81
Hill Gro. Romf—27Gd 48
Hillhouse. Wal A—5Hc 13
Hill Ho. Av. Stan—24Ha 38
Hill Ho. Clo. N21—17Qb 24
Hill Ho. Clo. Ger X—23A 34
Hill House Dri. Wey—83Q 158
Hill Ho. Rd. SW16—64Pb 126
Hill Ho. Rd. Dart—59Sd 112
Hillhurst Gdns. Cat—92Ub 181
Hilliard Rd. N'wd—25V 36
Hilliards Ct. E1—46Yb 84
Hilliards Rd. Uxb—44M 75
Hillier Clo. Barn—16Db 23
Hillier Gdns. Croy—78Qb 146
Hillier Rd. SW11—58Hb 103
Hilliers Av. Uxb—41Q 76
Hilliers La. Croy—76Nb 146
Hillingdale. West—90Kc 167
Hillingdon Av. Sev—93Ld 187
Hillingdon Av. Stai—60N 97
Hillingdon Hill. Uxb—41N 75
Hillingdon Rise. Sev—94Md 187
Hillingdon Rd. Bexh—55Ed 110
Hillingdon Rd. Grav—1D 136
Hillingdon Rd. Uxb—39M 55
Hillingdon Rd. Wat—6W 4
Hillingdon St.—51Rb 105
SE17 1-237 & 2-244
SE5 remainder
Hillington Gdns. Wfd G—26Mc 45
Hill La. Ruis—32S 56
Hill La. Tad—93Ab 178
Hillman Clo. Horn—27Md 49
Hillman Clo. Uxb—36N 55
Hillman St. E8—37Xb 63
Hillmarton Rd. N7—36Nb 62
Hillmead Dri. SW9—56Rb 105
Hillmont Rd. Esh—76Ga 142
Hillmore Gro. SE26—64Ac 128
Hill Oak Wlk. NW6—37Bb 61
Hill Path. SW16—64Pb 126
Hillreach. SE18—50Pc 86
Hill Rise. N9—16Xb 25
Hill Rise. NW11—28Db 41
Hill Rise. SE23—60Xb 105
Hill Rise. Dart—64Td 134
Hill Rise. Esh—75Ka 142
Hill Rise. Ger X—26A 34
Hill Rise. Gnfd—39Ea 58
Hill Rise. Pot B—6Eb 9
Hill Rise. Pot B—1Nb 10
(Cuffley)
Hill Rise. Rich—57Ma 101
Hill Rise. Rick—16K 17
Hill Rise. Ruis—32S 56
Hill Rise. Slou—51C 96
Hill Rise. Upm—33Qd 69
Hill Rise. W on T—73V 140
Hillrise Av. Wat—10Z 5
Hill Rise Cres. Ger X—26A 34
Hillrise Rd. N19—31Nb 62
Hillrise Rd. Romf—23Ed 48
Hill Rd. N10—25Hb 41
Hill Rd. NW8—40Eb 61 (3A 190)
Hill Rd. Brtwd—20Wd 32
Hill Rd. Cars—79Gb 145
Hill Rd. Dart—61Nd 133
Hill Rd. Epp—10Uc 14
Hill Rd. Harr—29Ja 38
Hill Rd. Lea—94Da 175
Hill Rd. Mitc—67Kb 126
Hill Rd. N'wd—23T 36
Hill Rd. Pinn—29Aa 37
Hill Rd. Purl—84Pb 164
Hill Rd. Sutt—78Db 145
Hill Rd. Wemb—34Ka 58
Hillsborough Grn. Wat—20W 18
Hillsborough Rd. SE22—57Ub 105
Hills Chace. Brtwd—21Yd 50
Hillside. NW9—28Ta 39
Hillside. NW10—38Sa 59
Hillside. SW19—65Za 124
Hillside. Bans—87Ab 162
Hillside. Barn—15Eb 23
Hillside. Dart—64Ud 134
Hillside. F'ham, Dart—73Pd 153
Hillside. Grays—49Fe 91
Hillside. Romf—21Md 49
Hillside. Slou—7J 73
Hillside. Uxb—29L 35
Hillside. Wok—8G 188
Hillside Av. N11—23Hb 41
Hillside Av. Borwd—14Ra 21
Hillside Av. Grav—1F 136
Hillside Av. Purl—85Rb 165
Hillside Av. Wal X—3Zb 12
Hillside Av. Wemb—35Pa 59
Hillside Av. Wfd G—23Lc 45
Hillside Clo. NW8—40Db 61

Hillside Clo.—Homestead Rd.

Hillside Clo. Abb L, Wat—4U 4
Hillside Clo. Bans—88Ab 162
Hillside Clo. Ger X—23A 34
Hillside Clo. Mord—70Ab 124
Hillside Clo. Wok—5A 188
Hillside Clo. Wfd G—22Lc 45
Hillside Cres. Enf—10Tb 11
Hillside Cres. Harr—32Ea 58
Hillside Cres. N'wd—25W 36
Hillside Cres. Wal X—3Zb 12
Hillside Cres. Wat—16Aa 19
Hillside Dri. Edgw—23Qa 39
Hillside Dri. Grav—1F 136
Hillside Est. N15—30Vb 43
Hillside Gdns. E17—27Fc 45
Hillside Gdns. N6—30Kb 42
Hillside Gdns. N11—23Lb 42
Hillside Gdns. Barn—14Ab 22
Hillside Gdns. Edgw—21Pa 39
Hillside Gdns. Harr—31Na 59
Hillside Gdns. N'wd—24W 36
Hillside Gdns. Wall—80Lb 146
Hillside Gdns. Wey—78H 139
Hillside Gro. N14—17Mb 24
Hillside Gro. NW7—24Wa 40
Hillside La. Brom—75Hc 149
Hillside Pas. SW2—61Pb 126
Hillside Rise. N'wd—24W 36
Hillside Rd. N15—31Ub 63
Hillside Rd. SW2—61Qb 126
Hillside Rd. W5—43Na 79
Hillside Rd. Asht—89Pa 161
Hillside Rd. Brom—69Hc 129
Hillside Rd. Bush, Wat—15Aa 19
Hillside Rd. Coul—90Pb 164
Hillside Rd. Croy—78Rb 147
Hillside Rd. Dart—58Jd 110
Hillside Rd. Eps—82Ya 162
Hillside Rd. N'wd & Pinn—24W 36
Hillside Rd. Rad—7Ka 6
Hillside Rd. Rick—15E 16
Hillside Rd. Sev—95Md 187
Hillside Rd. Sev—89Pd 171
(Kemsing)
Hillside Rd. S'hall—42Ca 77
Hillside Rd. Surb—70Qa 123
Hillside Rd. Sutt—80Bb 145
Hillside Rd. West—91Nc 184
Hillside Rd. Whyt—90Wb 165
Hillside, The. Orp—81Xc 169
Hillside Wlk. Brtwd—20Vd 32
Hills La. N'wd—25U 36
Hills La. Sev—85Rd 171
Hillsleigh Rd. W8—46Bb 81
Hillsmead Way. S Croy—85Xb 165
Hills Pl. W1—44Lb 82 (3B 198)
Hills Rd. Buck H—18Kc 27
Hillstowe St. E5—34Yb 64
Hill St. W1—46Jb 82 (6K 197)
Hill St. Rich—57Ma 101
Hill, The. Cat—96Vb 181
Hill, The. Grav—58Ee 113
Hill Top. NW11—28Db 41
Hill Top. Lou—12Qc 28
Hill Top. Mord—72Cb 145
Hill Top. Sutt—73Bb 145
Hill Top. Wfd G—23Pc 46
Hilltop Clo. Asc—8C 116
Hilltop Clo. Lea—95La 176
Hill Top Clo. Lou—13Qc 28
Hilltop Gdns. NW4—26Xa 40
Hilltop Gdns. Dart—57Pd 111
Hilltop Gdns. Orp—75Uc 150
Hilltop La. Cat & Red—98Qb 180
Hilltop Rise. Lea—98Ea 176
Hilltop Rd. NW6—38Cb 61
Hilltop Rd. Grays—51Xd 112
Hilltop Rd. Whyt—89Ub 165
Hilltop Wlk. Cat—92Ac 182
Hilltop Way. Stan—20Ja 20
Hillview. SW20—66Xa 124
★Hill View. Sev—92Ce
Hillview Av. Harr—29Na 39
Hillview Av. Horn—30Ld 49
Hillview Clo. Pinn—23Ba 37
Hillview Clo. Purl—83Rb 165
★Hill View Clo. Sev—92Ce
Hill View Clo. Tad—93Ya 178
Hill View Ct. Wok—90B 156
Hill View Cres. Ilf—30Pc 46
Hill View Cres. Orp—74Vc 151
Hill View Dri. Well—54Uc 108
Hillview Gdns. NW4—28Za 40
Hill View Gdns. NW9—29Ta 39
Hillview Gdns. Harr—27Ca 37
Hill View Rd. NW7—21Za 40
Hillview Rd. Chst—64Qc 130
Hill View Rd. Esh—80Ja 142
Hill View Rd. Long, Dart—69De 135
Hill View Rd. Orp—75Vc 151
Hillview Rd. Pinn—24Ba 37
Hillview Rd. Sutt—76Eb 145
Hill View Rd. Twic—58Ja 100
Hill View Rd. Wok—90B 156
Hillview Rd. Wray, Stai—8P 95
Hillway. N6—33Jb 62
Hillway. NW9—32Ua 60
Hill Waye. Ger X—30B 34
Hill Way, The. Brtwd—11Fe 33
Hillwood Clo. Brtwd—18De 33
Hillwood Gro. Brtwd—18De 33
Hillworth Rd. SW2—59Qb 104
Hillyard Rd. W7—43Ga 78
Hillyard St. SW9—53Qb 104
Hillydeal Rd. Sev—87Ld 171
Hillyfield. E17—26Ac 44
Hillyfields. Lou—12Qc 28
Hilly Fields Cres. SE4—55Cc 106
Hilperton Rd. Slou—7J 73
Hilsea St. E5—35Yb 64
Hilton Av. N12—22Fb 41
Hilton Clo. Uxb—40K 55
Hilton Way. S Croy—87Xb 165
Hilversum Cres. SE22—57Ub 105
Himley Rd. SW17—64Gb 125
Hinchcliffe Clo. Wall—80Pb 146
Hinchley Clo. Esh—77Ha 142
Hinchley Dri. Esh—76Ha 142
Hinchley Way. Esh—76Ja 142
Hinckley Rd. SE15—56Wb 105
Hind Clo. Chig—22Vc 47
Hind Ct. EC4—44Qb 82 (3A 200)
Hind Cres. Eri—51Fd 110
Hinde M. W1—(2J 197)
Hindes Rd. Harr—29Fa 38
Hinde St. W1—44Jb 82 (2J 197)
Hind Gro. E14—44Cc 84
Hindhead Clo. N16—32Ub 63
Hindhead Clo. Uxb—43R 76
Hindhead Gdns. N'holt—39Aa 57
Hindhead Grn. Wat—22Y 37
Hindhead Way. Wall—78Nb 146
Hindmans Rd. SE22—57Wb 105
Hindmans Way. Dag—42Bd 87
Hindmarsh Clo. E1—45Wb 83
Hindrey Rd. E5—36Xb 63
Hindsley's Pl. SE23—61Zb 128
Hinkler Clo. Wall—80Nb 146
Hinkler Rd. Harr—27Ma 39
Hinkley Clo. Uxb—28L 35
Hinksey Clo. Slou—48D 74
Hinksey Path. SE2—47Zc 87
Hinstock Rd. SE18—52Sc 108
Hinton Av. Houn—56Z 99
Hinton Clo. SE9—60Nc 108
Hinton Rd. N18—21Ub 43
Hinton Rd. SE24—55Rb 105
Hinton Rd. Slou—5C 72
Hinton Rd. Uxb—39L 55
Hinton Rd. Wall—79Lb 146
Hipley St. Wok—92D 172
Hippodrome Pl. W11—45Ab 80
Hitcham Rd. E17—31Bc 64
Hitchcock Clo. Shep—69P 119
Hitchen Hatch La. Sev—95Jd 186
Hitchin Clo. Romf—21Ld 49
Hitchin Sq. E3—40Ac 64
Hitherbroom Rd. Hay—46W 76
Hitherfield Rd. SW16—62Qb 126
Hitherfield Rd. Dag—33Ad 67
Hither Grn. La. SE13—57Ec 106
Hither Meadow. Ger X—25A 34
Hithermoor Rd. Stai—58H 97
Hitherwell Dri. Harr—25Fa 38
Hitherwood Clo. Horn—35Md 69
Hitherwood Dri. SE19—63Vb 127
Hive Clo. Bush, Wat—19Fa 20
Hive La. Grav—58De 113
Hive Rd. Bush, Wat—19Fa 20
Hoadly Rd. SW16—62Mb 126
Hobart Clo. N20—19Gb 23
Hobart Gdns. T Hth—69Tb 127
Hobart Pl. SW1—48Kb 82 (3K 203)
Hobart Pl. Rich—59Pa 101
Hobart Rd. Dag—35Zc 67
Hobart Rd. Hay—42Z 77
Hobart Rd. Ilf—26Sc 46
Hobart Rd. Til—3C 114
Hobart Rd. Wor Pk—76Xa 144
Hobarts Dri. Uxb—30H 35
Hobbayne Rd. W7—44Fa 78
Hobbes Wlk. SW15—57Xa 102
Hobbs Clo. Wal X—1Zb 12
Hobbs Clo. Wey—85K 157
Hobbs Grn. N2—27Eb 41
Hobbs Pl. N1—40Ub 63 (1H 195)
Hobbs Rd. SE27—63Sb 127
Hobday St. E14—44Dc 84
Hobill Wlk. Surb—72Pa 143
Hoblands End. Chst—65Uc 130
Hobury St. SW10—51Fb 103
Hockenden La. Swan—69Cd 132
Hockering Est. Wok—90D 156
Hockering Gdns. Wok—90D 156
Hockering Rd. Wok—90C 156
Hocker St. E2—41Vb 83 (4K 195)
Hockett Clo. SE8—49Ac 84
Hockley Av. E6—40Nc 66
Hockley Dri. Romf—26Ld 49
Hockley La. Slou—8M 53
Hocroft Av. NW2—34Bb 61
Hocroft Rd. NW2—34Bb 61
Hocroft Wlk. NW2—35Ab 60
Hodder Dri. Gnfd—40Ha 58
Hoddesdon Rd. Belv—50Cd 88
Hodford Rd. NW11—32Bb 61
Hodgkin Clo. SE28—45Zc 87
Hodister Clo. SE5—52Sb 105
Hodnet Gro. SE16—49Zb 84
Hodsoll Ct. Orp—71Zc 151
★Hodsoll St. Sev—81Fe
Hodson Clo. Harr—34Ba 57
Hodson Cres. Orp—71Zc 151
Hoe La. Enf—10Wb 11
Hoe La. Romf—13Xc 29
Hoe St. E17—28Cc 44
Hoe, The. Wat—19Z 19
Hofland Rd. W14—48Ab 80
Hoford Rd. Grays—9F 92
Hogan M. W2—43Fb 81 (7B 190)
Hogan Way. E5—33Wb 63
Hogarth Av. Ashf—65S 120
Hogarth Av. Brtwd—20Ae 33
Hogarth Clo. E16—43Mc 85
Hogarth Clo. W5—43Na 79
Hogarth Clo. Slou—5C 72
Hogarth Ct. EC3—44Ub 83 (4J 201)
Hogarth Ct. SE19—63Vb 127
Hogarth Ct. Bush, Wat—17Da 19
Hogarth Cres. SW19—67Fb 125
Hogarth Cres. Croy—73Sb 147
Hogarth Gdns. Houn—52Ca 99
Hogarth Hill. NW11—28Bb 41
Hogarth La. W4—51Ua 102
Hogarth Rd. SW5—49Db 81
Hogarth Rd. Edgw—26Qa 39
Hogarths Rd. Grays—46Ce 91
Hogarth Way. Hmptn—67Ea 122
Hogden Clo. Tad—97Bb 179
Hogfair. Slou—1A 72
Hogfair La. Slou—2B 72
Hoggin Rd. N9—19Ub 25
Hogg La. Grays—47Ce 91
Hog Hill Rd. Romf—24Bd 47
Hog La. Borwd—14Ja 20
★Hognore La. Sev—86Fe
Hogscross La. Coul—95Hb 179
Hogsden Clo. N1—40Sb 63 (1E 194)
Hogshill La. Cob—86X 159
Hogs La. Grav—62Fe 135
Hogsmill Way. Eps—77Sa 143
Hogtrough Hill. Sev & West —92Vc 185
Hogtrough La. God—99Cc 182
Hogtrough La. Oxt—100Dc 182
Holbeach Gdns. Sidc—58Vc 109
Holbeach Rd. SE6—59Cc 106
Holbeck Row. SE15—52Wb 105
Holbein Ga. N'wd—22U 36
Holbein M. SW1—50Jb 82 (7H 203)
Holbein Pl. SW1—49Jb 82 (6H 203)
Holberton Gdns. NW10—41Xa 80
Holborn. EC1—43Qb 82 (1A 200)
Holborn Bldgs. EC1—(1K 199)
Holborn Cir. EC1 —43Qb 82 (1A 200)
Holborn Pl. WC2—(1H 199)
Holborn Rd. E13—43Kc 85
Holborn Viaduct. EC1 —43Rb 83 (1A 200)
Holbrook Clo. N19—32Kb 62
Holbrook Clo. Enf—10Wb 11
Holbrooke Ct. N7—34Nb 62
Holbrooke Pl. Rich—57Ma 101
Holbrook La. Chst—66Tc 130
Holbrook Rd. E15—40Hc 65
Holbrook Way. Brom—72Pc 150
Holburne Clo. SE3—53Lc 107
Holburne Gdns. SE3—53Mc 107
Holburne Rd. SE3—53Lc 107
Holcombe Hill. NW7—20Wa 22
Holcombe Rd. N17—27Wb 43
Holcombe Rd. Ilf—31Qc 66
Holcombe St. W6—49Xa 80
Holcroft Rd. E9—38Yb 64
Holdbrook N. Wal X—6Bc 12
Holdbrook S. Wal X—6Bc 12
Holdbrook Way. Romf—26Pd 49
Holden Av. N12—22Db 41
Holden Av. NW9—32Sa 59
Holdenby Rd. SE4—57Ac 106
Holden Gdns. Brtwd—22Zd 51
Holden Rd. N12—22Db 41
Holden St. SW11—54Jb 104
Holden Way. Upm—32Td 70
Holdernesse Rd. SW17—61Jb 126
Holderness Way. SE27—64Rb 127
Holder's Hill Av. NW4—26Za 40
Holders Hill Cir. NW7—24Ab 40
Holder's Hill Cres. NW4—26Za 40
Holder's Hill Dri. NW4—27Za 40
Holders Hill Gdns. NW4—26Ab 40
Holders Hill Rd. NW4 & NW7 —26Za 40
Holdgate St. SE7—48Mc 85
Holecroft. Wal A—6Gc 13
Hole Farm La. Brtwd—25Wd 50
Holford Pl. WC1—41Pb 82 (3J 193)
Holford Rd. NW3—34Eb 61
Holford St. WC1—41Qb 82 (3K 193)
Holgate Av. SW11—55Fb 103
Holgate Gdns. Dag—37Cd 68
Holgate Rd. Dag—36Cd 68
Holland Av. SW20—67Va 124
Holland Av. Sutt—81Cb 163
Holland Clo. N20—17Fb 23
Holland Clo. Brom—75Hc 149
Holland Clo. Stan—22Ka 38
Holland Ct. NW7—23Wa 40
Holland Ct. Surb—73Ma 143
Holland Gdns. W14—48Ab 80
Holland Gdns. Egh—68H 119
Holland Gdns. Wat—7Y 5
Holland Gro. SW9—52Qb 104
Holland La. W14—48Bb 81
Holland Pk. W11—46Ab 80
Holland Pk. Av. W11—46Ab 80
Holland Pk. Av. Ilf—30Uc 46
Holland Pk. Gdns. W14—47Ab 80
Holland Pk. M. W11—46Bb 81
Holland Pk. Rd. W14—48Bb 81
Holland Rd. E6—39Pc 66
Holland Rd. E15—41Gc 85
Holland Rd. NW10—39Wa 60
Holland Rd. SE25—71Wb 147
Holland Rd. W14—47Ab 80
Holland Rd. Wemb—37Ma 59
Hollands Clo. Grav—4N 137
(in two parts)
Hollands, The. Felt—63Z 121
Hollands, The. Wor Pk—74Va 144
Holland St. SE1—46Rb 83 (6C 200)
Holland St. W8—47Cb 81
Holland Vs. Rd. W14—47Ab 80
Holland Wlk. N19—32Mb 62
Holland Wlk. W8—46Bb 81
Holland Wlk. Stan—22Ja 38
Holland Way. Brom—75Hc 149
Hollar Rd. N16—34Vb 63
Hollen St. W1—44Mb 82 (2D 198)
Holles Clo. Hmptn—65Ca 121
Holles St. W1—44Kb 82 (2A 198)
Holley Rd. W3—47Ua 80
Hollick Wood Av. N12—23Hb 41
Hollidge Way. Dag—38Dd 68
Hollies Av. Sidc—61Vc 131
Hollies Av. Wey—85H 157
Hollies Clo. Twic—61Ha 122
Hollies Ct. Wey—78L 139
Hollies End. NW7—22Xa 40
Hollies Rd. W5—49La 78
Hollies, The. N20—18Fb 23
Hollies, The. Grav—5F 136
Hollies Way. SW12—59Jb 104
Hollies Way. Pot B—4Eb 9
Holligrave Rd. Brom—67Jc 129
Hollingbourne Av. Bexh —53Bd 109
Hollingbourne Gdns. W13 —43Ka 78
Hollingbourne Rd. SE24—57Sb 105
Hollingsworth Ct. Surb—73Ma 143
Hollingsworth Rd. Croy—79Xb 147
Hollington Cres. N Mald —72Va 144
Hollington Rd. E6—41Pc 86
Hollington Rd. N17—26Wb 43
Hollingworth Rd. Orp—73Rc 150
Hollingworth Way. West —98Tc 184
Hollis Pl. Grays—49Ce 91
Hollman Gdns. SW16—65Rb 127
Holloway Clo. W Dray—50N 75
Holloway Hill. Cher—76E 138
Holloway La. Rick—9E 2
Holloway La. W Dray—51N 97
Holloway Rd. E6—41Pc 86
Holloway Rd. E11—34Gc 65
Holloway Rd.—33Mb 62
N7 31-479 & 2-596
N19 remainder
Holloway St. Houn—55Da 99
Hollowfield Av. Grays—49Fe 91
Hollowfield Wlk. N'holt—38Aa 57
Hollow Hill La. Iver—45D 74
Hollow La. Vir W—9N 117
Hollows, The. Bren—51Pa 101
Hollow, The. Wfd G—21Hc 45
Holly Av. Stan—26Na 39
Holly Av. W on T—74Z 141
Holly Av. Wey—82J 157
Hollybank Clo. Hmptn—64Ca 121
Holly Bank Rd. Wey—86J 157
Holly Bank Rd. Wok—9E 188
Hollybrake Clo. Chst—66Tc 130
Hollybush Clo. E11—29Jc 45
Hollybush Clo. Harr—25Ga 38
Hollybush Gdns. E2—41Xb 83
Hollybush Hill. E11—30Hc 45
Holly Bush Hill. NW3—35Eb 61
Hollybush Hill. Slou—8L 53
Holly Bush La. Hmptn—66Ba 121
Hollybush La. Iver—44D 74
Holly Bush La. Orp—79Cd 152
Holly Bush La. Sev—96Ld 187
Hollybush La. Uxb—33E 54
Hollybush La. Wok—91M 173
Hollybush Pl. E2—41Xb 83
Hollybush Rd. Grav—1E 136
Hollybush Rd. King—64Na 123
Hollybush St. E13—41Kc 85
Holly Bush Vale. NW3—35Eb 61
Holly Clo. NW10—38Ua 60
Holly Clo. Buck H—20Mc 27
Holly Clo. Felt—64Aa 121
Holly Clo. Egh—5M 117
Holly Clo. Slou—5G 52
Holly Clo. Wok—7E 188
Hollycombe. Egh—3N 117
Holly Cres. Beck—71Bc 148
Holly Cres. Wind—4B 94
Holly Cres. Wfd G—24Fc 45
Hollycroft Av. NW3—34Cb 61
Hollycroft Av. Wemb—34Pa 59
Hollycroft Clo. W Dray—51Q 98
Hollycroft Gdns. W Dray—51Q 98
Hollydale Dri. Brom—76Pc 150
Hollydale Rd. SE15—54Yb 106
Hollydene. SE15—53Xb 105
Hollydown Way. E11—34Fc 65
Holly Dri. E4—17Dc 26
Holly Dri. Pot B—5Db 9
Holly Dri. Wind—7J 95
Hollyfarm Rd. S'hall—50Aa 77
Hollyfield Av. N11—22Hb 41
Hollyfield Rd. Surb—73Pa 143
Holly Gro. NW9—31Sa 59
Holly Gro. SE15—54Vb 105
Hollygrove. Bush, Wat—17Fa 20
Hollyhedge Rd. Cob—86X 159
Holly Hedges La. Hem & Rick —2E 2
Holly Hedge Ter. SE13—57Fc 107
Holly Hill. N21—16Pb 24
Holly Hill. NW3—35Eb 61
Holly Hill Dri. Bans—89Cb 163
Holly Hill Rd. Belv & Eri—50Dd 88
Holly La. Bans—88Cb 163
Holly La. E. Bans—88Db 163
Holly La. W. Bans—89Db 163
Holly Lea. Guild—100A 172
Holly Lodge Gdns. N6—33Jb 62
Hollymead. Cars—76Hb 145
Hollymead Rd. Coul—90Jb 164
Hollymeoak Rd. Coul—91Kb 180
Holly M. SW10—(7A 202)
Hollymoor La. Eps—82Ta 161
Holly Mt. NW3—35Eb 61
Hollymount Clo. SE10—53Ec 106
Hollyoak Ter. Sev—96Jd 186
Holly Pk. N3—27Bb 41
Holly Pk. N4—31Pb 62
(in two parts)
Holly Pk. Est. N4—31Pb 62
Holly Pk. Gdns. N3—27Cb 41
Holly Pk. Rd. N11—22Jb 42
Holly Pk. Rd. W7—46Ha 78
Holly Rd. E11—31Hc 65
Holly Rd. W4—49Ta 79
Holly Rd. Dart—60Md 111
Holly Rd. Enf—8Zb 12
Holly Rd. Hmptn—65Ea 122
Holly Rd. Houn—56Da 99
Holly Rd. Orp—80Wc 151
Holly Rd. Twic—60Ha 100
Holly St. E8—38Vb 63
Holly St. Est. E8—38Vb 63
Holly Ter. N6—32Jb 62
Holly Ter. N20—19Eb 23
Holly Tree Av. Swan—68Gd 132
Holly Tree Clo. SW19—60Za 102
Hollytree Clo. Ger X—22A 34
Holly Tree Rd. Cat—94Ub 181
Holly Village. N6—33Jb 62
Holly Wlk. NW3—35Eb 61
Holly Wlk. Enf—13Tb 25
Holly Wlk. Wind—3C 116
Holly Way. Mitc—70Mb 126
Hollywood Ct. Borwd—14Qa 21
Hollywood Gdns. Hay—44X 77
★Hollywood La. Sev—83Vd
Hollywood M. SW10—51Eb 103
Hollywood Rd. E4—22Ac 44
Hollywood Rd. SW10—51Eb 103
Hollywoods. Croy—81Bc 166
Hollywood Way. Wfd G—24Fc 45
Holman Rd. SW11—54Fb 103
Holman Rd. Eps—78Sa 143
Holmbank Dri. Shep—70U 120
Holmbridge Gdns. Enf—14Zb 26
Holmbrook Dri. NW4—29Za 40
Holmbury Clo. Bush, Wat—19Ga 20
Holmbury Ct. SW17—62Hb 125
Holmbury Ct. S Croy—78Ub 147
Holmbury Gdns. Hay—46V 76
Holmbury Gro. Croy—80Bc 148
Holmbury Pk. Brom—66Nc 130
Holmbury View. E5—32Xb 63
Holmbush Rd. SW15—58Ab 102
Holm Clo. Wey—84G 156
Holmcote Gdns. N5—36Sb 63
Holmcroft Way. Brom—71Pc 150
Holmdale Clo. Borwd—12Pa 21
Holmdale Gdns. NW4—29Za 40
Holmdale Rd. NW6—36Cb 61
Holmdale Rd. Chst—64Sc 130
Holmdale Ter. N15—30Ub 43
Holmdene Av. NW7—23Wa 40
Holmdene Av. SE24—57Sb 105
Holmdene Av. Harr—27Da 37
Holmdene Clo. Beck—68Ec 128
Holmead Rd. SW6—52Db 103
Holme Chase. Wey—79S 140
Holme Clo. Wal X—3Ac 12
Holmedale. Slou—5N 73
Holme Lacey Rd. SE12—58Hc 107
Holme Lea. Wat—6Y 5
Holme Pk. Borwd—12Pa 21
Holme Rd. E6—39Nc 66
Holme Rd. Horn—32Qd 69
Holmes Av. E17—27Bc 44
Holmes Av. NW7—22Ab 40
Holmesdale. Wal X—7Zb 12
Holmesdale Av. SW14—56Ra 101
Holmesdale Clo. SE25—69Vb 127
Holmesdale Clo. Iver—44H 75
Holmesdale Rd. N6—31Kb 62
Holmesdale Rd.—71Tb 147
SE25 45-387 & 62-326
Croy remainder
Holmesdale Rd. Bexh—54Zc 109
Holmesdale Rd. Rich—53Pa 101
Holmesdale Rd. Sev—95Md 187
Holmesdale Rd. Tedd—66La 122
Holmesley Rd. SE23—58Ac 106
Holmes Pl. SW10—51Eb 103
Holmes Rd. NW5—36Kb 62
Holmes Rd. SW19—66Eb 125
Holmes Rd. Twic—61Ha 122
Holmes Ter. SE1—(1K 205)
Holmeswood Ct. N22—26Qb 42
Holme Way. Stan—23Ha 38
Holmewood Gdns. SW2—59Pb 104
Holmewood Rd. SE25—69Ub 127
Holmewood Rd. SW2—59Pb 104
Holmfield. NW11—28Cb 41
Holmfield Av. NW4—29Za 40
Holmfield Ct. NW3—37Gb 61
Holm Gro. Uxb—38Q 56
Holmhurst Rd. Belv—50Dd 88
Holmlea Rd. Slou—3P 95
Holmlea Wlk. Slou—3N 95
Holmleigh Av. Dart—57Ld 111
Holmleigh Rd. N16—32Ub 63
Holmoak Clo. SW15—58Bb 103
Holmoaks Ho. Beck—68Ec 128
Holmsdale Gro. Bexh—55Gd 110
Holmsdale Hill. S Dar, Dart —67Sd 134
Holmsdale Rd. S Dar, Dart —67Sd 134
Holmshaw Clo. SE26—63Ac 128
Holmshill La. Borwd—8Ua 8
Holmside Rise. Wat—20X 19
Holmside Rd. SW12—58Jb 104
Holmsley Clo. N Mald—73Va 144
Holmstall Av. Edgw—27Sa 39
Holm Wlk. SE3—54Jc 107
Holmwood Av. Brtwd—16Ce 33
Holmwood Av. S Croy—85Vb 165
Holmwood Clo. Harr—27Ea 38
Holmwood Clo. Lea—100U 174
Holmwood Clo. N'holt—37Da 57
Holmwood Clo. Sutt—81Za 162
Holmwood Clo. Wey—78J 139
Holmwood Gdns. N3—26Cb 41
Holmwood Gdns. Wall—79Kb 146
Holmwood Gro. NW7—22Ta 39
Holmwood Rd. Chess—78Na 143
Holmwood Rd. Enf—8Zb 12
Holmwood Rd. Ilf—33Uc 66
Holmwood Rd. Sutt—81Ya 162
Holne Chase. N2—30Eb 41
Holne Chase. Mord—72Bb 145
Holness Rd. E15—37Hc 65
Holroyd Clo. Esh—81Ha 160
Holroyd Rd. SW15—56Ya 102
Holroyd Rd. Esh—81Ha 160
Holstein Av. Wey—77Q 140
Holstein Way. Eri—48Zc 87
Holstock Rd. Ilf—33Sc 66
Holsworth Clo. Harr—29Ea 38
Holsworthy Ho. Romf—25Md 49
Holsworthy Sq. WC1—(6J 193)
Holsworthy Way. Chess —78La 142
Holt Clo. N10—28Jb 42
Holt Clo. SE28—45Yc 87
Holt Clo. Borwd—14Pa 21
Holton St. E1—42Zb 84
Holt Rd. E16—46Nc 86
Holt Rd. Wemb—34Ka 58
Holtsmere Clo. Wat—7Y 5
Holt, The. Ilf—23Sc 46
Holt, The. Wall—77Lb 146
Holt Way. Chig—22Vc 47
Holtwhite Av. Enf—12Sb 25
Holtwhite's Hill. Enf—11Rb 25
Holtwood Rd. Lea—85Ea 160
Holwell Pl. Pinn—28Aa 37
Holwood Clo. W on T—75Y 141
Holwood Pk. Av. Orp—77Pc 150
Holwood Pl. SW4—56Mb 104
Holwood Rd. Brom—68Jc 129
Holybourne Av. SW15—59Wa 102
Holybush Wlk. SW9—56Rb 105
Holyfield Rd. Wal A—1Ec 12
Holyhead Clo. E3—41Cc 84
Holyoake Av. Wok—5F 188
Holyoake Cres. Wok—5F 188
Holyoake Wlk. N2—27Eb 41
Holyoake Wlk. W5—42La 78
Holyoak Rd. SE11 —49Rb 83 (5B 206)
Holyport Rd. SW6—52Za 102
Holyrood Av. Harr—35Aa 57
Holyrood Gdns. Edgw—27Ra 39
Holyrood Gdns. Grays—9E 92
Holyrood Rd. Barn—16Eb 23
Holyrood St. SE1 —46Ub 83 (7H 201)
Holywell Clo. SE3—51Jc 107
Holywell Clo. Stai—60N 97
Holywell La. EC2 —42Ub 83 (5J 195)
Holywell Rd. Wat—15W 18
Holywell Row. EC2 —42Ub 83 (6H 195)
Holywell Way. Stai—60N 97
Home Clo. Cars—75Hb 145
Home Clo. Lea—93Fa 176
Home Clo. N'holt—41Ba 77
Home Ct. Felt—60W 98
Homecroft Gdns. Lou—14Rc 28
Homecroft Rd. N22—25Sb 43
Homecroft Rd. SE26—64Yb 128
Homedean Rd. Sev—95Ed 186
Home Farm Clo. Eps—89Za 162
Home Farm Clo. Esh—79Da 141
Home Farm Clo. Shep—70U 120
Homefarm Clo. Th Dit—73Ha 142
Home Farm Gdns. W on T —75Y 141
Homefarm Rd. W7—44Ha 78
Home Farm Rd. Brtwd—25Ae 51
Home Farm Rd. Rick—21Q 36
Home Farm Way. Slou—9N 53
Home Field. Barn—15Bb 23
Homefield. Wal A—4Jc 13
Homefield. W on T—77Z 141
Homefield Av. Ilf—29Uc 46
Homefield Clo. NW10—38Sa 59
Homefield Clo. Epp—2Wc 15
Homefield Clo. Lea—93La 176
Homefield Clo. Swan—69Hd 132
Homefield Clo. Wey—84G 156
Homefield Gdns. N2—27Fb 41
Homefield Gdns. Mitc—68Eb 125
Homefield Gdns. Tad—92Ya 178
Homefield Pk. Sutt—79Db 145
Homefield Rise. Orp—74Wc 151
Homefield Rd. SW19—65Ab 124
Homefield Rd. W4—50Va 80
Homefield Rd. Brom—67Lc 129
Homefield Rd. Bush, Wat—15Ca 19
Homefield Rd. Coul & Cat —91Rb 181
Homefield Rd. Edgw—23Ta 39
Homefield Rd. Rad—9Ha 6
Homefield Rd. Rick—14F 16
Homefield Rd. Sev—94Gd 186
Homefield Rd. W on T—73Aa 141
Homefield Rd. Warl—91Yb 182
Homefield Rd. Wemb—35Ka 58
Homefield St. N1 —40Ub 63 (2H 195)
Home Gdns. Dag—34Ed 68
Home Gdns. Dart—58Nd 111
Home Hill. Swan—66Hd 132
Homeland Dri. Sutt—81Db 163
Homelands. Lea—93La 176
Homelands Dri. SE19—66Ub 127
Home Lea. Orp—78Vc 151
Homeleigh Rd. SE15—57Zb 106
Home Mead. Stan—25La 38
Homemead Clo. Grav—9D 114
Home Meadow. Slou—10G 52
Homemead Rd. Brom—71Pc 150
Homemead Rd. Croy—72Lb 146
Home Orchard. Dart—58Nd 111
Homepark Cotts. K Lan—2R 4
Home Pk. Industrial Est. K Lan —3R 4
Home Pk. Rd. SW19—63Bb 125
Home Pk. Wlk. King—70Ma 123
Homer Clo. Bexh—53Ed 110
Home Rd. SW11—54Gb 103
Homer Rd. E9—37Ac 64
Homer Rd. Croy—72Zb 148
Homer Row. W1—43Gb 81 (1E 196)
Homersham Rd. King—68Qa 123
Homers Rd. Wind—3B 94
Homer St. W1—43Gb 81 (1E 196)
Homerton Gro. E9—36Zb 64
Homerton High St. E9—36Zb 64
Homerton Rd. E9—36Bc 64
Homerton Row. E9—36Yb 64
Homerton Ter. E9—37Yb 64
Homesdale Clo. E11—29Jc 45
Homesdale Rd. Brom—70Lc 129
Homesdale Rd. Cat—95Tb 181
Homesdale Rd. Orp—73Uc 150
Homestall Rd. SE22—57Yb 106
Homestead Gdns. Esh—78Ga 142
Homestead Paddock. N14 —15Kb 24
Homestead Pk. NW2—34Va 60
Homestead Rd. SW6—52Bb 103
Homestead Rd. Cat—95Tb 181
Homestead Rd. Dag—33Bd 67
Homestead Rd. Orp—80Xc 151
Homestead Rd. Rick—17M 1

Homestead Rd.—Hyde Rd.

Homestead Rd. Stai—65K 119
Homestead, The. Dart—58Ld 111
Homestead Way. Croy—83Ec 166
Homewaters Av. Sun—67V 120
Home Way. Rick—18H 17
Homeway. Romf—23Rd 49
Homewood. Slou—4P 73
Homewood Clo. Hmptn—65Ba 121
Homewood Cres. Chst—65Uc 130
Homildon Ho. SE26—62Wb 127
Honduras St. EC1
—42Sb 83 (5D 194)
Honeybourne Rd. NW6—36Db 61
Honeybourne Way. Orp—74Tc 150
Honeybrook. Wal A—5Gc 13
Honeybrook Rd. SW12—59Lb 104
★Honey Clo. Brtwd—7Zd
Honeycroft. Lou—14Rc 28
Honeycroft Hill. Uxb—38N 55
Honeyden Rd. Sidc—65Ad 131
Honey Hill. Uxb—38P 55
Honey La. EC2—(3E 200)
Honey La. Wal A—5Gc 13
Honeypot Clo. NW9—28Pa 39
Honeypot La. Brtwd—20Wd 32
Honeypot La. Sev—91Rd 187
Honeypot La. Sev
Honeypot La. Stan & NW9
—24Ma 39
Honeypots Rd. Wok—94A 172
Honeypots Rd. Wok—10G 188
Honeysett Rd. N17—26Vb 43
Honeysuckle Clo. Brtwd—15Xd 32
Honeysuckle Clo. Romf—23Md 49
Honeysuckle Gdns. Croy
—74Zb 148
Honeysuckle La. N22—26Sb 43
Honeywell Rd. SW11—58Hb 103
Honeywood Clo. Pot B—5Fb 9
Honeywood Rd. NW10—40Va 60
Honeywood Rd. Iswth—56Ja 100
Honeywood Wlk. Cars—77Hb 145
Honister Clo. Stan—25Ka 38
Honister Gdns. Stan—24Ka 38
Honister Heights. Purl—86Tb 165
Honister Pl. Stan—25Ka 38
Honiton Rd. NW6—40Bb 61
Honiton Rd. Romf—30Fd 48
Honiton Rd. Well—54Vc 109
Honley Rd. SE6—59Dc 106
Honnor Rd. Stai—66M 119
Honor Oak Pk. SE23—58Yb 106
Honor Oak Rise. SE23—58Yb 106
Honor Oak Rd. SE23—60Yb 106
Hood Av. N14—16Kb 24
Hood Av. SW14—57Sa 101
Hood Av. Orp—71Xc 151
Hood Clo. Croy—74Rb 147
Hoodcote Gdns. N21—17Rb 25
Hood Ct. EC4—(3A 200)
Hood Rd. SW20—66Va 124
Hood Rd. Rain—40Hd 68
Hood Wlk. Romf—25Dd 48
★Hook End La. Brtwd—7Yd
★Hook End Rd. Brtwd—7Xd
Hooke Rd. Lea—97V 174
Hookers Rd. E17—27Zb 44
Hook Farm Rd. Brom—71Mc 149
Hookfield. Eps—85Sa 161
Hookfields. Grav—2A 136
Hook Gate. Enf—9Xb 11
Hook Grn. La. Dart—62Hd 132
Hook Grn. Rd. Grav—66Ae 135
Hook Heath Av. Wok—7E 188
Hook Heath Gdns. Wok—9C 188
Hook Heath Rd. Wok—9C 188
Hook Hill. S Croy—82Ub 165
Hook Hill La. Wok—9E 188
Hook Hill Pk. Wok—9E 188
Hooking Grn. Harr—29Da 37
Hook La. Pot B—4Hb 9
Hook La. Pot B—3Hb 9
Hook La. Romf—16Bd 29
Hook La. Well—56Vc 109
Hook Rise N. Surb—76Qa 143
Hook Rise S. Surb—76Qa 143
Hook Rd. Chess—78Ma 143
Hook Rd. Eps—80Sa 143
Hook Rd. Surb—75Na 143
Hooks Clo. SE15—53Xb 105
Hooks Hall Dri. Dag—34Ed 68
Hook, The. Barn—16Fb 23
Hook Wlk. Edgw—24Sa 39
Hookwood Rd. Orp—83Yc 169
Hooper Rd. E16—44Jc 85
Hooper's Ct. SW3
—47Hb 81 (2F 203)
Hooper St. E1—44Wb 83
Hoopers Yd. Sev—98Ld 187
Hoop La. NW11—31Bb 61
Hope Clo. SE12—62Kc 129
Hope Clo. Brtwd—11Fe 33
Hope Clo. Wfd G—23Lc 45
Hopedale Rd. SE7—51Kc 107
Hopefield Av. NW6—40Ab 60
Hopefield Av. Wey—84N 157
Hope Grn. Wat—5W 4
Hope Pk. Brom—66Hc 129
Hope Rd. Swans—58Be 113
Hope St. SW11—55Fb 103
Hopewell Dri. Grav—4H 137
Hopewell St. SE5—52Tb 105
Hopfields. Wok—88A 156
Hopgarden La. Sev—100Jd 186
Hop Gdns. WC2—45Nb 82 (4F 199)
Hopgood St. W12—46Ya 80
Hopkinsons Pl. NW1—39Jb 62
Hopkins St. W1—44Lb 82 (3C 198)
Hoppers Rd. N21—19Qb 24
Hoppett Rd. E4—19Gc 27
Hoppety, The. Tad—94Za 178
Hopping La. N1—37Rb 63
Hoppingwood Av. N Mald
—69Ua 124
Hoppit Rd. Wal A—5Dc 12
Hoppner Rd. Hay—40T 56
Hopton Gdns. N Mald—72Wa 144
Hopton Rd. SW16—64Nb 126
Hopton St. SE1—46Rb 83 (6C 200)
Hopwood Rd. SE17—51Tb 105
Hopwood Wlk. E8—38Wb 63
Horace Av. Romf—32Ed 68
Horace Rd. E7—35Kc 65
Horace Rd. Ilf—27Sc 46
Horace Rd. King—69Pa 123
Horatio St. E2—40Wb 63
Horatius Way. Croy—79Pb 146
Horbury Cres. W11—45Cb 81
Horbury M. W11—45Bb 81
Horder Rd. SW6—53Ab 102
Hordle Promenade E. SE15
—52Vb 105
Hordle Promenade N. SE15
—52Vb 105
Hordle Promenade S. SE15
—52Vb 105
Hordle Promenade W. SE15
—52Ub 105
Horizon Way. SE7—49Kc 85
Horley Clo. Bexh—57Cd 110
Horley Rd. SE9—63Nc 130
Hormead Rd. W9—42Bb 81
Hornbeam Av. Upm—35Qd 69
Hornbeam Clo. Borwd—11Qa 21
Hornbeam Clo. Brtwd—20De 33
Hornbeam Clo. Epp—9Uc 14
Hornbeam Cres. Bren—52Ka 100
Hornbeam Gro. E4—20Gc 27
Hornbeam La. E4—15Gc 27
Hornbeam La. Bexh—54Ed 110
Hornbeam Rd. Buck H—20Mc 27
Hornbeam Rd. Epp—9Tc 14
Hornbeam Rd. Hay—43Y 77
Hornbeams. St Alb—2Ba 5
Hornbeams Av. Enf—7Yb 12
Hornbeam Wlk. Rich—62Pa 123
Hornbeam Wlk. W on T—81V 158
Hornbeam Way. Brom—72Qc 150
Hornbill Clo. Uxb—44M 75
Hornbuckle Clo. Harr—33Fa 58
Hornby Clo. NW3—38Gb 61
Horncastle Clo. SE12—59Jc 107
Horncastle Rd. SE12—59Jc 107
Hornchurch Hill. Whyt—90Vb 165
Hornchurch Rd. Horn—32Jd 68
Horndean Clo. SW15—60Wa 102
Horndon Clo. Romf—25Ed 48
Horndon Grn. Romf—25Ed 48
Horndon Rd. Romf—25Ed 48
Horndon Rd. Stanf—2J 93
Horne Rd. Shep—70Q 120
Hornets, The. Wat—14X 19
Horne Way. SW15—54Ya 102
Hornfair Rd. SE7—51Mc 107
Hornford Way. Romf—31Gd 68
Horn Hill La. Ger X—22B 34
Hornhill Rd. Ger X & Rick—22E 34
Horniman Dri. SE23—60Xb 105
Horning Clo. SE9—63Nc 130
Horn La. SE10—49Jc 85
Horn La. W3—45Sa 79
Horn La. Wfd G—23Jc 45
Hornminster Glen. Horn—33Qd 69
Hornpark La. SE12—57Kc 107
Hornsby Rd. Grays—7C 92
Horns End Pl. Pinn—28Y 37
Hornsey La. N6—32Lb 62
Hornsey La. Gdns. N6—31Lb 62
Hornsey Pk. Rd. N8—27Pb 42
Hornsey Rise. N19—31Mb 62
Hornsey Rise Gdns. N19—31Mb 62
Hornsey Rd.—33Nb 62
N7 1-281 & 2-352
N19 remainder
Hornsey St. N7—36Pb 62
Hornshay St. SE15—51Yb 106
Horns Rd. Ilf—29Sc 46
Hornton Pl. W8—47Db 81
Hornton St. W8—47Cb 81
Horsa Clo. Wall—80Nb 146
Horsa Rd. SE12—59Lc 107
Horsa Rd. Eri—52Ed 110
Horse & Dolphin Yd. W1—(4E 198)
Horsecroft. Bans—89Bb 163
Horsecroft Clo. Orp—74Xc 151
Horsecroft Rd. Edgw—24Ta 39
Horse Fair. King—68Ma 123
Horseferry Pl. SE10—51Ec 106
Horseferry Rd. SW1
—49Mb 82 (4D 204)
Horseguards Av. SW1
—46Nb 82 (7F 199)
Horse Guards Rd. SW1
—46Mb 82 (7E 198)
Horse Hill. Che—4A 2
Horseleys. Rick—22F 34
Horsell Birch. Wok—3E 188
(in two parts)
Horsell Comn. Rd. Wok—2F 188
Horsell Ct. Cher—73K 139
Horsell Moor. Wok—89A 156
Horsell Moor. Wok—5G 188
Horsell Pk. Wok—89A 156
Horsell Pk. Wok—4G 188
Horsell Pk. Clo. Wok—4G 188
Horsell Rise. Wok—87A 156
Horsell Rise. Wok—3G 188
Horsell Rise. Clo. Wok—3G 188
Horsell Rd. N5—36Qb 62
Horsell Rd. Orp—67Xc 131
Horsell Vale. Wok—88A 156
Horsell Way. Wok—4F 188
Horselydown La. SE1
—46Vb 83 (1K 207)
★Horseman Ct. Brtwd—9Ud
Horseman Side. Brtwd—17Jd 30
Horsemoor Clo. Slou—49C 74
Horsenden Av. Gnfd—36Ha 58
Horsenden Cres. Gnfd—36Ha 58
Horsenden La. N. Gnfd—37Ga 58
Horsenden La. S. Gnfd—39Ja 58
Horse Ride. SW1—(1C 204)
Horse Ride. Cars—83Hb 163
Horse Ride. Epp—7Rc 14
Horse Shoe All. SE1—(6E 200)
Horseshoe Clo. NW2—33Xa 60
Horse Shoe Cres. N'holt—40Ca 57
Horse Shoe Grn. Sutt—75Db 145
Horseshoe Hill. Slou—5A 52
Horseshoe Hill. Wal A—5Lc 13
Horseshoe La. N20—18Za 22
Horse Shoe La. Enf—13Sb 25
Horseshoe La. Wat—4X 5
Horseshoe, The. Bans—87Cb 163
Horseshoe, The. Coul—85Mb 164
Horse Shoe Yd. W1—(4A 198)
Horsfeld Gdns. SE9—57Nc 108
Horsfeld Rd. SE9—57Mc 107
Horsford Rd. SW2—57Pb 104
Horsham Av. N12—22Gb 41
Horsham Clo. Orp—73Vc 151
Horsham Rd. Bexh—57Cd 110
Horsham Rd. Felt—58S 98
Horsley Clo. Eps—85Ta 161
Horsley Dri. Croy—80Ec 148
Horsley Rd. E4—19Ec 26
Horsley Rd. Brom—67Kc 129
Horsley Rd. Cob—94W 174
Horsley St. SE17—51Tb 105
Horsman St. SE5—51Sb 105
Horsmonden Rd. SE4—58Bc 106
Hortensia Rd. SW10—52Eb 103
Horticultural Pl. W4—50Ta 79
Horton Av. NW2—35Ab 60
Horton Bri. Rd. W Dray—46P 75
Horton Clo. W Dray—46Q 76
Horton Footpath. Eps—83Sa 161
Horton Gdns. Eps—83Sa 161
Horton Gdns. Slou—55B 96
Horton Hill. Eps—83Sa 161
Horton La. Eps—83Qa 161
Horton Rd. E8—37Xb 63
Horton Rd. Slou—54A 96
(Datchet)
Horton Rd. Slou—3N 95
(Datchet)
Horton Rd. Slou—54C 96
(Horton)
Horton Rd. Slou—55G 96
(Poyle)
Horton Rd. S Dar, Dart—69Sd 134
Horton Rd. Stai—56H 97
Horton Rd. W Dray—46N 75
Horton St. SE13—55Dc 106
Hortons Way. West—98Tc 184
Horton Way. F'ham, Dart
—73Pd 153
Hortus Rd. E4—19Ec 26
Hortus Rd. S'hall—47Ba 77
Hosack Rd. SW17—61Jb 126
Hoselands View. Long, Dart
—70Ae 135
Hoser Av. SE12—61Jc 129
Hosey Comn. Rd. West
—100Uc 184
Hosey Hill. West—99Uc 184
Hosier La. EC1—43Rb 83 (1B 200)
Hoskins Clo. E16—44Lc 85
Hoskins Clo. Hay—50V 76
Hoskins Rd. Oxt—100Gc 183
Hoskins St. SE10—50Fc 85
Hospital Bri. Rd. Twic—59Da 99
Hospital La. Iswth—57Ha 100
Hospital Rd. Houn—55Ca 99
Hospital Rd. Sev—93Ld 187
Hospital Rd. Sutt—83Db 163
Hotham Clo. E Mol—69Ca 121
Hotham Rd. SW15—55Ya 102
Hotham Rd. SW19—66Eb 125
Hotham St. E15—39Gc 65
Hothfield Pl. SE16—48Yb 84
Hotspur Rd. N'holt—40Ca 57
Hotspur St. SE11
—50Qb 82 (6K 205)
Hottsfield. Long, Dart—69Ae 135
Houblon Rd. Rich—57Na 101
Houblons Hill. Epp—3Yc 15
Houghton Clo. E8—37Vb 63
Houghton Clo. Hmptn—65Aa 121
Houghton Rd. N15—28Vb 43
Houghton St. WC2
—44Pb 82 (3J 199)
Houlder Cres. Croy—79Rb 147
Houndsden Rd. N21—16Pb 24
Houndsditch. EC3
—44Ub 83 (2J 201)
Houndsfield Rd. N9—17Xb 25
Hounslow Av. Houn—57Da 99
Hounslow Gdns. Houn—57Da 99
Hounslow Rd. Felt—60X 99
Hounslow Rd. Felt—63Z 121
(Hanworth)
Hounslow Rd. Twic—58Da 99
Houseman Way. SE5—52Tb 105
Houston Rd. SE23—61Ac 128
Hove Av. E17—29Bc 44
Hoveden Rd. NW2—36Ab 60
Hove Gdns. Sutt—74Db 145
Hoveton Rd. SE28—44Yc 87
Howard Av. Bex—60Yc 109
Howard Av. Eps—82Wa 162
Howard Av. Slou—3H 73
Howard Clo. N11—19Jb 24
Howard Clo. NW2—35Ab 60
Howard Clo. W3—44Ra 79
Howard Clo. Asht—90Pa 161
Howard Clo. Bush, Wat—17Ga 20
Howard Clo. Hmptn—66Ea 122
Howard Clo. Lea—95La 176
Howard Clo. Sun—65V 120
Howard Clo. Tad—97Va 178
Howard Clo. Wat—9W 4
Howard Dri. Borwd—14Ta 21
★Howard Lodge Rd. Brtwd—9Sd
Howard Pl. SW1—48Lb 82 (4B 204)
Howard Rd. E6—40Pc 66
Howard Rd. E11—34Gc 65
Howard Rd. E17—27Dc 44
Howard Rd. N15—30Ub 43
Howard Rd. N16—35Tb 63
Howard Rd. NW2—35Za 60
Howard Rd. SE20—67Yb 128
Howard Rd. SE25—71Wb 147
Howard Rd. Ashf—63M 119
Howard Rd. Bark—39Tc 66
Howard Rd. Brom—66Jc 129
Howard Rd. Coul—87Lb 164
Howard Rd. Dart—58Qd 111
Howard Rd. Ilf—35Rc 66
Howard Rd. Iswth—55Ha 100
Howard Rd. Lea—95W 174
Howard Rd. Lea
Howard Rd. N Mald—69Ua 124
Howard Rd. S'hall—44Da 77
Howard Rd. Surb—72Pa 143
Howard Rd. Upm—33Sd 70
Howards Clo. Lea—97T 174
Howards Clo. Pinn—26X 37
Howards Clo. Wok—92C 172
Howard's La. SW15—56Xa 102
Howards La. Wey—80H 139
Howards Rd. E13—41Jc 85
Howards Rd. Wok—92B 172
Howards Thicket. Ger X—3N 53
Howard St. Th Dit—73Ka 142
Howards Wood Dri. Ger X—33A 54
Howards Wood Dri. Ger X—3P 53
Howard Wlk. N2—28Eb 41
Howarth Rd. SE2—50Wc 87
Howberry Clo. Edgw—23Ma 39
Howberry Rd. Stan & Edgw
—23Ma 39
Howberry Rd. T Hth—67Tb 127
Howbury La. Eri—54Jd 110
Howbury Rd. SE15—55Yb 106
Howcroft Cres. N3—24Cb 41
Howcroft La. Gnfd—41Fa 78
Howden Clo. SE28—45Zc 87
Howden Ho. Houn—59Aa 99
Howden Rd. SE25—68Vb 127
Howden St. SE15—55Wb 105
Howe Clo. Romf—25Cd 48
Howell Clo. Romf—29Zc 47
Howell Hill Clo. Eps—83Ya 162
Howell Hill Gro. Eps—82Ya 162
Howells Clo. Sev—79Ud 154
Howell Wlk. SE17
—49Rb 83 (6C 206)
Howfield Pl. N17—27Vb 43
Howgate Rd. SW14—55Ta 101
Howick Pl. SW1—48Lb 82 (4C 204)
Howie St. SW11—52Gb 103
Howitt Rd. NW3—37Gb 61
Howland M. E. W1
—43Lb 82 (7C 192)
Howland St. W1—43Lb 82 (7B 192)
How La. Coul—91Hb 179
Howletts La. Ruis—29S 36
Howlett's Rd. SE24—58Sb 105
Howley Pl. W2—43Eb 81 (7A 190)
Howley Rd. Croy—76Rb 147
Hows Clo. Uxb—39L 55
Howsman Rd. SW13—51Wa 102
Howson Rd. SE4—56Ac 106
Howson Ter. Rich—58Na 101
Hows Rd. Uxb—39L 55
How's St. E2—40Vb 63 (1K 195)
Howton Pl. Bush, Wat—18Fa 20
How Wood. St Alb—1Da 5
Hoxton Mkt. N1—(4H 195)
Hoxton Sq. N1—41Ub 83 (4H 195)
Hoxton St. N1—39Ub 63 (1H 195)
Hoylake Cres. Uxb—33Q 56
Hoylake Gdns. Mitc—69Lb 126
Hoylake Gdns. Romf—24Qd 49
Hoylake Gdns. Ruis—32X 57
Hoylake Gdns. Wat—21Z 37
Hoylake Rd. W3—44Ua 80
Hoyland Clo. SE15—52Xb 105
Hoyle Rd. SW17—64Gb 125
Hoy St. E16—44Hc 85
Hubbard Rd. SE27—63Sb 127
Hubbards Chase. Horn—29Qd 49
Hubbards Clo. Horn—29Qd 49
Hubbards Rd. Rick—15F 16
Hubbard St. E15—39Gc 65
Hubert Gro. SW9—55Nb 104
Hubert Rd. E6—41Mc 85
Hubert Rd. Brtwd—20Xd 32
Hubert Rd. Rain—41Hd 88
Hubert Rd. Slou—8P 73
Hucknall Clo. Romf—23Pd 49
Huddart St. E3—43Bc 84
(in two parts)
Huddlestone Cres. Red
—100Mb 180
Huddlestone Rd. E7—35Hc 65
Huddlestone Rd. N7—34Lb 62
Huddlestone Rd. NW2—37Xa 60
Hudson Clo. Wat—8V 4
Hudson Pl. SE18—50Sc 86
Hudson Rd. Bexh—54Bd 109
Hudson Rd. Hay—51T 98
Hudson Rd. King—67Na 123
Hudsons Clo. Stanf—1M 93
Hudson's Pl. SW1
—49Kb 82 (5B 204)
Huggin Ct. EC4—(4E 200)
Huggin Hill. EC4—45Sb 83 (4E 200)
Hughan Rd. E15—36Fc 65
Hughenden Av. Harr—29Ka 38
Hughenden Gdns. N'holt—41Y 77
Hughenden Rd. N Mald—73Wa 144
Hughenden Rd. Slou—4H 73
Hughendon Ter. E15—35Ec 64
Hughes Rd. Ashf—65S 120
Hughes Rd. Grays—8C 92
Hughes Rd. Hay—45X 77
Hughes Wlk. Croy—73Sb 147
Hugh M. SW1—49Kb 82 (6A 204)
Hugh St. SW1—49Kb 82 (6A 204)
Hugo Gdns. Rain—37Jd 68
Hugon Rd. SW6—55Db 103
Hugo Rd. N19—35Lb 62
Huguenot Pl. SW18—57Eb 103
Huguenot Sq. SE15—55Xb 105
Hullbridge M. N1—39Tb 63
Hullets La. Brtwd—13Ud 32
Hull St. EC1—41Sb 83 (4D 194)
Hulse Av. Bark—37Tc 66
Hulse Av. Romf—25Dd 48
Hulsewood Clo. Dart—62Kd 133
Hulton Clo. Lea—95La 176
Hulverston Clo. Sutt—82Db 163
Humber Av. S Ock—44Vd 90
Humber Dri. Upm—30Td 50
Humber Rd. NW2—33Xa 60
Humber Rd. SE3—51Hc 107
Humberstone Rd. E13—41Lc 85
Humberton Clo. E9—36Ac 64
Humber Trading Est. NW2
—33Xa 60
Humber Way. Slou—49C 74
Humbolt Rd. W6—51Ab 102
Hume Av. Til—5D 114
Humes Av. W7—48Ga 78
Hume Way. Ruis—30W 36
Hummer Rd. Egh—63C 118
Humphrey Clo. Ilf—25Pc 46
Humphrey Clo. Lea—94Ea 176
Humphrey St. SE1
—50Vb 83 (7K 207)
Humphries Clo. Dag—35Bd 67
Hundred Acre. NW9—26Va 40
Hungerdown. E4—18Ec 26
Hungerford Av. Slou—3J 73
Hungerford La. WC2—(6F 199)
(in two parts)
Hungerford Rd. N7—37Mb 62
Hungry Hill La. Wok—96M 173
Hungry Hill La. Wok—98L 173
Hunsdon Clo. Dag—37Ad 67
Hunsdon Dri. Sev—95Kd 187
Hunsdon Rd. SE14—52Zb 106
Hunslett St. E2—41Yb 84
Hunston Rd. Mord—74Db 145
Hunter Av. Brtwd—16Ce 33
Hunter Clo. SE1—48Tb 83 (4G 207)
Hunter Clo. Borwd—15Sa 21
Hunter Clo. Pot B—5Db 9
Huntercombe Clo. M'head—4A 72
Huntercombe La. N. Slou &
M'head—3A 72
Huntercombe La. S. M'head
—6A 72
Huntercombe Spur. Slou—6A 72
Hunter Ct. Slou—3A 72
Huntercrombe Gdns. Wat—22Y 37
Hunter Dri. Horn—35Ld 69
Hunter Rd. SW20—67Ya 124
Hunter Rd. Ilf—36Rc 66
Hunter Rd. T Hth—69Tb 127
Hunters Clo. SW12—60Jb 104
Hunters Clo. Eps—85Sa 161
Hunters Clo. Hem—1C 2
Hunters Gro. Harr—28La 38
Hunters Gro. Hay—46W 76
Hunters Gro. Romf—22Dd 48
Hunters Hall Rd. Dag—35Cd 68
Hunters Hill. Ruis—34Y 57
Hunter's La. Wat—5V 4
Hunters Meadows. SE19
—63Ub 127
Hunters Ride. St Alb—3Ca 5
Hunter's Rd. Chess—76Na 143
Hunters Sq. Dag—35Cd 68
Hunter St. WC1—42Nb 82 (5G 193)
Hunter's Way. Croy—77Ub 147
Hunters Way. Enf—11Qb 24
Hunter Wlk. E13—40Jc 65
Hunter Wlk. Borwd—15Ta 21
Hunting Clo. Esh—77Ca 141
Huntingdon Clo. Mitc—69Nb 126
Huntingdon Gdns. Wor Pk
—76Ya 144
Huntingdon Rd. N2—27Gb 41
Huntingdon Rd. N9—18Yb 26
Huntingdon St. E16—44Hc 85
Huntingdon St. N1—38Pb 62
Huntingfield. Croy—80Bc 148
Huntingfield Rd. SW15—56Wa 102
Huntingfield Way. Egh—65F 118
Hunting Ga. Dri. Chess—80Na 143
Huntings Rd. Dag—37Cd 68
Huntley Av. Grav—58De 113
Huntley St. WC1—42Lb 82 (6D 192)
Huntley Way. SW20—68Wa 124
Huntly Dri. N3—23Cb 41
Huntly Rd. SE25—70Ub 127
Hunton Bri. Hill. K Lan—5S 4
Hunton St. E1—43Wb 83
Hunt Rd. Grav—2A 136
Hunt Rd. S'hall—48Ca 77
Hunt's Clo. SE3—54Jc 107
Hunt's Ct. WC2—45Mb 82 (5E 198)
Hunts La. E15—40Ec 64
Huntsman Rd. Ilf—23Wc 47
Huntsmans Clo. Felt—63X 121
Huntsmans Clo. Lea—96Fa 176
Huntsmans Dri. Upm—36Sd 70
Huntsman St. SE17
—49Ub 83 (6H 207)
Hunts Mead. Enf—13Zb 26
Huntsmead Clo. Chst—66Pc 130
Huntsmoor Rd. Eps—78Ta 143
Huntspill St. SW17—62Eb 125
Hunts Slip Rd. SE21—62Ub 127
Hunt St. W11—46Za 80
Huntsworth M. NW1
—42Hb 81 (5F 191)
Hurley Clo. W on T—75X 141
Hurley Rd. Gnfd—43Da 77
Hurlfield. Dart—62Ld 133
Hurlingham Gdns. SW6—55Bb 103
Hurlingham Rd. SW6—54Bb 103
Hurlingham Rd. Bexh—52Bd 109
Hurlock St. N5—34Rb 63
Hurlstone Rd. SE25—71Ub 147
Hurn Ct. Houn—54Z 99
Hurn Ct. Rd. Houn—54Z 99
Hurnford Clo. S Croy—82Ub 165
Huron Rd. SW17—61Jb 126
Hurren Clo. SE3—55Gc 107
Hurry Clo. E15—38Gc 65
Hurst Av. E4—21Cc 44
Hurst Av. N6—30Lb 42
Hurst Av. Stai—65K 119
Hurstbourne. Esh—79Ha 142
Hurstbourne Gdns. Bark—37Uc 66
Hurstbourne Rd. SE23—60Ac 106
Hurst Clo. E4—20Cc 26
Hurst Clo. NW11—30Db 41
Hurst Clo. Brom—74Hc 149
Hurst Clo. Chess—78Qa 143
Hurst Clo. N'holt—36Ba 57
Hurst Clo. Wok—8F 188
Hurstcourt Rd. Sutt—75Db 145
Hurstdene Av. Brom—74Hc 149
Hurstdene Gdns. N15—31Ub 63
Hurst Dri. Tad—98Wa 178
Hurst Dri. Wal X—6Zb 12
Hurstfield. Brom—71Jc 149
Hurstfield Cres. Hay—42U 76
Hurstfield Dri. M'head—4A 72
Hurstfield Rd. E Mol—69Ca 121
Hurst Gro. W on T—74V 140
Hurstlands Clo. Horn—31Ld 69
Hurst La. SE2—50Zc 87
Hurst La. E Mol—70Ea 122
Hurst La. Egh—68C 118
Hurst La. Eps—96Sa 177
Hurst La. Est. SE2—50Zc 87
Hurstleigh Gdns. Ilf—25Pc 46
Hurst Lodge. Wey—79T 140
Hurstmead Ct. Edgw—21Ra 39
Hurst Pk. Av. Horn—35Nd 69
Hurst Pl. Dart—58Ld 111
Hurst Rise. Barn—13Cb 23
Hurst Rd. E17—27Dc 44
Hurst Rd. N21—18Qb 24
Hurst Rd. Buck H—18Mc 27
Hurst Rd. Croy—77Tb 147
Hurst Rd. Eps—83Ta 161
Hurst Rd. Eps & Tad—95Ta 177
Hurst Rd. Eri—53Ed 110
Hurst Rd. Sidc & Bex—61Wc 131
Hurst Rd. Slou—3B 72
Hurst Rd. W on T & E Mol—71Y 141
Hurst Springs. Bex—60Ad 109
Hurst St. SE24—58Rb 105
Hurst View Rd. S Croy—80Ub 147
Hurst Way. Sev—99Ld 187
Hurst Way. S Croy—79Ub 147
Hurstway. Wok—86G 156
Hurstway Wlk. W11—45Za 80
Hurstwood Av. E18—28Kc 45
Hurstwood Av. Bex—60Ad 109
Hurstwood Av. Brtwd—17Xd 32
Hurstwood Av. Eri & Bexh
—53Gd 110
Hurstwood Dri. Brom—69Pc 130
Hurstwood Rd. NW11—28Ab 40
Hurtwood Rd. W on T—73Ba 141
Hurworth Rd. Slou—8N 73
Huson Clo. NW3—38Gb 61
Husseywell Cres. Brom—74Jc 149
Hutchings St. E14—47Cc 84
Hutchings Wlk. NW11—28Db 41
Hutchins Clo. E15—38Ec 64
Hutchinson Ter. Wemb—34Ma 59
Hutton Clo. Gnfd—36Fa 58
Hutton Clo. Wfd G—23Kc 45
Hutton Dri. Brtwd—17Ee 33
Hutton Gdns. Harr—24Ea 38
Hutton Gro. N12—22Db 41
Hutton La. Harr—24Ea 38
Hutton Rd. Brtwd—17Be 33
Hutton St. EC4—44Rb 83 (3B 200)
Hutton Village. Brtwd—17Fe 33
Hutton Wlk. Harr—24Ea 38
Huxbear St. SE4—57Bc 106
Huxley Clo. E10—33Ec 64
Huxley Clo. N'holt—39Aa 57
Huxley Clo. Uxb—42M 75
Huxley Dri. Romf—31Xc 67
Huxley Gdns. NW10—41Pa 79
Huxley Pde. N18—22Tb 43
Huxley Pl. N13—20Rb 25
Huxley Rd. E10—33Ec 64
Huxley Rd. N18—21Tb 43
Huxley Rd. Well—55Vc 109
Huxley Sayze. N18—22Tb 43
Huxley S. N18—22Tb 43
Huxley St. W10—41Ab 80
Hyacinth Clo. Hmptn—65Ca 121
Hyacinth Ct. Pinn—27Y 37
Hyacinth Rd. SW15—60Wa 102
Hyburn Clo. St Alb—2Ba 5
Hycliffe Gdns. Chig—21Sc 46
Hyde Av. Pot B—5Db 9
Hyde Clo. E13—40Jc 65
Hyde Clo. Barn—13Bb 23
Hyde Cres. NW9—29Ua 40
Hydefield Clo. N21—18Tb 25
Hydefield Ct. N9—19Ub 25
Hyde La. SW11—53Gb 103
Hyde La. Hem—1C 2
Hyde La. St Alb—1Fa 6
Hyde La. Wok—92R 174
Hyde Pk. Av. N21—19Sb 25
Hyde Pk. Corner. SW1 & W1
—47Jb 82 (1J 203)
Hyde Pk. Cres. W2
—44Gb 81 (3D 196)
Hyde Pk. Gdns. N21—18Sb 25
Hyde Pk. Gdns. W2
—45Fb 81 (4C 196)
Hyde Pk. Gdns. M. W2
—45Fb 81 (4C 196)
Hyde Pk. Ga. SW7
—47Eb 81 (2A 202)
(in two parts)
Hyde Pk. Ga. M. SW7
—47Eb 81 (2A 202)
Hyde Pk. Pl. W2—45Gb 81 (4E 196)
Hyde Pk. Sq. W2—44Gb 81 (3D 196)
Hyde Pk. Sq. M. W2—(3D 196)
Hyde Pk. St. W2—44Gb 81 (3D 196)
Hyde Pk. Towers. W2—(5A 196)
Hyde Pl. Twic—58Ma 101
Hyde Rd. N1—39Tb 63
(in two parts)

Hyde Rd.—Josephine Av.

Hyde Rd. Bexh—54Bd 109
Hyde Rd. Rich—57Pa 101
Hyde Rd. S Croy—85Ub 165
Hyde Rd. Wat—12W 18
Hyder Rd. Grays—8E 92
Hydeside Gdns. N9—19Vb 25
Hydes Pl. N1—38Rb 63
Hyde St. SE8—51Cc 106
Hyde Ter. Ashf—65U 120
Hyde, The. NW9—29Ua 40
Hydethorpe Av. N9—19Vb 25
Hydethorpe Rd. SW12—60Lb 104
Hyde Vale. SE10—52Ec 106
Hyde Wlk. Mord—73Cb 145
Hyde Way. N9—19Vb 25
Hyde Way. Hay—49V 76
Hyland Clo. Horn—31Kd 69
Hylands Clo. Eps—87Sa 161
Hylands M. Eps—87Sa 161
Hylands Rd. E17—26Fc 45
Hylands Rd. Eps—87Sa 161
Hyland Way. Horn—31Kd 69
Hylle Clo. Wind—3C 94
Hylton St. SE18—49Vc 87
Hyndewood. SE23—62Zb 128
Hyndman St. SE15—51Xb 105
Hynton Rd. Dag—33Yc 67
Hyperion Pl. Eps—81Ta 161
Hyrstdene. S Croy—78Rb 147
Hyson Rd. SE16—50Xb 83
Hythe Av. Bexh—52Ad 109
Hythe Clo. N18—21Wb 43
Hythe Clo. Orp—70Yc 131
Hythe End Rd. Wray, Stai—61B 118
Hythe Field Av. Egh—65F 118
Hythe Pk. Rd. Egh—64E 118
Hythe Rd. NW10—41Va 80
Hythe Rd. Stai—64F 118
Hythe Rd. T Hth—68Tb 127
Hythe St. Dart—58Nd 111
Hythe, The. Stai—64G 118
Hyver Hill. NW7—16Ta 21

Ian Sq. Enf—11Zb 26
Ibbetson Path. Lou—13Rc 28
Ibbotson Av. E16—44Hc 85
Ibbott St. E1—42Yb 84
Iberian Av. Wall—77Mb 146
Ibis La. W4—53Sa 101
Ibscott Clo. Dag—37Ed 68
Ibsley Gdns. SW15—60Wa 102
Ibsley Way. Barn—14Gb 23
Iceland Rd. E3—39Cc 64
Ickburgh Rd. E5—34Xb 63
Ickenham Clo. Ruis—33T 56
Ickenham Grn. Uxb—32R 56
Ickenham Rd. Uxb—33S 56
Ickleton Rd. SE9—63Nc 130
Icklingham Rd. Cob—84Y 159
Icknield Dri. Ilf—29Rc 46
Ickworth Pk. Rd. E17—28Ac 44
Ida Rd. N15—28Tb 43
Ida St. E14—44Ec 84
Iden Clo. Brom—69Gc 129
Idlecombe Rd. SW17—65Jb 126
Idleigh Ct. Rd. Long, Dart & Grav—75De 155
Idmiston Rd. E15—35Hc 65
Idmiston Rd. SE27—62Sb 127
Idmiston Rd. Wor Pk—73Va 144
Idmiston Sq. Wor Pk—73Va 144
Idol La. EC3—45Ub 83 (5H 201)
Idonia St. SE8—52Cc 106
Iffley Clo. Uxb—38M 55
Iffley Rd. W6—48Xa 80
Ifield Rd. SW10—51Db 103
Ifield Rd. Grav—78Fe 155
Ifield Way. Grav—5F 136
★Ightham By-Pass. Sev—93Yd
Ightham Rd. Eri—52Cd 110
Ikona Ct. Wey—78S 140
Ilbert St. W10—41Za 80
Ilchester Gdns. W2—45Db 81
Ilchester Pl. W14—48Bb 81
Ilchester Rd. Dag—36Xc 67
Ildersley Gro. SE21—61Tb 127
Ilderton Rd.—50Yb 84
SE16 1-187 & 2-132
SE15 remainder
Ilex Clo. Egh—6M 117
Ilex Clo. Sun—68Y 121
Ilex Rd. NW10—37Va 60
Ilex Way. SW16—64Qb 126
Ilford Hill. Ilf—34Qc 66
Ilford La. Ilf—34Rc 66
Ilfracombe Cres. Horn—35Ld 69
Ilfracombe Gdns. Romf—31Xc 67
Ilfracombe Rd. Brom—62Hc 129
Iliffe St. SE17—50Rb 83 (7C 206)
Iliffe Yd. SE17—(7C 206)
Ilkley Clo. SE19—65Tb 127
Ilkley Rd. E16—43Lc 85
Ilkley Rd. Wat—22Z 37
Illingworth. Wind—5C 94
Illingworth Clo. Mitc—69Fb 125
Illingworth Way. Enf—15Ub 25
Ilmington Rd. Harr—30Ma 39
Ilminster Gdns. SW11—56Gb 103
Imber Clo. N14—17Lb 24
Imber Gro. Esh—73Fa 142
Imber Pk. Rd. Esh—74Fa 142
Imber St. N1—39Tb 63 (1F 195)
Imperial Clo. Harr—30Ca 37
Imperial Dri. Grav—4H 137
Imperial Dri. Harr—31Ca 57
Imperial M. E6—40Mc 65
Imperial Rd. N22—25Nb 42
Imperial Rd. SW6—53Db 103
Imperial Rd. Felt—59U 98
Imperial Rd. Wind—5E 94
Imperial Sq. SW6—53Db 103
Imperial St. E3—41Ec 84
Imperial Way. Chst—63Sc 130
Imperial Way. Croy—79Qb 146
Imperial Way. Harr—30Na 39
Imperial Way. Wat—11Y 19

Inca Dri. SE9—59Rc 108
Ince Rd. W on T—79U 140
Inchmery Rd. SE6—61Dc 128
Inchwood. Croy—77Dc 148
Independents Rd. SE3—55Hc 107
Inderwick Rd. N8—29Pb 42
Indescon Ct. E14—47Dc 84
India Rd. Slou—7M 73
India St. EC3—44Vb 83 (3K 201)
India Way. W12—45Xa 80
Indus Rd. SE7—52Lc 107
Industry Ter. SW9—55Qb 104
Ingal Rd. E13—42Jc 85
Ingate Pl. SW8—53Kb 104
Ingatestone Rd. E12—32Lc 65
Ingatestone Rd. SE25—70Xb 127
★Ingatestone Rd. Ing—4Be
Ingatestone Rd. Wfd G—24Kc 45
Ingelow Rd. SW8—54Kb 104
Ingels Mead. Epp—1Vc 15
Ingersoll Rd. W12—46Xa 80
Ingersoll Rd. Enf—10Yb 12
Ingestre Pl. W1—44Lb 82 (3C 198)
Ingestre Rd. E7—35Jc 65
Ingestre Rd. NW5—35Kb 62
Ingham Clo. S Croy—81Zb 166
Ingham Rd. NW6—35Cb 61
Ingham Rd. S Croy—81Yb 166
Inglebert St. EC1 —41Qb 82 (3K 193)
Ingleboro Dri. Purl—85Tb 165
Ingleborough St. SW9—54Qb 104
Ingleby Dri. Harr—34Fa 58
Ingleby Gdns. Chig—20Xc 29
Ingleby Rd. N7—34Nb 62
Ingleby Rd. Dag—37Dd 68
Ingleby Rd. Grays—8D 92
Ingleby Rd. Ilf—32Rc 66
Ingleby Way. Chst—64Qc 130
Ingleby Way. Wall—81Mb 164
Ingle Clo. Pinn—27Aa 37
Ingledew Rd. SE18—50Tc 86
Inglefield. Pot B—2Cb 9
Ingleglen. Horn—31Qd 69
Ingleglen. Slou—6F 52
Inglehurst. Wey—82K 157
Inglehurst Gdns. Ilf—29Pc 46
Inglemere Rd. SE23—62Zb 128
Inglemere Rd. Mitc—66Hb 125
Inglesham Wlk. E9—37Bc 64
Ingleside Clo. Beck—66Cc 128
Ingleside Gro. SE3—51Hc 107
Inglethorpe St. SW6—53Za 102
Ingleton Av. Well—57Wc 109
Ingleton Rd. N18—23Wb 43
Ingleton Rd. Cars—81Gb 163
Ingleton St. SW9—54Qb 104
Ingleway. N12—23Fb 41
Inglewood. Croy—81Ac 166
Inglewood. Ilf—23Vc 47
Inglewood. Wok—6E 188
Inglewood Clo. Horn—35Md 69
Inglewood Copse. Brom —68Pc 130
Inglewood Rd. NW6—36Cb 61
Inglewood Rd. Bexh—56Fd 110
Inglis Rd. W5—45Pa 79
Inglis Rd. Croy—74Vb 147
Inglis St. SE5—53Rb 105
Ingoldsby Rd. Grav—10G 114
Ingram Av. NW11—31Eb 61
Ingram Clo. SE11 —49Pb 82 (5J 205)
Ingram Clo. Stan—22La 38
Ingram Rd. N2—28Gb 41
Ingram Rd. Dart—60Nd 111
Ingram Rd. Grays—49Ee 91
Ingram Rd. T Hth—67Sb 127
Ingrams Clo. W on T—78Y 141
Ingram Way. Gnfd—39Fa 58
Ingrave Rd. Brtwd—19Zd 33
Ingrave Rd. Romf—28Gd 48
Ingrave St. SW11—55Fb 103
Ingrebourne Gdns. Upm—32Sd 70
Ingrebourne Rd. Rain—42Kd 89
Ingress Gdns. Grnh—57Zd 113
Ingress St. W4—50Ua 80
Ingreway. Romf—23Rd 49
Inigo Jones Rd. SE7—52Nc 108
Inigo Pl. WC2—(4F 199)
Inkerman Rd. NW5—37Kb 62
Inkerman Rd. Wind—9D 72
Inkerman Rd. Wok—6B 188
Inkerman Way. Wok—6B 188
Inks Grn. E4—22Ec 44
Inman Rd. NW10—39Ua 60
Inman Rd. SW18—59Eb 103
Inmans Row. Wfd G—21Jc 45
Inner Circ. NW1—41Jb 82 (4H 191)
Inner Pk. Rd. SW19—61Za 124
Inner Ring E. Houn—55R 98
Inner Ring W. Houn—55Q 98
Inner Temple La. EC4 —44Qb 82 (3K 199)
Innes Clo. SW20—68Ab 124
Innes Gdns. SW15—58Xa 102
Innis Ho. SE17—(7H 207)
Inniskilling Rd. E13—40Lc 65
Innis Yd. Croy—76Sb 147
Inskip Clo. E10—33Dc 64
Inskip Dri. Horn—32Nd 69
Inskip Rd. Dag—32Zc 67
Institute Pl. E8—36Xb 63
Institute Rd. Epp—1Zc 15
Instone Clo. Wall—80Nb 146
Instone Rd. Dart—59Md 111
Insurance St. WC1 —41Qb 82 (4K 193)
Integer Gdns. E11—31Fc 65
International Av. Houn—50Y 77
International Trading Est. S'hall—48X 77
Inverary Pl. SE18—51Tc 108
Inver Clo. E5—33Yb 64
Inverclyde Gdns. Romf—28Zc 47
Inver Ct. W2—44Db 81
Inveresk Gdns. Wor Pk—76Wa 144

Inverforth Clo. NW3—33Eb 61
Inverforth Rd. N11—22Kb 42
Inverine Rd. SE7—50Kc 85
Invermore Pl. SE18—49Sc 86
Inverness Dri. Ilf—23Uc 46
Inverness Gdns. W8—46Db 81
Inverness M. W2—45Db 81
Inverness Pl. W2—45Db 81
Inverness Rd. N18—22Xb 43
Inverness Rd. Enf—11Ub 25
Inverness Rd. Houn—56Ba 99
Inverness Rd. S'hall—49Aa 77
Inverness Rd. Wor Pk—74Za 144
Inverness St. NW1—39Kb 62
Inverness Ter. W2—44Db 81
Inverton Rd. SE15—56Zb 106
Invicta Clo. Chst—64Qc 130
Invicta Gro. N'holt—41Ba 77
Invicta Rd. SE3—52Jc 107
Invicta Rd. Dart—58Rd 111
Inville Rd. SE17—50Tb 83 (7G 207)
Inville Wlk. SE17—50Tb 83
Inwood Av. Coul—92Qb 180
Inwood Av. Houn—55Ea 100
Inwood Clo. Croy—75Ac 148
Inwood Ct. W on T—75Y 141
Inwood Rd. Houn—56Da 99
Inworth St. SW11—54Gb 103
Iona Clo. SE6—59Cc 106
Iona Cres. Slou—4C 72
Ion Sq. E2—40Wb 63
Ipswich Rd. SW17—65Jb 126
Ipswich Rd. Slou—4D 72
Ireland Yd. EC4—44Rb 83 (3C 200)
Irene Rd. SW6—53Cb 103
Irene Rd. Cob—86Da 159
Irene Rd. Orp—73Vc 151
Ireton Av. W on T—75U 140
Ireton Ho. SW9—54Qb 104
Ireton Pl. Grays—49Ce 91
Ireton Rd. N19—33Mb 62
Iris Av. Bexh & Bex—57Ad 109
Iris Clo. Brtwd—15Xd 32
Iris Clo. Croy—74Zb 148
Iris Clo. Surb—73Pa 143
Iris Ct. Pinn—27Y 37
Iris Cres. Bexh—51Bd 109
Iris Path. Romf—24Ld 49
Iris Rd. Eps—78Ra 143
Iris Way. E4—23Bc 44
Irkdale Av. Enf—11Vb 25
Iron Bri. Rd. W Dray—46Q 76
Iron Mill La. Dart—56Gd 110
Iron Mill Pl. SW18—58Db 103
Iron Mill Pl. Dart—56Hd 110
Iron Mill Rd. SW18—58Db 103
Ironmonger La. EC2 —44Tb 83 (3E 200)
Ironmonger Row. EC1 —41Sb 83 (4E 194)
Irons Way. Romf—24Ed 48
Irvine Av. Harr—27Ja 38
Irvine Clo. N20—19Gb 23
Irvine Gdns. S Ock—44Vd 90
Irvine Way. Orp—73Vc 151
Irving Av. N'holt—39Z 57
Irving Gro. SW9—54Pb 104
Irving Rd. W14—48Za 80
Irving St. WC2—45Mb 82 (5E 198)
Irving Wlk. Swans—59Ae 113
Irving Way. NW9—30Va 40
Irving Way. Swan—68Fd 132
Irwin Av. SE18—52Uc 108
Irwin Gdns. NW10—39Xa 60
Isabella Dri. Orp—77Sc 150
Isabella Rd. E9—36Yb 64
Isabella St. SE1—46Rb 83 (7B 200)
Isabel St. SW9—53Pb 104
Isambard Clo. Uxb—42M 75
Isard Ho. Brom—74Kc 149
Isel Way. SE22—57Ub 105
Isham Rd. SW16—68Nb 126
Isis Clo. SW15—56Ya 102
Isis Clo. Ruis—30S 36
Isis Dri. Upm—30Ud 50
Isis St. SW18—61Eb 125
Island Clo. Stai—63G 118
Island Farm Av. E Mol—71Ba 141
Island Farm Rd. E Mol—71Ba 141
Island Rd. Mitc—66Hb 125
Island Row. E14—44Bc 84
Isla Rd. SE18—51Sc 108
Islay Gdns. Houn—57Z 99
Islay Wlk. N1—37Sb 63
Isledon Rd. N7—34Qb 62
Islehurst Clo. Chst—67Qc 130
Isleworth Promenade. Twic —56Ka 100
Islington Grn. N1 —39Rb 63 (1B 194)
Islington High St. N1 —40Qb 62 (2A 194)
Islington Pk. St. N1—38Qb 62
Islip Gdns. Edgw—24Ta 39
Islip Gdns. N'holt—38Aa 57
Islip Mnr. Rd. N'holt—38Aa 57
Islip St. NW5—36Lb 62
Ismailia Rd. E7—38Kc 65
★Ismays Rd. Sev—96Xd
Isom Clo. E13—41Kc 85
Istead Rise. Grav—6B 136
Ivanhoe Clo. Uxb—43M 75
Ivanhoe Dri. Harr—27Ja 38
Ivanhoe Rd. SE5—55Vb 105
Ivanhoe Rd. Houn—55Z 99
Ivatt Pl. W14—50Bb 81
Ivatt Way. N17—27Rb 43
Iveagh Av. NW10—40Qa 59
Iveagh Clo. E9—39Zb 64
Iveagh Clo. NW10—40Qa 59
Iveagh Clo. N'wd—25R 36
Iveagh Ct. Beck—69Ec 128
Iveagh Rd. Wok—6C 188
Ivedon Rd. Well—54Yc 109
Ive Farm Clo. E10—33Cc 64
Ive Farm La. E10—33Cc 64
Iveley Rd. SW4—54Lb 104

Iverdale Clo. Iver—45E 74
Ivere Dri. Barn—16Db 23
Iverhurst Clo. Bexh—57Zc 109
Iver La. Iver & Uxb—44J 75
Iverna Ct. W8—48Cb 81
Iverna Gdns. W8—48Cb 81
Iverna Gdns. Felt—57T 98
Iver Rd. Brtwd—16Xd 32
Iver Rd. Iver—44J 75
Iverson Rd. NW6—37Bb 61
Ivers Way. Croy—80Dc 148
Ives Gdns. Romf—28Hd 48
Ives Rd. E16—43Gc 85
Ives Rd. Slou—48B 74
Ives St. SW3—49Gb 81 (5E 202)
Ivestor Ter. SE23—59Yb 106
Ivimey St. E2—41Wb 83
Ivinghoe Clo. Enf—11Ub 25
Ivinghoe Clo. Wat—7Z 5
Ivinghoe Rd. Bush, Wat—17Fa 20
Ivinghoe Rd. Dag—36Xc 67
Ivinghoe Rd. Rick—17J 17
Ivor Gro. SE9—60Rc 108
Ivor Pl. NW1—42Hb 81 (6F 191)
Ivor St. NW1—38Lb 62
Ivorydown. Brom—63Jc 129
Ivybridge La. WC2 —45Nb 82 (5G 199)
Ivy Chimneys Rd. Epp—4Uc 14
Ivychurch Clo. SE20—66Yb 128
Ivychurch La. SE17 —50Vb 83 (7K 207)
Ivy Clo. Dart—58Qd 111
Ivy Clo. Grav—2E 136
Ivy Clo. Harr—35Ba 57
Ivy Clo. Pinn—31Y 57
Ivy Clo. Sun—68Y 121
Ivy Cres. W4—49Sa 79
Ivy Cres. Slou—5D 72
Ivydale Rd. SE15—55Zb 106
Ivydale Rd. Cars—75Hb 145
Ivyday Gro. SW16—62Pb 126
Ivydene. E Mol—71Ba 141
Ivydene Clo. Sutt—77Eb 145
Ivydene Rd. E8—38Wb 63
Ivy Gdns. N8—30Nb 42
Ivy Gdns. Mitc—69Mb 126
Ivy Ho. La. Sev—90Fd 170
Ivyhouse Rd. Dag—37Zc 67
Ivyhouse Rd. Uxb—34R 56
Ivy La. Houn—56Ba 99
Ivy La. Sev—88Ad 169
Ivy La. Wok—90D 156
Ivy Lodge La. Romf—25Rd 49
Ivymount Rd. SE27—62Qb 126
Ivy Rd. E16—44Jc 85
Ivy Rd. E17—30Cc 44
Ivy Rd. N14—17Lb 24
Ivy Rd. NW2—35Ya 60
Ivy Rd. SE4—56Bc 106
Ivy Rd. Houn—56Da 99
Ivy Rd. Surb—74Qa 143
Ivy St. N1—40Ub 63 (1H 195)
Ivy Vs. Grnh—57Wd 112
Ivy Wlk. Dag—37Ad 67
Ixworth Pl. SW3—50Gb 81 (7D 202)
Izane Rd. Bexh—56Bd 109

Jackass La. Kes—78Kc 149
Jack Barnett Way. N22—26Pb 42
Jack Cornwell St. E12—35Qc 66
Jackets La. Uxb & N'wd—24Q 36
Jacketts Field. Abb L, Wat—3V 4
Jacklin Grn. Wfd G—21Jc 45
Jackman M. NW10—34Ua 60
Jackmans La. Wok—7D 188
Jackman St. E8—39Xb 63
Jackson Clo. Eps—86Ta 161
Jackson Clo. Uxb—38N 55
Jackson Rd. N7—35Pb 62
Jackson Rd. Bark—39Tc 66
Jackson Rd. Barn—16Gb 23
Jackson Rd. Brom—75Pc 150
Jackson Rd. Gnfd—39Ja 58
Jackson Rd. Uxb—38N 55
Jacksons La. N6—31Kb 62
Jackson's Pl. Croy—74Ub 147
Jackson St. SE18—51Qc 108
Jackson Way. S'hall—47Da 77
Jack Walker Ct. N5—35Rb 63
Jacob Clo. Wind—3C 94
Jacob's Ladder. Warl—91Xb 181
Jacob St. SE1—47Wb 83
Jacob's Well M. W1 —44Jb 82 (2J 197)
Jacob's Well Rd. Guild—100A 172
Jacqueline Clo. N'holt—39Aa 57
Jaffray Rd. Brom—70Mc 129
Jaggard Way. SW12—59Hb 103
Jago Clo. SE18—51Sc 108
Jago Wlk. SE5—52Tb 105
Jail La. West—87Mc 167
Jamacia Rd. T Hth—72Rb 147
Jamaica Rd. SE1 & SE16 —47Vb 83 (2K 207)
Jamaica St. E1—43Yb 84
James Av. NW2—36Ya 60
James Av. Dag—32Bd 67
James Bedford Clo. Pinn—26Y 37
James Boswell Clo. SW16 —63Qb 126
James Clo. E13—40Jc 65
James Clo. NW11—30Ab 40
James Clo. Bush, Wat—15Aa 19
James Clo. Romf—29Jd 48
James Gdns. N22—24Rb 43
James La.—31Ec 64
E11 27-55
E10 remainder
James Martin Clo. Uxb—30J 35
Jameson St. W8—46Cb 81
James Pl. N17—25Vb 43
James Rd. Dart—59Jd 110
James's Cotts. Rich—52Qa 101
James St. W1—44Jb 82 (2J 197)
James St. WC2—45Nb 82 (3G 199)

James St. Bark—38Sc 66
James St. Enf—15Vb 25
James St. Epp—1Wc 15
James St. Houn—55Fa 100
James St. Wind—3H 95
Jamestown Rd. NW1—39Kb 62
Jamnagar Clo. Stai—65H 119
Jane St. E1—44Xb 83
Janet St. E14—48Cc 84
Janeway Pl. SE16—47Xb 83
Janeway St. SE16—47Wb 83
Janmead. Brtwd—17De 33
Janoway Hill La. Wok—7F 188
Jansen Wlk. SW11—55Fb 103
Janson Clo. E15—36Gc 65
Janson Rd. E15—36Gc 65
Jansons Rd. N15—27Ub 43
Japan Cres. N4—31Pb 62
Japan Rd. Romf—30Zc 47
Japonica Clo. Wok—6F 188
Jarrah Cotts. Purf—51Td 112
Jarrett Clo. SW2—60Rb 105
Jarrow Clo. Mord—71Db 145
Jarrow Rd. N17—28Xb 43
Jarrow Rd. SE16—49Yb 84
Jarrow Rd. Romf—30Yc 47
Jarrow Way. E9—35Bc 64
Jarvis Clo. Barn—15Za 22
Jarvis Rd. SE22—56Ub 105
Jarvis Rd. S Croy—79Tb 147
Jasmine Clo. Orp—75Rc 150
Jasmine Clo. Wok—4C 188
Jasmine Gdns. Croy—76Dc 148
Jasmine Gdns. Harr—33Ca 57
Jasmine Gro. SE20—67Xb 127
Jasmine Ter. W Dray—47Q 76
Jasmine Way. E Mol—70Ga 122
Jasmin Rd. Eps—78Ra 143
Jason Clo. Brtwd—21Vd 50
Jason Clo. Wey—78S 140
Jason Ct. W1—(2J 197)
Jason Wlk. SE9—63Qc 130
Jasper Clo. Enf—10Yb 12
Jasper Pas. SE19—65Vb 127
Jasper Rd. SE19—65Vb 127
Javelin Way. N'holt—41Z 77
Jaycroft. Enf—11Qb 24
Jay M. SW7—47Eb 81 (2A 202)
Jebb Av. SW2—58Nb 104
Jebb St. E3—40Cc 64
Jedburgh Rd. E13—41Lc 85
Jedburgh St. SW11—56Jb 104
Jeddo Rd. W12—47Va 80
Jefferson Clo. W13—48Ka 78
Jefferson Clo. Ilf—29Rc 46
Jefferson Clo. Slou—49C 74
Jeffreys Rd. SW4—54Nb 104
Jeffreys Rd. Enf—14Ac 26
Jeffrey's St. NW1—38Lb 62
Jeffreys Wlk. SW4—54Nb 104
Jeffs Rd. Sutt—77Bb 145
Jegrove Ct. EC1—(1A 200)
Jeken Rd. SE9—56Lc 107
Jelf Rd. SW2—57Qb 104
Jellicoe Av. Grav—2E 136
Jellicoe Gdns. Stan—23Ja 38
(in two parts)
Jellicoe Rd. E13—42Jc 85
Jellicoe Rd. N17—24Tb 43
Jengar Clo. Sutt—77Db 145
Jenkins Av. St Alb—2Aa 5
Jenkins La. Bark—40Sc 66
Jenkins Rd. E13—42Kc 85
Jenner Pl. SW13—51Xa 102
Jenner Rd. N16—34Vb 63
Jennery La. Slou—1A 72
Jennett Rd. Croy—76Qb 146
Jennifer Rd. Brom—62Hc 129
Jenningham Dri. Grays—46Ce 91
Jennings Rd. SE22—58Vb 105
Jennings Way. Barn—13Ya 22
Jenningtree Rd. Eri—52Kd 111
Jenningtree Way. Belv—47Ed 88
Jenny Path. Romf—24Md 49
Jenson Way. SE19—66Vb 127
Jenton Av. Bexh—54Ad 109
Jephson Rd. E7—38Lc 65
Jephson St. SE5—53Tb 105
Jephtha Rd. SW18—58Cb 103
Jeppos La. Mitc—70Hb 125
Jerdan Pl. SW6—52Cb 103
Jeremiah St. E14—44Dc 84
Jeremy's Grn. N18—21Xb 43
Jermyn St. SW1—46Lb 82 (6B 198)
Jernigham Av. Ilf—26Rc 46
Jerningham Rd. SE14—54Ac 106
Jerome Cres. NW8 —42Gb 81 (5D 190)
Jerome St. E1—42Vb 83 (7K 195)
Jerrard St. SE13—55Dc 106
Jerrold St. N1—40Ub 63 (2J 195)
Jersey Av. Stan—26La 38
Jersey Dri. Orp—72Tc 150
Jersey Ho. N1—37Sb 63
Jersey Rd. E11—32Fc 65
Jersey Rd. E16—44Kc 85
Jersey Rd. SW17—65Kb 126
Jersey Rd. W7—47Ja 78
Jersey Rd. Houn & Islwth—53Da 99
Jersey Rd. Ilf—35Rc 66
Jersey Rd. Rain—38Jd 68
Jersey St. E2—41Xb 83
Jerusalem Pas. EC1 —42Rb 83 (6B 194)
Jervis Av. Enf—7Ac 12
Jervis Ct. W1—(3A 198)
Jerviston Gdns. SW16—65Qb 126
Jeskyns Rd. Grav—9E 136
Jesmond Av. Wemb—37Pa 59
Jesmond Rd. Croy—73Vb 147
Jesmond Rd. Grays—46Fe 91
Jesmond Way. Stan—22Na 39
Jessam Av. E5—32Xb 63
Jessamine Pl. Dart—59Sd 112
Jessamine Rd. W7—46Ha 78
Jessamy Rd. Wey—76R 140
Jessel Dri. Lou—11Sc 28

Jesse Rd. E10—32Ec 64
Jessica Rd. SW18—58Eb 103
Jessiman Ter. Shep—71Q 140
Jessop Rd. SE24—56Sb 105
Jessops Way. Croy—72Lb 146
Jessup Clo. SE18—49Sc 86
Jetstar Way. N'holt—41Aa 77
Jevington Way. SE12—60Kc 107
Jewel Rd. E17—27Cc 44
Jewels Hill. Warl—85Jc 167
Jewry St. EC3—44Vb 83 (3K 201)
Jew's Row. SW18—56Eb 103
Jews Wlk. SE26—63Xb 127
Jeymer Av. NW2—36Xa 60
Jeymer Dri. Gnfd—39Ea 58
(in two parts)
Jeypore Pas. SW18—58Eb 103
Jeypore Rd. SW18—58Eb 103
Jillian Clo. Hmptn—66Ca 121
Joan Cres. SE9—59Mc 107
Joan Gdns. Dag—33Ad 67
Joan Rd. Dag—33Ad 67
Joan St. SE1—46Rb 83 (7B 200)
Jocelyn Rd. Rich—55Na 101
Jockey's Fields. WC1 —43Pb 82 (7J 193)
Jodrell Rd. E3—39Bc 64
Joel St. N'wd & Pinn—27W 36
Johanna St. SE1—47Qb 82 (2K 205)
John Adam St. WC2 —45Nb 82 (5G 199)
John Aird Ct. W2—(7A 190)
John Barnes Wlk. E15—37Hc 65
John Bradshaw Rd. N14—18Mb 24
John Burns Dri. Bark—38Uc 66
Johnby Clo. Enf—9Ac 12
John Campbell Rd. N16—36Ub 63
John Carpenter St. EC4 —45Rb 83 (4B 200)
John Clay Gdns. Grays—45De 91
John Cobb Rd. Wey—80Q 140
John Felton Rd. SE16—47Wb 83
John Fisher St. E1—45Wb 83
John Islip St. SW1 —49Mb 82 (7E 204)
John McKenna Wlk. SE16 —48Wb 83
John Newton Ct. Well—55Xc 109
John Parker Clo. Dag—38Dd 68
John Parker Sq. SW11—55Fb 103
John Penn St. SE13—53Dc 106
John Perrin Pl. Harr—31Na 59
John Prince's St. W1 —44Kb 82 (2A 198)
John Rennie Wlk. E1—46Xb 83
John Roll Way. SE16—48Wb 83
John Ruskin St. SE5—52Rb 105
John's Av. NW4—28Ya 40
John's Clo. Ashf—63S 120
John's Clo. Long, Dart—71Be 155
Johns La. Mord—71Eb 145
John's M. WC1—42Pb 82 (6J 193)
Johnson Clo. E8—39Wb 63
Johnson Clo. Grav—62Fe 135
Johnson Rd. Brom—71Mc 149
Johnson Rd. Croy—73Tb 147
Johnson Rd. Houn—52Y 99
Johnson's Av. Sev—82Dd 170
Johnsons Clo. Cars—75Hb 145
Johnson's Ct. EC4 —44Qb 82 (3A 200)
Johnsons Dri. Hmptn—67Ea 122
Johnson's Pl. SW1 —50Lb 82 (7B 204)
Johnson St. E1—45Yb 84
Johnson St. S'hall—48Y 77
Johnsons Way. NW10—42Ra 79
Johnson's Yd. Uxb—38L 55
John Spencer Sq. N1—37Rb 63
John's Pl. E1—44Xb 83
John's Rd. Grav—10B 136
John's Rd. West—92Mc 183
John's Ter. Croy—74Ub 147
John's Ter. Romf—23Rd 49
Johnstone Rd. E6—41Pc 86
Johnston Rd. Wfd G—23Jc 45
Johnston Ter. NW2—34Za 60
John St. E15—39Hc 65
John St. SE25—70Wb 127
John St. WC1—42Pb 82 (6J 193)
John St. Enf—15Vb 25
John St. Grays—51Ee 113
John St. Houn—54Aa 99
Johns Wlk. Whyt—91Wb 181
John Taylor Ct. Slou—6G 72
John Trundle Ct. EC2—(7D 194)
John Wilson St. SE18—48Qc 86
John Woolley Clo. SE13—56Fc 107
Joiners Clo. Ger X—24B 34
Joiner's La. Ger X—25A 34
Joiner St. SE1—46Tb 83 (7G 201)
Joiners Way. Ger X—24A 34
Jolliffe Rd. Red—98Lb 180
Jollys La. Harr—32Fa 58
Jolly's La. Hay—43Z 77
Jonathan St. SE11 —50Pb 82 (7H 205)
Jones Rd. E13—42Kc 85
Jones Rd. Wal X—2Rb 11
Jones St. W1—45Kb 82 (5K 197)
Jones Wlk. Rich—58Pa 101
Jones Way. Slou—3H 53
Jonquil Gdns. Hmptn—65Ca 121
Jonson Clo. Hay—43W 76
Jonson Clo. Mitc—70Kb 126
Joram Way. SE16—50Xb 83
Jordan Clo. Dag—35Dd 68
Jordan Clo. Harr—34Ba 57
Jordan Clo. Islwth—53Ga 100
Jordan Clo. S Croy—83Vb 165
Jordan Clo. Wat—7V 4
Jordan Rd. Gnfd—39Ka 58
Jordans Clo. Stai—59L 97
Jordans Way. Rain—40Md 69
Jordan's Way. St Alb—2Ba 5
Josephine Av. SW2—57Pb 104
Josephine Av. Tad—99Bb 179

Josephine Clo. Tad—99Bb 179
Josepn Powell Clo. SW12 —58Kb 104
Joseph St. E3—42Bc 84
Joshua St. E14—44Ec 84
Joslin Rd. Purf—50Sd 90
Joubert St. SW11—54Hb 103
Journeys End. Slou—3J 73
Jowett St. SE15—52Vb 105
Joyce Av. N18—22Vb 43
Joyce Ct. Wal A—6Fc 13
Joyce Grn. La. Dart—53Nd 111
Joyce Grn. Wlk. Dart—56Pd 111
Joydens Wood Rd. Bex & Dart —63Fd 132
Joydon Dri. Romf—30Xc 47
Joy Rd. Grav—10E 114
Jubb Powell Ho. N15—30Ub 43
Jubilee Av. E4—23Ec 44
Jubilee Av. Romf—29Dd 48
Jubilee Av. Twic—60Ea 100
Jubilee Clo. NW9—30Ta 39
Jubilee Clo. Grnh—58Yd 112
Jubilee Clo. Pinn—26Y 37
Jubilee Clo. Romf—29Dd 48
Jubilee Clo. Stai—59L 97
Jubilee Cotts. Sev—92Kd 187
Jubilee Cres. E14—48Ec 84
Jubilee Cres. N9—18Wb 25
Jubilee Cres. Grav—1G 136
Jubilee Cres. Wey—78M 139
Jubilee Dri. Ruis—35Z 57
Jubilee Gdns. Barn—14Za 22
Jubilee Gdns. S'hall—43Ca 77
Jubilee Pl. SW3—50Gb 81 (7E 202)
Jubilee Rise. Sev—93Pd 187
Jubilee Rd. Grays—51Xd 112
Jubilee Rd. Gnfd—39Ka 58
Jubilee Rd. Orp—79Cd 152
Jubilee Rd. Sutt—80Za 144
Jubilee Rd. Wat—10W 4
Jubilee St. E1—44Yb 84
Jubilee Ter. N1—40Tb 63 (1G 195)
Jubilee Way. SW19—67Db 125
Jubilee Way. Chess—77Qa 143
Jubilee Way. Sidc—61Wc 131
Judd St. WC1—41Nb 82 (3F 193)
Jude St. E16—44Hc 85
Judge Heath La. Hay—44S 76
Judge's Hill. Pot B—1Gb 9
Judge St. Wat—10X 5
Judges Wlk. NW3—34Eb 61
Judith Anne Ct. Upm—33Ud 70
Judith Av. Romf—23Dd 48
Judith Gdns. Grav—4G 136
Juer St. SW11—52Gb 103
Jug Hill. West—88Mc 167
Juglans Rd. Orp—74Wc 151
Julia Gdns. Bark—40Zc 67
Julian Av. W3—45Ra 79
Julian Clo. Barn—13Db 23
Julian Clo. Wok—6F 188
Julian Hill. Harr—33Ga 58
Julian Hill. Wey—80Q 140
Julian Pl. E14—50Dc 84
Julian Rd. Orp—79Wc 151
Julians Clo. Sev—99Jd 186
Julians Way. Sev—99Jd 186
Julia St. NW5—35Jb 62
Julien Rd. W5—48La 78
Julien Rd. Coul—87Mb 164
Junction App. SE13—55Ec 106
Junction M. W2—44Gb 81 (2D 196)
Junction Pl. W2—(2D 196)
Junction Rd. E13—40Kc 65
Junction Rd. N9—18Wb 25
Junction Rd. N17—27Wb 43
Junction Rd. N19—34Lb 62
Junction Rd. W5—49La 78
Junction Rd. Ashf—64S 120
Junction Rd. Brtwd—21Yd 50
Junction Rd. Dart—58Md 111
Junction Rd. Harr—30Ga 38
Junction Rd. Romf—28Hd 48
Junction Rd. S Croy—78Tb 147
Junction Rd. E. Romf—31Ad 67
Junction Rd. W. Romf—31Ad 67
June Clo. Coul—86Kb 164
Junewood Clo. Wey—83H 157
Juniper Av. St Alb—3Ca 5
Juniper Clo. Rick—20M 17
Juniper Clo. West—89Nc 168
Juniper Ct. Harr—25Ha 38
Juniper Gdns. SW16—67Lb 126
Juniper Ga. Rick—20M 17
Juniper Gro. Wat—10W 4
Juniper Rd. Ilf—34Qc 66
Juniper St. E1—45Yb 84
Juniper Wlk. Swan—68Fd 132
Juniper Way. Hay—45T 76
Juniper Way. Romf—25Nd 49
Juno Way. SE14—51Zb 106
Jupiter Way. N7—37Pb 62
Jupp Rd. E15—38Fc 65
Jupp Rd. W. E15—39Fc 65
Justin Clo. Bren—52Ma 101
Justin Rd. E4—24Cc 44
Jute La. Enf—13Ac 26
Jutland Gdns. Coul—92Pb 180
Jutland Rd. E13—42Jc 85
Jutland Rd. SE6—59Ec 106
Jutsums Av. Romf—30Dd 48
Jutsums La. Romf—30Dd 48
Juxon Clo. Harr—25Da 37
Juxon St. SE11—49Pb 82 (5J 205)

Kaduna Clo. Pinn—29W 36
Kale Rd. Eri—48Ad 87
Kambala Rd. SW11—55Fb 103
Kandlewood. Brtwd—17De 33
Kangley Bri. Rd. SE26—64Bc 128
Karen Clo. Brtwd—17Yd 32
Karen Clo. Rain—40Gd 68
Kashgar Rd. SE18—49Vc 87
Kashmir Clo. Wey—81M 157
Kashmir Rd. SE7—52Mc 107
Kassala Rd. SW11—53Hb 103
Katherine Clo. Wey—79J 139
Katherine Gdns. SE9—56Mc 107
Katherine Gdns. Ilf—24Sc 46
Katherine Rd.—37Lc 65
E6 1-239 & 2-224
E7 remainder
Katherine Rd. Twic—60Ja 100
Katherine St. Croy—76Sb 147
Kathleen Av. W3—43Sa 79
Kathleen Av. Wemb—38Na 59
Kathleen Rd. SW11—55Hb 103
Kavanaghs Rd. Brtwd—20Wd 32
Kavanaghs Ter. Brtwd—20Xd 32
Kayemoor Rd. Sutt—79Fb 145
Kay Rd. SW9—54Nb 104
Kay St. E2—40Wb 63
Kay St. E15—38Fc 65
Kay St. Well—53Xc 109
Kaywood Clo. Slou—8P 73
Kean St. WC2—44Pb 82 (3H 199)
Kearsley M. SW11—53Hb 103
Kearton Clo. Kenl—89Sb 165
Keary Rd. Swans—59Ae 113
Keats Av. Romf—24Kd 49
Keats Clo. Chig—23Sc 46
Keats Clo. Hay—43W 76
Keats Gdns. Til—4D 114
Keat's Gro. NW3—35Gb 61
Keats La. Wind—1G 94
Keats Pl. EC2—(1F 201)
Keats Rd. Belv—48Ed 88
Keats Rd. Well—53Uc 108
Keats Wlk. Brtwd—17Fe 33
Keats Way. Croy—72Yb 148
Keats Way. Gnfd—43Da 77
Keats Way. W Dray—49P 75
Keble Clo. N'holt—36Ea 58
Keble Clo. Wor Pk—74Va 144
Keble St. SW17—63Eb 125
Keble Ter. Abb L, Wat—4V 4
Kechill Gdns. Brom—73Jc 149
Kedleston Dri. Orp—71Vc 151
Kedleston Wlk. E2—41Xb 83
Keedonwood Rd. Brom—64Gc 129
Keel Dri. Slou—7F 72
Keeler Clo. Wind—5C 94
Keeley Rd. Croy—75Sb 147
Keeley St. WC2—44Pb 82 (3H 199)
Keeling Rd. SE9—57Mc 107
Keemor Clo. SE18—52Qc 108
Keensacre. Iver—40F 54
Keens Rd. Croy—77Sb 147
Keen's Yd. N1—37Rb 63
Keepers Farm Clo. Wind—4C 94
(in two parts)
Keepers Wlk. Vir W—10P 117
Keep, The. SE3—54Jc 107
Keep, The. King—66Pa 123
Keeton's Rd. SE16—48Xb 83
Keevil Dri. SW19—59Za 102
Keighley Clo. N7—35Nb 62
Keighley Rd. Romf—24Nd 49
Keightley Dri. SE9—60Sc 108
Keilder Clo. Uxb—40Q 56
Keildon Rd. SW11—56Hb 103
Keir Hardie Ho. Grays—6A 92
Keir Hardie Way. Bark—38Wc 67
Keir Hardie Way. Hay—41W 76
Keith Av. S at H, Dart—65Rd 133
Keith Gro. W12—47Wa 80
Keith Pk. Cres. West—84Kc 167
Keith Pk. Rd. Uxb—38P 55
Keith Rd. E17—25Bc 44
Keith Rd. Bark—40Tc 66
Keith Rd. Hay—48U 76
Keith Way. Horn—31Nd 69
Kelbrook Rd. SE3—54Nc 108
Kelburn Way. Rain—41Jd 88
Kelby Path. SE9—62Rc 130
Kelceda Clo. NW2—33Wa 60
Kelday Rd. E9—38Cc 64
Kelf Gro. Hay—44V 76
Kelfield Gdns. W10—44Ya 80
Kelland Rd. E13—42Jc 85
Kellaway Rd. SE3—54Mc 107
Kellerton Rd. SE13—57Gc 107
Kellett Rd. SW2—56Qb 104
Kelling Gdns. Croy—73Rb 147
Kellino St. SW17—63Hb 125
Kellner Rd. SE28—48Vc 87
Kell St. SE1—48Rb 83 (3C 206)
Kelly Clo. Shep—68U 120
Kelly Rd. NW7—23Ab 40
Kelly St. NW1—37Kb 62
Kelly Way. Romf—30Ad 47
Kelman Clo. SW4—54Mb 104
Kelmore Gro. SE22—56Wb 105
Kelmscott Clo. E17—25Bc 44
Kelmscott Clo. Wat—15W 18
Kelmscott Cres. Wat—15W 18
Kelmscott Gdns. W12—48Wa 80
Kelmscott Rd. SW11—57Gb 103
Kelpatrick Rd. Slou—4B 72
Kelross Rd. N5—35Sb 63
Kelsall Clo. SE3—54Kc 107
Kelsey La. Beck—68Cc 128
Kelsey Pk. Av. Beck—69Dc 128
Kelsey Pk. Rd. Beck—68Cc 128
Kelsey Rd. Orp—68Xc 131
Kelsey Sq. Beck—68Cc 128
Kelsey St. E2—42Wb 83
Kelsey Way. Beck—69Cc 128
Kelshall. Wat—8Aa 5
Kelsie Way. Ilf—23Uc 46
Kelso Dri. Grav—3H 137
Kelso Pl. W8—48Db 81
Kelso Rd. Cars—73Eb 145
Kelston Rd. Ilf—26Rc 46
Kelvedon Av. W on T—80U 140
Kelvedon Clo. Brtwd—16Fe 33
Kelvedon Clo. King—65Qa 123
★Kelvedon Grn. Brtwd—9Ud
★Kelvedon Hall La. Brtwd—8Rd
Kelvedon Rd. SW6—52Bb 103
Kelvedon Wlk. Rain—39Hd 68
Kelvedon Way. Wfd G—23Pc 46
Kelvin Av. N13—23Pb 42
Kelvin Av. Lea—92Ha 176
Kelvin Av. Tedd—65Ga 122
Kelvinbrook. E Mol—69Da 121
Kelvin Clo. Eps—79Qa 143
Kelvin Cres. Harr—24Ga 38
Kelvin Dri. Twic—58Ka 100
Kelvin Gdns. S'hall—44Ca 77
Kelvin Gro. SE26—62Xb 127
Kelvin Gro. Chess—76Ma 143
Kelvington Clo. Croy—73Ac 148
Kelvington Rd. SE15—57Zb 106
Kelvin Pde. Orp—74Uc 150
Kelvin Rd. N5—35Sb 63
Kelvin Rd. Til—4C 114
Kelvin Rd. Well—55Wc 109
Kember St. N1—38Pb 62
Kemble Clo. Pot B—5Fb 9
Kemble Clo. Wey—77T 140
Kemble Dri. Brom—76Nc 150
Kemble Pde. Pot B—4Eb 9
Kemble Rd. N17—25Wb 43
Kemble Rd. SE23—62Zb 106
Kemble Rd. Croy—76Rb 147
Kembleside Rd. West—90Lc 167
Kemble St. WC2—44Pb 82 (3H 199)
Kemerton Rd. SE5—55Sb 105
Kemerton Rd. Beck—68Dc 128
Kemerton Rd. Croy—73Vb 147
Kemeys St. E9—36Ac 64
Kemnal Rd. Chst—66Sc 130
Kempe Rd. NW6—40Za 60
Kempe Rd. Enf—8Xb 11
Kemp Gdns. Croy—72Sb 147
Kempis Way. SE22—57Ub 105
Kemplay Rd. NW3—35Fb 61
Kemp Pl. Bush, Wat—16Ca 19
Kemp Rd. Dag—32Zc 67
Kemp's Ct. W1—(3D 198)
Kemps Dri. E14—45Cc 84
Kemps Dri. N'wd—24V 36
Kempsford Gdns. SW5—50Cb 81
Kempsford Rd. SE11 —49Qb 82 (6A 206)
Kempshott Rd. SW16—66Mb 126
Kempson Rd. SW6—52Cb 103
Kempthorne Rd. SE8—49Bc 84
Kempthorne St. Grav—8D 114
Kempton Av. Horn—35Pd 69
Kempton Av. N'holt—37Ca 57
Kempton Av. Sun—67X 121
Kempton Clo. Eri—51Ed 110
Kempton Clo. Uxb—35S 56
Kempton Rd. E6—39Pc 66
Kempton Rd. Hmptn—68Ba 121
Kempton Wlk. Croy—72Ac 148
Kempt St. SE18—51Qc 108
Kemsing Clo. Bex—59Ad 109
Kemsing Clo. Brom—75Hc 149
Kemsing Clo. T Hth—70Sb 127
Kemsing Rd. SE10—50Jc 85
★Kemsing Rd. Sev—88Vd
Kemsley Clo. Grav—3B 136
Kemsley Clo. Grnh—58Xd 112
Kemsley Rd. West—91Mc 183
Kenbury Clo. Uxb—34Q 56
Kenbury St. SE5—54Sb 105
Kenchester Clo. SW8—52Nb 104
Kendal Av. N18—21Tb 43
Kendal Av. W3—42Qa 79
Kendal Av. Bark—39Uc 66
Kendal Av. Epp—2Wc 15
Kendal Clo. Hay—40U 56
Kendal Clo. Slou—5L 73
Kendal Clo. Wfd G—19Hc 27
Kendal Croft. Horn—36Jd 68
Kendal Dri. Slou—5L 73
Kendale Rd. Brom—64Gc 129
Kendal Gdns. N18—21Tb 43
Kendal Gdns. Sutt—75Eb 145
Kendall Av. Beck—68Ac 128
Kendall Av. S Croy—81Tb 165
Kendall Av. S. S Croy—82Sb 165
Kendall Pl. W1—43Jb 82 (1H 197)
Kendall Rd. Beck—68Ac 128
Kendall Rd. Iswth—54Ja 100
Kendal Pde. N18—21Tb 43
Kendal Rd. NW10—35Wa 60
Kendals Clo. Rad—8Ga 6
Kendal St. W2—44Gb 81 (3E 196)
Kender St. SE14—52Yb 106
Kendoa Rd. SW4—56Mb 104
Kendon Clo. E11—29Kc 45
Kendor Av. Eps—83Sa 161
Kendra Hall Rd. S Croy—80Rb 147
Kendrey Gdns. Twic—59Ga 100
Kendrick M. SW7 —49Fb 81 (6B 202)
Kendrick Pl. SW7 —49Fb 81 (6B 202)
Kendrick Rd. Slou—8M 73
Kenelm Clo. Harr—34Ja 58
Kenerne Dri. Barn—15Ab 22
Kenford Clo. Wat—4X 5
Kenia Wlk. Grav—2H 137
Kenilford Rd. SW12—59Kb 104
Kenilworth Av. E17—26Cc 44
Kenilworth Av. SW19—64Cb 125
Kenilworth Av. Cob—86Da 159
Kenilworth Av. Harr—35Ba 57
Kenilworth Av. N'holt—41Ba 77
Kenilworth Av. Romf—23Rd 49
Kenilworth Clo. Bans—88Db 163
Kenilworth Clo. Borwd—13Sa 21
Kenilworth Clo. Slou—8K 73
Kenilworth Ct. Wat—11W 18
Kenilworth Cres. Enf—11Ub 25
Kenilworth Dri. Borwd—13Sa 21
Kenilworth Dri. Rick—14R 18
Kenilworth Dri. W on T—76Z 141
Kenilworth Gdns. SE18—54Rc 108
Kenilworth Gdns. Hay—43V 76
Kenilworth Gdns. Horn—34Ld 69
Kenilworth Gdns. Ilf—33Vc 67
Kenilworth Gdns. Lou—16Pc 28
Kenilworth Gdns. Stai—64L 119
Kenilworth Gdns. Wat—22Y 37
Kenilworth Rd. E3—40Ac 64
Kenilworth Rd. NW6—39Bb 61
Kenilworth Rd. SE20—67Zb 128
Kenilworth Rd. W5—46Na 79
Kenilworth Rd. Ashf—62M 119
Kenilworth Rd. Edgw—20Sa 21
Kenilworth Rd. Eps—78Wa 144
Kenilworth Rd. Orp—72Sc 150
Kenley Av. NW9—25Ua 40
Kenley Clo. Barn—14Gb 23
Kenley Clo. Bex—59Cd 110
Kenley Clo. Cat—92Ub 181
Kenley Clo. Chst—69Uc 130
Kenley Gdns. Horn—33Pd 69
Kenley Gdns. T Hth—70Rb 127
Kenley La. Kenl—86Sb 165
Kenley Rd. SW19—68Cb 125
Kenley Rd. King—68Ra 123
Kenley Rd. Twic—58Ka 100
Kenley Wlk. W11—46Ab 80
Kenley Wlk. Sutt—77Za 144
Kenlor Rd. SW17—64Fb 125
Kenmare Dri. Mitc—66Hb 125
Kenmare Gdns. N13—21Sb 43
Kenmare Rd. T Hth—72Qb 146
Kenmere Gdns. Wemb—39Qa 59
Kenmere Rd. Well—54Yc 109
Kenmont Gdns. NW10—41Xa 80
Kenmore Av. Harr—28Ja 38
Kenmore Clo. Rich—52Qa 101
Kenmore Cres. Hay—41V 76
Kenmore Gdns. Edgw—26Ra 39
Kenmore Rd. Harr—27Ma 39
Kenmore Rd. Kenl—86Rb 165
Kenmure Rd. E8—36Xb 63
Kenmure Yd. E8—36Xb 63
Kennard Rd. E15—38Fc 65
Kennard Rd. N11—22Hb 41
Kennard St. E16—46Pc 86
Kennard St. SW11—53Jb 104
Kenneally. Wind—4A 94
Kenneally Clo. Wind—4A 94
Kenneally Wlk. Wind—4A 94
Kennedy Av. Enf—16Yb 26
Kennedy Clo. E13—40Jc 65
Kennedy Clo. Orp—74Tc 150
Kennedy Clo. Pinn—23Ba 37
Kennedy Clo. Slou—7G 52
Kennedy Ct. Croy—72Bc 148
Kennedy Gdns. Sev—94Md 187
Kennedy Path. W7—42Ha 78
Kennedy Rd. W7—43Ga 78
Kennedy Rd. Bark—39Uc 66
Kennel Clo. Lea—96Ea 176
Kennel La. Brtwd—11Ud 32
Kennel La. Lea—94Da 175
(in two parts)
Kennel Wood Cres. Croy —83Fc 167
Kennet Clo. SW11—56Fb 103
Kennet Clo. Upm—30Ud 50
Kennet Grn. S Ock—45Xd 90
Kenneth Av. Ilf—35Rc 66
Kenneth Cres. NW2—36Xa 60
Kenneth Gdns. Stan—23Ja 38
Kenneth More Rd. Ilf—34Rc 66
Kenneth Rd. Bans—87Fb 163
Kenneth Rd. Romf—31Zc 67
Kennet Rd. W9—42Bb 81
Kennet Rd. Dart—55Jd 110
Kennet Rd. Iswth—55Ha 100
Kennet Rd. Slou—48D 74
Kennet Wharf La. EC4—(4E 200)
Kenninghall Rd. E5—34Wb 63
Kenninghall Rd. N18—22Yb 44
Kenning St. SE16—47Yb 84
Kennings Way. SE11 —50Qb 82 (7B 206)
Kenning Ter. N1—39Ub 63
Kennington Grn. SE11—50Qb 82
Kennington Gro. SE11—51Pb 104
Kennington La. SE11 —50Pb 82 (7J 205)
Kennington Oval. SE11—51Pb 104
Kennington Pk. Gdns. SE11 —51Rb 105
Kennington Pk. Pl. SE11 —51Qb 104
Kennington Pk. Rd. SE11 —51Qb 104 (7B 206)
Kennington Rd.—48Qb 82 (3K 205)
SE1 1-69 & 2-64
SE11 remainder
Kennylands Rd. Ilf—24Wc 47
Kenny Rd. NW7—23Ab 40
Kenrick Pl. W1—43Jb 82 (1H 197)
Kensal Rd. W10—42Ab 80
Kensington Av. E12—37Nc 66
Kensington Av. T Hth—67Qb 126
Kensington Av. Wat—14V 18
Kensington Chu. St. W8—46Cb 81
Kensington Ct. W8—47Db 81
Kensington Ct. Pl. W8—48Db 81
Kensington Dri. Wfd G—26Mc 45
Kensington Gdns. Ilf—32Pc 66
Kensington Gdns. Sq. W2 —44Db 81
Kensington Ga. W8 —48Eb 81 (3A 202)
Kensington Gore. SW7 —47Fb 81 (2B 202)
Kensington High St.—48Bb 81
W8 1-353 & 2-280
W14 remainder
Kensington Mall. W8—46Cb 81
Kensington Pal. Gdns. W8 —46Db 81
Kensington Pk. Gdns. W11 —45Bb 81
Kensington Pk. M. W11—44Bb 81
Kensington Pk. Rd. W11—44Bb 81
Kensington Pl. W8—46Cb 81
Kensington Rd. W8 & SW7 —47Eb 81 (2A 202)
Kensington Rd. Brtwd—16Wd 32
Kensington Rd. N'holt—41Ca 77
Kensington Rd. Romf—30Ed 48
Kensington Sq. W8—47Db 81
Kensington Ter. S Croy—80Tb 147
Kent Av. W13—43Ka 78
Kent Av. Dag—42Cd 88
Kent Av. Slou—3G 72
Kent Av. Well—57Vc 109
Kent Clo. Borwd—10Ta 7
Kent Clo. Mitc—70Nb 126
Kent Clo. Orp—79Uc 150
Kent Clo. Stai—65M 119
Kent Dri. Barn—14Jb 24
Kent Dri. Horn—35Md 69
Kent Dri. Tedd—64Ga 122
Kentford Way. N'holt—39Aa 57
Kent Gdns. W13—43Ka 78
Kent Gdns. Ruis—30W 36
Kent Ga. Way. Croy—79Bc 148
Kent Ho. Ger X—22A 34
Kent Ho. La. Beck—64Ac 128
Kent Ho. Rd.—67Zb 128
SE26 1-95 & 2-72
Beck remainder
Kentish Bldgs. SE1—(7F 201)
Kentish Rd. Belv—49Cd 88
Kentish Town Rd.—38Kb 62
NW1 1-187 & 2-158
NW5 remainder
Kentmere Rd. SE18—49Uc 86
Kenton Av. Harr—31Ha 58
Kenton Av. S'hall—45Ca 77
Kenton Av. Sun—68Z 121
Kenton Ct. Harr—30Ka 38
Kentone Ct. SE25—70Xb 127
Kenton Gdns. Harr—29La 38
Kenton La. Harr—23Ha to 29La 38
Kenton Pk. Av. Harr—28Ma 39
Kenton Pk. Clo. Harr—28La 38
Kenton Pk. Cres. Harr—28Ma 39
Kenton Pk. Rd. Harr—28La 38
Kenton Rd. E9—37Zb 64
Kenton Rd. Harr—31Ha 58
Kentons La. Wind—4C 94
Kenton St. WC1—42Nb 82 (5F 193)
Kenton Way. Hay—41U 76
Kenton Way. Wok—5C 188
Kent Pas. NW1—41Hb 81 (5F 191)
Kent Rd. N21—18Tb 25
Kent Rd. W4—48Sa 79
Kent Rd. Dag—36Dd 68
Kent Rd. Dart—58Nd 111
Kent Rd. E Mol—70Ea 122
Kent Rd. Grav—10C 114
Kent Rd. Grays—51Ee 113
Kent Rd. King—69Ma 123
Kent Rd. Long, Dart—68Zd 135
Kent Rd. Orp—72Xc 151
Kent Rd. Rich—52Qa 101
Kent Rd. W Wick—74Dc 148
Kent Rd. Wok—88D 156
Kent's Pas. Hmptn—67Ba 121
Kent St. E2—40Vb 63 (1K 195)
Kent St. E13—41Lc 85
Kent Ter. NW1—41Gb 81 (4E 190)
Kent View. S Ock—47Sd 90
Kent View Gdns. Ilf—33Uc 66
Kent Wlk. SW9—56Rb 105
Kent Way. SE15—53Vb 105
Kent Way. Surb—76Na 143
Kentwode Grn. SW13—52Wa 102
Kent Yd. SW7—47Gb 81 (2E 202)
Kenver Av. N12—23Fb 41
Kenward Rd. SE9—57Lc 107
Kenway. Rain—41Md 89
Kenway. Romf—26Ed 48
Ken Way. Wemb—34Sa 59
Kenway Clo. Rain—41Ld 89
Kenway Rd. SW5—49Db 81
Kenway Wlk. Rain—41Md 89
Kenwood Av. N14—15Mb 24
Kenwood Av. SE14—53Zb 106
Kenwood Av. Long, Dart—69Ee 135
Kenwood Clo. NW3—32Fb 61
Kenwood Clo. W Dray—51Q 98
Kenwood Dri. Beck—69Ec 128
Kenwood Dri. Rick—19H 17
Kenwood Dri. W on T—79X 141
Kenwood Gdns. E18—27Kc 45
Kenwood Gdns. Ilf—28Qc 46
Kenwood Pk. Wey—79T 140
Kenwood Rd. N6—30Hb 41
Kenwood Rd. N9—18Wb 25
Kenworth Clo. Wal X—5Zb 12
Kenworthy Rd. E9—36Ac 64
Kenwyn Dri. NW2—33Ua 60
Kenwyn Rd. SW4—56Mb 104
Kenwyn Rd. SW20—67Ya 124
Kenya Rd. SE7—52Mc 107
Kenyngton Ct. Sun—64W 120
Kenyngton Dri. Sun—64W 120
Kenyngton Pl. Harr—29La 38
Kenyons. Lea—100R 174
Kenyon St. SW6—53Za 102
Keogh Rd. E15—37Gc 65
Kepler Rd. SW4—56Nb 104
Keppel Rd. E6—38Pc 66
Keppel Rd. Dag—35Ad 67
Keppel Row. SE1 —46Sb 83 (7D 200)
Keppel Spur. Wind—9M 95
Keppel St. WC1—43Mb 82 (7E 192)
Keppel St. Wind—4H 95
Kerbela St. E2—42Wb 83
Kerby St. E14—44Dc 84
Kerdistone Clo. Pot B—2Db 9
Kerfield Cres. SE5—53Tb 105
Kerfield Pl. SE5—53Tb 105
Kernow Clo. Horn—33Nd 69
Kerri Clo. Barn—14Ya 22
Kerrill Av. Coul—91Qb 180
Kerrison Pl. W5—46Ma 79
Kerrison Rd. E15—39Fc 65
Kerrison Rd. SW11—55Gb 103
Kerrison Rd. W5—46Ma 79
Kerry Av. Stan—21Ma 39
Kerry Clo. E16—44Kc 85
Kerry Clo. Upm—31Vd 70
Kerry Ct. Stan—21Ma 39
Kerry Dri. Upm—31Vd 70
Kerry Path. SE14—51Bc 106
Kerry Rd. Grays—46Fe 91
Kerry Ter. Wok—88D 156
Kersey Dri. S Croy—84Yb 166
Kersey Gdns. SE9—63Nc 130
Kersey Gdns. Romf—24Nd 49
Kersfield Rd. SW15—58Za 102
Kershaw Clo. SW18—58Fb 103
Kershaw Rd. Dag—34Cd 68
Kerslake Ho. Ger X—22A 34
Kersley Rd. N16—34Ub 63
Kersley St. SW11—54Hb 103
Kerstin Clo. Hay—45V 76
Kerswell Clo. N15—29Ub 43
Kerwick Clo. N7—38Nb 62
Keslake Rd. NW6—40Za 60
Kessock Clo. N17—29Xb 43
Kesteven Clo. Ilf—23Vc 47
Kestlake Rd. Bex—58Yc 109
Keston Av. Coul—91Qb 180
Keston Av. Kes—78Lc 149
Keston Av. Wey—83J 157
Keston Clo. N18—20Tb 25
Keston Clo. Well—52Yc 109
Keston Gdns. Kes—77Lc 149
Keston Pk. Clo. Kes—76Pc 150
Keston Rd. N17—27Tb 43
Keston Rd. SE15—55Wb 105
Keston Rd. T Hth—72Qb 146
Kestrel Av. SE24—57Sb 105
Kestrel Av. Stai—62H 119
Kestrel Clo. Ilf—21Yc 47
Kestrel Clo. Rain—38Kd 69
Kestrel Clo. Wat—6Aa 5
Kestrel Ct. E17—26Zb 44
Kestrel Path. Slou—2C 72
Kestrel Way. Croy—81Fc 167
Keswick Av. SW15—64Ua 124
Keswick Av. SW19—68Cb 125
Keswick Av. Horn—32Md 69
Keswick Clo. Sutt—77Eb 145
Keswick Ct. Slou—5K 73
Keswick Dri. Enf—8Yb 12
Keswick Gdns. Ilf—28Nc 46
Keswick Gdns. Ruis—30T 36
Keswick Gdns. Wemb—36Na 59
Keswick M. W5—46Na 79
Keswick Rd. SW15—57Ab 102
Keswick Rd. Bexh—53Cd 110
Keswick Rd. Lea—96Ea 176
Keswick Rd. Lea—97Ea 176
Keswick Rd. Orp—74Vc 151
Keswick Rd. Twic—58Ea 100
Keswick Rd. W Wick—75Gc 149
Kettering Rd. Enf—9Zb 12
Kettering Rd. Romf—24Nd 49
Kettering St. SW16—65Lb 126
Kett Gdns. SW2—57Pb 104
Kettlebaston Rd. E10—32Bc 64
Kettlewell Clo. Wok—87A 156
Kettlewell Ct. Swan—68Hd 132
Kettlewell Dri. Wok—86A 156
Kettlewell Hill. Wok—86A 156
Ketton Grn. Red—100Mb 180
Kevan Dri. Wok—97G 172
Kevelioc Rd. N17—25Sb 43
Kevin Clo. Houn—54Z 99
Kevington Clo. Orp—70Vc 131
Kevington Dri. Chst & Orp —70Vc 131
Kew Bri. Bren & Rich—51Qa 101
Kew Bri. Ct. W4—50Qa 79
Kew Bri. Rd. Bren—51Pa 101
Kew Cres. Sutt—76Ab 144
Kewferry Dri. N'wd—22R 36
Kewferry Rd. N'wd—23S 36
Kew Foot Rd. Rich—56Na 101
Kew Gdns. Rd. Rich—52Pa 101
Kew Grn. Rich—51Pa 101
Kew Meadow Path. Rich —53Ra 101
Kew Rd. Rich—55Na 101
Key Clo. E1—42Yb 84
Keyes Rd. NW2—36Za 60
Keyes Rd. Dart—56Pd 111
Keymer Clo. West—88Nc 167
Keymer Rd. SW2—61Pb 126
Keynes Clo. N2—28Hb 41
Keynsham Av. Wfd G—21Gc 45
Keynsham Gdns. SE9—57Nc 108
Keynsham Rd. SE9—57Mc 107
Keynsham Rd. Mord—74Db 145
Keynsham Wlk. Mord—74Db 145
Keyse Rd. SE1—48Vb 83 (4K 207)
Keysham Av. Houn—53W 98
Keystone Cres. N1 —40Nb 62 (2G 193)
Keywood Dri. Sun—65W 120
Keyworth Pl. SE1—(3C 206)
Keyworth St. SE1 —48Rb 83 (3C 206)
Kezia St. SE8—50Ac 84
Khama Rd. SW17—63Gb 125
Khartoum Rd. E13—41Kc 85
Khartoum Rd. SW17—63Fb 125
Khartoum Rd. Ilf—36Rc 66
Khyber Rd. SW11—54Gb 103
Kibworth St. SW8—52Pb 104
Kidborough Down. Lea—99Ca 175
Kidbrooke Gdns. SE3—54Jc 107
Kidbrooke Gro. SE3—53Jc 107
Kidbrooke La. SE9—56Nc 108
Kidbrooke Pk. Clo. SE3—53Kc 107
Kidbrooke Pk. Rd. SE3—53Kc 107
Kidbrooke Way. SE3—54Kc 107
Kidderminster Rd. Croy—74Rb 147
Kidderminster Rd. Slou—1E 72
Kidderpore Av. NW3—35Cb 61
Kidderpore Gdns. NW3—35Cb 61
Kidd Pl. SE7—50Nc 86
Kidlington Way. NW9—25Ta 39
Kidron Way. E9—39Yb 64
Kielder Clo. Ilf—23Vc 47
Kier Pk. Asc—9A 116
Kiffen St. EC2—42Tb 83 (5G 195)

Kilburn High Rd.—Knapdale Clo.

Kilburn High Rd. NW6—38Bb 61
Kilburn La.—41Za 80
W10 1-271 & 2-300
W9 remainder
Kilburn Pk. Rd. NW6—41Cb 81
Kilburn Pl. NW6—39Cb 61
Kilburn Priory. NW6—39Db 61
Kilburn Sq. NW6—39Cb 61
Kilburn Vale. NW6—39Db 61
Kilby Clo. Wat—7Z 5
Kilcorral Clo. Eps—86Wa 162
Kildare Clo. Ruis—32Y 57
Kildare Gdns. W2—44Cb 81
Kildare Rd. E16—43Jc 85
Kildare Ter. W2—44Cb 81
Kildare Wlk. E14—44Cc 84
Kildonan Clo. Wat—11V 18
Kildoran Rd. SW2—57Nb 104
Kildowan Rd. Ilf—32Wc 67
Kilgour Rd. SE23—58Ac 106
Kilkie St. SW6—54Eb 103
Killarney Rd. SW18—58Eb 103
Killaser Ct. Tad—95Ya 178
Killearn Rd. SE6—60Fc 107
Killester Gdns. Wor Pk—77Xa 144
Killewarren Way. Orp—72Yc 151
Killick St. N1—40Pb 62 (1H 193)
Killieser Av. SW2—61Nb 126
Killigarth Ct. Sidc—63Wc 131
Killip Clo. E16—44Hc 85
Killowen Av. N'holt—36Ea 58
Killowen Rd. E9—37Zb 64
Killyon Rd. SW8—54Lb 104
Killyon Ter. SW8—54Lb 104
Kilmaine Rd. SW6—52Ab 102
Kilmarnock Rd. Wat—21Z 37
Kilmarsh Rd. W6—49Ya 80
Kilmartin Av. SW16—69Qb 126
Kilmartin Rd. Ilf—33Wc 67
Kilmartin Way. Horn—36Kd 69
Kilmeston Way. SE15—52Vb 105
Kilmington Clo. Brtwd—19De 33
Kilmington Rd. SW13—51Wa 102
Kilmiston Av. Shep—72S 140
Kilmorey Gdns. Iswth—57Ka 100
Kilmorey Rd. Twic—56Ka 100
Kilmorie Rd. SE23—60Ac 106
Kiln Clo. Hay—51T 98
Kilndown. Grav—5F 136
Kilner St. E14—43Cc 84
★Kiln Field. Brtwd—7Zd
Kiln La. Asc—10E 116
Kiln La. Eps—83Ua 162
Kiln La. Slou—2G 52
Kiln La. Wind—5A 116
Kiln La. Wok—96J 173
Kiln Pl. NW5—36Jb 62
Kilnside. Esh—80Ja 142
Kiln Way. N'wd—23U 36
Kilravock St. W10—41Ab 80
Kilrue La. W on T—77V 140
Kilrush Ter. Wok—88C 156
Kilsby Wlk. Dag—37Xc 67
Kilsha Rd. W on T—72Y 141
Kilsmore La. Wal X—1Zb 12
Kilvinton Dri. Enf—10Tb 11
Kilworth Av. Brtwd—16Ce 33
Kimbell Gdns. SW6—53Ab 102
Kimber Clo. Wind—5E 94
Kimberley Av. E6—40Nc 66
Kimberley Av. SE15—54Yb 106
Kimberley Av. Ilf—31Uc 66
Kimberley Av. Romf—30Ed 48
Kimberley Clo. Slou—49B 74
Kimberley Dri. Sidc—61Zc 131
Kimberley Gdns. N4—29Rb 43
Kimberley Gdns. Enf—13Vb 25
Kimberley Pl. Purl—83Qb 164
Kimberley Ride. Cob—85Da 159
Kimberley Rd. E4—18Gc 27
Kimberley Rd. E11—33Fc 65
Kimberley Rd. E16—42Hc 85
Kimberley Rd. E17—25Bc 44
Kimberley Rd. N17—26Wb 43
Kimberley Rd. N18—23Xb 43
Kimberley Rd. NW6—39Ab 60
Kimberley Rd. SW9—55Nb 104
Kimberley Rd. Beck—68Zb 128
Kimberley Rd. Croy—72Rb 147
Kimberley Way. E4—18Gc 27
Kimber Rd. SW18—59Cb 103
Kimble Cres. Bush, Wat—17Ea 20
Kimble Rd. SW19—65Fb 125
Kimbolton Clo. SE12—58Hc 107
Kimbolton Grn. Borwd—14Sa 21
Kimmeridge Gdns. SE9—63Nc 130
Kimmeridge Rd. SE9—63Nc 130
Kimpton Av. Brtwd—17Xd 32
Kimpton Pl. Wat—6Z 5
Kimpton Rd. SE5—53Tb 105
Kimpton Rd. Sutt—75Bb 145
(in two parts)
Kimptons Clo. Pot B—4Za 8
Kimptons Mead. Pot B—5Za 8
Kinburn Dri. Egh—64A 118
Kinburn St. SE16—47Zb 84
Kincaid Rd. SE15—52Xb 105
Kinch Gro. Harr—31Pa 59
Kincraig Dri. Sev—95Jd 186
Kinder Clo. SE28—45Zc 87
Kindersley Way. Abb L, Wat —3S 4
Kinder St. E1—44Xb 83
Kinfauns Av. Horn—30Ld 49
Kinfauns Rd. SW2—61Qb 126
Kinfauns Rd. Ilf—32Wc 67
Kingaby Gdns. Rain—38Jd 68
King Alfred Av. SE6—63Cc 128
King Alfred Rd. Romf—26Pd 49
King & Queen St. SE17 —50Sb 83 (7E 206)
King Arthur Clo. SE15—52Yb 106
King Charles Cres. Surb —73Pa 143
King Charles Rd. Surb—71Pa 143
King Charles St. SW1 —47Nb 82 (1E 204)
King Charles Wlk. SW19 —60Ab 102
Kingcup Clo. Croy—74Zb 148
King David La. E1—45Yb 84
Kingdon Rd. NW6—37Cb 61
King Edward Av. Dart—58Md 111
King Edward Av. Rain—41Md 89
King Edward Ct. Shopping—3H 95
Centre. Wind
King Edward Dri. Chess—76Na 143
King Edward Dri. Grays—7A 92
King Edward M. SW13—53Wa 102
King Edward Rd. E10—32Ec 64
King Edward Rd. E17—27Ac 44
King Edward Rd. Barn—14Cb 23
King Edward Rd. Brtwd—20Yd 32
King Edward Rd. Grnh—57Wd 112
King Edward Rd. Romf—30Hd 48
King Edward Rd. Shen, Rad—5Pa 7
King Edward Rd. Wal X—5Ac 12
King Edward Rd. Wat—16Aa 19
King Edward VII Av. Wind—2J 95
King Edward's Gdns. W3—46Qa 79
King Edwards Gro. Tedd —65Ka 122
King Edward's Rd. E9—39Xb 63
King Edward's Rd. N9—17Xb 25
King Edward's Rd. Bark—39Tc 66
King Edward's Rd. Enf—14Zb 26
King Edward's Rd. Ruis—32T 56
King Edward's Rd. Stanf—3M 93
King Edward St. EC1 —44Sb 83 (2D 200)
King Edward St. Slou—7H 73
King Edward Wlk. SE1 —48Qb 82 (3A 206)
Kingfield Clo. Wok—92B 172
Kingfield Dri. Wok—92B 172
Kingfield Gdns. Wok—92B 172
Kingfield Rd. W5—42Ma 79
Kingfield Rd. Wok—92B 172
Kingfield St. E14—49Ec 84
Kingfisher Clo. SE28—45Yc 87
Kingfisher Clo. Brtwd—17Ce 33
Kingfisher Clo. W on T—78Aa 141
Kingfisher Dri. Rich—63Ka 122
Kingfisher Dri. Stai—63H 119
Kingfisher Gdns. S Croy —82Zb 166
Kingfisher Lure. K Lan—1R 4
Kingfisher Lure. Rick—14K 17
Kingfisher Pl. N22—26Pb 42
Kingfisher Rd. Upm—32Vd 70
King Gdns. Croy—78Rb 147
King George Av. E16—44Mc 85
King George Av. Bush, Wat —16Da 19
King George Av. W on T—74Z 141
King George Clo. Romf—27Ed 48
King George Rd. Wal A—6Ec 12
King George's Av. Wat—15U 18
King George's Dri. S'hall—43Ba 77
King George's Dri. Wey—82J 157
King George VI Av. Grays—9K 93
King George VI Av. Mitc—70Hb 125
King George VI Av. West —88Mc 167
King Georges Rd. Brtwd—16Xd 32
King George's Trading Est. Chess—77Qa 143
King George St. SE10—52Ec 106
Kingham Clo. SW18—59Eb 103
Kingham Clo. W11—47Ab 80
King Harolds Way. Bexh —52Zc 109
King Henry's Dri. Croy—81Ec 166
King Henry's Rd. NW3—38Fb 61
King Henry's Rd. King—69Ra 123
King Henry St. N16—36Ub 63
King Henry's Wlk. N1—37Ub 63
Kinghorn St. EC1 —43Sb 83 (1D 200)
King James & Tinker Rd. Enf —7Tb 11
King James' Av. Pot B—1Nb 10
King James St. SE1 —47Rb 83 (2C 206)
King John Ct. EC2 —42Ub 83 (5J 195)
King John's Clo. Wray, Stai—8N 95
King John St. E1—43Zb 84
King John's Wlk. SE9—59Nc 108
Kinglake Ct. Wok—6B 188
Kinglake St. SE17 —50Ub 83 (7H 207)
Kingly Ct. W1—(4C 198)
Kingly St. W1—44Lb 82 (3B 198)
Kingsand Rd. SE12—61Jc 129
Kings Arbour. S'hall—50Aa 77
Kings Arms Yd. EC2 —44Tb 83 (2F 201)
Kings Arms Yd. Romf—29Gd 48
Kingsash Dri. Hay—42Aa 77
King's Av. N10—27Jb 42
King's Av. N21—18Rb 25
Kings Av.—59Mb 104
SW4 1-147 & 2-118
SW12 remainder
Kings Av. W5—44Ma 79
Kings Av. Brom—65Hc 129
King's Av. Buck H—19Mc 27
King's Av. Cars—80Gb 145
King's Av. Gnfd—44Da 77
Kings Av. Houn—53Da 99
Kings Av. N Mald—70Ua 124
Kings Av. Romf—30Bd 47
King's Av. Sun—64V 120
King's Av. Wat—14V 18
Kings Av. Wey—84M 157
King's Av. Wfd G—23Kc 45
King's Bench St. SE1 —47Rb 83 (1C 206)
King's Bench Wlk. EC4 —45Qb 82 (4A 200)
Kingsbridge Av. W3—47Pa 79
Kingsbridge Cir. Romf—23Nd 49
Kingsbridge Clo. Romf—23Nd 49
Kingsbridge Cres. S'hall—43Ba 77
Kingsbridge Rd. W10—44Ya 80
Kingsbridge Rd. Bark—40Tc 66
Kingsbridge Rd. Mord—73Za 144
Kingsbridge Rd. Romf—23Nd 49
Kingsbridge Rd. S'hall—49Ba 77
Kingsbridge Rd. W on T—73X 141
Kingsbrook. Lea—90Ja 160
Kingsbury Circ. NW9—29Qa 39
Kingsbury Dri. Wind—9L 95
Kingsbury Rd. N1—37Ub 63
Kingsbury Rd. NW9—29Qa 39
Kingsbury Ter. N1—37Ub 63
Kingsbury Trading Est. NW9 —30Ta 39
King's Chase. Brtwd—20Yd 32
Kingsclere Clo. SW15—59Wa 102
Kingscliffe Gdns. SW19—60Bb 103
King's Clo. E10—31Dc 64
King's Clo. NW4—28Za 40
Kings Clo. Chal—19A 16
King's Clo. Dart—56Gd 110
King's Clo. K Lan—3K 3
Kings Clo. N'wd—23V 36
Kings Clo. Stai—65M 119
Kings Clo. W on T—74X 141
King's Clo. Wat—14X 19
King's College Rd. NW3—38Gb 61
Kings College Rd. Ruis—30V 36
Kingscote Rd. W4—48Ta 79
Kingscote Rd. Croy—73Xb 147
Kingscote Rd. N Mald—69Ta 123
Kingscote St. EC4 —45Rb 83 (4B 200)
King's Ct. E13—39Kc 65
King's Ct. Tad—94Ya 178
King's Ct. Wok—88B 156
Kingscourt Rd. SW16—62Mb 126
King's Cres. N4—34Sb 63
King's Cres. Est. N4—33Sb 63
Kingscroft Rd. NW2—37Bb 61
Kingscroft Rd. Bans—87Fb 163
Kingscroft Rd. Lea—92Ka 176
King's Cross Bri. WC1—(3G 193)
King's Cross Rd. WC1 —41Pb 82 (3H 193)
Kingsdale Gdns. W11—46Za 80
Kingsdale Rd. SE18—51Vc 109
Kingsdale Rd. SE20—66Zb 128
Kingsdene. Tad—93Xa 178
Kingsdown Av. W3—45Ua 80
Kingsdown Av. W13—47Ka 78
Kingsdown Av. S Croy—82Rb 165
Kingsdown Clo. W11—44Za 80
Kingsdown Rd. E11—34Gc 65
Kingsdown Rd. N19—33Nb 62
Kingsdown Rd. Eps—85Wa 162
Kingsdown Rd. Surb—73Na 143
Kingsdown Rd. Sutt—78Ab 144
Kingsdown Way. Brom—72Jc 149
King's Dri. Edgw—21Pa 39
Kings Dri. Grav—2D 136
Kings Dri. Surb—73Qa 143
Kings Dri. Tedd—64Fa 122
Kings Dri. Th Dit—72Ka 142
Kings Dri. Wemb—33Ra 59
Kings Dri., The. W on T—81V 158
Kingsend. Ruis—32U 56
Kings Farm Av. Rich—56Qa 101
Kings Farm Rd. Rick—16F 16
Kingsfield. Wind—3B 94
Kingsfield Av. Harr—28Da 37
Kingsfield Ct. Wat—17Z 19
Kingsfield Dri. Enf—7Zb 12
Kingsfield Rd. Harr—31Fa 58
Kingsfield Rd. Wat—17Z 19
Kingsfield Ter. Dart—57Md 111
Kingsfield Ter. Harr—31Fa 58
Kingsfield Way. Enf—7Zb 12
Kingsford Av. Wall—80Nb 146
Kingsford St. NW5—36Hb 61
Kings Gdns. Ilf—32Tc 66
Kings Gdns. Upm—31Ud 70
Kingsgate. Wemb—34Sa 59
Kingsgate Av. N3—27Cb 41
Kingsgate Clo. Bexh—53Ad 109
Kingsgate Clo. Orp—68Yc 131
Kingsgate Pde. SW1—(4C 204)
Kingsgate Pl. NW6—38Cb 61
Kingsgate Rd. NW6—38Cb 61
Kings Grn. Lou—13Nc 28
Kingsground. SE9—59Mc 107
King's Gro. SE15—53Xb 105
Kings Gro. Romf—29Jd 48
King's Hall Rd. Beck—66Ac 128
King's Head Ct. EC3—(5G 201)
Kings Head Hill. E4—17Dc 26
Kingshead La. Wey—83M 157
King's Head Yd. SE1 —46Tb 83 (7F 201)
King's Highway. SE18—51Uc 108
Kings Hill. Lou—12Nc 28
Kingshill Av. Harr—28Ka 38
Kingshill Av. Hay & N'holt—41V 76
Kingshill Av. N Mald—73Wa 144
Kingshill Av. Romf—23Ed 48
Kingshill Dri. Harr—27Ka 38
Kingshold Rd. E9—38Yb 64
Kingsholm Gdns. SE9—56Mc 107
Kingshurst Rd. SE12—59Jc 107
Kingsingfield Clo. Sev—80Ud 154
Kingsingfield Rd. Sev—80Ud 154
★Kingsingfield Rd. Sev—81Ud
Kings Keep. King—70Na 123
Kingsland Grn. E8—37Ub 63
Kingsland High St. E8—37Vb 63
Kingsland Pas. E8—37Ub 63
Kingsland Rd.—41Ub 83 (3J 195)
E2 1-283 & 2-240
E8 remainder
Kingsland Rd. E13—41Lc 85
Kings La. Egh—4L 117
King's La. K Lan—3J 3
Kings La. Sutt—78Fb 145
Kingslawn Clo. SW15—57Xa 102
Kingslea. Lea—92Ja 176
Kingsleigh Wlk. Brom—70Hc 129
Kingsley Av. W13—44Ja 78
Kingsley Av. Bans—87Cb 163
Kingsley Av. Borwd—12Pa 21
Kingsley Av. Dart—57Qd 111
Kingsley Av. Egh—5M 117
Kingsley Av. Houn—54Ea 100
Kingsley Av. S'hall—45Ca 77
Kingsley Av. Sutt—77Fb 145
Kingsley Av. Wal X—1Xb 11
Kingsley Clo. N2—29Eb 41
Kingsley Clo. Dag—35Dd 68
Kingsley Dri. Wor Pk—75Va 144
Kingsley Gdns. E4—22Cc 44
Kingsley Gdns. Horn—28Md 49
Kingsley M. W8—48Db 81
Kingsley Path. Slou—2B 72
Kingsley Pl. N6—31Jb 62
Kingsley Rd. E7—38Jc 65
Kingsley Rd. E17—26Ec 44
Kingsley Rd. N13—21Rb 43
Kingsley Rd. NW6—39Bb 61
Kingsley Rd. SW19—64Db 125
Kingsley Rd. Brtwd—17Fe 33
Kingsley Rd. Croy—74Qb 146
Kingsley Rd. Harr—35Ea 58
Kingsley Rd. Houn—53Da 99
Kingsley Rd. Ilf—25Sc 46
Kingsley Rd. Lou—13Tc 28
Kingsley Rd. Orp—80Vc 151
Kingsley Rd. Pinn—28Ba 37
Kingsley St. SW11—55Hb 103
Kingsley Wlk. Grays—9C 92
Kingsley Way. N2—29Eb 41
Kingsley Wood Dri. SE9—62Pc 130
Kingslyn Cres. SE19—67Ub 127
Kings Lynn Clo. Romf—23Md 49
Kings Lynn Dri. Romf—23Md 49
Kings Lynn Path. Romf—23Md 49
Kings Mall. W6—49Ya 80
Kingsman Dri. Grays—45De 91
Kingsman Pde. SE18—48Pc 86
Kingsman Rd. Stanf—2K 93
Kingsman St. SE18—48Pc 86
Kingsmead. Barn—14Cb 23
Kingsmead. Pot B—1Nb 10
Kingsmead. West—88Mc 167
Kingsmead Av. N9—18Xb 25
Kingsmead Av. NW9—31Ta 59
Kingsmead Av. Mitc—69Lb 126
Kingsmead Av. Romf—30Hd 48
Kingsmead Av. Sun—68Y 121
Kingsmead Av. Surb—75Qa 143
Kingsmead Av. Wor Pk—76Xa 144
Kingsmead Clo. Eps—80Ta 143
Kingsmead Clo. Sidc—61Wc 131
Kingsmead Ct. N6—31Mb 62
Kingsmead Dri. N'holt—38Ba 57
Kings Meadow. K Lan—1Q 4
Kingsmead Rd. SW2—61Qb 126
King's Mead Way. E9—35Ac 64
Kingsmere Pk. NW9—32Ra 59
Kingsmere Rd. SW19—61Za 124
King's M. SW4—57Nb 104
King's M. WC1—42Pb 82 (6J 193)
Kings M. Chig—19Sc 28
Kingsmill Gdns. Dag—36Bd 67
Kingsmill Rd. Dag—36Bd 67
Kingsmill Ter. NW8 —40Fb 61 (1C 190)
Kingsnympton Pk. King—65Ra 123
King's Orchard. SE9—58Nc 108
King's Paddock. Hmptn—67Ea 122
Kingspark Ct. E18—27Jc 45
Kings Pas. King—68Ma 123
King's Pl. SE1—47Sb 83 (2D 206)
King's Pl. W4—50Sa 79
Kings Pl. Buck H—19Lc 27
King Sq. EC1—41Sb 83 (4D 194)
Kings Ride Ga. Rich—56Qa 101
Kingsridge. SW19—61Ab 124
Kingsridge Gdns. Dart—58Ld 111
Kings Rd. E4—18Fc 27
Kings Rd. E6—39Lc 65
Kings Rd. E11—31Gc 65
King's Rd. N17—25Vb 43
King's Rd. N18—22Wb 43
Kings Rd. N22—25Pb 42
Kings Rd. NW10—38Xa 60
Kings Rd. SE25—69Wb 127
King's Rd.—52Db 103 (7E 202)
SW3 1-363 & 2-392
SW10 365-539 & 394-552
SW6 remainder
Kings Rd. SW14—55Ta 101
King's Rd. SW19—65Cb 125
Kings Rd. W5—43Ma 79
King's Rd. Asc—10B 116
Kings Rd. Bark—38Sc 66
Kings Rd. Barn—13Ya 22
Kings Rd. Brtwd—19Yd 32
Kings Rd. Chal—18A 16
Kings Rd. Egh—63C 118
King's Rd. Felt—60Y 99
King's Rd. Harr—33Ba 57
King's Rd. King—66Na 123
Kings Rd. Mitc—69Jb 126
Kings Rd. Orp—77Vc 151
Kings Rd. Rich—57Pa 101
King's Rd. Romf—29Jd 48
King's Rd. Slou—8J 73
King's Rd. Surb—74Ka 142
King's Rd. Sutt—82Cb 163
King's Rd. Tedd—64Fa 122
Kings Rd. Twic—58Ka 100
Kings Rd. Uxb—40M 55
Kings Rd. Wal X—6Ac 12
Kings Rd. W on T—75X 141
King's Rd. W Dray—47P 75
Kings Rd. West—88Lc 167
Kings Rd. Wey—82K 157
King's Rd. Wind—6H 95
(in two parts)
Kings Rd. Wok—88C 156
King's Scholar's Pas. SW1 —(4B 204)
King's Shade Wlk. Eps—85Ta 161
Kingstable St. Wind—2H 95
King's Ter. NW1—39Lb 62 (1B 192)
Kingsthorpe Rd. SE26—63Zb 128
Kingston Av. Felt—58U 98
Kingston Av. Lea—93Ka 176
Kingston Av. Lea—98U 174
(East Horsley)
Kingston Av. Sutt—76Ab 144
Kingston Av. W Dray—45P 75
(in two parts)
Kingston Bri. King—68Ma 123
Kingston By-Pass—75Ga 142 to 62Ua 124
Esh—75Ga 142
Surb—76Ja 142
N Mald—73Sa 143
SW20—69Wa 124
SW15—64Ua 124
Kingston Clo. N'holt—39Ba 57
Kingston Clo. Romf—27Ad 47
Kingston Clo. Tedd—65Ka 122
Kingston Ct. Grav—57De 113
Kingston Cres. Ashf—64L 119
Kingston Cres. Beck—67Bc 128
Kingston Hall Rd. King—69Ma 123
Kingston Hill. King—67Qa 123
Kingston Hill Av. Romf—27Ad 47
Kingston Ho. Gdns. Lea—93Ka 176
Kingston La. Lea—99Q 174
Kingston La. Tedd—64Ja 122
Kingston La. Uxb—41N 75
Kingston La. W Dray—47P 75
Kingston Rise. Wey—82J 157
Kingston Rd. N9—19Wb 25
Kingston Rd. SW15—61Wa 124
Kingston Rd.—68Za 124
SW19 1-277 & 2-216
SW20 remainder
Kingston Rd. Barn—15Fb 23
Kingston Rd. Eps—81Va 162
Kingston Rd. Ilf—35Sc 66
Kingston Rd. King & N Mald —69Ra 123
Kingston Rd. Lea—90Ja 160
Kingston Rd. Lea—88Ja 160
(Pachesham Park)
Kingston Rd. Romf—28Hd 48
Kingston Rd. S'hall—47Ba 77
Kingston Rd. Stai & Ashf—63J 119
Kingston Rd. Surb, Wor Pk & Eps—75Ra 143
Kingston Rd. Tedd—64Ka 122
Kingston Sq. SE19—64Tb 127
Kingston Vale. SW15—63Ta 123
Kingstown St. NW1—39Jb 62
King St. E13—42Jc 85
King St. EC2—44Sb 83 (3E 200)
King St. N2—27Fb 41
King St. N17—25Vb 43
King St. SW1—46Lb 82 (7C 198)
King St. W3—46Sa 79
King St. W6—49Wa 80
King St. WC2—45Nb 82 (4F 199)
King St. Cher—74J 139
King St. Grav—8D 114
King St. Rich—57Ma 101
King St. S'hall—48Aa 77
King St. Stanf—2L 93
King St. Twic—60Ja 100
King St. Wat—14Y 19
Kingsville Ct. W Dray—45M 75
Kings Wlk. Grays—51Ce 113
King's Wlk. King—67Ma 123
Kings Wlk. S Croy—86Xb 165
Kingsway. N12—23Eb 41
Kingsway. SW14—55Ra 101
Kingsway. WC2—44Pb 82 (2H 199)
Kings Way. Croy—78Pb 146
Kingsway. Enf—15Xb 25
Kingsway. Ger X—27A 34
Kings Way. Harr—28Ga 38
Kingsway. Hay—43S 76
Kingsway. Iver—44G 74
Kingsway. N Mald—71Ya 144
Kingsway. Orp—71Tc 150
Kingsway. Pot B—2Nb 10
Kingsway. Slou—7F 52
Kingsway. Stai—60M 97
Kingsway. Wemb—35Na 59
Kingsway. W Wick—76Gc 149
Kingsway. Wok—6G 188
Kings Way. Wfd G—22Lc 45
Kingsway Av. S Croy—81Yb 166
Kingsway Av. Wok—6G 188
Kingsway Cres. Harr—28Ea 38
Kingsway N. Orbital Rd. Wat—7V 4
Kingsway Rd. Sutt—80Ab 144
Kingsway, The. Eps—82Va 162
Kingswear Rd. NW5—34Kb 62
Kingswear Rd. Ruis—33W 56
Kingswell Ride. Pot B—2Nb 10
Kingswick Dri. Asc—10B 116
Kingswood Av. NW6—39Ab 60
Kingswood Av. Belv—49Bd 87
Kingswood Av. Brom—70Gc 129
Kingswood Av. Hmptn—65Da 121
Kingswood Av. Houn—54Ba 99
Kingswood Av. S Croy—87Xb 165
Kingswood Av. Swan—70Hd 132
Kingswood Av. T Hth—71Qb 146
Kingswood Clo. N20—17Eb 23
Kingswood Clo. SW8—52Nb 104
Kingswood Clo. Dart—58Ld 111
Kingswood Clo. Egh—3P 117
Kingswood Clo. N Mald—72Va 144
Kingswood Clo. Orp—73Uc 150
Kingswood Clo. Surb—73Na 143
Kingswood Clo. Wey—80R 140
Kingswood Creek. Wray, Stai —7P 95
Kingswood Dri. SE19—63Ub 127
Kingswood Dri. Cars—74Hb 145
Kingswood Ho. Slou—3G 72
Kingswood La. Warl & S Croy —87Yb 166
Kingswood Pk. N3—25Bb 41
Kingswood Pl. SE13—56Gc 107
Kingswood Rise. Egh—4P 117
Kingswood Rd. SE20—65Yb 128
Kingswood Rd. SW2—58Nb 104
Kingswood Rd. SW19—66Bb 125
Kingswood Rd. W4—48Sa 79
Kingswood Rd. Brom—69Gc 129
Kingswood Rd. Ilf—32Wc 67
Kingswood Rd. Sev—92Gd 186
Kingswood Rd. Tad—93Xa 178
Kingswood Rd. Wat—6X 5
Kingswood Way. S Croy (in two parts) —85Yb 166
Kingswood Way. Wall—78Nb 146
Kingsworth Clo. Beck—71Ac 148
Kingthorpe Rd. NW10—38Ta 59
Kingwell Rd. Barn—10Fb 9
King William IV Gdns. SE20 —65Yb 128
King William St. EC4 —45Tb 83 (4G 201)
King William Wlk. SE10—51Ec 106
Kingwood Rd. SW6—53Ab 102
Kinlet Rd. SE18—53Sc 108
Kinloch Dri. NW9—31Ta 59
Kinloch St. N7—34Pb 62
Kinloss Gdns. N3—27Bb 41
Kinloss Rd. Cars—73Eb 145
Kinnaird Av. W4—52Sa 101
Kinnaird Av. Brom—65Hc 129
Kinnaird Clo. Brom—65Hc 129
Kinnaird Way. Wfd G—23Pc 46
Kinnear Rd. W12—47Va 80
Kinnerton Pl. N. SW1—(2G 203)
Kinnerton Pl. S. SW1—(2G 203)
Kinnerton St. SW1 —47Jb 82 (2H 203)
Kinnerton Yd. SW1—(2H 203)
Kinnoul Rd. W6—51Ab 102
Kinross Av. Wor Pk—75Wa 144
Kinross Clo. Harr—29Pa 39
Kinross Clo. Sun—64V 120
Kinross Dri. Sun—64V 120
Kinross St. SE1—47Ub 83 (2J 207)
Kinsale Rd. SE15—55Wb 105
Kintore Way. SE1 —49Vb 83 (5K 207)
Kintyre Clo. SW16—68Pb 126
Kinveachy Gdns. SE7—50Nc 86
Kinver Rd. SE26—63Yb 128
Kipling Av. Til—3D 114
Kipling Pl. Stan—23Ha 38
Kipling Rd. Bexh—53Ad 109
Kipling Rd. Dart—57Rd 111
Kipling St. SE1—47Tb 83 (2G 207)
Kipling Ter. N9—20Tb 25
Kippington Dri. SE9—60Mc 107
Kippington Rd. Sev—96Jd 186
Kirby Clo. Eps—78Va 144
Kirby Clo. Ilf—23Uc 46
Kirby Clo. Lou—17Nc 28
Kirby Clo. N'wd—23V 36
Kirby Gro. SE1—47Ub 83 (1H 207)
Kirby Rd. Dart—59Td 112
Kirby Rd. Wok—5F 188
Kirby St. EC1—43Qb 82 (7A 194)
Kirby Way. W on T—72Y 141
Kirchen Rd. W13—45Ka 78
Kirkcaldy Grn. Wat—20Y 19
Kirkcourt. Sev—95Jd 186
Kirkdale. SE26—61Xb 127
Kirkdale Rd. E11—32Gc 65
Kirkham Rd. E6—44Nc 86
Kirkham St. SE18—51Uc 108
Kirkland Av. Ilf—26Qc 46
Kirkland Av. Wok—4B 188
Kirkland Clo. Sidc—58Uc 108
Kirkland Wlk. E8—37Vb 63
Kirkland Way. Orp—69Zc 131
Kirk La. SE18—51Sc 108
Kirklees Rd. Dag—36Yc 67
Kirklees Rd. Surb—74Na 143
Kirklees Rd. T Hth—71Qb 146
Kirkley Rd. SW19—67Cb 125
Kirkly Clo. S Croy—81Ub 165
Kirkman Pl. W1—(1D 198)
Kirkmichael Rd. E14—44Ec 84
Kirk Rd. E17—30Bc 44
Kirkside Rd. SE3—51Jc 107
Kirk's Pl. E14—43Bc 84
Kirkstall Av. N17—28Tb 43
Kirkstall Gdns. SW2—60Nb 104
Kirkstall Rd. SW2—60Mb 104
Kirksted Rd. Mord—74Db 145
Kirkstone Way. Brom—66Gc 129
Kirk St. WC1—(6J 193)
Kirkton Rd. N15—28Ub 43
Kirkwall Pl. E2—41Yb 84
Kirkwood Pl. NW1—38Jb 62
Kirkwood Rd. SE15—54Xb 105
Kirn Rd. W13—45Ka 78
Kirtley Rd. SE26—63Ac 128
Kirtling St. SW8—52Lb 104
Kirton Clo. W4—49Ta 79
Kirton Clo. Horn—37Ld 69
Kirton Gdns. E2—41Vb 83 (4K 195)
Kirton Rd. E13—40Lc 65
Kirton Wlk. Edgw—24Sa 39
Kirwyn Way. SE5—52Sb 105
Kitcat Ter. E3—41Cc 84
Kitchener Av. Grav—2E 136
Kitchener Ho. Ger X—22A 34
Kitchener Rd. E7—37Kc 65
Kitchener Rd. E17—25Dc 44
Kitchener Rd. N2—27Gb 41
Kitchener Rd. N17—27Ub 43
Kitchener Rd. Dag—37Ed 68
Kitchener Rd. T Hth—69Tb 127
Kitley Gdns. SE19—67Vb 127
Kitsmead La. Cher—75A 138
Kitson Rd. SE5—52Tb 105
Kitson Rd. SW13—53Wa 102
Kitswell Way. Rad—5Ha 6
Kittiwake Clo. S Croy—82Ac 166
Kittiwake Rd. N'holt—41Z 77
Kitto Rd. SE14—54Zb 106
Kitts End Rd. Barn—8Za 8
Kiver Rd. N19—33Mb 62
Klea Av. SW4—58Lb 104
Knapdale Clo. SE23—61Xb 127

Knapmill Rd. SE6—61Cc **128**
Knapmill Way. SE6—61Dc **128**
Knapp Clo. NW10—37Ua **60**
Knapp Rd. E3—42Cc **84**
Knapp Rd. Ashf—63P **119**
Knapton M. SW17—65Jb **126**
Knaresborough Pl. SW5—49Db **81**
Knatchbull Rd. NW10—39Ta **59**
Knatchbull Rd. SE5—54Rb **105**
★Knatts La. Sev—83Td
Knatts Valley Rd. Sev—79Sd **154**
★Knatts Valley Rd. Sev—85Sd
Knave Wood Rd. Sev—89Nd **171**
Knebworth Av. E17—25Cc **44**
Knebworth Path. Borwd—14Ta **21**
Knebworth Rd. N16—35Ub **63**
Knee Hill. SE2—49Yc **87**
Knee Hill Cres. SE2—49Yc **87**
Kneller Gdns. Iswth—58Fa **100**
Kneller Rd. SE4—56Ac **106**
Kneller Rd. N Mald—73Ua **144**
Kneller Rd. Twic—58Ea **100**
Knightland Rd. E5—33Xb **63**
Knighton Clo. Romf—30Fd **48**
Knighton Clo. S Croy—81Rb **165**
Knighton Clo. Wfd G—21Kc **45**
Knighton Dri. Wfd G—21Kc **45**
Knighton La. Buck H—19Kc **27**
Knighton Pk. Rd. SE26—64Zb **128**
Knighton Rd. E7—34Jc **65**
Knighton Rd. Romf—30Ed **48**
Knighton Rd. Sev—88Hd **170**
Knighton Way La. Uxb—37K **55**
Knightrider Ct. EC4—(4D 200)
Knightrider St. EC4
—44Rb **83** (4C **200**)
Knights Av. W5—47Na **79**
Knightsbridge—47Hb **81** (2E **202**)
SW1 1-161 & 2-124
SW7 remainder
Knightsbridge Ct. SW1—(2G 203)
Knightsbridge Cres. Stai—65K **119**
Knightsbridge Gdns. Romf
—29Fd **48**
Knightsbridge Grn. SW1
—47Hb **81** (2F **203**)
Knight's Clo. E9—36Yb **64**
Knights Clo. Egh—65F **118**
Knights Clo. Wind—3B **94**
Knights Croft. Long, Dart
—76Be **155**
(in two parts)
Knights Hill. SE27—64Rb **127**
Knights Hill Sq. SE27—63Rb **127**
Knights La. N9—20Wb **25**
Knights Pk. King—69Na **123**
Knights Ridge. Orp—78Xc **151**
Knight's Rd. E16—47Jc **85**
Knights Rd. Stan—21La **38**
Knight's Wlk. SE11
—49Rb **83** (6B **206**)
Knights Wlk. Romf—13Xc **29**
Knights Way. Brtwd—20Ce **33**
Knights Way. Ilf—23Sc **46**
Knightswood. Wok—6C **188**
Knightswood Clo. Edgw—19Sa **21**
Knightswood Ct. N6—31Mb **62**
Knightswood Ho. N12—23Eb **41**
Knightwood Cres. N Mald
—72Ua **144**
Knipp Hill Cob—85Ba **159**
Knivet Rd. SW6—51Cb **103**
Knobs Hill Rd. E15—39Dc **64**
Knockhall Chase. Grnh—57Xd **112**
Knockhall Rd. Grnh—58Yd **112**
Knockholt Main Rd. Sev
—91Vc **185**
Knockholt Rd. SE9—57Mc **107**
Knockholt Rd. Sev—86Bd **169**
★Knock Mill La. Sev—85Wd
Knole Clo. Croy—72Yb **148**
Knole La. Sev—98Ld **187**
Knole Rd. Dart—59Jd **110**
Knole Rd. Sev—95Md **187**
Knole, The. SE9—63Qc **130**
Knole, The. Grav—6A **136**
Knole Way. Sev—97Ld **187**
Knoll Cres. N'wd—25U **36**
Knoll Dri. N14—17Jb **24**
Knollmead. Surb—74Sa **143**
Knoll Rise. Orp—74Vc **151**
Knoll Rd. SW18—57Eb **103**
Knoll Rd. Bex—59Cd **110**
Knoll Rd. Sidc—64Xc **131**
Knolls Clo. Wor Pk—76Xa **144**
Knolls, The. Eps—88Ya **162**
Knoll, The. W5—43La **78**
Knoll, The. Beck—67Dc **128**
Knoll, The. Brom—74Jc **149**
Knoll, The. Cob—85Ca **159**
Knollys Clo. SW16—62Qb **126**
Knollys Rd. SW16—62Qb **126**
Knolton Way. Slou—4M **73**
Knottisford St. E2—41Yb **84**
Knotts Grn. Rd. E10—30Dc **44**
Knotts Pl. Sev—96Jd **186**
Knowland Way. Uxb—30H **35**
Knowle Av. Bexh—52Ad **109**
Knowle Clo. SW9—55Qb **104**
Knowle Gdns. Wey—85H **157**
Knowle Grn. Stai—64J **119**
Knowle Pk. Cob—87Aa **159**
Knowle Pk. Av. Stai—65K **119**
Knowle Rd. Brom—75Pc **150**
Knowle Rd. Twic—60Ga **100**
Knowles Hill Cres. SE13—57Fc **107**
Knowles Wlk. SW4—55Lb **104**
Knowl Hill. Wok—91D **172**
Knowl Pk. Borwd—15Na **21**
Knowlton Grn. Brom—71Hc **149**
Knowl Way. Borwd—15Pa **21**
Knowsley Av. S'hall—46Da **77**
Knowsley Rd. SW11—54Hb **103**
Knox Rd. E7—37Hc **65**
Knox St. W1—43Hb **81** (7F **191**)
Knoyle St. SE14—51Ac **106**
Knutsford Av. Wat—10Z **5**
Kohat Rd. SW19—64Db **125**
Koh-i-noor Av. Bush, Wat
—16Ca **19**
Koonowla Clo. West—87Mc **167**
Kooringa. Warl—91Xb **181**
Korda Clo. Shep—60P **97**
Kossuth St. SE10—50Gc **85**
Kotree Way. SE1—49Wb **83**
Kramer M. SW5—50Cb **81**
Kreisel Wlk. Rich—51Pa **101**
Krupnik Pl. EC2—(5J 195)
Kuala Gdns. SW16—67Pb **126**
Kuhn Way. E7—36Jc **65**
Kydbrook Clo. Orp—73Sc **150**
Kylemore Clo. E6—40Mc **65**
Kylemore Rd. NW6—38Cb **61**
Kymberley Rd. Harr—30Ga **38**
Kyme Rd. Horn—30Hd **48**
Kynance Clo. Romf—21Ld **49**
Kynance Gdns. Stan—25La **38**
Kynance M. SW7
—48Eb **81** (4A **202**)
Kynance Pl. SW7
—48Eb **81** (4A **202**)
Kynaston Av. N16—34Vb **63**
Kynaston Av. T Hth—71Sb **147**
Kynaston Clo. Harr—24Fa **38**
Kynaston Cres. T Hth—71Sb **147**
Kynaston Rd. N16—34Ub **63**
Kynaston Rd. Brom—64Jc **129**
Kynaston Rd. Enf—11Tb **25**
Kynaston Rd. Orp—73Xc **151**
Kynaston Rd. T Hth—71Sb **147**
Kynaston Wood. Harr—24Fa **38**
Kynnersley Clo. Cars—76Hb **145**
Kynoch Rd. N18—21Yb **44**
Kyrle Rd. SW11—58Jb **104**
Kytes Dri. Wat—5Z **5**
Kytes Est. Wat—5Z **5**
Kyverdale Rd. N16—32Vb **63**

★Labour in Vain Rd. Sev—85Zd
Laburnham Clo. N11—23Jb **42**
Laburnham Clo. Upm—31Wd **70**
Laburnham Gdns. Upm—31Vd **70**
Laburnham Rd. Cher—74J **139**
Laburnum Av. N9—19Vb **25**
Laburnum Av. N17—24Tb **43**
Laburnum Av. Dart—60Ld **111**
Laburnum Av. Horn—33Jd **68**
Laburnum Av. Sutt—76Gb **145**
Laburnum Av. Swan—69Fd **132**
Laburnum Av. W Dray—45P **75**
Laburnum Clo. E4—23Bc **44**
Laburnum Clo. SE15—52Yb **106**
Laburnum Clo. Wal X—3Zb **12**
Laburnum Ct. Stan—21La **38**
Laburnum Cres. Sun—67X **121**
Laburnum Gdns. N21—19Sb **25**
Laburnum Gdns. Croy—74Zb **148**
Laburnum Gro. N21—19Sb **25**
Laburnum Gro. NW9—31Sa **59**
Laburnum Gro. Grav—59Fe **113**
Laburnum Gro. Houn—56Ba **99**
Laburnum Gro. N Mald—68Ta **123**
Laburnum Gro. Ruis—30T **36**
Laburnum Gro. Slou—51D **96**
Laburnum Gro. S'hall—42Ba **77**
Laburnum Pl. Egh—5M **117**
Laburnum Rd. SW19—66Eb **125**
Laburnum Rd. Epp—1Yc **15**
Laburnum Rd. Eps—85Ua **162**
Laburnum Rd. Hay—49V **76**
Laburnum Rd. Mitc—68Jb **126**
Laburnum Rd. Wok—8G **188**
Laburnum St. E2
—39Vb **63** (1K **195**)
Laburnum Wlk. Horn—36Ld **69**
Laburnum Way. Brom—73Qc **150**
Laburnum Way. Stai—60P **97**
Lacey Av. Coul—92Qb **180**
Lacey Clo. Egh—66F **118**
Lacey Dri. Coul—92Rb **181**
Lacey Dri. Edgw—21Pa **39**
Lacey Dri. Hmptn—67Ba **121**
Lacey Grn. Coul—92Qb **180**
Lacey Wlk. E3—40Cc **64**
Lackford Rd. Coul—90Hb **163**
Lackington St. EC2
—43Tb **83** (7G **195**)
Lackmore Rd. Enf—7Yb **12**
Lacock Clo. SW19—65Eb **125**
Lacon Rd. SE22—56Wb **105**
Lacy Rd. SW15—56Za **102**
Ladas Rd. SE27—63Sb **127**
Ladbroke Cres. W11—44Ab **80**
Ladbroke Gdns. W11—45Bb **81**
Ladbroke Gro.—42Za **80**
W11 1-137 & 2-108
W10 remainder
Ladbroke M. W11—46Ab **80**
Ladbroke Rd. W11—46Bb **81**
Ladbroke Rd. Enf—16Vb **25**
Ladbroke Rd. Eps—86Ta **161**
Ladbroke Sq. W11—45Bb **81**
Ladbroke Ter. W11—45Bb **81**
Ladbroke Wlk. W11—46Bb **81**
Ladbrook Clo. Pinn—29Ba **37**
Ladbrooke Clo. Pot B—4Cb **9**
Ladbrooke Cres. Sidc—62Zc **131**
Ladbrooke Dri. Pot B—4Cb **9**
Ladbrooke Rd. Slou—8H **73**
Ladbrook Rd. SE25—70Tb **127**
Ladderstile Ride. King—64Ra **123**
Ladderswood Way. N11—22Lb **42**
Ladds Way. Swan—70Fd **132**
Ladycroft Gdns. Orp—78Sc **150**
Ladycroft Rd. SE13—55Dc **106**
Ladycroft Wlk. Stan—25Ma **39**
Ladycroft Way. Orp—78Sc **150**
Ladyday Pl. Slou—6G **72**
Lady Dock Wlk. SE16—47Ac **84**
Ladyfields. Grav—3B **136**
Ladyfields. Lou—14Sc **28**
Ladyfields Clo. Lou—14Sc **28**
Ladygate La. Ruis—30R **36**
Ladygrove. Croy—81Ac **166**
Lady Hay. Wor Pk—75Va **144**
Lady Margaret Rd.—36Lb **62**
NW5 1-83 & 2-70
N19 remainder
Lady Margaret Rd. S'hall
—45Ba **77**
Lady's Clo. Wat—14Y **19**
Lady Shaw Ct. N13—19Pb **24**
Ladyship Ter. SE22—59Wb **105**
Ladysmith Av. E6—40Nc **66**
Ladysmith Av. Ilf—31Uc **66**
Ladysmith Rd. E16—41Hc **85**
Ladysmith Rd. N17—26Wb **43**
Ladysmith Rd. N18—22Xb **43**
Ladysmith Rd. SE9—58Qc **108**
Ladysmith Rd. Enf—13Ub **25**
Ladysmith Rd. Harr—26Ga **38**
Lady Somerset Rd. NW5—35Kb **62**
★Ladys Wlk. Sev—96Wd
Ladythorpe Clo. Wey—77K **139**
Ladywell Rd. SE13—57Cc **106**
Ladywell St. E15—39Hc **65**
Ladywood Av. Orp—71Uc **150**
Ladywood Clo. Rick—13L **17**
Ladywood Rd. Dart—64Ud **134**
Ladywood Rd. Surb—75Qa **143**
Lafone Av. Felt—61Y **121**
Lafone St. SE1—47Vb **83** (1K **207**)
Lagonda Av. Ilf—23Vc **47**
Lagoon Rd. Orp—71Yc **151**
Laing Clo. Ilf—23Tc **46**
Laing Dean. N'holt—39Y **57**
Laings Av. Mitc—68Hb **125**
Lainlock Pl. Houn—53Da **99**
Lainson St. SW18—59Cb **103**
Lairdale Clo. SE21—60Sb **105**
Laird Av. Grays—47Fe **91**
Lairs Clo. N7—36Nb **62**
Laitwood Rd. SW12—60Kb **104**
Lake Av. Brom—65Jc **129**
Lake Av. Rain—40Md **69**
Lake Av. Slou—5H **73**
Lake Clo. Wey—84M **157**
Lakedale Rd. SE18—51Uc **108**
Lake End Rd. M'head & Wind
—5A **72**
Lakefield Rd. N22—26Rb **43**
Lakefields Clo. Rain—40Md **69**
Lake Footpath. SE2—47Zc **87**
Lake Gdns. Dag—36Cd **68**
Lake Gdns. Rich—61Ka **122**
Lake Gdns. Wall—76Kb **146**
Lakehall Gdns. T Hth—71Rb **147**
Lakehall Rd. T Hth—71Rb **147**
Lake Ho. Rd. E11—34Jc **65**
Lakehurst Rd. Eps—78Ua **144**
Lakeland Clo. Chig—21Xc **47**
Lakeland Clo. Harr—23Fa **38**
Lakeman Ho. Ger X—22B **34**
Lakenheath. N14—15Mb **24**
Lake Rise. Romf—27Hd **48**
Lake Rd. SW19—64Bb **125**
Lake Rd. Croy—75Bc **148**
Lake Rd. Romf—28Zc **47**
Lake Rd. Vir W—10M **117**
Laker Pl. SW15—58Ab **102**
Lakers Rise. Bans—88Gb **163**
Lakeside. W13—44La **78**
Lakeside. Beck—69Dc **128**
Lakeside. Enf—14Mb **24**
Lakeside. Rain—40Nd **69**
Lakeside. Wall—77Kb **146**
Lakeside. Wey—75U **140**
Lakeside. Wok—7B **188**
Lakeside Av. Ilf—28Mc **45**
Lakeside Clo. SE25—68Wb **127**
Lakeside Clo. Ruis—28T **36**
Lakeside Clo. Sidc—57Yc **109**
Lakeside Clo. Wok—7B **188**
Lakeside Ct. N4—33Sb **63**
Lakeside Ct. Borwd—15Qa **21**
Lakeside Cres. Barn—15Hb **23**
Lakeside Cres. Brtwd—20Zd **33**
Lakeside Dri. Brom—76Nc **150**
Lakeside Dri. Esh—79Fa **142**
Lakeside Dri. Slou—9J **53**
Lakeside Rd. N13—21Pb **42**
Lakeside Rd. W14—48Za **80**
Lakeside Rd. Slou—52H **97**
Lakeside Ter. EC2—(7E 194)
Lakeside Way. Wemb—35Qa **59**
Lakes Rd. Kes—78Lc **149**
Lakestreet Grn. Oxt—100Mc **183**
Lake, The. Bush, Wat—18Fa **20**
Lake View. Edgw—22Pa **39**
Lake View. Pot B—5Eb **9**
(in two parts)
Lakeview Rd. SE27—64Qb **126**
Lake View Rd. Sev—95Jd **186**
Lake View Rd. Well—56Xc **109**
Lakewood Rd. Orp—72Rc **150**
Lakis Clo. NW3—35Eb **61**
Laleham Av. NW7—20Ta **21**
Laleham Ct. Wok—88A **156**
Laleham Rd. SE6—59Ec **106**
Laleham Rd. Shep—70P **119**
Laleham Rd. Stai—64H **119**
Lalor St. SW6—54Ab **102**
Lambarde Av. SE9—63Qc **130**
Lambarde Dri. Sev—95Jd **186**
Lambarde Rd. Sev—94Jd **186**
Lambardes. Long, Dart—75Be **155**
Lamb Clo. Til—4E **114**
Lamberhurst Clo. Orp—74Zc **151**
Lamberhurst Rd. SE27—63Qb **126**
Lamberhurst Rd. Dag—32Bd **67**
Lambert Av. Rich—55Qa **101**
Lambert Av. Slou—48A **74**
Lambert Clo. West—88Mc **167**
Lambert Ct. Bush, Wat—14Z **19**
Lambert Jones M. EC2—(7D 194)
Lamberton Ct. Borwd—11Qa **21**
Lambert Rd. E16—44Kc **85**
Lambert Rd. N12—22Eb **41**
Lambert Rd. SW2—57Nb **104**
Lambert Rd. Bans—86Cb **163**
Lamberts Pl. Croy—74Tb **147**
Lamberts Rd. Surb—71Pa **143**
Lambert St. N1—38Qb **62**
Lambert Wlk. Wemb—34Ma **59**
Lambert Way. N12—22Eb **41**
Lambeth Bri. SW1 & SE1
—49Nb **82** (5G **205**)
Lambeth High St. SE1
—49Pb **82** (5H **205**)
Lambeth Hill. EC4
—45Sb **83** (4D **200**)
Lambeth Pal. Rd. SE1
—48Pb **82** (4H **205**)
Lambeth Rd. SE1
—48Pb **82** (5H **205**)
Lambeth Rd. Croy—74Qb **146**
Lambeth Wlk. SE11
—49Pb **82** (5J **205**)
(in two parts)
Lamb La. E8—38Xb **63**
Lamble St. NW5—36Jb **62**
Lambley Rd. Dag—37Xc **67**
Lambolle Pl. NW3—37Gb **61**
Lambolle Rd. NW3—37Gb **61**
Lambourn Clo. W7—47Ha **78**
Lambourne. Grays—9L **93**
Lambourne Av. SW19—63Bb **125**
Lambourne Cres. Chig—19Xc **29**
Lambourne Cres. Wok—85F **156**
Lambourne Dri. Brtwd—16Fe **33**
Lambourne Gdns. E4—19Cc **26**
Lambourne Gdns. Bark—38Uc **67**
Lambourne Gdns. Enf—12Vb **25**
Lambourne Gdns. Horn—33Md **69**
Lambourne Pl. SE3—53Kc **107**
Lambourne Rd. E11—31Ec **64**
Lambourne Rd. Bark—38Uc **66**
Lambourne Rd. Chig—20Vc **29**
Lambourne Rd. Ilf—33Uc **66**
Lambourn Gro. King—68Ra **123**
Lambourn Rd. SW4—55Kb **104**
Lambrook Ter. SW6—53Ab **102**
Lamb's Bldgs. EC1
—42Tb **83** (6F **195**)
Lambs Clo. N9—19Wb **25**
Lambs Clo. Pot B—1Pb **10**
Lamb's Conduit Pas. WC1
—43Pb **82** (7H **193**)
Lamb's Conduit St. WC1
—42Pb **82** (6H **193**)
Lambscroft Av. SE9—62Lc **129**
Lambscroft Way. Ger X—26A **34**
Lamb's La. Rain—43Kd **89**
Lambs Meadow. Wfd G—26Mc **45**
Lamb's M. N1—39Rb **63** (1B **194**)
Lamb's Pas. EC1—42Tb **83** (7F **195**)
Lamb's Pas. Bren—51Pa **101**
Lambs Ter. N9—19Tb **25**
Lamb St. E1—43Vb **83** (7K **195**)
Lamb's Wlk. Enf—12Sb **25**
Lambton Av. Wal X—5Zb **12**
Lambton Pl. W11—45Bb **81**
Lambton Rd. N19—32Nb **62**
Lambton Rd. SW20—67Ya **124**
Lamb Wlk. SE1—47Ub **83** (2H **207**)
Lamerock Rd. Brom—63Hc **129**
Lamerton Rd. Ilf—26Rc **46**
Lamerton St. SE8—51Cc **106**
Lamford Clo. N17—24Tb **43**
Lamington St. W6—49Xa **80**
Lamlash St. SE11
—49Rb **83** (5B **206**)
Lammas Av. Mitc—68Jb **126**
Lammas Ct. Stai—61F **118**
Lammas Ct. Wind—4G **94**
Lammas Dri. Stai—63F **118**
Lammas Grn. SE26—62Xb **127**
Lammas La. Esh—78Ca **141**
Lammas Pk. Gdns. W5—46La **78**
Lammas Pk. Rd. W5—47Ma **79**
Lammas Rd. E9—38Zb **64**
Lammas Rd. E10—33Ac **64**
Lammas Rd. Rich—63La **122**
Lammas Rd. Slou—3B **72**
Lammas Rd. Wat—15Y **19**
Lammermoor Rd. SW12
—59Kb **104**
Lamont Rd. SW10—51Eb **103**
Lamorbey Clo. Sidc—61Vc **131**
Lamorna Av. Grav—1F **136**
Lamorna Clo. Orp—73Wc **151**
Lamorna Clo. Rad—6Ka **6**
Lamorna Gro. Stan—25Ma **39**
Lampard Gro. N16—32Vb **63**
Lampern Sq. E2—41Wb **83**
Lampeter Clo. Wok—90A **156**
Lampeter Sq. W6—51Ab **102**
Lampmead Rd. SE12—57Hc **107**
Lamport Clo. SE18—49Pc **86**
Lampton Av. Houn—53Da **99**
Lampton Ho. Clo. SW19—63Za **124**
Lampton Pk. Rd. Houn—54Da **99**
Lampton Rd. Houn—54Da **99**
Lamson Rd. Rain—43Hd **88**
Lanacre Av. NW9—25Ua **40**
Lanark Clo. W5—43La **78**
Lanark Pl. W9—42Eb **81** (5A **190**)
Lanark Rd. W9—40Db **61** (4A **190**)
Lanbury Rd. SE15—56Zb **106**
Lancashire Ct. W1—(4A 198)
Lancaster Av. E18—28Kc **45**
Lancaster Av. SE27—61Rb **127**
Lancaster Av. SW19—64Za **124**
Lancaster Av. Bark—38Uc **66**
Lancaster Av. Barn—10Fb **9**
Lancaster Av. Mitc—71Nb **146**
Lancaster Av. Slou—2G **72**
Lancaster Clo. N17—24Wb **43**
Lancaster Clo. SE27—61Rb **127**
Lancaster Clo. Brtwd—15Wd **32**
Lancaster Clo. Brom—70Hc **129**
Lancaster Clo. Croy—75Nb **146**
Lancaster Clo. King—64Ma **123**
Lancaster Cotts. Rich—58Na **101**
Lancaster Ct. SW6—52Bb **103**
Lancaster Ct. Bans—86Bb **163**
Lancaster Ct. W on T—73W **140**
Lancaster Dri. NW3—37Gb **61**
Lancaster Dri. Horn—36Kd **69**
Lancaster Garages. NW3
—37Gb **61**
Lancaster Gdns. SW19—64Ab **124**
Lancaster Gdns. W13—47Ka **78**
Lancaster Gdns. King—64Ma **123**
Lancaster Ga. W2
—45Eb **81** (5A **196**)
Lancaster Gro. NW3—37Fb **61**
Lancaster M. W2
—45Eb **81** (4A **196**)
Lancaster M. Rich—58Na **101**
Lancaster Pk. Rich—57Na **101**
Lancaster Pl. SW19—64Za **124**
Lancaster Pl. WC2
—45Pb **82** (4H **199**)
Lancaster Pl. Houn—54Z **99**
Lancaster Pl. Twic—58Ja **100**
Lancaster Rd. E7—38Jc **65**
Lancaster Rd. E11—33Gc **65**
Lancaster Rd. E17—26Zb **44**
Lancaster Rd. N4—31Qb **62**
Lancaster Rd. N11—23Mb **42**
Lancaster Rd. N18—22Vb **43**
Lancaster Rd. NW10—36Wa **60**
Lancaster Rd. SE25—68Vb **127**
Lancaster Rd. SW19—64Za **124**
Lancaster Rd. W11—44Ab **80**
Lancaster Rd. Barn—15Fb **23**
Lancaster Rd. Enf—11Tb **25**
Lancaster Rd. Harr—29Ca **37**
Lancaster Rd. N'holt—37Ea **58**
Lancaster Rd. S'hall—45Aa **77**
Lancaster Rd. Uxb—37M **55**
Lancaster St. SE1
—47Rb **83** (2C **206**)
Lancaster Ter. W2
—45Fb **81** (4B **196**)
Lancaster Wlk. W2 & SW7
—46Eb **81** (5A **196**)
Lancaster Wlk. Hay—44S **76**
Lance Croft. Long, Dart—75Be **155**
Lancefield St. W10—41Bb **81**
(in two parts)
Lancell St. N16—33Ub **63**
Lancelot Av. Wemb—35Ma **59**
Lancelot Cres. Wemb—35Ma **59**
Lancelot Gdns. Barn—17Jb **24**
Lancelot Pl. SW7
—47Hb **81** (2F **203**)
Lancelot Rd. Ilf—24Uc **46**
Lancelot Rd. Well—56Wc **109**
Lancelot Rd. Wemb—36Ma **59**
Lance Rd. Harr—31Ea **58**
Lancey Clo. SE7—49Nc **86**
Lanchester Rd. N6—29Hb **41**
Lancing Gdns. N9—18Vb **25**
Lancing Rd. W13—45Ka **78**
Lancing Rd. Croy—73Pb **146**
Lancing Rd. Felt—61V **120**
Lancing Rd. Ilf—30Tc **46**
Lancing Rd. Orp—75Wc **151**
Lancing Rd. Romf—24Nd **49**
Lancing St. NW1
—41Mb **82** (4D **192**)
Lancing Way. Rick—15R **18**
Lancresse Clo. Uxb—37M **55**
Landau Way. Eri—50Md **89**
Landcroft Rd. SE22—57Vb **105**
Landells Rd. SE22—58Vb **105**
Lander Rd. Grays—50Fe **91**
Landford Clo. Rick—19N **17**
Landford Rd. SW15—55Ya **102**
Landgrove Rd. SW19—64Cb **125**
Landmann Way. SE14—50Zb **84**
Landmead Rd. Wal X—1Ac **12**
Landon Pl. SW1—48Hb **81** (3F **203**)
Landon Wlk. E14—45Dc **84**
Landon Way. Ashf—65R **120**
Landor Rd. SW9—55Nb **104**
Landor Wlk. W12—47Wa **80**
Landport Way. SE15—52Vb **105**
Landra Gdns. N21—16Rb **25**
Landridge Rd. SW6—54Bb **103**
Landrock Rd. N8—30Pb **42**
Landscape Rd. Warl—91Xb **181**
Landscape Rd. Wfd G—24Kc **45**
Landseer Av. E12—36Qc **66**
Landseer Av. Grav—62Fe **135**
Landseer Clo. SW19—67Eb **125**
Landseer Clo. Edgw—26Qa **39**
Landseer Rd. N19—34Nb **62**
Landseer Rd. Enf—15Wb **25**
Landseer Rd. N Mald—73Ta **143**
Landseer Rd. Sutt—79Cb **145**
Landstead Rd. SE18—52Tc **108**
Landway. Sev—92Pd **187**
Landway, The. Orp—69Yc **131**
Landway, The. Sev—90Qd **171**
★Landway, The. Sev—92Be
Lane App. NW7—22Ab **40**
Lane Av. Grnh—58Yd **112**
Lane Clo. NW2—34Xa **60**
Lane Clo. Wey—78K **139**
Lane End. Bexh—55Dd **110**
Lane End. Eps—86Ra **161**
Lane End Dri. Wok—5A **188**
Lane Gdns. Bush, Wat—17Ga **20**
Lanercost Clo. SW2—61Qb **126**
Lanercost Gdns. N14—17Nb **24**
Lanercost Rd. SW2—61Qb **126**
Lanes Av. Grav—2B **136**
Laneside. Chst—64Sc **130**
Laneside. Edgw—22Sa **39**
Laneside Av. Dag—31Bd **67**
Lane, The. NW8—40Eb **61**
Lane, The. SE3—55Jc **107**
Lane, The. Cher—69J **118**
Lane, The. Vir W—69B **118**
Laneway. SW15—57Xa **102**
Lanfranc Rd. E3—40Ac **64**
Lanfranc St. SE1—(3A 206)
Lanfrey Pl. W14—50Bb **81**
Langafel Clo. Long, Dart
—68Ae **135**
Langaller La. Lea—94Da **175**
Langbourne Av. N6—33Jb **62**
Langbourne Way. Esh—79Ja **142**
Langbrook Rd. SE3—55Mc **107**
Lang Clo. Lea—95Da **175**
Langcroft Clo. Cars—76Hb **145**
Langdale Av. Mitc—69Hb **125**
Langdale Clo. SE17—51Sb **105**
Langdale Clo. Orp—76Rc **150**
Langdale Clo. Wok—4F **188**
Langdale Cres. Bexh—52Cd **110**
Langdale Dri. Hay—40U **56**
Langdale Gdns. Gnfd—41Ka **78**
Langdale Gdns. Horn—36Jd **68**
Langdale Gdns. Wal X—7Zb **12**
Langdale Rd. SE10—52Ec **106**
Langdale Rd. T Hth—70Qb **126**
Langdale St. E1—44Xb **83**
Langdale Wlk. Grav—2A **136**
Langdon Ct. NW10—39Ua **60**
Langdon Cres. E6—40Qc **66**
Langdon Dri. NW9—32Sa **59**
Langdon Pk. Rd. N6—31Lb **62**
Langdon Pl. SW14—55Sa **101**
Langdon Rd. E6—39Qc **66**
Langdon Rd. Brom—69Kc **129**
Langdon Rd. Mord—71Eb **145**
Langdons Ct. S'hall—48Ca **77**
Langdon Shaw. Sidc—64Vc **131**
Langdon Wlk. Mord—71Eb **145**
Langdon Way. SE1—49Wb **83**
Langford Clo. E8—36Wb **63**
Langford Clo. N15—30Ub **43**
Langford Clo. NW8
—40Eb **61** (1A **190**)
Langford Cres. Barn—14Hb **23**
Langford Grn. SE5—55Ub **105**
Langford Pl. NW8
—40Eb **61** (1A **190**)
Langford Pl. Sidc—62Wc **131**
Langford Rd. SW6—54Db **103**
Langford Rd. Barn—14Hb **23**
Langford Rd. Wfd G—23Lc **45**
Langfords. Buck H—19Mc **27**
Langham Ct. Horn—31Md **69**
Langham Dene. Kenl—87Rb **165**
Langham Dri. Romf—30Xc **47**
Langham Gdns. N21—15Qb **24**
Langham Gdns. W13—45Ka **78**
Langham Gdns. Edgw—24Sa **39**
Langham Gdns. Rich—63La **122**
Langham Gdns. Wemb—33La **58**
Langham Ho. Clo. Rich—63Ma **123**
Langham Pl. N15—27Rb **43**
Langham Pl. W1—43Kb **82** (1A **198**)
Langham Pl. Egh—64B **118**
Langham Rd. N15—27Rb **43**
Langham Rd. SW20—67Ya **124**
Langham Rd. Edgw—23Sa **39**
Langham Rd. Tedd—64Ka **122**
Langham St. W1
—43Kb **82** (1A **198**)
Langhedge Clo. N18—23Vb **43**
Langhedge La. N18—23Vb **43**
Langholm Clo. SW12—59Mb **104**
Langholme. Bush, Wat—18Ea **20**
Langhorne Rd. Dag—38Cd **68**
Langland Ct. N'wd—24S **36**
Langland Cres. E. Stan—26Ma **39**
Langland Cres. W. Stan—26Ma **39**
Langland Dri. Pinn—24Aa **37**
Langland Gdns. NW3—36Db **61**
Langland Gdns. Croy—75Bc **148**
Langlands Dri. Dart—64Ud **134**
Langlands Rise. Eps—85Sa **161**
Langler Rd. NW10—40Ya **60**
Langley Av. Ruis—33X **57**
Langley Av. Surb—74Ma **143**
Langley Av. Wor Pk—75Za **144**
Langley Broom. Slou—50B **74**
Langleybury La. Wat & K Lan
—9R **4**
Langley Clo. Eps—91Ta **177**
Langley Clo. Romf—24Md **49**
Langley Clo. Wok—90A **156**
Langley Ct. WC2—(4F 199)
Langley Cres. E11—31Lc **65**
Langley Cres. Dag—38Yc **67**
Langley Cres. Edgw—20Sa **21**
Langley Cres. Hay—52V **98**
Langley Cres. K Lan—2Q **4**
Langley Dri. E11—31Kc **65**
Langley Dri. W3—47Ra **79**
Langley Dri. Brtwd—20Wd **32**
Langley Gdns. Brom—70Lc **129**
Langley Gdns. Dag—38Zc **67**
Langley Gdns. Orp—72Rc **150**
Langley Gro. N Mald—68Ua **124**
Langley Hill. K Lan—1P **3**
Langley Hill Clo. K Lan—1Q **4**
Langley La. SW8—51Pb **104**
Langley La. Abb L, Wat—4V **4**
Langley La. Dor & Eps—97Ra **177**
Langley Meadow. Lou—12Tc **28**
Langley Oaks Av. S Croy
—82Wb **165**
Langley Pk. NW7—23Ua **40**
Langley Pk. Rd. Slou & Iver
—46C **74**
Langley Pk. Rd. Sutt—79Eb **145**
Langley Rd. SW19—67Bb **125**
Langley Rd. Abb L, Wat—3U **4**
Langley Rd. Beck—70Ac **128**
Langley Rd. Iswth—54Ha **100**
Langley Rd. K Lan—2K **3**
Langley Rd. Slou—47A **74**
Langley Rd. Slou—7N **73**
Langley Rd. S Croy—81Zb **166**
Langley Rd. Stai—65H **119**
Langley Rd. Surb—73Na **143**
Langley Rd. Wat—11W **18**
Langley Rd. Well—51Yc **109**
Langley St. WC2
—44Nb **82** (3F **199**)
Langley Vale Rd. Eps—91Sa **177**
Langley Wlk. Wok—91A **172**
Langley Way. Wat—12U **18**
Langley Way. W Wick—74Fc **149**
Langmans Way. Wok—4B **188**

Langmead Dri. Bush, Wat —18Ga 20
Langmead St. SE27—63Sb 127
Langmore Ct. Bexh—55Zc 109
Langport Ct. W on T—74Y 141
Langroyd Rd. SW17—61Hb 125
Langshot Clo. Wey—83G 156
Langside Av. SW15—56Wa 102
Langside Cres. N14—20Mb 24
Langston Rd. Lou—15Sc 28
Lang St. E1—42Yb 84
Langthorn Ct. EC2—(2G 201)
Langthorne Cres. Grays—49Ee 91
Langthorne Rd. E11—34Ec 64
Langthorne St. SW6—52Za 102
Langton Av. E6—41Qc 86
Langton Av. N20—17Eb 23
Langton Av. Eps—83Va 162
Langton Clo. WC1 —42Pb 82 (5J 193)
Langton Clo. Wey—76K 139
Langton Clo. Wok—5C 188
Langton Gro. N'wd—22S 36
Langton Rise. SE23—59Xb 105
Langton Rd. NW2—34Ya 60
Langton Rd. SW9—52Rb 105
Langton Rd. E Mol—70Ea 122
Langton Rd. Harr—24Ea 38
Langton's Meadow. Slou—7G 52
Langton St. SW10—51Eb 103
Langton Way. SE3—53Jc 107
Langton Way. Croy—77Ub 147
Langton Way. Egh—65E 118
Langton Way. Grays—9E 92
Langtry Rd. NW8—39Db 61
Langtry Rd. N'holt—40Z 57
Langtry Wlk. NW8—39Eb 61
Langwood Chase. Tedd—65La 122
Langwood Gdns. Wat—11W 18
Langworth Clo. Dart—62Md 133
Langworth Dri. Hay—44X 77
Langworthy. Pinn—23Ca 37
Lanhill Rd. W9—42Cb 81
Lanier Rd. SE13—58Fc 107
Lankaster Gdns. N2—25Fb 41
Lankers Dri. Harr—30Ba 37
Lankton Clo. Beck—67Ec 128
Lannock Rd. Hay—46V 76
Lannoy Rd. SE9—60Sc 108
Lanrick Rd. E14—44Fc 85
Lanridge Rd. SE2—48Zc 87
Lansbury Av. N18—22Tb 43
Lansbury Av. Bark—38Wc 67
Lansbury Av. Felt—58X 99
Lansbury Av. Romf—29Ad 47
Lansbury Clo. NW10—36Sa 59
Lansbury Cres. Dart—57Qd 111
Lansbury Dri. Hay—43V 76
Lansbury Est. E14—44Dc 84
Lansbury Gdns. E14—44Fc 85
Lansbury Rd. Enf—11Zb 26
Lansbury Way. N18—22Ub 43
Lanscombe Wlk. SW8—53Nb 104
Lansdell Rd. Mitc—68Jb 126
Lansdown Clo. W on T—74Y 141
Lansdown Clo. Wok—7C 188
Lansdowne Av. Orp—74Rc 150
Lansdowne Av. Slou—6J 73
Lansdowne Av. Well—52Zc 109
Lansdowne Clo. SW20—66Za 124
Lansdowne Clo. Twic—60Ha 100
Lansdowne Clo. Wat—7Z 5
Lansdowne Ct. Purl—82Rb 165
Lansdowne Ct. Slou—6J 73
Lansdowne Ct. Wor Pk—75Wa 144
Lansdowne Cres. W11—45Ab 80
Lansdowne Dri. E8—38Wb 63
Lansdowne Gdns. SW8—53Nb 104
Lansdowne Gro. NW10—35Ua 60
Lansdowne Hill. SE27—62Rb 127
Lansdowne La. SE7—50Mc 85
Lansdowne M. SE7—50Mc 85
Lansdowne M. W11—46Bb 81
Lansdowne Pl. SE1 —48Tb 83 (3G 207)
Lansdowne Pl. SE19—66Vb 127
Lansdowne Rise. W11—45Ab 80
Lansdowne Rd. E4—19Cc 26
Lansdowne Rd. E11—33Hc 65
Lansdowne Rd. E17—30Cc 44
Lansdowne Rd. E18—27Jc 45
Lansdowne Rd. N3—24Cb 41
Lansdowne Rd. N10—26Lb 42
Lansdowne Rd. N17—25Wb 43
Lansdowne Rd. SW20—66Ya 124
Lansdowne Rd. W11—45Ab 80
Lansdowne Rd. Brom—66Jc 129
Lansdowne Rd. Croy—75Tb 147
Lansdowne Rd. Eps—80Ta 143
Lansdowne Rd. Harr—31Ga 58
Lansdowne Rd. Houn—55Da 99
Lansdowne Rd. Ilf—32Vc 67
Lansdowne Rd. Purl—84Qb 164
Lansdowne Rd. Stai—66K 119
Lansdowne Rd. Stan—23La 38
Lansdowne Rd. Til—4B 114
Lansdowne Rd. Uxb—44S 76
Lansdowne Row. W1 —46Kb 82 (6A 198)
Lansdowne Ter. WC1 —42Nb 82 (6G 193)
Lansdowne Wlk. W11—46Bb 81
Lansdowne Way. SW8—53Mb 104
Lansdown Pl. Grav—10B 114
Lansdown Rd. E7—38Lc 65
Lansdown Rd. Sidc—62Xc 131
Lansdown Sq. Grav—8B 114
Lansfield Av. N18—21Wb 43
Lantern Clo. SW15—56Wa 102
Lantern Clo. Wemb—36Ma 59
Lant St. SE1—47Sb 83 (1D 206)
Lanvanor Rd. SE15—54Yb 106
Lapford Clo. W9—42Bb 81
Lapis Clo. Grav—10K 115
La Plata Gro. Brtwd—20Xd 32
Lapponum Wlk. Hay—42Z 77
Lapse Wood Wlk. SE23—61Xb 127
Lapstone Gdns. Harr—30La 38
Lapwing Clo. S Croy—82Ac 166
Lapwings. Long, Dart—69De 135
Lapworth Clo. Orp—75Yc 151
Lara Clo. Chess—80Na 143
Larbert Rd. SW16—66Lb 126
Larby Pl. Eps—82Ua 162
Larch Av. W3—46Ua 80
Larch Av. Asc—10C 116
Larch Av. St Alb—2Aa 5
Larch Clo. N11—24Jb 42
Larch Clo. SW12—61Kb 126
Larch Clo. Slou—3F 72
Larch Clo. Tad—93Eb 179
Larch Clo. Warl—91Ac 182
Larch Cres. Eps—79Ra 143
Larch Cres. Hay—43Y 77
Larch Dene. Orp—75Qc 150
Larches Av. SW14—56Ta 101
Larches Av. Enf—7Yb 12
Larches, The. N13—20Sb 25
Larches, The. Uxb—40R 56
Larches, The. Wat—15Z 19
Larch Grn. NW9—25Ua 40
Larch M. N19—33Lb 62
Larchmoor Pk. Slou—5L 53
Larch Rd. NW2—35Ya 60
Larch Rd. Dart—59Md 111
Larch Tree Way. Croy—76Cc 148
Larch Way. Brom—73Qc 150
Larch Way. Swan—68Fd 132
Larchwood Av. Romf—23Dd 48
Larchwood Clo. Bans—87Ab 162
Larchwood Clo. Romf—23Ed 48
Larchwood Dri. Egh—5M 117
Larchwood Gdns. Brtwd —16Wd 32
Larchwood Rd. SE9—61Rc 130
Larchwood Rd. Wok—8A 188
Larcom St. SE17—49Sb 83 (6E 206)
Larden Rd. W3—47Ua 80
Largewood Av. Surb—75Qa 143
Lark Av. Stai—62H 119
Larkbere Rd. SE26—63Ac 128
Larken Dri. Bush, Wat—18Ea 20
Larkfield. Cob—85W 158
Larkfield Av. Harr—27Ka 38
Larkfield Clo. Brom—75Hc 149
Larkfield Rd. Rich—56Na 101
Larkfield Rd. Sev—95Ed 186
Larkfield Rd. Sidc—62Vc 131
Larkfields. Grav—2A 136
Larkhall Clo. W on T—79Y 141
Larkhall La. SW4—54Mb 104
Larkhall Rise. SW4—55Lb 104
Larkings La. Slou—9M 53
Lark Row. E2—39Yb 64
Larksfield. Egh—6N 117
Larks Field. Long, Dart—70Be 135
Larksfield Gro. Enf—11Xb 25
Larkshall Ct. Romf—26Ed 48
Larkshall Cres. E4—21Ec 44
Larkshall Rd. E4—22Ec 44
Larkspur Clo. N17—24Tb 43
Larkspur Clo. Orp—75Yc 151
Larkspur Clo. S Ock—41Yd 90
Larkspur Way. Eps—78Sa 143
Larks Way. Wok—4A 188
Larkswood Ct. E4—22Fc 45
Larkswood Rise. Pinn—28Y 37
Larkswood Rd. E4—21Cc 44
Larkway Clo. NW9—28Ta 39
Larmans Rd. Enf—8Zb 12
Larnach Rd. W6—51Za 102
Larne Rd. Ruis—31V 56
Larner Rd. Eri—52Gd 110
La Roche Clo. Slou—8N 73
Larpent Av. SW15—57Ya 102
Larsen Dri. Wal A—6Fc 13
Larwood Clo. Gnfd—36Fa 58
Lascelles Av. Harr—31Fa 58
Lascelles Clo. E11—33Fc 65
Lascelles Clo. Brtwd—15Wd 32
Lascelles Rd. Slou—8M 73
Lascotts Rd. N22—23Pb 42
Lassa Rd. SE9—57Nc 108
Lassell St. SE10—50Fc 85
Lasswade Rd. Cher—73H 139
Latchett Rd. E18—25Kc 45
Latchford Pl. Chig—21Xc 47
Latchingdon Gdns. Wfd G —23Nc 46
Latchmere Clo. Rich—64Na 123
Latchmere La. King & Rich —65Pa 123
Latchmere Pas. SW11—54Hb 103
Latchmere Rd. SW11—54Hb 103
Latchmere Rd. King—66Na 123
Latchmere St. SW11—54Hb 103
Latchmoor Av. Ger X—28A 34
Latchmoor Gro. Ger X—28A 34
Latchmoor Way. Ger X—28A 34
Lateward Rd. Bren—51Ma 101
Latham Clo. E6—43Nc 86
Latham Clo. Twic—59Ja 100
Latham Clo. West—88Lc 167
Latham Rd. Bexh—57Cd 110
Latham Rd. Twic—59Ha 100
Latham's Way. Croy—74Nb 146
Lathkill Clo. Enf—17Wb 25
Lathom Rd. E6—38Nc 66
Latimer Av. E6—39Pc 66
Latimer Clo. Pinn—25Y 37
Latimer Clo. Wor Pk—77Xa 144
Latimer Gdns. Pinn—25Y 37
Latimer Pl. W10—44Ya 80
Latimer Rd. E7—35Kc 65
Latimer Rd. N15—30Ub 43
Latimer Rd. SW19—65Db 125
Latimer Rd. W10—43Ya 80
Latimer Rd. Barn—13Db 23
Latimer Rd. Che & Rick—10A 2
Latimer Rd. Croy—76Rb 147
Latimer Rd. Tedd—64Ha 122
Latona Dri. Grav—4H 137
Latona Rd. SE15—51Wb 105
La Tourne Gdns. Orp—76Sc 150
Latton Clo. Esh—77Da 141
Latton Clo. W on T—73Aa 141
Latymer Clo. Wey—77S 140
Latymer Ct. W6—49Za 80
Latymer Gdns. N3—26Ab 40
Latymer Rd. N9—18Vb 25
Latymer Way. N9—19Ub 25
Lauder Clo. N'holt—40Z 57
Lauder Ct. N14—17Nb 24
Lauderdale Dri. Rich—62Ma 123
Lauderdale Rd. W9—41Db 81
Lauderdale Rd. K Lan—5S 4
Lauderdale Tower. EC2—(7D 194)
Laud St. SE11—50Pb 82 (7H 205)
Laud St. Croy—76Sb 147
Laughton Rd. N'holt—39Z 57
Launcelot Rd. Brom—63Jc 129
Launcelot St. SE1 —47Qb 82 (2K 205)
Launceston Clo. Romf—25Ld 49
Launceston Gdns. Gnfd—38La 58
Launceston Pl. W8 —48Eb 81 (3A 202)
Launceston Rd. Gnfd—39La 58
Launch St. E14—48Ec 84
Launder's La. Rain—43Nd 89
Laundry La. Brtwd—11Fe 33
Laundry Rd. E4—18Fc 27
Laundry Rd. W6—51Ab 102
Laura Clo. E11—29Lc 45
Laura Clo. Enf—15Ub 25
Lauradale Rd. N2—28Hb 41
Laura Dri. Swan—66Jd 132
Laura Pl. E5—35Yb 64
Laurel Av. Egh—4M 117
Laurel Av. Grav—1E 136
Laurel Av. Pot B—4Bb 9
Laurel Av. Slou—47A 74
Laurel Av. Twic—60Ha 100
Laurel Bank Gdns. SW6—54Bb 103
Laurel Bank Rd. Enf—11Tb 25
Laurel Clo. N19—33Lb 62
Laurel Clo. Brtwd—15De 33
Laurel Clo. Dart—60Ld 111
Laurel Clo. Ilf—23Tc 46
Laurel Clo. Sidc—62Wc 131
Laurel Clo. Slou—52G 96
Laurel Ct. Pot B—1Pb 10
Laurel Cres. Croy—76Cc 148
Laurel Cres. Romf—32Gd 68
Laurel Cres. Wok—85E 156
Laurel Dri. N21—17Qb 24
Laurel Gdns. E4—17Dc 26
Laurel Gdns. NW7—20Ta 21
Laurel Gdns. W7—46Ga 78
Laurel Gdns. Houn—56Aa 99
Laurel Gro. SE20—66Yb 128
Laurel Gro. SE26—63Zb 128
Laurel La. W Dray—49N 75
Laurel Lodge La. Barn—8Ya 8
Laurel Pk. Harr—24Ha 38
Laurel Rd. SW13—54Wa 102
Laurel Rd. SW20—67Xa 124
Laurel Rd. Ger X—25A 34
Laurel Rd. Tedd—64Fa 122
Laurels Rd. Iver—40F 54
Laurels, The. Dart—62Ld 133
Laurels, The. Long, Dart—69Fe 135
Laurels, The. Wey—76T 140
Laurel St. E8—37Vb 63
Laurel View. N12—20Db 23
Laurel Way. E18—28Hc 45
Laurel Way. N20—20Cb 23
Laurence M. W12—47Wa 80
Laurence Pountney Hill. EC4 —45Tb 83 (4F 201)
Laurence Pountney La. EC4 —45Tb 83 (4G 201)
Laurie Gro. SE14—53Ac 106
Laurie Rd. W7—43Ga 78
Laurier Rd. NW5—34Kb 62
Laurier Rd. Croy—73Vb 147
Laurie Wlk. Romf—29Gd 48
Laurimel Clo. Stan—23Ka 38
Lauriston Rd. E9—38Yb 64
Lauriston Rd. SW19—65Za 124
Lausanne Rd. N8—28Qb 42
Lausanne Rd. SE15—53Yb 106
Lauser Rd. Stai—59L 97
Lavell St. N16—35Tb 63
Lavender Av. NW9—32Sa 59
Lavender Av. Brtwd—15Xd 32
Lavender Av. Mitc—67Gb 125
Lavender Av. Wor Pk—76Ya 144
Lavender Clo. SW3—51Fb 103
Lavender Clo. Cars—77Kb 146
Lavender Clo. Romf—24Md 49
Lavender Gdns. SW11—56Hb 103
Lavender Gdns. Enf—11Rb 25
Lavender Gro. E8—38Wb 63
Lavender Gro. Mitc—67Gb 125
Lavender Hill. SW11—55Hb 103
Lavender Hill. Enf—11Qb 24
Lavender Hill. Swan—69Fd 132
Lavender Pde. Slou—6N 73
Lavender Pk. Rd. Wey—85J 157
Lavender Rise. W Dray—47Q 76
Lavender Rd. SE16—46Ac 84
Lavender Rd. SW11—55Fb 103
Lavender Rd. Cars—77Jb 146
Lavender Rd. Croy—72Pb 146
Lavender Rd. Enf—11Tb 25
Lavender Rd. Eps—78Ra 143
Lavender Rd. Sutt—77Fb 145
Lavender Rd. Uxb—43P 75
Lavender Rd. Wok—88D 156
Lavender St. E15—37Gc 65
Lavender Sweep. SW11 —56Hb 103
Lavender Ter. SW11—55Gb 103
Lavender Vale. Wall—79Mb 146
Lavender Wlk. SW11—56Hb 103
Lavender Wlk. Mitc—69Jb 126
Lavender Way. Croy—72Zb 148
Lavengro Rd. SE27—61Sb 127
Lavenham Rd. SW18—61Bb 125
Lavernock Rd. Bexh—54Cd 110
Lavers Rd. N16—34Ub 63
Laverstoke Gdns. SW15 —59Va 102
Laverton Pl. SW5—49Db 81
Lavidge Rd. SE9—61Nc 130
Lavina Gro. N1—40Pb 62 (1H 193)
Lavington Rd. W13—46Ka 78
Lavington Rd. Croy—76Pb 146
Lavington St. SE1 —46Rb 83 (7C 200)
Lavinia Av. Wat—6Z 5
Lavinia Rd. Dart—58Pd 111
Lawdons Gdns. Croy—77Rb 147
Lawford Av. Rick—16E 16
Lawford Clo. Horn—35Ld 69
Lawford Clo. Rick—16E 16
Lawford Clo. Wall—81Nb 164
Lawford Gdns. Dart—57Ld 111
Lawford Rd. NW5—37Lb 62
Lawford Rd. N1—38Ub 63
Lawford Rd. W4—52Sa 101
Lawkland. Slou—1G 72
Lawless St. E14—45Dc 84
Lawley Rd. N14—17Kb 24
Lawley St. E5—35Yb 64
Lawn Av. W Dray—47L 75
Lawn Clo. N9—17Vb 25
Lawn Clo. Brom—66Kc 129
Lawn Clo. N Mald—68Ua 124
Lawn Clo. Ruis—34V 56
Lawn Clo. Slou—2N 95
Lawn Clo. Swan—68Ed 132
Lawn Cres. Rich—54Qa 101
Lawn Farm Gro. Romf—28Ad 47
Lawn Gdns. W7—46Ga 78
Lawn La. SW8—51Pb 104
Lawn Rd. NW3—36Hb 61
Lawn Rd. Beck—66Bc 128
Lawn Rd. Grav—57Ee 113
(in two parts)
Lawn Rd. Uxb—38L 55
Lawns Cres. Grays—51Fe 113
Lawnside. SE3—56Hc 107
Lawns Pl. Grays—51Fe 113
Lawns, The. E4—22Cc 44
Lawns, The. SE3—55Hc 107
Lawns, The. SE19—67Tb 127
Lawns, The. Pinn—24Da 37
Lawns, The. Sidc—63Yc 131
Lawns, The. Sutt—80Ab 144
Lawnsway. Romf—24Ed 48
Lawn Ter. SE3—55Gc 107
Lawn, The. S'hall—50Ca 77
Lawn Vale. Pinn—26Aa 37
Lawrance Sq. Grav—2B 136
Lawrence Av. E12—35Qc 66
Lawrence Av. E17—25Zb 44
Lawrence Av. N13—21Rb 43
Lawrence Av. NW7—21Ua 40
Lawrence Av. N Mald—72Ta 143
Lawrence Bldgs. N16—34Vb 63
Lawrence Campe Clo. N20 —20Fb 23
Lawrence Clo. E3—41Cc 84
Lawrence Clo. N15—27Ub 43
Lawrence Ct. NW7—22Ua 40
Lawrence Cres. Dag—34Dd 68
Lawrence Cres. Edgw—26Qa 39
Lawrence Dri. Grav—10J 137
Lawrence Dri. Uxb—35S 56
Lawrence Gdns. NW7—20Va 22
Lawrence Gdns. Wal X—1Zb 12
Lawrence Hill. E4—19Cc 26
Lawrence Hill Gdns. Dart —58Ld 111
Lawrence Hill Rd. Dart—58Ld 111
Lawrence La. EC2 —44Sb 83 (3E 200)
Lawrence Rd. E6—39Nc 66
Lawrence Rd. E13—39Kc 65
Lawrence Rd. N15—28Ub 43
Lawrence Rd. N18—21Xb 43
Lawrence Rd. SE25—70Vb 127
Lawrence Rd. W5—49Ma 79
Lawrence Rd. Hmptn—66Ba 121
Lawrence Rd. Hay—40S 56
Lawrence Rd. Houn—56Y 99
Lawrence Rd. Pinn—29Z 37
Lawrence Rd. Rich—63La 122
Lawrence Rd. Romf—29Kd 49
Lawrence Rd. W Wick—77Jc 149
Lawrence St. E16—43Hc 85
Lawrence St. NW7—22Va 40
Lawrence St. SW3—51Gb 103
Lawrence Way. Gnfd—39Ja 58
Lawrence Way. Slou—3B 72
Lawrence Weaver Clo. Mord —72Cb 145
Lawrence Yd. N15—28Ub 43
Lawrie Pk. Av. SE26—64Xb 127
Lawrie Pk. Cres. SE26—64Xb 127
Lawrie Pk. Gdns. SE26—63Xb 127
Lawrie Pk. Rd. SE26—65Xb 127
Lawson Clo. E16—43Lc 85
Lawson Clo. SW19—62Za 124
Lawson Ct. Surb—73Ma 143
Lawson Rd. Dart—56Md 111
Lawson Rd. Enf—11Yb 26
Lawson Rd. S'hall—42Ca 77
Law St. SE1—48Tb 83 (3G 207)
Lawton Rd. E3—41Ac 84
Lawton Rd. E10—32Ec 64
Lawton Rd. Barn—13Fb 23
Lawton Rd. Lou—12Rc 28
Laxey Rd. Orp—79Vc 151
Laxley Clo. SE5—52Rb 105
Laxton Gdns. Red—100Mb 180
Laxton Pl. NW1—42Kb 82 (5A 192)
Layard Rd. SE16—49Xb 83
Layard Rd. Enf—11Vb 25
Layard Rd. T Hth—68Tb 127
Layard Sq. SE16—49Xb 83
Layburn Cres. Slou—51D 96
Laycock St. N1—37Qb 62
Layer Gdns. W3—45Qa 79
Layfield Clo. NW4—31Xa 60
Layfield Cres. NW4—31Xa 60
Layfield Rd. NW4—31Xa 60
Layhams Rd. W Wick, Kes & Warl —77Gc 149
Laymarsh Clo. Belv—48Bd 87
Laymead Clo. N'holt—37Aa 57
Layrock La. Rick—17P 17
Laystall St. EC1—42Qb 82 (6K 193)
Layters Way. Ger X—29A 34
Layton Ct. Wey—77R 140
Layton Cres. Croy—78Qb 146
Layton Rd. N1—40Qb 62 (1A 194)
Layton Rd. Bren—50Ma 79
Layton Rd. Houn—56Da 99
Layton's Bldgs. SE1 —47Tb 83 (1F 207)
Layton's La. Sun—68V 120
Layzell Wlk. SE9—60Mc 107
Lazar Wlk. N7—33Pb 62
Lazenby Ct. WC2—(4F 199)
Leabank Clo. Harr—34Ga 58
Leabank View. N15—30Wb 43
Leabourne Rd. N16—31Wb 63
Lea Bri. Rd.—34Yb 64
E5 1-49 & 2-148
E10 51-713 & 150-738
E17 remainder
Lea Bushes. Wat—7Aa 5
Leach Gro. Lea—94La 176
Lea Clo. Bush, Wat—15Da 19
Lea Cres. Ruis—35V 56
Leacroft. Asc—10E 116
Leacroft. Stai—63K 119
Leacroft Av. SW12—59Hb 103
Leacroft Clo. Kenl—88Sb 165
Leacroft Clo. Stai—63K 119
Leacroft Clo. W Dray—44N 75
Leacroft Rd. Iver—44G 74
Leadale Av. E4—19Cc 26
Leadale Rd.—30Wb 43
N16 1-81 & 2-46
N15 remainder
Leadenhall Av. EC3—(3H 201)
Leadenhall Pl. EC3 —44Ub 83 (3H 201)
Leadenhall St. EC3 —44Ub 83 (3H 201)
Leader Av. E12—36Qc 66
Leadings, The. Wemb—34Sa 59
Leaf Clo. N'wd—24T 36
Leaf Clo. Th Dit—71Ga 142
Leaf Gro. SE27—64Qb 126
Leafield Clo. SW16—65Rb 127
Leafield Clo. Wok—6E 188
Leafield La. Sidc—62Bd 131
Leafield Rd. SW20—69Bb 125
Leafield Rd. Sutt—75Cb 145
Leaford Cres. Wat—9V 4
Leafy Gro. Kes—78Lc 149
Leafy Oak Rd. SE12—63Lc 129
Leafy Wlk. Croy—75Vb 147
Leafy Way. Brtwd—18Fe 33
Lea Gdns. Wemb—35Na 59
Leagrave St. E5—34Yb 64
Lea Hall Rd. E10—32Cc 64
Leaholme Gdns. Slou—3A 72
Leaholme Waye. Ruis—30S 36
Leahurst Rd. SE13—57Fc 107
Leake Ct. SE1—47Pb 82 (2J 205)
Leake St. SE1—47Pb 82 (1J 205)
Lealand Rd. N15—30Vb 43
Lealand Rd. W13—46Ja 78
Leamington Av. E17—29Cc 44
Leamington Av. Brom—64Lc 129
Leamington Av. Mord—70Ab 124
Leamington Av. Orp—77Uc 150
Leamington Clo. E12—36Nc 66
Leamington Clo. Brom—64Lc 129
Leamington Clo. Houn—57Ea 100
Leamington Clo. Romf—23Qd 49
Leamington Cres. Harr—34Aa 57
Leamington Gdns. Ilf—33Vc 67
Leamington Pk. W3—43Ta 79
Leamington Pl. Hay—42V 76
Leamington Rd. Romf—22Qd 49
Leamington Rd. S'hall—49Z 77
Leamington Rd. Vs. W11—43Bb 81
Leamore St. W6—49Ya 80
Leamouth Rd. E6—43Nc 86
Leamouth Rd. E14—44Fc 85
Leander Ct. SE8—53Cc 106
Leander Ct. Surb—73Ma 143
Leander Dri. Grav—3H 137
Leander Gdns. Wat—9Aa 5
Leander Rd. SW2—58Pb 104
Leander Rd. N'holt 40Ca 57
Leander Rd. T Hth—70Pb 126
Lea Rd. Beck—68Cc 128
Lea Rd. Enf—11Tb 25
Lea Rd. Grays—10C 92
Lea Rd. Sev—99Ld 187
Lea Rd. S'hall—49Aa 77
Lea Rd. Wal A—6Cc 12
Lea Rd. Wat—10X 5
Learoyd Gdns. E6—45Qc 86
Leas Clo. Chess—80Qa 143
Leas Dale. SE9—62Qc 130
Leas Dri. Iver—44G 74
Leas Grn. Chst—65Vc 131
Leaside. Lea—95Ca 175
Leaside Av. N10—27Jb 42
Leaside Rd. E5—32Yb 64
Leas La. Warl—90Zb 166
Leasowes Rd. E10—32Cc 64
Leas Rd. Warl—90Zb 166
Leas, The. Bush, Wat—11Ba 19
Leas, The. Upm—31Td 70
Leasway. Brtwd—20Zd 33
Leasway. Grays—46Ee 91
Leasway. Upm—35Sd 70
Lea, The. Egh—66E 118
Leatherbottle Grn. Eri—48Bd 87
Leather Bottle La. Belv—49Ad 87
Leather Clo. Mitc—68Jb 126
Leatherdale St. E1—41Zb 84
Leather Gdns. E15—39Gc 65
Leatherhead By-Pass Rd. Lea —92Ka 176
Leatherhead Clo. N16—32Vb 63
Leatherhead Industrial Est. Lea—93Ja 176
Leatherhead Rd. Chess—86Ka 160
Leatherhead Rd. Lea—98Da 175
(Great Bookham)
Leatherhead Rd. Lea—86Fa 160
(Oxshott)
Leatherhead Rd. Lea & Asht —93Ma 177
Leather La. EC1—43Qb 82 (7K 193)
Leathermarket St. SE1 —47Ub 83 (2H 207)
Leathsail Rd. Harr—34Da 57
Leathwaite Rd. SW11—56Hb 103
Leathwell Rd. SE8—54Dc 106
Lea Vale. Dart—56Fd 110
Lea Valley Rd. Enf & E4—15Ac 26
Lea Valley Viaduct. N18 & E4 —22Zb 44
Leaveland Clo. Beck—70Cc 128
Leaver Gdns. Gnfd—40Fa 58
Leavesden Rd. Stan—23Ja 38
Leavesden Rd. Wat—10X 5
Leavesden Rd. Wey—78R 140
Leaves Grn. Cres. Kes—83Lc 167
Leaves Grn. Rd. Kes—83Mc 167
Lea View. Wal A—5Dc 12
Leaway. E10—32Zb 64
Leazes Av. Cat—95Qb 180
Leazes La. Cat—95Qb 180
Lebanon Av. Felt—64Z 121
Lebanon Clo. Wat—8T 4
Lebanon Dri. Cob—85Ca 159
Lebanon Gdns. SW18—58Cb 103
Lebanon Gdns. West—89Mc 167
Lebanon Pk. Twic—59Ka 100
Lebanon Rd. SW18—57Cb 103
Lebanon Rd. Croy—74Ub 147
Lebrun Sq. SE3—56Kc 107
Lechmere App. Wfd G—26Mc 45
Lechmere Av. Chig—21Sc 46
Lechmere Av. Wfd G—26Mc 45
Lechmere Rd. NW2—37Xa 60
Leckford Rd. SW18—61Eb 125
Leckwith Av. Bexh—51Ad 109
Lecky St. SW7—50Fb 81 (7B 202)
Leconfield Av. SW13—55Va 102
Leconfield Rd. N5—35Tb 63
Leconfield Wlk. Horn—37Ld 69
Leda Av. Enf—10Zb 12
Leda Rd. SE18—48Pc 86
Ledbury M. N. W11—45Cb 81
Ledbury M. W. W11—45Cb 81
Ledbury Pl. Croy—77Tb 147
Ledbury Rd. W11—44Bb 81
Ledbury Rd. Croy—77Tb 147
Ledbury St. SE15—52Wb 105
Ledger Dri. Wey—79H 139
Ledgers Rd. Slou—7H 73
Ledgers Rd. Warl—89Dc 166
Ledrington Rd. SE19—65Wb 127
Ledway Dri. Wemb—31Pa 59
Lee Av. Romf—30Ad 47
Lee Bri. SE13—55Ec 106
Leechcroft Av. Sidc—57Vc 109
Leechcroft Av. Swan—69Hd 132
Leechcroft Rd. Wall—76Jb 146
Leech La. Dor & Eps—98Sa 177
Lee Chu. St. SE13—56Gc 107
Lee Clo. E17—25Zb 44
Lee Conservancy Rd. E9—36Bc 64
Leecroft Rd. Barn—15Ab 22
Leeds Clo. Orp—75Zc 151
Leeds Pl. N4—32Pb 62
Leeds Rd. Ilf—32Tc 66
Leeds Rd. Slou—5J 73
Leeds St. N18—22Wb 43
Leefern Rd. W12—47Wa 80
Lee Gdns. App. Horn—32Qd 69
Lee Ga. SE12—57Hc 107
Lee Grn. SE12—57Hc 107
Lee Grn. La. Eps—96Ra 177
Lee Gro. Chig—19Rc 28
Lee High Rd.—55Ec 106
SE13 1-231 & 2-332
SE12 Remainder
Lee Ho. EC2—(1E 200)
Leeke St. WC1—41Pb 82 (3H 193)
Leeland Ter. W13—46Ka 78
Leeland Way. NW10—35Va 60
Leeming Rd. Borwd—11Pa 21
Leemount Clo. NW4—28Za 40
Lee Pk. SE3—56Hc 107
Lee Pk. Way. E4, N18 & N9 —22Zb 44
Lee Rd. NW7—24Za 40
Lee Rd. SE3—55Hc 107
Lee Rd. SW19—67Db 125
Lee Rd. Enf—16Wb 25
Lee Rd. Gnfd—39La 58
Lees Av. N'wd—25V 36
Leeside. Barn—15Ab 22
Leeside Cres. NW11—30Ab 40
Leeside Rd. N17—23Xb 43
Leeson Gdns. Wind—9C 72
Leeson Rd. SE24—56Qb 104
Leeson's Hill. Chst & Orp —69Vc 131
Leeson's Way. Orp—68Vc 131
Lees Pl. W1—45Jb 82 (4H 197)
Lees Rd. Uxb—42R 76
Lees, The. Croy—75Bc 148
Lee St. E8—39Vb 63
Lee Ter. SE3—55Gc 107
Lee Valley Trading Est. N18 & E4—23Zb 44
Lee View. Enf—11Rb 25
Leeward Gdns. SW19—64Ab 124
Leeway. SE8—50Bc 84
Leeway Clo. Pinn—24Ba 37
Leewood Pl. Swan—70Fd 132
Leewood Way. Lea—99Y 175
Lefevre Wlk. E3—39Bc 64
Lefroy Rd. W12—47Va 80
Legard Rd. N5—34Rb 63
Legatt Rd. SE9—57Mc 107
Leggatt Rd. E15—40Ec 64

Leggatts Clo. Wat—8V 4
Leggatts Rise. Wat—7W 4
Leggatts Way. Wat—8V 4
Leggatts Wood Av. Wat—8X 5
Legge St. SE13—57Ec 106
Leghorn Rd. NW10—40Va 60
Leghorn Rd. SE18—50Tc 86
Legion Clo. N1—38Qb 62
Legion Ct. Mord—72Cb 145
Legion Rd. Gnfd—40Fa 58
Legon Av. Romf—32Ed 68
Legrace Av. Houn—54Z 99
Leicester Av. Mitc—70Nb 126
Leicester Clo. Wor Pk—77Ya 144
Leicester Ct. WC2—(4E 198)
Leicester Gdns. Ilf—31Uc 66
Leicester Pl. WC2
—45Mb 82 (4E 198)
Leicester Rd. E11—29Kc 45
Leicester Rd. N2—27Gb 41
Leicester Rd. Barn—15Db 23
Leicester Rd. Croy—73Ub 147
Leicester Rd. Til—3B 114
Leicester Sq. WC2
—45Mb 82 (5E 198)
Leicester St. WC2
—45Mb 82 (4E 198)
Leigham Av. SW16—62Nb 126
Leigham Ct. Rd. SW16—61Nb 126
Leigham Dri. Iswth—52Ga 100
Leigham Vale—62Pb 126
SW16 8-91
SW2 remainder
Leigh Av. Ilf—28Mc 45
Leigh Clo. N Mald—70Ta 123
Leigh Clo. Wey—80H 139
Leigh Ct. Harr—32Ga 58
Leigh Ct. Clo. Cob—86Y 159
Leigh Cres. Croy—80Dc 148
Leigh Dri. Romf—21Md 49
Leigh Gdns. NW10—40Ya 60
Leigh Hill Rd. Cob—87Y 159
Leigh Hunt St. SE1
—47Sb 83 (1D 206)
Leigh Orchard Clo. SW16
—62Pb 126
Leigh Pk. Slou—2N 95
Leigh Pl. EC1—43Qb 82 (7K 193)
Leigh Pl. Cob—87Y 159
Leigh Pl. Well—54Wc 109
Leigh Rd. E6—37Qc 66
Leigh Rd. E10—31Ec 64
Leigh Rd. N5—35Rb 63
Leigh Rd. Cob—86X 159
Leigh Rd. Grav—1D 136
Leigh Rd. Houn—56Fa 100
Leigh Rd. Slou—5F 72
Leigh Rd. Wat—20Ba 19
Leigh Sq. Wind—4B 94
Leigh St. WC1—41Nb 82 (4F 193)
Leighton Av. E12—36Qc 66
Leighton Av. Pinn—27Aa 37
Leighton Clo. Edgw—26Qa 39
Leighton Cres. NW5—36Lb 62
Leighton Gdns. NW10—40Xa 60
Leighton Gdns. S Croy—85Xb 165
Leighton Gro. NW5—36Lb 62
Leighton Pl. NW5—36Lb 62
Leighton Rd. NW5—36Lb 62
Leighton Rd. W13—47Ja 78
Leighton Rd. Enf—15Vb 25
Leighton Rd. Harr—26Fa 38
Leighton St. Croy—74Rb 147
Leighton Way. Eps—86Ta 161
Leinster Av. SW14—55Sa 101
Leinster Gdns. W2
—44Eb 81 (3A 196)
Leinster M. W2—45Eb 81 (4A 196)
Leinster Pl. W2—44Eb 81
Leinster Rd. N10—28Kb 42
Leinster Rd. NW6—41Cb 81
Leinster Sq. W2—44Db 81
Leinster Ter. W2—45Eb 81 (4A 196)
Leiston Spur. Slou—4J 73
Leith Clo. NW9—32Ta 59
Leithcote Gdns. SW16—63Pb 126
Leithcote Path. SW16—62Pb 126
Leith Hill. Orp—67Wc 131
Leith Hill Grn. Orp—67Wc 131
Leith Pk. Rd. Grav—10D 114
Leith Rd. N22—25Rb 43
Leith Rd. Eps—84Ua 162
Lela Av. Houn—54Y 99
Lelitia Clo. E8—39Wb 63
Leman St. E1—44Vb 83
Lemark Clo. Stan—22La 38
Le May Av. SE12—62Kc 129
Lemmon Rd. SE10—51Gc 107
Lemna Rd. E11—31Gc 65
Lemonfield Dri. Wat—4Aa 5
Lemonwell Dri. SE9—58Sc 108
Lemsford Clo. N15—30Wb 43
Lemsford Ct. Borwd—14Sa 21
Lemuel St. SW18—58Eb 103
Lena Gdns. W6—48Ya 80
Lendal Ter. SW4—55Mb 104
★Lendon Rd. Sev—93Be
Lenelby Rd. Surb—74Qa 143
Lenham Rd. SE12—56Hc 107
Lenham Rd. Bexh—51Bd 109
Lenham Rd. Sutt—77Db 145
Lenham Rd. T Hth—68Tb 127
Lenmore Av. Grays—48Ee 91
Lennard Av. W Wick—75Gc 149
Lennard Clo. W Wick
—75Gc 149
Lennard Rd.—65Zb 128
SE20 1-89 & 2-98
Beck remainder
Lennard Rd. Brom—74Pc 150
Lennard Rd. Croy—74Sb 147
Lennard Rd. Sev—92Gd 186
Lennard Row. S Ock—46Td 90
Lennon Rd. NW2—36Ya 60
Lennox Av. Grav—8C 114
Lennox Clo. Romf—30Hd 48
Lennox Gdns. NW10—35Va 60
Lennox Gdns. SW1
—49Hb 81 (4F 203)
Lennox Gdns. Croy—77Rb 147
Lennox Gdns. Ilf—32Pc 66
Lennox Gdns. M. SW1
—49Hb 81 (4F 203)
Lennox Rd. E17—30Bc 44
Lennox Rd. N4—33Pb 62
Lennox Rd. Grav—8B 114
Lennox Rd. E. Grav—9C 114
Lenor Clo. Bexh—56Ad 109
Lensbury Clo. Wal X—1Ac 12
Lensbury Way. SE2—48Yc 87
Lens Rd. E7—38Lc 65
Lent Grn. Slou—2A 72
Lent Grn. La. Slou—2A 72
Lenthall Av. Grays—47Ce 91
Lenthall Pl. SW7—(5A 202)
Lenthall Rd. E8—38Wb 63
Lenthall Rd. Lou—14Tc 28
Lenthorp Rd. SE10—49Hc 85
Lentmead Rd. Brom—62Hc 129
Lenton Rise. Rich—55Na 101
Lenton St. SE18—49Tc 86
Lenton Ter. N4—33Qb 62
Lenville Way. SE16—50Wb 83
Leof Cres. SE6—64Dc 128
Leominster Rd. Mord—72Eb 145
Leominster Wlk. Mord—72Eb 145
Leonard Av. Mord—71Eb 145
Leonard Av. Romf—32Fd 68
Leonard Av. Sev—88Kd 171
Leonard Av. Swans—59Ae 113
Leonard Rd. E4—23Cc 44
Leonard Rd. E7—35Jc 65
Leonard Rd. N9—20Vb 25
Leonard Rd. SW16—67Lb 126
Leonard Rd. S'hall—49Z 77
Leonard St. E16—46Nc 86
Leonard St. EC2—42Tb 83 (5G 195)
Leonard Way. Brtwd—21Ud 50
Leontine Clo. SE15—52Wb 105
Leopards Ct. EC1—(7K 193)
Leopold Av. SW19—64Bb 125
Leopold Rd. E17—29Cc 44
Leopold Rd. N2—27Fb 41
Leopold Rd. N18—22Xb 43
Leopold Rd. NW10—38Ua 60
Leopold Rd. SW19—63Bb 125
Leopold Rd. W5—46Pa 79
Leopold St. E3—43Bc 84
Leo St. SE15—52Xb 105
Leo Yd. EC1—(6C 194)
Le Personne Rd. Cat—94Tb 181
Leppoc Rd. SW4—57Mb 104
Leret Way. Lea—93Ka 176
Leroy St. SE1—49Ub 83 (5H 207)
Lescombe Clo. SE23—62Ac 128
Lescombe Rd. SE23—62Ac 128
Lesley Clo. Bex—59Dd 110
Lesley Clo. Grav—7B 136
Lesley Clo. Swan—69Fd 132
Leslie Gdns. Sutt—80Cb 145
Leslie Gro. Croy—74Ub 147
Leslie Pk. Rd. Croy—74Ub 147
Leslie Rd. E11—35Ec 64
Leslie Rd. E16—44Kc 85
Leslie Rd. N2—27Fb 41
Leslie Smith Sq. SE18—51Qc 108
Lesney Farm Est. Eri—52Fd 110
Lesney Pk. Eri—51Fd 110
Lesney Pk. Rd. Eri—51Fd 110
Lessar Av. SW4—58Lb 104
Lessingham Av. SW17—63Hb 125
Lessingham Av. Ilf—27Qc 46
Lessing St. SE23—59Ac 106
Lessington Av. Romf—30Ed 48
Lessness Av. Bexh—52Zc 109
Lessness Pk. Belv—50Cd 88
Lessness Rd. Belv—51Cd 110
Lessness Rd. Mord—72Eb 145
Lester Av. E15—41Gc 85
Leswin Pl. N16—34Vb 63
Leswin Rd. N16—34Vb 63
Letchford Gdns. NW10—41Wa 80
Letchford M. NW10—41Wa 80
Letchford Ter. Harr—25Da 37
Letchmore Rd. Rad—8Ja 6
Letchworth Av. Felt—59V 98
Letchworth Clo. Brom—71Jc 149
Letchworth Clo. Wat—23Z 37
Letchworth Dri. Brom—71Jc 149
Letchworth St. SW17—63Hb 125
Lethbridge Clo. SE13—53Ec 106
Letter Box La. Sev—100Md 187
Letterstone Rd. SW6—52Bb 103
Lettice St. SW6—53Bb 103
Lett Rd. E15—38Fc 65
Lettsom St. SE5—54Ub 105
Lettsom Wlk. E13—40Jc 65
Leucha Rd. E17—29Ac 44
Levana Clo. SW19—60Ab 102
Levehurst Way. SW4—54Nb 104
Leven Clo. Wal X—5Zb 12
Leven Clo. Wat—22Z 37
Levendale Rd. SE23—61Ac 128
Leven Dri. Wal X—5Zb 12
Leven Rd. E14—43Ec 84
Leven Way. Hay—44U 76
Leveret Clo. Croy—83Fc 167
Leveret Clo. Wat—6W 4
Leverett St. SW3
—49Gb 81 (5E 202)
Leverholme Gdns. SE9—63Qc 130
Leverington Pl. N1—(4H 195)
Leverson St. SW16—65Lb 126
Lever Sq. Grays—9B 92
Lever St. EC1—41Rb 83 (4C 194)
Leverton Pl. NW5—36Lb 62
Leverton St. NW5—36Lb 62
Leverton Way. Wal A—5Ec 12
Leveson Rd. Grays—8D 92
Levett Gdns. Ilf—35Vc 67
Levett Rd. Bark—37Uc 66
Levett Rd. Lea—92Ka 176
Levett Rd. Stanf—1N 93
Levine Gdns. Bark—40Zc 67
Levison Way. N19—32Mb 62
Lewen's Ct. EC1—(5D 194)
Lewes Clo. N'holt—37Ca 57
Lewesdon Clo. SW19—60Za 102
Lewes Rd. N12—22Gb 41
Lewes Rd. Brom—68Mc 129
Lewes Rd. Romf—21Md 49
Leweston Pl. N16—31Vb 63
Lewes Way. Rick—14S 18
Lewgars Av. NW9—30Sa 39
Lewin Rd. SW14—55Ta 101
Lewin Rd. SW16—65Mb 126
Lewin Rd. Bexh—56Ad 109
Lewins Rd. Eps—86Ra 161
Lewins Rd. Ger X—27A 34
Lewins Way. Slou—5D 72
Lewis Av. E17—25Cc 44
Lewis Clo. Brtwd—17Be 33
Lewis Clo. Wey—77L 139
Lewis Cres. NW10—36Ta 59
Lewis Gdns. N2—26Fb 41
Lewis Gro. SE13—55Ec 106
Lewisham High St. SE13
—58Dc 106
Lewisham Hill. SE13—54Ec 106
Lewisham Pk. SE13—57Ec 106
Lewisham Rd. SE13—53Dc 106
Lewisham St. SW1
—47Mb 82 (2E 204)
Lewisham Way—53Bc 106
SE14 1-169 & 2-158a
SE4 remainder
Lewis La. Ger X—25A 34
Lewis Rd. Grav—7B 136
Lewis Rd. Horn—30Ld 49
Lewis Rd. Mitc—68Fb 125
Lewis Rd. Rich—57Ma 101
Lewis Rd. Sidc—62Yc 131
Lewis Rd. S'hall—47Aa 77
Lewis Rd. Sutt—77Db 145
Lewis Rd. Swans—58Ae 113
Lewis Rd. Well—55Yc 109
Lewis St. NW1—38Kb 62
Lexden Dri. Romf—30Xc 47
Lexden Rd. W3—46Ra 79
Lexden Rd. Mitc—70Mb 126
Lexham Gdns. W8—49Cb 81
Lexham Gdns. M. W8—48Db 81
Lexham M. W8—49Cb 81
Lexington Clo. Borwd—13Pa 21
Lexington Ct. Purl—83Sb 165
Lexington St. W1
—45Lb 82 (4C 198)
Lexington Way. Barn—14Za 22
Lexington Way. Upm—30Vd 50
Lexton Gdns. SW12—60Mb 104
Leybourne Av. W13—47Ka 78
Leyborne Pk. Rich—53Qa 101
Leybourne Av. Wey—85P 157
Leybourne Clo. Brom—72Jc 149
Leybourne Clo. Wey—85P 157
Leybourne Rd. E11—32Hc 65
Leybourne Rd. NW1—38Kb 62
(in two parts)
Leybourne Rd. NW9—29Qa 39
Leybourne Rd. Uxb—39S 56
Leybourne St. NW1—38Kb 62
Leybridge Ct. SE12—57Jc 107
Leyburn Clo. E17—28Dc 44
Leyburn Cres. Romf—24Nd 49
Leyburn Gdns. Croy—75Ub 147
Leyburn Gro. N18—23Wb 43
Leyburn Rd. N18—23Wb 43
Leyburn Rd. Romf—24Nd 49
Leycroft Clo. Lou—15Qc 28
Leycroft Gdns. Eri—53Kd 111
Leydenhatch La. Swan
—67Ed 132
Leyden St. E1—43Vb 83 (1K 201)
Leyes Rd. E16—44Lc 85
Leyfield. Wor Pk—74Ua 144
Leyhill Clo. Swan—70Gd 132
Leyland Av. Enf—12Ac 26
Leyland Clo. Wal X—1Yb 12
Leyland Gdns. Wfd G—22Lc 45
Leyland Rd. SE12—57Jc 107
Leylands La. Stai—56H 97
Leylang Rd. SE14—52Zb 106
Leys Av. Dag—39Ed 68
Leys Clo. Dag—38Ed 68
Leys Clo. Harr—29Fa 38
Leys Clo. Uxb—25M 35
Leysdown Av. Bexh—56Ed 110
Leysdown Rd. SE9—61Nc 130
Leysfield Rd. W12—48Wa 80
Leys Gdns. Barn—15Jb 24
Leyspring Rd. E11—32Hc 65
Leys Rd. Lea—84Fa 160
Leys Rd. E. Enf—11Ac 26
Leys Rd. W. Enf—11Ac 26
Leys Sq. N3—25Db 41
Leys, The. N2—28Eb 41
Leys, The. Harr—30Pa 39
Ley St. Ilf—33Rc 66
Leyswood Dri. Ilf—29Uc 46
Leythe Rd. W3—47Sa 79
Leyton Ct. SE23—60Yb 106
Leyton Cross Rd. Dart—62Hd 132
Leyton Grange Est. E10—32Dc 64
Leyton Grn. Rd. E10—30Ec 44
Leyton Pk. Rd. E10—34Ec 64
Leyton Rd. E15—36Ec 64
Leyton Rd. SW19—66Eb 125
Leytonstone Rd. E15—36Gc 65
Leyton Way. E11—31Gc 65
Leywick St. E15—40Gc 65
Lezayre Rd. Orp—79Vc 151
Liardet St. SE14—51Ac 106
Liberia Rd. N5—37Rb 63
Liberty Av. SW19—67Fb 125
Liberty Hall Rd. Wey—78J 139
Liberty La. Wey—78J 139
Liberty Rise. Wey—79J 139
Liberty St. SW9—53Pb 104
Liberty, The. Romf—29Gd 48
Libra Rd. E3—40Bc 64
Libra Rd. E13—40Jc 65
Library Hill. Brtwd—19Zd 33
Library Pl. E1—45Xb 83
Library St. SE1—47Rb 83 (2B 206)
Lichfield Gdns. Rich—56Na 101
Lichfield Gro. N3—25Cb 41
Lichfield Rd. E3—41Ac 84
Lichfield Rd. E6—41Mc 85
Lichfield Rd. N9—19Wb 25
Lichfield Rd. NW2—35Ab 60
Lichfield Rd. Dag—35Xc 67
Lichfield Rd. Houn—55Y 99
Lichfield Rd. N'wd—27W 36
Lichfield Rd. Rich—53Pa 101
Lichfield Rd. Wfd G—21Gc 45
Lichfield Ter. Upm—33Ud 70
Lichfield Way. S Croy—82Zb 166
Lichlade Clo. Orp—77Vc 151
Lidbury Rd. NW7—23Ab 40
Lidcote Gdns. SW9—54Qb 104
Liddall Way. W Dray—46P 75
Liddell Gdns. NW10—40Ya 60
Liddell Pl. Wind—5A 94
Liddell Rd. NW6—37Cb 61
Liddell Sq. Wind—4A 94
Liddell Way. Wind—5A 94
Lidding Rd. Harr—29Ma 39
Liddington Rd. E15—39Hc 65
Liddon Rd. E13—41Kc 85
Liddon Rd. Brom—69Lc 129
Lidell Clo. Harr—27Ma 39
Lidfield Rd. N16—35Tb 63
Lidiard Rd. SW18—61Eb 125
Lidlington Pl. NW1
—40Lb 62 (2C 192)
Lidstone Clo. Wok—5E 188
Lidyard Rd. N19—32Lb 62
Liffler Rd. SE18—50Uc 86
Liffords Pl. SW13—54Va 102
Lifford St. SW15—56Za 102
Lightcliffe Rd. N13—21Qb 42
Lighterman's Rd. E14—47Cc 84
Lightfoot Rd. N8—29Nb 42
Lightley Clo. Wemb—39Na 59
Ligonier St. E2—42Vb 83 (5K 195)
Lilac Av. Wok—8G 188
Lilac Clo. E4—23Bc 44
Lilac Clo. Brtwd—15Xd 32
Lilac Clo. Wal X—3Xb 11
Lilac Gdns. W5—48Ma 79
Lilac Gdns. Croy—76Cc 148
Lilac Gdns. Hay—44U 76
Lilac Gdns. Romf—32Gd 68
Lilac Gdns. Swan—69Fd 132
Lilac Pl. SE11—49Pb 82 (6H 205)
Lilac Pl. W Dray—45P 75
Lilacs Av. Enf—8Yb 12
Lilac St. W12—45Wa 80
Lila Pl. Swan—70Gd 132
Lilburne Gdns. SE9—57Nc 108
Lilburne Rd. SE9—57Nc 108
Lilburne Wlk. NW10—37Sa 59
Lile Cres. W7—43Ga 78
Lilestone St. NW8
—42Gb 81 (5D 190)
Lilford Rd. SE5—54Rb 105
Lilian Board Way. Gnfd—36Fa 58
Lilian Clo. N16—34Ub 63
Lilian Cres. Brtwd—19Ee 33
Lilian Gdns. Wfd G—25Kc 45
Lilian Rd. SW16—67Lb 126
Lillechurch Rd. Dag—37Xc 67
Lilley Clo. Brtwd—21Vd 50
Lilley Dri. Tad—94Db 179
Lilley La. NW7—22Ta 39
Lillian Av. W3—47Qa 79
Lillian Rd. SW13—51Xa 102
Lillie Rd. SW6—51Ab 102
Lillie Rd. West—90Mc 167
Lillieshall Rd. SW4—55Kb 104
Lillieshall Rd. Mord—72Fb 145
Lillie Yd. SW6—51Cb 103
Lillington Gdns. Est. SW1
—49Lb 82 (6C 204)
Lilliput Av. N'holt—39Aa 57
Lilliput Ct. SE12—57Kc 107
Lilliput Rd. Romf—31Fd 68
Lillyville Rd. SW6—53Bb 103
Lily Clo. W14—49Za 80
Lily Gdns. Wemb—40La 58
Lily Pl. EC1—43Qb 82 (7A 194)
Lily Rd. E17—30Cc 44
Limbourne Av. Dag—31Bd 67
Limburg Rd. SW11—56Gb 103
Lime Av. Brtwd—20Be 33
Lime Av. Grav—59Fe 113
Lime Av. Upm—35Qd 69
Lime Av. W Dray—45P 75
Lime Av. Wind—3K 95
Lime Av. Wind—2D 116
(Windsor Great Park)
Limebush. Wey—81L 157
Lime Clo. Buck H—19Mc 27
Lime Clo. Cars—75Hb 145
Lime Clo. Guild—100K 173
Lime Clo. Romf—28Ed 48
Lime Clo. S Ock—41Yd 90
Lime Clo. Wat—17Z 19
Lime Cres. Sun—68Y 121
Limecroft Clo. Eps—80Ta 143
Limedene Clo. Pinn—25Z 37
Lime Gro. N20—18Bb 23
Lime Gro. W12—47Ya 80
★Lime Gro. Brtwd—9Yd
Lime Gro. Guild—100K 173
Lime Gro. Hay—45T 76
Lime Gro. Ilf—23Vc 47
Lime Gro. N Mald—69Ta 123
Lime Gro. Orp—75Rc 150
Lime Gro. Ruis—30X 37
Lime Gro. Sidc—58Vc 109
Lime Gro. Twic—58Ha 100
Lime Gro. Warl—90Ac 166
Lime Gro. Wey—77J 139
Lime Gro. Wok—93A 172
Limeharbour. E14—40Dc 84
Limehouse Causeway. E14
—45Bc 84
Limehouse Fields Est. E14
—43Ac 84
Lime Meadow Av. S Croy
—85Wb 165
Lime Pit La. Sev—89Ed 170
Limerick Clo. SW12—59Lb 104
Limerick Gdns. Upm—31Vd 70
Lime Rd. Epp—3Vc 15
Lime Rd. Rich—56Pa 101
Lime Rd. Swan—69Fd 132
Lime Row. Eri—48Bd 87
Limerston St. SW10—51Eb 103
Limes Av. E11—28Kc 45
Limes Av. N12—21Eb 41
Limes Av. NW7—23Ua 40
Limes Av. NW11—31Ab 60
Limes Av. SE20—66Xb 127
Limes Av. SW13—54Va 102
Limes Av. Cars—74Hb 145
Limes Av. Chig—22Sc 46
Limes Av. Croy—76Qb 146
Limes Av., The. N11—22Lb 42
Limes Clo. Ashf—64Q 120
Limesdale Gdns. Edgw—26Sa 39
Limes Field Rd. SW14—55Ua 102
Limesford Rd. SE15—56Zb 106
Limes Gdns. SW18—58Cb 103
Limes Gro. SE13—56Ec 106
Limes Pl. Croy—73Tb 147
Limes Rd. Beck—68Dc 128
Limes Rd. Croy—73Tb 147
Limes Rd. Egh—64B 118
Limes Rd. Wal X—4Ac 12
Limes Rd. Wey—77Q 140
Limes, The. Brtwd—20Be 33
Limes, The. Brom—75Nc 150
Limestone Wlk. Eri—47Zc 87
Lime St. E17—28Ac 44
Lime St. EC3—45Ub 83 (4H 201)
Lime St. Pas. EC3
—44Ub 83 (3H 201)
Limes Wlk. SE15—56Yb 106
Limes Wlk. W5—47Ma 79
Lime Ter. W7—45Ga 78
Lime Tree Av. SE20—67Xb 127
Lime Tree Av. Esh & Th Dit
—74Ga 142
Limetree Clo. SW2—60Pb 104
Lime Tree Clo. Lea—96Ca 175
Lime Tree Ct. Pinn—24Ca 37
Lime Tree Gro. Croy—76Bc 148
Lime Tree Pl. Mitc—67Kb 126
Lime Tree Rd. Houn—53Da 99
Lime Tree Wlk. Bush, Wat
—19Ga 20
Lime Tree Wlk. Enf—10Sb 11
Lime Tree Wlk. Rick—15K 17
Lime Tree Wlk. Sev—97Kd 187
Lime Tree Wlk. W Wick—77Hc 149
Lime Wlk. Uxb—36L 55
Limewood Clo. W13—44Ka 78
Limewood Clo. Wok—8A 188
Limewood Rd. Eri—52Ed 110
Lime Works Rd. Red—98Lb 180
Limpsfield Av. SW19—61Za 124
Limpsfield Av. T Hth—71Pb 146
Limpsfield Rd. S Croy & Warl
—84Wb 165
Linacre Rd. NW2—37Xa 60
Linberry Wlk. SE8—49Bc 84
Linchfield Rd. Slou—3N 95
Linchmere Rd. SE12—59Hc 107
Lincoln Av. N14—20Lb 24
Lincoln Av. SW19—62Za 124
Lincoln Av. Romf—32Gd 68
Lincoln Av. Twic—61Ea 122
Lincoln Clo. Eri—54Hd 110
Lincoln Clo. Gnfd—39Ea 58
Lincoln Clo. Harr—29Ba 37
Lincoln Clo. Horn—29Qd 49
Lincoln Ct. Borwd—15Ta 21
Lincoln Cres. Enf—15Ub 25
Lincoln Dri. Rick—14R 18
Lincoln Dri. Wat—20Y 19
Lincoln Dri. Wok—87G 156
Lincoln Gdns. Ilf—31Nc 66
Lincoln Grn. Rd. Orp—71Vc 151
Lincoln Hatch La. Slou—2A 72
Lincoln M. NW6—39Bb 61
Lincoln Rd. E7—37Mc 65
Lincoln Rd. E13—42Kc 85
Lincoln Rd. E18—25Jc 45
Lincoln Rd. N2—27Gb 41
Lincoln Rd. SE25—69Xb 127
Lincoln Rd. Enf—14Ub 25
Lincoln Rd. Eri—54Hd 110
Lincoln Rd. Felt—62Ba 121
Lincoln Rd. Ger X—25A 34
Lincoln Rd. Harr—29Ba 37
Lincoln Rd. Mitc—71Nb 146
Lincoln Rd. N Mald—69Sa 123
Lincoln Rd. N'wd—27V 36
Lincoln Rd. Sidc—64Xc 131
Lincoln Rd. Wemb—37Ma 59
Lincoln Rd. Wor Pk—74Xa 144
Lincolns Field. Epp—2Vc 15
Lincoln's Inn Fields. WC2
—44Pb 82 (2H 199)
Lincolns La. Brtwd—15Sd 32
Lincolns, The. NW7—20Va 22
Lincoln St. E11—33Gc 65
Lincoln St. SW3—49Hb 81 (6F 203)
Lincoln Wlk. Eps—82Ta 161
(in two parts)
Lincoln Way. Enf—15Xb 25
Lincoln Way. Rick—14R 18
Lincoln Way. Slou—5B 72
Lincoln Way. Sun—67U 120
Lincombe Rd. Brom—62Hc 129
Lindal Cres. Enf—14Nb 24
Lindale Clo. Vir W—10K 117
Lindal Rd. SE4—57Bc 106
Lindbergh Rd. Wall—80Nb 146
Linden Av. NW10—40Za 60
Linden Av. Coul—88Kb 164
Linden Av. Dart—60Ld 111
Linden Av. Enf—11Wb 25
Linden Av. Houn—57Da 99
Linden Av. Ruis—32W 56
Linden Av. T Hth—70Rb 127
Linden Av. Wemb—36Pa 59
Linden Chase Rd. Sev—94Kd 187
Linden Clo. N14—16Lb 24
Linden Clo. Lea—100Aa 175
Linden Clo. Orp—78Wc 151
Linden Clo. Purf—51Sd 112
Linden Clo. Ruis—32W 56
Linden Clo. Stan—22Ka 38
Linden Clo. Th Dit—73Ha 142
Linden Clo. Wey—83J 157
Linden Ct. W12—46Ya 80
Linden Ct. Egh—5M 117
Linden Ct. Lea—93Ka 176
Linden Ct. Sidc—63Uc 130
Linden Cres. Gnfd—37Ha 58
Linden Cres. King—68Pa 123
Linden Cres. Wfd G—23Kc 45
Linden Dri. Cat—96Sb 181
Linden Dri. Slou—9G 52
Lindenfield. Chst—68Rc 130
Linden Gdns. W2—45Cb 81
Linden Gdns. W4—50Ua 80
Linden Gdns. Enf—11Wb 25
Linden Gdns. Lea—93La 176
Linden Gro. SE15—55Xb 105
Linden Gro. SE26—65Yb 128
Linden Gro. N Mald—69Ua 124
Linden Gro. Tedd—64Ha 122
Linden Gro. W on T—75V 140
Linden Gro. Warl—90Ac 166
Linden Lea. N2—29Eb 41
Linden Lea. Wat—5W 4
Linden Leas. W Wick—75Fc 149
Linden M. W2—45Cb 81
Linden Pit Path. Lea—93Ka 176
(in two parts)
Linden Pl. Eps—84Ua 162
Linden Rd. E17—29Bc 44
Linden Rd. N10—28Kb 42
Linden Rd. N11—19Hb 23
Linden Rd. N15—28Sb 43
Linden Rd. Hmptn—67Ca 121
Linden Rd. Lea—93Ka 176
Linden Rd. Wey—81S 158
Lindens Lawns. Wemb—35Pa 59
Linden Sq. Sev—94Gd 186
Lindens, The. W4—53Sa 101
Lindens, The. Croy—79Ec 148
Lindens, The. Lou—15Qc 28
Linden St. Romf—28Fd 48
Linden Way. N14—16Lb 24
Linden Way. Purl—82Lb 164
Linden Way. Shep—71S 140
Linden Way. Wok—93B 172
Linden Way. Wok—96H 173
(Send Marsh)
Linden Way. Wok—97H 173
(Send Marsh)
Lindfield Gdns. NW3—36Eb 61
Lindfield Rd. W5—42La 78
Lindfield Rd. Croy—72Vb 147
Lindfield Rd. Romf—22Nd 49
Lindfield St. E14—44Cc 84
Lindisfarne Clo. Grav—1G 136
Lindisfarne Rd. SW20—66Wa 124
Lindisfarne Rd. Dag—34Yc 67
Lindisfarne Way. E9—35Ac 64
Lindley Rd. E10—33Ec 64
Lindley Rd. W on T—75Z 141
Lindley St. E1—43Yb 84
Lindore Rd. SW11—56Hb 103
Lindores Rd. Cars—74Eb 145
Lind Rd. Sutt—78Eb 145
Lindrop St. SW6—54Eb 103
Lindsay Clo. Chess—80Na 143
Lindsay Clo. Eps—85Sa 161
Lindsay Clo. Stai—57M 97
Lindsay Dri. Harr—30Na 39
Lindsay Dri. Shep—72T 140
Lindsay Rd. Hmptn—63Da 121
Lindsay Rd. Wey—83J 157
Lindsay Rd. Wor Pk—75Xa 144
Lindsell St. SE10—53Ec 106
Lindsey Clo. Brtwd—21Wd 50
Lindsey Clo. Brom—69Nc 130
Lindsey Clo. Mitc—70Nb 126
Lindsey Gdns. Felt—59T 98
Lindsey M. N1—38Sb 63
Lindsey Rd. Dag—35Yc 67
Lindsey St. EC1—43Rb 83 (7C 194)
Lindsey St. Epp—1Vc 15
Lindsey Way. Horn—29Ld 49
Lind St. SE8—54Cc 106
Lindum Rd. Tedd—66La 122
Lindway. SE27—64Rb 127
Linfield Clo. W on T—78X 141
Linford Rd. E17—27Ec 44
Linford Rd. Grays—10D 92
Linford St. SW8—53Lb 104
Lingards Rd. SE13—56Ec 106
Lingey Clo. Sidc—61Vc 131
★Lingfield. Sev—92De
Lingfield Av. Dart—59Rd 111
Lingfield Av. King—70Na 123
Lingfield Av. Upm—34Pd 69
Lingfield Clo. Enf—16Ub 25
Lingfield Clo. N'wd—24U 36
Lingfield Cres. SE9—56Tc 108
Lingfield Gdns. N9—17Xb 25
Lingfield Gdns. Coul—91Rb 181
Lingfield Rd. SW19—64Za 124
Lingfield Rd. Grav—1D 136
Lingfield Rd. Wor Pk—76Ya 144
Lingham St. SW9—54Nb 104
Lingholm Way. Barn—15Za 22
Lingmere Clo. Chig—19Sc 28
Ling Rd. E16—43Jc 85
Ling Rd. Eri—51Ed 110
Lingrove Gdns. Buck H—19Kc 27
Lings Coppice. SE21—61Tb 127
Lingwell Rd. SW17—62Gb 125
Lingwood. Bexh—54Dd 110
Lingwood Gdns. Iswth—52Ga 100
Lingwood Rd. E5—31Wb 63

Linhope St. NW1
—42Hb 81 (5F 191)
Link Av. Wok—87F 156
Linkfield. Brom—72Jc 149
Linkfield. E Mol—69Da 121
Linkfield Rd. Iswth—54Ha 100
Link La. Wall—79Mb 146
Linklea Clo. NW9—24Ua 40
Link Rd. N8—27Qb 42
Link Rd. N11—21Jb 42
Link Rd. Dag—40Dd 68
Link Rd. Felt—59V 98
Link Rd. Slou—3N 95
Link Rd. Wall—74Jb 146
Link Rd. Wat & Bush, Wat—12Z 19
Link Rd. Wey—77N 139
Links Av. Mord—70Cb 125
Links Av. Romf—26Kd 49
Links Brow. Lea—96Ga 176
Links Clo. Asht—89La 160
Linkscroft Av. Ashf—65R 120
Links Dri. N20—18Cb 23
Links Dri. Borwd—13Pa 21
Links Dri. Rad—5Ha 6
Links Gdns. SW16—66Qb 126
Links Grn. Way. Cob—86Ca 159
Linkside. N12—23Cb 41
Linkside. Chig—22Sc 46
Linkside. N Mald—68Ua 124
Linkside Clo. Enf—13Ob 24
Linkside Gdns. Enf—13Pb 24
Links Pl. Asht—89Ma 161
Links Rd. NW2—33Va 60
Links Rd. SW17—65Jb 126
Links Rd. W3—44Qa 79
Links Rd. Ashf—64N 119
Links Rd. Asht—90La 160
Links Rd. Eps—85Wa 162
Links Rd. W Wick—74Ec 148
Links Rd. Wfd G—22Jc 45
Links Side. Enf—13Qb 24
Links, The. E17—28Ac 44
Links, The. W on T—75W 140
Link St. E9—37Yb 64
Links View. N3—24Bb 41
Links View. Dart—60Ld 111
Links View Clo. Stan—23Ja 38
Links View Rd. Croy—76Cc 148
Links View Rd. Hmptn—64Ea 122
Linksway. NW4—26Za 40
Links Way. Beck—72Cc 148
Links Way. Lea—100Aa 175
Links Way. N'wd—24S 36
Links Way. Rick—13S 18
Linkswood Rd. Slou—10A 52
Link, The. W3—44Ra 79
Link, The. Enf—11Ac 26
Link, The. N'holt—36Ba 57
Link, The. Pinn—31Y 57
Link, The. Slou—4M 73
Link, The. Wemb—32La 58
Linkway. N4—31Sb 63
Linkway. SW20—69Xa 124
Link Way. Brom—73Nc 150
Linkway. Dag—35Yc 67
Link Way. Horn—32Nd 69
Link Way. Pinn—25Z 37
Linkway. Rich—61Ka 122
Link Way. Stai—65K 119
Link Way. Uxb—30J 35
Linkway. Wok—89E 156
Linkway Rd. Brtwd—20Vd 32
Linkway, The. Barn—16Db 23
Linkway, The. Sutt—81Eb 163
Linley Cres. Romf—27Dd 48
Linley Rd. N17—26Ub 43
Linnell Clo. NW11—30Db 41
Linnell Dri. NW11—30Db 41
Linnell Rd. N18—22Wb 43
Linnell Rd. SE5—54Ub 105
Linnet Clo. SE28—45Yc 87
Linnet Clo. Bush, Wat—17Ea 20
Linnet Clo. S Croy—82Zb 166
Linnet M. SW12—59Jb 104
Linnett Clo. E4—21Ec 44
Linom Rd. SW4—56Nb 104
Linscott Rd. E5—35Yb 64
Linsdell Rd. Bark—39Sc 66
Linsey St. SE16—49Wb 83
(in two parts)
Linslade Rd. Orp—79Wc 151
Linstead St. NW6—38Cb 61
Linstead Way. SW18—59Ab 102
Linster Gro. Borwd—15Sa 21
Lintaine Clo. W6—51Ab 102
Linthorpe Av. Wemb—37La 58
Linthorpe Rd. N16—31Ub 63
Linthorpe Rd. Barn—13Gb 23
Linton Av. Borwd—12Pa 21
Linton Clo. Well—53Xc 109
Linton Ct. Romf—26Gd 48
Linton Gdns. E6—43Nc 86
Linton Glade. Croy—81Ac 166
(in two parts)
Linton Gro. SE27—64Sb 127
Linton Rd. Bark—38Sc 66
Lintons La. Eps—84Ua 162
Linton St. N1—39Sb 63 (1E 194)
Lintott Ct. Stai—58M 97
Linver Rd. SW6—54Cb 103
Linwood Clo. E6—43Pc 86
Linzee Rd. N8—28Nb 42
Lion Av. Twic—60Ha 100
Lion Clo. Shep—69N 119
Lionel Gdns. SE9—57Mc 107
Lionel M. W10—43Ab 80
Lionel Rd. SE9—57Mc 107
Lionel Rd. Bren—48Na 79
(in two parts)
Lion Ga. Gdns. Rich—55Pa 101
Lion Grn. Rd. Coul—88Mb 164
Lion Pk. Av. Chess—77Qa 143
Lion Rd. N9—19Wb 25
Lion Rd. Bexh—56Ad 109
Lion Rd. Croy—71Sb 147
Lion Rd. Twic—60Ha 100
Lions Clo. SE9—62Mc 129

Lion Way. Bren—52Ma 101
Lion Wharf. Iswth—55Ka 100
Liphook Clo. Horn—35Hd 68
Liphook Cres. SE23—59Yb 106
Liphook Rd. Wat—21Z 37
Lippitts Hill. Lou—11Gc 27
Lipsham Clo. Bans—85Fb 163
Lipton Clo. SE28—45Yc 87
Lipton Rd. E1—44Zb 84
Lisbon Av. Twic—61Ea 122
Lisburne Rd. NW3—35Hb 61
Lisford St. SE15—53Vb 105
Lisgar Ter. W14—49Bb 81
Liskeard Clo. Chst—65Sc 130
Liskeard Gdns. SE3—53Jc 107
Lisle Clo. Grav—1K 137
Lisle Pl. Grays—48Ce 91
Lisle St. WC2—45Mb 82 (4E 198)
Lismore Clo. Iswth—54Ja 100
Lismore Rd. N17—27Tb 43
Lismore Rd. S Croy—79Ub 147
Lissenden Gdns. NW5—35Jb 62
Lissoms Rd. Coul—90Jb 164
Lisson Gro.—42Fb 81 (4C 190)
NW1 1-135 & 2-116
NW8 remainder
Lisson St. NW1—43Gb 81 (7D 190)
Liss Way. SE15—52Vb 105
Lister Gdns. N18—22Sb 43
Lister M. N7—35Pb 62
Lister Rd. E11—32Gc 65
Lister Rd. Til—4C 114
Lister St. E13—41Jc 85
Lister Wlk. SE28—45Zc 87
Liston Rd. N17—25Wb 43
Liston Rd. SW4—55Lb 104
Liston Way. Wfd G—24Lc 45
Listowel Clo. SW9—52Rb 105
Listowel Rd. Dag—34Cd 68
Listria Pk. N16—33Ub 63
Litcham Spur. Slou—4H 73
Litchfield Av. E15—37Gc 65
Litchfield Av. Mord—73Bb 145
Litchfield Gdns. NW10—37Wa 60
Litchfield Rd. Sutt—77Eb 145
Litchfield St. WC2
—45Mb 82 (4E 198)
Litchfield Way. NW11—29Db 41
Lithgow's Rd. Houn—56U 98
Lithos Rd. NW3—37Db 61
Lit. Acre. Beck—69Cc 128
Lit. Albany St. NW1—(3A 192)
(in two parts)
Lit. Argyll St. W1
—44Lb 82 (3B 198)
Lit. Aston Rd. Romf—24Pd 49
Lit. Belhus Clo. S Ock—42Wd 90
Lit. Benty. W Dray—50M 75
Lit. Birch Clo. Wey—81M 157
Lit. Birches. Sidc—61Uc 130
Lit. Boltons, The. SW10—50Db 81
Lit. Bookham St. Lea—95Ba 175
Lit. Bornes. SE21—63Ub 127
Lit. Britain. EC1—43Rb 83 (1C 200)
Littlebrook Gdns. Wal X—2Zb 12
Littlebrook Mnr. Way. Dart
—57Qd 111
Lit. Brownings. SE23—61Xb 127
Lit. Buntings. Wind—5D 94
★Littlebury Ct. Brtwd—9Ud
Littlebury Rd. SW4—55Mb 104
Lit. Bury St. N9—17Ub 25
Lit. Bushey La. Bush, Wat
—13Ca 19
Lit. Cedars. N12—21Eb 41
Lit. Chester St. SW1
—48Kb 82 (3K 203)
Lit. College La. EC4—(4F 201)
Lit. College St. SW1
—48Nb 82 (3F 205)
Littlecombe. SE7—51Kc 107
Littlecombe Clo. SW15—58Za 102
Littlecote Clo. SW19—59Ab 102
Littlecote Pl. Pinn—25Aa 37
Little Ct. W Wick—75Gc 149
Lit. Court Rd. Sev—96Jd 186
Lit. Cranmore La. Lea—100R 174
Lit. Croft. SE9—55Qc 108
Littlecroft. Grav—6A 136
Littlecroft Rd. Egh—64B 118
Littledale. SE2—51Wc 109
Lit. Dean's Yd. SW1—(3F 205)
Lit. Dimocks. SW12—61Kb 126
Lit. Dorrit Ct. SE1
—47Sb 83 (1E 206)
Littledown Rd. Slou—6K 73
Lit. Dragons. Lou—14Mc 27
Lit. Ealing La. W5—49La 78
Lit. Edward St. NW1
—41Kb 82 (3A 192)
Lit. Elms. Hay—52T 98
Lit. Essex St. WC2—(4K 199)
Lit. Ferry Rd. Twic—60Ka 100
Littlefield Clo. N19—35Lb 62
Littlefield Rd. Edgw—24Sa 39
Lit. Friday Hill. E4—19Gc 27
Lit. Gaynes Gdns. Upm—35Rd 69
Lit. Gaynes La. Upm—35Qd 69
Lit. Gearies. Ilf—28Rc 46
Lit. George St. SW1
—47Nb 82 (2F 205)
Lit. Gerpins La. Upm—39Pd 69
Lit. Graylings. Abb L, Wat—5U 4
Lit. Green. Rich—56Ma 101
Lit. Green La. Cher—76G 138
Lit. Green La. Rick—13Q 18
Lit. Green La. Farm Est. Cher
—77F 138
Lit. Green St. NW5—35Kb 62
Littlegrove. Barn—16Gb 23
Lit. Grove. Bush, Wat—14Da 19
Lit. Hayes. K Lan—1Q 4
Lit. Heath. SE7—51Nc 108
Lit. Heath. Romf—28Xc 47
Littleheath La. Cob—86Ca 159
Lit. Heath Rd. Bexh—53Bd 109
Littleheath Rd. S Croy—80Xb 147

Lit. Hill. Rick—16E 16
Lit. Holt. E11—29Jc 45
Lit. How Croft. Abb L, Wat—3S 4
Lit. Ilford La. E12—35Pc 66
Lit. John Rd. W7—44Ha 78
Littlejohn Rd. Orp—72Wc 151
Lit. Julians Hill. Sev—99Jd 186
Lit. Marlborough St. W1—(3B 198)
Lit. Martins. Bush, Wat—15Da 19
Littlemead. Esh—77Fa 142
Littlemede. SE9—62Pc 130
Lit. Montague Ct. EC1—(1D 200)
Littlemoor Rd. Ilf—34Tc 66
Littlemore Rd. SE2—47Wc 87
Lit. Moss La. Pinn—26Aa 37
Lit. Newport St. WC2
—45Mb 82 (4E 198)
Lit. New St. EC4—44Qb 82 (2A 200)
Lit. Orchard. Wey—83J 157
Lit. Orchard. Wok—86C 156
Lit. Orchard Clo. Pinn—26Aa 37
Lit. Oxhey La. Wat—22Z 37
Lit. Park Dri. Felt—61Aa 121
Lit. Park Gdns. Enf—13Tb 25
Lit. Pastures. Brtwd—21Vd 50
Lit. Pipers Clo. Wal X—1Rb 11
Lit. Pluckett's Way. Buck H
—18Mc 27
Lit. Portland St. W1
—44Lb 82 (2B 198)
Littleport Spur. Slou—4J 73
Lit. Potters. Bush, Wat—17Fa 20
Lit. Queen's Rd. Tedd—65Ha 122
Lit. Queen St. Dart—59Pd 111
Lit. Redlands. Brom—68Nc 130
Little Rd. Hay—47V 76
Lit. Roke Av. Kenl—86Rb 165
Lit. Roke Rd. Kenl—86Sb 165
Littlers Clo. SW19—67Fb 125
Lit. Russell St. WC1
—43Nb 82 (1F 199)
Lit. Saint James's St. SW1
—46Lb 82 (7B 198)
Lit. Saint Leonard's. SW14
—55Sa 101
Lit. Sanctuary. SW1
—47Mb 82 (2E 204)
Lit. Smith St. SW1
—48Mb 82 (3E 204)
Lit. Somerset St. E1
—44Vb 83 (3K 201)
Littlestone Clo. Beck—65Cc 128
Lit. Strand. NW9—26Va 40
Lit. Stream Clo. N'wd—22U 36
Lit. Sutton La. Slou—50E 74
Lit. Thrift. Orp—70Sc 130
Lit. Titchfield St. W1
—43Lb 82 (1B 198)
Littleton Av. E4—18Hc 27
Littleton Cres. Harr—33Ha 58
Littleton La. Shep—72M 139
Littleton Rd. Ashf—66S 120
Littleton Rd. Harr—33Ha 58
Littleton St. SW18—61Eb 125
Lit. Trinity La. EC4
—45Sb 83 (4E 200)
Lit. Turnstile. WC1
—43Pb 82 (1H 199)
Lit. Venice. W2—43Eb 81 (7A 190)
Lit. Warley Hall La. Brtwd &
Upm—26Ae 51
Littlewick Rd. Wok—4B 188
Lit. Windmill Hill. K Lan—4H 3
Littlewood. SE13—58Ec 106
Lit. Wood. Sev—94Ld 187
Littlewood Clo. W13—48Ka 78
Lit. Woodcote La. Cars & Purl
—84Kb 164
Littleworth Av. Esh—78Fa 142
Littleworth Comn. Rd. Esh
—76Fa 142
Littleworth La. Esh—77Fa 142
Littleworth Rd. Esh—78Fa 142
Littleworth Rd. Slou—4A 52
Livermere Rd. E8—39Vb 63
Liverpool Gro. SE17
—50Tb 83 (7F 207)
Liverpool Rd. E10—30Ec 44
Liverpool Rd. E16—43Gc 85
Liverpool Rd.—37Qb 62 (1A 194)
N1 1-393 & 2-296
N7 remainder
Liverpool Rd. W5—47Ma 79
Liverpool Rd. King—66Qa 123
Liverpool Rd. Slou—4F 72
Liverpool Rd. T Hth—69Sb 127
Liverpool Rd. Wat—15X 19
Liverpool St. EC2
—43Ub 83 (1H 201)
Livesey Pl. SE15—51Wb 105
Livingstone Gdns. Grav—4F 136
Livingstone Pl. E14—50Ec 84
Livingstone Rd. E15—39Ec 64
Livingstone Rd. E17—30Dc 44
Livingstone Rd. N13—23Nb 42
Livingstone Rd. SW11—55Fb 103
Livingstone Rd. Cat—94Tb 181
Livingstone Rd. Grav—4F 136
Livingstone Rd. Houn—56Ea 100
Livingstone Rd. S'hall—45Z 77
Livingstone Rd. T Hth—68Tb 127
Livingstone Ter. Rain—39Gd 68
Livonia St. W1—44Lb 82 (3C 198)
Lizard St. EC1—41Sb 83 (4E 194)
Lizban St. SE3—52Kc 107
Llanbury Clo. Ger X—24A 34
Llanelly Rd. NW2—33Bb 61
Llanover Rd. SE18—51Qc 108
Llanover Rd. Wemb—34Ma 59
Llanthony Rd. Mord—71Fb 145
Llanvanor Rd. NW2—33Bb 61
Llewellyn St. SE16—47Wb 83
Lloyd Av. SW16—67Nb 126
Lloyd Av. Coul—86Jb 164
Lloyd Baker St. WC1
—41Qb 82 (4K 193)
Lloyd Ct. Pinn—29Z 37

Lloyd Pk. Av. Croy—77Vb 147
Lloyd Rd. E6—39Pc 66
Lloyd Rd. E17—28Zb 44
Lloyd Rd. Dag—38Bd 67
Lloyd Rd. Wor Pk—76Ya 144
Lloyd's Av. EC3—44Ub 83 (3J 201)
Lloyd's Pl. SE3—54Gc 107
Lloyd Sq. WC1—41Qb 82 (3K 193)
Lloyd's Row. EC1
—41Qb 82 (3B 194)
Lloyd St. WC1—41Qb 82 (3K 193)
Lloyds Way. Beck—71Ac 148
Loampit Hill. SE13—54Cc 106
Loampit Vale. SE13—55Dc 106
Loates La. Wat—13Y 19
Loats Rd. SW2—58Nb 104
Local Board Rd. Wat—15Y 19
Locarno Rd. W3—46Sa 79
Locarno Rd. Gnfd—42Fa 78
Lochaber Rd. SE13—56Gc 107
Lochaline St. W6—51Ya 102
Lochan Clo. Hay—42Aa 77
Lochinvar St. SW12—59Kb 104
Lochmere Clo. Eri—51Dd 110
Lochnagar St. E14—43Ec 84
Lock Chase. SE3—55Gc 107
Lock Clo. Wey—84G 156
Locke Clo. Rain—37Hd 68
Locke Gdns. Slou—7N 73
Locke King Clo. Wey—80Q 140
Locke King Rd. Wey—80Q 140
Locker Wlk. Wemb—34Ma 59
Lockesley Dri. Orp—72Vc 151
Lockesley Sq. Surb—72Ma 143
Locket Rd. Harr—27Ga 38
Lockets Clo. Wind—3B 94
Lockfield Av. Enf—12Ac 26
Lockfield Dri. Wok—4B 188
Lockfields. SE17—(6G 207)
Lockhart Clo. N7—37Pb 62
Lockhart Rd. Cob—85Y 159
Lockhart St. E3—42Bc 84
Lockhurst St. E5—35Zb 64
Lockington Rd. SW8—53Kb 104
Lock La. Wok—88K 157
Lockmead Rd. N15—30Wb 43
Lockmead Rd. SE13—55Ec 106
Lock Path. Wind—1B 94
Lock Rd. Rich—63La 122
Locks La. Mitc—67Jb 126
Locksley Est. E14—44Bc 84
Locksley St. E14—43Bc 84
Locksmeade Rd. Rich—63La 122
Lockwood Clo. SE26—63Zb 128
Lockwood Path. Wok—85G 156
Lockwood Sq. SE16—48Xb 83
Lockwood Wlk. Romf—29Gd 48
Lockwood Way. E17—26Zb 44
Lockwood Way. Chess—78Qa 143
Lockyer Est. SE1—(1G 207)
Lockyer Rd. Purf—51Sd 112
Lockyer St. SE1—47Tb 83 (2G 207)
Loddiges Rd. E9—38Yb 64
Loddon Spur. Slou—5J 73
Loder Clo. Wok—85F 156
Loder St. SE15—52Yb 106
Lodge Av. SW14—55Ua 102
Lodge Av. Borwd—15Pa 21
Lodge Av. Croy—76Qb 146
Lodge Av. Dag—39Wc 67
Lodge Av. Dart—58Ld 111
Lodge Av. Harr—28Na 39
Lodge Av. Romf—28Jd 48
Lodgebottom Rd. Dor—99Qa 177
Lodge Clo. N18—22Sb 43
Lodge Clo. Chig—20Wc 29
Lodge Clo. Cob—88Ba 159
Lodge Clo. Edgw—23Pa 39
Lodge Clo. Egh—4P 117
Lodge Clo. Iswth—53Ka 100
Lodge Clo. Lea—94Fa 176
Lodge Clo. Orp—74Xc 151
Lodge Clo. Slou—7G 72
Lodge Clo. Uxb—42L 75
Lodge Clo. Wall—74Jb 146
Lodge Ct. Horn—33Nd 69
Lodge Cres. Orp—74Xc 151
Lodge Cres. Wal X—6Zb 12
Lodge Dri. N13—21Qb 42
Lodge End. Rad—6Ka 6
Lodge End. Rick—14T 18
Lodge Gdns. Beck—71Bc 148
Lodge Hill. Ilf—28Nc 46
Lodge Hill. Purl—87Qb 164
Lodge Hill. Well—52Xc 109
Lodge La. N12—22Eb 41
Lodge La. Amer & Chal—11A 16
Lodge La. Bex—58Zc 109
Lodge La. Croy—79Cc 148
Lodge La. Grav—10K 137
Lodge La. Grays—47Ce 91
Lodge La. Romf—24Cd 48
Lodge La. Wal A—7Fc 13
Lodge La. West—99Sc 184
Lodge Pl. Sutt—78Db 145
Lodge Rd. NW4—28Ya 40
Lodge Rd. NW8—41Fb 81 (4C 190)
Lodge Rd. Brom—66Lc 129
Lodge Rd. Croy—72Rb 147
Lodge Rd. Epp—6Qc 14
Lodge Rd. Lea—94Ea 176
Lodge Rd. Wall—78Kb 146
Lodge Vs. Wfd G—24Hc 45
Lodge Way. Ashf—61N 119
Lodge Way. Shep—68S 120
Lodge Way. Wind—5C 94
Lodore Gdns. NW9—29Ua 40
Lodore Grn. Uxb—34N 55
Lodore St. E14—44Ec 84
Loewen Rd. Grays—8C 92
Loftie St. SE16—47Wb 83
Lofting Rd. N1—38Qb 62
Loftus Rd. W12—46Xa 80
Logan Clo. Enf—11Zb 26
Logan Clo. Houn—55Ba 99
Logan M. W8—49Cb 81
Logan Pl. W8—49Cb 81

Logan Rd. N9—19Xb 25
Logan Rd. Wemb—33Ma 59
Logs Hill. Chst—66Nc 130
Logs Hill Clo. Chst—67Nc 130
Lois Dri. Shep—71R 140
Lolesworth Clo. E1
—43Vb 83 (1K 201)
Lollard St. SE11—49Pb 82 (5J 205)
Lollesworth La. Lea—98S 174
Loman Path. S Ock—44Vd 90
Loman St. SE1—47Rb 83 (1C 206)
Lomas St. E1—43Wb 83
Lombard Av. Enf—11Yb 26
Lombard Av. Ilf—32Uc 66
Lombard Ct. EC3
—45Tb 83 (4G 201)
Lombard La. EC4
—44Qb 82 (3A 200)
Lombard Rd. N11—22Kb 42
Lombard Rd. SW11—54Fb 103
Lombard Rd. SW19—68Db 125
Lombards Chase. Brtwd—30Fe 51
Lombard St. EC3
—44Tb 83 (3G 201)
Lombard St. S Dar, Dart—71Sd 154
Lombard Wall. SE7—48Kc 85
(in two parts)
Lombardy Pl. W2—45Db 81
Lombardy Way. Borwd—11Na 21
Lomond Clo. N15—29Ub 43
Lomond Clo. Wemb—38Pa 59
Lomond Gro. SE5—52Tb 105
Lomond Ho. SE15—52Vb 105
Loncin Mead Av. Wey—81L 157
Loncroft Rd. SE5—51Ub 105
Londesborough Rd. N16—35Ub 63
Londesdale Clo. SE9—62Mc 129
London Bri. SE1 & EC4
—46Tb 83 (6G 201)
London Bri. St. SE1
—46Tb 83 (7G 201)
London Fields E. Side. E8
—38Xb 63
London Fields W. Side. E8
—38Wb 63
London Industrial Pk. E6—43Qc 86
London La. E8—38Xb 63
London La. Brom—66Hc 129
London M. W2—44Fb 81 (3C 196)
London Rd. E13—40Jc 65
London Rd. SE1—48Rb 83 (3B 206)
London Rd. SE23—60Xb 105
London Rd.—67Pb 126
SW16 1102-1544 & 1109-1599
T Hth & Croy remainder
London Rd.—70Gb 125
SW17 1-59 & 2-66
Mitc remainder
London Rd. Asc—9A 116
London Rd. Asc, Vir W & Egh
—10H 117
London Rd. Ashf & Felt—63J 119
London Rd. Bark—38Rc 66
London Rd. Brtwd—21Vd 50
London Rd. Brom—66Hc 129
London Rd. Bush, Wat—16Aa 19
London Rd. Cat—95Tb 181
London Rd. Dart—57Fd 110
London Rd. Dart, Grnh & Swans
—59Rd 111
London Rd. Enf—15Tb 25
London Rd. Eps & Wor Pk
—80Wa 144
London Rd. Grav—58Fe 113
London Rd. Grays—51Zd 113
London Rd. Guild & Wok
—100E 172
London Rd. Harr—33Ga 58
London Rd. Houn, Iswth & Bren
—55Ea 100
London Rd. King—68Pa 123
London Rd. Mitc & Wall—73Jb 146
London Rd. Mord—71Cb 145
★London Rd. Ong & Stap T, Romf
—10Hd
London Rd. Purf & Grays—50Qd 89
London Rd. Rain & Purf—46Pd 89
London Rd. Rick—19N 17
London Rd. Romf—30Cd 48
London Rd. Romf—14Vc 29
(Abridge)
London Rd. Sev—95Hd 186
London Rd. Sev—81Ad 169
(Badger's Mount)
London Rd. Sev—90Fd 170
(Dunton Green)
★London Rd. Sev—83Xd
(Stansted)
London Rd. Sev—78Td 154
(West Kingsdown)
★London Rd. Sev—88De
(Wrotham)
London Rd. Shen, Rad & Borwd
—5Pa 7
London Rd. Slou—49A 74
London Rd. Slou—7M 73
London Rd. Slou—2M 95
(Datchet)
London Rd. Stanf—2K 93
London Rd. Stan—22Ja 38
London Rd. Stap T, Romf—11Fd 30
London Rd. Swan—68Fd 132
London Rd. Swan & F'ham, Dart
—70Hd 132
London Rd. Til—4D 114
London Rd. Twic—59Ja 100
London Rd. West—95Sc 184
London Rd. West—98Tc 184
London Rd. N. Red—98Kb 180
London Rd. S. Red—100Kb 180
London Rd. West Thurrock.
Grays—51Vd 112
Londons Clo. Upm—36Sd 70
London Stile. W4—50Qa 79
London St. EC3—45Ub 83 (4J 201)
London St. W2—44Fb 81 (2B 196)
London St. Cher—73J 139

London Wall. EC2
—43Sb 83 (1E 200)
Long Acre. WC2—45Nb 82 (4F 199)
Long Acre. Orp—75Zc 151
Longacre Pl. Cars—79Jb 146
Longacre Rd. E17—25Fc 45
Longaford Way. Brtwd—18Ee 33
Long Barn Clo. Wat—4W 4
Longbeach Rd. SW11—55Hb 103
Longberrys. NW2—34Bb 61
Longbourne Way. Cher—72H 139
Longbridge Rd. Bark & Dag
—37Tc 66
Longbridge Way. SE13—57Ec 106
Longbridge Way. Uxb—40K 55
Longbury Dri. Orp—69Xc 131
Longcliffe Path. Wat—20W 18
Long Clo. Slou—8F 52
Long Copse Clo. Lea—95Da 175
Longcroft. SE9—62Pc 130
Longcroft. Wat—17X 19
Longcroft Av. Bans—86Eb 163
Longcroft Dri. Wal X—6Bc 12
Longcrofte Rd. Edgw—24Ma 39
Long Croft La. Hem—1E 2
Longcroft Rise. Lou—15Qc 28
Longcroft Rd. Rick—22F 34
Longcrofts. Wal A—6Gc 13
Longcross Rd. Cher—76A 138
Long Deacon Rd. E4—18Gc 27
Longdon Wood. Kes—77Nc 150
Longdown La. N. Eps—86Wa 162
Longdown La. S. Eps—87Wa 162
Longdown Rd. SE6—63Cc 128
Longdown Rd. Eps—86Wa 162
Long Dri. W3—44Ua 80
Long Dri. Gnfd—39Da 57
Long Dri. Ruis—35Y 57
Long Dri. Slou—1A 72
Long Elmes. Harr—25Da 37
Long Elms. Abb L, Wat—5T 4
Long Elms Clo. Abb L, Wat—5T 4
Longfellow Dri. Brtwd—17Ee 33
Longfellow Rd. E3—41Ac 84
Longfellow Rd. E17—30Bc 44
Longfellow Rd. Wor Pk—74Wa 144
Long Field. NW9—24Ua 40
Longfield. Brom—67Hc 129
Longfield. Lou—15Mc 27
Longfield. Slou—4H 53
Longfield Av. E17—28Ac 44
Longfield Av. NW7—24Wa 40
Longfield Av. W5—45La 78
Longfield Av. Enf—9Yb 12
Longfield Av. Horn—31Hd 68
Longfield Av. Long, Dart—68Ee 135
Longfield Av. Wall—74Jb 146
Longfield Av. Wemb—32Na 59
Longfield Cres. SE26—62Yb 128
Longfield Cres. Tad—92Ya 178
Longfield Dri. SW14—57Ra 101
Longfield Rd. W5—44La 78
Longfield Rd. Long, Dart—71Fe 155
Longfield St. SW18—59Cb 103
Longfield Wlk. W5—44La 78
Longford Av. Felt—58U 98
Longford Av. S'hall—45Da 77
Longford Av. Stai—60N 97
Longford Cir. W Dray—53K 97
Longford Clo. Hmptn—63Ca 121
Longford Clo. Hay—45Z 77
Longford Ct. Eps—77Sa 143
Longford Gdns. Hay—45Z 77
Longford Gdns. Sutt—75Eb 145
Longford Rd. Twic—60Da 99
Longford St. NW1
—42Kb 82 (5A 192)
Longford Wlk. SW2—59Qb 104
Longford Way. Stai—60N 97
Long Furlong Dri. Slou—2C 72
Long Grn. Chig—21Uc 46
Long Grove Rd. Eps—82Ra 161
Longhayes Av. Romf—28Zc 47
Longheath Gdns. Croy—71Yb 148
Longhedge St. SW11—54Jb 104
Long Hedges. Houn—53Ca 99
Long Hill. Cat—93Zb 182
(in three parts)
Longhill Rd. SE6—61Fc 129
Longhook Gdns. N'holt—41X 77
Longhouse Rd. Grays—8D 92
Longhurst Rd. SE13—57Fc 107
Longhurst Rd. Croy—72Xb 147
Longland Ct. SE1—50Wb 83
Longland Dri. N20—20Db 23
Longlands Av. Coul—86Jb 164
Longlands Clo. Wal X—4Zb 12
Longlands Pk. Cres. Sidc—62Uc 130
Longlands Rd. Sidc—62Uc 130
Long La. EC1—43Rb 83 (1C 200)
Long La.—25Db 41
N3 1-223 & 2-280
N2 remainder
Long La. SE1—47Tb 83 (2F 207)
Long La. Bexh—52Zc 109
Long La. Croy—72Yb 148
Long La. Grays—47Ce 91
Long La. Hem—4C 2
Long La. Hem—3B 2
Long La. Rick—16E 16
(in two parts)
Long La. Stai—61P 119
Long La. Uxb—41Q 76
Longleat Rd. Enf—15Ub 25
Longleat Way. Felt—59T 98
Longlees. Rick—22F 34
Longleigh La. SE2 & Bex H
—51Yc 109
Longley Av. Wemb—39Pa 59
Longley Rd. SW17—65Gb 125
Longley Rd. Croy—73Rb 147
Longley Rd. Harr—29Ea 38
Long Leys. E4—23Ec 44
Longley St. SE1—49Wb 83
Long Lodge Dri. W on T—76Y 141
Longmarsh View. S at H, Dart
—67Rd 133

Long Mead. NW9—25Va 40
Longmead. Chst—68Qc 130
Longmead. Wind—3C 94
Longmead Clo. Brtwd—18Ae 33
Longmead Clo. Cat—94Ub 181
Longmead Dri. Sidc—61Zc 131
Longmead Ho. SE27—64Sb 127
Longmead La. Slou—8B 52
Long Meadow. NW5—36Mb 62
Long Meadow. Brtwd—19Ee 33
Longmeadow. Lea—97Ba 175
Longmeadow Rd. Sidc—60Uc 108
Longmead Rd. SW17—64Hb 125
Longmead Rd. Eps—83Ta 161
Longmead Rd. Hay—45V 76
Longmead Rd. Th Dit—73Ga 142
Longmere Gdns. Tad—91Ya 178
★Long Mill La. Sev—96De
Long Moor. Wal X—1Ac 12
Longmoore St. SW1 —49Lb 82 (6B 204)
Longmore Av. Barn—16Eb 23
Longmore Clo. Rick—21H 35
Longmore Rd. W on T—77Aa 141
Longnor Est. E1—41Zb 84
Longnor Rd. E1—41Zb 84
Long Pond Rd. SE3—53Gc 107
Longport Clo. Ilf—23Wc 47
Long Reach. Wok & Lea—95Q 174
Long Reach Rd. Bark—42Vc 87
Longreach Rd. Eri—52Kd 111
Long Readings La. Slou—1F 72
Longridge Gro. Wok—86H 157
Longridge La. S'hall—44Da 77
Longridge Rd. SW5—49Cb 81
Long Ridings Av. Brtwd—15De 33
Long Rd. SW4—56Lb 104
Longs Clo. Wok—88J 157
Long's Ct. WC2—(5E 198)
Long Shaw. Lea—92Ja 176
Longshaw Rd. E4—20Fc 27
Longshore. SE8—49Bc 84
Longside Clo. Egh—67E 118
Longspring. Wat—9X 5
Longstaff Cres. SW18—59Cb 103
Longstaff Rd. SW18—58Cb 103
★Longstead La. Sev—95Xd
Lohgstone Av. NW10—38Va 60
Longstone Rd. SW17—64Kb 126
Longstone Rd. Iver—40E 54
Long St. E2—41Vb 83 (3K 195)
(in two parts)
Long St. Wal A—4Nc 14
Long St. Wal A—3Nc 14
Longthornton Rd. SW16 —68Lb 126
Longton Av. SE26—63Wb 127
Longton Gro. SE26—63Xb 127
Longtown Clo. Romf—22Ld 49
Longtown Rd. Romf—22Ld 49
Longview Way. Romf—25Fd 48
Longville Rd. SE11 —49Rb 83 (5C 206)
Long Wlk. SE1—48Ub 83 (3J 207)
Long Wlk. SE18—51Rc 108
Long Wlk. SW13—54Va 102
Long Wlk. Chal—13A 16
Long Wlk. Eps—91Ya 178
Longwalk. Grav—7A 136
Long Wlk. Guild—100P 173
Long Wlk. N Mald—69Sa 123
Long Wlk. Wal A—2Cc 12
Long Wlk. Wey—86L 157
Long Wlk. Wind—7H 95
Long Wall. E15—41Fc 85
Longways, The. Stai—67G 118
Longwood Clo. Upm—36Sd 70
Longwood Dri. SW15—58Wa 102
Longwood Gdns. Ilf—28Pc 46
Longwood Rd. Kenl—88Tb 165
Long Yd. WC1—42Pb 82 (6H 193)
Loning, The. NW9—28Va 40
Loning, The. Enf—10Yb 12
Lonsdale Av. E6—42Mc 85
Lonsdale Av. Brtwd—16Fe 33
Lonsdale Av. Romf—30Ed 48
Lonsdale Av. Wemb—36Na 59
Lonsdale Clo. E6—42Nc 86
Lonsdale Clo. Pinn—24Aa 37
Lonsdale Clo. Uxb—43S 76
Lonsdale Ct. Surb—73Ma 143
Lonsdale Cres. Ilf—30Rc 46
Lonsdale Dri. Enf—14Mb 24
Lonsdale Gdns. T Hth—70Pb 126
Lonsdale M. Rich—53Qa 101
Lonsdale Pl. N1—38Qb 62
Lonsdale Rd. E11—31Hc 65
Lonsdale Rd. NW6—39Bb 61
Lonsdale Rd. SE25—70Xb 127
Lonsdale Rd. SW13—53Va 102
Lonsdale Rd. W4—49Va 80
Lonsdale Rd. W11—44Bb 81
Lonsdale Rd. Bexh—54Bd 109
Lonsdale Rd. Dart—60Sd 112
Lonsdale Rd. S'hall—48Z 77
Lonsdale Rd. Wey—80Q 140
Lonsdale Sq. N1—38Qb 62
Loobert Rd. N15—27Ub 43
Looe Gdns. Ilf—27Rc 46
Loom La. Rad—9Ha 6
Loom Pl. Rad—8Ja 6
Loop Rd. Chst—65Sc 130
Loop Rd. Eps—88Sa 161
Loop Rd. Wal A—4Dc 12
Loop Rd. Wok—92B 172
Lopen Rd. N18—21Ub 43
Loraine Clo. Enf—15Yb 26
Loraine Gdns. Asht—89Na 161
Loraine Rd. N7—35Pb 62
Loraine Rd. W4—51Ra 101
Lord Av. Ilf—28Pc 46
Lord Chancellor Wlk. King —67Sa 123
Lorden Wlk. E2—41Wb 83
Lord Gdns. Ilf—28Nc 46
Lord Hills Bri. W2—43Db 81
Lord Hill's Rd. W2—43Db 81
Lord Holland La. SW9—54Qb 104
Lord Knyvett Clo. Stai—58M 97
Lord Mayors Dri. Slou—6E 52
Lord Napier Pl. W6—50Wa 80
Lord North St. SW1 —48Nb 82 (4F 205)
Lord Roberts M. SW6—52Db 103
Lord Robert's Ter. SE18—50Qc 86
Lordsbury Field. Wall—82Lb 164
Lord's Clo. SE21—61Sb 127
Lords Clo. Felt—61Aa 121
Lordship Clo. Brtwd—17Fe 33
Lordship Gro. N16—33Tb 63
Lordship La.—26Qb 42
N17 1-421 & 2-470
N22 remainder
Lordship La. SE22—57Vb 105
Lordship Pk. N16—33Sb 63
Lordship Pk. M. N16—33Sb 63
Lordship Pl. SW3—51Gb 103
Lordship Rd. N16—32Tb 63
Lordship Rd. N'holt—38Aa 57
Lordship Rd. Wal X—2Xb 11
Lordship Ter. N16—33Tb 63
Lordsmead Rd. N17—26Ub 43
Lord St. E16—46Nc 86
Lord St. Grav—9D 114
Lord St. Wat—13Y 19
Lordswood Clo. Dart—63Ud 134
Lord Warwick St. SE18—48Pc 86
Lorenzo St. WC1 —41Pb 82 (3H 193)
Loretto Gdns. Harr—28Na 39
Lorian Clo. N12—21Db 41
Loring Rd. N20—19Gb 23
Loring Rd. Iswth—54Ha 100
Loring Rd. Wind—3D 94
Loris Rd. W6—48Ya 80
Lorn Ct. SW9—53Qb 104
Lorne Av. Croy—73Zb 148
Lorne Clo. NW8—41Gb 81 (4E 190)
Lorne Clo. Slou—8F 72
Lorne Ct. Slou—8F 72
Lorne Gdns. E11—28Lc 45
Lorne Gdns. W11—47Ab 80
Lorne Gdns. Croy—73Zb 148
Lorne Rd. E7—35Kc 65
Lorne Rd. E17—29Cc 44
Lorne Rd. N4—32Pb 62
Lorne Rd. Brtwd—21Yd 50
Lorne Rd. Harr—26Ha 38
Lorne Rd. Rich—57Pa 101
Lorne Ter. N3—26Bb 41
Lorne, The. Lea—98Ca 175
Lorn Rd. SW9—54Pb 104
Lorraine Pk. Harr—24Ga 38
Lorrimore Rd. SE17—51Rb 105
Lorrimore Sq. SE17—51Rb 105
Lorton Clo. Grav—1G 136
Lorton Rd. Grav—1G 136
Losberne Way. SE16—50Wb 83
Loseberry Rd. Esh—78Fa 142
Losfield Rd. Wind—3C 94
Lossie Dri. Iver—45D 74
Lothair Rd. N4—31Rb 63
Lothair Rd. W5—47Ma 79
Lothair Rd. N. N4—30Rb 43
Lothbury. EC2—44Tb 83 (2F 201)
Lothian Av. Hay—43X 77
Lothian Rd. SW9—53Rb 105
Lothian Wood. Tad—94Xa 178
Lothrop St. W10—41Ab 80
Lots Rd. SW10—52Eb 103
Lotus Rd. West—90Pc 168
Loubet St. SW17—65Hb 125
Loudhams Wood La. Chal—12A 16
Loudoun Av. Ilf—29Rc 46
Loudoun Rd. NW8 —39Eb 61 (1A 190)
Loudwater Clo. Sun—70W 120
Loudwater Dri. Rick—14L 17
Loudwater Heights. Rick—13K 17
Loudwater Hill. Rick—15L 17
Loudwater La. Rick—14M 17
Loudwater Rd. Sun—70W 120
Loughborough Pk. SW9 —56Rb 105
Loughborough Rd. SW9 —54Qb 104
Loughborough St. SE11 —50Pb 82 (7J 205)
Lough Rd. N7—36Pb 62
Loughton Ct. Wal A—5Kc 13
Loughton La. Epp—10Tc 14
Loughton Way. Buck H & Lou —18Mc 27
Louisa St. E1—42Zb 84
Louise Ct. N22—25Qb 42
Louise Gdns. Rain—41Gd 88
Louise Rd. E15—37Gc 65
Louisville Rd. SW17—62Jb 126
Louvaine Rd. SW11—56Fb 103
Louvain Rd. Grnh—59Ud 112
Louvain Way. Wat—4X 5
Lovat Clo. NW2—34Va 60
Lovat Clo. Edgw—23Ra 39
Lovat Dri. Ruis—29W 36
Lovat La. EC3—45Ub 83 (5H 201)
Lovat Wlk. Houn—52Aa 99
Loveday Rd. W13—47Ka 78
Love Grn. La. Iver—43G 74
Lovegrove St. SE1—50Wb 83
Love Hill La. Slou—45C 74
Lovejoy La. Wind—4B 94
Lovekyn Clo. King—68Na 123
Lovelace Av. Brom—72Qc 150
Lovelace Clo. Lea—95W 174
Lovelace Clo. Sev—79Ud 154
Lovelace Dri. Wok—88H 157
Lovelace Gdns. Bark—35Wc 67
Lovelace Gdns. Surb—73Ma 143
Lovelace Gdns. W on T—78Y 141
Lovelace Grn. SE9—55Pc 108
Lovelace Rd. SE21—61Sb 127
Lovelace Rd. Barn—17Gb 23
Lovelace Rd. Surb—73La 142
Lovelands La. Chob—1A 188
Lovelands La. Tad—99Db 179
Love La. EC2—44Sb 83 (2E 200)
Love La. N17—24Vb 43
Love La. SE18—49Qc 86
Love La. SE25—69Xb 127
Love La. Abb L, Wat—2V 4
Love La. Bex—58Bd 109
Love La. Brom—68Kc 129
Love La. Grav—9E 114
Love La. Grays—1L 115
Love La. Hat—1Xa 8
Love La. Iver—44F 74
Love La. K Lan—1N 3
Love La. Mitc—69Gb 125
Love La. Mord—73Cb 145
Love La. Pinn—27Aa 37
Love La. S Ock—47Sd 90
Love La. Surb—75La 142
Love La. Sutt—79Ab 144
(in two parts)
Love La. Tad—98Va 178
Love La. Wfd G—23Pc 46
Lovel Av. Well—54Wc 109
Lovelinch Clo. SE15—51Yb 106
Lovel La. Wind—4A 116
Lovell Pl. SE16—48Ac 84
Lovell Rd. Enf—7Xb 11
Lovell Rd. Rich—62La 122
Lovell Rd. S'hall—44Da 77
Lovell Wlk. Rain—37Jd 68
Loveridge Rd. NW6—37Bb 61
Lovers La. Grnh—56Yd 112
Lovers Wlk. NW7—23Bb 41
Lovers Wlk. SE10—51Fc 107
Lovers Wlk. Romf—22Fd 48
Lovett Dri. Cars—73Eb 145
Lovett Rd. Stai—63E 118
Lovett Rd. Uxb—27L 35
Lovetts. Rick—14Q 18
Lovett Way. NW10—36Sa 59
Love Wlk. SE5—54Tb 105
Lovibonds Av. Orp—76Rc 150
Lowbrook Rd. Ilf—35Rc 66
Low Cross Wood La. SE21 —62Vb 127
Lowdell Clo. W Dray—44N 75
Lowden Rd. N9—18Xb 25
Lowden Rd. SE24—56Rb 105
Lowden Rd. S'hall—45Aa 77
Lowe Av. E16—43Jc 85
Lowe Clo. Chig—22Wc 47
Lowell St. E14—44Ac 84
Lowen Rd. Rain—40Fd 68
Lwr. Addiscombe Rd. Croy —74Ub 147
Lwr. Addison Gdns. W14—47Ab 80
Lwr. Barn Rd. Purl—84Sb 165
Lwr. Bedfords Rd. Romf—23Gd 48
Lwr. Belgrave St. SW1 —48Kb 82 (4K 203)
Lwr. Boston Rd. W7—46Ga 78
Lwr. Britwell Rd. Slou—2B 72
(in two parts)
Lwr. Broad St. Dag—39Cd 68
Lwr. Bury La. Epp—3Uc 14
Lwr. Camden. Chst—66Pc 130
Lwr. Church Hill. Grnh—57Ud 112
Lwr. Church St. Croy—75Rb 147
Lwr. Cippenham La. Slou—6C 72
Lwr. Clapton Rd. E5—34Xb 63
Lwr. Common S. SW15—55Xa 102
Lwr. Coombe St. Croy—77Sb 147
Lwr. Court Rd. Eps—83Sa 161
Lower Cres. Stanf—8J 93
Lwr. Croft. Swan—70Hd 132
Lwr. Downs Rd. SW20—67Za 124
Lwr. Drayton Pl. Croy—75Rb 147
Lwr. Farm Rd. Lea—96X 175
Lwr. Fore St. N9—21Wb 43
Lwr. George St. Rich—57Ma 101
Lwr. Gravel Rd. Brom—74Nc 150
Lwr. Green Rd. Esh—75Da 141
Lwr. Green W. Mitc—69Gb 125
Lwr. Grosvenor Pl. SW1 —48Kb 82 (3A 204)
Lwr. Grove Rd. Rich—58Pa 101
Lwr. Guildford Rd. Wok—5A 188
Lwr. Hall La. E4—22Ac 44
Lwr. Hampton Rd. Sun—69Y 121
Lwr. Ham Rd. King—65Ma 123
Lwr. Higham Rd. Grav—10H 115
Lwr. High St. Wat—15Z 19
Lwr. Hill Rd. Eps—84Ra 161
Lwr. Hythe St. Dart—57Nd 111
Lwr. Island Way. Wal A—7Dc 12
Lwr. James St. W1 —45Lb 82 (4C 198)
Lwr. John St. W1 —45Lb 82 (4C 198)
Lwr. Kenwood Av. Enf—15Nb 24
Lwr. Lees Rd. Slou—1F 72
Lwr. Maidstone Rd. N11—23Lb 42
Lwr. Mall. W6—50Xa 80
Lwr. Mardyke Av. Rain—40Ed 68
Lwr. Marsh. SE1 —47Qb 82 (2K 205)
Lwr. Marsh La. King—70Pa 123
Lwr. Mead. Iver—41F 74
Lwr. Merton Rise. NW3—38Gb 61
Lwr. Morden La. Mord—72Za 144
Lwr. Mortlake Rd. Rich—56Na 101
Lwr. Noke Clo. Romf—19Nd 31
Lwr. Paddock Rd. Wat—16Aa 19
Lwr. Park Rd. N11—22Kb 42
Lwr. Park Rd. Bans—90Gb 163
Lwr. Park Rd. Belv—49Cd 88
Lwr. Park Rd. Lou—15Nc 28
Lwr. Peryers. Lea—100U 174
Lwr. Pillory Downs. Coul & Cars—85Kb 164
Lwr. Pyrford Rd. Wok—88K 157
Lwr. Queen's Rd. Buck H—19Mc 27
Lwr. Range Rd. Grav—9G 114
Lwr. Richmond Rd. SW15 —55Xa 102
Lwr. Richmond Rd. Rich & SW14 —55Qa 101
Lower Rd.—48Yb 84
SE16 1-245 & 2-196
SE8 remainder
Lower Rd. Belv & Eri—48Dd 88
Lower Rd. Brtwd—12Fe 33
Lower Rd. Ger X—25A 34
Lower Rd. Grav—1N 137
(Lower Shorne)
Lower Rd. Grav—56Be 113
(Northfleet)
Lower Rd. Harr—32Fa 58
Lower Rd. Kenl—85Rb 165
Lower Rd. Lea—96Ea 176
Lower Rd. Lea—99Z 175
Lower Rd. Lou—11Qc 28
Lower Rd. Orp—72Xc 151
Lower Rd. Rick—14E 16
Lower Rd. Sutt—77Eb 145
Lower Rd. Swan—66Jd 132
Lower Rd. Uxb—31E 54
Lwr. Robert St. WC2—(5G 199)
Lwr. Sandfields. Wok—96F 172
Lwr. Shott. Lea—98Ca 175
Lwr. Sloane St. SW1 —49Jb 82 (6H 203)
Lower Sq. Iswth—55Ka 100
Lower Sq., The. Sutt—78Db 145
Lwr. Station Rd. Dart—58Gd 110
Lwr. Strand. NW9—26Va 40
Lwr. Sunbury Rd. Hmptn —68Ba 121
Lwr. Swaines. Epp—2Uc 14
Lwr. Tail. Wat—20Aa 19
Lwr. Teddington Rd. King —67Ma 123
Lower Ter. NW3—34Eb 61
Lwr. Thames St. EC3 —45Ub 83 (5G 201)
Lower Tub. Bush, Wat—17Fa 20
Lwr. Village Rd. Asc—10A 116
Lwr. Wood Rd. Esh—79Ka 142
Lowestoft Rd. Wat—11X 19
Loweswater Clo. Wemb—33Ma 59
Lowe, The. Chig—22Wc 47
Lowfield Rd. NW6—38Cb 61
Lowfield Rd. W3—44Sa 79
Lowfield St. Dart—59Nd 111
Low Hall Clo. E4—17Dc 26
Lowhall La. E17—30Ac 44
Lowick Rd. Harr—28Ga 38
Lowlands Gdns. Romf—30Dd 48
Lowlands Rd. Harr—31Ga 58
Lowlands Rd. Pinn—30Y 37
Lowlands Rd. S Ock—46Sd 90
Lowman Rd. N7—35Pb 62
Lowndes Clo. SW1 —48Jb 82 (4J 203)
Lowndes Pl. SW1 —48Jb 82 (4H 203)
Lowndes Sq. SW1 —47Hb 81 (2G 203)
Lowndes St. SW1 —48Jb 82 (3G 203)
Lownds Av. Brom—68Jc 129
Lowood St. E1—45Xb 83
Lowshoe La. Romf—25Dd 48
Lowson Gro. Wat—17Aa 19
Low St. La. Grays—9H 93
Lowswood Clo. N'wd—25S 36
Lowther Clo. Borwd—15Pa 21
Lowther Dri. Enf—14Nb 24
Lowther Hill. SE23—59Ac 106
Lowther Rd. E17—26Ac 44
Lowther Rd. N7—36Qb 62
Lowther Rd. SW13—53Va 102
Lowther Rd. King—67Pa 123
Lowther Rd. Stan—27Pa 39
Lowthorpe. Wok—6D 188
Lowth Rd. SE5—54Sb 105
Loxford Av. E6—40Mc 65
Loxford La. Ilf—36Sc 66
Loxford Rd. Bark—37Rc 66
Loxford Rd. Cat—97Vb 181
Loxford Way. Cat—97Vb 181
Loxham Rd. E4—24Dc 44
Loxham St. WC1—41Nb 82 (4G 193)
Loxley Clo. SE9—64Zb 128
Loxley Rd. SW18—60Fb 103
Loxley Rd. Hmpton—63Ba 121
Loxton Rd. SE23—60Zb 106
Loxwood Clo. Orp—75Zc 151
Loxwood Rd. N17—27Ub 43
Lubbock Rd. Chst—66Pc 130
Lubbock St. SE14—52Yb 106
Lucan Dri. Stai—66M 119
Lucan Pl. SW3—49Gb 81 (6D 202)
Lucan Rd. Barn—13Ab 22
Lucas Av. E13—39Kc 65
Lucas Av. Harr—33Ca 57
Lucas Ct. Wal A—5Hc 13
Lucas Rd. SE20—65Yb 128
Lucas Rd. Grays—48Ce 91
Lucas St. SE8—53Cc 106
Lucerne Clo. N13—20Nb 24
Lucerne Clo. Wok—91A 172
Lucerne Ct. Eri—48Ad 87
Lucerne Gro. E17—28Fc 45
Lucerne M. W8—46Cb 81
Lucerne Rd. N5—35Rb 63
Lucerne Rd. Orp—74Vc 151
Lucerne Rd. T Hth—70Sb 127
Lucerne Way. Romf—23Md 49
Lucey Rd. SE16—48Wb 83
Lucey Way. SE16—48Wb 83
Lucie Av. Ashf—65R 120
Lucien Rd. SW17—63Jb 126
Lucien Rd. SW19—61Db 125
Lucknow St. SE18—52Uc 108
Lucorn Clo. SE12—58Hc 107
Luctons Av. Buck H—18Lc 27
Lucy Cres. W3—43Sa 79
Lucy Gdns. Dag—34Bd 67
Luddesdon Rd. Eri—52Cd 110
Luddington Av. Vir W—68B 118
Ludford Clo. NW9—26Ua 40
Ludgate B'way. EC4 —44Rb 83 (3B 200)
Ludgate Cir. EC4 —44Rb 83 (3B 200)
Ludgate Ct. EC4—(3B 200)
Ludgate Hill. EC4 —44Rb 83 (3B 200)
Ludgate Sq. EC4—(3C 200)
Ludham Clo. SE28—44Yc 87
Ludlow Clo. Harr—35Ba 57
Ludlow Mead. Wat—20X 19
Ludlow Pl. Grays—48De 91
Ludlow Rd. W5—42La 78
Ludlow Rd. Felt—63W 120
Ludlow St. EC1—42Sb 83 (5D 194)
Ludlow Way. N2—28Eb 41
Ludlow Way. Rick—14S 18
Ludovick Wlk. SW15—56Ua 102
Ludwick M. SE14—52Ac 106
Luff Clo. Wind—5C 94
Luffield Rd. SE2—48Xc 87
Luffman Rd. SE12—62Kc 129
Lugard Rd. SE15—54Xb 105
Luke St. EC2—42Ub 83 (5H 195)
Lukin Cres. E4—20Fc 27
Lukin St. E1—44Yb 84
Lullarook Clo. West—88Lc 167
Lullingstone Av. Swan—69Hd 132
Lullingstone Clo. Orp—66Xc 131
Lullingstone Cres. Orp—66Wc 131
Lullingstone La. Eyns, Dart —76Ld 153
Lullingstone Rd. Belv—51Bd 109
Lullington Garth. N12—22Bb 41
Lullington Garth. Borwd—15Ra 21
Lullington Garth. Brom—66Gc 129
Lullington Rd. SE20—66Wb 127
Lullington Rd. Dag—38Ad 67
Lulot Gdns. N19—33Kb 62
Lulworth Av. Houn—52Ea 100
Lulworth Av. Wal X—1Rb 11
Lulworth Av. Wemb—31La 58
Lulworth Clo. Harr—34Ba 57
Lulworth Clo. Stanf—3K 93
Lulworth Dri. Pinn—31Z 57
Lulworth Dri. Romf—22Dd 48
Lulworth Gdns. Harr—33Aa 57
Lulworth Rd. SE9—61Nc 130
Lulworth Rd. SE15—54Xb 105
Lulworth Rd. Well—54Vc 109
Lulworth Waye. Hay—44Y 77
Lumley Clo. Belv—50Cd 88
Lumley Ct. WC2—45Nb 82 (5G 199)
Lumley Gdns. Sutt—78Ab 144
Lumley Rd. Sutt—78Ab 144
Lumley St. W1—44Jb 82 (3J 197)
Lunar Clo. West—88Mc 167
Luna Rd. T Hth—69Sb 127
Lundin Wlk. Wat—21Z 37
Lundy Dri. Hay—49U 76
Lundy Wlk. N1—37Sb 63
Lunedale Rd. Dart—60Sd 112
Lunghurst Rd. Cat—92Bc 182
Lunham Rd. SE19—65Ub 127
Lupin Clo. SW2—61Rb 127
Lupin Clo. Croy—74Zb 148
Lupin Clo. W Dray—50M 75
Luppit Clo. Brtwd—18Ce 33
Lupton Clo. SE12—62Kc 129
Lupton Rd. NW5—35Lb 62
Lupus St. SW1—50Kb 82 (7A 204)
Luralda Gdns. E14—50Fc 85
Lurgan Av. W6—51Za 102
Lurgan St. W6—50Za 80
Lurline Gdns. SW11—53Jb 104
Luscombe Ct. Brom—68Gc 129
Luscombe Way. SW8—52Nb 104
Lushes Rd. Lou—15Rc 28
Lushington Dri. Cob—86X 159
Lushington Rd. NW10—40Xa 60
Lushington Rd. SE6—64Dc 128
Lushington Ter. E8—36Wb 63
Lusted Hall La. West—92Lc 183
Lusted Rd. Sev—92Gd 186
Luther Clo. Edgw—19Sa 21
Luther Rd. Tedd—64Ha 122
★Luthers Clo. Brtwd—9Ud
Luton Pl. SE10—52Ec 106
Luton Rd. E17—27Bc 44
Luton Rd. Sidc—62Yc 131
Luton St. NW8—42Fb 81 (6C 190)
Luttrell Av. SW15—57Xa 102
Lutwyche Rd. SE6—61Bc 128
Luxborough La. Chig—20Nc 28
Luxborough St. W1 —43Jb 82 (7H 191)
Luxemburg Gdns. W6—49Za 80
Luxfield Rd. SE9—60Nc 108
Luxford St. SE16—49Zb 84
Luxmore Gdns. SE4—54Bc 106
Luxmore St. SE4—53Bc 106
Luxor St. SE5—55Sb 105
Luxted Rd. Orp—84Qc 168
Lyall Av. SE21—63Ub 127
Lyall M. SW1—48Jb 82 (4H 203)
Lyall M. W. SW1—48Jb 82 (4H 203)
Lyall St. SW1—48Jb 82 (4H 203)
Lyal Rd. E3—40Ac 64
Lycett Pl. W12—47Wa 80
Lych Ga. Orp—74Wc 151
Lych Ga. Wat—5Z 5
Lych Ga. Wlk. Hay—45V 76
(in two parts)
Lych Way. Wok—4G 188
Lyconby Gdns. Croy—73Ac 148
Lydd Clo. Sidc—62Uc 130
Lydden Gro. SW18—59Db 103
Lydden Rd. SW18—59Db 103
Lydd Rd. Bexh—52Bd 109
Lydeard Rd. E6—38Pc 66
Lydele Clo. Wok—87B 156
Lydford Av. Slou—3H 73
Lydford Rd. N15—29Tb 43
Lydford Rd. NW2—37Za 60
Lydford Rd. W9—42Bb 81
Lydhurst Av. SW2—61Pb 126
Lydia Rd. Eri—51Hd 110
Lydney Clo. SE15—52Ub 105
Lydney Clo. SW19—61Ab 124
Lydon Rd. SW4—55Lb 104
Lydsey Clo. Slou—1E 72
Lydstep Rd. Chst—63Qc 130
Lye La. St Alb—2Ca 5
Lyell. Wind—5A 94
Lyell Pl. E. Wind—5A 94
Lyfield. Lea—86Da 159
Lyford Rd. SW18—59Fb 103
(in two parts)
Lygon Pl. SW1—48Kb 82 (4K 203)
Lyham Clo. SW2—58Nb 104
Lyham Rd. SW2—57Nb 104
Lyle Pk. Sev—95Kd 187
Lymbourne Clo. Sutt—82Cb 163
Lyme Farm Rd. SE12—56Jc 107
Lyme Gro. E9—38Yb 64
Lymer Av. SE19—64Vb 127
Lyme Regis Rd. Bans—89Bb 163
Lyme Rd. Well—53Xc 109
Lymescote Gdns. Sutt—75Cb 145
Lyme St. NW1—38Lb 62
Lyme Ter. NW1—38Lb 62
Lyminge Clo. Sidc—63Vc 131
Lyminge Gdns. SW18—60Gb 103
Lymington Av. N22—26Qb 42
Lymington Clo. SW16—68Mb 126
Lymington Dri. Ruis—33T 56
Lymington Gdns. Eps—78Va 144
Lymington Rd. NW6—37Db 61
Lymington Rd. Dag—32Zc 67
Lympstone Gdns. SE15 —52Wb 105
Lynbridge Gdns. N13—21Rb 43
Lynbrook Clo. SE15—52Ub 105
Lynbrook Clo. Rain—40Fd 68
Lynceley Grange. Epp—1Wc 15
Lynch Clo. Uxb—38L 55
Lynchen Clo. Houn—53X 99
Lynch Hill La. Slou—2C 72
Lynch, The. Uxb—38L 55
Lynch Wlk. SE8—51Bc 106
Lyncott Cres. SW4—56Kb 104
Lyncroft Av. Pinn—29Aa 37
Lyncroft Gdns. NW6—36Cb 61
Lyncroft Gdns. W13—47La 78
Lyncroft Gdns. Eps—81Va 162
Lyncroft Gdns. Houn—57Ea 100
Lyndale. NW2—35Bb 61
★Lyndale. Brtwd—9Vd
Lyndale Av. NW2—34Bb 61
Lyndale Clo. SE3—51Hc 107
Lyndale Ct. Wey—85J 157
Lynden Way. Swan—69Ed 132
Lyndhurst Av. N12—23Hb 41
Lyndhurst Av. NW7—23Ua 40
Lyndhurst Av. SW16—68Mb 126
Lyndhurst Av. Pinn—25X 37
Lyndhurst Av. S'hall—46Da 77
Lyndhurst Av. Sun—69W 120
Lyndhurst Av. Surb—74Ra 143
Lyndhurst Av. Twic—60Ba 99
Lyndhurst Clo. NW10—34Ta 59
Lyndhurst Clo. Bexh—55Dd 110
Lyndhurst Clo. Croy—76Vb 147
Lyndhurst Clo. Wok—3G 188
Lyndhurst Ct. E18—25Jc 45
Lyndhurst Dri. E10—31Ec 64
Lyndhurst Dri. Horn—32Ld 69
Lyndhurst Dri. N Mald—73Ua 144
Lyndhurst Dri. Sev—96Gd 186
Lyndhurst Gdns. N3—25Ab 40
Lyndhurst Gdns. NW3—36Fb 61
Lyndhurst Gdns. Bark—37Uc 66
Lyndhurst Gdns. Enf—14Ub 25
Lyndhurst Gdns. Ilf—30Tc 46
Lyndhurst Gdns. Pinn—25X 37
Lyndhurst Gro. SE15—54Ub 105
Lyndhurst Rise. Chig—21Qc 46
Lyndhurst Rd. E4—24Ec 44
Lyndhurst Rd. N18—21Wb 43
Lyndhurst Rd. N22—23Qb 42
Lyndhurst Rd. NW3—36Fb 61
Lyndhurst Rd. Bexh—55Dd 110
Lyndhurst Rd. Coul—88Jb 164
Lyndhurst Rd. Gnfd—42Da 77
Lyndhurst Rd. T Hth—70Qb 126
Lyndhurst Sq. SE15—53Vb 105
Lyndhurst Ter. NW3—36Fb 61
Lyndhurst Way. SE15—53Vb 105
Lyndhurst Way. Brtwd—17Ee 33
Lyndhurst Way. Cher—76G 138
Lyndhurst Way. Grav—7B 136
Lyndhurst Way. Sutt—81Cb 163
Lyndon Av. Pinn—23Aa 37
Lyndon Av. Sidc—57Vc 109
Lyndon Av. Wall—76Jb 146
Lyndon Rd. Belv—49Cd 88
Lyndwood Dri. Wind—8L 95
Lyne Clo. Vir W—72B 138
Lyne Cres. E17—25Bc 44
Lyne Crossing Rd. Cher—72C 138
Lynegrove Av. Ashf—64S 120
Lyneham Wlk. E5—36Ac 64
Lyne La. Cher, Vir W & Egh —72C 138
Lyne Rd. Vir W—72A 138
Lynette Av. SW4—58Lb 104
Lynett Rd. Dag—33Zc 67
Lynford Clo. Edgw—24Sa 39
Lynford Gdns. Edgw—20Ra 21
Lynford Gdns. Ilf—33Vc 67
Lynford Ter. N9—17Vb 25
Lynhurst Cres. Uxb—38S 56
Lynhurst Rd. Uxb—38S 56
Lynmere Rd. Well—54Xc 109
Lynmouth Av. Enf—16Vb 25
Lynmouth Av. Mord—73Za 144
Lynmouth Dri. Ruis—33X 57
Lynmouth Gdns. Gnfd—39Ka 58
Lynmouth Gdns. Houn—52Z 99
Lynmouth Rise. Orp—70Xc 131
Lynmouth Rd. E17—30Ac 44
Lynmouth Rd. N2—28Hb 41
Lynmouth Rd. N16—32Vb 63
Lynmouth Rd. Gnfd—39Ka 58
Lynn Clo. Ashf—64T 120
Lynn Clo. Harr—26Fa 38

Lynne Clo.—Manor Rd.

Lynne Clo. Orp—79Vc 151
Lynne Clo. S Croy—83Yb 166
Lynne Wlk. Esh—78Ea 142
Lynne Way. NW10—37Ua 60
Lynne Way. N'holt—40Z 57
Lynn Rd. E11—33Gc 65
Lynn Rd. SW12—59Kb 104
Lynn Rd. Ilf—31Tc 66
Lynn St. Enf—11Tb 25
Lynross Clo. Romf—26Pd 49
Lynsted Clo. Bexh—57Dd 110
Lynsted Clo. Brom—68Lc 129
Lynsted Ct. Beck—68Ac 128
Lynsted Gdns. SE9—56Mc 107
Lynton Av. N12—21Fb 41
Lynton Av. NW9—28Va 40
Lynton Av. W13—44Ja 78
Lynton Av. Orp—70Xc 131
Lynton Av. Romf—25Dd 48
Lynton Clo. Chess—77Na 143
Lynton Clo. Iswth—56Ha 100
Lynton Cres. Ilf—30Rc 46
Lynton Crest. Pot B—4Cb 9
Lynton Gdns. Enf—17Ub 25
Lynton Mead. N20—20Cb 23
Lynton Rd. E4—22Dc 44
Lynton Rd. E11—35Fc 65
Lynton Rd. N8—29Mb 42
Lynton Rd. N11—23Mb 42
Lynton Rd. NW6—40Bb 61
Lynton Rd. SE1—49Vb 83 (6K 207)
Lynton Rd. W3—45Qa 79
Lynton Rd. Croy—72Qb 146
Lynton Rd. Grav—10C 114
Lynton Rd. Harr—33Aa 57
Lynton Rd. N Mald—71Ta 143
Lynton Rd. S. Grav—10C 114
Lynton Wlk. Hay—41U 76
Lynwood Av. Coul—87Kb 164
Lynwood Av. Egh—65A 118
Lynwood Av. Eps—86Va 162
Lynwood Av. Slou—8P 73
Lynwood Clo. E18—25Lc 45
Lynwood Clo. Romf—23Dd 48
Lynwood Clo. Ruis—34Aa 57
Lynwood Clo. Wok—85F 156
Lynwood Ct. King—68Ra 123
Lynwood Dri. N'wd—25V 36
Lynwood Dri. Romf—23Dd 48
Lynwood Dri. Wor Pk—75Wa 144
Lynwood Gdns. Croy—77Pb 146
Lynwood Gdns. S'hall—44Ba 77
Lynwood Gro. N21—18Qb 24
Lynwood Gro. Orp—73Uc 150
Lynwood Heights. Rick—15K 17
Lynwood Rd. SW17—63Hb 125
Lynwood Rd. W5—41Na 79
Lynwood Rd. Eps—86Va 162
Lynwood Rd. Th Dit—75Ha 142
Lynx Hill. Lea—100V 174
Lyon Industrial Est. NW2
—33Xa 60
Lyon Meade. Stan—25La 38
Lyon Pk. Av. Wemb—37Na 59
(in two parts)
Lyon Rd. SW19—67Eb 125
Lyon Rd. Harr—30Ha 38
Lyon Rd. Romf—31Hd 68
Lyon Rd. W on T—75Aa 141
Lyonsdene. Tad—99Bb 179
Lyonsdown Av. Barn—16Eb 23
Lyonsdown Rd. Barn—16Eb 23
Lyons Pl. NW8—42Fb 81 (6B 190)
Lyon St. N1—38Pb 62
Lyon Way. Gnfd—39Ga 58
Lyoth Rd. Orp—75Sc 150
Lyric Rd. SW13—53Va 102
Lysander Gro. N19—32Mb 62
Lysander Rd. Croy—79Pb 146
Lysander Rd. Ruis—33T 56
Lysander Way. Orp—76Sc 150
Lysias Rd. SW12—58Kb 104
Lysia St. SW6—52Za 102
Lysons Wlk. SW15—56Wa 102
Lytchet Rd. Brom—66Kc 129
Lytchet Way. Enf—11Yb 26
Lytchgate Clo. S Croy—80Ub 147
Lytcott Gro. SE22—57Vb 105
Lytham Av. Wat—22Z 37
Lytham Gro. W5—41Pa 79
Lytham St. SE17—50Tb 83
Lyttelton Clo. NW3—38Gb 61
Lyttelton Rd. E10—34Dc 64
Lyttleton Rd. N2—29Eb 41
Lyttleton Rd. N8—27Qb 42
Lytton Av. N13—19Qb 24
Lytton Av. Enf—10Ac 12
Lytton Clo. N2—29Fb 41
Lytton Clo. Lou—13Tc 28
Lytton Clo. N'holt—38Ba 57
Lytton Gdns. Wall—77Mb 146
Lytton Gro. SW15—57Za 102
Lytton Rd. E11—31Gc 65
Lytton Rd. Barn—14Eb 23
Lytton Rd. Grays—9C 92
Lytton Rd. Pinn—24Aa 37
Lytton Rd. Romf—29Kd 49
Lytton Rd. Wok—88D 156
Lytton Strachey Path. SE28
—45Xc 87
Lyveden Rd. SE3—52Kc 107
Lyveden Rd. SW17—65Hb 125
Lywood Clo. Tad—94Ya 178

Mabbutt Clo. St Alb—2Aa 5
Mabel Rd. Swan—65Jd 132
Mabel St. Wok—5G 188
Maberley Cres. SE19—66Wb 127
Maberley Rd. SE19—67Vb 127
Maberley Rd. Beck—69Zb 128
Mabledon Pl. WC1
—41Mb 82 (4E 192)
Mablethorpe Rd. SW6—52Ab 102
Mabley St. E9—36Ac 64
McAdam Dri. Enf—12Rb 25
Macaret Way. N20—17Eb 23
Macarthur Ter. SE7—51Mc 107
Macaulay Rd. E6—40Mc 65
Macaulay Rd. SW4—55Kb 104
Macaulay Rd. Cat—94Ub 181
Macaulay Sq. SW4—56Kb 104
Macaulay Way. SE28—46Xc 87
Macauley Av. Esh—75Ha 142
McAuley Clo. SE1
—48Qb 82 (3K 205)
Macauley M. SE13—54Ec 106
McAuliffe Dri. Slou—5D 52
Macbean St. SE18—48Rc 86
Macbeth St. W6—50Xa 80
McCall Clo. SW4—54Nb 104
McCall Cres. SE7—50Nc 86
McCarthy Rd. Felt—64Z 121
Macclesfield Rd. EC1
—41Sb 83 (3D 194)
Macclesfield Rd. SE25—71Yb 148
Macclesfield St. W1
—45Mb 82 (4E 198)
McClouds M. SW7—49Db 81
MacCoid Way. SE1
—47Sb 83 (2D 206)
McCrone M. NW3—37Fb 61
McCullum Rd. E3—40Bc 64
McDermott Clo. SW11—55Gb 103
McDermott Rd. SE15—55Wb 105
★McDermott Rd. Sev—92Be
Macdonald Av. Dag—34Dd 68
Macdonald Av. Horn—28Nd 49
Macdonald Rd. E7—35Jc 65
Macdonald Rd. E17—26Ec 44
Macdonald Rd. N11—22Hb 41
Macdonald Rd. N19—33Lb 62
Macdonald Way. Horn—28Nd 49
Macdonnell Gdns. Wat—7V 4
McDonough Clo. Chess—77Na 143
McDowall Rd. SE5—53Sb 105
McDowell Clo. E16—43Hc 85
Macduff Rd. SW11—53Jb 104
Mace Ct. Grays—1A 114
Mace La. Sev—85Tc 168
McEntee Av. E17—25Ac 44
Mace St. E2—40Zb 64
McEwan Way. E15—39Fc 65
Macfarlane Pl. W12—46Ya 80
Macfarlane Rd. W12—46Ya 80
Macfarren Pl. NW1
—42Jb 82 (6J 191)
McGrath Rd. E15—37Hc 65
McGredy. Wal X—1Xb 11
Macgregor Rd. E16—43Lc 85
McGregor Rd. W11—43Bb 81
Machell Rd. SE15—55Yb 106
McIntosh Clo. Romf—27Gd 48
McIntosh Clo. Wall—80Nb 146
McIntosh Rd. Romf—27Gd 48
Mackay Rd. SW4—55Kb 104
McKay Rd. SW20—66Xa 124
McKellar Clo. Bush, Wat—19Ea 20
Mackennal St. NW8
—40Gb 61 (1E 190)
Mackenzie Mall. Slou—7K 73
Mackenzie Rd. N7—37Pb 62
Mackenzie Rd. Beck—68Yb 128
Mackenzie Way. Grav—5F 136
McKerrell Rd. SE15—53Wb 105
Mackeson Rd. NW3—35Hb 61
Mackie Rd. SW2—59Qb 104
Mackintosh La. E9—36Zb 64
Macklin St. WC2
—44Nb 82 (2G 199)
Mackrow Wlk. E14—45Ec 84
Mack's Rd. SE16—49Wb 83
Mackworth St. NW1
—41Lb 82 (3B 192)
Maclean Rd. SE23—58Ac 106
Maclennan Av. Rain—41Md 89
Macleod Clo. Grays—49Fe 91
McLeod Rd. SE2—49Xc 87
McLeod St. SE17—50Sb 83
Maclise Rd. W14—48Ab 80
Macmillan Gdns. Dart—56Qd 111
McMillan St. SE8—51Cc 106
McNeil Rd. SE5—54Ub 105
Macoma Rd. SE18—51Tc 108
Macoma Ter. SE18—51Tc 108
Macon Way. Upm—31Ud 70
Macquarie Way. E14—49Dc 84
Macready Pl. N7—35Nb 62
Macroom Rd. W9—41Bb 81
Madan Rd. West—97Tc 184
Madans Wlk. Eps—86Ta 161
Mada Rd. Orp—76Rc 150
Maddams St. E3—42Dc 84
Madden Clo. Swans—58Zd 113
Maddison Clo. Tedd—65Ha 122
Maddocks Clo. Sidc—64Ad 131
Maddock Way. SE17—51Rb 105
Maddox La. Lea—95Aa 175
Maddox Pk. Lea—95Aa 175
Maddox St. W1—45Kb 82 (4A 198)
Madeira Av. Brom—66Gc 129
Madeira Clo. Wey—85J 157
Madeira Cres. Wey—85J 157
Madeira Gro. Wfd G—23Lc 45
Madeira Rd. E11—32Fc 65
Madeira Rd. N13—20Rb 25
Madeira Rd. SW16—64Nb 126
Madeira Rd. Mitc—70Hb 125
Madeira Rd. Wey—85H 157
Madeira Wlk. Brtwd—20Ae 33
Madeira Wlk. Wind—3H 95
Madeley Rd. W5—44Na 79
Madeline Rd. SE20—66Wb 127
Madells. Epp—3Vc 15
Madison Cres. Well—52Yc 109
Madison Gdns. Brom—69Hc 129
Madison Gdns. Well—52Yc 109
Madison Way. Sev—95Hd 186
Madras Pl. N7—37Qb 62
Madras Rd. Ilf—35Rc 66
Madrid Rd. SW13—53Wa 102
Madron St. SE17
—50Ub 83 (7J 207)
Maesmaur Rd. West—93Mc 183
Mafeking Av. E6—40Nc 66
Mafeking Av. Ilf—31Tc 66
Mafeking Rd. E16—42Hc 85
Mafeking Rd. N17—26Wb 43
Mafeking Rd. Bren—51Na 101
Mafeking Rd. Enf—13Vb 25
Mafeking Rd. Wray, Stai—61D 118
Magazine Pl. Lea—94Ka 176
Magazine Rd. Cat—94Rb 181
Magdala Av. N19—33Lb 62
Magdala Rd. Iswth—55Ja 100
Magdala Rd. S Croy—80Tb 147
Magdalen Clo. Wey—86N 157
Magdalen Cres. Wey—86N 157
Magdalene Clo. SE15—54Xb 105
Magdalene Gdns. E6—42Qc 86
Magdalene Rd. Shep—69P 119
Magdalen Pas. E1—45Vb 83
Magdalen Rd. SW18—60Eb 103
Magdalen St. SE1
—46Ub 83 (7H 201)
Magee St. SE11—51Qb 104
Magna Carta La. Wray, Stai
—60A 96
Magna Carta La. Wray, Stai
—10P 95
Magna Rd. Egh—5M 117
Magnaville Rd. Bush, Wat
—17Ga 20
Magnin Clo. E8—39Wb 63
Magnolia Clo. King—65Ra 123
Magnolia Ct. SW4—57Nb 104
Magnolia Ct. Harr—31Pa 59
Magnolia Dri. West—88Mc 167
Magnolia Rd. W4—51Ra 101
Magnolia St. W Dray—49M 75
Magnolia Way. Brtwd—15Xd 32
Magnolia Way. Eps—78Sa 143
Magnum Clo. Rain—42Ld 89
Magpie All. EC4—44Qb 82 (3A 200)
Magpie Bottom. Sev—85Md 171
Magpie Clo. Coul—90Lb 164
Magpie Hall Clo. Brom—72Nc 150
Magpie Hall La. Brom—73Nc 150
Magpie Hall Rd. Bush, Wat
—19Ga 20
Magpie La. Brtwd—26Zd 51
Magpie Way. Slou—2C 72
Maguire Dri. Rich—63La 122
Maguire St. SE1—47Vb 83 (1K 207)
Mahlon Av. Ruis—36X 57
Mahogany Clo. SE16—46Ac 84
Maida Av. E4—17Dc 26
Maida Av. W2—43Eb 81 (7A 190)
Maida Rd. Belv—48Cd 88
Maida Vale. W9—40Db 61 (4A 190)
Maida Vale Rd. Dart—57Jd 110
Maida Way. E4—17Dc 26
Maiden Erlegh Av. Bex—60Ad 109
Maidenhead Rd. Wind—2A 94
Maiden La. NW1—38Mb 62
Maiden La. WC2—45Nb 82 (5G 199)
Maiden La. Dart—55Jd 110
Maiden Rd. E15—38Gc 65
Maidenshaw Rd. Eps—84Ta 161
Maidenstone Hill. SE10—53Ec 106
Maids of Honour Row. Rich
—57Ma 101
Maidstone Av. Romf—26Ed 48
Maidstone Bldgs. SE1
—46Sb 83 (7E 200)
Maidstone Rd. N11—23Mb 42
Maidstone Rd. Grays—51Ce 113
Maidstone Rd. Sev—93Qd 187
★Maidstone Rd. Sev—92Ce
(Borough Green)
Maidstone Rd. Sev—94Gd 186
(Riverhead)
Maidstone Rd. Sidc—65Zc 131
Mail Coach Yd. N1—41Ub 83 (3J 195)
Main Av. Enf—15Vb 25
Main Av. N'wd—20S 18
Main Dri. Iver—49G 74
Main Pde. Rick—14E 16
Mainridge Rd. Chst—63Qc 130
Main Rd. Brtwd—11Fe 33
Main Rd. F'ham, Dart—73Qd 153
Main Rd. Kes & West—85Lc 167
Main Rd. Long, Dart—68Zd 135
Main Rd. Orp—69Yc 131
Main Rd. Romf—28Hd 48
Main Rd. Sev—96Zc 185
Main Rd. Sidc—62Tc 130
Main Rd. S at H, Dart—65Rd 133
Main Rd. Swan—72Fd 152
(Crockenhill)
Main Rd. Swan—66Hd 132
(Hextable)
Main St. Felt—64Z 121
Maisie Webster Clo. Stai—59L 97
Maismore St. SE15—52Wb 105
Maitland Clo. Houn—55Ba 99
Maitland Clo. Wey—85J 157
Maitland Pk. Est. NW3—37Hb 61
Maitland Pk. Rd. NW3—37Hb 61
Maitland Pk. Vs. NW3—37Hb 61
Maitland Rd. E15—37Hc 65
Maitland Rd. SE26—65Zb 128
Maize Row. E14—45Bc 84
Maizey Ct. Brtwd—15Wd 32
Majendie Rd. SE18—50Tc 86
Major Rd. E15—36Fc 65
Major Rd. SE16—48Wb 83
Majors Farm Rd. Slou—52A 96
Majors Farm Rd. Slou—2P 95
Makepeace Av. N6—33Jb 62
Makepeace Rd. N'holt—40Aa 57
Makins St. SW3—49Gb 81 (6E 202)
Malabar St. E14—47Cc 84
Malacca Farm. Guild—100K 173
Malam Gdns. E14—45Dc 84
Malan Clo. West—89Nc 168
Malan Sq. Rain—37Kd 69
Malbrook Rd. SW15—56Xa 102
Malcolm Ct. Stan—22La 38
Malcolm Cres. NW4—30Wa 40
Malcolm Dri. Surb—74Ma 143
Malcolm Pl. E2—42Yb 84
Malcolm Rd. E1—42Yb 84
Malcolm Rd. SE20—66Yb 128
Malcolm Rd. SE25—73Wb 147
Malcolm Rd. SW19—65Ab 124
Malcolm Rd. Coul—87Mb 164
Malcolm Rd. Uxb—35P 55
Malcolm Way. E11—28Jc 45
Malden Av. SE25—69Xb 127
Malden Av. Gnfd—36Ga 58
Malden Ct. N Mald—69Xa 124
Malden Cres. NW1—37Jb 62
Malden Grn. Av. Wor Pk
—74Va 144
Malden Hill. N Mald—69Va 124
Malden Hill Gdns. N Mald
—69Va 124
Malden Pk. N Mald—72Va 144
Malden Pl. NW5—36Jb 62
Malden Rd. NW5—36Jb 62
Malden Rd. Borwd—13Qa 21
Malden Rd. N Mald & Wor Pk
—71Ua 144
Malden Rd. Sutt—77Za 144
Malden Rd. Wat—12X 19
Malden Way N. Surb & N Mald
—73Sa 143
Malden Way S. Surb & Mald
—73Sa 143
Maldon Clo. N1—39Sb 63
Maldon Clo. SE5—55Ub 105
Maldon Rd. N9—20Vb 25
Maldon Rd. W3—45Sa 79
Maldon Rd. Romf—31Ed 68
Maldon Rd. Wall—78Kb 146
Maldon Wlk. Wfd G—23Lc 45
Malet Clo. Egh—65F 118
Malet Pl. WC1—42Mb 82 (6D 192)
Malet St. WC1—42Mb 82 (6D 192)
Maley Av. SE27—61Rb 127
Malford Ct. E18—26Jc 45
Malford Gro. E18—28Hc 45
Malfort Rd. SE5—55Ub 105
Malham Rd. SE23—60Zb 106
Malins Clo. Barn—15Xa 22
Mallams M. SW9—55Rb 105
Mallard Clo. E9—37Bc 64
Mallard Clo. Barn—16Fb 23
Mallard Clo. Twic—59Ca 99
Mallard Clo. Upm—31Vd 70
Mallard Dri. Slou—5D 72
Mallard Pl. N22—26Pb 42
Mallard Pl. Twic—62Ja 122
Mallard Rd. S Croy—82Zb 166
Mallards Reach. Wey—75T 140
Mallards Rd. Wfd G—24Kc 45
Mallards, The. Stai—68K 119
Mallard Wlk. Sidc—65Yc 131
Mallard Way. NW9—31Sa 59
Mallard Way. Brtwd—17De 33
Mallard Way. N'wd—24S 36
Mallard Way. Wat—9Aa 5
Mallet Dri. N'holt—36Ba 57
Mallet Rd. SE13—58Fc 107
Malling Clo. Croy—72Yb 148
Malling Gdns. Mord—72Eb 145
Malling Way. Brom—73Hc 149
Mallinson Rd. SW11—57Gb 103
Mallinson Rd. Croy—76Mb 146
Mallion Ct. Wal A—5Hc 13
Mallord St. SW3—51Fb 103
Mallory Clo. SE4—56Ac 106
Mallory Gdns. Barn—17Jb 24
Mallory St. NW8—42Gb 81 (5E 190)
Mallow Clo. Croy—74Zb 148
Mallow Ct. Grays—51Fe 113
Mallow Mead. NW7—24Ab 40
Mallows, The. Uxb—34R 56
Mallow St. EC1—42Tb 83 (5F 195)
Mall Rd. W6—50Xa 80
Mall, The. E15—38Fc 65
Mall, The. N14—19Nb 24
Mall, The. SW1—46Mb 82 (6E 198)
Mall, The. SW14—57Sa 101
Mall, The. W5—45Na 79
Mall, The. Bexh—56Cd 110
Mall, The. Brom—69Jc 129
Mall, The. Croy—75Sb 147
Mall, The. Dag—37Cd 68
Mall, The. Harr—30Pa 39
Mall, The. Surb—72Ma 143
Malmains Clo. Beck—70Fc 129
Malmains Way. Beck—70Ec 128
Malm Clo. Rick—19M 17
Malmesbury Clo. Pinn—28W 36
Malmesbury Rd. E3—41Bc 84
Malmesbury Rd. E16—43Gc 85
Malmesbury Rd. E18—25Hc 45
Malmesbury Rd. Mord—73Eb 145
Malmesbury Ter. E16—43Hc 85
Malmstone Av. Red—100Lb 180
Malpas Dri. Pinn—29Z 37
Malpas Rd. E8—36Xb 63
Malpas Rd. SE4—54Bc 106
Malpas Rd. Dag—37Zc 67
Malpas Rd. Grays—8E 92
Malpas Rd. Slou—5M 73
Malta Rd. E10—31Cc 64
Malta Rd. Til—4B 114
Malta St. EC1—42Rb 83 (5C 194)
Maltby Clo. Orp—74Wc 151
Maltby Rd. Chess—79Qa 143
Maltby St. SE1—47Vb 83 (2K 207)
Malt Hill. Egh—64A 118
Malthouse Clo. Wind—9M 95
Malthouse Dri. Felt—64Z 121
Malthouse La. Grav—4N 137
Malthouse Rd. Sev—80Be 155
Malthus Path. SE28—46Yc 87
Malting La. Grays—2C 92
Maltings Clo. SW13—54Va 102
Maltings Dri. Epp—1Wc 15
Maltings La. Epp—1Wc 15
Maltings Pl. SW6—53Db 103
Maltings, The. K Lan—6S 4
Maltings, The. Orp—74Vc 151
Maltings, The. Wey—85P 157
Malt La. Rad—7Ja 6
Malton Av. Slou—4F 72
Malton M. W10—44Ab 80
Malton Rd. W10—44Ab 80
Malton St. SE18—51Uc 108
Maltravers St. WC2
—45Pb 82 (4K 199)
Malt St. SE1—51Wb 105
Malus Clo. Wey—80H 139
Malus Dri. Wey—80H 139
Malva Clo. SW18—57Db 103
Malvern Av. E4—24Fc 45
Malvern Av. Bexh—52Ad 109
Malvern Av. Ruis—34Aa 57
Malvern Clo. SE20—68Wb 127
Malvern Clo. W10—43Bb 81
Malvern Clo. Cher—79E 138
Malvern Clo. Mitc—69Lb 126
Malvern Clo. Surb—74Na 143
Malvern Clo. Uxb—33Q 56
Malvern Ct. Slou—51C 96
Malvern Dri. Felt—64Z 121
Malvern Dri. Ilf—35Vc 67
Malvern Dri. Wfd G—22Lc 45
Malvern Gdns. NW2—33Ab 60
Malvern Gdns. NW6—40Bb 61
Malvern Gdns. Harr—28Na 39
Malvern Gdns. Lou—16Pc 28
Malvern Ho. N16—32Vb 63
Malvern M. NW6—41Cb 81
Malvern Pl. NW6—41Bb 81
Malvern Rd. E6—39Nc 66
Malvern Rd. E8—38Wb 63
Malvern Rd. E11—33Gc 65
Malvern Rd. N8—27Qb 42
Malvern Rd. N17—27Wb 43
Malvern Rd. NW6—41Cb 81
Malvern Rd. Enf—8Ac 12
Malvern Rd. Grays—9A 92
Malvern Rd. Hmptn—66Ca 121
Malvern Rd. Hay—52U 98
Malvern Rd. Horn—30Jd 48
Malvern Rd. Orp—77Xc 151
Malvern Rd. Surb—75Na 143
Malvern Rd. T Hth—70Qb 126
Malvern Ter. N1—39Qb 62
Malvern Ter. N9—18Vb 25
Malvern Way. W13—43Ka 78
Malvern Way. Rick—15R 18
Malvina Av. Grav—1D 136
Malwood Rd. SW12—58Kb 104
Malyons Rd. SE13—57Dc 106
Malyons Rd. Swan—66Hd 132
Malyons Ter. SE13—57Dc 106
Managers St. E14—46Ec 84
Manaton Clo. SE15—55Xb 105
Manaton Cres. S'hall—44Ca 77
Manbey Gro. E15—37Gc 65
Manbey Pk. Rd. E15—37Gc 65
Manbey Rd. E15—37Gc 65
Manbey St. E15—37Gc 65
Manbrough Av. E6—41Qc 86
Manchester Dri. W10—42Ab 80
Manchester Gro. E14—50Ec 84
Manchester M. W1—(1H 197)
Manchester Rd. E14—50Ec 84
Manchester Rd. N15—30Tb 43
Manchester Rd. T Hth—69Sb 127
Manchester Sq. W1
—44Jb 82 (2J 197)
Manchester St. W1
—43Jb 82 (1H 197)
Manchester Way. Dag—35Dd 68
Manchuria Rd. SW11—58Jb 104
Manciple St. SE1
—47Tb 83 (2F 207)
Mandalay Rd. SW4—57Lb 104
Mandarin St. E14—45Cc 84
Mandela Clo. NW10—38Sa 59
Mandela St. NW1—39Lb 62
Mandeville Clo. SE3—52Jc 107
Mandeville Clo. Wat—10V 4
Mandeville Ct. Egh—63C 118
Mandeville Dri. Surb—74Ma 143
Mandeville Pl. W1
—44Jb 82 (2J 197)
Mandeville Rd. N14—19Kb 24
Mandeville Rd. Enf—8Ac 12
Mandeville Rd. Iswth—54Ja 100
Mandeville Rd. N'holt—38Ca 57
Mandeville Rd. Pot B—4Eb 9
Mandeville Rd. Shep—71Q 140
Mandeville St. E5—34Ac 64
Mandrake Rd. SW17—62Hb 125
Mandrell Rd. SW2—57Nb 104
Manette St. W1—44Mb 82 (3E 198)
Manfield Clo. Slou—1E 72
Manford Clo. Chig—21Wc 47
Manford Cross. Chig—22Wc 47
Manford Way. Chig—22Uc 46
Manfred Rd. SW15—57Bb 103
Manger Rd. N7—37Nb 62
Mangold Way. Eri—48Zc 87
Manilla St. E14—47Cc 84
Manister Rd. SE2—48Wc 87
Manley Ct. N16—34Vb 63
Manley St. NW1—39Jb 62
Manly Dixon Dri. Enf—9Ac 12
Manningford Clo. EC1
—41Rb 83 (3B 194)
Manning Gdns. Harr—31Ma 59
Manning Rd. E17—29Ac 44
Manning Rd. Dag—37Cd 68
Manning Rd. Orp—71Zc 151
Manning St. S Ock—46Sd 90
Manningtree Clo. SW19
—60Ab 102
Manningtree Rd. Ruis—35X 57
Manningtree St. E1—44Wb 83
Mannin Rd. Romf—31Xc 67
Mannley's Yd. SW11—55Jb 104
Mannock Dri. Lou—12Sc 28
Mannock Rd. N22—27Rb 43
Mann's Clo. Iswth—57Ha 100
Manns Rd. Edgw—23Qa 39
Manoel Rd. Twic—61Ea 122
Manor Av. SE4—54Bc 106
Manor Av. Cat—96Ub 181
Manor Av. Horn—29Ld 49
Manor Av. Houn—55Z 99
Manor Av. N'holt—38Ba 57
Manor Brook. SE3—56Jc 107
Manor Chase. Wey—78R 140
Manor Clo. NW7—22Ta 39
Manor Clo. NW9—29Ra 39
Manor Clo. SE28—44Yc 87
Manor Clo. Barn—14Ab 22
Manor Clo. Dag—37Fd 68
Manor Clo. Dart—56Fd 110
(Crayford)
Manor Clo. Dart—62Jd 132
(Wilmington)
Manor Clo. Grav—1K 137
Manor Clo. Lea—100U 174
Manor Clo. Romf—29Jd 48
Manor Clo. Ruis—32V 56
Manor Clo. S Ock—46Sd 90
Manor Clo. Warl—89Ac 166
Manor Clo. Wok—89H 157
Manor Clo. Wor Pk—74Ua 144
Manor Cotts. N'wd—25V 36
Manor Cotts. App. N2—26Eb 41
Manor Ct. Enf—8Xb 11
Manor Ct. Twic—61Ea 122
Manor Ct. Wey—77R 140
Manor Ct. Rd. W7—45Ga 78
Manor Cres. Horn—29Ld 49
Manor Cres. Surb—72Qa 143
Manor Cres. Wey—85P 157
Manorcrofts Rd. Egh—65C 118
Manor Dene. SE28—44Yc 87
Manordene Clo. Th Dit—74Ja 142
Manordene Rd. SE28—44Zc 87
Manor Dri. N14—18Kb 24
Manor Dri. N20—21Gb 41
Manor Dri. NW7—22Ta 39
Manor Dri. Eps—79Ua 144
Manor Dri. Esh—76Ha 142
Manor Dri. Felt—64Z 121
Manor Dri. Long, Dart—72Ce 155
Manor Dri. Sun—68W 120
Manor Dri. Surb—72Pa 143
Manor Dri. Wemb—35Pa 59
Manor Dri. Wey—82J 157
Manor Dri. N. N Mald & Wor Pk
—73Ta 143
Manor Dri., The. Wor Pk—74Va 144
Manor Farm Av. Shep—72R 140
Manor Farm Clo. Wind—5D 94
Manor Farm Dri. E4—20Gc 27
Manor Farm Est. Wey—86P 157
Manor Farm La. Egh—64C 118
Manor Farm Rd. SW16—68Qb 126
Manor Farm Rd. Enf—7Xb 11
Manor Farm Rd. Wemb—40Ma 59
Manor Fields. SW15—58Za 102
Manor Forstal. Long, Dart
—76Be 155
Manor Gdns. N7—34Nb 62
Manor Gdns. SW20—68Bb 125
Manor Gdns. W3—49Qa 79
Manor Gdns. Hmptn—66Da 121
Manor Gdns. Lea—100Z 175
Manor Gdns. Rich—56Pa 101
Manor Gdns. Ruis—36Y 57
Manor Gdns. S Croy—79Vb 147
Manor Gdns. Sun—68W 120
Manor Ga. N'holt—38Aa 57
Manorgate Rd. King—67Qa 123
Manor Grn. Rd. Eps—85Ra 161
Manor Gro. SE15—51Yb 106
Manor Gro. Beck—68Dc 128
Manor Gro. Rich—56Qa 101
Manor Hall Av. NW4—26Za 40
Manor Hall Dri. NW4—26Za 40
Manorhall Gdns. E10—32Cc 64
Manor Hill. Bans—87Hb 163
Manor Ho. Ct. Eps—85Sa 161
Manor Ho. Ct. Shep—73R 140
Manor Ho. Dri. NW6—38Za 60
Manor Ho. Gdns. Abb L, Wat
—3T 4
Manorhouse La. Lea—98Aa 175
Manor Ho. La. Slou—2M 95
Manor La.—57Gc 107
SE13 1-59 & 2-86
SE12 remainder
Manor La. Felt—61W 120
Manor La. Ger X—31A 54
Manor La. Ger X—1P 53
Manor La. Hay—51T 98
Manor La. Long, Dart—73Yd 154
(Fawkham Green)
Manor La. Long, Dart—72Ce 155
(Hartley)
Manor La. Sun—68W 120
Manor La. Sutt—78Eb 145
Manor La. Tad—100Cb 179
Manor La. Ter. SE13—57Gc 107
Manor Leaze. Egh—64D 118
Manor M. SE4—54Bc 106
Manor Mt. SE23—60Yb 106
Manor Pk. SE13—56Fc 107
Manor Pk. Chst—68Tc 130
Manor Pk. Rich—56Pa 101
Manor Pk. Clo. W Wick—74Dc 148
Manor Pk. Cres. Edgw—23Qa 39
Manor Pk. Dri. Harr—27Da 37
Manor Pk. Gdns. Edgw—22Qa 39
Manor Pk. Rd. E12—35Mc 65
Manor Pk. Rd. N2—27Eb 41
Manor Pk. Rd. NW10—39Va 60
Manor Pk. Rd. Chst—67Sc 130
Manor Pk. Rd. Sutt—78Eb 145
Manor Pk. Rd. W Wick—74Dc 148
Manor Pl. SE17—50Rb 83 (7C 206)
Manor Pl. Chst—68Tc 130
Manor Pl. Dart—60Nd 111
Manor Pl. Felt—60W 98
Manor Pl. Mitc—69Lb 126
Manor Pl. Stai—64K 119
Manor Pl. Sutt—77Db 145
Manor Pl. W on T—73V 140
Manor Rd. E10—31Cc 64

Manor Rd.—Maryatt Av.

Manor Rd.—42Gc 85
E15 1-347 & 2-118
E16 remainder
Manor Rd. E17—26Ac 44
Manor Rd. N16—32Ub 63
Manor Rd. N17—25Wb 43
Manor Rd. N22—23Nb 42
Manor Rd. SE25—70Wb 127
Manor Rd. SW20—68Bb 125
Manor Rd. W13—45Ja 78
Manor Rd. Ashf—64P 119
Manor Rd. Bark—37Vc 67
Manor Rd. Barn—14Ab 22
Manor Rd. Beck—68Dc 128
Manor Rd. Bex—60Dd 110
Manor Rd. Dag—37Ed 68
Manor Rd. Dart—56Gd 110
Manor Rd. E Mol—70Fa 122
Manor Rd. Enf—12Sb 25
Manor Rd. Eri—51Hd 110
Manor Rd. Grav—8D 114
Manor Rd. Grav—10E 136
(Sole Street)
Manor Rd. Grays—51Yd 112
Manor Rd. Harr—30Ja 38
Manor Rd. Hay—44W 76
Manor Rd. Long, Dart—71Ee 155
Manor Rd. Lou—16Kc 27
Manor Rd. Lou—11Kc 27
(High Beach)
Manor Rd. Mitc—70Lb 126
Manor Rd. Pot B—3Bb 9
Manor Rd. Red—100Lb 180
Manor Rd. Rich—56Qa 101
Manor Rd. Romf—29Jd 48
Manor Rd. Romf—30Zc 47
(Chadwell Heath)
Manor Rd. Romf—19Yc 29
(Lambourne End)
Manor Rd. Ruis—32T 56
Manor Rd. Sev—96Zc 185
Manor Rd. Sidc—62Wc 131
Manor Rd. Stanf—2M 93
Manor Rd. Sutt—80Bb 145
Manor Rd. Swans—58Zd 113
Manor Rd. Tedd—64Ja 122
(in two parts)
Manor Rd. Til—4C 114
Manor Rd. Twic—61Ea 122
Manor Rd. Wall—77Kb 146
Manor Rd. Wal A—5Fc 13
Manor Rd. W on T—73V 140
Manor Rd. Wat—11X 19
Manor Rd. West—92Nc 184
Manor Rd. W Wick—75Dc 148
Manor Rd. Wind—4C 94
Manor Rd. Wok—4F 188
Manor Rd. Wok—95H 173
(Send Marsh)
Manor Rd. Wfd G & Chig—23Pc 46
Manor Rd. N. Esh & Th Dit —76Ha 142
Manor Rd. N. Wall—77Kb 146
Manor Rd. S. Esh—77Ga 142
Manorside. Barn—14Ab 22
Manorside Clo. SE2—49Yc 87
Manor Sq. Dag—33Zc 67
Manor Vale. Bren—50La 78
Manor View. N3—26Db 41
Manor Wlk. Wey—78R 140
Manor Way. E4—21Fc 45
Manor Way. NW9—28Ua 40
Manor Way. SE3—56Hc 107
Manor Way. Bans—88Hb 163
Manor Way. Beck—68Cc 128
Manor Way. Bex—60Cd 110
Manor Way. Bexh—55Fd 110
Manor Way. Borwd—13Sa 21
Manor Way. Brtwd—20Wd 32
Manor Way. Brom—72Nc 150
Manor Way. Egh—65B 118
Manorway. Enf—17Ub 25
Manor Way. Grays—52De 113
Manor Way. Harr—28Da 37
Manor Way. Lea—88Ea 160
Manor Way. Mitc—69Lb 126
Manor Way. Orp—70Sc 130
Manor Way. Pot B—2Cb 9
Manor Way. Purl—84Nb 164
Manor Way. Rain—44Gd 88
Manor Way. Rick—14Q 18
Manor Way. Ruis—31U 56
Manor Way. S'hall—49Z 77
Manor Way. S Croy—79Ub 147
Manor Way. Swans & Grav —56Zd 113
Manor Way. Wal X—3Ac 12
Manor Way. Wok—93D 172
Manor Way. Wfd G—22Lc 45
Manor Way. Wor Pk—74Ua 144
Manor Waye. Uxb—39M 55
Manorway Gdns. SE28—45Yc 87
Manorway, The. Stanf—1N 93
Manor Way, The. Wall—77Kb 146
Manor Wood Rd. Purl—85Nb 164
Manresa Rd. SW3 —50Gb 81 (7D 202)
Mansard Beeches. SW17 —64Jb 126
Mansard Clo. Pinn—27Z 37
Manse Clo. Hay—51T 98
Mansel Clo. Slou—3M 73
Mansel Gro. E17—25Cc 44
Mansell Clo. Wind—3C 94
Mansell Rd. W3—47Ta 79
Mansell Rd. Gnfd—43Da 77
Mansell St. E1—44Vb 83 (3K 201)
Mansel Rd. SW19—65Ab 124
Mansergh Clo. SE18—52Nc 108
Manse Rd. N16—34Vb 63
Manser Rd. Rain—41Gd 88
Manse Way. Swan—70Jd 132
Mansfield Av. N15—28Tb 43
Mansfield Av. Barn—16Hb 23
Mansfield Clo. N9—16Wb 25
Mansfield Clo. Orp—73Zc 151
Mansfield Clo. Wey—78R 140
Mansfield Dri. Hay—42U 76
Mansfield Dri. Red—100Mb 180
Mansfield Gdns. Horn—33Md 69
Mansfield Hill. E4—18Dc 26
Mansfield M. W1 —43Kb 82 (1K 197)
Mansfield Pl. NW3—35Eb 61
Mansfield Rd. E11—30Kc 45
Mansfield Rd. E17—28Bc 44
Mansfield Rd. NW3—36Hb 61
Mansfield Rd. W3—42Ra 79
Mansfield Rd. Chess—78La 142
Mansfield Rd. Ilf—33Qc 66
Mansfield Rd. S Croy—79Tb 147
Mansfield Rd. Swan—65Gd 132
Mansfield St. W1 —43Kb 82 (1K 197)
Mansford St. E2—40Wb 63
Manship Rd. Mitc—66Jb 126
Mansion Gdns. NW3—34Db 61
Mansion Ho. Pl. EC4 —44Tb 83 (3F 201)
Mansion Ho. St. EC2—(3F 201)
Mansion La. Iver—46E 74
Manson M. SW7—49Eb 81 (5A 202)
Manson Pl. SW7—49Fb 81 (6B 202)
Manstead Gdns. Rain—44Kd 89
Mansted Gdns. Romf—31Yc 67
Manston Av. S'hall—49Ca 77
Manston Clo. SE20—67Yb 128
Manston Clo. Wal X—2Yb 12
Manstone Rd. NW2—36Ab 60
Manston Way. Horn—37Kd 69
Manthorp Rd. SE18—50Sc 86
Mantilla Rd. SW17—63Jb 126
Mantle Rd. SE4—55Ac 106
Manton Av. W7—47Ha 78
Manton Clo. Hay—45U 76
Manton Rd. SE2—49Wc 87
Mantua St. SW11—55Fb 103
Mantus Clo. E1—42Yb 84
Mantus Rd. E1—42Yb 84
Manus Way. N20—19Eb 23
Manville Gdns. SW17—62Kb 126
Manville Rd. SW17—61Jb 126
Manwood Rd. SE4—57Bc 106
Manwood St. E16—46Pc 86
Manygate La. Shep—73S 140
Manygates. SW12—61Kb 126
Mapesbury Rd. NW2—38Ab 60
Mape St. E2—42Xb 83
Maple Av. E4—22Bc 44
Maple Av. W3—46Ua 80
Maple Av. Harr—33Da 57
Maple Av. Upm—34Rd 69
Maple Av. W Dray—45N 75
Maple Clo. N16—30Wb 43
Maple Clo. SW4—58Mb 104
Maple Clo. Brtwd—20Be 33
Maple Clo. Buck H—20Mc 27
Maple Clo. Bush, Wat—12Aa 19
Maple Clo. Horn—34Kd 69
Maple Clo. Mitc—67Kb 126
Maple Clo. Orp—71Tc 150
Maple Clo. Ruis—30X 37
Maple Clo. Whyt—89Vb 165
Maple Ct. Egh—5M 117
Maple Ct. N Mald—69Ta 123
Maple Ct. Wok—4F 188
Maple Cres. Sidc—58Wc 109
Maple Cres. Slou—5M 73
Maplecroft Clo. E6—44Mc 85
Mapledale Av. Croy—75Wb 147
Mapledene. Chst—64Sc 130
Mapledene Rd. E8—38Wb 63
Maplefield. St Alb—1Ea 6
Maple Gdns. Edgw—24Ua 40
Maple Gro. NW9—31Sa 59
Maple Gro. W5—48Ma 79
Maple Gro. Bren—52Ka 100
Maple Gro. S'hall—43Ba 77
Maple Gro. Wat—11W 18
Maple Gro. Wok—93A 172
Maplehurst Clo. King—70Na 123
Mapleleafe Gdns. Ilf—27Rc 46
Maplelodge Clo. Rick—21G 34
Maple Pl. W1—43Lb 82 (6C 192)
Maple Pl. Bans—86Za 162
Maple Pl. W Dray—46N 75
Maple Rd. E11—30Gc 45
Maple Rd. SE20—67Xb 127
Maple Rd. Asht—91Ma 177
Maple Rd. Dart—60Ld 111
Maple Rd. Grav—3E 136
Maple Rd. Grays—51Ee 113
Maple Rd. Hay—41Y 77
Maple Rd. Surb—72Ma 143
Maple Rd. Whyt—89Vb 165
Maple Rd. Wok—96J 173
Maples. Stanf—1N 93
Maplescombe La. Farn, Dart & Sev—77Rd 153
Maples Pl. E1—43Xb 83
Maplesprings. Wal A—5Jc 13
Maplestead Rd. SW2—59Pb 104
Maplestead Rd. Dag—39Xc 67
Maples, The. Bans—86Db 163
Maples, The. Cher—79E 138
Maple St. W1—43Lb 82 (7B 192)
Maple St. Romf—28Ed 48
Maplethorpe Rd. T Hth—70Rb 127
Mapleton Clo. Brom—72Jc 149
Mapleton Cres. SW18—58Db 103
Mapleton Cres. Enf—10Yb 12
Mapleton Rd. E4—20Ec 26
Mapleton Rd. SW18—58Db 103
Mapleton Rd. Enf—12Xb 25
★Mapletree La. Ing—4De
Maple Wlk. W10—41Za 80
Maple Wlk. Sutt—82Db 163
Maple Way. Coul—93Kb 180
Maple Way. Felt—62W 120
Maplin Clo. N21—16Pb 24
Maplin Rd. E16—44Jc 85
Maplin St. E3—42Bc 84
Mapperley Dri. Wfd G—24Gc 45
Maran Way. Eri—48Zc 87
Marban Rd. W9—41Bb 81
Marbeck Clo. Wind—3B 94
Marble Arch. W2 —45Hb 81 (4G 197)
Marble Clo. W3—46Ra 79
Marble Hill Clo. Twic—59Ka 100
Marble Hill Gdns. Twic—59Ka 100
Marbles Way. Tad—91Za 178
Marbrook Ct. SE12—62Lc 129
Marcellina Way. Orp—76Vc 151
Marcet Rd. Dart—57Ld 111
Marchant Rd. E11—33Fc 65
Marchbank Rd. W14—51Bb 103
Marchmont Rd. Rich—57Pa 101
Marchmont Rd. Wall—80Lb 146
Marchmont St. WC1 —42Nb 82 (5F 193)
March Rd. Twic—59Ja 100
March Rd. Wey—78Q 140
Marchwood Clo. SE5—52Ub 105
Marchwood Cres. W5—44Ma 79
Marcia Rd. SE1—49Ub 83 (6J 207)
Marcilly Rd. SW18—57Fb 103
Marconi Rd. Grav—62Fe 135
Marconi Way. S'hall—44Da 77
Marcon Pl. E8—36Xb 63
Marco Rd. W6—48Ya 80
Marcus Ct. E15—39Gc 65
Marcus Garvey Way. SW9 —56Qb 104
Marcus Rd. Dart—59Jd 110
Marcus St. E15—39Gc 65
Marcus St. SW18—58Db 103
Mardale Dri. NW9—29Ta 39
Mardell Rd. Croy—71Zb 148
Marden Av. Brom—72Jc 149
Marden Cres. Bexh—57Ed 110
Marden Cres. Croy—72Pb 146
Marden Rd. N17—26Ub 43
Marden Rd. Croy—72Pb 146
Marden Rd. Romf—30Gd 48
Marden Sq. SE16—48Xb 83
Marder Rd. W13—47Ja 78
Mardyke Wlk. Grays—46Ce 91
Marechal Niel Av. Sidc—62Tc 130
Marescroft Rd. Slou—2C 72
Mares Field. Croy—76Ub 147
Maresfield Gdns. NW3—36Eb 61
Mare St. E8—39Xb 63
Margaret Av. E4—16Dc 26
Margaret Av. Brtwd—16Ce 33
Margaret Bondfield Av. Bark —38Wc 67
Margaret Bldgs. N16—32Vb 63
Margaret Clo. Pot B—5Eb 9
Margaret Clo. Romf—29Kd 49
Margaret Clo. Stai—65M 119
Margaret Clo. Wal A—5Fc 13
Margaret Ct. W1—(2B 198)
Margaret Dri. Horn—32Pd 69
Margaret Rd. N16—32Vb 63
Margaret Rd. Barn—14Fb 23
Margaret Rd. Bex—58Zc 109
Margaret Rd. Epp—1Wc 15
Margaret Rd. Romf—29Kd 49
Margaret Sq. Uxb—39L 55
Margaret St. W1—44Lb 82 (2A 198)
Margaretta Ter. SW3—51Gb 103
Margaretting Rd. E12—32Lc 65
Margaret Way. Coul—91Rb 181
Margaret Way. Ilf—30Nc 46
Margate Rd. SW2—57Nb 104
Margeholes. Wat—19Aa 19
Margery Gro. Tad—100Ab 178
Margery La. Tad—100Bb 179
Margery Pk. Rd. E7—37Jc 65
Margery Rd. Dag—34Zc 67
Margery St. WC1 —41Qb 82 (4K 193)
Margin Dri. SW19—64Za 124
Margravine Gdns. W6—50Za 80
Margravine Rd. W6—50Za 80
Marham Gdns. SW18—60Gb 103
Marham Gdns. Mord—72Eb 145
Maria Clo. SE1—49Wb 83
Mariam Gdns. Horn—33Pd 69
Marian Clo. Grays—46Ae 91
Marian Clo. Hay—42Z 77
Marian Ct. Sutt—78Db 145
Marian Pl. E2—40Xb 63
Marian Rd. SW16—67Lb 126
Marian St. E2—40Xb 63
Marian Way. NW10—38Va 60
Maria Ter. E1—43Zb 84
Maria Theresa Clo. N Mald —71Ta 143
Maricas Av. Harr—25Fa 38
Mariette Way. Wall—81Nb 164
Marigold All. SE1—(5B 200)
Marigold St. SE16—47Xb 83
Marigold Way. E4—23Bc 44
Marigold Way. Croy—74Zb 148
Marina Av. N Mald—71Xa 144
Marina Clo. Brom—69Jc 129
Marina Dri. Dart—60Qd 111
Marina Dri. Grav—9B 114
Marina Dri. Well—54Uc 108
Marina Gdns. Romf—29Ed 48
Marina Gdns. Wal X—2Yb 12
Marina Way. Iver—45J 75
Marina Way. Slou—5B 72
Marina Way. Tedd—66Ma 123
Marine Dri. SE18—49Pc 86
Marinefield Rd. SW6—54Db 103
Mariner Gdns. Rich—62La 122
Mariner Rd. E12—35Qc 66
Marine St. SE16—48Wb 83
Marion Av. Shep—71R 140
Marion Clo. Bush, Wat—11Ba 19
Marion Clo. Ilf—24Tc 46
Marion Cres. Orp—71Wc 151
Marion Gro. Wfd G—21Gc 45
Marion Rd. NW7—22Wa 40
Marion Rd. T Hth—71Sb 147
Marion Sq. E2—40Xb 63
Marischal Rd. SE13—55Fc 107
Marisco Clo. Grays—9D 92
Marish La. Uxb—28E 34
Marish Wharf. Slou—47A 74
Maritime St. E3—42Bc 84
Marius Pas. SW17—61Jb 126
Marius Rd. SW17—61Jb 126
Marjorams Av. Lou—12Qc 28
Marjorie Gro. SW11—56Hb 103
Markab Rd. N'wd—22V 36
Mark Av. E4—16Dc 26
Mark Clo. Bexh—53Ad 109
Mark Clo. S'hall—45Da 77
Marke Clo. Kes—77Nc 150
Markedge La. Coul & Red —96Hb 179
Markeston Grn. Wat—21Z 37
Market Centre, The. S'hall—49X 77
Market Ct. W1—(2B 198)
Market Entrance. SW8—52Lb 104
Market Hill. SE18—48Qc 86
Market La. Edgw—25Sa 39
Market La. Slou—48E 74
Market Link. Romf—28Gd 48
Market Meadow. Orp—70Yc 131
Market M. W1—46Kb 82 (7K 197)
Market Pl. N2—27Gb 41
Market Pl. NW11—28Db 41
Market Pl. SE16—49Wb 83
Market Pl. W1—44Lb 82 (2B 198)
Market Pl. W3—46Sa 79
Market Pl. Bexh—56Cd 110
Market Pl. Bren—52La 100
Market Pl. Dart—59Nd 111
Market Pl. Enf—13Tb 25
Market Pl. Ger X—25A 34
Market Pl. King—68Ma 123
Market Pl. Romf—29Gd 48
Market Pl. Romf—13Xc 29
(Abridge)
Market Rd. E14—45Cc 84
Market Rd. N7—37Nb 62
Market Rd. Rich—55Qa 101
Market Sq. E14—44Dc 84
Market Sq. N9—20Wb 25
Market Sq. Brom—68Jc 129
Market Sq. Stai—63G 118
Market Sq. Uxb—38L 55
Market Sq. West—98Tc 184
Market Sq. Wok—89A 156
Market St. E6—40Pc 66
Market St. SE18—49Qc 86
Market St. Dart—59Nd 111
Market St. Wat—14X 19
Market St. Wind—3H 95
Market Way. E14—44Dc 84
Market Way. West—98Tc 184
Markfield. Croy—82Bc 166
(in two parts)
Markfield Gdns. E4—17Dc 26
Markfield Rd. N15—28Wb 43
Markfield Rd. Cat—98Xb 181
Markhams. Stanf—1P 93
Markham Sq. SW3 —50Hb 81 (7F 203)
Markham St. SW3 —50Gb 81 (7E 202)
Markhole Clo. Hmptn—66Ba 121
Markhouse Av. E17—30Ac 44
Markhouse Rd. E17—30Bc 44
Mark La. EC3—45Ub 83 (4J 201)
Mark La. Grav—9G 114
(in two parts)
Markmanor Av. E17—31Ac 64
Mark Oak La. Lea—94Ca 175
Mark Rd. N22—26Rb 43
Marksbury Av. Rich—55Qa 101
Marks Rd. Romf—29Ed 48
Marks Rd. Warl—90Ac 166
Marks Sq. Grav—3B 136
Mark St. E15—38Gc 65
Mark St. EC2—42Ub 83 (5H 195)
Markville Gdns. Cat—97Wb 181
Markway. Sun—68Y 121
Mark Way. Swan—71Jd 152
Markwell Clo. SE26—63Xb 127
Markyate Rd. Dag—36Xc 67
Marlands Rd. Ilf—27Nc 46
Marlborough Av. E8—39Wb 63
(in three parts)
Marlborough Av. N14—20Lb 24
Marlborough Av. Edgw—20Ra 21
Marlborough Av. Ruis—30S 36
Marlborough Bldgs. SW3 —(5E 202)
Marlborough Clo. N20—20Hb 23
Marlborough Clo. SE17 —49Sb 83 (6C 206)
Marlborough Clo. SW19 —65Gb 125
Marlborough Clo. Grays—47Ee 91
Marlborough Clo. Orp—73Vc 151
Marlborough Clo. Upm—32Ud 70
Marlborough Clo. W on T—76Z 141
Marlborough Ct. W1—(3B 198)
Marlborough Cres. W4—48Ua 80
Marlborough Cres. Sev—96Gd 186
Marlborough Dri. Ilf—27Nc 46
Marlborough Dri. Wey—76S 140
Marlborough Gdns. N20—20Hb 23
Marlborough Gdns. Surb —73Ma 143
Marlborough Gdns. Upm—32Td 70
Marlborough Ga. Stables. W2 —(4B 196)
Marlborough Gro. SE1—50Wb 83
Marlborough Hill. NW8 —39Eb 61 (1A 190)
Marlborough Hill. Harr—28Ga 38
Marlborough La. SE7—52Lc 107
Marlborough Pk. Av. Sidc —59Wc 109
Marlborough Pl. NW8 —40Eb 61 (2A 190)
Marlborough Rd. E4—23Dc 44
Marlborough Rd. E7—38Lc 65
Marlborough Rd. E15—35Gc 65
Marlborough Rd. E18—26Jc 45
Marlborough Rd. N9—18Vb 25
Marlborough Rd. N19—33Mb 62
Marlborough Rd. N22—24Pb 42
Marlborough Rd. SW1 —46Lb 82 (7C 198)
Marlborough Rd. SW19—65Gb 125
Marlborough Rd. W4—50Sa 79
Marlborough Rd. W5—47Ma 79
Marlborough Rd. Ashf—64M 119
Marlborough Rd. Bexh—55Zc 109
Marlborough Rd. Brtwd—16Wd 32
Marlborough Rd. Brom—70Lc 129
Marlborough Rd. Dag—35Xc 67
Marlborough Rd. Dart—58Ld 111
Marlborough Rd. Felt—61Z 121
Marlborough Rd. Hmptn —65Ca 121
Marlborough Rd. Iswth—53Ka 100
Marlborough Rd. Rich—58Pa 101
Marlborough Rd. Romf—28Cd 48
Marlborough Rd. Slou—49A 74
Marlborough Rd. Slou—9P 73
Marlborough Rd. S'hall—48Y 77
Marlborough Rd. S Croy —80Sb 147
Marlborough Rd. Sutt—75Cb 145
Marlborough Rd. Uxb—42R 76
Marlborough Rd. Wat—14X 19
Marlborough Rd. Wok—88C 156
Marlborough St. SW3 —49Gb 81 (6D 202)
Marlborough Yd. N19—33Mb 62
Marld, The. Asht—90Pa 161
Marle Gdns. Wal A—4Ec 12
Marler Rd. SE23—60Ac 106
Marlescroft Way. Lou—15Rc 28
Marley Av. Bexh—51Zc 109
Marley Clo. Gnfd—41Ca 77
Marley Clo. Wey—79H 139
Marlingdene Clo. Hmptn —65Ca 121
Marlings Clo. Chst—70Uc 130
Marlings Clo. Whyt—89Ub 165
Marlings Pk. Av. Chst—70Uc 130
Marling Way. Grav—5G 136
Marlin Sq. Abb L, Wat—3V 4
Marloes Clo. Wemb—35Ma 59
Marloes Rd. W8—48Db 81
Marlow Clo. SE20—69Xb 127
Marlow Ct. NW9—27Va 40
Marlow Cres. Twic—58Ha 100
Marlow Dri. Sutt—75Za 144
Marlowe Clo. Chst—65Tc 130
Marlowe Clo. Ilf—25Sc 46
Marlowe Gdns. SE9—58Qc 108
Marlowe Gdns. Romf—25Ld 49
Marlowe Rd. E17—28Ec 44
Marlowe Sq. Mitc—70Lb 126
Marlowes, The. NW8—39Fb 61
Marlowes, The. Dart—56Fd 110
Marlow Gdns. Hay—48T 76
Marlow Rd. E6—41Pc 86
Marlow Rd. SE20—69Xb 127
Marlow Rd. S'hall—48Ba 77
Marlpit Av. Coul—89Nb 164
Marlpit La. Coul—88Mb 164
Marl Rd. SW18—56Db 103
Marlton St. SE10—50Hc 85
Marlyon Rd. Ilf—22Xc 47
Marmadon Rd. SE18—49Vc 87
Marmion App. E4—21Cc 44
Marmion Av. E4—21Bc 44
Marmion Clo. E4—21Bc 44
Marmion M. SW11—55Jb 104
Marmion Rd. SW11—56Jb 104
Marmont Rd. SE15—53Wb 105
Marmora Rd. SE22—58Yb 106
Marmott Rd. Houn—55Z 99
Marne Av. N11—21Kb 42
Marne Av. Well—55Wc 109
Marnell Way. Houn—55Z 99
Marne St. W10—41Ab 80
Marney Rd. SW11—56Jb 104
Marneys Clo. Eps—87Qa 161
Marnham Av. NW2—35Ab 60
Marnham Cres. Gnfd—41Da 77
Marnock Rd. SE4—57Bc 106
Maroon St. E14—43Ac 84
Maroons Way. SE6—64Cc 128
Marquess Rd. N1—37Tb 63
Marquis Clo. Wemb—38Pa 59
Marquis Rd. N4—32Pb 62
Marquis Rd. N22—23Pb 42
Marquis Rd. NW1—37Mb 62
Marram Ct. Grays—1A 114
Marrick Clo. SW15—56Wa 102
Marrilyne Av. Enf—10Bc 12
Marriot Lodge Clo. Wey—77L 139
Marriots Clo. NW9—30Va 40
Marriott Clo. Felt—58T 98
Marriott Rd. E15—39Gc 65
Marriott Rd. N4—32Pb 62
Marriott Rd. N10—25Hb 41
Marriott Rd. Barn—13Za 22
Marriott Rd. Dart—59Qd 111
Mar Rd. S Ock—42Yd 90
Marrowells. Wey—76V 140
Marryat Pl. SW19—63Ab 124
Marryat Rd. SW19—64Za 124
Marryat Rd. Enf—7Xb 11
Marsala Rd. SE13—56Dc 106
Marsden Rd. N9—19Xb 25
Marsden St. NW5—37Jb 62
Marsden St. SE15—55Vb 105
Marsden Way. Orp—76Vc 151
Marshall Clo. SW18—58Eb 103
Marshall Clo. Harr—31Fa 58
Marshall Clo. Houn—57Ba 99
Marshall Dri. Hay—43V 76
Marshall Ho. SE1—(4J 207)
Marshall Path. SE28—45Xc 87
Marshall Rd. N17—25Tb 43
Marshalls Clo. N11—21Kb 42
Marshalls Clo. Eps—85Sa 161
Marshalls Dri. Romf—27Gd 48
Marshall's Gro. SE18—49Nc 86
Marshalls Rd. Romf—28Fd 48
Marshall's Rd. Sutt—77Db 145
Marshall St. W1—44Lb 82 (3C 198)
Marshalsea Rd. SE1 —47Sb 83 (1E 206)
Marsham Clo. Chst—64Rc 130
Marsham La. Ger X—30A 34
Marsham Lodge. Ger X—30A 34
Marsham St. SW1 —48Mb 82 (4E 204)
Marsham Way. Ger X—29A 34
Marsh Av. Eps—82Ua 162
Marsh Av. Mitc—68Hb 125
Marshbrook Clo. SE3—55Mc 107
Marsh Clo. NW7—20Va 22
Marsh Clo. Wal X—5Ac 12
Marsh Ct. E8—38Wb 63
Marshcroft Dri. Wal X—2Ac 12
Marsh Dri. NW9—30Va 40
Marshe Clo. Pot B—4Fb 9
Marsh Farm Rd. Twic—60Ha 100
Marshfield St. E14—48Ec 84
Marshfoot Rd. Grays—10B 92
Marshgate La. E15—39Dc 64
Marshgate Path. SE18—48Sc 86
Marsh Grn. Rd. Dag—39Cd 68
Marsh Hill. E9—36Ac 64
Marsh La. E10—33Bc 64
Marsh La. N17—25Xb 43
Marsh La. NW7—20Ua 22
Marsh La. Stan—22La 38
Marsh La. Wey—77K 139
Marsh Rd. Pinn—28Aa 37
Marsh Rd. Wemb—41Ma 79
Marsh St. E14—49Dc 84
Marsh St. Dart—54Qd 111
(in two parts)
Marsh Wall. E14—46Cc 84
Marsland Clo. SE17 —50Rb 83 (7C 206)
Marston. Eps—83Sa 161
Marston Av. Chess—79Na 143
Marston Av. Dag—33Cd 68
Marston Clo. NW6—38Eb 61
Marston Clo. Dag—34Cd 68
Marston Dri. Warl—90Ac 166
Marston Ho. SW9—54Qb 104
Marston Rd. Ilf—25Nc 46
Marston Rd. Tedd—64Ka 122
Marston Rd. Wok—5E 188
Marston Way. SE19—66Sb 127
Marsworth Av. Pinn—25Z 37
Martaban Rd. N16—33Vb 63
Martello St. E8—38Xb 63
Martello Ter. E8—38Xb 63
Martell Rd. SE21—62Tb 127
Martel Pl. E8—37Vb 63
Marten Rd. E17—26Cc 44
Martens Av. Bexh—56Dd 110
Martens Clo. Bexh—56Ed 110
Martha Ct. E2—40Xb 63
Martha Rd. E15—37Gc 65
Martha St. E1—44Yb 84
Marthorne Cres. Harr—26Fa 38
Martinau Est. E1—44Yb 84
Martin Bowes Rd. SE9—55Pc 108
Martinbridge Trading Est. Enf —15Wb 25
Martin Clo. S Croy—83Zb 166
Martin Clo. Warl—88Xb 165
Martin Clo. Wind—3A 94
Martin Cres. Croy—74Qb 146
Martindale. SW14—57Sa 101
Martindale Av. Orp—78Wc 151
Martindale Rd. SW12—59Kb 104
Martindale Rd. Houn—55Aa 99
Martindale Rd. Wok—6D 188
Martin Dene. Bexh—57Bd 109
Martin Dri. N'holt—36Ba 57
Martin Dri. Rain—42Kd 89
Martineau Clo. Esh—77Fa 142
Martineau Ho. Ger X—22B 34
Martineau Rd. N5—35Rb 63
Martingale Clo. Sun—70W 120
Martingales Clo. Rich—62Ma 123
Martin Gdns. Dag—35Zc 67
Martin Gro. Mord—69Cb 125
Martin Ho. Grav—2B 136
Martin La. EC4—45Tb 83 (4G 201)
Martin Rise. Bexh—57Bd 109
Martin Rd. Dag—35Yc 67
Martin Rd. Dart—62Ld 133
Martin Rd. Slou—8J 73
Martin Rd. S Ock—46Td 90
Martins Clo. Orp—69Zc 131
Martins Clo. Stanf—1M 93
Martins Dri. Wal X—1Ac 12
Martins Mt. Barn—14Cb 23
Martins Plain. Slou—1K 73
Martins Rd. Brom—68Hc 129
Martins Shaw. Sev—94Ed 186
Martins Wlk. N10—25Jb 42
Martin Way—69Ab 124
SW20 267-347 & 274-358
Mord remainder
Martin Way. Wok—6D 188
Martlesham Clo. Horn—36Ld 69
Martlett Ct. WC2 —44Nb 82 (3G 199)
Martley Dri. Ilf—29Rc 46
Martock Clo. Harr—28Ja 38
Marton Clo. SE6—62Cc 128
Marton Rd. N16—34Ub 63
Mart St. WC2—45Nb 82 (4G 199)
Martyrs La. Wok—84D 156
Marunden Grn. Slou—1D 72
Marvell Av. Hay—43W 76
Marvels Clo. SE12—61Kc 129
Marvels La. SE12—61Kc 129
Marville Rd. SW6—52Bb 103
Marvin St. E8—37Xb 63
Marwell. West—98Rc 184
Marwood Clo. K Lan—1P 3
Marwood Clo. Well—55Xc 109
Marwood Way. SE16—50Xb 83
Mary Adelaide Clo. SW15 —63Ua 124
Mary Ann Gdns. SE8—51Cc 106
Maryatt Av. Harr—33Da 57

Mary Bank—Melcombe Gdns.

Mary Bank. SE18—49Pc **86**
Mary Burrows Gdns. Sev —89Rd **171**
Mary Clo. Stan—28Pa **39**
Mary Datchelor Clo. SE5 —53Tb **105**
Maryfield Clo. Bex—62Gd **132**
Maryhill Clo. Kenl—89Sb **165**
Maryland Pk. E15—36Gc **65**
Maryland Rd. E15—36Fc **65**
Maryland Rd. N22—23Qb **42**
Maryland Rd. T Hth—67Rb **127**
Maryland Sq. E15—36Gc **65**
Marylands Rd. W9—42Cb **81**
Maryland St. E15—36Fc **65**
Maryland Way. Sun—68W **120**
Marylebone Fly-over. W2 & NW1 —43Gb **81** (1D 196)
Marylebone High St. W1 —43Jb **82** (7J 191)
Marylebone La. W1 —44Jb **82** (2J 197)
Marylebone M. W1 —43Kb **82** (1K 197)
Marylebone Pas. W1 —44Lb **82** (2C 198)
Marylebone Rd. NW1 —43Gb **81** (7F 191)
Marylebone St. W1 —43Jb **82** (1J 197)
Marylee Way. SE11 —49Pb **82** (6J 205)
Mary Morgan Ct. Slou—3H **73**
Maryon Gro. SE7—49Nc **86**
Maryon M. NW3—35Gb **61**
Maryon Rd. SE7 & SE18—49Nc **86**
Mary Peters Dri. Gnfd—36Fa **58**
Mary Pl. W11—45Ab **80**
Mary Rose Clo. Hmptn—67Ca **121**
Maryside. Slou—47A **74**
Mary's Ter. Twic—59Ja **100**
Mary St. E16—43Hc **85**
Mary St. N1—39Sb **63**
Mary Ter. NW1—39Lb **62** (1A 192)
Maryville. Well—54Vc **109**
Masbro Rd. W14—48Za **80**
Mascalls Gdns. Brtwd—21Vd **50**
Mascalls La. Brtwd—21Vd **50**
Mascalls Rd. SE7—51Lc **107**
Mascotte Rd. SW15—56Za **102**
Mascotts Clo. NW2—34Xa **60**
Masefield Av. Borwd—15Ra **21**
Masefield Av. S'hall—45Ca **77**
Masefield Av. Stan—22Ha **38**
Masefield Clo. Eri—53Hd **110**
Masefield Clo. Romf—25Ld **49**
Masefield Ct. Brtwd—21Yd **50**
Masefield Ct. Surb—73Ma **143**
Masefield Cres. N14—15Lb **24**
Masefield Cres. Romf—25Ld **49**
Masefield Dri. Upm—31Sd **70**
Masefield Gdns. E6—42Qc **86**
Masefield La. Hay—42X **77**
Masefield Rd. Dart—57Rd **111**
Masefield Rd. Grav—62Fe **135**
Masefield Rd. Grays—7A **92**
Masefield Rd. Hmptn—63Ba **121**
Masefield View. Orp—76Sc **150**
Mashie Rd. W3—44Ua **80**
Mashiters Hill. Romf—25Fd **48**
Mashiters Wlk. Romf—27Gd **48**
Maskell Clo. SW2—60Qb **104**
Maskell Rd. SW17—62Eb **125**
Maskelyne Clo. SW11—53Gb **103**
Mason Clo. E16—45Jc **85**
Mason Clo. Bexh—55Dd **110**
Mason Clo. Hmptn—67Ba **121**
Masonic Hall Rd. Cher—72H **139**
Mason Rd. Wfd G—21Gc **45**
Mason's Arms M. W1 —44Kb **82** (3A 198)
Mason's Av. EC2 —44Tb **83** (2F 201)
Masons Av. Croy—76Sb **147**
Masons Av. Harr—28Ha **38**
Masons Ct. Slou—5C **72**
Masons Grn. La. W5 & W3 —42Qa **79**
Masons Hill. SE18—49Rc **86**
Masons Hill. Brom—69Kc **129**
Mason's Pl. EC1—41Sb **83** (3D 194)
Masons Pl. Mitc—67Hb **125**
Masons Rd. Enf—8Xb **11**
Masons Rd. Slou—5C **72**
Mason St. SE17—49Tb **83** (5G 207)
Mason's Yd. SW1 —46Lb **82** (6C 198)
Mason's Yd. SW19—64Za **124**
Mason Way. Wal A—5Gc **13**
Massey Clo. N11—22Kb **42**
Massie Rd. E8—37Wb **63**
Massinger St. SE17 —49Ub **83** (6H 207)
Massingham St. E1—42Zb **84**
Masson Av. Ruis—37Y **57**
Master Clo. Oxt—100Gc **183**
Master Gunners Pl. SE18 —52Nc **108**
Masterman Rd. E6—41Nc **86**
Master's St. E1—43Zb **84**
Mast Ho. Ter. E14—49Cc **84**
Mastmaker Rd. E14—47Cc **84**
Maswell Pk. Cres. Houn—57Ea **100**
Maswell Pk. Rd. Houn—57Da **99**
Matcham Rd. E11—34Gc **65**
★Matching Field. Brtwd—9Vd
Matfield Clo. Brom—71Jc **149**
Matfield Rd. Belv—51Cd **110**
Matham Gro. SE22—56Vb **105**
Matham Rd. E Mol—71Fa **142**
Matheson Rd. W14—49Bb **81**
Mathew Ct. E17—27Ec **44**
Mathews Av. E6—40Qc **66**
Mathews La. Stai—63H **119**
Mathews Pk. Av. E15—37Hc **65**
Mathews Yd. WC2 —44Nb **82** (3F 199)
Mathias Clo. Eps—85Sa **161**
Matilda St. N1—39Pb **62**
Matlock Clo. SE24—56Sb **105**
Matlock Cres. Sutt—77Ab **144**
Matlock Cres. Wat—20Y **19**
Matlock Gdns. Horn—34Nd **69**
Matlock Gdns. Sutt—77Ab **144**
Matlock Pl. Sutt—77Ab **144**
Matlock Rd. E10—30Ec **44**
Matlock Rd. Cat—93Ub **181**
Matlock St. E14—44Ac **84**
Matlock Way. N Mald—67Ta **123**
Matrimony Pl. SW4—54Lb **104**
Matthew Arnold Clo. Cob —86W **158**
Matthew Clo. W10—42Za **80**
Matthew Parker St. SW1 —47Mb **82** (2E 204)
Matthews Clo. Romf—26Pd **49**
Matthews Gdns. Croy—83Fc **167**
Matthews Rd. Gnfd—36Fa **58**
Matthews St. SW11—54Hb **103**
Matthias Rd. N16—36Ub **63**
Mattison Rd. N4—30Qb **42**
Mattock La.—46Ka **78**
W13 37-81
W5 remainder
Maude Cres. Wat—10X **5**
Maude Rd. E17—29Ac **44**
Maude Rd. SE5—53Ub **105**
Maude Rd. Swan—65Jd **132**
Maude Ter. E17—29Ac **44**
Maud Gdns. E13—40Hc **65**
Maud Gdns. Bark—40Vc **67**
Maudlin's Grn. E1—46Wb **83**
Maud Rd. E10—34Ec **64**
Maud Rd. E13—40Hc **65**
Maudslay Rd. SE9—55Pc **108**
Maud St. E16—43Hc **85**
Maudsville Cotts. W7—46Ga **78**
Mauleverer Rd. SW2—57Nb **104**
Maundeby Wlk. NW10—37Ua **60**
Maunder Rd. W7—46Ha **78**
Maunsel St. SW1 —49Mb **82** (5D 204)
Maureen Ct. Beck—68Zb **128**
Maurice Av. N22—26Rb **43**
Maurice Av. Cat—94Tb **181**
Maurice Brown Clo. NW7 —22Za **40**
Maurice St. W12—44Xa **80**
Maurice Wlk. NW11—28Eb **41**
Maurier Clo. N'holt—39Y **57**
Mauritius Rd. SE10—49Gc **85**
Maury Rd. N16—34Wb **63**
Mavelstone Clo. Brom—67Nc **130**
Mavelstone Rd. Brom—67Nc **130**
Maverton Rd. E3—39Cc **64**
Mavis Av. Eps—78Ua **144**
Mavis Clo. Eps—78Ua **144**
Mavis Gro. Horn—33Nd **69**
Mawbey Pl. SE1—50Vb **83** (7K 207)
Mawbey Pl. SW8—52Nb **104**
Mawbey Rd. SE1—50Vb **83**
Mawney Clo. Romf—26Dd **48**
Mawney Rd. Romf—26Dd **48**
Mawson Clo. SW20—68Ab **124**
Mawson La. W4—51Va **102**
Maxey Gdns. Dag—35Ad **67**
Maxey Rd. SE18—49Sc **86**
Maxey Rd. Dag—35Ad **67**
Maxilla Wlk. W11—44Za **80**
Maximfeldt Rd. Eri—50Gd **88**
Maxim Rd. N21—16Qb **24**
Maxim Rd. Dart—57Gd **110**
Maxim Rd. Eri—49Fd **88**
Maxted Pk. Harr—31Ga **58**
Maxted Rd. SE15—55Vb **105**
Maxwell Clo. Rick—19J **17**
Maxwell Dri. Wey—83L **157**
Maxwell Gdns. Orp—76Vc **151**
Maxwell Rise. Wat—17Aa **19**
Maxwell Rd. SW6—52Db **103**
Maxwell Rd. Ashf—65S **120**
Maxwell Rd. Borwd—13Ra **21**
Maxwell Rd. N'wd—24T **36**
Maxwell Rd. Well—55Vc **109**
Maxwell Rd. W Dray—49P **75**
Maxwelton Av. NW7—22Ta **39**
Maxwelton Clo. NW7—22Ta **39**
Mayall Rd. SE24—57Rb **105**
Maya Rd. N2—28Eb **41**
May Av. Grav—10B **114**
May Av. Orp—71Xc **151**
Maybank Av. E18—26Kc **45**
Maybank Av. Horn—36Kd **69**
Maybank Av. Wemb—36Ja **58**
Maybank Gdns. Pinn—29W **36**
Maybank Lodge. Horn—36Ld **69**
Maybank Rd. E18—25Kc **45**
Mayberry Pl. Surb—73Pa **143**
Maybourne Clo. SE26—65Xb **127**
Maybourne Rise. Wok—96A **172**
Maybrick Rd. Horn—30Ld **49**
Maybury Av. Dart—60Sd **112**
Maybury Av. Wal X—1Xb **11**
Maybury Clo. Orp—71Rc **150**
Maybury Clo. Slou—4D **72**
Maybury Clo. Tad—91Ab **178**
Maybury Est. Wok—88E **156**
Maybury Gdns. NW10—37Xa **60**
Maybury Hill. Wok—88D **156**
Maybury Rd. E13—42Lc **85**
Maybury Rd. Bark—40Vc **67**
Maybury Rd. Wok—88C **156**
Maybury St. SW17—64Gb **125**
Maybush Rd. Horn—31Nd **69**
Maychurch Clo. Stan—24Ma **39**
May Clo. Chess—79Pa **143**
Maycock Gro. N'wd—23V **36**
May Ct. Grays—1A **114**
Maycroft. Pinn—26X **37**
Maycroft Av. Grays—50Fe **91**
Maycroft Gdns. Grays—50Fe **91**
Maycross Av. Mord—69Bb **125**
Mayday Gdns. SE3—54Nc **108**
Mayday Rd. T Hth—72Rb **147**
Maydwell Lodge. Borwd—12Pa **21**
Mayell Clo. Lea—95La **176**
Mayerne Rd. SE9—57Mc **107**
Mayesbrook Rd. Bark—39Vc **67**
Mayesbrook Rd. Ilf & Dag —34Wc **67**
Mayes Clo. Swan—70Jd **132**
Mayes Clo. Warl—90Zb **166**
Mayesford Rd. Romf—31Yc **67**
Mayes Rd. N22—26Pb **42**
Mayeswood Rd. SE12—63Lc **129**
Mayfair. Rick—15T **18**
Mayfair Av. Bexh—53Zc **109**
Mayfair Av. Ilf—33Pc **66**
Mayfair Av. Romf—30Zc **47**
Mayfair Av. Twic—59Ea **100**
Mayfair Av. Wor Pk—74Wa **144**
Mayfair Clo. Beck—67Dc **128**
Mayfair Clo. Surb—74Na **143**
Mayfair Gdns. N17—23Tb **43**
Mayfair Gdns. Wfd G—24Jc **45**
Mayfair Pl. W1—46Kb **82** (6A 198)
Mayfair Rd. Dart—57Md **111**
Mayfair Ter. N14—17Mb **24**
Mayfield. Bexh—55Bd **109**
Mayfield. Wal A—6Fc **13**
Mayfield Av. N12—21Eb **41**
Mayfield Av. N14—19Mb **24**
Mayfield Av. W4—49Ua **80**
Mayfield Av. W13—47Ka **78**
Mayfield Av. Harr—29Ka **38**
Mayfield Av. Orp—74Vc **151**
Mayfield Av. Wey—82K **157**
Mayfield Av. Wfd G—23Jc **45**
Mayfield Clo. E8—38Vb **63**
Mayfield Clo. SE20—67Xb **127**
Mayfield Clo. Ashf—65R **120**
Mayfield Clo. Th Dit—74Ka **142**
Mayfield Clo. Uxb—41R **76**
Mayfield Clo. W on T—77W **140**
Mayfield Clo. Wey—82L **157**
Mayfield Cres. N9—16Xb **25**
Mayfield Cres. T Hth—70Pb **126**
Mayfield Dri. Pinn—28Ba **37**
Mayfield Gdns. NW4—30Za **40**
Mayfield Gdns. W7—44Fa **78**
Mayfield Gdns. Brtwd—18Xd **32**
Mayfield Gdns. Stai—65H **119**
Mayfield Gdns. W on T—77W **140**
Mayfield Rd. E4—19Ec **26**
Mayfield Rd. E8—38Vb **63**
Mayfield Rd. E13—42Hc **85**
Mayfield Rd. E17—26Ac **44**
Mayfield Rd. N8—29Pb **42**
Mayfield Rd. SW19—67Bb **125**
Mayfield Rd. W3—45Ra **79**
Mayfield Rd. W12—47Ua **80**
Mayfield Rd. Belv—49Ed **88**
Mayfield Rd. Brom—71Nc **150**
Mayfield Rd. Dag—32Yc **67**
Mayfield Rd. Enf—12Zb **26**
Mayfield Rd. Grav—9B **114**
Mayfield Rd. S Croy—81Tb **165**
Mayfield Rd. Sutt—79Fb **145**
Mayfield Rd. T Hth—70Pb **126**
Mayfield Rd. W on T—77W **140**
Mayfield Rd. Wey—78P **139**
Mayfields. Grays—47Ee **91**
Mayfields. Wemb—33Qa **59**
Mayfields Clo. Wemb—33Qa **59**
Mayflower Clo. Ruis—30S **36**
Mayflower Clo. S Ock—42Yd **90**
Mayflower Ho. Brtwd—23Yd **50**
Mayflower Path. Brtwd—23Yd **50**
Mayflower Rd. SW9—55Nb **104**
Mayflower St. SE16—47Yb **84**
Mayflower Way. Slou—6G **52**
Mayford Clo. SW12—59Hb **103**
Mayford Clo. Beck—69Zb **128**
Mayford Clo. Wok—10G **188**
Mayford Rd. SW12—59Hb **103**
May Gdns. Wemb—41La **78**
Maygoods Clo. Uxb—43M **75**
Maygoods Grn. Uxb—43M **75**
Maygoods La. Uxb—43M **75**
Maygood St. N1—40Qb **62** (1K 193)
Maygoods View. Uxb—43L **75**
Maygreen Cres. Horn—31Jd **68**
Maygrove Rd. NW6—37Bb **61**
Mayhew Clo. E4—20Cc **26**
Mayhill Rd. SE7—51Kc **107**
Mayhill Rd. Barn—16Ab **22**
Mayhurst Av. Wok—88E **156**
Mayhurst Clo. Wok—88E **156**
Mayhurst Cres. Wok—88E **156**
Maylands Av. Horn—35Kd **69**
Maylands Dri. Sidc—62Zc **131**
Maylands Dri. Uxb—37M **55**
Maylands Rd. Wat—21Y **37**
Maylands Way. Romf—23Sd **50**
Maynard Clo. SW6—52Db **103**
Maynard Clo. Eri—52Hd **110**
Maynard Ct. Wal A—6Hc **13**
Maynard Pl. Pot B—1Nb **10**
Maynard Rd. E17—29Ec **44**
Maynards. Horn—31Nd **69**
Mayo Clo. Wal X—1Yb **12**
Mayo Ct. W13—48Ka **78**
Mayola Rd. E5—35Yb **64**
Mayo Rd. NW10—37Ua **60**
Mayo Rd. Croy—71Tb **147**
Mayo Rd. W on T—73V **140**
Mayow Rd.—63Zb **128**
SE23 1-69 & 2-24
SE26 remainder
Mayplace Av. Dart—56Jd **110**
Mayplace Clo. Bexh—55Dd **110**
Mayplace La. SE18—52Rc **108**
Mayplace Rd. E. Bexh—55Dd **110**
Mayplace Rd. W. Bexh—56Cd **110**
Maypole Cres. Eri—51Md **111**
Maypole Cres. Ilf—24Tc **46**
Maypole Dri. Chig—20Wc **29**
Maypole Rd. Orp—78Bd **151**
May Rd. E4—23Cc **44**
May Rd. E13—40Jc **65**
May Rd. Dart—63Pd **133**
May Rd. Twic—60Ga **100**
Mayroyd Av. Surb—75Qa **143**
Mays Ct. WC2—45Nb **82** (5F 199)
Maysfield Rd. Wok—95F **172**
Mays Gro. Wok—95F **172**
Mays Hill Rd. Brom—68Gc **129**
Mays La. Barn—17Xa **22**
Maysoule Rd. SW11—56Fb **103**
Mays Rd. Tedd—64Fa **122**
May St. W14—50Bb **81**
Mayswood Gdns. Dag—37Ed **68**
Maythorne Clo. Wat—14U **18**
Mayton St. N7—34Pb **62**
Maytree Clo. Edgw—20Sa **21**
Maytree Clo. Rain—40Gd **68**
Maytree Ct. N'holt—41Aa **77**
Maytree Cres. Wat—8V **4**
May Tree La. Stan—24Ja **38**
May Tree Wlk. SW2—61Qb **126**
Mayville Rd. E11—33Gc **65**
Mayville Rd. Ilf—36Rc **66**
May Wlk. E13—40Kc **65**
Maywater Clo. S Croy—83Ub **165**
Maywin Dri. Horn—32Pd **69**
Maywood Clo. Beck—66Dc **128**
Maze Hill—51Gc **107**
SE10 1-119 & 2-40
SE3 remainder
Mazenod Av. NW6—38Cb **61**
Maze Rd. Rich—52Qa **101**
Mead Av. Slou—47D **74**
Mead Clo. Egh—65D **118**
Mead Clo. Grays—47De **91**
Mead Clo. Harr—25Fa **38**
Mead Clo. Romf—26Jd **48**
Mead Clo. Slou—47D **74**
Mead Clo. Swan—71Jd **152**
Mead Clo. Uxb—33J **55**
Mead Ct. NW9—29Ta **39**
Mead Ct. Wal A—6Dc **12**
Mead Ct. Wok—4B **188**
Mead Cres. E4—21Ec **44**
Mead Cres. Dart—60Md **111**
Mead Cres. Lea—97Ca **175**
Mead Cres. Sutt—76Gb **145**
Meadcroft Rd. SE11—51Rb **105**
Meade Clo. W4—51Qa **101**
Mead End. Asht—89Pa **161**
Meader Ct. SE14—52Zb **106**
Meadfield. Edgw—19Ra **21**
Meadfield Av. Slou—48C **74**
Meadfield Rd. Slou—48C **74**
Meadfoot Rd. SW16—66Lb **126**
Meadgate Av. Wfd G—22Nc **46**
Mead Gro. Romf—27Zc **47**
Mead Ho. Rd. Hay—42T **76**
Meadhurst Rd. Cher—74K **139**
Meadlands Dri. Rich—61Ma **123**
Mead La. Cher—73K **139**
Meadow Av. Croy—72Zb **148**
Meadoway. N14—19Nb **24**
Meadow Bank. N21—16Pb **24**
Meadowbank. NW3—38Hb **61**
Meadow Bank. SE3—55Hc **107**
Meadow Bank. Lea—99V **174**
Meadowbank. Surb—72Pa **143**
Meadowbank. Wat—17Y **19**
Meadowbank Clo. SW6—52Ya **102**
Meadow Bank Clo. Sev—80Vd **154**
Meadowbank Gdns. Houn—53X **99**
Meadowbank Rd. NW9—31Ta **59**
Meadow Brook Clo. Slou—53H **97**
Meadow Clo. E4—18Dc **26**
Meadow Clo. SE6—64Cc **128**
Meadow Clo. SW20—70Ya **124**
Meadow Clo. Barn—16Bb **23**
Meadow Clo. Chst—64Rc **130**
Meadow Clo. Enf—10Ac **12**
Meadow Clo. Esh—76Ha **142**
Meadow Clo. Houn—58Ca **99**
Meadow Clo. N'holt—40Ca **57**
Meadow Clo. Purl—85Mb **164**
Meadow Clo. Rich—60Na **101**
Meadow Clo. Ruis—30V **36**
Meadow Clo. Sev—95Jd **186**
Meadow Clo. Sutt—75Eb **145**
Meadow Clo. W on T—77Ba **141**
Meadow Clo. Wind—7M **95**
Meadow Ct. Eps—85Sa **161**
Meadow Ct. Stai—62G **118**
Meadowcourt Rd. SE3—56Hc **107**
Meadowcroft. Brom—69Pc **130**
Meadowcroft. Ger X—26A **34**
Meadowcroft Clo. N13—19Rb **25**
Meadowcroft Rd. N13—19Qb **24**
Meadowcross. Wal A—6Gc **13**
Meadow Dri. N10—26Kb **42**
Meadow Dri. NW4—26Ya **40**
Meadow Dri. Wok—95H **173**
Meadow Gdns. Edgw—23Ra **39**
Meadow Gdns. Stai—64F **118**
Meadow Garth. NW10—37Sa **59**
Meadow Hill. Coul & Purl —86Lb **164**
Meadow Hill. N Mald—72Ua **144**
Meadowlands. Cob—85W **158**
Meadowlands. Horn—31Nd **69**
Meadowlands. Sev—92Pd **187**
Meadow La. Lea—94Ea **176**
Meadow La. Stai—63H **119**
Meadow La. Wind—2G **94**
Meadow Leigh Clo. Wey—76S **140**
Meadow Mead. Rad—5Ha **6**
Meadow M. SW8—51Pb **104**
Meadow Pl. SW8—52Nb **104**
Meadow Rise. Coul—85Mb **164**
Meadow Rise. Wok—5A **188**
Meadow Rd. SW8—52Pb **104**
Meadow Rd. SW19—66Eb **125**
Meadow Rd. Ashf—64T **120**
Meadow Rd. Asht—89Na **161**
Meadow Rd. Bark—38Vc **67**
Meadow Rd. Borwd—12Ra **21**
Meadow Rd. Brom—68Gc **129**
Meadow Rd. Bush, Wat—15Da **19**
Meadow Rd. Dag—37Bd **67**
Meadow Rd. Epp—1Vc **15**
Meadow Rd. Esh—79Ga **142**
Meadow Rd. Felt—61Aa **121**
Meadow Rd. Grav—1C **136**
Meadow Rd. Grav—60Ee **113**
(Northfleet)
Meadow Rd. Grays—48Ee **91**
Meadow Rd. Lou—15Nc **28**
Meadow Rd. Pinn—28Z **37**
Meadow Rd. Romf—32Ed **68**
Meadow Rd. Slou—48A **74**
Meadow Rd. S'hall—45Ba **77**
Meadow Rd. Sutt—77Gb **145**
Meadow Rd. Vir W—10J **117**
Meadow Rd. Wat—6W **4**
Meadow Row. SE1 —48Sb **83** (4D 206)
Meadows Clo. E10—33Cc **64**
Meadows Clo. Brtwd—23Ee **51**
Meadows End. Sun—67W **120**
Meadowside. SE9—56Lc **107**
Meadowside. Dart—60Md **111**
Meadowside. Lea—95Ca **175**
Meadowside. W on T—75Y **141**
Meadowside Rd. Sutt—81Ab **162**
Meadowside Rd. Upm—36Sd **70**
Meadows, The. Brtwd—23Ee **51**
Meadows, The. Orp—79Yc **151**
Meadows, The. Sev—85Bd **169**
Meadow Stile. Croy—76Sb **147**
Meadow, The. Chst—65Sc **130**
Meadow View. Orp—69Yc **131**
Meadow View. Sev—90Fd **170**
Meadow View. Sidc—59Xc **109**
Meadowview Rd. SE6—64Cc **128**
Meadowview Rd. Bex—58Ad **109**
Meadowview Rd. Eps—81Ua **162**
Meadow View Rd. Hay—42T **76**
Meadow View Rd. T Hth—71Rb **147**
Meadow Wlk. E18—28Jc **45**
Meadow Wlk. Dag—37Bd **67**
Meadow Wlk. Dart—63Ld **133**
Meadow Wlk. Eps—79Ua **144**
Meadow Wlk. Tad—96Xa **178**
Meadow Wlk. Wall—76Kb **146**
Meadow Way. NW9—29Ta **39**
Meadow Way. Chess—78Na **143**
Meadow Way. Chig—20Sc **28**
Meadow Way. Dart—59Sd **112**
Meadow Way. K Lan—2Q **4**
Meadow Way. Lea—95Da **175**
(Great Bookham)
Meadow Way. Lea—97T **174**
(West Horsley)
Meadow Way. Orp—76Qc **150**
Meadow Way. Pot B—6Cb **9**
Meadow Way. Rick—17L **17**
Meadow Way. Ruis—30X **37**
Meadow Way. Tad—89Ab **162**
Meadow Way. Upm—34Sd **70**
Meadow Way. Wemb—35Ma **59**
Meadow Way. Wey—77K **139**
Meadow Way. Wind—8M **95**
Meadow Waye. Houn—51Aa **99**
Meadow Way, The. Harr—25Ga **38**
Mead Path. SW17 & SW19 —63Eb **125**
Mead Pl. E9—37Yb **64**
Mead Pl. Croy—74Sb **147**
Mead Pl. Rick—18K **17**
Mead Plat. NW10—37Sa **59**
Mead Rd. Cat—95Vb **181**
Mead Rd. Chst—65Sc **130**
Mead Rd. Dart—60Md **111**
Mead Rd. Edgw—23Qa **39**
Mead Rd. Grav—1D **136**
Mead Rd. Rich—62La **122**
Mead Rd. Shen, Rad—5Pa **7**
Mead Rd. Uxb—38M **55**
Mead Rd. W on T—77Aa **141**
Mead Row. SE1—48Qb **82** (3K 205)
Meads La. Ilf—31Uc **66**
Meads Rd. N22—26Rb **43**
Meads Rd. Enf—11Ac **26**
Meads, The. Edgw—23Ta **39**
Meads, The. St Alb—2Ca **5**
Meads, The. Sutt—76Ab **144**
Meads, The. Upm—33Ud **70**
Meads, The. Uxb—42N **75**
Meadsway. Brtwd—23Xd **50**
Mead, The. N2—26Eb **41**
Mead, The. W13—43Ka **78**
Mead, The. Asht—91Na **177**
Mead, The. Beck—67Ec **128**
Mead, The. Romf—13Xc **29**
Mead, The. Uxb—33Q **56**
Mead, The. Wall—79Mb **146**
Mead, The. Wal X—1Yb **12**
Mead, The. Wat—20Aa **19**
Mead, The. W Wick—74Fc **149**
Meadvale Rd. W5—42Ka **78**
Meadvale Rd. Croy—73Vb **147**
Mead Wlk. Slou—47D **74**
Meadway. NW11—30Db **41**
Meadway. SW20—70Ya **124**
Meadway. Ashf—63Q **120**
Meadway. Barn—14Cb **23**
Meadway. Beck—67Ec **128**
Mead Way. Brom—72Hc **149**
Mead Way. Bush, Wat—12Aa **19**
Mead Way. Coul—90Nb **164**
Mead Way. Croy—75Ac **148**
Meadway. Enf—8Yb **12**
Meadway. Eps—84Sa **161**
Meadway. Esh—81Da **159**
Meadway. Grays—49Fe **91**
Meadway. Ilf—35Uc **66**
Meadway. Lea—100Aa **175**
(Effingham)
Meadway. Lea—86Ga **160**
(Oxshott)
Meadway. Orp—79Xc **151**
Meadway. Romf—26Jd **48**
Mead Way. Ruis—30T **36**
Meadway. Sev—85Bd **169**
Mead Way. Slou—3B **72**
Meadway. Stai—66J **119**
Meadway. Surb—74Sa **143**
Meadway. Twic—60Fa **100**
Meadway. Warl—88Yb **166**
Mead Way. Wfd G—22Lc **45**
Meadway Clo. NW11—30Db **41**
Meadway Clo. Barn—14Cb **23**
Meadway Clo. Pinn—23Da **37**
Meadway Clo. Stai—66J **119**
Meadway Ct. Dag—33Bd **67**
Meadway Dri. Wey—80L **139**
Meadway Dri. Wok—4F **188**
Meadway Gdns. Ruis—30T **36**
Meadway Ga. NW11—30Cb **41**
Meadway Pk. Ger X—2P **53**
Meadway, The. SE3—54Fc **107**
Meadway, The. Buck H—18Mc **27**
Meadway, The. Lou—16Pc **28**
Meadway, The. Pot B—1Pb **10**
Meadway, The. Sev—94Hd **186**
Meaford Way. SE20—66Xb **127**
Meakin Est. SE1—48Ub **83** (3H 207)
Meanley Rd. E12—35Nc **66**
Meard St. W1—44Mb **82** (3D 198)
Meath Clo. Orp—71Xc **151**
Meath Rd. E15—40Hc **65**
Meath Rd. Ilf—34Sc **66**
Meath St. SW11—53Kb **104**
Mechanic's Path. SE18—52Cc **106**
Mecklenburgh Pl. WC1 —42Pb **82** (5H 193)
Mecklenburgh Sq. WC1 —42Pb **82** (5H 193)
Mecklenburgh St. WC1 —42Pb **82** (5H 193)
Medburn St. NW1 —40Mb **62** (1D 192)
Medcalfe Pl. N1—40Qb **62** (2A 194)
Medcalf Rd. Enf—9Bc **12**
Medcroft Gdns. SW14—56Sa **101**
Medebourne Clo. SE3—55Jc **107**
Mede Clo. Wray, Stai—10P **95**
Mede Ct. Stai—62G **118**
Mede Field. Lea—96Fa **176**
Medesenge Way. N13—23Rb **43**
Medfield St. SW15—59Xa **102**
Medhurst Cres. Grav—2H **137**
Medhurst Gdns. Grav—2H **137**
Medhurst Rd. E3—40Ac **64**
Median Rd. E5—36Yb **64**
Medick Ct. Grays—1A **114**
Medina Av. Esh—76Ga **142**
Medina Gro. N7—34Qb **62**
Medina Rd. N7—34Qb **62**
Medina Rd. Grays—49Fe **91**
Medlake Rd. Egh—65E **118**
Medland Clo. Wall—74Jb **146**
Medlar Clo. N'holt—40Z **57**
Medlar Rd. Grays—51Fe **113**
Medlar St. SE5—53Sb **105**
Medley Rd. NW6—37Cb **61**
Medman Clo. Uxb—40L **55**
Medora Rd. SW2—59Pb **104**
Medora Rd. Romf—28Fd **48**
Medusa Rd. SE6—58Dc **106**
Medway Clo. Croy—72Yb **148**
Medway Clo. Ilf—36Sc **66**
Medway Clo. Wat—6Y **5**
Medway Dri. Gnfd—40Ha **58**
Medway Gdns. Wemb—35Ja **58**
Medway M. E3—40Ac **64**
Medway Pde. Gnfd—40Ha **58**
Medway Rd. E3—40Ac **64**
Medway Rd. Dart—54Jd **110**
Medway St. SW1 —48Mb **82** (4D 204)
Medwin St. SW4—56Pb **104**
Meerbrook Rd. SE3—55Lc **107**
Meeson Rd. E15—38Hc **65**
Meeson's La. Grays—49Be **91**
Meeson St. E5—35Ac **64**
Meeting Field Path. E9—37Yb **64**
Meetinghouse All. E1—46Xb **83**
Meeting Ho. La. SE15—53Xb **105**
Megg La. K Lan—2K **3**
Mehetabel Rd. E9—36Yb **64**
Melancholy Wlk. Rich—61La **122**
Melanda Clo. Chst—64Pc **130**
Melanie Clo. Bexh—53Ad **109**
Melba Gdns. Til—2C **114**
Melba Way. SE13—53Dc **106**
Melbourne Av. N13—23Pb **42**
Melbourne Av. W13—46Ja **78**
Melbourne Av. Pinn—27Da **37**
Melbourne Av. Slou—4G **72**
Melbourne Clo. SE20—66Wb **127**
Melbourne Clo. Orp—73Uc **150**
Melbourne Clo. Uxb—35Q **56**
Melbourne Clo. Wall—78Lb **146**
Melbourne Gdns. Romf—29Ad **47**
Melbourne Gro. SE22—56Ub **105**
Melbourne M. SW9—53Qb **104**
Melbourne Pl. WC2 —44Pb **82** (3J 199)
Melbourne Rd. E6—40Pc **66**
Melbourne Rd. E10—31Dc **64**
Melbourne Rd. E17—28Ac **44**
Melbourne Rd. SW19—67Cb **125**
Melbourne Rd. Bush, Wat —16Da **19**
Melbourne Rd. Ilf—32Rc **66**
Melbourne Rd. Tedd—65La **122**
Melbourne Rd. Til—3A **114**
Melbourne Rd. Wall—78Kb **146**
Melbourne Sq. SW9—53Qb **104**
Melbourne Way. Enf—16Vb **25**
Melbury Av. S'hall—48Da **77**
Melbury Clo. Cher—73J **139**
Melbury Clo. Chst—65Pc **130**
Melbury Clo. Esh—79Ka **142**
Melbury Clo. Wey—86J **157**
Melbury Ct. W8—48Cb **81**
Melbury Dri. SE5—52Ub **105**
Melbury Gdns. SW20—67Xa **124**
Melbury Rd. W14—48Bb **81**
Melbury Rd. Harr—29Pa **39**
Melbury Ter. NW1 —42Gb **81** (6E 190)
Melcombe Gdns. Harr—30Pa **39**

Melcombe Pl.—Milne Pk. W.

Melcombe Pl. NW1
—43Hb 81 (7F 191)
Melcombe St. NW1
—42Hb 81 (6G 191)
Meldon Clo. SW6—53Db 103
Meldrum Clo. Orp—72Yc 151
Meldrum Rd. Ilf—33Wc 67
Melfield Gdns. SE6—64Ec 128
Melford Av. Bark—37Uc 66
Melford Rd. E6—41Pc 86
Melford Rd. E11—33Gc 65
Melford Rd. E17—28Bc 44
Melford Rd. SE22—59Wb 105
Melford Rd. Ilf—33Tc 66
Melfort Av. T Hth—69Rb 127
Melfort Rd. T Hth—69Rb 127
Melgund Rd. N5—36Qb 62
Melina Clo. Hay—43T 76
Melina Pl. NW8—41Fb 81 (4B 190)
Melina Rd. W12—47Xa 80
Melior Pl. SE1—47Ub 83 (1H 207)
Melior St. SE1—47Ub 83 (1H 207)
Meliot Rd. SE6—61Fc 129
Melksham Clo. Romf—24Pd 49
Melksham Dri. Romf—24Pd 49
Melksham Gdns. Romf—24Nd 49
Melksham Grn. Romf—24Pd 49
Meller Clo. Croy—76Nb 146
Melling St. SE18—51Uc 108
Mellish Clo. Bark—39Vc 67
Mellish St. E14—48Cc 84
Mellison Rd. SW17—64Gb 125
Mellitus St. W12—44Va 80
Mellor Clo. W on T—73Ba 141
Mellow Clo. Bans—86Db 163
Mellow La. E. Hay—42S 76
Mellow La. W. Uxb—41S 76
Mellows Rd. Ilf—27Pc 46
Mellows Rd. Wall—78Mb 146
Mells Cres. SE9—63Pc 130
Mell St. SE10—50Gc 85
Melody Rd. SW18—57Eb 103
Melody Rd. W4—50Ra 79
Melody Rd. West—90Lc 167
Melon Pl. W8—47Cb 81
Melon Rd. SE15—53Wb 105
Melrose Av. N22—25Rb 43
Melrose Av. NW2—36Xa 60
Melrose Av. SW16—69Qb 126
Melrose Av. SW19—61Bb 125
Melrose Av. Borwd—15Ra 21
Melrose Av. Gnfd—40Da 57
Melrose Av. Mitc—66Kb 126
Melrose Av. Pot B—4Cb 9
Melrose Av. Twic—59Da 99
Melrose Clo. SE12—60Jc 107
Melrose Clo. Gnfd—40Da 57
Melrose Clo. Hay—43W 76
Melrose Cres. Orp—77Tc 150
Melrose Dri. S'hall—46Ca 77
Melrose Gdns. W6—48Ya 80
Melrose Gdns. Edgw—26Ra 39
Melrose Gdns. N Mald—69Ta 123
Melrose Gdns. W on T—78Y 141
Melrose Pl. Wat—10V 4
Melrose Rd. SW13—54Va 102
Melrose Rd. SW18—58Bb 103
Melrose Rd. SW19—68Cb 125
Melrose Rd. W3—48Sa 79
Melrose Rd. Coul—87Kb 164
Melrose Rd. Pinn—28Ba 37
Melrose Rd. West—88Lc 167
Melrose Rd. Wey—78Q 140
Melrose Ter. W6—48Ya 80
Melsa Rd. Mord—72Eb 145
Melstock Av. Upm—35Sd 70
Meltham Way. SE16—50Xb 83
Melthorne Dri. Ruis—34Y 57
Melthorpe Gdns. SE3—53Nc 108
Melton Clo. Ruis—32Y 57
Melton Ct. SW7—49Fb 81 (6C 202)
Melton Gdns. Romf—31Hd 68
Melton Pl. Eps—81Ta 161
Melton St. NW1—41Mb 82 (4C 192)
Melville Av. SW20—66Wa 124
Melville Av. Gnfd—36Ha 58
Melville Av. S Croy—78Vb 147
Melville Clo. Uxb—33T 56
Melville Gdns. N13—22Rb 43
Melville Rd. E17—27Bc 44
Melville Rd. NW10—38Ta 59
Melville Rd. SW13—53Wa 102
Melville Rd. Rain—42Jd 88
Melville Rd. Romf—25Dd 48
Melville Rd. Sidc—61Yc 131
Melville St. N1—38Sb 63
Melville Vs. Rd. W3—46Ta 79
Melvin Rd. SE20—67Yb 128
Melvinshaw. Lea—93La 176
Melyn Clo. N7—35Lb 62
Memel Ct. EC1—(6D 194)
Memel St. EC1—42Sb 83 (6D 194)
Memess Path. SE18—51Qc 108
Memorial Av. E15—41Gc 85
Memorial Clo. Houn—51Ba 99
Mendip Clo. SE26—63Yb 128
Mendip Clo. SW19—61Ab 124
Mendip Clo. Hay—52T 98
Mendip Clo. Slou—50C 74
Mendip Dri. NW2—33Ab 60
Mendip Rd. SW11—55Eb 103
Mendip Rd. Bexh—53Gd 110
Mendip Rd. Bush, Wat—16Ea 20
Mendip Rd. Horn—31Jd 68
Mendip Rd. Ilf—29Uc 46
Mendora Rd. SW6—52Ab 102
Mendoza Clo. Horn—29Nd 49
Menelik Rd. NW2—35Ab 60
Menlo Gdns. SE19—66Tb 127
Menotti St. E2—42Wb 83
Menthone Pl. Horn—31Md 69
Mentmore Clo. Harr—30La 38
Mentmore Ter. E8—38Xb 63
Meon Clo. Tad—94Xa 178
Meon Ct. Iswth—54Ga 100
Meon Rd. W3—47Sa 79
Meopham Rd. Mitc—67Lb 126
Mepham Cres. Harr—24Ea 38
Mepham Gdns. Harr—24Ea 38
Mepham St. SE1—46Qb 82 (7J 199)
Mera Dri. Bexh—56Cd 110
Mercator Rd. SE13—56Fc 107
Mercer Av. WC2—44Nb 82 (3G 199)
Mercer Clo. Th Dit—73Ha 142
Merceron St. E1—42Xb 83
Mercer Pl. Pinn—26Y 37
Mercers Clo. SE10—49Hc 85
Mercers Pl. W6—49Ya 80
Mercers Rd. N19—34Mb 62
Mercer St. WC2—44Nb 82 (3F 199)
Mercer Wlk. Uxb—38L 55
Merchant Industrial Ter. NW10
—42Sa 79
Merchant St. E3—41Bc 84
Merchiston Rd. SE6—61Fc 129
Merchland Rd. SE9—60Sc 108
Mercia Gro. SE13—56Ec 106
Mercian Way. Slou—6B 72
Mercia Wlk. Wok—89B 156
Mercier Rd. SW15—57Ab 102
Mercury Gdns. Romf—29Gd 48
Mercury Rd. Bren—50La 78
Mercury Way. SE14—51Zb 106
Mercy Ter. SE13—57Dc 106
Merebank La. Croy—78Nb 146
Mere Clo. SW15—59Za 102
Mere Clo. Orp—75Qc 150
Meredith Av. NW2—36Ya 60
Meredith Clo. Pinn—24Z 37
Meredith Rd. Grays—9C 92
Meredith St. E13—41Jc 85
Meredith St. EC1
—41Rb 83 (4B 194)
Meredyth Rd. SW13—54Wa 102
Mere End. Croy—73Zb 148
Merefield Gdns. Tad—91Za 178
Mere Rd. Shep—72R 140
Mere Rd. Slou—8K 73
Mere Rd. Tad—96Xa 178
Mere Rd. Wey—76T 140
Mere Side. Orp—75Qc 150
Meretone Clo. SE4—56Ac 106
Merevale Cres. Mord—72Eb 145
Mereway Rd. Twic—60Fa 100
Merewood Clo. Brom—68Qc 130
Merewood Rd. Bexh—54Ed 110
Mereworth Clo. Brom—71Hc 149
Mereworth Dri. SE18—52Rc 108
Merganser Gdns. SE28—48Tc 86
Meriden Clo. Brom—66Nc 129
Meriden Clo. Ilf—25Sc 46
Meriden Way. Wat—8Aa 5
Meridian Rd. SE7—52Mc 107
Meridian View. E14—46Ec 84
Meridian Wlk. N17—23Ub 43
Merifield Rd. SE9—56Lc 107
Merino Pl. Sidc—58Wc 109
Merivale Rd. SW15—56Ab 102
Merivale Rd. Harr—31Ea 58
Merland Grn. Tad—92Ya 178
Merland Rise. Eps & Tad
—91Ya 178
Merle Av. Uxb—26K 35
Merlewood. Sev—95Kd 187
Merlewood Clo. Cat—92Tb 181
Merlewood Dri. Chst—67Pc 130
Merlewood Pl. SE9—58Pc 108
Merley Ct. NW9—32Sa 59
Merlin Clo. Croy—77Ub 147
Merlin Clo. Ilf—22Yc 47
Merlin Clo. N'holt—41Y 77
Merlin Clo. Romf—23Fd 48
Merlin Clo. Slou—51D 96
Merlin Ct. Brom—70Hc 129
Merlin Cres. Edgw—25Pa 39
Merlin Gdns. Brom—62Jc 129
Merlin Gdns. Romf—23Fd 48
Merlin Gro. Beck—70Bc 128
Merlin Gro. Ilf—24Rc 46
Merlin Rd. E12—33Mc 65
Merlin Rd. Romf—23Fd 48
Merlin Rd. Well—56Wc 109
Merlin Rd. N. Well—56Wc 109
Merlins Av. Harr—34Ba 57
Merlin St. WC1—41Qb 82 (4K 193)
Mermagen Dri. Rain—38Kd 69
Mermaid Ct. SE1—47Tb 83 (1F 207)
Mermers Gdns. Grav—3H 137
Merredene St. SW2—58Pb 104
Merrick Rd. S'hall—48Ba 77
Merrick Sq. SE1—48Tb 83 (3F 207)
Merridene. N21—16Rb 25
Merrielands Cres. Dag—40Bd 67
Merrilands Rd. Wor Pk—74Ya 144
Merrilees Rd. Sidc—59Uc 108
Merrilyn Clo. Esh—79Ja 142
Merriman Rd. SE3—53Lc 107
Merrington Rd. SW6—51Cb 103
Merrion Av. Stan—22Ma 39
Merritt Rd. SE4—57Bc 106
Merritt's Bldgs. EC2—(6H 195)
Merrivale. N14—16Mb 24
Merrivale Av. Ilf—28Mc 45
Merrow La. Guild—100E 172
Merrow Rd. Sutt—81Za 162
Merrows Clo. N'wd—23S 36
Merrow St. SE17
—50Tb 83 (7G 207)
Merrow Wlk. SE17
—50Tb 83 (7G 207)
Merrow Way. Croy—79Ec 148
Merrydown Way. Chst—67Nc 130
Merryfield. SE3—54Hc 107
Merryfield Gdns. Stan—22La 38
Merryfields. Uxb—40M 55
(in two parts)
Merryhill Clo. E4—17Dc 26
Merry Hill Mt. Bush, Wat—18Da 19
Merry Hill Rd. Bush, Wat—16Ba 19
Merryhills Clo. West—88Mc 167
Merryhills Ct. N14—15Lb 24
Merryhills Dri. Enf—14Mb 24
Merrylands. Cher—76G 138
Merrylands Rd. Lea—96Ba 175
Merry Meet. Bans—86Hb 163
Mersey Av. Upm—30Td 50
Mersey Rd. E17—27Bc 44
Mersham Dri. NW9—29Qa 39
Mersham Rd. T Hth—68Tb 127
Merten Rd. Romf—31Ad 67
Merthyr Ter. SW13—51Xa 102
Merton Av. W4—49Va 80
Merton Av. Long, Dart—70Ae 135
Merton Av. N'holt—36Ea 58
Merton Av. Uxb—38R 56
Merton Gdns. Orp—71Rc 150
Merton Gdns. Tad—91Za 178
Merton Hall Gdns. SW20
—67Ab 124
Merton Hall Rd. SW19—67Ab 124
Merton High St. SW19—66Db 125
Merton La. N6—33Hb 61
Merton Mans. SW20—68Za 124
Merton Pl. Grays—9C 92
Merton Rise. NW3—38Gb 61
Merton Rd. E17—29Ec 44
Merton Rd. SE25—71Wb 147
Merton Rd. SW18—58Cb 103
Merton Rd. SW19—66Db 125
Merton Rd. Bark—38Vc 67
Merton Rd. Enf—10Tb 11
Merton Rd. Harr—32Ea 58
Merton Rd. Ilf—31Vc 67
Merton Rd. Slou—8L 73
Merton Rd. Wat—14X 19
Merton Wlk. Lea—90Ja 160
Merton Way. E Mol—70Da 121
Merton Way. Lea—91Ja 176
Merton Way. Uxb—38R 56
Merttins Rd. SE15—57Zb 106
Mervan Rd. SW2—56Qb 104
Mervin Rd. Shep—73S 140
Mervyn Av. SE9—62Sc 130
Mervyn Rd. W13—48Ja 78
Merwin Way. Wind—4B 94
Meryfield Rd. Borwd—12Pa 21
Mesne Way. Sev—84Hd 170
Messaline Av. W3—44Sa 79
Messent Rd. SE9—57Lc 107
Messeter Pl. SE9—58Qc 108
Messina Av. NW6—38Cb 61
Metcalfe Wlk. Felt—63Aa 121
Metcalf Rd. Ashf—64R 120
Meteor St. SW11—56Jb 104
Meteor Way. Wall—80Nb 146
Metheringham Way. NW9
—25Ua 40
Methley St. SE11
—50Qb 82 (7A 206)
Methuen Clo. Edgw—24Qa 39
Methuen Pk. N10—27Kb 42
Methuen Rd. Belv—49Dd 88
Methuen Rd. Bexh—56Bd 109
Methuen Rd. Edgw—24Qa 39
Methwold Rd. W10—43Za 80
Meux Clo. Wal X—3Wb 11
Mews End. West—90Mc 167
Mews St. E1—46Wb 83
Mews, The. N1—39Sb 63
Mews, The. Ilf—29Mc 45
Mews, The. Romf—28Gd 48
Mews, The. Slou—8J 73
Mews, The. Twic—58Ka 100
Mexfield Rd. SW15—57Bb 103
Meyer Gro. Enf—10Wb 11
Meyer Rd. Eri—51Fd 110
Meymott St. SE1
—46Rb 83 (7B 200)
Meynell Cres. E9—38Zb 64
Meynell Gdns. E9—38Zb 64
Meynell Rd. E9—38Zb 64
Meynell Rd. Romf—24Kd 49
Meyrick Clo. Wok—4B 188
Meyrick Rd. NW10—37Wa 60
Meyrick Rd. SW11—55Fb 103
Mezen Clo. N'wd—22T 36
Miall Wlk. SE26—63Ac 128
Micawber Av. Uxb—42Q 76
Micawber St. N1—41Sb 83 (3E 194)
Michael Gdns. Grav—4G 136
Michael Gdns. Horn—28Md 49
Michael Gaynor Clo. W7—46Ha 78
Michael Rd. E11—32Hc 65
Michael Rd. SE25—69Ub 127
Michael Rd. SW6—53Db 103
Michael's Clo. SE13—56Gc 107
Michaels La. Long, Dart—75Xd 154
Micheldever Rd. SE12—58Hc 107
Michelham Gdns. Tad—92Ya 178
Michelham Gdns. Twic—62Ha 122
Michel's Row. Rich—56Na 101
Michigan Av. E12—35Nc 66
Michleham Down. N12—21Bb 41
Micholls Av. Ger X—21A 34
Micklefield Way. Borwd—10Na 7
Mickleham By-Pass. Dor
—99Ka 176
Mickleham Clo. Orp—68Vc 131
Mickleham Dri. Dor—98La 176
Mickleham Gdns. Sutt—79Ab 144
Mickleham Rd. Orp—67Vc 131
Mickleham Way. Croy—80Fc 149
Micklethwaite Rd. SW6—51Cb 103
Midas Industrial Est. Uxb—40K 55
Midcroft. Ruis—32U 56
Midcroft. Slou—2F 72
Mid Cross La. Ger X—22B 34
Middle Boy. Romf—13Yc 29
Middle Clo. Coul—92Qb 180
Middle Clo. Eps—84Ua 162
Middle Cres. Uxb—31F 54
Middle Dene. NW7—20Ta 21
Middle Field. NW8—39Fb 61
Middlefielde. W13—43Ka 78
Middlefields. Croy—81Ac 166
Middle Furlong. Bush, Wat
—14Da 19
★Middle Grn. Brtwd—9Yd
Middle Grn. Slou—46A 74
Middle Grn. Stai—66M 119
Middle Grn. Clo. Surb—72Pa 143
Middlegreen Rd. Slou—46A 74
Middlegreen Rd. Slou—7P 73
Middleham Gdns. N18—23Wb 43
Middleham Rd. N18—23Wb 43
Middle Hill. Egh—64A 118
Middle Hill. Egh—3N 117
Middle La. N8—29Nb 42
Middle La. Eps—84Ua 162
Middle La. Hem—1C 2
Middle La. Sev—93Pd 187
Middle La. Tedd—65Ha 122
Middlemead Clo. Lea—97Ca 175
Middlemead Rd. Lea—97Ba 175
Middle Ope. Wat—9X 5
Middle Pk. Av. SE9—58Mc 107
Middle Path. Harr—32Fa 58
Middle Rd. E13—40Jc 65
Middle Rd. SW16—68Mb 126
Middle Rd. Barn—16Gb 23
Middle Rd. Brtwd—22Ee 51
Middle Rd. Harr—33Fa 58
Middle Rd. Lea—93Ka 176
Middle Rd. Uxb—31E 54
Middle Rd. Wal A—4Dc 12
Middle Row. W10—42Ab 80
Middlesborough Rd. N18
—23Wb 43
Middlesex Ct. W4—50Va 80
Middlesex Pas. EC1—(1C 200)
Middlesex Rd. Mitc—71Nb 146
Middlesex St. E1
—43Ub 83 (1J 201)
Middlesex Wharf. E5—33Yb 64
Middle St. EC1—43Sb 83 (7D 194)
Middle St. Croy—75Sb 147
Middle Temple La. EC4
—44Qb 82 (3K 199)
Middleton Av. E4—21Bc 44
Middleton Av. Gnfd—40Fa 58
Middleton Av. Sidc—65Yc 131
Middleton Bldgs. W1—(1B 198)
Middleton Clo. E4—20Bc 26
Middleton Dri. Pinn—27W 36
Middleton Gdns. Ilf—30Rc 46
Middleton Gro. N7—36Nb 62
Middleton Hall La. Brtwd
—19Ae 33
Middleton M. N7—36Nb 62
Middleton Rd. E8—38Vb 63
Middleton Rd. NW11—31Cb 61
Middleton Rd. Brtwd—18Ae 33
Middleton Rd. Cob—91Y 175
Middleton Rd. Eps—82Ta 161
Middleton Rd. Hay—43T 76
Middleton Rd. Mord & Cars
—72Db 145
Middleton Rd. N Mald—68Sa 123
Middleton Rd. Rick—18J 17
Middleton St. E2—41Xb 83
Middleton Way. SE13—56Fc 107
Middle Wlk. Slou—1A 72
Middle Wlk. Wok—89A 156
Middleway. NW11—29Db 41
Middle Way. SW16—68Mb 126
Middle Way. Hay—42Y 77
Middle Way. Wat—9X 5
Middle Way, The. Harr—26Ha 38
Middle Yd. SE1—46Ub 83 (6H 201)
Middlings Rise. Sev—98Hd 186
Middlings, The. Sev—97Hd 186
Middlings Wood. Sev—97Hd 186
Midfield Av. Bexh—55Ed 110
Midfield Av. Swan—65Jd 132
Midfield Pde. Bexh—55Ed 110
Midfield Way. Orp—67Xc 131
Midford Pl. W1—42Lb 82 (6C 192)
Midholm. NW11—28Db 41
Midholm. Wemb—32Qa 59
Midholm Clo. NW11—28Db 41
Midholm Rd. Croy—75Ac 148
Midhope Clo. Wok—91A 172
Midhope Gdns. Wok—91A 172
Midhope Rd. Wok—91A 172
Midhope St. WC1
—41Nb 82 (4G 193)
Midhurst Av. N10—27Jb 42
Midhurst Av. Croy—73Qb 146
Midhurst Clo. Horn—35Jd 68
Midhurst Gdns. Uxb—39S 56
Midhurst Hill. Bexh—58Cd 110
Midhurst Rd. W13—47Ja 78
Midland Pl. E14—50Ec 84
Midland Rd. E10—31Ec 64
Midland Rd. NW1
—40Mb 62 (2E 192)
Midland Ter. NW2—34Za 60
Midland Ter. NW10—42Ua 80
Midmoor Rd. SW12—60Lb 104
Midmoor Rd. SW19—67Ab 124
Midstrath Rd. NW10—35Ua 60
Midsummer Av. Houn—56Ba 99
Midway. Sutt—73Bb 145
Midway. W on T—75X 141
Midway Av. Cher—69J 119
Midway Av. Egh—69D 118
Midwood Clo. NW2—34Xa 60
Miena Way. Asht—89Ma 161
Miers Clo. E6—39Qc 66
Mighell Av. Ilf—29Mc 45
Mike Spring Ct. Grav—3F 136
Milborne Gro. SW10—50Eb 81
Milborne St. E9—37Yb 64
Milborough Cres. SE12—58Gc 107
Milbourne La. Esh—79Ea 142
Milbrook. Esh—79Ea 142
Milburn Wlk. Eps—87Ua 162
Milbury Grn. Warl—90Fc 167
Milby Ct. Borwd—11Pa 21
Milcombe Clo. Wok—6F 188
Milcote St. SE1—47Rb 83 (2B 206)
Mildenhall Rd. E5—35Yb 64
Mildenhall Rd. Slou—4J 73
Mildmay Av. N1—37Tb 63
Mildmay Gro. N1—36Tb 63
(in two parts)
Mildmay Pk. N1—36Tb 63
Mildmay Pl. Sev—83Hd 170
Mildmay Rd. N1—36Tb 63
Mildmay Rd. Ilf—34Rc 66
Mildmay Rd. Romf—29Ed 48
Mildmay St. N1—37Tb 63
Mildred Av. Borwd—14Qa 21
Mildred Av. Hay—49T 76
Mildred Av. N'holt—36Da 57
Mildred Av. Wat—14V 18
Mildred Clo. Dart—58Qd 111
Mildred Rd. Eri—50Gd 88
Mile Clo. Wal A—5Ec 12
Mile End Pl. E1—42Zb 84
Mile End Rd.—43Yb 84
E1 1-357 & 2-510
E3 remainder
Mile End, The. E17—25Zb 44
Mile Path. Wok—8E 188
(in two parts)
Mile Rd. Wall—74Kb 146
Miles La. Cob—85Aa 159
Milespit Hill. NW7—22Xa 40
Miles Pl. NW8—(7D 190)
Miles Pl. Surb—70Pa 123
Miles Rd. N8—27Nb 42
Miles Rd. Eps—84Ta 161
Miles Rd. Mitc—69Gb 125
Miles St. SW8—51Nb 104
(in two parts)
Milestone Clo. Sutt—80Fb 145
Milestone Clo. Wok—94J 173
Milestone Rd. SE19—65Vb 127
Milestone Rd. Dart—58Rd 111
Miles Way. N20—19Gb 23
Milfoil St. W12—45Wa 80
Milford Clo. SE2—51Ad 109
Milford Gdns. Edgw—24Qa 39
Milford Gdns. Wemb—36Ma 59
Milford Gro. Sutt—77Eb 145
Milford La. WC2—45Qb 82 (4K 199)
Milford M. SW16—62Pb 126
Milford Rd. W13—46Ka 78
Milford Rd. Grays—46Fe 91
Milford Rd. S'hall—45Ca 77
Milford Towers. SE6—59Dc 106
Milford Way. SE15—53Vb 105
Milking La. Kes—83Mc 167
Milking La. Orp—84Nc 168
Milk St. E16—46Rc 86
Milk St. EC2—44Sb 83 (3E 200)
Milk St. Brom—65Kc 129
Milkwell Gdns. Wfd G—24Kc 45
Milkwood Rd. SE24—57Rb 105
Milk Yd. E1—45Yb 84
Millais Av. E12—36Qc 66
Millais Gdns. Edgw—26Qa 39
Millais Rd. E11—35Ec 64
Millais Rd. Enf—15Vb 25
Millais Rd. N Mald—73Ua 144
Millais Way. Eps—77Sa 143
Millard Clo. N16—36Ub 63
Millard Ter. Dag—37Cd 68
Mill Av. Uxb—40L 55
Millbank. SW1—49Nb 82 (7F 205)
Millbank Way. SE12—57Jc 107
Millbourne Rd. Felt—63Aa 121
Mill Bridge. Barn—16Bb 23
Millbro. Swan—67Jd 132
Millbrook. Wey—77U 140
Millbrook Av. Well—56Tc 108
Millbrook Gdns. Romf—26Gd 48
Millbrook Gdns. Romf—30Bd 47
(Chadwell Heath)
Millbrook Rd. N9—18Xb 25
Millbrook Rd. SW9—55Rb 105
Millbrook Rd. Bush, Wat—11Ba 19
Mill Brook Rd. Orp—70Yc 131
Mill Clo. Cars—75Jb 146
Mill Clo. Lea—96Ca 175
Mill Clo. W Dray—48M 75
Mill Corner. Barn—11Bb 23
Mill Ct. E10—34Ec 64
Millcrest Rd. Wal X—1Rb 11
Mill Dri. SW16—69Pb 126
Millen Clo. Wey—82K 157
Millender Wlk. SE16—49Yb 84
Miller Clo. Pinn—26Y 37
Miller Rd. SW19—65Fb 125
Miller Rd. Croy—74Pb 146
Miller Rd. Grav—1J 137
Millers Av. E8—36Vb 63
Miller's Clo. Chig—19Xc 29
Millers Copse. Eps—91Ta 177
Miller's Ct. W6—50Va 80
Millers Grn. Enf—13Rb 25
Miller's La. Chig—18Xc 29
Miller's La. Wind—8K 95
Millers Ter. E8—36Vb 63
Miller St. NW1—40Lb 62 (1B 192)
Millet Rd. Gnfd—41Da 77
Mill Farm Av. Sun—66U 120
Mill Farm Clo. Pinn—26Y 37
Mill Farm Cres. Houn—60Aa 99
Millfield. Long, Dart—75Ae 155
Millfield. Sun—67T 120
Millfield Av. E17—25Ac 44
Millfield La. N6—33Hb 61
Millfield La. Long, Dart—75Ae 155
Millfield La. Tad—97Bb 179
Millfield Pl. N6—33Jb 62
Millfield Rd. Edgw—26Sa 39
Millfield Rd. Houn—60Aa 99
Millfield Rd. Sev—79Td 154
Millfields Clo. Orp—70Xc 131
Millfields Rd. E5—35Yb 64
Mill Gdns. SE26—62Xb 127
Mill Grn. Rd. Mitc—73Hb 146
Millgrove St. SW11—54Jb 104
Millharbour. E14—48Cc 84
Millhedge Clo. Cob—88Aa 159
Mill Hill. Brtwd—17Ae 33
Mill Hill Cir. NW7—22Va 40
Mill Hill Gro. W3—46Ra 79
Mill Hill La. Grav—4M 137
Mill Hill Rd. SW13—54Wa 102
Mill Hill Rd. W3—47Ra 79
Mill Hill Ter. W3—46Ra 79
Millhoo Ct. Wal A—6Hc 13
Mill Ho. La. Egh—64F 118
Mill Ho. La. Egh & Cher—70D 118
Millhouse Pl. SE27—63Rb 127
Millicent Rd. E10—32Bc 64
Milligan St. E14—45Bc 84
Milling Rd. Edgw—24Ta 39
Millington Rd. Hay—48U 76
Mill La. E4—13Dc 26
Mill La. NW6—36Bb 61
Mill La. SE18—50Qc 86
Mill La. Asc—8D 116
★Mill La. Brtwd—7Zd
(Hook End)
★Mill La. Brtwd—9Ud
(Kelvedon Hatch)
Mill La. Cars—77Hb 145
Mill La. Croy—76Pb 146
Mill La. Egh—70E 118
Mill La. Eps—81Va 162
Mill La. Eyns, Dart—74Nd 153
Mill La. Ger X—30B 34
Mill La. Grays—3C 92
(Orsett)
Mill La. Grays—48Zd 91
(South Stifford)
Mill La. K Lan—1Q 4
Mill La. Lea—94Ja 176
Mill La. Orp—82Qc 168
Mill La. Romf—30Ad 47
(Chadwell Heath)
Mill La. Romf—11Kd 31
(Navestock Heath)
Mill La. Sev—93Ld 187
★Mill La. Sev—94Zd
(Ightham)
Mill La. Sev—82Hd 170
(Shoreham)
Mill La. Slou—55D 96
Mill La. West—99Sc 184
Mill La. Wey—85P 157
Mill La. Wind—2E 94
Mill La. Wok—91M 173
Mill La. Wfd G—22Hc 45
Millman M. WC1—42Pb 82 (6H 193)
Millman St. WC1
—42Pb 82 (6H 193)
Millmark Gro. SE14—54Ac 106
Millmarsh La. Enf—12Bc 26
Mill Mead. Stai—63H 119
Millmead. Wey—84P 157
Millmead Industrial Centre.
N17—27Xb 43
Mill Mead Rd. N17—27Xb 43
Mill Pk. Av. Horn—33Nd 69
Mill Pl. E14—44Ac 84
Mill Pl. Chst—67Rc 130
Mill Pl. Dart—56Jd 110
Mill Pl. King—69Pa 123
Mill Pl. Slou—4P 95
Mill Plat. Iswth—54Ja 100
Mill Plat Av. Iswth—54Ja 100
Mill Pond Rd. Dart—58Nd 111
Mill Ridge. Edgw—22Pa 39
Mill Rd. E16—46Kc 85
Mill Rd. SE13—55Ec 106
Mill Rd. SW19—66Eb 125
Mill Rd. Cob—87Y 159
Mill Rd. Dart—63Pd 133
Mill Rd. Eps—84Va 162
Mill Rd. Eri—52Ed 110
Mill Rd. Esh—75Ca 141
Mill Rd. Grav—9A 114
Mill Rd. Ilf—34Qc 66
Mill Rd. Purf—51Rd 111
Mill Rd. Sev—93Gd 186
Mill Rd. S Ock—45Sd 90
Mill Rd. Tad—95Za 178
Mill Rd. Twic—61Ea 122
Mill Rd. W Dray—48L 75
Mill Row. N1—39Ub 63 (1J 195)
Mills Clo. Uxb—40Q 56
Mills Ct. EC2—(4H 195)
Mills Cres. Sev—91Pd 187
Mills Gro. E14—44Ec 84
Mills Gro. NW4—27Za 40
Mill Shot Clo. SW6—53Ya 102
Millside. Cars—75Hb 145
Millsmead Way. Lou—12Pc 28
Millson Clo. N20—19Fb 23
Mills Rd. W4—49Ta 79
Mills Rd. W on T—78Y 141
Mills Row. W4—49Ta 79
Mills Spur. Wind—9M 95
Millstead Clo. Tad—95Xa 178
Millstream La. Slou—6C 72
Millstream Rd. SE1
—47Vb 83 (2K 207)
Mill St. SE1—47Vb 83 (2K 207)
Mill St. W1—45Lb 82 (4B 198)
Mill St. King—69Na 123
Mill St. Slou—6K 73
Mill St. Slou—52F 96
(Colnbrook)
Mill St. West—99Tc 184
Mills Way. Brtwd—18Ee 33
Millthorn Clo. Rick—15P 17
Mill Vale. Brom—68Hc 129
Mill View Gdns. Croy—76Zb 148
Millwall Dock Rd. E14—48Cc 84
Mill Way. NW7—21Ua 40
Mill Way. Bush, Wat—12Aa 19
Mill Way. Dor—96Pa 177
Mill Way. Felt—57X 99
Mill Way. Rick—18H 17
Millway Gdns. N'holt—37Ba 57
Millwell Cres. Chig—22Tc 46
Millwood Rd. Houn—57Ea 100
Millwood Rd. Orp—69Yc 131
Millwood St. W10—43Ab 80
Milman Clo. Pinn—27Z 37
Milman Rd. NW6—40Ab 60
Milman's St. SW10—51Fb 103
Milne Est. SE18—49Pc 86
Milne Feild. Pinn—24Ca 37
Milne Gdns. SE9—57Nc 108
Milne Pk. E. Croy—83Fc 167
Milne Pk. W. Croy—83Fc 167

Milner App. Cat—93Wb 181
Milner Clo. Cat—94Wb 181
Milner Clo. Wat—6X 5
Milner Ct. Bush, Wat—16Da 19
Milner Dri. Cob—84Ba 159
Milner Dri. Twic—59Fa 100
Milner Pl. N1—39Rb 63
Milner Pl. Cars—77Jb 146
Milner Rd. E15—41Gc 85
Milner Rd. SW19—67Db 125
Milner Rd. Cat—94Wb 181
Milner Rd. Dag—33Yc 67
Milner Rd. King—69Ma 123
Milner Rd. Mord—71Fb 145
Milner Rd. T Hth—69Tb 127
Milner Sq. N1—38Rb 63
Milner St. SW3—49Hb 81 (5F 203)
Milne Way. Uxb—25K 35
Milnthorpe Rd. W4—51Ta 101
Milo Rd. SE22—58Vb 105
Milroy Av. Grav—1A 136
Milroy Wlk. SE1—46Rb 83 (6B 200)
Milson Rd. W14—48Za 80
Milton Av. E6—38Mc 65
Milton Av. N6—31Lb 62
Milton Av. NW9—27Sa 39
Milton Av. NW10—39Sa 59
Milton Av. Barn—15Bb 23
Milton Av. Croy—73Tb 147
Milton Av. Ger X—28A 34
Milton Av. Grav—10E 114
Milton Av. Horn—33Hd 68
Milton Av. Sev—82Dd 170
Milton Av. Sutt—76Fb 145
Milton Clo. N2—29Eb 41
Milton Clo. Hay—44W 76
Milton Clo. Pinn—24Aa 37
Milton Clo. Slou—55C 96
Milton Clo. Sutt—76Fb 145
Milton Ct. EC2—43Tb 83 (7F 195)
Milton Ct. Uxb—34R 56
Milton Ct. Wal A—6Ec 12
Milton Ct. Rd. SE14—51Ac 106
Milton Cres. Ilf—31Sc 66
Milton Dri. Borwd—15Ra 21
Milton Dri. Shep—70N 119
Milton Gdns. Eps—86Ua 162
Milton Gdns. Til—3D 114
Milton Gro. N11—22Lb 42
Milton Gro. N16—35Ub 63
Milton Hall Rd. Grav—10F 114
Milton Ho. Ger X—21A 34
Milton Pk. N6—31Lb 62
Milton Pl. N7—36Qb 62
Milton Pl. Grav—8E 114
Milton Rd. E17—28Cc 44
Milton Rd. N6—31Lb 62
Milton Rd. N15—28Rb 43
Milton Rd. NW7—22Wa 40
Milton Rd. NW9—31Wa 60
Milton Rd. SE24—57Rb 105
Milton Rd. SW14—55Ta 101
Milton Rd. SW19—65Eb 125
Milton Rd. W3—46Ta 79
Milton Rd. W7—45Ha 78
Milton Rd. Belv—49Cd 88
Milton Rd. Brtwd—21Yd 50
Milton Rd. Cat—93Tb 181
Milton Rd. Croy—73Tb 147
Milton Rd. Egh—64B 118
Milton Rd. Grav—8E 114
Milton Rd. Grays—50De 91
Milton Rd. Hmptn—66Ca 121
Milton Rd. Harr—28Ga 38
Milton Rd. Mitc—66Jb 126
Milton Rd. Romf—30Jd 48
Milton Rd. Sev—93Gd 186
Milton Rd. Slou—2H 73
Milton Rd. Sutt—76Cb 145
Milton Rd. Swans—59Ae 113
Milton Rd. Uxb—35R 56
Milton Rd. Wall—79Lb 146
Milton Rd. W on T—76Z 141
Milton Rd. Well—53Vc 109
Milton Rd. Wey—79J 139
Milton St. EC2—43Tb 83 (7F 195)
Milton St. Swans—58Zd 113
Milton St. Wal A—6Ec 12
Milton St. Wat—11X 19
Milton Way. W Dray—49P 75
Milverton Dri. Uxb—35S 56
Milverton Gdns. Ilf—33Vc 67
Milverton Rd. NW6—38Ya 60
Milverton St. SE11 —50Qb 82 (7A 206)
Milverton Way. SE9—63Qc 130
Milward St. E1—43Xb 84
Milward Wlk. SE18—51Qc 108
Mimms Hall Rd. Pot B—4Za 8
Mimms Hall Rd. Pot B—3Za 8
Mimms La. Shen, Rad & Pot B —5Ja 7
Mimosa Clo. Brtwd—15Xd 32
Mimosa Clo. Orp—75Yc 151
Mimosa Clo. Romf—24Ld 49
Mimosa Rd. Hay—43Y 77
Mimosa St. SW6—53Bb 103
Mina Av. Slou—7P 73
Minard Rd. SE6—59Gc 107
Mina Rd. SE17—50Ub 83 (7J 207)
Mina Rd. SW19—67Cb 125
Minchenden Cres. N14—20Mb 24
Minchin Clo. Lea—94Ja 176
Mincing La. EC3—45Ub 83 (4H 201)
Minden Rd. SE20—67Xb 127
Minehead Rd. SW16—64Pb 126
Minehead Rd. Harr—34Ca 57
Mineral St. SE18—49Uc 86
Minera M. SW1—49Jb 82 (5J 203)
Minerva Dri. Wat—8U 4
Minerva Rd. E4—24Dc 44
Minerva Rd. NW10—42Sa 79
Minerva Rd. King—68Pa 123
Minerva Rd. Sidc—63Uc 130
Minerva St. E2—40Xb 63
Minet Av. NW10—40Ua 60
Minet Dri. Hay—46W 76
Minet Gdns. NW10—40Ua 60
Minet Gdns. Hay—46X 77
Minet Rd. SW9—54Rb 105
Minford Gdns. W14—47Za 80
Mingard Wlk. N7—33Pb 62
Ming St. E14—45Cc 84
Miniver Pl. EC4—(4E 200)
Miniver St. SE1—(2C 206)
Mink Ct. Houn—54Y 99
Minniecroft Rd. Slou—1A 72
Minniedale. Surb—71Pa 143
Minnis, The. Long, Dart—76Be 155
Minnow Wlk. SE17 —49Ub 83 (6J 207)
Minorca Rd. Wey—77Q 140
Minories. EC3—44Vb 83 (3K 201)
Minshull St. SW8—53Mb 104
Minson Rd. E9—39Zb 64
Minstead Gdns. SW15—59Va 102
Minstead Way. N Mald—72Ua 144
Minster Av. Sutt—75Cb 145
Minster Dri. Croy—77Ub 147
Minster Gdns. E Mol—70Ba 121
Minsterley Av. Shep—70U 120
Minster Rd. NW2—36Ab 60
Minster Rd. Brom—66Kc 129
Minster Wlk. N8—28Nb 42
Minster Way. Horn—32Pd 69
Minster Way. Slou—47B 74
Minstrel Gdns. Surb—70Pa 123
Mintern Clo. N13—20Rb 25
Minterne Av. S'hall—49Ca 77
Minterne Rd. Harr—29Pa 39
Minterne Waye. Hay—44Y 77
Mintern St. N1—40Tb 63 (1G 195)
Mint La. Tad—100Cb 179
Minton M. NW6—37Db 61
Minton Rise. M'head—4A 72
Mint Rd. Bans—88Eb 163
Mint Rd. Wall—77Kb 146
Mint St. SE1—47Sb 83 (1D 206)
Mint Wlk. Croy—76Sb 147
Mint Wlk. Warl—89Zb 166
Mint Wlk. Wok—5B 188
Mirabel Rd. SW6—52Bb 103
Mirador Cres. Slou—5M 73
Miramar Way. Horn—36Md 69
Miranda Rd. N19—32Lb 62
Mirfield St. SE7—49Mc 85
Miriam Rd. SE18—50Uc 86
Mirrie La. Uxb—29E 34
Mirror Path. SE9—62Lc 129
Misbourne Av. Ger X—22A 34
Misbourne Clo. Ger X—22A 34
Misbourne Ct. Slou—49C 74
Misbourne Rd. Uxb—40Q 56
Misbourne Vale. Ger X—22A 34
Miskin Rd. Dart—59Ld 111
Miskin Way. Grav—5F 136
Missenden Gdns. Mord—72Eb 145
Mission Gro. E17—29Ac 44
Mission Pl. SE15—53Wb 105
Mission Sq. Bren—51Na 101
Mistletoe Clo. Croy—74Zb 148
Mitcham Garden Village. Mitc —71Jb 146
Mitcham La. SW16—65Kb 126
Mitcham Pk. Mitc—70Gb 125
Mitcham Rd. E6—41Nc 86
Mitcham Rd. SW17—64Hb 125
Mitcham Rd. Croy—72Nb 146
Mitcham Rd. Ilf—31Vc 67
Mitchell Av. Grav—61Fe 135
Mitchell Clo. SE2—49Yc 87
Mitchell Clo. Dart—61Nd 133
Mitchell Rd. N13—22Sb 43
Mitchell Rd. Orp—77Vc 151
Mitchell St. EC1—42Sb 83 (5D 194)
Mitchell Wlk. E6—43Nc 86
Mitchell Wlk. Swans—59Ae 113
Mitchell Way. NW10—37Sa 59
Mitchell Way. Brom—67Jc 129
Mitchison Rd. N1—37Tb 63
Mitchley Av. Purl & S Croy —85Tb 165
Mitchley Gro. S Croy—85Wb 165
Mitchley Hill. S Croy—85Vb 165
Mitchley Rd. N17—27Wb 43
Mitchley View. S Croy—85Wb 165
Mitford Rd. N19—33Nb 62
Mitre Clo. Sutt—80Eb 145
Mitre Ct. EC2—(2E 200)
Mitre Rd. E15—40Gc 65
Mitre Rd. SE1—47Qb 82 (1A 206)
Mitre Sq. EC3—44Ub 83 (3J 201)
Mitre St. EC3—44Ub 83 (3J 201)
Mitre, The. E14—45Bc 84
Mixbury Gro. Wey—79T 140
Mixnams La. Cher—69J 119
Mizen Clo. Cob—86Z 159
Mizen Way. Cob—87Y 159
Moat Clo. Bush, Wat—15Da 19
Moat Ct. Asht—89Na 161
Moat Cres. N3—27Db 41
Moat Dri. E13—40Lc 65
Moat Dri. Harr—28Ea 38
Moat Dri. Ruis—31U 56
Moat Dri. Slou—3N 73
Moat Farm Rd. N'holt—37Ba 57
Moatfield Rd. Bush, Wat—15Da 19
Moat La. Eri—53Jd 110
Moat Pl. SW9—55Pb 104
Moat Pl. W3—44Ra 79
Moatside. Enf—14Zb 26
Moatside. Felt—63Y 121
Moat, The. N Mald—67Ua 124
Moberley Rd. SW4—59Mb 104
Modbury Gdns. NW5—37Jb 62
Modder Pl. SW15—56Za 102
Model Bldgs. WC1—(4J 193)
Model Cotts. SW14—56Sa 101
Model Cotts. W13—47Ka 78
Model Farm Clo. SE9—62Nc 130
Modern Ct. EC4—(2B 200)
Moelwyn Hughes Ct. N7—36Mb 62
Moelyn M. Harr—29Ja 38
Moffat Gdns. Mitc—69Gb 125
Moffat Rd. N13—23Nb 42
Moffat Rd. SW17—63Hb 125
Moffat Rd. T Hth—68Sb 127
Mogador Rd. Tad—100Ab 178
Mogden La. Iswth—57Ha 100
Moiety Rd. E14—47Cc 84
Moira Clo. N17—26Ub 43
Moira Rd. SE9—56Pc 108
Moir Clo. S Croy—81Wb 165
Moland Mead. SE16—50Zb 84
Molash Rd. Orp—70Zc 131
Mole Abbey Gdns. E Mol —69Da 121
Mole Business Pk. Lea—93Ja 176
Mole Ct. Eps—77Sa 143
Molember Rd. E Mol—71Ga 142
Mole Rd. Lea—93Fa 176
Mole Rd. W on T—78Z 141
Molescroft. SE9—62Sc 130
Molesey Av. E Mol—71Ba 141
Molesey Clo. W on T—77Aa 141
Molesey Dri. Sutt—75Ab 144
Molesey Pk. Av. E Mol—71Da 141
Molesey Pk. Clo. E Mol—71Ea 142
Molesey Pk. Rd. E Mol—71Da 141
Molesey Rd. W on T & E Mol —78Z 141
Molesford Rd. SW6—53Cb 103
Molesham Clo. E Mol—69Da 121
Molesham Way. E Mol—69Da 121
Moles Hill. Lea—83Fa 160
Molesworth Rd. Cob—85W 158
Molesworth St. SE13—55Ec 106
Mole Valley Pl. Asht—91Ma 177
Moliner Ct. Beck—66Cc 128
Mollands La. S Ock—42Yd 90
Mollison Av. Enf—14Ac 26
Mollison Dri. Wall—80Mb 146
Mollison Way. Edgw—26Pa 39
Molteno Rd. Wat—11W 18
Molyneux Rd. Wey—78Q 140
Molyneux St. W1 —43Gb 81 (1E 196)
Monahan Av. Purl—84Pb 164
Monarch Clo. Felt—59U 98
Monarch Clo. Til—4D 114
Monarch Clo. W Wick—77Hc 149
Monarch Rd. Belv—48Cd 88
Monarchs Way. Ruis—32U 56
Monarchs Way. Wal X—5Ac 12
Mona Rd. SE15—54Yb 106
Monastery Gdns. Enf—12Tb 25
Mona St. E16—43Hc 85
Monaveen Gdns. E Mol—69Da 121
Monck St. SW1—48Mb 82 (4E 204)
Monclar Rd. SE5—56Tb 105
Moncorvo Clo. SW7 —47Gb 81 (2D 202)
Moncrieff Clo. E6—44Nc 86
Moncrieff St. SE15—54Wb 105
Monega Rd.—37Lc 65
E7 1-203 & 2-204
E12 remainder
Money Av. Cat—94Ub 181
Money Hill Rd. Rick—18L 17
Money La. W Dray—48M 75
Money Rd. Cat—94Tb 181
Mongers La. Eps—82Va 162
Monica James Ho. Sidc —62Wc 131
Monical Clo. Wat—12Y 19
Monier Rd. E3—38Cc 64
Monivea Rd. Beck—66Bc 128
Monkchester Clo. Lou—11Pc 28
Monk Dri. E16—45Jc 85
Monkfrith Av. N14—16Kb 24
Monkfrith Clo. N14—17Kb 24
Monkfrith Way. N14—17Jb 24
Monkham's Av. Wfd G—22Kc 45
Monkham's Dri. Wfd G—22Kc 45
Monkham's La. Buck H—20Kc 27
Monkham's La. Wfd G—21Kc 45
Monkleigh Rd. Mord—69Ab 124
Monks Av. Barn—16Eb 23
Monks Av. E Mol—71Ba 141
Monks Chase. Brtwd—22Ee 51
Monks Clo. SE2—49Zc 87
Monks Clo. Enf—12Sb 25
Monks Clo. Ruis—35Z 57
Monks Cres. W on T—74X 141
Monksdene Gdns. Sutt—76Db 145
Monks Dri. W3—43Qa 79
Monksfield Way. Slou—1E 72
Monks Grn. Lea—93Ea 176
Monksgrove. Lou—15Qc 28
Monks Haven. Stanf—1N 93
Monksmead. Borwd—14Sa 21
Monks Orchard. Dart—61Md 133
Monks Orchard Rd. Beck —74Cc 148
Monks Pk. Wemb—37Ra 59
Monks Pk. Gdns. Wemb—38Ra 59
Monks Pl. Cat—94Xb 181
Monks Rd. Bans—89Cb 163
Monks Rd. Enf—12Sb 25
Monks Rd. Vir W—10P 117
Monks Rd. Wind—4B 94
Monk St. SE18—49Qc 86
Monks Wlk. Grav—65Ce 135
Monks Way. NW11—28Bb 41
Monks Way. Beck—72Cc 148
Monks Way. Orp—75Sc 150
Monks Way. Stai—66M 119
Monks Way. W Dray—51N 97
Monkswell La. Coul—96Db 179
Monkswood Av. Wal A—5Fc 13
Monkswood Gdns. Borwd —15Ta 21
Monkswood Gdns. Ilf—27Qc 46
★Monkton Rd. Sev—92Be
Monkton Rd. Well—54Vc 109
Monkton St. SE11 —49Qb 82 (5A 206)
Monkville Av. NW11—28Bb 41
Monkwell Sq. EC2 —43Sb 83 (1E 200)
Monmouth Av. E18—27Kc 45
Monmouth Av. King—66La 122
Monmouth Clo. Mitc—70Nb 126
Monmouth Clo. Well—56Wc 109
Monmouth Rd. E6—41Pc 86
Monmouth Rd. N9—19Xb 25
Monmouth Rd. W2—44Cb 81
Monmouth Rd. Dag—36Bd 67
Monmouth Rd. Hay—49V 76
Monmouth Rd. Wat—13X 19
Monmouth St. WC2 —44Nb 82 (3F 199)
Monnery Rd. N19—34Lb 62
Monnow Grn. S Ock—45Sd 90
Monnow Rd. SE1—49Wb 83
Monnow Rd. S Ock—45Sd 90
Monnow Ter. Wok—6D 188
Mono La. Felt—61X 121
Monoux Gro. E17—25Cc 44
Monpelier Rd. Purl—82Rb 165
Monroe Cres. Enf—11Xb 25
Monroe Dri. SW14—57Ra 101
Monro Gdns. Harr—24Ga 38
Monsell Gdns. Stai—64G 118
Monsell Rd. N4—34Rb 63
Monson Rd. NW10—40Wa 60
Monson Rd. SE14—52Zb 106
Mons Way. Brom—72Nc 150
Montacute Rd. SE6—59Bc 106
Montacute Rd. Bush, Wat—17Ga 20
Montacute Rd. Croy—81Ec 166
Montacute Rd. Mord—72Fb 145
Montagu Cres. N18—21Xb 43
Montague Av. SE4—56Bc 106
Montague Av. W7—46Ha 78
Montague Av. S Croy—84Ub 165
Montague Clo. SE1 —46Tb 83 (6F 201)
Montague Clo. W on T—73W 140
Montague Gdns. W3—45Qa 79
Montague Pl. WC1 —43Mb 82 (7E 192)
Montague Rd. E8—36Wb 63
Montague Rd. E11—33Hc 65
Montague Rd. N8—29Pb 42
Montague Rd. N15—28Wb 43
Montague Rd. SW19—66Db 125
Montague Rd. W7—47Ha 78
Montague Rd. W13—44Ka 78
Montague Rd. Croy—74Rb 147
Montague Rd. Houn—55Da 99
Montague Rd. Rich—58Na 101
Montague Rd. Slou—5K 73
Montague Rd. S'hall—49Aa 77
Montague Rd. Swan—70Hd 132
Montague Rd. Uxb—38M 55
Montague Sq. SE15—52Yb 106
Montague St. WC1 —43Nb 82 (7F 193)
Montague Waye. S'hall—48Aa 77
Montagu Gdns. N18—21Xb 43
Montagu Gdns. Wall—77Lb 146
Montagu Mans. W1 —43Hb 81 (7G 191)
Montagu M. N. W1 —43Hb 81 (1G 197)
Montagu M. S. W1 —44Hb 81 (2G 197)
Montagu M. W. W1 —44Hb 81 (2G 197)
Montagu Pl. W1—43Hb 81 (1F 197)
Montagu Rd.—22Xb 43
N18 1-219 & 2-228
N9 remainder
Montagu Rd. NW4—30Wa 40
Montagu Rd. Slou—3M 95
Montagu Row. W1 —43Hb 81 (1G 197)
Montagu Sq. W1 —43Hb 81 (1G 197)
Montagu St. W1—44Hb 81 (2G 197)
Montalt Rd. Wfd G—22Hc 45
Montana Clo. S Croy—82Tb 165
Montana Rd. SW17—62Jb 126
Montana Rd. SW20—67Ya 124
Montayne Rd. Wal X—4Zb 12
Montbelle Rd. SE9—62Rc 130
Montcalm Clo. Brom—72Jc 149
Montcalm Clo. Hay—41X 77
Montcalm Rd. SE7—52Mc 107
Montclare St. E2 —42Vb 83 (5K 195)
Monteagle Av. Bark—37Sc 66
Monteagle Ct. N1 —40Ub 63 (1J 195)
Monteagle Way. E5—34Wb 63
Monteagle Way. SE15—55Xb 105
Montefiore St. SW8—54Kb 104
Monteith Rd. E3—39Bc 64
Montem La. Slou—6H 73
Montem Rd. SE23—59Bc 106
Montem Rd. N Mald—70Ua 124
Montem St. N4—32Pb 62
Montenotte Rd. N8—29Lb 42
Monterey Clo. Bex—61Ed 132
Montesole Ct. Pinn—26Y 37
Montford Pl. SE11—50Qb 82
Montford Rd. Sun—70W 120
Montfort Gdns. Ilf—23Sc 46
Montfort Pl. SW19—60Za 102
Montfort Rd. Sev—89Nd 171
Montgolfier Wlk. N'holt—41Aa 77
Montgomery Av. Esh—75Ga 142
Montgomery Clo. Grays—47Ee 91
Montgomery Clo. Mitc—70Nb 126
Montgomery Clo. Sidc—58Vc 109
Montgomery Cres. Romf—22Ld 49
Montgomery Rd. W4—49Sa 79
Montgomery Rd. Edgw—23Pa 39
Montgomery Rd. S Dar, Dart —67Td 134
Montholme Rd. SW11—58Hb 103
Monthope Rd. E1—43Wb 83
Montolieu Gdns. SW15—57Xa 102
Montpelier. Wind—4G 94
Montpelier Av. W5—43La 78
Montpelier Av. Bex—59Zc 109
Montpelier Clo. Uxb—39Q 56
Montpelier Gdns. E6—41Mc 85
Montpelier Gdns. Romf—31Yc 67
Montpelier Gro. NW5—36Lb 62
Montpelier M. SW7 —48Gb 81 (3E 202)
Montpelier Pl. SW7 —48Gb 81 (3E 202)
Montpelier Rise. NW11—31Ab 60
Montpelier Rise. Wemb—32Ma 59
Montpelier Rd. N3—25Eb 41
Montpelier Rd. SE15—53Xb 105
Montpelier Rd. W5—43Ma 79
Montpelier Rd. Sutt—77Eb 145
Montpelier Row. SE3—54Hc 107
Montpelier Row. Twic—59La 100
Montpelier Sq. SW7 —47Gb 81 (2E 202)
Montpelier St. SW7 —48Gb 81 (3E 202)
Montpelier Ter. SW7 —47Gb 81 (2E 202)
Montpelier Vale. SE3—54Hc 107
Montpelier Wlk. SW7 —48Gb 81 (3E 202)
Montpelier Way. NW11—31Ab 60
Montrave Rd. SE20—65Yb 128
Montreal Pl. WC2 —45Pb 82 (4H 199)
Montreal Rd. Ilf—31Sc 66
Montreal Rd. Sev—95Gd 186
Montreal Rd. Til—5C 114
Montrell Rd. SW2—60Nb 104
Montrose Av. NW6—40Ab 60
Montrose Av. Edgw—26Sa 39
Montrose Av. Romf—26Ld 49
Montrose Av. Sidc—59Wc 109
Montrose Av. Slou—4F 72
Montrose Av. Slou—2N 95
(Datchet)
Montrose Av. Twic—59Da 99
Montrose Av. Well—55Tc 108
Montrose Clo. Ashf—65S 120
Montrose Clo. Well—55Vc 109
Montrose Clo. Wfd G—21Jc 45
Montrose Ct. SW7 —47Fb 81 (2C 202)
Montrose Cres. N12—23Eb 41
Montrose Cres. Wemb—37Na 59
Montrose Gdns. Lea—84Fa 160
Montrose Gdns. Mitc—68Hb 125
Montrose Gdns. Sutt—75Db 145
Montrose Pl. SW1 —47Jb 82 (2J 203)
Montrose Rd. Felt—58T 98
Montrose Rd. Harr—26Ga 38
Montrose Wlk. Wey—76R 140
Montrose Way. SE23—60Zb 106
Montrose Way. Slou—3P 95
Montrouge Cres. Eps—88Ya 162
Montserrat Av. Wfd G—24Fc 45
Montserrat Clo. SE19—64Tb 127
Montserrat Rd. SW15—56Ab 102
Monument Grn. Wey—76R 140
Monument Hill. Wey—77R 140
Monument La. Ger X—23A 34
Monument Rd. Wey—77R 140
Monument Rd. Wok—86C 156
Monument St. EC3 —45Tb 83 (4G 201)
Monument Way. N17—27Vb 43
Monument Way E. Wok—87D 156
Monument Way W. Wok—87C 156
Monza St. E1—45Yb 84
Moodkee St. SE16—48Yb 84
Moody St. E1—41Zb 84
Moon La. Barn—13Bb 23
Moon St. N1—39Rb 63
Moorcroft La. Uxb—43Q 76
Moorcroft Rd. SW16—62Nb 126
Moorcroft Way. Pinn—29Aa 37
Moordown. SE18—53Rc 108
Moore Av. Til—4D 114
Moore Clo. SW14—55Sa 101
Moore Clo. Mitc—68Kb 126
Moore Clo. Wall—80Nb 146
Moore Clo. Wey—78K 139
Moore Cres. Dag—39Xc 67
Moore Gro. Cres. Egh—66A 118
Moorehead Way. SE3—55Kc 107
Mooreland Rd. Brom—66Hc 129
Moor End Rd. Twic—58Ja 100
Moore Pk. Rd. SW6—52Db 103
Moore Rd. SE19—65Sb 127
Moore Rd. Swans—58Ae 113
★Moorescroft. Brtwd—9Ud
Moores La. Wind—9D 72
Moore's Pl. Brtwd—19Zd 33
Moore St. SW3—49Hb 81 (5F 203)
Moore Wlk. E7—35Jc 65
Moorey Clo. E15—39Hc 65
Moorfield Av. W5—42Ma 79
Moorfield Rd. N17—26Vb 43
Moorfield Rd. Chess—78Na 143
Moorfield Rd. Enf—11Yb 26
Moorfield Rd. Orp—73Wc 151
Moorfield Rd. Uxb—31J 55
(Denham)
Moorfield Rd. Uxb—44M 75
Moorfields. EC2—43Tb 83 (1F 201)
Moorfields Clo. Stai—67G 118
Moorfields Highwalk. EC2 —(1F 201)
Moorgate. EC2—44Tb 83 (2F 201)
Moorgate Pl. EC2—(2F 201)
Moorhall Rd. Uxb—30K 35
Moorhayes Dri. Stai—69L 119
Moor Hill La. St Alb—1Ga 6
Moorholme. Wok—91A 172
Moorhouse Rd. W2—44Cb 81
Moorhouse Rd. Harr—27Ma 39
Moorhouse Rd. West—100Qc 184
Moorhurst Av. Wal X—1Qb 10
Moorland Clo. Romf—24Dd 48
Moorland Clo. Twic—59Ca 99
Moorland Rd. SW9—56Rb 105
Moorland Rd. W Dray—51L 97
Moorlands Av. NW7—23Xa 40
Moorlands, The. Wok—93B 172
Moor La. EC2—43Tb 83 (1F 201)
Moor La. Chess—77Na 143
Moor La. Rick—8G 2
(Sarratt)
Moor La. Rick—18P 17
Moor La. Stai—61F 118
Moor La. Upm—32Ud 70
Moor La. W Dray—51L 97
Moor La. Wok—94A 172
Moor La. Crossing. Wat—17S 18
Moormead Dri. Eps—78Ua 144
Moormede Cres. Stai—63H 119
Moor Pk. Rd. N'wd—23T 36
Moor Pl. EC2—43Tb 83 (1F 201)
Moor Rd. Sev—92Kd 187
Moorside Rd. Brom—62Gc 129
Moorsom Way. Coul—89Mb 164
Moor St. W1—44Mb 82 (3E 198)
Moortown Rd. Wat—21Y 37
Moor View. Wat—16W 18
Moot Ct. NW9—29Qa 39
Morant Gdns. Romf—22Dd 48
Morant Pl. N22—25Pb 42
Morant Rd. Grays—8D 92
Morants Ct. Rd. Sev—90Ed 170
Morant St. E14—45Cc 84
Mora Rd. NW2—35Ya 60
Mora St. EC1—41Sb 83 (4E 194)
Morat St. SW9—53Pb 104
Moravian Pl. SW10—51Fb 103
Moravian St. E2—41Yb 84
Moray Av. Hay—46V 76
Moray Clo. Romf—24Gd 48
Moray M. N7—33Pb 62
Moray Rd. N4—33Pb 62
Moray Way. Romf—24Fd 48
Mordaunt Gdns. Dag—38Ad 67
Mordaunt Rd. NW10—39Ta 59
Mordaunt St. SW9—55Pb 104
Morden Clo. Tad—92Za 178
Morden Ct. Mord—70Db 125
Morden Gdns. Gnfd—36Ha 58
Morden Gdns. Mitc—70Fb 125
Morden Hall Rd. Mord—69Db 125
Morden Hill. SE13—54Ec 106
Morden La. SE13—53Ec 106
Morden Rd. SE3—54Jc 107
Morden Rd. SW19—67Db 125
Morden Rd. Mord & Mitc —70Eb 125
Morden Rd. Romf—31Ad 67
Morden Rd. M. SE3—54Jc 107
Morden St. SE13—53Dc 106
Morden Way. Sutt—73Cb 145
Morden Wharf Rd. SE10—48Gc 85
Mordon Rd. Ilf—31Vc 67
Mordred Rd. SE6—61Gc 129
Moreau Wlk. Slou—44A 74
More Av. Grays—50Ae 91
Morecambe Clo. E1—43Zb 84
Morecambe Clo. Horn—36Kd 69
Morecambe Gdns. Stan—21Ma 39
Morecambe St. SE17 —50Sb 83 (6E 206)
Morecambe Ter. N18—21Tb 43
More Clo. E16—44Hc 85
More Clo. W14—49Za 80
More Clo. Purl—83Qb 164
Morecoombe Clo. King—66Ra 123
Moree Way. N18—21Wb 43
Moreland Av. Grays—47Ee 91
Moreland Av. Slou—52E 96
Moreland Clo. NW11—32Db 61
Moreland Dri. Ger X—31B 54
Moreland St. EC1 —41Rb 83 (3C 194)
Moreland Way. E4—20Ec 26
More La. Esh—76Da 141
Morella Clo. Vir W—10P 117
Morella Rd. SW12—59Hb 103
Morello Av. Uxb—43R 76
Moremead Rd. SE6—63Bc 128
Morena St. SE6—59Dc 106
Moresby Av. Surb—73Ra 143
Moresby Rd. E5—32Xb 63
Moresby Wlk. SW8—54Lb 104
Mores La. Brtwd—14Sd 32
Moretaine Rd. Ashf—62M 119
Moreton Av. Iswth—53Ga 100
Moreton Clo. E5—33Xb 63
Moreton Clo. N15—30Tb 43
Moreton Clo. Swan—68Gd 132
Moreton Gdns. Wfd G—22Nc 46
Moreton Pl. SW1 —50Lb 82 (7C 204)
Moreton Rd. N15—30Tb 43
Moreton Rd. S Croy—78Tb 147
Moreton Rd. Wor Pk—75Wa 144
Moreton St. SW1 —50Lb 82 (7C 204)
Moreton Ter. SW1 —50Lb 82 (7C 204)
Moreton Ter. M. N. SW1 —50Lb 82 (7C 204)
Moreton Ter. M. S. SW1 —50Lb 82 (7C 204)
Moreton Way. Slou—6B 72
Morewood Clo. Sev—95Hd 186
Morford Clo. Ruis—31X 57
Morford Way. Ruis—31X 57
Morgan Av. E17—28Cc 45
Morgan Clo. Dag—38Cd 68
Morgan Clo. N'wd—23V 36
Morgan Cres. Epp—8Tc 14
Morgan Dri. Grnh—59Ud 112
Morgan Rd. N7—36Qb 62
Morgan Rd. W10—43Bb 81
Morgan Rd. Brom—66Jc 129
Morgan's La. SE1 —46Ub 83 (7H 201)
Morgan's La. Hay—43T 76
Morgan St. E3—41Ac 84
Morgan St. E16—43Hc 85
Morgan Way. Rain—41Ld 89
Morgan Way. Wfd G—23Nc 46
Morie St. SW18—57Db 103

Morieux Rd.—Navarino Gro.

Morieux Rd. E10—32Bc 64
Moring Rd. SW17—63Jb 126
Morkyns Wlk. SE21—62Ub 127
Morland Av. Croy—74Ub 147
Morland Clo. Hmptn—64Ba 121
Morland Gdns. NW10—38Ta 59
Morland Gdns. S'hall—46Da 77
Morland M. N1—38Qb 62
Morland Rd. E17—29Zb 44
Morland Rd. SE20—65Zb 128
Morland Rd. Croy—74Ub 147
Morland Rd. Dag—38Cd 68
Morland Rd. Dart—57Kd 111
Morland Rd. Harr—29Na 39
Morland Rd. Ilf—33Rc 66
Morland Rd. Sutt—78Eb 145
Morland Way. Wal X—1Ac 12
Morley Av. E4—24Fc 45
Morley Av. N18—21Wb 43
Morley Av. N22—26Qb 42
Morley Clo. Orp—75Rc 150
Morley Clo. Ruis—33Y 57
Morley Clo. Slou—47B 74
Morley Ct. Brom—70Hc 129
Morley Cres. Edgw—19Sa 21
Morley Cres. E. Stan—26La 38
Morley Cres. W. Stan—27La 38
Morley Hill. Enf—10Tb 11
Morley Ho. N16—33Wb 63
Morley Rd. E10—32Ec 64
Morley Rd. E15—40Hc 65
Morley Rd. SE13—56Ec 106
Morley Rd. Bark—39Tc 66
Morley Rd. Chst—67Sc 130
Morley Rd. Romf—29Ad 47
Morley Rd. S Croy—82Vb 165
Morley Rd. Sutt—74Bb 145
Morley Rd. Twic—58Ma 101
Morley Sq. Grays—9C 92
Morley St. SE1—48Qb 82 (3A 206)
Mormead. Wal A—5Fc 13
Morna Rd. SE5—54Sb 105
Morning La. E9—37Yb 64
Morning Rise. Rick—13M 17
Morningside Rd. Wor Pk
—75Ya 144
Mornington Av. W14—49Bb 81
Mornington Av. Brom—69Lc 129
Mornington Av. Ilf—31Qc 66
Mornington Clo. Wfd G—21Jc 45
Mornington Ct. Bex—60Fd 110
Mornington Cres. NW1
—40Lb 62 (1B 192)
Mornington Cres. Houn—53X 99
Mornington Gro. E3—41Cc 84
Mornington M. SE5—53Sb 105
Mornington Pl. NW1
—40Lb 62 (1B 192)
Mornington Rd. E4—17Fc 27
Mornington Rd. E11—31Hc 65
Mornington Rd. SE8—52Bc 106
Mornington Rd. Ashf—64S 120
Mornington Rd. Gnfd—43Da 77
Mornington Rd. Lou—13Sc 28
Mornington Rd. Rad—6Ka 6
Mornington Rd. Wfd G—21Hc 45
Mornington St. NW1
—40Kb 62 (1A 192)
Mornington Ter. NW1
—40Kb 62 (1A 192)
Mornington Wlk. Rich—63La 122
Morocco St. SE1
—47Ub 83 (2H 207)
Morpeth Av. Borwd—10Pa 7
Morpeth Gro. E9—39Zb 64
Morpeth Rd. E9—39Zb 64
Morpeth St. E2—41Zb 84
Morpeth Ter. SW1
—48Lb 82 (4B 204)
Morpeth Wlk. N17—24Xb 43
Morrab Gdns. Ilf—34Vc 67
Morrell Clo. Barn—13Eb 23
Morrice Clo. Slou—49B 74
Morris Av. E12—36Pc 66
Morris Clo. Ger X—25B 34
Morris Clo. Orp—76Uc 150
Morris Ct. Wal A—6Hc 13
Morris Gdns. SW18—59Cb 103
Morris Gdns. Dart—57Qd 111
Morrish Rd. SW2—59Nb 104
Morrison Av. N17—27Ub 43
Morrison Rd. Bark—40Ad 67
Morrison Rd. Hay—41X 77
Morrison St. SW11—55Jb 104
Morris Pl. N4—33Qb 62
Morris Rd. E14—43Dc 84
Morris Rd. E15—35Gc 65
Morris Rd. Dag—33Bd 67
Morris Rd. Iswth—55Ha 100
Morris Rd. Romf—24Kd 49
Morris St. E1—44Xb 83
Morriston Clo. Wat—22Y 37
Morse Clo. E13—41Jc 85
Morshead Rd. W9—41Cb 81
Morston Gdns. SE9—63Pc 130
Morten Clo. SW4—58Mb 104
Morten Gdns. Uxb—31J 55
Morteyne Rd. N17—25Tb 43
Mortham St. E15—39Gc 65
Mortimer Clo. NW2—33Bb 61
Mortimer Clo. SW16—61Mb 126
Mortimer Clo. Bush, Wat—16Da 19
Mortimer Cres. NW6—39Db 61
Mortimer Cres. Wor Pk—76Ta 143
Mortimer Mkt. WC1
—42Lb 82 (6C 192)
Mortimer Pl. NW6—39Db 61
Mortimer Rd. E6—41Pc 86
Mortimer Rd. N1—38Ub 63
Mortimer Rd. NW10—41Ya 80
Mortimer Rd. W13—44La 78
Mortimer Rd. Eri—51Fd 110
Mortimer Rd. Mitc—67Hb 125
Mortimer Rd. Orp—74Wc 151
Mortimer Rd. Slou—8P 73
Mortimer Rd. West—84Lc 167
Mortimer Sq. W11—45Za 80
Mortimer St. W1—43Lb 82 (2B 198)
Mortimer Ter. NW5—35Kb 62
Mortlake Clo. Croy—76Nb 146
Mortlake High St. SW14
—55Ta 101
Mortlake Rd. E16—44Kc 85
Mortlake Rd. Ilf—35Sc 66
Mortlake Rd. Rich—52Qa 101
Mortlock Clo. SE15—53Xb 105
Mortlock Ct. E12—35Mc 65
Morton Clo. Wok—3G 188
Morton Cres. N14—21Mb 42
Morton Dri. Slou—6C 52
Morton Gdns. Wall—78Lb 146
Morton Pl. SE1—48Qb 82 (4K 205)
Morton Rd. E15—38Hc 65
Morton Rd. N1—38Sb 63
Morton Rd. Mord—71Fb 145
Morton Rd. Wok—3G 188
Morton Way. N14—20Lb 24
Morvale Clo. Belv—49Bd 87
Morval Rd. SW2—57Qb 104
Morven Clo. Pot B—3Eb 9
Morven Rd. SW17—62Hb 125
Morville St. E3—40Cc 64
Morwell St. WC1
—43Mb 82 (1D 198)
Mosbach Gdns. Brtwd—19De 33
Moscow Pl. W2—45Db 81
Moscow Rd. W2—45Cb 81
Moselle Av. N22—26Qb 42
Moselle Clo. N8—27Pb 42
Moselle Rd. West—90Nc 168
Moselle St. N17—24Vb 43
Mospey Cres. Eps—87Va 162
Mossborough Clo. N12—23Db 41
Mossbury Rd. SW11—55Gb 103
Moss Clo. E1—43Wb 83
Moss Clo. Pinn—26Ba 37
Moss Clo. Rick—19M 17
Mossdown Clo. Belv—49Cd 88
Mossenden Clo. Uxb—25M 35
Mossfield. Cob—85W 158
Mossford Ct. Ilf—27Rc 46
Mossford Grn. Ilf—27Rc 46
Mossford La. Ilf—26Rc 46
Mossford St. E3—42Bc 84
Moss Gdns. S Croy—80Zb 148
Moss Hall Cres. N12—23Db 41
Moss Hall Gro. N12—23Db 41
Mossington Gdns. SE16—49Yb 84
Moss La. Pinn—25Aa 37
Moss La. Romf—30Hd 48
Mosslea Rd. SE20—65Yb 128
Mosslea Rd. Brom—71Mc 149
Mosslea Rd. Orp—76Sc 150
Mosslea Rd. Whyt—88Vb 165
Mossop St. SW3—49Gb 81 (5E 202)
Moss Rd. Dag—38Cd 68
Moss Rd. S Ock—43Yd 90
Moss Rd. Wat—6X 5
Moss Side. St Alb—2Ba 5
Mossville Gdns. Mord—69Bb 125
Moston Clo. Hay—50V 76
Mostyn Av. Wemb—36Pa 59
Mostyn Gdns. NW10—41Za 80
Mostyn Gro. E3—40Cc 64
Mostyn Rd. SW9—53Qb 104
Mostyn Rd. SW19—67Bb 125
Mostyn Rd. Bush, Wat—15Ea 20
Mostyn Rd. Edgw—24Ua 40
Mosul Way. Brom—72Nc 150
Mosyer Dri. Orp—75Zc 151
Motcomb St. SW1
—48Jb 82 (3H 203)
Motherwell Way. Grays—50Wd 90
Motley Av. EC2—(5H 195)
Motspur Pk. N Mald—72Va 144
Mottingham Gdns. SE9—60Mc 107
Mottingham La.—60Lc 107
SE12 2-48
SE9 remainder
Mottingham Rd. N9—16Zb 26
Mottingham Rd. SE9—61Nc 130
Mottisfont Rd. SE2—48Wc 87
Motts Hill La. Tad—95Wa 178
Mott St. E4 & Lou—10Fc 13
Mouchotte Clo. West—84Kc 167
Moulins Rd. E9—38Zb 64
Moultain Hill. Swan—70Jd 132
Moulton Av. Houn—54Aa 99
Moultrie Way. Upm—31Ud 70
Moundfield Rd. N16—30Wb 43
Mound, The. SE9—62Qc 130
Mountacre Clo. SE26—63Wb 127
Mt. Adon Pk. SE22—59Wb 105
Mountague Pl. E14—45Ec 84
Mt. Angelus Rd. SW15—59Va 102
Mt. Ararat Rd. Rich—57Na 101
Mt. Ash Rd. SE26—62Xb 127
Mount Av. E4—20Cc 26
Mount Av. W5—43La 78
Mount Av. Brtwd—17De 33
Mount Av. Cat—96Sb 181
Mount Av. Romf—23Sd 50
Mount Av. S'hall—44Ca 77
Mountbatten Clo. SE18—51Uc 108
Mountbatten Clo. SE19—64Ub 127
Mountbatten Clo. Slou—8L 73
Mountbatten M. SW18—59Eb 103
Mountbatten Sq. Wind—3G 94
Mountbel Rd. Stan—26Ja 38
Mount Clo. W5—43La 78
Mount Clo. Barn—14Jb 24
Mount Clo. Brom—67Nc 130
Mount Clo. Cars—81Jb 164
Mount Clo. Kenl—88Tb 165
Mount Clo. Lea—95Ga 176
Mount Clo. Sev—95Hd 186
Mount Clo. Wok—9F 188
Mountcombe Clo. Surb—73Na 143
Mount Cotts. Slou—5G 52
Mount Ct. W Wick—75Gc 149
Mount Cres. Brtwd—21Zd 51
Mt. Culver Av. Sidc—65Zc 131
Mount Dri. Bexh—57Ad 109
Mount Dri. Harr—29Ba 37
Mount Dri. Wemb—33Sa 59
Mountearl Gdns. SW16—62Pb 126
Mt. Echo Av. E4—18Dc 26
Mt. Echo Dri. E4—18Dc 26
Mt. Ephraim La. SW16—62Mb 126
Mt. Ephraim Rd. SW16—62Mb 126
Mt. Felix. W on T—73V 140
★Mountfield. Sev—92Ce
Mountfield Clo. Stanf—1N 93
Mountfield Rd. E6—40Qc 66
Mountfield Rd. N3—27Bb 41
(in two parts)
Mountfield Rd. W5—44Ma 79
Mountfield Way. Orp—70Yc 131
Mountfort Cres. N1—38Qb 62
Mountfort Ter. N1—38Qb 62
Mount Gdns. SE26—62Xb 127
Mt. Grace Rd. Pot B—3Cb 9
Mount Gro. Edgw—20Sa 21
Mountgrove Rd. N5—34Sb 63
Mt. Harry Rd. Sev—95Jd 186
Mt. Hermon Clo. Wok—90A 156
Mt. Hermon Rd. Wok—90A 156
Mt. Hermon Rd. Wok—7G 188
Mount Hill. Sev—89Wc 169
Mount Hill. Wind—1A 116
Mt. Hill La. Ger X—2M 53
Mounthurst Rd. Brom—73Hc 149
Mountjoy Clo. SE2—47Xc 87
Mt. Joy Ho. EC2—(1E 200)
Mount La. Uxb—33F 54
Mt. Lee. Egh—64B 118
Mt. Mills. EC1—41Rb 83 (4C 194)
Mountnessing By-Pass. Brtwd
—13Fe 33
Mountnessing La. Brtwd—11Zd 33
★Mountnessing La. Brtwd—9Ae
★Mountnessing Rd. Ing & Brtwd
—5Be
Mt. Nod Rd. SW16—62Pb 126
Mt. Olive Ct. W7—47Ga 78
Mount Pk. Cars—81Jb 164
Mount Pk. Av. Harr—33Fa 58
Mount Pk. Av. S Croy—81Rb 165
Mount Pk. Cres. W5—44Ma 79
Mount Pk. Rd. W5—43Ma 79
Mount Pk. Rd. Harr—34Fa 58
Mount Pk. Rd. Pinn—29W 36
Mt. Pleasant. SE27—63Sb 127
Mt. Pleasant. WC1
—42Qb 82 (6K 193)
Mt. Pleasant. Barn—14Hb 23
Mt. Pleasant. Eps—82Va 162
Mt. Pleasant. Lea—100A 175
(Effingham)
Mt. Pleasant. Lea—100R 174
(West Horsley)
Mt. Pleasant. Ruis—33Y 57
Mt. Pleasant. Uxb—25J 35
Mt. Pleasant. Wemb—39Na 59
Mt. Pleasant. West—89Mc 167
Mt. Pleasant. Wey—76Q 140
Mt. Pleasant Av. Brtwd—16Fe 33
Mt. Pleasant Cres. N4—31Pb 62
Mt. Pleasant Hill. E5—33Yb 64
Mt. Pleasant La. E5—33Xb 63
Mt. Pleasant La. St Alb—2Aa 5
Mt. Pleasant Rd. E17—26Ac 44
Mt. Pleasant Rd. N17—26Ub 43
Mt. Pleasant Rd. NW10—38Ya 60
Mt. Pleasant Rd. SE13—58Dc 106
Mt. Pleasant Rd. W5—42La 78
Mt. Pleasant Rd. Cat—95Wb 181
Mt. Pleasant Rd. Chig—21Tc 46
Mt. Pleasant Rd. Dart—58Pd 111
Mt. Pleasant Rd. N Mald
—69Sa 123
Mt. Pleasant Rd. Romf—23Fd 48
Mt. Pleasant Vs. N4—31Pb 62
Mt. Pleasant Wlk. Bex—57Ed 110
Mount Rd. NW2—34Ya 60
Mount Rd. NW4—30Wa 40
Mount Rd. SW19—61Cb 125
Mount Rd. Barn—15Gb 23
Mount Rd. Bexh—57Zc 109
Mount Rd. Chess—78Pa 143
Mount Rd. Chob—1E 188
Mount Rd. Dag—32Bd 67
Mount Rd. Dart—58Hd 110
Mount Rd. Epp—4Zc 15
Mount Rd. Felt—62Aa 121
Mount Rd. Hay—47W 76
Mount Rd. Ilf—36Rc 66
Mount Rd. Mitc—68Fb 125
Mount Rd. N Mald—69Ta 123
Mount Rd. Wok—9E 188
Mount Row. W1—45Kb 82 (5K 197)
Mountsfield Clo. Stai—58J 97
Mountsfield Ct. SE13—58Fc 107
Mountside. Stan—25Ja 38
Mounts Pond Rd. SE3—54Fc 107
Mount Sq., The. NW3—34Eb 61
Mounts Rd. Grnh—57Xd 112
Mt. Stewart Av. Harr—31Ma 59
Mount St. W1—45Jb 82 (5H 197)
Mount, The. N20—19Eb 23
Mount, The. NW3—35Eb 61
Mount, The. Brtwd—20Yd 32
Mount, The. Coul—86Kb 164
Mount, The. Eps—82Va 162
Mount, The. Esh—79Ca 141
Mount, The. Lea—96Ga 176
Mount, The. N Mald—69Va 124
Mount, The. Pot B—2Db 9
Mount, The. Rick—16L 17
Mount, The. Romf—20Ld 31
Mount, The. Stanf—1P 93
Mount, The. Tad—98Bb 179
Mount, The. Wemb—33Sa 59
Mount, The. Wey—75U 140
Mount, The. Wok—6G 188
(Mount Hermon)
Mount, The. Wok—7D 188
(St John's)
Mount, The. Wor Pk—77Xa 144
Mt. Vernon. NW3—35Eb 61
Mount View. NW7—20Ta 21
Mount View. Enf—10Pb 10
Mount View. N'wd—23V 36
Mount View. Rick—18K 17
Mountview Ct. N15—28Rb 43
Mt. View Rd. E4—17Fc 27
Mt. View Rd. N4—31Nb 62
Mt. View Rd. NW9—29Ta 39
Mt. View Rd. Esh—80Ka 142
Mountview Rd. Orp—73Wc 151
Mount Vs. SE27—62Rb 127
Mount Way. Cars—81Jb 164
Mountway. Pot B—2Cb 9
Mount Wood. E Mol—69Da 121
Mountwood Clo. S Croy
—82Xb 165
Movers La. Bark—39Tc 66
Mowatt Clo. N19—33Mb 62
Mowbray Av. Wey—85N 157
Mowbray Pde. Edgw—21Qa 39
Mowbray Rd. NW6—38Ab 60
Mowbray Rd. SE19—67Vb 127
Mowbray Rd. Barn—15Eb 23
Mowbray Rd. Edgw—21Qa 39
Mowbray Rd. Rich—62La 122
Mowbrays Clo. Romf—25Ed 48
Mowbrays Rd. Romf—26Ed 48
Mowbrey Gdns. Lou—11Sc 28
Mowlem St. E2—40Xb 63
Mowlem Trading Est. N17
—24Yb 44
Mowll St. SW9—52Qb 104
Moxon Clo. E13—40Hc 65
Moxon St. W1—43Jb 82 (1H 197)
Moxon St. Barn—13Bb 23
Moye Clo. E2—40Wb 63
Moyers Rd. E10—31Ec 64
Moylan Rd. W6—51Ab 102
Moyne Ct. Wok—6C 188
Moyne Pl. NW10—40Qa 59
Moyser Rd. SW16—64Kb 126
Mozart St. W10—41Bb 81
Muchelney Rd. Mord—72Eb 145
Muckhatch La. Egh—69D 118
Muckingford Rd. Grays—9G 92
Mucking Wharf Rd. Stanf
—4L 93
Muddy La. Dart—59Rd 111
Muddy La. Slou—3J 73
Muggeridge Rd. Dag—35Dd 68
Muggins La. Grav—3L 137
Muirdown Av. SW14—56Ta 101
Muirfield. W3—44Ua 80
Muirfield Clo. Wat—22Y 37
Muirfield Grn. Wat—21X 37
Muirfield Rd. Wat—21X 37
Muirfield Rd. Wok—6D 188
Muirkirk Rd. SE6—60Ec 106
Muir Rd. E5—35Wb 63
Muir St. E16—46Pc 86
Mulberry Av. Stai—60N 97
Mulberry Av. Wind—5K 95
Mulberry Clo. E4—19Cc 26
Mulberry Clo. NW3—35Fb 61
Mulberry Clo. NW4—27Ya 40
Mulberry Clo. SW16—63Lb 126
Mulberry Clo. N'holt—40Aa 57
Mulberry Clo. Romf—28Ld 49
Mulberry Clo. St Alb—1Da 5
Mulberry Clo. Wey—76R 140
Mulberry Clo. Wok—86A 156
Mulberry Ct. Bark—38Vc 67
Mulberry Ct. Surb—73Ma 143
Mulberry Cres. Bren—52La 100
Mulberry Cres. W Dray—47Q 76
Mulberry Dri. Purf—49Pd 89
Mulberry Dri. Slou—50A 74
Mulberry Hill. Brtwd—17Be 33
Mulberry La. Croy—74Vb 147
Mulberry M. Wall—79Lb 146
Mulberry Pl. W6—50Wa 80
Mulberry Rd. Grav—2A 136
Mulberry St. E1—44Wb 83
Mulberry Trees. Shep—73T 140
Mulberry Wlk. SW3—51Fb 103
Mulberry Way. E18—26Kc 45
Mulberry Way. Belv—47Ed 88
Mulberry Way. Ilf—28Sc 46
Mulgrave Rd. NW10—35Va 60
Mulgrave Rd. SW6—51Bb 103
Mulgrave Rd. W5—42Ma 79
Mulgrave Rd. Croy—76Tb 147
Mulgrave Rd. Harr—33Ja 58
Mulgrave Rd. Sutt—80Bb 145
Mulgrave Way. Wok—6B 188
Mulholland Clo. Mitc—68Kb 126
Mulkern Rd. N19—32Mb 62
Mullein Ct. Grays—51Fe 113
Mullens Rd. Egh—64E 118
Muller Rd. SW4—58Mb 104
Mullins Path. SW14—55Ta 101
Mullion Clo. Harr—25Da 37
Mullion Wlk. Wat—21Z 37
Mulready St. NW8
—42Gb 81 (6D 190)
Multi Way. W3—47Ua 80
Multon Rd. SW18—59Fb 103
Multon Rd. Sev—79Ud 154
Mulvaney Way. SE1
—47Tb 83 (2G 207)
Mumford Ct. EC2
—44Sb 83 (2E 200)
Mumford Rd. SE24—57Rb 105
Muncaster Clo. Ashf—63Q 120
Muncaster Rd. SW11—57Hb 103
Muncaster Rd. Ashf—64R 120
Mundania Rd. SE22—58Xb 105
Munday Rd. E16—45Jc 85
Munden Dri. Wat—9Aa 5
Munden Gro. Wat—10Y 5
Munden St. W14—49Ab 80
Mundesley Spur. Slou—4J 73
Mundesly Clo. Wat—21Y 37
Mundford Rd. E5—33Yb 64
Mundon Gdns. Ilf—32Tc 66
Mund St. W14—50Bb 81
Mundy St. N1—41Ub 83 (3H 195)
Munford Dri. Swans—59Ae 113
Mungo Pk. Clo. Bush, Wat
—19Ea 20
Mungo Pk. Rd. Grav—4F 136
Mungo Pk. Rd. Rain—37Jd 68
Mungo Pk. Way. Orp—73Yc 151
Munnings Gdns. Iswth—57Fa 100
Munro Dri. N11—23Lb 42
Munro M. W10—43Ab 80
Munro Rd. Bush, Wat—15Da 19
Munro Ter. SW10—51Fb 103
Munster Av. Houn—57Aa 99
Munster Gdns. N13—21Rb 43
Munster Rd. SW6—52Ab 102
Munster Rd. Tedd—65La 122
Munster Sq. NW1
—42Kb 82 (4A 192)
Munton Rd. SE17
—49Sb 83 (5E 206)
Murchison Av. Bex—60Zc 109
Murchison Rd. E10—33Ec 64
Murdoch Clo. Stai—64J 119
Murdock Cotts. E3—41Ac 84
Murdock St. SE15—51Xb 105
Murfett Clo. SW19—61Ab 124
Murfitt Way. Upm—35Qd 69
Muriel Av. Wat—15Y 19
Muriel St. N1—40Pb 62 (1J 193)
(in two parts)
Murillo Rd. SE13—56Fc 107
Murphy St. SE1—47Qb 82 (2K 205)
Murray Av. Brom—69Kc 129
Murray Av. Houn—57Da 99
Murray Ct. Twic—61Fa 122
Murray Cres. Pinn—25Z 37
Murray Grn. Wok—86E 156
Murray Gro. N1—40Sb 63 (2E 194)
Murray M. NW1—38Mb 62
Murray Rd. SW19—65Za 124
Murray Rd. W5—49La 78
Murray Rd. Cher—79E 138
Murray Rd. N'wd—24U 36
Murray Rd. Orp—69Xc 131
Murray Rd. Rich—61Ka 122
Murray Sq. E16—44Jc 85
Murray St. NW1—38Mb 62
Murray Ter. NW3—35Fb 61
Murrell's Wlk. Lea—95Ca 175
Murreys Ct. Asht—90Ma 161
Murreys, The. Asht—90La 160
Murthering La. Romf—17Hd 30
Murtwell Dri. Chig—23Sc 46
Musard Rd. W6—51Ab 102
Musbury St. E1—44Yb 84
Muschamp Rd. SE15—55Vb 105
Muschamp Rd. Cars—75Gb 145
Muscovy St. EC3
—45Ub 83 (4J 201)
Museum Pas. E2—41Yb 84
Museum St. WC1
—43Nb 82 (1F 199)
Musgrave Clo. Barn—11Eb 23
Musgrave Cres. SW6—53Cb 103
Musgrave Rd. Iswth—53Ha 100
Musgrove Rd. SE14—53Zb 106
Musjid Rd. SW11—54Fb 103
Musquash Way. Houn—54Y 99
Mussenden La. S Dar & Long,
Dart—71Sd 154
Mustard Mill Rd. Stai—63G 118
Muston Rd. E5—33Xb 63
Muswell Av. N10—25Kb 42
Muswell Hill. N10—27Kb 42
Muswell Hill B'way. N10—27Kb 42
Muswell Hill Pl. N10—28Kb 42
Muswell Hill Rd.—30Jb 42
N6 1 & 2-40
N10 remainder
Muswell M. N10—27Kb 42
Muswell Rd. N10—27Kb 42
Mutchetts Clo. Wat—5Aa 5
Mutrix Rd. NW6—39Cb 61
Mutton La. Pot B—4Bb 9
Mutton La. Pot B—3Ya 8
Mutton Pl. NW1—37Jb 62
★Mutton Row. Ong—4Ld
Muybridge Rd. N Mald—68Sa 123
Myatt Rd. SW9—53Rb 105
Mycenae Rd. SE3—52Jc 107
Myddelton Av. Enf—10Ub 11
Myddelton Clo. Enf—11Vb 25
Myddelton Gdns. N21—17Sb 25
Myddelton Ho. WC1—(2J 193)
Myddelton Pk. N20—20Fb 23
Myddelton Pas. EC1
—41Qb 82 (3A 194)
Myddelton Rd. N8—28Nb 42
Myddelton Sq. EC1
—41Qb 82 (3A 194)
Myddelton St. EC1
—41Qb 82 (4A 194)
Myddleton Path. Wal X—3Xb 11
Myddleton Rd. N22—24Nb 42
Myddleton Rd. Uxb—39L 55
Mygrove Clo. Rain—40Md 69
Mygrove Gdns. Rain—40Md 69
Mygrove Rd. Rain—40Md 69
Mylis Clo. SE26—63Xb 127
Mylne St. EC1—41Qb 82 (3K 193)
Mylor Clo. Wok—86A 156
Mynn's Clo. Eps—86Ra 161
Myra St. SE2—49Wc 87
Myrdle St. E1—43Wb 83
Myrke, The. Slou—9K 73
Myrna Clo. Mitc—66Gb 125
Myron Pl. SE13—55Ec 106
Myrtle Av. Felt—57U 98
Myrtle Av. Ruis—31W 56
Myrtle Clo. Barn—18Hb 23
Myrtle Clo. Eri—52Gd 110
Myrtle Clo. Slou—53G 96
Myrtle Clo. Uxb—43P 75
Myrtle Clo. W Dray—48P 75
Myrtle Cres. Slou—5K 73
Myrtledene Rd. SE2—50Wc 87
Myrtle Gdns. W7—46Ga 78
Myrtle Gro. Enf—10Tb 11
Myrtle Gro. N Mald—68Sa 123
Myrtle Gro. S Ock—47Sd 90
Myrtle Pl. Dart—57Td 112
Myrtle Rd. E6—39Nc 66
Myrtle Rd. E17—30Ac 44
Myrtle Rd. N13—20Sb 25
Myrtle Rd. W3—46Sa 79
Myrtle Rd. Brtwd—21Yd 50
Myrtle Rd. Croy—76Cc 148
Myrtle Rd. Dart—60Md 111
Myrtle Rd. Hmptn—65Ea 122
Myrtle Rd. Houn—54Ea 100
Myrtle Rd. Ilf—33Rc 66
Myrtle Rd. Romf—23Ld 49
Myrtle Rd. Sutt—78Eb 145
Myrtleside Clo. N'wd—24T 36
Myrtle Wlk. N1—40Ub 63 (2H 195)
Mysore Rd. SW11—56Hb 103
Myton Rd. SE21—62Tb 127

Nadine St. SE7—50Lc 85
Nagle Clo. E17—26Fc 45
Nags Head Ct. EC1—(6E 194)
Nags Head La. Upm & Brtwd
—25Sd 50
Nags Head La. Well—55Xc 109
Nags Head Rd. Enf—14Yb 26
Nailsworth Cres. Red—100Mb 180
Nailzee Clo. Ger X—31A 54
Nairne Gro. SE24—57Tb 105
Nairn Grn. Wat—20W 18
Nairn Rd. Ruis—37Y 57
Nairn St. E14—43Ec 84
Naish Ct. N1—39Nb 62
Nallhead Rd. Felt—64Y 121
Namton Dri. T Hth—70Pb 126
Nan Clark's La. NW7—19Va 22
Nancy Downs. Wat—17Y 19
Nankin St. E14—44Cc 84
Nansen Rd. SW11—55Jb 104
Nansen Rd. Grav—3F 136
Nansen Village. N12—21Db 41
Nantes Clo. SW18—56Eb 103
Nantes Pas. E1—43Vb 83 (7K 195)
Nant Rd. NW2—33Bb 61
Nant St. E2—41Xb 83
Napier Av. SW6—55Bb 103
Napier Clo. SE8—52Bc 106
Napier Clo. W14—48Bb 81
Napier Dri. Bush, Wat—14Aa 19
Napier Gro. N1—40Sb 63 (1E 194)
Napier Pl. W14—48Bb 81
Napier Rd. E6—39Qc 66
Napier Rd. E11—35Gc 65
Napier Rd. E15—40Gc 65
Napier Rd. N17—27Ub 43
Napier Rd. NW10—41Xa 80
Napier Rd. SE25—70Xb 127
Napier Rd. W14—48Bb 81
Napier Rd. Ashf—66T 120
Napier Rd. Belv—49Bd 87
Napier Rd. Brom—70Kc 129
Napier Rd. Enf—15Zb 26
Napier Rd. Grav—10B 114
Napier Rd. Houn—53M 97
Napier Rd. Iswth—56Ja 100
Napier Rd. S Croy—80Tb 147
Napier Rd. Wemb—37Ma 59
Napier Rd. W Dray—48P 75
Napier Ter. N1—38Rb 63
Napoleon Rd. E5—34Xb 63
Napoleon Rd. Twic—59Ka 100
Nap, The. K Lan—1Q 4
Napton Clo. Hay—42Aa 77
Narbonne Av. SW4—57Lb 104
Narboro Ct. Romf—30Jd 48
Narborough Clo. Uxb—33S 56
Narborough St. SW6—54Db 103
Narcissus Rd. NW6—36Cb 61
Nare Rd. S Ock—45Sd 90
Naresby Fold. Stan—23La 38
Narford Rd. E5—34Wb 63
Narrow La. Warl—91Xb 181
Narrow St. E14—45Ac 84
Narrow St. W3—46Ra 79
Narrow Way. Brom—72Nc 150
Nascot Pl. Wat—12X 19
Nascot Rd. Wat—12X 19
Nascot St. W12—44Ya 80
Nascot St. Wat—12X 19
Nascot Wood Rd. Wat—9V 4
Naseby Clo. NW6—38Eb 61
Naseby Clo. Iswth—53Ga 100
Naseby Ct. W on T—75Y 141
Naseby Rd. SE19—65Tb 127
Naseby Rd. Dag—34Cd 68
Naseby Rd. Ilf—25Qc 46
Nash Bank. Grav—8B 136
Nash Clo. Borwd—14Pa 21
Nashdom La. Slou—7A 52
Nash Grn. Brom—65Jc 129
Nash La. Kes—80Jc 149
Nash Rd. N9—19Yb 26
Nash Rd. SE4—57Ac 106
Nash Rd. Romf—28Zc 47
Nash Rd. Slou—49C 74
Nash St. NW1—41Kb 82 (3A 192)
Nash St. Grav—8C 136
Nash's Yd. Uxb—38M 55
Nasmyth St. W6—48Xa 80
Nassau Path. SE28—46Yc 87
Nassau Rd. SW13—53Va 102
Nassau St. W1—43Lb 82 (1B 198)
Nassington Rd. NW3—35Hb 61
Natalie Clo. Felt—59T 98
Natal Rd. N11—23Nb 42
Natal Rd. SW16—65Mb 126
Natal Rd. Ilf—35Rc 66
Natal Rd. T Hth—69Tb 127
Nathaniel Clo. E1
—43Vb 83 (1K 201)
Nathans Rd. Wemb—32La 58
Nathan Way. SE28, Eri & Belv
—49Uc 86
Nation Way. E4—18Ec 26
Naval Row. E14—45Ec 84
Navarino Gro. E8—37Wb 63

Navarino Rd.—Nine Acres Clo.

Navarino Rd. E8—37Wb 63
Navarre Gdns. Romf—22Dd 48
Navarre Rd. E6—40Nc 66
Navarre St. E2—42Vb 83 (5K 195)
Navenby Wlk. E3—42Cc 84
Navestock Clo. E4—20Ec 26
Navestock Cres. Wfd G—24Lc 45
Navestockside. Brtwd—12Sd 32
Navy St. SW4—55Mb 104
Naylor Gro. Enf—15Zb 26
Naylor Rd. N20—19Eb 23
Naylor Rd. SE15—52Xb 105
Nazeing Wlk. Rain—38Hd 68
Neagle Clo. Borwd—11Sa 21
Neal Av. S'hall—42Ba 77
Neal Clo. Ger X—32D 54
Neal Clo. N'wd—25W 36
Neal Ct. Wal A—5Hc 13
Nealden St. SW9—55Pb 104
Neale Clo. N2—27Eb 41
Neal Rd. Sev—79Ud 154
Neal St. WC2—44Nb 82 (3F 199)
Neal St. Wat—15Y 19
Neal's Yd. WC2—44Nb 82 (3F 199)
Near Acre. NW9—25Va 40
Neasden Clo. NW10—36Ua 60
Neasden La. NW10—35Ua 60
(in two parts)
Neasden La. N. NW10—34Ta 59
Neasham Rd. Dag—36Xc 67
Neate St. SE5—51Ub 105
Neath Gdns. Mord—72Eb 145
Neathouse Pl. SW1
—49Lb 82 (5B 204)
Neats Acre. Ruis—31T 56
Neatscourt Clo. E6—43Mc 85
Neave Cres. Romf—25Ld 49
Nebraska St. SE1
—47Tb 83 (2F 207)
Neckinger. SE1—48Vb 83 (3K 207)
Neckinger St. SE1—47Vb 83
Nectarine Way. SE13—54Dc 106
Needham Clo. Wind—3C 94
Needham Rd. W11—44Cb 81
Needham Ter. NW2—34Za 60
Neela Clo. Uxb—35R 56
Neeld Cres. NW4—29Xa 40
Neeld Cres. Wemb—36Qa 59
Neil Clo. Ashf—64S 120
Nelgarde Rd. SE6—59Cc 106
Nella Rd. W6—51Za 102
Nelldale Rd. SE16—49Yb 84
Nellgrove Rd. Uxb—42R 76
Nell Gwynne Av. Asc—10B 116
Nell Gwynne Av. Shep—72T 140
Nelmes Clo. Horn—29Pd 49
Nelmes Cres. Horn—29Pd 49
Nelmes Rd. Horn—31Nd 69
Nelmes Way. Horn—28Nd 49
Nelson Clo. Brtwd—22Zd 51
Nelson Clo. Croy—74Rb 147
Nelson Clo. Romf—25Dd 48
Nelson Clo. Slou—9P 73
Nelson Clo. Uxb—41R 76
Nelson Clo. W on T—74X 141
Nelson Clo. West—89Nc 168
Nelson Ct. SE1—(1C 206)
Nelson Gdns. E2—41Wb 83
Nelson Gdns. Houn—58Ca 99
Nelson Gro. Rd. SW19—67Eb 125
Nelson Industrial Est. SW19
—67Db 125
Nelson La. Uxb—41R 76
Nelson Pas. EC1—41Sb 83 (3E 194)
Nelson Pl. N1—40Rb 63 (2C 194)
Nelson Pl. W3—46Ra 79
Nelson Pl. Sidc—63Wc 131
Nelson Rd. E4—23Dc 44
Nelson Rd. E11—28Jc 45
Nelson Rd. N8—29Pb 42
Nelson Rd. N9—19Xb 25
Nelson Rd. N15—28Ub 43
Nelson Rd. SE10—51Ec 106
Nelson Rd. SW19—66Eb 125
Nelson Rd. Ashf—64N 119
Nelson Rd. Belv—50Bd 87
Nelson Rd. Brom—70Lc 129
Nelson Rd. Cat—95Tb 181
Nelson Rd. Dart—58Ld 111
Nelson Rd. Enf—16Zb 26
Nelson Rd. Grav—1B 136
Nelson Rd. Grays—4F 92
Nelson Rd. Harr—32Ga 58
Nelson Rd. Houn—53P 97
Nelson Rd. Houn & Twic—58Ca 99
Nelson Rd. N Mald—71Ta 143
Nelson Rd. Rain—40Hd 68
Nelson Rd. Sidc—63Wc 131
Nelson Rd. S Ock—40Yd 70
Nelson Rd. Stan—23La 38
Nelson Rd. Uxb—41R 76
Nelson Rd. Wind—5D 94
Nelson Sq. SE1—47Rb 83 (1B 206)
Nelson's Row. SW4—56Mb 104
Nelson St. E1—44Xb 83
Nelson St. E6—40Pc 66
(in two parts)
Nelson St. E16—45Hc 85
(in two parts)
Nelson Ter. N1—40Rb 63 (2C 194)
Nelson Wlk. SE16—46Ac 84
Nelwyn Av. Horn—29Pd 49
Nemoure Rd. W3—45Sa 79
Nene Gdns. Felt—61Ba 121
Nene Rd. Houn—53R 98
Nepaul Rd. SW11—55Gb 103
Nepean St. SW15—58Wa 102
★Nepicar La. Sev—87Ee
Neptune Rd. Harr—30Fa 38
Neptune Rd. Houn—53S 98
Neptune St. SE16—48Yb 84
Nesbit Clo. SE3—55Gc 107
Nesbit Rd. SE9—56Mc 107
Nesbitts All. Barn—13Bb 23
Ness Rd. Eri—51Md 111
Ness St. SE16—48Wb 83
Nesta Rd. Wfd G—23Gc 45
Nestles Av. Hay—48V 76
Neston Rd. Wat—9Y 5
Neston St. SE16—47Yb 84
Nestor Av. N21—16Rb 25
Nethan Dri. S Ock—45Sd 90
Netheravon Rd. W7—46Ha 78
Netheravon Rd. N. W4—49Va 80
Netheravon Rd. S. W4—50Va 80
Netherbury Rd. W5—48Ma 79
Netherby Gdns. Enf—14Nb 24
Netherby Pk. Wey—78U 140
Netherby Rd. SE23—59Yb 106
Nether Clo. N3—24Cb 41
Nethercote Av. Wok—5C 188
Nethercourt Av. N3—23Cb 41
Netherfield Gdns. Bark—38Tc 66
Netherfield Rd. N12—22Db 41
Netherfield Rd. SW17—62Jb 126
Netherford Rd. SW4—54Lb 104
Netherhall Gdns. NW3—37Eb 61
Netherhall Way. NW3—36Eb 61
Netherlands Rd. Barn & N20
—16Fb 23
Netherlands, The. Coul—91Lb 180
Netherleigh Clo. N6—32Lb 62
Nethern Ct. Rd. Cat—95Cc 182
Netherne La. Coul—95Lb 180
Netherpark Dri. Romf—26Hd 48
Nether St.—25Cb 41
N12 1-175 & 2-124
N3 remainder
Netherton Gro. SW10—51Eb 103
Netherton Rd. N15—30Tb 43
Netherton Rd. Twic—57Ja 100
Netherwood Rd. W14—48Za 80
Netherwood St. NW6—38Bb 61
Netley Clo. Croy—80Ec 148
Netley Clo. Sutt—78Za 144
Netley Dri. W on T—73Ba 141
Netley Gdns. Mord—73Eb 145
Netley Rd. E17—29Bc 44
Netley Rd. Bren—51Na 101
Netley Rd. Houn—53T 98
Netley Rd. Ilf—29Tc 46
Netley Rd. Mord—73Eb 145
Netley St. NW1—41Lb 82 (4B 192)
Nettlecombe Clo. Sutt—81Db 163
Nettleden Av. Wemb—37Qa 59
Nettlefold Pl. SE27—62Rb 127
Nettlestead Clo. Beck—66Bc 128
Nettleton Rd. SE14—53Zb 106
Nettleton Rd. Houn—53R 98
Nettleton Rd. Uxb—35P 55
Nettlewood Rd. SW16—66Mb 126
Neuchatel Rd. SE6—61Bc 128
Nevada St. SE10—51Ec 106
Nevern Pl. SW5—49Cb 81
Nevern Rd. SW5—49Cb 81
Nevern Sq. SW5—49Cb 81
Neville Av. N Mald—67Ta 123
Neville Clo. E11—34Hc 65
Neville Clo. NW1
—40Mb 62 (2E 192)
Neville Clo. NW6—40Bb 61
Neville Clo. SE15—53Wb 105
Neville Clo. W3—47Sa 79
Neville Clo. Esh—79Ba 141
Neville Clo. Houn—54Da 99
Neville Clo. Pot B—3Bb 9
Neville Clo. Sidc—63Vc 131
Neville Clo. Slou—7K 53
Neville Dri. N2—30Eb 41
Neville Gdns. Dag—34Zc 67
Neville Gill Clo. SW18
—58Cb 103
Neville Pl. N22—25Pb 42
Neville Rd. E7—38Jc 65
Neville Rd. NW6—40Bb 61
Neville Rd. W5—42Ma 79
Neville Rd. Croy—73Tb 147
Neville Rd. Dag—34Zc 67
Neville Rd. Ilf—25Sc 46
Neville Rd. King—68Qa 123
Neville Rd. Rich—62La 122
Nevilles Ct. NW2—34Wa 60
Neville St. SW7—50Fb 81 (7B 202)
Neville Ter. SW7—50Fb 81 (7B 202)
Neville Wlk. Cars—73Gb 145
Nevill Gro. Wat—11X 19
Nevill Rd. N16—35Ub 63
Nevill Way. Lou—16Nc 28
Nevin Dri. E4—18Dc 26
Nevis Clo. Romf—23Gd 48
Nevis Rd. SW17—61Jb 126
Newall Rd. Houn—53S 98
Newark Clo. Wok—93J 173
Newark Ct. W on T—74Y 141
Newark Cres. NW10—41Ta 79
Newark Grn. Borwd—13Ta 21
Newark La. Wok—91H 173
Newark Rd. S Croy—79Tb 147
Newark St. E1—43Xb 83
(in two parts)
Newark Way. NW4—28Wa 40
New Ash Clo. N2—27Fb 41
New Barn La. West & Sev
—90Sc 168
New Barn La. Whyt—88Ub 165
New Barn Rd. Grav & Long, Dart
—63De 135
New Barn Rd. Swan—67Gd 132
New Barns Av. Mitc—70Mb 126
New Barn St. E13—42Jc 85
New Barns Way. Chig—20Rc 28
Newberries Av. Rad—7Ka 6
New Berry La. W on T—78Z 141
Newbery Rd. Eri—53Hd 110
Newbery Way. Slou—7H 73
Newbiggin Path. Wat—21Y 37
Newbolt Av. Sutt—78Ya 144
Newbolt Rd. Stan—22Ha 38
New Bond St. W1
—44Kb 82 (4A 198)
Newborough Grn. N Mald
—70Ta 123
New Brent St. NW4—29Ya 40
New Bri. St. EC4—44Rb 83 (3B 200)
New Broad St. EC2
—43Ub 83 (1H 201)
New B'way. W5—45Ma 79
Newburgh Rd. W3—46Sa 79
Newburgh St. W1
—44Lb 82 (3B 198)
New Burlington M. W1
—45Lb 82 (4B 198)
New Burlington Pl. W1
—45Lb 82 (4B 198)
New Burlington St. W1
—45Lb 82 (4B 198)
Newburn St. SE11
—50Pb 82 (7J 205)
Newbury Av. Enf—10Bc 12
Newbury Clo. N'holt—37Ba 57
Newbury Clo. Romf—23Md 49
Newbury Cres. Wind—3A 94
Newbury Gdns. Eps—77Va 144
Newbury Gdns. Romf—23Md 49
Newbury Gdns. Upm—34Pd 69
Newbury M. NW5—37Jb 62
Newbury Rd. E4—23Ec 44
Newbury Rd. Brom—69Jc 129
Newbury Rd. Houn—53P 97
Newbury Rd. Ilf—30Uc 46
Newbury Rd. Romf—23Md 49
Newbury St. EC1
—43Sb 83 (1D 200)
Newbury Wlk. Romf—22Md 49
Newbury Way. N'holt—37Aa 57
New Butt La. SE8—52Cc 106
Newby Clo. Enf—12Ub 25
Newby St. E14—45Ec 84
Newby St. SW8—55Kb 104
Newcastle Av. Ilf—23Wc 47
Newcastle Clo. EC4
—44Rb 83 (2B 200)
Newcastle Ct. EC4—(4E 200)
Newcastle Pl. W2
—43Fb 81 (7C 190)
Newcastle Row. EC1
—42Qb 82 (6A 194)
New Cavendish St. W1
—43Jb 82 (1J 197)
New Change. EC4
—44Sb 83 (3D 200)
New Chapel Sq. Felt—60X 99
New Chu. Rd. SE5—52Tb 105
Newchurch Rd. Slou—3D 72
New City Rd. E13—41Lc 85
New Clo. SW19—69Eb 125
New Clo. Felt—64Aa 121
New College M. N1—38Qb 62
Newcombe Gdns. SW16
—63Nb 126
Newcombe Pk. NW7—22Ua 40
Newcombe Pk. Wemb—39Pa 59
Newcombe St. W8—46Cb 81
Newcomen Rd. E11—34Hc 65
Newcomen Rd. SW11—55Fb 103
Newcomen St. SE1
—47Tb 83 (1F 207)
Newcome Path. Shen. Rad—6Qa 7
Newcome Rd. Shen. Rad—6Qa 7
New Compton St. WC2
—44Mb 82 (3E 198)
New Ct. EC4—(4F 201)
(Bank)
New Ct. EC4—(4K 199)
(Temple)
New Ct. Dart—58Nd 111
Newcourt. Uxb—43L 75
New Ct. Wey—76L 139
Newcourt St. NW8
—40Gb 61 (2D 190)
New Coventry St. W1
—45Mb 82 (5E 198)
Newcroft Clo. Uxb—43P 75
New Cross Rd. SE14—52Zb 106
Newdales Clo. N9—19Wb 25
Newdene Av. N'holt—40Z 57
Newdigate Grn. Uxb—25M 35
Newdigate Rd. Uxb—25L 35
Newdigate Rd. E. Uxb—25M 35
Newell St. E14—44Bc 84
New End. NW3—34Eb 61
New End Sq. NW3—35Fb 61
Newenham Rd. Lea—98Ca 175
Newent Clo. SE15—52Ub 105
Newent Clo. Cars—74Hb 145
New Farm Av. Brom—70Jc 129
New Farm Dri. Romf—13Yc 29
New Farm La. N'wd—25U 36
New Fetter La. EC4
—44Qb 82 (2A 200)
Newfield Clo. Hmptn—67Ca 121
Newfield Rise. NW2—34Xa 60
New Ford Rd. Wal X—6Bc 12
New Forest La. Chig—23Qc 46
Newgale Gdns. Edgw—25Pa 39
New Garden Dri. W Dray—47N 75
Newgate. Croy—74Sb 147
Newgate Clo. Felt—62Aa 121
Newgate St. E4—20Gc 27
Newgate St. EC1
—44Rb 83 (2C 200)
Newgatestreet Rd. Wal X—1Sb 11
New Goulston St. E1
—44Vb 83 (2K 201)
New Hall Ct. Wal A—5Hc 13
New Hall Dri. Romf—25Nd 49
Newham Pl. Grays—9C 92
Newham's Row. SE1
—47Ub 83 (2J 207)
Newham Way—43Hc 85
E16 55-413
E6 remainder
Newhaven Clo. Hay—49V 76
Newhaven Cres. Ashf—64T 120
Newhaven Gdns. SE9—56Mc 107
Newhaven Rd. SE25—71Tb 147
New Haw Rd. Wey—78L 139
New Heston Rd. Houn—52Ba 99
Newhouse Av. Romf—27Zc 47
Newhouse Clo. N Mald—73Ua 144
Newhouse Cres. Wat—4X 5
New Ho. La. Grav—2B 136
★New Ho. La. Sev—88Ae
Newhouse Wlk. Mord—73Eb 145
Newick Clo. Bex—58Dd 110
Newick Rd. E5—35Xb 63
Newing Grn. Brom—66Mc 129
Newington Barrow Way. N7
—34Pb 62
Newington Butts
—49Rb 83 (6C 206)
SE1 2-22
SE11 remainder
Newington Causeway. SE1
—48Sb 83 (4C 206)
Newington Grn. N1 & N16
—36Tb 63
Newington Grn. Rd. N1—36Tb 63
New Inn B'way. EC2
—42Ub 83 (5J 195)
New Inn Pas. WC2—(3J 199)
New Inn Sq. EC2—(5J 195)
New Inn St. EC2—42Ub 83 (5J 195)
New Inn Yd. EC2—42Ub 83 (5J 195)
New Kent Rd. SE1
—49Sb 83 (4D 206)
New Kings Rd. SW6—54Bb 103
New King St. SE8—51Cc 106
Newland Clo. Pinn—23Aa 37
Newland Dri. Enf—11Xb 25
Newland Gdns. W13—47Ja 78
Newland Rd. N8—27Nb 42
Newlands Av. Rad—6Ha 6
Newlands Av. Th Dit—74Ga 142
Newlands Av. Wok—93B 172
Newlands Clo. Brtwd—17Fe 33
Newlands Clo. Edgw—20Na 21
Newlands Clo. S'hall—50Aa 77
Newlands Clo. W on T—77Aa 141
Newlands Clo. Wemb—37La 58
Newlands Ct. SE9—58Qc 108
Newlands Pk. SE26—65Yb 128
Newlands Pl. Barn—15Za 22
Newlands Rd. SW16—68Nb 126
Newlands Rd. Wfd G—19Hc 27
Newlands, The. Wall—80Mb 146
Newland St. E16—46Nc 86
Newlands Wlk. Wat—5Z 5
Newlands Way. Chess—78La 142
Newlands Wood. Croy—81Bc 166
New La. Wok & Guild—95A 172
Newling Clo. E6—44Pc 86
New Lodge Dri. Oxt—100Hc 183
New London St. EC3—(4J 201)
New Lydenburgh St. SE7—48Lc 85
Newlyn Clo. St Alb—2Aa 5
Newlyn Clo. Uxb—43Q 76
Newlyn Gdns. Harr—31Ba 57
Newlyn Rd. N17—25Vb 43
Newlyn Rd. Barn—14Bb 23
Newlyn Rd. Well—54Vc 109
Newman Clo. Horn—29Nd 49
New Mnr. Rd. E15—40Gc 65
Newman Pas. W1
—43Lb 82 (1C 198)
Newman Rd. E13—41Kc 85
Newman Rd. E17—29Zb 44
Newman Rd. Brom—67Jc 129
Newman Rd. Croy—74Pb 146
Newman Rd. Hay—45X 77
Newmans Clo. Lou—13Qc 28
Newman's Ct. EC3—(3G 201)
Newmans Dri. Brtwd—17Ee 33
Newmans La. Lou—13Qc 28
Newmans Rd. Grav—1B 136
Newman's Row. WC2
—43Pb 82 (1J 199)
Newman St. W1—43Lb 82 (1C 198)
Newman's Way. Barn—11Eb 23
Newman Yd. W1
—44Mb 82 (2D 198)
Newmarket Av. N'holt—36Ca 57
Newmarket Grn. SE9—59Mc 107
Newmarket Way. Horn—35Nd 69
New Mile Rd. Asc—8A 116
Newminster Rd. Mord—72Eb 145
New Mount St. E15—38Fc 65
Newnes Path. SW15—56Xa 102
Newnham Av. Ruis—32Y 57
Newnham Clo. Lou—16Mc 27
Newnham Clo. N'holt—37Ea 58
Newnham Clo. Slou—6L 73
Newnham Clo. T Hth—68Sb 127
Newnham Gdns. N'holt—37Ea 58
Newnham Ho. Lou—16Mc 27
Newnham Pde. Wal X—2Zb 12
Newnham Rd. N22—25Pb 42
Newnhams Clo. Brom—69Pc 130
Newnham Ter. SE1
—48Qb 82 (3K 205)
Newnham Way. Harr—29Na 39
New North Pl. EC2
—42Ub 83 (5H 195)
New North Rd. N1—38Sb 63
New North Rd. Ilf—24Tc 46
New North St. WC1
—43Pb 82 (7H 193)
Newnton Clo. N4—31Tb 63
New Oak Rd. N2—26Fb 41
New Orleans Wlk. N19—31Mb 62
New Oxford St. WC1
—44Mb 82 (2E 198)
New Pde. Ashf—63P 119
New Pk. Av. N13—20Sb 25
New Pk. Clo. N'holt—37Aa 57
New Pk. Rd. SW2—60Mb 104
New Pk. Rd. Ashf—64S 120
New Pk. Rd. Uxb—25L 35
New Peachey La. Uxb—44M 75
Newpiece. Lou—13Rc 28
New Pl. Croy—79Cc 148
New Pl. Gdns. Upm—33Td 70
New Pl. Sq. SE16—48Xb 83
New Plaistow Rd. E15—39Gc 65
Newport Av. E13—42Kc 85
Newport Ct. WC2
—45Mb 82 (4E 198)
Newport Mead. Wat—21Z 37
Newport Pl. W1—45Mb 82 (4E 198)
Newport Rd. E10—33Ec 64
Newport Rd. E17—28Ac 44
Newport Rd. SW13—53Wa 102
Newport Rd. Hay—43T 76
Newport Rd. Houn—53Q 98
Newport Rd. Slou—2C 72
Newports. Swan—73Fd 152
Newport St. SE11
—49Pb 82 (6H 205)
Newquay Cres. Harr—33Aa 57
Newquay Gdns. Wat—19X 19
Newquay Rd. SE6—61Dc 128
New Quebec St. W1
—44Hb 81 (3G 197)
New River Ct. Wal X—3Xb 11
New River Cres. N13—21Rb 43
New River Wlk. N1—37Sb 63
New Rd. E1—43Xb 83
New Rd. E4—21Dc 44
New Rd. N8—29Nb 42
New Rd. N9—20Wb 25
New Rd. N17—25Vb 43
New Rd. N22—25Sb 43
New Rd. NW7—24Ab 40
(Bittacy Hill)
New Rd. NW7—17Va 22
(Hendon Wood La.)
New Rd. SE2—49Zc 87
New Rd. Borwd—16Ma 21
New Rd. Bren—51Ma 101
New Rd. Brtwd—19Zd 33
New Rd. Chal—13A 16
New Rd. Dag & Rain—40Cd 68
New Rd. E Mol—70Ca 121
New Rd. Esh—76Ea 142
New Rd. Felt—60X 99
New Rd. Felt—58T 98
(Bedfont)
New Rd. Felt—64Aa 121
(Hanworth)
New Rd. Grav—8D 114
New Rd. Grays—51De 113
(in two parts)
New Rd. Harr—35Ha 58
New Rd. Hay—52S 98
New Rd. Houn—56Da 99
New Rd. Ilf—33Uc 66
New Rd. K Lan—2H 3
New Rd. King—66Qa 123
New Rd. Lea—83Ha 160
New Rd. Mitc—74Jb 146
New Rd. Orp—73Wc 151
New Rd. Pot B—5Wa 8
New Rd. Rad—8Ga 6
New Rd. Rich—63La 122
New Rd. Rick—15Q 18
New Rd. Rick—11H 17
(Sarratt)
New Rd. Romf—16Zc 29
New Rd. Sev—96Zc 185
New Rd. Shen, Rad—6Qa 7
New Rd. Shep—69Q 120
New Rd. Slou—48C 74
New Rd. Slou—3P 95
(Datchet)
New Rd. S Dar, Dart—68Sd 134
New Rd. Stai—64E 118
New Rd. Swan—69Hd 132
New Rd. Swan—66Hd 132
(Hextable)
New Rd. Tad—95Ya 178
New Rd. Uxb—42S 76
New Rd. Wat—14Y 19
New Rd. Wat—11Ga 20
(Letchmore Heath)
New Rd. Well—54Xc 109
New Rd. Hill. Kes & Orp—81Nc 168
New Rochford St. NW5—36Hb 61
New Row. WC2—45Nb 82 (4F 199)
Newry Rd. Twic—57Ja 100
Newsam Av. N15—29Tb 43
Newsham Rd. Wok—5D 188
New Spring Gdns. Wlk. SE11
—50Nb 82 (7G 205)
New Sq. WC2—44Qb 82 (2K 199)
New Sq. Slou—7K 73
Newstead Av. Orp—76Tc 150
Newstead Rise. Cat—98Xb 181
Newstead Rd. SE12—59Hc 107
Newstead Wlk. Cars—73Eb 145
Newstead Way. SW19—63Ab 124
New St. EC2—43Ub 83 (1J 201)
New St. Stai—63J 119
New St. Wat—14Y 19
New St. West—99Sc 184
New St. Hill. Brom—64Kc 129
New St. Rd. Grav & Sev—76Ee 155
New St. Sq. EC4—44Qb 82 (2A 200)
Newteswell Dri. Wal A—4Fc 13
Newton Abbot Rd. Grav—1B 136
Newton Av. N10—25Jb 42
Newton Av. W3—47Sa 79
Newton Clo. Slou—47B 74
Newton Gro. W4—49Ua 80
Newton La. Wind—8M 95
Newton Rd. E15—36Fc 65
Newton Rd. N15—29Wb 43
Newton Rd. NW2—35Ya 60
Newton Rd. SW19—66Ab 124
Newton Rd. W2—44Db 81
Newton Rd. Chig—22Xc 47
Newton Rd. Harr—26Ga 38
Newton Rd. Isleth—55Ha 100
Newton Rd. Purl—84Lb 164
Newton Rd. Til—5C 114
Newton Rd. Well—55Wc 109
Newton Rd. Wemb—38Pa 59
Newtons Clo. Rain—38Hd 68
Newton St. WC2—44Nb 82 (2G 199)
Newton's Yd. SW18—57Cb 103
Newton Wlk. Edgw—25Ra 39
Newton Way. N18—22Sb 43
Newton Wood Rd. Asht—88Pa 161
Newtown Rd. Uxb—37K 55
Newtown St. SW11—53Kb 104
New Trinity Rd. N2—27Fb 41
New Turnstile. WC1—(1H 199)
New Union Clo. E14—48Ec 84
New Union St. EC2
—43Tb 83 (1F 201)
★New Wlk. Sev—88Be
New Wanstead. E11—30Hc 45
New Way Rd. NW9—28Ua 40
New Wharf Rd. N1
—40Nb 62 (1G 193)
New Wickham La. Egh—66C 118
New Windsor St. Uxb—39L 55
Newyears Grn. La. Uxb—30N 35
New Years La. Sev & Orp
—88Vc 169
New Zealand Av. W on T—74V 140
New Zealand Way. W12—45Xa 80
New Zealand Way. Rain—41Hd 88
Niagara Av. W5—49La 78
Niagara Clo. Wal X—1Zb 12
Nibthwaite Rd. Harr—29Ga 38
Nicholas Clo. Gnfd—40Da 57
Nicholas Clo. S Ock—41Yd 90
Nicholas Clo. Wat—9X 5
Nicholas Gdns. W5—47Ma 79
Nicholas Gdns. Wok—88H 157
Nicholas La. EC4
—45Tb 83 (4G 201)
Nicholas Pas. EC4—(4G 201)
Nicholas Rd. E1—42Yb 84
Nicholas Rd. Borwd—15Pa 21
Nicholas Rd. Croy—77Nb 146
Nicholas Rd. Dag—33Bd 67
Nicholas Wlk. Grays—7D 92
Nicholas Way. N'wd—25S 36
Nicholay Rd. N19—32Mb 62
Nichol Clo. N14—18Mb 24
Nicholes Rd. Houn—56Ca 99
Nichol La. Brom—66Jc 129
Nicholl Rd. Epp—3Vc 15
Nicholls. Wind—5A 94
Nicholls Av. Uxb—42Q 76
Nichollsfield Wlk. N7—36Pb 62
Nicholl St. E2—39Wb 63
Nicholls Wlk. Wind—5A 94
Nichol Rd. Ger X—25A 34
Nichols Grn. W5—43Na 79
Nicholson Rd. Croy—74Vb 147
Nicholson St. SE1
—46Rb 83 (7B 200)
Nicholson Wlk. Egh—64C 118
Nichol's Sq. E2—40Vb 63 (2K 195)
Nickleby Clo. Uxb—44R 76
Nickleby Rd. Grav—10J 115
Nicola Clo. Harr—26Fa 38
Nicola Clo. S Croy—79Sb 147
Nicol Clo. Twic—58Ka 100
Nicoll Pl. NW4—30Xa 40
Nicoll Rd. NW10—39Ua 60
Nicoll Way. Borwd—15Ta 21
Nicolson Dri. Bush, Wat—19Ea 20
Nicolson Rd. Orp—73Zc 151
Nicolson Way. Sev—94Md 187
Nicosia Rd. SW18—59Gb 103
Niederwald Rd. SE26—63Ac 128
Nield Rd. Hay—47V 76
Nigel Clo. N'holt—39Aa 57
Nigel M. Ilf—35Rc 66
Nigel Playfair Av. W6—50Xa 80
Nigel Rd. E7—36Lc 65
Nigel Rd. SE15—55Wb 105
Nigeria Rd. SE7—52Mc 107
Nightingale Av. E4—22Gc 45
Nightingale Av. Lea—96T 174
Nightingale Av. Upm—32Vd 70
Nightingale Clo. E4—21Gc 45
Nightingale Clo. W4—51Sa 101
Nightingale Clo. Cars—75Jb 146
Nightingale Clo. Cob—83Z 159
Nightingale Clo. Grav—2A 136
Nightingale Cres. Lea—97S 174
Nightingale Dri. Eps—79Ra 143
Nightingale Gro. SE13—57Fc 107
Nightingale Gro. Dart—56Qd 111
Nightingale La. E11—29Kc 45
Nightingale La. N8—28Nb 42
Nightingale La.—59Hb 103
SW4 1-25
SW12 remainder
Nightingale La. Brom—68Lc 129
Nightingale La. Rich—59Na 101
Nightingale Pl. SE18—51Qc 108
Nightingale Pl. Rick—17M 17
Nightingale Rd. E5—34Xb 63
Nightingale Rd. N9—16Yb 26
Nightingale Rd. N22—24Nb 42
Nightingale Rd. NW10—40Va 60
Nightingale Rd. W7—46Ha 78
Nightingale Rd. Bush, Wat
—15Ca 19
Nightingale Rd. Cars—76Hb 145
Nightingale Rd. E Mol—71Da 141
Nightingale Rd. Esh—79Ba 141
Nightingale Rd. Hmptn—64Ca 121
Nightingale Rd. Lea—97V 174
Nightingale Rd. Orp—72Sc 150
Nightingale Rd. Rick—17L 17
Nightingale Rd. Sev—89Md 171
Nightingale Rd. S Croy—83Zb 166
Nightingales. Wal A—6Gc 13
Nightingales La. Chal—14A 16
Nightingales La. Chal—17A 16
Nightingale Sq. SW12—59Jb 104
Nightingale Vale. SE18—51Qc 108
Nightingale Wlk. SW4—58Kb 104
Nightingale Way. Swan
—69Gd 132
Nightingale Way. Uxb—30H 35
Nile Path. SE18—51Qc 108
Nile Rd. E13—40Lc 65
Nile St. N1—41Tb 83 (3F 195)
Nile Ter. SE15—50Vb 83 (7K 207)
Nimbus Rd. Eps—82Ta 161
Nimegan Way. SE22—57Ub 105
Nimmo Dri. Bush, Wat—17Fa 20
Nimrod Clo. N'holt—41Z 77
Nimrod Rd. SW16—65Kb 126
Nine Acres Clo. E12—36Nc 66

Nine Ashes Rd.—Nunnington Clo.

★Nine Ashes Rd. Brtwd—5Xd
Nine Elms Av. Uxb—43M 75
Nine Elms Clo. Uxb—43M 75
Nine Elms Gro. Grav—9C 114
Nine Elms La. SW8—52Lb 104
Ninefields. Wal A—5Hc 13
Ninehams Clo. Cat—92Tb 181
Ninehams Gdns. Cat—92Tb 181
Ninehams Rd. Cat—93Tb 181
Ninehams Rd. West—93Lc 183
Nine Stiles Clo. Uxb—37K 55
Nineteenth Rd. Mitc—70Nb 126
Ninhams Wood. Orp—77Qc 150
Ninnings Rd. Ger X—24B 34
Ninnings Way. Ger X—24B 34
Ninth Av. Hay—45W 76
Nita Rd. Brtwd—22Yd 50
Nithdale Rd. SE18—52Rc 108
Nithsdale Gro. Uxb—34S 56
Niton Clo. Barn—16Za 22
Niton Rd. Rich—55Qa 101
Niton St. SW6—52Za 102
Nixey Clo. Slou—7L 73
Noah's Ark. Sev—90Rd 171
Noak Hill Rd. Romf—21Ld 49
Nobel Rd. N18—22Yb 44
Noble St. EC2—44Sb 83 (2D 200)
Nobles Way. Egh—65A 118
Noel Pk. Rd. N22—26Qb 42
Noel Rd. E6—42Nc 86
Noel Rd. N1—40Rb 63 (1B 194)
Noel Rd. W3—45Qa 79
Noel Sq. Dag—35Yc 67
Noel St. W1—44Lb 82 (3C 198)
Nolan Way. E5—35Wb 63
Nolton Pl. Edgw—25Pa 39
Nonsuch Clo. Ilf—23Rc 46
Nonsuch Ct. Av. Eps—82Xa 162
Nonsuch Industrial Est. Eps
—83Ua 162
Nonsuch Wlk. Sutt—82Za 162
(in two parts)
Nora Gdns. NW4—28Za 40
Nora Ter. Harr—32Ga 58
Norbiton Av. King—68Qa 123
Norbiton Comn. Rd. King
—69Ra 123
Norbiton Rd. E14—44Bc 84
Norbreck Gdns. W5—41Pa 79
Norbreck Pde. W5—41Na 79
Norbroke St. W12—45Va 80
Norburn St. W10—43Ab 80
Norbury Av.—67Pb 126
SW16 245-319 & 236-328
T Hth remainder
Norbury Av. Houn—56Fa 100
Norbury Clo. SW16—67Qb 126
Norbury Ct. Rd. SW16—68Nb 126
Norbury Cres. SW16—67Pb 126
Norbury Cross. SW16—69Nb 126
Norbury Gdns. Romf—29Zc 47
Norbury Gro. NW7—20Ua 22
Norbury Hill. SW16—66Qb 126
Norbury Rise. SW16—69Nb 126
Norbury Rd. E4—22Cc 44
Norbury Rd. T Hth—68Sb 127
Norbury Trading Est. SW16
—68Pb 126
Norbury Way. Lea—97Ea 176
Norcombe Gdns. Harr—30La 38
Norcott Clo. Hay—42Y 77
Norcott Rd. N16—33Wb 63
Norcroft Gdns. SE22—59Wb 105
Norcutt Rd. Twic—60Ga 100
Nordenfeldt Rd. Eri—50Fd 88
Norelands Dri. Slou—10A 52
Norfield Rd. Dart—63Ed 132
Norfolk Av. N13—23Rb 43
Norfolk Av. N15—30Vb 43
Norfolk Av. Slou—3G 72
Norfolk Av. S Croy—82Wb 165
Norfolk Av. Wat—10Y 5
Norfolk Clo. N2—27Gb 41
Norfolk Clo. N13—23Rb 43
Norfolk Clo. Barn—14Jb 24
Norfolk Clo. Twic—58Ka 100
Norfolk Cres. W2
—44Gb 81 (2E 196)
Norfolk Cres. Sidc—59Uc 108
Norfolk Farm Clo. Wok—88F 156
Norfolk Farm Rd. Wok—87F 156
Norfolk Gdns. Bexh—53Bd 109
Norfolk Gdns. Borwd—14Ta 21
Norfolk Gdns. Houn—57Ba 99
Norfolk Ho. Rd. SW16—62Mb 126
Norfolk Pl. W2—44Fb 81 (2C 196)
Norfolk Pl. Well—54Wc 109
Norfolk Rd. E6—39Pc 66
Norfolk Rd. E17—26Zb 44
Norfolk Rd. NW8
—39Fb 61 (1C 190)
Norfolk Rd. NW10—38Ua 60
Norfolk Rd. SW19—66Gb 125
Norfolk Rd. Bark—38Uc 66
Norfolk Rd. Barn—13Cb 23
Norfolk Rd. Dag—36Dd 68
Norfolk Rd. Enf—15Xb 25
Norfolk Rd. Esh—78Ga 142
Norfolk Rd. Felt—60Y 99
Norfolk Rd. Grav—8F 114
(in two parts)
Norfolk Rd. Harr—29Da 37
Norfolk Rd. Ilf—32Uc 66
Norfolk Rd. Rick—18N 17
Norfolk Rd. Romf—30Ed 48
Norfolk Rd. T Hth—69Sb 127
Norfolk Rd. Upm—34Qd 69
Norfolk Rd. Uxb—37M 55
Norfolk Row. SE11
—49Pb 82 (5H 205)
Norfolk Sq. W2—44Fb 81 (3C 196)
Norfolk Sq. M. W2—(3C 196)
Norfolk St. E7—36Jc 65
Norfolk Ter. W6—50Ab 80
Norgrove St. SW12—59Jb 104
Norheads La. Warl & West
—91Jc 183
Norhyrst Av. SE25—69Vb 127
Nork Gdns. Bans—86Ab 162
Nork Rise. Bans—88Za 162
Nork Way. Bans—88Ya 162
Norland Pl. W11—46Ab 80
Norland Rd. W11—46Za 80
Norlands Cres. Chst—67Rc 130
Norlands La. Egh—69G 118
Norland Sq. W11—46Ab 80
Norley Vale. SW15—60Wa 102
Norlington Rd.—32Ec 64
E11 1-55 & 2-28
E10 remainder
Norman Av. N22—25Sb 43
Norman Av. Eps—84Va 162
Norman Av. Felt—61Aa 121
Norman Av. S'hall—45Aa 77
Norman Av. S Croy—82Sb 165
Norman Av. Twic—59La 100
Normanby Clo. SW15—57Bb 103
Normanby Rd. NW10—35Va 60
Norman Clo. N22—25Sb 43
Norman Clo. Orp—76Sc 150
Norman Clo. Romf—25Dd 48
Norman Clo. Wal A—5Fc 13
Norman Ct. N4—31Qb 62
Norman Ct. Ilf—31Tc 66
Norman Ct. Pot B—3Eb 9
Norman Cres. Brtwd—20Ce 33
Norman Cres. Houn—52Z 99
Norman Cres. Pinn—25Y 37
Normand M. W14—51Ab 102
Normand Rd. W14—51Bb 103
Normandy Av. Barn—15Bb 23
Normandy Dri. Hay—44S 76
Normandy Rd. SW9—53Qb 104
Normandy Ter. E16—44Kc 85
Normandy Way. Eri—53Gd 110
Norman Gro. E3—40Ac 64
Normanhurst. Ashf—64Q 120
Normanhurst. Brtwd—16Ee 33
Normanhurst Av. Well & Bex H
—53Zc 109
Normanhurst Dri. Twic—57Ka 100
Normanhurst Rd. SW2—61Pb 126
Normanhurst Rd. Orp—68Xc 131
★Normanhurst Rd. Sev—92Ce
Normanhurst Rd. W on T—75Z 141
Norman Rd. E6—42Pc 86
Norman Rd. E11—33Fc 65
Norman Rd. N15—29Vb 43
Norman Rd. SE10—52Dc 106
Norman Rd. SW19—66Eb 125
Norman Rd. Ashf—65T 120
Norman Rd. Belv—48Dd 88
Norman Rd. Dart—60Nd 111
Norman Rd. Horn—31Jd 68
Norman Rd. Ilf—36Rc 66
Norman Rd. Sutt—78Cb 145
Norman Rd. T Hth—71Rb 147
Norman's Bldgs. EC1
—41Sb 83 (4D 194)
Normans Clo. NW10—37Ta 59
Norman's Clo. Grav—9C 114
Norman's Clo. Uxb—42P 75
Normansfield Av. Tedd—66La 122
Normansfield Clo. Bush, Wat
—17Da 19
Normanshire Av. E4—21Ec 44
Normanshire Dri. E4—21Cc 44
Normans Mead. NW10—37Ta 59
Normans, The. Slou—4M 73
Norman St. EC1—41Sb 83 (4D 194)
Norman Ter. NW6—36Bb 61
Normanton Av. SW19—61Cb 125
Normanton Pk. E4—19Gc 27
Normanton Rd. S Croy—79Ub 147
Normanton St. SE23—61Zb 128
Norman Way. N14—19Nb 24
Norman Way. W3—43Ra 79
Normington Clo. SW16—64Qb 126
Norrels Dri. Lea—98V 174
Norrels Ride. Lea—97V 174
Norrice Lea. N2—29Fb 41
Norris Rd. Stai—63H 119
Norris St. SW1—45Mb 82 (5D 198)
Norris Way. Dart—55Hd 110
Norroy Rd. SW15—56Za 102
Norry's Clo. Barn—14Hb 23
Norry's Rd. Barn—14Hb 23
Norseman Way. Gnfd—39Da 57
Norstead Pl. SW15—61Wa 124
Norsted La. Orp—84Wc 169
(in two parts)
N. Access Rd. E17—30Zb 44
North Acre. NW9—25Ua 40
North Acre. Bans—88Bb 163
N. Acton Rd. NW10—40Ta 59
Northallerton Way. Romf
—22Md 49
Northall Rd. Bexh—54Ed 110
Northampton Av. Slou—4G 72
Northampton Gro. N1—36Tb 63
Northampton Pk. N1—37Sb 63
Northampton Rd. EC1
—42Qb 82 (5A 194)
Northampton Rd. Croy—75Wb 147
Northampton Rd. Enf—14Ac 26
Northampton Row. EC1—(5A 194)
Northampton Sq. EC1
—41Rb 83 (4B 194)
Northampton St. N1—38Sb 63
Northanger Rd. SW16—65Nb 126
North App. N'wd—19S 18
North App. Wat—6W 4
N. Ash Rd. Long, Dart—76Ae 155
N. Audley St. W1
—45Jb 82 (3H 197)
North Av. N18—21Wb 43
North Av. W13—43Ka 78
North Av. Cars—80Jb 146
North Av. Harr—30Da 37
North Av. Hay—45W 76
North Av. Rich—53Qa 101
North Av. Shen, Rad—4Na 7
North Av. S'hall—45Ba 77
North Av. W on T—81U 158
Northaw Rd. E. Pot B—3Mb 10
Northaw Rd. W. Pot B—2Hb 9
North Bank. NW8
—41Gb 81 (4D 190)
Northbank Rd. E17—26Ec 44
N. Birkbeck Rd. E11—34Fc 65
Northborough Rd. SW16
—69Mb 126
Northborough Rd. Slou—2E 72
Northbourne. Brom—73Jc 149
Northbourne Rd. SW4—57Mb 104
Northbrook Dri. N'wd—25U 36
Northbrook Rd. N22—24Nb 42
Northbrook Rd. SE13—57Gc 107
Northbrook Rd. Barn—16Ab 22
Northbrook Rd. Croy—71Tb 147
Northbrook Rd. Ilf—33Qc 66
Northburgh St. EC1
—42Rb 83 (5C 194)
N. Burnham Clo. Slou—10A 52
N. Carriage Dri. W2—(4E 196)
Northchurch. SE17
—50Tb 83 (7G 207)
Northchurch Rd. N1—38Tb 63
(in two parts)
N. Church Rd. Wemb—37Qa 59
Northchurch Ter. N1—38Ub 63
N. Circular Rd. E4—24Bc 44
N. Circular Rd. E6—38Nc 66
N. Circular Rd. E18—26Hc 45
N. Circular Rd.—41Pa 79 to 24Hb 41
NW10—41Pa 79
NW2—34Ua 60
NW4—32Xa 60
NW11—30Za 40
N3—28Bb 41
N12—25Fb 41
N. Circular Rd. N13—22Qb 42
Northcliffe Clo. Wor Pk—76Ua 144
Northcliffe Dri. N20—18Bb 23
North Clo. Barn—15Ya 22
North Clo. Bexh—56Zc 109
North Clo. Chig—22Wc 47
North Clo. Dag—39Cd 68
North Clo. Felt—58T 98
North Clo. Mord—70Ab 124
North Clo. Wind—3D 94
North Comn. Wey—77S 140
N. Common Rd. W5—45Na 79
N. Common Rd. Uxb—36M 55
Northcote. Lea—87Ea 160
Northcote. Pinn—26Y 37
Northcote. Wey—77M 139
Northcote Av. W5—45Na 79
Northcote Av. Iswth—57Ja 100
Northcote Av. S'hall—45Aa 77
Northcote Av. Surb—73Ra 143
Northcote Cres. Lea—97S 174
Northcote Rd. E17—28Ac 44
Northcote Rd. NW10—38Ua 60
Northcote Rd. SW11—57Gb 103
Northcote Rd. Croy—72Tb 147
Northcote Rd. Grav—10B 114
Northcote Rd. Lea—97S 174
Northcote Rd. N Mald—69Ta 123
Northcote Rd. Sidc—63Uc 130
Northcote Rd. Twic—57Ja 100
Northcott Av. N22—25Nb 42
N. Countess Rd. E17—25Bc 44
North Ct. W1—43Lb 82 (7C 192)
N. Cray Rd. Sidc & Bex—65Ad 131
North Cres. N3—26Bb 41
North Cres. WC1
—43Mb 82 (7D 192)
Northcroft. Slou—2F 72
Northcroft Clo. Egh—4M 117
Northcroft Gdns. Egh—4M 117
Northcroft Rd. W13—47Ka 78
Northcroft Rd. Egh—4M 117
Northcroft Rd. Eps—80Ua 144
North Crofts. SE23—60Xb 105
Northcroft Vs. Egh—4M 117
N. Cross Rd. SE22—57Vb 105
N. Cross Rd. Ilf—28Sc 46
North Dene. NW7—20Ta 21
Northdene. Chig—22Tc 46
North Dene. Houn—54Ea 100
Northdene Gdns. N15—30Vb 43
North Down. S Croy—83Ub 165
Northdown Clo. Ruis—34V 56
Northdown Gdns. Ilf—29Uc 46
Northdown Rd. Cat—96Ac 182
Northdown Rd. Ger X—23A 34
Northdown Rd. Horn—31Kd 69
Northdown Rd. Long, Dart
—68Zd 135
Northdown Rd. Sev—89Nd 171
Northdown Rd. Sutt—82Cb 163
Northdown Rd. Well—54Xc 109
N. Downs Cres. Croy—82Dc 166
(in two parts)
N. Downs Rd. Croy—82Dc 166
Northdown St. N1
—40Pb 62 (2H 193)
North Dri. SW16—63Lb 126
North Dri. Houn—54Ea 100
North Dri. Orp—77Uc 150
North Dri. Romf—27Ld 49
North Dri. Slou—1J 73
North Dri. Vir W—10J 117
Northeast Pl. N1—(1A 194)
North End. NW3—33Eb 61
Northend. Brtwd—22Yd 50
North End. Buck H—17Lc 27
North End. Croy—75Sb 147
N. End Av. NW3—33Eb 61
N. End Cres. W14—49Bb 81
N. End La. Orp—83Qc 168
N. End Rd. NW11—32Cb 61
N. End Rd.—49Ab 80
W14 1-311 & 2-234
SW6 remainder
Northend Rd. Eri—53Hd 110
N. End Rd. Wemb—34Qa 59
N. End Way. NW3—33Eb 61
Northern Av. N9—19Vb 25
Northernhay Wlk. Mord—70Ab 124
Northern Perimeter Rd. Houn
—53R 98
Northern Perimeter Rd. W. Houn
—53N 97
Northern Rd. E13—40Kc 65
Northern Rd. Slou—2H 73
Northey Av. Sutt—82Za 162
N. Eyot Gdns. W6—50Va 80
Northey St. E14—45Ac 84
N. Feltham Trading Est. Felt
—57X 99
Northfield. Long, Dart—69Be 135
Northfield Av.—46Ka 78
W13 1-249 & 2-242
W5 remainder
Northfield Av. Orp—72Yc 151
Northfield Av. Pinn—28Z 37
Northfield Clo. Hay—48V 76
Northfield Cres. Sutt—77Ab 144
Northfield Gdns. Dag—35Bd 67
Northfield Gdns. Wat—9Y 5
Northfield Industrial Est.
NW10—41Qa 79
Northfield Industrial Est.
Wemb—39Qa 59
Northfield Pde. Hay—48U 76
Northfield Pk. Hay—48V 76
Northfield Path. Dag—35Bd 67
Northfield Pl. Wey—80R 140
Northfield Rd. E6—38Pc 66
Northfield Rd. N16—31Ub 63
Northfield Rd. W13—47Ka 78
Northfield Rd. Barn—13Gb 23
Northfield Rd. Borwd—11Ra 21
Northfield Rd. Cob—85X 159
Northfield Rd. Dag—35Bd 67
Northfield Rd. Enf—15Xb 25
Northfield Rd. Houn—51Z 99
Northfield Rd. Stai—67K 119
Northfield Rd. Wal X—4Ac 12
Northfield Rd. Wind—9D 72
Northfields. SW18—56Cb 103
Northfields. Asht—90Na 161
(in two parts)
Northfields Rd. W3—43Ra 79
Northfleet Industrial Est.
Grav—56Be 113
N. Flock St. SE16—47Wb 83
North Gdns. SW19—66Fb 125
Northgate. N'wd—24S 36
Northgate Path. Borwd—10Pa 7
North Glade, The. Bex—60Bd 109
N. Gower St. NW1
—41Lb 82 (4C 192)
North Grn. NW9—24Ua 40
North Grn. Slou—5J 73
North Gro. N6—31Jb 62
North Gro. N15—29Tb 43
North Gro. Cher—72H 139
N. Hatton Rd. Houn—53T 98
North Hill. N6—30Hb 41
North Hill. Rick—12G 16
N. Hill Av. N6—30Jb 42
N. Hill Dri. Romf—21Md 49
N. Hill Grn. Romf—21Md 49
N. Hyde Gdns. Hay—49W 76
N. Hyde La. S'hall & Houn
—50Aa 77
N. Hyde Rd. Hay—48U 76
(in two parts)
Northiam. N12—21Cb 41
Northiam St. E8—39Xb 63
Northington St. WC1
—42Pb 82 (6J 193)
N. Kent Av. Grav—58Ee 113
N. Kent Gro. SE18—49Pc 86
Northlands. Pot B—3Fb 9
Northlands Av. Orp—77Uc 150
Northlands St. SE5—54Sb 105
North La. Tedd—65Ha 122
N. Lodge Clo. SW15—57Za 102
North Mall. N9—19Xb 25
North Mall. Stai—63H 119
Northmead Rd. Slou—3D 72
North M. WC1—42Pb 82 (6J 193)
Northolm. Edgw—21Ta 39
Northolme Clo. Grays—48Ee 91
Northolme Gdns. Edgw—25Qa 39
Northolme Rise. Orp—75Uc 150
Northolme Rd. N5—35Sb 63
Northolt Av. Ruis—36X 57
Northolt Gdns. Gnfd—36Ha 58
Northolt Rd. Harr—35Da 57
Northolt Rd. Houn—53M 97
Northolt Way. Horn—37Ld 69
N. Orbital Rd. Rick—22G 34
N. Orbital Rd. Uxb—29J 35
N. Orbital Rd. Wat—5Z 5
N. Orbital Rd. Wat & St Alb—3Z 5
Northover. Brom—62Hc 129
North Pde. Chess—78Pa 143
North Pk. SE9—58Pc 108
North Pk. Ger X—27A 34
N. Park Av. NW10 & NW2—36Xa 60
N. Park Rd. Iver—48F 74
North Pas. SW18—56Cb 103
North Pl. Mitc—66Hb 125
North Pl. Tedd—65Ha 122
North Pl. Wal A—5Dc 12
N. Pole La. Kes—79Hc 149
N. Pole Rd. W10—43Ya 80
Northport St. N1—39Tb 63 (1G 195)
N. Ridge Rd. Grav—2E 136
N. Riding. St Alb—2Ca 5
North Rd. N6—31Jb 62
North Rd. N7—37Nb 62
North Rd. N9—18Xb 25
North Rd. SE18—49Uc 86
North Rd. SW19—65Eb 125
North Rd. W5—48Ma 79
North Rd. Belv—48Dd 88
North Rd. Bren—51Na 101
North Rd. Brtwd—18Yd 32
North Rd. Brom—67Kc 129
North Rd. Dart—58Hd 110
North Rd. Edgw—25Ra 39
North Rd. Felt—58T 98
North Rd. Hav, Romf—20Gd 30
North Rd. Hay—43T 76
North Rd. Ilf—33Uc 66
North Rd. Purf—49Sd 90
North Rd. Rich—55Qa 101
North Rd. Rick—15F 16
North Rd. Romf—29Ad 47
North Rd. Ruis—31U 56
North Rd. S'hall—45Ca 77
North Rd. S Ock & Upm—40Yd 70
North Rd. Surb—72Ma 143
North Rd. Wal X—5Ac 12
North Rd. W on T—78Y 141
North Rd. W Dray—48P 75
North Rd. W Wick—74Dc 148
North Rd. Wok—88C 156
North Rd. Av. Brtwd—19Yd 32
North Row. W1—45Hb 81 (4G 197)
N. Service Rd. Brtwd—19Yd 32
North Several. SE3—54Fc 107
Northside Rd. Brom—67Jc 129
Northspur Rd. Sutt—76Cb 145
North Sq. N9—19Xb 25
North Sq. NW11—29Cb 41
Northstead Rd. SW2—61Qb 126
North St. E13—40Kc 65
North St. NW4—29Ya 40
North St. SW4—55Lb 104
North St. Bark—38Sc 66
North St. Bexh—56Cd 110
North St. Brom—67Jc 129
North St. Cars—76Hb 145
North St. Dart—59Md 111
North St. Egh—64B 118
North St. Grav—9D 114
North St. Horn—32Md 69
North St. Iswth—55Ja 100
North St. Lea—93Ja 176
North St. Romf—27Fd 48
North St. Wind—1A 116
North St. Pas. E13—40Kc 65
N. Tenter St. E1—44Vb 83 (3K 201)
North Ter. SW3—48Gb 81 (4D 202)
North Ter. Wind—2H 95
Northumberland All. EC3
—44Ub 83 (3J 201)
Northumberland Av. E12—32Lc 65
Northumberland Av. WC2
—46Nb 82 (6F 199)
Northumberland Av. Enf—11Xb 25
Northumberland Av. Horn
—29Ld 49
Northumberland Av. Iswth
—53Ha 100
Northumberland Av. Well
—55Uc 108
Northumberland Clo. Eri
—52Ed 110
Northumberland Clo. Stai—58N 97
Northumberland Cres. Felt
—58U 98
Northumberland Gdns. N9
—20Vb 25
Northumberland Gdns. Iswth
—52Ja 100
Northumberland Gdns. Mitc
Northumberland Gro. N17
—24Xb 43
Northumberland Pk. N17—24Wb 43
Northumberland Pk. Eri—52Ed 110
Northumberland Pl. W2—44Cb 81
Northumberland Pl. Rich
—57Ma 101
Northumberland Rd. E6—44Pc 86
Northumberland Rd. E17—31Cc 64
Northumberland Rd. Barn
—16Eb 23
Northumberland Rd. Grav—6B 136
Northumberland Rd. Harr
—29Ba 37
Northumberland Rd. Stanf—7H 93
Northumberland Row. Twic
—60Ga 100
Northumberland St. WC2
—46Nb 82 (6F 199)
Northumberland Way. Eri
—53Ed 110
Northumbria St. E14—44Cc 84
N. Verbena Gdns. W6—50Wa 80
North View. SW19—64Ya 124
North View. W5—42La 78
North View. Ilf—24Wc 47
North View. Pinn—31Y 57
Northview. Swan—68Gd 132
N. View Av. Til—3C 114
N. View Cres. NW10—35Va 60
N. View Cres. Eps—89Ya 162
N. View Dri. Wfd G—26Mc 45
N. View Rd. N8—27Mb 42
N. View Rd. Sev—93Ld 187
North Vs. NW1—37Mb 62
North Wlk. Croy—79Dc 148
(in two parts)
North Wlk. Sutt—83Za 162
(in two parts)
North Way. N9—19Zb 26
North Way. N11—23Lb 42
North Way. NW9—27Ra 39
Northway. NW11—29Db 41
Northway. Mord—70Ab 124
North Way. Pinn—28Z 37
Northway. Rick—17M 17
North Way. Uxb—38N 55
Northway. Wall—77Lb 146
Northway Cir. NW7—21Ta 39
Northway Cres. NW7—21Ta 39
Northway Gdns. NW11—29Db 41
Northway Rd. SE5—55Sb 105
Northway Rd. Croy—72Vb 147
N. Western Av. Wat—7U 4
Northwest Pl. N1
—40Qb 62 (1A 194)
N. Wharf Rd. W2—43Fb 81 (1B 196)
Northwick Av. Harr—30Ja 38
Northwick Circ. Harr—30La 38
Northwick Clo. NW8
—42Fb 81 (5B 190)
Northwick Pk. Rd. Harr—30Ha 38
Northwick Rd. Wat—21Y 37
Northwick Rd. Wemb—39Ma 59
Northwick Sq. Houn—53S 98
Northwick Ter. NW8
—42Fb 81 (5B 190)
Northwick Wlk. Harr—31Ha 58
Northwold Dri. Pinn—26Y 37
Northwold Est. E5—33Wb 63
Northwold Rd.—33Vb 63
N16 1-67 & 2-34
E5 remainder
Northwood. Grays—7D 92
Northwood Av. Horn—35Jd 68
Northwood Av. Purl & Kenl
—85Qb 164
Northwood Av. Wok—6A 188
N. Wood Ct. SE25—69Wb 127
Northwood Gdns. N12—22Fb 41
Northwood Gdns. Gnfd—36Ha 58
Northwood Gdns. Ilf—28Qc 46
Northwood Pl. Eri—48Bd 87
Northwood Rd. N6—31Kb 62
Northwood Rd. SE23—60Bc 106
Northwood Rd. Cars—79Jb 146
Northwood Rd. Houn—53M 97
Northwood Rd. T Hth—68Sb 127
Northwood Rd. Uxb—25M 35
Northwood Way. SE19—65Tb 127
Northwood Way. N'wd—24W 36
Northwood Way. Uxb—25M 35
N. Woolwich Rd. E16—46Kc 85
(in two parts)
N. Worple Way. SW14—55Ta 101
Nortoft Rd. Ger X—23B 34
Norton Av. Surb—73Ra 143
Norton Clo. E4—22Cc 44
Norton Clo. Enf—12Xb 25
Norton Folgate. E1
—43Ub 83 (7J 195)
Norton Gdns. SW16—68Nb 126
Norton La. Cob—91V 174
Norton Rd. E10—32Bc 64
Norton Rd. Dag—37Fd 68
Norton Rd. Uxb—41M 75
Norton Rd. Wemb—37Ma 59
Norval Rd. Wemb—33Ka 58
Norway Dri. Slou—3M 73
Norway Pl. E14—44Bc 84
Norway St. SE10—51Dc 106
Norway Wlk. Rain—42Ld 89
Norwich M. Ilf—32Wc 67
Norwich Pl. Bexh—56Cd 110
Norwich Rd. E7—36Jc 65
Norwich Rd. Dag—40Cd 68
Norwich Rd. Gnfd—39Da 57
Norwich Rd. N'wd—27V 36
Norwich Rd. T Hth—69Sb 127
Norwich St. EC4—44Qb 82 (2K 199)
Norwich Wlk. Edgw—24Sa 39
Norwich Way. Rick—13R 18
Norwood Av. Romf—31Gd 68
Norwood Av. Wemb—39Pa 59
Norwood Clo. Lea—100Aa 175
Norwood Clo. S'hall—49Ca 77
Norwood Cres. Houn—53S 98
Norwood Dri. Harr—30Ca 37
Norwood Farm La. Cob—83X 159
Norwood Gdns. Hay—42Y 77
Norwood Gdns. S'hall—49Ba 77
Norwood Grn. Rd. S'hall—49Ca 77
Norwood High St. SE27—62Rb 127
Norwood La. Iver—42F 74
Norwood Pk. Rd. SE27—64Sb 127
Norwood Rd.—60Rb 105
SE24 1-339 & 2-150
SE27 remainder
Norwood Rd. Lea—100Aa 175
Norwood Rd. S'hall—48Aa 77
Noss Clo. Sutt—78Gb 145
Notley End. Egh—6N 117
Notley St. SE5—52Tb 105
Notson Rd. SE25—70Xb 127
Notting Barn Rd. W10—42Za 80
Nottingham Av. E16—43Lc 85
Nottingham Clo. Wat—5W 4
Nottingham Clo. Wok—6C 188
Nottingham Ct. WC2
—44Nb 82 (3F 199)
Nottingham Pl. W1
—43Jb 82 (6H 191)
Nottingham Rd. E10—30Ec 44
Nottingham Rd. SW17—60Hb 103
Nottingham Rd. Iswth—54Ha 100
Nottingham Rd. Rick—17E 16
Nottingham Rd. S Croy—78Sb 147
Nottingham St. W1
—43Jb 82 (7H 191)
Nottingham Ter. NW1—(6H 191)
Notting Hill Ga. W11—46Cb 81
Nova M. Sutt—74Ab 144
Novar Clo. Orp—73Vc 151
Nova Rd. Croy—73Rb 147
Novar Rd. SE9—60Sc 108
Novello St. SW6—53Cb 103
Nowell Rd. SW13—51Wa 102
Nower Hill. Pinn—28Ba 37
Nower, The. Sev—92Vc 185
Noyna Rd. SW17—62Hb 125
Nuding Clo. SE13—55Cc 106
Nuffield Lodge. N6—30Kb 42
Nuffield Rd. Swan—65Jd 132
Nugent Industrial Pk. Orp
—70Yc 131
Nugent Rd. N19—32Nb 62
Nugent Rd. SE25—69Vb 127
Nugents Pk. Pinn—25Aa 37
Nugent Ter. NW8
—40Eb 61 (2A 190)
Nun Ct. EC2—(2F 201)
Nuneaton Rd. Dag—38Ad 67
Nunfield. K Lan—3K 3
Nunhead Cres. SE15—55Xb 105
Nunhead Grn. SE15—55Xb 105
Nunhead Gro. SE15—55Yb 106
Nunhead La. SE15—55Xb 105
Nunnington Clo. SE9—62Nc 130

Nunns Rd.—Old Fox Clo.

Nunns Rd. Enf—12Sb 25
Nunns Way. Grays—49Fe 91
Nuns Wlk. Vir W—10P 117
Nupton Dri. Barn—16Ya 22
Nursery App. N12—23Gb 41
Nursery Av. N3—26Eb 41
Nursery Av. Bexh—55Bd 109
Nursery Av. Croy—75Zb 148
Nursery Clo. SW15—56Za 102
Nursery Clo. Croy—75Zb 148
Nursery Clo. Dart—59Sd 112
Nursery Clo. Enf—11Zb 26
Nursery Clo. Eps—82Ua 162
Nursery Clo. Felt—59X 99
Nursery Clo. Orp—73Wc 151
Nursery Clo. Romf—30Zc 47
Nursery Clo. Sev—94Ld 187
Nursery Clo. S Ock—42Yd 90
Nursery Clo. Swan—68Ed 132
Nursery Clo. Tad—97Xa 178
Nursery Clo. Wey—82H 157
Nursery Clo. Wok—4F 188
Nursery Clo. Wfd G—22Kc 45
Nursery Ct. N17—24Vb 43
Nursery Gdns. Enf—11Zb 26
Nursery Gdns. Stai—65K 119
Nursery Gdns. Sun—68V 120
Nursery La. E7—37Jc 65
Nursery La. W10—43Ya 80
Nursery La. Slou—6P 73
Nursery La. Uxb—42M 75
Nursery Pl. Sev—94Fd 186
Nursery Rd. E9—37Yb 64
Nursery Rd. N2—25Fb 41
Nursery Rd. N14—17Lb 24
Nursery Rd. SW9—56Pb 104
Nursery Rd. SW19—68Db 125
(Merton)
Nursery Rd. SW19—66Ab 124
(Wimbledon)
★Nursery Rd. Brtwd—6Yd
Nursery Rd. Grav—10C 136
Nursery Rd. Lou—15Lc 27
Nursery Rd. Lou—11Lc 27
(High Beach)
Nursery Rd. M'head—4A 72
Nursery Rd. Pinn—27Y 37
Nursery Rd. Stanf—1N 93
Nursery Rd. Sun—68U 120
Nursery Rd. Sutt—77Eb 145
Nursery Rd. Tad—97Xa 178
Nursery Rd. T Hth—70Tb 127
Nursery Rd. Wok—5A 188
Nursery Row. Barn—13Ab 22
Nursery St. N17—24Vb 43
Nursery, The. Eri—52Hd 110
Nursery, The. West—99Sc 184
Nursery Wlk. NW4—27Ya 40
Nursery Wlk. Romf—31Fd 68
Nursery Way. Wray, Stai—8P 95
Nursery Waye. Uxb—39M 55
Nurstead Av. Long, Dart—70Fe 135
Nurstead La. Long, Dart—70Fe 135
Nurstead Rd. Eri—52Cd 110
Nutberry Av. Grays—47Ce 91
Nutbourne St. W10—41Ab 80
Nutbrook St. SE15—55Wb 105
Nutbrowne Rd. Dag—39Bd 67
Nutcroft Gro. Lea—93Ga 176
Nutcroft Rd. SE15—52Xb 105
Nutfield Clo. N17—23Wb 43
Nutfield Gdns. Ilf—33Wc 67
Nutfield Gdns. N'holt—40Y 57
Nutfield Rd. E15—35Ec 64
Nutfield Rd. NW2—34Wa 60
Nutfield Rd. SE22—56Vb 105
Nutfield Rd. Coul—88Jb 164
Nutfield Rd. Red—100Lb 180
Nutfield Rd. T Hth—70Rb 127
Nutfield Way. Orp—75Rc 150
Nutford Pl. W1—44Hb 81 (2E 196)
Nuthatch. Long, Dart—69De 135
Nuthatch Gdns. SE28—47Tc 86
Nuthatch M. SE28—47Tc 86
Nuthurst Av. SW2—61Pb 126
Nutley Clo. Swan—67Hd 132
Nutley Ter. NW3—37Eb 61
Nutmead Clo. Bex—60Ed 110
Nuttall St. N1—40Ub 63 (1J 195)
Nutter La. E11—30Lc 45
Nuttfield Clo. Rick—16R 18
Nutt Gro. Edgw—19Na 20
Nut Tree Clo. Orp—76Zc 151
Nutt St. SE15—52Vb 105
Nutty La. Shep—69S 120
Nutwell St. SW17—64Gb 125
Nuxley Rd. Belv—51Bd 109
Nyanza St. SE18—51Tc 108
Nyefield Pk. Tad—98Wa 178
Nylands Av. Rich—54Qa 101
Nymans Gdns. SW20—69Xa 124
Nynehead St. SE14—52Ac 106
Nyon Gro. SE6—61Bc 128
Nyssia Clo. Wfd G—23Pc 46
Nyth Clo. Upm—30Td 50
Nyton Clo. N19—32Nb 62

Oakapple Clo. S Croy—86Xb 165
Oak Av. N8—28Nb 42
Oak Av. N10—24Kb 42
Oak Av. N17—24Tb 43
Oak Av. Croy—75Cc 148
Oak Av. Egh—66E 118
Oak Av. Enf—10Pb 10
Oak Av. Hmptn—64Aa 121
Oak Av. Houn—52Z 99
Oak Av. St Alb—2Ca 5
Oak Av. Sev—100Kd 187
Oak Av. Upm—34Rd 69
Oak Av. Uxb—33R 56
Oak Av. W Dray—48Q 76
Oak Bank. Croy—79Ec 148
Oakbank. Wok—91A 172
Oakbank Av. W on T—73Ba 141
Oakbank Gro. SE24—56Sb 105
Oakbrook Clo. Brom—63Kc 129
Oakbury Rd. SW6—54Db 103
Oak Clo. N14—17Kb 24
Oak Clo. Sutt—75Eb 145
Oak Clo. Wal A—6Fc 13
Oakcombe Clo. N Mald—67Ua 124
Oak Cottage Clo. SE6—60Hc 107
Oak Cotts. W7—47Ga 78
Oak Cres. E16—43Gc 85
Oakcroft Clo. Pinn—26X 37
Oakcroft Clo. Wey—86H 157
Oakcroft Rd. SE13—54Fc 107
Oakcroft Rd. Chess—77Pa 143
Oakcroft Rd. Wey—86H 157
Oakcroft Vs. Chess—77Pa 143
Oakdale. N14—18Kb 24
Oakdale Av. Harr—29Na 39
Oakdale Av. N'wd—26W 36
Oakdale Clo. Wat—21Y 37
Oakdale Rd. E7—38Kc 65
Oakdale Rd. E11—33Fc 65
Oakdale Rd. E18—26Kc 45
Oakdale Rd. N4—30Sb 43
Oakdale Rd. SE4—55Yb 106
Oakdale Rd. SW16—64Nb 126
Oakdale Rd. Eps—81Ta 161
Oakdale Rd. Wat—21Y 37
Oakdale Rd. Wey—76Q 140
Oak Dene. SE15—53Xb 105
Oak Dene. W13—43Ka 78
Oakdene. Tad—92Ab 178
Oakdene. Wal X—2Ac 12
Oakdene Av. Chst—64Qc 130
Oakdene Av. Eri—51Ed 110
Oakdene Av. Th Dit—74Ja 142
Oakdene Clo. Horn—30Kd 49
Oakdene Clo. Lea—99Ea 176
Oakdene Clo. Pinn—24Ba 37
Oakdene Dri. Surb—73Sa 143
Oakdene Pde. Cob—86X 159
Oakdene Pk. N3—24Bb 41
Oakdene Rd. Cob—86X 159
Oakdene Rd. Lea—96Ba 175
Oakdene Rd. Orp—71Vc 151
Oakdene Rd. Sev—94Jd 186
Oakdene Rd. Uxb—40R 56
Oakdene Rd. Wat—8X 5
Oakden St. SE11
—49Qb 82 (5A 206)
Oaken Coppice. Asht—91Qa 177
Oaken Dri. Esh—79Ha 142
Oakend Way. Ger X—29B 34
Oak End Way. Wey—84H 157
Oaken La. Esh—77Ga 142
Oakenshaw Clo. Surb—73Na 143
Oakes Clo. E6—44Pc 86
Oakeshott Av. N6—33Jb 62
Oakey La. SE1—48Qb 82 (3K 205)
Oak Farm. Borwd—15Sa 21
Oakfield. E4—22Dc 44
Oakfield. Rick—17H 17
Oakfield. Wok—5B 188
Oakfield Av. Harr—27Ka 38
Oakfield Av. Slou—6F 72
Oakfield Clo. N Mald—71Va 144
Oakfield Clo. Wey—77S 140
Oakfield Ct. N8—31Nb 62
Oakfield Gdns. N18—21Ub 43
Oakfield Gdns. SE19—64Vb 127
(in two parts)
Oakfield Gdns. Beck—71Dc 148
Oakfield Gdns. Cars—74Gb 145
Oakfield Gdns. Gnfd—42Fa 78
Oakfield Glade. Wey—77S 140
Oakfield La. Dart—61Hd 132
Oakfield La. Kes—77Lc 149
Oakfield Pk. Rd. Dart—61Md 133
Oakfield Pl. Dart—61Md 133
Oakfield Rd. E6—39Nc 66
Oakfield Rd. E17—26Ac 44
Oakfield Rd. N3—25Db 41
Oakfield Rd. N4—30Qb 42
Oakfield Rd. N14—19Nb 24
Oakfield Rd. SE20—66Xb 127
Oakfield Rd. SW19—62Za 124
Oakfield Rd. Ashf—64R 120
Oakfield Rd. Asht—90Na 161
Oakfield Rd. Cob—86X 159
Oakfield Rd. Croy—74Sb 147
Oakfield Rd. Ilf—34Rc 66
Oakfield Rd. Orp—73Wc 151
Oakfield Rd. Th Dit—71Ha 142
Oakfields. Sev—98Kd 187
Oakfields. W on T—74W 140
Oakfields. Wey—86K 157
Oakfields Rd. NW11—30Ab 40
Oakfield St. SW10—51Eb 103
Oakford Rd. NW5—35Lb 62
Oak Gdns. Croy—75Cc 148
Oak Gdns. Edgw—26Ra 39
Oak Glade. N'wd—25R 36
Oak Glen. Horn—27Nd 49
Oak Grange Rd. Guild—100K 173
Oak Grn. Abb L, Wat—4U 4
Oak Grn. Way. Abb L, Wat—4U 4
Oak Gro. NW2—35Ab 60
Oak Gro. Ruis—31X 57
Oak Gro. Sun—66X 121
Oak Gro. W Wick—74Ec 148
Oak Gro. Rd. SE20—67Yb 128
Oakhall Dri. Sun—64V 120
Oak Hall Rd. E11—30Jc 45
Oakham Clo. SE6—61Bc 128
Oakham Dri. Brom—70Hc 129
Oakhampton Rd. NW7—24Za 40
Oak Hill. Eps—88Ta 161
Oakhill. Esh—79Ja 142
Oak Hill. Sev—96Jd 186
Oak Hill. Surb—73Na 143
Oak Hill. Wfd G—24Fc 45
Oakhill Av. NW3—35Db 61
Oakhill Av. Pinn—26Aa 37
Oakhill Clo. Asht—90La 160
Oak Hill Clo. Wfd G—24Fc 45
Oakhill Ct. E11—30Kc 45
Oakhill Cres. Surb—73Na 143
Oak Hill Cres. Wfd G—24Fc 45
Oakhill Dri. Surb—73Na 143
Oakhill Gdns. Wey—75U 140
Oak Hill Gdns. Wfd G—25Gc 45
Oakhill Gro. Surb—72Na 143
Oak Hill Pk. NW3—35Db 61
Oak Hill Pk. M. NW3—35Eb 61
Oakhill Path. Surb—72Na 143
Oakhill Pl. SW15—57Cb 103
Oakhill Rd. SW15—57Bb 103
Oakhill Rd. SW16—67Pb 126
Oakhill Rd. Asht—90La 160
Oakhill Rd. Beck—68Ec 128
Oakhill Rd. Orp—74Vc 151
Oakhill Rd. Rick—21F 34
Oak Hill Rd. Romf—17Fd 30
Oakhill Rd. Sev—96Jd 186
Oakhill Rd. Surb—72Na 143
Oakhill Rd. Sutt—76Db 145
Oakhill Rd. Wey—79H 139
Oak Hill Way. NW3—35Db 61
Oakhouse Rd. Bexh—57Cd 110
Oakhurst Av. Barn—17Gb 23
Oakhurst Av. Bexh—52Ad 109
Oakhurst Clo. E17—28Gc 45
Oakhurst Clo. Tedd—64Ga 122
Oakhurst Gdns. E4—18Hc 27
Oakhurst Gdns. E17—28Gc 45
Oakhurst Gdns. Bexh—52Ad 109
Oakhurst Gro. SE22—56Wb 105
Oakhurst Rise. Cars—82Gb 163
Oakhurst Rd. Enf—8Zb 12
Oakhurst Rd. Eps—79Ta 143
Oakington Av. Amer—11A 16
Oakington Av. Harr—31Ca 57
Oakington Av. Hay—49T 76
Oakington Av. Wemb—34Pa 59
Oakington Dri. Sun—68Y 121
Oakington Mnr. Dri. Wemb
—36Qa 59
Oakington Rd. W9—42Cb 81
Oakington Way. N8—31Nb 62
Oakland Ct. Wey—76K 139
Oakland Gdns. Brtwd—15Ee 33
Oaklands. N21—19Pb 24
Oaklands. Beck—67Dc 128
Oaklands. Kenl—86Sb 165
Oaklands. Lea—96Fa 176
Oaklands Av. N9—16Xb 25
Oaklands Av. Esh—74Fa 142
Oaklands Av. Iswth—51Ha 100
Oaklands Av. Romf—27Gd 48
Oaklands Av. Sidc—59Vc 109
Oaklands Av. T Hth—70Qb 126
Oaklands Av. Wat—18X 19
Oaklands Av. W Wick—76Dc 148
Oaklands Clo. Bexh—57Bd 109
Oaklands Clo. Orp—72Uc 150
Oaklands Clo. Sev—79Ud 154
Oaklands Clo. Wemb—36Ma 59
Oaklands Ct. Wat—11W 18
Oaklands Ct. Wemb—36Ma 59
Oaklands Dri. S Ock—43Yd 90
Oaklands Dri. Twic—59Ea 100
Oaklands Gdns. Kenl—86Sb 165
Oaklands Ga. N'wd—23U 36
Oaklands Gro. W12—46Wa 80
Oaklands La. Barn—14Xa 22
Oaklands La. West—85Kc 167
Oaklands Pk. Av. Ilf—33Sc 66
Oaklands Pl. SW4—56Lb 104
Oaklands Rd. N20—17Bb 23
Oaklands Rd. NW2—35Za 60
Oaklands Rd. SW14—55Ta 101
Oaklands Rd. W7—47Ha 78
Oaklands Rd. Bexh—56Bd 109
Oaklands Rd. Brom—66Gc 129
Oaklands Rd. Dart—60Sd 112
Oaklands Rd. Grav—3B 136
Oakland Way. Eps—79Ua 144
Oak La. E14—45Bc 84
Oak La. N2—26Fb 41
Oak La. N11—23Mb 42
Oak La. Egh—2N 117
Oak La. Iswth—56Ga 100
Oak La. Pot B—1Pb 10
Oak La. Sev—100Hd 186
Oak La. Twic—59Ja 100
Oak La. Wind—3E 94
Oak La. Wok—88D 156
Oak La. Wfd G—21Hc 45
Oaklawn Rd. Lea—90Ga 160
Oakleafe Gdns. Ilf—27Rc 46
Oaklea Pas. King—69Ma 123
Oakleigh Av. N20—19Fb 23
Oakleigh Av. Edgw—26Ra 39
Oakleigh Av. Surb—74Qa 143
Oakleigh Clo. N20—20Hb 23
Oakleigh Ct. Edgw—26Sa 39
Oakleigh Cres. N20—20Gb 23
Oakleigh Dri. Rick—16S 18
Oakleigh Gdns. N20—18Eb 23
Oakleigh Gdns. Edgw—22Pa 39
Oakleigh Gdns. Orp—77Uc 150
Oakleigh M. N20—18Eb 23
Oakleigh Pk. Av. Chst—67Qc 130
Oakleigh Pk. N. N20—18Fb 23
Oakleigh Pk. S. N20—18Gb 23
Oakleigh Rise. Epp—4Wc 15
Oakleigh Rd. Pinn—23Ba 37
Oakleigh Rd. Uxb—38S 56
Oakleigh Rd. N. N20—19Fb 23
Oakleigh Rd. S. N11—20Jb 24
Oakleigh Way. Mitc—67Kb 126
Oakleigh Way. Surb—74Qa 143
Oakley Av. W5—45Qa 79
Oakley Av. Bark—38Vc 67
Oakley Av. Croy—77Pb 146
Oakley Clo. E4—20Ec 26
Oakley Clo. E6—44Nc 86
Oakley Clo. W7—45Ga 78
Oakley Clo. Iswth—53Fa 100
Oakley Clo. Wey—77M 139
Oakley Cres. EC1
—40Rb 63 (2C 194)
Oakley Cres. Slou—5J 73
Oakley Dri. SE9—60Tc 108
Oakley Dri. Brom—76Nc 150
Oakley Dri. Romf—22Qd 49
Oakley Gdns. N8—29Pb 42
Oakley Gdns. SW3—51Gb 103
Oakley Gdns. Bans—87Db 163
Oakley Grn. Rd. Wind—4A 94
Oakley Pk. Sidc—59Yc 109
Oakley Pl. SE1—50Vb 83 (7K 207)
Oakley Rd. N1—38Tb 63
Oakley Rd. SE25—71Xb 147
Oakley Rd. Brom—76Nc 150
Oakley Rd. Harr—30Ga 38
Oakley Rd. Warl—90Wb 165
Oakley Sq. NW1—40Lb 62 (1C 192)
Oakley St. SW3—51Gb 103
Oakley Wlk. W6—51Za 102
Oak Lodge. E11—30Jc 45
Oak Lodge Av. Chig—22Tc 46
Oak Lodge Clo. Stan—22La 38
Oak Lodge Clo. W on T—78Y 141
Oak Lodge Dri. W Wick—73Dc 148
Oak Lodge La. West—97Tc 184
Oakmead Av. Brom—72Jc 149
Oak Meade. Pinn—23Ca 37
Oakmead Gdns. Edgw—21Ta 39
Oakmead Rd. SW12—60Kb 104
Oakmead Rd. Croy—72Mb 146
Oakmere Av. Pot B—5Eb 9
Oakmere Clo. Pot B—3Fb 9
Oakmere La. Pot B—4Eb 9
Oakmere Rd. SE2—51Wc 109
Oakmont Pl. Orp—74Tc 150
Oakmoor Way. Chig—22Uc 46
Oak Pk. Wey—85G 156
Oakridge Av. Rad—6Ha 6
Oakridge Dri. N2—27Fb 41
Oakridge La. Wat & St Alb—9Fa 6
Oakridge Rd. Brom—63Gc 129
Oak Rise. Buck H—20Mc 27
Oak Rd. W5—45Ma 79
Oak Rd. Cat—94Ub 181
Oak Rd. Cob—87Z 159
Oak Rd. Epp—2Vc 15
Oak Rd. Eri—52Ed 110
(Northumberland Heath)
Oak Rd. Eri—54Jd 110
(Slade Green)
Oak Rd. Grav—2E 136
Oak Rd. Grays—51Ee 113
Oak Rd. Grnh—58Ud 112
Oak Rd. Lea—91Ja 176
Oak Rd. N Mald—68Ta 123
Oak Rd. Orp—80Wc 151
Oak Rd. Romf—25Pd 49
Oak Rd. West—97Tc 184
Oak Row. SW16—68Lb 126
Oakroyd Av. Pot B—5Bb 9
Oakroyd Clo. Pot B—5Bb 9
Oaks Av. SE19—64Ub 127
Oaks Av. Felt—61Aa 121
Oaks Av. Romf—26Ed 48
Oaks Av. Wor Pk—76Xa 144
Oaks Clo. Lea—93Ja 176
Oaksford Av. SE26—62Xb 127
Oaks Gro. E4—19Gc 27
Oakshade Rd. Brom—63Fc 129
Oakshade Rd. Lea—86Ea 160
Oakshaw. Oxt—99Fc 183
Oakshaw Rd. SW18—59Db 103
Oakside. Uxb—37K 55
Oaks La. Croy—76Yb 148
Oaks La. Ilf—29Uc 46
Oaks Rd. Croy—78Xb 147
Oaks Rd. Kenl—86Rb 165
Oaks Rd. Stai—58M 97
Oaks Rd. Wok—89A 156
Oaks Sq. Sev—98Ld 187
Oaks, The. N12—21Db 41
Oaks, The. SE18—50Sc 86
Oaks, The. Eps—86Ua 162
Oaks, The. Hay—40S 56
Oaks, The. Ruis—31U 56
Oaks, The. Wey—86J 157
Oaks, The. Wfd G—24Gc 45
Oaks Track. Cars & Wall
—83Hb 163
Oak St. Romf—29Ed 48
Oaks Way. Cars—80Hb 145
Oaks Way. Eps—91Xa 178
Oaks Way. Kenl—86Sb 165
Oaksway. Surb—74Ma 143
Oakthorpe Pk. Est. N13—22Sb 43
Oakthorpe Rd. N13—22Qb 42
Oaktree Av. N13—20Rb 25
Oak Tree Clo. W5—44La 78
Oak Tree Clo. Brtwd—20Be 33
Oak Tree Clo. Stan—24La 38
Oaktree Clo. Wal X—1Rb 11
Oak Tree Ct. N'holt—40Z 57
Oak Tree Dell. NW9—29Ta 39
Oak Tree Dri. N20—18Db 23
Oak Tree Dri. Egh—4N 117
Oak Tree Gdns. Brom—64Kc 129
Oak Tree Rd. NW8
—41Gb 81 (4D 190)
Oakview Clo. Wal X—1Xb 11
Oakview Gdns. N2—28Fb 41
Oakview Gro. Croy—74Ac 148
Oakview Rd. SE6—64Dc 128
Oak Village. NW5—35Jb 62
Oak Way. N14—17Kb 24
Oakway. SW20—70Ya 124
Oak Way. W3—46Ua 80
Oak Way. Asht—88Qa 161
Oakway. Brom—68Fc 129
Oak Way. Croy—72Zb 148
Oak Way. Felt—60U 98
Oakway. Grays—46De 91
Oakway. Wok—7B 188
Oakway Clo. Bex—58Ad 109
Oakways. SE9—58Rc 108
Oakwood. Wall—81Kb 164
Oakwood. Wal A—6Gc 13
Oakwood Av. N14—17Mb 24
Oakwood Av. Beck—68Ec 128
Oakwood Av. Borwd—14Ra 21
Oakwood Av. Brom—69Kc 129
Oakwood Av. Mitc—68Fb 125
Oakwood Av. Purl—84Rb 165
Oakwood Av. S'hall—45Ca 77
Oakwood Chase. Horn—31Pd 69
Oakwood Clo. N14—16Lb 24
Oakwood Clo. Chst—65Pc 130
Oakwood Clo. Dart—60Rd 111
Oakwood Clo. Lea—99U 174
Oakwood Clo. Wfd G—23Nc 46
Oakwood Ct. W14—48Bb 81
Oakwood Cres. N21—16Nb 24
Oakwood Cres. Gnfd—37Ja 58
Oakwood Dri. SE19—65Tb 127
Oakwood Dri. Bexh—56Ed 110
Oakwood Dri. Edgw—23Sa 39
Oakwood Dri. Lea—99U 174
Oakwood Gdns. Ilf—33Vc 67
Oakwood Gdns. Orp—75Sc 150
Oakwood Gdns. Sutt—75Cb 145
Oakwood Hill. Lou—16Pc 28
Oakwood Hill Industrial Est.
Lou—15Rc 28
Oakwood La. W14—48Bb 81
Oakwood Pde. Enf—15Vb 25
Oakwood Pk. Rd. N14—16Nb 24
Oakwood Pl. Croy—72Qb 146
Oakwood Rise. Long, Dart
—69Ae 135
Oakwood Rd. NW11—29Cb 41
Oakwood Rd. SW20—67Wa 124
Oakwood Rd. Croy—72Qb 146
Oakwood Rd. Orp—75Sc 150
Oakwood Rd. Pinn—26X 37
Oakwood Rd. Red—100Qb 180
Oakwood Rd. St Alb—1Ba 5
Oakwood Rd. Vir W—10N 117
Oakwood Rd. Wok—7B 188
Oakwood View. N14—16Mb 24
Oakworth Rd. W10—43Za 80
Oast Cotts. Sev—94Jd 186
Oast Ho. Clo. Wray, Stai—59A 96
Oasthouse Way. Orp—70Xc 131
Oast Way. Long, Dart—72Ae 155
Oates Rd. Romf—22Dd 48
Oatfield Rd. Orp—74Vc 151
Oatfield Rd. Tad—93Xa 178
Oatland Rise. E17—26Ac 44
Oatlands Av. Wey—78T 140
Oatlands Chase. W on T—76U 140
Oatlands Clo. Wey—77S 140
Oatlands Dri. Slou—4H 73
Oatlands Dri. Wey—77S 140
Oatlands Grn. Wey—76T 140
Oatlands Mere. Wey—76T 140
Oatlands Rd. Enf—11Yb 26
Oatlands Rd. Tad—91Ab 178
Oat La. EC2—44Sb 83 (2E 200)
Oban Rd. E13—41Lc 85
Oban Rd. SE25—70Tb 127
Oban St. E14—44Fc 85
Oberon Way. Shep—69N 119
Oberstein Rd. SW11—56Fb 103
Oborne Clo. SE24—57Rb 105
Observatory Gdns. W8—47Cb 81
Observatory Rd. SW14—56Sa 101
Occupation La. SE18—53Rc 108
Occupation La. W5—49Ma 79
Occupation Rd. SE17
—50Sb 83 (7D 206)
Occupation Rd. W7—49Ja 78
Occupation Rd. W13—47Ka 78
Occupation Rd. Wat—15X 19
Ocean Est. E1—43Ac 84
(in two parts)
Ocean St. E1—43Zb 84
Ockenden Clo. Wok—90B 156
Ockenden Gdns. Wok—90B 156
Ockenden Rd. Wok—90B 156
Ockendon Rd. N1—37Tb 63
Ockendon Rd. Upm—36Sd 70
Ockham Dri. Lea—96T 174
Ockham Dri. Orp—66Wc 131
Ockham La. Wok & Cob—93Q 174
Ockham Rd. N. Wok & Lea
—92N 173
Ockham Rd. S. Lea—98U 174
Ockley Rd. SW16—63Nb 126
Ockley Rd. Croy—73Pb 146
Octagon Rd. W on T—81U 158
Octavia Clo. Mitc—71Gb 145
Octavia Rd. Iswth 55Ga 100
Octavia St. SW11—53Gb 103
Octavia Way. SE28—45Xc 87
Octavia Way. Stai—65J 119
Octavius St. SE8—52Cc 106
Odard Rd. E Mol—70Ca 121
Oddesey Rd. Borwd—11Ra 21
Odencroft Rd. Slou—1E 72
Odessa Rd. E7—35Hc 65
Odessa Rd. NW10—40Wa 60
Odessa St. SE16—47Bc 84
Odger St. SW11—54Hb 103
Offa's Mead. E9—35Bc 64
Offenham Rd. SE9—63Pc 130
Offerton Rd. SW4—55Lb 104
Offham Slope. N12—22Bb 41
Offley Rd. SW9—52Qb 104
Offord Clo. N17—23Wb 43
Offord Rd. N1—38Pb 62
Offord St. N1—38Pb 62
Ogilby St. SE18—49Pc 86
Oglander Rd. SE15—55Vb 105
Ogle St. W1—43Lb 82 (7B 192)
Oglethorpe Rd. Dag—34Cd 68
Ohio Rd. E13—42Hc 85
Oil Mill La. W6—50Wa 80
Okeburn Rd. SW17—64Jb 126
Okehampton Clo. N12—22Fb 41
Okehampton Cres. Well—53Xc 109
Okehampton Rd. NW10—39Ya 60
Okehampton Rd. Romf—23Ld 49
Okehampton Sq. Romf—23Ld 49
Okemore Gdns. Orp—70Yc 131
Olaf St. W11—45Za 80
Old Acre. Wey—86J 157
Old Av. Wey—81S 158
Old Av. Wey—85G 156
(West Byfleet)
Old Av. Clo. Wey—85G 156
Old Bailey. EC4—44Rb 83 (3C 200)
Old Barge Ho. All. SE1—(5A 200)
Old Barn Clo. Sutt—80Ab 144
Old Barn La. Rick—15P 17
Old Barn La. Whyt—88Vb 165
Old Barn Rd. Eps—89Sa 161
Old Barn Way. Bexh—56Fd 110
Old Barrack Yd. SW1
—47Jb 82 (2H 20)
Old Barrowfield. E15—39Gc 65
Oldberry Rd. Edgw—23Ta 39
Old Bethnal Grn. Rd. E2—41Wb 83
Old Bexley La. Bex & Dart
—61Fd 132
Old Bond St. W1—45Lb 82 (5B 198)
Oldborough Rd. Wemb—34La 58
Old Brewer's Yd. WC2
—44Nb 82 (3F 199)
Old Brewery M. NW3—35Fb 61
Old Bri. Clo. N'holt—40Ca 57
Old Bri. St. King—68Ma 123
(in two parts)
Old Broad St. EC2
—44Tb 83 (3G 201)
Old Bromley Rd. Brom—64Fc 129
Old Brompton Rd.
—50Db 81 (7A 202)
SW7 1-125 & 2-146
SW5 remainder
Old Bldgs. WC2—(2K 199)
Old Burlington St. W1
—45Lb 82 (4B 198)
Oldbury Clo. Cher—73G 138
Oldbury Clo. Orp—70Yc 131
★Oldbury Clo. Sev—94Xd
★Oldbury La. Sev—93Xd
Oldbury Pl. W1—43Jb 82 (7J 191)
Oldbury Rd. Cher—73G 138
Oldbury Rd. Enf—12Wb 25
Old Carriageway, The. Sev
—94Ed 186
Old Castle St. E1—44Vb 83 (2K 201)
Old Cavendish St. W1
—44Kb 82 (3K 197)
Old Change Ct. EC4—(3D 200)
Old Chapel Rd. Swan—73Ed 152
Old Charlton Rd. Shep—71S 140
Old Chestnut Av. Esh—79Ca 141
Oldchurch Gdns. Romf—31Fd 68
Old Chu. La. NW9—33Ta 59
Old Chu. La. Gnfd—41Ja 78
Old Chu. La. Stan—22Ka 38
Old Chu. Path. Esh—77Ea 142
Oldchurch Rise. Romf—31Gd 68
Old Chu. Rd. E1—44Zb 84
Old Chu. Rd. E4—21Cc 44
Oldchurch Rd. Romf—31Fd 68
Old Chu. St. SW3
—50Fb 81 (7C 202)
Old Claygate La. Esh—79Ja 142
Old Coach Rd. Cher—71F 138
Old Comn. Rd. Cob—85X 159
Old Compton St. W1
—45Mb 82 (4D 198)
Old Cote Dri. Houn—51Ca 99
Old Cotts. St Alb—1Na 7
Old Ct. Asht—91Na 177
Old Ct. Pl. W8—47Db 81
Old Crown Centre. Slou—7K 73
Old Crown La. Brtwd—11Td 32
Old Deer Pk. Gdns. Rich—55Na 101
Old Devonshire Rd. SW12
—59Kb 104
Old Dock Clo. Rich—51Qa 101
Old Dover Rd. SE3—52Jc 107
Old Downs. Long, Dart—71Ae 155
Oldenhurst Av. N12—24Eb 41
Olden La. Purl—84Qb 164
Old Esher Clo. W on T—78Z 141
Old Esher Rd. W on T—78Z 141
Old Farleigh Rd. S Croy & Warl
—82Yb 166
Old Farm Av. N14—17Lb 24
Old Farm Av. Sidc—60Tc 108
Old Farm Clo. Houn—56Ba 99
Old Farm Gdns. Swan—69Hd 132
Old Farm Ho. Dri. Lea—87Ea 160
Old Farm Pas. Hmptn—67Ea 122
Old Farm Rd. N2—25Fb 41
Old Farm Rd. Hmptn—65Ba 121
Old Farm Rd. W Dray—47M 75
Old Farm Rd. E. Sidc—61Wc 131
Old Farm Rd. W. Sidc—61Vc 131
Old Ferry Dri. Wray, Stai—8N 95
Oldfield Clo. Amer—11A 16
Oldfield Clo. Brom—70Pc 130
Oldfield Clo. Gnfd—36Ga 58
Oldfield Clo. Stan—22Ja 38
Oldfield Farm Gdns. Gnfd
—39Fa 58
Oldfield Gdns. Asht—90Ma 161
Oldfield Gro. SE16—49Zb 84
Oldfield La. N. Gnfd—39Fa 58
Oldfield La. S. Gnfd—41Ea 78
Oldfield M. N6—31Lb 62
Oldfield Rd. N16—34Ub 63
Oldfield Rd. NW10—38Va 60
Oldfield Rd. SW18—56Db 103
Oldfield Rd. SW19—65Ab 124
Oldfield Rd. W3—47Va 80
Oldfield Rd. Bexh—54Ad 109
Oldfield Rd. Brom—70Pc 130
Oldfield Rd. Hmptn—67Ba 121
Oldfields Cir. N'holt—37Ea 58
Oldfields Rd. Sutt—76Bb 145
Old Fold Clo. Barn—11Bb 23
Old Fold La. Barn—11Bb 23
Old Fold View. Barn—13Ya 22
Old Ford Rd.—40Yb 64
E2 1-211 & 2-316
E3 remainder
Old Forge Clo. Stan—21Ja 38
Old Forge Clo. Wat—5W 4
Old Forge Cres. Shep—72R 140
Old Forge Rd. Enf—10Vb 11
Old Forge Way. Sidc—63Xc 131
Old Fox Clo. Cat—93Rb 181

Old Gannon Clo.—Overmead

Old Gannon Clo. N'wd—21S 36
Old Gdns., The. Sev—95Fd 186
Old Gloucester St. WC1
—43Nb 82 (7G 193)
Old Hall Clo. Pinn—25Aa 37
Old Hall Dri. Pinn—25Aa 37
Oldhams Ter. W3—47Sa 79
Old Harrow La. West—91Sc 184
Old Hatch Mnr. Ruis—31W 56
Old Hill. Chst—67Qc 130
Old Hill. Orp—79Tc 150
Old Hill. Wok—8G 188
Old Hill Est. Wok—8G 188
Oldhill St. N16—32Wb 63
Old Homesdale Rd. Brom
—70Lc 129
Old Ho. Clo. SW19—64Ab 124
Old Ho. Clo. Eps—82Va 162
Oldhouse La. K Lan—7N 3
Old Jamaica Rd. SE16—48Wb 83
Old James St. SE15—55Xb 105
Old Jewry. EC2—44Tb 83 (3F 201)
Old Kenton La. NW9—29Ra 39
Old Kent Rd. SE1
—49Ub 83 (5H 207)
Old Kingston Rd. Wor Pk
—76Sa 143
Old La. West—92Mc 183
Old La. Wok & Cob—90R 158
Old La. Gdns. Cob—94W 174
Old Lodge La. Purl & Kenl
—85Pb 164
Old Lodge Way. Stan—22Ja 38
Old London Rd. Dor—99La 176
Old London Rd. Eps—89Wa 162
Old London Rd. Lea—98W 174
Old London Rd. Sev—87Ad 169
(Knockholt)
★Old London Rd. Sev—87Be
(Wrotham)
Old Maidstone Rd. Sidc—66Bd 131
Old Malden La. Wor Pk—75Ta 143
Old Malt Way. Wok—5G 188
Old Mnr. Rd. Iswth—58Ea 100
Old Mnr. Way. Bexh—54Fd 110
Old Mnr. Yd. SW5—49Db 81
Old Marylebone Rd. NW1
—43Gb 81 (1E 196)
Old Mead. Ger X—23A 34
Old Mill Clo. E18—27Lc 45
Old Mill La. Red—100Kb 180
Old Mill La. Uxb—44K 75
Old Mill Rd. SE18—51Tc 108
Old Mill Rd. K Lan—6S 4
Old Mill Rd. Uxb—34J 55
Old Mitre Ct. EC4
—44Qb 82 (3A 200)
Old Montague St. E1—43Wb 83
Old Nichol St. E2—42Vb 83 (5K 195)
Old North St. WC1—(7H 193)
Old Oak Av. Coul—91Gb 179
Old Oak Common La.—43Ua 80
W3 51-189 & 82-240
NW10 remainder
Old Oak La. NW10—41Ua 80
Old Oak Rd. W3—45Va 80
Old Orchard. Sun—68Y 121
Old Orchard. Wey—84P 157
Old Orchard, The. NW3—35Hb 61
Old Otford Rd. Sev—90Kd 171
Old Pal. Gdns. Wey—76R 140
Old Pal. La. Rich—57La 100
Old Pal. Rd. Croy—76Sb 147
Old Pal. Ter. Rich—57Ma 101
Old Pal. Yd. SW1—48Nb 82 (3F 205)
Old Pal. Yd. Rich—57Ma 101
Old Paradise St. SE11
—49Pb 82 (5H 205)
Old Pk. Av. SW12—58Jb 104
Old Pk. Av. Enf—14Sb 25
Old Pk. Gro. Enf—14Sb 25
Old Pk. La. W1—46Kb 82 (7K 197)
Old Pk. M. Houn—52Ba 99
Oldpark Ride. Wal X—4Tb 11
Oldpark Ride. Wal X—3Rb 11
Old Pk. Ridings. N21—16Rb 25
Old Pk. Rd. N13—21Pb 42
Old Pk. Rd. SE2—50Wc 87
Old Pk. Rd. Enf—13Rb 25
Old Pk. Rd. S. Enf—14Rb 25
Old Pk. View. Enf—13Qb 24
Old Perry St. Chst—65Uc 130
Old Perry St. Grav—1A 136
Old Polhill. Sev—86Ed 170
Old Pye St. SW1—48Mb 82 (3D 204)
Old Quebec St. W1
—44Hb 81 (3G 197)
Old Queen St. SW1
—47Mb 82 (2E 204)
Old Rectory Clo. Tad—96Wa 178
Old Rectory Gdns. Edgw—23Qa 39
Old Rectory La. Lea—98U 174
Old Rectory La. Uxb—31G 54
★Old Rectory Rd. Ong—5Ld
Old Redding. Harr—22Da 37
Oldridge Rd. SW12—59Jb 104
Old Rd. SE13—56Gc 107
Old Rd. Dart—57Fd 110
Old Rd. Enf—11Yb 26
Old Rd. Romf & Brtwd—12Md 31
Old Rd. Wey—80H 139
Old Rd. E. Grav—10D 114
Old Rd. W. Grav—10B 114
Old Ruislip Rd. N'holt—40Y 57
Olds App. Wat—18S 18
Old School Ct. Sev—94Ld 187
Old Schools La. Eps—81Va 162
Old Seacoal La. EC4
—44Rb 83 (3B 200)
Old Shire La. Rick—16C 16
Old Slade La. Iver—48G 74
Old S. Lambeth Rd. SW8
—52Nb 104
Old Sq. WC2—44Qb 82 (2K 199)
Old Sta. App. Lea—93Ja 176
Old Sta. Rd. Hay—48V 76
Old Sta. Rd. Lou—15Nc 28
Oldstead Rd. Brom—63Fc 129
Old Stockley Rd. W Dray—47R 76
Old St. E13—40Lc 65
Old St. EC1—42Sb 83 (6D 194)
Old Swan Yd. Cars—77Hb 145
★Old Terry's Lodge Rd. Sev—88Vd
Old Town. SW4—55Lb 104
Old Town. Croy—76Rb 147
Old Tye Av. West—88Nc 168
Old Uxbridge Rd. Rick—22G 34
Old Wlk., The. Sev—89Ld 171
Old Watford Rd. St Alb—2Aa 5
Old Watling St. Grav—4C 136
Oldway La. Slou—6B & 7B 72
Old Westhall Clo. Warl—91Yb 182
Old Woking Rd. Wok & Wey
—90D 156
Old Woolwich Rd. SE10—51Fc 107
Oleander Clo. Orp—78Tc 150
O'Leary Sq. E1—43Yb 84
Olga St. E3—40Ac 64
Olinda Rd. N16—30Vb 43
Oliphant St. W10—41Za 80
Oliver Av. SE25—69Vb 127
Oliver Clo. E10—33Dc 64
Oliver Clo. W4—51Ra 101
Oliver Clo. Wey—77K 139
Oliver Ct. SE18—49Sc 86
Oliver Cres. F'ham, Dart—73Pd 153
Oliver Gdns. E6—43Nc 86
Oliver Gro. SE25—70Vb 127
Olive Rd. E13—41Lc 85
Olive Rd. NW2—35Ya 60
Olive Rd. SW19—66Eb 125
Olive Rd. W5—48Ma 79
Olive Rd. Dart—60Md 111
Oliver Rd. E10—33Dc 64
Oliver Rd. E17—29Ec 44
Oliver Rd. Brtwd—15Ce 33
Oliver Rd. Grays—53Vd 112
Oliver Rd. N Mald—68Sa 123
Oliver Rd. Rain—39Hd 68
Oliver Rd. Sutt—77Fb 145
Oliver Rd. Swan—69Fd 132
Olivers Mill. Long, Dart—75Ae 155
Olivers Yd. EC1—42Tb 83 (5G 195)
Olive St. Romf—29Fd 48
Olivette St. SW15—56Za 102
Ollard's Gro. Lou—14Mc 27
Olleberrie La. Rick—4F 2
Ollerton Grn. E3—39Bc 64
Ollerton Rd. N11—22Mb 42
Olley Clo. Wall—80Nb 146
Ollgar Clo. W12—46Va 80
Olliffe St. E14—48Ec 84
Olmar St. SE1—51Wb 105
Olney Rd. SE17—51Rb 105
Olron Cres. Bexh—57Zc 109
Olven Rd. SE18—51Sc 108
Olveston Wlk. Cars—72Fb 145
Olyffe Av. Well—54Wc 109
Olyffe Dri. Beck—67Ec 128
Olympia Way. W14—48Ab 80
Olympia Yd. W2—45Db 81
Olympic Industrial Est. Wemb
—35Ra 59
Olympic Way. Gnfd—39Ea 58
Olympic Way. Wemb—34Qa 59
Olympus Sq. E5—34Wb 63
Oman Av. NW2—35Xa 60
O'Meara St. SE1—46Sb 83 (7E 200)
Omega Pl. N1—(2G 193)
Omega Rd. Wok—88C 156
Omega St. SE14—53Cc 106
Ommaney Rd. SE14—53Zb 106
Ondine Rd. SE15—56Vb 105
O'Neill Path. SE18—51Qc 108
One Pin La. Slou—5G 52
One Tree Clo. SE23—58Yb 106
Ongar Clo. Romf—29Yc 47
Ongar Clo. Wey—79H 139
Ongar Hill. Wey—79J 139
Ongar Pl. Brtwd—19Zd 33
Ongar Pl. Wey—79J 139
Ongar Rd. SW6—51Cb 103
Ongar Rd. Brtwd—13Td 32
★Ongar Rd. Brtwd—4Rd
(Kelvedon Hatch)
★Ongar Rd. Brtwd—4Ud
(Stondon Massey)
Ongar Rd. Romf & Stap T, Romf
—12Yc 29
Ongar Rd. Wey—78J 139
Ongar Way. Rain—39Gd 68
Onra Rd. E17—31Cc 64
Onslow Av. Rich—57Na 101
Onslow Av. Sutt—82Bb 163
Onslow Clo. E4—19Ec 26
Onslow Clo. Th Dit—74Ga 142
Onslow Clo. Wok—89C 156
Onslow Cres. Chst—67Rc 130
Onslow Cres. Wok—89C 156
Onslow Dri. Sidc—61Zc 131
Onslow Gdns. E18—27Kc 45
Onslow Gdns. N10—29Kb 42
Onslow Gdns. N21—15Qb 24
Onslow Gdns. SW7
—50Fb 81 (7B 202)
Onslow Gdns. S Croy—84Wb 165
Onslow Gdns. Th Dit—74Ga 142
Onslow Gdns. Wall—79Lb 146
Onslow M. SW7—49Fb 81 (6B 202)
Onslow M. E. SW7
—49Fb 81 (6B 202)
Onslow Rd. Croy—73Qb 146
Onslow Rd. N Mald—70Wa 124
Onslow Rd. Rich—57Na 101
Onslow Rd. W on T—77V 140
Onslow Sq. SW7—49Fb 81 (6C 202)
Onslow St. EC1—42Qb 82 (6A 194)
Onslow Way. Th Dit—74Ga 142
Onslow Way. Wok—87H 157
Ontario St. SE1—48Rb 83 (4C 206)
On the Hill. Wat—19Aa 19
Opal St. SE11—50Rb 83 (6B 206)
Opel M. Ilf—33Rc 66
Opendale Rd. Slou—3A 72
Openshaw Rd. SE2—49Xc 87
Openview. SW18—60Eb 103
Ophir Ter. SE15—53Wb 105
Opossum Way. Houn—55Y 99
Oppidans M. NW3—38Hb 61
Oppidans Rd. NW3—38Hb 61
Orange Ct. E1—46Wb 83
Orange Ct. La. Orp—81Qc 168
Orange Hill Rd. Edgw—24Sa 39
Orange Pl. SE16—48Yb 84
Orangery La. SE9—57Pc 108
Orangery, The. Rich—61La 122
Orange St. WC2—45Mb 82 (5E 198)
Orange Tree Hill. Hav, Romf
—21Gd 48
Orange Yd. W1—(3E 198)
Oran Pl. SE16—47Yb 84
Oratory La. SW3—(7D 202)
Orbain Rd. SW6—52Ab 102
Orbel St. SW11—53Gb 103
Orbital Cres. Wat—7V 4
Orb St. SE17—49Tb 83 (6F 207)
Orchard Av. N3—27Cb 41
Orchard Av. N14—17Lb 24
Orchard Av. N20—19Fb 23
Orchard Av. Ashf—65S 120
Orchard Av. Belv—51Ad 109
Orchard Av. Brtwd—20Be 33
Orchard Av. Croy—74Ac 148
Orchard Av. Dart—59Kd 111
Orchard Av. Felt—57T 98
Orchard Av. Grav—4D 136
Orchard Av. Houn—52Aa 99
Orchard Av. Mitc—74Jb 146
Orchard Av. N Mald—69Ua 124
Orchard Av. Rain—42Ld 89
Orchard Av. Slou—3B 72
Orchard Av. S'hall—46Ba 77
Orchard Av. Th Dit—74Ja 142
Orchard Av. Wat—3X 5
Orchard Av. Wey—83H 157
Orchard Av. Wind—3E 94
Orchard Clo. SE23—58Yb 106
Orchard Clo. SW20—70Ya 124
Orchard Clo. W10—43Bb 81
Orchard Clo. Ashf—65S 120
Orchard Clo. Bans—86Db 163
Orchard Clo. Bexh—53Ad 109
Orchard Clo. Borwd—14Pa 21
Orchard Clo. Bush, Wat—18Fa 20
Orchard Clo. Edgw—23Na 39
Orchard Clo. Egh—64D 118
Orchard Clo. Lea—94Fa 176
Orchard Clo. Lea—96V 174
(East Horsley)
Orchard Clo. Long, Dart—68De 135
(in two parts)
Orchard Clo. N'holt—37Ea 58
Orchard Clo. Rad—9Ga 6
Orchard Clo. Rick—14F 16
Orchard Clo. Ruis—31S 56
Orchard Clo. Sev—92Ld 187
Orchard Clo. S Ock—42Yd 90
Orchard Clo. Surb—74Ka 142
Orchard Clo. Uxb—37K 55
Orchard Clo. Wat—12V 18
Orchard Clo. Wemb—39Na 59
Orchard Clo. Wok—88D 156
Orchard Ct. Twic—61Ea 122
Orchard Ct. Wor Pk—74Wa 144
Orchard Cres. Croy—73Ac 148
Orchard Cres. Edgw—22Sa 39
Orchard Cres. Enf—11Vb 25
Orchard Dri. SE3—54Fc 107
Orchard Dri. Asht—92Ma 177
Orchard Dri. Edgw—22Pa 39
Orchard Dri. Epp—8Uc 14
Orchard Dri. Grav—10B 136
Orchard Dri. Grays—47Ce 91
Orchard Dri. Rick—13E 16
Orchard Dri. Uxb—42M 75
Orchard Dri. Wat—11V 18
Orchard Dri. Wok—87A 156
Orchard End. Lea—96Ea 176
Orchard End. Wey—75U 140
Orchard Gdns. Chess—77Na 143
Orchard Gdns. Eps—87Sa 161
Orchard Gdns. Lea—100Aa 175
Orchard Gdns. Sutt—78Cb 145
Orchard Gdns. Wal A—6Ec 12
Orchard Ga. NW9—28Ua 40
Orchard Ga. Esh—74Fa 142
Orchard Ga. Gnfd—37Ka 58
Orchard Grn. Orp—75Uc 150
Orchard Gro. Edgw—25Qa 39
Orchard Gro. Harr—29Pa 39
Orchard Gro. Orp—75Vc 151
Orchard Hill. SE13—54Dc 106
Orchard Hill. Cars—78Hb 145
Orchard Hill. Dart—57Gd 110
Orchard La. SW20—67Xa 124
Orchard La. Brtwd—15Vd 32
Orchard La. E Mol—72Fa 142
Orchard La. Wfd G—21Lc 45
Orchard Lea Clo. Wok—87G 156
Orchard Leigh. Lea—94Ka 176
Orchardleigh Av. Enf—12Yb 26
Orchard Mains. Wok—7F 188
Orchardmede. N21—16Tb 25
Orchard M. N1—38Tb 63
Orchard Pde. Pot B—3Za 8
Orchard Pl. E14—45Gc 85
Orchard Pl. N17—24Vb 43
Orchard Pl. Sev—96Ad 185
Orchard Rise. Croy—74Ac 148
Orchard Rise. King—67Sa 123
Orchard Rise. Rich—56Ra 101
Orchard Rise E. Sidc—57Vc 109
Orchard Rise W. Sidc—57Uc 108
Orchard Rd. N6—31Kb 62
Orchard Rd. SE3—54Gc 107
Orchard Rd. SE18—49Tc 86
Orchard Rd. Barn—14Bb 23
Orchard Rd. Belv—49Cd 88
Orchard Rd. Bren—51La 100
Orchard Rd. Brom—67Lc 129
Orchard Rd. Chess—77Na 143
Orchard Rd. Dag—39Cd 68
Orchard Rd. Enf—15Yb 26
Orchard Rd. Grav—61Ee 135
Orchard Rd. Hmptn—66Ba 121
Orchard Rd. Hay—45W 76
Orchard Rd. Houn—57Ba 99
Orchard Rd. King—68Na 123
Orchard Rd. Mitc—74Jb 146
Orchard Rd. Orp—78Rc 150
(Farnborough)
Orchard Rd. Orp—82Yc 169
(Pratt's Bottom)
Orchard Rd. Rich—55Qa 101
Orchard Rd. Romf—25Dd 48
Orchard Rd. Sev—88Hd 170
(Otford)
Orchard Rd. Sev—94Gd 186
(Riverhead)
Orchard Rd. Sidc—63Uc 130
Orchard Rd. S Croy—86Xb 165
Orchard Rd. S Ock—42Yd 90
Orchard Rd. Sun—66X 121
Orchard Rd. Sutt—78Cb 145
Orchard Rd. Swans—57Ae 113
Orchard Rd. Twic—57Ja 100
Orchard Rd. Well—55Xc 109
Orchard Rd. Wind—8M 95
Orchards N., The. Epp—4Wc 15
Orchardson St. NW8
—42Fb 81 (6B 190)
Orchards S., The. Epp—4Wc 15
Orchard St. E17—28Ac 44
Orchard St. W1—44Jb 82 (3H 197)
Orchard St. Dart—58Nd 111
Orchard Ter. Enf—16Wb 25
Orchard, The. N21—16Tb 25
Orchard, The. NW11—29Cb 41
Orchard, The. SE3—54Fc 107
Orchard, The. W4—49Ta 79
Orchard, The. Houn—54Ea 100
Orchard, The. K Lan—1Q 4
Orchard, The. Swan—68Fd 132
Orchard, The. Vir W—71A 138
Orchard, The. Wok—94A 172
Orchard View. Uxb—42M 75
Orchardville. Slou—2A 72
Orchard Way. Ashf—61P 119
Orchard Way. Croy & Beck
—73Ac 148
Orchard Way. Dart—62Md 133
Orchard Way. Enf—13Ub 25
Orchard Way. Esh—79Ea 142
Orchard Way. Pot B—1Db 9
Orchard Way. Rick—17J 17
Orchard Way. Sev—89Qd 171
Orchard Way. Sutt—77Fb 145
Orchard Way. Tad—98Bb 179
Orchard Way. Wey—79K 139
Orchard Way. Wok—97E 172
Orchard Waye. Uxb—40M 55
Orchehill Av. Ger X—28A 34
Orchehill Rise. Ger X—29A 34
Orchid Rd. N14—17Lb 24
Orchid St. W12—45Wa 80
Orchis Way. Romf—23Pd 49
Orde Hall St. WC1
—43Pb 82 (7H 193)
Ordell Rd. E3—40Bc 64
Ordnance Clo. Felt—61W 120
Ordnance Cres. SE10—47Gc 85
Ordnance Hill. NW8
—39Fb 61 (1C 190)
Ordnance M. NW8
—40Fb 61 (1C 190)
Ordnance Rd. E16—43Hc 85
Ordnance Rd. SE18—51Qc 108
Ordnance Rd. Enf—9Zb 12
Ordnance Rd. Grav—8E 114
Oregon Av. E12—35Pc 66
Oregon Sq. Orp—74Tc 150
Orestan La. Lea—99X 175
Oreston Rd. Rain—41Md 89
Orford Gdns. Twic—61Ha 122
Orford Rd. E17—29Dc 44
Orford Rd. E18—27Kc 45
Organ Hall Rd. Borwd—11Na 21
Organ La. E4—19Ec 26
Oriel Clo. Mitc—70Mb 126
Oriel Ct. Croy—74Tb 147
Oriel Gdns. Ilf—27Pc 46
Oriel Pl. NW3—35Eb 61
Oriel Rd. E9—37Zb 64
Oriel Way. N'holt—38Da 57
Oriental Clo. Wok—89B 156
Oriental Rd. E16—46Mc 85
Oriental Rd. Asc—10B 116
Oriental Rd. Wok—89B 156
Oriental St. E14—45Cc 84
Orient Industrial Pk. E10—33Cc 64
Orient Rd. Til—5C 114
Orient St. SE11—49Rb 83 (5B 206)
Orient Way. E5—34Zb 64
Oriole Way. SE28—45Xc 87
Orion Way. N'wd—21V 36
Orissa Rd. SE18—50Uc 86
Orkney St. SW11—54Jb 104
Orlando Gdns. Eps—82Ta 161
Orlando Rd. SW4—55Lb 104
Orleans Rd. SE19—65Tb 127
Orleans Rd. Twic—59Ka 100
Orleston Gdns. Orp—78Ad 151
Orleston M. N7—37Qb 62
Orleston Rd. N7—37Qb 62
Orley Farm Rd. Harr—34Ga 58
Orlick Rd. Grav—10K 115
Orlop St. SE10—50Gc 85
Ormanton Rd. SE26—63Wb 127
Orme Ct. W2—45Db 81
Orme La. W2—45Db 81
Ormeley Rd. SW12—60Kb 104
Orme Rd. King—68Ra 123
Ormerod Gdns. Mitc—68Jb 126
Ormesby Clo. SE28—45Zc 87
Ormesby Dri. Pot B—4Za 8
Ormesby Way. Harr—30Pa 39
Orme Sq. W2—45Db 81
Ormiston Gro. W12—46Xa 80
Ormiston Rd. SE10—50Jc 85
Ormond Av. Hmptn—67Da 121
Ormond Clo. WC1
—43Nb 82 (7G 193)
Ormond Cres. Hmptn—67Da 121
Ormond Dri. Hmptn—66Da 121
Ormonde Av. Eps—82Ta 161
Ormonde Av. Orp—75Sc 150
Ormonde Ga. SW3—50Hb 81
Ormonde Pl. SW1
—49Jb 82 (6H 203)
Ormonde Rise. Buck H—18Lc 27
Ormonde Rd. SW14—55Sa 101
Ormonde Rd. N'wd—21T 36
Ormonde Rd. Wok—4F 188
Ormonde Ter. NW8
—39Hb 61 (1F 191)
Ormond M. WC1—42Nb 82 (6H 193)
Ormond Rd. N19—32Nb 62
Ormond Rd. Rich—57Ma 101
Ormond Yd. SW1
—46Lb 82 (6C 198)
Ormsby Gdns. Gnfd—40Ea 58
Ormsby Pl. N16—34Vb 63
Ormsby St. E2—40Vb 63 (1K 195)
Ormside St. SE15—51Yb 106
Ormskirk Rd. Wat—22Z 37
Ornan Rd. NW3—36Gb 61
Oronsay Wlk. N1—38Sb 63
Orpen Wlk. N16—34Ub 63
Orphanage Rd. Wat—12Y 19
Orpheus St. SE5—53Tb 105
Orpington By-Pass. Orp—75Xc 151
Orpington By-Pass Rd. Orp &
Sev—81Cd 170
Orpington Gdns. N18—20Ub 25
Orpington Rd. N21—18Rb 25
Orpington Rd. Chst—69Uc 130
Orpwood Clo. Hmptn—65Ba 121
Orsett Heath Cres. Grays—8C 92
Orsett Rd. Grays—50De 91
Orsett Rd. Grays & Stanf—2E 92
Orsett St. SE11—50Pb 82 (7J 205)
Orsett Ter. W2—44Eb 81 (2A 196)
Orsett Ter. Wfd G—24Lc 45
Orsman Rd. N1—39Ub 63
Orton St. E1—46Wb 83
Orville Rd. SW11—54Fb 103
Orwell. Grays—9L 93
Orwell Clo. Wind—5H 95
Orwell Rd. E13—40Lc 65
Osbaldeston Rd. N16—33Wb 63
Osberton Rd. SE12—57Jc 107
Osbert St. SW1—49Mb 82 (6D 204)
Osborn Clo. E8—39Wb 63
Osborne Av. Stai—60P 97
Osborne Clo. Beck—70Ac 128
Osborne Clo. Felt—64Z 121
Osborne Clo. Horn—30Kd 49
Osborne Ct. Wind—4G 94
Osborne Gdns. T Hth—68Sb 127
Osborne Gro. E17—28Bc 44
Osborne Gro. N4—32Qb 62
Osborne M. Wind—4G 94
Osborne Pl. Sutt—78Fb 145
Osborne Rd. E7—36Kc 65
Osborne Rd. E9—37Bc 64
Osborne Rd. E10—33Dc 64
Osborne Rd. N4—32Qb 62
Osborne Rd. N13—20Qb 24
Osborne Rd. NW2—37Xa 60
Osborne Rd. W3—48Ra 79
Osborne Rd. Belv—50Bd 87
Osborne Rd. Brtwd—16Wd 32
Osborne Rd. Buck H—18Kc 27
Osborne Rd. Dag—36Bd 67
Osborne Rd. Egh—65B 118
Osborne Rd. Enf—12Ac 26
Osborne Rd. Horn—30Kd 49
Osborne Rd. Houn—55Ba 99
Osborne Rd. King—66Na 123
Osborne Rd. Pot B—2Db 9
Osborne Rd. S'hall—44Ea 78
Osborne Rd. T Hth—68Sb 127
Osborne Rd. Uxb—38L 55
Osborne Rd. W on T—74W 140
Osborne Rd. Wat—10Y 5
Osborne Rd. Wind—4G 94
Osborne Sq. Dag—35Bd 67
Osborne St. Slou—7K 73
Osborn Gdns. NW7—24Za 40
Osborn La. SE23—59Ac 106
Osborn St. E1—43Vb 83
Osborn Ter. SE3—56Hc 107
Osbourne Av. K Lan—1P 3
Oscar St. SE8—53Cc 106
Oseney Cres. NW5—36Lb 62
Osgood Av. Orp—78Vc 151
Osgood Gdns. Orp—78Vc 151
O'Shea Gro. E3—39Bc 64
Osidge La. N14—18Jb 24
Osiers Rd. SW18—56Cb 103
Osier St. E1—42Yb 84
Osier Way. E10—34Dc 64
Osier Way. Bans—86Ab 162
Osier Way. Mitc—71Hb 145
Oslac Rd. SE6—64Dc 128
Oslo Ct. NW8—(2D 190)
Osman Clo. N15—30Tb 43
Osman Rd. N9—20Wb 25
Osman Rd. W6—48Ya 80
Osmond Clo. Harr—33Ea 58
Osmond Gdns. Wall—78Lb 146
Osmund St. W12—43Va 80
Osnaburgh St. NW1
—42Kb 82 (5A 192)
Osnaburgh Ter. NW1
—42Kb 82 (5A 192)
Osney Wlk. Cars—72Fb 145
Osney Way. Grav—1H 137
Osprey Est. SE16—49Zb 84
Osprey Gdns. S Croy—82Ac 166
Ospringe Rd. NW5—35Lb 62
Ossian Rd. N4—31Pb 62
Ossington Bldgs. W1
—43Jb 82 (7H 191)
Ossington Clo. W2—45Cb 81
Ossington St. W2—45Db 81
Ossory Rd. SE1—51Wb 105
Ossulston St. NW1
—40Mb 62 (2E 192)
Ossulton Pl. N2—27Eb 41
Ossulton Way. N2—28Eb 41
Ostade Rd. SW2—59Pb 104
Osten M. SW7—48Db 81
Osterberg Rd. Dart—56Pd 111
Osterley Av. Iswth—52Fa 100
Osterley Clo. Orp—67Wc 131
Osterley Cres. Iswth—53Ha 100
Osterley Gdns. T Hth—68Sb 127
Osterley La. S'hall & Iswth
—50Ca 77
Osterley Pk. Rd. S'hall—48Ba 77
Osterley Pk. View Rd. W7
—47Ga 78
Osterley Rd. N16—35Ub 63
Osterley Rd. Iswth—52Ga 100
Oswald Clo. Lea—94Ea 176
Oswald Rd. Lea—94Ea 176
Oswald Rd. S'hall—46Aa 77
Oswald's Mead. E9—35Ac 64
Oswald St. E5—34Zb 64
Osward. Croy—82Bc 166
(in three parts)
Osward Pl. N9—19Xb 25
Osward Rd. SW17—61Hb 125
Oswin St. SE11—49Rb 83 (5C 206)
Oswyth Rd. SE5—54Ub 105
Otford Clo. Bex—58Dd 110
Otford Clo. Brom—69Qc 130
Otford Cres. SE4—58Bc 106
Otford La. Sev—84Bd 169
Otford Rd. Sev—91Kd 187
Othello Clo. SE11
—50Rb 83 (7B 206)
Otis St. E3—41Ec 84
Otley App. Ilf—30Rc 46
Otley Dri. Ilf—30Rc 46
Otley Rd. E16—44Lc 85
Otley Ter. E5—34Zb 64
Otley Way. Wat—20Y 19
Otlinge Clo. Orp—70Zc 131
Ottawa Gdns. Dag—38Fd 68
Ottawa Rd. Til—4C 114
Ottaway Ct. E5—34Wb 63
Ottaway St. E5—34Wb 63
Otterbourne Rd. E4—20Fc 27
Otterbourne Rd. Croy—75Sb 147
Otterburn Gdns. Iswth—52Ja 100
Otterburn St. SW17—65Hb 125
Otter Clo. Cher—79D 138
Otterden Clo. Orp—77Uc 150
Otterden St. SE6—63Cc 128
Otterfield Rd. W Dray—45N 75
Ottermead La. Cher—79E 138
Otter Rd. Gnfd—42Ea 78
Otterspool La. Wat—10Aa 5
Otterspool Way. Wat—11Ca 19
Otto Clo. SE26—62Xb 127
Ottoman Ter. Wat—13Y 19
Otto St. SE17—51Rb 105
(in two parts)
Ottway's Av. Asht—91Ma 177
Ottways La. Asht—92Ma 177
Otways Clo. Pot B—4Db 9
Oulton Clo. E5—33Yb 64
Oulton Clo. SE28—44Yc 87
Oulton Cres. Bark—37Vc 67
Oulton Cres. Pot B—4Za 8
Oulton Rd. N15—29Tb 43
Oulton Way. Wat—21Ba 37
Oundle Av. Bush, Wat—16Ea 20
Ousden Clo. Wal X—2Ac 12
Ousden Dri. Wal X—2Ac 12
Ouseley Rd. Wind—9N 95
Ouseley Rd. Wray, Stai—9N 95
Ousley Rd. SW12—60Hb 104
Outer Circ. NW1—40Gb 61 (1F 191)
Outfield Rd. Ger X—24A 34
Outgate Rd. NW10—38Va 60
★Outings La. Brtwd—7Xd
Outram Pl. N1—39Nb 62
Outram Pl. Wey—78S 140
Outram Rd. E6—39Nc 66
Outram Rd. N22—25Mb 42
Outram Rd. Croy—75Vb 147
Outwich St. EC3—(2J 201)
Outwood La. Tad & Coul
—94Db 179
Oval Gdns. Grays—48Ee 91
Oval Pl. SW8—52Pb 104
Oval Rd. NW1—39Kb 62
Oval Rd. Croy—74Ub 147
Oval Rd. N. Dag—39Dd 68
Oval Rd. S. Dag—40Dd 68
Oval, The. E2—40Xb 63
Oval, The. Bans—86Cb 163
Oval, The. Long, Dart—69Ee 135
Oval, The. Sidc—59Wc 109
Oval Way. SE11—50Pb 82
Oval Way. Ger X—23A 34
Ovenden Rd. Sev—92Zc 185
Overbrae. Beck—64Cc 128
Overbrook. Lea—100R 174
Overbrook Wlk. Edgw—24Qa 39
Overbury Av. Beck—69Dc 128
Overbury Cres. Croy—82Ec 166
Overbury Rd. N15—30Tb 43
Overbury St. E5—35Zb 64
Overcliff. Grav—8C 114
Overcliff Rd. SE13—55Cc 106
Overcliff Rd. Grays—50Fe 91
(in two parts)
Overcourt Clo. Sidc—58Xc 109
Overdale. Asht—88Na 161
Overdale Av. N Mald—68Ta 123
Overdale Rd. W5—48La 78
Overdown Rd. SE6—63Cc 128
Overhill. Warl—91Yb 182
Overhill Rd. SE22—59Wb 105
Overhill Rd. Purl—81Qb 164
Overhill Way. Beck—71Fc 149
Overlea Rd. E5—31Wb 63
Overmead. Sidc—59Tc 108

Overmead—Parkmead

Overmead. Swan—71Gd 152
Over Minnis. Long, Dart—76Be 155
Overstand Clo. Beck—71Cc 148
Overstone Gdns. Croy—73Bc 148
Overstone Rd. W6—49Ya 80
Overstream. Rick—14K 17
Over the Misbourne. Ger X—30C 34
Over the Misbourne. Uxb—30D 34
Overthorpe Clo. Wok—5B 188
Overton Clo. NW10—37Sa 59
Overton Clo. Iswth—53Ha 100
Overton Ct. E11—31Jc 65
Overton Dri. E11—31Jc 65
Overton Dri. Romf—31Yc 67
Overton Rd. E10—32Ac 64
Overton Rd. N14—15Nb 24
Overton Rd. SE2—48Yc 87
Overton Rd. SW9—54Qb 104
Overton Rd. Sutt—80Cb 145
Overton Rd. E. SE2—48Zc 87
Overtons Yd. Croy—76Sb 147
Overy St. Dart—58Nd 111
Ovesdon Av. Harr—32Ba 57
Oveton Way. Lea—98Da 175
Ovett Clo. SE19—65Ub 127
Ovex Clo. E14—47Ec 84
Ovington Ct. Wok—4C 188
Ovington Gdns. SW3
—48Gb 81 (4E 202)
Ovington M. SW3—(4E 202)
Ovington Sq. SW3
—48Gb 81 (4E 202)
Ovington St. SW3
—49Gb 81 (5E 202)
Owen Clo. SE28—46Yc 87
Owen Clo. Hay—41X 77
Owen Gdns. Wfd G—23Nc 46
Owenite St. SE2—49Xc 87
Owen Pl. Lea—94Ka 176
Owen Rd. N13—21Sb 43
Owen Rd. Hay—41X 77
Owen's Ct. EC1—(3B 194)
Owen's Row. EC1
—41Rb 83 (3B 194)
Owen St. EC1—40Rb 63 (2B 194)
Owens Way. SE23—59Ac 106
Owens Way. Rick—15Q 18
Owen Wlk. SE20—67Wb 127
Owen Way. NW10—36Sa 59
Owgan Clo. SE5—52Tb 105
Owl Clo. S Croy—82Zb 166
Owlets Hall Clo. Horn—27Pd 49
Ownstead Gdns. S Croy—83Vb 165
Ownsted Hill. Croy—82Ec 166
Oxberry Av. SW6—54Ab 102
Oxdowne Clo. Cob—86Da 159
Oxenden Wood Rd. Orp—80Yc 151
Oxendon St. SW1
—45Mb 82 (5D 198)
Oxenford St. SE15—55Vb 105
Oxenhill Rd. Sev—89Nd 171
Oxenpark Av. Wemb—32Na 59
Oxestall's Rd. SE8—50Ac 84
Oxford Av. NW10—41Ya 80
Oxford Av. SW20—68Ab 124
Oxford Av. Grays—9C 92
Oxford Av. Hay—52V 98
Oxford Av. Horn—28Qd 49
Oxford Av. Houn—50Ca 77
Oxford Av. Slou—3D 72
Oxford Av. Slou—10A 52
(Burnham)
Oxford Cir. W1—(3B 198)
Oxford Cir. Av. W1—(3B 198)
Oxford Clo. N9—19Xb 25
Oxford Clo. Ashf—66S 120
Oxford Clo. Grav—1H 137
Oxford Clo. Mitc—69Lb 126
Oxford Clo. Wal X—1Zb 12
Oxford Cotts. Felt—61U 120
Oxford Ct. EC4—(4F 201)
Oxford Ct. Brtwd—21Zd 50
Oxford Ct. Felt—63Z 121
Oxford Cres. N Mald—72Ta 143
Oxford Dri. Ruis—33Y 57
Oxford Gdns. N20—18Fb 23
Oxford Gdns. N21—17Sb 25
Oxford Gdns. W4—50Ra 79
Oxford Gdns. W10—44Za 80
Oxford Gdns. Uxb—34H 55
Oxford M. Bex—59Cd 110
Oxford Rd. E15—37Fc 65
(in two parts)
Oxford Rd. N4—32Qb 62
Oxford Rd. N9—19Xb 25
Oxford Rd. N20—18Fb 23
Oxford Rd. NW6—40Cb 61
Oxford Rd. SE19—65Tb 127
Oxford Rd. SW15—56Ab 102
Oxford Rd. W5—45Ma 79
Oxford Rd. Cars—79Gb 145
Oxford Rd. Enf—15Xb 25
Oxford Rd. Ger X & Uxb—31A 54
Oxford Rd. Harr—27Ha 38
(Wealdstone)
Oxford Rd. Harr—30Ea 38
(West Harrow)
Oxford Rd. Ilf—36Sc 66
Oxford Rd. Romf—23Pd 49
Oxford Rd. Sidc—64Xc 131
Oxford Rd. Stanf—2K 93
Oxford Rd. Tedd—64Fa 122
Oxford Rd. Uxb—36K 55
Oxford Rd. Wall—78Lb 146
Oxford Rd. Wind—3G 94
(in two parts)
Oxford Rd. Wfd G—22Mc 45
Oxford Rd. N. W4—50Ra 79
Oxford Rd. S. W4—50Ra 79
Oxford Sq. W2—44Gb 81 (3E 196)
Oxford St. W1—44Jb 82 (3G 197)
Oxford St. Wat—15X 19
Oxford Wlk. W1—44Lb 82 (2C 198)
Oxford Wlk. S'hall—46Ba 77
Oxford Way. Felt—63Z 121
Oxgate Gdns. NW2—34Xa 60
Oxgate La. NW2—33Xa 60
Oxhawth Cres. Brom—72Qc 150
Oxhey Av. Wat—17Z 19
Oxhey Dri. N'wd & Wat—22X 37
Oxhey La. Wat & Pinn—18Aa 19
Oxhey Rd. Wat—17Y 19
Ox La. Eps—81Wa 162
Oxleas Clo. Well—54Tc 108
Oxleay Rd. Harr—32Ca 57
Oxleigh Clo. N Mald—71Ua 144
Oxley Clo. Romf—26Ld 49
Oxleys Rd. NW2—34Xa 60
Oxleys Rd. Wal A—4Jc 13
Oxlip Clo. Croy—74Zb 148
Oxlow La. Dag—35Bd 67
Oxonian St. SE22—56Vb 105
Oxshott Rise. Cob—85Z 159
Oxshott Rd. Lea—88Ha 160
Oxshott Way. Cob—87Aa 159
Oxted Clo. Mitc—69Fb 125
Oxtoby Way. SW16—67Mb 126
Oyster La. Wey—82M 157
Ozolins Way. E16—44Jc 85
Pachesham Dri. Lea—88Ha 160
Pachesham Pk. Lea—88Ja 160
Pacific Rd. E16—44Jc 85
Packet Boat La. Uxb—44K 75
Packham Rd. Grav—2B 136
Packhorse La. Borwd—9Ua 8
Packhorse La. Pot B—4Ta 7
Packhorse La. Pot B—2Ta 7
Packhorse Rd. Ger X—28A 34
Packhorse Rd. Sev—95Ed 186
Packington Rd. W3—48Sa 79
Packington Sq. N1
—39Sb 63 (1D 194)
Packington St. N1
—39Rb 63 (1D 194)
Packmores Rd. SE9—57Tc 108
Padbury. SE17—(7J 207)
Padbury Ct. E2—41Vb 83 (4K 195)
Padcroft Rd. W Dray—46M 75
Paddenswick Rd. W6—48Wa 80
Paddington Clo. Hay—42Z 77
Paddington Grn. W2
—43Fb 81 (7C 190)
Paddington St. W1
—43Jb 82 (7H 191)
Paddock Clo. SE3—55Jc 107
Paddock Clo. SE26—63Zb 128
Paddock Clo. Grays—3D 92
Paddock Clo. Harr—35Da 57
Paddock Clo. N'holt—40Ca 57
Paddock Clo. Orp—77Rc 150
Paddock Clo. S Dar, Dart
—67Sd 134
Paddock Clo. Wor Pk—74Ua 144
Paddock Gdns. SE19—65Ub 127
Paddock Rd. NW2—34Wa 60
Paddock Rd. Bexh—56Ad 109
Paddock Rd. Ruis—34Z 57
Paddocks Clo. Asht—90Na 161
Paddocks Clo. Cob—86Y 159
Paddocks Clo. Orp—75Zc 151
Paddocks Mead. Wok—4B 188
Paddocks, The. Barn—13Hb 23
Paddocks, The. Croy—79Cc 148
Paddocks, The. Lea—98Da 175
Paddocks, The. Wemb—33Ra 59
Paddocks, The. Wey—76U 140
Paddocks Way. Asht—90Na 161
Paddocks Way. Cher—74K 139
Paddock, The. Ger X—22A 34
Paddock, The. Slou—3M 95
Paddock, The. Uxb—35R 56
Paddock, The. West—98Sc 184
Paddock Wlk. Warl—91Xb 181
Paddock Way. Chst—66Tc 130
Paddock Way. Wok—86D 156
Padfield Rd. SE5—55Sb 105
Padnall Rd. Romf—27Zc 47
Padstow Rd. Enf—12Rb 25
Padua Rd. SE20—67Yb 128
Pagden St. SW8—53Kb 104
Pageant Clo. Til—3E 114
Pageant Wlk. Croy—76Ub 147
Page Clo. Dart—62Yd 134
Page Clo. Hmptn—65Aa 121
Page Clo. Harr—30Pa 39
Page Cres. Croy—78Rb 147
Page Cres. Eri—52Hd 110
Page Grn. N15—29Vb 43
Page Grn. Rd. N15—29Wb 43
Page Heath La. Brom—69Mc 129
Page Heath Vs. Brom—69Mc 129
Pagehurst Rd. Croy—73Xb 147
Page Meadow. NW7—24Wa 40
Page Pl. E1—44Xb 83
Page Rd. Felt—58T 98
Pages Hill. N10—26Jb 42
Pages La. N10—26Jb 42
Page St. NW7—25Wa 40
Page St. SW1—49Mb 82 (5E 204)
Page's Wlk. SE1—49Ub 83 (5H 207)
Pages Yd. W4—51Ua 102
Paget Av. Sutt—76Fb 145
Paget Clo. Hmptn—63Fa 122
Paget Gdns. Chst—67Rc 130
Paget Rise. SE18—51Qc 108
Paget Rd. N16—32Tb 63
Paget Rd. Ilf—35Rc 66
Paget Rd. Slou—49B 74
Paget Rd. Uxb—42S 76
Paget St. EC1—41Rb 83 (3B 194)
Paget Ter. SE18—51Rc 108
Paglesfield. Brtwd—16Ee 33
Pagnell St. SE14—52Bc 106
Pagoda Av. Rich—55Pa 101
Pagoda Gdns. SE3—54Fc 107
Pagoda Vista. Rich—53Pa 101
Paignton Rd. N15—30Ub 43
Paignton Rd. Ruis—34W 56
Paines Brook Rd. Romf—23Pd 49
Paines Brook Way. Romf—23Pd 49
Paines Clo. Pinn—27Aa 37
Paines La. Pinn—25Aa 37
Pain's Clo. Mitc—68Kb 126
Painsthorpe Rd. N16—34Ub 63
Painters Ash La. Grav—62Fe 135
Painters La. Enf—7Ac 12
Painters Rd. Ilf—27Vc 47
Paisley Rd. N22—25Rb 43
Paisley Rd. Cars—74Fb 145
Pakeman St. N7—34Pb 62
Pakenham Clo. SW12—60Jb 104
Pakenham St. WC1
—42Pb 82 (4J 193)
Pakes Way. Epp—9Uc 14
Palace Av. W8—47Db 81
Palace Clo. K Lan—2P 3
Palace Ct. NW3—36Db 61
Palace Ct. W2—45Db 81
Palace Ct. Harr—30Na 39
Palace Ct. Gdns. N10—27Lb 42
Palace Gdns. Buck H—18Mc 27
Palace Gdns. Enf—14Tb 25
Palace Gdns. M. W8—46Db 81
Palace Gdns. Ter. W8—46Cb 81
Palace Ga. W8—47Eb 81 (2A 202)
Palace Gates Rd. N22—25Mb 42
Palace Grn. W8—46Db 81
Palace Grn. Croy—80Bc 148
Palace Grn. SE19—66Vb 127
Palace Gro. Brom—67Kc 129
Palace M. SW1—(6J 203)
Palace M. Enf—13Tb 25
Palace Pl. SW1—48Lb 82 (3B 204)
Palace Rd. N8—29Mb 42
(in two parts)
Palace Rd. N11—24Nb 42
Palace Rd. SE19—66Vb 127
Palace Rd. SW2—60Pb 104
Palace Rd. Brom—67Kc 129
Palace Rd. E Mol—69Fa 122
Palace Rd. King—70Ma 123
Palace Rd. Ruis—35Aa 57
Palace Rd. West—93Qc 184
Palace Sq. SE19—66Vb 127
Palace St. SW1—48Lb 82 (3B 204)
Palace View. SE12—61Jc 129
Palace View. Brom—69Kc 129
Palace View. Croy—77Bc 148
Palace View Rd. E4—22Dc 44
Palamos Rd. E10—32Cc 64
Palatine Av. N16—35Ub 63
Palatine Rd. N16—35Ub 63
Palermo Rd. NW10—40Wa 60
Palestine Gro. SW19—67Fb 125
Palewell Clo. Orp—68Xc 131
Palewell Comn. Dri. SW14
—57Ta 101
Palewell Pk. SW14—57Ta 101
Paley Gdns. Lou—13Rc 28
Palfrey Pl. SW8—52Pb 104
Palgrave Av. S'hall—45Ca 77
Palgrave Rd. W12—48Va 80
Palins Way. Grays—46Ce 91
Palissy St. E2—41Vb 83 (4K 195)
Pallant Way. Orp—76Qc 150
Pallet Way. SE18—53Nc 108
Palliser Rd. W14—50Ab 80
Pall Mall. SW1—46Lb 82 (7C 198)
Pall Mall E. SW1
—46Mb 82 (6E 198)
Pall Mall Pl. SW1—(7C 198)
Palmar Cres. Bexh—55Cd 110
Palmar Rd. Bexh—54Cd 110
Palmarsh Clo. Orp—70Zc 131
Palm Av. Sidc—65Zc 131
Palmeira Rd. Bexh—55Zc 109
Palmer Av. Bush, Wat—15Da 19
Palmer Av. Grav—3F 136
Palmer Av. Sutt—77Ya 144
Palmer Clo. Houn—53Ca 99
Palmer Cres. King—69Na 123
Palmer Pl. N7—36Qb 62
Palmer Rd. E13—42Kc 85
Palmer Rd. Borwd—11Ra 21
Palmers. Stanf—1P 93
Palmers Av. Grays—50Ee 91
Palmers Dri. Grays—49Fe 91
Palmersfield Rd. Bans—86Cb 163
Palmers Gdns. Barn—15Za 22
Palmers Gro. E Mol—70Ca 121
Palmers Hill. Epp—1Wc 15
Palmers La. Enf—11Xb 25
Palmer's Moor La. Iver—42K 75
Palmers Orchard. Sev—83Hd 170
Palmers Pas. SW14—55Sa 101
Palmer's Rd. E2—40Zb 64
Palmer's Rd. N11—22Lb 42
Palmers Rd. SW14—55Sa 101
Palmers Rd. SW16—68Pb 126
Palmerston Clo. Wok—86C 156
Palmerston Ct. Surb—73Ma 143
Palmerston Cres. N13—22Pb 42
Palmerston Cres. SE18—51Sc 108
Palmerston Gdns. Grays—50Zd 91
Palmerston Gro. SW19—66Cb 125
Palmerston Rd. E7—37Kc 65
Palmerston Rd. E17—28Bc 44
Palmerston Rd. N22—24Pb 42
Palmerston Rd. NW6—38Bb 61
(in two parts)
Palmerston Rd. SW14—56Sa 101
Palmerston Rd. SW19—66Cb 125
Palmerston Rd. W3—48Sa 79
Palmerston Rd. Buck H—19Kc 27
Palmerston Rd. Cars—77Hb 145
Palmerston Rd. Grays—50Zd 91
Palmerston Rd. Harr—27Ha 38
Palmerston Rd. Orp—78Sc 150
Palmerston Rd. Rain—40Ld 69
Palmerston Rd. Slou—8M 73
Palmerston Rd. Sutt—78Eb 145
Palmerston Rd. T Hth—71Tb 147
Palmerston Rd. Twic—58Ha 100
Palmerston Way. SW8—52Lb 104
Palmer St. SW1—48Mb 82 (3D 204)
Palmers Way. Wal X—1Ac 12
Palm Gro. W5—48Na 79
Palm Rd. Romf—29Ed 48
Pamber St. W10—44Za 80
Pamela Gdns. Pinn—29X 37
Pamela Wlk. E8—39Wb 63
Pampisford Rd. Purl & S Croy
—83Qb 164
Pam's Way. Eps—78Ta 143
Pancras La. EC4—44Sb 83 (3F 201)
Pancras Rd. NW1
—40Mb 62 (1D 192)
Pancroft. Romf—13Xc 29
Pandora Rd. NW6—37Cb 61
Panfield M. Ilf—30Qc 46
Panfield Rd. SE2—48Wc 87
Pangbourne Av. W10—43Ya 80
Pangbourne Dri. Stan—22Ma 39
Panhard Pl. S'hall—45Da 77
Pank Av. Barn—15Eb 23
Panmuir Rd. SW20—67Xa 124
Panmure Clo. N5—35Rb 63
Panmure Rd. SE26—62Xb 127
Pansy Gdns. W12—45Wa 80
Panter's. Swan—66Hd 132
Pantile Rd. Wey—77T 140
Pantile Row. Slou—49C 74
Pantiles Clo. Wok—6E 188
Pantiles, The. Bexh—52Bd 109
Pantiles, The. Brom—69Nc 130
Pantiles, The. Bush, Wat—18Fa 20
Pantiles Wlk. Uxb—38L 55
Panton St. SW1—45Mb 82 (5D 198)
Panyer All. EC4—(2D 200)
Papercourt La. Wok—93H 173
Papillons Wlk. SE3—55Jc 107
Papworth Gdns. N7—36Pb 62
Papworth Way. SW2—59Qb 104
Parade M. SE27—61Rb 127
Parade, The. N4—32Qb 62
Parade, The. SW11—52Hb 103
Parade, The. Brtwd—20Yd 32
Parade, The. Dart—57Hd 110
Parade, The. Eps—85Ua 162
Parade, The. Esh—79Ga 142
Parade, The. Romf—23Rd 49
Parade, The. Sev—89Nd 171
Parade, The. Sun—66V 120
Parade, The. Wat—13X 19
Parade, The. Wat—20Aa 19
(Carpenders Park)
Parade, The. Wat—20Z 19
(South Oxhey)
Parade, The. Wind—3B 94
Paradise Pas. N7—36Qb 62
Paradise Pl. SE18—49Nc 86
Paradise Rd. SW4—54Nb 104
Paradise Rd. Rich—57Na 101
Paradise Rd. Wal A—6Ec 12
Paradise St. SE16—47Xb 83
Paradise Wlk. SW3—51Hb 103
Paragon All. SE1
—48Ub 83 (4H 207)
Paragon Gro. Surb—72Pa 143
Paragon M. SE1—49Tb 83 (5G 207)
Paragon Pl. SE3—54Hc 107
Paragon Pl. Surb—72Pa 143
Paragon Rd. E9—37Yb 64
Paragon Row. SE17
—49Tb 83 (5F 207)
Paragon, The. SE3—54Jc 107
Parbury Rise. Chess—79Na 143
Parbury Rd. SE23—58Ac 106
Parchmore Rd. T Hth—68Rb 127
Parchmore Way. T Hth—68Rb 127
Pardoner St. SE1
—48Tb 83 (3G 207)
Pardon St. EC1—42Rb 83 (5C 194)
Pares Clo. Wok—4G 188
Parfett St. E1—43Wb 83
Par Four Dri. Kenl—88Sb 165
Parfrey St. W6—51Ya 102
Parham Dri. Ilf—30Rc 46
Parham Way. N10—26Lb 42
Parisfal Rd. NW6—36Cb 61
Paris Garden. SE1
—46Rb 83 (6B 200)
Parish Ga. Dri. Sidc—58Uc 108
Parish La. SE20—65Zb 128
Parish La. Slou—3F 52
Park App. SE16—48Xb 83
Park App. Well—56Xc 109
Park Av. E6—39Qc 66
Park Av. E15—37Gc 65
Park Av. N3—25Db 41
Park Av. N13—20Qb 24
Park Av. N18—21Wb 43
Park Av. N22—26Nb 42
Park Av. NW10—36Xa 60
(Dudden Hill)
Park Av. NW10—40Pa 59
(Park Royal)
Park Av. NW11—32Db 61
Park Av. SW14—56Ta 101
Park Av. Bark—37Sc 66
Park Av. Brtwd—18Ee 33
Park Av. Brom—65Hc 129
Park Av. Bush, Wat—12Aa 19
Park Av. Cars—79Jb 146
Park Av. Cat—96Ub 181
Park Av. Egh—65E 118
Park Av. Enf—15Tb 25
Park Av. Grav—10E 114
Park Av. Grav—10A 114
(Northfleet)
Park Av. Houn—58Da 99
Park Av. Ilf—32Qc 66
Park Av. Mitc—66Kb 126
Park Av. Orp—75Wc 151
Park Av. Orp—76Pc 150
(Locksbottom)
Park Av. Pot B—6Eb 9
Park Av. Rad—5Ka 6
Park Av. Rick—15J 17
Park Av. Ruis—30T 36
Park Av. S'hall—47Ba 77
Park Av. Stai—65H 119
Park Av. Upm—31Ud 70
Park Av. Wat—14W 18
Park Av. W Wick—75Ec 148
Park Av. Wfd G—22Kc 45
Park Av. Wray, Stai—7P 95
Park Av. E. Eps—79Wa 144
Park Av. M. Mitc—66Kb 126
Park Av. N. N8—28Mb 42
Park Av. Rd. N17—24Xb 43
Park Av. S. N8—28Mb 42
Park Av. St. Grays—51Wd 112
Park Av. W. Eps—79Wa 144
Park Boulevd. Romf—25Hd 48
Park Chase. Wemb—35Pa 59
Park Clo. E9—39Yb 64
Park Clo. NW2—34Xa 60
Park Clo. NW10—41Pa 79
Park Clo. SE7—50Nc 86
Park Clo. SW1—47Hb 81 (2F 203)
Park Clo. W4—50Ta 79
Park Clo. W14—48Bb 81
Park Clo. Bush, Wat—13Z 19
Park Clo. Cars—79Hb 145
Park Clo. Esh—79Ca 141
Park Clo. Hmptn—67Ea 122
Park Clo. Harr—25Ga 38
Park Clo. Houn—57Ea 100
Park Clo. Lea—96Fa 176
Park Clo. Rick—21R 36
Park Clo. W on T—75V 140
Park Clo. Wey—82K 157
Park Clo. Wind—4H 95
Park Corner. Wind—5C 94
Park Corner Dri. Lea—100U 174
Park Corner Rd. Grav—63Be 135
Park Ct. N17—24Wb 43
Park Ct. Harr—31Na 59
Park Ct. King—67La 122
Park Ct. N Mald—70Ta 123
Park Ct. Wemb—36Na 59
Park Ct. Wok—90B 156
Park Cres. N3—24Eb 41
Park Cres. W1—42Kb 82 (6K 191)
Park Cres. Borwd—13Pa 21
Park Cres. Enf—14Tb 25
Park Cres. Eri—51Ed 110
Park Cres. Harr—25Ga 38
Park Cres. Horn—31Jd 68
Park Cres. Twic—60Fa 100
Park Cres. M. E. W1
—42Kb 82 (6A 192)
Park Cres. M. W. W1
—42Kb 82 (6K 191)
Parkcroft. Edgw—25Sa 39
Parkcroft Rd. SE12—59Hc 107
Parkdale Cres. Wor Pk—76Ta 143
Parkdale Rd. SE18—50Uc 86
Park Dri. N21—16Sb 25
Park Dri. NW11—32Db 61
Park Dri. SE7—51Nc 108
Park Dri. SW14—57Ta 101
Park Dri. W3—48Qa 79
Park Dri. Asht—90Qa 161
Park Dri. Dag—34Ed 68
Park Dri. Harr—23Fa 38
(Harrow Weald)
Park Dri. Harr—31Ca 57
(Rayners Lane)
Park Dri. Long, Dart—69Ae 135
Park Dri. Pot B—3Db 9
Park Dri. Romf—28Fd 48
Park Dri. Upm—35Rd 69
Park Dri. Wok—90B 156
Park End. NW3—35Gb 61
Park End. Brom—67Hc 129
Park End Rd. Romf—28Gd 48
Parker Av. Til—3E 114
Parker Clo. E16—46Nc 86
Parke Rd. SW13—53Wa 102
Parke Rd. Sun—70W 120
Parker Rd. Croy—77Sb 147
Parker Rd. Grays—50Be 91
Parker's Clo. Asht—91Na 177
Parker's Hill. Asht—91Na 177
Parker's La. Asht—91Na 177
Parkers Row. SE1—47Vb 83
Parker St. E16—46Nc 86
Parker St. WC2—44Nb 82 (2G 199)
Parker St. Wat—11X 19
Parkes Rd. Chig—22Uc 46
Park Farm Clo. N2—27Eb 41
Park Farm Clo. Pinn—29X 37
Park Farm Rd. Brom—67Mc 129
Park Farm Rd. King—66Na 123
Park Farm Rd. Upm—36Pd 69
Parkfield. Long, Dart—70Ae 135
Parkfield. Rick—14H 17
Parkfield. Sev—95Pd 187
Parkfield Av. SW14—56Ua 102
Parkfield Av. Felt—62W 120
Parkfield Av. Harr—26Ea 38
Parkfield Av. N'holt—40Z 57
Parkfield Av. Uxb—41R 76
Parkfield Clo. Edgw—23Ra 39
Parkfield Clo. N'holt—40Aa 57
Parkfield Cres. Felt—62W 120
Parkfield Cres. Harr—26Ea 38
Parkfield Cres. Ruis—33Aa 57
Parkfield Dri. N'holt—40Z 57
Parkfield Gdns. Harr—27Da 37
Parkfield Rd. NW10—38Xa 60
Parkfield Rd. SE14—53Bc 106
Parkfield Rd. Felt—62W 120
Parkfield Rd. Harr—34Ea 58
Parkfield Rd. N'holt—40Aa 57
Parkfield Rd. Uxb—33R 56
Parkfields. SW15—56Ya 102
Parkfields. Croy—74Bc 148
Parkfields. Lea—83Fa 160
Parkfields Av. NW9—32Ta 59
Parkfields Av. SW20—67Xa 124
Park Fields Rd. King—64Pa 123
Parkfield St. N1—40Qb 62 (1A 194)
Parkfield Way. Brom—72Pc 150
Park Gdns. NW9—27Ra 39
Park Gdns. Eri—49Fd 88
Park Gdns. King—64Pa 123
Park Ga. N2—27Fb 41
Park Ga. N21—17Pb 24
Park Ga. SE3—55Hc 107
Park Ga. W5—43Ma 79
Parkgate Av. Barn—11Eb 23
Park Ga. Clo. King—65Ra 123
Parkgate Cres. Barn—11Eb 23
Parkgate Gdns. SW14—57Ta 101
Parkgate Rd. SW11—52Gb 103
Parkgate Rd. Orp—77Dd 152
Parkgate Rd. Wall—78Kb 146
Parkgate Rd. Wat—9Y 5
Park Grange Gdns. Sev—99Ld 187
Park Grn. Lea—96Da 175
Park Gro. E15—39Jc 65
Park Gro. N11—24Mb 42
Park Gro. Bexh—56Ed 110
Park Gro. Brom—67Kc 129
Park Gro. Chal—13A 16
Park Gro. Edgw—22Pa 39
Park Gro. Rd. E11—33Gc 65
Park Hall Rd. N2—28Gb 41
Park Hall Rd. SE21—62Tb 127
Parkham Ct. Brom—68Gc 129
Parkham St. SW11—53Gb 103
Park Hill. SE23—60Xb 105
Park Hill. SW4—57Mb 104
Park Hill. W5—43Ma 79
Park Hill. Brom—70Nc 130
Park Hill. Cars—79Gb 145
Park Hill. Grav—10A 136
Park Hill. Lou—15Mc 27
Park Hill. Rich—58Pa 101
Park Hill Clo. Cars—78Gb 145
Parkhill Clo. Horn—33Ld 69
Park Hill Ct. SW17—62Hb 125
Park Hill Rise. Croy—75Ub 147
Parkhill Rd. E4—17Ec 26
Parkhill Rd. NW3—36Hb 61
Parkhill Rd. Bex—59Bd 109
Park Hill Rd. Brom—68Gc 129
Park Hill Rd. Croy—77Ub 147
Parkhill Rd. Eps—83Va 162
Park Hill Rd. Sev—89Nd 171
Parkhill Rd. Sidc—62Uc 130
Park Hill Rd. Wall—80Kb 146
Parkhill Wlk. NW3—36Hb 61
Parkholme Rd. E8—37Wb 63
Park Ho. N21—17Pb 24
Park Ho. Gdns. Twic—57La 100
Parkhouse St. SE5—52Tb 105
Parkhurst. Eps—82Sa 161
Parkhurst Gdns. Bex—59Cd 110
Parkhurst Rd. E12—35Qc 66
Parkhurst Rd. E17—28Ac 44
Parkhurst Rd. N7—35Nb 62
Parkhurst Rd. N11—22Jb 42
Parkhurst Rd. N17—26Wb 43
Parkhurst Rd. N22—23Pb 42
Parkhurst Rd. Bex—59Cd 110
Parkhurst Rd. Sutt—77Fb 145
Parking Ct. E6—44Nc 86
Parkland Av. Romf—26Hd 48
Parkland Av. Slou—9P 73
Parkland Av. Upm—36Rd 69
Parkland Clo. Sev—100Ld 187
Parkland Gro. Ashf—63Q 120
Parkland Rd. N22—26Pb 42
Parkland Rd. Ashf—63Q 120
Parkland Rd. Wfd G—24Kc 45
Parklands. Chig—20Sc 28
Parklands. Epp—1Zc 15
(in two parts)
Parklands. Surb—71Pa 143
Parklands. Wal A—4Fc 13
Parklands. Wey—78L 139
Parklands Clo. Chig—20Sc 28
Parklands Ct. Houn—54Z 99
Parklands Dri. N3—27Ab 40
Parklands Pde. Houn—54Z 99
Parklands Rd. SW16—64Kb 126
Parklands Way. Wor Pk
—75Ua 144
Park La. E15—39Fc 65
Park La. N9—20Vb 25
Park La. N17—24Wb 43
Park La. W1—45Hb 81 (4G 197)
Park La. Asht—90Pa 161
Park La. Brtwd—24Fe 51
Park La. Cars & Wall—78Jb 146
Park La. Coul—93Mb 180
Park La. Croy—76Tb 147
Park La. Harr—34Da 57
Park La. Hay—43U 76
Park La. Horn—30Hd 48
Park La. Horn—37Kd 69
(Elm Park)
Park La. Houn—52W 98
Park La. Rich—56Ma 101
Park La. Romf—30Zc 47
Park La. Sev—96Ld 187
Park La. Sev—90Qd 171
(Kemsing)
Park La. Sev—93Qd 187
(Seal)
Park La. Slou—8M 73
Park La. Slou—3C 52
(Burnham)
Park La. Slou—55C 96
(Horton)
Park La. S Ock—46Td 90
(in two parts)
Park La. Sutt—79Ab 144
Park La. Swan—68Ld 133
Park La. Tedd—65Ha 122
Park La. Uxb—25J 35
Park La. Wal X—5Yb 12
Park La. Wemb—36Na 59
Park La. Wind—10A 94
Park La. Clo. N17—24Wb 43
Parklawn Av. Eps—85Ra 161
Park Lawn Rd. Wey—77S 140
Park Lawns. Wemb—35Pa 59
Parklea Clo. NW9—25Ua 40
Parkleigh Rd. SW19—68Db 125
Park Ley Rd. Cat—92Zb 182
Parkleys. Rich—63Ma 123
Park Mans. Arc. SW1—(2F 203)
Parkmead. SW15—58Xa 102
Park Mead. Harr—34Da 57
Parkmead. Lou—15Qc 28

Park Mead—Penderry Rise

Park Mead. Sidc—57Xc **109**
Parkmead Gdns. NW7—23Va **40**
Parkmore Clo. Wfd G—21Jc **45**
Park Nook Gdns. Enf—9Tb **11**
Park Pde. NW10—40Va **60**
Park Pde. W5—48Qa **79**
Park Pl. SW1—46Lb **82** (7B **198**)
Park Pl. W3—49Qa **79**
Park Pl. W5—46Ma **79**
Park Pl. Grav—8E **114**
Park Pl. Hmptn—65Ea **122**
Park Pl. Wemb—35Pa **59**
Park Pl. Gdns. W2
—43Eb **81** (7A **190**)
Park Pl. Vs. W2—43Eb **81** (7A **190**)
Park Ride. Wind—9B **94**
Park Ridings. N8—27Qb **42**
Park Rise. SE23—60Ac **106**
Park Rise. Harr—25Ga **38**
Park Rise. Lea—93Ka **176**
Park Rise Clo. Lea—93Ka **176**
Park Rise Rd. SE23—60Ac **106**
Park Rd. E6—39Lc **65**
Park Rd. E10—32Cc **64**
Park Rd. E12—32Kc **65**
Park Rd. E15—39Jc **65**
Park Rd. E17—29Bc **44**
Park Rd. N2—27Fb **41**
Park Rd. N8—28Lb **42**
Park Rd. N11—24Mb **42**
Park Rd. N14—18Mb **24**
Park Rd. N15—28Rb **43**
Park Rd. N18—21Wb **43**
Park Rd.—41Gb **81** (4E **190**)
NW1 1-71 & 2-98
NW8 remainder
Park Rd. NW4—31Wa **60**
Park Rd. NW9—31Ta **59**
Park Rd. NW10—39Ua **60**
Park Rd. SE25—70Ub **127**
Park Rd. SW19—65Fb **125**
Park Rd. W4—52Sa **101**
Park Rd. W7—45Ha **78**
Park Rd. Ashf—64R **120**
Park Rd. Asht—90Na **161**
Park Rd. Bans—87Db **163**
Park Rd. Barn—14Fb **23**
(East Barnet)
Park Rd. Barn—14Bb **23**
(High Barnet)
Park Rd. Beck—66Bc **128**
Park Rd. Brtwd—18Xd **32**
Park Rd. Brom—67Kc **129**
Park Rd. Bush, Wat—16Ca **19**
Park Rd. Cat—95Ub **181**
Park Rd. Chst—65Rc **130**
Park Rd. Dart—59Qd **111**
Park Rd. E Mol—70Ea **122**
Park Rd. Egh—63C **118**
Park Rd. Enf—8Ac **12**
Park Rd. Esh—77Da **141**
Park Rd. Felt—63Z **121**
Park Rd. Grav—10D **114**
Park Rd. Grays—50De **91**
Park Rd. Hmptn—64Da **121**
Park Rd. Hay—43U **76**
Park Rd. Houn—57Da **99**
Park Rd. Ilf—34Tc **66**
Park Rd. Iswth—53Ka **100**
Park Rd. Kenl—87Sb **165**
Park Rd. King—64Pa **123**
Park Rd. King—67La **122**
(Hampton Wick)
Park Rd. N Mald—70Ta **123**
Park Rd. Orp—71Yc **151**
Park Rd. Oxt—100Hc **183**
Park Rd. Pot B—2Jb **10**
Park Rd. Rad—7Ja **6**
Park Rd. Rich—58Pa **101**
Park Rd. Rick—17N **17**
Park Rd. Shep—74Q **140**
Park Rd. Slou—10G **52**
Park Rd. Stai—58K **97**
Park Rd. Stanf—2K **93**
Park Rd. Sun—66X **121**
Park Rd. Surb—72Pa **143**
Park Rd. Sutt—79Ab **144**
Park Rd. Swan—69Hd **132**
Park Rd. Swans—58Ae **113**
Park Rd. Tedd—65Ha **122**
Park Rd. Twic—58La **100**
Park Rd. Uxb—38N **55**
Park Rd. Wall—78Kb **146**
Park Rd. Wall—75Kb **146**
(Hackbridge)
Park Rd. Wal X—5Zb **12**
Park Rd. Warl—86Gc **167**
Park Rd. Wat—11W **18**
Park Rd. Wemb—37Na **59**
Park Rd. Wok—89B **156**
Park Rd. E. W3—47Sa **79**
Park Rd. E. Uxb—40M **55**
Park Rd. N. W3—47Ra **79**
Park Rd. N. W4—50Ta **79**
Park Row. SE10—50Fc **85**
Park Royal Rd. NW10 & W3
—41Sa **79**
Parkshot. Rich—56Ma **101**
Parkside. N3—25Db **41**
Parkside. NW2—34Wa **60**
Parkside. NW7—23Wa **40**
Parkside. SW19—63Za **124**
Parkside. Buck H—19Kc **27**
Parkside. Grays—48Fe **91**
Parkside. Hmptn—64Fa **122**
Parkside. Pot B—4Eb **9**
Parkside. Sev—85Bd **169**
Parkside. Sidc—61Xc **131**
Parkside. Sutt—79Ab **144**
Parkside. Wat—16Z **19**
Park Side. Wey—83K **157**
Parkside Av. SW19—64Za **124**
Parkside Av. Bexh—54Fd **110**
Parkside Av. Brom—70Nc **130**
Parkside Av. Romf—27Fd **48**
Parkside Av. Til—4D **114**
Parkside Clo. Lea—97V **174**
Parkside Ct. Wey—77Q **140**
Parkside Cres. Surb—72Sa **143**
Parkside Cross. Bexh—54Gd **110**
Parkside Dri. Edgw—20Qa **21**
Parkside Dri. Wat—12U **18**
Parkside Gdns. SW19—63Za **124**
Parkside Gdns. Barn—18Hb **23**
Parkside Gdns. Coul—89Kb **164**
Parkside Pl. Lea—97V **174**
Parkside Rd. SW11—53Jb **104**
Parkside Rd. Belv—49Dd **88**
Parkside Rd. Houn—57Da **99**
Parkside Rd. N'wd—22V **36**
Parkside Ter. N18—21Tb **43**
Parkside Way. Harr—28Da **37**
Parkspring Gro. Iver—37C **54**
Park Sq. Esh—77Da **141**
Park Sq. E. NW1—42Kb **82** (5K **191**)
Park Sq. M. NW1—(6K **191***)*
Park Sq. W. NW1
—42Kb **82** (6K **191**)
Parkstead Rd. SW15—57Xa **102**
Parkstone Av. N18—22Vb **43**
Parkstone Av. Horn—30Nd **49**
Parkstone Rd. E17—27Ec **44**
Parkstone Rd. SE15—54Wb **105**
Park St. SE1—46Sb **83** (6D **200**)
Park St. W1—45Jb **82** (4H **197**)
Park St. Croy—75Sb **147**
Park St. Slou—8K **73**
Park St. Slou—53F **96**
(Colnbrook)
Park St. Tedd—65Ga **122**
Park St. Wind—3H **95**
Park St. La. St Alb—2Da **5**
Park Ter. Enf—10Ac **12**
Park Ter. Grnh—57Yd **112**
Park Ter. Sev—96Zc **185**
Park Ter. Wor Pk—74Wa **144**
Park, The. N6—30Jb **42**
Park, The. NW11—32Db **61**
Park, The. SE19—66Ub **127**
Park, The. SE23—60Yb **106**
Park, The. W5—46Ma **79**
Park, The. Cars—79Hb **145**
Park, The. Lea—96Ca **175**
Park, The. Sidc—63Wc **131**
Parkthorne Clo. Harr—30Da **37**
Parkthorne Dri. Harr—30Ca **37**
Parkthorne Rd. SW12—59Mb **104**
Park Towers. W2
—45Eb **81** (5A **196**)
Park View. N21—17Pb **24**
Park View. W3—43Sa **79**
Park View. Lea—97Ca **175**
Park View. N Mald—69Va **124**
Park View. Pinn—25Ba **37**
Park View. Pot B—5Eb **9**
Park View. Sev—80Ee **155**
Park View. S Ock—46Td **90**
Park View. Wemb—36Ra **59**
Parkview Chase. Slou—4C **72**
Park View Cres. N11—21Kb **42**
Park View Est. E2—40Zb **64**
Park View Gdns. N22—25Qb **42**
Park View Gdns. NW4—29Ya **40**
Park View Gdns. Bark—40Uc **66**
Park View Gdns. Grays—50De **91**
Park View Gdns. Ilf—28Pc **46**
Park View Rd. N3—25Db **41**
Park View Rd. N17—27Wb **43**
Park View Rd. NW10—35Va **60**
Parkview Rd. SE9—61Rc **130**
Park View Rd. W5—43Na **79**
Park View Rd. Cat—94Ac **182**
Park View Rd. Croy—74Wb **147**
Park View Rd. Pinn—24X **37**
Park View Rd. S'hall—46Ca **77**
Park View Rd. Well—55Yc **109**
Park Village E. NW1
—40Kb **62** (1K **191**)
Park Village W. NW1
—40Kb **62** (1K **191**)
Park Vs. Romf—30Zc **47**
Parkville Rd. SW6—52Bb **103**
Park Vista. SE10—51Fc **107**
Park Wlk. N6—31Jb **62**
Park Wlk. SW10—51Eb **103**
Park Wlk. Asht—91Pa **177**
Park Wlk. Barn—13Fb **23**
Parkway. N14—19Nb **24**
Park Way. N20—21Hb **41**
Parkway. NW1—39Kb **62** (1K **191**)
Park Way. NW11—29Ab **40**
Parkway. SW20—70Za **124**
Park Way. Brtwd—18Be **33**
Parkway. Croy—81Dc **166**
Park Way. Dart—62Gd **132**
Park Way. E Mol—69Da **121**
Park Way. Edgw—25Ra **39**
Park Way. Enf—12Qb **24**
Parkway. Eri—48Ad **87**
Park Way. Felt—59X **99**
Parkway. Grays—3C **92**
Park Way. Ilf—34Vc **67**
Park Way. Lea—95Ca **175**
Parkway. Rain—42Jd **88**
Park Way. Rick—18L **17**
Parkway. Romf—26Hd **48**
Park Way. Ruis—32W **56**
Parkway. Uxb—38Q **56**
Park Way. Wey—77T **140**
Park Way. Wfd G—22Lc **45**
Parkway, The. Houn & S'hall
—54X **99**
Parkway, The. Iver—39E **54**
Parkway Trading Est. Houn
—51Y **99**
Park W. Pl. W2—44Gb **81** (2E **196**)
Park Wood. N20—20Hb **23**
Parkwood. Beck—66Cc **128**
★Parkwood. Brtwd—10Zd
Parkwood Av. Esh—74Ea **142**
Park Wood Clo. Bans—87Za **162**
Parkwood Gro. Sun—69W **120**
Parkwood Rd. SW19—64Bb **125**
Park Wood Rd. Bans—87Za **162**
Park Wood Rd. Bex—59Bd **109**
Parkwood Rd. Iswth—53Ha **100**
Parkwood Rd. West—93Nc **184**
Park Wood View. Bans—88Za **162**
Parlaunt Rd. Slou & Iver—49C **74**
Parley Dri. Wok—5F **188**
Parliament Ct. E1—(1J **201***)*
Parliament Hill. NW3—35Gb **61**
Parliament Sq. SW1
—47Nb **82** (2F **205**)
Parliament St. SW1
—47Nb **82** (1F **205**)
Parma Cres. SW11—56Hb **103**
Parmiter St. E2—40Xb **63**
Parnell Clo. Abb L, Wat—2V **4**
Parnell Clo. Edgw—21Ra **39**
Parnell Rd. E3—39Bc **64**
Parnham St. E14—44Ac **84**
Parolles Rd. N19—32Lb **62**
Paroma Rd. Belv—48Cd **88**
Parr Av. Eps—82Xa **162**
Parr Clo. Lea—92Ha **176**
Parr Ct. Felt—63Y **121**
Parrock Av. Grav—10E **114**
Parrock Rd. Grav—10E **114**
Parrock St. Grav—8D **114**
Parrots Clo. Rick—14Q **18**
Parr Rd. E6—39Mc **65**
Parr Rd. Stan—25Na **39**
Parrs Clo. S Croy—81Tb **165**
Parrs Pl. Hmptn—66Ca **121**
Parr St. N1—40Tb **63** (1F **195**)
Parry Av. E6—44Pc **86**
Parry Clo. Eps—80Xa **144**
Parry Grn. Slou—49B **74**
Parry Pl. SE18—49Rc **86**
Parry Rd. SE25—69Ub **127**
Parsley Gdns. Croy—74Zb **148**
Parsloes Av. Dag—35Zc **67**
Parsonage Clo. Abb L, Wat—2U **4**
Parsonage Clo. Hay—44V **76**
Parsonage Clo. Slou—7G **52**
Parsonage Clo. Warl—88Bc **166**
★Parsonage Field. Brtwd—9Zd
Parsonage Gdns. Enf—12Sb **25**
Parsonage La. Enf—12Tb **25**
Parsonage La. Sidc—63Bd **131**
Parsonage La. Slou—7G **52**
Parsonage La. S at H, Dart
—65Rd **133**
Parsonage La. Wind—3E **94**
Parsonage Manorway. Belv
—51Cd **110**
Parsonage Rd. Egh—4P **117**
Parsonage Rd. Rain—41Ld **89**
Parsonage Rd. Rick—17M **17**
Parsonage St. E14—49Ec **84**
Parson's Cres. Edgw—20Qa **21**
Parsonsfield Clo. Bans—87Za **162**
Parsonsfield Rd. Bans—87Za **162**
Parson's Grn. SW6—54Cb **103**
Parson's Grn. La. SW6—53Cb **103**
Parson's Gro. Edgw—20Qa **21**
Parsons La. Dart—62Kd **133**
★Parsons La. Sev—82Ae
Parsons Mead. Croy—74Rb **147**
Parsons Mead. E Mol—69Ea **122**
Parson's Rd. E13—40Lc **65**
Parson St. NW4—28Ya **40**
Parthenia Rd. SW6—53Cb **103**
Partingdale La. NW7—22Za **40**
Partington Clo. N19—32Mb **62**
Partridge Clo. E16—43Mc **85**
Partridge Clo. Bush, Wat—18Da **19**
Partridge Ct. EC1—(5B **194***)*
Partridge Dri. Orp—76Sc **150**
Partridge Grn. SE9—62Qc **130**
Partridge Knoll. Purl—85Rb **165**
Partridge Mead. Bans—87Ya **162**
Partridge Rd. Hmptn—65Ba **121**
Partridge Rd. Sidc—62Uc **130**
Partridge Vs. Uxb—39M **55**
Partridge Way. N22—25Nb **42**
Parvills Rd. Wal A—4Fc **13**
Parvin St. SW8—53Mb **104**
Parvis Rd. Wey—85K **157**
Pasadena Clo. Hay—47W **76**
Pascal St. SW8—52Mb **104**
Pascoe Rd. SE13—57Fc **107**
Pasfield. Wal A—5Fc **13**
Pasley Clo. SE17
—50Sb **83** (7D **206**)
Pasquier Rd. E17—27Ac **44**
Passey Pl. SE9—58Pc **108**
Passfield Dri. E14—43Dc **84**
Passfield Path. SE28—45Xc **87**
Passing All. EC1—(6C **194***)*
Passmore Edwards Ho. Ger X
—22A **34**
Passmore Gdns. N11—23Mb **42**
Passmore St. SW1
—50Jb **82** (7H **203**)
Pasteur Gdns. N18—22Rb **43**
Paston Clo. E5—34Zb **64**
Paston Cres. SE12—59Kc **107**
Pastor St. SE11—49Rb **83** (5C **206**)
Pasture Clo. Bush, Wat—17Ea **20**
Pasture Clo. Wemb—34Ka **58**
Pasture Rd. SE6—60Hc **107**
Pasture Rd. Dag—36Bd **67**
Pasture Rd. Wemb—33Ka **58**
Pastures Mead. Uxb—37Q **56**
Pastures, The. N20—18Bb **23**
Patcham Ter. SW8—53Kb **104**
Patch, The. E4—18Hc **27**
Patch, The. Sev—94Gd **186**
Paternoster Clo. Wal A—5Hc **13**
Paternoster Hill. Wal A—4Hc **13**
Paternoster Row. EC4
—44Sb **83** (3D **200**)
Paternoster Row. Hav, Romf
—18Ld **31**
Paternoster Sq. EC4
—44Rb **83** (2C **200**)
Paterson Rd. Ashf—64M **119**
Pater St. W8—48Cb **81**
Pates Mnr. Dri. Felt—59T **98**
Pathfield Rd. SW16—65Mb **126**
Path, The. SW19—67Db **125**
Pathway, The. Rad—8Ha **6**
Pathway, The. Wat—18Z **19**
Pathway, The. Wok—97H **173**
Patience Rd. SW11—54Gb **103**
Patio Clo. SW4—58Mb **104**
Patmore La. W on T—79V **140**
Patmore Rd. Wal A—6Gc **13**
Patmore St. SW8—53Lb **104**
Patmore Way. Romf—22Dd **48**
Patmos Rd. SW9—52Rb **105**
Paton Clo. E3—41Cc **84**
Patricia Clo. Slou—5C **72**
Patricia Ct. Chst—67Tc **130**
Patricia Ct. Well—52Xc **109**
Patricia Dri. Horn—32Nd **69**
Patricia Gdns. Sutt—83Cb **163**
Patrick Connolly Gdns. E3
—41Dc **84**
Patrick Pas. SW11—54Gb **103**
Patrick Rd. E13—41Lc **85**
Patrington.Clo. Uxb—41L **75**
Patriot Sq. E2—40Yb **64**
Patrol Pl. SE6—58Dc **106**
Patrons Dri. Uxb—29H **35**
Patshull Pl. NW5—37Lb **62**
Patshull Rd. NW5—37Lb **62**
Patten All. Rich—57Ma **101**
Pattenden Rd. SE6—60Bc **106**
Patten Rd. SW18—59Gb **103**
Patterdale Clo. Brom—65Hc **129**
Patterdale Rd. SE15—52Yb **106**
Patterdale Rd. Dart—60Td **112**
Patterson Ct. SE19—66Vb **127**
Patterson Ct. Dart—57Qd **111**
Patterson Rd. SE19—65Vb **127**
Pattison Rd. NW2—34Cb **61**
Pattison Wlk. SE18—50Sc **86**
Paulet Rd. SE5—54Rb **105**
Paul Gdns. Croy—75Vb **147**
Paulhan Rd. Harr—28Ma **39**
Paulin Dri. N21—17Qb **24**
Pauline Cres. Twic—60Ea **100**
Paulinus Clo. Orp—68Yc **131**
Pauls Grn. Wal X—5Ac **12**
Paul's Pl. Asht—91Ra **177**
Paul St. E15—39Gc **65**
Paul St. EC2—42Tb **83** (6G **195**)
Paul's Wlk. EC4—45Sb **83** (4C **200**)
Paultons Sq. SW3—51Fb **103**
Paultons St. SW3—51Fb **103**
Pauntley St. N19—32Lb **62**
Paved Ct. Rich—57Ma **101**
Paveley Dri. SW11—52Gb **103**
Paveley St. NW8—41Gb **81** (4E **190**)
Pavement M. Romf—31Zc **67**
Pavement Sq. Croy—74Wb **147**
Pavement, The. SW4—56Lb **104**
Pavement, The. W5—48Na **79**
Pavet Clo. Dag—37Dd **68**
Pavilion Gdns. Stai—66K **119**
(in two parts)
Pavilion Rd. E15—41Gc **85**
Pavilion Rd. SW1
—48Hb **81** (2G **203**)
Pavilion Rd. Ilf—31Pc **66**
Pavilion St. SW1
—48Hb **81** (4G **203**)
Pavilion Ter. Ilf—29Uc **46**
Pavilion Way. Ruis—33Y **57**
Pavinia Clo. Wfd G—23Pc **46**
Pawleyne Clo. SE20—66Yb **128**
Pawsey Clo. E13—39Kc **65**
Pawsons Rd. Croy—72Sb **147**
Paxford Rd. Wemb—33Ka **58**
Paxton Av. Slou—8G **72**
Paxton Clo. Rich—54Pa **101**
Paxton Gdns. Wok—84G **156**
Paxton Pl. SE27—63Ub **127**
Paxton Rd. N17—24Wb **43**
Paxton Rd. W4—51Ua **102**
Paxton Rd. Brom—66Jc **129**
Paynell Ct. SE3—55Gc **107**
Payne Rd. E3—40Dc **64**
Paynesfield Av. SW14—55Ta **101**
Paynesfield Rd. Bush, Wat
—17Ha **20**
Paynesfield Rd. West—93Lc **183**
Payne St. SE8—52Bc **106**
Paynes Wlk. W6—51Ab **102**
Peabody Av. SW1
—50Kb **82** (7K **203**)
Peabody Bldgs. SE1—(7D **200***)*
Peabody Cotts. N17—25Ub **43**
Peabody Est. EC1
—42Sb **83** (6E **194**)
Peabody Est. SE1—(1E **206***)*
Peabody Est. SE24—59Rb **105**
Peabody Est. SW11—56Gb **103**
Peabody Est. W6—50Ya **80**
Peabody Hill. SE21—60Rb **105**
Peabody Sq. SE1
—47Rb **83** (2B **206**)
Peabody Yd. N1—39Sb **63**
Peace Clo. Wal X—1Xb **11**
Peaceful Row. Grays—51Yd **112**
Peace Gro. Wemb—33Ra **59**
Peace Rd. Iver—41B **74**
Peace St. E1—42Wb **83**
Peace St. SE18—51Qc **108**
Peaches Clo. Sutt—80Ab **144**
Peachey Clo. Uxb—44M **75**
Peachey La. Uxb—43M **75**
Peach Rd. W10—41Za **80**
Peach Tree Av. W Dray—44P **75**
Peachum Rd. SE3—51Hc **107**
Peacock Av. Felt—60T **98**
Peacock Clo. Horn—28Nd **49**
Peacock Gdns. S Croy—82Ac **166**
Peacock St. SE17
—49Rb **83** (6C **206**)
Peacock St. Grav—9E **114**
Peacock Yd. SE17—(6C **206***)*
Peaketon Av. Ilf—28Mc **45**
Peak Hill. SE26—63Yb **128**
Peak Hill Av. SE26—63Yb **128**
Peak Hill Gdns. SE26—63Yb **128**
Peaks Hill. Purl—82Mb **164**
Peaks Hill Rise. Purl—82Nb **164**
Peak, The. SE26—62Yb **128**
Pea La. Upm—37Wd **70**
Peal Gdns. W13—42Ja **78**
Peall Rd. Croy—72Pb **146**
Pearcefield Av. SE23—60Yb **106**
Pearce Rd. E Mol—69Da **121**
Pear Clo. NW9—28Ta **39**
Pearcroft Rd. E11—33Fc **65**
Peardon St. SW8—54Kb **104**
Peareswood Gdns. Stan—25Ma **39**
Peareswood Rd. Eri—53Hd **110**
Pearfield Rd. SE23—62Ac **128**
Pearl Ct. Wok—4B **188**
Pearl Rd. E17—27Cc **44**
Pearl St. E1—46Xb **83**
Pearmain Clo. Shep—71R **140**
Pearman St. SE1
—48Qb **82** (3A **206**)
Pear Pl. SE1—47Qb **82** (1K **205**)
Pearscroft Ct. SW6—53Db **103**
Pearscroft Rd. SW6—53Db **103**
Pearsons. Stanf—1P **93**
Pearson's Av. SE14—53Cc **106**
Pearson St. E2—40Vb **63** (1K **195**)
Pears Rd. Houn—55Ea **100**
Pear Tree Av. W Dray—44P **75**
★Peartree Clo. Brtwd—10Zd
Peartree Clo. Eri—53Fd **110**
Peartree Clo. Mitc—68Gb **125**
Peartree Clo. S Croy—86Xb **165**
Peartree Clo. S Ock—40Yd **70**
Pear Tree Clo. Swan—68Fd **132**
Pear Tree Ct. E18—25Kc **45**
Pear Tree Ct. EC1
—42Qb **82** (6A **194**)
Peartree Gdns. Dag—35Xc **67**
Peartree Gdns. Romf—26Dd **48**
Peartree La. E1—45Yb **84**
★Peartree La. Brtwd—9Yd
Peartree La. Grav—6P **137**
Pear Tree Rd. Ashf—64S **120**
Peartree Rd. Enf—13Ub **25**
Pear Tree Rd. Wey—78J **139**
Pear Trees. Brtwd—23Ee **51**
Pear Tree St. EC1
—42Sb **83** (5D **194**)
Peary Pl. E2—41Yb **84**
Peascod Pl. Wind—3H **95**
Peascod St. Wind—3H **95**
Pease Hill. Sev—79Be **155**
Peas Mead Ter. E4—21Ec **44**
Peatmore Av. Wok—88J **157**
Peatmore Clo. Wok—88J **157**
Pebble Clo. Tad—100Ua **178**
Pebble La. Eps—94Qb **180**
Pebble La. Lea & Eps—96Pa **177**
Pebworth Rd. Harr—33Ja **58**
Peckarmans Wood. SE26
—62Wb **127**
Peckett Sq. N5—35Sb **63**
Peckford Clo. SW9—54Qb **104**
Peckford Pl. SW9—54Qb **104**
Peckham Gro. SE15—52Ub **105**
Peckham High St. SE15
—53Wb **105**
Peckham Hill St. SE15—52Wb **105**
Peckham Pk. Rd. SE15—52Wb **105**
Peckham Rd.—53Ub **105**
SE5 1-93 & 2-84
SE15 remainder
Peckham Rye—55Wb **105**
SE15 1-261 & 2-132
SE22 remainder
Peckwater St. NW5—36Lb **62**
Pedham Pl. Est. Swan—72Jd **152**
Pedhoulas. N14—20Nb **24**
Pedlars Wlk. N7—36Pb **62**
Pedley Rd. Dag—32Yc **67**
Pedley St. E1—42Vb **83**
Pedro St. E5—34Zb **64**
Pedworth Gdns. SE16—49Yb **84**
Peek Cres. SW19—64Za **124**
Peel Clo. Wind—5F **94**
Peel Dri. NW9—27Va **40**
Peel Dri. Ilf—27Nc **46**
Peel Gro. E2—40Yb **64**
Peel Pl. Ilf—26Nc **46**
Peel Precinct. NW6—40Cb **61**
Peel Rd. E18—25Hc **45**
Peel Rd. NW6—41Bb **81**
Peel Rd. Harr—27Ha **38**
Peel Rd. Orp—78Sc **150**
Peel Rd. Wemb—34Ma **58**
Peel St. W8—46Cb **81**
Peel Way. Romf—26Pd **49**
Peel Way. Uxb—43N **75**
Peerage Way. Horn—31Pd **69**
Peerless Dri. Uxb—28L **35**
Peerless St. EC1—41Tb **83** (4F **195**)
Pegamoid Rd. N9—20Yb **26**
Pegasus Ct. King—69Ma **123**
Pegasus Pl. SE11—51Qb **104**
Pegasus Rd. Croy—79Qb **146**
Pegelm Gdns. Horn—31Pd **69**
Peggotty Way. Uxb—44R **76**
Pegg Rd. Houn—52Z **99**
Pegley Gdns. SE12—61Jc **129**
Pegmire La. Wat—11Ea **20**
Pegwell St. SE18—52Uc **108**
Peket Clo. Stai—67G **118**
Pekin Clo. E14—44Cc **84**
Pekin St. E14—44Cc **84**
Peldon Ct. Rich—57Pa **101**
Peldon Pas. Rich—56Pa **101**
Pelham Av. Bark—39Vc **67**
Pelham Clo. SE5—55Ub **105**
Pelham Ct. Sidc—62Wc **131**
Pelham Cres. SW7
—49Gb **81** (6D **202**)
Pelham Pl. SW7—49Gb **81** (6D **202**)
Pelham Rd. E18—27Kc **45**
Pelham Rd. N15—28Vb **43**
Pelham Rd. N22—26Qb **42**
Pelham Rd. SW19—66Cb **125**
Pelham Rd. Beck—68Yb **128**
Pelham Rd. Bexh—55Cd **110**
Pelham Rd. Grav—10B **114**
Pelham Rd. Ilf—33Tc **66**
Pelham Rd. S. Grav—10B **114**
Pelham's Clo. Esh—77Ca **141**
Pelhams, The. Wat—7Z **5**
Pelham St. SW7—49Fb **81** (5C **202**)
Pelham's Wlk. Esh—77Ca **141**
Pelham Ter. Grav—9B **114**
Pelham Way. Lea—98Ea **176**
Pelican Est. SE15—53Vb **105**
Pelican Pas. E1—42Yb **84**
Pelican Wlk. SW9—56Rb **105**
Pelier St. SE17—51Sb **105**
Pelinore Rd. SE6—61Gc **129**
Pellant Rd. SW6—52Ab **102**
Pellatt Gro. N22—25Qb **42**
Pellatt Rd. SE22—57Vb **105**
Pellerin Rd. N16—36Ub **63**
Pelling Hill. Wind—10M **95**
Pelling St. E14—44Cc **84**
Pellipar Clo. N13—20Qb **24**
Pellipar Gdns. SE18—50Pc **86**
★Pells La. Sev—84Wd
Pelly Ct. Epp—3Vc **15**
Pelly Rd. E13—39Jc **65**
Pelter St. E2—41Vb **83** (3K **195**)
Pelton Av. Sutt—82Db **163**
Pelton Rd. SE10—50Gc **85**
Pembar Av. E17—27Ac **44**
Pember Rd. NW10—41Za **80**
Pemberton Av. Romf—27Kd **49**
Pemberton Gdns. N19—34Lb **62**
Pemberton Gdns. Romf—29Ad **47**
Pemberton Gdns. Swan—69Gd **132**
Pemberton Pl. E9—38Yb **64**
Pemberton Rd. N4—29Qb **42**
Pemberton Rd. E Mol—70Ea **122**
Pemberton Rd. Slou—2C **72**
Pemberton Row. EC4
—44Qb **82** (2A **200**)
Pemberton Ter. N19—34Lb **62**
Pembrey Way. Horn—37Ld **69**
Pembridge Av. Twic—60Ba **99**
Pembridge Chase. Hem—1C **2**
Pembridge Clo. Hem—1C **2**
Pembridge Cres. W11—45Cb **81**
Pembridge Gdns. W2—45Cb **81**
Pembridge M. W11—45Cb **81**
Pembridge Pl. W2—45Cb **81**
Pembridge Rd. W11—45Cb **81**
Pembridge Rd. Hem—1C **2**
Pembridge Sq. W2—45Cb **81**
Pembridge Vs. W11—45Cb **81**
Pembroke Av. Enf—11Xb **25**
Pembroke Av. Harr—27Ja **38**
Pembroke Av. Surb—71Ra **143**
Pembroke Av. W on T—77Z **141**
Pembroke Clo. SW1
—47Jb **82** (2J **203**)
Pembroke Clo. Bans—89Db **163**
Pembroke Clo. Horn—28Pd **49**
Pembroke Dri. Wal X—1Rb **11**
Pembroke Gdns. W8—49Bb **81**
Pembroke Gdns. Dag—34Dd **68**
Pembroke Gdns. Wok—90C **156**
Pembroke Gdns. Clo. W8—48Cb **81**
Pembroke M. W8—48Cb **81**
Pembroke Pl. W8—48Cb **81**
Pembroke Pl. Edgw—24Qa **39**
Pembroke Pl. Iswth—54Ga **100**
Pembroke Pl. S at H, Dart
—67Rd **133**
Pembroke Rd. E17—29Dc **44**
Pembroke Rd. N8—28Nb **42**
Pembroke Rd. N10—25Jb **42**
Pembroke Rd. N13—20Sb **25**
Pembroke Rd. N15—29Vb **43**
Pembroke Rd. SE25—70Ub **127**
Pembroke Rd. W8—49Cb **81**
Pembroke Rd. Brom—68Lc **129**
Pembroke Rd. Eri—50Ed **88**
Pembroke Rd. Gnfd—42Da **77**
Pembroke Rd. Ilf—32Vc **67**
Pembroke Rd. Mitc—68Jb **126**
Pembroke Rd. N'wd—20S **18**
Pembroke Rd. Ruis—32V **56**
Pembroke Rd. Sev—97Kd **187**
Pembroke Rd. Wemb—34Ma **59**
Pembroke Rd. Wok—89C **156**
Pembroke Sq. W8—48Cb **81**
Pembroke St. N1—38Nb **62**
Pembroke Vs. W8—49Cb **81**
Pembroke Vs. Rich—56Ma **101**
Pembroke Wlk. W8—49Cb **81**
Pembury Av. Wor Pk—74Wa **144**
Pembury Clo. Brom—73Hc **149**
Pembury Clo. Coul—86Jb **164**
Pembury Ct. Hay—51T **98**
Pembury Cres. Sidc—61Ad **131**
Pembury Pl. E5—36Xb **63**
Pembury Rd. E5—36Xb **63**
Pembury Rd. N17—25Vb **43**
Pembury Rd. SE25—70Wb **127**
Pembury Rd. Bexh—52Ad **109**
Pemdevon Rd. Croy—73Qb **146**
Pemell Clo. E1—42Yb **84**
Pemerich Clo. Hay—50V **76**
Penally Pl. N1—39Tb **63**
Penang St. E1—46Xb **83**
Penarth St. SE15—51Yb **106**
Penberth Rd. SE6—61Ec **128**
Penbury Rd. S'hall—50Ba **77**
Pencombe M. W11—45Bb **81**
Pencraig Way. SE15—51Xb **105**
Penda Rd. Eri—52Dd **110**
Pendarves Rd. SW20—67Ya **124**
Penda's Mead. E9—35Ac **64**
Pendell Av. Hay—52V **98**
Pendennis Clo. Wey—86J **157**
Pendennis Rd. N17—27Tb **43**
Pendennis Rd. SW16—63Nb **126**
Pendennis Rd. Orp—75Yc **151**
Pendennis Rd. Sev—95Kd **187**
Penderel Rd. Houn—57Ca **99**
Penderry Rise. SE6—61Fc **129**

Penderyn Way—Pitt Pl.

Penderyn Way. N7—35Mb 62
Pendle Ho. SE26—62Wb 127
Pendle Rd. SW16—65Kb 126
Pendlestone Rd. E17—29Dc 44
Pendragon Rd. Brom—62Hc 129
Pendrell Rd. SE4—54Ac 106
Pendrell St. SE18—51Tc 108
Pendula Dri. Hay—42Z 77
Penenden. Long, Dart—74Be 155
Penerley Rd. SE6—60Dc 106
Penerley Rd. Rain—43Kd 89
Penfold La. Bex—61Zc 131
Penfold Pl. NW1—43Gb 81 (7D 190)
Penfold Rd. N9—18Zb 26
Penfold St.—42Fb 81 (6C 190)
NW1 1-11 & 2-28
NW8 remainder
Penford Gdns. SE9—55Mc 107
Penford St. SE5—54Rb 105
Pengarth Rd. Bex—58Zc 109
Penge La. SE20—66Yb 128
Pengelly Clo. Wal X—2Xb 11
Penge Rd. E13—39Lc 65
Penge Rd.—69Wb 127
SE25 1-81 & 2-70
SE20 remainder
Penhall Rd. SE7—49Mc 85
Penhill Rd. Bex—58Yc 109
Penhurst. Wok—86B 156
Penhurst Rd. Ilf—24Rc 46
Penifather La. Gnfd—41Fa 78
Peninsular Clo. Felt—58T 98
Peninsular Rd. Til—5C 114
Penistone Rd. SW16—66Nb 126
Penistone Wlk. Romf—23Ld 49
Penketh Dri. Harr—34Fa 58
Penley Ct. WC2—(4J 199)
Penmon Rd. SE2—48Wc 87
Pennack Rd. SE15—51Vb 105
Pennant M. W8—49Db 81
Pennant Ter. E17—26Bc 44
Pennard Rd. W12—47Ya 80
Pennards, The. Sun—69Y 121
Penn Clo. Grays—2D 92
Penn Clo. Gnfd—40Da 57
Penn Clo. Harr—28La 38
Penn Clo. Rick—16F 16
Penn Clo. Uxb—42M 75
Penn Dri. Uxb—30H 35
Penner Clo. SW19—61Ab 124
Pennethorne Clo. E9—39Yb 64
Pennethorne Rd. SE15—52Xb 105
Penney Clo. Dart—59Md 111
Penn Gdns. Chst—68Rc 130
Penn Gdns. Romf—24Cd 48
Penn Gaskell La. Ger X—22B 34
Penn Ho. Ger X—22A 34
Pennine Dri. NW2—33Za 60
Pennine La. NW2—33Ab 60
Pennine Rd. Slou—3E 72
Pennine Way. Bexh—53Gd 110
Pennine Way. Grav—2A 136
Pennine Way. Hay—52T 98
Pennington Clo. SE27—63Tb 127
Pennington Clo. Romf—22Cd 48
Pennington Dri. Wey—76U 140
Pennington Rd. Ger X—24A 34
Pennington St. E1—45Xb 83
Pennis La. Long, Dart—72Zd 155
Penn La. Bex—58Zc 109
Penn Meadow. Slou—9K 53
Penn Rd. N7—36Nb 62
Penn Rd. Ger X—25A 34
Penn Rd. Rick—18H 17
Penn Rd. Slou—2H 73
Penn Rd. Slou—3P 95
(Datchet)
Penn Rd. Wat—11X 19
Penn St. N1—39Tb 63 (1G 195)
Penn Way. Rick—16F 16
Pennycroft. Croy—81Ac 166
Pennyfield. Cob—85W 158
Pennyfields. E14—45Cc 84
Pennyfields. Brtwd—21Yd 50
Penny La. Shep—73U 140
Pennylets Grn. Slou—8K 53
Pennymead Dri. Lea—99V 174
Pennymead Rise. Lea—99V 174
Pennymoor Wlk. W9—41Bb 81
Pennypot La. Chob—1A 188
Penny Rd. NW10—41Ra 79
Penpoll Rd. E8—37Xb 63
Penpool La. Well—55Xc 109
Penrhyn Av. E17—25Cc 44
Penrhyn Cres. E17—25Cc 44
Penrhyn Cres. SW14—56Sa 101
Penrhyn Gro. E17—25Cc 44
Penrhyn Rd. King—70Na 123
Penrith Clo. SW15—57Ab 102
Penrith Clo. Beck—67Dc 128
Penrith Clo. Uxb—38M 55
Penrith Cres. Horn—36Jd 68
Penrith Pl. SE27—61Rb 127
Penrith Rd. N15—29Tb 43
Penrith Rd. Ilf—23Vc 47
Penrith Rd. N Mald—70Ta 123
Penrith Rd. Romf—23Qd 49
Penrith Rd. T Hth—68Sb 127
Penrith St. SW16—65Lb 126
Penrose Av. Wat—19Aa 19
Penrose Gro. SE17
—50Sb 83 (7D 206)
Penrose Rd. Lea—94Ea 176
Penrose St. SE17
—50Sb 83 (7D 206)
Penryn Ho. SE11—(7B 206)
Penryn St. NW1—40Mb 62 (1D 192)
Penry St. SE1—49Ub 83 (6J 207)
Pensbury Pl. SW8—54Lb 104
Pensbury St. SW8—54Lb 104
Penscroft Gdns. Borwd—14Ta 21
Pensford Av. Rich—54Qa 101
Penshurst Av. Sidc—58Wc 109
Penshurst Clo. Sev—79Ud 154
Penshurst Gdns. Edgw—22Ra 39
Penshurst Grn. Brom—71Hc 149
Penshurst Rd. E9—38Zb 64
Penshurst Rd. N17—24Vb 43
Penshurst Rd. Bexh—53Bd 109
Penshurst Rd. Pot B—4Fb 9
Penshurst Rd. T Hth—71Rb 147
Penshurst Wlk. Brom—71Hc 149
Penshurst Way. Sutt—81Cb 163
Pentelow Gdns. Felt—58W 98
Pentire Clo. Upm—30Ud 50
Pentire Rd. E17—25Fc 45
Pentland Av. Shep—71Q 140
Pentland Clo. NW11—33Ab 60
Pentland Gdns. SW18—58Eb 103
Pentland Rd. Bush, Wat—16Ea 20
Pentland Rd. Slou—3E 72
Pentlands Clo. Mitc—69Kb 126
Pentland St. SW18—58Eb 103
Pentland Way. Uxb—34S 56
Pentlow St. SW15—55Ya 102
Pentlow Way. Buck H—17Nc 28
Pentney Rd. E4—18Fc 27
Pentney Rd. SW12—60Lb 104
Pentney Rd. SW19—67Ab 124
Penton Av. Stai—66H 119
Penton Dri. Wal X—1Zb 12
Penton Gro. N1—40Qb 62 (2K 193)
Penton Hall Dri. Stai—67J 119
Penton Hook Rd. Stai—66J 119
Penton Pl. SE17—50Rb 83 (7C 206)
Penton Rise. WC1
—41Pb 82 (3J 193)
Penton Rd. Stai—66H 119
Penton St. N1—40Qb 62 (1K 193)
Pentonville Rd. N1
—40Pb 62 (2G 193)
Pentrich Av. Enf—10Wb 11
Pentridge St. SE15—52Vb 105
Pentyre Av. N18—22Tb 43
Penwerris Av. Iswth—52Ea 100
Penwith Rd. SW18—61Db 125
Penwood End. Wok—9E 188
Penwortham Ct. N22—26Pb 42
Penwortham Rd. SW16—65Lb 126
Penwortham Rd. S Croy
—82Tb 165
Penylan Pl. Edgw—24Qa 39
Penywern Rd. SW5—50Cb 81
Penzance Clo. Uxb—25M 35
Penzance Gdns. Romf—23Qd 49
Penzance Ho. SE11—(7B 206)
Penzance Pl. W11—46Ab 80
Penzance Rd. Romf—23Qd 49
Penzance St. W11—46Ab 80
Peony Clo. Brtwd—16Xd 32
Peony Ct. Wfd G—24Gc 45
Peony Gdns. W12—45Wa 80
Peploe Rd. NW6—40Za 60
Pepper All. Lou—12Hc 27
Pepperhill. Grav—62Ee 135
Pepperhill La. Grav—62Ee 135
Pepper St. SE1—47Sb 83 (1D 206)
Pepys Clo. Asht—89Qa 161
Pepys Clo. Dart—56Qd 111
Pepys Clo. Grav—62Fe 135
Pepys Clo. Slou—51D 96
Pepys Clo. Til—3E 114
Pepys Clo. Uxb—35R 56
Pepys Cres. Barn—15Ya 22
Pepys Rise. Orp—74Vc 151
Pepys Rd. SE14—53Zb 106
Pepys Rd. SW20—67Ya 124
Pepys St. EC3—45Ub 83 (4J 201)
Perceval Av. NW3—36Gb 61
Percheron Rd. Borwd—16Ta 21
Perch St. E8—35Vb 63
Percival Ct. N17—24Vb 43
Percival Gdns. Romf—30Zc 47
Percival Rd. SW14—56Sa 101
Percival Rd. Enf—14Vb 25
Percival Rd. Felt—61V 120
Percival Rd. Horn—30Ld 49
Percival Rd. Orp—75Rc 150
Percival St. EC1—42Rb 83 (5B 194)
Percival Way. Eps—77Ta 143
Percy Av. Ashf—64Q 120
Percy Bryant Rd. Sun—66U 120
Percy Cir. WC1—41Pb 82 (3J 193)
Percy Gdns. Enf—15Zb 26
Percy Gdns. Hay—41U 76
Percy Gdns. Iswth—55Ja 100
Percy Gdns. Wor Pk—74Ua 144
Percy M. W1—(1D 198)
Percy Pas. W1—(1D 198)
Percy Pl. Slou—3M 95
Percy Rd. E11—31Gc 65
Percy Rd. E16—43Gc 85
Percy Rd. N12—22Eb 41
Percy Rd. N21—17Sb 25
Percy Rd. NW6—41Cb 81
Percy Rd. SE20—67Zb 128
Percy Rd. SE25—71Wb 147
Percy Rd. W12—47Wa 80
Percy Rd. Bexh—54Ad 109
Percy Rd. Dag—42Cd 88
Percy Rd. Hmptn—66Ca 121
Percy Rd. Ilf—31Wc 67
Percy Rd. Iswth—56Ja 100
Percy Rd. Mitc—73Jb 146
Percy Rd. Romf—27Dd 48
Percy Rd. Twic—60Da 99
Percy Rd. Wat—14X 19
Percy St. W1—43Mb 82 (1D 198)
Percy St. Grays—51Ee 113
Percy Way. Twic—60Ea 100
Percy Yd. WC1—41Pb 82 (3J 193)
Peregrine Clo. Wat—6Aa 5
Peregrine Rd. Ilf—22Xc 47
Peregrine Rd. Sun—68V 120
Peregrine Way. SW19—66Ya 124
Perham Rd. W14—50Ab 80
Perifield. SE21—60Sb 105
Perimeade Rd. Gnfd—40La 58
Perimeter Rd. Wind—3H 95
Periton Rd. SE9—56Mc 107
Perivale Gdns. W13—42Ka 78
Perivale Gdns. Wat—6X 5
Perivale Industrial Pk. Gnfd
—39Ka 58
Perivale La. Gnfd—41Ja 78
Perkin Clo. Wemb—36Ka 58
Perkins Ct. Ashf—64P 119
Perkin's Rents. SW1
—48Mb 82 (4D 204)
Perkins Rd. Ilf—27Tc 46
Perks Clo. SE3—55Gc 107
Perpins Rd. SE9—58Uc 108
Perran Clo. Long, Dart—70Be 135
Perran Rd. SW2—60Rb 105
Perran Wlk. Bren—50Na 79
Perren St. NW5—37Kb 62
Perrers Rd. W6—49Xa 80
Perrin Clo. Ashf—64P 119
Perrin Rd. Wemb—35Ka 58
Perrin's La. NW3—35Eb 61
Perrin's Wlk. NW3—35Eb 61
Perrott St. SE18—49Sc 86
Perry Av. W3—44Ta 79
Perry Clo. Rain—40Fd 68
Perry Clo. Uxb—44R 76
Perry Ct. N15—30Ub 43
Perrycroft. Wind—5C 94
Perryfield Way. NW9—30Va 40
Perryfield Way. Rich—62Ka 122
Perry Gdns. N9—20Tb 25
Perry Garth. N'holt—39Y 57
Perry Gro. Dart—56Qd 111
Perry Hall Clo. Orp—73Wc 151
Perry Hall Rd. Orp—72Vc 151
Perry Hill. SE6—62Bc 128
Perry How. Wor Pk—74Va 144
Perrymans Farm Rd. Ilf—30Tc 46
Perryman Way. Slou—1D 72
Perry Mead. Bush, Wat—16Ea 20
Perry Mead. Enf—12Rb 25
Perrymead St. SW6—53Db 103
Perryn Rd. W3—46Ta 79
Perry Oaks Dri. W Dray & Houn
—54K 97
Perry Rise. SE23—62Ac 128
Perry Rd. S Ock—45Sd 90
Perrys La. Orp—85Xc 169
Perry's Pl. W1—44Mb 82 (2D 198)
Perry St. Chst—65Tc 130
Perry St. Dart—56Gd 110
Perry St. Grav—10B 114
Perry St. Gdns. Chst—65Uc 130
Perry St. Shaw. Chst—66Uc 130
Perry Vale. SE23—61Yb 128
Persant Rd. SE6—61Gc 129
Perseverance Pl. Rich—56Na 101
Persfield Clo. Eps—82Wa 162
Pershore Clo. Ilf—29Rc 46
Pershore Gro. Cars—72Fb 145
Pert Clo. N10—23Kb 42
Perth Av. NW9—31Ta 59
Perth Av. Hay—42Y 77
Perth Av. Slou—4F 72
Perth Clo. SW20—68Wa 124
Perth Rd. E10—32Ac 64
Perth Rd. E13—40Kc 65
Perth Rd. N4—32Qb 62
Perth Rd. N22—25Rb 43
Perth Rd. Bark—39Tc 66
Perth Rd. Beck—68Ec 128
Perth Rd. Ilf—30Qc 46
Perth Ter. Ilf—31Sc 66
Perwell Av. Harr—32Ba 57
Pescot Av. Long, Dart—69Ce 135
Peter Av. NW10—38Xa 60
Peterborough Av. Upm—32Ud 70
Peterborough Ct. EC4
—44Qb 82 (3A 200)
Peterborough Gdns. Ilf—31Nc 66
Peterborough M. SW6—54Cb 103
Peterborough Rd. E10—29Ec 44
Peterborough Rd. SW6—54Cb 103
Peterborough Rd. Cars—72Gb 145
Peterborough Rd. Harr—32Ga 58
Peterborough Vs. SW6—53Db 103
Petergate. SW11—56Eb 103
Peterhill Clo. Ger X—22A 34
Peters Clo. Stan—23Ma 39
Petersfield Av. Romf—23Nd 49
Petersfield Av. Slou—6L 73
Petersfield Av. Stai—65L 119
Petersfield Clo. N18—22Sb 43
Petersfield Clo. Romf—23Qd 49
Petersfield Cres. Coul—87Nb 164
Petersfield Rise. SW15—60Xa 102
Petersfield Rd. W3—47Sa 79
Petersfield Rd. Stai—64L 119
Petersham Av. Wey—84N 157
Petersham Clo. Rich—61Ma 123
Petersham Clo. Sutt—78Cb 145
Petersham Clo. Wey—84N 157
Petersham Dri. Orp—68Vc 131
Petersham Gdns. Orp—68Vc 131
Petersham La. SW7
—48Eb 81 (3A 202)
Petersham M. SW7
—48Eb 81 (4A 202)
Petersham Pl. SW7
—48Eb 81 (4A 202)
Petersham Rd. Rich—58Ma 101
Peters Hill. EC4—45Sb 83 (4D 200)
Peter's La. EC1—43Rb 83 (7C 194)
Peter's Path. SE26—63Xb 127
Peterstone Rd. SE2—47Xc 87
Peterstow Clo. SW19—61Ab 124
Peter St. W1—45Mb 82 (4D 198)
Petherton Rd. N5—36Sb 63
Petley Rd. W6—51Za 102
Peto Pl. NW1—42Kb 82 (5A 192)
Peto St. N. E16—44Hc 85
Peto St. S. E16—45Hc 85
Petre Clo. Brtwd—30Ee 51
Petrie Clo. NW2—37Ab 60
Petten Clo. Orp—74Zc 151
Petten Gro. Orp—74Zc 151
Petters Rd. Asht—88Pa 161
Petticoat La. E1—43Ub 83 (2K 201)
Petticoat Sq. E1—44Vb 83 (2K 201)
Pettits Boulevd. Romf—25Gd 48
Pettits Clo. Romf—26Gd 48
★Pettits La. Brtwd—10Ae
Pettits La. Romf—26Gd 48
Pettits La. N. Romf—25Fd 48
Pettits Pl. Dag—36Cd 68
Pettits Rd. Dag—36Cd 68
Pettiward Clo. SW15—56Ya 102
Pettley Gdns. Romf—29Fd 48
Pettman Cres. SE28—48Tc 86
Pettsgrove Av. Wemb—36La 58
Pett's Hill. N'holt—36Da 57
Petts La. Shep—70Q 120
Pett St. SE18—49Nc 86
Petts Wood Rd. Orp—71Tc 150
Petty France. SW1
—48Lb 82 (3C 204)
Petworth Clo. N'holt—38Ba 57
Petworth Clo. Sutt—76Db 145
Petworth Gdns. SW20—69Xa 124
Petworth Gdns. Uxb—39S 56
Petworth Rd. N12—22Gb 41
Petworth Rd. Bexh—57Cd 110
Petworth St. SW11—53Gb 103
Petworth Way. Horn—35Hd 68
Petyt Pl. SW3—51Gb 103
Petyward. SW3—49Gb 81 (6E 202)
Pevensey Av. N11—22Mb 42
Pevensey Av. Enf—12Ub 25
Pevensey Clo. Iswth—52Ea 100
Pevensey Rd. E7—35Hc 65
Pevensey Rd. SW17—63Fb 125
Pevensey Rd. Felt—60Aa 99
Pevensey Rd. Slou—3E 72
Peverett Clo. N11—22Kb 42
Peveril Dri. Tedd—64Fa 122
Pewsey Clo. E4—22Cc 44
Peyton Pl. SE10—52Ec 106
Pheasant Clo. Purl—85Rb 165
Pheasants Way. Rick—17K 17
Phelps Clo. Sev—79Ud 154
Phelp St. SE17—51Tb 105
Phelps Way. Hay—49V 76
Phene St. SW3—51Gb 103
Philan Way. Romf—23Fd 48
Philbeach Gdns. SW5—50Cb 81
Philchurch Pl. E1—44Wb 83
Philip Av. Romf—32Fd 68
Philip Av. Swan—70Fd 132
Philip Clo. Brtwd—16Xd 32
Philip Clo. Romf—32Fd 68
Philip Gdns. Croy—75Bc 148
Philip La. N15—28Tb 43
Philipot Path. SE9—58Pc 108
Philippa Gdns. SE9—57Mc 107
Philip Rd. SE15—55Wb 105
Philip Rd. Rain—41Gd 88
Philip Rd. Stai—65M 119
Philip St. E13—42Jc 85
Philip Wlk. SE15—55Xb 105
Phillida Rd. Romf—26Qd 49
Phillimore Gdns. NW10—39Ya 60
Phillimore Gdns. W8—47Cb 81
Phillimore Gdns. Clo. W8—48Cb 81
Phillimore Pl. W8—47Cb 81
Phillimore Pl. Rad—8Ga 6
Phillimore Wlk. W8—48Cb 81
Phillipers. Wat—7Aa 5
Phillipp St. N1—39Ub 63 (1H 195)
Phillips Clo. Dart—58Kd 111
Philpot La. EC3—45Ub 83 (4H 201)
Philpot La. Chob—1E 188 &
83A 156
Philpot Path. Ilf—34Sc 66
Philpots Clo. W Dray—45M 75
Philpot Sq. SW6—55Db 103
Philpot St. E1—44Xb 83
(in two parts)
Phineas Pett Rd. SE9—55Nc 108
Phipps Bri. Rd. —68Eb 125
SW19 97-273 & 84-176
Mitc remainder
Phipps Hatch La. Enf—10Sb 11
Phipp's M. SW1—49Kb 82 (4K 203)
Phipps Rd. Slou—3B 72
Phipp St. EC2—42Ub 83 (5H 195)
Phoebeth Rd. SE4—57Cc 106
Phoenix Ct. EC1—(2C 200)
Phoenix Dri. Kes—77Mc 149
Phoenix Pl. Dart—59Md 111
Phoenix Rd. NW1
—41Mb 82 (3D 192)
Phoenix Rd. SE20—65Yb 128
Phoenix St. WC2
—44Mb 82 (3E 198)
Phoenix Trading Pk. Bren
—50Ma 79
Phoenix Way. Houn—51Z 99
Phoenix Way. N'wd—21V 36
Phygtle, The. Ger X—23A 34
Phyllis Av. N Mald—71Xa 144
Picardy Manorway. Belv
—48Dd 88
Picardy Rd. Belv—50Cd 88
Picardy St. Belv—48Cd 88
Piccadilly. W1—46Kb 82 (7A 198)
Piccadilly Arc. SW1—(6B 198)
Piccadilly Cir. W1
—45Mb 82 (5D 198)
Piccadilly Pl. W1—(5C 198)
Pickard St. EC1—41Rb 83 (3C 194)
Pickering Av. E6—40Qc 66
Pickering M. W2—44Db 81
Pickering Pl. SW1—(7C 198)
Pickering St. N1—39Rb 63
Pickets Clo. Bush, Wat—18Fa 20
Pickets St. SW12—59Kb 104
Pickett Croft. Stan—25Ma 39
Picketts Lock La. N9—19Zb 26
Pickford Clo. Bexh—54Ad 109
Pickford La. Bexh—54Ad 109
Pickford Rd. Bexh—55Ad 109
Pickfords Yd. N17—23Vb 43
Pick Hill. Wal A—4Hc 13
Pickhurst Grn. Brom—73Hc 149
Pickhurst La. W Wick & Brom
—71Gc 149
Pickhurst Mead. Brom—73Hc 149
Pickhurst Pk. Brom—71Gc 149
Pickhurst Rise. W Wick—74Fc 149
Pickins Piece. Slou—54C 96
Pickle Herring St. SE1
—46Ub 83 (7J 201)
Pickmoss La. Sev—88Jd 170
Pickwick Gdns. Grav—62Fe 135
Pickwick M. N18—22Ub 43
Pickwick Pl. Harr—31Ga 58
Pickwick Rd. SE21—59Tb 105
Pickwick St. SE1
—47Sb 83 (2D 206)
Pickwick Way. Chst—65Sc 130
Pickworth Clo. SW8—52Nb 104
Picquets Way. Bans—89Bb 163
Picton Pl. W1—44Jb 82 (3J 197)
Picton St. SE5—52Tb 105
Piedmont Rd. SE18—50Tc 86
Pield Heath Av. Uxb—42Q 76
Pield Heath Rd. Uxb—42N 75
Piercing Hill. Epp—7Tc 14
Piermont Rd. SE22—57Xb 105
Pierrepoint Rd. W3—45Ra 79
Pierrepont Arc. N1—(1B 194)
Pierrepont Row. N1—(1B 194)
Pier Rd. E16—47Qc 86
Pier Rd. Eri—51Gd 110
(in two parts)
Pier Rd. Felt—57X 99
Pier Rd. Grav—8B 114
Pier Rd. Grnh—56Xd 112
Pierson Rd. Wind—3B 94
Pier St. E14—49Ec 84
Pier Ter. SW18—56Db 103
Pigeon Ho. La. Coul—96Eb 179
Pigeon Ho. La. Coul—97Eb 179
Pigeon La. Hmptn—63Ca 121
Piggy La. Rick—16D 16
Pigott St. E14—44Cc 84
Pike Clo. Brom—64Kc 129
Pike La. Upm—36Vd 70
Pike Rd. NW7—21Ta 39
Pike's End. Pinn—28X 37
Pikes Hill. Eps—85Ua 162
Pikestone Clo. Hay—42Aa 77
Pilgrimage St. SE1
—47Tb 83 (2F 207)
Pilgrim Hill. SE27—63Sb 127
Pilgrim's Clo. Brtwd—15Vd 32
Pilgrims Clo. Wat—5Z 5
Pilgrim's La. NW3—35Fb 61
Pilgrim's La. Brtwd—14Td 32
Pilgrim's La. Cat—98Pb 180
Pilgrims La. Grays—46Yd 90
Pilgrims La. Oxt & West—96Lc 183
Pilgrim's Pl. NW3—35Fb 61
Pilgrims Rise. Barn—15Gb 23
Pilgrims Rd. Swans—56Ae 113
Pilgrim St. EC4—44Rb 83 (3B 200)
Pilgrims Way. N19—32Mb 62
Pilgrims Way. Dart—60Qd 111
Pilgrims Way. Sev—88Nd 171
(Kemsing)
★Pilgrims Way. Sev—87Be
(Wrotham, in two parts)
Pilgrims Way. S Croy—78Vb 147
Pilgrim's Way. Wemb—32Ra 59
Pilgrims Way. West & Sev
—95Qc 184
Pilgrims Way E. Sev—87Ld 171
Pilgrims Way W. Sev—88Fd 170
Pilkington Rd. SE15—54Xb 105
Pilkington Rd. Orp—75Sc 150
★Pillar Box Rd. Sev—94Ud
Pillions, The. Hay—42T 76
Pillmans Clo. Sidc—65Yc 131
Pilot Industrial Centre. NW10
—42Ta 79
Pilsden Clo. SW19—60Za 102
Piltdown Rd. Wat—21Z 37
Pimlico Rd. SW1—50Jb 82 (7H 203)
Pimlico Wlk. N1—41Ub 83 (3H 195)
Pimpernel Way. Romf—23Md 49
Pinchbeck Rd. Orp—79Vc 151
Pinchfield. Rick—22F 34
Pinchin St. E1—45Wb 83
Pincott La. Lea—100R 174
Pincott Rd. SW19—66Eb 125
Pincott Rd. Bexh—57Cd 110
Pincroft Wood. Long, Dart
—69Ee 135
Pindar St. EC2—43Ub 83 (7H 195)
Pindock M. W9—42Db 81
Pine Apple Ct. SW1—(3C 204)
Pine Av. Grav—10F 114
Pine Av. W Wick—74Dc 148
Pine Clo. N14—17Lb 24
Pine Clo. N19—33Lb 62
Pine Clo. Kenl—89Tb 165
Pine Clo. S Ock—41Vd 90
Pine Clo. Stan—21Ka 38
Pine Clo. Swan—70Hd 132
Pine Clo. Wal X—1Zb 12
Pine Clo. Wey—83K 157
Pine Clo. Wok—4F 188
Pine Coombe. Croy—77Zb 148
Pine Ct. N'holt—42Aa 77
Pine Ct. Upm—35Rd 69
Pine Cres. Brtwd—15Fe 33
Pine Cres. Cars—83Fb 163
Pinecroft. Brtwd—17De 33
Pine Dean. Lea—97Da 175
Pine Dene. SE15—53Xb 105
Pinefield Clo. E14—45Cc 84
Pine Gdns. Ruis—32X 57
Pine Gdns. Surb—72Qa 143
Pine Glade. Orp—77Pc 150
Pine Gro. N4—33Nb 62
Pine Gro. N20—18Bb 23
Pine Gro. SW19—64Bb 125
Pine Gro. Bush, Wat—12Ba 19
Pine Gro. St Alb—2Ba 5
Pine Gro. Wey—78R 140
Pine Gro. M. Wey—78S 140
Pine Hill. Eps—87Ta 161
Pinehurst Wlk. Orp—74Uc 150
Pineneedles La. Sev—95Kd 187
Pine Pl. Bans—86Za 162
Pine Pl. Hay—42V 76
Pine Ridge. Cars—81Jb 164
Pine Rd. N11—19Jb 24
Pine Rd. NW2—35Ya 60
Pine Rd. Wok—8F 188
Pines Av. Enf—8Yb 12
Pines Clo. N'wd—23U 36
Pines Rd. Brom—68Nc 130
Pines, The. Coul—90Kb 164
Pines, The. Grays—46De 91
Pines, The. Purl—85Sb 165
Pines, The. Sun—69W 120
Pines, The. Wfd G—20Jc 27
Pine St. EC1—42Qb 82 (5K 193)
Pine Tree Clo. Houn—53X 99
Pine Tree Hill. Wok—88F 156
Pine Trees Dri. Uxb—35N 55
★Pine View. Sev—92Ee
Pine View Mnr. Epp—2Wc 15
Pine Wlk. Bans—89Hb 163
Pine Wlk. Cars—82Fb 163
Pine Wlk. Cat—94Vb 181
Pine Wlk. Cob—86Z 159
Pine Wlk. Lea—100V 174
(East Horsley)
Pine Wlk. Lea—97Da 175
(Great Bookham)
Pine Wlk. Surb—72Qa 143
Pine Wlk. E. Cars—83Fb 163
Pine Wlk. W. Cars—82Fb 163
Pine Way. Egh—5M 117
Pine Wood. Sun—67W 120
Pinewood Av. Pinn—23Da 37
Pinewood Av. Rain—42Kd 89
Pinewood Av. Sev—93Md 187
Pinewood Av. Sidc—60Uc 108
Pinewood Av. Uxb—44P 75
Pinewood Av. Wey—81L 157
Pinewood Clo. Borwd—11Ta 21
Pinewood Clo. Croy—76Ac 148
Pinewood Clo. Ger X—31A 54
Pinewood Clo. Iver—38E 54
Pinewood Clo. Orp—74Tc 150
Pinewood Clo. Pinn—23Da 37
Pinewood Clo. Stanf—8K 93
Pinewood Clo. Wok—87C 156
Pinewood Dri. Orp—78Uc 150
Pinewood Dri. Stai—64J 119
Pinewood Grn. Iver—38E 54
Pinewood Gro. W5—44La 78
Pinewood Gro. Wey—82K 157
Pinewood Pk. Wey—83K 157
Pinewood Rd. SE2—51Zc 109
Pinewood Rd. Brom—70Jc 129
Pinewood Rd. Felt—62X 121
Pinewood Rd. Hav, Romf—21Ed 48
Pinewood Rd. Iver—37D 54
Pinewood Rd. Vir W—10L 117
Pinewood Way. Brtwd—15Fe 33
Pinfold Rd. SW16—63Nb 126
Pinfold Rd. Bush, Wat—12Ba 19
Pinglestone Clo. W Dray—52N 97
Pinkcoat Clo. Felt—62X 121
Pinkerton Pl. SW16—63Mb 126
Pinkham Way. N11—24Jb 42
Pink La. Slou—10A 52
Pinks Hill. Swan—71Gd 152
Pinkwell Av. Hay—49T 76
Pinkwell La. Hay—49S 76
Pinley Gdns. Dag—39Xc 67
Pinnacle Hill. Bexh—56Dd 110
Pinnacle Hill N. Bexh—56Dd 110
Pinnacles. Wal A—6Gc 13
Pinn Clo. Uxb—44M 75
Pinnell Rd. SE9—56Mc 107
Pinner Grn. Pinn—26Y 37
Pinner Gro. Pinn—28Aa 37
Pinner Hill. Pinn—24X 37
Pinner Hill Rd. Pinn—24X 37
Pinner Pk. Av. Harr—27Da 37
Pinner Pk. Gdns. Harr—26Ea 38
Pinner Rd. N'wd & Pinn—25V 36
Pinner Rd. Pinn & Harr—28Ba 37
Pinner Rd. Wat—16Z 19
Pinner View. Harr—28Ea 38
Pinnocks Av. Grav—10D 114
Pinn Way. Ruis—31T 56
Pinstone Way. Ger X—33D 54
Pintail Rd. Wfd G—24Kc 45
Pinto Clo. Borwd—16Ta 21
Pinto Way. SE3—56Kc 107
Piper Clo. N7—36Pb 62
Piper Rd. King—69Qa 123
Pipers Clo. Cob—87Z 159
Pipers Clo. Slou—1A 72
Piper's End. Vir W—9P 117
Pipers Grn. NW9—29Sa 39
Pipers Grn. La. Edgw—20Na 21
Piper's Grn. Rd. West—100Wc 185
Pipers La. West—99Xc 185
Pipewell Rd. Cars—72Gb 145
Pippin Clo. Croy—74Bc 148
Pippins Clo. W Dray—48M 75
Pippins Ct. Ashf—65R 120
Piquet Rd. SE20—68Yb 128
Pirbright Cres. Croy—79Ec 148
Pirbright Rd. SW18—60Bb 103
Pirie St. E16—46Kc 85
Pirrip Clo. Grav—1H 137
Pitcairn Clo. Romf—28Cd 48
Pitcairn Rd. Mitc—66Hb 125
Pitchfont La. Oxt—96Hc 183
Pitchfont La. Oxt—97Jc 183
Pitchford St. E15—38Fc 65
Pitfield. Long, Dart—70Be 135
Pitfield St. N1—41Ub 83 (4H 195)
Pitfield Way. NW10—37Sa 59
Pitfield Way. Enf—11Yb 26
Pitfold Clo. SE12—58Kc 107
Pitfold Rd. SE12—58Jc 107
Pitlake. Croy—75Rb 147
Pitman St. SE5—52Sb 105
Pitsea Pl. E1—44Zb 84
Pitsea St. E1—44Zb 84
Pitshanger La. W5—42Ka 78
Pitt Cres. SW19—63Db 125
Pittman Clo. Brtwd—22Ee 51
Pitt Pl. Eps—86Ua 162

Pitt Rd.—Primrose Gdns.

Pitt Rd. Eps—86Ua 162
Pitt Rd. Orp—77Sc 150
Pitt Rd. T Hth—71Sb 147
Pitt's Ct. SE1—(7H 201)
Pitt's Head M. W1
—46Jb 82 (7J 197)
Pittsmead Av. Brom—73Jc 149
Pitts Rd. Slou—6G 72
Pitt St. SE15—53Vb 105
Pitt St. W8—47Cb 81
Pittville Gdns. SE25—69Wb 127
Pitwood Grn. Tad—92Ya 178
Pitwood Pk. Tad—92Xa 178
Pixley St. E14—44Bc 84
Pixton Way. Croy—81Ac 166
Place Farm Av. Orp—74Tc 150
★Place Farm La. Brtwd—9Wd
Placehouse La. Coul—91Pb 180
Plackett Way. Slou—6B 72
Plain Ride. Wind—10A 94
Plain, The. Epp—1Xc 15
Plaistow Clo. Stanf—1M 93
Plaistow Gro. E15—39Hc 65
Plaistow Gro. Brom—66Kc 129
Plaistow La. Brom—66Kc 129
Plaistow Pk. Rd. E13—40Kc 65
Plaistow Rd. E15—39Hc 65
Plaitford Clo. Rick—19N 17
Plane Av. Grav—59Fe 113
Planes, The. Cher—73L 139
Plane St. SE26—62Xb 127
Plane Tree Cres. Felt—62X 121
Plane Tree Wlk. SE19—65Ub 127
Plantagenet Clo. Wor Pk
—77Ta 143
Plantagenet Gdns. Romf—31Zc 67
Plantagenet Pl. Romf—31Zc 67
Plantagenet Rd. Barn—14Eb 23
Plantain Pl. SE1—47Tb 83 (1F 207)
Plantation Dri. Orp—74Zc 151
Plantation La. Cat & Warl
—91Ac 182
Plantation Rd. Eri—53Jd 110
Plantation Rd. Swan—66Jd 132
Plantation, The. SE3—54Jc 107
Plashet Gdns. Brtwd—21Ce 51
Plashet Gro. E6—39Lc 65
Plashet Rd. E13—39Jc 65
Plassy Rd. SE6—59Dc 106
Platford Grn. Horn—28Nd 49
Platina St. EC2—(5G 195)
Plato Rd. SW2—56Nb 104
★Platt Comn. Sev—92Ee
★Platt Ho. La. Sev—85Ee
★Platt Industrial Est. Sev—92Ee
Platts Av. Wat—13X 19
Platt's La. NW3—34Cb 61
Platts Rd. Enf—11Yb 26
Platt St. NW1—40Mb 62 (1D 192)
Platt, The. SW15—55Za 102
(in two parts)
Plawsfield Rd. Beck—67Zb 128
★Plaxdale Grn. Rd. Sev—85Zd
Plaxtol Clo. Brom—67Lc 129
Plaxtol Rd. Eri—52Cd 110
Playfield Av. Romf—25Ed 48
Playfield Cres. SE22—57Vb 105
Playfield Rd. Edgw—26Sa 39
Playford Rd. N4—33Pb 62
(in two parts)
Playgreen Way. SE6—62Cc 128
Playground Clo. Beck—68Zb 128
Playhouse Yd. EC4
—44Rb 83 (3C 200)
Pleasance Rd SW15—57Xa 102
Pleasance Rd. Orp—68Xc 131
Pleasance, The. SW15—56Xa 102
Pleasant Gro. Croy—76Bc 148
Pleasant Pl. N1—38Rb 63
Pleasant Pl. Harr—33Fa 58
Pleasant Pl. W on T—79Y 141
Pleasant Row. NW1—39Kb 62
Pleasant View. Eri—50Gd 88
Pleasant View Pl. Orp—78Rc 150
Pleasant Way. Wemb—40La 58
Pleasure Pit Rd. Asht—90Ra 161
Plender Pl. NW1—(1C 192)
Plender St. NW1—39Lb 62 (1B 192)
Pleshey Rd. N7—35Mb 62
Plesman Way. Wall—81Nb 164
Plevna Cres. N15—30Ub 43
Plevna Rd. N9—20Wb 25
Plevna Rd. Hmptn—67Da 121
Plevna St. E14—48Ec 84
Pleydell Av. SE19—66Vb 127
Pleydell Av. W6—49Va 80
Pleydell Ct. EC4—(3A 200)
Pleydell St. EC4—(3A 200)
Plimsoll Clo. E14—44Dc 84
Plimsoll Rd. N4—34Rb 63
Plough Ct. EC3—45Tb 83 (4G 201)
Plough Farm Clo. Ruis—30T 36
Plough Hill. Pot B—1Nb 10
★Plough Hill. Sev—95Be
Plough La. SE22—58Vb 105
Plough La.—64Db 125
SW19 2-56
SW17 remainder
Plough La. Cob—89W 158
Plough La. Purl—81Pb 164
Plough La. Rick—5H 3
Plough La. Slou—9M 53
Plough La. Uxb—23L 35
Plough La. Wall—77Nb 146
Plough La. Clo. Wall—78Nb 146
Plough Lees La. Slou—5J 73
Ploughmans Clo. NW1—39Mb 62
Ploughmans End. Iswth—57Fa 100
Plough Pl. EC4—44Qb 82 (2A 200)
Plough Rise. Upm—31Ud 70
Plough Rd. SW11—55Fb 103
Plough Rd. Eps—81Ta 161
Plough Ter. SW11—56Fb 103
Plough Way. SE16—49Zb 84
Plough Yd. EC2—42Ub 83 (6J 195)
Plover Clo. Stai—62H 119
Plover Gdns. Upm—32Vd 70
★Plovers Barrow. Brtwd—8Zd
★Plovers Mead. Brtwd—8Zd
Plumber's Row. E1—44Wb 83
Plumbridge St. SE10—53Ec 106
Plum Garth. Bren—49Ma 79
Plum La. SE18—52Rc 108
Plummer La. Mitc—68Hb 125
Plummer Rd. SW4—59Mb 104
Plumpton Av. Horn—35Nd 69
Plumpton Clo. N'holt—37Ca 57
Plumpton Way. Cars—76Gb 145
Plumstead Comn. Rd. SE18
—51Rc 108
Plumstead High St. SE18—49Tc 86
Plumstead Rd. SE18—49Rc 86
Plumtree Clo. Wall—80Mb 146
Plumtree Ct. EC4
—44Rb 83 (2B 200)
Plumtree Mead. Lou—13Qc 28
Plybrook Rd. Sutt—76Cb 145
Plymouth Dri. Sev—96Ld 187
Plymouth Pk. Sev—96Ld 187
Plymouth Rd. E16—43Jc 85
Plymouth Rd. Brom—67Kc 129
Plympton Av. NW6—38Bb 61
Plympton Pl. NW8
—42Gb 81 (6D 190)
Plympton Rd. NW6—38Bb 61
Plympton St. NW8
—42Gb 81 (6D 190)
Plymstock Rd. Well—52Yc 109
Pocketsdell La. Hem—1A 2
Pocklington Clo. NW9—26Ua 40
Pococks La. Wind—10J 73
Pocock St. SE1—47Rb 83 (1B 206)
Podmore Rd. SW18—56Eb 103
Poets' Corner. SW1
—48Nb 82 (3F 205)
Poet's Rd. N5—36Tb 63
Pointalls Clo. N3—26Eb 41
Point Clo. SE10—53Ec 106
Pointers Cotts. Rich—61La 122
Pointers Rd. Cob—88S 158
Point Hill. SE10—53Ec 106
Point Pleasant. SW18—56Cb 103
Point, The. Ruis—35W 56
Poland St. W1—44Lb 82 (2C 198)
Polebrook Rd. SE3—55Lc 107
Pole Cat All. Brom—75Hc 149
Polecroft La. SE6—61Bc 128
Pole Hill Rd. E4—17Ec 26
Pole Hill Rd. Uxb—42R 76
Polesden Gdns. SW20—68Xa 124
Polesden La. Lea—100Da 175
Polesden La. Wok—95H 173
Poles Hill. Rick—5G 2
Polesteeple Hill. West—89Mc 167
Polesworth Rd. Dag—38Zc 67
Poley Rd. Stanf—2L 93
Polhill. Sev—87Ed 170
Police Sta. La. Bush, Wat—17Da 19
Police Sta. Rd. W on T—79Y 141
Pollard Av. Uxb—30H 35
Pollard Clo. E16—45Jc 85
Pollard Clo. N7—35Pb 62
Pollard Clo. Chig—22Wc 47
Pollard Clo. Wind—7M 95
Pollard Rd. N20—19Gb 23
Pollard Rd. Mord—71Fb 145
Pollard Rd. Wok—88D 156
Pollard Row. E2—41Wb 83
Pollards. Rick—22F 34
Pollards Clo. Lou—15Lc 27
Pollards Clo. Wal X—1Sb 11
Pollards Cres. SW16—69Nb 126
Pollards Hill E. SW16—69Pb 126
Pollards Hill N. SW16—69Nb 126
Pollards Hill S. SW16—69Nb 126
Pollards Hill W. SW16—69Pb 126
Pollard St. E2—41Wb 83
Pollards Wood Rd. SW16
—69Nb 126
Pollard Wlk. Sidc—65Yc 131
Pollen St. W1—44Lb 82 (3B 198)
Pollitt Dri. NW8—42Fb 81 (5C 190)
Pollyhaugh. Eyns, Dart—76Nd 153
Polperro Clo. Orp—72Vc 151
Polsted Rd. SE6—59Bc 106
Polthorne Gro. SE18—49Tc 86
Polworth Rd. SW16—64Nb 126
Polygon Rd. NW1
—40Mb 62 (2D 192)
Polygon, The. SW4—56Lb 104
Polytechnic St. SE18—49Qc 86
Pomell Way. E1—44Vb 83 (2K 201)
Pomeroy Cres. Wat—8X 5
Pomeroy St. SE14—52Yb 106
Pomfret Rd. SE5—55Rb 105
Pompadour Clo. Brtwd—22Yd 50
Pond Clo. SE3—54Hc 107
Pond Clo. Uxb—26L 35
Pond Clo. W on T—79W 140
Pond Cotts. SE21—60Ub 105
Ponders End Industrial Est.
Enf—15Ac 26
Ponder St. N7—38Pb 62
Pondfield Ho. SE27—64Sb 127
Pondfield La. Brtwd—21Ce 51
Pondfield La. Grav—6N 137
Pondfield Rd. Brom—74Fc 149
Pondfield Rd. Dag—36Dd 68
Pondfield Rd. Kenl—88Rb 165
Pondfield Rd. Orp—76Rc 150
Pond Grn. Ruis—33U 56
Pondhead La. W on T—81V 158
Pond Hill Gdns. Sutt—79Ab 144
Pondmead. SE21—58Tb 105
Pond Piece. Lea—85Da 159
Pond Pl. SW3—49Gb 81 (6D 202)
Pond Pl. Asht—89Na 161
Pond Rd. E15—40Gc 65
Pond Rd. SE3—54Hc 107
Pond Rd. Egh—65E 118
Pond Rd. Wok—8D 188
Pondside Clo. Hay—51T 98
Pond Sq. N6—32Jb 62
Pond St. NW3—36Gb 61
Pond Wlk. Upm—33Ud 70
Pond Way. Chst—65Rc 130
Pond Way. Tedd—65La 122
Pondwood Rise. Orp—73Uc 150
Ponler St. E1—44Xb 83
Ponsard Rd. NW10—41Xa 80
Ponsford St. E9—37Yb 64
Ponsonby Bldgs. SE1—(7B 200)
Ponsonby Pl. SW1
—50Mb 82 (7E 204)
Ponsonby Rd. SW15—59Xa 102
Ponsonby Ter. SW1
—50Mb 82 (7E 204)
Pontefract Rd. Brom—64Hc 129
Pontoise Clo. Sev—94Hd 186
Ponton Rd. SW8—52Mb 104
Pont St. SW1—48Hb 81 (4F 203)
Pont St. M. SW1—48Hb 81 (4F 203)
Pontypool Pl. SE1—(1B 206)
Pontypool Wlk. Romf—23Ld 49
Pony Chase. Cob—85Ba 159
Pool Clo. Beck—64Cc 128
Pool Clo. E Mol—71Ba 141
Poole Clo. Ruis—33U 56
Poole Ct. Rd. Houn—54Aa 99
Poole Rd. E9—37Zb 64
Poole Rd. Eps—79Ta 143
Poole Rd. Horn—31Pd 69
Poole Rd. Wok—90A 156
Pooles Bldgs. EC1—(6K 193)
Pooles Cotts. Rich—61Ma 123
Pooles La. SW10—52Eb 103
Pooles La. Dag—40Ad 67
Pooles Pk. N4—33Qb 62
Poole St. N1—39Tb 63 (1F 195)
Poole Way. Hay—41U 76
Pooley Av. Egh—64D 118
Pooley Grn. Clo. Egh—64E 118
Pooley Grn. Rd. Egh—64D 118
Poolmans Rd. Wind—5B 94
Pool Rd. E Mol—71Ba 141
Poolsford Rd. NW9—28Ua 40
Poonah St. E1—44Yb 84
Pope Rd. Brom—71Mc 149
Popes Av. Twic—61Ga 122
Popes Clo. Slou—52D 96
Pope's Rd. N3—25Cb 41
Popes Gro. Croy—76Bc 148
Popes Gro. Twic—61Ha 122
Pope's Head All. EC3
—44Tb 83 (3G 201)
Popes La. W5—48Ma 79
Popes La. Wat—10X 5
Pope's Rd. SW9—55Qb 104
Pope's Rd. Abb L, Wat—3U 4
Pope St. SE1—47Ub 83 (2J 207)
Popham Clo. Felt—62Ba 121
Popham Gdns. Rich—55Qa 101
Popham Rd. N1—39Sb 63
(in two parts)
Popham St. N1—39Sb 63
Poplar Av. Grav—3E 136
Poplar Av. Lea—94La 176
Poplar Av. Mitc—67Hb 125
Poplar Av. Orp—75Rc 150
Poplar Av. S'hall—48Da 77
Poplar Av. W Dray—45P 75
Poplar Bath St. E14—45Dc 84
Poplar Clo. Pinn—25Z 37
Poplar Clo. Slou—53G 96
Poplar Ct. SW19—64Cb 125
Poplar Cres. Eps—79Sa 143
Poplar Dri. Bans—86Ab 162
Poplar Farm Clo. Eps—79Sa 143
Poplar Gdns. SE28—44Yc 87
Poplar Gdns. N Mald—68Ta 123
Poplar Gro. N11—23Jb 42
Poplar Gro. W6—47Ya 80
Poplar Gro. N Mald—68Ta 123
Poplar Gro. Wemb—34Sa 59
Poplar Gro. Wok—91A 172
Poplar High St. E14—45Dc 84
Poplar Mt. Belv—49Ed 88
Poplar Pl. SE28—46Yc 87
Poplar Pl. W2—45Db 81
Poplar Pl. Hay—45W 76
Poplar Rd. SE24—56Sb 105
Poplar Rd. SW19—68Cb 125
Poplar Rd. Ashf—64S 120
Poplar Rd. Lea—94Ka 176
Poplar Rd. Sutt—74Bb 145
Poplar Rd. Uxb—37L 55
Poplar Rd. S. SW19—69Cb 125
Poplar Row. Epp—9Uc 14
Poplars Av. NW2—37Ya 60
Poplars Clo. Long, Dart—69Ee 135
Poplars Clo. Ruis—32U 56
Poplars Clo. Wat—4X 5
Poplar Shaw. Wal A—5Hc 13
Poplars Rd. E17—30Dc 44
Poplars, The. N14—15Kb 24
Poplars, The. Romf—13Xc 29
Poplar St. Romf—28Ed 48
Poplar Wlk. SE24—56Sb 105
Poplar Wlk. Croy—74Sb 147
Poplar Way. Felt—62X 121
Poplar Way. Ilf—28Sc 46
Poppins Ct. EC4—44Rb 83 (3B 200)
Poppleton Rd. E11—30Gc 45
Poppy Clo. Brtwd—15Xd 32
Poppy La. Croy—74Yb 148
Porchester Clo. SE5—56Tb 105
Porchester Clo. Horn—30Nd 49
Porchester Clo. Long, Dart
—70Be 135
Porchester Gdns. W2—45Db 81
Porchester Gdns. M. W2—44Db 81
Porchester Mead. Beck—65Cc 128
Porchester M. W2—44Db 81
Porchester Pl. W2
—44Gb 81 (3E 196)
Porchester Rd. W2—44Db 81
Porchester Rd. King—68Ra 123
Porchester Sq. W2—44Db 81
Porchester Ter. W2
—45Eb 81 (4A 196)
Porchester Ter. N. W2—44Db 81
Porchfield Clo. Grav—1E 136
Porchfield Clo. Sutt—82Db 163
Porch Way. N20—20Hb 23
Porcupine Clo. SE9—61Nc 130
Porden Rd. SW2—56Pb 104
Porlock Av. Harr—34Ea 58
Porlock Ho. SE26—62Wb 127
Porlock Rd. Enf—17Vb 25
Porlock St. SE1—47Tb 83 (1G 207)
Porrington Clo. Chst—67Qc 130
Portal Clo. SE27—62Qb 126
Portal Clo. Ruis—35W 56
Portal Clo. Uxb—38N 55
Port Av. Grnh—58Xd 112
Portbury Clo. SE15—53Wb 105
Port Cres. E13—42Kc 85
Portcullis Lodge Rd. Enf—13Tb 25
Portelet Rd. E1—41Zb 84
Porten Rd. W14—48Ab 80
Porter Rd. E6—44Pc 86
Porters Av. Dag—37Xc 67
Porters Clo. Brtwd—18Wd 32
Porter St. W1—43Hb 81 (7G 191)
Porters Way. W Dray—48P 75
Porteus Rd. W2—43Eb 81 (7B 190)
Portgate Clo. W9—42Bb 81
Porthcawe Rd. SE26—63Ac 128
Port Hill. Orp—84Xc 169
Porthkerry Av. Well—56Wc 109
Portia Way. E3—42Bc 84
Portinscale Rd. SW15—57Ab 102
Portland Av. N16—31Vb 63
Portland Av. Grav—1D 136
Portland Av. N Mald—73Va 144
Portland Av. Sidc—58Wc 109
Portland Cres. SE9—61Nc 130
Portland Cres. Felt—63T 120
Portland Cres. Gnfd—43Da 77
Portland Cres. Stan—26Ma 39
Portland Dri. Red—100Mb 180
Portland Dri. Wal X—3Wb 11
Portland Gdns. N4—30Rb 43
Portland Gdns. Romf—29Zc 47
Portland Gro. SW8—53Pb 104
Portland M. W1—(3C 198)
Portland Pl. W1—43Kb 82 (6K 191)
Portland Pl. Eps—84Ua 162
Portland Rise. N4—32Rb 63
Portland Rise. Est. N4—32Sb 63
Portland Rd. N15—28Vb 43
Portland Rd. SE9—61Nc 130
Portland Rd. SE25—70Wb 127
Portland Rd. W11—45Ab 80
Portland Rd. Ashf—62N 119
Portland Rd. Brom—63Lc 129
Portland Rd. Grav—10D 114
Portland Rd. Grav—58Fe 113
(Northfleet)
Portland Rd. Hay—41U 76
Portland Rd. King—69Na 123
Portland Rd. Mitc—68Gb 125
Portland Rd. S'hall—48Ba 77
Portland St. SE17
—50Tb 83 (7F 207)
Portland Ter. Rich—56Ma 101
Portley La. Cat—93Ub 181
Portley Wood Rd. Cat—93Vb 181
Portman Av. SW14—55Ta 101
Portman Bldgs. NW1—(6E 190)
Portman Clo. W1
—44Jb 82 (2G 197)
Portman Clo. Bex—60Gd 110
Portman Clo. Bexh—55Ad 109
Portman Dri. Wfd G—26Mc 45
Portman Gdns. NW9—26Ta 39
Portman M. S. W1
—44Jb 82 (3H 197)
Portman Pl. E2—41Yb 84
Portman Rd. King—68Pa 123
Portman Sq. W1—44Jb 82 (2H 197)
Portman St. W1—44Jb 82 (3H 197)
Portmeadow Wlk. SE2—47Zc 87
Portmeers Clo. E17—30Bc 44
Portmore Gdns. Romf—22Cd 48
Portmore Pk. Rd. Wey—77Q 140
Portnall Dri. Vir W—10K 117
Portnall Rd. W9—41Bb 81
Portnall Rd. Vir W—10K 117
Portnalls Clo. Coul—88Kb 164
Portnalls Rise. Coul—88Lb 164
Portnalls Rd. Coul—90Kb 164
Portnoi Clo. Romf—26Fd 48
Portobello M. W11—45Cb 81
Portobello Rd.—43Ab 80
W11 1-275 & 2-262
W10 remainder
Portpool La. EC1
—43Qb 82 (7K 193)
Portree Clo. N22—24Pb 42
Portree St. E14—44Fc 85
Portsdown. Edgw—22Qa 39
Portsdown Av. NW11—30Bb 41
Portsea M. W2—(3E 196)
Portsea Pl. W2—44Gb 81 (3E 196)
Portsea Rd. Til—3E 114
Portslade Rd. SW8—54Lb 104
Portsmouth Av. Th Dit
—73Ja 142
Portsmouth Bldgs. SE1—(4H 207)
Portsmouth Rd. SW15—59Xa 102
Portsmouth Rd. Cob & Esh
—85X 159
Portsmouth Rd. Esh, Th Dit,
Surb & King—79Ca 141
Portsmouth Rd. Wok—96J 173
Portsmouth Rd. Wok & Cob
—91P 173
Portsmouth St. WC2
—44Pb 82 (3H 199)
Portsoken St. E1
—45Vb 83 (4K 201)
Portswood Pl. SW15—59Va 102
Portugal Gdns. Twic—61Ea 122
Portugal Rd. Wok—88B 156
Portugal St. WC2
—44Pb 82 (3H 199)
Portway. E15—39Hc 65
Portway. Eps—81Wa 162
Portway Cres. Eps—81Wa 162
Portway Gdns. SE18—52Mc 107
Postern Grn. Enf—13Qb 24
Postern, The. EC2—(1E 200)
Post Ho. La. Lea—97Ca 175
Post La. Twic—60Fa 100
Post Meadow. Iver—41F 74
Post Office All. Hmptn—68Da 121
Post Office App. E7—36Kc 65
Post Office Ct. EC3—(3G 201)
Post Office La. Slou—4P 73
Post Office Way. SW8—51Mb 104
Postway M. Ilf—34Rc 66
(in two parts)
Potier St. SE1—48Tb 83 (4G 207)
Potter Clo. Mitc—68Kb 126
Potterne Clo. SW19—59Za 102
Potters Clo. Lou—12Nc 28
Potters Cross. Iver—41G 74
Potters' Fields. SE1
—46Ub 83 (7J 201)
Potters Gro. N Mald—70Sa 123
Potters Heights Clo. Pinn—24X 37
Potter's La. SW16—65Mb 126
Potters La. Barn—14Cb 23
Potters La. Borwd—11Sa 21
Potters La. Wok—95D 172
Potters La. Wok—98E 172
Potters Rd. Barn—14Db 23
Potter St. N'wd & Pinn—25W 36
Potter St. Hill. Pinn—23X 37
Pottery La. W11—46Ab 80
Pottery Rd. Bex—61Ed 132
Pottery Rd. Bren—51Na 101
Pottery St. SE16—47Xb 83
Pott St. E2—41Xb 83
Poulcott. Wray, Stai—58A 96
Poulett Gdns. Twic—60Ja 100
Poulett Rd. E6—40Pc 66
Poulner Way. SE15—52Wb 105
Poulters Wood. Kes—78Mc 149
Poulton Av. Sutt—76Fb 145
Poulton Clo. E8—37Xb 63
Poultry. EC2—44Tb 83 (3F 201)
Pound Bank Clo. Sev—80Vd 154
Pound Clo. Orp—75Tc 150
Pound Clo. Surb—74La 142
Pound Ct. Asht—90Pa 161
Pound Ct. Dri. Orp—75Tc 150
Pound Cres. Lea—93Fa 176
Poundfield. Wat—7V 4
Poundfield Gdns. Wok—92E 172
Poundfield Rd. Lou—15Qc 28
Pound La. NW10—37Wa 60
Pound La. Eps—83Ta 161
(in two parts)
Pound La. Grays—2C 92
Pound La. Sev—96Ld 187
Pound La. Sev—87Zc 169
(Knockholt Pound)
Pound La. Shen, Rad—5Pa 7
Pound Pk. Rd. SE7—49Mc 85
Pound Pl. SE9—58Qc 108
Pound Rd. Bans—89Bb 163
Pound Rd. Cher—73K 139
Pound St. Cars—78Hb 145
Pound, The. Slou—2B 72
Pounsley Rd. Sev—93Gd 186
Pountney Rd. SW11—55Jb 104
Poverest Rd. Orp—71Vc 151
Powder Mill La. Dart—61Nd 133
Powder Mill La. Twic—59Ba 99
Powdermill La. Wal A—5Dc 12
Powdermill Way. Wal A—5Dc 12
Powell Clo. Edgw—23Pa 39
Powell Clo. Wall—80Nb 146
Powell Gdns. Dag—35Cd 68
Powell Rd. E5—34Xb 63
Powell Rd. Buck H—17Lc 27
Powell's Wlk. W4—51Ua 102
Power Industrial Est. Eri
—53Jd 110
Power Rd. W4—49Qa 79
Powers Ct. Twic—59Ma 101
Powerscroft Rd. E5—35Yb 64
Powerscroft Rd. Sidc—65Yc 131
Powis Ct. Pot B—6Eb 9
Powis Gdns. NW11—31Bb 61
Powis Gdns. W11—44Bb 81
Powis M. W11—44Bb 81
Powis Pl. WC1—42Nb 82 (6G 193)
Powis Rd. E3—41Dc 84
Powis Sq. W11—44Bb 81
Powis St. SE18—48Qc 86
Powis Ter. W11—44Bb 81
Powlett Pl. NW1—38Kb 62
Pownall Gdns. Houn—56Da 99
Pownall Rd. E8—39Wb 63
Pownall Rd. Houn—56Da 99
Powster Rd. Brom—64Jc 129
Powys Clo. Bexh—51Zc 109
Powys Ct. N13—22Nb 42
Powys La.—21Nb 42
N14 2-46
N13 remainder
Poyle Industrial Est. Slou—54G 96
Poyle La. Slou—10A 52
Poyle Rd. Slou—55G 96
Poynder Rd. Til—3D 114
Poynders Gdns. SW4—59Lb 104
Poynders Rd. SW4—58Lb 104
Poynings Clo. Orp—75Yc 151
Poynings Rd. N19—34Lb 62
Poynings, The. Iver—49H 75
Poynings Way. N12—22Cb 41
Poynings Way. Romf—25Nd 49
Poyntell Cres. Chst—67Tc 130
Poynter Rd. Enf—15Wb 25
Poynton Rd. N17—26Wb 43
Poyntz Rd. SW11—54Hb 103
Poyser St. E2—40Xb 63
Praed M. W2—44Fb 81 (2C 196)
Praed St. W2—44Fb 81 (3B 196)
Prae, The. Wok—90H 157
Pragel St. E13—40Lc 65
Pragnell Rd. SE12—61Kc 129
Prague Pl. SW2—57Nb 104
Prah Rd. N4—33Qb 62
Prairie Clo. Wey—76K 139
Prairie Rd. Wey—76K 139
Prairie St. SW8—54Kb 104
Pratt M. NW1—39Lb 62
Pratts La. W on T—77Z 141
Pratt St. NW1—39Lb 62
Pratt Wlk. SE11—49Pb 82 (5J 205)
Prayle Gro. NW2—32Za 60
Prebend Gdns.—49Va 80
W4 1-37 & 2-40
W6 remainder
Prebend St. N1—39Sb 63 (1D 194)
Precinct Rd. Hay—45W 76
Precincts, The. Slou—2A 72
Precinct, The. Egh—64C 118
Premier Av. Grays—47Ee 91
Premier Lodge. N3—25Cb 41
Prendergast Rd. SE3—55Gc 107
Prentis Rd. SW16—63Mb 126
Prentiss Ct. SE7—49Mc 85
Presburg Rd. N Mald—71Ua 144
Prescelly Pl. Edgw—25Pa 39
Prescot Rd. Slou—54G 96
Prescot St. E1—45Vb 83 (4K 201)
Prescott Av. Orp—72Rc 150
Prescott Clo. SW16—66Nb 126
Prescott Grn. Lou—13Sc 28
Prescott Pl. SW4—56Mb 104
President St. EC1—(3D 194)
Press Rd. NW10—34Ta 59
Press Rd. Uxb—37M 55
Prestage St. E14—45Fc 85
Prestbury Ct. Wok—6D 188
Prestbury Cres. Bans—88Hb 163
Prestbury Rd. E7—38Lc 65
Prestbury Sq. SE9—63Pc 130
Prested Rd. SW11—56Gb 103
Preston Av. E4—23Fc 45
Preston Clo. SE1
—49Ub 83 (5H 207)
Preston Clo. Twic—62Ga 122
Preston Ct. W on T—74Y 141
Preston Dri. E11—29Lc 45
Preston Dri. Bexh—53Zc 109
Preston Dri. Eps—79Ua 144
Preston Gdns. NW10—37Ua 60
Preston Gdns. Enf—9Ac 12
Preston Gdns. Ilf—30Nc 46
Preston Gro. Asht—89La 160
Preston Hill. Harr—31Na 59
Preston La. Tad—93Xa 178
Preston Pl. NW2—37Wa 60
Preston Pl. Rich—57Na 101
Preston Rd. E11—30Gc 45
Preston Rd. SE19—65Rb 127
Preston Rd. SW20—66Va 124
Preston Rd. Grav—10A 114
Preston Rd. Romf—21Md 49
Preston Rd. Shep—71Q 140
Preston Rd. Slou—5N 73
Preston Rd. Wemb & Harr
—33Na 59
Preston's Rd. E14—45Ec 84
Prestons Rd. Brom—76Jc 149
Preston Waye. Harr—32Na 59
Prestwick Rd. Wat—22X 37
Prestwood. Slou—4M 73
Prestwood Av. Harr—28Ka 38
Prestwood Clo. Harr—28Ka 38
Prestwood Dri. Romf—22Ed 48
Prestwood Gdns. Croy—73Sb 147
Prestwood St. N1
—40Sb 63 (2E 194)
Pretoria Av. E17—28Ac 44
Pretoria Clo. N17—24Vb 43
Pretoria Cres. E4—18Ec 26
Pretoria Rd. E4—18Ec 26
Pretoria Rd. E11—32Fc 65
Pretoria Rd. E16—42Hc 85
Pretoria Rd. N17—24Vb 43
Pretoria Rd. SW16—65Kb 126
Pretoria Rd. Cher—74H 139
Pretoria Rd. Ilf—36Rc 66
Pretoria Rd. Romf—28Ed 48
Pretoria Rd. Wat—14W 18
Pretoria Rd. N. N18—23Vb 43
Prevost Rd. N11—19Jb 24
Price Clo. NW7—23Ab 40
Price Clo. SW17—62Hb 125
Price Rd. Croy—78Rb 147
Price's St. SE1—46Rb 83 (7C 200)
Price's Yd. N1—39Pb 62
Price Way. Hmptn—65Aa 121
Pricklers Hill. Barn—16Db 23
Prickley Wood. Brom—74Hc 149
Priddy's Yd. Croy—75Sb 147
Prideaux Pl. WC1
—41Pb 82 (3J 193)
Prideaux Rd. SW9—55Nb 104
Pridham Rd. E. T Hth—70Tb 127
Priestfield Rd. SE23—62Ac 128
Priest Hill. Egh & Wind—2N 117
Priestlands Pk. Rd. Sidc
—62Vc 131
Priestley Clo. N16—31Vb 63
Priestley Gdns. Romf—30Xc 47
Priestley Rd. Mitc—68Jb 126
Priestley St. E9—36Zb 64
Priestley Way. E17—27Zb 44
Priestley Way. NW2—32Wa 60
Priests Av. Romf—26Fd 48
Priests Bri.—55Ua 102
SW15 2-20
SW14 remainder
Priest's Ct. EC2—(2D 200)
Priest's Field. Brtwd—22Ee 51
Priests La. Brtwd—19Ae 33
Priest Wlk. Grav—1J 137
Prima Rd. SW9—52Qb 104
Primrose Av. Enf—11Ub 25
Primrose Av. Romf—31Xc 67
Primrose Clo. Harr—34Ba 57
Primrose Gdns. NW3—37Gb 61
Primrose Gdns. Bush, Wat
—17Da 19

Primrose Gdns.—Queens Mead Rd.

Primrose Gdns. Ruis—36Y 57
Primrose Glen. Horn—28Nd 49
Primrose Hill. EC4
—44Qb 82 (3A 200)
Primrose Hill. Brtwd—20Yd 32
Primrose Hill. K Lan—1R 4
Primrose Hill Rd. NW3—38Hb 61
Primrose La. Croy—74Zb 148
Primrose Path. Wal X—3Wb 11
Primrose Rd. E10—32Dc 64
Primrose Rd. E18—26Kc 45
Primrose Rd. W on T—78Y 141
Primrose St. EC2
—43Ub 83 (7H 195)
Primrose Way. Wemb—40Ma 59
Primula St. W12—44Wa 80
Prince Albert Rd.
—40Gb 61 (3D 190)
NW1 1-23
NW8 remainder
Prince Albert's Wlk. Wind—3L 95
Prince Arthur M. NW3—35Eb 61
Prince Arthur Rd. NW3—36Eb 61
Prince Charles Av. Grays—2D 92
Prince Charles Av. S Dar, Dart
—68Td 134
Prince Charles Dri. NW4—31Ya 60
Prince Charles Rd. SE3—54Hc 107
Prince Charles Way. Wall
—76Kb 146
Prince Consort Cotts. Wind—4H 95
Prince Consort Dri. Chst
—67Tc 130
Prince Consort Rd. SW7
—48Fb 81 (3A 202)
Prince Consort's Dri. Wind—8D 94
Princedale Rd. W11—46Ab 80
Prince Edward Rd. E9—37Bc 64
Prince George Av. N14—15Mb 24
Prince George Rd. N16—35Ub 63
Prince George's Av. SW20
—68Ya 124
Prince George's Rd. SW19
—67Fb 125
Prince Henry Rd. SE7—52Mc 107
Prince Imperial Rd. SE18
—53Pc 108
Prince Imperial Rd. Chst
—66Rc 130
Prince John Rd. SE9—57Nc 108
Princelet St. E1—43Vb 83 (7K 195)
Prince of Orange La. SE10
—52Ec 106
Prince of Wales Clo. NW4
—28Xa 40
Prince of Wales Dri. SW11 &
SW8—53Hb 103
Prince of Wales Footpath. Enf
—10Ac 12
Prince of Wales Ho. Ger X—22B 34
Prince of Wales Pas. NW1
—(4B 192)
Prince of Wales Rd. E16—44Lc 85
Prince of Wales Rd. NW5—37Jb 62
Prince of Wales Rd. SE3—53Hc 107
Prince of Wales Rd. Sutt
—75Fb 145
Prince of Wales Ter. W4—50Ua 80
Prince of Wales Ter. W8—47Db 81
Prince Philip Av. Grays—46Ce 91
Prince Regent La.—41Kc 85
E13 1-279 & 2-250
E16 remainder
Prince Regent Rd. Houn—55Ea 100
Prince Rd. SE25—71Ub 147
Prince Rupert Rd. SE9—56Pc 108
Princes Arc. SW1—(6C 198)
Princes Av. N3—25Cb 41
Princes Av. N10—27Kb 42
Princes Av. N13—22Qb 42
Princes Av. N22—25Mb 42
Princes Av. NW9—28Qa 39
Princes Av. W3—48Qa 79
Princes Av. Cars—80Hb 145
Princes Av. Dart—60Rd 111
Princes Av. Enf—8Ac 12
Prince's Av. Gnfd—44Da 77
Princes Av. Orp—71Uc 150
Princes Av. S Croy—87Xb 165
Princes Av. Surb—74Qa 143
Prince's Av. Wat—15V 18
Princes Av. Wfd G—21Kc 45
Princes Cir. WC2—(2F 199)
Princes Clo. NW9—28Qa 39
Princes Clo. Edgw—22Qa 39
Princes Clo. Sidc—62Zc 131
Princes Clo. S Croy—87Xb 165
Prince's Clo. Tedd—63Fa 122
Princes Clo. Wind—10D 72
Princes Ct. Wemb—36Na 59
Princes Dri. Harr—27Ga 38
Prince's Dri. Lea—84Ga 160
Princesfield Rd. Wal A—5Kc 13
Prince's Gdns. SW7
—48Fb 81 (3C 202)
Princes Gdns. W3—43Qa 79
Princes Gdns. W5—42La 78
Prince's Ga. SW7
—47Fb 81 (2D 202)
(in three parts)
Prince's Ga. Ct. SW7
—47Fb 81 (2C 202)
Prince's Ga. M. SW7
—48Fb 81 (3C 202)
Princes La. N10—27Kb 42
Prince's M. W2—45Db 81
Princes Pk. Rain—38Jd 68
Princes Pk. Av. NW11—30Ab 40
Princes Pk. Av. Hay—45T 76
Princes Pk. Circ. Hay—45T 76
Princes Pk. Clo. Hay—45T 76
Princes Pk. La. Hay—45T 76
Princes Pk. Pde. Hay—45T 76
Princes Pl. SW1—(6C 198)
Princes Pl. W11—46Ab 80
Prince's Plain. Brom—73Nc 150
Prince's Rise. SE13—54Ec 106
Princes Rd. N18—21Yb 44
Princes Rd. SE20—65Zb 128
Princes Rd. SW14—55Ta 101
Prince's Rd. SW19—65Cb 125
Princes Rd. W13—46Ka 78
Princes Rd. Ashf—64P 119
Prince's Rd. Brtwd—11Nd 31
Princes Rd. Buck H—19Lc 27
Princes Rd. Dart—58Jd 110
Princes Rd. Egh—65B 118
Princes Rd. Felt—62V 120
Princes Rd. Grav—2E 136
Princes Rd. Ilf—28Tc 46
Princes Rd. King—66Qa 123
Princes Rd. Pot B—4Db 9
Princes Rd. Rich—57Pa 101
Princes Rd. Rich—53Pa 101
(Kew)
Prince's Rd. Romf—29Jd 48
Prince's Rd. Tedd—63Fa 122
Princes Rd. Wey—78R 140
Princess Av. Grays—9L 93
Princess Av. Wemb—33Na 59
Princess Av. Wind—5F 94
Princess Ct. N6—31Lb 62
Princess Cres. N4—33Rb 63
Princess Gdns. Wok—88D 156
Princess Margaret Rd. Grays
—9K 93
Princess Mary's Rd. Wey—77L 139
Princess May Rd. N16—35Ub 63
Princess M. NW3—36Fb 61
Princess Pde. Orp—76Qc 150
Prince's Sq. W2—45Db 81
Princess Rd. NW1—39Jb 62
Princess Rd. NW6—40Cb 61
Princess Rd. Croy—72Sb 147
Princess Rd. Swan—65Jd 132
Princess Rd. Wok—88D 156
Princess St. SE1—48Rb 83 (4C 206)
Prince's St. EC2—44Tb 83 (3F 201)
Princes St. N17—23Ub 43
Princes St. W1—44Kb 82 (3A 198)
Princes St. Bexh—56Bd 109
Princes St. Grav—8D 114
Princes St. Rich—56Na 101
Princes St. Slou—7M 73
Princes St. Sutt—77Fb 145
Princes Ter. E13—39Kc 65
Prince St. SE8—51Bc 106
Prince St. Wat—13Y 19
Princes View. Dart—60Qd 111
Princes Way. SW19—59Za 102
Princes Way. Brtwd—18Ce 33
Princes Way. Buck H—19Lc 27
Princes Way. Croy—78Pb 146
Princes Way. Ruis—35Aa 57
Princes Way. W Wick—77Hc 149
Princethorpe Rd. SE26—63Zb 128
Princeton St. WC1
—43Pb 82 (7H 193)
Pringle Gdns. SW16—63Lb 126
(in two parts)
Printer St. EC4—44Qb 82 (2A 200)
Printinghouse La. Hay—47U 76
Printing Ho. Yd. E2
—41Ub 83 (4J 195)
Priolo Rd. SE7—50Lc 85
Prior Av. Sutt—80Gb 145
Prior Bolton St. N1—37Rb 63
Prioress Rd. SE27—62Rb 127
Prioress St. SE1—48Ub 83 (4G 207)
Priors Ct. Wok—6D 188
Priors Croft. E17—26Ac 44
Prior's Croft. Wok—92C 172
Priors Field. N'holt—37Aa 57
Priorsford Av. Orp—70Wc 131
Priors Gdns. Ruis—36Y 57
Priors Mead. Enf—11Ub 25
Priors Mead. Lea—97Ea 176
Priors Pk. Horn—34Ld 69
Priors Rd. Wind—5B 94
Priors, The. Asht—91Ma 177
Prior St. SE10—52Ec 106
Priory Av. E4—20Bc 26
Priory Av. E17—29Cc 44
Priory Av. N8—28Mb 42
Priory Av. W4—49Ua 80
Priory Av. Orp—72Tc 150
Priory Av. Sutt—77Za 144
Priory Av. Uxb—28L 35
Priory Av. Wemb—35Ha 58
Priory Clo. E4—20Bc 26
Priory Clo. E18—25Jc 45
Priory Clo. N3—25Bb 41
Priory Clo. N14—15Kb 24
Priory Clo. N20—18Bb 23
Priory Clo. SW19—67Db 125
Priory Clo. Beck—69Ac 128
Priory Clo. Brtwd—15Wd 32
Priory Clo. Chst—67Pc 130
Priory Clo. Dart—57Md 111
Priory Clo. Hmptn—67Ba 121
Priory Clo. Ruis—32V 56
Priory Clo. Stan—20Ha 20
Priory Clo. Sun—66W 120
Priory Clo. Uxb—34J 55
(Denham)
Priory Clo. Uxb—28L 35
(Harefield)
Priory Clo. W on T—76W 140
Priory Clo. Wemb—35Ha 58
Priory Clo. Wok—85F 156
Priory Ct. E17—26Bc 44
Priory Ct. SW8—53Mb 104
Priory Ct. Est. E17—26Bc 44
Priory Cres. SE19—66Sb 127
Priory Cres. Sutt—77Za 144
Priory Cres. Wemb—34Ja 58
Priory Dri. SE2—50Zc 87
Priory Dri. Stan—20Ha 20
Priory Gdns. N6—30Kb 42
Priory Gdns. SW13—55Va 102
Priory Gdns. W4—49Ua 80
Priory Gdns. W5—41Na 79
Priory Gdns. Dart—57Md 111
Priory Gdns. Hmptn—66Ba 121
Priory Gdns. Uxb—28L 35
Priory Gdns. Wemb—35Ja 58
Priory Grn. Stai—64K 119
Priory Gro. SW8—53Nb 104
Priory Gro. Romf—20Nd 31
Priory Hill. Dart—58Md 111
Priory Hill. Wemb—35Ja 58
Priory La. SW15—58Ua 102
Priory La. E Mol—70Da 121
Priory La. F'ham, Dart—74Pd 153
Priory La. Rich—52Qa 101
★Priory Mead. Brtwd—8Yd
Priory M. SW8—53Mb 104
Priory Pk. SE3—55Hc 107
Priory Pk. Rd. NW6—39Bb 61
Priory Pk. Rd. Wemb—35Ja 58
Priory Path. Romf—20Nd 31
Priory Pl. Dart—58Md 111
Priory Rd. E6—39Mc 65
Priory Rd. N8—28Mb 42
Priory Rd. NW6—39Db 61
Priory Rd. SW19—66Fb 125
Priory Rd. W4—48Ta 79
Priory Rd. Bark—38Tc 66
Priory Rd. Chess—76Na 143
Priory Rd. Croy—73Qb 146
Priory Rd. Dart—57Md 111
(in two parts)
Priory Rd. Hmptn—66Ba 121
Priory Rd. Houn—57Ea 100
Priory Rd. Lou—14Nc 28
Priory Rd. Rich—51Qa 101
Priory Rd. Romf—20Nd 31
Priory Rd. Slou—3A 72
Priory Rd. Stanf—1N 93
Priory Rd. Sutt—77Za 144
Priory St. E3—41Dc 84
Priory Ter. NW6—39Db 61
Priory Ter. Sun—66W 120
Priory, The. SE3—56Hc 107
Priory View. Bush, Wat—17Ga 20
Priory Wlk. SW10
—50Eb 81 (7A 202)
Priory Way. Harr—28Da 37
Priory Way. Slou—2M 95
Priory Way. S'hall—48Z 77
Priory Way. W Dray—51N 97
Pritchard's Rd. E2—40Wb 63
Priter Rd. SE16—48Wb 83
Priter Way. SE16—48Wb 83
Private Rd. Enf—15Tb 25
Probert Rd. SW2—57Qb 104
Probyn Rd. SW2—61Rb 127
Procter Gdns. Lea—97Da 175
Procter St. WC1—43Pb 82 (1H 199)
Proctors Clo. Felt—60W 98
Profumo Rd. W on T—78Z 141
Progress Way. N22—25Qb 42
Progress Way. Croy—75Pb 146
Progress Way. Enf—15Wb 25
Promenade App. Rd. W4
—52Ua 102
Promenade de Verdun. Purl
—83Mb 164
Promenade, The. W4—53Ua 102
Prospect Av. Stanf—2K 93
Prospect Clo. SE26—63Xb 127
Prospect Clo. Belv—49Cd 88
Prospect Clo. Houn—53Ba 99
Prospect Clo. Ruis—31Z 57
Prospect Cotts. SW18—56Cb 103
Prospect Cres. Twic—58Ea 100
Prospect Gro. Grav—9F 114
Prospect Hill. E17—28Dc 44
Prospect La. Egh—4L 117
Prospect Pl. N2—28Fb 41
Prospect Pl. N17—24Ub 43
Prospect Pl. NW2—34Bb 61
Prospect Pl. W4—50Ta 79
Prospect Pl. Brom—69Kc 129
Prospect Pl. Eps—84Ua 162
Prospect Pl. Grav—9F 114
Prospect Pl. Grays—51De 113
Prospect Pl. Romf—26Ed 48
Prospect Pl. Stai—64H 119
Prospect Ring. N2—27Fb 41
Prospect Rd. NW2—34Bb 61
Prospect Rd. Barn—14Cb 23
Prospect Rd. Horn—27Pd 49
Prospect Rd. Sev—95Ld 187
Prospect Rd. Surb—72La 142
Prospect Rd. Wal X—1Yb 12
Prospect Rd. Wfd G—23Lc 45
Prospect St. SE16—48Xb 83
Prospect Vale. SE18—49Nc 86
Prospero Rd. N19—32Mb 62
Protheroe Rd. SW6—52Bb 103
Prothero Gdns. NW4—29Xa 40
Prout Gro. NW10—35Ua 60
Prout Rd. E5—34Xb 63
Provence St. N1—40Sb 63 (1D 194)
Providence Ct. W1
—45Jb 82 (4J 197)
Providence La. Hay—52T 98
Providence Pl. N1—39Rb 63
Providence Pl. Eps—84Ua 162
Providence Pl. Romf—26Bd 47
Providence Pl. Wok—86K 157
Providence Rd. W Dray—46N 75
Providence Row. N1—(2H 193)
Providence St. Grnh—57Wd 112
Provident Industrial Est. Hay
—47W 76
Provost Rd. NW3—38Hb 61
Provost St. N1—41Tb 83 (2F 195)
Prowse Av. Bush, Wat—18Ea 20
Prowse Pl. NW1—38Lb 62
Pruden Clo. N14—19Lb 24
Prudent Pas. EC2—(3E 200)
Prune Hill. Egh—66A 118
Prune Hill. Egh—6P 117
Prusom St. E1—46Xb 83
Pryor Clo. Abb L, Wat—4V 4
Pryors, The. NW3—34Fb 61
Puck La. Wal A—1Gc 13
Puckshill. Wok—5A 188
Pudding La. EC3—45Tb 83 (5G 201)
Pudding La. Chig—16Uc 28
Pudding La. Sev—93Pd 187
Pudding Mill La. E15—39Dc 64
Puddle Dock. EC4
—45Rb 83 (4C 200)
Puddledock La. Dart & Swan
—64Gd 132
Pulborough Rd. SW18—59Bb 103
Pulborough Way. Houn—56Y 99
Pulford Rd. N15—30Tb 43
Pulham Av. N2—28Eb 41
Puller Rd. Barn—12Ab 22
Pulleyns Av. E6—41Nc 86
Pullman Gdns. SW15—58Ya 102
Pulross Rd. SW9—55Pb 104
Pulteney Clo. E3—39Bc 64
Pulteney Rd. E18—27Kc 45
Pulteney Ter. N1—39Pb 62
Pulton Pl. SW6—52Cb 103
Puma Ct. E1—43Vb 83 (7K 195)
Pump All. Bren—52Ma 101
Pump Clo. N'holt—40Ca 57
Pump Ct. EC4—44Qb 82 (3K 199)
Pump Hill. Lou—12Pc 28
Pumping Sta. Rd. W4—52Ua 102
Pumpkin Hill. Slou—7C 52
Pump La. Asc—7C 116
Pump La. Hay—47V 76
Pump La. Orp—78Dd 152
Pump Pail N. Croy—76Sb 147
Pump Pail S. Croy—76Sb 147
Pump St. Stanf—1J 93
Punch Croft. Long, Dart—76Ae 155
Punderson's Gdns. E2—41Xb 83
Purbeck Av. N Mald—72Va 144
Purbeck Clo. Red—100Mb 180
Purbeck Dri. NW2—33Za 60
Purbeck Dri. Wok—86B 156
Purbeck Rd. Horn—31Jd 68
Purberry Gro. Eps—82Va 162
Purbrock Av. Wat—8Y 5
Purbrook St. SE1
—48Ub 83 (3J 207)
Purcell Clo. Borwd—11Ma 21
Purcell Clo. Stanf—1L 93
Purcell Cres. SW6—52Ab 102
Purcell Rd. Gnfd—43Da 77
Purcells Av. Edgw—22Qa 39
Purcell's Clo. Asht—90Pa 161
Purcell St. N1—40Ub 63 (1H 195)
Purchese St. NW1
—40Mb 62 (1E 192)
Purdy St. E3—42Dc 84
Purfleet By-Pass. Purf—49Rd 89
Purfleet Rd. S Ock—47Qd 89
Purland Clo. Dag—32Bd 67
Purland Way. SE28—47Vc 87
Purleigh Av. Wfd G—23Nc 46
Purley Av. NW2—33Ab 60
Purley Bury Av. Purl—83Sb 165
Purley Bury Clo. Purl—83Sb 165
Purley Clo. Ilf—26Qc 46
Purley Downs Rd. Purl & S Croy
—82Sb 165
Purley Hill Rd. Purl—84Rb 165
Purley Knoll. Purl—83Pb 164
Purley Oaks Rd. S Croy—81Tb 165
Purley Pk. Rd. Purl—82Rb 165
Purley Pl. N1—38Rb 63
Purley Rise. Purl—84Pb 164
Purley Rd. N9—20Ub 25
Purley Rd. Purl—83Qb 164
Purley Rd. S Croy—80Tb 147
Purley Vale. Purl—85Rb 165
Purley Way. Croy & Purl
—73Pb 146
Purlieu Way. Epp—7Uc 14
Purlings Rd. Bush, Wat—15Da 19
Purneys Rd. SE9—56Mc 107
Purrett Rd. SE18—50Vc 87
Purser's Cross Rd. SW6—53Bb 103
Pursewardens Clo. W13—46La 78
Pursley Gdns. Borwd—10Qa 7
Pursley Rd. NW7—24Xa 40
Purton La. Slou—8G 52
Purves Rd. NW10—40Xa 60
Putney Bri. SW15 & SW6
—55Ab 102
Putney Bri. App. SW6—55Ab 102
Putney Bri. Rd.—56Ab 102
SW18 1-73 & 2-114
SW15 remainder
Putney Comn. SW15—55Ya 102
Putney Heath. SW15—58Xa 102
Putney Heath La. SW15—58Za 102
Putney High St. SW15—56Ab 102
Putney Hill. SW15—58Za 102
Putney Pk. Av. SW15—56Wa 102
Putney Pk. La. SW15—56Xa 102
Putney Rd. Enf—8Zb 12
Puttenham Clo. Wat—20Y 19
Pyecombe Corner. N12—21Bb 41
Pyghtle Footpath. Uxb—32J 55
Pyghtle, The. Uxb—31J 55
Pylbrook Rd. Sutt—76Cb 145
Pyle Hill. Wok—96A 172
Pym Clo. Barn—15Fb 23
Pymers Mead. SE21—60Sb 105
Pym Ho. SW9—54Qb 104
Pymmes Clo. N13—22Pb 42
Pymmes Gdns. N. N9—20Vb 25
Pymmes Gdns. S. N9—20Vb 25
Pymmes Grn. Rd. N11—21Kb 42
Pymmes Rd. N13—23Nb 42
Pymms Brook Dri. Barn—14Gb 23
Pym Orchard. West—96Yc 185
Pym Pl. Grays—49Ce 91
Pynchester Clo. Uxb—33Q 56
Pyne Rd. Surb—74Qa 143
Pynest Grn. La. Wal A—10Jc 13
Pynham Clo. SE2—48Xc 87
Pynnacles Clo. Stan—22Ka 38
Pyrcroft La. Wey—78R 140
Pyrcroft Rd. Cher—73G 138
Pyrford Bottom Rd. Wok—88F 156
Pyrford Heath. Wok—88H 157
Pyrford Rd. Wey & Wok—85J 157
Pyrford Wood Est. Wok—88G 156
Pyrford Woods. Wok—87G 156
Pyrford Woods Clo. Wok—87H 157
Pyrland Rd. N5—36Tb 63
Pyrland Rd. Rich—58Pa 101
Pyrles Grn. Lou—11Rc 28
Pyrles La. Lou—12Rc 28
Pyrmont Gro. SE27—62Rb 127
Pyrmont Rd. W4—51Qa 101
Pytchley Cres. SE19—65Sb 127
Pytchley Rd. SE5—55Ub 105

Quadrant Arc. W1—(5C 198)
Quadrant Arc. Romf—29Gd 48
Quadrant Gro. NW5—36Hb 61
Quadrant Rd. Rich—56Ma 101
Quadrant Rd. T Hth—70Rb 127
Quadrant, The. NW4—28Ya 40
Quadrant, The. SW20—67Ab 124
Quadrant, The. Bexh—52Zc 109
Quadrant, The. Purf—49Sd 90
Quadrant, The. Rich—56Na 101
Quadrant, The. Sutt—79Eb 145
Quadrant, The. Wey—77Q 140
Quaggy Wlk. SE3—56Jc 107
Quail Gdns. S Croy—82Ac 166
Quainton St. NW10—34Ta 59
Quaker Clo. Long, Dart—69Ae 135
Quaker La. Iswth—52Ja 100
(in two parts)
Quaker La. S'hall—48Ca 77
Quaker La. Wal A—6Ec 12
Quakers Clo. Sev—95Md 187
Quakers Course. NW9—25Va 40
Quakers Hall La. Sev—94Ld 187
Quakers La. Pot B—2Db 9
Quaker St. E1—42Vb 83 (6K 195)
Quakers Wlk. N21—16Tb 25
Quality Ct. WC2—(2K 199)
Quality St. Red—100Kb 180
Quantock Clo. Hay—52T 98
Quantock Clo. Slou—50C 74
Quantock Gdns. NW2—33Za 60
Quantock Rd. Bexh—54Gd 110
Quarles Clo. Romf—24Cd 48
Quarley Way. SE15—52Vb 105
Quarrendon St. SW6—54Cb 103
Quarr Rd. Cars—72Gb 145
Quarry Cotts. Sev—95Jd 186
Quarry Hill. Grays—50Ce 91
Quarry Hill. Sev—95Md 187
★Quarry Hill Rd. Sev—94Ae
Quarry Pk. Rd. Sutt—79Bb 145
Quarry Rise. Sutt—79Bb 145
Quarry Rd. SW18—58Eb 103
Quartermaine Av. Wok—94B 172
Quarter Mile La. E10 & E15
—35Dc 64
Quaves Rd. Slou—8M 73
Quebec Av. West—98Tc 184
Quebec Cotts. West—99Tc 184
Quebec M. W1—44Hb 81 (3G 197)
Quebec Rd. Hay—45Y 77
Quebec Rd. Ilf—31Rc 66
Quebec Rd. Til—4C 114
Quebec Sq. West—98Tc 184
Quebec Way. SE16—47Ac 84
Queen Adelaide Ct. SE20
—65Yb 128
Queen Adelaide Rd. SE20
—66Yb 128
Queen Adelaide's Ride. Wind
—8B 94
Queen Anne Av. N15—29Vb 43
Queen Anne Av. Brom—69Hc 129
Queen Anne Dri. Esh—80Ga 142
Queen Anne M. W1
—43Kb 82 (1A 198)
Queen Anne Rd. E9—37Zb 64
Queen Anne's Clo. Twic—62Fa 122
Queen Anne's Gdns. W4—48Ua 80
Queen Anne's Gdns. W5—47Na 79
Queen Anne's Gdns. Enf—16Ub 25
Queen Anne's Gdns. Lea
—93Ka 176
Queen Anne's Gdns. Mitc
—69Hb 125
Queen Anne's Ga. SW1
—47Mb 82 (2D 204)
Queen Anne's Ga. Bexh—55Zc 109
Queen Anne's Gro. W4—48Ua 80
Queen Anne's Gro. W5—47Na 79
Queen Anne's Gro. Enf—17Tb 25
Queen Anne's Pl. Enf—16Vb 25
Queen Anne's Ride. Wind—4E 116
Queen Anne's Rd. Wind—6G 94
Queen Anne's Ter. Lea—93Ka 176
Queen Anne St. W1
—43Kb 82 (1K 197)
Queen Anne's Wlk. WC1—(6G 193)
Queenborough Gdns. Ilf—28Qc 46
Queen Caroline St. W6—50Ya 80
Queendale Ct. Wok—4C 188
Queen Elizabeth Av. Grays—9K 93
Queen Elizabeth Gdns. Mord
—70Cb 125
Queen Elizabeth Ho. SW12
—59Jb 104
Queen Elizabeth Pl. Til—6C 114
Queen Elizabeth Rd. E17—27Ac 44
Queen Elizabeth Rd. King
—68Pa 123
Queen Elizabeth's Clo. N16
—33Tb 63
Queen Elizabeth's Dri. N14
—18Nb 24
Queen Elizabeth's Dri. Croy
—81Fc 167
Queen Elizabeth's Gdns. Croy
—82Fc 167
Queen Elizabeth St. SE1
—47Vb 83 (1K 207)
Queen Elizabeth's Wlk. N16
—33Tb 63
Queen Elizabeth's Wlk. Wind
—4J 95
Queen Elizabeth Wlk. SW13
—53Xa 102
Queen Elizabeth Wlk. Wall
—77Mb 146
Queen Elizabeth Way. Wok
—91B 172
Queenhill Rd. S Croy—82Xb 165
Queenhithe. EC4—45Sb 83 (4E 200)
Queenhythe Rd. Guild—100A 172
Queen Margaret's Gro. N1
—36Ub 63
Queen Mary Av. Grays—9L 93
Queen Mary Av. Mord—71Za 144
Queen Mary Clo. Wok—88E 156
Queen Mary Rd. SE19—65Rb 127
Queen Mary Rd. Shep—68S 120
Queen Mary's Av. Cars—80Hb 145
Queen Mary's Av. Wat—14U 18
Queen Mary's Dri. Wey—82H 157
Queen Mothers Dri. Uxb—30H 35
Queens Acre. Sutt—80Ab 144
Queens Av. N3—24Eb 41
Queens Av. N10—27Jb 42
Queens Av. N20—19Fb 23
Queens Av. N21—18Rb 25
Queens Av. Felt—63Y 121
Queen's Av. Gnfd—44Da 77
Queens Av. Stan—27La 38
Queen's Av. Wat—14V 18
Queen's Av. Wey—84M 157
Queen's Av. Wfd G—22Kc 45
Queensberry M. W. SW7
—49Fb 81 (5B 202)
Queensberry Pl. SW7
—49Fb 81 (5B 202)
Queensberry Way. SW7
—49Fb 81 (5B 202)
Queensborough M. W2—45Eb 81
Queensborough Ter. W2—45Db 81
Queensbridge Pk. Iswth
—58Ga 100
Queensbridge Rd.—37Vb 63
E2 1-173 & 2-120
E8 remainder
Queensbury Ho. Rich—57Ma 101
Queensbury Rd. NW9—31Ta 59
Queensbury Rd. Wemb—40Pa 59
Queensbury Sta. Pde. Edgw
—27Pa 39
Queensbury St. N1—38Sb 63
Queen's Cir. SW8—52Kb 104
Queen's Clo. Edgw—22Qa 39
Queens Clo. Esh—77Da 141
Queens Clo. Tad—96Wa 178
Queens Clo. Wall—78Kb 146
Queen's Clo. Wind—7L 95
Queen's Club Gdns. W14
—51Ab 102
Queens Ct. SE23—61Yb 128
Queens Ct. Harr—26La 38
Queens Ct. Rich—58Pa 101
Queenscourt. Wemb—35Na 59
Queens Ct. Wey—79U 140
Queens Ct. Ride. Cob—85W 158
Queen's Cres. NW5—37Jb 62
Queen's Cres. Rich—57Pa 101
Queenscroft Rd. SE9—58Mc 107
Queensdale Cres. W11—46Za 80
Queensdale Pl. W11—46Ab 80
Queensdale Rd. W11—46Ab 80
Queensdale Wlk. W11—46Ab 80
Queensdown Rd. E5—35Xb 63
Queens Dri. E10—31Cc 64
Queen's Dri. N4—33Rb 63
Queens Dri. W3—44Pa 79
Queens Dri. Abb L, Wat—4V 4
Queen's Dri. Lea—83Ea 160
Queen's Dri. Sev—92Ld 187
Queen's Dri. Slou—39B 54
Queen's Dri. Surb—73Qa 143
Queen's Dri. Th Dit—72Ja 142
Queen's Dri. Wal X—6Cc 12
Queen's Dri., The. Rick—17H 17
Queen's Elm Sq. SW3
—50Fb 81 (7C 202)
Queen's Farm Rd. Grav—1N 137
Queensferry Wlk. N17—28Xb 43
Queen's Gdns. NW4—29Ya 40
Queen's Gdns. SW1
—47Lb 82 (1B 204)
Queen's Gdns. W2
—45Eb 81 (4A 196)
Queen's Gdns. W5—42La 78
Queens Gdns. Dart—60Rd 111
Queens Gdns. Houn—53Aa 99
Queen's Gdns. Rain—40Fd 68
Queens Gdns. Upm—30Vd 50
Queen's Ga. SW7
—48Eb 81 (2A 202)
Queen's Ga. Gdns. SW7
—48Eb 81 (4A 202)
Queens Ga. Gdns. SW15—56Xa 102
Queensgate Gdns. Chst—67Tc 130
Queen's Ga. M. SW7
—48Eb 81 (3A 202)
Queensgate Pl. NW6—38Cb 61
Queen's Ga. Pl. SW7
—48Eb 81 (4A 202)
Queen's Ga. Pl. M. SW7
—48Eb 81 (4A 202)
Queen's Ga. Ter. SW7
—48Eb 81 (3A 202)
Queen's Gro. NW8
—39Fb 61 (1B 190)
Queens Gro. Rd. E4—18Fc 27
Queen's Head St. N1—39Rb 63
Queens Head Yd. SE1—(7F 201)
Queens Hill Rise. Asc—9A 116
Queen's Ho. Tedd—65Ha 122
Queensland Av. N18—23Sb 43
Queensland Av. SW19—67Db 125
Queensland Pl. N7—35Qb 62
Queensland Rd. N7—35Qb 62
Queens La. N10—27Kb 42
Queens La. Ashf—63P 119
Queensmead. NW8—39Fb 61
Queensmead. Slou—3M 95
Queensmead Av. Eps—82Xa 162
Queens Mead Rd. Brom—68Hc 129

Queensmere—Rays Hill

Queensmere. Slou—7K 73
Queensmere Clo. SW19—61Za 124
Queensmere Rd. SW19—61Za 124
Queensmere Rd. Slou—7L 73
Queen's M. W2—45Db 81
Queensmill Rd. SW6—52Za 102
Queens Pde. N8—28Rb 43
Queen's Pde. N11—22Hb 41
Queens Pde. W5—44Pa 79
Queens Pk. Gdns. Felt—62V 120
Queen's Pk. Rd. Cat—95Ub 181
Queen's Pk. Rd. Romf—25Qd 49
Queens Pl. Mord—70Cb 125
Queen's Pl. Wat—13Y 19
Queen's Promenade. King
—70Ma 123
Queen Sq. WC1—42Nb 82 (6G 193)
Queen Sq. Pl. WC1—(6G 193)
Queens Ride. SW13 & SW15
—55Wa 102
Queens Rise. Rich—58Pa 101
Queens Rd. E11—31Gc 65
Queens Rd. E13—39Kc 65
Queen's Rd. E17—30Bc 44
Queens Rd. N3—25Eb 41
Queens Rd. N9—19Xb 25
Queen's Rd. N11—24Nb 42
Queens Rd. NW4—29Ya 40
Queen's Rd.—53Xb 105
SE15 1-289 & 2-222
SE14 remainder
Queen's Rd. SW14—55Ta 101
Queens Rd. SW19—65Cb 125
Queen's Rd. W5—44Na 79
Queen's Rd. Asc—10B 116
Queens Rd. Bark—38Sc 66
Queens Rd. Barn—13Za 22
Queens Rd. Beck—68Ac 128
Queens Rd. Brtwd—20Yd 32
Queens Rd. Brom—68Jc 129
Queen's Rd. Buck H—19Kc 27
Queens Rd. Chst—65Rc 130
Queens Rd. Croy—72Rb 147
Queen's Rd. Egh—65B 118
Queen's Rd. Enf—14Ub 25
Queen's Rd. Eri—51Gd 110
Queen's Rd. Felt—60X 99
Queens Rd. Grav—2E 136
Queen's Rd. Hmptn—63Da 121
Queen's Rd. Hay—44U 76
Queen's Rd. Houn—55Da 99
Queen's Rd. King—66Qa 123
Queens Rd. Lou—13Nc 28
Queen's Rd. Mitc—69Fb 125
Queens Rd. Mord—70Cb 125
Queens Rd. N Mald—70Va 124
Queen's Rd. Rich—59Pa 101
Queen's Rd. Slou—5K 73
Queen's Rd. Slou—2M 95
(Datchet)
Queens Rd. S'hall—47Z 77
Queens Rd. Sutt—83Cb 163
Queen's Rd. Tedd—65Ha 122
Queen's Rd. Th Dit—71Ha 142
Queens Rd. Twic—60Ja 100
Queen's Rd. Uxb—41L 75
Queens Rd. Wall—78Kb 146
Queen's Rd. Wal X—5Ac 12
Queen's Rd. W on T—78X 141
Queen's Rd. Wat—13Y 19
(in two parts)
Queen's Rd. Well—54Xc 109
Queens Rd. W Dray—47P 75
Queens Rd. Wey & W on T
—78S 140
Queen's Rd. Wind—4G 94
Queen's Rd. Wind—10D 72
(Eton Wick)
Queen's Rd. Wok—6A 188
Queens Rd. W. E13—40Jc 65
Queen's Row. SE17—51Tb 105
Queen's St. Eri—51Gd 110
Queen's Ter. E13—39Kc 65
Queen's Ter. NW8
—40Fb 61 (1B 190)
Queens Ter. Iswth—56Ja 100
Queen's Ter. Cotts. W7—47Ga 78
Queensthorpe Rd. SE26—63Zb 128
Queenstown Gdns. Rain—41Hd 88
Queenstown Rd. SW8—55Kb 104
Queen St. EC4—45Sb 83 (4E 200)
Queen St. N17—23Ub 43
Queen St. Bexh—55Bd 109
Queen St. Brtwd—22Yd 50
Queen St. Cher—74J 139
Queen St. Croy—77Sb 147
Queen St. Grav—8D 114
Queen St. K Lan—4J 3
Queen St. Romf—30Fd 48
Queen St. Mayfair. W1
—46Kb 82 (6K 197)
Queen St. Pl. EC4
—45Sb 83 (5E 200)
Queensville Rd. SW12—59Mb 104
Queens Wlk. E4—18Fc 27
Queens Wlk. NW9—33Sa 59
Queen's Wlk. SW1
—46Lb 82 (7B 198)
Queen's Wlk. W5—42La 78
Queen's Wlk. Ashf—63M 119
Queens Wlk. Harr—28Ga 38
Queens Wlk. Ruis—33Y 57
Queen's Way. NW4—29Ya 40
Queensway. W2—44Db 81
Queensway. Croy—78Pb 146
Queensway. Enf—14Xb 25
Queens Way. Felt—63Y 121
Queensway. Orp—71Sc 150
Queens Way. Shen, Rad—4Na 7
Queensway. Sun—68W 120
Queensway. Wal X—6Bc 12
Queensway. W Wick—77Hc 149
Queensway N. W on T—77Y 141
Queensway S. W on T—78Y 141
(in two parts)
Queensway, The. Ger X—28A 34
Queenswell Av. N20—21Gb 41
Queenswood Av. E17—25Ec 44
Queenswood Av. Brtwd—15Fe 33
Queenswood Av. Hmptn
—65Da 121
Queenswood Av. Houn—54Ba 99
Queenswood Av. T Hth—71Qb 146
Queenswood Av. Wall—77Mb 146
Queenswood Ct. SE27—63Tb 127
Queenswood Cres. Wat—5W 4
Queenswood Gdns. E11—32Kc 65
Queens Wood Pk. N3—26Ab 40
Queens Wood Rd. N10—30Kb 42
Queenswood Rd. SE23—62Zb 128
Queenswood Rd. Sidc—58Vc 109
Queenswood Rd. Wok—7A 188
Queen Victoria Av. Wemb
—38Ma 59
Queen Victoria St. EC4
—45Rb 83 (4B 200)
Queen Victoria Wlk. Wind—3J 95
Quelmans Head Ride. Wind
—1B 116
Quemerford Rd. N7—36Pb 62
Quendon Dri. Wal A—5Fc 13
Quennell Clo. Asht—91Pa 177
Quennell Way. Brtwd—17Fe 33
Quentin Pl. SE13—55Gc 107
Quentin Rd. SE13—55Gc 107
Quentin Way. Vir W—10M 117
Quernmore Clo. Brom—65Jc 129
Quernmore Rd. N4—30Qb 42
Quernmore Rd. Brom—65Jc 129
Querrin St. SW6—54Eb 103
Quex M. NW6—39Cb 61
Quex Rd. NW6—39Cb 61
Quickley La. Rick—16E 16
(in two parts)
Quickley Rise. Rick—16E 16
Quickmoor La. K Lan—5K 3
Quick Pl. N1—39Rb 63
Quick Rd. W4—50Ua 80
Quicksilver Pl. N22—26Pb 42
Quicks Rd. SW19—66Db 125
Quick St. N1—40Rb 63 (2C 194)
Quickswood. NW3—38Gb 61
Quickwood Clo. Rick—16J 17
Quiet Clo. Wey—77J 139
Quiet Nook. Kes—76Mc 149
Quill La. SW15—56Za 102
Quillot, The. W on T—78V 140
Quilp St. SE1—47Sb 83 (1D 206)
Quilter Gdns. Orp—74Yc 151
Quilter Rd. Orp—74Yc 151
Quilter St. E2—41Wb 83
Quinbrookes. Slou—4N 73
Quince Tree Clo. S Ock—41Yd 90
Quinta Dri. Barn—15Xa 22
Quintin Av. SW20—67Bb 125
Quinton Clo. Beck—69Ec 128
Quinton Clo. Wall—77Kb 146
Quinton Rd. Th Dit—74Ja 142
Quinton St. SW18—61Eb 125
Quinton Way. Wal A—7Ec 12
Quintrell Clo. Wok—5E 188
Quixley St. E14—45Fc 85
Quorn Rd. SE22—56Ub 105

Rabbit La. W on T—80W 140
Rabbit Row. W8—46Cb 81
Rabbits Rd. E12—35Nc 66
Rabbits Rd. S Dar, Dart—68Ud 134
Rabbs Mill Ho. Uxb—40L 55
Raby Rd. N Mald—70Ta 123
Raby St. E14—44Ac 84
Raccoon Way. Houn—54Y 99
Racefield Clo. Grav—6N 137
Racton Rd. SW6—51Cb 103
Radbourne Av. W5—49La 78
Radbourne Clo. E5—35Zb 64
Radbourne Cres. E17—27Fc 45
Radbourne Rd. SW12—59Lb 104
Radbroke. Lea—94La 176
Radcliffe Av. NW10—40Wa 60
Radcliffe Av. Enf—11Sb 25
Radcliffe Gdns. Cars—80Gb 145
Radcliffe Rd. N21—18Rb 25
Radcliffe Rd. Croy—75Vb 147
Radcliffe Rd. Stan—26Ja 38
Radcliffe Sq. SW15—58Za 102
Radcliffe Way. N'holt—41Z 77
Radcot Av. Slou—48D 74
Radcot St. SE11—50Qb 82 (7A 206)
Raddington Rd. W10—43Ab 80
Radfield Way. Sidc—59Tc 108
Radford Rd. SE13—58Ec 106
Radford Way. Bark—41Vc 87
Radipole Rd. SW6—53Bb 103
Radland Rd. E16—44Hc 85
Radlett Av. SE26—61Xb 127
Radlett Clo. E7—37Hc 65
Radlett La. Shen, Rad—6Ma 7
Radlett Pk. Rd. Rad—6Ja 6
Radlett Pl. NW8—39Gb 61
Radlett Rd. St Alb—1Ga 6
Radlett Rd. Wat—13Y 19
Radlett Rd. Wat—10Da 5
(Aldenham)
Radley Av. Ilf—35Wc 67
Radley Gdns. Harr—28Na 39
Radley M. W8—48Db 81
Radley Rd. N17—26Ub 43
Radley's La. E18—26Jc 45
Radleys Mead. Dag—37Dd 68
Radley Sq. E5—33Xb 64
Radlix Rd. E10—32Cc 64
Radnor Av. Harr—29Ga 38
Radnor Av. Well—57Xc 109
Radnor Clo. Chst—65Uc 130
Radnor Clo. Mitc—70Nb 126
Radnor Cres. Ilf—29Pc 46
Radnor Gdns. Enf—11Ub 25
Radnor Gdns. Twic—61Ha 122
Radnor Gro. Uxb—40Q 56
Radnor M. W2—44Fb 81 (3C 196)
Radnor Pl. W2—44Gb 81 (3D 196)
Radnor Rd. NW6—39Ab 60
Radnor Rd. SE15—52Wb 105
Radnor Rd. Harr—29Fa 38
Radnor Rd. Twic—61Ha 122
(in two parts)
Radnor Rd. Wey—76Q 140
Radnor St. EC1—41Sb 83 (4E 194)
Radnor Ter. W14—49Bb 81
Radnor Wlk. SW3
—50Gb 81 (7E 202)
Radnor Wlk. Croy—72Bc 148
Radnor Way. NW10—42Ra 79
Radnor Way. Slou—49A 74
Radstock Av. Harr—27Ja 38
Radstock St. SW11—52Gb 103
Radstock Way. Red—100Mb 180
Radstone Ct. Wok—90B 156
Radwell Path. Borwd—11Na 21
Raebarn Gdns. Barn—15Xa 22
Raeburn Av. Dart—57Kd 111
Raeburn Av. Surb—74Ra 143
Raeburn Clo. NW11—30Eb 41
Raeburn Clo. King—66Ma 123
Raeburn Ct. Wok—7D 188
Raeburn Rd. Edgw—25Qa 39
Raeburn Rd. Hay—40T 56
Raeburn Rd. Sidc—58Uc 108
Raeburn St. SW2—56Nb 104
Rafford Way. Brom—68Kc 129
Ragge Way. Sev—92Pd 187
Raggleswood. Chst—67Qc 130
Rag Hill Clo. West—93Nc 184
Rag Hill Rd. West—93Mc 183
Raglan Av. Wal X—6Zb 12
Raglan Ct. SE12—57Jc 107
Raglan Ct. S Croy—78Rb 147
Raglan Gdns. Wat—18X 19
Raglan Precinct. Cat—94Ub 181
Raglan Rd. E17—29Ec 44
Raglan Rd. SE18—50Sc 86
Raglan Rd. Belv—49Bd 87
Raglan Rd. Brom—70Lc 129
Raglan Rd. Enf—17Vb 25
Raglan Rd. Wok—6B 188
Raglan St. NW5—37Kb 62
Raglan Ter. Harr—35Da 57
Raglan Way. N'holt—37Ea 58
Ragley Clo. W3—47Sa 79
Ragstone Rd. Slou—8J 73
Rahn Rd. Epp—3Wc 15
Raider Clo. Romf—25Dd 48
Railey M. NW5—36Lb 62
Railpit La. Warl—87Gc 167
Railshead Rd. Twic—56Ka 100
Railton Rd. SE24—56Qb 104
Railway App. SE1
—46Tb 83 (7G 201)
Railway App. Cher—74H 139
Railway App. Harr—28Ha 38
Railway App. Twic—59Ja 100
Railway App. Wall—78Kb 146
Railway Av. SE16—47Yb 84
Railway Cotts. Houn—58Ca 99
Railway Cotts. Rad—7Ja 6
Railway Cotts. Wat—11X 19
Railway M. W10—44Ab 80
Railway Pde. Brtwd—17Ce 33
Railway Pas. Tedd—65Ja 122
Railway Pl. EC3—45Ub 83 (4J 201)
Railway Pl. SW19—65Bb 125
Railway Pl. Belv—48Cd 88
Railway Pl. Grav—8D 114
Railway Rise. SE22—56Ub 105
Railway Rd. Tedd—63Ha 122
Railway Rd. Wal X—5Ac 12
Railway Side. SW13—55Va 102
Railway Sq. Brtwd—20Yd 32
Railway St. N1—40Nb 62 (2G 193)
Railway St. Grav—57Ce 113
Railway St. Romf—31Yc 67
Railway Ter. E17—25Ec 44
Railway Ter. SE13—57Dc 106
Railway Ter. Felt—60W 98
Railway Ter. Slou—6K 73
Railway Ter. Stai—64F 118
Railway Ter. West—97Tc 184
Rainborough Clo. NW10—37Sa 59
Rainbow Ct. Wat—16Y 19
Rainbow Ct. Wok—4B 188
Rainbow La. Stanf—1P 93
Rainbow St. SE5—52Ub 105
Rainer Clo. Wal X—1Zb 12
Raine St. E1—46Xb 83
Rainham Clo. SE9—58Uc 108
Rainham Clo. SW11—58Gb 103
Rainham Rd. NW10—41Ya 80
Rainham Rd. Rain & Horn
—41Jd 88
Rainham Rd. N. Dag—33Dd 68
Rainham Rd. S. Dag—35Dd 68
Rainhill Way. E3—41Dc 84
Rainsborough Av. SE8—49Ac 84
Rainsford Clo. Stan—21La 38
Rainsford Rd. NW10—40Ra 59
Rainsford Way. Horn—32Jd 68
Rainton Rd. SE7—50Jc 85
Rainville Rd. W6—51Ya 102
Raisins Hill. Pinn—27Y 37
Raith Av. N14—20Mb 24
Raleana Rd. E14—46Ec 84
Raleigh Av. Hay—43X 77
Raleigh Av. Wall—77Mb 146
Raleigh Clo. NW4—29Ya 40
Raleigh Clo. Pinn—31Z 57
Raleigh Clo. Ruis—33V 56
Raleigh Ct. Stai—63J 119
Raleigh Ct. Wall—79Kb 146
Raleigh Dri. N20—20Gb 23
Raleigh Dri. Esh—78Fa 142
Raleigh Dri. Surb—74Sa 143
Raleigh Gdns. Mitc—69Hb 125
Raleigh Rd. N8—28Qb 42
Raleigh Rd. SE20—66Zb 128
Raleigh Rd. Enf—14Tb 25
Raleigh Rd. Felt—62V 120
Raleigh Rd. Rich—55Pa 101
Raleigh Rd. S'hall—50Aa 77
Raleigh St. N1—39Rb 63 (1C 194)
Raleigh Way. N14—18Mb 24
Raleigh Way. Felt—64Y 121
Ralliwood Rd. Asht—91Qa 177
Ralph St. SE1—48Sb 83 (3E 206)
Ralston St. SW3—50Hb 81
Ralston Way. Wat—19Z 19
Rama Ct. Harr—33Ga 58
Rambler Clo. SW16—63Lb 126
Rambler Clo. M'head—4A 72
Rambler La. Slou—8N 73
Ramilles Clo. SW2—58Nb 104
Ramillies Pl. W1—44Lb 82 (3B 198)
Ramillies Rd. NW7—19Ua 22
Ramillies Rd. W4—49Ta 79
Ramillies Rd. Sidc—58Xc 109
Ramillies St. W1—44Lb 82 (3B 198)
Ramney Dri. Enf—8Ac 12
Ramornie Clo. W on T—77Ba 141
Rampart St. E1—44Xb 83
Ram Pas. King—68Ma 123
Rampayne St. SW1
—50Mb 82 (7D 204)
Ram Pl. E9—37Yb 64
Rampton Clo. E4—20Cc 26
Ramsay Gdns. Romf—25Ld 49
Ramsay Rd. E7—35Gc 65
Ramscroft Clo. N9—17Ub 25
Ramsdale Rd. SW17—64Jb 126
Ramsden Clo. Orp—74Yc 151
Ramsden Dri. Romf—24Cd 48
Ramsden Rd. N11—22Hb 41
Ramsden Rd. SW12—58Jb 104
Ramsden Rd. Eri—52Fd 110
Ramsden Rd. Orp—74Xc 151
Ramsey Clo. Gnfd—36Fa 58
Ramsey Rd. W3—48Sa 79
Ramsey Rd. T Hth—72Pb 146
Ramsey St. E2—42Wb 83
Ramsey Wlk. N1—37Tb 63
Ramsey Way. N14—17Lb 24
Ramsgate St. E8—37Vb 63
Ramsgill App. Ilf—28Vc 47
Ramsgill Dri. Ilf—29Vc 47
Rams Gro. Romf—28Ad 47
Ramulis Dri. Hay—42Aa 77
Ramus Wood Av. Orp—78Uc 150
Rancliffe Gdns. SE9—56Nc 108
Rancliffe Rd. E6—40Nc 66
Randall Av. NW2—33Ua 60
Randall Clo. SW11—53Gb 103
Randall Clo. Eri—51Ed 110
Randall Clo. Slou—50B 74
Randall Ct. NW7—24Wa 40
Randall Dri. Horn—35Ld 69
Randall Farm La. Lea—91Ja 176
Randall Pl. SE10—52Ec 106
Randall Rd. SE11
—49Pb 82 (6H 205)
Randall Rd. Romf—30Hd 48
Randall Row. SE11
—49Pb 82 (6H 205)
Randalls Cres. Lea—92Ja 176
Randalls Dri. Brtwd—16Fe 33
Randalls Pk. Av. Lea—92Ja 176
Randalls Pk. Dri. Lea—93Ja 176
Randalls Rd. Lea—91Ga 176
Randalls Way. Lea—93Ja 176
★Randell Hill Rd. Sev—88Be
Randell's Rd. N1—39Nb 62
Randle Rd. Rich—63La 122
Randlesdown Rd. SE6—63Cc 128
Randles La. Sev—86Zc 169
Randolph App. E16—44Lc 85
Randolph Av. W9
—41Db 81 (5A 190)
Randolph Clo. Bexh—55Ed 110
Randolph Clo. Cob—87Ca 159
Randolph Clo. King—64Sa 123
Randolph Clo. Wok—5B 188
Randolph Cres. W9
—42Eb 81 (6A 190)
Randolph Gdns. NW6—40Db 61
Randolph M. W9—42Eb 81 (6A 190)
Randolph Rd. E17—29Dc 44
Randolph Rd. W9
—42Eb 81 (6A 190)
Randolph Rd. Eps—86Va 162
Randolph Rd. Slou—48A 74
Randolph Rd. S'hall—47Ba 77
Randolph's La. West—98Rc 184
Randolph St. NW1—38Lb 62
Randon Clo. Harr—26Da 37
Ranelagh Av. SW6—55Bb 103
Ranelagh Av. SW13—54Wa 102
Ranelagh Bri. W2—43Db 81
Ranelagh Clo. Edgw—21Qa 39
Ranelagh Dri. Edgw—21Qa 39
Ranelagh Dri. Iswth—57Ka 100
Ranelagh Gdns. E11—29Lc 45
Ranelagh Gdns. SW6—55Ab 102
Ranelagh Gdns. W4—52Sa 101
Ranelagh Gdns. Grav—9B 114
Ranelagh Gdns. Ilf—32Pc 66
Ranelagh Gro. SW1
—50Jb 82 (7J 203)
Ranelagh M. W5—47Ma 79
Ranelagh Pl. N Mald—71Ua 144
Ranelagh Rd. E6—39Qc 66
Ranelagh Rd. E11—35Gc 65
Ranelagh Rd. E15—40Gc 65
Ranelagh Rd. N17—27Ub 43
Ranelagh Rd. N22—25Pb 42
Ranelagh Rd. NW10—40Va 60
Ranelagh Rd. SW1
—50Lb 82 (7C 204)
Ranelagh Rd. W5—47Ma 79
Ranelagh Rd. S'hall—46Z 77
Ranelagh Rd. Wemb—37Ma 59
Ranfurly Rd. Sutt—75Cb 145
Rangefield Rd. Brom—64Gc 129
Rangemoor Rd. N15—29Vb 43
Range Rd. Grav—9G 114
Rangers Rd. E4 & Lou—17Hc 27
Rangers Sq. SE10—53Fc 107
Range Way. Shep—73Q 140
Rangoon St. EC3
—44Vb 83 (3K 201)
Rankin Clo. NW9—27Ua 40
Ranleigh Gdns. Bexh—52Bd 109
Ranmere St. SW12—60Kb 104
Ranmoor Clo. Harr—28Fa 38
Ranmoor Gdns. Harr—28Fa 38
Ranmore Av. Croy—76Vb 147
Ranmore Path. Orp—70Wc 131
Ranmore Rd. Sutt—81Za 162
Rannoch Rd. W6—51Ya 102
Rannock Av. NW9—31Ta 59
Ranskill Rd. Borwd—11Qa 21
Ransom Rd. SE7—50Lc 85
Ransom Wlk. SE7—49Lc 85
Ranston St. NW1
—43Gb 81 (7D 190)
Ranulf Rd. NW2—35Bb 61
Ranwell Clo. E3—39Bc 64
Ranworth Clo. Eri—54Gd 110
Ranworth Rd. N9—19Yb 26
Raphael Av. Romf—27Hd 48
Raphael Av. Til—2C 114
Raphael Dri. Wat—12Z 19
Raphael Rd. Grav—9F 114
Raphael St. SW7
—47Hb 81 (2F 203)
Rapier Clo. Purf—49Qd 89
Raquet Ct. EC4—(3B 200)
Rasehill Clo. Rick—15L 17
Rashleigh Way. S Dar, Dart
—70Sd 134
Rasper Rd. N20—19Eb 23
Rastell Av. SW2—60Mb 104
Ratcliffe Clo. Uxb—41M 75
Ratcliffe Cross St. E1—44Zb 84
Ratcliffe La. E14—44Ac 84
Ratcliffe Orchard. E1—45Zb 84
Ratcliff Gro. EC1—41Sb 83 (4E 194)
Ratcliff Rd. E7—36Lc 65
Rathbone Pl. W1
—44Mb 82 (1D 198)
Rathbone St. E16—44Hc 85
Rathbone St. W1
—43Lb 82 (1C 198)
Rathcoole Av. N8—29Pb 42
Rathcoole Gdns. N8—29Pb 42
Rathfern Rd. SE6—60Bc 106
Rathgar Av. W13—46Ka 78
Rathgar Clo. N3—26Bb 41
Rathgar Rd. SW9—55Rb 105
Rathmell Dri. SW4—58Mb 104
Rathmore Rd. SE7—50Kc 85
Rathmore Rd. Grav—9D 114
Rats La. Lou—10Kc 13
Rattray Rd. SW2—56Qb 104
Raul Rd. SE15—54Wb 105
Raveley St. NW5—35Lb 62
Ravel Gdns. S Ock—43Sd 90
Ravel Rd. S Ock—44Sd 90
Raven Clo. Rick—17M 17
Ravendale Rd. Sun—68W 120
Ravenet St. SW11—53Kb 104
Ravenfield. Egh—5N 117
Ravenfield Rd. SW17—62Hb 125
Ravenhill Rd. E13—40Lc 65
Ravenna Rd. SW15—57Za 102
Ravenor Pk. Rd. Gnfd—41Da 77
Raven Rd. E18—26Lc 45
Raven Row. E1—43Xb 83
Ravensbourne Av. Brom
—66Fc 129
Ravensbourne Av. Stai—60P 97
Ravensbourne Cres. Romf
—27Pd 49
Ravensbourne Gdns. W13
—43Ka 78
Ravensbourne Gdns. Ilf—25Qc 46
Ravensbourne Pk. SE6—59Cc 106
Ravensbourne Pk. Cres. SE6
—59Bc 106
Ravensbourne Pl. SE13—54Dc 106
Ravensbourne Rd. SE6—59Bc 106
Ravensbourne Rd. Brom
—69Jc 129
Ravensbourne Rd. Dart—55Jd 110
Ravensbourne Rd. Twic—58La 100
Ravensbury Av. Mord—71Eb 145
Ravensbury Clo. Mitc—68Hb 125
Ravensbury Gro. Mitc—70Fb 125
Ravensbury La. Mitc—70Fb 125
Ravensbury Path. Mitc—70Fb 125
Ravensbury Rd. SW18—61Db 125
Ravensbury Rd. Orp—70Wc 131
Ravensbury Ter. SW18—60Db 103
Ravenscar Rd. Brom—63Gc 129
Ravenscar Rd. Surb—75Pa 143
Ravens Clo. Brom—68Hc 129
Ravens Clo. Enf—12Ub 25
Ravens Clo. Wok—4A 188
Ravenscourt. Sun—67V 120
Ravenscourt Av. W6—49Wa 80
Ravenscourt Clo. Horn—34Nd 69
Ravens Ct. Clo. Ruis—31S 56
Ravenscourt Dri. Horn—34Nd 69
Ravenscourt Gdns. W6—49Wa 80
Ravenscourt Gro. Horn—33Nd 69
Ravenscourt Pk. W6—49Wa 80
Ravenscourt Pl. W6—49Xa 80
Ravenscourt Rd. W6—49Xa 80
Ravenscourt Rd. Orp—69Wc 131
Ravenscourt Sq. W6—48Wa 80
Ravenscraig Rd. N11—21Lb 42
Ravenscroft Av. NW11—31Bb 61
Ravenscroft Av. Wemb—32Na 59
Ravenscroft Clo. E16—43Jc 85
Ravenscroft Pk. Barn—13Za 22
Ravenscroft Rd. E16—43Jc 85
Ravenscroft Rd. W4—49Sa 79
Ravenscroft Rd. Beck—68Yb 128
Ravenscroft Rd. Wey—83S 158
Ravenscroft St. E2
—40Vb 63 (2K 195)
Ravensdale Av. N12—21Eb 41
Ravensdale Clo. SE19—66Tb 127
Ravensdale Rd. N16—31Vb 63
Ravensdale Rd. Houn—55Aa 99
Ravensdon St. SE11
—50Qb 82 (7A 206)
Ravensfield. Slou—7P 73
Ravensfield Clo. Dag—35Zc 67
Ravensfield Gdns. Eps—78Ua 144
Ravenshaw St. NW6—36Bb 61
Ravenshead Clo. S Croy
—83Yb 166
Ravenshill. Chst—67Rc 130
Ravenshurst Av. NW4—28Ya 40
Ravenslea Rd. SW12—59Hb 103
Ravensmead. Ger X—22B 34
Ravensmead Rd. Brom—66Fc 129
Ravensmede Way. W4—49Va 80
Ravensmere. Epp—3Wc 15
Ravenstone. SE17—(7J 207)
Ravenstone Rd. N8—27Qb 42
Ravenstone Rd. NW9—30Va 40
Ravenstone St. SW12—60Jb 104
Ravens Way. SE12—57Jc 107
Ravens Wold. Kenl—87Sb 165
Ravenswood. Bex—60Ad 109
Ravenswood Av. Surb—75Pa 143
Ravenswood Av. W Wick
—74Ec 148
Ravenswood Clo. Romf—22Dd 48
Ravenswood Ct. King—65Ra 123
Ravenswood Ct. Wok—90B 156
Ravenswood Cres. Harr—33Ba 57
Ravenswood Cres. W Wick
—74Ec 148
Ravenswood Gdns. Iswth
—53Ga 100
Ravenswood Pk. N'wd—23W 36
Ravenswood Rd. E17—28Ec 44
Ravenswood Rd. SW12—59Kb 104
Ravenswood Rd. Croy—76Rb 147
Ravensworth Rd. NW10—41Xa 80
Ravensworth Rd. SE9—63Pc 130
Ravensworth Rd. Slou—1E 72
Ravent Rd. SE11—49Pb 82 (6H 205)
Ravey St. EC2—42Ub 83 (5H 195)
Ravine Gro. SE18—51Uc 108
Rawchester Clo. SW18—60Bb 103
Rawlings Clo. Orp—78Vc 151
Rawlings St. SW3
—49Hb 81 (5F 203)
Rawlins Clo. N3—27Ab 40
Rawlins Clo. S Croy—80Bc 148
Rawnsley Av. Mitc—71Fb 145
Rawson St. SW11—53Jb 104
Rawstone Wlk. E13—40Jc 65
Rawstorne Pl. EC1
—41Rb 83 (3B 194)
Rawstorne St. EC1
—41Rb 83 (3B 194)
Raybell Ct. Iswth—54Ha 100
Rayburn Rd. Horn—31Qd 69
Raydean Rd. Barn—15Db 23
Raydene Rd. SE18—51Uc 108
Raydon Rd. Wal X—4Zb 12
Raydons Gdns. Dag—36Ad 67
Raydons Rd. Dag—36Ad 67
Raydon St. N19—33Kb 62
Ray Field. Epp—2Vc 15
Rayfield Clo. Brom—72Nc 150
Rayford Av. SE12—59Hc 107
Rayford Clo. Dart—57Ld 111
Ray Gdns. Bark—40Wc 67
Ray Gdns. Stan—22Ka 38
Rayleas Clo. SE18—53Rc 108
Rayleigh Av. Tedd—65Ga 122
Rayleigh Clo. N13—20Tb 25
Rayleigh Clo. Brtwd—16Ee 33
Rayleigh Ct. King—68Qa 123
Rayleigh Rise. S Croy—79Ub 147
Rayleigh Rd. N13—20Sb 25
Rayleigh Rd. SW19—67Bb 125
Rayleigh Rd. Brtwd—16De 33
Rayleigh Rd. Stanf—2K 93
Rayleigh Rd. Wfd G—23Lc 45
Ray Lodge Rd. Wfd G—23Lc 45
Raymead. NW4—28Ya 40
Raymead Av. T Hth—71Qb 146
Raymead Clo. Lea—94Ga 176
Raymead Way. Lea—94Ga 176
Raymere Gdns. SE18—52Tc 108
Raymond Av. E18—27Hc 45
Raymond Av. W13—48Ja 78
Raymond Bldgs. WC1
—43Pb 82 (7J 193)
Raymond Clo. SE26—64Yb 128
Raymond Clo. Abb L, Wat—4T 4
Raymond Clo. Slou—53G 96
Raymond Gdns. Chig—20Xc 29
Raymond Postgate Ct. SE28
—45Xc 87
Raymond Rd. E13—39Lc 65
Raymond Rd. SW19—65Ab 124
Raymond Rd. Beck—70Ac 128
Raymond Rd. Ilf—31Tc 66
Raymond Rd. Slou—48C 74
Raymond Way. Esh—79Ja 142
Raymouth Rd. SE16—49Xb 83
Rayne Ct. E18—28Hc 45
Rayners Clo. Slou—52E 96
Rayners Clo. Wemb—36Ma 59
Rayner's Ct. Grav—58De 113
Rayners Cres. N'holt—41X 77
Rayners Gdns. N'holt—41X 77
Rayners La. Pinn & Harr—29Ba 37
to 34Da 57
Rayners Rd. SW15—57Ab 102
Raynes Av. E11—31Lc 65
Raynham Av. N18—23Wb 43
Raynham Rd. N18—22Wb 43
Raynham Rd. W6—49Xa 80
Raynham Ter. N18—22Wb 43
Raynor Clo. S'hall—46Ba 77
Raynor Pl. N1—38Sb 63
Raynton Clo. Harr—32Aa 57
Raynton Clo. Hay—42V 76
Raynton Dri. Hay—42V 76
Raynton Rd. Enf—9Zb 12
Ray Rd. E Mol—71Da 141
Ray Rd. Romf—22Dd 48
Rays Av. N18—21Yb 44
Ray's Av. Wind—2D 94
Rays Hill. S Dar, Dart—70Sd 134

Rays Rd.—Ridgeway, The

Rays Rd. N18—21Yb 44
Ray St. EC1—42Qb 82 (6A 194)
Ray St. Bri. EC1—(6A 194)
Ray Wlk. N7—33Pb 62
Read Ct. Wal A—5Jc 13
Readens, The. Bans—88Gb 163
Reade Wlk. NW10—38Ua 60
Reading La. E8—37Xb 63
Reading Rd. N'holt—36Da 57
Reading Rd. Sutt—78Eb 145
Readings, The. Rick—13H 17
Reading Way. NW7—22Za 40
Read Rd. Asht—89Ma 161
Reads Rest La. Tad—92Cb 179
Reads Way. Ilf—34Qc 66
Read Way. Grav—4G 136
Reapers Clo. NW1—39Mb 62
Reapers Way. Iswth—57Fa 100
Reardon Path. E1—46Xb 83
Reardon St. E1—46Xb 83
Reaston St. SE14—52Zb 106
Rebecca Ter. SE16—48Yb 84
Reckitt Rd. W4—50Ua 80
Record St. SE15—51Yb 106
Recovery St. SW17—64Gb 125
Recreation Av. Romf—29Ed 48
Recreation Av. Romf—26Pd 49
(Harold Wood)
Recreation Rd. SE26—63Zb 128
Recreation Rd. Brom—68Hc 129
Recreation Rd. S'hall—49Aa 77
Recreation Way. Mitc—69Nb 126
Rector St. N1—39Sb 63
★Rectory Chase. Brtwd—9Yd
(Doddinghurst)
Rectory Chase. Brtwd—28Zd 51
(Little Warley)
Rectory Clo. E4—20Cc 26
Rectory Clo. N3—25Bb 41
Rectory Clo. SW20—69Ya 124
Rectory Clo. Asht—91Pa 177
Rectory Clo. Dart—56Gd 110
Rectory Clo. Shep—69Q 120
Rectory Clo. Sidc—63Xc 131
Rectory Clo. Slou—1G 72
Rectory Clo. Stan—22Ka 38
Rectory Clo. Surb—74La 142
Rectory Clo. Wey—85N 157
Rectory Clo. Wind—3E 94
Rectory Cres. E11—30Lc 45
Rectory Farm Rd. Enf—10Pb 10
Rectory Field Cres. SE7—52Lc 107
Rectory Gdns. N8—28Nb 42
Rectory Gdns. SW4—55Lb 104
Rectory Gdns. N'holt—39Ba 57
Rectory Gdns. Upm—33Td 70
Rectory Grn. Beck—67Bc 128
Rectory Gro. SW4—55Lb 104
Rectory Gro. Croy—76Rb 147
Rectory Gro. Hmptn—63Ba 121
Rectory La. SW17—64Jb 126
Rectory La. Asht—91Pa 177
Rectory La. Bans—87Hb 163
Rectory La. Brtwd—24Fe 51
Rectory La. Edgw—23Qa 39
Rectory La. K Lan—1Q 4
Rectory La. Lea—98Ba 175
Rectory La. Lou—12Qc 28
Rectory La. Rick—18M 17
Rectory La. Sev—98Ld 187
★Rectory La. Sev—94Yd
(Ightham)
Rectory La. Shen, Rad—5Pa 7
Rectory La. Sidc—63Xc 131
Rectory La. Stan—22Ka 38
Rectory La. Surb—74La 142
Rectory La. Wall—77Lb 146
Rectory La. West—96Yc 185
(Brasted)
Rectory La. West—95Nc 184
(Tatsfield)
Rectory La. Wey—85N 157
Rectory Meadow. Grav—65Ce 135
Rectory Orchard. SW19—63Ab 124
Rectory Pk. S Croy—85Ub 165
Rectory Pk. Av. N'holt—41Ba 77
Rectory Pl. SE18—49Qc 86
Rectory Rd. E12—36Pc 66
Rectory Rd. E17—28Dc 44
Rectory Rd. N16—34Vb 63
Rectory Rd. SW13—54Wa 102
Rectory Rd. W3—46Ra 79
Rectory Rd. Beck—67Cc 128
Rectory Rd. Coul—97Eb 179
Rectory Rd. Dag—38Dd 68
Rectory Rd. Grays—48Fe 91
Rectory Rd. Grays—3D 92
(Orsett)
Rectory Rd. Grays—1F 114
(West Tilbury)
Rectory Rd. Hay—44W 76
Rectory Rd. Houn—54Y 99
Rectory Rd. Kes—80Mc 149
Rectory Rd. Rick—18M 17
Rectory Rd. Sev—78De 155
Rectory Rd. S'hall—48Ba 77
Rectory Rd. Stanf—2M 93
Rectory Rd. Sutt—76Cb 145
Rectory Rd. Swans—59Ae 113
Rectory Sq. E1—43Zb 84
Rectory Way. Uxb—33R 56
Reculver M. N18—21Wb 43
Reculver Rd. SE16—50Zb 84
Red Anchor Clo. SW3—51Fb 103
Redan Pl. W2—44Db 81
Redan St. W14—48Za 80
Redan Ter. SE5—54Rb 105
Redbarn Clo. Purl—83Rb 165
Red Barracks Rd. SE18—49Pc 86
Redberry Gro. SE26—62Yb 128
Redbourne Av. N3—25Cb 41
Redbridge Gdns. SE5—52Ub 105
Redbridge La. E. Ilf—30Mc 45
Redbridge La. W. E11—30Kc 45
Redburn St. SW3—51Hb 103
Redbury Clo. Rain—42Ld 89
Redcar Clo. N'holt—36Da 57
Redcar Rd. Romf—22Pd 49
Redcar St. SE5—52Sb 105
Redcastle Clo. E1—45Yb 84
Red Cedars Rd. Orp—73Uc 150
Redchurch St. E2
—42Vb 83 (5K 195)
Redcliffe Gdns. SW10—50Db 81
Redcliffe Gdns. Ilf—32Qc 66
Redcliffe M. SW10—50Db 81
Redcliffe Pl. SW10—51Eb 103
Redcliffe Rd. SW10—51Eb 103
Redcliffe Sq. SW10—50Db 81
Redcliffe St. SW10—51Db 103
Redclose Av. Mord—71Cb 145
Redclyffe Rd. E6—39Lc 65
Red Cottage M. Slou—8N 73
Red Ct. Slou—6J 73
Red Ct. Wok—87F 156
Redcroft Rd. S'hall—45Ea 78
Redcross Way. SE1
—47Sb 83 (1E 206)
Redden Ct. Rd. Romf—27Nd 49
Reddings Av. Bush, Wat—15Da 19
Reddings Clo. NW7—21Va 40
Reddings, The. NW7—20Va 22
Reddings, The. Borwd—13Pa 21
Reddington Clo. S Croy—81Tb 165
Reddington Dri. Slou—49A 74
Reddins Rd. SE15—52Wb 105
Reddons Rd. Beck—66Ac 128
Reddown Rd. Coul—90Mb 164
Reddy Rd. Eri—51Hd 110
Rede Pl. W2—44Cb 81
Redesdale Gdns. Iswth—52Ja 100
Redesdale St. SW3—51Hb 103
Redfern Av. Houn—59Ca 99
Redfern Clo. Uxb—39L 55
Redfern Gdns. Romf—26Md 49
Redfern Rd. NW10—38Ua 60
Redfern Rd. SE6—59Ec 106
Redfield La. SW5—49Cb 81
Redford Av. Coul—87Kb 164
Redford Av. T Hth—70Pb 126
Redford Av. Wall—79Nb 146
Redford Rd. Wind—3B 94
Redford Way. Uxb—38M 55
Redgate Dri. Brom—75Kc 149
Redgate Ter. SW15—58Za 102
Redgrave Rd. SW15—55Za 102
Redhall La. Rick—11N 17
Redheath Clo. Wat—7V 4
Red Hill. Chst—64Rc 130
Red Hill. Uxb—33F 54
Redhill Ct. SW2—61Qb 126
Redhill Dri. Edgw—26Sa 39
Redhill Rd. Cob—85R 158
Redhill Rd. Long, Dart—77Ae 155
Redhill St. NW1—40Kb 62 (3A 192)
Redhill Wood. Long, Dart
(in two parts) —76Ce 155
Red Ho. Cotts. Sev—97Ld 187
Red Ho. La. Bexh—56Ad 109
Red Ho. La. W on T—75W 140
Redhouse Rd. Croy—72Mb 146
Redhouse Rd. West—93Lc 183
Redington Gdns. NW3—35Db 61
Redington Rd. NW3—34Db 61
Redlands. Coul—88Nb 164
Redlands Ct. Brom—66Hc 129
Redlands Gdns. E Mol—70Ba 121
Redlands Rd. Enf—11Ac 26
Redlands Rd. Sev—96Hd 186
Redlands Way. SW2—59Pb 104
Red La. Esh—79Ja 142
Redlaw Way. SE16—50Wb 83
Redleaf Clo. Belv—51Cd 110
Redleaves Av. Ashf—65R 120
Redlees Clo. Iswth—56Ja 100
Red Lion Clo. Orp—72Yc 151
Red Lion Ct. EC4—44Qb 82 (3A 200)
Red Lion Hill. N2—26Fb 41
Red Lion La. SE18—53Qc 108
Red Lion La. Rick—7J 3
Red Lion Pl. SE18—53Qc 108
Red Lion Rd. Surb—75Pa 143
Red Lion Sq. WC1
—43Pb 82 (1H 199)
Red Lion St. WC1
—43Pb 82 (7H 193)
Red Lion St. Rich—57Ma 101
Red Lion Way. SE17—51Sb 105
Red Lion Yd. W1—(6K 197)
Red Lion Yd. Wat—14Y 19
Red Lodge Cres. Bex—62Gd 132
Red Lodge Rd. Bex—62Fd 132
Red Lodge Rd. W Wick—73Ec 148
Redmans La. Sev—79Ed 152
Redman's Rd. E1—43Yb 84
Redmead La. E1—46Wb 83
Redmead Rd. Hay—49U 76
Redmore Rd. W6—49Xa 80
Red Oak Clo. Orp—75Rc 150
Red Oaks Mead. Epp—9Tc 14
Red Pl. W1—45Jb 82 (4H 197)
Redpoll Way. Eri—48Zc 87
Red Post Hill—56Tb 105
SE21 1-9 & 2-12
SE24 remainder
Redriffe Rd. E13—39Hc 65
Redriff Rd. SE16—48Zb 84
Redriff Rd. Romf—26Dd 48
Red Rd. Borwd—13Pa 21
Red Rd. Brtwd—21Xd 50
Redruth Clo. N22—24Pb 42
Redruth Gdns. Romf—22Pd 49
Redruth Rd. E9—39Yb 64
Redruth Rd. Romf—22Pd 49
Redruth Wlk. Romf—22Pd 49
Redstart Clo. Croy—82Fc 167
Redston Rd. N8—28Mb 42
Red St. Grav—64Ce 135
Redvers Rd. N22—26Qb 42
Redvers Rd. Warl—90Zb 166
Redvers St. N1—41Ub 83 (3J 195)
Redwald Rd. E5—35Zb 64
Redway Dri. Twic—59Ea 100
Redwing Clo. S Croy—83Zb 166
Redwing Path. SE28—48Tc 86
Redwood. Egh—68G 118
Redwood Clo. N14—17Mb 24
Redwood Clo. SE16—46Ac 84
Redwood Clo. Kenl—86Sb 165
Redwood Clo. Uxb—40R 56
Redwood Clo. Wat—21Z 37
Redwood Ct. N'holt—41Aa 77
Redwood Ct. Surb—73Ma 143
Redwood Est. Houn—51X 99
Redwood Gdns. Chig—22Wc 47
Redwood Rise. Borwd—9Qa 7
Redwoods. SW15—60Wa 102
Reece M. SW7—49Fb 81 (5B 202)
Reed Av. Orp—76Uc 150
Reed Clo. E16—43Jc 85
Reed Clo. SE12—57Jc 107
Reed Clo. Iver—44G 74
Reede Gdns. Dag—36Dd 68
Reede Rd. Dag—37Cd 68
Reede Way. Dag—37Dd 68
Reedham Clo. N17—28Xb 43
Reedham Clo. St Alb—1Ca 5
Reedham Dri. Purl—85Pb 164
Reedham Pk. Av. Purl—88Qb 164
Reedham St. SE15—55Wb 105
Reedholm Vs. N16—35Tb 63
Reed Pond Wlk. Romf—26Hd 48
Reed Rd. N17—26Vb 43
Reedsfield Rd. Ashf—63R 120
Reed's Pl. NW1—38Lb 62
Reeds Wlk. Wat—12Y 19
Reedworth St. SE11
—49Qb 82 (6A 206)
Reenglass Rd. Stan—21Ma 39
Rees Gdns. Croy—72Vb 147
Reesland Clo. E12—37Qc 66
Rees St. N1—39Sb 63
Reets Farm Clo. NW9—30Ua 40
Reeves Av. NW9—31Ta 59
★Reeves Clo. Brtwd—6Xd
Reeves Corner. Croy—75Rb 147
Reeves Cres. Swan—69Fd 132
Reeves M. W1—45Jb 82 (5H 197)
Reeves Path. Hay—50V 76
Reeves Rd. E3—42Dc 84
Reeves Rd. SE18—51Rc 108
Reform Row. N17—26Vb 43
Reform St. SW11—54Hb 103
Regal Clo. E1—43Wb 83
Regal Clo. W5—43Ma 79
Regal Ct. N18—22Vb 43
Regal Cres. Wall—76Kb 146
Regal La. NW1—39Jb 62
Regal Way. Harr—30Na 39
Regan Way. N1—40Ub 63 (1H 195)
Regarder Rd. Chig—22Xc 47
Regarth Av. Romf—30Gd 48
Regency Clo. W5—44Na 79
Regency Clo. Chig—22Sc 46
Regency Clo. Hmptn—64Ba 121
Regency Clo. Sev—79Ud 154
Regency Ct. Brtwd—19Yd 32
Regency Dri. Ruis—32U 56
Regency Dri. Wey—85H 157
Regency M. Iswth—57Ga 100
Regency Pl. SW1
—49Mb 82 (5E 204)
Regency St. SW1
—49Mb 82 (5D 204)
Regency Wlk. Croy—72Bc 148
Regency Way. Bexh—55Zc 109
Regency Way. Wok—87F 156
Regent Av. Uxb—38R 56
Regent Clo. N12—22Eb 41
Regent Clo. Grays—47Ee 91
Regent Clo. Harr—30Na 39
Regent Clo. Houn—53X 99
Regent Clo. Wey—81M 157
Regent Ct. N20—19Eb 23
Regent Ct. Slou—4J 73
Regent Pl. W1—45Lb 82 (4C 198)
Regent Pl. Croy—74Vb 147
Regent Rd. SE24—57Rb 105
Regent Rd. Epp—2Vc 15
Regent Rd. Surb—71Pa 143
Regents Av. N13—22Qb 42
Regents Clo. Rad—6Ja 6
Regents Clo. S Croy—79Ub 147
Regents Clo. Whyt—90Vb 165
Regents Ct. Edgw—21Na 39
Regents Dri. Kes—78Mc 149
Regents M. NW8—40Eb 61 (1A 190)
Regent's Pk. Est. NW1—(3B 192)
Regent's Pk. Gdns. M. NW1
—39Jb 62
Regents Pk. Rd. N3—27Bb 41
Regent's Pk. Rd. NW1—39Hb 61
Regent's Pk. Ter. NW1—39Kb 62
Regent's Pl. SE3—54Jc 107
Regent Sq. E3—41Dc 84
Regent Sq. WC1—41Nb 82 (4G 193)
Regent Sq. Belv—49Dd 88
Regent's Row. E8—39Wb 63
Regent St. NW10—41Za 80
Regent St.—44Kb 82 (2A 198)
SW1 1-37 & 2-36
W1 remainder
Regent St. W4—50Qa 79
Regent St. Wat—10X 5
Regina Clo. Barn—13Za 22
Reginald Rd. E7—37Jc 65
Reginald Rd. SE8—52Cc 106
Reginald Rd. N'wd—25V 36
Reginald Rd. Romf—25Qd 49
Reginald Sq. SE8—52Cc 106
Regina Rd. N4—32Pb 62
Regina Rd. SE25—69Wb 127
Regina Rd. W13—46Ja 78
Regina Rd. S'hall—49Aa 77
Regina Ter. W13—46Ka 78
Regis Rd. NW5—36Kb 62
Regnart Bldgs. NW1—(4C 192)
Reid Av. Cat—93Tb 181
Reid Clo. Pinn—28W 36
Reidhaven Rd. SE18—49Uc 86
Reigate Av. Sutt—74Cb 145
Reigate Rd. Brom—62Hc 129
Reigate Rd. Eps & Tad—82Wa 162
Reigate Rd. Ilf—33Vc 67
Reigate Rd. Lea—95La 176
Reigate Way. Wall—78Nb 146
Reighton Rd. E5—34Wb 63
Relay Rd. W12—46Ya 80
Relf Rd. SE15—55Wb 105
Reliance Sq. EC2—(5J 195)
Relko Ct. Eps—83Ta 161
Relko Gdns. Sutt—78Fb 145
Relton M. SW7—48Gb 81 (3E 202)
Rembrandt Clo. SW1—(7H 203)
Rembrandt Dri. Grav—62Fe 135
Rembrandt Rd. SE13—56Gc 107
Rembrandt Rd. Edgw—26Qa 39
Rembrandt Way. W on T—75X 141
Remington Rd. E6—44Nc 86
Remington Rd. N15—30Tb 43
Remington St. N1
—40Rb 63 (2C 194)
Remnant St. WC2
—44Pb 82 (2H 199)
Rempstone M. N1
—40Tb 63 (1G 195)
Remus Rd. E3—38Cc 64
Rendlesham Av. Rad—9Ha 6
Rendlesham Rd. E5—35Wb 63
Rendlesham Rd. Enf—11Rb 25
Rendlesham Way. Rick—16E 16
Renforth St. SE16—47Yb 84
Renfrew Clo. E6—45Qc 86
Renfrew Ct. Houn—54Aa 99
Renfrew Rd. SE11
—49Rb 83 (5B 206)
Renfrew Rd. Houn—54Aa 99
Renfrew Rd. King—66Ra 123
Renmans, The. Asht—88Ma 161
Renmuir St. SW17—65Hb 125
Rennell St. SE13—55Ec 106
Renness Rd. E17—27Ac 44
Rennets Clo. SE9—57Uc 108
Rennets Wood Rd. SE9—57Tc 108
Rennie Clo. Ashf—62M 119
Rennies Est. SE16—49Xb 83
Rennie St. SE1—46Rb 83 (6B 200)
Renown Clo. Croy—74Rb 147
Renown Clo. Romf—25Cd 48
Rensburg Rd. E17—30Zb 44
Renshaw Clo. Belv—51Bd 109
Renters Av. NW4—30Ya 40
Renton Dri. Orp—73Zc 151
Renwick Clo. Orp—70Zc 131
Renwick Rd. Bark—42Xc 87
Repens Way. Hay—42Z 77
Rephidim St. SE1
—48Ub 83 (4H 207)
Replingham Rd. SW18—60Bb 103
Reporton Rd. SW6—52Ab 102
Repository Rd. SE18—51Pc 108
Repton Av. Hay—49T 76
Repton Av. Romf—27Jd 48
Repton Av. Wemb—35La 58
Repton Clo. Cars—78Gb 145
Repton Ct. Beck—67Dc 128
Repton Ct. Ilf—25Pc 46
Repton Dri. Romf—28Jd 48
Repton Gdns. Romf—27Jd 48
Repton Gro. Ilf—25Pc 46
Repton Rd. Harr—28Pa 39
Repton Rd. Orp—76Wc 151
Repton St. E14—44Ac 84
Repton Way. Rick—15Q 18
Repulse Clo. Romf—25Cd 48
Reservoir Rd. N14—15Lb 24
Reservoir Rd. SE4—54Ac 106
Reservoir Rd. Lou—11Kc 27
Reservoir Rd. Ruis—28T 36
Resolution Wlk. SE18—48Pc 86
Restell Clo. SE3—51Gc 107
Reston Clo. Borwd—10Qa 7
Reston Path. Borwd—10Qa 7
Reston Pl. SW7—47Eb 81 (2A 202)
Restons Cres. SE9—58Tc 108
Restormel Clo. Houn—57Ca 99
Retcar Clo. N19—33Kb 62
Retford Clo. Romf—23Qd 49
Retford Path. Romf—23Qd 49
Retford Rd. Romf—23Pd 49
Retford St. N1—40Ub 63 (2J 195)
Retingham Way. E4—19Dc 26
Retreat. Brtwd—18Xd 32
Retreat Clo. Harr—29La 38
Retreat Pl. E9—37Yb 64
Retreat Rd. Rich—57Ma 101
Retreat, The. NW9—29Ta 39
Retreat, The. SW14—55Ua 102
Retreat, The. Abb L, Wat—3S 4
Retreat, The. Amer—11A 16
Retreat, The. Brtwd—16De 33
Retreat, The. Egh—4P 117
Retreat, The. Grays—51De 113
Retreat, The. Harr—31Ca 57
Retreat, The. Orp—79Xc 151
Retreat, The. Sev—96Kd 187
Retreat, The. Surb—72Pa 143
Retreat, The. T Hth—70Tb 127
Retreat, The. Wor Pk—76Xa 144
Retreat Way. Chig—20Xc 29
Reubens Rd. Brtwd—16De 33
Revell Clo. Lea—94Da 175
Revell Dri. Lea—94Da 175
Revell Rise. SE18—51Vc 109
Revell Rd. King—68Ra 123
Revell Rd. Sutt—79Bb 145
Revelon Rd. SE4—55Ac 106
Revelstoke Rd. SW18—61Bb 125
Reventlow Rd. SE9—60Sc 108
Reverdy Rd. SE1—49Wb 83
Revesby Rd. Cars—72Gb 145
Review Rd. NW2—33Va 60
Review Rd. Dag—40Dd 68
Rewell St. SW6—52Eb 103
Rewley Rd. Cars—72Fb 145
Rex Av. Ashf—65Q 120
Rex Clo. Romf—24Dd 48
Rex Pl. W1—45Jb 82 (5J 197)
Reydon Av. E11—30Lc 45
Reynard Clo. Brom—69Pc 130
Reynard Dri. SE19—66Vb 127
Reynardson Rd. N17—24Sb 43
Reynards Way. St Alb—1Ba 5
Reynolds Av. E12—36Qc 66
Reynolds Av. Chess—80Na 143
Reynolds Av. Romf—31Yc 67
Reynolds Clo. NW11—31Db 61
Reynolds Clo. Cars—74Hb 145
Reynolds Dri. Edgw—27Pa 39
Reynold's Pl. SE3—52Kc 107
Reynolds Pl. Rich—58Pa 101
Reynolds Rd. SE15—56Yb 106
Reynolds Rd. W4—48Sa 79
Reynolds Rd. Hay—42Y 77
Reynolds Rd. N Mald—73Ta 143
Reynolds Way. Croy—77Ub 147
Rheidol M. N1—40Sb 63 (1D 194)
Rheidol Ter. N1—39Sb 63 (1C 194)
Rheingold Way. Wall—81Nb 164
Rheola Clo. N17—25Vb 43
Rhoda St. E2—42Vb 83 (5K 195)
Rhodes Av. N22—25Lb 42
Rhodesia Rd. E11—33Fc 65
Rhodesia Rd. SW9—54Nb 104
Rhodesmoor Ho. Ct. Mord
—72Cb 145
Rhodes St. N7—36Pb 62
Rhodes Way. Wat—12Z 19
Rhodeswell Rd. E14—44Bc 84
Rhododendron Ride. Egh—5K 117
Rhodrons Av. Chess—78Na 143
Rhondda Gro. E3—41Ac 84
Rhyl Rd. Gnfd—40Ha 58
Rhyl St. NW5—37Jb 62
Rhys Av. N11—24Mb 42
Rialto Rd. Mitc—68Jb 126
Ribble Clo. Wfd G—23Lc 45
Ribblesdale Av. N'holt—37Da 57
Ribblesdale Rd. N8—28Pb 42
Ribblesdale Rd. SW16—65Kb 126
Ribblesdale Rd. Dart—60Sd 112
Ribchester Av. Gnfd—41Ha 78
Ribston Clo. Brom—74Bc 148
Ricardo Path. SE28—46Yc 87
Ricardo Rd. Wind—8M 95
Ricardo St. E14—44Dc 84
Ricards Rd. SW19—64Bb 125
Richard Clo. SE18—49Nc 86
Richards Av. Romf—30Ed 48
Richards Clo. Harr—29Ja 38
Richards Clo. Hay—51T 98
Richards Clo. Uxb—39Q 56
Richardson Rd. E15—40Gc 65
Richardson's M. W1—(6B 192)
Richards Pl. E17—27Cc 44
Richard's Pl. SW3
—49Gb 81 (5E 202)
Richards Rd. Cob—86Da 159
Richard St. E1—44Xb 83
(in two parts)
Richbell Clo. Asht—90Ma 161
Richbell Pl. WC1—43Pb 82 (7H 193)
Richborne Ter. SW8—52Pb 104
Richborough Clo. Orp—70Zc 131
Richborough Rd. NW2—35Ab 60
Riches Rd. Ilf—33Sc 66
Richfield Rd. Bush, Wat—17Ea 20
Richford Rd. E15—39Hc 65
Richford St. W6—47Ya 80
Richings Way. Iver—48H 75
Richland Av. Coul—86Jb 164
Richlands Av. Eps—77Wa 144
Rich La. SW5—50Db 81
Richmer Rd. Eri—52Jd 110
Richmond Av. E4—22Fc 45
Richmond Av. N1—39Pb 62
Richmond Av. NW10—37Ya 60
Richmond Av. SW20—67Ab 124
Richmond Av. Uxb—37R 56
Richmond Bri. Twic & Rich
—58Ma 101
Richmond Bldgs. W1
—44Mb 82 (3D 198)
Richmond Clo. E17—30Bc 44
Richmond Clo. Eps—86Ua 162
Richmond Clo. Lea—96Ea 176
Richmond Clo. Wal X—1Yb 12
Richmond Clo. West—91Kc 183
Richmond Ct. Pot B—3Eb 9
Richmond Cres. E4—22Fc 45
Richmond Cres. N1—39Qb 62
Richmond Cres. N9—18Wb 25
Richmond Cres. Slou—6L 73
Richmond Cres. Stai—64H 119
Richmond Dri. Shep—72T 140
Richmond Dri. Wat—12U 18
Richmond Gdns. NW4—29Wa 40
Richmond Gdns. Harr—24Ha 38
Richmond Grn. Croy—76Nb 146
Richmond Gro. N1—38Rb 63
Richmond Gro. Surb—72Pa 143
Richmond Hill. Rich—58Na 101
Richmond Hill Ct. Rich—58Na 101
Richmond M. W1
—44Mb 82 (3D 198)
Richmond M. Tedd—64Ha 122
Richmond Pk. Rd. SW14
—57Sa 101
Richmond Pk. Rd. King—66Na 123
Richmond Pl. SE18—49Sc 86
Richmond Rd. E4—18Fc 27
Richmond Rd. E7—36Kc 65
Richmond Rd. E8—38Vb 63
Richmond Rd. E11—33Fc 65
Richmond Rd. N2—26Eb 41
Richmond Rd. N11—23Nb 42
Richmond Rd. N15—30Ub 43
Richmond Rd. SW20—67Xa 124
Richmond Rd. W5—47Na 79
Richmond Rd. Barn—15Db 23
Richmond Rd. Coul—87Kb 164
Richmond Rd. Croy—76Nb 146
Richmond Rd. Felt—58U 98
Richmond Rd. Grays—50Ee 91
Richmond Rd. Ilf—34Sc 66
Richmond Rd. Iswth—55Ja 100
Richmond Rd. King—64Ma 123
Richmond Rd. Pot B—3Eb 9
Richmond Rd. Romf—30Hd 48
Richmond Rd. Stai—64H 119
Richmond Rd. T Hth—69Rb 127
Richmond Rd. Twic—59Ka 100
Richmond St. E13—40Jc 65
Richmond Ter. SW1
—47Nb 82 (1F 205)
Richmond Ter. M. SW1
—47Nb 82 (1F 205)
Richmond Way. E11—33Jc 65
Richmond Way—47Za 80
W12 1-15 & 2-52
W14 remainder
Richmond Way. Lea—95Da 175
(in two parts)
Richmount Gdns. SE3—55Jc 107
Rich St. E14—45Bc 84
Rickard Clo. SW2—60Qb 104
Rickard Clo. W Dray—48M 75
Rickards Clo. Surb—74Na 143
Ricketts Hill Rd. West—90Mc 167
Rickett St. SW6—51Cb 103
Rickfields. Harr—33Fa 58
Rickman Cres. Wey—76K 139
Rickman Hill. Coul—89Kb 164
Rickman Hill Rd. Coul—90Kb 164
Rickman's La. Slou—7J 53
Rickman St. E1—42Yb 84
Rickmansworth La. Ger X—23A 34
Rickmansworth Rd. N'wd—22R 36
Rickmansworth Rd. Pinn—26X 37
Rickmansworth Rd. Rick—14H 17
Rickmansworth Rd. Uxb—25L 35
Rickmansworth Rd. Wat—14U 18
Ricksons La. Lea—99R 174
Rickthorne Rd. N19—33Nb 62
Rickyard Path. SE9—56Nc 108
Ridding La. Gnfd—36Ha 58
Riddlesdown Av. Purl—84Sb 165
Riddlesdown Rd. Purl & Kenl
—83Sb 165
Riddons Rd. SE12—62Lc 129
Rideout St. SE18—49Pc 86
Rider Clo. Sidc—58Sc 108
Ride, The. Bren—50Ka 78
Ride, The. Enf—14Zb 26
Ridge Av. N21—17Sb 25
Ridge Av. Dart—58Hd 110
Ridgebank. Slou—5D 72
Ridgebrook Rd. SE3—55Mc 107
Ridge Clo. NW4—26Za 40
Ridge Clo. NW9—28Ta 39
Ridge Clo. Wok—9E 188
Ridge Crest. Enf—11Pb 24
Ridgecroft Clo. Bex—60Ed 110
Ridgedale St. E3—40Dc 64
Ridge Hill. NW11—32Ab 60
Ridgehurst Av. Wat—6V 4
Ridgelands. Lea—96Fa 176
Ridge La. Wat—9V 4
Ridge Langley. S Croy—82Wb 165
Ridgemead Rd. Egh—2M 117
Ridgemont Gdns. Edgw—21Sa 39
Ridgemount. Wey—75U 140
Ridgemount Av. Coul—89Kb 164
Ridgemount Av. Croy—74Zb 148
Ridgemount Clo. SE20—66Xb 127
Ridgemount End. Ger X—22A 34
Ridgemount Gdns. Enf—12Rb 25
Ridge Pk. Purl—82Mb 164
Ridge Rd. N8—30Pb 42
Ridge Rd. N21—18Sb 25
Ridge Rd. NW2—34Bb 61
Ridge Rd. Mitc—66Kb 126
Ridge Rd. Sutt—74Ab 144
Ridge St. Wat—10X 5
Ridge, The. Barn—15Bb 23
Ridge, The. Bex—59Bd 109
Ridge, The. Cat—97Ec 182
Ridge, The. Coul—86Nb 164
Ridge, The. Eps—90Sa 161
Ridge, The. Lea—96Fa 176
Ridge, The. Orp—75Tc 150
Ridge, The. Purl—82Mb 164
Ridge, The. Surb—71Qa 143
Ridge, The. Twic—59Fa 100
Ridge, The. Wok—89D 156
Ridgeview Clo. Barn—16Za 22
Ridgeview Rd. N20—20Bb 23
Ridgeway. SE19—65Ub 127
Ridgeway. Brtwd—18De 33
Ridgeway. Brom—75Jc 149
Ridge Way. Dart—58Hd 110
(Crayford)
Ridgeway. Dart—64Ud 134
(Lane End)
Ridgeway. Eps—84Sa 161
Ridge Way. Felt—62Aa 121
Ridgeway. Grays—9A 92
Ridge Way. Iver—45H 75
Ridge Way. Rick—17K 17
Ridgeway. Wok—87A 156
Ridgeway. Wok—3G 188
Ridge Way. Wfd G—21Lc 45
Ridgeway Av. Barn—16Hb 23
Ridgeway Av. Grav—2D 136
Ridgeway Clo. Lea—86Ea 160
Ridgeway Clo. Wok—3G 188
Ridgeway Cres. Orp—76Uc 150
Ridgeway Cres. Gdns. Orp—76Uc 150
Ridgeway Dri. Brom—64Kc 129
Ridgeway E. Sidc—57Vc 109
Ridgeway Gdns. Ilf—29Nc 46
Ridgeway Gdns. Wok—3G 188
Ridgeway Rd. Iswth—52Ga 100
Ridgeway Rd. N. Iswth—52Ga 100
Ridgeway, The. E4—18Ec 26
Ridgeway, The. N3—24Db 41
Ridgeway, The. N11—21Hb 41
Ridgeway, The. N14—19Nb 24
Ridgeway, The. NW7—21Xa 40
Ridgeway, The. NW9—28Ta 39
Ridgeway, The. NW11—32Bb 61
Ridgeway, The. W3—48Qa 79

Ridgeway, The—Romney Gdns.

Ridgeway, The. Croy—76Pb 146
Ridgeway, The. Enf & Pot B —12Rb 25
Ridgeway, The. Ger X—27A 34
Ridgeway, The. Grav—6N 137
Ridgeway, The. Harr—30La 38 (Kenton)
Ridgeway, The. Harr—29Ba 37 to 31Da 57 (North Harrow)
Ridgeway, The. Lea—96Ga 176 (Fetcham)
Ridgeway, The. Lea—86Ea 160 (Oxshott)
Ridgeway, The. Pot B—1Mb 10
Ridgeway, The. Rad—9Ja 6
Ridgeway, The. Romf—28Jd 48
Ridgeway, The. Romf—25Pd 49 (Harold Wood)
Ridgeway, The. Ruis—31W 56
Ridge Way, The. S Croy—82Ub 165
Ridgeway, The. Stan—23La 38
Ridgeway, The. Sutt—79Fb 145
Ridgeway, The. W on T—74V 140
Ridgeway, The. Wat—9U 4
Ridgeway W. Sidc—57Uc 108
Ridgewell Av. Grays—2C 92
Ridgewell Clo. N1—39Sb 63
Ridgewell Clo. Dag—39Dd 68
Ridgmount Gdns. WC1 —43Mb 82 (7D 192)
Ridgmount Pl. WC1 —43Mb 82 (7D 192)
Ridgmount Rd. SW18—57Db 103
Ridgmount St. WC1 —43Mb 82 (7D 192)
Ridgway. SW19—66Ya 124
Ridgway. Wok—87J 157
Ridgway Gdns. SW19—66Za 124
Ridgway Pl. SW19—65Ab 124
Ridgway Rd. SW9—55Rb 105
Ridgway Rd. Wok—87H 157
Ridgwell Rd. E16—43Lc 85
Riding Ct. Rd. Slou—51A 96
Riding Ct. Rd. Slou—2N 95
Riding Hill. S Croy—85Wb 165
Riding Ho. St. W1 —43Lb 82 (1A 198)
Ridings Av. N21—15Sb 25
Ridings Clo. N6—31Lb 62
Ridings La. Wok—95R 174
Ridings, The. W5—42Pa 79
Ridings, The. Asht—89Ma 161
Ridings, The. Barn—17Fb 23
Ridings, The. Che—8A 2
Ridings, The. Cob—84Ca 159
Ridings, The. Eps—87Ua 162
Ridings, The. Iver—49H 75
Ridings, The. Lea—97V 174
Ridings, The. Sun—67W 120
Ridings, The. Surb—71Qa 143
Ridings, The. Tad—92Bb 179
Ridings, The. West.—89Nc 168
Ridings, The. Wey—79G 138
Ridings, The. Wok—95J 173
Riding, The. NW11—31Bb 61
Riding, The. Wok—86D 156
Ridler Rd. Enf—10Ub 11
Ridley Av. W13—48Ka 78
Ridley Clo. Romf—25Kd 49
Ridley Rd. E7—35Lc 65
Ridley Rd. E8—36Vb 63
Ridley Rd. NW10—40Wa 60
Ridley Rd. SW19—66Db 125
Ridley Rd. Brom—69Hc 129
Ridley Rd. Warl—90Yb 166
Ridley Rd. Well—53Xc 109
Ridley Several. SE3—54Jc 107
Ridsdale Rd. SE20—67Xb 127
Ridsdale Rd. Wok—5E 188
Riefield Rd. SE9—56Sc 108
Riesco Dri. Croy—79Yb 148
Riffel Rd. NW2—36Ya 60
Riffhams. Brtwd—20De 33
Rifle Butts All. Eps—87Va 162
Rifle Ct. SE11—51Qb 104
Rifle Pl. W11—46Za 80
Rifle St. E14—43Dc 84
Rigault Rd. SW6—54Ab 102
Rigby Clo. Croy—76Qb 146
Rigby Gdns. Grays—9D 92
Rigby La. Hay—47S 76
Rigby M. Ilf—33Qc 66
Rigden St. E14—44Dc 84
Rigeley Rd. NW10—41Wa 80
Rigg App. E10—32Zb 64
Rigge Pl. SW4—56Mb 104
Riggindale Rd. SW16—64Mb 126
★Riggs Way. Sev—88Be
Riley Rd. SE1—48Vb 83 (3K 207)
Riley Rd. Enf—10Yb 12
Riley St. Sw10—52Fb 103
Ring Clo. Brom—66Kc 129
Ringcroft St. N7—36Qb 62
Ringers Rd. Brom—69Jc 129
Ringford Rd. SW18—57Bb 103
Ringlewell Clo. Enf—12Xb 25
Ringmer Av. SW6—53Ab 102
Ringmer Gdns. N19—33Nb 62
Ringmer Pl. N21—15Tb 25
Ringmer Way. Brom—71Pc 150
Ringmore Rise. SE23—59Xb 105
Ringmore Rd. W on T—76Y 141
Ringshall Rd. Orp—69Wc 131
Ringslade Rd. N22—26Pb 42
Ringstead Rd. SE6—59Dc 106
Ringstead Rd. Sutt—77Fb 145
Ring, The. W2—46Gb 81 (6D 196)
Ring Way. N11—23Lb 42
Ringway. S'hall—50Aa 77
Ringwold Clo. Beck—66Ac 128
Ringwood Av. N2—26Hb 41
Ringwood Av. Croy—73Nb 146
Ringwood Av. Horn—33Md 69
Ringwood Av. Orp—82Yc 169
Ringwood Clo. Pinn—27Y 37
Ringwood Gdns. SW15—60Wa 102
Ringwood Rd. E17—30Bc 44
Ringwood Way. N21—17Rb 25
Ringwood Way. Hmptn—63Ca 121
Ripley Av. Egh—65A 118
Ripley By-Pass. Wok—95L 173
Ripley Clo. Brom—71Pc 150
Ripley Clo. Croy—79Ec 148
Ripley Clo. Slou—49A 74
Ripley Gdns. SW14—55Ta 101
Ripley Gdns. Sutt—77Eb 145
Ripley La. Lea—98Q 174
Ripley La. Wok—95N 173
Ripley Rd. E16—44Lc 85
Ripley Rd. Belv—49Cd 88
Ripley Rd. Enf—11Sb 25
Ripley Rd. Hmptn—66Ca 121
Ripley Rd. Ilf—33Vc 67
Ripley Rd. Wok & Guild—98L 173
Ripley View. Lou—10Rc 14
Ripley Way. Wal X—2Xb 11
Ripon Clo. N'holt—37Ca 57
Ripon Gdns. Chess—78Ma 143
Ripon Rd. N9—17Xb 25
Ripon Rd. N17—27Tb 43
Ripon Rd. SE18—51Rc 108
Ripon Way. Borwd—15Ta 21
Rippersley Rd. Well—53Wc 109
Ripple Rd. Bark & Dag—39Tc 66
Ripplevale Gro. N1—38Pb 62
Rippolson Rd. SE18—50Vc 87
Rippon Gdns. Ilf—31Nc 66
Ripston Rd. Asht—64T 120
Risborough Dri. N Mald —73Wa 144
Risborough St. SE1 —47Rb 83 (1C 206)
Risdon St. SE16—47Yb 84
Risebridge Chase. Romf—24Hd 48
Risebridge Rd. Romf—26Hd 48
Risedale Rd. Bexh—55Ed 110
Riseholme St. E9—37Bc 64
Riseldine Rd. SE23—58Ac 106
Rise Pk. Boulevd. Romf—25Hd 48
Rise Pk. Pde. Romf—26Gd 48
Rise, The. E11—29Jc 45
Rise, The. N13—21Qb 42
Rise, The. NW7—23Va 40
Rise, The. NW10—35Ta 59
Rise, The. Bex—59Yc 109
Rise, The. Borwd—15Pa 21
Rise, The. Buck H—17Mc 27
Rise, The. Dart—56Hd 110
Rise, The. Edgw—22Ra 39
Rise, The. Eps—82Va 162
Rise, The. Grav—3G 136
Rise, The. Gnfd—36Ja 58
Rise, The. Lea—98U 174
Rise, The. Sev—100Ld 187
Rise, The. S Croy—81Yb 166
Rise, The. Uxb—40P 55
Riseway. Brtwd—20Ae 33
Rising Hill Clo. N'wd—23S 36
Risinghill St. N1—40Qb 62 (1K 193)
Rising Holme Clo. Bush, Wat —17Da 19
Risingholme Clo. Harr—25Ga 38
Risingholme Rd. Harr—26Ga 38
Risings, The. E17—28Fc 45 (in two parts)
Rising Sun Ct. EC1—(1C 200)
Risley Av. N17—25Sb 43
Rita Rd. SW8—51Nb 104
Ritches Rd. N15—29Sb 43
Ritchie Rd. Croy—72Xb 147
Ritchie St. N1—40Qb 62 (1A 194)
Ritchings Av. E17—28Ac 44
Ritherdon Rd. SW17—61Jb 126
Ritson Rd. E8—37Wb 63
Ritter St. SE18—51Qc 108
Ritz Ct. Pot B—3Cb 9
Rivaz Pl. E9—37Yb 64
Rivenhall Gdns. E18—28Hc 45
River Av. N13—20Rb 25
River Av. Th Dit—73Ja 142
River Bank. N21—17Sb 25
River Bank. E Mol—69Ga 122
River Bank. E Mol—69Ca 121 (West Molesey)
Riverbank. Stai—65H 119
River Bank. Th Dit—71Ha 142
River Barge Clo. E14—47Ec 84
River Clo. E11—30Lc 45
River Clo. Rain—43Kd 89
River Clo. Ruis—30V 36
River Clo. S'hall—49Ea 78
River Clo. Wal X—6Cc 12
River Ct. Sev—94Gd 186
Rivercourt Rd. W6—49Xa 80
Riverdale. SE13—55Ec 106
Riverdale Dri. Wok—93B 172
Riverdale Gdns. Twic—57La 100
Riverdale Rd. SE18—50Vc 87
Riverdale Rd. Bex—59Bd 109
Riverdale Rd. Eri—50Dd 88
Riverdale Rd. Felt—63Ba 121
Riverdale Rd. Twic—58La 100
Riverdene. Edgw—20Sa 21
Riverdene Industrial Est. W on T —78Z 141
Riverdene Rd. Ilf—34Qc 66
River Dri. Upm—30Sd 50
Riverfield Rd. Stai—65H 119
River Front. Enf—13Ub 25
River Gdns. Cars—75Jb 146
River Gdns. Felt—57X 99
River Gro. Pk. Beck—67Bc 128
Riverhead Clo. E17—26Zb 44
River Hill. Cob—87X 159
Riverholme Dri. Eps—81Ua 162
River Ho. SE26—62Xb 127
River La. Cob—88Aa 159
River La. Lea—93Fa 176
River La. Rich—60Ma 101
Rivermead. Wey—85P 157
Rivermead Clo. Tedd—64Ka 122
Rivermead Clo. Wey—80L 139
River Meads Av. Twic—62Da 121
River Mt. W on T—73V 140
Rivernook Clo. W on T—71Y 141
River Pde. Sev—94Gd 186
River Pk. Av. Stai—63F 118
River Pk. Gdns. Brom—66Fc 129
River Pk. Rd. N22—26Pb 42
River Pl. N1—38Sb 63
River Reach. Tedd—64La 122
River Rd. Bark—40Uc 66
River Rd. Brtwd—21Vd 50
River Rd. Buck H—18Nc 28
River Rd. Stai—67H 119
Riversdale. Grav—1A 136
Riversdale Rd. N5—34Rb 63
Riversdale Rd. Romf—24Dd 48
Riversdale Rd. Th Dit—72Ja 142
Riversdell Clo. Cher—73H 139
Riversfield Rd. Enf—13Ub 25
Riverside. NW4—31Xa 60
Riverside. SE7—48Lc 85
Riverside. Cher—68K 119
Riverside. Egh—62C 118
Riverside. Eyns, Dart—75Md 153
Riverside. Rich—57Ma 101
Riverside. Shep—73U 140
Riverside. Stai—64H 119
Riverside. Twic—60Ka 100
Riverside. Wray, Stai—9N 95
Riverside Av. E Mol—71Fa 142
River Side Av. Rich—52Na 101
Riverside Clo. W7—42Ga 78
Riverside Clo. K Lan—1R 4
Riverside Clo. King—70Ma 123
Riverside Clo. Stai—67H 119
Riverside Clo. Wall—76Kb 146
Riverside Ct. SW8—51Mb 104
Riverside Dri. NW11—30Ab 40
Riverside Dri. W4—52Ta 101
Riverside Dri. Esh—77Ca 141
Riverside Dri. Mitc—71Gb 145
Riverside Dri. Rich—62Ka 122
Riverside Dri. Rick—18M 17
Riverside Dri. Stai—64G 118 (Chertsey La.)
Riverside Dri. Stai—67H 119 (Wheatsheaf La.)
Riverside Gdns. W6—50Xa 80
Riverside Gdns. Enf—12Tb 25
Riverside Gdns. Wemb—40Na 59
Riverside Gdns. Wok—93D 172
Riverside Industrial Est. Enf —16Ac 26
Riverside Industrial Est. Dart
Riverside Path. Wal X—1Yb 12
Riverside Pl. Stai—58M 97
Riverside Rd. E15—40Ec 64
Riverside Rd. N15—30Wb 43
Riverside Rd. SW17—63Db 125
Riverside Rd. Sidc—62Ad 131
Riverside Rd. Stai—66H 119
Riverside Rd. Stai—57M 97 (Stanwell)
Riverside Rd. W on T—77Aa 141
Riverside Rd. Wat—16X 19
Riverside Wlk. N12 & N20 —20Db 23
Riverside Wlk. SE1 —46Pb 82 (6J 199)
Riverside Wlk. Barn—16Za 22
Riverside Wlk. Iswth—55Ga 100
Riverside Way. Dart—57Nd 111
Riverside Way. Uxb—39K 55
River St. EC1—41Qb 82 (3K 193)
River St. Wind—2H 95
River Ter. W6—50Ya 80
Riverton Clo. W9—41Bb 81
River View. Enf—13Sb 25
River View. Grays—9C 92
Riverview Gdns. SW13—51Xa 102
River View Gdns. Twic—61Ha 122
Riverview Gro. W4—51Ra 101
Riverview Pk. SE6—61Cc 128
Riverview Rd. W4—52Ra 101
Riverview Rd. Eps—77Sa 143
River View Rd. Grnh—57Wd 112
River Wlk. Uxb—36L 55
River Wlk. W on T—72W 140
Riverway. N13—21Qb 42
River Way. SE10—48Hc 85
River Way. Eps—78Ta 143
River Way. Lou—16Pc 28
Riverway. Stai—67K 119
River Way. Twic—61Da 121
Riverwood La. Chst—68Tc 130
Rivey Clo. Wey—86H 157
Rivington Av. Wfd G—26Mc 45
Rivington Bldgs. EC2 —41Ub 83 (4H 195)
Rivington Ct. NW10—39Wa 60
Rivington Cres. NW7—24Va 40
Rivington Pl. EC2 —41Ub 83 (4J 195)
Rivington St. EC2 —41Ub 83 (4H 195)
Rivington Wlk. E8—39Wb 63
Rivulet Rd. N17—24Sb 43
Rixon Clo. Slou—44A 74
Rixsen Rd. E12—36Nc 66
Roach Rd. E3—38Cc 64
Roads Pl. N19—33Nb 62
Roakes Av. Wey—75K 139
Roan St. SE10—52Dc 106
Roasthill La. Wind—10B 72
Robbins Ct. Beck—68Fc 129
★Robbins, The. Brtwd—7Zd
Robb Rd. Stan—23Ja 38
Robert Adam St. W1 —44Jb 82 (2H 197)
Roberta St. E2—41Wb 83
Robert Clo. W9—42Eb 81 (6A 190)
Robert Clo. Chig—22Vc 47
Robert Clo. Pot B—5Ab 8
Robert Clo. W on T—78X 141
Robert Dashwood Way. SE17 —49Sb 83 (6D 206)
Robert Keen Clo. SE15—53Wb 105
Robert Lowe Clo. SE14—52Zb 106
Roberton Dri. Brom—67Lc 129
Robert Rd. Slou—3H 53
Roberts All. W5—47Ma 79
Robertsbridge Rd. Cars—73Eb 145
Roberts Clo. Romf—25Kd 49
Roberts Clo. Stai—58L 97
Roberts Clo. Sutt—80Za 144
Roberts Clo. W Dray—46N 75
Roberts Ct. Ger X—22C 34
Roberts M. SW1—48Jb 82 (4H 203)
Robertson Ct. Wok—6B 188
Robertson St. SW8—55Kb 104
Roberts Pl. EC1—42Qb 82 (5A 194)
Roberts Rd. E17—25Dc 44
Roberts Rd. NW7—23Ab 40
Roberts Rd. Belv—50Cd 88
Roberts Rd. Wat—15Y 19
Robert St. E16—46Rc 86
Robert St. NW1—41Kb 82 (4A 192)
Robert St. SE18—50Tc 86
Robert St. WC2—45Nb 82 (5G 199)
Robert St. Croy—76Sb 147
Roberts Way. Egh—6N 117
Roberts Wood Dri. Ger X—22B 34
Robeson St. E3—43Bc 84
Robina Clo. Bexh—56Zc 109
Robina Clo. Ilf—23Uc 46
Robin Clo. Romf—24Fd 48
Robin Clo. Wey—78M 139
Robin Gro. N6—33Jb 62
Robin Gro. Bren—51La 100
Robin Gro. Harr—30Pa 39
Robin Hill Dri. Chst—65Nc 130
Robinhood Clo. Mitc—69Lb 126
Robin Hood Clo. Slou—6D 72
Robin Hood Clo. Wok—6C 188
Robin Hood Cres. Wok—5B 188
Robin Hood Dri. Bush, Wat —11Ba 19
Robin Hood Dri. Harr—24Ha 38
Robin Hood Grn. Orp—71Wc 151
Robin Hood La. E14—45Ec 84
Robin Hood La. SW15—63Ua 124
Robin Hood La. Bexh—57Ad 109
Robinhood La. Mitc—69Lb 126
Robin Hood La. Sutt—78Cb 145
Robin Hood La. Wok & Guild —96B 172
Robin Hood Rd. SW19—64Wa 124
Robin Hood Rd. Brtwd—17Yd 32
Robin Hood Rd. Wok—5B 188
Robin Hood Way. SW15 & SW20 —64Ua 124
Robin Hood Way. Gnfd—37Ha 58
Robinia Av. Grav—59Fe 113
Robins Clo. Uxb—43L 75
Robins Ct. SE12—62Lc 129
Robins Dale. Wok—5A 188
Robins Gro. W Wick—76Jc 149
Robinson Av. Wal X—1Rb 11
Robinson Cres. Bush, Wat —18Ea 20
Robinson Rd. E2—40Yb 64
Robinson Rd. SW17—65Gb 125
Robinson Rd. Dag—35Cd 68
Robinson's Clo. W13—43Ja 78
Robinson St. SW3—51Hb 103
Robins Orchard. Ger X—24A 34
Robins Way. Wal A—6Gc 13
Robinsway. W on T—77Y 141
Robin Way. Orp—69Xc 131
Robin Way. Stai—62H 119
Robinwood Pl. SW15—63Ta 123
Roborough Wlk. Horn—37Ld 69
Robsart St. SW9—54Qb 104
Robson Av. NW10—39Wa 60
Robson Clo. E6—44Nc 86
Robson Clo. Enf—12Rb 25
Robson Clo. Ger X—22A 34
Robson Rd. SE27—62Sb 127
Robsons Clo. Wal X—1Yb 12
Robyns Way. Sev—94Hd 186
Roch Av. Edgw—26Pa 39
Rochdale Rd. E17—31Cc 64
Rochdale Rd. SE2—50Xc 87
Rochdale Way. SE8—52Cc 106
Rochelle Clo. SW11—56Fb 103
Rochelle St. E2—41Vb 83 (4K 195)
Roche Rd. SW16—67Pb 126
Rochester Av. E13—39Lc 65
Rochester Av. Brom—68Kc 129
Rochester Av. Felt—61V 120
Rochester Clo. SE3—55Lc 107
Rochester Clo. SW16—66Nb 126
Rochester Clo. Enf—10Ub 25
Rochester Clo. Sidc—58Xc 109
Rochester Dri. Bex—58Cd 110
Rochester Dri. Pinn—29Z 37
Rochester Gdns. Cat—94Ub 181
Rochester Gdns. Croy—76Ub 147
Rochester Gdns. Ilf—31Pc 66
Rochester M. NW1—38Lb 62
Rochester Pl. NW1—37Lb 62 (in two parts)
Rochester Rd. NW1—37Lb 62
Rochester Rd. Cars—77Hb 145
Rochester Rd. Dart—59Od 111
Rochester Rd. Grav—9G 114
Rochester Rd. N'wd—27V 36
Rochester Row. SW1 —49Lb 82 (5C 204)
Rochester Sq. NW1—38Lb 62
Rochester St. SW1 —49Mb 82 (4D 204)
Rochester Ter. NW1—37Lb 62
Rochester Wlk. SE1—(6F 201)
Rochester Way.—53Kc 107
SE3 1-325 & 2-364
SE9 remainder
Rochester Way. Bex & Dart —59Gd 110
Rochester Way. Rick—14R 18
Roche Wlk. Cars—72Fb 145
Rochford Av. Brtwd—15Ce 33
Rochford Av. Lou—13Sc 28
Rochford Av. Romf—29Yc 47
Rochford Av. Wal A—6Fc 13
Rochford Clo. E6—40Mc 65
Rochford Clo. Horn—37Kd 69
Rochford Gdns. Slou—6N 73
Rochford Grn. Lou—13Sc 28
Rochford Wlk. E8—38Wb 63
Rochford Way. Croy—72Nb 146
Rock Av. SW14—55Ta 101
Rockbourne Rd. SE23—60Zb 106
Rockchase Gdns. Horn—30Nd 49
Rockdale Rd. Sev—97Ld 187
Rockell's Pl. SE22—58Xb 105
Rockford Av. Gnfd—40Ka 58
Rock Gdns. Dag—36Dd 68
Rockhall Rd. NW2—35Za 60
Rockhampton Clo. SE27 —63Qb 126
Rockhampton Rd. SE27—63Qb 126
Rockhampton Rd. S Croy —79Ub 147
Rock Hill. SE26—63Vb 127
Rock Hill. Orp—79Dd 152
Rockingham Av. Horn—30Kd 49
Rockingham Clo. SW15—56Va 102
Rockingham Clo. Uxb—39L 55
Rockingham Pde. Uxb—38L 55
Rockingham Rd. Uxb—39K 55
Rockingham St. SE1 —48Sb 83 (4D 206)
Rockland Rd. SW15—56Ab 102
Rocklands Dri. Stan—26Ka 38
Rockley Rd. W14—47Za 80
Rockliffe Av. K Lan—2Q 4
Rockmount Rd. SE18—50Xc 87
Rockmount Rd. SE19—65Tb 127
★Rock Rd. Sev—92Be
Rockshaw Rd. Red—99Lb 180
Rocks La. SW13—55Wa 102
Rock St. N4—33Qb 62
Rockware Av. Gnfd—39Fa 58
Rockways. Barn—16Va 22
Rockwell Rd. Dag—36Dd 68
Rockwood Pl. W12—47Ya 80
Rocky La. Red—100Hb 179
Rocliffe St. N1—40Rb 63 (2C 194)
Rocombe Cres. SE23—59Yb 106
Rocque La. SE3—55Hc 107
Rodborough Rd. NW11—32Cb 61
Roden Gdns. Croy—72Ub 147
Rodenhurst Rd. SW4—58Lb 104
Roden St. N7—34Pb 62
Roden St. Ilf—34Qc 66
Roderick Rd. NW3—35Hb 61
Rodgers Ct. Swan—70Jd 132
Roding Av. Wfd G—23Nc 46
★Roding Dri. Brtwd—9Vd
Roding La. Buck H & Chig —18Nc to 19Sc 28
Roding La. N. Wfd G—26Mc 45
Roding La. S. Ilf & Wfd G—28Mc 45
Roding Rd. E5—35Zb 64
Roding Rd. E6—43Rc 86
Roding Rd. Lou—15Nc 28
Rodings, The. Upm—30Td 50
Rodings, The. Wfd G—23Lc 45
Roding Trading Est. Bark —38Rc 66
Roding View. Buck H—18Mc 27
Roding Way. Rain—40Md 69
Rodmarton St. W1 —43Hb 81 (1G 197)
Rodmell Slope. N12—22Bb 41
Rodmere St. SE10—50Gc 85
Rodmill La. SW2—59Nb 104
Rodney Clo. Croy—74Rb 147
Rodney Clo. N Mald—71Ua 144
Rodney Clo. Pinn—31Aa 57
Rodney Clo. W on T—74Y 141
Rodney Ct. W9—(5A 190)
Rodney Ct. Barn—13Bb 23
Rodney Gdns. Pinn—29X 37
Rodney Gdns. W Wick—77Jc 149 (in two parts)
Rodney Grn. W on T—75Y 141
Rodney Pl. E17—26Ac 44
Rodney Pl. SE17—49Sb 83 (5E 206)
Rodney Pl. SW19—67Eb 125
Rodney Rd. E11—28Kc 45
Rodney Rd. SE17 —49Tb 83 (5E 206)
Rodney Rd. Mitc—69Gb 125
Rodney Rd. N Mald—71Ua 144
Rodney Rd. Twic—58Ca 99
Rodney Rd. W on T—75Y 141
Rodney St. N1—40Pb 62 (1J 193)
Rodney Way. Romf—25Dd 48
Rodney Way. Slou—53G 96
Rodona Rd. Wey—83T 158
Rodsley St. SE1—51Wb 105
Rodway Rd. SW15—59Wa 102
Rodway Rd. Brom—67Kc 129
Rodwell Clo. Ruis—32Y 57
Rodwell Rd. SE22—58Vb 105
Roebourne Way. E16—46Qc 86
Roebuck Clo. Asht—92Na 177
Roebuck Clo. Felt—63X 121
Roebuck Grn. Slou—6C 72
Roebuck La. N17—23Vb 43
Roebuck La. Buck H—17Lc 27
Roebuck Rd. Chess—78Qa 143
Roebuck Rd. Ilf—23Xc 47
Roedean Av. Enf—11Yb 26
Roedean Clo. Enf—11Yb 26
Roedean Cres. SW15—58Ua 102
Roe End. NW9—28Sa 39
Roe Grn. NW9—29Sa 39
Roehampton Clo. SW15 —56Wa 102
Roehampton Clo. Grav—9G 114
Roehampton Dri. Chst—65Sc 130
Roehampton Ga. SW15—58Ua 102
Roehampton High St. SW15 —59Wa 102
Roehampton La. SW15—56Wa 102
Roehampton Vale. SW15 —62Va 124
Roe La. NW9—28Ra 39
Roe Way. Wall—79Nb 146
Rofant Rd. N'wd—23U 36
Roffe's La. Cat—96Tb 181
Roffey Clo. Purl—88Rb 165
Roffey St. E14—47Ec 84
Roffords. Wok—5E 188
Rogers Clo. Borwd—16Ma 21
Rogers Clo. Cat—94Xb 181
Rogers Clo. Coul—90Rb 165
Rogers Gdns. Dag—36Cd 68
Roger Simmons Ct. Lea—96Ba 175
Rogers La. Slou—8K 53
Rogers La. Warl—90Bc 166
Rogers Rd. E16—44Hc 85
Rogers Rd. SW17—63Fb 125
Rogers Rd. Dag—36Cd 68
Rogers Rd. Grays—49Ge 91
Rogers Ruff. N'wd—25S 36
Roger St. WC1—42Pb 82 (6J 193)
Rogers Wlk. N12—20Db 23
Rogers Wood La. Long, Dart —77Wd 154
Rojack Rd. SE23—60Zb 106
Rokeby Ct. Wok—5C 188
Rokeby Gdns. Wfd G—25Jc 45
Rokeby Pl. SW20—66Xa 124
Rokeby Rd. SE4—54Bc 106
Rokeby Rd. Harr—27Fa 38
Rokeby St. E15—39Gc 65
Roke Clo. Kenl—86Sb 165
Roke Lodge Rd. Kenl—85Rb 165
Roke Rd. Kenl—87Sb 165
Roker Pk. Av. Uxb—35N 55
Rokesby Clo. Well—54Tc 108
Rokesby Pl. Wemb—36Ma 59
Rokesby Rd. Slou—1D 72
Rokesly Av. N8—29Nb 42
Roland Gdns. SW7 —50Eb 81 (7A 202)
Roland Rd. E17—28Fc 45
Roland Way. SE17—50Tb 83
Roland Way. SW7 —50Eb 81 (7A 202)
Roland Way. Wor Pk—75Va 144
Roles Gro. Romf—28Zc 47
Rolfe Clo. Barn—14Gb 23
Rolinsden Way. Kes—78Mc 149
Rollesby Rd. Chess—79Qa 143
Rollesby Way. SE28—44Yc 87
Rolleston Av. Orp—72Rc 150
Rolleston Rd. Orp—73Rc 150
Rolleston Rd. S Croy—80Tb 147
Roll Gdns. Ilf—29Qc 46
Rollins St. SE15—51Yb 106
Rollit Cres. Houn—57Ca 99
Rollit St. N7—36Qb 62
Rollo Rd. Swan—66Hd 132
Rolls Bldgs. EC4—44Qb 82 (2A 200)
Rollscourt Av. SE24—57Sb 105
Rolls Pk. Av. E4—22Cc 44
Rolls Pk. Rd. E4—22Dc 44
Rolls Pas. EC4—(2K 199)
Rolls Rd. SE1—50Vb 83 (7K 207)
Rolt St. SE8—51Ac 106
Rolvenden Gdns. Brom—66Mc 129
Roman Clo. W3—47Ra 79
Roman Clo. Felt—57Y 99
Roman Clo. Rain—40Fd 68
Roman Clo. Uxb—25K 35
Roman Gdns. K Lan—2R 4
Roman Ho. EC2—(1E 200)
Romanhurst Av. Brom—70Gc 129
Romanhurst Gdns. Brom —70Gc 129
Roman Industrial Est. Croy —73Ub 147
Roman Rise. SE19—65Tb 127
Roman Rd.—41Yb 84
E2 1-229 & 2-256
E3 remainder
Roman Rd. E6—42Nc 86
Roman Rd. N10—24Kb 42
Roman Rd. W4—49Va 80
Roman Rd. Brtwd—13Ee 33
Roman Rd. Grav—62Ee 135
Roman Rd. Ilf—37Rc 66
Romans Way. Wok—87J 157
Roman Villa Rd. Dart & S Dar, Dart—64Sd 134
Roman Way. N7—37Pb 62
Roman Way. SE15—52Yb 106
Roman Way. Croy—75Rb 147
Roman Way. Enf—15Vb 25
Romany Gdns. E17—25Ac 44
Romany Gdns. Sutt—73Cb 145
Romany Rise. Orp—74Sc 150
Romany Rd. Wok—3A 188
Roma Rd. E17—27Ac 44
Romberg Rd. SW17—62Jb 126
Romborough Gdns. SE13 —57Ec 106
Romborough Way. SE13 —57Ec 106
Rom Cres. Romf—31Hd 68
Romeland. Wal A—5Ec 12
Romero Sq. SE3—56Lc 107
Romeyn Rd. SW16—62Pb 126
Romford Rd.—37Gc 65
E15 1-191 & 2-166a
E7 193-607 & 168-544
E12 remainder
Romford Rd. Chig & Romf —20Xc 29
Romford Rd. S Ock—45Sd 90
Romford St. E1—43Xb 83
Romilly Dri. Wat—21Aa 37
Romilly Rd. N4—33Rb 63
Romilly St. W1—45Mb 82 (4E 198)
Romily Ct. SW6—54Bb 103
Rommany Rd. SE27—63Tb 127
Romney Chase. Horn—30Qd 49
Romney Clo. N17—25Xb 43
Romney Clo. NW11—32Eb 61
Romney Clo. SE14—52Yb 106
Romney Clo. Ashf—64S 120
Romney Clo. Chess—77Na 143
Romney Clo. Harr—31Ca 57
Romney Dri. Brom—66Mc 129
Romney Dri. Harr—31Ca 57
Romney Gdns. Bexh—53Bd 109

Romney Lock Rd.—Runnel Field

Romney Lock Rd. Wind—2H 95
Romney Rd. SE10—51Fc 107
Romney Rd. Grav—2A 136
Romney Rd. Hay—40T 56
Romney Rd. N Mald—72Ta 143
Romney St. SW1
—48Nb 82 (4F 205)
Romney St. Sev—83Qd 171
Romola Rd. SE24—60Rb 105
Romsey Clo. Slou—48B 74
Romsey Dri. Slou—4H 53
Romsey Gdns. Dag—39Zc 67
Romsey Rd. W13—45Ja 78
Romsey Rd. Dag—39Zc 67
Rom Valley Way. Romf—31Gd 68
Ronald Av. E15—41Gc 85
Ronald Clo. Beck—71Bc 148
Ronald Rd. Romf—25Qd 49
Ronalds Rd. N5—36Qb 62
Ronalds Rd. Brom—67Jc 129
Ronaldstone Rd. Sidc—58Uc 108
Ronald St. E1—44Yb 84
Rona Rd. NW3—35Jb 62
Rondu Rd. NW2—36Ab 60
Ronelean Rd. Surb—76Pa 143
Roneo Corner. Horn—32Hd 68
Ronfearn Av. Orp—71Zc 151
Ronneby Clo. Wey—76U 140
Ronson Way. Lea—93Ja 176
Ronver Rd. SE12—60Hc 107
Rood La. EC3—45Ub 83 (4H 201)
Rookby Ct. N21—19Rb 25
Rook Clo. Rain—38Jd 68
Rookdean. Sev—94Ed 186
Rookeries Clo. Felt—62Y 121
Rookery Clo. NW9—29Va 40
Rookery Clo. Lea—96Ga 176
Rookery Clo. Stanf—2K 93
Rookery Cres. Dag—38Dd 68
Rookery Dri. Chst—67Qc 130
Rookery Gdns. Orp—71Yc 151
Rookery Hill. Asht—90Qa 161
Rookery La. Brom—72Mc 149
Rookery Rd. SW4—56Lb 104
Rookery Rd. Orp—82Pc 168
Rookery Rd. Stai—64K 119
Rookery, The. Grays—51Wd 112
Rookery View. Grays—50Fe 91
Rookery Way. NW9—29Va 40
Rookery Way. Tad—99Bb 179
Rookesley Rd. Orp—73Zc 151
Rooke Way. SE10—50Hc 85
Rookfield Av. N10—28Lb 42
Rookfield Clo. N10—28Lb 42
Rook La. Cat—96Qb 180
Rook La. Cat—97Pb 180
Rookley Clo. Sutt—81Db 163
Rooks Hill. Rick—14M 17
Rooksmead Rd. Sun—68W 120
Rookstone Rd. SW17—64Hb 125
Rook Wlk. E6—44Mc 85
Rookwood Av. Lou—13Sc 28
Rookwood Av. N Mald—70Wa 124
Rookwood Av. Wall—77Mb 146
Rookwood Clo. Grays—50De 91
Rookwood Clo. Red—100Kb 180
Rookwood Gdns. E4—19Hc 27
Rookwood Gdns. Lou—13Sc 28
Rookwood Rd. N16—31Wb 63
Roosevelt Way. Dag—37Fd 68
Ropemaker Rd. SE16—48Ac 84
Ropemakers' Fields. E14—45Bc 84
Ropemaker St. EC2
—43Tb 83 (7F 195)
Roper La. SE1—47Ub 83 (2J 207)
Ropers Av. E4—22Dc 44
Roper St. SE9—58Pc 108
Ropers Wlk. SW2—59Qb 104
Roper Way. Mitc—68Jb 126
Ropery St. E3—42Bc 84
Rope Wlk. Sun—69Y 121
Rope Wlk. Gdns. E1—44Wb 83
Rope Yd. Rails. SE18—48Rc 86
Ropley St. E2—40Wb 63
Rosa Alba M. N5—35Sb 63
Rosa Av. Ashf—63Q 120
Rosaline Rd. SW6—52Ab 102
Rosamond St. SE26—62Xb 127
Rosary Clo. Houn—54Aa 99
Rosary Ct. Pot B—2Db 9
Rosary Gdns. SW7
—49Eb 81 (6A 202)
Rosary Gdns. Ashf—63R 120
Rosaville Rd. SW6—52Bb 103
Rosbery Rd. N9—20Wb 25
Roscoe St. EC1—42Sb 83 (6E 194)
Roscoff Clo. Edgw—25Sa 39
Roseacre Clo. W13—43Ka 78
Roseacre Clo. Horn—31Pd 69
Roseacre Clo. Shep—71Q 140
Roseacre Rd. Well—55Xc 109
Rose All. EC2—(1J 201)
Rose All. SE1—46Sb 83 (6E 200)
Rose & Crown Ct. EC2—(2D 200)
Rose & Crown Pas. Iswth
—53Ja 100
Rose & Crown Yd. SW1
—46Lb 82 (7C 198)
Roseary Clo. W Dray—49M 75
Rose Av. E18—26Kc 45
Rose Av. Grav—10G 114
Rose Av. Mitc—67Hb 125
Rose Av. Mord—71Eb 145
Rosebank. SE20—66Xb 127
Rose Bank. Brtwd—20Zd 33
Rosebank. Eps—86Sa 161
Rosebank. Wal A—5Gc 13
Rosebank Av. Horn—36Ld 69
Rosebank Av. Wemb—35Ha 58
Rose Bank Cotts. Wok—94A 172
Rosebank Gdns. E3—40Bc 64
Rosebank Gro. E17—27Bc 44
Rosebank Rd. E17—30Dc 44
Rosebank Rd. W7—47Ga 78
Rosebank Vs. E17—28Cc 44
Rosebank Wlk. NW1—38Mb 62
Rosebank Way. W3—44Ta 79
Roseberry Av. N Mald—68Va 124
Roseberry Clo. Upm—30Vd 50
Roseberry Ct. Wat—11W 18
Roseberry Gdns. N4—30Rb 43
Roseberry Gdns. Dart—59Ld 111
Roseberry Gdns. Orp—76Uc 150
Roseberry Gdns. Upm—30Ud 50
Roseberry Pl. E8—37Vb 63
Roseberry Rd. SW2—58Nb 104
Roseberry St. SE16—49Xb 83
Rosebery Av. E12—37Nc 66
Rosebery Av. EC1
—42Qb 82 (6K 193)
Rosebery Av. N17—26Wb 43
Rosebery Av. Eps—86Ua 162
Rosebery Av. Harr—35Aa 57
Rosebery Av. Sidc—59Uc 108
Rosebery Av. T Hth—68Sb 127
Rosebery Clo. Mord—72Za 144
Rosebery Cres. Wok—92B 172
Rosebery Gdns. N8—29Nb 42
Rosebery Gdns. W13—44Ja 78
Rosebery Gdns. Sutt—77Db 145
Rosebery M. N10—26Lb 42
Rosebery Rd. N10—26Lb 42
Rosebery Rd. Bush, Wat—17Da 19
Rosebery Rd. Eps—91Ta 177
Rosebery Rd. Grays—51Ae 113
Rosebery Rd. Houn—57Ea 100
Rosebery Rd. King—68Ra 123
Rosebery Rd. Sutt—79Bb 145
Rosebery Sq. EC1—(6K 193)
Rosebery Sq. King—68Ra 123
Rosebine Av. Twic—59Fa 100
Rose Briar Clo. Wok—88J 157
Rosebriars. Cat—92Ub 181
Rosebriar Wlk. Wat—8V 4
Rosebury Rd. SW6—54Db 103
Rosebury Vale. Ruis—33W 56
Rosebushes. Eps—88Ya 162
Rose Ct. Pinn—27Y 37
Rosecourt Rd. Croy—72Pb 146
Rosecroft Av. NW3—34Cb 61
Rosecroft Clo. Orp—72Yc 151
Rosecroft Dri. Wat—8U 4
Rosecroft Gdns. NW2—34Wa 60
Rosecroft Gdns. Twic—60Fa 100
Rosecroft Rd. S'hall—42Ca 77
Rosecroft Wlk. Pinn—29Z 37
Rosecroft Wlk. Wemb—36Ma 59
Rosedale. Asht—90La 160
Rose Dale. Orp—75Rc 150
Rosedale Av. Hay—43T 76
Rosedale Av. Wal X—1Vb 11
Rosedale Clo. SE2—48Xc 87
Rosedale Clo. W7—47Ha 78
Rosedale Clo. Dart—58Nd 111
Rosedale Clo. St Alb—2Aa 5
Rosedale Clo. Stan—23Ka 38
Rosedale Ct. N5—35Rb 63
Rosedale Gdns. Dag—38Xc 67
Rosedale Rd. E7—36Lc 65
Rosedale Rd. SE21—60Sb 105
Rosedale Rd. Dag—38Xc 67
Rosedale Rd. Eps—78Wa 144
Rosedale Rd. Grays—50Fe 91
Rosedale Rd. Rich—56Na 101
Rosedale Rd. Romf—27Ed 48
Rosedale Way. Wal X—1Wb 11
Rosedene Av. SW16—62Pb 126
Rosedene Av. Croy—73Nb 146
Rosedene Av. Gnfd—41Ca 77
Rosedene Av. Mord—71Cb 145
Rosedene Ct. Dart—59Ld 111
Rosedene Ct. Ruis—32U 56
Rosedene Gdns. Ilf—28Qc 46
Rosedene Ter. E10—33Dc 64
Rosedew Rd. W6—51Za 102
Rose End. Wor Pk—74Za 144
Rosefield. Sev—96Jd 186
Rosefield Gdns. E14—45Cc 84
Rosefield Gdns. Cher—79F 138
Rosefield Rd. Stai—63J 119
Rose Garden Clo. Edgw—23Na 39
Rose Gdns. W5—48Ma 79
Rose Gdns. Felt—61W 120
Rose Gdns. S'hall—42Ca 77
Rose Gdns. Wat—15W 18
Rosegarth. Grav—7A 136
Rose Glen. NW9—28Ta 39
Rose Glen. Romf—32Gd 68
Rosehart M. W11—44Cb 81
Rosehatch Av. Romf—27Zc 47
Rose Heath Rd. Houn—57Ba 99
Rosehill. Esh—79Ja 142
Rosehill. Hmptn—67Ca 121
Rose Hill. Sutt—76Db 145
Rosehill Av. Sutt—74Eb 145
Rosehill Av. Wok—4F 188
Rosehill Ct. Slou—8L 73
Rosehill Gdns. Abb L, Wat—4S 4
Rosehill Gdns. Gnfd—36Ha 58
Rosehill Gdns. Sutt—75Db 145
Rosehill Pk. W. Sutt—74Eb 145
Rosehill Rd. SW18—58Eb 103
Rosehill Rd. West—89Lc 167
Roseland Clo. N17—24Tb 43
Rose La. Romf—27Zc 47
Rose La. Wok—93L 173
Rose Lawn. Bush, Wat—18Ea 20
Roseleigh Av. N5—35Rb 63
Roseleigh Clo. Twic—58Ma 101
Rosemary Av. N3—26Db 41
Rosemary Av. N9—18Xb 25
Rosemary Av. E Mol—69Ca 121
Rosemary Av. Enf—11Ub 25
Rosemary Av. Houn—54Z 99
Rosemary Av. Romf—27Hd 48
Rosemary Clo. S Ock—41Yd 90
Rosemary Clo. Uxb—43Q 76
Rosemary Dri. Ilf—29Mc 45
Rosemary Gdns. Chess—77Na 143
Rosemary Gdns. Dag—32Bd 67
Rosemary La. SW14—55Sa 101
Rosemary La. Egh—69D 118
Rosemary La. Sev—80Fe 155
Rosemary Rd. SE15—52Vb 105
Rosemary Rd. Well—53Vc 109
Rosemary St. N1—39Tb 63
Rosemead. NW9—31Va 60
Rose Mead. Pot B—2Eb 9
Rosemead Av. Felt—61V 120
Rosemead Av. Mitc—69Lb 126
Rosemead Av. Wemb—36Na 59
Rosemead Gdns. Brtwd—14Fe 33
Rosemont Av. N12—23Eb 41
Rosemont Rd. NW3—37Eb 61
Rosemont Rd. W3—45Ra 79
Rosemont Rd. N Mald—69Sa 123
Rosemont Rd. Rich—58Na 101
Rosemont Rd. Wemb—39Na 59
Rosemoor St. SW3
—49Hb 81 (6F 203)
Rosemount Av. Wey—85J 157
Rosemount Dri. Brom—70Pc 130
Rosemount Rd. W13—44Ja 78
Rosenau Cres. SW11—53Hb 103
Rosenau Rd. SW11—53Gb 103
Rosendale Rd.—59Sb 105
SE21 1-245 & 2-248
SE24 remainder
Roseneath Av. N21—18Rb 25
Roseneath Clo. Orp—80Yc 151
Roseneath Rd. SW11—58Jb 104
Roseneath Wlk. Enf—14Ub 25
Rosen's Wlk. Edgw—20Ra 21
Rosenthal Rd. SE6—58Dc 106
Rosenthorpe Rd. SE15—57Zb 106
Roserton St. E14—47Ec 84
Rosery, The. Croy—72Zb 148
Rosery, The. Egh—68G 118
Roses La. Wind—4B 94
Roses, The. Wfd G—24Hc 45
Rose St. WC2—45Nb 82 (4F 199)
Rose St. Grav—58De 113
Rosetta Clo. SW8—52Nb 104
Rose Valley. Brtwd—20Yd 32
Roseveare Rd. SE12—63Lc 129
Rose Vs. Dart—59Rd 111
Roseville Av. Houn—57Ca 99
Roseville Rd. Hay—50W 76
Rosevine Rd. SW20—67Ya 124
Rose Wlk. Purl—83Mb 164
Rose Wlk. Slou—3F 72
Rose Wlk. Surb—71Ra 143
Rose Wlk. W Wick—75Ec 148
Rose Wlk., The. Rad—9Ka 6
Rosewarne Clo. Wok—6D 188
Rose Way. SE12—57Jc 107
Roseway. SE21—58Tb 105
Rosewood. Dart—63Gd 132
Rosewood Av. Gnfd—36Ja 58
Rosewood Av. Horn—36Jd 68
Rosewood Clo. Sidc—62Yc 131
Rosewood Ct. Brom—67Mc 129
Rosewood Dri. Enf—7Qb 10
Rosewood Dri. Shep—71P 139
Rosewood Gdns. SE13—54Ec 106
Rosewood Gro. Sutt—75Eb 145
Rosewood Sq. W12—44Wa 80
Rosewood Way. Slou—6G 52
Rosher Clo. E15—38Fc 65
Rosina St. E9—37Zb 64
Roskell Rd. SW15—55Za 102
Rosken Gdns. Slou—10F 52
Roslin Rd. W3—48Ra 79
Roslin Way. Brom—64Jc 129
Roslyn Clo. Mitc—68Fb 125
Roslyn Gdns. Romf—26Hd 48
Roslyn Rd. N15—29Tb 43
Rosmead Rd. W11—45Ab 80
Rosoman Pl. EC1
—42Qb 82 (5A 194)
Rosoman St. EC1
—41Qb 82 (4A 194)
Rossall Clo. Horn—30Jd 48
Rossall Cres. NW10—41Pa 79
Ross Av. NW7—22Ab 40
Ross Av. Dag—32Bd 67
Ross Clo. Harr—24Ea 38
Ross Clo. Hay—49T 76
Ross Ct. NW9—27Ua 40
Ross Cres. Wat—7W 4
Rossdale. Sutt—78Gb 145
Rossdale Dri. N9—16Yb 26
Rossdale Dri. NW9—32Sa 59
Rossdale Rd. SW15—56Ya 102
Rosse M. SE3—53Kc 107
Rossendale St. E5—33Xb 63
Rossendale Way. NW1—38Lb 62
Rossindel Rd. Houn—57Ca 99
Rossington Av. Borwd—10Na 7
Rossington St. E5—33Wb 63
Rossiter Clo. Slou—49A 74
Rossiter Rd. SW12—60Kb 104
Rossland Clo. Bexh—57Dd 110
Rosslyn Av. E4—19Hc 27
Rosslyn Av. SW13—55Ua 102
Rosslyn Av. Barn—16Gb 23
Rosslyn Av. Dag—31Bd 67
Rosslyn Av. Felt—58W 98
Rosslyn Av. Romf—26Nd 49
Rosslyn Clo. Hay—43T 76
Rosslyn Clo. W Wick—76Hc 149
Rosslyn Ct. Wok—6D 188
Rosslyn Cres. Harr—28Ha 38
Rosslyn Cres. Wemb—35Na 59
Rosslyn Cres. N. Harr—28Ha 38
Rosslyn Cres. S. Harr—29Ha 38
Rosslyn Hill. NW3—35Fb 61
Rosslyn M. NW3—35Fb 61
Rosslyn Pk. M. NW3—36Fb 61
Rosslyn Rd. E17—28Ec 44
Rosslyn Rd. Bark—38Tc 66
Rosslyn Rd. Twic—58La 100
Rosslyn Rd. Wat—13X 19
Rossmore Rd. NW1
—42Gb 81 (6E 190)
Ross Pde. Wall—79Kb 146
Ross Rd. SE25—69Tb 127
Ross Rd. Cob—85Y 159
Ross Rd. Dart—58Jd 110
Ross Rd. Twic—60Da 99
Ross Rd. Wall—78Lb 146
Ross Way. SE9—55Nc 108
Ross Way. N'wd—21V 36
Rossway Dri. Bush, Wat—15Fa 20
Rosswood Gdns. Wall—79Lb 146
Rostella Rd. SW17—63Fb 125
Rostrevor Av. N15—30Vb 43
Rostrevor Gdns. Hay—46U 76
Rostrevor Gdns. Iver—40F 54
Rostrevor Gdns. S'hall—50Aa 77
Rostrevor M. SW6—53Bb 103
Rostrevor Rd. SW6—53Bb 103
Rostrevor Rd. SW19—64Cb 125
Roswell Clo. Wal X—2Ac 12
Rotary St. SE1—48Rb 83 (3C 206)
Rothbury Av. Rain—43Kd 89
Rothbury Gdns. Iswth—52Ja 100
Rothbury Rd. E9—38Bc 64
Rothbury Wlk. N17—24Wb 43
Roth Dri. Brtwd—19De 33
Rother Clo. Wat—6Y 5
Rotherfield Rd. Cars—78Jb 146
Rotherfield Rd. Enf—9Zb 12
Rotherfield St. N1—38Sb 63
Rotherhill Av. SW16—65Mb 126
Rotherhithe New Rd. SE16
—50Xb 83
Rotherhithe Old Rd. SE16—49Zb 84
Rotherhithe St. SE16—47Yb 84
Rotherhithe Tunnel. SE16
—47Yb 84
Rothermere Rd. Croy—78Pb 146
Rotherwick Hill. W5—42Pa 79
Rotherwick Rd. NW11—31Cb 61
Rotherwood Rd. SW15—55Za 102
Rothesay Av. SW20—68Ab 124
Rothesay Av. Gnfd—37Ea 58
Rothesay Av. Rich—56Ra 101
Rothesay Rd. SE25—70Tb 127
Rothsay Rd. E7—38Lc 65
Rothsay St. SE1—48Ub 83 (3H 207)
Rothschild Rd. W4—48Sa 79
Rothschild St. SE27—63Rb 127
Roth Wlk. N7—33Pb 62
Rothwell Gdns. Dag—38Yc 67
Rothwell Rd. Dag—39Yc 67
Rothwell St. NW1—39Hb 61
Rotten Row. NW3—32Eb 61
Rouel Rd. SE16—48Wb 83
Rouge La. Grav—10D 114
Rougemont Av. Mord—72Cb 145
Roughets La. Red—100Ub 181
Roughlands. Wok—87G 156
Rough Rd. Wok—10A 188
Roughs, The. N'wd—20U 18
Roughwood Clo. Wat—10U 4
Roughwood La. Chal—16A 16
Roundacre. SW19—61Za 124
Round Ash Way. Long, Dart
—72Ae 155
Roundaway Rd. Ilf—26Pc 46
Round Gro. Croy—73Zb 148
Roundhay Clo. SE23—61Zb 128
Roundhedge Way. Enf—10Pb 10
Round Hill. SE26—62Yb 128
Roundhill. Wok—91D 172
Roundhill Dri. Enf—14Pb 24
Roundhill Dri. Wok—90D 156
Roundhills. Wal A—6Gc 13
Roundhill Way. Cob—83Da 159
Roundmead Av. Lou—13Qc 28
Roundmead Clo. Lou—13Qc 28
Roundmoor Dri. Wal X—1Ac 12
Round Oak Rd. Wey—77P 139
Round St. Grav—9E 136
Roundtable Rd. Brom—62Hc 129
Roundthorn Way. Wok—4C 188
Roundtree Rd. Wemb—36Ka 58
Roundway. Egh—64E 118
Roundway. West—88Lc 167
Roundways. Ruis—34V 56
Roundway, The. N17—25Tb 43
Roundway, The. Esh—79Ha 142
Roundway, The. Wat—16V 18
Roundwood. Chst—68Rc 130
Roundwood Av. Brtwd—18Ce 33
Roundwood Clo. Ruis—31T 56
Roundwood Gro. Brtwd—17De 33
Roundwood Rd. NW10—37Va 60
Roundwood View. Bans
—87Za 162
Roundwood Way. Bans—87Za 162
Rounton Dri. Wat—10V 4
Rounton Rd. E3—42Cc 84
Rounton Rd. Wal A—5Gc 13
Roupell Rd. SW2—60Pb 104
Roupell St. SE1—46Qb 82 (7A 200)
Rousden St. NW1—38Lb 62
Rousebarn La. Rick—10P 3
Rouse Gdns. SE21—63Ub 127
Rous Rd. Buck H—18Nc 28
Routh Rd. SW18—59Gb 103
Routledge Clo. N19—32Mb 62
Rover Av. Ilf—23Vc 47
Rowallan Rd. SW6—52Ab 102
Rowan Av. E4—23Bc 44
Rowan Av. Egh—64E 118
Rowan Clo. SW16—67Lb 126
Rowan Clo. W5—47Na 79
Rowan Clo. N Mald—68Ua 124
Rowan Clo. St Alb—3Ca 5
Rowan Clo. Wemb—34Ja 58
Rowan Cres. SW16—67Lb 126
Rowan Cres. Dart—60Ld 111
Rowan Dri. NW9—27Wa 40
Rowan Gdns. Croy—76Vb 147
Rowan Grn. Wey—77T 140
Rowan Grn. E. Brtwd—20Be 33
Rowan Grn. W. Brtwd—20Be 33
Rowan Gro. Coul—93Kb 180
Rowanhurst Dri. Slou—6G 52
Rowan Pl. Hay—45V 76
Rowan Rd. SW16—68Lb 126
Rowan Rd. W6—49Za 80
Rowan Rd. Bexh—55Ad 109
Rowan Rd. Bren—52Ka 100
Rowan Rd. S Ock—41Yd 90
Rowan Rd. Swan—69Fd 132
Rowan Rd. W Dray—49M 75
Rowans, The. N13—20Sb 25
Rowans, The. Sun—64V 120
Rowantree Clo. N21—18Tb 25
Rowantree Rd. N21—18Tb 25
Rowantree Rd. Enf—12Rb 25
Rowan Wlk. N2—29Eb 41
Rowan Wlk. N19—33Lb 62
Rowan Wlk. W10—42Ab 80
Rowan Wlk. Brom—76Pc 150
Rowan Wlk. Horn—28Md 49
Rowanway. Lou—14Pc 28
Rowan Way. Romf—27Yc 47
Rowan Way. Slou—3F 72
Rowben Clo. N20—18Db 23
Rowberry Clo. SW6—52Ya 102
Rowcross Pl. SE1—(7K 207)
Rowcross St. SE1
—50Vb 83 (7K 207)
Rowdell Rd. N'holt—39Ca 57
Rowden Rd. E4—23Dc 44
Rowden Rd. Beck—67Ac 128
Rowden Rd. Eps—77Ra 143
Rowditch La. SW11—54Jb 104
Rowdon Av. NW10—38Xa 60
Rowdow. Sev—87Nd 171
Rowdow La. Sev—85Md 171
Rowdown Cres. Croy—81Fc 167
Rowdowns Rd. Dag—39Bd 67
Rowe Gdns. Bark—40Vc 67
Rowe La. E9—36Yb 64
Rowena Cres. SW11—54Gb 103
Rowe Wlk. Harr—34Ca 57
Rowfant Rd. SW17—60Jb 104
Rowhedge. Brtwd—20De 33
Row Hill. Wey—79H 139
Rowhill Rd. E5—35Xb 63
Rowhill Rd. Dart & Swan
—65Hd 132
Rowhurst Av. Lea—89Ha 160
Rowington Clo. W2—43Db 81
Rowland Av. Harr—27La 38
Rowland Clo. Wind—5B 94
Rowland Ct. E16—42Hc 85
Rowland Cres. Chig—21Uc 46
Rowland Gro. SE26—62Xb 127
Rowland Hill Av. N17—24Sb 43
Rowland Hill St. NW3—36Gb 61
Rowlands Av. Pinn—23Ca 37
Rowlands Clo. NW7—24Wa 40
Rowlands Clo. Wal X—2Zb 12
Rowlands Fields. Wal X—2Zb 12
Rowlands Rd. Dag—33Bd 67
Rowland Wlk. Hav, Romf—20Gd 30
Rowland Way. SW19—67Db 125
Rowland Way. Ashf—66S 120
Rowlatt Clo. Dart—63Ld 133
Rowlatt Rd. Dart—63Ld 133
Rowley Av. Sidc—59Xc 109
Rowley Clo. Wat—16Aa 19
Rowley Clo. Wemb—38Pa 59
Rowley Gdns. N4—31Sb 63
Rowley Gdns. Wal X—1Zb 12
Rowley Grn. Rd. Barn—15Wa 22
Rowley Industrial Pk. W3
—48Ra 79
Rowley La. Barn—14Ua 22
Rowley La. Borwd—11Ta 21
Rowley La. Slou—40A 54
Rowley La. Slou—9N 53
Rowley Rd. N15—29Sb 43
Rowley Rd. Grays—3C 92
Rowley Way. NW8—39Db 61
Rowlheys Pl. W Dray—48N 75
Rowlls Rd. King—69Pa 123
Rowney Gdns. Dag—37Yc 67
Rowney Rd. Dag—37Xc 67
Rowntree Path. SE28—46Xc 87
Rowntree Rd. Twic—60Ga 100
Rowse Clo. E15—39Ec 64
Rowsley Av. NW4—27Ya 40
Rowstock Gdns. N7—36Mb 62
Rowton Rd. SE18—52Sc 108
Rowtown. Wey—80H 139
Rowzill Rd. Swan—65Hd 132
Roxborough Av. Harr—31Ga 58
Roxborough Av. Iswth—52Ha 100
Roxborough Pk. Harr—31Ga 58
Roxborough Rd. Harr—30Fa 38
Roxbourne Clo. N'holt—37Aa 57
Roxburgh Av. Upm—34Sd 70
Roxburgh Rd. SE27—64Rb 127
Roxburn Way. Ruis—34V 56
Roxby Pl. SW6—51Cb 103
Roxeth Ct. Ashf—64Q 120
Roxeth Grn. Av. Harr—34Da 57
Roxeth Gro. Harr—35Da 57
Roxeth Hill. Harr—33Fa 58
Roxford Clo. Shep—71U 140
Roxley Rd. SE13—58Dc 106
Roxton Gdns. Croy—78Cc 148
Roxwell Clo. Slou—6C 72
Roxwell Rd. W12—47Wa 80
Roxwell Rd. Bark—40Wc 67
Roxwell Trading Pk. E10—31Ac 64
Roxwell Way. Wfd G—24Lc 45
Roxy Av. Romf—31Yc 67
Royal Arc. W1—(5B 198)
Royal Av. SW3—50Hb 81 (7F 203)
Royal Av. Wal X—5Ac 12
Royal Av. Wor Pk—75Ua 144
Royal Cir. SE27—62Qb 126
Royal Clo. Uxb—44P 75
Royal Clo. Wor Pk—75Ua 144
Royal College St. NW1
—38Lb 62 (1D 192)
Royal Cres. W11—46Za 80
Royal Cres. Ruis—35Aa 57
Royal Dri. Eps—90Xa 162
Royal Exchange Av. EC3—(3G 201)
Royal Exchange Bldgs. EC3
—(3G 201)
Royal Gdns. W7—48Ja 78
Royal Hill. SE10—52Ec 106
Royal Hospital Rd. SW3
—51Hb 103 (7G 203)
Royal La. Uxb & W Dray—43P 75
Royal London Est. N17—23Xb 43
Royal London Industrial Est.
NW10—40Ta 59
Royal Mint St. E1
—45Vb 83 (4K 201)
Royal Oak Hill. Sev—90Vc 169
Royal Oak Rd. E8—37Xb 63
Royal Oak Rd. Bexh—56Bd 109
Royal Oak Rd. Wok—6G 188
Royal Opera Arc. SW1
—46Mb 82 (6D 198)
Royal Pde. SE3—54Hc 107
Royal Pde. W5—41Na 79
Royal Pde. Chst—66Sc 130
Royal Pier Rd. Grav—8D 114
Royal Pl. SE10—52Ec 106
Royal Rd. E16—44Mc 85
Royal Rd. SE17—51Rb 105
Royal Rd. Dart—64Qd 133
Royal Rd. Sidc—62Zc 131
Royal Rd. Tedd—64Fa 122
Royal Route. Wemb—35Qa 59
Royal St. SE1—48Pb 82 (3J 205)
Royalty M. W1—(3D 198)
Royal Victoria Patriotic Building
SW18—58Fb 103
Royal Victor Pl. E3—40Zb 64
Royal Wlk. Wall—75Kb 146
Roycraft Av. Bark—40Vc 67
Roycroft Clo. E18—25Kc 45
Roycroft Clo. SW2—60Qb 104
Roydene Rd. SE18—51Uc 108
Roydon Clo. Lou—17Nc 28
Royds La. Brtwd—11Td 32
Roy Gdns. Ilf—28Uc 46
Roy Gro. Hmptn—65Da 121
Royle Clo. Ger X—24B 34
Royle Clo. Romf—29Kd 49
Royle Cres. W13—42Ja 78
Roy Rd. N'wd—24V 36
Royston Av. E4—22Cc 44
Royston Av. Sutt—76Fb 145
Royston Av. Wall—77Mb 146
Royston Av. Wey—84N 157
Royston Clo. Houn—53X 99
Royston Clo. W on T—74W 140
Royston Ct. SE24—58Sb 105
Royston Ct. Rich—53Pa 101
Royston Gdns. Ilf—30Mc 45
Royston Gro. Pinn—23Ca 37
Royston Pk. Rd. Pinn—23Ba 37
Royston Rd. SE20—67Zb 128
Royston Rd. Dart—58Hd 110
Royston Rd. Rich—57Na 101
Royston Rd. Romf—24Qd 49
Royston Rd. Wey—84N 157
Roystons, The. Surb—71Ra 143
Royston St. E2—40Yb 64
Royston Way. Slou—3B 72
Rozel Rd. SW4—55Lb 104
(in two parts)
Rubastic Rd. S'hall—48Y 77
Rubens Rd. N'holt—40Y 57
Rubens St. SE6—61Bc 128
Ruberoid Rd. Enf—13Bc 26
Ruby Rd. E17—27Cc 44
Ruby St. SE15—51Xb 105
Ruby Triangle. SE15—51Xb 105
Ruckholt Clo. E10—34Dc 64
Ruckholt Rd. E10—35Dc 64
Rucklidge Av. NW10—40Va 60
Rudall Cres. NW3—35Fb 61
Ruddlesway. Wind—3B 94
Ruddy Way. NW7—23Va 40
Ruden Way. Eps—88Xa 162
Rudge Rise. Wey—78H 139
Rudland Rd. Bexh—55Dd 110
Rudloe Rd. SW12—59Lb 104
Rudolph Rd. E13—40Hc 65
Rudolph Rd. NW6—40Cb 61
Rudolph Rd. Bush, Wat—16Ca 19
Rudost Pl. SE18—49Rc 86
Rudyard Gro. NW7—23Sa 39
Rue de St Lawrence. Wal A
—6Ec 12
Ruffets Wood. Grav—5E 136
Ruffetts Clo. S Croy—80Xb 147
Ruffetts, The. S Croy—80Xb 147
Ruffetts Way. Tad—90Ab 162
Rufford Clo. Harr—30Ja 38
Rufford St. N1—39Nb 62
Rufus Clo. Ruis—34Aa 57
Rufus St. N1—41Ub 83 (4H 195)
Rugby Av. N9—18Vb 25
Rugby Av. Gnfd—37Fa 58
Rugby Av. Wemb—36Ka 58
Rugby Clo. Harr—28Ga 38
Rugby Gdns. Dag—37Yc 67
Rugby La. Sutt—81Za 162
Rugby Rd. NW9—28Ra 39
Rugby Rd. W4—47Ua 80
Rugby Rd. Dag—38Xc 67
Rugby Rd. Twic & Iswth—58Ga 100
Rugby St. WC1—42Pb 82 (6H 193)
Rugby Way. Rick—15R 18
Rugged La. Wal A—5Mc 13
Ruggles-Brise Rd. Ashf—64M 119
Rugg St. E14—45Cc 84
Ruislip Clo. Gnfd—42Da 77
Ruislip Rd. N'holt & Gnfd
—39Y 57
Ruislip Rd. E.—42Fa 78
W13 1-33 & 80-82
W7 101-165
Gnfd remainder
Ruislip St. SW17—63Hb 125
Rumania Wlk. Grav—2H 137
Rumbold Rd. SW6—52Db 103
Rum Clo. E1—45Yb 84
Rumsey Clo. Hmptn—65Ba 121
Rumsey Rd. SW9—55Pb 104
Runbury Circ. NW9—33Ta 59
Runciman Clo. Orp—82Yc 169
Runcorn Clo. N17—28Xb 43
Runcorn Pl. W11—45Ab 80
Rundell Cres. NW4—29Xa 40
Runnel Field. Harr—34Ga 58

Runnemede Rd.—St George's Av.

Runnemede Rd. Egh—63C 118
(in two parts)
Running Horse Yd. Bren —51Na 101
Running Waters. Brtwd—21Ce 51
Runnymede. SW19—67Fb 125
Runnymede Clo. Twic—58Da 99
Runnymede Ct. Egh—63C 118
Runnymede Cres. SW16 —67Mb 126
Runnymede Gdns. Gnfd—40Ga 58
Runnymede Gdns. Twic—58Da 99
Runnymede Rd. Stanf—2L 93
Runnymede Rd. Twic—58Da 99
Runtley Wood La. Guild—97B 172
Runway, The. Ruis—36X 57
Rupack St. SE16—47Yb 84
Rupert Av. Wemb—36Na 59
Rupert Ct. W1—45Mb 82 (4D 198)
Rupert Gdns. SW9—54Rb 105
Rupert Rd. N19—34Mb 62
(in two parts)
Rupert Rd. NW6—40Bb 61
Rupert Rd. W4—48Ua 80
Rupert St. W1—45Mb 82 (4D 198)
Rural Av. Grav—9A 114
Rural Vale. Grav—9A 114
Rural Way. SW16—66Kb 126
Ruscoe Rd. E16—44Hc 85
Ruscombe Gdns. Slou—2L 95
Ruscombe Way. Felt—59V 98
Rusham Pk. Av. Egh—65B 118
Rusham Rd. SW12—58Hb 103
Rusham Rd. Egh—65B 118
Rushbrook Cres. E17—25Bc 44
Rushbrook Rd. SE9—61Sc 130
Rushcroft Rd. E4—24Dc 44
Rushcroft Rd. SW2—56Qb 104
Rushden Clo. SE19—66Tb 127
Rushdene. SE2—48Zc 87
Rushdene Av. Barn—17Gb 23
Rushdene Clo. N'holt—40Y 57
Rushdene Cres. N'holt—40X 57
Rushdene Rd. Brtwd—17Yd 32
Rushdene Rd. Pinn—30Z 37
Rushdene Wlk. West—89Mc 167
Rushden Gdns. NW7—23Ya 40
Rushden Gdns. Ilf—27Qc 46
Rushdon Clo. Grays—48Ce 91
Rushen Wlk. Cars—74Fb 145
Rushes Mead. Uxb—39L 55
Rushet Rd. Orp—68Wc 131
Rushett Clo. Th Dit—74Ka 142
Rushett La. Chess—83La 160
Rushett Rd. Th Dit—73Ka 142
Rushetts Rd. Sev—80Ud 154
Rushey Clo. N Mald—70Ta 123
Rushey Grn. SE6—59Dc 106
Rushey Hill. Enf—14Pb 24
Rushey Mead. SE4—57Cc 106
Rushfield. Pot B—5Za 8
Rushford Rd. SE4—58Bc 106
Rush Grn. Gdns. Romf—32Ed 68
Rush Grn. Rd. Romf—32Ed 68
Rushgrove Av. NW9—29Ua 40
Rushgrove Pde. NW9—29Ua 40
Rushgrove St. SE18—49Pc 86
Rush Hill Rd. SW11—55Jb 104
Rushleigh Av. Wal X—3Zb 12
Rushley Clo. Grays—46Fe 91
Rushley Clo. Kes—77Mc 149
Rushmead. E2—41Xb 83
Rushmead. Rich—62Ka 122
Rushmead Clo. Croy—77Vb 147
Rushmead Clo. Edgw—19Ra 21
Rushmere Av. Upm—34Sd 70
Rushmoor Clo. Pinn—28X 37
Rushmoor Clo. Rick—19M 17
Rushmore Clo. Brom—69Nc 130
Rushmore Ct. Wor Pk—75Wa 144
Rushmore Cres. E5—35Zb 64
Rushmore Hill. Orp & Sev —81Yc 169
Rushmore Rd. E5—35Yb 64
Rusholme Av. Dag—34Cd 68
Rusholme Gro. SE19—64Ub 127
Rusholme Rd. SW15—58Za 102
Rushout Av. Harr—30Ka 38
Rushton Av. Wat—7W 4
Rushton St. N1—40Tb 63 (1G 195)
Rushworth Av. NW4—27Wa 40
Rushworth Gdns. NW4—28Wa 40
Rushworth St. SE1 —47Rb 83 (1C 206)
Rushymead. Sev—90Qd 171
Ruskin Av. E12—37Nc 66
Ruskin Av. Felt—58V 98
Ruskin Av. Rich—52Qa 101
Ruskin Av. Upm—31Sd 70
Ruskin Av. Wal A—6Gc 13
Ruskin Av. Well—54Wc 109
Ruskin Clo. NW11—30Db 41
Ruskin Dri. Orp—76Uc 150
Ruskin Dri. Well—55Wc 109
Ruskin Dri. Wor Pk—75Xa 144
Ruskin Gdns. W5—42Ma 79
Ruskin Gdns. Harr—29Pa 39
Ruskin Gdns. Romf—24Kd 49
Ruskin Gro. Dart—57Qd 111
Ruskin Gro. Well—54Wc 109
Ruskin Pk. Ho. SE5—55Tb 105
Ruskin Rd. N17—25Vb 43
Ruskin Rd. Belv—49Cd 88
Ruskin Rd. Cars—78Jb 146
Ruskin Rd. Croy—75Rb 147
Ruskin Rd. Grays—9C 92
Ruskin Rd. Iswth—55Ha 100
Ruskin Rd. S'hall—45Aa 77
Ruskin Rd. Stai—65H 119
Ruskin Rd. Stanf—2L 93
Ruskin Wlk. N9—19Wb 25
Ruskin Wlk. SE24—57Sb 105
Ruskin Wlk. Brom—72Pc 150
Ruskin Way. SW19—67Fb 125
Rusland Av. Orp—76Tc 150
Rusland Pk. Rd. Harr—28Ga 38
Rusper Clo. Stan—21La 38
Rusper Rd. N22—27Sb 43
Rusper Rd. Dag—37Yc 67
Russell Av. N22—26Rb 43
Russell Clo. NW10—38Sa 59
Russell Clo. SE7—52Lc 107
Russell Clo. Amer—11A 16
Russell Clo. Beck—69Ec 128
Russell Clo. Bexh—56Cd 110
Russell Clo. Brtwd—17Xd 32
Russell Clo. Dart—56Jd 110
Russell Clo. Ruis—33Y 57
Russell Clo. Tad—97Wa 178
Russell Clo. Wok—3F 188
Russell Ct. N14—16Mb 24
Russell Ct. SW1—(7C 198)
Russell Ct. Lea—94Ka 176
Russell Ct. St Alb—2Ca 5
Russell Cres. Wat—7V 4
Russell Dri. Stai—58M 97
Russell Gdns. N20—19Gb 23
Russell Gdns. NW11—30Ab 40
Russell Gdns. W14—48Ab 80
Russell Gdns. Rich—61La 122
Russell Gdns. W Dray—50Q 76
Russell Gdns. M. W14—48Ab 80
Russell Grn. Clo. Purl—82Qb 164
Russell Gro. NW7—21Ua 40
Russell Gro. SW9—52Qb 104
Russell Hill. Purl—82Pb 164
Russell Hill Pl. Purl—83Qb 164
Russell Hill Rd. Purl—83Qb 164
Russell La. N20—19Gb 23
Russell La. Wat—8T 4
Russell Pl. S at H, Dart—67Qd 133
Russell Rd. E4—21Bc 44
Russell Rd. E10—30Dc 44
Russell Rd. E16—44Jc 85
Russell Rd. E17—27Bc 44
Russell Rd. N8—30Mb 42
Russell Rd. N13—23Pb 42
Russell Rd. N15—29Ub 43
Russell Rd. N20—19Gb 23
Russell Rd. NW9—30Va 40
Russell Rd. SW19—66Cb 125
Russell Rd. W14—48Ab 80
Russell Rd. Buck H—18Lc 27
Russell Rd. Enf—10Vb 11
Russell Rd. Grav—8F 114
Russell Rd. Mitc—69Gb 125
Russell Rd. N'holt—36Ea 58
Russell Rd. N'wd—21S 36
Russell Rd. Shep—73S 140
Russell Rd. Til—3A 114
Russell Rd. Twic—58Ha 100
Russell Rd. W on T—72W 140
Russell Rd. Wok—3F 188
Russell's Footpath. SW16 —64Nb 126
Russell Sq. WC1—43Nb 82 (6F 193)
Russell's Ride. Wal X—3Ac 12
Russell St. WC2—45Nb 82 (4G 199)
Russell St. Wind—3H 95
Russell Wlk. Rich—58Pa 101
Russel Rd. Grays—49Ce 91
Russet Clo. Stai—58H 97
Russet Clo. Uxb—42S 76
Russet Cres. N7—36Pb 62
Russets Clo. E4—21Fc 45
Russett Clo. Orp—78Xc 151
Russett Hill. Ger X—27A 34
Russett Way. SE13—54Dc 106
Russett Way. Swan—67Fd 132
Russia Ct. EC2—(3E 200)
Russia Dock Rd. SE16—46Ac 84
Russia La. E2—40Yb 64
Russia Row. EC2 —44Sb 83 (3E 200)
Russington Rd. Shep—72T 140
Rusthall Av. W4—49Ta 79
Rusthall Clo. Croy—72Yb 148
Rustic Av. SW16—66Kb 126
Rustic Clo. Upm—32Ud 70
Rustic Pl. Wemb—35Ma 59
Rustington Wlk. Mord—73Bb 145
Ruston Av. Surb—73Ra 143
Ruston M. W11—44Ab 80
Ruston St. E3—39Bc 64
Rust Sq. SE5—52Tb 105
Rutford Rd. SW16—64Nb 126
Ruth Clo. Stan—28Pa 39
Ruthen Clo. Eps—86Ra 161
Rutherford Clo. Sutt—79Fb 145
Rutherford St. SW1 —49Mb 82 (5D 204)
Rutherford Way. Bush, Wat —18Fa 20
Rutherford Way. Wemb—35Qa 59
Rutherglen Rd. SE2—51Wc 109
Rutherwick Rise. Coul—89Nb 164
Rutherwyke Clo. Eps—79Wa 144
Rutherwyk Rd. Cher—73G 138
Ruthin Rd. SE3—51Jc 107
Ruthven Av. Wal X—5Zb 12
Ruthven St. E9—39Zb 64
Rutland App. Horn—29Qd 49
Rutland Av. Sidc—59Wc 109
Rutland Av. Slou—3G 72
Rutland Clo. SW14—55Sa 101
Rutland Clo. SW19—66Gb 125
Rutland Clo. Bex—60Zc 109
Rutland Clo. Chess—79Pa 143
Rutland Clo. Dart—59Md 111
Rutland Clo. Eps—82Ta 161
Rutland Ct. EC1—(6D 194)
Rutland Dri. Horn—29Qd 49
Rutland Dri. Mord—72Bb 145
Rutland Dri. Rich—60Na 101
Rutland Gdns. N4—30Rb 43
Rutland Gdns. SW7 —47Gb 81 (2E 202)
Rutland Gdns. W13—43Ja 78
Rutland Gdns. Croy—77Ub 147
Rutland Gdns. Dag—36Yc 67
Rutland Gdns. M. SW7 —47Gb 81 (2E 202)
Rutland Ga. SW7 —47Gb 81 (2E 202)
Rutland Ga. Belv—50Dd 88
Rutland Ga. Brom—70Hc 129
Rutland Ga. M. SW7—(2D 202)
Rutland Gro. W6—50Xa 80
Rutland M. NW8—39Db 61
Rutland M. E. SW7—(3E 202)
Rutland M. S. SW7—(3D 202)
Rutland Pk. NW2—37Ya 60
Rutland Pk. SE6—61Bc 128
Rutland Pl. EC1—43Rb 83 (7C 194)
Rutland Pl. Bush, Wat—18Fa 20
Rutland Rd. E7—38Mc 65
Rutland Rd. E9—39Zb 64
Rutland Rd. E11—29Kc 45
Rutland Rd. E17—30Cc 44
Rutland Rd. SW19—66Gb 125
Rutland Rd. Harr—30Ea 38
Rutland Rd. Hay—49T 76
Rutland Rd. Ilf—34Rc 66
Rutland Rd. S'hall—43Ca 77
Rutland Rd. Twic—61Fa 122
Rutland St. SW7—48Gb 81 (3E 202)
Rutland Wlk. SE6—61Bc 128
Rutland Way. Orp—72Yc 151
Rutley Clo. SE17—51Rb 105
Rutlish Rd. SW19—67Cb 125
Rutson Rd. Wey—86P 157
Rutter Gdns. Mitc—70Eb 125
Rutters Clo. W Dray—47Q 76
Rutt's Ter. SE14—53Zb 106
Rutts, The. Bush, Wat—18Fa 20
Ruvigny Gdns. SW15—55Za 102
Ruxbury Rd. Cher—72E 138
Ruxley Clo. Eps—78Ra 143
Ruxley Clo. Sidc—65Ad 131
Ruxley Corner Industrial Est. Sidc—65Zc 131
Ruxley Cres. Esh—80Ka 142
Ruxley La. Eps—79Ra 143
Ruxley Ridge. Esh—80Ja 142
Ruxton Clo. Swan—69Gd 132
Ryan Clo. SE3—56Lc 107
Ryarsh Cres. Orp—77Uc 150
Rycott Path. SE22—59Wb 105
Rycroft. Wind—5D 94
Rycroft Way. N17—27Vb 43
Ryculf Sq. SE3—54Hc 107
Rydal Clo. NW4—26Za 40
Rydal Clo. Purl—85Tb 165
Rydal Cres. Gnfd—41Ka 78
Rydal Dri. Bexh—53Cd 110
Rydal Dri. W Wick—74Fc 149
Rydal Gdns. NW9—29Ua 40
Rydal Gdns. SW15—64Ua 124
Rydal Gdns. Houn—58Da 99
Rydal Gdns. Wemb—32La 58
Rydal Rd. SW16—63Mb 126
Rydal Way. Enf—16Yb 26
Rydal Way. Ruis—35Y 57
Ryde Bldgs. EC1—(4H 207)
Ryde Clo. Wok—93L 173
Ryde Heron. Wok—5B 188
Rydens Av. W on T—75Y 141
Rydens Clo. W on T—75Y 141
Rydens Gro. W on T—77Z 141
Rydens Pk. W on T—75Z 141
Rydens Rd. W on T—76X 141
Rydens Way. Wok—92C 172
Ryder Clo. Brom—64Kc 129
Ryder Clo. Bush, Wat—16Da 19
Ryder Ct. SW1—(6C 198)
Ryder Gdns. Rain—37Hd 68
Ryders Ter. NW8 —40Eb 61 (1A 190)
Ryder St. SW1—46Lb 82 (6C 198)
Ryder Yd. SW1—46Lb 82 (6C 198)
Rydes Clo. Wok—92E 172
Ryde, The. Stai—67K 119
Ryde Vale Rd. SW12—61Lb 126
Rydinghurst Ho. Ger X—22A 34
Rydings. Wind—5D 94
Rydons Clo. SE9—55Nc 108
Rydon's La. Coul—92Sb 181
Rydon St. N1—39Sb 63
Rydon's Wood Clo. Coul —92Sb 181
Rydston Clo. N7—38Nb 62
Ryebridge Clo. Lea—90Ja 160
Ryebrook Rd. Lea—90Ja 160
Rye Clo. Bex—58Dd 110
Rye Clo. Horn—36Ld 69
Ryecotes Mead. SE21—60Ub 105
Rye Cres. Orp—74Yc 151
Ryecroft Av. Ilf—26Rc 46
Ryecroft Av. Twic—60Da 99
Ryecroft Cres. Barn—15Xa 22
Ryecroft Rd. SE13—57Ec 106
Ryecroft Rd. SW16—65Qb 126
Ryecroft Rd. Orp—72Tc 150
Ryecroft Rd. Sev—88Jd 170
Ryecroft St. SW6—53Db 103
Ryedale. SE22—58Xb 105
Rye Field. Orp—74Zc 151
Ryefield Av. Uxb—38R 56
Ryefield Cres. N'wd—26W 36
Ryefield Path. SW15—60Wa 102
Ryefield Rd. SE19—65Sb 127
Rye Hill Pk. SE15—56Yb 106
Ryeland Clo. W Dray—44N 75
Ryelands Clo. Cat—93Ub 181
Ryelands Ct. Lea—90Ja 160
Ryelands Cres. SE12—58Lc 107
Rye La. SE15—54Wb 105
Rye La. Sev—92Hd 186
Rye Rd. SE15—56Zb 106
Rye, The. N14—17Lb 24
Rye Wlk. SW15—57Za 102
Rye Way. Edgw—23Pa 39
Ryfold Rd. SW19—62Cb 125
Ryhope Rd. N11—21Kb 42
Rykhill. Grays—8D 92
Ryland Clo. Felt—63V 120
Rylandes Rd. NW2—34Wa 60
Rylandes Rd. S Croy—82Xb 165
Ryland Rd. NW5—37Kb 62
Rylett Cres. W12—48Va 80
Rylett Rd. W12—47Va 80
Rylston Rd. N13—20Tb 25
Rylston Rd. SW6—51Bb 103
Rymer Rd. SW18—57Eb 103
Rymer Rd. Croy—73Ub 147
Rymer St. SE24—58Rb 105
Rymill St. E16—46Qc 86
Rysbrack St. SW3 —48Hb 81 (3F 203)
Rysted La. West—98Sc 184
Rythe Ct. Th Dit—73Ja 142
Rythe Rd. Esh—78Fa 142
Ryvers Rd. Slou—48B 74

Sabbarton St. E16—44Hc 85
Sabella Ct. E3—40Bc 64
Sabina Rd. Grays—9E 92
Sabine Rd. SW11—55Hb 103
Sabine's Rd. Romf—12Md 31
Sable Clo. Houn—55Y 99
Sable St. N1—38Rb 63
Sach Rd. E5—33Xb 63
Sackville Av. Brom—74Jc 149
Sackville Clo. Harr—34Fa 58
Sackville Clo. Sev—94Kd 187
Sackville Cres. Romf—25Nd 49
Sackville Gdns. Ilf—32Pc 66
Sackville Rd. Dart—61Nd 133
Sackville Rd. Sutt—80Cb 145
Sackville St. W1—45Lb 82 (5C 198)
Saddington St. Grav—9D 114
Saddlers Clo. Borwd—15Ta 21
Saddlers Clo. Pinn—23Ca 37
Saddlers M. Wemb—35Ha 58
Saddler's Pk. Eyns, Dart —76Md 153
Saddlers Ride. E Mol—69Da 121
Saddlers Way. Eps—91Ta 177
Saddlescombe Way. N12 —22Cb 41
Saddleworth Rd. Romf—23Ld 49
Saddleworth Sq. Romf—23Ld 49
Sadler Clo. Mitc—68Hb 125
Saffron Clo. NW11—29Bb 41
Saffron Clo. Brtwd—30Fe 51
Saffron Clo. Slou—3M 95
Saffron Hill. EC1 —43Qb 82 (7A 194)
Saffron Rd. Romf—26Fd 48
Saffron St. EC1—43Qb 82 (7A 194)
Saffron Way. Surb—74Ma 143
Sage St. E1—45Yb 84
Saigasso Clo. E16—44Mc 85
Sail St. SE11—49Pb 82 (5J 205)
Sainfoin Rd. SW17—61Jb 126
Sainsbury Rd. SE19—64Ub 127
St Agatha's Dri. King—65Pa 123
St Agatha's Gro. Cars—74Hb 145
St Agnes Clo. E9—39Yb 64
St Agnes Pl. SE11—51Rb 105
St Agnes Well. EC1—(5G 195)
St Aidan's Rd. SE22—58Xb 105
St Aidan's Rd. W13—47Ka 78
St Aidan's Way. Grav—2G 136
St Alban's Av. E6—41Qc 86
St Alban's Av. W4—48Ta 79
St Albans Av. Felt—64Z 121
St Alban's Av. Upm—33Ud 70
St Albans Av. Wey—76Q 140
St Albans Clo. NW11—32Cb 61
St Alban's Clo. Grav—2F 136
St Albans Ct. EC2—(2E 200)
St Alban's Cres. N22—25Qb 42
St Alban's Cres. Wfd G—24Jc 45
St Albans Gdns. Grav—2F 136
St Alban's Gdns. Tedd—64Ja 122
St Alban's Gro. W8—48Db 81
St Alban's Gro. Cars—73Gb 145
St Albans La. NW11—32Cb 61
St Alban's M. W2 —43Fb 81 (7C 190)
St Alban's Pl. N1—39Rb 63
St Albans Rd. NW5—34Jb 62
St Albans Rd. NW10—39Ua 60
St Albans Rd. Barn—7Xa 8
St Alban's Rd. Dart—58Pd 111
St Alban's Rd. Epp—1Zc 15
St Albans Rd. Ilf—32Vc 67
St Alban's Rd. King—65Na 123
St Albans Rd. Pot B—4Va 8
St Albans Rd. Pot B—3Ua 8
St Alban's Rd. Sutt—77Bb 145
St Albans Rd. Wat—12X 19
St Alban's Rd. Wfd G—24Jc 45
St Alban's St. SW1 —45Mb 82 (5D 198)
St Alban's St. Wind—3H 95
St Alban's Ter. W6—51Ab 102
St Alfege Pas. SE10—51Ec 106
St Alfege Rd. SE7—51Mc 107
St Alphage Garden. EC2 —43Sb 83 (1E 200)
St Alphage Highwalk. EC2 —(1E 200)
St Alphage Ho. EC2—(1F 201)
St Alphage Wlk. Edgw—26Sa 39
St Alphege Rd. N9—17Yb 26
St Alphonsus Rd. SW4—56Lb 104
St Amunds Clo. SE6—63Cc 128
St Andrew's Av. Horn—36Hd 68
St Andrew's Av. Wemb—35Ja 58
St Andrews Av. Wind—4D 94
St Andrew's Clo. N12—21Eb 41
St Andrew's Clo. NW2—34Xa 60
St Andrews Clo. Iswth—53Ga 100
St Andrew's Clo. Ruis—33Z 57
St Andrews Clo. Shep—70T 120
St Andrew's Clo. Stan—26La 38
St Andrews Clo. Wind—8L 95
St Andrew's Ct. SW18—61Eb 125
St Andrew's Cres. Wind—4D 94
St Andrew's Dri. Orp—73Xc 151
St Andrew's Dri. Stan—25La 38
St Andrew's Gro. N16—32Tb 63
St Andrew's Hill. EC4 —44Rb 83 (4C 200)
St Andrew's M. N16—32Ub 63
St Andrew's M. SE3—52Jc 107
St Andrew's Pl. NW1 —42Kb 82 (5A 192)
St Andrew's Pl. Brtwd—19Be 33
St Andrew's Rd. E11—30Gc 45
St Andrew's Rd. E13—41Kc 85
St Andrew's Rd. E17—26Zb 44
St Andrew's Rd. N9—17Yb 26
St Andrew's Rd. NW9—32Ta 59
St Andrew's Rd. NW10—37Xa 60
St Andrew's Rd. NW11—30Bb 41
St Andrew's Rd. W3—45Ua 80
St Andrew's Rd. W7—47Ga 78
St Andrew's Rd. W14—51Ab 102
St Andrew's Rd. Cars—76Gb 145
St Andrew's Rd. Coul—88Jb 164
St Andrew's Rd. Croy—77Sb 147
St Andrew's Rd. Enf—13Tb 25
St Andrew's Rd. Grav—9D 114
St Andrew's Rd. Ilf—31Pc 66
St Andrew's Rd. Romf—30Fd 48
St Andrew's Rd. Sidc—62Zc 131
St Andrew's Rd. Surb—72Ma 143
St Andrew's Rd. Til—3A 114
St Andrew's Rd. Uxb—39N 55
St Andrew's Rd. Wat—20Z 19
St Andrew's Sq. Surb—72Ma 143
St Andrew St. EC4 —43Qb 82 (2A 200)
St Andrew's Wlk. Cob—87X 159
St Andrew's Way. Slou—5B 72
St Anne's Av. Stai—59M 97
St Anne's Clo. N6—34Jb 62
St Anne's Ct. W1 —44Mb 82 (3D 198)
St Anne's Ct. W Wick—77Gc 149
St Anne's Pas. E14—44Bc 84
St Anne's Rd. E11—33Fc 65
St Anne's Rd. Brtwd—11Ee 33
St Anne's Rd. Uxb—27L 35
St Anne's Rd. Wemb—36Ma 59
St Anne's Row. E14—44Bc 84
St Anne St. E14—44Bc 84
St Ann's. Bark—39Sc 66
St Ann's Clo. Cher—72H 139
St Ann's Cres. SW18—58Eb 103
St Ann's Gdns. NW5—37Jb 62
St Ann's Gdns. NW10—41Pa 79
St Ann's Hill. SW18—58Db 103
St Ann's Hill Rd. Cher—72E 138
St Ann's La. SW1 —48Mb 82 (4E 204)
St Ann's Pk. Rd. SW18—58Eb 103
St Ann's Pas. SW13—55Ua 102
St Ann's Rd. N9—18Vb 25
St Ann's Rd. N15—29Sb 43
St Ann's Rd. SW13—54Va 102
St Ann's Rd. W11—45Za 80
St Ann's Rd. Bark—39Sc 66
St Ann's Rd. Cher—72H 139
(in two parts)
St Ann's Rd. Harr—30Ga 38
St Ann's St. SW1 —48Mb 82 (3E 204)
St Ann's Ter. NW8 —40Fb 61 (1C 190)
St Ann's Vs. W11—46Za 80
St Ann's Way. S Croy—79Rb 147
St Anselm's Pl. W1 —45Kb 82 (4K 197)
St Anselm's Rd. Hay—47V 76
St Anthony's Av. Wfd G—23Lc 45
St Anthony's Clo. E1—46Wb 83
St Anthony's Clo. SW17—61Gb 125
St Anthony's Way. Felt—56V 98
St Antony's Rd. E7—38Kc 65
St Arvan's Clo. Croy—76Ub 147
St Asaph Rd. SE4—55Zb 106
St Aubyn's Av. SW19—64Bb 125
St Aubyn's Av. Houn—57Ca 99
St Aubyn's Clo. Orp—76Vc 151
St Aubyn's Gdns. Orp—76Vc 151
St Aubyn's Rd. SE19—65Vb 127
St Audrey Av. Bexh—54Cd 110
St Augustine Rd. Grays—9D 92
St Augustine's Av. W5—40Na 59
St Augustine's Av. Brom —71Nc 150
St Augustine's Av. S Croy
St Augustine's Av. Wemb
St Augustine's Rd. NW1—38Mb 62
St Augustine's Rd. Belv—49Bd 87
St Austell Clo. Edgw—26Pa 39
St Austell Rd. SE13—54Ec 106
St Awdry's Rd. Bark—38Tc 66
St Awdry's Wlk. Bark—38Sc 66
St Barnabas Clo. Beck—68Ec 128
St Barnabas Rd. E17—30Cc 44
St Barnabas Rd. Mitc—66Jb 126
St Barnabas Rd. Sutt—78Fb 145
St Barnabas Rd. Wfd G—25Kc 45
St Barnabas St. SW1 —50Jb 82 (7J 203)
St Barnabas Ter. E9—36Zb 64
St Barnabas Vs. SW8—53Nb 104
St Bartholomew's Clo. SE26 —63Yb 128
St Bartholomew's Rd. E6—40Pc 66
St Benedict's Av. Grav—1G 137
St Benedict's Clo. SW17—64Jb 126
St Benet's Clo. SW17—61Gb 125
St Benet's Gro. Cars—73Eb 145
St Benet's Pl. EC3 —45Ub 83 (4G 201)
St Bernards. Croy—76Ub 147
St Bernard's Clo. SE27—63Tb 127
St Bernard's Rd. E6—39Mc 65
St Bernard's Rd. Slou—8N 73
St Blaise Av. Brom—68Kc 129
St Botolph Rd. Grav—62Fe 135
St Botolph Row. EC3 —44Vb 83 (3K 201)
St Botolph's Av. Sev—96Jd 186
St Botolph's Rd. Sev—96Kd 187
St Botolph St. EC3 —44Vb 83 (2K 201)
St Bride's Av. EC4—(3B 200)
St Bride's Av. Edgw—25Pa 39
St Bride's Clo. Eri—47Zc 87
St Bride's Pas. EC4—(3B 200)
St Bride St. EC4—44Rb 83 (2B 200)
St Catherine's. Wok—7F 188
St Catherine's Clo. SW17 —61Gb 125
St Catherine's Dri. SE14—54Zb 106
St Catherine's Farm Ct. Ruis —30S 36
St Catherine's Rd. E4—19Cc 26
St Catherine's Rd. Ruis—30T 36
St Cecilia Rd. Grays—9D 92
St Cedds Ct. Grays—46De 91
St Chad's Dri. Grav—2G 136
St Chad's Gdns. Romf—31Ad 67
St Chad's Pl. WC1 —41Pb 82 (3G 193)
St Chad's Rd. Romf—31Ad 67
St Chad's Rd. Til—4C 114
St Chad's St. WC1 —41Nb 82 (3G 193)
St Charles Pl. W10—43Ab 80
St Charles Rd. Brtwd—18Xd 32
St Charles Sq. W10—43Ab 80
St Christopher Rd. Uxb—44M 75
St Christopher's Clo. Iswth —53Ga 100
St Christopher's Pl. W1 —44Jb 82 (2J 197)
St Clair Dri. Wor Pk—76Xa 144
St Claire Clo. Ilf—26Pc 46
St Clair Rd. E13—40Kc 65
St Clair's Rd. Croy—75Ub 147
St Clare St. EC3—44Vb 83 (3K 201)
St Clement Clo. Uxb—44M 75
St Clement's Ct. EC4—(4G 201)
St Clement's Heights. SE26 —62Wb 127
St Clement's La. WC2 —44Pb 82 (3J 199)
St Clement's Rd. Grays—52Yd 112
St Clement St. N7—38Qb 62
★St Clere Hill Rd. Sev—84Vd
St Cloud Rd. SE27—63Sb 127
St Columba's Clo. Grav—2G 136
St Crispin's Clo. NW3—35Gb 61
St Crispin's Clo. S'hall—44Ba 77
St Crispin's Way. Cher—81E 156
St Cross St. EC1—43Qb 82 (7A 194)
St Cuthbert's Gdns. Pinn—24Ba 37
St Cuthbert's Rd. NW2—37Bb 61
St Cuthbert's Wlk. NW6—37Bb 61
St Cyprian's St. SW17—63Hb 125
St David Clo. Uxb—43M 75
St David's. Coul—89Pb 164
St David's Clo. Iver—39F 54
St David's Clo. Wemb—34Sa 59
St David's Clo. W Wick—73Dc 148
St David's Cres. Grav—3F 136
St David's Dri. Edgw—25Pa 39
St David's Pl. NW4—31Xa 60
St David's Rd. Swan—65Hd 132
St Denis Rd. SE27—63Tb 127
St Denys Clo. Wok—6A 188
St Dionis Rd. SW6—54Bb 103
St Donatt's Rd. SE14—53Bc 106
St Dunstan's All. EC3—(5H 201)
St Dunstan's Av. W3—45Ta 79
St Dunstan's Clo. Hay—50V 76
St Dunstan's Ct. EC4 —44Qb 82 (3A 200)
St Dunstan's Dri. Grav—2G 136
St Dunstan's Gdns. W3—45Ta 79
St Dunstan's Hill. EC3 —45Ub 83 (5H 201)
St Dunstan's Hill. Sutt—79Ab 144
St Dunstan's La. EC3 —45Ub 83 (5H 201)
St Dunstan's La. Beck—72Ec 148
St Dunstan's Rd. E7—37Lc 65
St Dunstan's Rd. SE25—70Vb 127
St Dunstan's Rd. W6—50Za 80
St Dunstan's Rd. W7—47Ga 78
St Dunstan's Rd. Felt—62V 120
St Dunstan's Rd. Houn—54Y 99
St Edith's Rd. Sev—89Qd 171
St Edmund's Av. Ruis—30T 36
St Edmund's Clo. NW8 —39Hb 61 (1F 191)
St Edmund's Clo. SW17—61Gb 125
St Edmund's Clo. Eri—47Zc 87
St Edmund's Dri. Stan—25Ja 38
St Edmund's La. Twic—59Da 99
St Edmund's Rd. N9—17Wb 25
St Edmund's Rd. Dart—56Qd 111
St Edmund's Rd. Ilf—30Pc 46
St Edmund's Ter. NW8 —39Gb 61 (1E 190)
St Edward's Clo. NW11—30Cb 41
St Edward's Clo. Croy—83Fc 167
St Edward's Way. Romf—29Fd 48
St Egbert's Way. E4—18Ec 26
St Elmo Clo. Slou—2H 73
St Elmo Cres. Slou—2H 73
St Elmo Rd. W12—47Va 80
St Erkenwald Rd. Bark—39Tc 66
St Ermin's Hill. SW1—(3D 204)
St Ervan's Rd. W10—43Bb 81
St Faith's Clo. Enf—11Sb 25
St Faith's Rd. SE21—60Rb 105
St Fidelis Rd. Eri—49Fd 88
St Fillans Rd. SE6—60Ec 106
St Francis Av. Grav—3G 136
St Francis Clo. Orp—72Uc 150
St Francis Clo. Pot B—6Eb 9
St Francis Clo. Wat—18X 19
St Francis Rd. SE22—56Ub 105
St Francis Rd. Eri—49Fd 88
St Francis Rd. Uxb—30H 35
St Francis Way. Grays—8E 92
St Gabriel's Rd. NW2—36Za 60
St Gabriel St. SE11—(5C 206)
St George's Av. E7—38Kc 65
St George's Av. N7—35Mb 62
St George's Av. NW9—28Ta 39
St George's Av. W5—47Ma 79
St George's Av. Grays—49Ee 91

St George's Av.—St Peter's Way

St George's Av. Horn—31Pd 69
St George's Av. S'hall—45Ba 77
St George's Av. Wey—79R 140
St George's Bldgs. SE1 —47Sb 83 (1E 206)
St George's Centre. Grav—8D 114
St George's Cir. SE1 —48Rb 83 (3B 206)
St George's Clo. NW11—30Bb 41
St George's Clo. Wemb—34Ja 58
St George's Clo. Wey—78S 140
St George's Clo. Wind—3C 94
St George's Ct. E6—42Pc 86
★St George's Ct. Sev—88Be
St George's Cres. Grav—3F 136
St George's Cres. Slou—5B 72
St George's Dri. SW1 —49Kb 82 (6A 204)
St George's Dri. Uxb—34P 55
St George's Dri. Wat—20Aa 19
St George's Fields. W2 —44Gb 81 (3E 196)
St George's Gdns. Eps—86Va 162
St George's Gdns. Surb—75Ra 143
St George's Gro. SW17—62Fb 125
St George's La. EC3—(4G 201)
St George's La. Asc—9A 116
St George's Lodge. Wey—78T 140
St George's M. NW1—38Hb 61
St George's Rd. E7—38Kc 65
St George's Rd. E10—34Ec 64
St George's Rd. N9—20Wb 25
St George's Rd. N13—19Pb 24
St George's Rd. NW11—30Bb 41
St George's Rd. SE1 —48Rb 83 (3A 206)
St George's Rd. SW19—65Bb 125
St George's Rd. W4—47Ta 79
St George's Rd. W7—46Ha 78
St George's Rd. Beck—67Dc 128
St George's Rd. Brom—68Pc 130
St George's Rd. Dag—36Ad 67
St George's Rd. Enf—10Vb 11
St George's Rd. Felt—63Z 121
St George's Rd. Ilf—31Pc 66
St George's Rd. King—66Qa 123
St George's Rd. Mitc—69Kb 126
St George's Rd. Orp—72Tc 150
St George's Rd. Rich—55Pa 101
St George's Rd. Sev—94Kd 187
St George's Rd. Sidc—65Zc 131
St George's Rd. Swan—70Hd 132
St George's Rd. Twic—57Ka 100
St George's Rd. Wall—78Kb 146
St George's Rd. Wat—10X 5
St George's Rd. Wey—79T 140
St George's Rd. Wey—77L 139 (Addlestone)
St George's Rd. W. Brom —68Nc 130
St George's Sq. E7—38Kc 65
St George's Sq. SW1 —50Mb 82 (7D 204)
St George's Sq. Long, Dart —69Ae 135
St George's Sq. N Mald—69Ua 124
St George's Sq. M. SW1 —50Mb 82 (7D 204)
St George's Stairs. SE16—49Bc 84
St George's Ter. NW1—38Hb 61
St George St. W1 —45Kb 82 (4A 198)
St George's Wlk. Croy—76Sb 147
St George's Way. SE15—51Ub 105
St Gerard's Clo. SW4—57Lb 104
St German's Pl. SE3—53Jc 107
St German's Rd. SE23—60Ac 106
St Giles Av. Dag—38Dd 68
St Giles Av. Pot B—4Xa 8
St Giles Av. Uxb—35S 56
St Giles Cir. W1, WC1 & WC2 —44Mb 82 (2E 198)
St Giles Clo. Dag—38Dd 68
St Giles Clo. Orp—78Tc 150
St Giles Ct. Enf—7Yb 12
St Giles High St. WC2 —44Mb 82 (2E 198)
St Giles Ho. Barn—14Eb 23
St Giles Pas. WC2—(3E 198)
St Giles Rd. SE5—52Ub 105
St Gothard Rd. SE27—63Tb 127
St Gregory's Cres. Grav—1G 136
St Helena Rd. SE16—49Zb 84
St Helena St. WC1 —41Qb 82 (4K 193)
St Helen Clo. Uxb—43M 75
St Helen's Ct. Epp—2Wc 15
St Helen's Ct. Rain—42Jd 88
St Helen's Cres. SW16—67Pb 126
St Helen's Gdns. W10—44Za 80
St Helen's Pl. EC3 —44Ub 83 (2H 201)
St Helen's Rd. SW16—67Pb 126
St Helen's Rd. W13—46La 78
St Helen's Rd. Eri—47Zc 87
St Helen's Rd. Ilf—30Pc 46
St Helier Av. Mord—73Eb 145
St Helier's Av. Houn—57Ca 99
St Helier's Rd. E10—30Ec 44
St Hilda's Av. Ashf—64N 119
St Hilda's Clo. NW6—39Za 60
St Hilda's Clo. SW17—61Gb 125
St Hilda's Clo. Wok—5A 188
St Hilda's Rd. SW13—51Xa 102
St Hilda's Way. Grav—3F 136
St Hubert's Clo. Ger X—33A 54
St Hubert's La. Ger X—33B 54
St Hughe's Clo. SW17—61Gb 125
St Hughes Rd. SE20—67Xb 127
St Ivian's Dri. Romf—27Jd 48
St James Av. N20—20Gb 23
St James Av. W13—46Ja 78
St James Av. Eps—83Va 162
St James Av. Sutt—78Cb 145
St James Clo. N20—20Gb 23
St James Clo. SE18—50Sc 86
St James Clo. Eps—86Ua 162
St James Clo. N Mald—71Va 144
St James Clo. Ruis—33Y 57
St James Clo. Wok—6D 188
St James' Ct. SW1 —48Lb 82 (3C 204)
St James' Gdns. Wemb—38Na 59
St James Ga. NW1—38Mb 62
St James Gro. SW11—54Hb 103
St James La. Grnh—60Ud 112
St James Pl. Dart—58Md 111
St James Pl. Slou—4A 72
St James' Rd. E15—36Hc 65
St James' Rd. N9—19Xb 25
St James Rd. Cars—76Gb 145
St James Rd. King—68Ma 123
St James Rd. Mitc—66Jb 126
St James Rd. Purl—85Sb 165
St James' Rd. Sev—94Kd 187
St James Rd. Sutt—78Cb 145
St James Rd. Wat—15X 19
St James's. SE14—53Ac 106
St James's App. EC2—(6H 195)
St James's Av. E2—40Yb 64
St James's Av. Beck—69Ac 128
St James's Av. Grav—9C 114
St James's Av. Hmptn—64Ea 122
St James's Clo. SW17—61Hb 125
St James's Cotts. Rich—57Ma 101
St James's Cres. SW9—55Qb 104
St James's Dri. SW17—60Hb 103
St James's Gdns. W11—46Ab 80
St James's La. N10—28Kb 42
St James's Mkt. SW1 —45Mb 82 (5D 198)
St James's Pk. Croy—73Sb 147
St James's Pas. EC3—(3J 201)
St James's Pl. SW1 —46Lb 82 (7B 198)
St James Sq. Long, Dart—69Ae 135
St James's Rd.—48Wb 83
SE16 1-167 & 2-144
SE1 remainder
St James's Rd. Brtwd—20Yd 32
St James's Rd. Croy—73Sb 147
St James's Rd. Grav—8C 114
St James's Rd. Hmptn—64Da 121
St James's Rd. Surb—72Ma 143
St James's Row. EC1 —42Rb 83 (5B 194)
St James's Sq. SW1 —46Lb 82 (6C 198)
St James's St. SW1 —46Lb 82 (6B 198)
St James's St. Grav—8C 114
St James's Ter. NW8—(1F 191)
St James's Ter. M. NW8 —39Hb 61 (1F 191)
St James St. E17—29Ac 44
St James St. W6—50Ya 80
St James's Wlk. EC1 —42Rb 83 (5B 194)
St James Wlk. Iver—47G 74
St James Way. Sidc—64Ad 131
St Jerome's Gro. Hay—44S 76
St Joan's Rd. N9—19Vb 25
St John's Av. N11—22Hb 41
St John's Av. NW10—39Va 60
St John's Av. SW15—57Za 102
St John's Av. Brtwd—21Zd 51
St John's Av. Eps—84Wa 162
St John's Av. Lea—93Ka 176
St John's Chu. Rd. E9—36Yb 64
St John's Clo. Pot B—5Eb 9
St John's Clo. Rain—38Jd 68
St John's Clo. Uxb—39K 55
St John's Clo. Wemb—36Na 59
St John's Cotts. SE20—66Yb 128
St John's Ct. Buck H—18Kc 27
St John's Ct. Iswth—54Ha 100
St John's Ct. N'wd—25U 36
St John's Ct. Sev—94Ld 187
St John's Ct. Wok—7D 188
St John's Cres. SW9—55Qb 104
St John's Dri. SW18—60Db 103
St John's Dri. W on T—74Y 141
St John's Dri. Wind—4E 94
St John's Est. N1 —40Tb 63 (2G 195)
St John's Est. SE1—(1K 207)
St John's Gdns. W11—45Bb 81
St John's Gro. N19—33Lb 62
St John's Gro. Rich—56Na 101
St John's Hill. SW11—56Fb 103
St John's Hill. Coul—89Qb 164
St John's Hill. Purl—88Qb 164
St John's Hill. Sev—94Ld 187
St John's Hill Gro. SW11 —56Fb 103
St John's Hill Rd. Wok—7D 188
St John's La. EC1 —42Rb 83 (6B 194)
St John's La. Long, Dart—72Be 155
St John's Lye. Wok—7C 188 (in two parts)
St John's Pk. SE3—52Hc 107
St John's Pas. SW19—65Ab 124
St John's Path. EC1—(6B 194)
St John's Pl. EC1 —42Rb 83 (6B 194)
St John's Rise. Wok—7E 188
St John's Rd. E4—21Dc 44
St John's Rd. E6—39Nc 66
St John's Rd. E16—44Jc 85
St John's Rd. E17—26Dc 44
St John's Rd. N15—30Ub 43
St John's Rd. NW11—30Bb 41
St John's Rd. SE20—65Yb 128
St John's Rd. SW11—56Gb 103
St John's Rd. SW19—66Ab 124
St John's Rd. Bark—39Uc 66
St John's Rd. Cars—76Gb 145
St John's Rd. Croy—76Rb 147
St John's Rd. Dart—59Sd 112
St John's Rd. E Mol—70Fa 122
St John's Rd. Epp—2Vc 15
St John's Rd. Eri—50Fd 88
St John's Rd. Felt—63Aa 121
St John's Rd. Grav—9F 114
St John's Rd. Grays—10D 92
St John's Rd. Harr—30Ha 38
St John's Rd. Ilf—31Uc 66
St John's Rd. Iswth—54Ha 100
St John's Rd. King—68La 122
St John's Rd. Lea—93La 176
St John's Rd. Lou—12Pc 28
St John's Rd. N Mald—69Sa 123
St John's Rd. Orp—72Tc 150
St John's Rd. Rich—56Na 101
St John's Rd. Romf—22Ed 48
St John's Rd. Sev—94Ld 187
St John's Rd. Sidc—63Xc 131
St John's Rd. Slou—5L 73
St John's Rd. S'hall—48Aa 77
St John's Rd. Sutt—75Db 145
St John's Rd. Uxb—39K 55
St John's Rd. Wat—12X 19
St John's Rd. Well—55Xc 109
St John's Rd. Wemb—35Ma 59
St John's Rd. Wind—4E 94
St John's Rd. Wok—6D 188
St John's Sq. EC1 —42Rb 83 (6B 194)
St John's Ter. E7—37Kc 65
St John's Ter. SE18—51Sc 108
St John's Ter. W10—42Za 80
St John's Ter. Enf—9Tb 11
St John St. EC1—41Rb 83 (2A 194)
St John's Vale. SE8—54Cc 106
St John's Vs. N19—33Mb 62
St John's Way. N19—33Lb 62
St John's Wood Ct. NW8—(4C 190)
St John's Wood High St. NW8 —40Gb 61 (2D 190)
St John's Wood Pk. NW8—39Fb 61
St John's Wood Rd. NW8 —42Fb 81 (5B 190)
St John's Wood Ter. NW8 —40Gb 61 (1C 190)
St John's Yd. N17—24Vb 43
St Joseph's Clo. Orp—76Vc 151
St Joseph's Dri. S'hall—46Aa 77
St Joseph's Rd. N9—17Xb 25
St Joseph's Rd. Wal X—5Ac 12
St Joseph's St. SW8—53Kb 104
St Jude's Clo. Egh—4N 117
St Jude's Rd. E2—40Xb 63
St Jude's Rd. Egh—3N 117
St Jude St. N16—36Ub 63
St Julian's Clo. SW16—63Qb 126
St Julian's Farm Rd. SE27 —63Qb 126
St Julian's Rd. NW6—39Cb 61
St Justin Clo. Orp—69Zc 131
St Katharine's Precinct. NW1 —40Kb 62 (1K 191)
St Katharine's Way. E1 —46Vb 83 (6K 201)
St Katherine's Rd. Eri—47Zc 87
St Katherine's Row. EC3—(4J 201)
St Keverne Rd. SE9—63Nc 130
St Kilda Rd. W13—47Ja 78
St Kilda Rd. Orp—74Vc 151
St Kilda's Rd. N16—32Tb 63
St Kilda's Rd. Brtwd—17Yd 32
St Kilda's Rd. Harr—30Ga 38
St Kitts Ter. SE19—64Ub 127
St Laurence Clo. Orp—69Zc 131
St Laurence Clo. NW6—39Za 60
St Laurence Way. Slou—8L 73
St Lawrence Clo. Abb L, Wat—2U 4
St Lawrence Clo. Edgw—24Pa 39
St Lawrence Clo. Uxb—43L 75
St Lawrence Dri. Pinn—29X 37
St Lawrence Rd. Upm—33Sd 70
St Lawrence St. E14—46Ec 84
St Lawrence Ter. W10—43Ab 80
St Lawrence Way. SW9—54Qb 104
St Lawrence Way. St Alb—2Ba 5
St Leonard's Av. E4—23Fc 45
St Leonard's Av. Harr—29La 38
St Leonard's Av. Wind—4G 94
St Leonard's Clo. Bush, Wat —14Aa 19
St Leonard's Clo. Well—55Wc 109
St Leonard's Ct. N1—(3G 195)
St Leonard's Gdns. Houn —53Aa 99
St Leonard's Gdns. Ilf—36Sc 66
St Leonard's Hill. Wind—6B 94
St Leonard's Rise. Orp—77Uc 150
St Leonard's Rd. E14—43Dc 84 (in two parts)
St Leonard's Rd. NW10—42Ta 79
St Leonard's Rd. SW14—55Sa 101
St Leonard's Rd. W13—45La 78
St Leonard's Rd. Croy—76Rb 147
St Leonard's Rd. Eps—91Ya 178
St Leonard's Rd. Esh—79Ha 142
St Leonard's Rd. Surb—71Ma 143
St Leonard's Rd. Th Dit—73Ja 142
St Leonard's Rd. Wind—5F 94 (in two parts)
St Leonard's Rd. Wind—8A 94 (Windsor Safari Park)
St Leonard's Sq. Surb—71Ma 143
St Leonard's St. E3—41Dc 84
St Leonard's Ter. SW3 —50Hb 81 (7F 203)
St Leonard St. NW5—37Jb 62
St Leonard's Wlk. SW16 —66Pb 126
St Leonard's Wlk. Iver—48H 75
St Loo Av. SW3—51Gb 103
St Louis Rd. SE27—63Tb 127
St Loy's Rd. N17—26Ub 43
St Luke Clo. Uxb—44M 75
St Luke's Av. SW4—56Mb 104
St Luke's Av. Enf—10Tb 11
St Luke's Av. Ilf—36Rc 66
St Luke's Clo. EC1 —42Sb 83 (5E 194)
St Luke's Clo. SE25—72Xb 147
St Luke's M. W11—44Bb 81
St Luke's Pas. King—67Pa 123
St Luke's Path. Ilf—36Rc 66
St Luke's Rd. W11—43Bb 81
St Luke's Rd. Uxb—38N 55
St Luke's Rd. Whyt—90Vb 165
St Luke's Rd. Wind—8L 95
St Luke's Sq. E16—44Hc 85
St Luke's St. SW3 —50Gb 81 (7E 202)
St Luke's Yd. W9—40Bb 61
St Malo Av. N9—20Yb 26
St Margarets. Bark—39Tc 66
St Margaret's Av. N15—28Rb 43
St Margaret's Av. N20—18Eb 23
St Margaret's Av. Ashf—64R 120
St Margaret's Av. Harr—34Ea 58
St Margaret's Av. Sidc—62Tc 130
St Margaret's Av. Stanf—3L 93
St Margaret's Av. Sutt—76Ab 144
St Margaret's Av. Uxb—42Q 76
St Margaret's Clo. EC2—(2F 201)
St Margaret's Clo. Iver—40F 54
St Margaret's Clo. Orp—77Xc 151
St Margaret's Ct. N11—21Jb 42
St Margaret's Ct. SE1 —46Tb 83 (7F 201)
St Margaret's Cres. SW15 —57Xa 102
St Margaret's Cres. Grav—2G 136
St Margaret's Dri. Iswth —57Ka 100
St Margaret's Ga. Iver—40F 54
St Margaret's Gro. SE18 —51Sc 108
St Margaret's Gro. Twic—58Ja 100
St Margaret's Pas. SE13 —55Gc 107
St Margaret's Rd. E12—33Lc 65
St Margaret's Rd. N17—27Ub 43
St Margaret's Rd. NW10—41Ya 80
St Margaret's Rd. SE4—56Bc 106
St Margaret's Rd. W7—47Ga 78
St Margaret's Rd. Beck—70Zb 128
St Margaret's Rd. Coul—93Kb 180
St Margaret's Rd. Edgw—22Ra 39
St Margaret's Rd. Grav—10A 114
St Margaret's Rd. Ruis—30T 36
St Margaret's Rd. S Dar, Dart & Dart—66Ud 134
St Margaret's Rd. Twic—56Ka 100
St Margaret's Sq. SE4—56Bc 106
St Margaret's Ter. SE18—50Sc 86
St Margaret St. SW1 —47Nb 82 (2F 205)
St Mark's Av. Grav—9A 114
St Mark's Clo. SE10—52Ec 106
St Mark's Clo. W11—44Ab 80
St Mark's Clo. Barn—13Db 23
St Mark's Cres. NW1—39Jb 62
St Mark's Ga. E9—38Bc 64
St Mark's Gro. SW10—51Db 103
St Mark's Hill. Surb—72Na 143
St Mark's Pl. SW19—65Bb 125
St Mark's Pl. W11—44Ab 80
St Mark's Pl. Wind—4G 94
St Mark's Rise. E8—36Vb 63
St Mark's Rd. SE25—70Wb 127
St Mark's Rd. W5—46Na 79
St Mark's Rd. W7—47Ga 78
St Mark's Rd.—43Za 80
W11 1-53a & 2-22
W10 remainder
St Mark's Rd. Brom—69Kc 129
St Mark's Rd. Enf—16Vb 25
St Mark's Rd. Eps—90Ya 162
St Mark's Rd. Mitc—68Hb 125
St Mark's Rd. Tedd—66Ka 122
St Mark's Rd. Wind—4G 94
St Mark's Sq. NW1—39Jb 62
St Mark St. E1—44Vb 83
St Martha's Av. Wok—93B 172
St Martin Clo. Uxb—44M 75
St Martin's App. Ruis—31U 56
St Martin's Av. E6—40Mc 65
St Martin's Av. Eps—86Ua 162
St Martin's Clo. NW1—39Lb 62
St Martin's Clo. Brtwd—19Ee 33
St Martin's Clo. Enf—11Xb 25
St Martin's Clo. Eps—85Va 162
St Martin's Clo. Eri—47Zc 87
St Martin's Clo. Lea—100U 174
St Martin's Clo. W Dray—48M 75
St Martin's Ct. WC2 —45Nb 82 (4F 199)
St Martin's Ct. Ashf—64L 119
St Martin's Dri. Eyns, Dart —76Md 153
St Martin's Dri. W on T—76Y 141
St Martin's La. WC2 —45Nb 82 (4F 199)
St Martin's le Grand. EC1 —44Sb 83 (2D 200)
St Martin's Meadow. West —95Yc 185
St Martin's Pl. WC2 —45Nb 82 (5F 199)
St Martin's Rd. N9—19Xb 25
St Martin's Rd. SW9—54Pb 104
St Martin's Rd. Dart—58Pd 111
St Martin's Rd. W Dray—48M 75
St Martin's St. WC2 —45Mb 82 (5E 198)
St Martin's Way. SW17—62Eb 125
St Mary Abbot's Pl. W8—48Bb 81
St Mary Abbot's Ter. W14 —48Bb 81
St Mary at Hill. EC3 —45Ub 83 (5H 201)
St Mary Av. Wall—76Kb 146
St Mary Axe. EC3 —44Ub 83 (2J 201)
St Marychurch St. SE16—47Yb 84
St Mary Rd. E17—28Cc 44
St Mary's. Bark—39Tc 66
St Mary's App. E12—36Pc 66
St Mary's Av. E11—31Kc 65
St Mary's Av. N3—26Ab 40
St Mary's Av. Brtwd—15Ce 33
St Mary's Av. Brom—69Gc 129
St Mary's Av. N'wd—22U 36
St Mary's Av. S'hall—49Da 77 (in two parts)
St Mary's Av. Stai—59M 97
St Mary's Av. Tedd—65Ha 122
St Mary's Clo. N17—25Wb 43
St Mary's Clo. Chess—80Pa 143
St Mary's Clo. Eps—80Va 144
St Mary's Clo. Grav—1E 136
St Mary's Clo. Lea—95Fa 176
St Mary's Clo. Orp—68Yc 131
St Mary's Clo. Oxt—100Gc 183
★St Mary's Clo. Sev—92Ee
St Mary's Clo. Stai—59M 97
St Mary's Clo. Sun—70W 120
St Mary's Clo. Uxb—27K 35
St Mary's Clo. Wat—14Y 19
St Mary's Ct. E6—42Pc 86
St Mary's Ct. SE7—52Mc 107
St Mary's Ct. W5—47Ma 79
St Mary's Cres. NW4—27Xa 40
St Mary's Cres. Hay—45V 76
St Mary's Cres. Iswth—52Fa 100
St Mary's Cres. Stai—59M 97
St Mary's Dri. Felt—59S 98
St Mary's Dri. Sev—95Gd 186
St Mary's Gdns. SE11 —49Qb 82 (5A 206)
St Mary's Grn. N2—26Eb 41
St Mary's Grn. West—90Lc 167
St Mary's Gro. N1—37Rb 63
St Mary's Gro. SW13—55Xa 102
St Mary's Gro. W4—51Ra 101
St Mary's Gro. Rich—56Pa 101
St Mary's Gro. West—90Lc 167
St Mary's La. Upm & Brtwd —33Rd 69 to 31Ee 71
St Mary's Mans. W2 —43Fb 81 (7B 190)
St Mary's M. NW6—38Db 61
St Mary's Path. N1—39Rb 63
St Mary's Rd. E10—34Ec 64
St Mary's Rd. E13—40Kc 65
St Mary's Rd. N8—28Nb 42
St Mary's Rd. N9—18Xb 25
St Mary's Rd. NW10—39Ua 60
St Mary's Rd. NW11—31Ab 60
St Mary's Rd. SE15—53Yb 106
St Mary's Rd. SE25—69Ub 127
St Mary's Rd. SW19—64Ab 124
St Mary's Rd. W5—47Ma 79
St Mary's Rd. Barn—17Hb 23
St Mary's Rd. Bex—60Ed 110
St Mary's Rd. E Mol—71Fa 142
St Mary's Rd. Grays—9D 92
St Mary's Rd. Grnh—57Ud 112
St Mary's Rd. Hay—45V 76
St Mary's Rd. Ilf—33Tc 66
St Mary's Rd. Lea—94Ka 176
★St Mary's Rd. Sev—89Ce
St Mary's Rd. Slou—46A 74
St Mary's Rd. S Croy—81Tb 165
St Mary's Rd. Surb—72Ma 143
St Mary's Rd. Surb—73La 142 (Long Ditton)
St Mary's Rd. Swan—70Fd 132
St Mary's Rd. Uxb—30H 35 (Denham)
St Mary's Rd. Uxb—27K 35 (Harefield)
St Mary's Rd. Wal X—1Yb 12
St Mary's Rd. Wat—14X 19
St Mary's Rd. Wey—77T 140
St Mary's Rd. Wok—5F 188
St Mary's Rd. Wor Pk—75Ua 144
St Mary's Sq. W2 —43Fb 81 (7B 190)
St Mary's Ter. W2 —43Fb 81 (7B 190)
St Mary St. SE18—49Pc 86
St Mary's Wlk. SE11 —49Qb 82 (5A 206)
St Mary's Wlk. Hay—45V 76
St Mary's Way. Chig—22Qc 46
St Mary's Way. Ger X—26A 34
St Mary's Way. Long, Dart —69Ae 135
St Matthew Clo. Uxb—44M 75
St Matthew's Av. Surb—74Na 143
St Matthew's Clo. Rain—38Jd 68
St Matthew's Clo. Wat—16Z 19
St Matthew's Dri. Brom—69Pc 130
St Matthew's Rd. SW2—57Pb 104
St Matthew's Rd. W5—46Na 79
St Matthew's Row. E2—42Wb 83
St Matthew St. SW1 —48Mb 82 (4D 204)
St Matthias Clo. NW9—29Va 40
St Maur Rd. SW6—53Bb 103
St Merryn Clo. SE18—52Tc 108
St Merryn Ct. Beck—66Cc 128
St Michael's All. EC3 —44Tb 83 (3G 201)
St Michael's Av. N9—17Yb 26
St Michael's Av. Wemb—37Qa 59
St Michael's Clo. N3—26Bb 41
St Michael's Clo. N12—22Gb 41
St Michael's Clo. Brom—69Nc 130
St Michael's Clo. Eri—47Zc 87
St Michael's Clo. W on T—75Y 141
St Michael's Ct. Slou—2B 72
St Michael's Cres. Pinn—30Aa 37
St Michael's Dri. Sev—88Md 171
St Michael's Gdns. W10—43Ab 80
St Michael's Rise. Well—53Xc 109
St Michael's Rd. NW2—35Ya 60
St Michael's Rd. SW9—54Pb 104
St Michael's Rd. Ashf—64Q 120
St Michael's Rd. Cat—94Tb 181
St Michael's Rd. Croy—74Sb 147
St Michael's Rd. Wall—79Lb 146
St Michael's Rd. Well—55Xc 109
St Michael's Rd. Wok—86F 156
St Michael's St. W2 —44Fb 81 (2C 196)
St Michael's Ter. N22—25Nb 42
St Michael's Way. Pot B—2Db 9
St Mildred's Ct. EC2 —44Tb 83 (3F 201)
St Mildred's Rd. SE12—59Hc 107
St Monica's Rd. Tad—93Bb 179
St Neot's Rd. Romf—24Pd 49
St Nicholas Av. Horn—34Jd 68
St Nicholas Av. Lea—97Da 175
St Nicholas Clo. Borwd—16Ma 21
St Nicholas Clo. Uxb—44M 75
St Nicholas Dri. Sev—98Kd 187
St Nicholas Dri. Shep—73Q 140
St Nicholas Glebe. SW17 —64Jb 126
St Nicholas Gro. Brtwd—22Ee 51
St Nicholas Hill. Lea—94Ka 176
St Nicholas Rd. SE18—50Vc 87
St Nicholas Rd. Sutt—78Db 145
St Nicholas Rd. Th Dit—72Ha 142
St Nicholas St. SE8—53Bc 106
St Nicholas Way. Sutt—77Db 145
St Nicolas La. Chst—67Nc 130
St Norbert Grn. SE4—56Ac 106
St Norbert Rd. SE4—57Zb 106
St Norman's Way. Eps—82Wa 162
St Olaf's Rd. SW6—52Ab 102
St Olave's Clo. Stai—66H 119
St Olave's Ct. EC2 —44Tb 83 (3F 201)
St Olave's Gdns. SE11 —49Qb 82 (5K 205)
St Olave's Rd. E6—39Qc 66
St Olave's Ter. SE1—(1J 207)
St Olave's Wlk. SW16—68Lb 126
St Oswald's Pl. SE11 —50Pb 82 (7H 205)
St Oswald's Rd. SW16—67Rb 127
St Oswulf St. SW1—(6E 204)
St Pancras Ct. N2—26Fb 41
St Pancras Way. NW1 —38Lb 62 (1D 192)
St Patrick's Ct. Wfd G—24Gc 45
St Patrick's Gdns. Grav—2F 136
St Paul Clo. Uxb—43M 75
St Paul's All. EC4—(3C 200)
St Paul's Av. NW2—37Ya 60
St Paul's Av. SE16—46Zb 84
St Paul's Av. Harr—28Pa 39
St Paul's Av. Slou—5K 73
St Paul's Chyd. EC4 —44Rb 83 (3C 200)
St Paul's Clo. W5—47Pa 79
St Paul's Clo. Ashf—64S 120
St Paul's Clo. Cars—74Gb 145
St Paul's Clo. Chess—77Ma 143
St Paul's Clo. Hay—50T 76
St Paul's Clo. Houn—54Aa 99
St Paul's Clo. S Ock—45Sd 90
St Paul's Cray Rd. Chst—67Tc 130
St Paul's Cres. NW1—38Mb 62
St Paul's Dri. E15—36Fc 65
St Paul's Pl. N1—37Tb 63
St Paul's Pl. S Ock—45Sd 90
St Paul's Rd. N1—37Rb 63
St Paul's Rd. N11—22Kb 42
St Paul's Rd. N17—25Wb 43
St Paul's Rd. Bark—39Sc 66
St Paul's Rd. Bren—51Ma 101
St Paul's Rd. Eri—52Ed 110
St Paul's Rd. Rich—55Pa 101
St Paul's Rd. Stai—64F 118
St Paul's Rd. T Hth—69Sb 127
St Paul's Rd. Wok—89D 156
St Paul's Sq. Brom—68Hc 129
St Paul St. N1—39Sb 63 (1D 194) (in two parts)
St Paul's Wlk. King—66Qa 123
St Paul's Way. E3—43Bc 84
St Paul's Way. N3—24Db 41
St Paul's Way. Wat—12Y 19
St Paul's Wood Hill. Orp—68Uc 130
St Peter's All. EC3—(3H 201)
St Peter's Av. E2—40Wb 63
St Peter's Av. E17—28Gc 45
St Peter's Av. N18—21Wb 43
St Petersburgh M. W2—45Db 81
St Petersburgh Pl. W2—45Db 81
St Peter's Clo. E2—40Wb 63
St Peter's Clo. SW17—61Gb 125
St Peter's Clo. Barn—15Xa 22
St Peter's Clo. Bush, Wat—18Fa 20
St Peter's Clo. Chst—66Tc 130
St Peter's Clo. Ger X—25A 34
St Peter's Clo. Ilf—28Vc 47
St Peter's Clo. Rick—18K 17
St Peter's Clo. Ruis—33Z 57
St Peter's Clo. Slou—2A 72
St Peter's Clo. Stai—65H 119
St Peter's Clo. Wind—7L 95
St Peter's Clo. Wok—92E 172
St Peter's Ct. NW4—29Ya 40
St Peter's Ct. Ger X—25A 34
St Peter's Gdns. SE27—62Qb 126
St Peter's Gro. W6—49Wa 80
St Peter's Rd. N9—18Xb 25
St Peter's Rd. W6—50Wa 80
St Peter's Rd. Brtwd—21Xd 50
St Peter's Rd. Croy—77Tb 147
St Peter's Rd. E Mol—70Ca 121
St Peter's Rd. Grays—9D 92
St Peter's Rd. Iswth—57Ka 100
St Peter's Rd. King—68Qa 123
St Peter's Rd. S'hall—43Ca 77
St Peter's Rd. Uxb—43M 75
St Peter's Rd. Wok—90D 172
St Peter's Sq. E2—40Wb 63
St Peter's Sq. W6—50Wa 80
St Peter's St. N1—39Rb 63 (1C 194)
St Peter's St. S Croy—78Tb 147
St Peter's St. M. N1—(1C 194)
St Peter's Ter. SW6—52Bb 103
St Peter's Vs. W6—49Wa 80
St Peter's Way. N1—38Ub 63
St Peter's Way. W5—43Ma 79
St Peter's Way. Cher & Wey —77F 138
St Peter's Way. Hay—50T 76

St Peter's Way—Scotscraig

St Peter's Way. Rick—14D 16
St Philip's Av. Wor Pk—75Xa 144
St Philip's Pl. W2 —43Fb 81 (7B 190)
St Philip Sq. SW8—54Kb 104
St Philip's Rd. E8—37Wb 63
St Philip's Rd. Surb—72Ma 143
St Philip St. SW8—54Kb 104
St Philip's Way. N1—39Sb 63
St Pinnock Av. Stai—67J 119
St Quentin Rd. Well—55Vc 109
St Quintin Av. W10—43Ya 80
St Quintin Gdns. W10—43Ya 80
St Quintin Rd. E13—41Kc 85
St Raphael's Way. NW10—36Sa 59
St Regis Clo. N10—26Kb 42
St Regis Heights. NW3—34Db 61
St Ronan's Clo. Barn—10Fb 9
St Ronan's Cres. Wfd G—24Jc 45
St Rule St. SW8—54Lb 104
St Saviour's Rd. SW2—57Pb 104
St Saviour's Rd. Croy—72Sb 147
Saints Dri. E7—36Mc 65
St Silas Pl. NW5—37Jb 62
St Simon's Av. SW15—57Ya 102
St Stephen's Av. E17—29Ec 44
St Stephen's Av. W12—47Xa 80
St Stephen's Av. W13—44Ka 78
St Stephen's Av. Asht—88Na 161
St Stephen's Clo. E17—29Dc 44
St Stephen's Clo. NW8—39Gb 61
St Stephen's Clo. S'hall—43Ca 77
St Stephen's Cres. W2—44Cb 81
St Stephen's Cres. Brtwd—21Ce 51
St Stephen's Cres. T Hth—69Qb 126
St Stephen's Gdns. SW15 —57Bb 103
St Stephen's Gdns. W2—44Cb 81 (in two parts)
St Stephen's Gdns. Twic —58La 100
St Stephen's Gro. SE13—55Ec 106
St Stephen's M. W2—43Cb 81
St Stephen's Pas. Twic—58La 100
St Stephen's Rd. E3—39Ac 64
St Stephen's Rd. E6—38Lc 65
St Stephen's Rd. E17—29Dc 44
St Stephen's Rd. W13—44Ka 78
St Stephen's Rd. Barn—15Za 22
St Stephen's Rd. Enf—9Zb 12
St Stephen's Rd. Houn—58Ca 99
St Stephen's Rd. W Dray—46M 75
St Stephen's Row. EC4—(3F 201)
St Stephen's Ter. SW8—52Pb 104
St Stephen's Wlk. SW7 —49Eb 81 (5A 202)
Saint's Wlk. Grays—9E 92
St Swithin's La. EC4 —45Tb 83 (4F 201)
St Swithun's Rd. SE13—58Fc 107
St Teresa Wlk. Grays—9D 92
St Theresa's Rd. Felt—56V 98
St Thomas Ct. Bex—59Cd 110
St Thomas Dri. Orp—74Sc 150
St Thomas' Dri. Pinn—25Aa 37
St Thomas Gdns. Bark—37Sc 66
St Thomas Pl. Grays—51De 113
St Thomas Rd. E16—44Jc 85
St Thomas Rd. N14—17Mb 24
St Thomas Rd. W4—51Sa 101
St Thomas Rd. Belv—47Ed 88
St Thomas Rd. Brtwd—19Zd 33
St Thomas's Av. Grav—10D 114
St Thomas's Clo. Wal A—5Kc 13
St Thomas's Gdns. NW5—37Jb 62
St Thomas's Pl. E9—38Yb 64
St Thomas's Rd. N4—33Qb 62
St Thomas's Rd. NW10—39Ua 60
St Thomas's Sq. E9—38Yb 64
St Thomas St. SE1 —46Tb 83 (7G 201)
St Thomas's Way. SW6—52Bb 103
St Ursula Gro. Pinn—29Z 37
St Ursula Rd. S'hall—44Ca 77
St Vincent Rd. Twic—58Ea 100
St Vincent Rd. W on T—76X 141
St Vincent's Av. Dart—57Qd 111
St Vincent's Rd. Dart—58Qd 111
St Vincent St. W1 —43Jb 82 (1J 197)
St Vincent's Way. Pot B—6Eb 9
St Wilfrid's Clo. Barn—15Gb 23
St Wilfrid's Rd. Barn—15Gb 23
St Winefride's Av. E12—36Pc 66
St Winifred's Clo. Chig—22Sc 46
St Winifred's Rd. Tedd—65Ka 122
St Winifred's Rd. West—90Pc 168
Saladin Dri. Purf—49Qd 89
Salamanca Pl. SE1 —49Pb 82 (6H 205)
Salamanca St. SE1 & SE11 —49Pb 82 (6H 205)
Salamons Way. Rain—44Gd 88
Salcombe Dri. Mord—74Za 144
Salcombe Dri. Romf—30Bd 47
Salcombe Gdns. NW7—23Ya 40
Salcombe Rd. E17—31Bc 64
Salcombe Rd. N16—36Ub 63
Salcombe Rd. Ashf—62N 119
Salcombe Way. Hay—41U 76
Salcombe Way. Ruis—33W 56
Salcot Cres. Croy—82Ec 166
Salcote Rd. Grav—4G 136
Salcott Rd. SW11—57Gb 103
Salcott Rd. Croy—76Nb 146
Salehurst Clo. Harr—29Na 39
Salehurst Rd. SE4—58Bc 106
Salem Pl. Croy—76Sb 147
Salem Pl. Grav—59Fe 113
Salem Rd. W2—45Db 81
Sale Pl. W2—44Gb 81 (1D 196)
Sale St. E2—42Wb 83
Salford Rd. SW2—60Mb 104
Salhouse Clo. SE28—44Yc 87
Salisbury Av. N3—27Bb 41
Salisbury Av. Bark—38Tc 66
Salisbury Av. Slou—2G 72
Salisbury Av. Sutt—79Bb 145
Salisbury Av. Swan—70Jd 132
Salisbury Clo. SE17 —49Tb 83 (6F 207)
Salisbury Clo. Pot B—4Eb 9
Salisbury Clo. Upm—33Ud 70
Salisbury Clo. Wor Pk—76Va 144
Salisbury Ct. EC4 —44Rb 83 (3B 200)
Salisbury Cres. Wal X—4Zb 12
Salisbury Gdns. SW19—66Ab 124
Salisbury Gdns. Buck H—19Mc 27
Salisbury Hall Gdns. E4—24Cc 44
Salisbury M. SW6—52Bb 103
Salisbury Pl. W1 —43Hb 81 (7G 191)
Salisbury Rd. E4—20Cc 26
Salisbury Rd. E7—37Jc 65
Salisbury Rd. E10—33Ec 64
Salisbury Rd. E12—36Mc 65
Salisbury Rd. E17—29Ec 44
Salisbury Rd. N4—29Rb 43
Salisbury Rd. N9—20Wb 25
Salisbury Rd. N22—26Rb 43
Salisbury Rd. SE25—72Wb 147
Salisbury Rd. SW19—66Ab 124
Salisbury Rd. W13—47Ka 78
Salisbury Rd. Bans—86Db 163
Salisbury Rd. Barn—13Ab 22
Salisbury Rd. Bex—60Cd 110
Salisbury Rd. Brom—71Nc 150
Salisbury Rd. Cars—79Hb 145
Salisbury Rd. Dag—37Dd 68
Salisbury Rd. Dart—60Sd 112
Salisbury Rd. Enf—9Bc 12
Salisbury Rd. Felt—60Y 99
Salisbury Rd. Grav—10B 114
Salisbury Rd. Grays—50Ee 91
Salisbury Rd. Harr—29Fa 38
Salisbury Rd. Houn—55Y 99
Salisbury Rd. Ilf—33Uc 66
Salisbury Rd. N Mald—69Ta 123
Salisbury Rd. Pinn—28W 36
Salisbury Rd. Rich—56Na 101
Salisbury Rd. Romf—29Kd 49
Salisbury Rd. S'hall—49Aa 77
Salisbury Rd. Uxb—40K 55
Salisbury Rd. Wat—10X 5
Salisbury Rd. Wok—91A 172
Salisbury Rd. Wor Pk—77Ta 143
Salisbury Sq. EC4 —44Qb 82 (3A 200)
Salisbury St. NW8 —42Gb 81 (6D 190)
Salisbury St. W3—47Sa 79
Salisbury Ter. SE15—55Yb 106
Salisbury Wlk. N19—33Lb 62
Salix Clo. Sun—66X 121
Salix Rd. Grays—51Fe 113
Salliesfield. Twic—58Fa 100
Sallows Shaw. Grav—10F 136
Salmen Rd. E13—40Hc 65
Salmond Clo. Stan—23Ja 38
Salmonds Gro. Brtwd—22Ee 51
Salmon La. E14—44Ac 84
Salmon Rd. Belv—50Cd 88
Salmons La. Cat & Whyt —92Ub 181
Salmons La. W. Cat—92Ub 181
Salmons Rd. N9—18Wb 25
Salmons Rd. Chess—79Na 143
Salmons Rd. Lea—100X 175
Salmon St. NW9—32Ra 59
Salomons Rd. E13—43Lc 85
Salop Rd. E17—30Zb 44
Saltash Clo. Sutt—77Bb 145
Saltash Ho. SE11—(7B 206)
Saltash Rd. Ilf—24Tc 46
Saltash Rd. Well—53Yc 109
Saltbox Hill. West—85Kc 167
Saltcoats Rd. W4—47Ua 80
Saltcroft Clo. Wemb—32Ra 59
Salterford Rd. SW17—65Jb 126
Salter Rd. SE16—46Zb 84
Salters Ct. EC4—(3E 200)
Salter's Hall Ct. EC4—(4F 201)
Salters Hill. SE19—64Tb 127
Salters Rd. E17—28Fc 45
Salters Rd. W10—42Za 80
Salter St. E14—45Cc 84
Salter St. NW10—41Wa 80
Salterton Rd. N7—34Pb 62
Saltford Clo. Eri—50Gd 88
Salt Hill Av. Slou—6G 72
Salt Hill Clo. Uxb—36N 55
Salt Hill Dri. Slou—6G 72
Salt Hill Mans. Slou—6G 72
Salt Hill Way. Slou—6G 72
Saltoun Rd. SW2—56Qb 104
Saltram Clo. N15—28Vb 43
Saltram Cres. W9—41Bb 81
Saltwell St. E14—45Cc 84
Saltwood Clo. Orp—77Yc 151
Saltwood Gro. SE17—50Tb 83
Salusbury Rd. NW6—39Ab 60
Salvador. SW17—64Gb 125
Salva Gdns. Gnfd—40Ja 58
Salvin Rd. SW15—55Za 102
Salway Clo. Wfd G—24Jc 45
Salway Pl. E15—37Fc 65
Salway Rd. E15—37Fc 65
Samantha Clo. E17—31Bc 64
Samantha M. Hav, Romf—20Gd 30
Sam Bartram Clo. SE7—50Lc 85
Samels Ct. W6—50Wa 80
Samford St. NW8 —42Gb 81 (6D 190)
Samos Rd. SE20—68Xb 127
Samphire Ct. Grays—1A 114
Sampson Av. Barn—15Za 22
Sampson's Grn. Slou—1D 72
Sampson St. E1—46Wb 83
Samson St. E13—40Lc 65
Samuda Est. E14—48Ec 84
Samuel Clo. E8—39Vb 63
Samuel Johnson Clo. SW16 —63Pb 126
Samuel Lewis Trust Dwellings. SW3—(6D 202)
Samuel St. SE18—49Pc 86
Sancroft Clo. NW2—34Xa 60
Sancroft Rd. Harr—26Ha 38
Sancroft St. SE11 —50Pb 82 (7J 205)
Sanctuary Clo. Dart—58Ld 111
Sanctuary Clo. Uxb—24L 35
Sanctuary St. SE1 —47Sb 83 (1E 206)
Sanctuary, The. SW1—(3E 204)
Sanctuary, The. Bex—58Zc 109
Sanctuary, The. Mord—72Cb 145
Sandale Clo. N16—34Tb 63
Sandall Clo. W5—42Na 79
Sandall Rd. NW5—37Lb 62
Sandall Rd. W5—42Na 79
Sandal Rd. N18—22Wb 43
Sandal Rd. N Mald—70Ua 124
Sandal St. E15—39Gc 65
Sandalwood Av. Cher—76G 138
Sandalwood Clo. E1—42Ac 84
Sandalwood Rd. Felt—62X 121
Sandbach Pl. SE18—50Sc 86
Sandbanks Hill. Dart—65Xd 134
Sandbourne Av. SW19—68Db 125
Sandbourne Rd. SE4—54Ac 106
Sandbrook Clo. Edgw—23Ta 39
Sandbrook Rd. N16—34Ub 63
Sandby Grn. SE9—55Nc 108
Sandcliff Rd. Eri—49Fd 88
Sandell's Av. Ashf—63S 120
Sandell St. SE1—47Qb 82 (1K 205)
Sanderling Ct. SE28—45Yc 87
Sanders Clo. Hmptn—64Ea 122
Sandersfield Gdns. Bans —87Cb 163
Sandersfield Rd. Bans—86Db 163
Sanders La. NW7—24Ya 40
Sanderson Av. Sev—82Cd 170
Sanderson Clo. NW5—35Kb 62
Sanderson Cres. Gnfd—40Ja 58
Sanderson Sq. Brom—69Pc 130
Sanderstead Av. NW2—33Ab 60
Sanderstead Clo. SW12—59Lb 104
Sanderstead Ct. Av. S Croy —85Wb 165
Sanderstead Hill. S Croy —83Ub 165
Sanderstead Rd. E10—32Ac 64
Sanderstead Rd. Orp—72Xc 151
Sanderstead Rd. S Croy —80Tb 147
Sanders Way. N19—32Mb 62
Sandes Pl. Lea—90Ja 160
Sandfield Gdns. T Hth—69Rb 127
Sandfield Rd. T Hth—69Rb 127
Sandfields. Wok—96F 172
Sandford Av. N22—25Sb 43
Sandford Av. Lou—13Sc 28
Sandford Clo. E6—42Pc 86
Sandford Rd. E6—41Nc 86
Sandford Rd. Bexh—56Ad 109
Sandford Rd. Brom—70Jc 129
Sandford St. SW6—52Db 103
Sandford Way. Cob—85Ca 159
Sandgate Rd. Well—52Yc 109
Sandgate St. SE15—51Xb 105
Sandhills. Wall—77Mb 146
Sandhills Ct. Vir W—71A 138
Sandhills La. Vir W—71A 138
Sandhurst Av. Harr—30Da 37
Sandhurst Av. Surb—73Ra 143
Sandhurst Clo. NW9—27Qa 39
Sandhurst Clo. S Croy—81Ub 165
Sandhurst Dri. Ilf—35Vc 67
Sandhurst Rd. N9—16Yb 26
Sandhurst Rd. NW9—27Qa 39
Sandhurst Rd. SE6—60Fc 107
Sandhurst Rd. Bex—57Zc 109
Sandhurst Rd. Orp—76Wc 151
Sandhurst Rd. Sidc—62Wc 131
Sandhurst Rd. Til—4E 114
Sandhurst Way. S Croy—80Ub 147
Sandiford Rd. Sutt—75Bb 145
Sandiland Cres. Brom—75Hc 149
Sandilands. Croy—75Wb 147
Sandilands. Sev—94Fd 186
Sandilands Rd. SW6—53Db 103
Sandison St. SE15—55Wb 105
Sandlands Gro. Tad—95Wa 178
Sandlands Rd. Tad—95Wa 178
Sandland St. WC1 —43Pb 82 (1J 199)
Sandlers End. Slou—2F 72
Sandling Rise. SE9—62Qc 130
Sandlings, The. N22—27Rb 43
Sandmere Rd. SW4—56Nb 104
Sandon Clo. Esh—73Fa 142
Sandon Rd. Wal X—2Yb 12
Sandow Cres. Hay—48V 76
Sandown Av. Dag—37Ed 68
Sandown Av. Esh—78Ea 142
Sandown Av. Horn—33Md 69
Sandown Clo. Houn—53W 98
Sandown Dri. Cars—81Jb 164
Sandown Industrial Pk. Esh —75Ca 141
Sandown Rd. SE25—71Xb 147
Sandown Rd. Coul—88Jb 164
Sandown Rd. Esh—77Ea 142
Sandown Rd. Grav—5E 136
Sandown Rd. Grays—3G 92
Sandown Rd. Slou—3D 72
Sandown Rd. Wat—10Y 5
Sandown Way. N'holt—37Aa 57
Sandpiper Rd. S Croy—83Zb 166
Sandpit Hall Rd. Chob—1E 188
Sandpit La. Brtwd—18Vd 32
Sandpit La. Wok—3A 188
Sandpit Rd. SE7—50Nc 86
Sandpit Rd. Brom—64Gc 129
Sandpit Rd. Dart—56Ld 111
Sandpits Rd. Croy—77Zb 148
Sandpits Rd. Rich—61Ma 123
Sandra Clo. N22—25Sb 43
Sandra Clo. Houn—57Da 99
Sandridge Clo. Harr—28Ga 38
Sandringham Av. SW20 —68Ab 124
Sandringham Clo. Enf—12Ub 25
Sandringham Clo. Ilf—27Sc 46
Sandringham Ct. W9—(4A 190)
Sandringham Ct. Slou—4B 72
Sandringham Ct. Sutt—81Cb 163
Sandringham Ct. Uxb—42S 76
Sandringham Cres. Harr—33Ca 57
Sandringham Dri. Ashf—63M 119
Sandringham Dri. Well—54Uc 108
Sandringham Gdns. N8—30Nb 42
Sandringham Gdns. N12—23Fb 41
Sandringham Gdns. Houn —53W 98
Sandringham Gdns. Ilf—27Sc 46
Sandringham M. W5—45Ma 79
Sandringham Rd. E7—36Lc 65
Sandringham Rd. E8—36Vb 63
Sandringham Rd. E10—30Fc 45
Sandringham Rd. N22—26Sb 43
Sandringham Rd. NW2—37Xa 60
Sandringham Rd. NW11—31Ab 60
Sandringham Rd. Bark—37Vc 67
Sandringham Rd. Brtwd—16Xd 32
Sandringham Rd. Brom—64Jc 129
Sandringham Rd. Houn—57N 97
Sandringham Rd. N'holt—38Ca 57
Sandringham Rd. Pot B—2Db 9
Sandringham Rd. T Hth—71Sb 147
Sandringham Rd. Wat—9Y 5
Sandringham Rd. Wor Pk —76Wa 144
Sandringham Way. Wal X—6Zb 12
Sandrock Pl. Croy—77Zb 148
Sandrock Rd. SE13—55Cc 106
Sandroyd Way. Cob—85Ca 159
Sand's End La. SW6—53Db 103
Sands Farm Dri. Slou—2A 72
Sandstone Pl. N19—33Kb 62
Sandstone Rd. SE12—61Kc 129
Sands Way. Wfd G—23Pc 46
Sandtoft Rd. SE7—51Kc 107
Sandway Rd. Orp—70Yc 131
Sandwell Cres. NW6—37Cb 61
Sandwich St. WC1 —41Nb 82 (4F 193)
Sandy Bank Rd. Grav—10D 114
Sandy Bury. Orp—76Tc 150
Sandy Clo. Wok—89E 156
Sandycombe Rd. Felt—60W 98
Sandycombe Rd. Rich—55Qa 101
Sandycombe Rd. Twic—58La 100
Sandycroft. SE2—51Wc 109
Sandy Dri. Cob—83Ca 159
Sandy Dri. Felt—60U 98
Sandy Hill Av. SE18—50Rc 86
Sandy Hill Rd. SE18—50Rc 86
Sandyhill Rd. Ilf—35Rc 66
Sandy Hill Rd. Wall—81Lb 164
Sandy La. Bush, Wat & Wat —13Ea 20
Sandy La. Cob & Lea—84Ba 159
Sandy La. Dart—61Yd 134 (in two parts)
Sandy La. Grays—1D 114 (Biggin)
Sandy La. Grays—51Xd 112 (West Thurrock)
Sandy La. Harr—30Pa 39
Sandy La. Mitc—67Jb 126
Sandy La. N'wd—19V 18
Sandy La. Orp—73Wc 151
Sandy La. Orp & Sidc—68Zc 131
Sandy La. Oxt—100Ec 182
Sandy La. Oxt—99Kc 183 (Limpsfield)
Sandy La. Rain & S Ock—45Pd 89
Sandy La. Rich—61La 122
Sandy La. Sev—95Ld 187
★Sandy La. Sev—96Xd (Ightham Common)
Sandy La. Sutt—81Ab 162
Sandy La. Tad—96Bb 179
Sandy La. Tedd & King—66Ja 122
Sandy La. Vir W—70A 118
Sandy La. W on T—72X 141
Sandy La. West—97Tc 184
Sandy La. Wok—89D 156
Sandy La. Wok—89J 157 (Pyrford Village)
Sandy La. Wok—95E 172 (Send)
Sandy La. N. Wall—78Mb 146
Sandy La. S. Wall—81Lb 164
Sandy Lodge La. N'wd—19T 18
Sandy Lodge Rd. Rick—19R 18
Sandy Lodge Way. N'wd—22Ua 38
Sandymount Av. Stan—22La 38
Sandy Ridge. Chst—65Qc 130
★Sandy Ridge. Sev—92Ce
Sandy Rise. Ger X—25A 34
Sandy Rd. NW3—33Db 61
Sandy Rd. Wey—79J 139
Sandys Row. E1—43Ub 83 (1J 201)
Sandy Way. Cob—84Ca 159
Sandy Way. Croy—76Bc 148
Sandy Way. W on T—74V 140
Sandy Way. Wok—89E 156
Sanford Clo. Ruis—30S 36
Sanford La. N16—33Vb 63
Sanford St. SE14—51Ac 106
Sanford Ter. N16—34Vb 63
Sanford Wlk. N16—33Vb 63
Sanford Wlk. SE14—51Ac 106
Sanger Av. Chess—78Na 143
Sangley Rd. SE6—59Dc 106
Sangley Rd. SE25—70Ub 127
Sangora Rd. SW11—56Fb 103
Sansom Rd. E11—33Hc 65
Sansom St. SE5—53Tb 105
Sans Wlk. EC1—42Qb 82 (5B 194)
Santers La. Pot B—5Ab 8
Santley St. SW4—56Pb 104
Santos Rd. SW18—57Cb 103
Santway, The. Stan—22Ga 38
Sanway Clo. Wey—86N 157
Sanway Rd. Wey—86N 157
Sapcote Trading Est. NW10 —37Va 60
Saperton Wlk. SE11—(5J 205)
Sapho Pk. Grav—3H 137
Saphora Clo. Orp—78Tc 150
Sapphire Rd. SE8—49Ac 84
Sappho Ct. Wok—4B 188
Saracen Clo. Croy—72Tb 147
Saracen's Head Yd. EC3—(3K 201)
Saracen St. E14—44Cc 84
Sarah St. N1—41Ub 83 (3J 195)
Sara Pk. Grav—3G 136
Saratoga Rd. E5—35Yb 64
Sardinia St. WC2 —44Pb 82 (2H 199)
Sargeant Clo. Uxb—41M 75
Sarita Clo. Harr—26Fa 38
Sarjant Path. SW19—61Za 124
Sark Clo. Houn—52Ca 99
Sark Wlk. E16—44Kc 85
Sarnesfield Rd. Enf—14Tb 25
Sarratt La. Rick—12K 17
Sarratt Rd. Rick—9K 3
Sarre Av. Horn—37Ld 69
Sarre Rd. NW2—36Bb 61
Sarre Rd. Orp—71Yc 151
Sarsen Av. Houn—54Ca 99
Sarsfeld Rd. SW12—60Hb 103
Sarsfield Rd. Gnfd—40Ka 58
Sartor Rd. SE15—56Zb 106
Sarum Grn. Wey—76U 140
Satchell Mead. NW9—25Va 40
Satchwell Rd. E2—41Wb 83
Sauls Grn. E11—34Gc 65
Saunders Clo. Grav—1A 136
Saunders Copse. Wok—10E 188
Saunders La. Wok—10C 188
Saunders Ness Rd. E14—50Ec 84
Saunders Rd. SE18—50Vc 87
Saunders Rd. Uxb—38P 55
Saunders Way. SE28—45Xc 87
Saunderton Rd. Wemb—36Ka 58
Saunton Av. Hay—52V 98
Saunton Rd. Horn—33Jd 68
Savage Gdns. E6—44Pc 86
Savage Gdns. EC3 —45Ub 83 (4J 201)
Savay Clo. Uxb—31J 55
Savay La. Uxb—30J 35
Savernake Rd. N9—16Wb 25
Savernake Rd. NW3—35Hb 61
Savile Clo. N Mald—71Ua 144
Savile Gdns. Croy—75Vb 147
Savile Row. W1—45Lb 82 (4B 198)
Saville Cres. Ashf—65T 120
Saville Rd. E16—46Nc 86
Saville Rd. W4—48Ta 79
Saville Rd. Romf—30Bd 47
Saville Rd. Twic—60Ha 100
Saville Row. Enf—12Zb 26
Savill Gdns. SW20—69Wa 124
Savill Row. Wfd G—23Hc 45
Savona Clo. SW19—66Za 124
Savona St. SW8—52Lb 104
Savoy Av. Hay—50U 76
Savoy Bldgs. WC2—(5H 199)
Savoy Clo. E15—39Gc 65
Savoy Clo. Edgw—22Qa 39
Savoy Clo. Uxb—26M 35
Savoy Ct. NW3—34Db 61
Savoy Ct. WC2—45Pb 82 (5G 199)
Savoy Hill. WC2—45Pb 82 (5H 199)
Savoy Pde. Enf—13Ub 25
Savoy Pl. WC2—45Nb 82 (5G 199)
Savoy Rd. Dart—57Md 111
Savoy Row. WC2—(4H 199)
Savoy Steps. WC2—(5H 199)
Savoy St. WC2—45Pb 82 (4H 199)
Savoy Way. WC2—(5H 199)
Sawkins Clo. SW19—61Ab 124
Sawley Rd. W12—46Wa 80
Sawtry Clo. Cars—73Gb 145
Sawyer's Chase. Romf—13Xc 29
Sawyers Clo. Dag—37Ed 68
Sawyers Clo. Wind—2C 94
Sawyers Hall La. Brtwd—17Yd 32
Sawyer's Hill. Rich—59Pa 101
Sawyers La. Borwd—11Ka 20
Sawyers La. Pot B—5Za 8
Sawyers Lawn. W13—44Ja 78
Sawyer St. SE1—47Sb 83 (1D 206)
★Saxbys Rd. Sev—94Td
Saxby Rd. SW2—59Nb 104
Saxham Rd. Bark—39Uc 66
Saxlingham Rd. E4—20Fc 27
Saxon Av. Felt—61Aa 121
Saxonbury Av. Sun—69X 121
Saxonbury Clo. Mitc—69Fb 125
Saxonbury Gdns. Surb—74La 142
Saxon Clo. Brtwd—20Ce 33
Saxon Clo. Grav—62Ee 135
Saxon Clo. Romf—26Pd 49
Saxon Clo. Slou—47B 74
Saxon Clo. Uxb—43P 75
Saxon Ct. Borwd—11Na 21
Saxon Dri. W3—44Qa 79
Saxon Gdns. S'hall—45Aa 77
Saxon Pl. S Dar, Dart—71Sd 154
Saxon Rd. E3—40Bc 64
Saxon Rd. E6—42Pc 86
Saxon Rd. N22—25Rb 43
Saxon Rd. SE25—71Tb 147
Saxon Rd. Ashf—65T 120
Saxon Rd. Brom—66Hc 129
Saxon Rd. Dart—63Nd 133
Saxon Rd. Ilf—37Rc 66
Saxon Rd. S'hall—45Aa 77
Saxon Rd. W on T—75Z 141
Saxon Rd. Wemb—34Sa 59
Saxon Shore Way. Grav—8L 115
Saxon Wlk. Sidc—65Yc 131
Saxon Way. N14—16Mb 24
Saxon Way. Wal A—5Ec 12
Saxon Way. W Dray—51L 97
Saxon Way. Wind—8M 95
Saxony Pde. Hay—43S 76
Saxton Clo. SE13—55Fc 107
Saxville Rd. Orp—69Xc 131
Sayer Ct. Wok—6B 188
Sayers Clo. Lea—95Ea 176
Sayer's Wlk. Rich—59Pa 101
Sayes Ct. SE8—50Bc 84
Sayes Ct. Wey—78L 139
Sayes Ct. Farm Dri. Wey—78K 139
Sayes Ct. Rd. Orp—70Wc 131
Sayes Ct. St. SE8—51Bc 106
Scads Hill Clo. Orp—72Vc 151
Scafell Rd. Slou—2D 72
Scala St. W1—43Lb 82 (7C 192)
Scales Rd. N17—27Wb 43
Scampston M. W10—44Za 80
Scampton Rd. Houn—58P 97
Scandrett St. E1—46Xb 83
Scarborough Clo. Sutt—83Bb 163
Scarborough Clo. West—90Lc 167
Scarborough Rd. E11—32Fc 65
Scarborough Rd. N4—32Qb 62
Scarborough Rd. N9—17Yb 26
Scarborough St. E1 —44Vb 83 (3K 201)
Scarbrook Rd. Croy—76Sb 147
Scarle Rd. Wemb—37Ma 59
Scarlet Rd. SE6—62Gc 129
Scarlett Clo. Wok—6C 188
Scarlette Mnr. Way. SW2 —59Qb 104
Scarsbrook Rd. SE3—55Mc 107
Scarsdale Pl. W8—48Db 81
Scarsdale Rd. Harr—34Ea 58
Scarsdale Vs. W8—48Cb 81
Scarth Rd. SW13—55Va 102
Scatterdells La. K Lan—2H 3
Scawen Rd. SE8—50Ac 84
Scawfell St. E2—40Vb 63 (2K 195)
Sceau Gdns. SE5—53Ub 105
Sceptre Rd. E2—41Yb 84
Sceynes Link. N12—21Cb 41
Schofield Wlk. SE3—52Kc 107
Scholars Rd. E4—18Fc 27
Scholars Rd. SW12—60Lb 104
Scholefield Rd. N19—33Mb 62
School All. Twic—60Ja 100
School Allotment Ride. Wind —9A 94
School App. E2—41Ub 83 (3J 195)
Schoolfield Rd. Grays—51Wd 112
School Hill. Red—100Lb 180
School Ho. La. E1—45Zb 84
School Ho. La. Tedd—66Ka 122
School La. SE23—61Xb 127
School La. Bush, Wat—17Da 19
School La. Dag—34Yc 67
School La. Dart—63Yd 134
School La. Dor—99La 176
School La. Egh—64C 118
School La. Ger X—26A 34
School La. Grays—3C 92
School La. King—67La 122
School La. Lea—94Fa 176
School La. Lea—100R 174 (West Horsley)
School La. Pinn—28Aa 37
School La. Sev—93Pd 187 (Seal)
★School La. Sev—84Ud (West Kingsdown)
School La. Shep—72R 140
School La. Slou—8M 53
School La. S Dar, Dart—70Sd 134
School La. Surb—74Qa 143
School La. Swan—67Kd 133
School La. Tad—97Wa 178
School La. Wat & St Alb—6Ba 5
School La. Well—55Xc 109
School La. Wey—78J 139
School La. Wok—94R 174
School Mead. Abb L, Wat—4U 4
School Pas. S'hall—45Ba 77
School Rd. E12—35Pc 66
School Rd. NW10—42Ta 79
School Rd. Asc—10B 116
School Rd. Ashf—65R 120
★School Rd. Brtwd—9Ud
School Rd. Chst—67Sc 130
School Rd. Dag—39Cd 68
School Rd. E Mol—70Fa 122
School Rd. Grav—2E 136
School Rd. Hmptn—65Ea 122
School Rd. Houn—55Ea 100
School Rd. King—67La 122
★School Rd. Ong—4Jd
School Rd. Pot B—2Eb 9
School Rd. W on T—78V 140
School Rd. W Dray—51M 97
School Rd. Av. Hmptn—65Ea 122
School Wlk. Slou—5M 73
School Wlk. Sun—70V 120
School Way. N12—23Fb 41
Schroder Ct. Egh—4M 117
Schubert Rd. SW15—57Bb 103
Schubert Rd. Borwd—16Ma 21
Scilla Ct. Grays—51Fe 113
Sclater St. E1—42Vb 83 (5K 195)
Scoble Pl. N16—35Vb 63
Scoles Cres. SW2—60Qb 104
Scoresby St. SE1 —46Rb 83 (7B 200)
Scorton Av. Gnfd—40Ja 58
Scotch Comn. W13—43Ja 78
Scoter Clo. Wfd G—24Kc 45
Scotland Bri. Rd. Wey—83J 157
Scotland Grn. N17—26Wb 43
Scotland Grn. Rd. Enf—15Zb 26
Scotland Grn. Rd. N. Enf—14Ac 26
Scotland La. Grav—8J 137
Scotland Pl. SW1 —46Nb 82 (7F 199)
Scotland Rd. Buck H—18Lc 27
Scotlands Dri. Slou—7F 52
Scotney Wlk. Horn—36Ld 69
Scots Clo. Stai—60M 97
Scotscraig. Rad—7Ha 6

Scotsdale Clo.—Shepherdess Wlk.

Scotsdale Clo. Orp—70Uc 130
Scotsdale Clo. Sutt—80Ab 144
Scotsdale Rd. SE12—57Kc 107
Scotshall La. Warl—87Ec 166
Scots Hill. Rick—16P 17
Scots Hill Clo. Rick—16P 17
Scotswood St. EC1
—42Qb 82 (5A 194)
Scotswood Wlk. N17—24Wb 43
Scott Clo. SW16—67Pb 126
Scott Clo. Eps—78Sa 143
Scott Clo. Slou—6G 52
Scott Clo. W Dray—49P 75
Scott Cres. Eri—53Hd 110
Scott Cres. Harr—32Da 57
Scott Ellis Gdns. NW8
—41Fb 81 (4B 190)
Scottes La. Dag—32Zc 67
Scott Gdns. Houn—52Z 99
Scott Gro. Pinn—24Z 37
Scott Lidgett Cres. SE16—47Wb 83
Scott Rd. Grav—4F 136
Scott Rd. Grays—9C 92
Scotts Av. Brom—68Fc 129
Scotts Av. Sun—66U 120
Scotts Clo. Horn—36Ld 69
Scotts Dri. Hmptn—66Da 121
Scotts Farm Dri. Eps—79Sa 143
Scott's Gro. Clo. Chob—1A 188
Scott's Gro. Rd. Chob—1A 188
Scotts La. Brom—69Fc 129
Scotts La. W on T—77Z 141
Scott's Rd. E10—32Ec 64
Scotts Rd. W12—47Xa 80
Scotts Rd. Brom—66Jc 129
Scott's Rd. S'hall—48Y 77
Scott St. E1—42Xb 83
Scotts Way. Sev—94Gd 186
Scotts Way. Sun—66U 120
Scottswood Clo. Bush, Wat
—12Aa 19
Scottswood Rd. Bush, Wat
—12Aa 19
Scoulding Rd. E16—44Jc 85
Scouler St. E14—45Fc 85
Scout App. NW10—35Ua 60
Scout La. SW4—55Lb 104
Scout Way. NW7—21Ta 39
Scovell Rd. SE1—47Sb 83 (2D 206)
Scratchers La. F'ham & Long,
Dart—75Td 154
Scratton Rd. Stanf—1M 93
Scrattons Ter. Bark—39Zc 67
Scriven St. E8—39Vb 63
Scrooby St. SE6—58Dc 106
Scrubbitts Pk. Rd. Rad—7Ja 6
Scrubs La. NW10—41Wa 80
Scrutton Clo. SW12—59Mb 104
Scrutton St. EC2
—42Ub 83 (6H 195)
Scudamore La. NW9—28Sa 39
Scudders Hill. Long, Dart
—72Xd 154
Scutari Rd. SE22—57Yb 106
Scylla Pl. Wok—7D 188
Scylla Rd. SE15—55Xb 105
(in two parts)
Scylla Rd. Houn—58R 98
Seaborough Rd. Grays—9E 92
Seabright St. E2—41Xb 83
Seabrook Dri. W Wick—75Gc 149
Seabrooke Rise. Grays—51De 113
Seabrook Gdns. Romf—31Cd 68
Seabrook Rd. Dag—34Zc 67
Seaburn Clo. Rain—41Gd 88
Seacoal La. EC4—44Rb 83 (3B 200)
Seacourt Rd. SE2—47Zc 87
Seacourt Rd. Slou—49D 74
Seacroft Gdns. Wat—20Z 19
Seafield Rd. N11—21Mb 42
Seaford Clo. Ruis—33T 56
Seaford Rd. E17—27Dc 44
Seaford Rd. N15—29Tb 43
Seaford Rd. W13—46Ka 78
Seaford Rd. Enf—14Ub 25
Seaford St. WC1
—41Nb 82 (4G 193)
Seaforth Av. N Mald—71Xa 144
Seaforth Clo. Romf—24Gd 48
Seaforth Cres. N5—36Sb 63
Seaforth Dri. Wal X—6Zb 12
Seaforth Gdns. N21—17Pb 24
Seaforth Gdns. Eps—77Va 144
Seaforth Gdns. Wfd G—22Lc 45
Seager Pl. E3—43Bc 84
Seagrave Rd. SW6—51Cb 103
Seagry Rd. E11—30Jc 45
Sealand Rd. Houn—58Q 98
Sealand Wlk. N'holt—41Z 77
Seal Dri. Sev—93Pd 187
Seal Hollow Rd. Sev—96Ld 187
Seal Rd. Sev—93Ld 187
Seal St. E8—35Vb 63
Searchwood Rd. Warl—90Xb 165
Searle Pl. N4—32Pb 62
Searles Clo. SW11—52Gb 103
Searles Rd. SE1—49Tb 83 (5G 207)
Sears St. SE5—52Tb 105
Seasprite Clo. N'holt—41Z 77
Seaton Av. Ilf—36Vc 67
Seaton Clo. E13—42Jc 85
Seaton Clo. SE11
—50Qb 82 (7A 206)
Seaton Clo. SW15—60Xa 102
Seaton Clo. Twic—58Fa 100
Seaton Dri. Ashf—61N 119
Seaton Gdns. Ruis—34W 56
Seaton Rd. Dart—59Jd 110
Seaton Rd. Hay—49T 76
Seaton Rd. Mitc—68Gb 125
Seaton Rd. Twic—58Ea 100
Seaton Rd. Well—52Yc 109
Seaton Rd. Wemb—40Na 59
Seaton St. N18—22Wb 43
Sebastian Av. Brtwd—16Ce 33
Sebastian St. EC1
—41Rb 83 (4C 194)
Sebastopol Rd. N9—21Wb 43
Sebbon St. N1—38Rb 63
Sebert Rd. E7—36Kc 65
Sebright Pas. E2—40Wb 63
Sebright Rd. Barn—12Za 22
Secker Cres. Harr—25Ea 38
Secker St. SE1—46Qb 82 (7K 199)
Second Av. E12—35Nc 66
Second Av. E13—41Jc 85
Second Av. E17—29Cc 44
Second Av. N18—21Yb 44
Second Av. NW4—28Za 40
Second Av. SW14—55Ua 102
Second Av. W3—46Va 80
Second Av. W10—42Ab 80
★Second Av. Brtwd—6Yd
Second Av. Cher—74L 139
Second Av. Dag—40Dd 68
Second Av. Enf—15Vb 25
Second Av. Grays—51Wd 112
Second Av. Hay—46V 76
Second Av. Romf—29Yc 47
Second Av. Stanf—1M 93
Second Av. W on T—72X 141
Second Av. Wat—7Z 5
Second Av. Wemb—33Ma 59
Second Clo. E Mol—70Ea 122
Second Cres. Slou—3G 72
Second Cross Rd. Twic—61Ga 122
Second Way. Wemb—35Ra 59
Sedan Way. SE17
—50Ub 83 (7H 207)
Sedcombe Clo. Sidc—63Yc 131
Sedcote Rd. Enf—15Zb 26
Sedding St. SW1
—49Jb 82 (5H 203)
Seddon Rd. Mord—71Fb 145
Seddon St. WC1—41Pb 82 (4J 193)
Sedgebrook Rd. SE3—55Mc 107
Sedgecombe Av. Harr—29La 38
Sedge Ct. Grays—52Fe 113
Sedgefield Clo. Romf—21Pd 49
Sedgefield Cres. Romf—21Pd 49
Sedgeford Rd. W12—46Va 80
Sedgehill Rd. SE6—63Cc 128
Sedgemere Av. N2—27Eb 41
Sedgemere Rd. SE2—48Yc 87
Sedgemoor Dri. Dag—35Cd 68
Sedgeway. SE6—60Hc 107
Sedgewick Av. Uxb—38R 56
Sedgewood Clo. Brom—73Hc 149
Sedgmoor Pl. SE5—52Ub 105
Sedgwick Rd. E10—33Ec 64
Sedgwick St. E9—36Zb 64
Sedleigh Rd. SW18—58Bb 103
Sedlescombe Rd. SW6—51Cb 103
Sedley. Grav—65Ce 135
Sedley Gro. Uxb—28L 35
Sedley Pl. W1—44Kb 82 (3K 197)
Sedley Rise. Lou—12Pc 28
Seeley Dri. SE21—63Ub 127
Seelig Av. NW9—31Wa 60
Seely Rd. SW17—65Jb 126
Seething La. EC3
—45Ub 83 (4J 201)
Seething Wells La. Surb
—72La 142
Sefton Av. NW7—22Ta 39
Sefton Av. Harr—25Fa 38
Sefton Clo. Orp—70Vc 131
Sefton Clo. Slou—9K 53
Sefton Paddock. Slou—8L 53
Sefton Rd. Croy—74Wb 147
Sefton Rd. Eps—82Ta 161
Sefton Rd. Orp—70Vc 131
Sefton St. SW15—55Ya 102
Sefton Way. Uxb—44L 75
Segal Clo. SE23—59Ac 106
Segrave Clo. Wey—80Q 140
Sekforde St. EC1
—42Rb 83 (6B 194)
Selan Gdns. Hay—43X 77
Selbie Av. NW10—36Va 60
Selborne Av. E12—35Qc 66
Selborne Av. Bex—60Ad 109
Selborne Gdns. NW4—28Wa 40
Selborne Gdns. Gnfd—40Ja 58
Selborne Rd. E17—29Bc 44
Selborne Rd. N14—20Nb 24
Selborne Rd. N22—25Pb 42
Selborne Rd. Croy—76Ub 147
Selborne Rd. Ilf—33Qc 66
Selborne Rd. N Mald—68Ua 124
Selborne Rd. Sidc—63Xc 131
Selbourne Av. Surb—75Pa 143
Selbourne Av. Wey—82K 157
Selbourne Clo. Long, Dart
—69Fe 135
Selbourne Clo. Wey—82K 157
Selby Chase. Ruis—33X 57
Selby Clo. E6—43Nc 86
Selby Clo. Chess—80Na 143
Selby Clo. Chst—65Qc 130
Selby Gdns. S'hall—42Ca 77
Selby Grn. Cars—73Gb 145
Selby Rd. E11—34Gc 65
Selby Rd. E13—43Kc 85
Selby Rd. N17—24Ub 43
Selby Rd. SE20—68Wb 127
Selby Rd. W5—42Ka 78
Selby Rd. Ashf—65S 120
Selby Rd. Cars—73Gb 145
Selby St. E1—42Wb 83
Selby Wlk. Wok—6E 188
Selcroft Rd. Purl—84Rb 165
Selden Rd. SE15—54Yb 106
Selden Wlk. N7—33Pb 62
Selhurst Clo. Wok—87B 156
Selhurst New Rd. SE25—72Ub 147
Selhurst Pl. SE25—72Ub 147
Selhurst Rd. N9—20Ub 25
Selhurst Rd. SE25—72Ub 147
Selinas La. Dag—31Ad 67
Selkirk Rd. SW17—63Gb 125
Selkirk Rd. Twic—61Ea 122
Sellers Hall Clo. N3—24Cb 41
Sellincourt Rd. SW17—64Gb 125
Sellindge Clo. Beck—66Bc 128
Sellon M. SE11—49Pb 82 (6J 205)
Sellons Av. NW10—39Va 60
Sellwood Dri. Barn—15Za 22
Selsdon Av. S Croy—79Tb 147
Selsdon Clo. Romf—25Ed 48
Selsdon Clo. Surb—71Na 143
Selsdon Cres. S Croy—81Yb 166
Selsdon Pk. Rd. S Croy & Croy
—81Zb 166
Selsdon Rd. E11—31Jc 65
Selsdon Rd. E13—39Lc 65
Selsdon Rd. NW2—33Va 60
Selsdon Rd. SE27—62Qb 126
Selsdon Rd. S Croy—78Tb 147
Selsdon Rd. Wey—83J 157
Selsea Pl. N16—36Ub 63
Selsey Cres. Well—53Zc 109
Selsey St. E14—43Cc 84
Selvage La. NW7—22Ta 39
Selway Clo. Pinn—27X 37
Selwin Clo. Houn—56Aa 99
Selwood Clo. Stai—58L 97
Selwood Gdns. Stai—58L 97
Selwood Pl. SW7
—50Fb 81 (7B 202)
Selwood Rd. Brtwd—20Vd 32
Selwood Rd. Chess—77Ma 143
Selwood Rd. Croy—75Xb 147
Selwood Rd. Sutt—74Bb 145
Selwood Rd. Wok—92D 172
Selwood Ter. SW7
—50Fb 81 (7B 202)
Selworthy Clo. E11—29Jc 45
Selworthy Rd. SE6—62Bc 128
Selwyn Av. E4—23Ec 44
Selwyn Av. Ilf—30Vc 47
Selwyn Av. Rich—55Na 101
Selwyn Ct. Edgw—24Ra 39
Selwyn Cres. Well—55Xc 109
Selwyn Pl. Orp—69Xc 131
Selwyn Rd. E3—40Bc 64
Selwyn Rd. E13—39Kc 65
Selwyn Rd. NW10—38Ua 60
Selwyn Rd. N Mald—71Ta 143
Selwyn Rd. Til—4B 114
Semley Ga. E9—37Bc 64
Semley Pl. SW1—49Jb 82 (6J 203)
Semley Rd. SW16—68Nb 126
Semper Clo. Wok—5B 188
Semper Rd. Grays—7E 92
Semples. Stanf—1P 93
Senate St. SE15—54Yb 106
Send Barns La. Wok—96F 172
Send Clo. Wok—95E 172
Send Hill. Wok—96E 172
Send Hill. Wok—97E 172
Send Marsh Rd. Wok—95G 172
Send Pde. Clo. Wok—95E 172
Send Rd. Wok—95D 172
Seneca Rd. SW4—56Nb 104
Seneca Rd. T Hth—70Sb 127
Senga Rd. Wall—74Jb 146
Senhouse Rd. Sutt—76Za 144
Senior St. W2—43Db 81
Senlac Rd. SE12—60Kc 107
Sennen Rd. Enf—17Vb 25
Senrab St. E1—44Zb 84
Sentinel Sq. NW4—28Ya 40
September Way. Stan—23Ka 38
Septimus Pl. Enf—15Wb 25
Sequoia Clo. Bush, Wat—18Fa 20
Sequoia Gdns. Orp—73Vc 151
Sequoia Pk. Pinn—23Da 37
Serbin Clo. E10—31Ec 64
Sergeantsgreen La. Wal A—5Lc 13
Serjeant's Inn. EC4
—44Qb 82 (3A 200)
Serle St. WC2—44Pb 82 (2J 199)
Sermon Dri. Swan—69Ed 132
Serpentine Grn. Red—100Mb 180
Serpentine Rd. W2
—46Gb 81 (7D 196)
Serpentine Rd. Sev—95Md 187
Service Rd., The. Pot B—4Cb 9
Serviden Dri. Brom—67Mc 129
Setchell Rd. SE1—49Vb 83 (5K 207)
Setchell Way. SE1
—49Vb 83 (5K 207)
Seth St. SE16—47Yb 84
Seton Gdns. Dag—38Yc 67
Settle Rd. E13—40Jc 65
Settle Rd. Romf—21Qd 49
Settles St. E1—43Wb 83
Settrington Rd. SW6—54Db 103
Seven Acres. Long, Dart—76Ae 155
Seven Arches Rd. Brtwd—20Zd 33
Seven Dials. WC2
—44Nb 82 (3F 199)
Seven Hills Clo. W on T—81U 158
Seven Hills Rd. Iver—36D 54
Seven Hills Rd. W on T & Cob
—81U 158
Seven Kings Rd. Ilf—33Vc 67
Sevenoaks By-Pass. Sev
—95Ed 186
Sevenoaks Clo. Bexh—56Dd 110
Sevenoaks Clo. Romf—21Ld 49
Sevenoaks Ct. N'wd—24S 36
Sevenoaks Rd. SE4—58Ac 106
Sevenoaks Rd. Orp & Sev
—77Vc 151
★Sevenoaks Rd. Sev—92Ae
★Sevenoaks Rd. Sev—95Wd
(Ightham)
Sevenoaks Rd. Sev—88Kd 171
(Otford)
Sevenoaks Way. Orp & Sidc
—66Yc 131
Sevenoaks Way Industrial Est.
Orp—69Yc 131
Seven Sisters Rd.—34Pb 62
N7 1a-163 & 2-188a
N4 165-437 & 190-486
N15 remainder
Seventh Av. E12—35Pc 66
Seventh Av. Hay—46W 76
★Seven Wents La. Sev—95Wd
Severn. Grays—8K 93
Severn Av. Romf—27Kd 49
Severn Cres. Slou—50D 74
Severn Dri. Enf—10Wb 11
Severn Dri. Esh—75Ja 142
Severn Dri. Upm—30Td 50
Severn Dri. W on T—75Z 141
Severn Rd. S Ock—44Sd 90
Severns Field. Epp—1Wc 15
Severn Way. NW10—36Va 60
Severn Way. Wat—6Y 5
Severus Rd. SW11—56Gb 103
Seville St. SW1—47Hb 81 (2G 203)
Sevington Rd. NW4—30Xa 40
Sevington St. W9—42Db 81
Seward Rd. W7—47Ja 78
Seward Rd. Beck—68Zb 128
Sewardstone Gdns. E4—15Dc 26
Sewardstone Rd. E2—40Yb 64
Sewardstone Rd. E4 & Wal A
—17Dc 26
Sewardstone St. Wal A—5Ec 12
Seward St. EC1—41Sb 83 (5C 194)
Sewdley St. E5—35Zb 64
Sewell Rd. SE2—48Wc 87
Sewell St. E13—41Jc 85
Sexton Clo. Rain—39Hd 68
Sexton Rd. Til—3B 114
Seymer Rd. Romf—27Fd 48
Seymour Av. N17—26Wb 43
Seymour Av. Eps—81Xa 162
Seymour Av. Mord—73Za 144
Seymour Clo. EC1
—42Rb 83 (6B 194)
Seymour Clo. E Mol—71Ea 142
Seymour Clo. Pinn—25Ba 37
Seymour Ct. E4—19Hc 27
Seymour Ct. NW2—33Xa 60
Seymour Gdns. Felt—63Y 121
Seymour Gdns. Ilf—32Pc 66
Seymour Gdns. Ruis—32Z 57
Seymour Gdns. Surb—71Pa 143
Seymour Gdns. Twic—59Ka 100
Seymour M. W1—44Jb 82 (2H 197)
Seymour Pl. SE25—70Xb 127
Seymour Pl. W1—43Hb 81 (1F 197)
Seymour Rd. E4—18Dc 26
Seymour Rd. E6—40Mc 65
Seymour Rd. E10—32Bc 64
Seymour Rd. N3—24Db 41
Seymour Rd. N8—29Qb 42
Seymour Rd. N9—19Xb 25
Seymour Rd. SW18—58Bb 103
Seymour Rd. SW19—62Za 124
Seymour Rd. W4—49Sa 79
Seymour Rd. Cars—78Jb 146
Seymour Rd. E Mol—71Fa 142
Seymour Rd. Grav—1B 136
Seymour Rd. Hmptn—64Ea 122
Seymour Rd. King—67Ma 123
Seymour Rd. Mitc—73Jb 146
Seymour Rd. Slou—7H 73
Seymours, The. Lou—11Qc 28
Seymour St.—44Hb 81 (3F 197)
W1 1-61 & 2-68
W2 remainder
Seymour Ter. SE20—67Xb 127
Seymour Vs. SE20—67Xb 127
Seymour Wlk. SW10—51Eb 103
Seymour Way. Sun—66U 120
Shaa Rd. W3—45Ta 79
Shab Hall Cotts. Sev—90Ed 170
Shacklands Rd. Sev—83Dd 170
Shackleford Rd. Wok—92C 172
Shacklegate La. Tedd—63Ga 122
Shackleton Clo. SE23—61Xb 127
Shackleton Rd. Slou—5K 73
Shackleton Rd. S'hall—45Ba 77
Shacklewell Grn. E8—35Vb 63
Shacklewell La. E8—36Vb 63
Shacklewell Rd. N16—35Vb 63
Shacklewell Row. E8—35Vb 63
Shacklewell St. E2
—41Vb 83 (4K 195)
Shadbolt Clo. Wor Pk—75Va 144
Shad Thames. SE1
—47Vb 83 (7K 201)
Shadwell Dri. N'holt—41Ba 77
Shadwell Pierhead. E1—45Yb 84
Shadwell Pl. E1—45Yb 84
Shadybush Clo. Bush, Wat
—17Ea 20
Shady La. Wat—12X 19
Shaef Way. Tedd—66Ja 122
Shafter Rd. Dag—37Fd 68
Shaftesbury. Lou—13Mc 27
Shaftesbury Av.
—45Mb 82 (4D 198)
W1 1-111 & 2-136
WC2 remainder
Shaftesbury Av. Barn—14Eb 23
Shaftesbury Av. Enf—12Zb 26
Shaftesbury Av. Felt—58W 98
Shaftesbury Av. Harr—32Da 57
Shaftesbury Av. Harr—29Ma 39
(Kenton)
Shaftesbury Av. S'hall—48Ca 77
Shaftesbury Cres. Stai—66M 119
Shaftesbury La. Dart—56Rd 111
Shaftesbury Rd. E4—18Fc 27
Shaftesbury Rd. E7—38Lc 65
Shaftesbury Rd. E10—32Cc 64
Shaftesbury Rd. E17—30Dc 44
Shaftesbury Rd. N18—23Ub 43
Shaftesbury Rd. N19—32Nb 62
Shaftesbury Rd. Beck—68Bc 128
Shaftesbury Rd. Cars—73Fb 145
Shaftesbury Rd. Epp—1Vc 15
Shaftesbury Rd. Rich—55Na 101
Shaftesbury Rd. Romf—30Hd 48
Shaftesbury Rd. Wat—13Y 19
Shaftesbury Rd. Wok—89D 156
Shaftesburys, The. Bark—40Sc 66
Shaftesbury St. N1
—40Sb 63 (2F 195)
Shaftesbury Way. Twic—62Fa 122
Shaftesbury Waye. Hay—44Y 77
Shafto M. SW1—48Hb 81 (4G 203)
Shafton Rd. E9—39Zb 64
Shafts Ct. EC3—44Ub 83 (3H 201)
Shaggy Calf La. Slou—5L 73
Shakespeare Av. N11—22Lb 42
Shakespeare Av. NW10—39Ta 59
Shakespeare Av. Felt—58W 98
Shakespeare Av. Hay—44W 76
(in two parts)
Shakespeare Av. Til—4D 114
Shakespeare Ct. Barn—13Db 23
Shakespeare Cres. E12—37Pc 66
Shakespeare Cres. NW10
—39Ta 59
Shakespeare Dri. Harr—30Pa 39
Shakespeare Gdns. N2—28Hb 41
Shakespeare Rd. E17—26Zb 44
Shakespeare Rd. N3—25Cb 41
Shakespeare Rd. NW7—21Wa 40
Shakespeare Rd. SE24—57Rb 105
Shakespeare Rd. W3—46Sa 79
Shakespeare Rd. W7—45Ha 78
Shakespeare Rd. Bexh—53Ad 109
Shakespeare Rd. Dart—56Qd 111
Shakespeare Rd. Romf—30Hd 48
Shakespeare Rd. Wey—77M 139
Shakespeare Sq. Ilf—23Sc 46
Shakespeare St. Wat—10X 5
Shakespeare Way. Felt—63Y 121
Shakspeare Wlk. N16—35Ub 63
Shalcomb St. SW10—51Eb 103
Shalcross Dri. Wal X—2Bc 12
Shaldon Dri. Mord—71Ab 144
Shaldon Dri. Ruis—34Y 57
Shaldon Rd. Edgw—26Pa 39
Shaldon Way. W on T—76Y 141
Shale Grn. Red—100Mb 180
Shalfleet Dri. W10—45Za 80
Shalford Clo. Orp—77Sc 150
Shalimar Gdns. W3—45Sa 79
Shalimar Rd. W3—45Sa 79
Shallons Rd. SE9—63Rc 130
Shalstone Rd. SW14—55Ra 101
Shalston Vs. Surb—72Pa 143
Shamrock Clo. Lea—93Fa 176
Shamrock Rd. Croy—72Pb 146
Shamrock Rd. Grav—9G 114
Shamrock St. SW4—55Mb 104
Shamrock Way. N14—18Kb 24
Shandon Rd. SW4—58Lb 104
Shand St. SE1—47Ub 83 (1H 207)
Shandy St. E1—43Zb 84
Shanklin Gdns. Wat—21Y 37
Shanklin Rd. N8—29Mb 42
Shanklin Rd. N15—28Wb 43
Shanklin Way. SE15—52Vb 105
Shannon Clo. S'hall—50Z 77
Shannon Gro. SW9—56Pb 104
Shannon Pl. NW8
—40Gb 61 (1E 190)
Shannon Way. Beck—65Dc 128
Shannon Way. S Ock—45Sd 90
Shantock Hall La. Hem—1A 2
Shantock La. Hem—2A 2
Shap Cres. Cars—74Hb 145
Shap St. E2—40Vb 63 (1K 195)
(in two parts)
Shardcroft Av. SE24—57Rb 105
Shardeloes Rd. SE14—54Bc 106
Shard's Sq. SE15—51Wb 105
Sharland Rd. Grav—1E 136
Sharman Ct. Sidc—63Wc 131
Sharnbrooke Clo. Well—55Yc 109
Sharney Av. Slou—48D 74
Sharon Clo. Eps—85Sa 161
Sharon Clo. Lea—96Ca 175
Sharon Clo. Surb—74Ma 143
Sharon Gdns. E9—39Yb 64
Sharon Rd. W4—50Ta 79
Sharon Rd. Enf—12Ac 26
Sharpleshall St. NW1—38Hb 61
Sharp's La. Ruis—31T 56
Sharp Way. Dart—55Pd 111
Sharratt St. SE15—51Yb 106
Sharsted St. SE17—50Rb 83
Sharvel La. N'holt—39X 57
Shaver's Pl. SW1—(5D 198)
Shaw Av. Bark—40Ad 67
Shawbrooke Rd. SE9—57Mc 107
Shawbury Rd. SE22—57Vb 105
Shaw Clo. SE28—46Xc 87
Shaw Clo. Bush, Wat—19Fa 20
Shaw Clo. Cher—79E 138
Shaw Clo. Eps—83Va 162
Shaw Clo. S Croy—84Vb 165
Shaw Clo. Wal X—1Yb 12
Shaw Ct. Wind—7L 95
Shaw Cres. Brtwd—14Fe 33
Shaw Cres. S Croy—84Vb 165
Shaw Cres. Til—3D 114
Shawfield Pk. Brom—68Mc 129
Shawfield St. SW3
—50Gb 81 (7E 202)
Shawford Ct. SW15—59Wa 102
Shawford Rd. Eps—79Ta 143
Shaw Gdns. Bark—40Ad 67
Shawley Cres. Eps—90Ya 162
Shawley Way. Eps—90Xa 162
Shaw Rd. Brom—62Hc 129
Shaw Rd. Enf—11Zb 26
Shaw Rd. West—92Lc 183
Shaw Sq. E17—25Ac 44
Shaw Way. Wall—80Nb 146
Shaxton Cres. Croy—81Ec 166
Shearing Dri. Cars—73Eb 145
Shearling Way. N7—37Nb 62
Shearman Rd. SE3—56Hc 107
Shears Ct. Grav—1C 136
Shearwater. Long, Dart—69De 135
Shearwood Cres. Dart—55Jd 110
Sheath's La. Lea—85Da 159
Sheaveshill Av. NW9—28Ua 40
Sheba St. E1—42Vb 83 (6K 195)
Sheehy Way. Slou—5M 73
Sheen Comn. Dri. Rich—56Qa 101
Sheen Ct. Rd. Rich—56Qa 101
Sheendale Rd. Rich—56Pa 101
Sheenewood. SE26—63Xb 127
Sheen Ga. Gdns. SW14—56Sa 101
Sheen Gro. N1—39Qb 62
Sheen La. SW14—57Sa 101
Sheen Pk. Rich—56Pa 101
Sheen Rd. Orp—70Vc 131
Sheen Rd. Rich—57Na 101
Sheen Way. Wall—78Pb 146
Sheen Wood. SW14—57Sa 101
Sheepbarn La. Warl—84Hc 167
Sheepcot Dri. Wat—6Y 5
Sheepcote Clo. Houn—52W 98
Sheepcote Gdns. Uxb—30J 35
Sheepcote La. SW11—54Hb 103
Sheepcote La. Orp—71Bd 151
Sheepcote Rd. Harr—30Ha 38
Sheepcote Rd. Wind—4C 94
Sheepcote Rd. Wind—10E 72
(Eton Wick)
Sheepcotes Rd. Romf—28Ad 47
Sheepcot La. Wat—5W 4
(in two parts)
Sheephouse Way. N Mald
—73Ua 144
Sheep La. E8—39Xb 63
Sheep Wlk. Eps—93Ta 177
Sheep Wlk. Shep—73P 139
Sheep Wlk. M. SW19—65Ab 124
Sheep Wlk., The. Wok—90G 156
Sheerwater Av. Wey—84H 157
Sheerwater Rd. E16—43Mc 85
Sheerwater Rd. Wey—84G 156
Sheet St. Wind—4H 95
Sheet Street Rd. Wind—2C 116
Sheffield Dri. Romf—22Qd 49
Sheffield Gdns. Romf—22Qd 49
Sheffield Rd. Slou—4G 72
Sheffield Sq. E3—41Bc 84
Sheffield St. WC2
—44Pb 82 (3H 199)
Sheffield Ter. W8—46Cb 81
Shefton Rise. N'wd—24W 36
Sheila Clo. Romf—24Dd 48
Sheila Rd. Romf—24Dd 48
Sheilings, The. Horn—29Pd 49
Shelbourne Clo. Pinn—27Ba 37
Shelbourne Rd. N17—25Xb 43
Shelburne Rd. N7—35Pb 62
Shelbury Clo. Sidc—62Wc 131
Shelbury Rd. SE22—57Xb 105
Sheldon Av. N6—31Gb 61
Sheldon Av. Ilf—26Rc 46
Sheldon Clo. SE20—67Xb 127
Sheldon Rd. N18—21Ub 43
Sheldon Rd. NW2—35Za 60
Sheldon Rd. Bexh—53Bd 109
Sheldon Rd. Dag—38Ad 67
Sheldon St. Croy—76Sb 147
Sheldrake Pl. W8—47Cb 81
Sheldrick Clo. Mitc—68Fb 125
Sheldwick Ter. Brom—72Nc 150
Shelford Pl. N16—34Tb 63
Shelford Rise. SE19—66Vb 127
Shelford Rd. Barn—16Ya 22
Shelgate Rd. SW11—57Gb 103
Shellbank La. Dart—64Wd 134
Shell Clo. Brom—72Nc 150
Shelley Av. E12—37Nc 66
Shelley Av. Gnfd—41Fa 78
Shelley Av. Horn—33Hd 68
Shelley Clo. Bans—87Ab 162
Shelley Clo. Edgw—21Qa 39
Shelley Clo. Gnfd—41Fa 78
Shelley Clo. Hay—43W 76
Shelley Clo. N'wd—22V 36
Shelley Clo. Orp—76Uc 150
Shelley Clo. Slou—50C 74
Shelley Cres. Houn—53Z 99
Shelley Cres. S'hall—44Ba 77
Shelley Dri. Well—53Uc 108
Shelley Gdns. Wemb—33La 58
Shelley Gro. Lou—14Pc 28
Shelley Rd. Brtwd—17Fe 33
Shelleys La. Sev—88Wc 169
Shellness Rd. E5—36Xb 63
Shell Rd. SE13—55Dc 106
Shellwood Rd. SW11—54Hb 103
Shelmerdine Clo. E3—43Cc 84
Shelson Av. Felt—62V 120
Shelton Av. Warl—89Yb 166
Shelton Clo. Warl—89Yb 166
Shelton Rd. SW19—67Cb 125
Shelton St. WC2—44Nb 82 (3F 199)
(in two parts)
Shelvers Grn. Tad—93Ya 178
Shelvers Hill. Tad—93Xa 178
Shelvers Spur. Tad—93Ya 178
Shelvers Way. Tad—93Ya 178
Shenden Way. Sev—100Ld 187
Shendon Clo. Sev—99Ld 187
Shenfield Cres. Brtwd—19Ae 33
Shenfield Gdns. Brtwd—16De 33
Shenfield Grn. Brtwd—17Ce 33
Shenfield Pl. Brtwd—17Ae 33
Shenfield Rd. Brtwd—19Zd 33
Shenfield Rd. Wfd G—24Kc 45
Shenfield St. N1—40Ub 63 (2J 195)
Shenley Av. Ruis—33V 56
Shenleybury Cotts. Shen, Rad
—3Na 7
Shenley Hill. Rad—7Ka 6
Shenley La. St Alb & Shen, Rad
—1Ma 7
Shenley Rd. SE5—53Ub 105
Shenley Rd. Borwd—14Qa 21
Shenley Rd. Dart—58Qd 111
Shenley Rd. Houn—53Aa 99
Shenley Rd. Rad—6Ka 6
Shenstone Clo. Dart—56Fd 110
Shenstone Dri. Slou—2B 72
Shenstone Gdns. Romf—25Ld 49
Shepherdess Pl. N1
—41Tb 83 (3F 195)
Shepherdess Wlk. N1
—40Sb 63 (1E 194)

Shepherd Mkt.—Smeaton Rd.

Shepherd Mkt. W1 —46Kb 82 (7K 197)
Shepherd's Bush Centre. W12 —47Za 80
Shepherd's Bush Grn. W12 —47Ya 80
Shepherd's Bush Mkt. W12 —47Ya 80
Shepherd's Bush Pl. W12—47Za 80
Shepherd's Bush Rd. W6—49Ya 80
Shepherd's Clo. N6—30Kb 42
Shepherd's Clo. Orp—76Vc 151
Shepherds Clo. Romf—29Zc 47
Shepherds Clo. Shep—72R 140
Shepherds Clo. Uxb—42L 75
Shepherds Grn. Chst—66Tc 130
Shepherd's Hill. N6—30Kb 42
Shepherd's Hill. Red—98Lb 180
Shepherds Hill. Romf—26Qd 49
Shepherd's La. E9—37Zb 64
Shepherd's La. Dart—60Jd 110
Shepherds La. Rick—16F 16
Shepherds Pl. W1 —45Jb 82 (4H 197)
Shepherd's Rd. Wat—14V 18
Shepherd St. W1 —46Kb 82 (7K 197)
Shepherd St. Grav—59Fe 113
Shepherd's Wlk. NW3—36Fb 61
Shepherd's Wlk. Eps—92Ra 177
Shepherds Way. Rick—17K 17
Shepherds Way. S Croy—80Zb 148
Shepiston La. W Dray & Hay —49R 76
Shepley Clo. Cars—76Jb 146
Shepley Clo. Horn—36Md 69
Sheppard Clo. Enf—11Xb 25
Sheppard Clo. King—70Na 123
Sheppard St. E16—42Hc 85
Shepperton Clo. Borwd—11Ta 21
Shepperton Rd. N1—39Tb 63
Shepperton Rd. Orp—72Sc 150
Shepperton Rd. Stai & Shep —69L 119
Sheppey Clo. Eri—52Kd 111
Sheppey Gdns. Dag—38Yc 67
Sheppey Rd. Dag—38Xc 67
Sheppey's La. K Lan & Abb L, Wat —1S 4
Sheppey Wlk. N1—37Sb 63
Sheppy Pl. Grav—9D 114
Sherard Rd. SE9—57Nc 108
Sheraton Clo. Borwd—15Pa 21
Sheraton Dri. Eps—85Sa 161
Sheraton St. W1 —44Mb 82 (3D 198)
Sherborne Av. Enf—12Yb 26
Sherborne Av. S'hall—49Ca 77
Sherborne Cres. Cars—73Gb 145
Sherborne Gdns. NW9—27Qa 39
Sherborne Gdns. W13—43Ka 78
Sherborne Gdns. Romf—22Cd 48
Sherborne La. EC4 —45Tb 83 (4F 201)
Sherborne Rd. Chess—78Na 143
Sherborne Rd. Felt—60T 98
Sherborne Rd. Orp—71Vc 151
Sherborne Rd. Sutt—75Cb 145
Sherborne St. N1—39Tb 63
Sherborne Way. Rick—14R 18
Sherbourne Clo. Eps—89Ya 162
Sherbourne Clo. Sev—79Ud 154
Sherbourne Clo. Slou—53G 96
Sherbourne Dri. Wind—6D 94
Sherbourne Wlk. Slou—5G 52
Sherbrooke Clo. Bexh—56Cd 110
Sherbrooke Rd. SW6—52Ab 102
Sherbrook Gdns. N21—17Rb 25
Shere Av. Sutt—82Ya 162
Shereboro Rd. N15—30Vb 43
Shere Clo. Chess—78Ma 143
Sheredan Rd. E4—22Gc 45
Shere Rd. Ilf—29Qc 46
Sherfield Av. Rick—19M 17
Sherfield Gdns. SW15—58Va 102
Sherfield Rd. Grays—51De 113
Sheridan Clo. Romf—24Ld 49
Sheridan Clo. Swan—70Hd 132
Sheridan Clo. Uxb—42S 76
Sheridan Ct. Dart—56Qd 111
Sheridan Cres. Chst—68Rc 130
Sheridan Gdns. Harr—30Ma 39
Sheridan Pl. Hmptn—67Da 121
Sheridan Rd. E7—34Hc 65
Sheridan Rd. E12—36Nc 66
Sheridan Rd. SW19—67Bb 125
Sheridan Rd. Belv—49Cd 88
Sheridan Rd. Bexh—55Ad 109
Sheridan Rd. Rich—62La 122
Sheridan Rd. Wat—17Z 19
Sheridans Rd. Lea—98Ea 176
Sheridan St. E1—44Xb 83
Sheridan Ter. N'holt—36Da 57
Sheridan Wlk. NW11—30Cb 41
Sheridan Wlk. Cars—78Hb 145
Sheriff Way. Wat—5W 4
Sheringham Av. E12—35Pc 66
Sheringham Av. N14—15Mb 24
Sheringham Av. Felt—62W 120
Sheringham Av. Romf—30Ed 48
Sheringham Av. Twic—60Ca 99
Sheringham Dri. Bark—36Vc 67
Sheringham Rd. N7—37Qb 62
Sheringham Rd. SE20—69Yb 128
Sherington Av. Pinn—24Ca 37
Sherington Rd. SE7—51Kc 107
Sherland Rd. Twic—60Ha 100
Sherlies Av. Orp—75Uc 150
Sherlock M. W1—43Jb 82 (7H 191)
Shermanbury Pl. Eri—52Hd 110
Sherman Rd. Brom—67Jc 129
Sherman Rd. Slou—3J 73
Shernbroke Rd. Wal A—6Hc 13
Shernhall St. E17—27Ec 44
Sherrard Rd.—37Lc 65
E7 1-195 & 2-210
E12 remainder
Sherrards Way. Barn—15Cb 23
Sherrick Grn. Rd. NW10—36Xa 60
Sherriff Rd. NW6—37Cb 61
Sherringham Av. N17—26Wb 43
Sherrock Gdns. NW4—28Wa 40
Sherwin Rd. SE14—53Zb 106
Sherwood. Grays—46Ae 91
Sherwood Av. E18—27Kc 45
Sherwood Av. SW16—66Mb 126
Sherwood Av. Gnfd—37Ga 58
Sherwood Av. Hay—42X 77
Sherwood Av. Pot B—4Ab 8
Sherwood Av. Ruis—30U 36
Sherwood Clo. SW15—55Xa 102
Sherwood Clo. W13—46Ka 78
Sherwood Clo. Bex—58Yc 109
Sherwood Clo. Slou—48A 74
Sherwood Ct. Slou—50B 74
Sherwood Gdns. Bark—38Tc 66
Sherwood Pk. Av. Sidc—59Wc 109
Sherwood Pk. Rd. Mitc—70Lb 126
Sherwood Pk. Rd. Sutt—78Cb 145
Sherwood Rd. NW4—27Ya 40
Sherwood Rd. SW19—66Bb 125
Sherwood Rd. Coul—88Lb 164
Sherwood Rd. Croy—73Xb 147
Sherwood Rd. Hmptn—64Ea 122
Sherwood Rd. Harr—33Ea 58
Sherwood Rd. Ilf—28Tc 46
Sherwood Rd. Well—54Uc 108
Sherwood Rd. Wok—5B 188
Sherwoods Rd. Wat—17Aa 19
Sherwood St. N20—20Fb 23
Sherwood St. W1 —45Lb 82 (4C 198)
Sherwood Ter. N20—20Fb 23
Sherwood Way. W Wick —75Ec 148
Shetland Clo. Borwd—16Ta 21
Shetland Rd. E3—40Bc 64
Shevon Way. Brtwd—21Vd 50
Shey Copse. Wok—89E 156
Shield Dri. Bren—51Ja 100
Shieldhall St. SE2—49Yc 87
Shield Rd. Ashf—63S 120
Shielings, The. Sev—92Pd 187
Shilburn Way. Wok—6D 188
Shilliber Wlk. Chig—20Vc 29
Shillingford St. N1—38Rb 63
Shillitoe Av. Pot B—4Za 8
Shillitoe Rd. N13—22Sb 43
Shinfield St. W12—44Ya 80
Shinford Path. SE23—62Zb 128
Shingle Ct. Wal A—5Jc 13
Shingle End. Bren—52La 100
Shinglewell Rd. Eri—52Cd 110
Ship & Half Moon Pas. SE18 —48Rc 86
Ship & Mermaid Row. SE1 —47Tb 83 (1G 207)
Shipfield Clo. West—93Lc 183
Ship Hill. Slou & High W—2C 52
Ship Hill. West—93Lc 183
Shipka Rd. SW12—60Kb 104
Ship La. SW14—54Sa 101
Ship La. S Ock & Grays—46Td 90
Ship La. S at H, Dart—67Md 133
Shipley Hills Rd. Grav—75Fe 155
Shipman Rd. E16—44Kc 85
Shipman Rd. SE23—61Zb 128
Ship St. SE8—53Cc 106
Ship Tavern Pas. EC3 —45Ub 83 (4H 201)
Shipton Clo. Dag—34Zc 67
Shipton Pl. NW5—37Jb 62
Shipton Rd. Uxb—35P 55
Shipton St. E2—41Vb 83
Shipway Ter. N16—34Vb 63
Shipwright Rd. SE16—47Ac 84
Shirbutt St. E14—45Dc 84
Shirebrook Rd. SE3—55Mc 107
Shirehall Clo. NW4—30Za 40
Shirehall Gdns. NW4—30Za 40
Shirehall La. NW4—30Za 40
Shirehall Pk. NW4—30Za 40
Shirehall Rd. Dart—64Ld 133
Shire La. Ger X & Chal—20D 16
Shire La. Kes & Orp—80Pc 150
Shire La. Orp—78Uc 150
Shire La. Rick—15D 16
Shire La. Path. Ger X & Uxb —24E 34
Shiremeade. Borwd—15Pa 21
Shires Ho. Wey—85N 157
Shires, The. Rich—63Na 123
Shirland M. W9—41Bb 81
Shirland Rd. W9—41Bb 81
Shirley Av. Bex—59Zc 109
Shirley Av. Coul—91Rb 181
Shirley Av. Croy—74Yb 148
Shirley Av. Sutt—77Fb 145
Shirley Av. Sutt—81Bb 163
(Belmont)
Shirley Av. Wind—3D 94
Shirley Chu. Rd. Croy—76Zb 148
Shirley Clo. E17—29Dc 44
Shirley Clo. Dart—56Ld 111
Shirley Clo. Grav—10K 115
Shirley Clo. Houn—57Ea 100
Shirley Clo. Wal X—1Yb 12
Shirley Ct. Lou—12Pc 28
Shirley Cres. Beck—70Ac 128
Shirley Dri. Houn—57Ea 100
Shirley Gdns. W7—46Ha 78
Shirley Gdns. Bark—37Uc 66
Shirley Gdns. Horn—33Ld 69
Shirley Gro. N9—17Zb 26
Shirley Gro. SW11—55Jb 104
Shirley Heights. Wall—81Lb 164
Shirley Hills Rd. Croy—78Yb 148
Shirley Ho. Dri. SE7—52Lc 107
Shirley Oaks Rd. Croy—74Zb 148
Shirley Pk. Rd. Croy—74Xb 147
Shirley Pl. Wok—5A 188
Shirley Rd. E15—38Gc 65
Shirley Rd. W4—47Ta 79
Shirley Rd. Abb L, Wat—4V 4
Shirley Rd. Croy—73Xb 147
Shirley Rd. Enf—13Sb 25
Shirley Rd. Sidc—62Uc 130
Shirley Rd. Wall—81Lb 164
Shirley St. E16—44Hc 85
Shirley Way. Croy—76Ac 148
Shirlock Rd. NW3—35Hb 61
Shobden Rd. N17—25Tb 43
Shoebury Rd. E6—38Pc 66
Shoe La. EC4—44Qb 82 (2A 200)
Sholden Gdns. Orp—71Yc 151
Shonks Mill Rd. Romf & Stap T, Romf—11Kd 31
★Shonks Mill Rd. Stap T, Romf —9Jd
Shooters Av. Harr—28La 38
Shooters Hill. SE18 & Well —53Qc 108
Shooters Hill Rd.—53Fc 107
SE3 1-311 & 2-238
SE18 remainder
Shooters Rd. Enf—11Rb 25
Shoot up Hill. NW2—36Ab 60
Shord Hill. Kenl—88Tb 165
Shordiche Clo. Uxb—34P 55
Shore Clo. Felt—59W 98
Shore Clo. Hmptn—65Aa 121
Shoreditch High St. E1 —42Ub 83 (4J 195)
Shore Gro. Felt—61Ca 121
Shoreham Clo. SW18—57Db 103
Shoreham Clo. Bex—60Zc 109
Shoreham Clo. Croy—71Yb 148
Shoreham La. Orp—79Cd 152
Shoreham La. Sev—84Bd 169
(Halstead)
Shoreham La. Sev—94Hd 186
(Riverhead)
Shoreham Pl. Sev—84Jd 170
Shoreham Rd. Orp—68Xc 131
Shoreham Rd. Sev—83Kd 171
Shoreham Rd. E. Houn—57N 97
Shoreham Rd. W. Houn—57N 97
Shoreham Way. Brom—72Jc 149
Shorehill La. Sev—88Pd 171
Shore Pl. E9—38Yb 64
Shore Rd. E9—38Yb 64
Shores Rd. Wok—86A 156
Shore, The. Grav—8B 114
Shore, The. Grav—57Fe 113
(Northfleet)
Shorncliffe Rd. SE1 —50Vb 83 (7K 207)
Shorndean St. SE6—60Ec 106
Shorne Clo. Orp—70Zc 131
Shorne Clo. Sidc—58Xc 109
Shornefield Clo. Brom—69Qc 130
Shorne Ifield Rd. Grav—5J 137
Shornells Way. SE2—50Yc 87
Shorrold's Rd. SW6—52Bb 103
★Short Croft. Brtwd—9Vd
Shortcroft Rd. Eps—80Va 144
Shortcrofts Rd. Dag—37Bd 67
Shorter Av. Brtwd—17Be 33
Shorter St. E1—45Vb 83 (4K 201)
Shortfern. Slou—4N 73
Short Ga. N12—21Bb 41
Short Hill. Harr—31Ga 58
Shortlands. W6—49Za 80
Shortlands. Hay—51T 98
Shortlands Clo. N18—20Tb 25
Shortlands Gdns. Brom—68Gc 129
Shortlands Gro. Brom—69Fc 129
Shortlands Rd. E10—31Dc 64
Shortlands Rd. Brom—69Fc 129
Shortlands Rd. King—66Pa 123
Short La. St Alb—1Aa 5
Short La. Stai—59P 97
Shortmead Dri. Wal X—3Ac 12
Short Path. SE18—51Rc 108
Short Rd. E11—33Gc 65
Short Rd. E15—39Fc 65
Short Rd. W4—51Ua 102
Short Rd. Houn—58N 97
Shorts Croft. NW9—28Ra 39
Shorts Gdns. WC2 —44Nb 82 (3F 199)
Shorts Rd. Cars—77Gb 145
Short St. NW4—28Ya 40
Short St. SE1—47Qb 82 (1A 206)
Short Wall. E15—41Ec 84
Short Way. N12—23Gb 41
Short Way. SE9—55Nc 108
Short Way. Twic—59Ea 100
Shortwood Av. Ashf—62K 119
Shotfield. Wall—79Kb 146
Shotfield Av. SW14—56Ua 102
Shottendane Rd. SW6—53Cb 103
Shottery Clo. SE9—62Nc 130
Shoulder of Mutton All. E14 —45Ac 84
Shouldham St. W1 —43Gb 81 (1E 196)
Showers Way. Hay—46W 76
Shrapnel Clo. SE18—52Nc 108
Shrapnel Rd. SE9—55Pc 108
Shrewsbury Av. SW14—56Ta 101
Shrewsbury Av. Harr—28Na 39
Shrewsbury Clo. Surb—75Na 143
Shrewsbury Cres. NW10—39Ta 59
Shrewsbury La. SE18—53Rc 108
Shrewsbury Rd. E7—36Mc 65
Shrewsbury Rd. N11—23Mb 42
Shrewsbury Rd. W2—44Cb 81
Shrewsbury Rd. Beck—69Ac 128
Shrewsbury Rd. Cars—73Gb 145
Shrewsbury Wlk. Iswth—55Ja 100
Shrewton Rd. SW17—66Hb 125
Shroffold Rd. Brom—63Gc 129
Shropshire Clo. Mitc—70Nb 126
Shropshire Pl. WC1 —42Lb 82 (6C 192)
Shropshire Rd. N22—24Pb 42
Shroton St. NW1 —43Gb 81 (7D 190)
Shrubberies, The. E18—26Jc 45
Shrubberies, The. Chig—22Sc 46
Shrubbery Gdns. N21—17Rb 25
Shrubbery Rd. N9—20Wb 25
Shrubbery Rd. SW16—63Nb 126
Shrubbery Rd. Grav—10D 114
Shrubbery Rd. S'hall—46Ca 77
Shrubbery Rd. S Dar, Dart —67Td 134
Shrubbery, The. Upm—34Sd 70
Shrubland Gro. Wor Pk—76Ya 144
Shrubland Rd. E8—39Wb 63
Shrubland Rd. E10—31Cc 64
Shrubland Rd. E17—29Cc 44
Shrubland Rd. Bans—88Bb 163
Shrublands Av. Croy—76Cc 148
Shrublands Clo. N20—18Fb 23
Shrublands Clo. Chig—23Sc 46
Shrublands, The. Pot B—5Ab 8
Shrubs Rd. Rick—23P 35
Shuna Wlk. N1—37Tb 63
Shurland Av. Barn—16Fb 23
Shurland Gdns. SE15—52Vb 105
Shurlock Av. Swan—68Fd 132
Shurlock Dri. Orp—77Sc 150
Shuttle Clo. Sidc—59Vc 109
Shuttlemead. Bex—59Bd 109
Shuttle Rd. Dart—55Jd 110
Shuttle St. E1—42Wb 83
Shuttleworth Rd. SW11—54Gb 103
Sibella Rd. SW4—54Mb 104
Sibley Clo. Bexh—57Ad 109
Sibley Gro. E12—38Nc 66
Sibthorpe Rd. SE12—59Kc 107
Sibthorp Rd. Mitc—68Hb 125
Sibton Rd. Cars—73Gb 145
Sickert Ct. N1—38Sb 63
Sickle Corner. Dag—42Dd 88
Sidbury St. SW6—53Ab 102
Sidcup By-Pass. Sidc—62Tc 130
Sidcup High St. Sidc—63Wc 131
Sidcup Hill. Sidc—63Xc 131
Sidcup Hill Gdns. Sidc—64Yc 131
Sidcup Rd.—58Lc 107
SE12 1-59 & 2-188
SE9 remainder
Siddons La. NW1 —42Hb 81 (6G 191)
Siddons Rd. N17—25Wb 43
Siddons Rd. SE23—61Ac 128
Siddons Rd. Croy—76Qb 146
Side Rd. E17—29Bc 44
Side Rd. Uxb—31F 54
Sidewood Rd. SE9—60Tc 108
Sidford Pl. SE1—48Qb 82 (4J 205)
Sidings, The. E11—32Fc 65
Sidmouth Av. Iswth—54Ga 100
Sidmouth Clo. Wat—19X 19
Sidmouth Dri. Ruis—34W 56
Sidmouth Rd. E10—34Ec 64
Sidmouth Rd. NW2—38Ya 60
Sidmouth Rd. SE15—53Vb 105
Sidmouth Rd. Orp—71Xc 151
Sidmouth Rd. Well—52Yc 109
Sidmouth St. WC1 —41Pb 82 (4G 193)
Sidney Av. N13—22Pb 42
Sidney Elson Way. E6—40Qc 66
Sidney Gdns. Bren—51Ma 101
Sidney Gdns. Sev—89Ld 171
Sidney Gro. EC1—40Rb 63 (3B 194)
Sidney Rd. E7—34Jc 65
Sidney Rd. N22—24Pb 42
Sidney Rd. SE25—71Wb 147
Sidney Rd. SW9—54Pb 104
Sidney Rd. Beck—68Ac 128
Sidney Rd. Epp—8Tc 14
Sidney Rd. Harr—27Ea 38
Sidney Rd. Stai—63J 119
Sidney Rd. Twic—58Ja 100
Sidney Rd. W on T—73W 140
Sidney Sq. E1—43Yb 84
Sidney St. E1—43Yb 84
Sidney St. Est. E1—43Yb 84
(in two parts)
Sidworth St. E8—38Xb 63
Siebert Rd. SE3—51Jc 107
Siemens Rd. SE18—48Mc 85
Sigdon Rd. E8—36Wb 63
Sigers, The. Pinn—30X 37
Silbury Ho. SE26—62Wb 127
Silbury St. N1—41Tb 83 (3F 195)
Silchester Rd. W10 & W11 —44Za 80
Silecroft Rd. Bexh—53Cd 110
Silesia Bldgs. E8—38Xb 63
Silex St. SE1—47Rb 83 (2C 206)
Silkfield Rd. NW9—29Ua 40
Silkham Rd. Oxt—99Gc 183
Silkin Clo. SE12—57Jc 107
Silk Mill Ct. Wat—17X 19
Silk Mill Rd. Wat—17X 19
Silk Mills Path. SE13—54Ec 106
Silkmill Way. Wat—17X 19
Silkmore La. Lea—98Q 174
Silkstream Rd. Edgw—25Sa 39
Silk St. EC2—43Sb 83 (7E 194)
Silsoe Rd. N22—26Pb 42
Silver Birch Av. E4—23Bc 44
Silverbirch Clo. N11—23Jb 42
Silver Birch Clo. Dart—63Gd 132
Silverbirch Clo. Uxb—35N 55
Silver Birch Clo. Wey—84G 156
Silver Birches. Brtwd—18Ce 33
Silvercliffe Gdns. Barn—14Gb 23
Silver Clo. Harr—24Fa 38
Silver Clo. Tad—96Bb 179
Silver Cres. W4—49Ra 79
Silverdale. SE26—63Yb 128
Silverdale. Enf—14Nb 24
Silverdale Av. Ilf—29Uc 46
Silverdale Av. Lea—86Ea 160
Silverdale Av. W on T—75V 140
Silverdale Clo. W7—46Ha 78
Silverdale Clo. N'holt—36Ba 57
Silverdale Clo. Stai—63K 119
Silverdale Clo. Sutt—77Bb 145
Silverdale Dri. Horn—36Kd 69
Silverdale Dri. Sun—68W 120
Silverdale Gdns. Hay—47W 76
Silverdale Rd. E4—23Fc 45
Silverdale Rd. Bexh—54Dd 110
Silverdale Rd. Bush, Wat—15Aa 19
Silverdale Rd. Croy—76Rb 147
Silverdale Rd. Hay—47V 76
Silverdale Rd. Orp—70Sc 130
(Petts Wood)
Silverdale Rd. Orp—69Wc 131
(St Mary Cray)
Silver Dell. Wat—8V 4
Silverhall St. Iswth—55Ja 100
Silver Hill. Borwd—8Sa 7
Silverholme. Harr—31Na 59
Silver Jubilee Way. Houn—54X 99
Silverland St. E16—46Pc 86
Silver La. Purl—84Mb 164
Silver La. W Wick—75Fc 149
Silverleigh Rd. T Hth—70Pb 126
Silverlocke Rd. Grays—51Fe 113
Silvermere Av. Romf—23Dd 48
Silvermere Rd. SE6—59Dc 106
Silver Pl. W1—(4C 198)
Silver Rd. W12—45Za 80
Silver Rd. Grav—1G 136
Silversmiths Way. Wok—6F 188
Silver Spring Clo. Eri—51Dd 110
Silversted La. West—93Tc 184
Silverston Way. Stan—23La 38
Silver St. N18—21Tb 43
Silver St. Enf—13Tb 25
Silver St. Wal A—6Ec 12
Silver St. Wal X—2Sb 11
Silverthorne Gdns. E4—19Cc 26
Silverthorne Rd. SW8—54Kb 104
Silverton Rd. W6—51Za 102
Silvertown Av. Stanf—1M 93
Silvertown By-Pass. E16—46Mc 85
Silvertown Way. E16—44Hc 85
Silver Tree Clo. W on T—76W 140
Silvertree La. Gnfd—41Fa 78
Silver Wlk. SE16—46Bc 84
Silver Way. Romf—27Dd 48
Silverwood Clo. Beck—66Cc 128
Silverwood Clo. Grays—45Ce 91
Silverwood Clo. N'wd—25S 36
Silvester Rd. SE22—57Vb 105
Silvester St. SE1—47Tb 83 (2F 207)
Silwood Clo. Asc—8B 116
Silwood Rd. Asc—10D 116
Silwood St. SE16—49Yb 84
Simla Clo. SE14—51Ac 106
Simmil Rd. Esh—78Ga 142
Simmons Clo. N20—19Gb 23
Simmons Clo. Slou—49C 74
Simmons La. E4—19Fc 27
Simmons Pl. Grays—46Ce 91
Simmons Rd. SE18—50Rc 86
Simmons Way. N20—19Gb 23
Simms Clo. Cars—75Gb 145
Simms Rd. SE1—49Wb 83
Simnel Rd. SE12—59Kc 107
Simon Clo. W11—45Bb 81
Simon Ct. Bush, Wat—16Ca 19
Simonds Rd. E10—33Cc 64
Simone Clo. Brom—67Nc 130
Simone Dri. Kenl—88Sb 165
Simon Peter Ct. Enf—12Rb 25
Simons Clo. Cher—79E 138
Simons Wlk. E15—36Fc 65
Simons Wlk. Egh—6N 117
Simplemarsh Ct. Wey—77K 139
Simplemarsh Rd. Wey—77J 139
Simpson Rd. Houn—58Ba 99
Simpson Rd. Rain—37Hd 68
Simpson Rd. Rich—63La 122
Simpson's Rd. E14—45Dc 84
Simpsons Rd. Brom—69Jc 129
Simpson St. SW11—54Gb 103
Simrose Ct. SW18—57Cb 103
Sims Clo. Romf—28Hd 48
Sims Wlk. SE3—56Hc 107
Sinclair Ct. Croy—75Vb 147
Sinclair Gdns. W14—47Za 80
Sinclair Gro. NW11—30Za 40
Sinclair Rd. E4—22Bc 44
Sinclair Rd. W14—47Za 80
Sinclair Way. Dart—63Td 134
Sinclare Clo. Enf—11Vb 25
Sindall Rd. Gnfd—40Ka 58
Sinderby Clo. Borwd—11Pa 21
Singapore Rd. W13—46Ja 78
Singer St. EC2—41Tb 83 (4G 195)
Singles Cross La. Sev—86Yc 169
Single St. West—87Rc 168
Singleton Clo. SW17—66Hb 125
Singleton Clo. Croy—73Sb 147
Singleton Clo. Horn—35Hd 68
Singleton Rd. Dag—36Bd 67
Singleton Scarp. N12—22Cb 41
Singlewell Rd. Grav—1D 136
Singret Pl. Uxb—42L 75
Sinnott Rd. E17—25Zb 44
Sion Rd. Twic—60Ka 100
Sipson Clo. W Dray—51Q 98
Sipson La. W Dray—52Q 98
Sipson La. W Dray & Hay—51Q 98
Sipson Rd. W Dray—48P 75 to 52R 98
Sir Alexander Clo. W3—46Va 80
Sir Alexander Rd. W3—46Va 80
Sirdar Rd. N22—27Rb 43
Sirdar Rd. W11—45Za 80
Sirdar Rd. Mitc—65Jb 126
Sirdar Strand. Grav—4H 137
Sir Francis Way. Brtwd—19Xd 32
Sir Henry Peeks Dri. Slou—7E 52
Sirus Rd. N'wd—22W 36
Sisley Rd. Bark—39Uc 66
Sispara Gdns. SW18—58Bb 103
Sissinghurst Rd. Croy—73Wb 147
Sister Mabel's Way. SE15 —52Wb 105
Sisters Av. SW11—55Hb 103
Sistova Rd. SW12—60Kb 104
Sittingbourne Av. Enf—16Tb 25
Sitwell Gro. Stan—22Ha 38
Siverst Clo. N'holt—37Da 57
Siviter Way. Dag—38Dd 68
Siward Rd. N17—25Tb 43
Siward Rd. SW17—62Eb 125
Siward Rd. Brom—69Kc 129
Six Bells La. Sev—98Ld 187
Sixth Av. E12—35Pc 66
Sixth Av. W10—41Ab 80
Sixth Av. Hay—46V 76
Sixth Av. Wat—7Z 5
Sixth Av. Wey—75L 139
Sixth Cross Rd. Twic—62Ea 122
Skardu Rd. NW2—36Ab 60
Skarning Ct. Wal A—5Jc 13
Skeena Hill. SW18—59Ab 102
Skeet Hill La. Orp—75Ad 151
Skeffington Rd. E6—39Pc 66
Skelbrook St. SW18—61Eb 125
Skelgill Rd. SW15—56Bb 103
Skelley Rd. E15—38Hc 65
Skelton Clo. E8—37Vb 63
Skelton Rd. E7—37Jc 65
Skelton's La. E10—31Dc 64
Skelwith Rd. W6—51Ya 102
Sketchley Gdns. SE16—50Zb 84
Sketty Rd. Enf—13Vb 25
Skibbs La. Orp—78Ad 152
Skid Hill La. Warl—85Hc 167
Skidmore Way. Rick—18N 17
Skiers St. E15—39Gc 65
Skiffington Clo. SW2—60Qb 104
Skillet Hill. Wal A—7Kc 13
Skinner Ct. E2—40Xb 63
Skinners Clo. SE25—71Wb 147
Skinners La. EC4 —45Sb 83 (4E 200)
Skinners La. Asht—90Ma 161
Skinner's Row. SE10—53Dc 106
Skinner St. EC1—42Qb 82 (4A 194)
Skipsey Av. E6—41Pc 86
Skipton Dri. Hay—48S 76
Skipton St. SE1—48Rb 83 (4C 206)
Skipworth Rd. E9—39Yb 64
Skomer Wlk. N1—37Sb 63
Skydmore Path. Slou—1D 72
Skylark Rd. Uxb—32E 54
Sky Peals Rd. Wfd G—24Fc 45
Skyport Dri. W Dray—52M 97
Sladebrook Rd. SE3—55Mc 107
Slade Ct. Cher—79F 138
Sladedale Rd. SE18—50Uc 86
Slade End. Epp—8Uc 14
Slade Gdns. Eri—53Hd 110
Slade Grn. Rd. Eri—52Jd 110
Slade Grn. Rd. Eri
Sladen Pl. E5—35Xb 63
Slade Oak La. Ger X & Uxb—27D 34
Slade Rd. Cher—79F 138
Slades Clo. Enf—13Qb 24
Slades Dri. Chst—63Sc 130
Slades Gdns. Enf—13Qb 24
Slades Hill. Enf—13Qb 24
Slades Rise. Enf—13Qb 24
Slade, The. SE18—51Uc 108
Slade Wlk. SE17—51Sb 105
Slagrove Pl. SE4 & SE13 —57Cc 106
Slaidburn St. SW10—51Eb 103
Slaithwaite Rd. SE13—56Ec 106
Slaney Pl. N7—36Qb 62
Slapleys. Wok—92A 172
Sleaford Grn. Wat—20Z 19
Sleaford St. SW8—52Lb 104
Sleepers Farm Rd. Grays—7D 92
Slewins Clo. Horn—29Ld 49
Slewins La. Horn—29Ld 49
Slindon Ct. N16—34Vb 63
Slines New Rd. Cat—92Zb 182
Slines Oak Rd. Warl & Cat —91Cc 182
Slingsby Pl. WC2 —45Nb 82 (4F 199)
Slippers Pl. SE16—48Xb 83
Slip, The. West—98Sc 184
Sloane Av. SW3—49Gb 81 (6E 202)
Sloane Ct. E. SW3 —50Jb 82 (7H 203)
Sloane Ct. W. SW3 —50Jb 82 (7H 203)
Sloane Gdns. SW1 —49Jb 82 (6H 203)
Sloane Gdns. Orp—76Sc 150
Sloane Sq. SW1—49Hb 81 (6H 203)
Sloane St. SW1—48Hb 81 (2G 203)
Sloane Ter. SW1—49Jb 82 (5H 203)
Sloane Wlk. Croy—72Bc 148
Slocum Clo. SE28—45Yc 87
Slough By-Pass. Slou—9H 73
Slough Industrial Est. Slou—4F 72
Slough La. NW9—29Sa 39
Slough La. Eps—97Sa 177
Slough Rd. Iver—41E 74
Slough Rd. Slou—10L 73
Slough Rd. Wind & Slou—10H 73
Slough Trading Est. Slou—3D 72
Sly St. E1—44Xb 83
Smallberry Av. Iswth—54Ha 100
Smallbrook M. W2 —44Fb 81 (3B 196)
Smalley Clo. N16—34Vb 63
Small Grains. Long, Dart —76Xd 154
Smallholdings Rd. Eps—86Ya 162
(in two parts)
Smallwood Rd. SW17—63Fb 125
Smardale Rd. SW18—57Eb 103
Smarden Clo. Belv—50Cd 88
Smarden Gro. SE9—63Pc 130
Smart Clo. Romf—25Kd 49
Smart's Heath La. Wok—10D 188
Smart's Heath Rd. Wok—10C 188
Smart's La. Lou—14Mc 27
Smarts Pl. N18—22Wb 43
Smart's Pl. WC2—44Nb 82 (2G 199)
Smarts Rd. Grav—1E 136
Smart St. E2—41Zb 84
Smeaton Rd. SW18—59Cb 103
Smeaton Rd. Wfd G—22Pc 46

Smedley St.—Spencer Wlk.

Smedley St.—54Mb 104
SW8 1-3
SW4 remainder
Smeed Rd. E3—38Cc 64
Smitham Bottom La. Purl —83Lb 164
Smitham Downs Rd. Purl —85Mb 164
Smithfield St. EC1 —43Rb 83 (1B 200)
Smithies Rd. SE2—49Xc 87
Smith's La. Wind—4C 94
Smithson Rd. N17—25Tb 43
Smith Sq. SW1—48Nb 82 (4F 205)
Smith St. SW3—50Hb 81 (7F 203)
Smith St. Surb—72Pa 143
Smith St. Wat—14Y 19
Smith Ter. SW3—50Hb 81 (7F 203)
Smithwood Clo. SW19—60Ab 102
Smithy Clo. Tad—98Bb 179
Smithy La. Tad—99Bb 179
Smithy St. E1—43Yb 84
Smock Wlk. Croy—72Sb 147
Smug Oak La. St Alb—2Da 5
Smyrk's Rd. SE17 —50Ub 83 (7J 207)
Smyrna Rd. NW6—38Cb 61
Smythe Rd. S at H, Dart—67Qd 133
Smythe St. E14—45Dc 84
Snag La. Sev & Orp—84Tc 168
Snakes Hill. Brtwd—12Sd 32
Snakes La. Barn—13Kb 24
Snakes La. E. Wfd G—23Lc 45
Snakes La. W. Wfd G—23Jc 45
Snape Spur. Slou—4J 73
Snaresbrook Dri. Stan—21Ma 39
Snaresbrook Rd. E11—28Gc 45
Snarsgate St. W10—43Ya 80
Snatts Hill. Oxt—100Hc 183
Sneath Av. NW11—31Bb 61
Snelgar Rd. Wok—90A 156
Snelling Av. Grav—1A 136
Snellings Rd. W on T—78Y 141
Snells Pk. N18—23Vb 43
Sneyd Rd. NW2—36Ya 60
Snodland Clo. Orp—82Qc 168
Snowbury Rd. SW6—54Db 103
Snowden Av. Uxb—40R 56
Snowden Cres. Hay—48S 76
Snowden St. EC2 —42Ub 83 (6H 195)
Snowdon Clo. Wind—6B 94
Snowdrop Clo. Hmptn—65Ca 121
Snowdrop Path. Romf—24Md 49
Snow Hill. EC1—43Rb 83 (1B 200)
Snow Hill Ct. EC1 —44Rb 83 (2C 200)
Snowsfields. SE1 —47Tb 83 (1G 207)
Snowshill Rd. E12—36Nc 66
★Soames Mead. Brtwd—5Wd
Soames St. SE15—55Vb 105
Soames Wlk. N Mald—67Ua 124
Socket La. Brom—72Kc 149
Soham Rd. Enf—9Bc 12
Soho Sq. W1—44Mb 82 (2D 198)
Soho St. W1—44Mb 82 (2D 198)
Solebay St. E1—42Ac 84
Solecote. Lea—97Ca 175
Sole Farm Av. Lea—97Ba 175
Sole Farm Rd. Lea—96Ba 175
Sole Farm Rd. Lea—97Ba 175
Solefields. Sev—99Ld 187
Solefields Rd. Sev—100Kd 187
Solent Rd. NW6—36Cb 61
Solent Rd. Houn—58P 97
Solesbridge Clo. Rick—13H 17
Solesbridge La. Rick—13H 17
Sole St. Grav—10F 136
Soley M. WC1—41Qb 82 (3K 193)
Solid La. Brtwd—11Vd 32
Solna Av. SW15—57Ya 102
Solna Rd. N21—18Tb 25
Solomon's Hill. Rick—17M 17
Solomon's Pas. SE15—56Xb 105
Solomons Ter. N20—19Eb 23
Soloms Ct. Rd. Bans—89Fb 163
Solon New Rd. SW4—56Nb 104
Solon Rd. SW2—56Nb 104
Solway. Grays—8L 83
Solway Clo. Houn—55Aa 99
Solway Rd. N22—25Rb 43
Solway Rd. SE22—56Wb 105
Somaford Gro. Barn—16Fb 23
Somali Rd. NW2—36Bb 61
Somerby Rd. Bark—38Tc 66
Somercoates Clo. Barn—13Gb 23
Somerden Rd. Orp—73Zc 151
Somerfield Clo. Tad—91Ab 178
Somerfield Rd. N4—33Rb 63
Somerford Clo. Pinn—28W 36
Somerford Est. N16—35Vb 63
Somerford Gro. N16—35Vb 63
Somerford Gro. N17—24Wb 43
Somerford St. E1—42Xb 83
Somerford Way. SE16—47Ac 84
Somerhill Av. Sidc—59Xc 109
Somerhill Rd. Well—54Xc 109
Somerleyton Rd. SW9—56Qb 104
Somersby Gdns. Ilf—29Pc 46
Somers Clo. NW1 —40Mb 62 (1D 192)
Somers Cres. W2 —44Gb 81 (3D 196)
Somerset Av. SW20—68Xa 124
Somerset Av. Chess—77Ma 143
Somerset Av. Well—56Vc 109
Somerset Clo. Eps—81Ta 161
Somerset Clo. N Mald—72Ua 144
Somerset Clo. W on T—78X 141
Somerset Clo. Wfd G—25Jc 45
Somerset Gdns. N6—31Jb 62
Somerset Gdns. SE13—54Dc 106
Somerset Gdns. SW16—69Pb 126
Somerset Gdns. Horn—32Qd 69
Somerset Gdns. Tedd—64Ga 122
Somerset Rd. E17—30Cc 44
Somerset Rd. N17—27Vb 43
Somerset Rd. N18—22Vb 43
Somerset Rd. NW4—28Ya 40
Somerset Rd. SW19—62Za 124
Somerset Rd. W4—48Ta 79
Somerset Rd. W13—46La 78
Somerset Rd. Barn—15Db 23
Somerset Rd. Bren—51La 100
Somerset Rd. Dart—58Kd 111
Somerset Rd. Enf—10Bc 12
Somerset Rd. Harr—29Ea 38
Somerset Rd. King—68Pa 123
Somerset Rd. Orp—73Wc 151
Somerset Rd. S'hall—43Ca 77
Somerset Rd. Stanf—7J 93
Somerset Rd. Tedd—64Ga 122
Somerset Sq. W14—47Ab 80
Somerset Way. Houn—51Aa 99
Somerset Way. Iver—47H 75
Somersham Rd. Bexh—54Ad 109
Somers M. W2—44Gb 81 (3D 196)
Somers Pl. SW2—59Pb 104
Somers Rd. E17—28Bc 44
Somers Rd. SW2—58Pb 104
Somers Way. Bush Wat—17Ea 20
Somerton Av. Rich—55Ra 101
Somerton Clo. Purl—88Qb 164
Somerton Rd. NW2—34Ab 60
Somerton Rd. SE15—56Xb 105
Somertrees Av. SE12—61Kc 129
Somervell Rd. Harr—36Ba 57
Somerville Rd. SE20—66Zb 128
Somerville Rd. Cob—86Ca 159
Somerville Rd. Dart—58Pd 111
Somerville Rd. Romf—30Yc 47
Somerville Rd. Wind—10G 72
Sonderburg Rd. N7—33Pb 62
Sondes St. SE17—51Tb 105
Sonia Ct. Harr—30Ha 38
Sonia Gdns. N12—21Eb 41
Sonia Gdns. NW10—35Va 60
Sonia Gdns. Houn—52Ca 99
Sonnet Wlk. West—90Kc 167
Sonning Rd. SE25—72Wb 147
Sopers Rd. Pot B—1Pb 10
Sophia Clo. N7—37Pb 62
Sophia Rd. E10—32Dc 64
Sophia Rd. E16—44Kc 85
Sopwith Av. Chess—78Na 143
Sopwith Rd. Houn—52Y 99
Sopwith Way. Wall—80Mb 146
Sorrel Bank. Croy—81Ac 166
Sorrel Clo. SE28—46Wc 87
Sorrel Ct. Grays—51Fe 113
Sorrell Clo. SW9—54Qb 104
Sorrells, The. Stanf—1P 93
Sorrel Wlk. Romf—27Hd 48
Sorrento Rd. Sutt—76Db 145
Sospel Ct. Slou—10G 52
Sotheby Rd. N5—34Rb 34
Sotheron Rd. SW6—52Db 103
Sotheron Rd. Wat—13Y 19
Soudan Rd. SW11—53Hb 103
Souldern Rd. W14—48Za 80
Souldern St. Wat—15X 19
Sounds Lodge. Swan—72Ed 152
S. Access Rd. E17—31Ac 64
South Acre. NW9—26Va 40
Southacre Way. Pinn—25Y 37
S. Africa Rd. W12—46Xa 80
Southall La. Houn & S'hall—51X 99
Southall Pl. SE1—47Tb 83 (2F 207)
Southall Way. Brtwd—21Vd 50
Southampton Bldgs. WC2 —43Qb 82 (1H 199)
Southampton Gdns. Mitc —71Nb 146
Southampton Pl. WC1 —43Nb 82 (1G 199)
Southampton Rd. NW5—36Hb 61
Southampton Rd. Houn—58N 97
Southampton Row. WC1 —43Nb 82 (7G 193)
Southampton St. WC2 —45Nb 82 (4G 199)
Southampton Way. SE5 —52Tb 105
Southam St. W10—42Ab 80
S. Approach. N'wd—20T 18
S. Ash Rd. Sev—80Zd 155
S. Audley St. W1—45Jb 82 (5J 197)
South Av. E4—17Dc 26
South Av. Cars—80Jb 146
South Av. Egh—65E 118
South Av. Rich—54Qa 101
South Av. S'hall—45Ba 77
South Av. W on T—82U 158
South Av. Wey—82Q 158
South Av. Gdns. S'hall—45Ba 77
South Bank. Chst—63Sc 130
South Bank. Surb—72Na 143
Southbank. Th Dit—73Ka 142
South Bank. West—98Tc 184
S. Bank Ter. Surb—72Na 143
S. Birkbeck Rd. E11—34Fc 65
S. Black Lion La. W6—50Wa 80
S. Bolton Gdns. SW5—50Eb 81
S. Border, The. Purl—83Nb 164
Southborough Clo. Surb —74Ma 143
Southborough La. Brom —71Nc 150
Southborough Rd. E9—39Zb 64
Southborough Rd. Brom —69Nc 130
Southborough Rd. Surb —74Na 143
Southbourne. Brom—73Jc 149
Southbourne Av. NW9—26Sa 39
Southbourne Clo. Pinn—31Aa 57
Southbourne Cres. NW4—28Ab 40
Southbourne Gdns. SE12 —57Kc 107
Southbourne Gdns. Ilf—36Sc 66
Southbourne Gdns. Ruis—32X 57
Southbridge Pl. Croy—77Sb 147
Southbridge Rd. Croy—77Sb 147
Southbridge Way. S'hall—47Aa 77
Southbrook M. SE12—58Hc 107
Southbrook Rd. SE12—58Hc 107
Southbrook Rd. SW16—67Nb 126
Southbury Av. Enf—14Wb 25
Southbury Clo. Horn—36Md 69
Southbury Rd. Enf—13Ub 25
S. Carriage Dri. SW7 & SW1 —47Fb 81 (2C 202)
Southchurch Rd. E6—40Pc 66
Southcliffe Dri. Ger X—22A 34
South Clo. N6—30Kb 42
South Clo. Barn—13Bb 23
South Clo. Bexh—56Zc 109
South Clo. Dag—39Cd 68
South Clo. Mord—72Cb 145
South Clo. Pinn—25Z 37 (Pinner Green)
South Clo. Pinn—31Ba 57 (Rayners Lane)
South Clo. Slou—5B 72
South Clo. Twic—62Ca 121
South Clo. W Dray—48P 75
South Clo. Wok—4F 188
South Clo. Grn. Red—100Kb 180
Southcombe St. W14—49Ab 80
S. Common Rd. Uxb—37N 55
Southcote. Wok—3G 188
Southcote Av. Felt—61W 120
Southcote Av. Surb—73Ra 143
Southcote Rise. Ruis—31T 56
Southcote Rd. E17—29Zb 44
Southcote Rd. N19—35Lb 62
Southcote Rd. SE25—72Xb 147
Southcote Rd. S Croy—82Ub 165
S. Cottage Dri. Rick—15H 17
S. Cottage Gdns. Rick—15H 17
S. Countess Rd. E17—27Bc 44
South Cres. WC1—(1D 198)
Southcroft. Slou—2F 72
Southcroft Av. Well—55Uc 108
Southcroft Av. W Wick—75Ec 148
Southcroft Rd.—65Jb 126
SW17 1-161 & 2-248
SW16 remainder
Southcroft Rd. Orp—76Uc 150
S. Cross Rd. Ilf—29Sc 46
S. Croxted Rd. SE21—62Tb 127
Southdale. Chig—23Tc 46
Southdean Gdns. SW19—61Bb 125
South Dene. NW7—20Ta 21
Southdene. Sev—85Bd 169 (in two parts)
Southdown Av. W7—48Ja 78
Southdown Cres. Harr—32Ea 58
Southdown Cres. Ilf—29Uc 46
Southdown Dri. SW20—66Za 124
Southdown Rd. SW20—67Za 124
Southdown Rd. Cars—81Jb 164
Southdown Rd. Cat—94Bc 182
Southdown Rd. Horn—31Kd 69
Southdown Rd. W on T—77Aa 141
South Dri. Bans—85Gb 163
South Dri. Brtwd—21Zd 51
South Dri. Coul—87Mb 164
South Dri. Orp—78Uc 150
South Dri. Pot B—2Nb 10
South Dri. Romf—27Ld 49
South Dri. Ruis—32U 56
South Dri. Sutt—82Ab 162
S. Ealing Rd. W5 & Bren—47Ma 79
S. Eastern Av. N9—20Vb 25
S. Eaton Pl. SW1—49Jb 82 (5J 203)
S. Eden Pk. Rd. Beck—72Dc 148
S. Edwardes Sq. W8—48Cb 81
South End. W8—48Db 81
South End. Croy—77Sb 147
South End. Lea—98Da 175
Southend Arterial Rd. Romf, Horn, Upm & Brtwd—26Md 49 to 28Fe 51
S. End Clo. NW3—35Gb 61
Southend Clo. SE9—58Rc 108
Southend Cres. SE9—58Rc 108
S. End Grn. NW3—35Gb 61
Southend La.—63Bc 128
SE6 1-299 & 2-298
SE26 remainder
Southend Rd. E6—38Pc 66
Southend Rd. E17—25Fc 45
Southend Rd. E18—25Jc 45
S. End Rd. NW3—35Gb 61
Southend Rd. Beck—67Cc 128
Southend Rd. Grays—49Ee 91
S. End Rd. Rain & Horn—39Jd 68
Southend Rd. Stanf—1M 93
Southend Rd. Wfd G—26Mc 45
S. End Row. W8—48Db 81
Southerland Clo. Wey—77S 140
Southern Av. SE25—69Vb 127
Southern Av. Felt—60W 98
Southern Clo. E8—39Wb 63
Southern Dri. Lou—16Pc 28
Southern Gro. E3—41Bc 84
Southernhay. Lou—15Mc 27
Southern Perimeter Rd. Houn & Stai—57N 97
Southern Pl. Swan—70Fd 132
Southern Rd. E13—40Kc 65
Southern Rd. N2—28Hb 41
Southern Row. W10—42Ab 80
Southerns La. Coul—96Eb 179
Southern St. N1—40Pb 62 (1H 193)
Southern Way. Romf—30Cd 48
Southerton Rd. W6—49Ya 80
S. Esk Rd. E7—37Lc 65
Southey Rd. N15—29Ub 43
Southey Rd. SE20—66Zb 128
Southey Rd. SW9—53Qb 104
Southey Rd. SW19—66Cb 125
Southey Wlk. Til—3D 114
Southfield. Barn—16Za 22
Southfield Av. Wat—10Y 5
Southfield Clo. Uxb—42Q 76
Southfield Clo. Wind—8A 72
Southfield Cotts. W7—47Ha 78
Southfield Ct. E11—34Fc 65
Southfield Gdns. Slou—3A 72
Southfield Gdns. Twic—63Ha 122
Southfield Pk. Harr—28Da 37
Southfield Pl. Wey—80R 140
Southfield Rd. N17—26Ub 43
Southfield Rd. W4—47Ta 79
Southfield Rd. Chst—69Wc 131
Southfield Rd. Enf—16Xb 25
Southfield Rd. Wal X—4Ac 12
Southfields. NW4—27Xa 40
Southfields. E Mol—72Ga 142
Southfields Av. Ashf—65R 120
Southfields Pas. SW18—58Cb 103
Southfields Rd. SW18—58Cb 103
Southfields Rd. Cat—94Dc 182
Southfields Rd. Sev—80Vd 154
Southfleet Av. Long, Dart —68De 135
Southfleet Rd. Dart—63Yd 134
Southfleet Rd. Grav—10B 114
Southfleet Rd. Orp—76Uc 150
Southfleet Rd. Swans—59Be 113
South Gdns. SW19—66Fb 125
Southgate. Purf—49Sd 90
Southgate Av. Felt—63T 120
Southgate Cir. N14—18Mb 24
Southgate Gro. N1—38Tb 63
Southgate Rd. N1—39Tb 63
Southgate Rd. Pot B—5Eb 9
S. Gipsy Rd. Well—55Zc 109
South Glade, The. Bex—60Bd 109
South Grn. NW9—25Ua 40
South Grn. Slou—5J 73
South Gro. E17—29Bc 44
South Gro. N6—32Jb 62
South Gro. N15—29Tb 43
South Gro. Cher—72H 139
S. Hall Clo. F'ham, Dart—73Pd 153
S. Hall Dri. Rain—43Kd 89
South Hill. Chst—65Pc 130
South Hill. Stanf—1J 93
S. Hill Av. Harr—34Ea 58
S. Hill Cres. Stanf—1J 93
S. Hill Gro. Harr—35Ga 58
S. Hill Pk. NW3—35Gb 61
S. Hill Pk. Gdns. NW3—35Gb 61
S. Hill Rd. Brom—69Gc 129
S. Hill Rd. Grav—10E 114
Southill La. Pinn—28X 37
Southill Rd. Chst—66Nc 130
S. Island Pl. SW9—52Qb 104
S. Kensington Sta. Arc. SW7 —(5C 202)
S. Kent Av. Grav—58Ee 113
S. Lambeth Pl. SW8—51Nb 104
S. Lambeth Rd. SW8—51Nb 104
Southland Rd. SE18—52Vc 109
Southlands Av. Orp—77Uc 150
Southlands Clo. Coul—89Pb 164
Southlands Gro. Brom—69Nc 130
Southlands Rd. Brom—70Mc 129
Southlands Rd. Uxb—36H 55 (in two parts)
Southland Way. Houn—57Fa 100
South La. King—69Ma 123
South La. N Mald—70Ta 123
South La. W. N Mald—70Ta 123
Southlea Rd. Wind & Slou—6L 95
S. Lodge Av. Mitc—70Nb 126
S. Lodge Cres. Enf—14Mb 24 (in two parts)
S. Lodge Dri. N14—14Mb 24
S. Lodge Rd. W on T—81W 158
Southly Clo. Sutt—76Cb 145
South Mall. Stai—63H 119
South Mall, The. N9—20Wb 25
South Mead. NW9—25Va 40
South Mead. Eps—80Va 144
Southmead Cres. Wal X—2Ac 12
S. Meadow La. Wind—1G 94
S. Meadows. Wemb—36Pa 59
Southmead Rd. SW19—60Ab 102
S. Molton La. W1 —45Kb 82 (3K 197)
S. Molton Rd. E16—44Jc 85
S. Molton St. W1 —44Kb 82 (3K 197)
Southmont Rd. Esh—75Ga 142
Southmoor Way. E9—37Bc 64
S. Norwood Hill. SE25—67Ub 127
S. Oak Rd. SW16—63Pb 126
Southold Rise. SE9—62Pc 130
Southolm St. SW11—53Kb 104
Southover. N12—20Cb 23
Southover. Brom—64Jc 129
South Pde. SW3—50Fb 81 (7C 202)
South Pde. W4—49Ta 79
South Pde. Wal A—5Ec 12
South Pk. Ger X—29B 34
South Pk. Sev—97Kd 187
S. Park Av. Rick—15H 17
S. Park Cres. SE6—60Hc 107
S. Park Cres. Ger X—28A 34
S. Park Cres. Ilf—34Tc 66
S. Park Dri. Bark & Ilf—36Uc 66
S. Park Dri. Ger X—28A 34
S. Park Gro. N Mald—70Sa 123
S. Park Hill Rd. S Croy—78Tb 147
S. Park Rd. SW19—65Cb 125
S. Park Rd. Ilf—34Tc 66
S. Park Ter. Ilf—34Uc 66
S. Park View. Ger X—28B 34
S. Park Way. Ruis—37Y 57
South Path. Wind—3G 94
South Pl. EC2—43Tb 83 (7G 195)
South Pl. Enf—15Yb 26
South Pl. Surb—73Pa 143
South Pl. M. EC2—43Tb 83 (1G 201)
Southport Rd. SE18—49Tc 86
South Ridge. Wey—82R 158
S. Riding. St Alb—2Ca 5
South Rise. Cars—81Gb 163
South Rd. N9—18Wb 25
South Rd. SE23—61Zb 128
South Rd. SW19—65Eb 125
South Rd. W5—49Ma 79
South Rd. Edgw—25Ra 39
South Rd. Egh—5N 117
South Rd. Eri—52Hd 110
South Rd. Felt—64Z 121
South Rd. Hmptn—65Aa 121
South Rd. Rick—15E 16
South Rd. Romf—30Ad 47 (Chadwell Heath)
South Rd. Romf—29Yc 47 (Little Heath)
South Rd. S'hall—47Ba 77
South Rd. S Ock—44Yd 90 (in three parts)
South Rd. Twic—62Fa 122
South Rd. W Dray—48Q 76
South Rd. Wey—78S 140
South Rd. Wey—82R 158 (St George's Hill)
South Rd. Wok—3F 188
South Row. SE3—54Hc 107
Southsea Av. Wat—14W 18
Southsea Rd. King—70Na 123
South Side. W6—48Va 80
South Side. Ger X—27A 34
Southside Comn. SW19—65Ya 124
Southspring. Sidc—59Tc 108
South Sq. NW11—30Db 41
South Sq. WC1—43Qb 82 (1K 199)
South St. W1—46Jb 82 (6J 197)
South St. Brtwd—19Yd 32
South St. Brom—68Jc 129
South St. Enf—15Yb 26
South St. Eps—85Ta 161
South St. Grav—9D 114
South St. Iswth—55Ja 100
South St. Rain—40Ed 68
South St. Romf—29Gd 48
South St. Stai—64H 119
S. Tenter St. E1—45Vb 83 (4K 201)
South Ter. SW7—49Gb 81 (5D 202)
South Ter. Surb—72Na 143
South Vale. SE19—65Ub 127
South Vale. Harr—35Ga 58
Southvale Rd. SE3—54Gc 107
Southview. Brom—68Lc 129
Southview Av. NW10—36Va 60
S. View Av. Til—3C 114
Southview Clo. Bex—58Bd 109
Southview Clo. Swan—70Jd 132
Southview Cotts. Mitc—68Hb 125
S. View Ct. Wok—90A 156
Southview Cres. Ilf—30Rc 46
S. View Dri. E18—27Kc 45
S. View Dri. Upm—34Qd 69
Southview Gdns. Wall—80Lb 146
S. View Rd. N8—27Mb 42
S. View Rd. Asht—91Ma 177
Southview Rd. Brom—63Fc 129
Southview Rd. Cat—96Dc 182
S. View Rd. Dart—62Md 133
S. View Rd. Grays—51Yd 112
S. View Rd. Lou—16Pc 28
S. View Rd. Pinn—23X 37
Southview Rd. Warl—91Wb 181 (in four parts)
Southviews. S Croy—81Zb 166
South Vs. NW1—37Mb 62
Southville. SW8—53Mb 104
Southville Clo. Eps—81Ta 161
Southville Clo. Felt—60U 98
Southville Cres. Felt—60U 98
Southville Rd. Felt—60U 98
Southville Rd. Th Dit—73Ka 142
South Wlk. Hay—43T 76
South Wlk. W Wick—76Gc 149
Southwark Bri. SE1 & EC4 —45Sb 83 (5E 200)
Southwark Bri. Rd. SE1 —47Sb 83 (3C 206)
Southwark Gro. SE1 —46Sb 83 (7D 200)
Southwark Pk. Rd. SE16 —49Vb to 48Xb 83 (5K 207)
Southwark Pl. Brom—69Pc 130
Southwark St. SE1 —46Rb 83 (6C 200)
Southwater Clo. E14—44Bc 84
South Way. N9—19Yb 26
South Way. N11—23Lb 42
Southway. N20—19Cb 23
Southway. NW11—30Db 41
Southway. SW20—70Ya 124
South Way. Brom—73Jc 149
South Way. Croy—76Ac 148
South Way. Harr—28Ca 37
South Way. K Lan & Abb L, Wat —5T 4
South Way. Sutt—82Fb 163
Southway. Wall—77Lb 146
South Way. Wal A—9Dc 12
South Way. Wemb—36Qa 59
Southweald Dri. Wal A—5Fc 13
S. Weald Rd. Brtwd—20Wd 32
Southwell Av. N'holt—37Da 57
Southwell Gdns. SW7 —48Eb 81 (5A 202)
Southwell Gro. Rd. E11—33Gc 65
Southwell Rd. SE5—55Sb 105
Southwell Rd. Croy—72Qb 146
Southwell Rd. Harr—30Ma 39
S. Western Rd. Twic—58Ja 100
Southwest Rd. E11—32Fc 65
S. Wharf Rd. W2—44Fb 81 (2B 196)
Southwick M. W2 —44Fb 81 (2C 196)
Southwick Pl. W2 —44Gb 81 (3D 196)
Southwick St. W2 —44Gb 81 (2D 196)
Southwold Dri. Bark—36Wc 67
Southwold Rd. E5—33Xb 63
Southwold Rd. Bex—58Dd 110
Southwold Rd. Wat—9Y 5
Southwood Av. N6—31Kb 62
Southwood Av. Cher—80E 138
Southwood Av. Coul—87Lb 164
Southwood Av. King—67Sa 123
Southwood Av. Wok—6A 188
Southwood Clo. Brom—70Pc 130
Southwood Clo. Wor Pk—74Za 144
Southwood Dri. Surb—73Sa 143
Southwood Gdns. Esh—76Ja 142
Southwood Gdns. Ilf—28Rc 46
Southwood Hall. N6—30Kb 42
Southwood La. N6—31Jb 62
Southwood Lawn Rd. N6—31Kb 62
Southwood Pk. N6—31Jb 62
Southwood Rd. SE9—61Rc 130
Southwood Rd. SE28—46Xc 87
S. Worple Av. SW14—55Ua 102
S. Worple Way. SW14—55Ta 101
Sovereign Clo. W5—43La 78
Sovereign Clo. Ruis—32U 56
Sowerby Clo. SE9—57Pc 108
Sowrey Av. Rain—37Hd 68
Space Way. Felt—57X 99
Spackmans Way. Slou—8G 72
Spa Clo. SE25—67Ub 127
Spa Dri. Eps—86Qa 161
Spafield St. EC1—(5K 193)
Spa Hill. SE19—67Tb 127
Spalding Rd. NW4—31Ya 60
Spalding Rd. SW17—64Kb 126
Spalt Clo. Brtwd—19De 33
Spanby Rd. E3—42Cc 84
Spaniards Clo. NW11—32Fb 61
Spaniards End. NW3—32Eb 61
Spaniards Rd. NW3—33Eb 61
Spanish Pl. W1—44Jb 82 (2J 197)
Spanish Rd. SW18—57Eb 103
Spanswick Lodge. N15—28Rb 43
Spareleaze Hill. Lou—14Pc 28
Sparepenny La. Eyns & F'ham, Dart—75Md 153
Sparkbridge Rd. Harr—28Ga 38
Sparks Clo. Hmptn—65Aa 121
Spa Rd. SE16—48Vb 83 (4K 207)
Sparrick's Row. SE1 —47Tb 83 (1G 207)
Sparrow Dri. Orp—74Tc 150
Sparrow Farm Dri. Felt—59Y 99
Sparrow Farm Rd. Eps—77Wa 144
Sparrow Grn. Dag—34Dd 68
Sparrows Herne. Bush, Wat —17Da 19
Sparrows La. SE9—60Sc 108
Sparrows Way. Bush, Wat —17Ea 20
Sparsholt Rd. N19—32Pb 62
Sparsholt Rd. Bark—39Uc 66
Sparta St. SE10—53Ec 106
Speaker's Corner. W2—(4G 197)
Spearman St. SE18—51Qc 108
Spear M. SW5—49Cb 81
Spearpoint Gdns. Ilf—29Vc 47
Spears Rd. N19—32Nb 62
Speart La. Houn—52Aa 99
Spedan Clo. NW3—34Eb 61
Speedgate Hill. Long, Dart —75Wd 154
Speed Ho. EC2—(7F 195)
Speedwell Ct. Grays—2A 114
Speedwell Pl. SE8—52Cc 106
Speedy Pl. WC1—(4F 193)
Speer Rd. Th Dit—72Ha 142
Speirs Clo. N Mald—72Va 144
Speke Hill. SE9—62Pc 130
Speke Rd. T Hth—68Tb 127
Speldhurst Clo. Brom—71Hc 149
Speldhurst Rd. E9—38Zb 64
Speldhurst Rd. W4—48Ta 79
Spellbrook Wlk. N1—39Sb 63
Spelman St. E1—43Wb 83
Spelthorne Gro. Sun—66V 120
Spelthorne La. Ashf—67S 120
Spence Av. Wey—86P 157
Spencer Av. N13—23Pb 42
Spencer Av. Hay—43W 76
Spencer Clo. N3—26Cb 41
Spencer Clo. NW10—41Pa 79
Spencer Clo. Croy—73Tb 147
Spencer Clo. Eps—91Ua 178
Spencer Clo. Orp—75Uc 150
Spencer Clo. Uxb—41L 75
Spencer Clo. Wok—85F 156
Spencer Clo. Wfd G—22Lc 45
Spencer Dri. N2—30Eb 41
Spencer Gdns. SE9—57Pc 108
Spencer Gdns. SW14—57Sa 101
Spencer Gdns. Egh—4P 117
Spencer Hill. SW19—65Ab 124
Spencer M. W6—51Ab 102
Spencer Pk. SW18—57Fb 103
Spencer Rise. NW5—34Kb 62
Spencer Rd. E6—39Mc 65
Spencer Rd. E17—26Ec 44
Spencer Rd. N8—29Pb 42 (in two parts)
Spencer Rd. N11—21Kb 42
Spencer Rd. N17—25Wb 43
Spencer Rd. SW18—57Fb 103
Spencer Rd. SW20—67Xa 124
Spencer Rd. W3—46Sa 79
Spencer Rd. W4—52Sa 101
Spencer Rd. Brom—66Hc 129
Spencer Rd. Cat—93Tb 181
Spencer Rd. Cob—87X 159
Spencer Rd. E Mol—70Ea 122
Spencer Rd. Harr—26Ga 38
Spencer Rd. Ilf—32Vc 67
Spencer Rd. Iswth—53Ea 100
Spencer Rd. Mitc—69Jb 126
Spencer Rd. Mitc—73Jb 146 (Beddington Corner)
Spencer Rd. Rain—41Fd 88
Spencer Rd. Slou—48B 74
Spencer Rd. S Croy—78Ub 147
Spencer Rd. Twic—62Ga 122
Spencer Rd. Wemb—36Ja 58
★Spencers Cotts. Sev—92Ce
Spencer St. EC1—41Rb 83 (4B 194)
Spencer St. Grav—9C 114
Spencer St. S'hall—47Z 77
Spencer Wlk. SW15—56Za 102
Spencer Wlk. Rick—15L 17
Spencer Wlk. Til—4D 114

Spenser Av.—Starts Clo.

Spenser Av. Wey—81Q 158
Spenser Cres. Upm—31Sd 70
Spenser Gro. N16—35Ub 63
Spenser Rd. SE24—57Rb 105
Spenser St. SW1 —48Lb 82 (3C 204)
Spensley Wlk. N16—34Tb 63
Speranza St. SE18—50Vc 87
Sperling Rd. N17—26Ub 43
Spert St. E14—45Ac 84
Spey Side. N14—16Lb 24
Spey St. E14—43Ec 84
Spey Way. Romf—24Gd 48
Spezia Rd. NW10—40Wa 60
Spicer Clo. SW9—54Rb 105
Spicers Field. Lea—85Fa 160
Spice's Yd. Croy—77Sb 147
Spielman Rd. Dart—56Pd 111
Spigurnell Rd. N17—25Tb 43
Spikes Bri. Rd. S'hall—45Aa 77
★Spillbutters. Brtwd—8Xd
Spilsby Clo. NW9—25Ua 40
Spilsby Rd. Romf—24Md 49
Spindles. Til—2C 114
Spindlewood Gdns. Croy —77Ub 147
Spindlewoods. Tad—95Xa 178
Spinel Clo. SE18—50Vc 87
Spingate Clo. Horn—36Ld 69
Spinnells Rd. Harr—32Ba 57
Spinners Wlk. Wind—3G 94
Spinney. Slou—7F 72
Spinney Clo. Cob—83Ca 159
Spinney Clo. N Mald—71Ua 144
Spinney Clo. W Dray—45N 75
Spinney Dri. Felt—59S 98
Spinney Gdns. SE19—64Vb 127
Spinney Gdns. Dag—36Ad 67
Spinney Hill. Wey—78G 138
Spinney Oak. Brom—68Nc 130
Spinneys, The. Brom—68Pc 130
Spinney, The. N21—17Qb 24
Spinney, The. SW16—62Lb 126
Spinney, The. Barn—12Db 23
Spinney, The. Brtwd—16Ee 33
Spinney, The. Eps—91Xa 178
Spinney, The. Grays—2C 92
Spinney, The. Lea—96Da 175
Spinney, The. Pot B—3Fb 9
Spinney, The. Purl—83Rb 165
Spinney, The. Sidc—64Ad 131
Spinney, The. Stan—21Na 39
Spinney, The. Sun—67W 120
Spinney, The. Sutt—77Ya 144
Spinney, The. Wat—11W 18
Spinney, The. Wemb—34Ja 58
Spinney, The. Wok—99L 173
Spinney Way. Sev—83Tc 168
Spire Clo. Grav—10D 114
Spires, The. Dart—61Md 133
Spital La. Brtwd—20Vd 32
Spital Sq. E1—43Ub 83 (7J 195)
Spital St. E1—43Wb 83
Spital St. Dart—58Md 111
Spital Yd. E1—43Ub 83 (7J 195)
Spitfire Rd. Houn—58S 98
Spitfire Way. Houn—50Y 77
Spode Wlk. NW6—36Db 61
Spondon Rd. N15—28Wb 43
Spooner Wlk. Wall—78Nb 146
Sportsbank St. SE6—59Ec 106
Spottons Gro. N17—25Sb 43
Spout Hill. Croy—78Cc 148
Spout La. Stai—56J 97
Spout La. N. Stai—56K 97
Spratt Hall Rd. E11—30Jc 45
Spratts All. Cher—79G 138
Spratts La. Cher—79G 138
Spray La. Twic—58Ga 100
Spray St. SE18—49Rc 86
Spreighton Rd. E Mol—70Da 121
Spriggs Oak. Epp—1Wc 15
Sprimont Pl. SW3 —49Hb 81 (7F 203)
Springall St. SE15—52Xb 105
Springate Field. Slou—47A 74
Spring Av. Egh—65A 118
Spring Bank. N21—16Pb 24
Springbank Av. Horn—36Ld 69
Springbank Rd. SE13—58Fc 107
Springbank Wlk. NW1—38Mb 62
Spring Bottom La. Red —99Qb 180
Springbourne Ct. Beck—67Ec 128
Spring Bri. M. W5—45Ma 79
Springbridge Rd. W5—45Ma 79
Spring Clo. Borwd—11Qa 21
Spring Clo. Uxb—25M 35
Spring Clo. La. Sutt—79Ab 144
Spring Corner. Felt—62W 120
Spring Cotts. Surb—71Ma 143
Spring Ct. Eps—81Va 162
Spring Ct. Rd. Enf—10Qb 10
Springcroft. Long, Dart—71Ce 155
Spring Croft. Long, Dart
Springcroft Av. N2—28Hb 41
Spring Crofts. Bush, Wat—15Ca 19
Spring Cross. Long, Dart (in two parts) —76Ce 155
Springdale Rd. N16—35Tb 63
Spring Dri. Pinn—30W 36
Springfield. E5—32Xb 63
Springfield. Bush, Wat—18Fa 20
Springfield. Epp—4Vc 15
Springfield Av. N10—27Lb 42
Springfield Av. SW20—69Bb 125
Springfield Av. Brtwd—17Fe 33
Springfield Av. Hmptn—65Da 121
Springfield Av. Swan—70Hd 132
Springfield Clo. Pot B—3Fb 9
Springfield Clo. Rick—15R 18
Springfield Clo. Stan—20Ja 20
Springfield Clo. Wind—4F 94
Springfield Clo. Wok—6B 188
Springfield Dri. Ilf—29Sc 46
Springfield Gdns. E5—32Xb 63
Springfield Gdns. NW9—29Ta 39
Springfield Gdns. Brom—70Pc 130
Springfield Gdns. Ruis—32X 57
Springfield Gdns. Upm—34Rd 69
Springfield Gdns. W Wick —75Dc 148
Springfield Gdns. Wfd G—24Lc 45
Springfield Gro. SE7—51Lc 107
Springfield Gro. Sun—67W 120
Springfield La. NW6—39Db 61
Springfield La. Wey—77R 140
Springfield Meadows. Wey —77R 140
Springfield Mt. NW9—29Ua 40
Springfield Rise. SE26—62Xb 127
Springfield Rd. E4—18Gc 27
Springfield Rd. E6—38Pc 66
Springfield Rd. E15—41Gc 85
Springfield Rd. E17—30Bc 44
Springfield Rd. N11—22Kb 42
Springfield Rd. N15—28Wb 43
Springfield Rd. NW8—39Eb 61
Springfield Rd. SE26—64Xb 127
Springfield Rd. SW19—64Bb 125
Springfield Rd. W7—46Ga 78
Springfield Rd. Ashf—64P 119
Springfield Rd. Bexh—56Dd 110
Springfield Rd. Brom—70Pc 130
Springfield Rd. Eps—82Ya 162
Springfield Rd. Grays—7A 92
Springfield Rd. Harr—30Ga 38
Springfield Rd. Hay—46Y 77
Springfield Rd. King—69Na 123
Springfield Rd. Slou—52D 96
Springfield Rd. Tedd—64Ja 122
Springfield Rd. T Hth—67Sb 127
Springfield Rd. Twic—60Ca 99
Springfield Rd. Wall—78Kb 146
Springfield Rd. Wal X—4Ac 12
Springfield Rd. Wat—6X 5
Springfield Rd. Well—55Xc 109
Springfield Rd. Wind—4F 94
Springfields. Wal A—6Gc 13
Springfield Wlk. NW6—39Db 61
Spring Gdns. N5—36Sb 63
Spring Gdns. SW1 —46Mb 82 (6E 198)
Spring Gdns. E Mol—71Da 141
Spring Gdns. Horn—35Kd 69
Spring Gdns. Orp—79Xc 151
Spring Gdns. Romf—29Ed 48
Spring Gdns. Wall—78Lb 146
Spring Gdns. Wat—7Y 5
Spring Gdns. West—90Lc 167
Spring Gdns. Wfd G—24Lc 45
Spring Gro. SE19—66Vb 127
Spring Gro. W4—50Qa 79
Spring Gro. Grav—10D 114
Spring Gro. Hmptn—67Da 121
Spring Gro. Lea—95Da 175
Spring Gro. Lou—16Mc 27
Spring Gro. Cres. Houn—53Ea 100
Spring Gro. Rd. Houn & Iswth —53Da 99
Spring Gro. Rd. Rich—57Pa 101
Springhead Enterprise Pk. Grav —60Ee 113
Springhead Rd. Eri—51Hd 110
Springhead Rd. Grav—61Ee 135
Springhead Rd. Sev—89Pd 171
Spring Hill. E5—31Wb 63
Spring Hill. SE26—63Yb 128
Springhill Clo. SE5—55Tb 105
Springholm Clo. West—90Lc 167
Spring Ho. La. Stanf—1P 93
Spring Ho. Rd. Stanf—1P 93
Spring Lake. Stan—21Ka 38
Spring La. E5—31Xb 63
Spring La. SE25—72Xb 147
★Spring La. Sev—94Xd
Spring La. Slou—6D 72 *(Cippenham)*
Spring La. Slou—8F 52 *(Farnham Park)*
Spring M. W1—43Hb 81 (7G 191)
Spring Pk. Av. Croy—75Zb 148
Spring Pk. Dri. N4—32Sb 63
Springpark Dri. Beck—69Ec 128
Spring Pk. Rd. Croy—75Zb 148
Spring Pl. NW5—36Kb 62
★Spring Pond Meadow. Brtwd —7Yd
Springpond Rd. Dag—36Ad 67
Springrice Rd. SE13—58Fc 107
Spring Rise. Egh—65A 118
Spring Rd. Felt—62V 120
Springshaw Clo. Sev—95Fd 186
Spring St. W2—44Fb 81 (3B 196)
Spring St. Eps—81Va 162
Spring Ter. Rich—57Na 101
Spring Vale. Bexh—56Dd 110
Spring Vale. Grnh—58Yd 112
Spring Vale Av. Bren—50Na 79
Spring Vale Clo. Swan—67Hd 132
Springvale Ct. Grav—61Ee 135
Spring Vale N. Dart—59Md 111
Spring Vale S. Dart—59Md 111
Spring Vale Ter. W14—48Za 80
Springvale Way. Orp—69Yc 131
Springvilla Rd. Edgw—24Qa 39
Springwater Clo. SE18—53Qc 108
Springwell Av. NW10—39Va 60
Springwell Av. Rick—19J 17
Springwell Clo. SW16—63Pb 126
Springwell Ct. Houn—54Z 99
Springwell La. Rick & Uxb—20J 17
Springwell Rd. SW16—63Qb 126
Springwell Rd. Houn—53Z 99
Springwood Clo. Uxb—25M 35
Springwood Ct. S Croy—77Ub 147
Springwood Cres. Edgw—19Ra 21
Spring Woods. Vir W—10M 117
Springwood Way. Romf—29Jd 48
Sprowston M. E7—37Jc 65
Sprowston Rd. E7—36Jc 65
Sprucedale Gdns. Croy—77Zb 148
Sprucedale Gdns. Wall—81Nb 164
Spruce Hills Rd. E17—26Ec 44
Spruce Rd. West—88Mc 167
Sprules Rd. SE4—54Ac 106
Spur Clo. Abb L, Wat—5T 4
Spur Clo. Romf—13Xc 29
Spurfield. E Mol—69Da 121
Spurgate. Brtwd—19Ce 33
Spurgeon Av. SE19—67Tb 127
Spurgeon Rd. SE19—67Tb 127
Spurgeon St. SE1 —48Tb 83 (3F 207)
Spurling Rd. SE22—56Vb 105
Spurling Rd. Dag—37Bd 67
Spurrell Av. Bex—63Fd 132
Spur Rd. N15—28Tb 43
Spur Rd. SW1—47Lb 82 (2B 204)
Spur Rd. Edgw—21Na 39
Spur Rd. Felt—56X 99
Spur Rd. Iswth—52Ka 100
Spur Rd. Orp—75Wc 151
Spurstowe Rd. E8—36Xb 63
Spurstowe Ter. E8—37Xb 63
Spur, The. Slou—3B 72
Squadrons App. Horn—37Ld 69
Square, The. Cars—78Jb 146
Square, The. Ilf—31Qc 66
Square, The. Rich—57Ma 101
Square, The. Wat—9X 5
Square, The. W Dray—53K 97
Square, The. West—92Lc 183
Square, The. Wey—78S 140
Square, The. Wok—88N 157
Square, The. Wfd G—22Jc 45
Squarey St. SW17—62Eb 125
Squire's Bri. Rd. Shep—70P 119
Squires La. N3—26Db 41
Squires Mt. NW3—34Fb 61
Squire's Rd. Shep—70P 119
Squires Way. Bex—63Fd 132
Squires Wood Dri. Chst—66Nc 130
Squirrel Clo. Houn—55Y 99
Squirrells Chase. Grays—7C 92
Squirrels Clo. N12—21Eb 41
Squirrels Clo. Uxb—38Q 56
Squirrels Grn. Lea—95Ca 175
Squirrels Grn. Wor Pk—75Va 144
Squirrels Heath Av. Romf —27Kd 49
Squirrels Heath La. Romf & Horn—28Ld 49
Squirrels Heath Rd. Romf —27Nd 49
Squirrel's La. Buck H—20Mc 27
Squirrels, The. Bush, Wat—16Fa 20
Squirrels, The. Pinn—27Ba 37
Squirrels Way. Eps—87Ta 161
Squirries St. E2—41Wb 83
Stable Clo. N'holt—40Ca 57
Stable M. SE27—64Sb 127
Stables End. Orp—76Sc 150
Stables, The. Buck H—17Lc 27
Stables Way. SE11 —50Qb 82 (7K 205)
Stable Wlk. N2—25Fb 41
Stable Way. W10—44Ya 80
Stable Yd. SW1—(1B 204)
Stable Yd. Rd. SW1 —47Lb 82 (1C 204)
Stacey Av. N18—21Yb 44
Stacey Clo. E10—29Fc 45
Stacey Clo. Grav—4G 136
Stacey St. WC2—44Mb 82 (3E 198)
Stackhouse St. SW3—(3F 203)
Stacklands Clo. Sev—79Ud 154
Stack La. Long, Dart—71Be 155
Stack La. S Dar, Dart—69Sd 134
Stack Rd. S Dar, Dart—70Td 134
Stacy Path. SE5—52Ub 105
Stadium Rd. NW4—31Ya 60
Stadium Rd. SE18—52Pc 108
Stadium Rd. Dart—57Gd 110
Stadium St. SW10—52Eb 103
Stadium Way. Wemb—35Qa 59
Staffa Rd. E10—32Ac 64
Stafford Av. Horn—27Md 49
Stafford Av. Ilf—26Qc 46
Stafford Av. Slou—2G 72
Stafford Clo. N14—15Lb 24
Stafford Clo. NW6—41Cb 81
Stafford Clo. Cat—95Vb 181
Stafford Clo. M'head—4A 72
Stafford Clo. Sutt—79Ab 144
Stafford Clo. Wal X—1Xb 11
Stafford Gdns. Croy—78Pb 146
Stafford M. Rich—59Pa 101
Stafford Pl. SW1—48Lb 82 (3B 204)
Stafford Rd. E3—40Bc 64
Stafford Rd. E7—37Mc 65
Stafford Rd. NW6—41Cb 81
Stafford Rd. Cat—94Vb 181
Stafford Rd. Harr—24Ea 38
Stafford Rd. N Mald—69Sa 123
Stafford Rd. Ruis—35V 56
Stafford Rd. Sidc—63Uc 130
Stafford Rd. Wall & Croy —79Lb 146
Staffordshire St. SE15—53Wb 105
Stafford Sq. Wey—77T 140
Stafford St. W1—46Lb 82 (6B 198)
Stafford Ter. W8—47Cb 81
Stafford Way. Sev—99Ld 187
Staff St. EC1—41Tb 83 (4G 195)
Stagbury Av. Coul—90Gb 163
Stagbury Clo. Coul—91Gb 179
Stagbury Ho. Coul—91Gb 179
Stag Clo. Edgw—26Ra 39
Stag Ct. Eps—83Va 162
Staggart Grn. Chig—23Vc 47
Stagg Hill. Barn—9Gb 9
Stag La. SW15—62Va 124
Stag La. Buck H—19Kc 27
Stag La. Edgw—26Ra 39
Stag La. Rick—16E 16
Stag Leys. Asht—92Na 177
Stag Pl. SW1—48Lb 82 (3B 204)
Stags Way. Iswth—51Ha 100
Stainash Cres. Stai—64K 119
Stainbank Rd. Mitc—69Kb 126
Stainby Clo. W Dray—48N 75
Stainby Rd. N15—28Vb 43
Stainer Rd. Borwd—11Ma 21
Stainer St. SE1—46Tb 83 (7G 201)
Staines Av. Sutt—75Za 144
Staines Bri. Stai—64G 118
Staines By-Pass. Stai & Ashf —62F 118
Staines Central Trading Est. Stai—63G 118
Staines La. Cher—72H 139
Staines La. Clo. Cher—72H 139
Staines Rd. Cher—72G 138
Staines Rd. Felt & Houn—60R 99
Staines Rd. Ilf—36Sc 66
Staines Rd. Stai—66J 119
Staines Rd. Twic—62Da 121
Staines Rd. Wray, Stai—59A 96
Staines Rd. E. Sun—66W 120
Staines Rd. W. Ashf & Sun —65R 120
Staines Wlk. Sidc—65Yc 131
Stainford Clo. Ashf—64T 120
Stainforth Rd. E17—28Cc 44
Stainforth Rd. Ilf—31Tc 66
Staining La. EC2—44Sb 83 (2E 200)
Stainmore Clo. Chst—67Tc 130
Stainsbury St. E2—40Yb 64
Stainsby Pl. E14—44Cc 84
Stainsby Rd. E14—44Cc 84
Stains Clo. Wal X—1Ac 12
Stainton Rd. SE6—58Fc 107
Stainton Rd. Enf—11Yb 26
Stainton Wlk. Wok—6F 188
Stairfoot La. Sev—94Ed 186
Staithes Way. Tad—92Ya 178
Stalbridge St. NW1 —43Gb 81 (7E 190)
★Staleys Rd. Sev—92Be
Stalham St. SE16—48Xb 83
Stalisfield Pl. Orp—82Qc 168
Stambourne Way. SE19 —66Ub 127
Stambourne Way. W Wick —75Ec 148
Stamford Brook Av. W6—48Va 80
Stamford Brook Rd. W6—48Va 80
Stamford Clo. N15—29Wb 43
Stamford Clo. Harr—24Ga 38
Stamford Clo. Pot B—4Fb 9
Stamford Clo. S'hall—45Ca 77
Stamford Dri. Brom—70Hc 129
Stamford Gdns. Dag—38Yc 67
Stamford Grn. Rd. Eps—85Ra 161
Stamford Gro. E. N16—32Wb 63
Stamford Gro. W. N16—32Wb 63
Stamford Hill. N16—33Vb 63
Stamford Hill Est. N16—32Vb 63
Stamford Rd. E6—39Nc 66
Stamford Rd. N1—38Ub 63
Stamford Rd. N15—29Wb 43
Stamford Rd. Dag—39Xc 67
Stamford Rd. W on T—76Z 141
Stamford Rd. Wat—12X 19
Stamford St. SE1 —46Qb 82 (7K 199)
Stamp Pl. E2—40Vb 63 (2K 195)
Stanborough Av. Borwd—9Qa 7
Stanborough Clo. Borwd—10Qa 7
Stanborough Clo. Hmptn —65Ba 121
Stanborough Rd. Houn—55Fa 100
Stanbridge Rd. SW15—55Ya 102
Stanbrook Rd. SE2—47Xc 87
Stanbrook Rd. Grav—9B 114
Stanbury Av. Wat—9U 4
Stanbury Rd. SE15—54Xb 105
Stancroft. NW9—29Ua 40
Standale Gro. Ruis—29S 36
Standard Clo. N16—31Ub 63
Standard Industrial Est. E16 —47Pc 86
Standard Pl. EC2—(4J 195)
Standard Rd. NW10—42Sa 79
Standard Rd. Belv—50Cd 88
Standard Rd. Bexh—56Ad 109
Standard Rd. Enf—9Ac 12
Standard Rd. Houn—55Aa 99
Standard Rd. Orp—82Qc 168
Standen Av. Horn—34Nd 69
Standen Rd. SW18—59Bb 103
Standfield. Abb L, Wat—3U 4
Standfield Gdns. Dag—37Cd 68
Standfield Rd. Dag—36Cd 68
Standish Rd. W6—49Wa 80
Stane Clo. SW19—66Db 125
Stane Pas. SW16—64Nb 126
Stane Way. SE18—52Mc 107
Stane Way. Eps—82Wa 162
Stanfield Rd. E3—40Ac 64
Stanford Clo. Hmptn—65Ba 121
Stanford Clo. Romf—30Dd 48
Stanford Clo. Wfd G—22Nc 46
Stanford Ct. SW6—53Db 103
Stanford Ct. Wal A—5Jc 13
Stanford Gdns. S Ock—46Ud 90
Stanford-le-Hope By-Pass. Stanf —1L 93
Stanford Pl. SE17 —49Ub 83 (6H 207)
Stanford Rd. N11—22Hb 41
Stanford Rd. SW16—68Mb 126
Stanford Rd. W8—48Db 81
Stanford Rd. Grays & Stanf—7A 92
Stanford St. SW1 —49Mb 82 (6D 204)
Stanford Way. SW16—68Mb 126
Stangate Cres. Borwd—15Ta 21
Stangate Gdns. Stan—21Ka 38
Stanger Rd. SE25—70Wb 127
Stanham Pl. Dart—56Jd 110
Stanham Rd. Dart—57Ld 111
Stanhope. Stanf—2N 93
Stanhope Av. N3—27Bb 41
Stanhope Av. Brom—74Jc 149
Stanhope Av. Harr—25Fa 38
Stanhope Gdns. N4—30Rb 43
Stanhope Gdns. N6—30Lb 42
Stanhope Gdns. NW7—22Va 40
Stanhope Gdns. SW7 —49Eb 81 (5A 202)
Stanhope Gdns. Dag—34Bd 67
Stanhope Gdns. Ilf—32Pc 66
Stanhope Ga. W1 —46Jb 82 (7J 197)
Stanhope Gro. Beck—71Bc 148
Stanhope Heath. Stai—58L 97
Stanhope M. E. SW7 —49Eb 81 (5A 202)
Stanhope M. S. SW7 —49Eb 81 (6A 202)
Stanhope M. W. SW7 —49Eb 81 (5A 202)
Stanhope Pde. NW1—(3B 192)
Stanhope Pk. Rd. Gnfd—42Ea 78
Stanhope Pl. W2—45Hb 81 (3F 197)
Stanhope Rd. E17—29Dc 44
Stanhope Rd. N6—30Lb 42
Stanhope Rd. N12—22Eb 41
Stanhope Rd. Barn—16Za 22
Stanhope Rd. Bexh—54Ad 109
Stanhope Rd. Cars—80Jb 146
Stanhope Rd. Croy—76Ub 147
Stanhope Rd. Dag—33Bd 67
Stanhope Rd. Gnfd—43Ea 78
Stanhope Rd. Rain—40Jd 68
Stanhope Rd. Sidc—63Wc 131
Stanhope Rd. Slou—4B 72
Stanhope Rd. Swans—58Be 113
Stanhope Row. W1 —46Kb 82 (7K 197)
Stanhopes. Oxt—100Kc 183
Stanhope St. NW1 —41Lb 82 (3B 192) (in two parts)
Stanhope Ter. W2 —45Fb 81 (4C 196)
Stanhope Way. Sev—93Fd 186
Stanhope Way. Stai—58L 97
Stanier Clo. W14—50Bb 81
Stanlake M. W12—46Ya 80
Stanlake Rd. W12—46Ya 80
Stanlake Vs. W12—46Ya 80
Stanley Av. Bark—40Vc 67
Stanley Av. Beck—69Ec 128
Stanley Av. Dag—32Bd 67
Stanley Av. Gnfd—39Ea 58
Stanley Av. N Mald—71Wa 144
Stanley Av. Romf—28Jd 48
Stanley Av. Wemb—38Na 59
Stanley Clo. SW8—51Pb 104
Stanley Clo. Coul—89Pb 164
Stanley Clo. Horn—33Ld 69
Stanley Clo. Romf—28Jd 48
Stanley Clo. Uxb—39M 55
Stanley Clo. Wemb—38Na 59
Stanley Cotts. Slou—6K 73
Stanley Cres. W11—45Bb 81
Stanley Cres. Grav—4F 136
Stanleycroft Clo. Iswth—53Ga 100
Stanley Gdns. NW2—36Ya 60
Stanley Gdns. W3—47Ua 80
Stanley Gdns. W11—45Bb 81
Stanley Gdns. Borwd—11Na 21
Stanley Gdns. Mitc—65Jb 126
Stanley Gdns. S Croy—84Wb 165
Stanley Gdns. Wall—79Lb 146
Stanley Gdns. Rd. Tedd—64Ga 122
Stanley Grn. Slou—49B 74
Stanley Gro. N17—24Vb 43
Stanley Gro. SW8—54Jb 104
Stanley Gro. Croy—72Qb 146
Stanley Pk. Dri. Wemb—39Pa 59
Stanley Pk. Rd. Cars—80Hb 145
Stanley Pk. Rd. Wall—79Kb 146
Stanley Pas. NW1 —40Nb 62 (2F 193)
Stanley Rd. E4—18Fc 27
Stanley Rd. E10—30Dc 44
Stanley Rd. E12—36Nc 66
Stanley Rd. E15—39Fc 65
Stanley Rd. E18—25Hc 45
Stanley Rd. N2—27Fb 41
Stanley Rd. N9—19Vb 25
Stanley Rd. N10—24Kb 42
Stanley Rd. N11—23Mb 42
Stanley Rd. N15—28Rb 43
Stanley Rd. NW9—31Wa 60
Stanley Rd. SW14—56Ra 101
Stanley Rd. SW19—65Cb 125
Stanley Rd. W3—48Sa 79
Stanley Rd. Ashf—64N 119
Stanley Rd. Brom—70Lc 129
Stanley Rd. Cars—80Jb 146
Stanley Rd. Croy—73Qb 146
Stanley Rd. Enf—13Ub 25
Stanley Rd. Grays—50De 91
Stanley Rd. Harr—33Ea 58
Stanley Rd. Horn—33Ld 69
Stanley Rd. Houn—56Ea 100
Stanley Rd. Ilf—33Tc 66
Stanley Rd. Mitc—66Jb 126
Stanley Rd. Mord—70Cb 125
Stanley Rd. N'wd—25W 36
Stanley Rd. Orp—74Wc 151
Stanley Rd. Sidc—62Wc 131
Stanley Rd. S'hall—45Aa 77
Stanley Rd. Sutt—79Db 145
Stanley Rd. Swans—58Be 113
Stanley Rd. Twic & Tedd —62Fa 122
Stanley Rd. Wat—14Y 19
Stanley Rd. Wemb—37Pa 59
Stanley Rd. Wok—89B 156
Stanley Rd. N. Rain—39Gd 68
Stanley Rd. S. Rain—40Hd 68
Stanley Sq. Cars—81Hb 163
Stanley St. SE8—52Bc 106
Stanley St. Cat—94Sb 181
Stanley Ter. N19—33Nb 62
Stanley Way. Orp—71Xc 151
Stanmer St. SW11—54Gb 103
Stanmore. Grays—9L 93
Stanmore Gdns. Rich—55Pa 101
Stanmore Gdns. Sutt—76Eb 145
Stanmore Hill. Stan—20Ja 20
Stanmore Pl. NW1—39Kb 62
Stanmore Rd. E11—32Hc 65
Stanmore Rd. N15—28Rb 43
Stanmore Rd. Belv—49Ed 88
Stanmore Rd. Rich—55Pa 101
Stanmore Rd. Wat—11X 19
Stanmore St. N1—39Pb 62
Stanmore Ter. Beck—68Cc 128
Stanmore Way. Lou—11Qc 28
Stannard Cres. E6—44Qc 86
Stannard Rd. E8—37Wb 63
Stannary St. SE11—51Qb 104
Stannington Path. Borwd —11Qa 21
Stansfeld Rd. E16 & E6—43Mc 85
Stansfield Rd. SW9—55Pb 104
Stansfield Rd. Houn—54X 99
Stansgate Rd. Dag—34Cd 68
Stanstead Clo. Brom—72Hc 149
Stanstead Cres. Bex—60Zc 109
Stanstead Gro. SE6—60Bc 106
Stanstead Mnr. Sutt—79Cb 145
Stanstead Rd. E11—29Kc 45
Stanstead Rd.—60Zb 106
SE23 1-319 & 2-302
SE6 remainder
Stanstead Rd. Cat—96Ub 181
Stanstead Rd. Cat—99Tb 181
Stanstead Rd. Houn—58P 97
Stansted Clo. Horn—37Kd 69
★Stansted Hill. Sev—82Be
★Stansted La. Sev—82Xd
Stanswood Gdns. SE5—52Ub 105
Stanthorpe Clo. SW16—64Nb 126
Stanthorpe Rd. SW16—64Nb 126
Stanton Av. Tedd—65Ga 122
Stanton Clo. Eps—78Ra 143
Stanton Clo. Wor Pk—74Za 144
Stanton Rd. SE26—63Bc 128
Stanton Rd. SW13—54Va 102
Stanton Rd. SW20—67Za 124
Stanton Rd. Croy—73Sb 147
Stanton St. SE15—53Wb 105
Stanton Way. SE26—63Bc 128
Stanton Way. Slou—49A 74
Stanway Clo. Chig—22Uc 46
Stanway Ct. N1—40Ub 63 (2J 195)
Stanway Gdns. W3—46Qa 79
Stanway Gdns. Edgw—22Sa 39
Stanway Rd. Wal A—5Jc 13
Stanway St. N1—40Ub 63 (1J 195)
Stanwell Clo. Stai—58M 97
Stanwell Gdns. Stai—58M 97
Stanwell Moor Rd. Stai & W Dray —62J 119 to 52K 97
Stanwell New Rd. Stai—62K 119
Stanwell Rd. Ashf—62N 119
Stanwell Rd. Felt—59R 98
Stanwell Rd. Slou—55C 96
Stanwick Rd. W14—49Bb 81
Stanworth St. SE1 —48Vb 83 (2K 207)
Stanwyck Dri. Chig—22Sc 46
Stanwyck Gdns. Romf—22Kd 49
Stapenhill Rd. Wemb—34Ka 58
Staple Clo. Bex—62Fd 132
Staplefield Clo. SW2—60Nb 104
Staplefield Clo. Pinn—24Aa 37
Stapleford Av. Ilf—29Uc 46
Stapleford Clo. E4—20Ec 26
Stapleford Clo. SW19—59Ab 102
Stapleford Clo. King—68Qa 123
Stapleford Ct. Sev—96Hd 186
Stapleford Gdns. Romf—23Cd 48
Stapleford Rd. Romf & Stap T, Romf—15Dd 30
Stapleford Rd. Wemb—38Ma 59
Stapleford Way. Bark—41Xc 87
Staplehurst Rd. SE13—57Gc 107
Staplehurst Rd. Cars—80Gb 145
Staple Inn. WC1—(1K 199)
Staple Inn Bldgs. WC1 —43Qb 82 (1K 199)
Staples Clo. SE16—46Ac 84
Staples Corner. NW2—32Xa 60
Staples Rd. Lou—13Mc 27
Staple St. SE1—47Tb 83 (2G 207)
Stapleton Clo. Pot B—3Gb 9
Stapleton Cres. Rain—37Jd 68
Stapleton Gdns. Croy—78Qb 146
Stapleton Hall Rd. N4—31Pb 62
Stapleton Rd. SW17—62Jb 126
Stapleton Rd. Bexh—52Bd 109
Stapleton Rd. Borwd—10Qa 7
Stapleton Rd. Orp—76Vc 151
Stapley Rd. Belv—50Cd 88
Stapylton Rd. Barn—13Ab 22
Star All. EC3—(4J 201)
Star & Garter Hill. Rich—60Na 101
Starboard Av. Grnh—58Xd 112
Starboard Way. E14—48Cc 84
Starch Ho. La. Ilf—26Tc 46
Starcross St. NW1 —41Lb 82 (4C 192)
Starfield Rd. W12—47Wa 80
Star Hill. Dart—57Gd 110
Star Hill. Wok—7F 188
Star Hill Rd. Sev—88Bd 169
Starkleigh Way. SE16—50Xb 83
Star La. E16—42Gc 85
Star La. Coul—93Jb 180
Star La. Epp—2Wc 15
Star La. Orp—70Yc 131
Starling Clo. Buck H—18Jc 27
Starling Clo. Long, Dart—69De 135
Starling Clo. Pinn—27Y 37
Starling M. SE28—47Tc 86
Star Rd. W14—51Bb 103
Star Rd. Iswth—54Fa 100
Star Rd. Uxb—42S 76
Starrock La. Coul—92Hb 179
Starrock Rd. Coul—91Kb 180
Star St. E16—43Hc 85
Star St. W2—44Gb 81 (2C 196)
Starts Clo. Orp—76Qc 150

Starts Hill Av.—Stratford Clo.

Starts Hill Av. Orp—77Rc 150
Starts Hill Rd. Orp—76Qc 150
Starwood Clo. Wey—83L 157
Starwood Ct. Slou—8N 73
Star Yd. WC2—44Qb 82 (2K 199)
State Farm Av. Orp—77Rc 150
Staten Gdns. Twic—60Ha 100
Statham Gro. N16—35Tb 63
Statham Gro. N18—22Ub 43
Station App. E7—35Kc 65
Station App. E11—29Jc 45
Station App. EC4—(4F 201)
Station App. N11—22Kb 42
Station App. NW10—41Va 80
Station App. SE26—63Yb 128
Station App. SW6—55Ab 102
Station App. SW16—64Mb 126
Station App. W7—46Ga 78
Station App. Ashf—63P 119
Station App. Bex—60Cd 110
Station App. Bexh—54Ed 110
(Barnehurst)
Station App. Bexh—54Ad 109
(Bexleyheath)
Station App. Brom—74Jc 149
Station App. Buck H—21Mc 45
Station App. Chst—67Qc 130
Station App. Chst—65Nc 130
(Elmstead Woods)
Station App. Coul—88Mb 164
Station App. Coul—90Hb 163
(Chipstead)
Station App. Dart—58Nd 111
Station App. Dart—58Hd 110
(Crayford)
Station App. Epp—8Vc 15
Station App. Eps—85Ta 161
Station App. Eps—82Xa 162
(Ewell East)
Station App. Eps—81Va 162
(Ewell West)
Station App. Eps—78Wa 144
(Stoneleigh)
Station App. Esh—76Ha 142
Station App. Ger X—29A 34
Station App. Grays—51Ce 113
Station App. Hmptn—67Ca 121
Station App. Harr—31Ga 58
Station App. Hay—48V 76
Station App. King—68Qa 123
Station App. Lea—93Ja 176
Station App. Lea—98U 174
(Horsley)
Station App. Lou—15Nc 28
Station App. Lou—14Sc 28
(Debden)
Station App. N'wd—24U 36
Station App. Orp—75Vc 151
Station App. Orp—78Xc 151
(Chelsfield)
Station App. Orp—70Xc 131
(St Mary Cray)
Station App. Oxt—100Gc 183
Station App. Pinn—27Aa 37
Station App. Rad—7Ja 6
Station App. Rich—53Qa 101
Station App. Rick—14F 16
Station App. Ruis—32U 56
Station App. Ruis—36X 57
(South Ruislip)
Station App. Shep—71S 140
Station App. S Croy—81Tb 165
Station App. Stai—63J 119
Station App. Sun—67W 120
Station App. Sutt—80Ab 144
Station App. Swan—70Gd 132
Station App. Uxb—31F 54
Station App. Vir W—10P 117
Station App. Wal X—6Ac 12
Station App. Wat—14V 18
Station App. Wat—20Z 19
(Carpenders Park)
Station App. Well—54Wc 109
Station App. Wemb—37Ka 58
Station App. Wey—79Q 140
Station App. Wey—85J 157
(West Byfleet)
Station App. Whyt—90Wb 165
Station App. Wind—3H 95
Station App. Wok—89B 156
Station App. N. Sidc—61Wc 131
Station App. Rd. W4—52Sa 101
Station App. Rd. Tad—94Ya 178
Station App. Rd. Til—6C 114
Station Av. SW9—55Rb 105
Station Av. Cat—96Wb 181
Station Av. Eps—81Ua 162
Station Av. N Mald—69Ua 124
Station Av. Rich—53Qa 101
Station Av. W on T—77W 140
Station Clo. N3—25Cb 41
Station Clo. Hmptn—67Da 121
Station Clo. Pot B—4Cb 9
Station Clo. Pot B—3Bb 9
Station Cres. N15—28Tb 43
Station Cres. SE3—50Jc 85
Station Cres. Ashf—62M 119
Station Cres. Wemb—37Ka 58
Stationer's Hall Ct. EC4
—44Rb 83 (3C 200)
Station Est. Beck—70Zb 128
Station Est. Rd. Felt—60X 99
Station Garage M. SW16
—65Mb 126
Station Gdns. W4—52Sa 101
Station Gro. Wemb—37Na 59
Station Hill. Brom—75Jc 149
Station La. Horn—34Md 69
Station Pde. E11—29Jc 45
Station Pde. NW2—37Ya 60
Station Pde. Bark—38Sc 66
Station Pde. Felt—60X 99
Station Pde. Horn—35Kd 69
Station Pde. Lea—98U 174
(in two parts)
Station Pde. Rich—53Qa 101
Station Pde. Uxb—31J 55
Station Pde. Vir W—71A 138
Station Pde. Vir W—10P 117
Station Path. Stai—63H 119
Station Pl. N4—33Qb 62
Station Rise. SE27—61Rb 127
Station Rd. E4—18Fc 27
Station Rd. E7—35Jc 65
Station Rd. E10—34Ec 64
Station Rd. E12—35Nc 66
Station Rd. E17—30Ac 44
Station Rd. N3—25Cb 41
Station Rd. N11—22Kb 42
Station Rd. N17—27Wb 43
Station Rd. N18—22Vb 43
Station Rd. N19—34Lb 62
Station Rd. N21—18Rb 25
Station Rd. N22—24Nb 42
(Bowes Park)
Station Rd. N22—26Pb 42
(Wood Green)
Station Rd. NW4—30Wa 40
Station Rd. NW7—23Ua 40
Station Rd. NW10—40Va 60
Station Rd. SE20—65Yb 128
Station Rd. SE25—70Vb 127
Station Rd. SW13—54Va 102
Station Rd. SW19—67Eb 125
Station Rd. W5—44Pa 79
Station Rd. W7—46Ga 78
Station Rd. Asc—10E 116
Station Rd. Ashf—63P 119
Station Rd. Barn—15Db 23
Station Rd. Belv—48Cd 88
Station Rd. Bexh—55Ad 109
Station Rd. Borwd—14Qa 21
Station Rd. Brtwd—30Ee 51
Station Rd. Brom—67Jc 129
Station Rd. Brom—68Gc 129
(Shortlands)
Station Rd. Cars—77Hb 145
Station Rd. Cat—94Ac 182
Station Rd. Cher—74H 139
Station Rd. Chess—78Na 143
Station Rd. Chig—20Rc 28
Station Rd. Chob—1D 188
Station Rd. Cob—88Aa 159
Station Rd. Croy—75Tb 147
(East Croydon)
Station Rd. Croy—74Sb 147
(West Croydon)
Station Rd. Dart—59Hd 110
Station Rd. Edgw—23Qa 39
Station Rd. Egh—64C 118
Station Rd. Epp—3Wc 15
Station Rd. Eri—50Gd 88
Station Rd. Esh—78Ga 142
(Claygate)
Station Rd. Esh—75Fa 142
(Esher)
Station Rd. Esh—73Ha 142
(Thames Ditton)
Station Rd. Eyns. Dart—76Md 153
Station Rd. Ger X—29A 34
Station Rd. Grav—63Be 135
(Betsham)
Station Rd. Grav—10C 136
(Meopham)
Station Rd. Grav—58De 113
(Northfleet)
Station Rd. Grays—1H 115
Station Rd. Grnh—57Wd 112
Station Rd. Hmptn—67Ca 121
Station Rd. Harr—28Ha 38
Station Rd. Harr—29Da 37
(North Harrow)
Station Rd. Hay—49U 76
Station Rd. Houn—56Da 99
Station Rd. Ilf—34Rc 66
Station Rd. Ilf—27Tc 46
(Barkingside)
Station Rd. Kenl—86Sb 165
Station Rd. K Lan—1R 4
Station Rd. King—67Ma 123
(Hampton Wick)
Station Rd. King—67Qa 123
(Norbiton)
Station Rd. Lea—93Ja 176
Station Rd. Long, Dart—69Ae 135
Station Rd. Lou—15Nc 28
Station Rd. N Mald—71Xa 144
Station Rd. Orp—75Vc 151
Station Rd. Orp—70Yc 131
(St Mary Cray)
Station Rd. Pot B—1Pb 10
Station Rd. Rad—7Ja 6
Station Rd. Red—100Lb 180
Station Rd. Rick—17M 17
Station Rd. Romf—31Zc 67
(Chadwell Heath)
Station Rd. Romf—28Kd 49
(Gidea Park)
Station Rd. Romf—25Pd 49
(Harold Wood)
Station Rd. St Alb—3Ca 5
★Station Rd. Sev—92Be
(Borough Green)
Station Rd. Sev—92Gd 186
(Dunton Green)
Station Rd. Sev—83Bd 169
(Halstead)
Station Rd. Sev—88Kd 171
(Otford)
Station Rd. Sev—83Jd 170
(Shoreham)
Station Rd. Shep—71S 140
Station Rd. Sidc—61Wc 131
Station Rd. Slou—4C 72
(Burnham)
Station Rd. Slou—48C 74
(Langley)
Station Rd. Sun—66W 120
Station Rd. Sutt—82Cb 163
Station Rd. S at H & S Dar,
Dart—68Rd 133
Station Rd. Swan—70Gd 132
Station Rd. Tedd—64Ha 122
Station Rd. Th Dit—73Ha 142
Station Rd. Twic—60Ha 100
Station Rd. Upm—33Sd 70
Station Rd. Uxb—42M 75
Station Rd. Wal A—6Cc 12
Station Rd. Wat—12X 19
Station Rd. W Dray—47N 75
Station Rd. West—95Xc 185
Station Rd. W Wick—74Ec 148
Station Rd. Wey—77L 139
(Addlestone)
Station Rd. Wey—84J 157
(West Byfleet)
Station Rd. Whyt—90Vb 165
Station Rd. Wray. Stai—58B 96
Station Rd. E. Oxt—100Gc 183
Station Rd. N. Belv—48Dd 88
Station Rd. N. Red—100Lb 180
Station Rd. S. Red—100Lb 180
Station Rd. W. Oxt—100Gc 183
Station Sq. SE26—63Bc 128
Station Sq. Orp—71Sc 150
(Petts Wood)
Station Sq. Orp—70Xc 131
(St Mary Cray)
Station St. E15—38Fc 65
Station St. E16—46Rc 86
Station Ter. NW10—40Za 60
Station Ter. SE5—53Sb 105
Station View. Gnfd—39Fa 58
Station Way. Buck H—21Lc 45
Station Way. Eps—85Ta 161
Station Way. Esh—79Ga 142
Station Way. Sutt—80Ab 144
Station Yd. Twic—59Ja 100
Staunton Rd. King—65Na 123
Staunton Rd. Slou—3H 73
Staunton St. SE8—51Bc 106
Staveley Clo. E9—36Yb 64
Staveley Clo. N7—35Nb 62
Staveley Clo. SE15—53Yb 106
Staveley Gdns. W4—53Ta 101
Staveley Rd. W4—51Sa 101
Staveley Rd. Ashf—65T 120
Staveley Way. Wok—5B 188
Staverton Rd. NW2—38Ya 60
Staverton Rd. Horn—30Md 49
Stave Yd. Rd. SE16—46Ac 84
Stavordale Rd. N5—35Rb 63
Stavordale Rd. Cars—73Eb 145
Stayne End. Vir W—10L 117
Stayners Rd. E1—42Zb 84
Stayton Rd. Sutt—76Cb 145
Stead St. SE17—49Tb 83 (6F 207)
Steam Farm La. Felt—56V 98
Stean St. E8—39Vb 63
Stebbing Way. Bark—40Wc 67
Stebondale St. E14—49Ec 84
Stedham Pl. WC1—(2F 199)
Stedman Clo. Bex—62Gd 132
Stedman Clo. Uxb—34Q 56
Steedman St. SE17
—49Sb 83 (6D 206)
Steeds Rd. N10—25Hb 41
Steeds Way. Lou—13Nc 28
Steele Rd. E11—35Gc 65
Steele Rd. N17—27Ub 43
Steele Rd. NW10—40Sa 59
Steele Rd. W4—48Sa 79
Steele Rd. Isleworth—56Ja 100
Steele's M. NW3—37Hb 61
Steele's Rd. NW3—37Hb 61
Steel's La. E1—44Yb 84
Steel's La. Lea—86Da 159
Steen Way. SE22—57Ub 105
Steep Clo. Orp—79Vc 151
Steep Hill. SW16—62Mb 126
Steep Hill. Croy—77Ub 147
Steeplands. Bush, Wat—17Da 19
Steeple Clo. SW6—54Ab 102
Steeple Clo. SW19—64Ab 124
Steeplestone Clo. N18—22Sb 43
★Steeple Way. Brtwd—9Xd
Steerforth St. SW18—61Eb 125
Steers Mead. Mitc—67Hb 125
Stella Rd. SW17—65Hb 125
Stelling Rd. Eri—52Fd 110
Stellman Clo. E5—34Wb 63
Stembridge Rd. SE20—68Xb 127
Stenning Av. Stanf—9J 93
Stents La. Cob—92Ba 175
Stepbridge Path. Wok—5G 188
Stepgates. Cher—73K 139
Stephan Clo. E8—39Wb 63
Stephen Av. Rain—37Jd 68
Stephen Clo. Egh—65E 118
Stephen Clo. Orp—76Vc 151
Stephendale Rd. SW6—54Db 103
Stephen M. W1—43Mb 82 (1D 198)
Stephen Rd. Bexh—55Ed 110
Stephens Clo. Romf—22Ld 49
Stephenson Av. Til—3C 114
Stephenson Ct. Slou—7K 73
Stephenson Rd. W7—44Ha 78
Stephenson Rd. Twic—59Ca 99
Stephenson St. E16—42Gc 85
Stephenson St. NW10—41Ua 80
Stephenson Way. NW1
—42Lb 82 (5C 192)
Stephen's Rd. E15—39Gc 65
Stephen St. W1—43Mb 82 (1D 198)
Stepney Causeway. E1—44Zb 84
Stepney Grn. E1—43Zb 84
Stepney High St. E1—43Zb 84
Stepney Way. E1—43Xb 83
Sterling Av. Edgw—21Pa 39
Sterling Av. Wal X—6Zb 12
Sterling Rd. Enf—11Tb 25
Sterling St. SW7—48Gb 81 (3E 202)
Sterling Way. N18—22Tb 43
Sterndale Rd. W14—48Za 80
Sterndale Rd. Dart—59Pd 111
Sterne St. W12—47Za 80
Sternhall La. SE15—55Wb 105
Sternhold Av. SW2—61Mb 126
Sterry Cres. Dag—36Cd 68
Sterry Dri. Eps—77Ua 144
Sterry Dri. Th Dit—72Ga 142
Sterry Gdns. Dag—37Cd 68
Sterry Rd. Bark—39Vc 67
Sterry Rd. Dag—35Cd 68
Sterry St. SE1—47Tb 83 (2F 207)
Steugers La. SE23—60Ac 106
Steve Biko La. SE6—63Cc 128
Stevedale Rd. Well—54Yc 109
Stevenage Cres. Borwd—11Na 21
Stevenage Rd. E6—37Qc 66
Stevenage Rd. SW6—53Za 102
Stevens Av. E9—37Yb 64
Stevens Clo. Beck—65Cc 128
Stevens Clo. Bex—63Fd 132
Stevens Clo. Eps—85Ua 162
Stevens Clo. Hmptn—64Aa 121
Stevens Clo. Pinn—29Y 37
Stevens Grn. Bush, Wat—18Ea 20
Stevens La. Esh—80Ja 142
Stevenson Clo. Eri—52Kd 111
Stevenson Dri. Wind—2F 94
Stevenson Rd. Slou—3H 53
Stevens Rd. Dag—34Xc 67
Stevens St. SE1—48Ub 83 (3J 207)
Stevens Way. Chig—21Uc 46
Steventon Rd. W12—45Va 80
Steward Clo. Wal X—2Ac 12
Stewards Clo. Epp—5Wc 15
Stewards Grn. La. Epp—4Xc 15
Stewards Grn. Rd. Epp—5Wc 15
Stewards Holte Wlk. N11
—21Kb 42
Steward St. E1—43Ub 83 (7J 195)
Stewards Wlk. Romf—29Gd 48
Stewart Av. Shep—70Q 120
Stewart Av. Slou—3K 73
Stewart Av. Upm—34Rd 69
Stewart Clo. NW9—30Sa 39
Stewart Clo. Hmptn—65Aa 121
Stewart Rd. E15—35Fc 65
Stewartsby Clo. N18—22Sb 43
Stewart's Dri. Slou—5F 52
Stewart's Gro. SW3
—50Fb 81 (7D 202)
Stewart's Rd. SW8—52Lb 104
Stewart St. E14—47Ec 84
Steyne Rd. W3—46Ra 79
Steyning Clo. Kenl—88Rb 165
Steyning Gro. SE9—63Pc 130
Steynings Way. N12—22Cb 41
Steyning Way. Houn—56Y 99
Steynton Av. Bex—61Zc 131
Stickland Rd. Belv—49Cd 88
Stickleton Clo. Gnfd—41Da 77
Stifford Clays Rd. Grays—46Be 91
(in three parts)
Stifford Hill. S Ock & Grays
—45Yd 90
Stifford Rd. S Ock—46Ud 90
Stilecroft Gdns. Wemb—34Ka 58
Stile Hall Gdns. W4—50Qa 79
Stile Path. Sun—70W 120
Stile Rd. Slou—8P 73
Stiles Clo. Brom—72Pc 150
Stillingfleet Rd. SW13—51Wa 102
Stillington St. SW1
—49Lb 82 (5C 204)
Stillness Rd. SE23—58Ac 106
Stilton Cres. NW10—38Ta 59
Stilton Path. Borwd—10Qa 7
Stipularis Dri. Hay—42Z 77
Stirling Clo. Bans—89Bb 163
Stirling Clo. Rain—41Kd 89
Stirling Clo. Uxb—41L 75
Stirling Clo. Wind—4B 94
Stirling Corner. Borwd & Barn
—16Ta 21
Stirling Dri. Orp—78Xc 151
Stirling Rd. E13—40Kc 65
Stirling Rd. E17—27Ac 44
Stirling Rd. N17—25Wb 43
Stirling Rd. N22—25Rb 43
Stirling Rd. SW9—54Nb 104
Stirling Rd. W3—48Ra 79
Stirling Rd. Harr—27Ha 38
Stirling Rd. Hay—45X 77
Stirling Rd. Houn—58P 97
Stirling Rd. Slou—3E 72
Stirling Rd. Twic—59Ca 99
Stirling Rd. Path. E17—27Ac 44
Stirling Wlk. Surb—72Ra 143
Stirling Way. Borwd—16Ta 21
Stirling Way. Croy—73Nb 146
Stites Hill Rd. Cat—92Rb 181
Stiven Cres. Harr—34Ba 57
Stoats Nest Rd. Coul—86Nb 164
Stoats Nest Village. Coul
—87Nb 164
Stockbury Rd. Croy—72Yb 148
Stockdale Rd. Dag—33Bd 67
Stockdales Rd. Wind—9D 72
Stockdove Way. Gnfd—41Ha 78
Stockers Farm Rd. Rick—20M 17
Stockers La. Wok—92B 172
Stockfield Rd. SW16—62Pb 126
Stockfield Rd. Esh—78Ga 142
Stock Hill. West—88Mc 167
Stockholm Rd. SE16—50Yb 84
Stockhurst Clo. SW15—54Za 102
Stockingswater La. Enf—13Bc 26
Stockland Rd. Romf—30Fd 48
Stock La. Dart—62Ld 133
Stockley Clo. W Dray—47R 76
Stockley Farm Rd. W Dray
—48R 76
Stockley Rd. Uxb & W Dray
—44Q 76
Stock Orchard Cres. N7—36Pb 62
Stock Orchard St. N7—36Pb 62
Stockport Rd. SW16—67Mb 126
Stockport Rd. Rick—17E 16
★Stocksfield. Brtwd—9Vd
Stocksfield Rd. E17—27Ec 44
★Stocks La. Brtwd—9Vd
Stocks Pl. E14—45Bc 84
Stock St. E13—40Jc 65
Stockton Gdns. N17—24Sb 43
Stockton Gdns. NW7—20Ua 22
Stockton Rd. N17—24Sb 43
Stockton Rd. N18—23Wb 43
Stockwell Av. SW9—55Pb 104
Stockwell Gdns. SW9—53Pb 104
Stockwell Grn. SW9—54Pb 104
Stockwell La. SW9—54Pb 104
Stockwell La. Wal X—1Wb 11
Stockwell Pk. Cres. SW9
—54Pb 104
Stockwell Pk. Rd. SW9—53Pb 104
Stockwell Pk. Wlk. SW9
—55Qb 104
Stockwell Rd. SW9—54Pb 104
Stockwell St. SE10—51Ec 106
Stockwell Ter. SW9—53Pb 104
Stodart Rd. SE20—67Yb 128
Stofield Gdns. SE9—62Mc 129
Stoford Clo. SW19—60Ab 102
Stoke Av. Ilf—23Wc 47
Stoke Clo. Cob—88Ba 159
Stoke Comn. Rd. Slou—5L 53
Stoke Ct. Dri. Slou—5J 53
Stoke Gdns. Slou—6J 73
Stoke Grn. Slou—2L 73
Stokenchurch St. SW6—53Db 103
Stoke Newington Chu. St. N16
—34Tb 63
Stoke Newington Comn. N16
—33Vb 63
Stoke Newington High St. N16
—34Vb 63
Stoke Newington Rd. N16
—36Vb 63
Stoke Pk. Av. Slou—1G 72
Stoke Pl. NW10—41Va 80
Stoke Poges La. Slou—6J 73
Stoke Rd. Cob—87Y 159
Stoke Rd. King—66Sa 123
Stoke Rd. Rain—40Md 69
Stoke Rd. Slou—6K 73
Stoke Rd. W on T—76Y 141
Stokesay. Slou—5K 73
Stokesby Rd. Chess—79Pa 143
Stokes Cotts. Ilf—25Sc 46
Stokesheath Rd. Lea—83Ea 160
Stokesley St. W12—44Va 80
Stokes Rd. E6—42Nc 86
Stokes Rd. Croy—72Zb 148
Stoke Wood. Slou—5K 53
Stompond La. W on T—75W 140
Stomp Rd. Slou—3A 72
Stoms Path. SE6—64Cc 128
Stonard Rd. N13—20Qb 24
Stonard Rd. Dag—35Xc 67
Stonards Hill. Epp—2Xc 15
Stonards Hill. Lou—16Pc 28
Stondon Pk. SE23—58Ac 106
Stondon Wlk. E6—40Mc 65
Stonebridge Pk. NW10—38Ta 59
Stonebridge Rd. N15—29Vb 43
Stonebridge Rd. Grav—57Ce 113
Stonebridge Way. Wemb
—37Ra 59
Stone Bldgs. WC2—(1J 199)
Stone Clo. Dag—33Bd 67
Stone Clo. W Dray—46P 75
Stonecot Clo. Sutt—74Ab 144
Stonecot Hill. Sutt—74Ab 144
Stonecroft Av. Iver—44G 74
Stonecroft Rd. Eri—52Ed 110
Stonecroft Way. Croy—73Nb 146
Stonecutter St. EC4
—44Rb 83 (2B 200)
Stonefield Clo. Bexh—55Cd 110
Stonefield Clo. Ruis—36Aa 57
Stonefield St. N1—39Qb 62
Stonefield Way. SE7—52Mc 107
Stonefield Way. Ruis—35Aa 57
Stonegate Clo. Orp—69Yc 131
Stonegrove. Edgw—21Na 39
Stonegrove Gdns. Edgw—22Pa 39
Stonehall Av. Ilf—30Nc 46
Stone Hall Rd. N21—17Pb 24
Stoneham Rd. N11—22Lb 42
Stonehill Clo. SW14—57Ta 101
Stonehill Clo. Lea—97Ca 175
Stonehill Cres. Cher—79A 138
Stonehill Rd. SW14—57Ta 101
Stonehill Rd. W4—50Qa 79
Stonehill Rd. Chob & Cher
—79A 138
Stonehills Ct. SE21—62Ub 127
Stonehorse Rd. Enf—15Yb 26
Stone Ho. Ct. EC3—(2J 201)
Stonehouse Gdns. Cat—97Ub 181
Stonehouse La. Grays—50Ud 90
Stonehouse La. Sev—81Zc 169
Stonehouse Rd. Sev—82Yc 169
Stoneings La. Sev—90Vc 169
Stoneleigh Av. Enf—11Xb 25
Stoneleigh Av. Wor Pk—77Wa 144
Stoneleigh Clo. Wal X—5Zb 12
Stoneleigh Cres. Eps—78Va 144
Stoneleigh Pk. Wey—79S 140
Stoneleigh Pk. Av. Croy—72Zb 148
Stoneleigh Pk. Rd. Eps—79Va 144
Stoneleigh Pl. W11—45Za 80
Stoneleigh Rd. N17—27Vb 43
Stoneleigh Rd. Cars—73Gb 145
Stoneleigh Rd. Ilf—27Nc 46
Stoneleigh St. W11—45Za 80
Stoneleigh Ter. N19—33Kb 62
Stonell's Rd. SW11—58Hb 103
Stone Ness Rd. Grays—51Xd 112
Stonenest St. N4—32Pb 62
Stone Pk. Av. Beck—70Cc 128
Stone Pl. Wor Pk—75Wa 144
Stone Pl. Rd. Grnh—57Ud 112
Stone Rd. Brom—71Hc 149
Stones All. Wat—14X 19
Stones Cross Rd. Swan—71Ed 152
Stones End St. SE1
—47Sb 83 (2D 206)
Stones Rd. Eps—84Ua 162
Stone St. Croy—78Qb 146
Stone St. Grav—8D 114
Stone St. Rd. Sev—96Rd 187
★Stone St. Rd. Sev—96Td
Stonewold Ct. W5—44Ma 79
Stonewood. Dart—62Yd 134
Stonewood Rd. Eri—50Gd 88
Stoney All. SE18—54Qc 108
Stoneyard La. E14—45Dc 84
Stoney Corner. Grav—10A 136
Stoneycroft Clo. SE12—59Hc 107
Stoneycroft Rd. Wfd G—23Nc 46
Stoneydeep. Tedd—63Ja 122
Stoneydown. E17—28Ac 44
Stoneydown Av. E17—28Ac 44
Stoneyfield Rd. Coul—89Pb 164
Stoneyfields Gdns. Edgw
—21Sa 39
Stoneyfields La. Edgw—21Sa 39
Stoneylands Ct. Egh—64B 118
Stoneylands Rd. Egh—64B 118
Stoney La. E1—44Ub 83 (2K 201)
Stoney La. SE19—65Vb 127
Stoney La. K Lan—2G 2
Stoney La. Slou—9E 52
Stoney Meade. Slou—6F 72
Stoney St. SE1—46Tb 83 (6F 201)
Stonhouse St. SW4—56Mb 104
Stonny Croft. Asht—89Pa 161
Stonor Rd. W14—49Bb 81
Stony Hill. Esh—80Ba 141
Stony La. Amer—10A 1
Stony Path. Lou—11Pc 28
Stonyshotts. Wal A—6Gc 13
Stopford Rd. E13—39Jc 65
Stopford Rd. SE17
—50Rb 83 (7C 206)
Store Rd. E16—47Qc 86
Store St. E15—36Fc 65
Store St. WC1—43Mb 82 (1D 198)
Storey Rd. E17—28Bc 44
Storey Rd. N6—30Hb 41
Storey's Ga. SW1
—47Mb 82 (2E 204)
Storey St. E16—46Qc 86
Stories Rd. SE5—55Ub 105
Stork Rd. E7—37Jc 65
Storksmead Rd. Edgw—24Ua 40
Stork's Rd. SE16—48Wb 83
Stormont Rd. N6—31Hb 61
Stormont Rd. SW11—55Jb 104
Stormont Way. Chess—78La 142
Stormount Dri. Hay—47S 76
Stornaway Strand. Grav—2H 137
Storr Gdns. Brtwd—15Fe 33
Storrington Rd. Croy—74Vb 147
Story St. N1—38Pb 62
Stothard Pl. EC2—43Ub 83 (7J 195)
Stothard St. E1—42Yb 84
Stoughton Av. Sutt—78Za 144
Stoughton Clo. SE11
—49Pb 82 (6J 205)
Stoughton Clo. SW15—60Wa 102
Stour Av. S'hall—48Ca 77
Stourcliffe St. W1
—44Hb 81 (3F 197)
Stour Clo. Kes—77Lc 149
Stour Clo. Slou—8F 72
Stourhead Clo. SW19—59Za 102
Stourhead Gdns. SW20
—69Wa 124
Stour Rd. E3—38Cc 64
Stour Rd. Dag—33Cd 68
Stour Rd. Dart—55Jd 110
Stour Rd. Grays—10C 92
Stourton Av. Felt—63Ba 121
Stour Way. Upm—30Ud 50
Stovell Rd. Wind—2F 94
Stowage. SE8—51Dc 106
Stow Cres. E17—24Ac 44
Stowe Cres. Ruis—30R 36
Stowe Gdns. N9—18Vb 25
Stowell Av. Croy—82Fc 167
Stowe Pl. N15—27Ub 43
Stowe Rd. W12—47Xa 80
Stowe Rd. Orp—77Xc 151
Stowe Rd. Slou—5C 72
Stowting Rd. Orp—77Uc 150
Stoxmead. Harr—25Fa 38
Stracey Rd. E7—35Jc 65
Stracey Rd. NW10—39Ta 59
Strachan Pl. SW19—65Ya 124
Stradbroke Dri. Chig—23Rc 46
Stradbroke Gro. Buck H—18Mc 27
Stradbroke Gro. Ilf—27Nc 46
Stradbroke Rd. N5—35Sb 63
Stradella Rd. SE24—58Sb 105
Strafford Clo. Pot B—4Cb 9
Strafford Ga. Pot B—4Cb 9
Strafford Rd. W3—47Sa 79
Strafford Rd. Barn—13Ab 22
Strafford Rd. Houn—55Ba 99
Strafford Rd. Twic—59Ja 100
Strafford St. E14—47Cc 84
Strahan Rd. E3—41Ac 84
Straight Rd. Romf—22Kd 49
Straight Rd. Wind—7L 95
Straightsmouth. SE10—52Ec 106
Straight, The. S'hall—47Aa 77
Strait Rd. E6—45Nc 86
Straits, The. Wal A—4Dc 12
Straker's Rd. SE15—56Xb 105
Strand. WC2—45Nb 82 (5G 199)
Strand Clo. Eps—91Ta 177
Strand Ct. SE18—50Uc 86
Strandfield Clo. SE18—50Uc 86
Strand La. WC2—45Pb 82 (4J 199)
Strand on the Grn. W4—51Qa 101
Strand Pl. N18—21Ub 43
Strand School App. W4—51Qa 101
Strangeways. Wat—8U 4
Strangways Ter. W14—48Bb 81
Stranraer Rd. Houn—58N 97
Stranraer Way. N1—38Pb 62
Stratfield Rd. Borwd—13Qa 21
Stratfield Rd. Slou—7L 73
Stratford Av. W8—48Cb 81
Stratford Av. Uxb—40P 55
Stratford Clo. Bark—38Wc 67
Stratford Clo. Dag—38Ed 68

Stratford Clo.—Swale Clo.

Stratford Clo. Slou—2C 72
Stratford Ct. N Mald—70Ta 123
Stratford Gdns. Stanf—1M 93
Stratford Gro. SW15—56Za 102
Stratford Pl. W1—44Kb 82 (3K 197)
Stratford Rd. E13—39Hc 65
Stratford Rd. W8—48Cb 81
Stratford Rd. Hay—42X 77
Stratford Rd. S'hall—49Aa 77
Stratford Rd. T Hth—70Qb 126
Stratford Rd. Wat—12W 18
Stratford Shopping Centre. E15
—38Fc 65
Stratford Vs. NW1—38Mb 62
Stratford Way. Wat—12V 18
Strathan Clo. SW18—58Bb 103
Strathaven Rd. SE12—58Kc 107
Strathblaine Rd. SW11—56Fb 103
Strathbrook Rd. SW16—66Pb 126
Strathcona Av. Lea—100Aa 175
Strathcona Rd. Wemb—33Ma 59
Strathdale. SW16—64Pb 126
Strathdon Dri. SW17—62Fb 125
Strathearn Av. Hay—52V 98
Strathearn Av. Twic—60Da 99
Strathearn Pl. W2
—44Gb 81 (3D 196)
Strathearn Rd. SW19—64Cb 125
Strathearn Rd. Sutt—78Cb 145
Stratheden Rd. SE3—52Jc 107
Strathfield Gdns. Bark—37Tc 66
Strathleven Rd. SW2—57Nb 104
Strathmore Clo. Cat—93Ub 181
Strathmore Gdns. N3—25Db 41
Strathmore Gdns. W8—46Cb 81
Strathmore Gdns. Edgw—26Ra 39
Strathmore Gdns. Horn—32Hd 68
Strathmore Rd. SW19—62Cb 125
Strathmore Rd. Croy—73Tb 147
Strathmore Rd. Tedd—63Ga 122
Strathnairn St. SE1—49Wb 83
Strathray Gdns. NW3—37Gb 61
Strath Ter. SW11—56Gb 103
Strathville Rd. SW18—61Cb 125
Strathyre Av. SW16—69Qb 126
Stratton Av. Enf—9Tb 11
Stratton Av. Wall—81Mb 164
Stratton Clo. SW19—68Cb 125
Stratton Clo. Bexh—55Ad 109
Stratton Clo. Edgw—23Pa 39
Stratton Clo. Houn—53Ca 99
Stratton Clo. W on T—74Y 141
Strattondale St. E14—48Ec 84
Stratton Dri. Bark—36Vc 67
Stratton Gdns. S'hall—44Ba 77
Stratton Rd. SW19—68Cb 125
Stratton Rd. Bexh—55Ad 109
Stratton Rd. Romf—22Qd 49
Stratton Rd. Sun—68V 120
Stratton St. W1—46Kb 82 (6A 198)
Stratton Ter. West—99Sc 184
Stratton Wlk. Romf—22Qd 49
Strauss Rd. W4—47Ta 79
Strawberry Hill. Twic—62Ha 122
Strawberry Hill Clo. Twic
—62Ha 122
Strawberry Hill Rd. Twic
—62Ha 122
Strawberry La. Cars—76Jb 146
Strawberry Vale. N2—25Fb 41
Strawberry Vale. Twic—62Ja 122
(in two parts)
Strayfield Rd. Enf—8Qb 10
Streamdale. SE2—51Xc 109
Stream La. Edgw—22Ra 39
Streamside Clo. Brom—70Jc 129
Stream Way. Belv—51Cd 110
Streatfeild Av. E6—39Pc 66
Streatfield Rd. Harr—27La 38
Streatham Clo. SW16—61Nb 126
Streatham Comn. N. SW16
—64Nb 126
Streatham Comn. S. SW16
—65Nb 126
Streatham High Rd. SW16
—63Nb 126
Streatham Hill. SW2—61Nb 126
Streatham Pl. SW2—59Nb 104
Streatham Rd.—67Jb 126
SW16 225-263 & 228-260
Mitc remainder
Streatham St. WC1
—44Nb 82 (2F 199)
Streatham Vale. SW16—67Lb 126
Streathbourne Rd. SW17
—62Jb 126
Streatley Pl. NW3—35Eb 61
Streatley Rd. NW6—38Bb 61
Streetfield M. SE3—55Jc 107
Street, The. Asht—90Pa 161
Street, The. Grav—10J 137
(Cobham)
Street, The. Grav—4N 137
(Shorne)
Street, The. Guild—100J 173
Street, The. K Lan—3J 3
Street, The. Lea—95Fa 176
Street, The. Lea—100Z 175
(Effingham)
Street, The. Lea—99S 174
(West Horsley)
Street, The. Sev—78Ae 155
(Ash)
★Street, The. Sev—93Zd
(Ightham)
Street, The. S Dar, Dart—70Sd 134
Streimer Rd. E15—40Ec 64
Strelley Way. W3—45Ua 80
Stretton Rd. Croy—73Ub 147
Stretton Rd. Rich—61La 122
Stretton Way. Borwd—10Na 7
Strickland Av. Dart—55Pd 111
(in two parts)
Strickland Row. SW18—59Fb 103
Strickland St. SE8—53Cc 106
Strickland Way. Orp—77Vc 151
Stride Rd. E13—40Hc 65
Stringer's Av. Guild—100A 172
Stringhams Copse. Wok—96J 173
Strode Clo. N10—24Jb 42
Strode Rd. E7—35Jc 65
Strode Rd. N17—26Ub 43
Strode Rd. NW10—37Wa 60
Strode Rd. SW6—52Ab 102
Strode's Cres. Stai—64L 119
Strode St. Egh—63C 118
Strone Rd.—37Lc 65
E7 1-209 & 2-216
E12 remainder
Strongbow Cres. SE9—57Pc 108
Strongbow Rd. SE9—57Pc 108
Strongbridge Clo. Harr—32Ca 57
Stronsa Rd. W12—47Va 80
Strood Av. Romf—32Fd 68
Strood La. Wind—5A 116
Stroud Clo. Wind—5B 94
Stroud Cres. SW15—62Wa 124
Stroude Rd. Vir W & Egh—70A 118
Stroudes Clo. Wor Pk—73Va 144
Stroud Field. N'holt—37Aa 57
Stroud Ga. Harr—35Da 57
Stroud Grn. Gdns. Croy—73Yb 148
Stroud Grn. Rd. N4—32Pb 62
Stroud Grn. Way. Croy—73Xb 147
Stroudley Wlk. E3—41Dc 84
Stroud Rd. SE25—72Wb 147
Stroud Rd. SW19—62Cb 125
Stroudwater Pk. Wey—79R 140
Stroud Way. Ashf—65R 120
Strouts Pl. E2—41Vb 83 (3K 195)
Strutton Ground. SW1
—48Mb 82 (3D 204)
Struttons Av. Grav—1B 136
Strype St. E1—43Vb 83 (1K 201)
Stuart Av. NW9—31Wa 60
Stuart Av. W5—46Pa 79
Stuart Av. Brom—74Jc 149
Stuart Av. Harr—34Ba 57
Stuart Av. W on T—74X 141
Stuart Clo. Brtwd—15Xd 32
Stuart Clo. Swan—66Hd 132
Stuart Clo. Uxb—37Q 56
Stuart Clo. Wind—4D 94
Stuart Ct. Borwd—16Ma 21
Stuart Cres. N22—25Pb 42
Stuart Cres. Croy—76Bc 148
Stuart Cres. Hay—44S 76
Stuart Evans Clo. Well—55Yc 109
Stuart Gro. Tedd—64Ga 122
Stuart Mantle Way. Eri—52Gd 110
Stuart Pl. Mitc—67Hb 125
Stuart Rd. NW6—41Cb 81
Stuart Rd. SE15—56Yb 106
Stuart Rd. SW19—62Cb 125
Stuart Rd. W3—46Sa 79
Stuart Rd. Bark—38Vc 67
Stuart Rd. Barn—17Gb 23
Stuart Rd. Grav—8C 114
Stuart Rd. Grays—50De 91
Stuart Rd. Harr—27Ha 38
Stuart Rd. Rich—61Ka 122
Stuart Rd. T Hth—70Sb 127
Stuart Rd. Warl—92Xb 181
Stuart Rd. Well—53Xc 109
Stuart Way. Stai—65K 119
Stuart Way. Vir W—10L 117
Stuart Way. Wal X—3Xb 11
Stuart Way. Wind—4C 94
Stubbers La. Upm—37Td 70
Stubbs Hill. Orp—85Yc 169
Stubbs La. Tad—100Bb 179
Stubbs Way. SW19—67Fb 125
Stucley Pl. NW1—38Kb 62
Stucley Rd. Houn—52Ea 100
Studdridge St. SW6—54Cb 103
Studd St. N1—39Rb 63
Stud Grn. Wat—4W 4
Studholme Ct. NW3—35Cb 61
Studholme St. SE15—52Xb 105
Studio Pl. SW1—(2G 203)
Studios Rd. Shep—69P 119
Studios, The. Bush. Wat
—16Ca 19
Studio Way. Borwd—12Sa 21
Studland Clo. Sidc—62Vc 131
Studland Rd. SE26—64Zb 128
Studland Rd. W7—44Fa 78
Studland Rd. King—65Na 123
Studland Rd. Wey—85P 157
Studland St. W6—49Xa 80
Studley Av. E4—24Fc 45
Studley Clo. E5—36Ac 64
Studley Ct. Sidc—64Xc 131
Studley Cres. Long, Dart—68Ee 135
Studley Dri. Ilf—30Mc 45
Studley Grange Rd. W7—47Ga 78
Studley Rd. E7—37Kc 65
Studley Rd. SW4—53Nb 104
Studley Rd. Dag—38Zc 67
Stukeley Rd. E7—38Kc 65
Stukeley St. WC2
—44Nb 82 (2G 199)
Stumps Hill La. Beck—65Cc 128
Stumps La. Whyt—89Ub 165
Sturdy Rd. SE15—54Xb 105
Sturge Av. E17—26Dc 44
Sturgeon Rd. SE17
—50Sb 83 (7D 206)
Sturges Field. Chst—65Tc 130
Sturgess Av. NW4—31Xa 60
Sturge St. SE1—47Sb 83 (1D 206)
Sturlas Way. Wal X—5Zb 12
Sturmer Way. N7—36Pb 62
Sturrock Clo. N15—28Tb 43
Sturry St. E14—44Dc 84
Sturt's La. Tad—99Va 178
Sturt St. N1—40Sb 63 (2E 194)
Stutfield St. E1—44Wb 83
★Styants Bottom Rd. Sev—94Vd
Stylecroft Rd. Chal—19A 16
Styles End. Lea—99Da 175
Styles Gdns. SW9—55Rb 105
Styles Way. Beck—70Ec 128
Styventon Pl. Cher—73H 139
Succombs Hill. Whyt & Warl
—92Xb 181
Sudbourne Rd. SW2—57Nb 104
Sudbrooke Rd. SW12—58Hb 103
Sudbrook Gdns. Rich—62Ma 123
Sudbrook La. Rich—61Na 123
Sudbury Av. Wemb—34La 58
Sudbury Ct. Dri. Harr—34Ha 58
Sudbury Ct. Rd. Harr—34Ja 58
Sudbury Cres. Brom—65Jc 129
Sudbury Cres. Wemb—36Ka 58
Sudbury Gdns. Croy—77Ub 147
Sudbury Gro. Wemb—35Ha 58
Sudbury Heights Av. Gnfd
—36Ha 58
Sudbury Hill. Harr—34Ga 58
Sudbury Hill Clo. Wemb—34Ha 58
Sudbury Rd. Bark—36Vc 67
Sudeley St. N1—40Rb 63 (2C 194)
Sudicamps Ct. Wal A—5Jc 13
Sudlow Rd. SW18—57Cb 103
Sudrey St. SE1—47Sb 83 (2D 206)
Suez Av. Gnfd—40Ha 58
Suez Rd. Enf—14Ac 26
Suffield Clo. S Croy—84Zb 166
Suffield Rd. E4—21Dc 44
Suffield Rd. N15—29Vb 43
Suffield Rd. SE20—68Yb 128
Suffolk Clo. Borwd—15Ta 21
Suffolk Clo. Slou—4C 72
Suffolk Ct. E10—31Cc 64
Suffolk La. EC4—45Tb 83 (4F 201)
Suffolk Pk. Rd. E17—28Ac 44
Suffolk Pl. SW1—46Mb 82 (6E 198)
Suffolk Rd. E13—41Jc 85
Suffolk Rd. N15—29Tb 43
Suffolk Rd. NW10—38Ua 60
Suffolk Rd. SE25—70Vb 127
Suffolk Rd. SW13—52Va 102
Suffolk Rd. Bark—38Tc 66
Suffolk Rd. Dag—36Ed 68
Suffolk Rd. Dart—58Nd 111
Suffolk Rd. Enf—15Xb 25
Suffolk Rd. Grav—8F 114
Suffolk Rd. Harr—30Ba 37
Suffolk Rd. Ilf—30Uc 46
Suffolk Rd. Pot B—4Ab 8
Suffolk Rd. Sidc—65Yc 131
Suffolk Rd. Wor Pk—75Va 144
Suffolk St. E7—35Jc 65
Suffolk St. SW1—45Mb 82 (5E 198)
Suffolk Way. Horn—28Qd 49
Suffolk Way. Sev—97Ld 187
Sugar Baker's Ct. EC3—(3J 201)
Sugar Ho. La. E15—40Ec 64
Sugar Loaf Ct. EC4—(4E 200)
Sugar Loaf Wlk. E2—41Yb 84
Sugden Rd. SW11—55Jb 104
Sugden Rd. Th Dit—74Ka 142
Sugden St. SE5—51Tb 105
Sugden Way. Bark—40Vc 67
Sulgrave Rd. W6—48Ya 80
Sulina Rd. SW2—59Nb 104
Sulivan Ct. SW6—54Cb 103
Sulivan Rd. SW6—55Cb 103
Sullivan Av. E16—43Mc 85
Sullivan Clo. SW11—55Gb 103
Sullivan Clo. E Mol—69Da 121
Sullivan Cres. Uxb—26M 35
Sullivan Rd. SE11
—49Rb 83 (5B 206)
Sullivan Rd. Til—3C 114
Sullivan Way. Borwd—16La 20
Sultan Rd. E11—28Kc 45
Sultan St. SE5—52Sb 105
Sultan St. Beck—68Zb 128
Sumatra Rd. NW6—36Cb 61
Sumburgh Rd. SW12—58Jb 104
Summer Av. E Mol—71Ga 142
Summercourt Rd. E1—44Yb 84
Summerfield Av. NW6—40Ab 60
Summerfield Clo. Wey—78H 139
Summerfield La. Surb—75Ma 143
Summerfield Rd. W5—42Ka 78
Summerfield Rd. Lou—16Mc 27
Summerfield Rd. Wat—7W 4
Summerfield St. SE12—59Hc 107
Summer Gdns. E Mol—71Ga 142
Summer Gro. Borwd—16Ma 21
Summerhayes Clo. Wok—86A 156
Summerhays. Cob—85Z 159
Summer Hill. Borwd—15Qa 21
Summer Hill. Chst—68Qc 130
Summerhill Clo. Orp—76Uc 150
Summerhill Gro. Enf—16Ub 25
Summerhill Rd. N15—28Tb 43
Summerhill Rd. Dart—59Md 111
Summerhill Vs. Chst—67Qc 130
Summerhouse Av. Houn—53Aa 99
Summerhouse Dri. Bex & Swan
—63Fd 132
Summerhouse La. Uxb—24J 35
Summerhouse La. Wat—11Ea 20
Summerhouse La. W Dray
—51M 97
Summerhouse Rd. N16—33Ub 63
Summerhouse Way. Abb L, Wat
—2V 4
Summerland Gdns. N10—27Kb 42
Summerlands Av. W3—45Sa 79
Summerlea. Slou—6F 72
Summerlee Av. N2—28Hb 41
Summerlee Gdns. N2—28Hb 41
Summerley St. SW18—61Db 125
Summer Rd. E Mol & Th Dit
—71Ga 142
Summersby Rd. N6—30Kb 42
Summers Clo. Wemb—32Ra 59
Summers Clo. Wey—83Q 158
Summers Ct. Sutt—80Cb 145
Summers La. N12—24Fb 41
Summers Rd. Slou—1A 72
Summers Row. N12—23Gb 41
Summers St. EC1
—42Qb 82 (6K 193)
Summerstown. SW17—63Eb 125
Summerswood La. Borwd—6Ua 8
Summer Trees. Sun—67X 121
Summerville Gdns. Sutt
—79Bb 145
Summerwood Rd. Iswth
—57Ha 100
Summit Av. NW9—29Ta 39
Summit Clo. N14—19Lb 24
Summit Clo. NW2—36Ab 60
Summit Clo. NW9—29Ta 39
Summit Clo. Edgw—24Qa 39
Summit Dri. Wfd G—26Mc 45
Summit Rd. E17—28Dc 44
Summit Rd. N'holt—38Ca 57
Summit, The. Lou—11Pc 28
Summit Way. N14—19Kb 24
Summit Way. SE19—66Ub 127
Sumner Av. SE15—53Vb 105
Sumner Bldgs. SE1—(6D 200)
Sumner Clo. Lea—96Fa 176
Sumner Clo. Orp—77Sc 150
Sumner Gdns. Croy—74Rb 147
Sumner Pl. SW7—49Fb 81 (6C 202)
Sumner Pl. M. SW7
—49Fb 81 (6C 202)
Sumner Rd. SE15—52Vb 105
Sumner Rd. Croy—74Rb 147
Sumner Rd. Harr—31Ea 58
Sumner Rd. S. Croy—74Rb 147
Sumner St. SE1—46Rb 83 (6C 200)
Sumpter Clo. NW3—37Eb 61
Sun All. Rich—56Na 101
Sunbeam Rd. NW10—42Sa 79
Sunbury Av. NW7—22Ta 39
Sunbury Av. SW14—56Ta 101
Sunbury Ct. Rd. Sun—68Y 121
Sunbury Cres. Felt—63V 120
Sunbury Cross Shopping Centre.
Sun—66V 120
Sunbury Gdns. NW7—22Ta 39
Sunbury La. SW11—53Fb 103
Sunbury La. W on T—72W 140
Sunbury Rd. Felt—62V 120
Sunbury Rd. Sutt—76Ab 144
Sunbury Rd. Wind—1H 95
Sunbury St. SE18—48Pc 86
Sunbury Way. Felt—64Y 121
Sun Ct. EC3—(3G 201)
Suncourt. Eri—54Hd 110
Suncroft Pl. SE26—62Yb 128
Sundale Av. S Croy—82Yb 166
Sunderland Rd. SE23—60Zb 106
Sunderland Rd. W5—48Ma 79
Sunderland Rd. Houn—58N 97
Sunderland Ter. W2—44Db 81
Sunderland Way. E12—33Mc 65
Sundew Av. W12—45Wa 80
Sundew Ct. Grays—51Fe 113
Sundial Av. SE25—69Vb 127
Sundorne Rd. SE7—50Lc 85
Sundown Av. S Croy—83Vb 165
Sundown Rd. Ashf—64S 120
Sundra Wlk. E1—42Zb 84
Sundridge Av. Brom & Chst
—67Mc 129
Sundridge Av. Well—54Tc 108
Sundridge Clo. Dart—58Qd 111
Sundridge Hill. Sev—90Yc 169
Sundridge La. Sev—89Xc 169
Sundridge Pl. Croy—74Wb 147
Sundridge Rd. Croy—74Vb 147
Sundridge Rd. Sev—92Cd 186
Sundridge Rd. Wok—91C 172
Sunfields Pl. SE3—52Kc 107
Sunflower Way. Romf—25Md 49
Sun Hill. Long, Dart—76Wd 154
Sun Hill. Wok—9D 188
Sunkist Way. Wall—81Nb 164
Sunland Av. Bexh—56Ad 109
Sun La. SE3—52Kc 107
Sun La. Grav—1E 136
Sunleigh Rd. Wemb—39Na 59
Sunley Gdns. Gnfd—39Ja 58
Sunmead Clo. Lea—94Ha 176
Sunmead Rd. Sun—69W 120
Sunna Gdns. Sun—68X 121
Sunningdale. N14—22Mb 42
Sunningdale Av. W3—45Ua 80
Sunningdale Av. Bark—38Tc 66
Sunningdale Av. Felt—61Aa 121
Sunningdale Av. Rain—42Kd 89
Sunningdale Av. Ruis—32Y 57
Sunningdale Clo. Stan—24Ja 38
Sunningdale Gdns. NW9—29Sa 39
Sunningdale Rd. Brom—70Nc 130
Sunningdale Rd. Rain—38Jd 68
Sunningdale Rd. Sutt—77Bb 145
Sunningfields Cres. NW4
—26Xa 40
Sunningfields Rd. NW4—27Xa 40
Sunning Hill. Grav—1A 136
Sunninghill Clo. Asc—10B 116
Sunninghill Rd. SE13—54Dc 106
Sunninghill Rd. Asc—10B 116
Sunninghill Rd. Wind & Asc
—4B 116
Sunnings La. Upm—37Sd 70
Sunningvale Av. West—87Lc 167
Sunningvale Clo. West—87Mc 167
Sunny Bank. SE25—69Wb 127
Sunnybank. Eps—88Sa 161
Sunnybank. Warl—89Ac 166
Sunnybank Rd. Pot B—5Cb 9
Sunny Cres. NW10—38Sa 59
Sunnycroft Gdns. Upm—31Vd 70
Sunnycroft Rd. SE25—70Wb 127
Sunnycroft Rd. Houn—54Da 99
Sunnycroft Rd. S'hall—43Ca 77
Sunnydale. Orp—75Qc 150
Sunnydale Gdns. NW7—23Ta 39
Sunnydale Rd. SE12—57Kc 107
Sunnydene Av. E4—22Fc 45
Sunnydene Av. Ruis—32W 56
Sunnydene Clo. Romf—24Pd 49
Sunnydene Gdns. Wemb—37La 58
Sunnydene Rd. Purl—85Rb 165
Sunnydene St. SE26—63Ac 128
Sunnyfield. NW7—21Va 40
Sunnyfield Rd. Chst—69Wc 131
Sunny Gdns. Rd. NW4—26Xa 40
Sunny Hill. NW4—27Xa 40
Sunnyhill Rd. SW16—63Nb 126
Sunnyhill Rd. Rick—23F 34
Sunnyhurst Clo. Sutt—76Cb 145
Sunnymead Av. Mitc—69Mb 126
Sunnymead Rd. NW9—31Ta 59
Sunnymead Rd. SW15—57Xa 102
Sunnymede. Chig—20Xc 29
Sunnymede Av. Cars—83Fb 163
Sunnymede Av. Eps—81Ua 162
Sunnymede Dri. Ilf—28Rc 46
Sunny Nook Gdns. S Croy
—79Tb 147
Sunny Rise. Cat—96Tb 181
Sunny Rd., The. Enf—11Zb 26
Sunnyside. NW2—34Bb 61
Sunnyside. SW19—65Ab 124
Sunny Side. W on T—71Y 141
Sunnyside Dri. E4—17Ec 26
Sunnyside Gdns. Upm—34Sd 70
Sunnyside Pas. SW19—65Ab 124
Sunnyside Rd. E10—32Cc 64
Sunnyside Rd. N19—31Mb 62
Sunnyside Rd. W5—46Ma 79
Sunnyside Rd. Epp—5Vc 15
Sunnyside Rd. Ilf—34Sc 66
Sunnyside Rd. Tedd—63Fa 122
Sunnyside Rd. E. N9—20Wb 25
Sunnyside Rd. N. N9—20Wb 25
Sunnyside Rd. S. N9—20Vb 25
Sunny View. NW9—29Ta 39
Sunny Way. N12—24Gb 41
Sun Pas. Wind—3H 95
Sun Ray Av. Brtwd—16Fe 33
Sunray Av. Brom—72Nc 150
Sunray Av. Surb—75Ra 143
Sunray Av. W Dray—47M 75
Sunrise Av. Horn—34Ld 69
Sunrise Clo. Felt—62Ba 121
Sunrise Cotts. Sev—94Hd 186
Sun Rd. W14—50Bb 81
Sun Rd. Swans—58Be 113
Sunset Av. E4—18Dc 26
Sunset Av. Wfd G—21Hc 45
Sunset Dri. Hav, Romf—22Kd 49
Sunset Gdns. SE25—68Vb 127
Sunset Rd. SE5—56Sb 105
Sunset View. Barn—12Ab 22
Sunshine Way. Mitc—68Hb 125
Sunstone Gro. Red—100Nb 180
Sun St. EC2—43Tb 83 (7G 195)
Sun St. Wal A—5Ec 12
Sun St. Pas. EC2—(1H 201)
Sunwell Clo. SE15—53Xb 105
Surbiton Ct. Surb—72Ma 143
Surbiton Cres. King—70Na 123
Surbiton Hall Clo. King—70Na 123
Surbiton Hill Pk. Surb—71Pa 143
Surbiton Hill Rd. Surb—71Na 143
Surbiton Rd. King—70Ma 123
Surley Hall Wlk. Wind—3D 94
Surlingham Clo. SE28—45Zc 87
Surman Cres. Brtwd—17Ee 33
Surrendale Pl. W9—42Cb 81
Surrey Av. Slou—3G 72
Surrey Canal Rd. SE15 & SE14
—51Yb 106
Surrey Cres. W4—50Qa 79
Surrey Dri. Horn—28Qd 49
Surrey Gdns. Cob—94W 174
Surrey Gro. SE17
—50Ub 83 (7H 207)
Surrey Gro. Sutt—76Fb 145
Surrey La. SW11—53Gb 103
Surrey M. SE27—63Ub 127
Surrey Mt. SE23—60Xb 105
Surrey Rd. SE15—57Zb 106
Surrey Rd. Bark—38Uc 66
Surrey Rd. Dag—36Dd 68
Surrey Rd. Harr—29Ea 38
Surrey Rd. W Wick—74Dc 148
Surrey Row. SE1
—47Rb 83 (1B 206)
Surrey Sq. SE17—50Ub 83 (7H 207)
Surrey St. E13—41Kc 85
Surrey St. WC2—45Pb 82 (4J 199)
Surrey St. Croy—76Sb 147
Surrey Ter. SE17
—50Ub 83 (7J 207)
Surridge Clo. Rain—41Ld 89
Surridge Gdns. SE19—65Tb 127
Surr St. N7—36Nb 62
Susan Clo. Romf—27Ed 48
Susannah St. E14—44Dc 84
Susan Rd. SE3—54Kc 107
Susan Wood. Chst—67Qc 130
Sussex Av. Iswth—55Ga 100
Sussex Av. Romf—24Pd 49
Sussex Clo. N19—33Nb 62
Sussex Clo. Ilf—29Pc 46
Sussex Clo. N Mald—70Ua 124
Sussex Clo. Slou—7M 73
Sussex Clo. Twic—58Ka 100
Sussex Clo. Wok—6A 188
Sussex Cres. N'holt—37Ca 57
Sussex Gdns. N4—29Sb 43
Sussex Gdns. N6—29Hb 41
Sussex Gdns. W2
—44Fb 81 (3C 196)
Sussex Gdns. Chess—79Ma 143
Sussex Keep. Slou—7M 73
Sussex M. E. W2—(3C 196)
Sussex M. W. W2—(4C 196)
Sussex Pl. NW1—42Hb 81 (5F 191)
(in two parts)
Sussex Pl. W2—44Fb 81 (3C 196)
Sussex Pl. W6—50Ya 80
Sussex Pl. Eri—52Dd 110
Sussex Pl. N Mald—70Ua 124
Sussex Pl. Slou—7M 73
Sussex Ring. N12—22Cb 41
Sussex Rd. E6—39Qc 66
Sussex Rd. Brtwd—21Xd 50
Sussex Rd. Cars—79Hb 145
Sussex Rd. Dart—59Qd 111
Sussex Rd. Eri—52Dd 110
Sussex Rd. Harr—29Ea 38
Sussex Rd. Mitc—71Nb 146
Sussex Rd. N Mald—70Ua 124
Sussex Rd. Orp—72Yc 151
Sussex Rd. Sidc—64Xc 131
Sussex Rd. S'hall—48Z 77
Sussex Rd. S Croy—79Tb 147
Sussex Rd. Uxb—35S 56
Sussex Rd. Wat—10W 4
Sussex Rd. W Wick—74Dc 148
Sussex Rd. Wok—6A 188
Sussex Sq. W2—45Fb 81 (4C 196)
Sussex St. E13—41Kc 85
Sussex St. SW1—50Kb 82 (7A 204)
Sussex Wlk. SW9—56Rb 105
Sussex Way—32Nb 62
N7 1-131 & 2-130
N19 remainder
Sussex Way. Barn—15Kb 24
Sutcliffe Clo. NW11—29Db 41
Sutcliffe Clo. Bush, Wat—14Ea 20
Sutcliffe Rd. SE18—51Uc 108
Sutcliffe Rd. Well—54Yc 109
Sutherland Av. W9
—42Cb 81 (4A 190)
Sutherland Av. W13—44Ka 78
Sutherland Av. Hay—49W 76
Sutherland Av. Orp—72Vc 151
Sutherland Av. Pot B—1Mb 10
Sutherland Av. Sun—68V 120
Sutherland Av. Well—56Uc 108
Sutherland Av. West—89Mc 167
Sutherland Clo. Barn—14Ab 22
Sutherland Clo. Grav—1K 137
Sutherland Ct. NW9—29Ra 39
Sutherland Dri. SW19—67Fb 125
Sutherland Gdns. SW14
—55Ua 102
Sutherland Gdns. Sun—68V 120
Sutherland Gdns. Wor Pk
—74Xa 144
Sutherland Gro. SW18—58Ab 102
Sutherland Gro. Tedd—64Ga 122
Sutherland Pl. W2—44Cb 81
Sutherland Rd. E3—40Bc 64
Sutherland Rd. E17—27Zb 44
Sutherland Rd. N9—18Xb 25
Sutherland Rd. N17—25Wb 43
Sutherland Rd. W4—51Ua 102
Sutherland Rd. W13—44Ja 78
Sutherland Rd. Belv—48Cd 88
Sutherland Rd. Croy—73Qb 146
Sutherland Rd. Enf—16Zb 26
Sutherland Rd. S'hall—44Ba 77
Sutherland Rd. Path. E17—27Zb 44
Sutherland Row. SW1
—50Kb 82 (7A 204)
Sutherland Sq. SE17—50Sb 83
Sutherland St. SW1
—50Kb 82 (7K 203)
Sutherland Wlk. SE17—50Sb 83
Sutherland Way. Pot B—1Mb 10
Sutlej Rd. SE7—52Lc 107
Sutterton St. N7—37Pb 62
Sutton Arc. Sutt—78Db 145
Sutton Av. Slou—7N 73
Sutton Av. Wok—7B 188
Sutton Clo. Beck—67Dc 128
Sutton Clo. Lou—17Nc 28
Sutton Clo. Pinn—29W 36
Sutton Comn. Rd. Sutt—73Bb 145
Sutton Ct. W4—51Sa 101
Sutton Ct. Rd. E13—41Lc 85
Sutton Ct. Rd. W4—52Sa 101
Sutton Ct. Rd. Sutt—79Eb 145
Sutton Ct. Rd. Uxb—39R 56
Sutton Cres. Barn—15Za 22
Sutton Dene. Houn—53Da 99
Sutton Dwellings. SW3—(7D 202)
Sutton Est. W10—43Ya 80
Sutton Gdns. Bark—39Uc 66
Sutton Gdns. Croy—71Vb 147
Sutton Grn. Rd. Guild—98A 172
Sutton Gro. Sutt—78Fb 145
Sutton Hall Rd. Houn—52Ca 99
Sutton La. Houn—54Ba 99
Sutton La. Slou—51D 96
Sutton La. Sutt & Bans—83Db 163
Sutton La. N. W4—50Sa 79
Sutton La. S. W4—51Sa 101
Sutton Pk. Rd. Sutt—79Db 145
Sutton Path. Borwd—13Qa 21
Sutton Pl. E9—36Yb 64
Sutton Pl. Slou—51D 96
Sutton Rd. E13—42Hc 85
Sutton Rd. E17—25Zb 44
Sutton Rd. N10—25Jb 42
Sutton Rd. Bark—39Uc 66
Sutton Rd. Houn—53Ca 99
Sutton Rd. Wat—13Y 19
(in two parts)
Sutton Row. W1—44Mb 82 (2E 198)
Suttons Av. Horn—34Ld 69
Suttons Gdns. Horn—34Md 69
Suttons La. Horn—36Md 69
Sutton Sq. Houn—53Ba 99
Sutton St. E1—45Yb 84
Sutton Way. W10—42Ya 80
Sutton Way. Houn—53Ba 99
Swabey Rd. Slou—49C 74
Swaby Rd. SW18—60Eb 103
Swaffham Way. N22—24Rb 43
Swaffield Rd. SW18—59Db 103
Swaffield Rd. Sev—94Ld 187
Swain Clo. W Dray—47N 75
Swain Rd. T Hth—71Sb 147
Swains La. N6—34Jb 62
Swainson Rd. W3—47Va 80
Swains Rd. SW17—66Hb 125
Swaisland Dri. Dart—57Hd 110
Swaisland Rd. Dart—58Kd 111
Swakeleys Dri. Uxb—35Q 56
Swakeleys Rd. Uxb—35N 55
Swalecliffe Rd. Belv—50Dd 88
Swale Clo. S Ock—44Sd 90

Swaledale Rd.—Tennyson Av.

Swaledale Rd. Dart—60Sd 112
Swale Rd. Dart—56Jd 110
Swallands Rd. SE6—63Dc 128 (in two parts)
Swallow Clo. SE14—53Zb 106
Swallow Clo. Bush, Wat—18Da 19
Swallow Clo. Rick—17L 17
Swallow Clo. Stai—63H 119
Swallow Ct. Ilf—29Rc 46
Swallowdale. Iver—41F 74
Swallowdale. S Croy—81Zb 166
Swallow Dri. N'holt—40Ca 57
Swallowfield. Egh—5N 117
Swallowfield Rd. SE7—50Kc 85
Swallowfields. Grav—2A 136
Swallowfield Way. Hay—47T 76
Swallow Pas. W1—(3A 198)
Swallow Pl. W1—44Kb 82 (3A 198)
Swallow Rise. Wok—5A 188
Swallows Cross Rd. Brtwd —11Ee 33
★Swallows Cross Rd. Brtwd—9Ce
Swallow St. W1—45Lb 82 (5C 198)
Swallow St. Iver—41F 74
Swallow Wlk. Rain—37Kd 69
Swanage Rd. E4—24Ec 44
Swanage Rd. SW18—58Eb 103
Swanage Waye. Hay—44Y 77
Swan & Pike Rd. Enf—10Cc 12
Swan Av. Upm—32Vd 70
Swanbourne Dri. Horn—36Md 69
Swanbridge Rd. Bexh—53Cd 110
Swan Centre, The. Lea—93Ka 176
Swan Clo. Felt—63Aa 121
Swan Clo. Orp—69Wc 131
Swanfield Rd. Wal X—5Ac 12
Swanfield St. E2—41Vb 83 (4K 195)
Swanland Rd. Pot B & Hat—5Xa 8
Swan La. EC4—45Tb 83 (5G 201)
Swan La. N20—20Eb 23
★Swan La. Brtwd—9Ud
Swan La. Dart—59Hd 110
Swanley Bar La. Pot B—1Db 9
Swanley By-Pass. Swan —68Ed 132
Swanley Centre. Swan—69Gd 132
Swanley Cres. Pot B—1Db 9
Swanley La. Swan—69Hd 132
Swanley Rd. Well—53Yc 109
Swanley Village Rd. Swan —67Kd 133
Swan Mead. SE1 —48Ub 83 (4H 207)
Swan M. SW9—53Pb 104
Swanns Meadow. Lea—98Ca 175
Swan Paddock. Brtwd—19Yd 32
Swan Pl. SW13—54Va 102
Swan Rd. SE16—47Yb 84
Swan Rd. SE18—48Mc 85
Swan Rd. Felt—64Aa 121
Swan Rd. Iver—44H 75
Swan Rd. S'hall—44Da 77
Swan Rd. W Dray—47M 75
Swanscombe Rd. W4—50Ua 80
Swanscombe Rd. W11—46Za 80
Swanscombe St. Swans —59Ae 113
Swansea Rd. Enf—14Yb 26
Swanshope. Lou—12Rc 28
Swansland Gdns. E17—25Ac 44
Swanston Path. Wat—20Y 19
Swan St. SE1—48Sb 83 (3E 206)
Swan St. Iswth—55Ka 100
Swan Ter. Wind—2F 94
Swanton Gdns. SW19—60Za 102
Swanton Rd. Eri—52Cd 110
Swan Wlk. SW3—51Hb 103
Swan Wlk. Romf—29Gd 48
Swan Way. Enf—12Zb 26
Swanwick Clo. SW15—59Va 102
Swanworth La. Dor—100Ka 176
Swan Yd. N1—37Rb 63
Swanzy Rd. Sev—92Ld 187
Sward Rd. Orp—72Wc 151
Swaton Rd. E3—42Cc 84
Swaylands Rd. Belv—51Cd 110
Swedeland Ct. E1—(1J 201)
Swedenborg Gdns. E1—45Xb 83
Sweeney Cres. SE1 —47Vb 83 (2K 207)
Sweeps La. Egh—64B 118
Sweeps La. Orp—71Zc 151
Sweet Briar Grn. N9—20Vb 25
Sweet Briar Gro. N9—20Vb 25
Sweet Briar La. Eps—86Ta 161
Sweet Briar Wlk. N18—21Vb 43
Sweetcroft La. Uxb—38Q 56
Sweetland Ct. Dag—37Xc 67
Sweetmans Av. Pinn—27Z 37
Sweets Way. N20—19Fb 23
Swetenham Wlk. SE18—50Sc 86
Swete St. E13—40Jc 65
Sweyne Rd. Swans—58Ae 113
Sweyn Pl. SE3—54Jc 107
Sweyn Rd. Grnh—57Yd 112
Swievelands Rd. West—91Kc 183
Swift Clo. Harr—33Da 57
Swift Clo. Hay—44V 76
Swift Clo. Upm—32Ud 70
Swift Ct. Sutt—80Db 145
Swift Rd. Felt—63Z 121
Swift Rd. S'hall—48Ca 77
Swiftsden Way. Brom—65Gc 129
Swift St. SW6—53Bb 103
Swift Way. Wall—81Mb 164
Swiller's La. Grav—4N 137
Swinbrook Rd. W10—43Ab 80
Swinburne Cres. Croy—72Yb 148
Swinburne Gdns. Til—4D 114
Swinburne Rd. SW15—56Wa 102
Swinderby Rd. Wemb—37Na 59
Swindon Clo. Ilf—33Uc 66
Swindon Clo. Romf—22Pd 49
Swindon Gdns. Romf—22Pd 49
Swindon La. Romf—22Pd 49
Swindon St. W12—46Ya 80
Swinfield Clo. Felt—62Aa 121
Swinford Gdns. SW9—55Rb 105
Swingate La. SE18—51Uc 108
Swinnerton St. E9—36Ac 64
Swinton Clo. Wemb—32Ra 59
Swinton Pl. WC1 —41Pb 82 (3H 193)
Swinton St. WC1 —41Pb 82 (3H 193)
Swires Shaw. Kes—78Mc 149
Swiss Av. Wat—13U 18
Swiss Clo. Wat—13U 18
Swiss Ter. NW6—38Fb 61
Swithland Gdns. SE9—63Qc 130
Swyncombe Av. W5—49Ka 78
Sybourn St. E17—31Bc 64
Sycamore App. Rick—15S 18
Sycamore Av. W5—48Ma 79
Sycamore Av. Hay—45U 76
Sycamore Av. Sidc—58Vc 109
Sycamore Av. Upm—34Qd 69
Sycamore Clo. E16—43Gc 85
Sycamore Clo. Barn—16Fb 23
Sycamore Clo. Bush, Wat —12Aa 19
Sycamore Clo. Cars—77Hb 145
Sycamore Clo. Felt—62W 120
Sycamore Clo. Grav—9F 114
Sycamore Clo. N'holt—39Aa 57
Sycamore Clo. Wat—7X 5
Sycamore Clo. W Dray—45P 75
Sycamore Dri. Brtwd—18Yd 32
Sycamore Dri. Swan—69Gd 132
Sycamore Gdns. W6—48Xa 80
Sycamore Gdns. Mitc—68Fb 125
Sycamore Gro. NW9—31Sa 59
Sycamore Gro. SE20—67Wb 127
Sycamore Gro. N Mald—69Ta 123
Sycamore Rise. Bans—86Za 162
Sycamore Rd. SW19—65Ya 124
Sycamore Rd. Dart—60Md 111
Sycamore Rd. Rick—15S 18
Sycamores, The. S Ock—46Td 90
Sycamore St. EC1 —42Sb 83 (6D 194)
Sycamore Wlk. W10—42Ab 80
Sycamore Wlk. Egh—5M 117
Sycamore Wlk. Ilf—28Sc 46
Sycamore Wlk. Slou—44A 74
Sycamore Way. T Hth—71Qb 146
Sydcote. SE21—60Sb 105
Sydenham Av. SE26—64Xb 127
Sydenham Hill—63Vb 127
SE26 1-135 & 2-48
SE23 remainder
Sydenham Pk. SE26—62Yb 128
Sydenham Pk. Rd. SE26 —62Yb 128
Sydenham Pl. SE27—62Rb 127
Sydenham Rise. SE23—61Xb 127
Sydenham Rd. SE26—63Yb 128
Sydenham Rd. Croy—74Tb 147
Sydner M. N16—35Vb 63
Sydner Rd. N16—35Vb 63
Sydney Av. Purl—84Pb 164
Sydney Clo. SW3 —49Fb 81 (6C 202)
Sydney Cres. Ashf—65R 120
Sydney Gro. NW4—29Ya 40
Sydney Gro. Slou—4G 72
Sydney M. SW3—49Fb 81 (6C 202)
Sydney Pl. SW7—49Fb 81 (6D 202)
Sydney Rd. E11—30Kc 45
Sydney Rd. N8—28Qb 42
Sydney Rd. N10—25Kb 42
Sydney Rd. SE2—48Zc 87
Sydney Rd. SW20—68Za 124
Sydney Rd. W13—46Ja 78
Sydney Rd. Bexh—56Zc 109
Sydney Rd. Enf—14Tb 25
Sydney Rd. Felt—60W 98
Sydney Rd. Ilf—26Sc 46
Sydney Rd. Rich—56Na 101
Sydney Rd. Sidc—63Uc 130
Sydney Rd. Sutt—77Cb 145
Sydney Rd. Tedd—64Ha 122
Sydney Rd. Til—4C 114
Sydney Rd. Wat—15U 18
Sydney Rd. Wfd G—21Jc 45
Sydney St. SW3—50Gb 81 (7D 202)
Sykecluan. Iver—47G 74
Sykeings. Iver—48G 74
Sykes Rd. Slou—4F 72
Sylvana Clo. Uxb—39P 56
Sylvan Av. N3—26Cb 41
Sylvan Av. N22—24Pb 42
Sylvan Av. NW7—23Va 40
Sylvan Av. Horn—30Nd 49
Sylvan Av. Romf—30Bd 47
Sylvan Clo. Grays—49Ae 91
Sylvan Clo. Oxt—100Kc 183
Sylvan Clo. S Croy—82Xb 165
Sylvan Clo. Wok—89D 156
Sylvan Ct. N12—20Db 23
Sylvan Gdns. Surb—73Ma 143
Sylvan Gro. SE15—51Xb 105
Sylvan Hill. SE19—67Ub 127
Sylvan Rd. E7—37Jc 65
Sylvan Rd. E11—29Jc 45
Sylvan Rd. E17—29Cc 44
Sylvan Rd. SE19—67Vb 127
Sylvan Way. Chig—20Xc 29
Sylvan Way. Dag—35Xc 67
Sylvan Way. W Wick—77Gc 149
Sylverdale Rd. Purl—85Rb 165
Sylvester Av. Chst—65Pc 130
Sylvester Gdns. Ilf—22Xc 47
Sylvester Path. E8—37Xb 63
Sylvester Rd. E8—37Xb 63
Sylvester Rd. E17—31Bc 64
Sylvester Rd. N2—26Fb 41
Sylvester Rd. Wemb—36La 58
Sylvestrus Clo. King—67Qa 123
Sylvia Av. Brtwd—19Ee 33
Sylvia Av. Pinn—23Aa 37
Sylvia Gdns. Wemb—38Ra 59
Symes M. NW1—(1B 192)
Symonds Clo. Sev—78Ud 154
Symons St. SW3 —49Hb 81 (6G 203)
Syon Ga. Way. Bren—52Ja 100
Syon La. Iswth—51Ha 100
Syon Pk. Gdns. Iswth—52Ha 100
Syon Vista. Rich—53Na 101
Syracuse Av. Rain—41Nd 89
Syringa Ct. Grays—52Fe 113
Sythwood. Wok—5E 188
Tabard St. SE1—47Tb 83 (2F 207)
Tabarn Way. Eps—88Ya 162
Tabernacle Av. E13—42Jc 85
Tabernacle St. EC2 —42Tb 83 (6G 195)
Tableer Av. SW4—57Mb 104
Tabley Rd. N7—35Nb 62
Tabor Gdns. Sutt—79Bb 145
Tabor Gro. SW19—66Bb 125
Tabor Rd. W6—48Xa 80
Tabrums Way. Upm—31Ud 70
Tachbrook Est. SW1 —50Mb 82 (7E 204)
Tachbrook M. SW1 —49Lb 82 (5B 204)
Tachbrook Rd. Felt—59V 98
Tachbrook Rd. S'hall—49Z 77
Tachbrook Rd. Uxb—40L 55
Tachbrook Rd. W Dray—46N 75
Tachbrook St. SW1 —49Lb 82 (6C 204)
Tack M. SE4—55Cc 106
Tadema Rd. SW10—52Eb 103
Tadlows Clo. Upm—36Rd 69
Tadmor Clo. Sun—70V 120
Tadmor St. W12—46Za 80
Tadorne Rd. Tad—93Ya 178
Tadworth Av. N Mald—71Va 144
Tadworth Pde. Horn—35Kd 69
Tadworth Rd. NW2—33Wa 60
Tadworth St. Tad—95Ya 178
Taffy's How. Mitc—69Gb 125
Taft Way. E3—41Dc 84
Tait Rd. Croy—73Ub 147
Taits. Stanf—1P 93
Takeley Clo. Romf—26Fd 48
Takeley Clo. Wal A—5Fc 13
Talacre Rd. NW5—37Jb 62
Talbot Av. N2—27Fb 41
Talbot Av. Slou—47B 74
Talbot Av. Wat—17Aa 19
Talbot Clo. N15—28Vb 43
Talbot Ct. EC3—(4G 201)
Talbot Cres. NW4—29Wa 40
Talbot Gdns. Ilf—33Wc 67
Talbot Pl. SE3—54Gc 107
Talbot Pl. Slou—3N 95
Talbot Rd. E6—40Qc 66
Talbot Rd. E7—35Jc 65
Talbot Rd. N6—30Jb 42
Talbot Rd. N15—28Vb 43
Talbot Rd. N22—26Lb 42
Talbot Rd.—44Bb 81
W2 1-97 & 2-102
W11 remainder
(in two parts)
Talbot Rd. W13—46Ja 78
Talbot Rd. Ashf—64N 119
Talbot Rd. Brom—69Kc 129
Talbot Rd. Cars—78Jb 146
Talbot Rd. Dag—37Bd 67
Talbot Rd. Harr—26Ha 38
Talbot Rd. Iswth—56Ja 100
Talbot Rd. Rick—18N 17
Talbot Rd. S'hall—49Aa 77
Talbot Rd. T Hth—70Tb 127
Talbot Rd. Twic—60Ga 100
Talbot Rd. Wemb—37Ma 59
Talbot Sq. W2—44Fb 81 (3C 196)
Talbot Wlk. NW10—37Ua 60
Talbot Yd. SE1—46Tb 83 (7F 201)
Talbrook. Brtwd—20Vd 32
Talcott Path. SW2—60Qb 104
Taleworth Clo. Asht—92Ma 177
Taleworth Rd. Asht—92Ma 177
Talfourd Pl. SE15—53Vb 105
Talfourd Rd. SE15—53Vb 105
Talgarth Rd.—50Za 80
W14 1-155
W6 remainder
Talisman Sq. SE26—63Wb 127
Talisman Way. Eps—88Ya 162
Talisman Way. Wemb—34Pa 59
Tallack Clo. Harr—24Ga 38
Tallack Rd. E10—32Bc 64
Tall Elms Clo. Brom—71Hc 149
Tallis Clo. Stanf—1L 93
Tallis Gro. SE7—51Kc 107
Tallis St. EC4—45Qb 82 (4A 200)
Tallis Way. Borwd—11Ma 21
Tallon Rd. Brtwd—15Fe 33
Talma Gdns. Twic—58Ga 100
Talman Gro. Stan—23Ma 39
Talma Rd. SW2—56Qb 104
Talwin St. E3—41Dc 84
Tamar Clo. Upm—30Ud 50
Tamar Dri. S Ock—44Sd 90
Tamarisk Clo. S Ock—42Yd 90
Tamarisk Rd. S Ock—41Yd 90
Tamarisk Sq. W12—45Va 80
Tamar Sq. Wfd G—23Kc 45
Tamar Way. N17—27Wb 43
Tamar Way. Slou—50D 74
Tamesis Gdns. Wor Pk—75Ua 144
Tamesis Strand. Grav—4G 136
Tamian Way. Houn—56Y 99
Tamworth Av. E4—23Gc 45
Tamworth La. Mitc—68Kb 126
Tamworth Pk. Mitc—69Kb 126
Tamworth Pl. Croy—75Sb 147
Tamworth Rd. Croy—75Rb 147
Tamworth St. SW6—51Cb 103
Tamworth Vs. Mitc—70Lb 126
Tancred Rd. N4—30Rb 43
Tandridge Dri. Orp—74Tc 150
Tandridge Gdns. S Croy —85Wb 165
Tandridge Hill La. God—100Bc 182
Tandridge Pl. Orp—74Tc 150
Tandridge Rd. Warl—91Zb 182
Tanfield Av. NW2—35Ua 60
Tanfield Ct. EC4—44Qb 82 (3A 200)
Tanfield Rd. Croy—77Sb 147
Tangent Rd. Romf—25Md 49
Tangier Ct. Wind—1H 95
Tangier La. Wind—1H 95
Tangier Rd. Rich—56Qa 101
Tangier Way. Tad—89Ab 162
Tangier Wood. Tad—90Ab 162
Tanglewood Clo. Croy—76Yb 148
Tanglewood Clo. Felt—62X 121
Tanglewood Clo. Stan—19Ga 20
Tanglewood Clo. Uxb—41Q 76
Tanglewood Clo. Wok—88F 156
Tangley Gro. SW15—58Va 102
Tangley Pk. Rd. Hmptn—64Ba 121
Tanglyn Av. Shep—71R 140
Tangmere Cres. Horn—37Kd 69
Tangmere Gdns. N'holt—40Y 57
Tangmere Way. NW9—26Ua 40
Tan Ho. La. Brtwd—14Pd 31
Tanhurst Wlk. SE2—48Zc 87
Tankerton Rd. Surb—75Pa 143
Tankerton St. WC1 —41Nb 82 (4G 193)
Tankerville Rd. SW16—66Mb 126
Tank Hill Rd. Purf—49Qd 89
Tank La. Purf—49Qd 89
Tankridge Rd. NW2—33Xa 60
Tanners Dean. Lea—94La 176
Tanners End La. N18—22Ub 43
Tanner's Hill. SE8—53Bc 106
Tanners Hill. Abb L, Wat—3V 4
Tanners La. Ilf—27Sc 46
Tanner St. SE1—47Ub 83 (2J 207)
Tanner St. Bark—37Sc 66
Tanners Wood. Abb L, Wat—4U 4
Tannery Clo. Beck—71Zb 148
Tannery Clo. Dag—34Dd 68
Tannery La. Wok—95F 172
Tannsfeld Rd. SE26—64Zb 128
Tansley Clo. N7—36Mb 62
Tansy Clo. Romf—23Nd 49
Tantallon Rd. SW12—60Jb 104
Tant Av. E16—44Hc 85
Tantony Gro. Romf—27Zc 47
Tanworth Clo. N'wd—23S 36
Tanworth Gdns. Pinn—26Y 37
Tanyard Hill. Grav—5N 137
Tanza Rd. NW3—35Hb 61
Tapestry Clo. Sutt—80Db 145
Taplow. SE17—(7G 207)
Taplow St. N1—40Sb 63 (2E 194)
Tappesfield Rd. SE15—55Yb 106
Tapp St. E1—42Xb 83
Tapster St. Barn—14Bb 23
Tarbay La. Wind—5A 94
Tarbert Rd. SE22—57Ub 105
Tarbert Wlk. E1—45Yb 84
Target Clo. Felt—58U 98
Tariff Av. N17—23Wb 43
Tariff Rd. N17—23Wb 43
Tarleton Ct. N22—26Qb 42
Tarleton Gdns. SE23—61Xb 127
Tarling Clo. Sidc—62Xc 131
Tarling Rd. E16—44Hc 85
Tarling Rd. N2—26Eb 41
Tarling St. E1—44Yb 84
Tarling St. Est. E1—44Yb 84
Tarn Bank. Enf—15Nb 24
Tarnwood Pk. SE9—60Pc 108
Tarnworth Rd. Romf—23Qd 49
Tarrington Clo. SW16—62Mb 126
Tarry La. SE8—49Ac 84
Tartar Hill. Cob—85Y 159
Tartar Rd. Cob—85Y 159
Tarver Rd. SE17—50Rb 83 (7C 206)
Tarves Way. SE10—52Dc 106
Tash Pl. N11—22Kb 42
Tasker Rd. NW3—36Hb 61
Tasker Rd. Grays—8D 92
Tasman Ct. Ashf—66U 120
Tasmania Ter. N18—23Sb 43
Tasman Rd. SW9—55Nb 104
Tasman Wlk. E16—44Mc 85
Tasso Rd. W6—51Ab 102
Tatam Rd. NW10—38Ta 59
Tate Clo. Lea—95La 176
Tate Ho. Ger X—21B 34
Tate Rd. E16—46Pc 86
Tate Rd. Ger X—22B 34
Tate Rd. Sutt—78Cb 145
Tatnell Rd. SE23—58Ac 106
Tatsfield La. West—93Pc 184
Tattenham Corner Rd. Eps —89Va 162
Tattenham Cres. Eps—90Xa 162
Tattenham Gro. Eps—90Xa 162
Tattenham Way. Tad—89Ab 162
Tattersall Clo. SE9—57Nc 108
Tatton Cres. N16—31Vb 63
Tatum St. SE17—49Tb 83 (6G 207)
Taunton Av. SW20—68Xa 124
Taunton Av. Cat—95Vb 181
Taunton Av. Houn—54Ea 100
Taunton Clo. Bexh—54Fd 110
Taunton Clo. Sutt—74Cb 145
Taunton Dri. Enf—13Qb 24
Taunton La. Coul—91Qb 180
Taunton M. NW1 —42Hb 81 (6F 191)
Taunton Pl. NW1 —42Hb 81 (5F 191)
Taunton Rd. SE12—57Gc 107
Taunton Rd. Grav—57Ce 113
Taunton Rd. Gnfd—39Da 57
Taunton Rd. Romf—21Ld 49
Taunton Vale. Grav—2F 136
Taunton Way. Stan—26Na 39
Taverners Clo. W11—46Ab 80
Taverner Sq. N5—35Sb 63
Taverners Way. E4—18Gc 27
Tavern La. SW9—54Qb 104
Tavistock Av. E17—27Zb 44
Tavistock Av. Gnfd—40Ja 58
Tavistock Clo. N16—36Ub 63
Tavistock Clo. Pot B—3Fb 9
Tavistock Clo. Romf—25Md 49
Tavistock Clo. Stai—66M 119
Tavistock Cres. W11—43Bb 81
Tavistock Cres. Mitc—70Nb 126
Tavistock Gdns. Ilf—35Uc 66
Tavistock Gro. Croy—73Tb 147
Tavistock M. E18—27Jc 45
Tavistock Pl. E18—27Jc 45
Tavistock Pl. N14—17Kb 24
Tavistock Pl. WC1 —42Nb 82 (5F 193)
Tavistock Rd. E7—35Hc 65
Tavistock Rd. E15—37Hc 65
Tavistock Rd. E18—27Jc 45
Tavistock Rd. N4—30Tb 43
Tavistock Rd. NW10—40Va 60
Tavistock Rd. W11—44Bb 81
Tavistock Rd. Brom—70Hc 129
Tavistock Rd. Cars—74Fb 145
Tavistock Rd. Croy—74Tb 147
Tavistock Rd. Edgw—25Qa 39
Tavistock Rd. Uxb—36T 56
Tavistock Rd. Wat—11Z 19
Tavistock Rd. Well—53Yc 109
Tavistock Rd. W Dray—46M 75
Tavistock Sq. WC1 —42Mb 82 (5E 192)
Tavistock St. WC2 —45Nb 82 (4G 199)
Tavistock Ter. N19—34Mb 62
Tavistock Wlk. Cars—74Fb 145
Taviton St. WC1 —42Mb 82 (5D 192)
Tavy Bri. SE2—47Yc 87
Tavy Bri. Centre. SE2—47Yc 87
Tavy Clo. SE11—(7A 206)
Tawney Comn. Epp—4Bd 15
★Tawney Comn. Epp—4Dd
Tawney Rd. SE28—45Xc 87
Tawny Av. Upm—36Rd 69
Tawny Way. SE16—49Zb 84
Tayben Av. Twic—58Ga 100
Taybridge Rd. SW11—55Jb 104
Tay Bldgs. SE1—(3H 207)
Tayburn Clo. E14—44Ec 84
Tayles Hill. Eps—82Va 162
Taylor Av. Rich—54Ra 101
Taylor Clo. N17—24Wb 43
Taylor Clo. Hmptn—64Ea 122
Taylor Clo. Orp—77Vc 151
Taylor Clo. Romf—24Cd 48
Taylor Rd. Asht—89Ma 161
Taylor Rd. Mitc—66Gb 125
Taylor Rd. Wall—78Kb 146
Taylors Bldgs. SE18—49Rc 86
Taylor's Bushes Ride. Wind —1A 116
Taylors Clo. Sidc—63Vc 131
Taylors Grn. W3—44Ua 80
Taylors La. NW10—38Ua 60
Taylor's La. SE26—63Xb 127
Taylors La. Barn—11Bb 23
Taylor St. SE18—49Rc 86
Taymount Rise. SE23—61Yb 128
Tayport Clo. N1—38Pb 62
Tay Way. Romf—25Hd 48
Taywood Rd. N'holt—41Ba 77
Teak Clo. SE16—46Ac 84
Teal Clo. S Croy—83Zb 166
Teale St. E2—40Wb 63
Tealing Dri. Eps—77Ta 143
Teasel Clo. Croy—74Zb 148
Teasel Way. E15—41Gc 85
Tebworth Rd. N17—24Vb 43
Tedder Clo. Chess—78La 142
Tedder Clo. Ruis—36W 56
Tedder Clo. Uxb—38P 55
Tedder Rd. S Croy—80Zb 148
Teddington Clo. Eps—82Ta 161
Teddington Pk. Tedd—64Ha 122
Teddington Pk. Rd. Tedd —63Ha 122
Tedworth Sq. SW3—50Hb 81
Tees Av. Gnfd—40Ha 58
Tees Clo. Upm—31Td 70
Teesdale Av. Iswth—53Ja 100
Teesdale Clo. E2—40Xb 63
Teesdale Gdns. SE25—68Ub 127
Teesdale Gdns. Iswth—53Ja 100
Teesdale Rd. E11—31Hc 65
Teesdale Rd. Dart—60Sd 112
Teesdale Rd. Slou—3D 72
Teesdale St. E2—40Xb 63
Tees Dri. Romf—20Md 31
Tee, The. W3—44Ua 80
Teevan Clo. Croy—73Wb 147
Teevan Rd. Croy—73Wb 147
Tegg's La. Wok—88H 157
Teignmouth Clo. SW4—56Mb 104
Teignmouth Clo. Edgw—26Pa 39
Teignmouth Gdns. Gnfd—40Ja 58
Teignmouth Rd. NW2—36Za 60
Teignmouth Rd. Well—54Yc 109
Telcote Way. Ruis—31Y 57
Telegraph Hill. NW3—34Db 61
Telegraph La. Esh—78Ha 142
Telegraph M. Ilf—32Wc 67
Telegraph Rd. SW15—59Xa 102
Telegraph St. EC2 —44Tb 83 (2F 201)
Telegraph Track. Cars & Wall —83Jb 164
Teleman Sq. SE3—56Kc 107
Telephone Pl. SW6—51Bb 103
Telferscot Rd. SW12—60Mb 104
Telford Av. SW2—60Mb 104
Telford Av. Slou—7E 72
Telford Clo. SE19—65Vb 127
Telford Clo. Wat—7Z 5
Telford Rd. N11—22Lb 42
Telford Rd. SE9—61Tc 130
Telford Rd. W10—43Ab 80
Telford Rd. S'hall—45Da 77
Telford Rd. Twic—59Ca 99
Telford Way. W3—43Ua 80
Telham Rd. E6—40Qc 66
Tell Gro. SE22—56Vb 105
Tellisford. Esh—77Da 141
Tellson Av. SE18—53Mc 107
Telscombe Clo. Orp—75Uc 150
Telston La. Sev—89Hd 170
Temeraire St. SE16—47Yb 84
Temperley Rd. SW12—59Jb 104
Tempest Av. Pot B—4Fb 9
Tempest Rd. Egh—65E 118
Tempest Way. Rain—37Jd 68
Templar Dri. Grav—4C 136
Templar Ho. NW2—37Bb 61
Templar Pl. Hmptn—66Ca 121
Templars Av. NW11—30Bb 41
Templars Cres. N3—26Cb 41
Templars Dri. Harr—23Fa 38
Templars Ho. E15—36Dc 64
Templar St. SE5—54Rb 105
Temple Av. EC4—45Qb 82 (4A 200)
Temple Av. N20—17Fb 23
Temple Av. Croy—75Bc 148
Temple Av. Dag—32Cd 68
Temple Bar Rd. Wok—7C 188
Temple Clo. N3—26Bb 41
Temple Clo. Wal X—3Wb 11
Temple Clo. Wat—12V 18
Templecombe Rd. E9—39Yb 64
Templecombe Way. Mord —71Ab 144
Templecroft. Ashf—65T 120
Templedene Av. Stai—66K 119
Temple Field Clo. Wey—79K 139
Temple Fortune Hill. NW11 —29Cb 41
Temple Fortune La. NW11 —30Cb 41
Temple Fortune Pde. NW11 —29Bb 41
Temple Gdns. N21—19Rb 25
Temple Gdns. NW11—30Bb 41
Temple Gdns. Dag—34Zc 67
Temple Gdns. Rick—21R 36
Temple Gdns. Stai—67H 119
Temple Gro. NW11—30Cb 41
Temple Gro. Enf—13Rb 25
Temple Hall Ct. E4—19Fc 27
Temple Hill. Dart—58Pd 111
Temple Hill Sq. Dart—57Pd 111
Templehof Av. NW4—31Ya 60
Temple La. EC4—44Qb 82 (3A 200)
Templeman Clo. Purl—88Rb 165
Templeman Rd. W7—43Ha 78
Templemead Clo. W3—44Ua 80
Temple Mead Clo. Stan—23Ka 38
Templemere. Wey—76T 140
Temple Mills La. E15—35Dc 64
Temple Mills Rd. E15—35Cc 64
Templepan La. Rick—9N 3
Temple Pk. Uxb—41Q 76
Temple Pl. WC2—45Pb 82 (4J 199)
Templer Av. Grays—9C 92
Temple Rd. E6—39Nc 66
Temple Rd. N8—28Pb 42
Temple Rd. NW2—35Ya 60
Temple Rd. W4—48Sa 79
Temple Rd. W5—48Ma 79
Temple Rd. Croy—77Tb 147
Temple Rd. Eps—84Ta 161
Temple Rd. Houn—56Da 99
Temple Rd. Rich—54Pa 101
Temple Rd. West—89Mc 167
Temple Rd. Wind—4G 94
Temple Sheen. SW14—57Sa 101
Temple Sheen Rd. SW14 —56Ra 101
Temple St. E2—40Xb 63
Templeton Av. E4—21Cc 44
Templeton Clo. N15—30Tb 43
Templeton Clo. N16—36Ub 63
Templeton Clo. SE19—67Tb 127
Templeton Pl. SW5—49Cb 81
Templeton Rd. N15—30Tb 43
Temple Way. Slou—6G 52
Temple Way. Sutt—76Fb 145
Temple W. M. SE11—(4B 206)
Templewood. W13—43Ka 78
Templewood Av. NW3—34Db 61
Templewood Gdns. NW3—34Db 61
Templewood La. Slou—6G 52
Tempsford Av. Borwd—14Ta 21
Tempsford Clo. Enf—13Sb 25
Temsford Clo. Harr—26Ea 38
Ten Acre. Wok—6D 188
Ten Acre La. Egh—68E 118
Ten Acres. Lea—96Fa 176
Tenbury Clo. E7—36Mc 65
Tenbury Ct. SW2—60Mb 104
Tenby Av. Harr—26Ka 38
Tenby Clo. N15—28Vb 43
Tenby Clo. Romf—30Ad 47
Tenby Gdns. N'holt—37Ca 57
Tenby Rd. E17—29Ac 44
Tenby Rd. Edgw—25Pa 39
Tenby Rd. Enf—14Yb 26
Tenby Rd. Romf—30Ad 47
Tenby Rd. Well—53Zc 109
Tench St. E1—46Xb 83
Tenda Rd. SE16—49Xb 83
Tendring Way. Romf—29Yc 47
Tenham Av. SW2—61Mb 126
Tenison Ct. W1—45Lb 82 (4B 198)
Tenison Way. SE1 —46Qb 82 (7J 199)
Tenniel Clo. W2—45Eb 81
Tennis Ct. La. Th Dit—70Ha 122
Tennison Av. Borwd—15Ra 21
Tennison Clo. Coul—92Rb 181
Tennison Rd. SE25—70Vb 127
Tennis St. SE1—47Tb 83 (1F 207)
Tenniswood Rd. Enf—11Ub 25
Tennyson Av. E11—31Jc 65
Tennyson Av. E12—38Nc 66
Tennyson Av. NW9—27Sa 39

Tennyson Av.—Tithe Clo.

Tennyson Av. Grays—48De 91
Tennyson Av. N Mald—71Xa 144
Tennyson Av. Twic—60Ha 100
Tennyson Av. Wal A—6Gc 13
Tennyson Clo. Felt—58V 98
Tennyson Clo. Well—53Uc 108
Tennyson Rd. E10—32Dc 64
Tennyson Rd. E15—38Gc 65
Tennyson Rd. E17—30Bc 44
Tennyson Rd. NW6—39Bb 61
Tennyson Rd. NW7—22Wa 40
Tennyson Rd. SE20—66Zb 128
Tennyson Rd. SW19—65Eb 125
Tennyson Rd. W7—45Ha 78
Tennyson Rd. Ashf—64N 119
Tennyson Rd. Brtwd—17Ee 33
Tennyson Rd. Dart—57Qd 111
Tennyson Rd. Houn—54Ea 100
Tennyson Rd. Romf—24Ld 49
Tennyson Rd. Wey—77N 139
Tennyson St. SW8—54Kb 104
Tennyson Wlk. Grav—62Fe 135
Tennyson Wlk. Til—4D 114
Tennyson Way. Horn—32Hd 68
Tennyson Way. Slou—2C 72
Tensing Av. Grav—2A 136
Tensing Rd. S'hall—48Ca 77
Tentelow La. S'hall—50Ca 77
Tenterden Clo. NW4—27Za 40
Tenterden Clo. SE9—63Pc 130
Tenterden Dri. NW4—27Za 40
Tenterden Gdns. NW4—27Za 40
Tenterden Gdns. Croy—73Wb 147
Tenterden Gro. NW4—27Za 40
Tenterden Rd. N17—24Vb 43
Tenterden Rd. Croy—73Wb 147
Tenterden Rd. Dag—33Bd 67
Tenterden St. W1
—44Kb 82 (3A 198)
Tenter Ground. E1
—43Vb 83 (1K 201)
Tent St. E1—42Xb 83
Terborch Way. SE22—57Ub 105
Tercel Path. Chig—21Xc 47
Terence Clo. Grav—1H 137
Teresa Wlk. N10—29Kb 42
Terling Clo. E11—34Hc 65
Terling Rd. Dag—33Cd 68
Terlings, The. Brtwd—20Wd 32
Terminus Pl. SW1
—48Kb 82 (4A 204)
Tern Gdns. Upm—32Ud 70
Tern Way. Brtwd—21Ud 50
Terrace Gdns. SW13—54Va 102
Terrace Gdns. Wat—12X 19
Terrace La. Rich—58Na 101
Terrace Rd. E9—38Zb 64
Terrace Rd. E13—39Jc 65
Terrace Rd. W on T—73W 140
Terrace St. Grav—8D 114
(in two parts)
Terrace, The. EC4—(3A 200)
Terrace, The. N3—26Bb 41
Terrace, The. NW6—39Cb 61
Terrace, The. SE8—49Bc 84
Terrace, The. SW1
—47Nb 82 (2G 205)
Terrace, The. SW13—54Ua 102
Terrace, The. Asc—10B 116
Terrace, The. Grav—8D 114
(in two parts)
Terrace, The. Sev—94Fd 186
Terrace, The. Wey—78N 139
Terrace, The. Wfd G—23Jc 45
Terrace Wlk. Dag—36Ad 67
Terrapin Rd. SW17—62Kb 126
Terretts Pl. N1—38Rb 63
Terrick Rd. N22—25Nb 42
Terrick St. W12—44Xa 80
Terrilands. Pinn—27Ba 37
Terront Rd. N15—28Sb 43
★Terry's Lodge Rd. Sev—86Xd
Testerton Wlk. W11—45Za 80
Testwood Rd. Wind—3B 94
Tetbury Pl. N1—39Rb 63 (1B 194)
Tetcott Rd. SW10—52Eb 103
Tetherdown. N10—26Jb 42
Tetterby Way. SE16—50Wb 83
Tetty Way. Brom—68Jc 129
Teversham La. SW8—53Nb 104
Teviot Av. S Ock—44Sd 90
Teviot Clo. Well—53Xc 109
Teviot St. E14—43Ec 84
Tewkesbury Av. SE23—59Xb 105
Tewkesbury Av. Pinn—29Aa 37
Tewkesbury Clo. N15—30Tb 43
Tewkesbury Clo. Wey—83M 157
Tewkesbury Gdns. NW9—27Ra 39
Tewkesbury Rd. N15—30Tb 43
Tewkesbury Rd. W13—46Ja 78
Tewkesbury Rd. Cars—74Fb 145
Tewkesbury Ter. N11—23Lb 42
Tewson Rd. SE18—50Uc 86
Teynham Av. Enf—16Tb 25
Teynham Grn. Brom—71Jc 149
Teynton Ter. N17—25Sb 43
Thackeray Av. N17—26Wb 43
Thackeray Av. Til—3D 114
Thackeray Clo. SW19—66Za 124
Thackeray Clo. Harr—32Ca 57
Thackeray Clo. Uxb—44R 76
Thackeray Dri. Romf—31Wc 67
Thackeray Rd. E6—40Mc 65
Thackeray Rd. SW8—54Kb 104
Thackeray St. W8—48Db 81
Thakeham Clo. SE26—64Xb 127
Thalia Clo. SE10—51Fc 107
Thalmassing Clo. Brtwd—19De 33
Thames Av. Dag—42Dd 88
Thames Av. Gnfd—40Ha 58
Thames Av. Wind—2H 95
Thames Bank. SW14—54Sa 101
Thames Clo. Cher—73L 139
Thames Clo. Hmptn—68Da 121
Thames Clo. Rain—44Kd 89
Thames Clo. Stanf—1P 93
Thames Dri. Grays—10C 92
Thames Dri. Ruis—30S 36
Thamesfield Ct. Shep—73S 140
Thamesfield M. Shep—73S 140
Thamesgate Clo. Rich—63Ka 122
Thameshill Av. Romf—26Ed 48
Thameside. Tedd—66Ma 123
Thameside Industrial Est. E16
—47Mc 85
Thamesmead. W on T—73W 140
Thames Mead. Wind—3C 94
Thames Meadow. E Mol
—68Ca 121
Thames Pl. E14—45Bc 84
Thames Rd. E16—46Mc 85
Thames Rd. W4—51Qa 101
Thames Rd. Bark—41Vc 87
Thames Rd. Dart—54Hd 110
Thames Rd. Grays—52De 113
Thames Rd. Slou—49C 74
Thames Side. King—67Ma 123
Thames Side. Stai & Cher
—70L 119
Thames Side. Wind—2H 95
Thames St. SE10—51Dc 106
Thames St. Hmptn—68Da 121
Thames St. King—68Ma 123
Thames St. Shep—75R 140
Thames St. Stai—64H 119
Thames St. Sun—70X 121
Thames St. W on T—73V 140
Thames St. Wind—2H 95
Thamesvale Clo. Houn—54Ca 99
Thames View. Grays—10C 92
Thames Village. W4—53Sa 101
Thanescroft Gdns. Croy
—76Ub 147
Thanet Dri. Kes—76Mc 149
Thanet Pl. Croy—77Sb 147
Thanet Rd. Bex—59Cd 110
Thanet Rd. Eri—52Gd 110
Thanet St. WC1—41Nb 82 (4F 193)
Thane Vs. N7—34Pb 62
Tharp Rd. Wall—78Mb 146
Thatcham Gdns. N20—17Eb 23
Thatcher Clo. W Dray—47N 75
Thatcher Ct. Dart—59Md 111
Thatchers Clo. Lou—12Sc 28
Thatchers Way. Iswth—57Fa 100
Thatches Gro. Romf—28Ad 47
Thavies Inn. EC1
—44Qb 82 (2A 200)
Thaxted Ho. Dag—38Dd 68
Thaxted Pl. SW20—66Za 124
Thaxted Rd. SE9—61Sc 130
Thaxted Rd. Buck H—17Nc 28
Thaxted Wlk. Rain—38Gd 68
Thaxted Way. Wal A—5Fc 13
Thaxton Rd. W14—51Bb 103
Thayers Farm Rd. Beck—67Ac 128
Thayer St. W1—44Jb 82 (1J 197)
Thaynesfield. Pot B—3Fb 9
Theatre St. SW11—55Hb 103
Theberton St. N1—39Qb 62
Theed St. SE1—46Qb 82 (7A 200)
Thelma Clo. Grav—4H 137
Thelma Gdns. SE3—53Mc 107
Thelma Gro. Tedd—65Ja 122
Thelusson Ct. Rad—7Ja 6
Theobald Cres. Harr—25Ea 38
Theobald Rd. E17—31Cc 64
Theobald Rd. Croy—75Rb 147
Theobalds Av. N12—21Eb 41
Theobalds Av. Grays—50Ee 91
Theobalds Clo. Pot B—2Pb 10
Theobalds La. Wal X—4Xb 11
Theobalds Pk. Rd. Enf—7Rb 11
Theobald's Rd. WC1
—43Pb 82 (7H 193)
Theobalds Rd. Pot B—2Nb 10
Theobald St. SE1—(4F 207)
Theobald St. Rad & Borwd—8Ka 6
Theodore Rd. SE13—58Fc 107
Therapia La. Croy—73Mb 146
(in two parts)
Therapia Rd. SE22—58Yb 106
Theresa Rd. W6—49Wa 80
Theresa's Wlk. S Croy—81Tb 165
Thermopylae Ga. E14—49Dc 84
Theseus Wlk. N1—(2C 194)
Thesiger Rd. SE20—66Zb 128
Thessaly Rd. SW8—52Lb 104
Thetford Clo. N13—23Rb 43
Thetford Gdns. Dag—38Ad 67
Thetford Rd. Ashf—62N 119
Thetford Rd. Dag—38Zc 67
Thetford Rd. N Mald—72Ta 143
Thetis Ter. Rich—51Qa 101
(in two parts)
Theydon Ct. Wal A—5Jc 13
Theydon Gdns. Rain—38Gd 68
Theydon Gro. Epp—2Wc 15
Theydon Gro. Wfd G—23Lc 45
Theydon Mt. Epp—6Bd 15
Theydon Pk. Rd. Epp—9Uc 14
Theydon Pl. Epp—3Vc 15
Theydon Rd. E5—33Yb 64
Theydon Rd. Epp—6Tc 14
Theydon St. E17—31Bc 64
Thicket Cres. Sutt—77Eb 145
Thicket Gro. Dag—37Yc 67
Thicket Rd. SE20—66Wb 127
Thicket Rd. Sutt—77Eb 145
Thicket, The. W Dray—44N 75
Thickthorne La. Stai—66L 119
Third Av. E12—35Nc 66
Third Av. E13—41Jc 85
Third Av. E17—29Cc 44
Third Av. W3—46Va 80
Third Av. W10—41Ab 80
Third Av. Cher—74L 139
Third Av. Dag—39Dd 68
Third Av. Enf—15Vb 25
Third Av. Grays—51Wd 112
Third Av. Hay—46V 76
Third Av. Romf—30Yc 47
Third Av. Wat—7Z 5
Third Av. Wemb—33Ma 59
Third Clo. E Mol—70Ea 122
Third Cres. Slou—3G 72
Third Cross Rd. Twic—61Fa 122
Third Way. Wemb—35Ra 59
Thirkleby Clo. Slou—6G 72
Thirleby Rd. SW1
—48Lb 82 (4C 204)
Thirleby Rd. Edgw—25Ta 39
Thirlmere Av. Gnfd—41La 78
Thirlmere Av. Slou—3A 72
Thirlmere Gdns. N'wd—22R 36
Thirlmere Gdns. Wemb—32La 58
Thirlmere Rise. Brom—65Hc 129
Thirlmere Rd. N10—25Kb 42
Thirlmere Rd. SW16—63Mb 126
Thirlmere Rd. Bexh—53Ed 110
Thirsk Clo. N'holt—37Ca 57
Thirsk Rd. SE25—70Tb 127
Thirsk Rd. SW11—55Jb 104
Thirsk Rd. Borwd—9Qa 7
Thirsk Rd. Mitc—66Jb 126
Thirza Rd. Dart—58Pd 111
Thistlebrook. SE2—47Yc 87
Thistlecroft Gdns. Stan—26Ma 39
Thistlecroft Rd. W on T—77Y 141
Thistledene. Th Dit—72Ga 142
Thistledene. Wey—85H 157
Thistledene Av. Harr—34Aa 57
Thistledene Av. Romf—22Dd 48
Thistledown. Grav—5F 136
Thistle Gro. SW10
—50Eb 81 (7A 202)
Thistlemead. Chst—68Rc 130
Thistle Mead. Lou—13Qc 28
Thistle Rd. Grav—9G 114
Thistlewaite Rd. E5—34Xb 63
Thistlewood Clo. N7—33Pb 62
Thistlewood Cres. Croy—84Fc 167
Thistleworth Clo. Iswth—52Fa 100
Thoby La. Brtwd—11Ee 33
Thomas a' Beckett Clo. Wemb
—35Ha 58
Thomas Av. Cat—93Sb 181
Thomas Baines Rd. SW11
—55Fb 103
Thomas Bata Av. Grays—9K 93
Thomas Clo. Brtwd—19Ae 33
Thomas Doyle St. SE1
—48Rb 83 (3C 206)
Thomas Dri. Grav—1F 136
Thomas La. SE6—59Cc 106
Thomas More Ho. EC2—(1D 200)
Thomas More St. E1—46Wb 83
Thomas More Way. N2—27Eb 41
Thomas Rd. E14—44Bc 84
Thomas Sims Ct. Horn—36Kd 69
Thomas St. SE18—49Rc 86
★Thomas Wyatt Way. Sev—88Be
Thompkins La. Slou—8E 52
Thompson Av. Rich—55Qa 101
Thompson Clo. Slou—49C 74
Thompson Rd. SE22—58Vb 105
Thompson Rd. Dag—34Bd 67
Thompson Rd. Uxb—38N 55
Thompson's Av. SE5—52Sb 105
Thompson's La. Lou—10Jc 13
Thompson Way. Ilf—33Sc 66
Thomson Cres. Croy—74Qb 146
Thomson Ho. SW1—(7E 204)
Thomson Rd. Harr—27Ga 38
Thong La. Grav—3H 137
Thorburn Sq. SE1—49Wb 83
Thorburn Way. SW19—67Fb 125
Thoresby St. N1—41Sb 83 (3E 194)
Thorkhill Gdns. Th Dit—74Ja 142
Thorkhill Rd. Th Dit—74Ja 142
Thorley Clo. Wey—86J 157
Thorley Gdns. Wey—86J 157
Thorley Rd. Grays—46Ce 91
Thornaby Gdns. N18—22Wb 43
Thornash Clo. Wok—3F 188
Thornash Rd. Wok—3F 188
Thornash Way. Wok—3F 188
Thorn Av. Bush, Wat—18Ea 20
Thornbank Clo. Stai—57J 97
Thornbridge Rd. Iver—39E 54
Thornbury Av. Iswth—52Fa 100
Thornbury Gdns. Borwd—14Sa 21
Thornbury Rd. SW2—58Nb 104
Thornbury Rd. Iswth—52Fa 100
Thornby Rd. E5—34Yb 64
Thorncliffe Rd. SW2—58Nb 104
Thorncliffe Rd. S'hall—50Ba 77
Thorn Clo. Brom—72Qc 150
Thorn Clo. N'holt—41Ba 77
Thorncombe Rd. SE22—57Ub 105
Thorncroft. Horn—30Kd 49
Thorncroft Clo. Coul—91Qb 180
Thorncroft Dri. Lea—95Ka 176
Thorncroft Rd. Sutt—78Db 145
Thorncroft St. SW8—52Nb 104
Thorndales. Brtwd—21Zd 51
Thorndean St. SW18—61Eb 125
Thorndene. SE28—45Yc 87
Thorndene Av. N11—18Jb 24
Thorndike. Slou—3E 72
Thorndike Av. N'holt—39Z 57
Thorndike Clo. SW10—52Eb 103
Thorndike St. SW1—(6D 204)
Thorndon App. Brtwd—24Fe 51
Thorndon Av. Brtwd—29Ee 51
Thorndon Clo. Orp—68Vc 131
Thorndon Gdns. Eps—78Ua 144
Thorndon Ga. Brtwd—22Ee 51
Thorndon Rd. Orp—68Vc 131
★Thorndyke. Sev—88Be
Thorndyke Ct. Pinn—24Ba 37
Thorne Clo. E11—35Gc 65
Thorne Clo. E16—44Jc 85
Thorne Clo. Ashf—66S 120
Thorne Clo. Eri—51Dd 110
Thorne Clo. N Mald—70Sa 123
Thorneloe Gdns. Croy—78Qb 146
Thorne Pas. SW13—54Ua 102
Thorne Rd. SW8—52Nb 104
Thorne Rd. N Mald—70Sa 123
Thornes Clo. Beck—69Ec 128
Thorne St. SW13—55Ua 102
Thornet Wood Rd. Brom
—69Qc 130
Thorney Cres. SW11—52Fb 103
Thorney Hedge Rd. W4—49Ra 79
Thorney La. N. Iver—44H 75
Thorney La. S. Iver—47H 75
Thorney Mill Rd. Iver & W Dray
—48J 75
Thorney St. SW1
—49Nb 82 (5F 205)
Thornfield Av. NW7—25Ab 40
Thornfield Rd. W12—47Xa 80
Thornfield Rd. Bans—89Cb 163
Thornford Rd. SE13—57Ec 106
Thorngate Rd. W9—42Cb 81
Thorngrove Rd. E13—39Kc 65
Thornham Gro. E15—36Fc 65
Thornham St. SE10—51Dc 106
Thornhaugh M. WC1
—42Mb 82 (6E 192)
Thornhaugh St. WC1
—42Mb 82 (6E 192)
Thornhill Av. SE18—52Uc 108
Thornhill Av. Surb—75Na 143
Thornhill Cres. N1—38Pb 62
Thornhill Gdns. E10—33Dc 64
Thornhill Gdns. Bark—38Uc 66
Thornhill Gro. N1—38Pb 62
Thornhill Rd. E10—33Dc 64
Thornhill Rd. N1—38Qb 62
Thornhill Rd. Croy—73Sb 147
Thornhill Rd. N'wd—21S 36
Thornhill Rd. Surb—75Na 143
Thornhill Rd. Uxb—35P 55
Thornhill Sq. N1—38Pb 62
Thornhill Way. Shep—71Q 140
Thorn La. Rain—40Md 69
Thornlaw Rd. SE27—63Qb 126
Thornley Clo. N17—24Xb 43
Thornley Dri. Harr—33Da 57
Thornley Pl. SE10—50Gc 85
Thornridge. Brtwd—18Xd 32
Thornsbeach Rd. SE6—60Ec 106
Thornsett Pl. SE20—68Xb 127
Thornsett Rd. SE20—68Xb 127
Thornsett Rd. SW18—60Db 103
Thorns Meadow. West—95Yc 185
Thorns, The. Brtwd—11Ud 32
Thornton Av. SW2—60Mb 104
Thornton Av. W4—49Ua 80
Thornton Av. Croy—72Pb 146
Thornton Av. W Dray—48P 75
Thornton Clo. W Dray—48P 75
Thornton Cres. Coul—91Qb 180
Thornton Dene. Beck—68Cc 128
Thornton Gdns. SW12—60Mb 104
Thornton Gro. Pinn—23Ca 37
Thornton Hill. SW19—66Ab 124
Thornton Pl. W1—43Hb 81 (7G 191)
Thornton Rd. E11—33Fc 65
Thornton Rd. SW12—59Mb 104
Thornton Rd. SW14—56Ta 101
Thornton Rd. SW19—65Za 124
Thornton Rd. Barn—13Ab 22
Thornton Rd. Belv—49Dd 88
Thornton Rd. Brom—64Jc 129
Thornton Rd. Cars—74Fb 145
Thornton Rd. Croy & T Hth
—72Pb 146
Thornton Rd. Ilf—35Rc 66
Thornton Rd. Pot B—2Eb 9
Thornton Rd. E. SW19—65Za 124
Thornton Row. T Hth—71Qb 146
Thornton's Farm Av. Romf
—32Fd 68
Thornton St. SW9—54Qb 104
Thornton Way. NW11—29Db 41
Thorntree Rd. SE7—50Mc 85
Thornville St. SE8—53Cc 106
Thornwood Clo. E18—26Kc 45
Thornwood Rd. SE13—57Gc 107
Thornwood Rd. Epp—1Xc 15
Thorogood Gdns. E15—36Gc 65
Thorogood Way. Rain—39Gd 68
Thorold Clo. S Croy—82Zb 166
Thorold Rd. N22—24Nb 42
Thorold Rd. Ilf—33Rc 66
Thoroughfare, The. Tad
—96Wa 178
Thorparch Rd. SW8—53Mb 104
Thorpebank Rd. W12—46Wa 80
Thorpe By-Pass. Egh—68D 118
Thorpe Clo. W10—44Ab 80
Thorpe Clo. Croy—83Ec 166
Thorpe Clo. Orp—75Uc 150
Thorpe Cres. E17—26Bc 44
Thorpe Cres. Wat—17Y 19
Thorpedale Gdns. Ilf—28Qc 46
Thorpedale Rd. N4—32Nb 62
Thorpe Hall Rd. E17—25Ec 44
Thorpe Industrial Est. Egh
—67E 118
Thorpe Lea Rd. Egh—65D 118
Thorpe Lodge. Horn—31Md 69
Thorpe Rd. E6—39Pc 66
Thorpe Rd. E7—35Hc 65
Thorpe Rd. E17—26Ec 44
Thorpe Rd. N15—30Ub 43
Thorpe Rd. Bark—38Tc 66
Thorpe Rd. Cher—71F 138
Thorpe Rd. King—66Na 123
Thorpe Rd. Stai—64F 118
Thorpewood Av. SE26—61Xb 127
Thorpland Av. Uxb—34S 56
Thorsden Clo. Wok—91A 172
Thorsden Ct. Wok—90A 156
Thorsden Way. SE19—64Ub 127
Thors Oak. Stanf—1N 93
Thorverton Rd. NW2—34Ab 60
Thoydon Rd. E3—40Ac 64
Thrale Rd. SW16—64Lb 126
Thrale St. SE1—46Sb 83 (7E 200)
Thrawl St. E1—43Vb 83 (1K 201)
Threadneedle St. EC2
—44Tb 83 (3G 201)
Three Colts La. E2—42Xb 83
Three Colt St. E14—44Bc 84
Three Corners. Bexh—54Dd 110
Three Cups Yd. WC1—(1J 199)
Three Gates Rd. Long, Dart
—74Wd 154
Three Kings Rd. Mitc—69Jb 126
Three Kings Yd. W1
—45Kb 82 (4K 197)
Three Mill La. E3—41Ec 84
Three Oak La. SE1
—47Vb 83 (1K 207)
Three Oaks Clo. Uxb—34P 55
Three Tuns Ct. SE1—(7F 201)
Threshers Pl. W11—45Ab 80
Thriffwood. SE23—62Zb 128
Thrift Farm La. Borwd—12Sa 21
Thrift Grn. Brtwd—20Ce 33
Thrifts Mead. Epp—9Uc 14
Thrift, The. Dart—62Yd 134
Thrigby Rd. Chess—79Pa 143
Thrisk Rd. SW11—55Jb 104
Throckmorten Rd. E16—44Kc 85
Throgmorton Av. EC2
—44Tb 83 (2G 201)
Throgmorton St. EC2
—44Tb 83 (2G 201)
Throwley Clo. SE2—48Yc 87
(in two parts)
Throwley Rd. Sutt—78Db 145
Throwley Way. Sutt—77Db 145
Thrums, The. Wat—9X 5
Thrupp Clo. Mitc—68Kb 126
Thrupp's Av. W on T—78Z 141
Thrupp's La. W on T—78Z 141
Thrush Grn. Rick—17L 17
Thrush St. SE17—50Sb 83 (7D 206)
Thruxton Way. SE15—52Vb 105
Thurbarn Rd. SE6—64Dc 128
Thurland Rd. SE16—48Wb 83
Thurlby Clo. Harr—30Ja 38
Thurlby Clo. Wfd G—22Pc 46
Thurlby Rd. SE27—63Qb 126
Thurlby Rd. Wemb—37Ma 59
Thurleigh Av. SW12—58Jb 104
Thurleigh Rd. SW12—58Hb 103
Thurleston Av. Mord—71Ab 144
Thurlestone Av. N12—23Hb 41
Thurlestone Av. Ilf—35Vc 67
Thurlestone Rd. SE27—63Qb 126
Thurloe Clo. SW7
—49Gb 81 (5D 202)
Thurloe Gdns. Romf—30Hd 48
Thurloe Pl. SW7—49Fb 81 (5C 202)
Thurloe Pl. M. SW7—(5C 202)
Thurloe Sq. SW7
—49Gb 81 (5D 202)
Thurloe St. SW7—49Fb 81 (5C 202)
Thurloe Wlk. Grays—48Ce 91
Thurlow Gdns. Ilf—23Tc 46
Thurlow Gdns. Wemb—36Ma 59
Thurlow Hill. SE21—60Sb 105
Thurlow Pk. Rd. SE21—61Rb 127
Thurlow Rd. NW3—36Fb 61
Thurlow Rd. W7—47Ja 78
Thurlow St. SE17
—50Tb 83 (7G 207)
Thurlow Ter. NW5—37Hb 61
Thurlow Wlk. SE17—50Ub 83
Thurlstone Clo. Shep—72S 140
Thurlston Rd. Ruis—34W 56
Thurlton Ct. Wok—88A 156
Thurrock Pk. Way. Til—53Fe 113
Thursby Rd. Wok—6D 188
Thursland Rd. Sidc—64Ad 131
Thursley Cres. Croy—80Fc 149
Thursley Gdns. SW19—61Za 124
Thursley Rd. SE9—62Pc 130
Thurso Clo. Romf—23Rd 49
Thurso St. SW17—63Fb 125
Thurstan Rd. SW20—66Xa 124
Thurston Path. Borwd—12Qa 21
Thurston Rd. SE13—54Dc 106
Thurston Rd. Slou—4J 73
Thurston Rd. S'hall—44Ba 77
Thurtle Rd. E2—40Vb 63 (1K 195)
Thwaite Clo. Eri—51Ed 110
Thyer Clo. Orp—77Sc 150
Thyra Gro. N12—23Db 41
Tibbatts Rd. E3—42Dc 84
Tibbenham Wlk. E13—40Hc 65
Tibberton Sq. N1—38Sb 63
Tibbet's Clo. SW19—60Za 102
Tibbet's Corner. SW19—60Za 102
Tibbet's Ride. SW15—59Za 102
Tibbles Clo. Wat—7Aa 5
Tibbs Hill Rd. Abb L, Wat—2V 4
Ticehurst Rd. SE23—61Ac 128
Tichmarsh. Eps—83Sa 161
Tickford Clo. SE2—47Yc 87
Tidal Basin Rd. E16—45Hc 85
Tidenham Gdns. Croy—76Ub 147
Tideswell Rd. SW15—56Va 102
Tideswell Rd. Croy—76Cc 148
Tideway Clo. Rich—63Ka 122
Tideway Wlk. SW8—51Lb 104
Tidey St. E3—43Cc 84
Tidford Rd. Well—54Vc 109
Tidworth Rd. E3—42Cc 84
Tidy's La. Epp—1Xc 15
Tiepigs La. W Wick—75Gc 149
Tierney Ct. Croy—75Vb 147
Tierney Rd. SW2—60Nb 104
Tiger Bay. SE16—48Zb 84
Tiger La. Brom—70Kc 129
Tiger Way. E5—35Xb 63
Tilbrook Rd. SE3—55Lc 107
Tilbury Clo. SE15—52Vb 105
Tilbury Clo. Orp—68Xc 131
Tilbury Gdns. Til—6C 114
Tilbury Hotel Rd. Til—6C 114
Tilbury Rd. E6—40Pc 66
Tilbury Rd. E10—31Ec 64
Tildesley Rd. SW15—58Ya 102
Tile Farm Rd. Orp—76Tc 150
Tilehouse La. Rick & Uxb—26G 34
Tilehouse Way. Uxb—31H 55
Tilehurst Rd. SW18—60Fb 103
Tilehurst Rd. Sutt—78Ab 144
Tile Kiln La. N6—32Lb 62
Tile Kiln La. N13—22Sb 43
Tile Kiln La. Bex—61Ed 132
Tile Kiln La. Dart—62Gd 132
Tile Kiln La. Uxb—31R 56
Tile Kiln Studios. N6—32Lb 62
Tile Yd. E14—44Bc 84
Tileyard Rd. N7—38Nb 62
Tilford Av. Croy—81Ec 166
Tilford Gdns. SW19—60Za 102
Tilia Rd. E5—35Xb 63
Till Av. F'ham, Dart—73Pd 153
Tiller Rd. E14—48Cc 84
Tillet Clo. NW10—37Sa 59
Tillet Way. E2—41Wb 83
Tilley La. Eps—95Sa 177
Tillingbourne Gdns. N3—27Bb 41
Tillingbourne Grn. Orp—70Wc 131
Tillingbourne Way. N3—28Bb 41
Tillingdown Hill. Cat—94Wb 181
(in two parts)
Tillingdown La. Cat—96Xb 181
Tillingdown La. Cat—97Xb 181
Tillingham Ct. Wal A—5Jc 13
Tillingham Way. N12—21Cb 41
Tilling Rd. NW4—32Ya 60
Tillman St. E1—44Xb 83
Tilloch St. N1—38Pb 62
Tillotson Rd. N9—19Vb 25
Tillotson Rd. Harr—24Da 37
Tillotson Rd. Ilf—31Qc 66
Tillys La. Stai—63H 119
Tilmans Mead. F'ham, Dart
—73Qd 153
Tilney Ct. EC1—42Sb 83 (5E 194)
Tilney Dri. Buck H—19Jc 27
Tilney Gdns. N1—37Tb 63
Tilney Rd. Dag—37Bd 67
Tilney Rd. S'hall—49Y 77
Tilney St. W1—46Jb 82 (6J 197)
Tilson Gdns. SW2—59Nb 104
Tilson Rd. N17—25Wb 43
Tilstone Av. Wind—10C 72
Tilstone Clo. Wind—10C 72
Tilt Clo. Cob—88Aa 159
Tilt Meadow. Cob—88Aa 159
★Tilton Rd. Sev—92Be
Tilton St. SW6—51Ab 102
Tilt Rd. Cob—87Z 159
Tiltwood, The. W3—45Sa 79
Tilt Yd. App. SE9—58Pc 108
Timber Clo. Chst—68Qc 130
Timber Clo. Lea—99Ea 176
Timbercroft. Eps—77Ua 144
Timbercroft La. SE18—51Uc 108
Timberdene. NW4—26Za 40
Timberhill. Asht—91Na 177
Timber Hill. Cat—96Wb 181
Timberland Rd. E1—44Xb 83
Timberling Gdns. S Croy
—82Tb 165
Timbermill Way. SW4—55Mb 104
Timberslip Dri. Wall—81Mb 164
Timber St. EC1—42Sb 83 (5D 194)
Timbertop Rd. West—90Lc 167
Timberwharf Rd. N16—30Wb 43
Times Sq. Sutt—78Db 145
Timsbury Wlk. SW15—60Wa 102
Timsway. Stai—64H 119
Tindale Clo. S Croy—83Tb 165
Tindall Clo. Romf—26Pd 49
Tindal St. SW9—53Rb 105
Tinderbox All. SW14—55Ta 101
Tine Rd. Chig—22Uc 46
Tinker Pot La. Sev—86Rd 171
★Tinker Pot La. Sev—85Ud
Tinkers La. Wind—4B 94
Tinsley Rd. E1—43Yb 84
Tintagel Clo. Eps—86Va 162
Tintagel Cres. SE22—56Vb 105
Tintagel Dri. Stan—21Ma 39
Tintagel Rd. Orp—75Yc 151
Tintells La. Lea—100R 174
Tintern Av. NW9—27Ra 39
Tintern Clo. SW15—57Ab 102
Tintern Clo. SW19—65Eb 125
Tintern Clo. Slou—8G 72
Tintern Gdns. N14—17Nb 24
Tintern Rd. N22—25Sb 43
Tintern Rd. Cars—74Fb 145
Tintern St. SW4—56Nb 104
Tintern Way. Harr—32Da 57
Tinto Rd. E16—42Jc 85
Tinworth St. SE11
—50Nb 82 (7G 205)
Tippetts Clo. Enf—11Sb 25
★Tipps Cross La. Brtwd—6Xd
★Tipps Cross Mead. Brtwd—7Xd
Tipthorpe Rd. SW11—55Jb 104
Tipton Dri. Croy—77Ub 147
Tiptree Clo. E4—20Ec 26
Tiptree Clo. Horn—32Qd 69
Tiptree Cres. Ilf—27Qc 46
Tiptree Dri. Enf—14Tb 25
Tiptree Rd. Ruis—35X 57
Tirlemont Rd. S Croy—80Sb 147
Tirrell Rd. Croy—72Sb 147
Tisbury Ct. W1—(4D 198)
Tisbury Rd. SW16—68Nb 126
Titan Rd. Grays—50Ce 91
Titchborne. Rick—22F 34
Titchborne Row. W2
—44Gb 81 (3D 196)
Titchfield Rd. NW8
—40Hb 61 (1F 191)
Titchfield Rd. Cars—74Fb 145
Titchfield Rd. Enf—9Ac 12
Titchfield Wlk. Cars—73Fb 145
Titchwell Rd. SW18—60Fb 103
Tite Hill. Egh—64A 118
Tite Hill. Egh—4P 117
Tite St. SW3—51Hb 103
Tithe Barn Clo. King—67Pa 123
Tithebarns La. Wok—98J 173
Tithe Barn Way. N'holt—40X 57
Tithe Clo. NW7—25Wa 40

Tithe Ct.—Tudor Dri.

Tithe Ct. Slou—49C 74
Tithe Farm Av. Harr—34Ca 57
Tithe Farm Clo. Harr—34Ca 57
Tithe La. Wray, Stai—58C 96
Tithepit Shaw La. Warl—89Xb 165
Tithe Wlk. NW7—25Wa 40
Titian Av. Bush, Wat—17Ga 20
Titley Clo. E4—22Cc 44
Titmus Clo. Uxb—44S 76
Titmuss Av. SE28—45Xc 87
Titmuss St. W12—47Xa 80
Titsey Hill. Oxt—95Jc 183
Titsey Rd. Oxt—97Kc 183
Tiverton Av. Ilf—27Qc 46
Tiverton Dri. SE9—60Sc 108
Tiverton Gro. Romf—22Qd 49
Tiverton Rd. N15—30Tb 43
Tiverton Rd. N18—22Ub 43
Tiverton Rd. NW10—39Za 60
Tiverton Rd. Edgw—26Pa 39
Tiverton Rd. Houn—54Ea 100
Tiverton Rd. Pot B—4Fb 9
Tiverton Rd. Pot B—3Fb 9
Tiverton Rd. Ruis—34W 56
Tiverton Rd. T Hth—71Qb 146
Tiverton Rd. Wemb—40Na 59
Tiverton St. SE1—48Sb 83 (4D 206)
Tiverton Way. Chess—78Ma 143
Tivoli Gdns. SE18—49Nc 86
Tivoli Rd. N8—29Mb 42
Tivoli Rd. SE27—64Sb 127
Tivoli Rd. Houn—56Aa 99
Tobago St. E14—47Cc 84
Tobin Clo. NW3—38Gb 61
Toby La. E1—42Ac 84
Tockley Rd. Slou—1A 72
Todds Wlk. N7—33Pb 62
Toft Av. Grays—49Fe 91
Tokenhouse Yd. EC2
—44Tb 83 (2F 201)
Tokyngton Av. Wemb—37Qa 59
Toland Sq. SW15—57Wa 102
Tolcarne Dri. N'wd—26W 36
Toley Av. Wemb—31Na 59
Tolldene Clo. Wok—5B 188
Tollers La. Coul—90Pb 164
Tollesbury Gdns. Ilf—27Tc 46
Tollet St. E1—42Zb 84
★Tollgate. Sev—91Ce
Tollgate Clo. Rick—14H 17
Tollgate Dri. SE21—61Ub 127
Tollgate Gdns. NW6—40Db 61
Tollgate Rd.—43Lc 85
E16 1-153 & 2-130
E6 remainder
Tollgate Rd. Dart—59Td 112
Tollgate Rd. Wal X—7Zb 12
Tollhouse Way. N19—33Lb 62
Tollington Pk. N4—33Pb 62
Tollington Pl. N4—33Pb 62
Tollington Rd. N7—35Pb 62
Tollington Way. N7—34Nb 62
Tolmers Gdns. Pot B—1Pb 10
Tolmers Rd. Pot B—1Nb 10
Tolmers Sq. NW1
—42Lb 82 (5C 192)
Tolpits Clo. Wat—15V 18
Tolpits La. Wat—18S 18
Tolsford Rd. E5—36Xb 63
Tolson Rd. Iswth—55Ja 100
Tolverne Rd. SW20—67Ya 124
Tolworth Clo. Surb—74Ra 143
Tolworth Gdns. Romf—29Zc 47
Tolworth Pk. Rd. Surb—75Pa 143
Tolworth Rise. N. Surb—74Ra 143
Tolworth Rise. S. Surb—74Ra 143
Tolworth Rd. Surb—75Na 143
Tom Coombs Clo. SE9—56Nc 108
Tom Cribb Rd. SE28—48Sc 86
Tomkins Clo. Borwd—11Na 21
Tomkins Clo. Stanf—1L 93
Tomkyns La. Upm—26Td 50
Tomlin Rd. Slou—2C 72
Tomlins All. Twic—60Jc 107
Tomlin's Gro. E3—41Cc 84
Tomlinson Clo. E2
—41Vb 83 (4K 195)
Tomlinson Clo. W4—50Ra 79
Tomlins Orchard. Bark—39Sc 66
Tomlins Ter. E14—44Ac 84
Tomlins Wlk. N7—33Pb 62
Tomlyns Clo. Brtwd—16Fe 33
Tom Mann Clo. Bark—39Uc 66
Tompion St. EC1
—41Rb 83 (4C 194)
Tom's Hill. Rick—8N 3
Tom's La. K Lan & Abb L, Wat
—1R 4
Tom Smith Clo. SE10—51Gc 107
Tomswood Ct. Ilf—25Sc 46
Tomswood Hill. Ilf—24Rc 46
Tomswood Rd. Chig—23Qc 46
Tonbridge Clo. Bans—86Hb 163
Tonbridge Cres. Harr—28Na 39
Tonbridge Rd. E Mol—70Ba 121
Tonbridge Rd. Romf—24Md 49
Tonbridge Rd. Sev—99Ld 187
★Tonbridge Rd. Sev—96Yd
(Ightham)
Tonbridge St. WC1
—41Nb 82 (3F 193)
Tonbridge Wlk. WC1—(3F 193)
Tonfield Rd. Sutt—74Bb 145
Tonge Clo. Beck—71Cc 148
Tonsley Hill. SW18—57Db 103
Tonsley Pl. SW18—57Db 103
Tonsley Rd. SW18—57Db 103
Tonsley St. SW18—57Db 103
Tonstall Rd. Eps—82Ta 161
Tonstall Rd. Mitc—68Jb 126
Tony Law Ho. SE20—67Xb 127
Tooke Clo. Pinn—25Aa 37
Took's Ct. EC4—44Qb 82 (2K 199)
Tooley St. SE1
—46Ub 83 (6G 201)
Tooley St. Grav—59Fe 113
Toorack Rd. Harr—26Fa 38
Tooting Bec Gdns. SW16
(in two parts) —63Mb 126
Tooting Bec Rd. SW17 & SW16
—62Jb 126
Tooting B'way. SW17—64Hb 125
Tooting Gro. SW17—64Gb 125
Tooting High St. SW17—64Gb 125
Tootswood Rd. Brom—71Gc 149
Tooveys Mill Clo. K Lan—1Q 4
Topaz St. SE11—49Pb 82 (5J 205)
Topcliffe Dri. Orp—77Tc 150
Top Dartford Rd. Swan—66Hd 132
Topham Sq. N17—25Sb 43
Topham St. EC1—42Qb 82 (5K 193)
Top Ho. Rise. E4—17Ec 26
Topiary Sq. Rich—55Pa 101
Toplands Rd. S Ock—46Sd 90
Topley St. SE9—56Lc 107
Top Pk. Beck—71Gc 149
Top Pk. Ger X—1N 53
Topp Wlk. NW2—33Ya 60
Topsfield Rd. N8—29Nb 42
Topsham Rd. SW17—62Hb 125
Torbay Rd. NW6—38Bb 61
Torbay Rd. Harr—33Aa 57
Torbay St. NW1—38Kb 62
Torbridge Clo. Edgw—24Na 39
Torbrook Clo. Bex—58Ad 109
Torcross Dri. SE23—61Yb 128
Torcross Rd. Ruis—34X 57
Tor Gdns. W8—47Cb 81
Tor Ho. N6—30Kb 42
Torin Ct. Egh—4N 117
Torland Dri. Lea—85Fa 160
Tor La. Wey—83T 158
Tormead Clo. Sutt—79Cb 145
Tormount Rd. SE18—51Uc 108
Toronto Av. E12—35Pc 66
Toronto Rd. E11—35Fc 65
Toronto Rd. Ilf—32Rc 66
Toronto Rd. Til—4C 114
Torquay Gdns. Ilf—28Mc 45
Torquay St. W2—43Db 81
Torrance Clo. Horn—32Ld 69
Torrens Rd. E15—37Hc 65
Torrens Rd. SW2—57Pb 104
Torrens Sq. E15—37Hc 65
Torrens St. EC1—40Rb 63 (2B 194)
Torrens Wlk. Grav—4G 136
Torre Wlk. Cars—74Gb 145
Torriano Av. NW5—36Mb 62
Torriano Cotts. NW5—36Lb 62
Torricon Clo. Wok—5E 188
Torridge. Grays—9L 93
Torridge Gdns. SE15—56Yb 106
Torridge Rd. Slou—51D 96
Torridge Rd. T Hth—71Rb 147
Torridon Rd.—59Fc 107
SE13 1 & 3
SE6 remainder
Torrington Av. N12—22Fb 41
Torrington Clo. Esh—79Ga 142
Torrington Dri. Harr—34Da 57
Torrington Dri. Lou—14Sc 28
Torrington Dri. Pot B—4Fb 9
Torrington Dri. Pot B—3Fb 9
Torrington Gdns. N11—23Lb 42
Torrington Gdns. Gnfd—38La 58
Torrington Gdns. Lou—14Sc 28
Torrington Gro. N12—22Gb 41
Torrington Pk. N12—22Eb 41
Torrington Pl. WC1
—43Mb 82 (7D 192)
Torrington Rd. E18—27Jc 45
Torrington Rd. Dag—32Bd 67
Torrington Rd. Esh—79Ga 142
Torrington Rd. Gnfd—39La 58
Torrington Rd. Ruis—34V 56
Torrington Sq. WC1
—42Mb 82 (6E 192)
Torrington Way. Mord—72Cb 145
Tor Rd. Well—53Yc 109
Torr Rd. SE20—66Zb 128
Torver Rd. Harr—28Ga 38
Torver Way. Orp—76Tc 150
Torwood La. Whyt—92Vb 181
Torwood Rd. SW15—57Wa 102
Torworth Rd. Borwd—11Pa 21
Tothill St. SW1—47Mb 82 (2D 204)
Totnes Rd. Well—52Xc 109
Totnes Wlk. N2—28Fb 41
Tottenhall Rd. N13—23Qb 42
Tottenham Ct. Rd. W1
—42Lb 82 (6C 192)
Tottenham Grn. E. N15—28Vb 43
Tottenham Grn. E. S. Side. N15
—28Vb 43
Tottenham La. N8—29Nb 42
Tottenham M. W1
—43Lb 82 (7C 192)
Tottenham Rd. N1—37Ub 63
Tottenham St. W1
—43Lb 82 (7C 192)
Totterdown St. SW17—63Hb 125
Totteridge Comn. N20—19Wa 22
Totteridge Grn. N20—19Cb 23
Totteridge La. N20—19Cb 23
Totteridge Rd. Enf—9Zb 12
Totteridge Village. N20—18Ab 22
Totternhoe Clo. Harr—29La 38
Totton Rd. T Hth—69Qb 126
Totty St. E3—40Ac 64
Toulmin St. SE1—47Sb 83 (2D 206)
Toulon St. SE5—52Sb 105
Tournay Rd. SW6—52Bb 103
Toussaint Wlk. SE16—48Wb 83
Tovil Clo. SE20—68Xb 127
Towcester Rd. E3—42Ec 84
Tower Bri. SE1 & E1
—46Vb 83 (7K 201)
Tower Bri. App. E1
—45Vb 83 (6K 201)
Tower Bri. Rd. SE1
—48Ub 83 (4H 207)
Tower Clo. NW3—36Fb 61
Tower Clo. SE20—66Xb 127
Tower Clo. Grav—4G 136
Tower Clo. Ilf—23Rc 46
Tower Clo. Orp—76Vc 151
Tower Clo. Wok—5G 188
Tower Ct. E5—31Vb 63
Tower Ct. WC2—(3F 199)
Tower Ct. Brtwd—19Yd 32
Tower Croft. Eyns, Dart—75Nd 153
Tower Gdns. Rd. N17—25Sb 43
Tower Gro. Wey—75U 140
Tower Hamlets Rd. E7—35Hc 65
Tower Hamlets Rd. E17—27Cc 44
Tower Hill. EC3—45Vb 83 (5K 201)
Tower Hill. Brtwd—19Yd 32
Tower Hill. K Lan—1G 2
Tower La. Red—100Gb 179
Tower M. E17—28Cc 44
Tower Pl. EC3—(5J 201)
Tower Ride. Wind—2C 116
Tower Rise. Rich—55Na 101
Tower Rd. NW10—38Wa 60
Tower Rd. Belv—49Ed 88
Tower Rd. Bexh—56Cd 110
Tower Rd. Epp—2Uc 14
Tower Rd. Grnh—58Ld 111
Tower Rd. Orp—75Vc 151
Tower Rd. Tad—95Ya 178
Tower Rd. Twic—62Ha 122
Tower Royal. EC4
—45Tb 83 (4F 201)
Towers Av. Uxb—41S 76
Towers Pl. Rich—57Na 101
Towers Rd. Pinn—25Aa 37
Towers Rd. S'hall—42Ca 77
Towers Rd. Industrial Est.
Grays—50Ee 91
Towers, The. Kenl—87Sb 165
Tower St. WC2—44Nb 82 (3E 198)
Towers Wlk. Wey—79R 140
Towers Wood. S Dar, Dart
—67Td 134
Tower Ter. N22—26Pb 42
Tower View. Croy—73Ac 148
Tower Yd. Rich—57Pa 101
Towfield Av. Felt—61Ba 121
Towgar Ct. N20—17Eb 23
Towncourt Cres. Orp—71Sc 150
Towncourt La. Orp—72Tc 150
Towncourt Path. N4—32Sb 63
Townend. Cat—94Ub 181
Townend Clo. Cat—94Ub 181
Towney Mead. N'holt—40Ba 57
Townfield. Rick—17L 17
Townfield Rd. Hay—46V 76
Townfield Sq. Hay—45V 76
Town Hall App. Rd. N15—28Vb 43
Town Hall Rd. SW11—55Hb 103
Townholm Cres. W7—48Ha 78
Town La. Stai—58M 97
Townley Ct. E15—37Hc 65
Townley Rd. SE22—57Ub 105
Townley Rd. Bexh—57Bd 109
Townley St. SE17
(in two parts) —50Tb 83 (7F 207)
Town Mead. Bren—51Ma 101
Townmead Rd. SW6—55Db 103
Townmead Rd. Rich—54Ra 101
Townmead Rd. Wal A—6Ec 12
Town Quay. Bark—39Rc 66
Town Rd. N9—19Xb 25
Townsend Av. N14—21Mb 42
Townsend Industrial Est. NW10
—40Sa 59
Townsend La. NW9—31Ta 59
Townsend La. Wok—93D 172
Townsend Rd. N15—29Vb 43
Townsend Rd. Ashf—64N 119
Townsend Rd. S'hall—46Aa 77
Townsend St. SE17
—49Ub 83 (6G 207)
Townsend Way. N'wd—24V 36
Townsend Yd. N6—32Kb 62
Townshend Rd. NW8
—39Gb 61 (1D 190)
Townshend Rd. Chst—64Rc 130
Townshend Rd. Rich—56Pa 101
Townshend Ter. Rich—56Pa 101
Townshott Clo. Lea—98Ca 175
Townslow La. Wok—88L 157
Townson Av. N'holt—40W 56
Townson Way. N'holt—40W 56
Town Sq. Eri—51Gd 110
Town, The. Enf—13Tb 25
Town Tree Rd. Ashf—64Q 120
Town Wharf. Iswth—55Ka 100
Towpath. Shep—75Q 140
Towton Rd. SE27—61Sb 127
Toynbee Rd. SW20—67Ab 124
Toynbee St. E1—43Vb 83 (1K 201)
Toyne Way. N6—30Hb 41
Tozer Wlk. Wind—5B 94
Tracery, The. Bans—87Db 163
Tracey Av. NW2—36Ya 60
Tracey St. SE11—49Qb 82 (6K 205)
(in two parts)
Tracious Clo. Wok—4E 188
Tracious La. Wok—4E 188
Tracy Ct. Stan—24La 38
Tradescant Rd. SW8—52Nb 104
Trading Est. Rd. NW10—42Sa 79
Trafalgar Av. N17—23Ub 43
Trafalgar Av. SE15
—50Vb 83 (7K 207)
Trafalgar Av. Wor Pk—74Za 144
Trafalgar Dri. W on T—76X 141
Trafalgar Gdns. E1—43Zb 84
Trafalgar Gro. SE10—51Fc 107
Trafalgar Pl. N18—22Wb 43
Trafalgar Rd. SE10—51Fc 107
Trafalgar Rd. SW19—66Eb 125
Trafalgar Rd. Dart—61Nd 133
Trafalgar Rd. Grav—9C 114
Trafalgar Rd. Rain—40Hd 68
Trafalgar Rd. Twic—61Fa 122
Trafalgar Sq. WC2 & SW1
—46Mb 82 (6E 198)
Trafalgar St. SE17
—50Tb 83 (7F 207)
Trafalgar Ter. Harr—32Ga 58
Trafford Clo. E15—36Dc 64
Trafford Rd. T Hth—71Pb 146
Tramway Av. E15—38Fc 65
Tramway Av. N9—17Yb 26
Tramway Path. Mitc—70Gb 125
(in two parts)
Tranby Pl. E9—36Zb 64
Tranley M. NW3—35Gb 61
Tranmere Rd. N9—17Vb 25
Tranmere Rd. SW18—61Eb 125
Tranmere Rd. Twic—59Da 99
Tranquil Pas. SE3—54Hc 107
Tranquil Rise. Eri—50Gd 88
Tranquil Vale. SE3—54Gc 107
Transay Wlk. N1—37Tb 63
Transept St. NW1
—43Gb 81 (1E 196)
Transmere Clo. Orp—72Sc 150
Transmere Rd. Orp—72Sc 150
Transport Av. Bren—50Ka 78
Tranton Rd. SE16—48Wb 83
Trap's Hill. Lou—13Pc 28
Traps La. N Mald—67Ua 124
Travellers Way. Houn—54Y 99
Travers Rd. N7—34Qb 62
Travic Rd. Slou—1D 72
Travis Ct. Slou—1F 72
Treacy Clo. Bush, Wat—19Ea 20
Treadgold St. W11—45Za 80
Treadway St. E2—40Xb 63
Treadwell Rd. Eps—88Ua 162
Treasury Pas. SW1—(1F 205)
Treaty Rd. Houn—55Da 99
Treaty St. N1—39Pb 62 (1H 193)
Trebble Rd. Swans—58Ae 113
Trebeck St. W1—46Kb 82 (6K 197)
Trebovir Rd. SW5—50Cb 81
Treby St. E3—42Bc 84
Trecastle Way. N7—35Mb 62
Tredegar Rd. E3—40Bc 64
Tredegar Rd. Dart—62Jd 132
Tredegar Sq. E3—41Bc 84
Tredegar Ter. E3—41Bc 84
Trede Rd. N11—24Mb 42
Trederwen Rd. E8—39Wb 63
Tredown Rd. SE26—64Yb 128
Tredwell Clo. Brom—70Nc 130
Tredwell Rd. SE27—63Rb 127
Treebourne Rd. West—90Lc 167
Treebys Av. Guild—100A 172
Tree Clo. Rich—60Ma 101
Treemount Ct. Eps—85Ua 162
Treen Av. SW13—55Va 102
Tree Rd. E16—44Lc 85
Treeside Clo. W Dray—49M 75
Tree Tops. Brtwd—18Yd 32
Treetops. Grav—4D 136
Treetops Clo. SE2—50Ad 87
Treetops Clo. N'wd—22T 36
Treewall Gdns. Brom—63Kc 129
Trefgarne Rd. Dag—33Cd 68
Trefil Wlk. N7—35Nb 62
Trefoil Rd. SW18—57Eb 103
Trefusis Wlk. Wat—11U 18
Tregaron Av. N8—30Nb 42
Tregaron Gdns. N Mald—70Ua 124
Tregarth Pl. Wok—5C 188
Tregarvon Rd. SW11—56Jb 104
Tregenna Av. Harr—35Ca 57
Tregenna Clo. N14—15Lb 24
Trego Rd. E9—38Cc 64
Tregothnan Rd. SW9—55Nb 104
Tregunter Rd. SW10
—51Eb 103 (7A 202)
Trehearn Rd. Ilf—24Tc 46
Treherne Ct. SW9—53Rb 105
Treherne Ct. SW17—63Jb 126
Trehern Rd. SW14—55Ta 101
Trehurst St. E5—36Ac 64
Trelawn Clo. Cher—80E 138
Trelawney Av. Slou—48A 74
Trelawney Av. Slou—8P 73
Trelawney Est. E9—37Yb 64
Trelawney Gro. Wey—79Q 140
Trelawney Rd. Ilf—24Tc 46
Trelawn Rd. E10—34Ec 64
Trelawn Rd. SW2—57Qb 104
Trellis Sq. E3—41Bc 84
Treloar Gdns. SE19—65Tb 127
Tremadoc Rd. SW4—56Mb 104
Tremaine Clo. SE4—54Cc 106
Tremaine Rd. SE20—68Xb 127
Tremlett Gro. N19—34Lb 62
Tremlett M. N19—34Lb 62
Trenance Gdns. Ilf—34Wc 67
Trenchard Av. Ruis—35X 57
Trenchard Clo. Stan—23Ja 38
Trenchard Clo. W on T—78Y 141
Trenchard Ct. NW4—29Wa 40
Trenchard Ct. Mord—72Cb 145
Trenchard St. SE10—50Fc 85
Trenches La. Slou—45C 74
Trenchold St. SW8—51Nb 104
Trenham Dri. Warl—88Yb 166
Trenholme Clo. SE20—66Xb 127
Trenholme Ct. Cat—94Wb 181
Trenholme Rd. SE20—66Xb 127
Trenholme Ter. SE20—66Xb 127
Trenmar Gdns. NW10—41Xa 80
Trent. Grays—9L 93
Trent Av. W5—48La 78
Trent Av. Upm—30Td 50
Trent Gdns. N14—16Kb 24
Trentham Cres. Wok—93C 172
Trentham Dri. Orp—70Wc 131
Trentham St. SW18—60Cb 103
Trent Rd. SW2—57Pb 104
Trent Rd. Buck H—18Kc 27
Trent Rd. Slou—51D 96
Trent Vs. Est. Slou—3N 95
Trent Way. Hay—40U 56
Trent Way. Wor Pk—76Ya 144
Trentwood Side. Enf—13Pb 24
Treport St. SW18—59Db 103
Tresco Clo. Brom—65Gc 129
Trescoe Gdns. Harr—31Aa 57
Trescoe Gdns. Romf—22Ed 48
Tresco Gdns. Ilf—33Wc 67
Tresco Rd. SE15—56Xb 105
Tresham Cres. NW8
—42Gb 81 (4D 190)
Tresham Rd. Bark—38Vc 67
Tresham Wlk. E9—36Yb 64
Tresillian Way. Wok—4D 188
Tressell Clo. N1—38Rb 63
Tressillian Cres. SE4—55Cc 106
Tressillian Rd. SE4—56Bc 106
Tresta Wlk. Wok—4D 188
Trestis Clo. Hay—42Z 77
Treswell Rd. Dag—39Ad 67
Tretawn Gdns. NW7—21Ua 40
Tretawn Pk. NW7—21Ua 40
Trevanion Rd. W14—50Ab 80
Treve Av. Harr—31Fa 58
Trevellance Way. Wat—5Z 5
Trevelyan Av. E12—35Pc 66
Trevelyan Clo. Dart—56Pd 111
Trevelyan Cres. Harr—31Ma 59
Trevelyan Gdns. NW10—39Ya 60
Trevelyan Rd. E15—35Hc 65
Trevelyan Rd. SW17—65Gb 125
Treveris St. SE1—46Rb 83 (7C 200)
Treverton St. W10—42Za 80
Treville St. SW15—59Xa 102
Treviso Rd. SE23—61Zb 128
Trevithick Dri. Dart—56Pd 111
Trevithick St. SE8—51Cc 106
Trevone Gdns. Pinn—30Aa 37
Trevor Clo. Barn—16Fb 23
Trevor Clo. Brom—73Hc 149
Trevor Clo. Harr—24Ha 38
Trevor Clo. Iswth—57Ha 100
Trevor Clo. N'holt—40Y 57
Trevor Cres. Ruis—35V 56
Trevor Gdns. Edgw—25Ta 39
Trevor Gdns. N'holt—40Y 57
Trevor Pl. SW7—47Gb 81 (2E 202)
Trevor Rd. SW19—66Ab 124
Trevor Rd. Edgw—25Ta 39
Trevor Rd. Hay—47U 76
Trevor Rd. Wfd G—24Jc 45
Trevor Sq. SW7—47Hb 81 (3E 202)
Trevor St. SW7—47Gb 81 (2E 202)
Trevose Av. Wey—86H 157
Trevose Rd. E17—25Fc 45
Trevose Way. Wat—20Y 19
Trewenna Dri. Chess—78Ma 143
Trewenna Dri. Pot B—4Fb 9
Trewince Rd. SW20—67Ya 124
Trewint St. SW18—61Eb 125
Trewsbury Rd. SE26—64Zb 128
Triandra Way. Hay—43Z 77
Triangle Ct. E16—43Lc 85
Triangle Pas. Barn—14Eb 23
Triangle Pl. SW4—56Mb 104
Triangle Rd. E8—39Xb 63
Triangle, The. E8—39Xb 63
Triangle, The. N13—21Qb 42
Triangle, The. Bark—37Sc 66
Triangle, The. King—68Sa 123
Triangle, The. Wok—6F 188
Trident Rd. Wat—6V 4
Trident St. SE16—49Zb 84
Trident Way. S'hall—48X 77
Trigg's Clo. Wok—7G 188
Trigg's La. Wok—7G 188
Trig La. EC4—45Sb 83 (4D 200)
Trigo Ct. Eps—83Ta 161
Trigon Rd. SW8—52Pb 104
Trilby Rd. SE23—61Zb 128
Trimmer Wlk. Bren—51Na 101
Trinder Gdns. N19—32Nb 62
Trinder Rd. N19—32Nb 62
Trinder Rd. Barn—15Ya 22
Tring Av. W5—46Pa 79
Tring Av. S'hall—44Ba 77
Tring Av. Wemb—37Qa 59
Tring Clo. Ilf—29Tc 46
Tring Clo. Romf—21Pd 49
Tring Gdns. Romf—21Nd 49
Tring Grn. Romf—21Nd 49
Tringham Clo. Cher—78E 138
Tring Wlk. Romf—21Nd 49
Trinidad Gdns. Dag—38Fd 68
Trinidad St. E14—45Bc 84
Trinity Av. N2—27Fb 41
Trinity Av. Enf—16Vb 25
Trinity Chu. Pas. EC4—(2A 200)
Trinity Chu. Rd. SW13—51Xa 102
Trinity Chu. Sq. SE1
—48Sb 83 (2E 206)
Trinity Clo. E11—33Gc 65
Trinity Clo. SE13—56Fc 107
Trinity Clo. Brom—74Nc 150
Trinity Clo. Houn—56Aa 99
Trinity Clo. N'wd—23U 36
Trinity Clo. S Croy—81Ub 165
Trinity Clo. Stai—58L 97
Trinity Cotts. Rich—55Pa 101
Trinity Ct. N1—39Ub 63
Trinity Ct. Croy—75Sb 147
Trinity Cres. SW17—61Hb 125
Trinity Gdns. E16—43Hc 85
Trinity Gdns. SW9—56Pb 104
Trinity Gro. SE10—53Ec 106
Trinity Hall Clo. Wat—13Y 19
Trinity La. Wal X—4Ac 12
Trinity Pl. EC3—45Vb 83 (4K 201)
Trinity Pl. Bexh—56Bd 109
Trinity Pl. Wind—4G 94
Trinity Rise. SW2—60Qb 104
Trinity Rd. N2—27Fb 41
Trinity Rd. N22—24Nb 42
Trinity Rd.—56Eb 103
SW17 1-259 & 4-226
SW18 remainder
Trinity Rd. SW19—65Cb 125
Trinity Rd. Grav—9E 114
Trinity Rd. Ilf—27Sc 46
Trinity Rd. Rich—55Pa 101
Trinity Rd. S'hall—46Aa 77
Trinity Sq. EC3—45Vb 83 (5J 201)
Trinity St. E16—43Hc 85
Trinity St. SE1—47Sb 83 (2E 206)
Trinity St. Enf—12Sb 25
Trinity Wlk. NW3—37Eb 61
Trinity Way. W3—45Ua 80
Trio Pl. SE1—47Sb 83 (2E 206)
Tristan Sq. SE3—55Gc 107
Tristram Clo. E17—27Fc 45
Tristram Rd. Brom—63Hc 129
Triton Sq. NW1—42Lb 82 (5B 192)
Tritton Av. Croy—77Nb 146
Tritton Rd. SE21—62Tb 127
Triumph Clo. Hay—53S 98
Trocadero Centre. W1—(5D 198)
Trojan Way. Croy—76Pb 146
Troon St. E1—44Ac 84
Trosley Av. Grav—1D 136
Trosley Rd. Belv—51Cd 110
Trossachs Rd. SE22—57Ub 105
Trothy Rd. SE1—49Wb 83
Trotsworth Av. Vir W—70A 118
Trotters Bottom. Borwd—9Wa 8
Trott Rd. N10—24Hb 41
Trotts La. West—99Sc 184
Trott St. SW11—53Gb 103
Trotwood. Chig—23Tc 46
Trotwood Clo. Brtwd—18Ae 33
Troughton Rd. SE7—50Kc 85
Troutbeck Ho. NW1—(4A 192)
Troutbeck Rd. SE14—53Ac 106
Trout La. W Dray—45L 75
Trout Rise. Rick—13K 17
Trout Rd. W Dray—46M 75
Troutstream Way. Rick—14K 17
Trouville Rd. SW4—58Lb 104
Trowbridge Rd. E9—37Bc 64
Trowbridge Rd. Romf—23Md 49
Trowley Rise. Abb L, Wat—3U 4
Trowlock Av. Tedd—65La 122
Trowlock Way. Tedd—65Ma 123
Troy Rd. SE19—65Tb 127
Troy Town. SE15—55Wb 105
Truesdale Dri. Uxb—28L 35
Truesdale Rd. E6—44Pc 86
Trulock Rd. N17—24Wb 43
Truman's Rd. N16—36Ub 63
Trumble Gdns. T Hth—70Rb 127
Trumpers Way. W7—48Ga 78
Trumper Way. Uxb—39L 55
Trumpington Rd. E7—35Hc 65
Trumpsgreen Av. Vir W—72A 138
Trumps Grn. Clo. Vir W—71A 138
Trumpsgreen Rd. Vir W—71A 138
Trumpsgreen Rd. Vir W—72A 138
Trumps Mill La. Vir W—72B 138
Trump St. EC2—44Sb 83 (3E 200)
Trundlers Way. Bush, Wat
—18Ga 20
Trundle St. SE1—(1D 206)
Trundley's Rd. SE8—50Zb 84
Trundley's Ter. SE8—49Zb 84
Trunks All. Swan—68Dd 132
Truro Gdns. Ilf—31Nc 66
Truro Rd. E17—28Bc 44
Truro Rd. N22—24Nb 42
Truro Rd. Grav—2F 136
Truro St. NW5—37Jb 62
Truro Wlk. Romf—23Ld 49
Truro Way. Hay—41U 76
Truslove Rd. SE27—64Qb 126
Truss Hill Rd. Asc—10A 116
Trussley Rd. W6—48Ya 80
Truston's Gdns. Horn—31Jd 68
Trust Rd. Wal X—6Ac 12
Trust Wlk. SE21—60Rb 105
★Trycewell La. Sev—93Zd
Tryfan Clo. Ilf—29Mc 45
Tryon St. SW3—50Hb 81 (7F 203)
Trystings Clo. Esh—79Ja 142
Tuam Rd. SE18—51Tc 108
Tubbenden Clo. Orp—76Uc 150
Tubbenden Dri. Orp—77Tc 150
Tubbenden La. Orp—77Tc 150
Tubbenden La. S. Orp—78Tc 150
Tubbs Rd. NW10—40Va 60
Tubs Hill. Sev—96Kd 187
Tubs Hill Ho. Sev—96Jd 186
Tubs Hill Pde. Sev—96Jd 186
Tubwell Rd. Slou—9M 53
Tucker St. Wat—15Y 19
Tuckey Gro. Wok—96H 173
Tuck Rd. Rain—37Jd 68
Tuckton Wlk. SW15—59Va 102
Tudor Av. Hmptn—66Ca 121
Tudor Av. Romf—27Jd 48
Tudor Av. Wal X—3Wb 11
Tudor Av. Wat—10Z 5
Tudor Av. Wor Pk—76Xa 144
Tudor Clo. N6—31Lb 62
Tudor Clo. NW3—36Gb 61
Tudor Clo. NW7—23Wa 40
Tudor Clo. NW9—33Sa 59
Tudor Clo. Ashf—63N 119
Tudor Clo. Bans—87Ab 162
Tudor Clo. Brtwd—16Ce 33
Tudor Clo. Chess—78Na 143
Tudor Clo. Chig—21Qc 46
Tudor Clo. Chst—67Pc 130
Tudor Clo. Cob—85Ba 159
Tudor Clo. Coul—90Qb 164
Tudor Clo. Dart—58Kd 111
Tudor Clo. Lea—96Ca 175
Tudor Clo. Pinn—29W 36
Tudor Clo. S Croy—87Xb 165
Tudor Clo. Sutt—78Za 144
Tudor Clo. Wall—80Lb 146
Tudor Clo. Wal X—3Xb 11
Tudor Clo. Wfd G—22Kc 45
Tudor Ct. E17—31Bc 64
Tudor Ct. Borwd—12Na 21
Tudor Ct. Felt—63Y 121
Tudor Ct. Romf—23Rd 49
Tudor Ct. N. Wemb—36Qa 59
Tudor Ct. S. Wemb—36Qa 59
Tudor Cres. Enf—11Sb 25
Tudor Cres. Ilf—23Rc 46
Tudor Cres. Sev—88Ld 171
Tudor Dri. King—64Ma 123

Tudor Dri.—Valley View

Tudor Dri. Mord—72Za 144
Tudor Dri. Romf—28Jd 48
Tudor Dri. Sev—88Ld 171
Tudor Dri. W on T—74Z 141
Tudor Dri. Wat—10Z 5
Tudor Gdns. NW9—33Sa 59
Tudor Gdns. SW13—55Ua 102
Tudor Gdns. W3—43Qa 79
Tudor Gdns. Harr—26Fa 38
Tudor Gdns. Romf—28Jd 48
Tudor Gdns. Slou—4A 72
Tudor Gdns. Twic—60Ha 100
Tudor Gdns. Upm—33Sd 70
Tudor Gdns. W Wick—76Ec 148
Tudor Gro. E9—38Yb 64
Tudor Leys. Wind—9N 95
Tudor Pl. Mitc—66Gb 125
Tudor Rd. E4—23Dc 44
Tudor Rd. E6—39Lc 65
Tudor Rd. E9—39Xb 63
Tudor Rd. N9—17Xb 25
Tudor Rd. SE19—66Vb 127
Tudor Rd. SE25—71Xb 147
Tudor Rd. Ashf—65T 120
Tudor Rd. Bark—39Vc 67
Tudor Rd. Barn—13Cb 23
Tudor Rd. Beck—69Ec 128
Tudor Rd. Hmptn—66Ca 121
Tudor Rd. Harr—26Fa 38
Tudor Rd. Hay—44T 76
Tudor Rd. Houn—56Fa 100
Tudor Rd. King—66Qa 123
Tudor Rd. Pinn—26Y 37
Tudor Rd. S'hall—45Aa 77
Tudor Sq. Hay—43T 76
Tudor St. EC4—45Qb 82 (4A 200)
Tudor Vs. Wal X—1Ub 11
(in two parts)
Tudor Wlk. Bex—58Ad 109
Tudor Wlk. Lea—92Ha 176
Tudor Wlk. Wat—9Z 5
Tudor Wlk. Wey—76R 140
Tudor Way. N14—18Mb 24
Tudor Way. W3—47Qa 79
Tudor Way. Orp—72Tc 150
Tudor Way. Rick—18J 17
Tudor Way. Uxb—37Q 56
Tudor Way. Wal A—5Fc 13
Tudor Way. Wind—3C 94
Tudor Well Clo. Stan—22Ka 38
Tudway Rd. SE3—55Kc 107
Tufnail Rd. Dart—58Pd 111
Tufnell Pk. Rd.—35Lb 62
N7 1-217 & 2-210
N19 remainder
Tufter Rd. Chig—22Vc 47
Tufton Gdns. E Mol—68Da 121
Tufton Rd. E4—21Cc 44
Tufton St. SW1—48Nb 82 (3E 204)
Tugela Rd. Croy—72Tb 147
Tugela St. SE6—61Bc 128
Tulip Clo. Brtwd—15Xd 32
Tulip Clo. Croy—74Zb 148
Tulip Clo. Hmptn—65Ba 121
Tulip Clo. Romf—23Md 49
Tulip Ct. Pinn—27Y 37
Tuliptree Av. Rich—53Na 101
Tulse Clo. Beck—69Ec 128
Tulse Hill. SW2—58Qb 104
Tulsemere Rd. SE27—61Sb 127
Tumber St. Eps—97Sa 177
★Tumblefield Rd. Sev—83Be
Tumblewood Rd. Bans—88Ab 162
Tumbling Bay. W on T—72W 140
Tuncombe Rd. N18—21Ub 43
Tunis Rd. W12—46Ya 80
Tunley Grn. E14—43Bc 84
Tunley Rd. NW10—39Ua 60
Tunley Rd. SW17—61Jb 126
Tunmarsh La. E13—41Lc 85
Tunnel App. E14—45Ac 84
Tunnel App. SE10—47Gc 85
Tunnel Av. SE10—47Fc 85
(in two parts)
Tunnel Gdns. N11—24Lb 42
Tunnel Rd. SE16—47Yb 84
Tunnel Wood Clo. Wat—9V 4
Tunnel Wood Rd. Wat—9V 4
Tuns La. Slou—8G 72
Tunstall Av. Ilf—23Wc 47
Tunstall Clo. Orp—77Uc 150
Tunstall Rd. SW9—56Pb 104
Tunstall Rd. Croy—74Ub 147
Tunstall Wlk. Bren—51Na 101
Tunworth Clo. NW9—30Sa 39
Tunworth Cres. SW15—58Va 102
Tupwood La. Cat—96Wb 181
Tupwood La. Cat—98Wb 181
Tupwood Scrubs Rd. Cat
—100Wb 181
Turenne Clo. SW18—56Eb 103
Turin Rd. N9—18Yb 26
Turin St. E2—41Wb 83
Turkey Oak Clo. SE19—67Ub 127
Turkey St. Enf—8Wb 11
Turks Clo. Uxb—41Q 76
Turk's Head Yd. EC1
—43Rb 83 (7B 194)
Turks Row. SW3
—50Hb 81 (7G 203)
Turle Rd. N4—33Pb 62
Turle Rd. SW16—68Nb 126
Turley Clo. E15—39Gc 65
Turnagain La. EC4—(2B 200)
Turnage Rd. Dag—32Ad 67
Turnberry Way. Orp—74Tc 150
Turnbull Clo. Grnh—59Ud 112
Turnchapel M. SW4—55Kb 104
Turner Av. N15—28Ub 43
Turner Av. Mitc—67Hb 125
Turner Av. Twic—62Ea 122
Turner Clo. NW11—30Db 41
Turner Clo. Hay—40S 56
Turner Dri. NW11—30Db 41
Turner Rd. E17—27Ec 44
Turner Rd. Bush, Wat—14Ea 20
Turner Rd. Dart—62Xd 134
Turner Rd. Edgw—26Na 39
Turner Rd. N Mald—73Ta 143
Turner Rd. Slou—7N 73
Turner Rd. West—84Lc 167
Turner's All. EC3
—45Ub 83 (4H 201)
Turner's Hill. Wal X—1Zb 12
Turners La. W on T—79X 141
Turner's Rd. E3—43Bc 84
Turner St. E1—43Xb 83
Turner St. E16—44Hc 85
Turners Wood. NW11—31Eb 61
Turneville Rd. W14—51Bb 103
Turney Rd. SE21—59Sb 105
Turnham Grn. Ter. W4—49Ua 80
Turnham Grn. Ter. M. W4
—49Ua 80
Turnham Rd. SE4—57Ac 106
Turnmill St. EC1—43Rb 83 (6B 194)
Turnoak Av. Wok—92A 172
Turnoak La. Wok—92A 172
Turnpike Clo. SE8—52Bc 106
Turnpike Dri. Orp—81Yc 169
Turnpike La. N8—28Pb 42
Turnpike La. Grays—10F 92
Turnpike La. Uxb—40N 55
Turnpike Link. Croy—75Ub 147
Turnpin La. SE10—51Ec 106
Turnstone. Long. Dart—69Ce 135
Turnstone Clo. S Croy—82Ac 166
Turnstones, The. Wat—8Aa 5
Turp Av. Grays—47Ee 91
Turpentine La. SW1
—50Kb 82 (7A 204)
Turpin Av. Romf—24Cd 48
Turpington Clo. Brom—73Nc 150
Turpington La. Brom—73Nc 150
Turpin Rd. Felt—58V 98
Turpin's La. Wfd G—22Pc 46
Turpin Way. N19—33Mb 62
Turpin Way. Wall—80Kb 146
Turquand St. SE17
—49Sb 83 (6E 206)
Turret Gro. SW4—55Lb 104
Turtlewray Clo. N4—32Pb 62
Turton Rd. Wemb—36Na 59
Turton Way. Slou—8H 73
Turville St. E2—42Vb 83 (5K 195)
Tuscan Rd. SE18—50Tc 86
Tuskar St. SE10—51Gc 107
Tustin Est. SE15—51Yb 106
Tuttlebee La. Buck H—19Jc 27
Tuxford Clo. Borwd—10Na 7
Tweed. Grays—9L 93
Tweeddale Gro. Uxb—34S 56
Tweeddale Rd. Cars—74Fb 145
Tweed Glen. Romf—24Fd 48
Tweed Grn. Romf—24Fd 48
Tweedmouth Rd. E13—40Kc 65
Tweed Rd. Slou—51D 96
Tweed Way. Romf—24Fd 48
Tweedy Rd. Brom—67Jc 129
Tweezer's All. WC2—(4K 199)
Twelve Acre Clo. Lea—96Ba 175
Twelvetrees Cres. E3—42Ec 84
Twentyman Clo. Wfd G—22Jc 45
Twickenham Bri. Twic & Rich
—57La 100
Twickenham Clo. Croy—76Pb 146
Twickenham Gdns. Gnfd—36Ja 58
Twickenham Gdns. Harr—24Ga 38
Twickenham Rd. E11—33Fc 65
Twickenham Rd. Felt—62Ba 121
Twickenham Rd. Iswth—57Ja 100
Twickenham Rd. Rich—56La 100
Twickenham Rd. Tedd—63Ja 122
(in two parts)
Twickenham Trading Est. Iswth
—58Ha 100
Twigg Clo. Eri—52Gd 110
Twilley St. SW18—59Db 103
Twinches La. Slou—6F 72
Twineham Grn. N12—21Cb 41
Twining Av. Twic—62Ea 122
Twinn Rd. NW7—23Ab 40
Twinoaks. Cob—85Ca 159
Twisden Rd. NW5—35Kb 62
Twitton Bungalows. Sev
—88Gd 170
Twitton La. Sev—87Fd 170
Twitton Stream Cotts. Sev
—88Gd 170
Twybridge Way. NW10—38Sa 59
Twyford Abbey Rd. NW10
—41Pa 79
Twyford Av. N2—27Hb 41
Twyford Av. W3—45Qa 79
Twyford Cres. W3—46Qa 79
Twyford Pl. WC2
—44Pb 82 (2H 199)
Twyford Rd. Cars—74Fb 145
Twyford Rd. Harr—32Da 57
Twyford Rd. Ilf—36Sc 66
Twyford St. N1—39Pb 62
Tyas Rd. E16—42Hc 85
Tybenham Rd. SW19—69Cb 125
Tyberry Rd. Enf—13Yb 26
Tyburn La. Harr—31Ha 58
Tyburns, The. Brtwd—19Ee 33
Tyburn Way. W1
—45Hb 81 (4G 197)
Tycehurst Hill. Lou—14Pc 28
Tydcombe Rd. Warl—91Yb 182
Tye La. Orp—78Sc 150
Tyers Ga. SE1—47Ub 83 (2H 207)
Tyers St. SE11—50Pb 82 (7H 205)
Tyers Ter. SE11—50Pb 82 (7H 205)
Tyeshurst Clo. SE2—50Ad 87
Tyfield Clo. Wal X—2Yb 12
Tykeswater La. Borwd—12La 20
Tylecroft Rd. SW16—68Nb 126
Tyle Grn. Horn—28Nd 49
Tylehurst Gdns. Ilf—36Sc 66
Tyle Pl. Wind—7L 95
Tyler Gdns. Wey—77L 139
Tyler Gro. Dart—56Pd 111
Tylers Clo. K Lan—1P 3
Tylers Clo. Lou—17Nc 28
Tylers Cres. Horn—36Ld 69
Tylers Ga. Harr—30Na 39
Tylers Grn. Rd. Swan—73Ed 152
Tylers Path. Cars—77Hb 145
Tyler St. SE10—50Gc 85
Tylers Way. Wat—14Fa 20
Tylney Av. SE19—64Vb 127
Tylney Rd. E7—35Lc 65
Tylney Rd. Brom—68Mc 129
Tynan Clo. Felt—60W 98
Tyndale La. N1—38Rb 63
Tyndale Ter. N1—38Rb 63
Tyndall Rd. E10—33Ec 64
Tyndall Rd. Well—55Vc 109
Tyne Clo. Upm—30Td 50
Tynedale Clo. Dart—60Td 112
Tyne Gdns. S Ock—45Sd 90
Tyneham Rd. SW11—54Jb 104
(in two parts)
Tynemouth Dri. Enf—10Wb 11
Tynemouth Rd. N15—28Vb 43
Tynemouth Rd. Mitc—66Jb 126
Tynemouth St. SW6—54Eb 103
Tyne St. E1—44Vb 83 (2K 201)
Tynwald Ho. SE26—62Wb 127
Type St. E2—40Zb 64
Tyrawley Rd. SW6—53Db 103
Tyrell Clo. Harr—35Ga 58
Tyrell Ct. Cars—77Hb 145
Tyrell Gdns. Wind—5D 94
Tyrell Rise. Brtwd—22Yd 50
Tyrells Clo. Upm—33Rd 69
Tyrone Rd. E6—40Pc 66
Tyron Way. Sidc—63Uc 130
Tyrrell Av. Well—57Wc 109
Tyrrell Rd. SE22—56Wb 105
Tyrrells Hall Clo. Grays—51Fe 113
Tyrrel Way. NW9—31Va 60
Tyrwhitt Rd. SE4—55Cc 106
Tysea Hill. Romf—18Hd 30
Tysoe Av. Enf—8Bc 12
Tysoe St. EC1—41Qb 82 (4A 194)
Tyson Rd. SE23—59Yb 106
Tyssen Pas. E8—37Vb 63
Tyssen Rd. N16—34Vb 63
Tyssen St. E8—37Vb 63
Tytherton Rd. N19—34Mb 62

Uamvar St. E14—43Dc 84
Uckfield Gro. Mitc—67Jb 126
Uckfield Rd. Enf—9Zb 12
Udall Gdns. Romf—23Cd 48
Udall St. SW1—49Lb 82 (6C 204)
Udney Pk. Rd. Tedd—65Ja 122
Uffington Rd. NW10—39Wa 60
Uffington Rd. SE27—63Qb 126
Ufford Clo. Harr—24Da 37
Ufford Rd. Harr—24Da 37
Ufford St. SE1—47Qb 82 (1A 206)
Ufton Gro. N1—38Tb 63
Ufton Rd. N1—38Ub 63
Ullathorne Rd. SW16—63Lb 126
Ullswater Rd. N14—20Nb 24
Ullin St. E14—43Ec 84
Ullswater Clo. SW15—63Ta 123
Ullswater Clo. Brom—66Gc 129
Ullswater Clo. Hay—40U 56
Ullswater Clo. Slou—3A 72
Ullswater Cres. SW15—63Ta 123
Ullswater Cres. Coul—88Nb 164
Ullswater Rd. SE27—61Rb 127
Ullswater Rd. SW13—52Wa 102
Ullswater Way. Horn—36Jd 68
Ulstan Clo. Cat—95Cc 182
Ulster Gdns. N13—21Sb 43
Ulster Pl. NW1—42Kb 82 (6K 191)
Ulster Ter. NW1—(5K 191)
Ulundi Rd. SE3—51Gc 107
Ulva Rd. SW15—57Za 102
Ulverscroft Rd. SE22—57Wb 105
Ulverstone Rd. SE27—61Rb 127
Ulverston Rd. E17—26Fc 45
Ulwin Av. Wey—85N 157
Ulysses Rd. NW6—36Bb 61
Umberston St. E1—44Wb 83
Umberville Way. Slou—1D 72
Umbria St. SW15—58Wa 102
Umfreville Rd. N4—30Rb 43
Underbridge Way. Enf—13Ac 26
Undercliffe Rd. SE13—55Cc 106
Underhill. Barn—15Cb 23
Underhill Rd. SE22—57Wb 105
Underhill St. NW1—39Kb 62
Underne Av. N14—19Kb 24
Undershaft. EC3
—44Ub 83 (3H 201)
Undershaw Rd. Brom—62Hc 129
Underwood. Croy—78Ec 148
Underwood Rd. E1—42Wb 83
Underwood Rd. E4—22Dc 44
Underwood Rd. Cat—98Ub 181
Underwood Row. N1
—41Sb 83 (3E 194)
Underwood St. N1
—41Sb 83 (3E 194)
Underwood, The. SE9—62Pc 130
Undine St. SW17—64Hb 125
Uneeda Dri. Gnfd—39Fa 58
Unicorn Pas. SE1
—46Ub 83 (7J 201)
Union Cotts. E15—38Gc 65
Union Ct. EC2—(2H 201)
Union Ct. Rich—57Na 101
Union Dri. E1—42Ac 84
Union Gro. SW8—54Mb 104
Union Rd. N11—23Mb 42
Union Rd.—54Mb 104
SW4 1-93 & 2-102
SW8 remainder
Union Rd. Brom—71Mc 149
Union Rd. Croy—73Sb 147
Union Rd. N'holt—40Ca 57
Union Rd. Wemb—37Na 59
Union Sq. N1—39Sb 63 (1E 194)
Union St. E15—39Ec 64
Union St. SE1—46Rb 83 (7B 200)
Union St. Barn—13Ab 22
Union St. King—68Ma 123
Union Wlk. E2—41Ub 83 (3J 195)
Union Yd. W1—44Kb 82 (3A 198)
Unity Rd. Enf—9Yb 12
Unity Way. SE18—48Mc 85
University Clo. NW7—24Va 40
University Pl. Eri—52Ed 110
University Rd. SW19—65Fb 125
University St. WC1
—42Lb 82 (6C 192)
Unwin Av. Felt—57T 98
Unwin Clo. SE15—51Wb 105
Unwin Rd. Iswth—55Ga 100
Upbrook M. W2—44Eb 81 (3A 196)
Upcerne Rd. SW10—52Eb 103
Upchurch Clo. SE20—66Xb 127
Upcroft. Wind—5F 94
Upcroft Av. Edgw—22Sa 39
Updale Clo. Pot B—5Ab 8
Updale Rd. Sidc—63Vc 131
Upfield. Croy—76Xb 147
Upfield Rd. W13—43Ha 78
Upgrove Mnr. Way. SW2
—59Qb 104
Uphall Rd. Ilf—36Rc 66
Upham Pk. Rd. W4—49Ua 80
Uphill Dri. NW7—22Ua 40
Uphill Dri. NW9—29Sa 39
Uphill Gro. NW7—21Ua 40
Uphill Rd. NW7—21Ua 40
Upland Ct. Rd. Romf—26Pd 49
Upland Rd. E13—42Jc 85
Upland Rd. SE22—59Wb 105
Upland Rd. Bexh—55Bd 109
Upland Rd. Cat—92Dc 182
(in two parts)
Upland Rd. S Croy—78Tb 147
Upland Rd. Sutt—80Fb 145
Uplands. Asht—92Ma 177
Uplands. Beck—68Cc 128
Uplands. Rick—16P 17
Uplands Av. E17—26Zb 44
Uplands Clo. SW14—57Ra 101
Uplands Clo. Ger X—32A 54
Uplands Clo. Sev—95Hd 186
Uplands End. Wfd G—24Nc 46
Uplands Pk. Rd. Enf—12Qb 24
Uplands Rd. N8—29Pb 42
Uplands Rd. Barn—18Jb 24
Uplands Rd. Brtwd—22Ae 51
Uplands Rd. Kenl—88Sb 165
Uplands Rd. Orp—74Xc 151
Uplands Rd. Romf—27Zc 47
Uplands Rd. Wfd G—24Nc 46
Uplands, The. Ger X—33A 54
Uplands, The. Lou—13Pc 28
Uplands, The. Ruis—31W 56
Uplands, The. St Alb—2Aa 5
Uplands Way. N21—15Qb 24
Uplands Way. Sev—95Hd 186
Upland Way. Eps—90Ya 162
Upminster Rd. Horn & Upm
—33Pd 69
Upminster Rd. N. Rain—41Ld 89
Upminster Rd. S. Rain—42Jd 88
Upney Clo. Horn—36Ld 69
Upney La. Bark—37Uc 66
Upnor Way. SE17
—50Ub 83 (7J 207)
Uppark Dri. Ilf—30Sc 46
Up. Abbey Rd. Belv—49Bd 87
Up. Addison Gdns. W14—47Ab 80
Up. Austin Lodge Rd. Eyns,
Dart & Sev—77Md 153
Upper Av. Grav—7A 136
Up. Belgrave St. SW1
—48Jb 82 (3J 203)
Up. Berkeley St. W1
—44Hb 81 (3F 197)
Up. Beulah Hill. SE19—67Ub 127
Up. Brentwood Rd. Romf—28Ld 49
Up. Brighton Rd. Surb—72Ma 143
Up. Brockley Rd. SE4—54Bc 106
Up. Brook St. W1
—45Jb 82 (4H 197)
Up. Butts. Bren—51La 100
Up. Cavendish Av. N3—27Cb 41
Up. Cheyne Row. SW3—51Gb 103
Up. Church Hill. Grnh—57Ud 112
Up. Clapton Rd. E5—33Xb 63
Up. Cornsland. Brtwd—20Zd 33
Up. Court Rd. Cat—95Ub 181
Up. Court Rd. Eps—83Sa 161
Upper Dri. West—90Lc 167
Up. Elmers End Rd. Beck
—70Ac 128
Up. Fairfield Rd. Lea—93Ka 176
Up. Farm Rd. E Mol—70Ba 121
Up. Fore St. N18—23Vb 43
Up. Green E. Mitc—69Hb 125
Up. Green W. Mitc—68Hb 125
Up. Grosvenor St. W1
—45Jb 82 (5H 197)
Up. Grotto Rd. Twic—61Ha 122
Up. Ground. SE1—46Qb 82 (6J 199)
Upper Gro. SE25—70Vb 127
Up. Grove Rd. Belv—51Bd 109
Up. Halliford By-Pass. Shep
—71U 140
Up. Halliford Grn. Shep—70U 120
Up. Halliford Rd. Shep—69U 120
Up. Ham Rd. Rich—63Ma 123
Up. Harley St. NW1
—42Jb 82 (6J 191)
Up. High St. Eps—85Ua 162
Up. Highway. K Lan & Abb L, Wat
—5T 4
Up. Hill Rise. Rick—16K 17
Up. Hitch. Wat—18Aa 19
Up. Holly Hill Rd. Belv—50Dd 88
Up. James St. W1
—45Lb 82 (4C 198)
Up. John St. W1—45Lb 82 (4C 198)
Up. Lambarde Rd. Sev—95Jd 186
Up. Lees Rd. Slou—1F 72
Up. Mall. W6—50Wa 80
Up. Marsh. SE1—48Pb 82 (3J 205)
Up. Montagu St. W1
—43Hb 81 (7F 191)
Up. Mulgrave Rd. Sutt—80Ab 144
Up. North St. E14—43Cc 84
Up. Paddock Rd. Wat—16Aa 19
Up. Palace Rd. E Mol—69Fa 122
Upper Pk. Lou—14Mc 27
Up. Park Rd. N11—22Lb 42
Up. Park Rd. NW3—36Hb 61
Up. Park Rd. Belv—49Dd 88
Up. Park Rd. Brom—67Kc 129
Up. Park Rd. King—65Qa 123
Up. Phillimore Gdns. W8—47Cb 81
Up. Pillory Downs. Cars—85Jb 164
Up. Pines. Bans—89Hb 163
Up. Rainham Rd. Horn—32Hd 68
Up. Richmond Rd. SW15
—56Va 102
Up. Richmond Rd. W. Rich &
SW14—56Qa 101
Upper Rd. E13—41Jc 85
Upper Rd. Uxb—31F 54
Upper Rd. Wall—78Mb 146
Up. Ryle. Brtwd—17Vd 32
Up. Saint Martin's La. WC2
—45Nb 82 (4F 199)
Up. Selsdon Rd. S Croy—81Vb 165
Up. Sheridan Rd. Belv—49Cd 88
Up. Shirley Rd. Croy—75Yb 148
★Up. Spring La. Sev—94Xd
Upper Sq. Iswth—55Ja 100
Up. Station Rd. Rad—7Ja 6
Upper St. N1—40Rb 63 (1A 194)
Up. Sunbury Rd. Hmptn
—67Aa 121
Up. Sutton La. Houn—53Ca 99
Up. Swaines. Epp—2Vc 15
Up. Tachbrook St. SW1
—49Lb 82 (5B 204)
Up. Tail. Wat—20Aa 19
Up. Teddington Rd. King
—67La 122
Upper Ter. NW3—34Eb 61
Up. Thames St. EC4
—45Rb 83 (4C 200)
Up. Tollington Pk. N4—32Qb 62
(in two parts)
Upperton Rd. Sidc—64Vc 131
Upperton Rd. E. E13—41Lc 85
Upperton Rd. W. E13—41Lc 85
Up. Tooting Pk. SW17—61Hb 125
Up. Tooting Rd. SW17—63Hb 125
Up. Town Rd. Gnfd—42Da 77
Up. Tulse Hill. SW2—59Pb 104
Up. Vernon Rd. Sutt—78Fb 145
Up. Village Rd. Asc—10A 116
Upper Wlk., The. Sutt—78Db 145
Up. Walthamstow Rd. E17
—27Fc 45
Up. Wickham La. Well—54Xc 109
Up. Wimpole St. W1
—43Jb 82 (7J 191)
Up. Woburn Pl. WC1
—41Mb 82 (4E 192)
Up. Woodcote Village. Purl
—84Mb 164
Uppingham Av. Stan—25Ka 38
Upsdell Av. N13—23Qb 42
Upshire Rd. Wal A—4Hc 13
Upshott La. Wok—89H 157
Upstall St. SE5—53Rb 105
Upton Av. E7—38Jc 65
Upton Clo. Bex—58Bd 109
Upton Clo. Slou—8K 73
Upton Clo. Stanf—1M 93
Upton Ct. Rd. Slou—8L 73
Upton Dene. Sutt—80Db 145
Upton Gdns. Harr—29Ka 38
Upton La. E7—38Jc 65
Upton Lea Pde. Slou—5M 73
Upton Lodge Clo. Bush, Wat
—17Ea 20
Upton Pk. Slou—8K 73
Upton Pk. Rd. E7—38Kc 65
Upton Rd. N18—22Xb 43
Upton Rd. SE18—51Sc 108
Upton Rd. Bexh & Bex—56Ad 109
Upton Rd. Houn—55Ca 99
Upton Rd. Slou—8L 73
Upton Rd. T Hth—68Tb 127
Upton Rd. Wat—13X 19
Upton Rd. S. Bex—58Bd 109
Upway. N12—23Gb 41
Upway. Ger X—25B 34
Upwood Rd. SE12—58Jc 107
Upwood Rd. SW16—67Nb 126
Urban Av. Horn—34Ld 69
Urlwin St. SE5—51Sb 105
Urlwin Wlk. SW9—53Qb 104
Urmston Dri. SW19—60Ab 102
Ursula St. SW11—53Gb 103
Urswick Gdns. Dag—38Ad 67
Urswick Rd. E9—36Yb 64
Urswick Rd. Dag—38Zc 67
Usher Rd. E3—40Bc 64
(in two parts)
Usk Rd. SW11—56Eb 103
Usk Rd. S Ock—43Sd 90
Usk St. E2—41Zb 84
Usk St. E16—45Hc 85
Utility Cotts. Sev—92Pd 187
Uvedale Clo. Croy—83Fc 167
Uvedale Cres. Croy—83Fc 167
Uvedale Rd. Dag—34Cd 68
Uvedale Rd. Enf—15Tb 25
Uverdale Rd. SW10—52Eb 103
Uxbridge Rd. W5 & W3—45Na 79
Uxbridge Rd. W12—46Wa 80
Uxbridge Rd. W13 & W5—46Ka 78
Uxbridge Rd. Felt—61Y 121
Uxbridge Rd. Hmptn—63Ca 121
Uxbridge Rd. King—70Ma 123
Uxbridge Rd. Pinn, Harr & Stan
—26Z 37
Uxbridge Rd. Rick—20H 17
Uxbridge Rd. Slou—7M 73
Uxbridge Rd. Slou & Iver—41C 74
Uxbridge Rd. S'hall—46Ca 77
Uxbridge Rd. Uxb & Hay—41Q 76
Uxbridge St. W8—46Cb 81
Uxendon Cres. Wemb—32Na 59
Uxendon Hill. Wemb—32Pa 59

Vaillant Rd. Wey—77S 140
Valance Av. E4—18Gc 27
Valan Leas. Brom—69Gc 129
Vale Av. Borwd—15Ra 21
Vale Border. Croy & S Croy
—83Zb 166
Vale Clo. W9—41Eb 81 (4A 190)
Vale Clo. Brtwd—15Vd 32
Vale Clo. Coul—86Nb 164
Vale Clo. Ger X—25A 34
Vale Clo. Orp—77Qc 150
Vale Clo. Wey—76T 140
Vale Cotts. Brom—69Jc 129
Vale Ct. W9—(4A 190)
Vale Ct. Wey—76T 140
Vale Cres. SW15—63Ua 124
Vale Croft. Pinn—29Aa 37
Vale Dri. Barn—14Bb 23
Vale End. SE22—56Vb 105
Vale Farm Rd. Wok—89A 156
Vale Gro. N4—31Sb 63
Vale Gro. W3—47Ta 79
Vale Gro. Slou—8J 73
Vale Industrial Pk. Rick—17S 18
Vale La. W3—43Qa 79
Valence Av. Dag—32Zc 67
Valence Cir. Dag—34Ad 67
Valence Dri. Wal X—1Wb 11
Valence Rd. Eri—52Fd 110
Valence Wood Rd. Dag—34Zc 67
Valencia Rd. Stan—21La 38
Valency Clo. N'wd—21V 36
Valentia Pl. SW9—56Qb 104
Valentine Av. Bex—60Ad 109
Valentine Pl. SE1
—47Rb 83 (1B 206)
Valentine Rd. E9—37Zb 64
Valentine Rd. Harr—34Da 57
Valentine Row. SE1
—47Rb 83 (2B 206)
Valentines Rd. Ilf—32Rc 66
Valentine's Way. Romf—33Gd 68
Valentine Way. Chal—19A 16
Vale Pl. W14—48Za 80
Valerian Way. E15—41Gc 85
Vale Rise. NW11—32Bb 61
Vale Rd. E7—37Kc 65
Vale Rd. N4—31Sb 63
Vale Rd. Brom—67Qc 130
Vale Rd. Bush, Wat—15Aa 19
Vale Rd. Dart—60Kd 111
Vale Rd. Esh—81Ga 160
Vale Rd. Grav—59Fe 113
Vale Rd. Mitc—70Mb 126
Vale Rd. Sutt—77Db 145
Vale Rd. Wey—76T 140
Vale Rd. Wind—3D 94
Vale Rd. Wor Pk & Eps—76Va 144
Vale Rd. N. Surb—75Na 143
Vale Rd. S. Surb—75Na 143
Vale Row. N5—34Rb 63
Vale Royal. N7—38Nb 62
Vale St. SE27—62Tb 127
Valeswood Rd. Brom—64Hc 129
Vale Ter. N4—30Sb 43
Vale, The. N10—25Jb 42
Vale, The. N14—16Pb 24
Vale, The. NW11—33Ab 60
Vale, The. SW3—51Fb 103
Vale, The. W3—46Va 80
Vale, The. Brtwd—18Yd 32
Vale, The. Coul—86Nb 164
Vale, The. Croy—75Zb 148
Vale, The. Felt—58X 99
Vale, The. Ger X—25A 34
Vale, The. Houn—51Aa 99
Vale, The. Ruis—35Y 57
Vale, The. Sun—65W 120
Vale, The. Wfd G—24Jc 45
Valetta Gro. E13—40Jc 65
Valetta Rd. W3—47Ua 80
Valette St. E9—37Yb 64
Valiant Clo. N'holt—41Z 77
Valiant Clo. Romf—26Dd 48
Vallance Rd.—42Wb 83
E1 1-121 & 2-168
E2 remainder
Vallance Rd. N22—26Lb 42
Vallentin Rd. E17—28Ec 44
Valley Av. N12—21Fb 41
Valley Clo. Dart—58Hd 110
Valley Clo. Lou—16Pc 28
Valley Clo. Pinn—26X 37
Valley Clo. Wal A—4Ec 12
Valley Dri. NW9—30Qa 39
Valley Dri. Grav—3F 136
Valley Dri. Sev—98Kd 187
Valleyfield Rd. SW16—64Pb 126
Valley Fields Cres. Enf—12Qb 24
Valley Gdns. SW19—66Fb 125
Valley Gdns. Wemb—38Pa 59
Valley Gro. SE7—50Lc 85
Valley Hill. Lou—16Nc 28
Valley M. Twic—61Ha 122
Valley Rise. Wat—5X 5
Valley Rd. SW16—64Pb 126
Valley Rd. Belv—49Dd 88
Valley Rd. Brom—68Gc 129
Valley Rd. Dart—58Fd 110
Valley Rd. Eri—49Fd 88
Valley Rd. Kenl—87Tb 165
Valley Rd. Long, Dart—74Xd 154
Valley Rd. Orp—67Xc 131
Valley Rd. Rick—15J 17
Valley Rd. Uxb—40N 55
Valley Side. E4—19Cc 26
Valley View. Barn—16Ab 22
Valley View. Grnh—58Xd 112

Valley View—Wakefield Cres.

Valley View. Wal X—1Sb 11
Valley View. West—90Lc 167
Valley View Gdns. Kenl—87Ub 165
Valley View Ter. F'ham, Dart —74Pd 153
Valley Wlk. Croy—75Yb 148
Valley Wlk. Rick—15S 18
Valley Way. Ger X—1N 53
Valliere Rd. NW10—41Wa 80
Valliers Wood Rd. Sidc—60Uc 108
Vallis Way. W13—43Ja 78
Vallis Way. Chess—77Ma 143
Valmar Av. Stanf—2K 93
Valmar Rd. SE5—53Sb 105
Valnay St. SW17—64Hb 125
Valognes Av. E17—25Ac 44
Valonia Gdns. SW18—58Bb 103
Vambery Rd. SE18—51Sc 108
Vanbrough Cres. N'holt—39Y 57
Vanbrugh Clo. E16—43Mc 85
Vanbrugh Fields. SE3—52Hc 107
Vanbrugh Hill—50Hc 85
SE3 1-31 & 2-44
SE10 remainder
Vanbrugh Pk. SE3—52Hc 107
Vanbrugh Pk. Rd. SE3—52Hc 107
Vanbrugh Pk. Rd. W. SE3 —52Hc 107
Vanbrugh Rd. W4—48Ta 79
Vanbrugh Ter. SE3—53Hc 107
Vanburgh Clo. Orp—74Uc 150
Vancouver Clo. Eps—83Sa 161
Vancouver Rd. SE23—61Ac 128
Vancouver Rd. Edgw—25Ra 39
Vancouver Rd. Hay—42X 77
Vancouver Rd. Rich—63La 122
Vanderbilt Rd. SW18—60Eb 103
Vandome Clo. E16—44Kc 85
Vandon Pas. SW1 —48Lb 82 (3C 204)
Vandon St. SW1—48Lb 82 (3C 204)
Van Dyck Av. N Mald—73Ta 143
Vandyke Clo. SW15—58Za 102
Vandyke Cross. SE9—57Nc 108
Vandy St. EC2—42Ub 83 (6H 195)
Vane Clo. NW3—35Fb 61
Vane Clo. Harr—30Pa 39
Vanessa Clo. Belv—50Cd 88
Vanessa Wlk. Grav—4H 137
Vanessa Way. Bex—62Fd 132
Vane St. SW1—49Lb 82 (5C 204)
Vanguard Clo. Croy—74Rb 147
Vanguard Clo. Romf—26Dd 48
Vanguard St. SE8—53Cc 106
Vanguard Way. Wall—80Nb 146
Vanners Pde. Wey—85N 157
Vanoc Gdns. Brom—63Jc 129
Vanquisher Wlk. Grav—2H 137
Vansittart Est. Wind—2G 94
Vansittart Rd. E7—35Hc 65
Vansittart Rd. Wind—3F 94
Vansittart St. SE14—51Ac 106
Vanston Pl. SW6—52Cb 103
Vantage Rd. Slou—6F 72
Vant Rd. SW17—64Hb 125
Varcoe Rd. SE16—50Xb 83
Vardens Rd. SW11—56Fb 103
Varden St. E1—44Xb 83
Varley Pde. NW9—28Ua 40
Varley Rd. E16—44Kc 85
Varna Rd. SW6—52Ab 102
Varna Rd. Hmptn—67Da 121
Varndell St. NW1 —41Lb 82 (3B 192)
Vartry Rd. N15—30Tb 43
Vassall Rd. SW9—52Qb 104
Vauban St. SE16 —48Vb 83 (4K 207)
Vaughan Av. NW4—29Wa 40
Vaughan Av. W6—49Va 80
Vaughan Av. Horn—35Md 69
Vaughan Clo. Hmptn—65Aa 121
Vaughan Est. E2—(3K 195)
Vaughan Gdns. Ilf—31Pc 66
Vaughan Gdns. Wind—9D 72
Vaughan Rd. E15—37Hc 65
Vaughan Rd. SE5—54Sb 105
Vaughan Rd. Harr—31Ea 58
Vaughan Rd. Th Dit—73Ka 142
Vaughan Rd. Well—54Vc 109
Vaughan Way. Slou—2C 72
Vaughan Williams Clo. SE8 —52Cc 106
Vaux Cres. W on T—79X 141
Vauxhall Bri. SW1 & SE1 —50Nb 82 (7F 205)
Vauxhall Bri. Rd. SW1 —49Lb 82 (4B 204)
Vauxhall Clo. Grav—9B 114
Vauxhall Cross. SE1—50Nb 82
Vauxhall Gdns. S Croy—79Sb 147
Vauxhall Gro. SW8—51Pb 104
Vauxhall Pl. Dart—59Nd 111
Vauxhall St. SE11 —50Pb 82 (7J 205)
Vauxhall Wlk. SE11 —50Pb 82 (7H 205)
Vawdrey Clo. E1—42Yb 84
Vectis Gdns. SW17—65Kb 126
Vectis Rd. SW17—65Kb 126
Veda Rd. SE13—56Cc 106
Vega Cres. N'wd—22V 36
Vegal Cres. Egh—4N 117
Vega Rd. Bush, Wat—17Ea 20
Velde Way. SE22—57Ub 105
Venables St. NW8 —42Fb 81 (7C 190)
Vencourt Pl. W6—49Wa 80
Venetian Rd. SE5—54Sb 105
Venetia Rd. N4—30Rb 43
Venetia Rd. W5—47Ma 79
Venette Clo. Rain—43Kd 89
Venner Rd. SE26—65Yb 128
Venners Clo. Bexh—54Gd 110
Venn St. SW4—56Lb 104
Ventnor Av. Stan—25Ka 38
Ventnor Dri. N20—20Db 23
Ventnor Gdns. Bark—37Uc 66
Ventnor Rd. SE14—52Zb 106
Ventnor Rd. Sutt—80Db 145
Venton Clo. Wok—5E 188
Venture Clo. Bex—59Ad 109
Venue St. E14—43Ec 84
Venus Hill. Hem—3C 2
Venus Rd. SE18—48Pc 86
Veny Cres. Horn—36Md 69
Vera Av. N21—15Qb 24
Vera Ct. Wat—17Z 19
Vera Rd. SW6—53Ab 102
Verbena Clo. S Ock—44Yd 90
Verbena Clo. W Dray—50M 75
Verbena Gdns. W6—50Wa 80
Verdant La. SE6—59Gc 107
Verdayne Av. Croy—75Zb 148
Verdayne Gdns. Warl—88Yb 166
Verderers Rd. Chig—21Wc 47
Verdun Rd. SE18—51Wc 109
Verdun Rd. SW13—51Wa 102
Vereker Dri. Sun—69W 120
Vereker Rd. W14—50Ab 80
Vere Rd. Lou—14Sc 28
Vere St. W1—44Kb 82 (3K 197)
Verity Clo. W11—45Ab 80
Vermont Rd. SE19—65Ub 127
Vermont Rd. SW18—58Db 103
Vermont Rd. Slou—2D 72
Vermont Rd. Sutt—76Db 145
Verney Gdns. Dag—35Ad 67
Verney Rd. SE16—50Xb 83
Verney Rd. Dag—35Ad 67
(in two parts)
Verney Rd. Slou—49C 74
Verney St. NW10—34Ta 59
Verney Way. SE16—50Xb 83
Vernham Rd. SE18—51Sc 108
Vernon Av. E12—35Pc 66
Vernon Av. SW20—68Za 124
Vernon Av. Enf—8Ac 12
Vernon Av. Wfd G—24Kc 45
Vernon Clo. Cher—79F 138
Vernon Clo. Eps—79Sa 143
Vernon Clo. Orp—69Xc 131
Vernon Clo. Sev—80Vd 154
Vernon Ct. W5—45La 78
Vernon Ct. Stan—25Ka 38
Vernon Cres. Barn—16Jb 24
Vernon Cres. Brtwd—20Ce 33
Vernon Dri. Stan—25Ja 38
Vernon Dri. Uxb—25L 35
Vernon Pl. WC1—43Nb 82 (1G 199)
Vernon Rise. WC1 —41Pb 82 (3J 193)
Vernon Rise. Gnfd—36Fa 58
Vernon Rd. E3—40Bc 64
Vernon Rd. E11—33Gc 65
Vernon Rd. E15—38Gc 65
Vernon Rd. E17—29Bc 44
Vernon Rd. N8—27Qb 42
Vernon Rd. SW14—55Ta 101
Vernon Rd. Bush, Wat—15Aa 19
Vernon Rd. Felt—61V 120
Vernon Rd. Ilf—32Vc 67
Vernon Rd. Romf—22Ed 48
Vernon Rd. Sutt—78Fb 145
Vernon Rd. Swans—58Ee 113
Vernon Sq. WC1—41Pb 82 (3J 193)
Vernon St. W14—49Ab 80
Vernon Wlk. Tad—92Za 178
Vernon Yd. W11—45Bb 81
Veroan Rd. Bexh—54Ad 109
Verona Clo. Uxb—43L 75
Verona Dri. Surb—75Na 143
Verona Gdns. Grav—3G 136
Verona Rd. E7—38Jc 65
Veronica Clo. Romf—24Ld 49
Veronica Rd. SW17—61Kb 126
Veronique Gdns. Ilf—29Sc 46
Verran Rd. SW12—59Kb 104
Versailles Rd. SE19—66Wb 127
Verulam Av. E17—31Bc 64
Verulam Av. Purl—84Lb 164
Verulam Bldgs. WC1—(7K 193)
Verulam Pas. Wat—12X 19
Verulam Rd. Gnfd—42Ca 77
Verulam St. WC1 —43Qb 82 (7K 193)
Verwood Rd. Harr—26Ea 38
Vesage Ct. EC1—(1A 200)
Vesey Path. E14—44Dc 84
Vespan Rd. W12—47Wa 80
Vesta Rd. SE4—54Ac 106
Vestris Rd. SE23—61Zb 128
Vestry Cotts. Sev—91Ld 187
Vestry Industrial Est. Sev —91Ld 187
Vestry M. SE5—53Ub 105
Vestry Rd. E17—28Dc 44
Vestry Rd. SE5—53Ub 105
Vestry Rd. Sev—91Ld 187
Vestry St. N1—41Tb 83 (3F 195)
Vevey St. SE6—61Bc 128
Veysey Gdns. Dag—34Cd 68
Viaduct Bldgs. EC1 —43Qb 82 (1A 200)
Viaduct Pl. E2—41Xb 83
Viaduct St. E2—41Xb 83
Viaduct, The. E18—26Kc 45
Vian Av. Enf—7Ac 12
Vian St. SE13—55Dc 106
Via Romana. Grav—10K 115
Vibart Gdns. SW2—59Pb 104
Vicarage Av. SE3—52Jc 107
Vicarage Av. Egh—64D 118
Vicarage Clo. Brtwd—21Ud 50
Vicarage Clo. Eri—51Ed 110
Vicarage Clo. Lea—97Ca 175
Vicarage Clo. N'holt—38Ba 57
Vicarage Clo. Pot B—2Hb 9
Vicarage Clo. Ruis—31T 56
Vicarage Clo. Tad—96Ab 178
Vicarage Ct. W8—47Db 81
Vicarage Ct. Egh—65D 118
Vicarage Ct. Felt—59S 98
Vicarage Ct. Ilf—36Rc 66
Vicarage Cres. SW11—53Fb 103
Vicarage Cres. Egh—64D 118
Vicarage Dri. SW14—57Ta 101
Vicarage Dri. Bark—38Sc 66
Vicarage Dri. Grav—58Ee 113
Vicarage Farm Rd. Houn—54Aa 99
Vicarage Fields. W on T—72Y 141
Vicarage Gdns. W8—46Cb 81
Vicarage Gdns. Mitc—69Gb 125
Vicarage Ga. W8—46Db 81
Vicarage Gro. SE5—53Tb 105
Vicarage Hill. West—98Tc 184
Vicarage La. E6—41Pc 86
Vicarage La. E15—38Gc 65
Vicarage La. Chig—19Sc 28
Vicarage La. Eps—81Wa 162
Vicarage La. Grav—1J 137
Vicarage La. Ilf—32Tc 66
Vicarage La. K Lan—1P 3
Vicarage La. Lea—94Ka 176
Vicarage La. Sev—91Fd 186
Vicarage La. Stai—69L 119
Vicarage La. Wok—98E 172
Vicarage La. Wray, Stai—60A 96
Vicarage Pk. SE18—50Sc 86
Vicarage Path. N8—31Mb 62
Vicarage Pl. Slou—8L 73
Vicarage Rd. E10—31Cc 64
Vicarage Rd. E15—38Hc 65
Vicarage Rd. N17—25Wb 43
Vicarage Rd. NW4—30Wa 40
Vicarage Rd. SE18—50Sc 86
Vicarage Rd. SW14—57Ta 101
Vicarage Rd. Bex—60Dd 110
Vicarage Rd. Croy—76Qb 146
Vicarage Rd. Dag—38Dd 68
Vicarage Rd. Egh—65D 118
Vicarage Rd. Epp—1Yc 15
Vicarage Rd. Horn—32Jd 68
Vicarage Rd. King—68Ma 123
Vicarage Rd. King—67La 122
(Hampton Wick)
Vicarage Rd. Stai—62G 118
Vicarage Rd. Sun—64V 120
Vicarage Rd. Sutt—76Db 145
Vicarage Rd. Tedd—64Ja 122
Vicarage Rd. Twic—61Ga 122
Vicarage Rd. Twic—58Ea 100
(Whitton)
Vicarage Rd. Wat—16W 18
Vicarage Rd. Wok—93B 172
Vicarage Rd. Wfd G—24Nc 46
Vicarage Wlk. SW11—53Fb 103
Vicarage Way. NW10—34Ta 59
Vicarage Way. Ger X—30B 34
Vicarage Way. Harr—31Ca 57
Vicarage Way. Slou—52F 96
Vicar's Clo. E9—39Yb 64
Vicars Clo. E15—39Jc 65
Vicars Clo. Enf—12Ub 25
Vicar's Hill. SE13—56Dc 106
Vicars Moor La. N21—17Rb 25
Vicars Oak Rd. SE19—65Ub 127
Vicar's Rd. NW5—36Jb 62
Vicars Wlk. Dag—34Xc 67
Viceroy Ct. Croy—74Tb 147
Viceroy Rd. SW8—53Nb 104
Vickers Rd. Eri—50Fd 88
Victor App. Horn—32Md 69
Victor Clo. Horn—32Md 69
Victor Gdns. Horn—32Md 69
Victor Gro. Wemb—38Na 59
Victoria Arc. SW1—(4A 204)
Victoria Av. E6—39Mc 65
Victoria Av. EC2—43Ub 83 (1J 201)
Victoria Av. N3—25Bb 41
Victoria Av. Barn—14Fb 23
Victoria Av. E Mol—69Da 121
Victoria Av. Grav—9D 114
Victoria Av. Grays—47Ee 91
Victoria Av. Houn—57Ca 99
Victoria Av. Romf—23Dd 48
Victoria Av. S Croy—82Sb 165
Victoria Av. Surb—72Ma 143
Victoria Av. Uxb—37R 56
Victoria Av. Wall—76Jb 146
Victoria Av. Wemb—37Ra 59
Victoria Clo. Barn—14Fb 23
Victoria Clo. E Mol—69Ca 121
Victoria Clo. Grays—47Ee 91
Victoria Clo. Hay—44T 76
Victoria Clo. Rick—17M 17
Victoria Clo. Wey—76T 140
Victoria Cotts. Rich—53Pa 101
Victoria Ct. Brtwd—21Yd 50
Victoria Ct. Wemb—37Qa 59
Victoria Cres. N15—29Ub 43
Victoria Cres. SE19—65Ub 127
Victoria Cres. SW19—66Bb 125
Victoria Cres. Iver—45H 75
Victoria Dock Rd. E16—44Gc 85
Victoria Dri. SW19—59Za 102
Victoria Dri. S Dar, Dart—68Td 134
Victoria Embkmt. SW1, WC2 & EC4—47Nb 82 (1G 205)
Victoria Gdns. W11—46Cb 81
Victoria Gdns. Houn—53Aa 99
Victoria Gdns. West—87Lc 167
Victoria Gro. N12—22Fb 41
Victoria Gro. W8—48Eb 81 (3A 202)
Victoria Hill Rd. Swan—67Jd 132
Victoria La. Barn—14Bb 23
Victoria La. Hay—50S 76
Victoria M. NW6—39Cb 61
Victoria M. SW4—56Kb 104
Victorian Gro. N16—34Ub 63
Victorian Rd. N16—34Vb 63
Victoria Pk. Rd. E9—39Yb 64
Victoria Pk. Sq. E2—41Yb 84
Victoria Pas. Wat—14X 19
Victoria Pl. Eps—84Ua 162
Victoria Pl. Rich—57Ma 101
Victoria Rise. SW4—55Kb 104
Victoria Rd. E4—18Gc 27
Victoria Rd. E11—35Gc 65
Victoria Rd. E13—40Jc 65
Victoria Rd. E17—26Ec 44
Victoria Rd. E18—27Kc 45
Victoria Rd. N4—31Pb 62
Victoria Rd. N15—28Wb 43
Victoria Rd.—21Vb 43
N18 1-55
N9 remainder
Victoria Rd. N22—25Lb 42
Victoria Rd. NW4—28Ya 40
Victoria Rd. NW6—40Bb 61
Victoria Rd. NW7—22Va 40
Victoria Rd. SW14—55Ta 101
Victoria Rd. W3—43Ta 79
Victoria Rd. W5—43Ka 78
Victoria Rd. W8—48Eb 81
Victoria Rd. Asc—10A 116
Victoria Rd. Bark—37Rc 66
Victoria Rd. Barn—14Fb 23
Victoria Rd. Bexh—56Cd 110
Victoria Rd. Brtwd—21Yd 50
Victoria Rd. Brom—71Mc 149
Victoria Rd. Buck H—19Mc 27
Victoria Rd. Bush, Wat—18Da 19
Victoria Rd. Chst—64Qc 130
Victoria Rd. Coul—87Mb 164
Victoria Rd. Dag—36Dd 68
Victoria Rd. Dart—57Md 111
Victoria Rd. Eri—51Gd 110
Victoria Rd. Felt—60X 99
Victoria Rd. Grav—10B 114
Victoria Rd. King—68Pa 123
Victoria Rd. Mitc—66Gb 125
Victoria Rd. Romf—30Hd 48
Victoria Rd. Ruis—32W 56
Victoria Rd. Sev—97Kd 187
Victoria Rd. Sidc—62Vc 131
Victoria Rd. Slou—6M 73
Victoria Rd. Slou—7G 52
(Farnham Common)
Victoria Rd. S'hall—48Ba 77
Victoria Rd. Stai—62G 118
Victoria Rd. Stanf—2L 93
Victoria Rd. Stanf—1H 93
(Horndon on the Hill)
Victoria Rd. Surb—72Ma 143
Victoria Rd. Sutt—78Fb 145
Victoria Rd. Tedd—65Ha 122
Victoria Rd. Twic—59Ka 100
Victoria Rd. Uxb—38L 55
Victoria Rd. Wal A—6Ec 12
Victoria Rd. Wat—10X 5
Victoria Rd. Wey—76T 140
Victoria Rd. Wey—77M 139
(Addlestone)
Victoria Rd. Wind—9C 72
Victoria Rd. Wok—90A 156
Victoria Rd. Wok—5A 188
(Knaphill)
Victoria Scott Ct. Dart—55Hd 110
Victoria Sq. SW1 —48Kb 82 (3A 204)
Victoria St. E15—38Gc 65
Victoria St. SW1—48Lb 82 (4A 204)
Victoria St. Belv—50Bd 87
Victoria St. Egh—5N 117
Victoria St. Slou—7K 73
Victoria St. Wind—3H 95
Victoria Ter. N4—32Qb 62
Victoria Ter. Harr—32Ga 58
Victoria Vs. Rich—56Pa 101
Victoria Way. SE7—50Kc 85
Victoria Way. Wey—76T 140
Victoria Way. Wok—89A 156
Victor Rd. NW10—41Xa 80
Victor Rd. SE20—66Zb 128
Victor Rd. Harr—27Ea 38
Victor Rd. Tedd—63Ga 122
Victor Rd. Wind—5G 94
Victors Cres. Brtwd—19De 33
Victors Dri. Hmptn—65Aa 121
Victor Vs. N9—20Tb 25
Victor Wlk. Horn—32Md 69
Victory Av. Mord—71Eb 145
Victory Pk. Rd. Wey—77L 139
Victory Pl. SE17—49Tb 83 (5F 207)
Victory Pl. SE19—66Ub 127
Victory Rd. SW19—66Eb 125
Victory Rd. Cher—74J 139
Victory Rd. Rain—40Jd 68
Victory Sq. SE5—51Tb 105
Victory Wlk. SE8—53Cc 106
Victory Way. SE16—47Ac 84
Victory Way. Houn—50Y 77
Victory Way. Romf—26Dd 48
View Clo. N6—31Hb 61
View Clo. Chig—22Tc 46
View Clo. Harr—28Fa 38
View Clo. West—88Lc 167
Viewfield Rd. SW18—58Bb 103
Viewfield Rd. Sidc—60Yc 109
Viewland Rd. SE18—50Vc 87
Viewlands Av. West—92Uc 184
View Rd. N6—31Hb 61
View Rd. Pot B—4Eb 9
View, The. SE2—50Ad 87
Viga Rd. N21—16Qb 24
Vigerons Way. Grays—9D 92
Viggory La. Wok—3F 188
Vigilant Clo. SE26—63Wb 127
Vigilant Way. Grav 4H 137
Vignoles Rd. Romf—31Cd 68
★Vigo Rd. Sev—83De
Vigo St. W1—45Lb 82 (5B 198)
Viking Rd. Grav—62Ee 135
Viking Rd. S'hall—45Aa 77
Viking Way. Brtwd—16Xd 32
Viking Way. Sev—78Ud 154
Villa Clo. Grav—1K 137
Villacourt Rd. SE18—52Wc 109
Village Clo. E4—22Ec 44
Village Grn. Av. West—89Nc 168
Village Grn. Rd. Dart—56Jd 110
Village Grn. Way. West—89Nc 168
Village La. Slou—2H 53
Village Rd. N3—26Ab 40
Village Rd. Egh—70D 118
Village Rd. Enf—17Tb 25
Village Rd. Uxb—33H 55
Village Rd. Wind—8A 72
Village Row. Sutt—80Cb 145
Village, The. SE7—51Mc 107
Village Way. NW10—35Ta 59
Village Way. SE21—58Tb 105
Village Way. Amer—12A 16
Village Way. Ashf—63P 119
Village Way. Beck—68Cc 128
Village Way. Pinn—31Aa 57
Village Way. S Croy—85Wb 165
Village Way E. Harr—31Ca 57
Villa Rd. SW9—55Qb 104
Villas Rd. SE18—49Sc 86
(in two parts)
Villa St. SE17—50Tb 83 (7G 207)
Villa Wlk. SE17—50Tb 83
Villiers Av. Surb—71Pa 143
Villiers Av. Twic—60Ba 99
Villiers Clo. E10—33Cc 64
Villiers Clo. Surb—70Pa 123
Villiers Path. Surb—71Na 143
Villiers Rd. NW2—37Wa 60
Villiers Rd. Beck—68Zb 128
Villiers Rd. Iswth—54Ga 100
Villiers Rd. King—70Pa 123
Villiers Rd. Slou—3H 73
Villiers Rd. S'hall—46Ba 77
Villiers Rd. Wat—16Aa 19
Villiers St. WC2—46Nb 82 (5F 199)
Villier St. Uxb—40M 55
Vincam Clo. Twic—59Ca 99
Vincent Av. Cars—83Fb 163
Vincent Av. Surb—75Sa 143
Vincent Clo. SE16—47Ac 84
Vincent Clo. Barn—13Db 23
Vincent Clo. Brom—70Kc 129
Vincent Clo. Cher—73G 138
Vincent Clo. Coul—92Hb 179
Vincent Clo. Esh—76Da 141
Vincent Clo. Ilf—23Sc 46
Vincent Clo. Lea—95Da 175
Vincent Clo. Sidc—60Uc 108
Vincent Clo. Wal X—1Ac 12
Vincent Clo. W Dray—51Q 98
Vincent Dri. Shep—69U 120
Vincent Gdns. NW2—34Va 60
Vincent Rd. E4—23Fc 45
Vincent Rd. N15—28Sb 43
Vincent Rd. N22—26Qb 42
Vincent Rd. SE18—49Rc 86
Vincent Rd. W3—48Sa 79
Vincent Rd. Cher—73G 138
Vincent Rd. Cob—88Aa 159
Vincent Rd. Coul—88Lb 164
Vincent Rd. Croy—73Ub 147
Vincent Rd. Dag—38Ad 67
Vincent Rd. Houn—55Z 99
Vincent Rd. Iswth—53Fa 100
Vincent Rd. King—69Qa 123
Vincent Rd. Rain—42Ld 89
Vincent Rd. Wemb—38Pa 59
Vincent Row. Hmptn—65Ea 122
Vincent Sq. SW1 —49Mb 82 (5C 204)
Vincent Sq. West—85Lc 167
Vincent St. E16—43Hc 85
Vincent St. SW1 —49Mb 82 (5D 204)
Vincent Ter. N1—40Rb 63 (1B 194)
Vince St. EC1—41Tb 83 (4G 195)
Vine Av. Sev—96Kd 187
Vine Clo. Stai—57J 97
Vine Clo. Surb—72Pa 143
Vine Clo. Sutt—76Eb 145
Vine Clo. W Dray—49Q 76
Vine Ct. E1—43Wb 83
Vine Ct. Harr—30Na 39
Vine Ct. Rd. Sev—96Ld 187
Vinegar All. E17—28Dc 44
Vine Gdns. Ilf—36Sc 66
Vinegar Yd. SE1—(1H 207)
Vine Gro. Uxb—38Q 56
Vine Hill. EC1—42Qb 82 (6K 193)
Vine La. SE1—46Ub 83 (7J 201)
Vine La. Uxb—39P 55
Vine Pl. Houn—56Da 99
Vineries Bank. NW7—22Xa 40
Vineries Clo. Dag—37Bd 67
Vineries Clo. W Dray—51Q 98
Vineries, The. N14—16Lb 24
Vineries, The. SE6—60Cc 106
Vineries, The. Enf—13Ub 25
Vine Rd. E15—38Hc 65
Vine Rd. SW13—55Va 102
Vine Rd. E Mol—70Fa 122
Vine Rd. Orp—79Vc 151
Vine Rd. Slou—7K 53
Vines Av. N3—25Db 41
Vine St. EC3—45Vb 83 (3K 201)
(in two parts)
Vine St. W1—45Lb 82 (5C 198)
Vine St. Romf—28Ed 48
Vine St. Uxb—39M 55
Vine St. Bri. EC1—42Qb 82 (6A 194)
Vine St. Bldgs. SE1—(7J 201)
Vine Way. Brtwd—18Yd 32
Vine Yd. SE1—(1E 206)
Vineyard Av. NW7—24Ab 40
Vineyard Clo. SE6—60Cc 106
Vineyard Hill. Pot B—1Jb 10
Vineyard Hill Rd. SW19—63Cb 125
Vineyard M. EC1—(5K 193)
Vineyard Pas. Rich—57Na 101
Vineyard Path. SW14—55Ta 101
Vineyard Rd. Felt—62W 120
Vineyard Row. King—67La 122
Vineyards Rd. Pot B—2Hb 9
Vineyard, The. Rich—57Na 101
Vineyard Wlk. EC1 —42Qb 82 (5K 193)
Viney Bank. Croy—81Bc 166
Viney Rd. SE13—55Dc 106
Vining St. SW9—56Qb 104
Vinlake Av. Uxb—34P 55
Vinson Clo. Orp—74Wc 151
Vintners Pl. EC4—45Sb 83 (4E 200)
Viola Av. SE2—49Xc 87
Viola Av. Felt—58Y 99
Viola Av. Stai—60N 97
Viola Clo. S Ock—41Yd 90
Viola Sq. W12—45Va 80
Violet Av. Enf—10Tb 11
Violet Av. Uxb—43P 75
Violet Gdns. Croy—78Rb 147
Violet Hill. NW8—40Eb 61 (2A 190)
Violet La. Croy—78Rb 147
Violet Rd. E3—42Dc 84
Violet Rd. E17—30Cc 44
Violet Rd. E18—26Kc 45
Violet St. E2—42Xb 83
Violet Way. Rick—14L 17
Virgil Pl. W1—43Hb 81 (1F 197)
Virgil St. SE1—48Pb 82 (3J 205)
Virginia Av. Vir W—10N 117
Virginia Clo. Asht—90Ma 161
Virginia Dri. Vir W—10N 117
Virginia Gdns. Ilf—26Tc 46
Virginia Rd. E2—41Vb 83 (4K 195)
Virginia Rd. T Hth—67Rb 127
Virginia St. E1—45Wb 83
Virginia Wlk. SW2—58Pb 104
Virginia Wlk. Grav—5F 136
Viscount Gro. N'holt—41Z 77
Viscount Rd. Stai—60N 97
Viscount St. EC1 —42Sb 83 (6D 194)
Viscount Way. Houn—56U 98
Vista Av. Enf—12Zb 26
Vista Dri. Ilf—29Mc 45
Vista, The. SE9—58Mc 107
Vista, The. Sidc—64Vc 131
Vista Way. Harr—30Na 39
Viveash Clo. Hay—48V 76
Vivian Av. NW4—29Xa 40
Vivian Av. Wemb—36Qa 59
Vivian Clo. Wat—18W 18
Vivian Gdns. Wat—18W 18
Vivian Gdns. Wemb—36Qa 59
Vivian Rd. E3—40Ac 64
Vivian Sq. SE15—55Xb 105
Vivian Way. N2—29Fb 41
Vivien Clo. Chess—80Na 143
Vivienne Clo. Twic—58Ma 101
Voce Rd. SE18—52Tc 108
Voewood Clo. N Mald—72Va 144
Voltaire Rd. SW4—55Mb 104
Voltaire Way. Hay—45U 76
Voluntary Pl. E11—30Jc 45
Vorley Rd. N19—33Lb 62
Voss Ct. SW16—65Nb 126
Voss St. E2—41Wb 83
Vulcan Clo. Wall—80Pb 146
Vulcan Ga. Enf—12Qb 24
Vulcan Rd. SE4—54Bc 106
Vulcan Ter. SE4—54Bc 106
Vulcan Way. N7—37Pb 62
Vulcan Way. Croy—82Gc 167
Vyner Rd. W3—45Ta 79
Vyner St. E2—39Xb 63
Vyner's Way. Uxb—36Q 56
Vyne, The. Bexh—55Dd 110
Vyse Clo. Barn—14Ya 22

Wadding St. SE17 —49Tb 83 (6F 207)
Waddington Av. Coul—92Qb 180
Waddington Clo. Coul—91Rb 181
Waddington Rd. E15—36Fc 65
Waddington St. E15—37Fc 65
Waddington Way. SE19—66Sb 127
Waddon Clo. Croy—76Qb 146
Waddon Ct. Rd. Croy—76Qb 146
Waddon Marsh Way. Croy —74Pb 146
Waddon New Rd. Croy—76Rb 147
Waddon Pk. Av. Croy—77Qb 146
Waddon Rd. Croy—76Qb 146
Waddon Way. Croy—79Qb 146
Wade Av. Orp—73Zc 151
Wade Dri. Slou—6E 72
Wade Rd. E16—44Lc 85
Wades Gro. N21—17Qb 24
Wades Hill. N21—16Qb 24
Wades La. Tedd—64Ja 122
Wadeson St. E2—40Xb 63
Wade's Pl. E14—45Dc 84
Wadeville Av. Romf—31Bd 67
Wadeville Clo. Belv—50Cd 88
Wadham Av. E17—24Dc 44
Wadham Clo. Shep—73S 140
Wadham Gdns. NW3—38Gb 61
Wadham Gdns. Gnfd—37Fa 58
Wadham Rd. E17—25Dc 44
Wadham Rd. SW15—56Ab 102
Wadham Rd. Abb L, Wat—3V 4
Wadhurst Clo. SE20—68Xb 127
Wadhurst Rd. SW8—53Lb 104
Wadhurst Rd. W4—48Ta 79
Wadley Rd. E11—31Gc 65
Wadsworth Clo. Enf—15Zb 26
Wadsworth Clo. Gnfd—40La 58
Wadsworth Rd. Gnfd—40Ka 58
Wager St. E3—42Bc 84
Waggon La. N17—23Wb 43
Waggon Rd. Barn—9Eb 9
Waghorn Rd. E13—39Lc 65
Waghorn Rd. Harr—27Ma 39
Waghorn St. SE15—55Wb 105
Wagner St. SE15—52Yb 106
Wagon Rd. Barn—8Db 9
Wagon Way. Rick—13L 17
Wagtail Gdns. S Croy—82Ac 166
Waid Clo. Dart—58Pd 111
Waights Ct. King—67Na 123
Wain Clo. Pot B—1Db 9
Wainfleet Av. Romf—26Ed 48
Wainford Clo. SW19—60Za 102
Wainwright Av. Brtwd—16Fe 33
Wainwright Gro. Iswth—56Fa 100
Waite Davies Rd. SE12—59Hc 107
Waite St. SE15—51Vb 105
Waithman St. EC4—(3B 200)
Wakefield Cres. Slou—7K 53

Westbourne Rd.—Whiston Rd.

Westbourne Rd. Uxb—42R 76
Westbourne St. W2
—45Fb 81 (4B 196)
Westbourne Ter. W2
—44Eb 81 (2A 196)
Westbourne Ter. M. W2
—44Eb 81 (2A 196)
Westbourne Ter. Rd. W2—43Eb 81
Westbourne Ter. Rd. Bri. W2
—(7A 190)
Westbridge Rd. SW11—53Fb 103
Westbrook Av. Hmptn—66Ba 121
Westbrook Clo. Barn—13Fb 23
Westbrook Cres. Barn—13Fb 23
Westbrook Dri. Orp—74Zc 151
Westbrooke Cres. Well—55Yc 109
Westbrooke Rd. Sidc—61Tc 130
Westbrooke Rd. Well—55Xc 109
Westbrook Rd. SE3—53Kc 107
Westbrook Rd. Houn—52Ba 99
Westbrook Rd. Stai—64H 119
Westbrook Rd. T Hth—68Tb 127
Westbrook Sq. Barn—13Fb 23
Westbury Av. N22—27Rb 43
Westbury Av. Esh—79Ha 142
Westbury Av. S'hall—42Ca 77
Westbury Av. Wemb—38Na 59
Westbury Clo. Ruis—31W 56
Westbury Clo. Shep—72R 140
Westbury Dri. Brtwd—19Yd 32
Westbury Gro. N12—23Cb 41
Westbury La. Buck H—19Lc 27
Westbury Lodge Clo. Pinn—27Z 37
Westbury Pl. Bren—51Ma 101
Westbury Rd. E7—37Kc 65
Westbury Rd. E17—28Cc 44
Westbury Rd. N11—23Nb 42
Westbury Rd. N12—22Cb 41
Westbury Rd. SE20—67Zb 128
Westbury Rd. W5—44Na 79
Westbury Rd. Bark—39Tc 66
Westbury Rd. Beck—69Ac 128
Westbury Rd. Brtwd—19Yd 32
Westbury Rd. Brom—67Mc 129
Westbury Rd. Buck H—18Lc 27
Westbury Rd. Croy—72Tb 147
Westbury Rd. Felt—60Z 99
Westbury Rd. Ilf—33Qc 66
Westbury Rd. N Mald—70Ta 123
Westbury Rd. N'wd—21U 36
Westbury Rd. Wat—15X 19
Westbury Rd. Wemb—38Na 59
Westbury St. SW8—54Lb 104
Westbury Ter. E7—37Kc 65
Westbury Ter. Upm—33Ud 70
Westbury Ter. West—99Sc 184
Westcar La. W on T—79X 141
W. Carriage Dri. W2—(5D 196)
W. Central St. WC1
—44Nb 82 (2F 199)
W. Centre Av. NW10—41Xa 80
West Chantry. Harr—25Da 37
Westchester Dri. NW4—27Za 40
West Clo. N9—20Vb 25
West Clo. Ashf—63N 119
West Clo. Barn—15Xa 22
West Clo. Barn—14Jb 24
(Cockfosters)
West Clo. Gnfd—40Ea 58
West Clo. Hmptn—65Aa 121
West Clo. Rain—42Kd 89
West Clo. Wemb—32Pa 59
Westcombe Av. SW20—67Va 124
Westcombe Av. Croy—73Nb 146
Westcombe Dri. Barn—15Cb 23
Westcombe Hill. SE3—52Jc 107
Westcombe Pk. Rd. SE3
—51Gc 107
West Comn. Ger X—29A 34
W. Common Clo. Ger X—29A 34
W. Common Rd. Brom—75Jc 149
W. Common Rd. Uxb—37M 55
Westcote Rise. Ruis—31S 56
Westcote Rd. SW16—64Lb 126
West Cotts. NW6—36Cb 61
Westcott Av. Grav—2C 136
Westcott Clo. N15—30Vb 43
Westcott Clo. Brom—71Nc 150
Westcott Clo. Croy—81Dc 166
Westcott Cres. W7—44Ga 78
Westcott Rd. SE17—51Rb 105
Westcott Way. Sutt—82Ya 162
West Ct. Wemb—33La 58
West Cres. Wind—3D 94
W. Crescent Rd. Grav—8D 114
Westcroft. Slou—2F 72
Westcroft Clo. NW2—35Ab 60
Westcroft Gdns. Mord—69Bb 125
Westcroft Rd. Cars & Wall
—77Jb 146
Westcroft Sq. W6—49Wa 80
Westcroft Way. NW2—35Ab 60
W. Cromwell Rd.—50Bb 81
SW5 1-87 & 2-94
W14 remainder
W. Cross Centre. Bren—51Ka 100
W. Cross Route.—45Za 80
W. Cross Way. Bren—51Ka 100
Westdale Pas. SE18—51Rc 108
Westdale Rd. SE18—51Rc 108
Westdean Av. SE12—60Kc 107
W. Dean Way. Wey—76U 140
West Dene. Sutt—79Ab 144
W. Dene Dri. Romf—22Md 49
West Down. Lea—99Da 175
Westdown Rd. E15—35Ec 64
Westdown Rd. SE6—59Cc 106
W. Drayton Pk. Av. W Dray
—48N 75
W. Drayton Rd. Uxb—44Q 76
West Dri. SW16—63Lb 126
West Dri. Cars—82Fb 163
West Dri. Harr—23Fa 38
West Dri. Sutt—81Za 162
West Dri. Tad—90Za 162
West Dri. Wat—8X 5
West Dri. Gdns. Harr—23Fa 38
W. Eaton Pl. SW1
—49Jb 82 (5H 203)
W. Eaton Pl. M. SW1—(5H 203)
Wested La. Swan—73Jd 152
W. Ella Rd. NW10—38Ua 60
West End. Sev—89Pd 171
West End. West—97Xc 185
W. End Av. E10—29Fc 45
W. End Av. Pinn—28Z 37
W. End Ct. Pinn—28Z 37
W. End Ct. Slou—9K 53
W. End Gdns. Esh—78Ba 141
W. End Gdns. N'holt—40Y 57
W. End La. NW6—36Cb 61
W. End La. Barn—14Za 22
W. End La. Esh—80Ba 141
W. End La. Hay—52S 98
W. End La. Pinn—27Z 37
W. End La. Slou—9J 53
W. End Rd. Ruis & N'holt—33U 56
W. End Rd. S'hall—46Aa 77
Westerdale Rd. SE10—50Jc 85
Westerdean Clo. SW18—57Db 103
Westerfield Rd. N15—29Vb 43
Westerfolds Clo. Wok—89E 156
Westergate Rd. SE2—51Ad 109
Westerham Av. N9—20Tb 25
Westerham Clo. Wey—79L 139
Westerham Dri. Sidc—58Yc 109
Westerham Hill. West—93Rc 184
Westerham Rd. E10—31Dc 64
Westerham Rd. Kes—79Mc 149
Westerham Rd. Oxt & West
—100Jc 183
Westerham Rd. Sev—95Dd 186
Westerham Rd. West—98Uc 184
Westerley Cres. SE26—64Bc 128
Western Av. NW11—30Za 40
Western Av. Brtwd—18Yd 32
Western Av. Cher—69J 119
Western Av. Dag—37Ed 68
Western Av. Egh—69D 118
Western Av. Epp—4Vc 15
Western Av. Romf—26Ld 49
Western Av.—35L 55 to 45Ua 80
Uxb 35L 55
Ruis—37S 56
N'holt—38Z 57
Gnfd—39Da 57
W5—41Ma 79
W3—42Qa 79
Western Ct. N3—23Cb 41
Western Dri. Shep—72T 140
Western Gdns. W5—45Qa 79
Western Gdns. Brtwd—19Yd 32
Western La. SW12—59Jb 104
Western Pde. Barn—15Cb 23
Western Perimeter Rd. Houn, Stai
& W Dray—57L to 53M 97
Western Rd. E13—40Lc 65
Western Rd. E17—29Ec 44
Western Rd. N2—28Hb 41
Western Rd. N22—26Pb 42
Western Rd. NW10—42Sa 79
Western Rd. SW9—55Qb 104
Western Rd.—67Fb 125
SW19 193-231 & 278-340
Mitc remainder
Western Rd. W5—45Ma 79
Western Rd. Brtwd—19Yd 32
Western Rd. Epp—4Vc 15
Western Rd. Romf—29Gd 48
★Western Rd. Sev—92Be
Western Rd. S'hall—49Y 77
Western Rd. Sutt—78Cb 145
Western View. Hay—47V 76
Westernville Gdns. Ilf—31Sc 66
Western Way. SE28—47Uc 86
Western Way. Barn—16Db 23
W. Farm Av. Asht—90La 160
W. Farm Clo. Asht—91La 176
W. Farm Dri. Asht—91Ma 177
Westferry Rd. E14—46Cc 84
West Field. Asht—90Pa 161
Westfield. Long, Dart—77Be 155
Westfield. Lou—15Mc 27
Westfield. Sev—94Ld 187
Westfield Av. S Croy—85Tb 165
Westfield Av. Wat—10Z 5
Westfield Av. Wok—93A 172
Westfield Clo. Enf—13Ac 26
Westfield Clo. Grav—4E 136
Westfield Clo. Sutt—77Bb 145
Westfield Clo. Wal X—3Bc 12
Westfield Comn. Wok—94A 172
Westfield Dri. Harr—28Ma 39
Westfield Dri. Lea—94Da 175
Westfield Gdns. Harr—28Ma 39
Westfield Gro. Wok—92A 172
Westfield La. Harr—28Ma 39
Westfield La. Slou—4P 73
Westfield Pde. Wey—82M 157
Westfield Pk. Pinn—24Ba 37
Westfield Rd. NW7—20Ua 22
Westfield Rd. W13—46Ja 78
Westfield Rd. Beck—68Bc 128
Westfield Rd. Bexh—55Ed 110
Westfield Rd. Croy—75Rb 147
Westfield Rd. Dag—35Ad 67
Westfield Rd. Mitc—68Hb 125
Westfield Rd. Slou—2F 72
Westfield Rd. Surb—71Ma 143
Westfield Rd. Sutt—77Bb 145
Westfield Rd. W on T—73Aa 141
Westfield Rd. Wok—94A 172
Westfields. SW13—55Va 102
Westfields Av. SW13—55Ua 102
Westfield Sq. Wok—94A 172
Westfields Rd. W3—43Ra 79
Westfield St. SE18—48Mc 85
Westfield Wlk. Wal X—3Bc 12
Westfield Way. Ruis—34U 56
Westfield Way. Wok—94B 172
W. Garden Pl. W2
—44Gb 81 (3E 196)
West Gdns. E1—45Xb 83
West Gdns. SW17—65Gb 125
West Gdns. Eps—82Ua 162
Westgate. W5—41Na 79
Westgate Clo. Eps—87Ta 161
Westgate Cres. Slou—5D 72
Westgate M. W10—42Za 80
Westgate Rd. SE25—70Xb 127
Westgate Rd. Beck—67Ec 128
Westgate Rd. Dart—58Md 111
Westgate St. E8—39Xb 63
Westgate Ter. SW10—51Db 103
Westglade Ct. Harr—29Ma 39
W. Green Rd. N15—28Rb 43
West Gro. SE10—53Ec 106
West Gro. W on T—77X 141
West Gro. Wfd G—23Lc 45
Westgrove La. SE10—53Ec 106
W. Halkin St. SW1
—48Jb 82 (3H 203)
W. Hallowes. SE9—60Nc 108
Westhall Pk. Warl—91Yb 182
W. Hall Rd. Rich—53Ra 101
Westhall Rd. Warl—90Wb 165
W. Ham La. E15—38Gc 65
W. Hampstead M. NW6—37Db 61
W. Harding St. EC4
—44Qb 82 (2A 200)
Westharold. Swan—69Fd 132
W. Hatch Mnr. Ruis—31V 56
Westhay Gdns. SW14—57Ra 101
W. Heath Av. NW11—32Cb 61
W. Heath Clo. NW3—34Cb 61
W. Heath Clo. Dart—58Hd 110
W. Heath Cotts. Sev—100Kd 187
W. Heath Dri. NW11—32Cb 61
W. Heath Gdns. NW3—34Cb 61
W. Heath La. Sev—100Kd 187
W. Heath Rd. NW3—33Cb 61
W. Heath Rd. SE2—51Zc 109
W. Heath Rd. Dart—58Hd 110
W. Hendon Broadway. NW9
—29Va 40
West Hill—59Za 102
SW18 1-81 & 2-70
SW15 remainder
West Hill. Dart—58Md 111
West Hill. Eps—85Ra 161
West Hill. Harr—33Ga 58
West Hill. Orp—84Pc 168
West Hill. S Croy—82Ub 165
West Hill. Wemb—32Pa 59
W. Hill Av. Eps—85Ra 161
Westhill Clo. Grav—10D 114
W. Hill Ct. N6—34Jb 62
W. Hill Dri. Dart—58Ld 111
W. Hill Pk. N6—33Hb 61
(in two parts)
W. Hill Rise. Dart—58Md 111
W. Hill Rd. SW18—58Bb 103
W. Hill Rd. Wok—91A 172
W. Hill Rd. Wok—7G 188
W. Hill Way. N20—18Db 23
Westholm. NW11—28Db 41
West Holme. Eri—53Ed 110
Westholme. Orp—73Vc 151
Westholme Gdns. Ruis—32W 56
Westhorne Av.—59Jc 107
SE12 1-421 & 2-320
SE9 remainder
Westhorpe Gdns. NW4—27Ya 40
Westhorpe Rd. SW15—55Ya 102
W. House Clo. SW19—60Ab 102
Westhurst Dri. Chst—64Rc 130
W. Hyde La. Ger X—24B 34
W. India Dock Rd. E14—45Cc 84
W. Kent Av. Grav—58Ee 113
Westlake Clo. N13—20Qb 24
Westland Av. Horn—32Nd 69
Westland Dri. Brom—75Hc 149
Westland Pl. N1—41Tb 83 (3F 195)
Westland Rd. Wat—12X 19
Westlands Av. Slou—4A 72
Westlands Clo. Hay—49W 76
Westlands Clo. Slou—4A 72
Westlands Ct. Eps—87Sa 161
Westlands Ter. SW12—58Lb 104
Westlands Way. Oxt—99Fc 183
Westland View. Grays—46Ce 91
Westland Way. Wal—80Mb 146
West La. SE16—47Xb 83
Westlea Av. Wat—9Aa 5
Westlea Rd. W7—48Ja 78
Westleigh Av. SW15—57Xa 102
Westleigh Av. Coul—88Kb 164
Westleigh Dri. Brom—67Nc 130
Westleigh Gdns. Edgw—25Qa 39
W. Lodge Av. W3—46Qa 79
Westlyn Clo. Rain—42Ld 89
W. Malling Way. Horn—36Ld 69
Westmead. SW15—58Xa 102
West Mead. Eps—79Ua 144
West Mead. Ruis—35Y 57
Westmead. Wind—5F 94
Westmead. Wok—5E 188
Westmeade Clo. Wal X—1Xb 11
Westmead Rd. Sutt—77Fb 145
Westmede. Chig—23Sc 46
Westmere Dri. NW7—20Ta 21
West M. N17—23Xb 43
West M. SW1—(6B 204)
Westminster Av. T Hth—68Rb 127
Westminster Bri. SW1 & SE1
—47Nb 82 (2G 205)
Westminster Bri. Rd. SE1
—48Qb 82 (2J 205)
Westminster Clo. Ilf—26Tc 46
Westminster Clo. Tedd—64Ja 122
Westminster Dri. N13—22Nb 42
Westminster Gdns. Bark—40Uc 66
Westminster Gdns. Ilf—26Sc 46
Westminster Industrial Est.
SE18—48Mc 85
Westminster Rd. N9—18Xb 25
Westminster Rd. W7—46Ga 78
Westminster Rd. Sutt—75Fb 145
W. Moat Clo. Beck—66Ec 128
Westmont Rd. Esh—75Ga 142
Westmoor Gdns. Enf—12Zb 26
Westmoor Rd. Enf—12Zb 26
Westmoor St. SE7—48Mc 85
Westmoreland Av. Horn—29Ld 49
Westmoreland Av. Well
—56Uc 108
Westmoreland Bldgs. EC1
—43Sb 83 (1D 200)
Westmoreland Dri. Sutt—80Db 145
Westmoreland Pl. SW1
—50Kb 82 (7A 204)
Westmoreland Pl. W5—43Ma 79
Westmoreland Rd. NW9—27Pa 39
Westmoreland Rd. SE17
—51Tb 105
Westmoreland Rd. SW13
—53Va 102
Westmoreland Rd. Brom
—71Gc 149
Westmoreland St. W1
—43Jb 82 (1J 197)
Westmoreland Ter. SW1
—50Kb 82 (7A 204)
Westmore Rd. West—93Lc 183
Westmorland Clo. E12—33Mc 65
Westmorland Clo. Eps—82Ua 162
Westmorland Clo. Twic—58Ka 100
Westmorland Ct. Surb—73Ma 143
Westmorland Rd. E17—30Cc 44
Westmorland Rd. Harr—29Da 37
Westmorland Way. Mitc
—71Nb 146
Westmount Rd. SE9—54Pc 108
West Oak. Beck—67Fc 129
Westoe Rd. N9—19Xb 25
Weston Av. E Mol—70Aa 121
Weston Av. Th Dit—73Ga 142
Weston Av. Wey—77K 139
Weston Clo. Brtwd—17Ee 33
Weston Clo. Coul—92Pb 180
Weston Dri. Stan—25Ka 38
West One Shopping Centre. W1
—(3J 197)
Weston Gdns. Iswth—53Ga 100
Weston Gdns. Wok—88G 156
Weston Grn. Dag—35Bd 67
Weston Grn. Th Dit—74Ga 142
(in two parts)
Weston Grn. Rd. Esh & Th Dit
—74Fa 142
Weston Gro. Brom—67Hc 129
Weston Pk. N8—30Nb 42
Weston Pk. King—68Na 123
Weston Pk. Th Dit—74Ga 142
Weston Pk. Clo. Th Dit—74Ga 142
Weston Rise. WC1
—41Pb 82 (3J 193)
Weston Rd. W4—48Sa 79
Weston Rd. Brom—66Hc 129
Weston Rd. Dag—35Ad 67
Weston Rd. Enf—12Tb 25
Weston Rd. Slou—3D 72
Weston Rd. Th Dit—74Ga 142
Weston St. SE1—47Ub 83 (1G 207)
Weston St. SE19—65Ub 127
Weston Wlk. E9—38Xb 63
Weston Way. Wok—88G 156
Weston Yd. SE1—47Tb 83 (1G 207)
Westover Clo. Sutt—81Db 163
Westover Hill. NW3—33Cb 61
Westover Rd. SW18—59Eb 103
Westow Hill. SE19—65Ub 127
W. Palace Gdns. Wey—76R 140
West Pk. SE9—61Nc 130
W. Park Av. Rich—53Ra 101
W. Park Clo. Romf—29Zc 47
W. Park Hill. Brtwd—20Wd 32
W. Park Rd. Eps—84Pa 161
W. Park Rd. Rich—53Qa 101
West Pier. E1—46Wb 83
West Pl. SW19—64Ya 124
West Point. Slou—6B 72
Westpoint Trading Est. W3
—43Qa 79
Westpole Av. Barn—14Jb 24
Westport Rd. E13—42Kc 85
Westport St. E1—44Zb 84
W. Poultry Av. EC1
—43Rb 83 (1B 200)
W. Quarters. W12—44Wa 80
West Ramp. Houn—53Q 98
W. Ridge Gdns. Gnfd—40Ea 58
W. Riding. St Alb—2Ba 5
West Rd. E15—39Hc 65
West Rd. N17—23Xb 43
West Rd. SW3—51Hb 103
West Rd. SW4—57Mb 104
West Rd. W5—43Na 79
West Rd. Barn—18Jb 24
West Rd. Chess—84La 160
West Rd. Felt—58T 98
West Rd. King—67Sa 123
West Rd. Romf—30Zc 47
(Chadwell Heath)
West Rd. Romf—31Fd 68
(Rush Green)
West Rd. S Ock—41Wd 90
West Rd. W Dray—48P 75
West Rd. Wey—81R 158
Westrow. SW15—58Ya 102
West Row. W10—42Ab 80
Westrow Dri. Bark—37Vc 67
Westrow Gdns. Ilf—33Vc 67
W. Sheen Vale. Rich—56Pa 101
West Side. NW4—26Xa 40
W. Side Comn. SW19—64Ya 124
W. Smithfield. EC1
—43Rb 83 (1B 200)
West Sq. SE11—48Rb 83 (4B 206)
West Sq. Iver—44H 75
West St. E2—40Xb 63
West St. E11—34Gc 65
West St. E17—29Dc 44
West St. WC2—44Mb 82 (3E 198)
West St. Bexh—55Bd 109
West St. Bren—51La 100
West St. Brom—67Jc 129
West St. Cars—76Hb 145
West St. Croy—77Sb 147
West St. Eps—85Sa 161
West St. Eps—82Ua 162
(Ewell)
West St. Eri—49Fd 88
West St. Grav—8C 114
West St. Grays—51Ce 113
West St. Harr—32Fa 58
★West St. Sev—88Be
West St. Sutt—78Db 145
West St. Wat—12X 19
West St. Wok—89B 156
West St. La. Cars—77Hb 145
W. Temple Sheen. SW14
—57Ra 101
W. Tenter St. E1—45Vb 83 (3K 201)
W. Thurrock Way. Grays—49Vd 90
West Towers. Pinn—30Z 37
West View. NW4—28Ya 40
West View. Felt—59S 98
West View. Lou—13Pc 28
W. View Av. Whyt—90Vb 165
W. View Clo. NW10—36Va 60
W. View Ct. Borwd—16Ma 21
W. View Cres. N9—17Ub 25
Westview Dri. Wfd G—26Mc 45
W. View Gdns. Borwd—16Ma 21
W. View Rd. Dart—58Pd 111
W. View Rd. Swan—70Jd 132
W. View Rd. Swan—72Fd 152
(Crockenhill)
W. View Rd. Warl—91Xb 181
Westville Rd. W12—47Wa 80
Westville Rd. Th Dit—73Ja 142
West Wlk. W5—43Na 79
West Wlk. Barn—17Jb 24
West Wlk. Hay—46W 76
W. Walkway, The. Sutt—78Db 145
Westward Rd. E4—22Bc 44
Westward Way. Harr—30Na 39
W. Warwick Pl. SW1
—49Lb 82 (6B 204)
Westway—45Va 80
Westway. N18—21Tb 43
West Way. NW10—34Ta 59
Westway. SW20—70Xa 124
West Way. Brtwd—20Wd 32
West Way. Cars—82Fb 163
Westway. Cat—94Tb 181
West Way. Croy—75Ac 148
West Way. Edgw—23Ra 39
West Way. Houn—53Ba 99
Westway. Orp—71Tc 150
West Way. Pinn—28Z 37
West Way. Rick—18K 17
West Way. Ruis—32V 56
West Way. Shep—72T 140
West Way. Wal A—8Dc 12
West Way. W Wick—72Fc 149
Westway Clo. SW20—69Xa 124
W. Way Gdns. Croy—75Zb 148
Westways. Eps—77Va 144
Westways. West—98Sc 184
Westwell Clo. Orp—74Zc 151
Westwell M. SW16—65Nb 126
Westwell Rd. SW16—65Nb 126
Westwell Rd. App. SW16
—65Nb 126
Westwick Gdns. W14—47Za 80
Westwick Gdns. Houn—54X 99
Westwood Av. SE19—66Tb 127
Westwood Av. Brtwd—21Wd 50
Westwood Av. Harr—35Da 57
Westwood Av. Wey—84H 157
Westwood Clo. Amer—11A 16
Westwood Clo. Brom—69Mc 129
Westwood Clo. Esh—76Fa 142
Westwood Clo. Pot B—2Cb 9
Westwood Clo. Ruis—30S 36
Westwood Dri. Amer—11A 16
Westwood Gdns. SW13—55Va 102
Westwood Hill. SE26—64Wb 127
Westwood La. Well & Sidc
—55Vc 109
Westwood Pk. SE23—59Xb 105
Westwood Rd. E16—46Kc 85
Westwood Rd. SW13—55Va 102
Westwood Rd. Coul—90Mb 164
Westwood Rd. Grav—65Ae 135
Westwood Rd. Ilf—32Vc 67
W. Woodside. Bex—60Ad 109
Westwood Way. Sev—94Hd 186
W. Yoke Rd. Long, Dart—76Ae 155
Wetheral Dri. Stan—25Ka 38
Wetherby Clo. N'holt—37Da 57
Wetherby Gdns. SW5
—49Eb 81 (6A 202)
Wetherby M. SW5—50Db 81
Wetherby Pl. SW7
—49Eb 81 (6A 202)
Wetherby Rd. Borwd—11Na 21
Wetherby Rd. Enf—11Sb 25
Wetherby Way. Chess—80Na 143
Wetherden St. E17—31Bc 64
Wethered Dri. Slou—3A 72
Wetherell Rd. E9—39Zb 64
Wetherill Rd. N10—25Jb 42
Wettern Clo. S Croy—82Ub 165
Wexford Rd. SW12—59Hb 103
Wexham Pk. La. Slou—42A 74
Wexham Pk. La. Slou—2N 73
Wexham Rd. Slou—7L 73
Wexham St. Slou—2M 73
Wexham Woods. Slou—3N 73
Weybank. Wok—88N 157
Weybarton. Wey—85P 157
Weybourne St. SW18—61Eb 125
Weybridge Pk. Wey—78Q 140
Weybridge Rd. T Hth—70Qb 126
Weybridge Rd. Wey—77N 139
Wey Clo. Wey—85K 157
Wey Ct. Eps—77Sa 143
Wey Ct. Wey—85L 157
Weydown Clo. SW19—60Ab 102
Weyhill Rd. E1—44Wb 83
Weylond Rd. Dag—34Bd 67
Wey Mnr. Rd. Wey—81M 157
Weyman Rd. SE3—53Lc 107
Weymead Clo. Cher—74L 139
Weymede. Wey—84P 157
Weymouth Av. NW7—22Ua 40
Weymouth Av. W5—48La 78
Weymouth Ct. Sutt—80Cb 145
Weymouth M. W1
—43Kb 82 (7K 191)
Weymouth Rd. Hay—41U 76
Weymouth St. W1
—43Jb 82 (7J 191)
Weymouth Ter. E2
—40Vb 63 (1K 195)
(in two parts)
Weymouth Wlk. Stan—23Ja 38
Wey Rd. Wey—77P 139
Weyside Clo. Wey—84P 157
Weystone Rd. Wey—77P 139
Whadcoat St. N4—33Qb 62
Whalebone Av. Romf—30Bd 47
Whalebone Ct. EC2—(2F 201)
Whalebone Gro. Romf—30Bd 47
Whalebone La. E15—38Gc 65
Whalebone La. N. Romf—24Ad 47
Whalebone La. S. Romf & Dag
—31Bd 67
Whaley Rd. Pot B—5Eb 9
Wharfdale Rd. N1
—40Nb 62 (1G 193)
Wharfedale Gdns. T Hth—70Pb 126
Wharfedale Rd. Dart—60Sd 112
Wharfedale St. SW10—50Db 81
Wharf La. Rick—18N 17
Wharf La. Twic—60Ja 100
Wharf La. Wok—95E 172
(Send)
Wharf La. Wok—90M 157
(Wisley)
Wharf Pl. E2—39Xb 63
Wharf Rd. E15—39Fc 65
Wharf Rd. N1—40Sb 63 (2D 194)
Wharf Rd. Brtwd—20Yd 32
Wharf Rd. Enf—16Ac 26
Wharf Rd. Grav—8G 114
Wharf Rd. Grays—51Be 113
Wharf Rd. Stanf—2M 93
Wharf Rd. Wray, Stai—9N 95
Wharfside Rd. E16—44Gc 85
Wharf St. E16—43Gc 85
Wharncliffe Dri. S'hall—46Fa 78
Wharncliffe Gdns. SE25
—68Ub 127
Wharncliffe Rd. SE25—68Ub 127
Wharton Clo. NW10—37Ua 60
Wharton Rd. Brom—67Kc 129
Wharton St. WC1
—41Pb 82 (4J 193)
★Whatcote Cotts. Sev—92Ee
Whateley Rd. SE20—66Zb 128
Whateley Rd. SE22—57Vb 105
Whatley Av. SW20—69Za 124
Whatman Rd. SE23—59Zb 106
Whatmore Clo. Stai—58J 97
Wheatash Rd. Wey—75K 139
Wheatcroft. Wal X—1Xb 11
Wheatfields. Enf—11Ac 26
Wheathill Rd. SE20—69Xb 127
Wheat Knoll. Kenl—88Sb 165
Wheatland Rd. Slou—8N 73
Wheatlands. Houn—51Ca 99
Wheatlands Rd. SW17—62Jb 126
Wheatley Clo. NW4—26Wa 40
Wheatley Cres. Hay—45W 76
Wheatley Gdns. N9—19Ub 25
Wheatley Rd. Iswth—55Ha 100
Wheatley St. W1—43Jb 82 (1J 197)
Wheatley Ter. Rd. Eri—51Hd 110
Wheatley Way. Ger X—23A 34
Wheatsheaf Clo. Cher—79F 138
Wheatsheaf Clo. Wok—88A 156
Wheatsheaf La. SW6—52Ya 102
Wheatsheaf La. SW8—52Nb 104
Wheatsheaf La. Stai—66H 119
Wheatsheaf Rd. Romf—30Hd 48
Wheatsheaf Ter. SW6—52Bb 103
Wheeler Av. Oxt—100Fc 183
Wheelers. Epp—1Vc 15
Wheelers Cross. Bark—40Tc 66
Wheelers Dri. Ruis—30S 36
Wheelers Farm Gdns. Ept—14Rd 31
Wheelers La. Eps—86Ra 161
Wheelers Orchard. Ger X—23A 34
Wheel Farm Dri. Dag—34Ed 68
Wheel Wright Clo. Bush, Wat
—17Da 19
Wheelwright St. N7—38Pb 62
Whelan Way. Wall—76Mb 146
Wheler St. E1—42Vb 83 (6K 195)
Whellock Rd. W4—48Ua 80
Whenman Av. Bex—62Ed 132
Whernside Clo. SE28—45Yc 87
Whetstone Clo. N20—19Fb 23
Whetstone Pk. WC2
—44Pb 82 (2H 199)
Whetstone Rd. SE3—54Lc 107
Whewell Rd. N19—33Nb 62
Whichcote St. SE1—(7K 199)
Whidborne St. WC1
—41Nb 82 (4G 193)
Whimbrel Clo. SE28—45Yc 87
Whimbrel Clo. S Croy—83Tb 165
Whinfell Clo. SW16—64Mb 126
Whinfell Way. Grav—3H 137
Whinyates Rd. SE9—55Nc 108
Whippendell Clo. Orp—67Xc 131
Whippendell Hill. K Lan—2L 3
Whippendell Rd. Wat—15U 18
Whippendell Way. Orp—67Xc 131
Whipps Cross. E17—29Fc 45
Whipps Cross Rd. E11—29Fc 45
Whiskin St. EC1—41Rb 83 (4B 194)
Whisper Wood. Rick—13K 17
Whistler Gdns. Edgw—26Pa 39
Whistlers Av. SW11—52Fb 103
Whistler St. N5—36Rb 63
Whistler Wlk. SW10—52Fb 103
Whiston Rd. E2—39Vb 63 (1K 195)

Whitakers Way—Wilsman Rd.

Whitakers Way. Lou—11Pc 28
Whitbread Clo. N17—25Wb 43
Whitbread Rd. SE4—56Ac 106
Whitburn Rd. SE13—56Ec 106
Whitby Av. NW10—41Ra 79
Whitby Av. Brtwd—23Fe 51
Whitby Clo. West—91Kc 183
Whitby Ct. N7—35Nb 62
Whitby Gdns. NW9—27Qa 39
Whitby Gdns. Sutt—75Fb 145
Whitby Rd. SE18—49Pc 86
Whitby Rd. Harr—34Ea 58
Whitby Rd. Ruis—34X 57
Whitby Rd. Slou—5G 72
Whitby Rd. Sutt—75Fb 145
Whitby St. E1—42Vb 83 (5K 195)
Whitcher Clo. SE14—51Ac 106
Whitcher Pl. NW1—37Lb 62
Whitchurch Av. Edgw—24Pa 39
Whitchurch Clo. Edgw—23Pa 39
Whitchurch Gdns. Edgw—23Pa 39
Whitchurch La. Edgw—24Ma 39
Whitchurch Rd. W11—45Za 80
Whitchurch Rd. Romf—21Md 49
Whitcomb Ct. WC2—(5E 198)
Whitcomb St. WC2
—45Mb 82 (5E 198)
White Acre. NW9—26Ua 40
Whitear Wlk. E15—37Fc 65
White Av. Grav—2B 136
Whitebarn La. Dag—39Cd 68
Whitebeam Av. Brom—73Qc 150
Whitebeam Clo. SW9—52Pb 104
White Beam Way. Tad—93Wa 178
Whitebridge Clo. Felt—58V 98
White Butts Rd. Ruis—34Z 57
Whitechapel High St. E1
—44Vb 83 (2K 201)
Whitechapel Rd. E1—43Wb 83
White Chu. La. E1—44Wb 83
White City Clo. W12—45Ya 80
White City Rd. W12—45Xa 80
White Clo. Slou—6H 73
White Conduit St. N1
—40Qb 62 (1A 194)
Whitecote Rd. S'hall—44Ea 78
White Craig Clo. Pinn—22Ca 37
Whitecroft Clo. Beck—70Fc 129
Whitecroft Way. Beck—70Ec 128
Whitecross Pl. EC2
—43Tb 83 (7G 195)
Whitecross St. EC1 & EC2
—42Sb 83 (5E 194)
Whitefield Av. NW2—32Ya 60
Whitefield Av. Purl—88Qb 164
Whitefield Clo. SW18—58Ab 102
Whitefield Clo. Orp—69Yc 131
Whitefields Rd. Wal X—1Yb 12
Whitefoot La. Brom—63Ec 128
Whitefoot Ter. Brom—62Hc 129
Whiteford Rd. Slou—3J 73
Whitefriars Av. Harr—26Ga 38
Whitefriars Dri. Harr—26Ga 38
Whitefriars St. EC4
—44Qb 82 (3A 200)
White Gdns. Dag—37Cd 68
Whitegate Gdns. Harr—24Ha 38
Whitegates. Whyt—91Wb 181
White Gates. Wok—92B 172
Whitegates Av. Sev—79Ud 154
White Gates Clo. Rick—14Q 18
Whitehall. SW1—46Nb 82 (7F 199)
Whitehall Clo. Chig—20Wc 29
Whitehall Clo. Uxb—39L 55
Whitehall Ct. SW1
—46Nb 82 (7F 199)
Whitehall Cres. Chess—78Ma 143
Whitehall Farm La. Vir W
—68A 118
Whitehall Gdns. E4—18Gc 27
Whitehall Gdns. SW1—(7F 199)
Whitehall Gdns. W3—46Qa 79
Whitehall Gdns. W4—51Ra 101
Whitehall La. Buck H—19Jc 27
Whitehall La. Egh—66B 118
Whitehall La. Eri—54Hd 110
Whitehall La. Grays—50Ee 91
Whitehall La. Wray, Stai—58C 96
Whitehall Pk. N19—32Lb 62
Whitehall Pk. Rd. W4—51Ra 101
Whitehall Pl. E7—36Jc 65
Whitehall Pl. SW1
—46Nb 82 (7F 199)
Whitehall Pl. Wall—77Kb 146
Whitehall Rd. E4 & Wfd G
—19Gc 27
Whitehall Rd. W7—47Ja 78
Whitehall Rd. Brom—71Mc 149
Whitehall Rd. Grays—49Ee 91
Whitehall Rd. Harr—31Ga 58
Whitehall Rd. T Hth—71Qb 146
Whitehall Rd. Uxb—39M 55
Whitehall St. N17—24Vb 43
White Hart Clo. Hay—51T 98
White Hart Clo. Sev—100Ld 187
White Hart Ct. EC2—(1H 201)
White Hart Ct. Wok—93L 173
White Hart La. N17—24Sb 43
White Hart La. N22—25Qb 42
White Hart La. NW10—37Va 60
White Hart La. SW13—55Ua 102
White Hart La. Brtwd—19Yd 32
White Hart La. Romf—25Cd 48
White Hart Meadows. Wok
—93L 173
White Hart Pde. Sev—94Gd 186
White Hart Rd. SE18—49Uc 86
White Hart Rd. Orp—73Wc 151
White Hart Rd. Slou—8H 73
Whitehart Row. Cher—73J 139
White Hart Slip. Brom—68Jc 129
White Hart St. SE11
—50Qb 82 (7A 206)
White Hart Wood. Sev—100Ld 187
White Hart Yd. SE1
—46Tb 83 (7F 201)
Whitehaven Clo. Brom—70Jc 129
Whitehaven St. NW8
—42Gb 81 (6D 190)
Whitehead Clo. SW18—59Eb 103
Whitehead Clo. Dart—62Ld 133
Whitehead's Gro. SW3
—49Gb 81 (7E 202)
White Heart Av. Uxb—43S 76
Whiteheath Av. Ruis—31S 56
White Hill. Coul—95Gb 179
White Hill. Rick—23Q 36
★White Hill. Sev—88De
(in two parts)
White Hill. S Croy—82Tb 165
Whitehill La. Cob—95S 174
Whitehill La. Grav—2E 136
Whitehill La. Red—99Tb 181
Whitehill Rd. Dart—57Jd 110
Whitehill Rd. Grav—1E 136
Whitehill Rd. Long, Dart &
Grav—68Zd 135
Whitehills Rd. Lou—13Qc 28
White Horse All. EC1—(7B 194)
White Horse Dri. Eps—86Sa 161
White Horse Hill. Chst—63Qc 130
White Horse La. E1—43Zb 84
Whitehorse La. SE25—70Tb 127
White Horse La. Wok—93L 173
White Horse Rd. E1—44Ac 84
(in two parts)
White Horse Rd. E6—41Pc 86
Whitehorse Rd. Croy & T Hth
—73Sb 147
White Horse Rd. Wind—5B 94
White Horse St. W1
—46Kb 82 (7A 198)
White Horse Yd. EC2
—44Tb 83 (2F 201)
Whitehouse Av. Borwd—13Ra 21
White Ho. Clo. Ger X—24A 34
White Ho. Dri. Stan—21La 38
Whitehouse La. Enf—11Sb 25
Whitehouse Way. N14—19Kb 24
Whitehouse Way. Iver—41F 74
White Kennett St. E1
—44Vb 83 (2K 201)
White Knights La. Wey—80S 140
White Knobs Way. Cat—97Wb 181
★Whitelands. Brtwd—7Zd
Whitelands Av. Rick—13D 16
Whitelands Way. Romf—25Md 49
White La. West & Oxt—95Kc 183
Whiteledges. W13—44La 78
Whitelegg Rd. E13—40Hc 65
Whiteley. Wind—2C 94
Whiteley Rd. SE19—64Tb 127
Whiteley Way. Felt—62Ca 121
White Lion Ct. EC3—(3H 201)
White Lion Hill. EC4
—45Rb 83 (4C 200)
White Lion St. N1
—40Qb 62 (2K 193)
White Lodge. SE19—66Rb 127
White Lodge. Sev—100Jd 186
White Lodge Clo. N2—30Fb 41
White Lodge Clo. Sutt—80Eb 145
White Lyon Ct. EC2—(7D 194)
White Lyons Rd. Brtwd—19Yd 32
White Oak Dri. Beck—68Ec 128
Whiteoaks La. Gnfd—41Fa 78
White Orchards. N20—17Bb 23
White Orchards. Stan—22Ja 38
White Post Hill. F'ham, Dart
—73Qd 153
White Post La. E9—37Cc 64
Whitepost La. SE13—55Cc 106
White Post La. Grav—10C 136
White Post St. SE15—52Yb 106
White Rd. E15—38Gc 65
Whiterose Ct. E1—(1J 201)
White Rose La. Wok—90B 156
Whites Av. Ilf—30Uc 46
White's Grounds. SE1
—47Ub 83 (2J 207)
White Shack La. Rick—9P 3
Whites La. Slou—1M 95
White's Row. E1—43Vb 83 (1K 201)
White's Sq. SW4—56Mb 104
Whitestile Rd. Bren—50La 78
Whitestone La. NW3—34Eb 61
White St. S'hall—47Z 77
White Swan M. W4—51Ua 102
Whitethorn Av. Coul—87Jb 164
Whitethorn Av. W Dray—45N 75
Whitethorn Gdns. Croy—75Xb 147
Whitethorn Gdns. Enf—15Tb 25
Whitethorn Gdns. Horn—30Ld 49
Whitethorn Pl. W Dray—46P 75
Whitethorn St. E3—43Cc 84
White Way. Lea—98Da 175
Whitewebbs La. Enf—7Ub 11
Whitewebbs Rd. Enf—7Rb 11
Whitewebbs Way. Orp—67Vc 131
Whitewood Cotts. West—92Lc 183
Whitfield Pl. W1—(6B 192)
Whitfield Rd. E6—38Lc 65
Whitfield Rd. SE3—53Fc 107
Whitfield Rd. Bexh—52Bd 109
Whitfields. Stanf—1P 93
Whitfield St. W1—42Lb 82 (6B 192)
Whitfield Way. Rick—18H 17
Whitford Gdns. Mitc—69Hb 125
Whitgift Av. S Croy—78Sb 147
Whitgift Centre. Croy—75Sb 147
Whitgift Sq. Croy—75Sb 147
Whitgift St. SE11
—49Pb 82 (5H 205)
Whitgift St. Croy—76Sb 147
Whiting Av. Bark—38Rc 66
Whitings Rd. Barn—15Ya 22
Whitings Way. E6—43Qc 86
Whitland Rd. Cars—74Fb 145
Whitlars Dri. K Lan—1P 3
Whitley Clo. Stai—58N 97
Whitley Rd. N17—26Ub 43
Whitlock Dri. SW19—59Ab 102
Whitman Rd. E3—42Ac 84
Whitmead Clo. S Croy—79Ub 147
Whitmoor La. Guild—98A 172
Whitmore Av. Grays—46De 91
Whitmore Clo. N11—22Kb 42
Whitmore Gdns. NW10—40Ya 60
Whitmore La. Asc—10E 116
Whitmore Rd. N1
—39Ub 63 (1H 195)
Whitmore Rd. Beck—69Bc 128
Whitmore Rd. Harr—31Ea 58
Whitmores Clo. Eps—87Sa 161
Whitnell Way. SW15—57Ya 102
Whitney Av. Ilf—28Mc 45
Whitney Rd. E10—31Dc 64
Whitney Wlk. Sidc—65Ad 131
Whitstable Clo. Beck—67Bc 128
Whitstable Clo. Ruis—33U 56
Whittaker Av. Rich—57Ma 101
Whittaker Rd. E6—38Mc 65
Whittaker Rd. Slou—2B 72
Whittaker Rd. Sutt—76Bb 145
Whittaker St. SW1
—49Jb 82 (6H 203)
Whittaker Way. SE1—49Wb 83
Whitta Rd. E12—35Mc 65
Whittell Gdns. SE26—62Yb 128
Whittenham Clo. Slou—6L 73
Whittingstall Rd. SW6—53Bb 103
Whittington Av. EC3
—44Ub 83 (3H 201)
Whittington Av. Hay—43V 76
Whittington Rd. N22—24Nb 42
Whittington Rd. Brtwd—16Ee 33
Whittington Way. Pinn—29Aa 37
Whittlebury Clo. Cars—80Hb 145
Whittle Clo. S'hall—44Da 77
Whittle Rd. Houn—52Y 99
Whittlesea Clo. Harr—24Ea 38
Whittlesea Path. Harr—25Ea 38
Whittlesea Rd. Harr—25Ea 38
Whittlesey St. SE1
—46Qb 82 (7A 200)
Whitton Av. E. Gnfd—36Ha 58
Whitton Av. W. N'holt & Gnfd
—36Da 57
Whitton Clo. Gnfd—37Ka 58
Whitton Dene. Houn & Iswth
—57Ea 100
Whitton Dene. Iswth—58Fa 100
Whitton Dri. Gnfd—37Ja 58
Whitton Mnr. Rd. Iswth—58Ea 100
Whitton Rd. Houn—56Da 99
Whitton Rd. Twic—58Ga 100
Whitton Wlk. E3—41Cc 84
Whitton Waye. Houn—58Ca 99
Whitwell Rd. E13—41Jc 85
Whitwell Rd. Wat—7Z 5
Whitworth Rd. SE18—52Qc 108
Whitworth Rd. SE25—69Ub 127
Whitworth St. SE10—50Gc 85
Whopshott Av. Wok—4F 188
Whopshott Clo. Wok—4F 188
Whopshott Dri. Wok—4F 188
Whorlton Rd. SE15—55Xb 105
Whybrews. Stanf—1P 93
Whybridge Clo. Rain—39Hd 68
Whymark Av. N22—27Rb 43
Whytecliffe Rd. Purl—83Qb 164
Whytecroft. Houn—52Z 99
Whyteleafe Hill. Whyt—91Ub 181
Whyteleafe Rd. Cat—92Ub 181
Whyteville Rd. E7—37Kc 65
Wichling Clo. Orp—74Zc 151
Wickenden Rd. Sev—94Ld 187
Wickersley Rd. SW11—54Jb 104
Wickers Oake. SE19—63Vb 127
Wicker St. E1—44Xb 83
Wicket, The. Croy—78Cc 148
Wickford Clo. Romf—22Pd 49
Wickford Dri. Romf—22Pd 49
Wickford St. E1—42Yb 84
Wickford Way. E17—28Zb 44
Wickham Av. Croy—75Ac 148
Wickham Av. Sutt—78Ya 144
Wickham Chase. W Wick
—74Fc 149
Wickham Clo. Enf—13Yb 26
Wickham Clo. N Mald—71Va 144
Wickham Clo. Uxb—25M 35
Wickham Ct. Rd. W Wick
—75Ec 148
Wickham Cres. W Wick—75Ec 148
Wickham Field. Sev—88Hd 170
Wickham Gdns. SE4—55Bc 106
Wickham La. SE2—50Wc 87
Wickham La. Egh—66C 118
Wickham M. SE4—54Bc 106
Wickham Rd. E4—24Ec 44
Wickham Rd. SE4—55Bc 106
Wickham Rd. Beck—68Dc 128
Wickham Rd. Croy—75Zb 148
Wickham Rd. Grays—7E 92
Wickham Rd. Harr—26Fa 38
Wickham St. SE11
—50Pb 82 (7H 205)
Wickham St. Well—54Uc 108
Wickham Way. Beck—70Ec 128
Wick La. E3—39Cc 64
(in two parts)
Wick La. Egh—5K 117
Wickliffe Av. N3—26Ab 40
Wickliffe Gdns. Wemb—33Ra 59
Wicklow St. WC1
—41Pb 82 (3H 193)
Wick Rd. E9—37Zb 64
Wick Rd. Egh—7L 117
Wick Rd. Tedd—66Ka 122
Wicks Clo. SE9—63Nc 129
Wick Sq. E9—37Bc 64
Wicksteed Clo. Bex—62Fd 132
Wickwood St. SE5—54Rb 105
Wid Clo. Brtwd—15Fe 33
Widdecombe Av. Harr—33Aa 57
Widdenham Rd. N7—35Pb 62
Widdin St. E15—38Gc 65
Widecombe Clo. Romf—25Md 49
Widecombe Gdns. Ilf—28Nc 46
Widecombe Rd. SE9—62Nc 130
Widecombe Way. N2—28Fb 41
Widecroft Rd. Iver—44G 74
Widegate St. E1—43Ub 83 (1J 201)
Widenham Clo. Pinn—29Y 37
Wide Way. Mitc—69Mb 126
Widgeon Way. Wat—9Aa 5
Widley Rd. W9—41Cb 81
Widmore Lodge Rd. Brom
—68Mc 129
Widmore Rd. Brom—68Jc 129
Widmore Rd. Uxb—42R 76
Widworthy Hayes. Brtwd
—18De 33
Wieland Rd. N'wd—24W 36
Wient, The. Slou—52E 96
Wigan Ho. E5—32Xb 63
Wigeon Path. SE28—48Tc 86
Wiggenhall Rd. Wat—15X 19
Wiggington Av. Wemb—37Ra 59
Wiggins Mead. NW9—24Va 40
Wightman Rd. N8—28Qb 42
Wigley Bush La. Brtwd—19Ud 32
Wigley Rd. Felt—61Z 121
Wigmore Pl. W1—44Kb 82 (2K 197)
Wigmore Rd. SE24—55Sb 105
Wigmore Rd. Cars—75Fb 145
Wigmore St. W1—44Jb 82 (2H 197)
Wigmore Wlk. Cars—75Fb 145
Wigram Rd. E11—30Lc 45
Wigram Sq. E17—27Ec 44
Wigston Rd. E13—42Kc 85
Wigton Gdns. Stan—25Na 39
Wigton Pl. SE11—50Qb 82 (7A 206)
Wigton Rd. E17—25Bc 44
Wigton Rd. Romf—21Nd 49
Wigton Way. Romf—21Nd 49
Wilberforce Rd. N4—33Rb 63
Wilberforce Rd. NW9—30Wa 40
Wilberforce Way. SW19
—65Za 124
Wilberforce Way. Grav—4F 136
Wilbraham Pl. SW1
—49Hb 81 (5H 203)
Wilbury Av. Sutt—82Bb 163
Wilbury Rd. Wok—5G 188
Wilbury Way. N18—22Tb 43
Wilby M. W11—46Bb 81
Wilcot Av. Wat—17Aa 19
Wilcox Clo. SW8—52Nb 104
Wilcox Clo. Borwd—11Sa 21
Wilcox Gdns. Shep—69N 119
Wilcox Pl. SW1—48Lb 82 (4C 204)
Wilcox Rd. SW8—52Nb 104
Wilcox Rd. Sutt—77Db 145
Wilcox Rd. Tedd—63Fa 122
Wild Acres. Wey—83L 157
Wild Ct. WC2—44Pb 82 (3H 199)
Wildcroft Gdns. Edgw—23Ma 39
Wildcroft Mnr. SW15—59Ya 102
Wildcroft Rd. SW15—59Ya 102
Wilde Clo. E8—39Wb 63
Wilde Clo. Til—4E 114
Wilde Pl. N13—23Rb 43
Wildernesse Av. Sev—94Nd 187
Wildernesse Mt. Sev—94Md 187
Wilderness Rd. Chst—66Rc 130
Wilderness, The. Hmptn—63Da 121
Wilders Clo. Wok—6F 188
Wilderton Rd. N16—31Ub 63
Wildfell Rd. SE6—59Dc 106
Wild Goose Dri. SE14—53Yb 106
Wildgreen. Slou—49C 74
Wild Hatch. NW11—30Cb 41
Wild Oaks Clo. N'wd—23W 36
Wild's Rents. SE1
—48Ub 83 (3H 207)
Wild St. WC2—44Nb 82 (3G 199)
Wildwood. N'wd—23T 36
Wildwood Av. St Alb—2Ba 5
Wildwood Clo. SE12—59Hc 107
Wildwood Clo. Lea—97V 174
Wildwood Clo. Wok—87H 157
Wildwood Ct. Kenl—87Tb 165
Wildwood Gro. NW3—32Eb 61
Wildwood Rise. NW11—32Eb 61
Wildwood Rd. NW11—30Eb 41
Wilford Clo. Enf—13Tb 25
Wilford Clo. N'wd—24T 36
Wilford Rd. Slou—49A 74
Wilfred Av. Rain—43Jd 88
Wilfred St. SW1—48Lb 82 (3B 204)
Wilfred St. Grav—8D 114
Wilfred Way. Wok—6G 188
Wilfrid Gdns. W3—43Sa 79
Wilhelmina Av. Coul—91Lb 180
Wilkes Rd. Brtwd—15Fe 33
Wilkes St. E1—43Vb 83 (7K 195)
(in two parts)
Wilkins Clo. Hay—50V 76
Wilkinson Clo. Dart—56Pd 111
Wilkinson Rd. E16—44Lc 85
Wilkinson St. SW8—52Pb 104
Wilkinson Way. W4—47Ta 79
Wilkin St. NW5—37Kb 62
Wilkin St. M. NW5—37Kb 62
Wilks Pl. N1—40Ub 63 (2J 195)
Willan Rd. N17—26Ub 43
Willan Wall. E16—45Hc 85
Willard St. SW8—55Kb 104
Willcocks Clo. Chess—76Na 143
Willcott Rd. W3—46Ra 79
Willcrooks Gdns. SE9—56Mc 107
Willenhall Av. Barn—16Eb 23
Willenhall Rd. SE18—50Rc 86
Willersley Av. Orp—76Tc 150
Willersley Av. Sidc—60Vc 109
Willersley Clo. Sidc—60Vc 109
Willesden La.—37Ya 60
NW6 1-221 & 2-218
NW2 remainder
Willes Rd. NW5—37Kb 62
Willet Clo. N'holt—41Y 77
Willett Clo. Orp—72Uc 150
Willett Pl. T Hth—71Qb 146
Willett Rd. T Hth—71Qb 146
Willetts La. Uxb—35H 55
Willett Way. Orp—71Tc 150
Willet Way. SE16—50Xb 83
Willey Broom La. Cat—97Qb 180
Willey Farm La. Cat—98Sb 181
Willey La. Cat—97Tb 181
William Barefoot Dri. SE9
—63Qc 130
William Booth Rd. SE20
—67Wb 127
William Clo. Romf—25Fd 48
William Cory Prom. Eri—50Gd 88
William Ct. W5—43La 78
William Covell Clo. Enf—10Pb 10
William Ellis Clo. Wind—7L 95
William Ellis Way. SE16—48Wb 83
William IV St. WC2
—45Nb 82 (5F 199)
William Gdns. SW15—57Xa 102
William Gunn Ho. NW3—36Gb 61
William Guy Gdns. E3—41Dc 84
William Margrie Clo. SE15
—54Wb 105
William M. SW1—47Hb 81 (2G 203)
William Morley Clo. E6—39Mc 65
William Morris Clo. E17—27Bc 44
William Pl. Orp—70Yc 131
William Rd. NW1
—41Lb 82 (4B 192)
William Rd. SW19—66Ab 124
William Rd. Cat—94Tb 181
William Rd. Sutt—78Eb 145
William Russell Ct. Wok—6B 188
Williams Av. E17—25Bc 44
William's Bldgs. E2—42Yb 84
Williams Gro. N22—25Qb 42
William's La. SW14—55Sa 101
Williams La. Mord—71Eb 145
Williamson Clo. SE10—50Hc 85
Williamson Rd. N4—30Rb 43
Williamson St. N7—35Nb 62
Williamson Way. NW7—23Ab 40
Williams Rd. W13—46Ja 78
Williams Rd. S'hall—49Aa 77
Williams Ter. Croy—79Qb 146
William St. E10—30Dc 44
William St. N17—24Vb 43
William St. SW1—47Hb 81 (2G 203)
William St. Bark—38Sc 66
William St. Bush, Wat—13Z 19
William St. Cars—76Gb 145
William St. Grav—9D 114
William St. Grays—51Ee 113
William St. Grays—51Yd 112
(West Thurrock)
William St. Slou—6K 73
William St. Wind—3H 95
Williams Way. Rad—7Ka 6
Willifield Way. NW11—28Bb 41
Willingale Clo. Brtwd—16Fe 33
Willingale Clo. Lou—12Sc 28
Willingale Clo. Wfd G—23Lc 45
Willingale Rd. Lou—13Sc 28
Willingdon Rd. N22—26Rb 43
Willinghall Clo. Wal A—4Fc 13
Willingham Clo. NW5—36Lb 62
Willingham Ter. NW5—36Lb 62
Willingham Way. King—69Qa 123
Willington Rd. SW9—55Nb 104
Willis Av. Sutt—79Gb 145
Willis Clo. Eps—86Ra 161
Willis Hill. Stanf—1M 93
Willis Rd. E15—40Hc 65
Willis Rd. Croy—73Sb 147
Willis Rd. Eri—49Fd 88
Willis St. E14—44Dc 84
Willmore End. SW19—67Db 125
Willoners. Slou—2E 72
Willoughby Av. Croy—77Pb 146
Willoughby Gro. N17—24Xb 43
Willoughby Ho. EC2—(1F 201)
Willoughby La. N17—23Xb 43
Willoughby Pk. Rd. N17—24Xb 43
Willoughby Rd. N8—27Qb 42
Willoughby Rd. NW3—35Fb 61
Willoughby Rd. King—67Pa 123
Willoughby Rd. Rain—38Gd 68
Willoughby Rd. Slou—48C 74
Willoughby Rd. Twic—57La 100
Willoughby St. WC1—(1F 199)
Willow Av. SW13—54Va 102
Willow Av. Sidc—58Wc 109
Willow Av. Swan—70Hd 132
Willow Av. Uxb—37L 55
Willow Av. W Dray—45P 75
Willow Bank. Rich—62Ka 122
Willow Dri. Rd. N1—37Sb 63
Willowbrook. Wind—9H 73
Willowbrook Rd. SE15—51Vb 105
Willowbrook Rd. S'hall—48Ca 77
Willowbrook Rd. Stai—61N 119
Willow Clo. Bex—58Bd 109
Willow Clo. Bren—51La 100
★Willow Clo. Brtwd—10Zd
(Doddinghurst)
Willow Clo. Brtwd—16De 33
(Hutton)
Willow Clo. Brom—71Pc 150
Willow Clo. Buck H—20Mc 27
Willow Clo. Horn—34Kd 69
Willow Clo. Orp—73Xc 151
Willow Clo. Slou—52E 96
Willow Clo. Wey—83H 157
Willow Cotts. N16—33Vb 63
Willow Cotts. Rich—51Qa 101
Willow Ct. EC2—(5H 195)
Willow Ct. Edgw—21Na 39
Willowcourt Av. Harr—29Ka 38
Willow Cres. E. Uxb—36L 55
Willow Cres. W. Uxb—36L 55
Willowdene. N6—31Hb 61
Willowdene. Brtwd—15Vd 32
Willow Dene. Bush, Wat—17Ga 20
Willow Dene. Pinn—26Z 37
Willowdene Clo. Twic—59Ea 100
Willowdene Ct. Brtwd—21Yd 50
Willow Dri. Barn—14Ab 22
Willow Dri. Wok—96J 173
Willow Edge. K Lan—1Q 4
Willow End. N20—19Cb 23
Willow End. Surb—74Na 143
Willow Gdns. Houn—53Ca 99
Willow Gdns. Ruis—33V 56
Willow Grange. Sidc—62Xc 131
Willow Grn. NW9—25Ua 40
Willow Grn. Borwd—15Ta 21
Willow Gro. Chst—65Qc 130
Willow Gro. Ruis—33V 56
Willow Hayne Dri. W on T
—73X 141
Willow Hayne Gdns. Wor Pk
—77Ya 144
Willowherb Wlk. Romf—24Ld 49
Willow La. Mitc—71Hb 145
Willow La. Wat—15W 18
Willow La. Industrial Est.
Mitc—72Hb 145
Willow Mead. Chig—20Wc 29
Willowmead Clo. W5—43Ma 79
Willowmead Clo. Wok—4D 188
Willow Mere. Esh—77Ea 142
Willow Mt. Croy—76Ub 147
Willow Pde. Slou—48C 74
Willow Pk. Sev—89Hd 170
Willow Pk. Slou—8L 53
Willow Path. Wal A—6Gc 13
Willow Pl. SW1—49Lb 82 (5C 204)
Willow Pl. Wind—1G 94
Willow Rd. NW3—35Fb 61
Willow Rd. W5—47Na 79
Willow Rd. Dart—60Ld 111
Willow Rd. Enf—13Ub 25
Willow Rd. Eri—53Jd 110
Willow Rd. N Mald—70Sa 123
Willow Rd. Romf—30Ad 47
Willow Rd. Slou—54G 96
Willow Rd. Wall—80Kb 146
Willows Av. Mord—71Db 145
Willows Clo. Pinn—26Y 37
Willows Path. Eps—86Ra 161
Willows, The. Grays—51Fe 113
Willows, The. Wat—17X 19
Willows, The. Wey—76Q 140
Willows, The. Wey—85N 157
(Byfleet)
Willow St. E4—18Fc 27
Willow St. EC2—42Ub 83 (5H 195)
Willow St. Romf—28Ed 48
Willow Tree Clo. SW18—60Db 103
Willowtree Clo. Hay—42Y 77
Willowtree Clo. Uxb—34S 56
Willow Tree La. Hay—42Y 77
Willow Vale. W12—46Wa 80
Willow Vale. Chst—65Rc 130
Willow Vale. Lea—95Da 175
(in two parts)
Willow View. SW19—67Fb 125
Willow Wlk. E17—29Bc 44
Willow Wlk. N2—26Fb 41
Willow Wlk. N15—28Rb 43
Willow Wlk. N21—16Pb 24
Willow Wlk. SE1—49Ub 83 (5J 207)
Willow Wlk. Cher—73J 139
Willow Wlk. Dart—56Ld 111
Willow Wlk. Egh—4N 117
Willow Wlk. Orp—76Rc 150
Willow Wlk. Sutt—76Bb 145
Willow Wlk. Upm—32Ud 70
Willow Way. N3—24Db 41
Willow Way. SE26—62Yb 128
Willow Way. Eps—79Ta 143
Willow Way. Pot B—5Db 9
Willow Way. Rad—8Ga 6
Willow Way. Romf—23Rd 49
Willow Way. Sun—70W 120
Willow Way. Twic—61Da 121
Willow Way. Wemb—34Ja 58
Willow Way. Wey—83L 157
Willow Way. Wok—93A 172
Willow Way. Wok—9G 188
Willow Wood Cres. SE25
—72Ub 147
Willrose Cres. SE2—50Xc 87
Wills Cres. Houn—58Da 99
Wills Gro. NW7—22Wa 40
Willson Rd. Egh—4M 117
Willson's Wharf. SE1—(6H 201)
Wilman Gro. E8—38Wb 63
Wilmar Clo. Hay—42T 76
Wilmar Clo. Uxb—38M 55
Wilmar Gdns. W Wick—74Dc 148
Wilmar Way. Sev—92Pd 187
Wilmer Clo. King—64Pa 123
Wilmer Cres. King—64Pa 123
Wilmer Gdns. N1
—39Ub 63 (1J 195)
(in two parts)
Wilmerhatch La. Eps—89Ra 161
Wilmer Lea Clo. E15—38Fc 65
Wilmer Way. N14—22Mb 42
Wilmington Av. W4—52Ta 101
Wilmington Av. Orp—75Yc 151
Wilmington Ct. Rd. Dart—62Jd 132
Wilmington Gdns. Bark—37Tc 66
Wilmington Sq. WC1
—41Qb 82 (4K 193)
Wilmington St. WC1
—41Qb 82 (4K 193)
Wilmot Clo. N2—26Eb 41
Wilmot Clo. SE15—52Wb 105
Wilmot Grn. Brtwd—23Yd 50
Wilmot Pl. NW1—38Lb 62
Wilmot Pl. W7—46Ga 78
Wilmot Rd. E10—33Dc 64
Wilmot Rd. N17—27Tb 43
Wilmot Rd. Cars—78Hb 145
Wilmot Rd. Dart—57Kd 111
Wilmot Rd. Purl—84Qb 164
Wilmot Rd. Slou—1A 72
Wilmot St. E2—42Xb 83
Wilmot Way. Bans—86Cb 163
Wilmount St. SE18—49Rc 86
Wilna Rd. SW18—59Eb 103
Wilsham St. W11—46Ab 80
Wilshaw St. SE14—53Cc 106
Wilsman Rd. S Ock—40Yd 70

Wilsmere Dri.—Woodend Rd.

Wilsmere Dri. Harr—24Ga 38
Wilsmere Dri. Ruis—36Aa 57
Wilson Av. Mitc—67Gb 125
Wilson Clo. Stanf—3L 93
Wilson Gdns. Harr—31Ea 58
Wilson Gro. SE16—47Xb 83
Wilson Rd. E6—41Mc 85
Wilson Rd. SE5—53Ub 105
Wilson Rd. Chess—79Pa 143
Wilson Rd. Ilf—31Pc 66
Wilson's Pl. E14—44Bc 84
Wilson St. E17—29Ec 44
Wilson St. EC2—43Tb 83 (7G 195)
Wilson St. N21—17Qb 24
Wilson Way. Wok—4G 188
Wilthorne Gdns. Dag—38Dd 68
Wilton Av. W4—50Ua 80
Wilton Cres. SW1
—47Jb 82 (2H 203)
Wilton Cres. SW19—67Bb 125
Wilton Cres. Wind—5B 94
Wilton Dri. Romf—24Ed 48
Wilton Gdns. E Mol—69Ca 121
Wilton Gdns. W on T—74Z 141
Wilton Gro. SW19—67Bb 125
Wilton Gro. N Mald—72Va 144
Wilton M. SW1—48Jb 82 (3J 203)
Wilton Pl. SW1—47Jb 82 (2H 203)
Wilton Rd. N10—26Jb 42
Wilton Rd. SE2—49Yc 87
Wilton Rd. SW1—49Lb 82 (4A 204)
Wilton Rd. SW19—66Gb 125
Wilton Rd. Barn—14Hb 23
Wilton Rd. Houn—55Z 99
Wilton Row. SW1
—47Jb 82 (2H 203)
Wilton Sq. N1—39Tb 63
Wilton St. SW1—48Kb 82 (3K 20)
Wilton Ter. SW1—48Jb 82 (3H 203)
Wilton Way. E8—37Wb 63
Wiltshire Av. Horn—28Pd 49
Wiltshire Av. Slou—2G 72
Wiltshire Clo. SW3
—49Hb 81 (6F 203)
Wiltshire Gdns. Twic—60Ea 100
Wiltshire La. Pinn—27V 36
Wiltshire Rd. SW9—55Qb 104
Wiltshire Rd. Orp—73Wc 151
Wiltshire Rd. T Hth—69Qb 126
Wiltshire Row. N1—39Tb 63
Wiltstone Clo. Hay—42Aa 77
Wilverley Cres. N Mald—72Ua 144
Wimbart Rd. SW2—59Pb 104
Wimbledon Hill Rd. SW19
—65Ab 124
Wimbledon Pk. Rd.—61Ab 124
SW18 1-257 & 2-218
SW19 remainder
Wimbledon Pk. Side. SW19
—61Za 124
Wimbledon Rd. SW17—63Eb 125
Wimbolt St. E2—41Wb 83
Wimborne Av. Hay—44X 77
Wimborne Av. Orp & Chst
—70Vc 131
Wimborne Av. S'hall—49Ca 77
Wimborne Clo. SE12—57Hc 107
Wimborne Clo. Buck H—19Kc 27
Wimborne Clo. Eps—85Va 162
Wimborne Clo. Wor Pk—74Ya 144
Wimborne Dri. NW9—27Qa 39
Wimborne Dri. Pinn—31Z 57
Wimborne Gdns. W13—43Ka 78
Wimborne Gro. Wat—9U 4
Wimborne Rd. N9—19Wb 25
Wimborne Rd. N17—26Ub 43
Wimborne Way. Beck—69Zb 128
Wimbourne St. N1
—40Tb 63 (1F 195)
Wimpole Clo. King—68Pa 123
Wimpole M. W1—43Kb 82 (7K 191)
Wimpole Rd. W Dray—46M 75
Wimpole St. W1—43Kb 82 (1K 197)
Winans Wlk. SW9—54Qb 104
Wincanton Cres. N'holt—36Ca 57
Wincanton Gdns. Ilf—26Rc 46
Wincanton Rd. SW18—59Bb 103
Wincanton Rd. Romf—20Md 31
Winchat Rd. SE28—48Tc 86
Winchcombe Rd. Cars—73Fb 145
Winchcomb Gdns. SE9
—55Mc 107
Winchelsea Av. Bexh—52Bd 109
Winchelsea Clo. SW15—57Za 102
Winchelsea Rd. E7—35Jc 65
Winchelsea Rd. N17—27Ub 43
Winchelsea Rd. NW10—39Ta 59
Winchelsey Rise. S Croy
—79Vb 147
Winchendon Rd. SW6—53Bb 103
Winchendon Rd. Tedd—63Fa 122
Winchester Av. NW6—39Ab 60
Winchester Av. NW9—27Qa 39
Winchester Av. Houn—51Ba 99
Winchester Av. Upm—32Vd 70
Winchester Clo. E6—44Pc 86
Winchester Clo. SE17
—49Rb 83 (6C 206)
Winchester Clo. Brom—69Hc 129
Winchester Clo. Enf—16Ub 25
Winchester Clo. Esh—77Ca 141
Winchester Clo. King—66Ra 123
Winchester Clo. Slou—53G 96
Winchester Cres. Grav—2F 136
Winchester Dri. Pinn—29Z 37
Winchester Pk. Brom—69Hc 129
Winchester Pl. E8—36Vb 63
Winchester Pl. N6—32Kb 62
Winchester Rd. E4—24Ec 44
Winchester Rd. N6—31Kb 62
Winchester Rd. N9—18Vb 25
Winchester Rd. NW3—38Fb 61
Winchester Rd. Bexh—54Zc 109
Winchester Rd. Brom—69Hc 129
Winchester Rd. Felt—62Ba 121
Winchester Rd. Harr—28Na 39
Winchester Rd. Hay—52U 98
Winchester Rd. Ilf—34Tc 66
Winchester Rd. N'wd—27W 36
Winchester Rd. Orp—77Yc 151
Winchester Rd. Twic—58Ka 100
Winchester Rd. W on T—74W 140
Winchester Sq. SE1—(6F 201)
Winchester St. SW1
—50Kb 82 (7A 204)
Winchester St. W3—47Sa 79
Winchester Wlk. SE1
—46Tb 83 (6F 201)
Winchester Way. Rick—15R 18
Winchet Wlk. Croy—72Yb 148
Winchfield Clo. Harr—30La 38
Winchfield Rd. SE26—64Ac 128
Winchfield Way. Rick—17L 17
Winchilsea Cres. E Mol—68Ea 122
Winchmore Hill Rd.—18Mb 24
N14 1-173 & 2-136
N21 remainder
Winchstone. Shep—70P 119
Winckley Clo. Harr—29Pa 39
Wincott St. SE11
—49Qb 82 (5A 206)
Wincrofts Dri. SE9—56Tc 108
Windborough Rd. Cars—80Jb 146
Windermere Av. N3—27Cb 41
Windermere Av. NW6—39Ab 60
Windermere Av. SW19—69Db 125
Windermere Av. Horn—36Jd 68
Windermere Av. Ruis—31Y 57
Windermere Av. Wemb—31La 58
Windermere Clo. Dart—60Kd 111
Windermere Clo. Orp—76Rc 150
Windermere Ct. Kenl—87Rb 165
Windermere Gdns. Ilf—29Nc 46
Windermere Gro. Wemb—32La 58
Windermere Ho. Barn—14Db 23
Windermere Rd. N10—25Kb 42
Windermere Rd. N19—33Lb 62
Windermere Rd. SW15—63Ua 124
Windermere Rd. SW16—67Lb 126
Windermere Rd. W5—48La 78
Windermere Rd. Bexh—54Ed 110
Windermere Rd. Coul—87Nb 164
Windermere Rd. Croy—74Vb 147
Windermere Rd. S'hall—43Ba 77
Windermere Rd. W Wick
—75Gc 149
Windermere Way. Slou—3A 72
Winders Rd. SW11—54Gb 103
Windfield. Lea—93Ka 176
Windfield Clo. SE26—63Zb 128
Windham Av. Croy—82Fc 167
Windham Rd. Rich—55Pa 101
Windings, The. S Croy—83Vb 165
Winding Way. Dag—34Yc 67
Winding Way. Harr—35Ga 58
Windlass Pl. SE8—49Ac 84
Windlesham Gro. SW19—60Za 102
Windley Clo. SE23—61Yb 128
Windmill Av. Eps—83Va 162
Windmill Clo. SE1—49Wb 83
Windmill Clo. Cat—93Sb 181
Windmill Clo. Eps—84Va 162
Windmill Clo. Sun—66U 120
Windmill Clo. Surb—74La 142
Windmill Clo. Upm—33Qd 69
Windmill Clo. Wal A—6Gc 13
Windmill Clo. Wind—4F 94
Windmill Ct. NW2—37Ab 60
Windmill Dri. SW4—57Kb 104
Windmill Dri. Kes—77Lc 149
Windmill Dri. Lea—95La 176
Windmill Dri. Rick—16P 17
Windmill End. Eps—84Va 162
Windmill Gdns. Enf—13Qb 24
Windmill Gro. Croy—72Sb 147
Windmill Hill. NW3—34Eb 61
Windmill Hill. Enf—13Rb 25
Windmill Hill. Ruis—31V 56
★Windmill Hill Rd. Sev—93Fe
Windmill La. E15—37Fc 65
Windmill La. Barn—16Va 22
Windmill La. Bush, Wat—18Ga 20
Windmill La. Eps—84Va 162
Windmill La. Gnfd—43Ea 78
Windmill La. S'hall & Iswth
—47Ea 78
Windmill La. Surb—73Ka 142
Windmill La. Wal X—2Ac 12
Windmill M. W4—49Ua 80
Windmill Pas. W4—49Ua 80
Windmill Rd. N18—21Tb 43
Windmill Rd. SW18—58Fb 103
Windmill Rd. SW19—63Xa 124
Windmill Rd. W4—49Ua 80
Windmill Rd.—49La 78
W5 143a-245 & 158-366
Bren remainder
Windmill Rd. Croy—73Sb 147
Windmill Rd. Hmptn—64Da 121
Windmill Rd. Mitc—71Lb 146
Windmill Rd. Slou—6H 73
Windmill Rd. Slou—6P 53
(Fulmer)
Windmill Rd. Sun—67U 120
Windmill Rd. W. Sun—68U 120
Windmill Row. SE11
—50Qb 82 (7K 205)
Windmill St. W1
—43Mb 82 (1D 198)
(in two parts)
Windmill St. Bush, Wat—18Ga 20
Windmill St. Grav—9D 114
Windmill Wlk. SE1
—46Qb 82 (7A 200)
Windmill Way. Ruis—32V 56
Windmore Av. Pot B—3Ya 8
Windover Av. NW9—28Ta 39
Windover Way. Grav—3G 136
Windrush. SE28—46Xc 87
Windrush Av. Slou—48D 74
Windrush Clo. SW11—56Fb 103
Windrush Clo. W4—53Sa 101
Windrush Clo. Uxb—35P 55
Windrush La. SE23—62Zb 128
Windsor & Eton Relief Rd. Wind
—3F 94
Windsor Av. E17—26Ac 44
Windsor Av. SW19—67Eb 125
Windsor Av. E Mol—69Ca 121
Windsor Av. Edgw—21Ra 39
Windsor Av. Grays—47De 91
Windsor Av. N Mald—71Sa 143
Windsor Av. Sutt—76Ab 144
Windsor Av. Uxb—39R 56
Windsor Clo. N3—26Ab 40
Windsor Clo. Borwd—11Qa 21
Windsor Clo. Bren—51Ka 100
Windsor Clo. Harr—34Ca 57
Windsor Clo. Hem—1C 2
Windsor Clo. N'wd—26W 36
Windsor Clo. Slou—2A 72
Windsor Clo. Wal X—2Wb 11
Windsor Ct. N14—17Lb 24
Windsor Ct. Sun—66W 120
Windsor Cres. Harr—34Ca 57
Windsor Cres. Wemb—34Ra 59
Windsor Dri. Ashf—63M 119
Windsor Dri. Barn—16Hb 23
Windsor Dri. Dart—58Jd 110
Windsor Dri. Orp—79Wc 151
Windsor Gdns. W9—43Cb 81
Windsor Gdns. Hay—48T 76
Windsor Gro. SE27—63Sb 127
Windsor La. Slou—2A 72
Windsor Pk. Rd. Hay—52V 98
Windsor Pl. SW1
—49Lb 82 (5C 204)
Windsor Rd. E4—21Dc 44
Windsor Rd. E7—36Kc 65
Windsor Rd. E10—33Dc 64
Windsor Rd. E11—33Jc 65
Windsor Rd. N3—26Ab 40
Windsor Rd. N7—34Nb 62
Windsor Rd. N13—20Qb 24
Windsor Rd. N17—26Wb 43
Windsor Rd. NW2—37Xa 60
Windsor Rd. W5—45Na 79
Windsor Rd. Barn—16Za 22
Windsor Rd. Bexh—56Ad 109
Windsor Rd. Brtwd—16Xd 32
Windsor Rd. Dag—34Ad 67
Windsor Rd. Enf—8Zb 12
Windsor Rd. Grav—2D 136
Windsor Rd. Harr—25Fa 38
Windsor Rd. Horn—31Ld 69
Windsor Rd. Houn—54Y 99
Windsor Rd. Ilf—35Rc 66
Windsor Rd. King—66Na 123
Windsor Rd. Rich—54Pa 101
Windsor Rd. Sidc—65Xc 131
Windsor Rd. Slou—8J 73
Windsor Rd. Slou—2L 95
(Datchet)
Windsor Rd. Slou & Ger X—5L 53
Windsor Rd. S'hall—48Ba 77
Windsor Rd. Sun—65W 120
Windsor Rd. Tedd—64Fa 122
Windsor Rd. T Hth—68Rb 127
Windsor Rd. Wat—10Y 5
Windsor Rd. Wind—2A 94
Windsor Rd. Wind—10N 95
(Old Windsor)
Windsor Rd. Wind—5A 116
(Woodside)
Windsor Rd. Wind & Egh—61A 118
Windsor Rd. Wor Pk—75Wa 144
Windsor Rd. Wray, Stai—58A 96
Windsor St. N1—39Rb 63
Windsor St. Cher—72J 139
Windsor St. Uxb—38L 55
(in two parts)
Windsor Ter. N1—41Sb 83 (3E 194)
Windsor Wlk. SE5—54Tb 105
Windsor Wlk. Wey—78R 140
Windsor Way. Rick—18J 17
Windsor Way. Wok—88E 156
Windspoint Dri. SE15—51Xb 105
Winds Ridge. Wok—97E 172
Windus Rd. N16—32Vb 63
Windus Wlk. N16—32Vb 63
Windward Clo. Enf—7Zb 12
Windy Hill. Brtwd—18Ee 33
Windy Ridge. Brom—67Nc 130
Windy Ridge Clo. SW19—64Za 124
Wine Clo. E1—45Yb 84
Wine Office Ct. EC4
—44Qb 82 (2A 200)
Winern Glebe. Wey—85M 157
★Winfield La. Sev—96Be
Winforton St. SE10—53Ec 106
Winfred Gro. SW11—56Hb 103
Winfrith Rd. SW18—60Eb 103
Wingate Cres. Croy—72Nb 146
Wingate Rd. W6—48Xa 80
Wingate Rd. Ilf—36Rc 66
Wingate Rd. Sidc—65Yc 131
Wingfield Clo. Brtwd—20Ce 33
Wingfield Clo. Wey—82K 157
Wingfield Gdns. Upm—30Ud 50
Wingfield Rd. E15—36Gc 65
Wingfield Rd. E17—29Dc 44
Wingfield Rd. Grav—9D 114
Wingfield Rd. King—65Qa 123
Wingfield St. SE15—55Wb 105
Wingfield Way. Ruis—37X 57
Wingford Rd. SW2—58Nb 104
Wingletye La. Horn—28Pd 49
Wingrave Rd. W6—51Ya 102
Wingrove Rd. SE6—61Gc 129
Wing Way. Brtwd—18Yd 32
Winifred Av. Horn—35Md 69
Winifred Rd. SW19—67Cb 125
Winifred Rd. Coul—88Jb 164
Winifred Rd. Dag—33Ad 67
Winifred Rd. Dart—57Kd 111
Winifred Rd. Eri—50Gd 88
Winifred Rd. Hmptn—63Ca 121
Winifred St. E16—46Pc 85
Winifred Ter. Enf—17Vb 25
Winkers Clo. Ger X—25B 34
Winkers La. Ger X—24B 34
Winkfield Plain. Wind—10A 94
Winkfield Rd. E13—40Kc 65
Winkfield Rd. N22—25Qb 42
Winkfield Rd. Asc—9A 116
Winkfield Rd. Wind—10A 94
Winkley St. E2—40Xb 63
Winkworth Pl. Bans—86Bb 163
Winkworth Rd. Bans—86Bb 163
Winlaton Rd. Brom—63Fc 129
Winmill Rd. Dag—34Bd 67
Winnards. Wok—6E 188
Winnett St. W1—45Mb 82 (4D 198)
Winnington Clo. N2—30Fb 41
Winnington Rd. N2—30Fb 41
Winnington Rd. Enf—10Yb 12
Winnington Way. Wok—6E 188
Winnock Rd. W Dray—46M 75
Winn Rd. SE12—60Jc 107
Winns Av. E17—27Bc 44
Winns Comn. Rd. SE18—51Uc 108
Winns M. N15—28Ub 43
Winns Ter. E17—27Cc 44
Winsbeach. E17—26Fc 45
Winscombe Cres. W5—42Ma 79
Winscombe St. N19—33Kb 62
Winscombe Way. Stan—22Ja 38
Winsford Rd. SE6—62Bc 128
Winsford Ter. N18—22Tb 43
Winsham Gro. SW11—57Jb 104
Winslade Rd. SW2—57Nb 104
Winslade Way. SE6—59Dc 106
Winsland M. W2—44Fb 81 (2B 196)
Winsland St. W2—44Fb 81 (2B 196)
Winsley St. W1—44Lb 82 (2C 198)
Winslow. SE17—(7H 207)
Winslow Clo. NW10—34Ua 60
Winslow Clo. Pinn—30X 37
Winslow Gro. E4—19Gc 27
Winslow Rd. W6—51Ya 102
Winslow Way. Felt—62Aa 121
Winslow Way. W on T—76Y 141
Winsor Ter. E6—43Qc 86
Winstanley Clo. Cob—86X 159
Winstanley Rd. SW11—55Fb 103
Winstead Gdns. Dag—36Ed 68
Winston Av. NW9—31Ua 60
Winston Clo. Harr—23Ha 38
Winston Clo. Romf—28Dd 48
Winston Ct. Harr—24Da 37
Winston Dri. Cob—88Aa 159
Winston Rd. N16—35Tb 63
Winston Wlk. W4—49Ta 79
Winston Way. Ilf—34Rc 66
Winston Way. Pot B—5Cb 9
Winston Way. Wok—92D 172
Winstre Rd. Borwd—11Qa 21
Winter Av. E6—39Nc 66
Winterborne Av. Orp—76Tc 150
Winterbourne Gro. Wey—79S 140
Winterbourne Rd. SE6—60Bc 106
Winterbourne Rd. Dag—33Yc 67
Winterbourne Rd. T Hth—70Qb 126
Winter Box Wlk. Rich—57Pa 101
Winterbrook Rd. SE24—58Sb 105
Winterdown Gdns. Esh—79Ba 141
Winterdown Rd. Esh—79Ba 141
Winterfold Clo. SW19—61Ab 124
Winters Croft. Grav—5F 136
Wintersells Rd. Wey—82M 157
Winters Rd. Th Dit—73Ka 142
Winterstoke Gdns. NW7—22Wa 40
Winterstoke Rd. SE6—60Bc 106
Winters Way. Wal A—5Jc 13
Winterton Ct. SE20—68Wb 127
Winterton Pl. SW10—51Eb 103
Winterwell Rd. SW2—57Nb 104
Winthorpe Rd. SW15—56Ab 102
Winthrop St. E1—43Xb 83
Winthrop Wlk. Wemb—34Na 59
Winton App. Rick—15S 18
Winton Av. N11—24Lb 42
Winton Clo. N9—17Zb 26
Winton Cres. Rick—15R 18
Winton Dri. Rick—15R 18
Winton Dri. Wal X—1Ac 12
Winton Gdns. Edgw—24Pa 39
Winton Pl. Wey—81M 157
Winton Rd. Orp—77Rc 150
Winton Way. SW16—64Qb 126
Wintoun Path. Slou—2C 72
Winvale. Slou—8J 73
Winwood. Slou—4N 73
Wirgrave Cres. Brtwd—21Ud 50
Wirrall Ho. SE26—62Wb 127
Wisbeach Rd. Croy—71Tb 147
Wisborough Rd. S Croy—81Vb 165
Wisdons Clo. Dag—32Dd 68
Wise La. NW7—22Wa 40
Wise La. W Dray—48M 75
Wiseman Rd. E10—33Cc 64
Wise Rd. E15—39Fc 65
Wises La. Sev—80Ae 155
Wiseton Rd. SW17—60Gb 103
Wishart Rd. SE3—54Mc 107
Wishford Ct. Asht—90Pa 161
Wisley La. Wok—88L 157
Wisley Rd. SW11—57Jb 104
Wisley Rd. Orp—66Wc 131
Wistaria Clo. Orp—75Rc 150
Wistari Clo. Brtwd—15Xd 32
Wisteria Gdns. Swan—68Fd 132
Wisteria Rd. SE13—56Fc 107
Witan St. E2—41Xb 83
Witches La. Sev—95Fd 186
Witham Clo. Lou—16Nc 28
Witham Gdns. Brtwd—30Fe 51
Witham Rd. SE20—69Yb 128
Witham Rd. W13—46Ja 78
Witham Rd. Dag—36Cd 68
Witham Rd. Iswth—53Fa 100
Witham Rd. Romf—29Kd 49
Withens Clo. Orp—70Yc 131
Witherby Clo. Croy—77Ub 147
Witherfield Way. SE16—50Xb 83
Witherings, The. Horn—29Nd 49
Witherington Rd. N5—36Qb 62
Withers Mead. NW9—25Va 40
Withers Pl. EC1—42Sb 83 (5E 194)
Witherston Way. SE9—61Qc 130
Witheygate Av. Stai—65K 119
Withies, The. Lea—92Ka 176
Withybed Corner. Tad—95Xa 178
Withy Clo. Wind—3C 94
Withycombe Rd. SW19—59Za 102
Withycroft. Slou—44A 74
Withy La. Ruis—29S 36
Withy Mead. E4—20Fc 27
Witley Cres. Croy—79Ec 148
Witley Gdns. S'hall—49Ba 77
Witley Rd. N19—33Lb 62
Witney Clo. Pinn—23Ba 37
Witney Clo. Uxb—35P 55
Witney Path. SE23—62Zb 128
Wittenham Way. E4—20Fc 27
Wittering Way. Horn—37Ld 69
Wittersham Rd. Brom—64Hc 129
Wivenhoe Clo. SE15—55Xb 105
Wivenhoe Ct. Houn—56Ba 99
Wivenhoe Rd. Bark—40Wc 67
Wiverton Rd. SE26—65Yb 128
Wix Rd. Dag—39Zc 67
Wix's La. SW4—55Kb 104
Woburn Av. Epp—9Uc 14
Woburn Av. Horn—35Jd 68
Woburn Av. Purl—83Qb 164
Woburn Clo. SW19—65Eb 125
Woburn Clo. Bush, Wat—16Ea 20
Woburn Hill. Wey—75L 139
Woburn Pl. WC1—42Nb 82 (5E 192)
Woburn Rd. Cars—74Gb 145
Woburn Rd. Croy—74Sb 147
Woburn Sq. WC1
—42Mb 82 (6E 192)
Woburn Wlk. WC1
—41Mb 82 (4E 192)
Woffington Clo. King—67La 122
Wokindon Rd. Grays—8D 92
Woking Clo. SW15—56Va 102
Woldham Rd. Brom—70Lc 129
Woldingham Rd. Cat—96Gc 183
Woldingham Rd. Cat—97Fc 183
Woldingham Rd. Cat—92Xb 181
(Woldingham)
Wolds Dri. Orp—77Qc 150
Wold, The. Cat—94Cc 182
Wolfe Clo. Brom—72Jc 149
Wolfe Clo. Hay—41X 77
Wolfe Cotts. West—99Tc 184
Wolfe Cres. SE7—50Mc 85
Wolfe Gdns. E15—37Hc 65
Wolferton Rd. E12—35Pc 66
Wolfington Rd. SE27—63Rb 127
Wolf La. Wind—5B 94
Wolfram Clo. SE13—57Gc 107
Wolftencroft Clo. SW11—55Gb 103
Wollaston Clo. SE1
—49Sb 83 (5D 206)
Wolmer Clo. Edgw—21Qa 39
Wolmer Gdns. Edgw—20Qa 21
Wolseley Av. SW19—61Cb 125
Wolseley Gdns. W4—51Ra 101
Wolseley Rd. E7—38Kc 65
Wolseley Rd. N8—30Mb 42
Wolseley Rd. N22—25Pb 42
Wolseley Rd. W4—49Sa 79
Wolseley Rd. Harr—27Ga 38
Wolseley Rd. Mitc—73Jb 146
Wolseley Rd. Romf—31Fd 68
Wolseley St. SE1—47Wb 83
Wolsey Av. E6—41Qc 86
Wolsey Av. E17—27Bc 44
Wolsey Av. Th Dit—71Ha 142
Wolsey Av. Wal X—1Vb 11
Wolsey Clo. SW20—66Xa 124
Wolsey Clo. Houn—56Ea 100
Wolsey Clo. King—67Ra 123
Wolsey Clo. S'hall—48Ea 78
Wolsey Clo. Wor Pk—77Wa 144
Wolsey Cres. Croy—81Ec 166
Wolsey Cres. Mord—73Ab 144
Wolsey Dri. King—64Na 123
Wolsey Dri. W on T—74Z 141
Wolsey Gdns. Ilf—23Rc 46
Wolsey Gro. Edgw—24Ta 39
Wolsey Gro. Esh—77Da 141
Wolsey M. NW5—37Lb 62
Wolsey Rd. N1—36Tb 63
Wolsey Rd. Ashf—63N 119
Wolsey Rd. E Mol—70Fa 122
Wolsey Rd. Enf—12Xb 25
Wolsey Rd. Esh—77Da 141
Wolsey Rd. Hmptn—65Da 121
Wolsey Rd. N'wd—19S 18
Wolsey Rd. Sun—66V 120
Wolsey St. E1—43Yb 84
Wolsey Wlk. Wok—89A 156
Wolsey Way. Chess—78Qa 143
Wolsley Clo. Dart—57Gd 110
Wolstonbury. N12—22Cb 41
Wolvercote Rd. SE2—47Zc 87
Wolverley St. E2—41Xb 83
Wolverton. SE17—50Ub 83 (7H 207)
Wolverton Av. King—67Qa 123
Wolverton Gdns. W5—45Pa 79
Wolverton Gdns. W6—49Za 80
Wolverton Rd. Stan—23Ka 38
Wolverton Way. N14—15Lb 24
Wolves La.—24Qb 42
N13 1-37 & 2-40
N22 remainder
Womersly Rd. N8—30Pb 42
Wonersh Way. Sutt—81Za 162
Wonford Clo. King—67Ua 124
Wonford Clo. Tad—98Wa 178
Wontford Rd. Purl—87Rb 165
Wontner Rd. SW17—61Hb 125
Wooburn Clo. Uxb—42R 76
Wooburn Comn. Rd. Slou—3A 52
Woodall Clo. E14—45Dc 84
Woodall Rd. Enf—16Zb 26
Wood Av. Purf—49Sd 90
Woodbank Rd. Brom—62Hc 129
Woodbastwick Rd. SE26
—64Zb 128
Woodberry Av. N21—19Qb 24
Woodberry Av. Harr—28Ea 38
Woodberry Clo. Sun—65W 120
Woodberry Cres. N10—27Kb 42
Woodberry Down. N4—31Sb 63
Woodberry Down. Epp—1Wc 15
Woodberry Gdns. N12—23Eb 41
Woodberry Gro. N4—31Sb 63
Woodberry Gro. N12—23Eb 41
Woodberry Gro. Bex—62Fd 132
Woodberry Way. E4—17Ec 26
Woodberry Way. N12—23Eb 41
Woodbine Clo. Twic—61Fa 122
Woodbine Gro. SE20—66Xb 127
Woodbine Gro. Enf—10Tb 11
Woodbine La. Wor Pk—76Ya 144
Woodbine Pl. E11—30Jc 45
Woodbine Rd. Sidc—60Uc 108
Woodbines Av. King—69Ma 123
Woodbine Ter. E9—37Yb 64
Woodborough Rd. SW15
—56Xa 102
Woodbourne Av. SW16
—62Mb 126
Woodbourne Dri. Esh—79Ha 142
Woodbourne Gdns. Wall
—80Kb 146
Woodbridge Av. Lea—90Ja 160
Woodbridge Clo. N7—33Pb 62
Woodbridge Clo. Romf—21Md 49
Woodbridge Ct. Wfd G—24Nc 46
Woodbridge Gro. Lea—90Ja 160
Woodbridge La. Romf—20Md 31
Woodbridge Rd. Bark—36Vc 67
Woodbridge St. EC1
—42Rb 83 (5B 194)
Woodbrook Gdns. Wal A—5Gc 13
Woodbrook Rd. SE2—51Wc 109
Woodburn Clo. NW4—29Za 40
Woodbury Clo. E11—28Kc 45
Woodbury Clo. Croy—75Vb 147
Woodbury Clo. West—90Pc 168
Woodbury Dri. Sutt—82Eb 163
Woodbury Hill. Lou—13Nc 28
Woodbury Hollow. Lou—12Nc 28
Woodbury Ho. SE26—62Wb 127
Woodbury Pk. Rd. W13—42Ka 78
Woodbury Rd. E17—28Dc 44
Woodbury Rd. West—90Pc 168
Woodbury St. SW17—64Gb 125
Woodchester Sq. W2—43Db 81
Woodchurch Clo. Sidc—62Uc 130
Woodchurch Dri. Brom—66Mc 129
Woodchurch Rd. NW6—38Db 61
Wood Clo. E2—42Wb 83
Wood Clo. NW9—31Ta 59
Wood Clo. Bex—62Gd 132
Wood Clo. Harr—31Fa 58
Wood Clo. Wind—6G 94
Woodclyffe Dri. Chst—68Qc 130
Woodcock Dell Av. Harr—31Ma 59
Woodcock Hill. Borwd—16Pa 21
Woodcock Hill. Harr—29La 38
Woodcock Hill Trading Est.
Rick—21N 35
Woodcombe Cres. SE23
—60Yb 106
Woodcote Av. NW7—23Ya 40
Woodcote Av. Horn—35Jd 68
Woodcote Av. T Hth—70Rb 127
Woodcote Av. Wall—81Kb 164
Woodcote Clo. Enf—16Yb 26
Woodcote Clo. Eps—86Ta 161
Woodcote Clo. King—64Pa 123
Woodcote Clo. Wal X—2Yb 12
Woodcote Dri. Orp—73Tc 150
Woodcote Dri. Purl—82Mb 164
Woodcote End. Eps—87Ta 161
Woodcote Grn. Wall—81Lb 164
Woodcote Grn. Rd. Eps—87Sa 161
Woodcote Gro. Cars—84Kb 164
Woodcote Gro. Rd. Coul
—87Mb 164
Woodcote Hurst. Eps—88Sa 161
Woodcote La. Purl—83Mb 164
Woodcote M. Wall—79Kb 146
Woodcote Pk. Av. Purl—84Lb 164
Woodcote Pk. Rd. Eps—87Sa 161
Woodcote Pl. SE27—64Rb 127
Woodcote Rd. E11—31Jc 65
Woodcote Rd. Eps—86Ta 161
Woodcote Rd. Wall & Purl
—79Kb 146
Woodcote Side. Eps—87Ra 161
Woodcote Valley Rd. Purl
—85Mb 164
Woodcrest Rd. Purl—85Nb 164
Woodcroft. N21—18Qb 24
Woodcroft. SE9—62Pc 130
Woodcroft. Gnfd—37Ja 58
Woodcroft Av. NW7—23Ua 40
Woodcroft Av. Stan—25Ja 38
Woodcroft Cres. Uxb—39R 56
Woodcroft Rd. T Hth—71Rb 147
Woodcutters Av. Grays—47Ee 91
Wood Dri. Chst—65Nc 130
Wood Dri. Sev—98Hd 186
Woodedge Clo. E4—18Hc 27
Woodend. SE19—65Sb 127
Woodend. Esh—75Ea 142
Wood End. Hay—44U 76
Woodend. Lea—97La 176
Wood End. St Alb—1Ea 6
Woodend. Sutt—75Eb 145
Wood End Av. Harr—35Da 57
Wood End Clo. N'holt—36Ea 58
Wood End Clo. Slou—4H 53
Woodend Clo. Wok—7D 188
Woodend Dri. Asc—10A 116
Woodend Gdns. Enf—14Nb 24
Wood End Gdns. N'holt—36Ea 58
Wood End Grn. Rd. Hay—43T 76
Wood End La. N'holt—36Da 57
Woodend Pk. Cob—87Z 159
Woodend Rd. E17—26Ec 44
Wood End Rd. Harr—35Fa 58
Woodend Rd. Wind—5A 116

Woodend, The—Wroxham Gdns.

Woodend, The. Wall—81Kb **164**
Woodend Way. Mord—70Bb **125**
Wood End Way. N'holt—36Ea **58**
Wooder Gdns. E7—35Jc **65**
Woodfall Av. Barn—15Bb **23**
Woodfall Rd. N4—33Qb **62**
Woodfall St. SW3
—50Hb **81** (7F **203**)
Woodfarrs. SE5—56Tb **105**
Woodfield. Asht—89Ma **161**
Woodfield Av. NW9—28Ua **40**
Woodfield Av. SW16—62Mb **126**
Woodfield Av. W5—42La **78**
Woodfield Av. Cars—79Jb **146**
Woodfield Av. Grav—10D **114**
Woodfield Av. N'wd—21U **36**
Woodfield Av. Wemb—34La **58**
Woodfield Clo. SE19—66Sb **127**
Woodfield Clo. Asht—89Ma **161**
Woodfield Clo. Coul—91Lb **180**
Woodfield Cres. W5—42Ma **79**
Woodfield Dri. Barn—18Jb **24**
Woodfield Dri. Romf—28Jd **48**
Woodfield Gdns. W9—43Cb **81**
Woodfield Gdns. N Mald
—71Va **144**
Woodfield Gro. SW16—62Mb **126**
Woodfield Hill. Coul—91Kb **180**
Woodfield La. SW16—62Mb **126**
Woodfield La. Asht—89Na **161**
Woodfield Pl. W9—42Bb **81**
Woodfield Rise. Bush, Wat
—17Fa **20**
Woodfield Rd. W5—42La **78**
Woodfield Rd. W9—43Bb **81**
Woodfield Rd. Asht—89Ma **161**
Woodfield Rd. Houn—54X **99**
Woodfield Rd. Rad—8Ja **6**
Woodfield Rd. Th Dit—75Ha **142**
Woodfields. Sev—95Fd **186**
Woodfields, The. S Croy—83Vb **165**
Woodfield Ter. Uxb—26K **35**
Woodfield Way. N11—24Mb **42**
Woodfield W. Horn—32Md **69**
Woodfines, The. Horn—30Md **49**
Woodford Av. Ilf—27Nc **46**
Woodford Bri. Rd. Ilf—27Mc **45**
Woodford Ct. Wal A—5Jc **13**
Woodford Cres. Pinn—26X **37**
Woodforde Ct. Hay—50T **76**
Woodford New Rd. E17, E18 &
Wfd G—28Gc **45**
Woodford Pl. Wemb—32Na **59**
Woodford Rd. E7—35Kc **65**
Woodford Rd. E18—28Jc **45**
Woodford Rd. Wat—12Y **19**
Woodford Trading Est. Wfd G
—27Mc **45**
Woodford Way. Slou—1E **72**
Woodgate. Wat—5X **5**
Woodgate Av. Chess—78Ma **143**
Woodgate Cres. N'wd—23W **36**
Woodgavil. Bans—88Bb **163**
Woodger Rd. W12—47Ya **80**
Woodgers Gro. Swan—68Hd **132**
Woodget Clo. E6—44Nc **86**
Woodgrange Av. N12—23Fb **41**
Woodgrange Av. W5—46Qa **79**
Woodgrange Av. Enf—16Wb **25**
Woodgrange Av. Harr—29La **38**
Woodgrange Clo. Harr—29Ma **39**
Woodgrange Gdns. Enf—16Wb **25**
Woodgrange Rd. E7—36Kc **65**
Woodgrange Ter. Enf—16Wb **25**
Woodgreen Rd. Wal A—5Lc **13**
Wood Green Shopping City. N22
—26Qb **42**
Wood Grn. Way. Wal X—3Ac **12**
Woodhall Av. SE21—62Vb **127**
Woodhall Av. Pinn—25Aa **37**
Woodhall Clo. Uxb—36M **55**
Woodhall Cres. Horn—31Pd **69**
Woodhall Dri. SE21—62Vb **127**
Woodhall Dri. Pinn—25Z **37**
Woodhall Ga. Pinn—24Z **37**
Woodhall La. Shen, Rad—7Na **7**
Woodhall La. Wat—20Z **19**
Woodhall Rd. Pinn—24Z **37**
Woodham Ct. E18—28Hc **45**
Woodham Hall Est. Wok—86D **156**
Woodham La. Wey—84G **156**
Woodham La. Wok—85D **156**
Woodham Pk. Rd. Wey—82H **157**
Woodham Pk. Way. Wey—83H **157**
Woodham Rise. Wok—87C **156**
Woodham Rd. SE6—62Ec **128**
Woodham Rd. Wok—87A **156**
Woodham Waye. Wok—86D **156**
Woodhatch Clo. E6—43Nc **86**
Woodhatch Spinney. Coul
—88Nb **164**
Woodhaven Gdns. Ilf—28Sc **46**
Woodhaw. Egh—63D **118**
Woodhayes Rd. SW19—66Ya **124**
Woodhead Dri. Orp—76Uc **150**
Woodheyes Rd. NW10—36Ta **59**
Woodhill. SE18—49Nc **86**
Woodhill. Wok—98F **172**
Woodhill Av. Ger X—30C **34**
Woodhill Cres. Harr—30Ma **39**
Woodhouse Av. Gnfd—40Ha **58**
Woodhouse Clo. Gnfd—40Ha **58**
Woodhouse Clo. Hay—48U **76**
Woodhouse Eaves. N'wd—22W **36**
Woodhouse Gro. E12—37Nc **66**
Woodhouse Rd. E11—34Hc **65**
Woodhouse Rd. N12—23Fb **41**
Woodhurst Av. Orp—72Sc **150**
Woodhurst Av. Wat—6Z **5**
Woodhurst Dri. Uxb—29H **35**
Woodhurst Rd. SE2—50Wc **87**
Woodhurst Rd. W3—45Sa **79**
Woodhyrst Gdns. Kenl—87Rb **165**
Woodington Clo. SE9—58Qc **108**
Woodison St. E3—42Ac **84**
Woodknoll Dri. Chst—67Pc **130**
Woodland App. Gnfd—37Ja **58**
Woodland Av. Brtwd—15Ee **33**
Woodland Av. Slou—5H **73**
Woodland Av. Wind—6D **94**
Woodland Clo. NW9—30Sa **39**
Woodland Clo. SE19—65Ub **127**
Woodland Clo. Brtwd—15Ee **33**
Woodland Clo. Eps—79Ua **144**
Woodland Clo. Long, Dart
—69Ee **135**
Woodland Clo. Uxb—33R **56**
Woodland Clo. Wey—77T **140**
Woodland Clo. Wfd G—20Kc **27**
Woodland Ct. Oxt—100Fc **183**
Woodland Cres. SE10—51Gc **107**
Woodland Dri. Lea—99V **174**
Woodland Dri. Wat—11V **18**
Woodland Gdns. N10—29Kb **42**
Woodland Gdns. Iswth—55Ga **100**
Woodland Gdns. S Croy
—83Yb **166**
Woodland Glade. Slou—4H **53**
Woodland Gro. SE10—50Gc **85**
Woodland Gro. Wey—77T **140**
Woodland Hill. SE19—65Ub **127**
Woodland La. Rick—13F **16**
Woodland Rise. N10—28Kb **42**
Woodland Rise. Gnfd—37Ja **58**
Woodland Rise. Sev—95Nd **187**
Woodland Rd. E4—18Ec **26**
Woodland Rd. N11—22Kb **42**
Woodland Rd. SE19—64Ub **127**
Woodland Rd. Lou—13Nc **28**
Woodland Rd. Rick—22F **34**
Woodland Rd. T Hth—70Qb **126**
Woodlands. NW11—29Ab **40**
Woodlands. SW20—70Ya **124**
Woodlands. Harr—28Ca **37**
Woodlands. Lea—94Ja **176**
Woodlands. Rad—6Ja **6**
Woodlands. Wok—91B **172**
Woodlands Av. E11—32Kc **65**
Woodlands Av. N3—24Eb **41**
Woodlands Av. W3—46Ra **79**
Woodlands Av. Horn—29Md **49**
Woodlands Av. Long, Dart
—71Be **155**
Woodlands Av. N Mald—67Sa **123**
Woodlands Av. Romf—31Ad **67**
Woodlands Av. Ruis—31Y **57**
Woodlands Av. Sidc—60Uc **108**
Woodlands Av. Wey—85H **157**
Woodlands Av. Wor Pk
—75Wa **144**
Woodlands Clo. NW11—29Ab **40**
Woodlands Clo. Borwd—14Ra **21**
Woodlands Clo. Brom—68Pc **130**
Woodlands Clo. Cher—82D **156**
Woodlands Clo. Esh—80Ha **142**
Woodlands Clo. Ger X—30C **34**
Woodlands Clo. Grays—8A **92**
Woodlands Clo. Swan—69Hd **132**
Woodlands Ct. SE22—59Xb **105**
Woodlands Ct. Wok—91A **172**
Woodlands Dri. Stan—23Ha **38**
Woodlands Dri. Sun—68Y **121**
Woodlands Est. Wok—6A **188**
Woodlands Gro. Coul—89Kb **164**
Woodlands Gro. Iswth—54Ga **100**
Woodlands Hill. High W—1C **52**
Woodlands La. Cob & Lea
—89Ca **159**
Woodlands Pde. Ashf—65S **120**
Woodlands Pk. Bex—63Fd **132**
Woodlands Pk. Wey—78H **139**
Woodlands Pk. Clo. SE10
—51Gc **107**
Woodlands Pk. Rd. N15—29Sb **43**
Woodlands Pk. Rd. SE10
—51Gc **107**
Woodlands Rise. Swan—68Hd **132**
Woodlands Rd. E11—33Gc **65**
Woodlands Rd. E17—27Ec **44**
Woodlands Rd. N9—18Yb **26**
Woodlands Rd. SW13—55Va **102**
Woodlands Rd. Bexh—55Ad **109**
Woodlands Rd. Brom—68Nc **130**
Woodlands Rd. Bush, Wat
—15Aa **19**
Woodlands Rd. Enf—11Tb **25**
Woodlands Rd. Eps—87Qa **161**
Woodlands Rd. Grav—6M **137**
Woodlands Rd. Harr—29Ha **38**
Woodlands Rd. Ilf—34Sc **66**
Woodlands Rd. Iswth—55Fa **100**
Woodlands Rd. Lea—89Fa **160**
Woodlands Rd. Lea—100Aa **175**
(Effingham)
Woodlands Rd. Orp—79Wc **151**
Woodlands Rd. Romf—27Hd **48**
Woodlands Rd. Romf—25Qd **49**
(Harold Wood)
Woodlands Rd. S'hall—46Z **77**
Woodlands Rd. Surb—73Ma **143**
Woodlands Rd. Vir W—10N **117**
Woodlands Rd. Wey—86H **157**
Woodlands Rd. E. Vir W—10N **117**
Woodlands Rd. W. Vir W—10N **117**
Woodlands St. SE13—59Fc **107**
Woodlands, The. N14—18Kb **24**
Woodlands, The. SE13—59Fc **107**
Woodlands, The. SE19—66Sb **127**
Woodlands, The. Esh—74Fa **142**
Woodlands, The. Ger X—30B **34**
Woodlands, The. Iswth—54Ha **100**
Woodlands, The. Orp—79Xc **151**
Woodlands, The. Wall—81Kb **164**
Woodlands Way. SW15—57Bb **103**
Woodlands Way. Asht—88Qa **161**
Woodlands Way. Wey—78T **140**
Woodland Ter. SE7—49Nc **86**
Woodland Wlk. SE10—50Gc **85**
Woodland Wlk. Brom—63Gc **129**
Woodland Way. N21—19Qb **24**
Woodland Way. NW7—23Va **40**
Woodland Way. SE2—49Zc **87**
Woodland Way. Cat—100Ub **181**
Woodland Way. Croy—74Ac **148**
Woodland Way. Epp—7Uc **14**
Woodland Way. Mitc—66Jb **126**
Woodland Way. Mord—70Bb **125**
Woodland Way. Orp—70Sc **130**
Woodland Way. Purl—85Qb **164**
Woodland Way. Surb—75Ra **143**
Woodland Way. Tad—94Ab **178**
Woodland Way. W Wick
—77Dc **148**
Woodland Way. Wfd G—20Kc **27**
Wood La. N6—30Kb **42**
Wood La. NW9—31Ta **59**
Wood La. W12—44Ya **80**
Wood La. Cat—96Tb **181**
Wood La. Dag—35Zc **67**
Wood La. Dart—63Td **134**
Wood La. Horn—36Jd **68**
Wood La. Iswth—51Ga **100**
Wood La. Iver—41E **74**
Wood La. Ruis—32T **56**
Wood La. Slou—8D **72**
Wood La. Stan—20Ja **20**
Wood La. Tad—89Bb **163**
Wood La. Wey—81S **158**
Wood La. Wok—6A **188**
Wood La. Wfd G—22Gc **45**
Wood La. Clo. Iver—41D **74**
Woodlawn Cres. Twic—61Da **121**
Woodlawn Dri. Felt—61Z **121**
Woodlawn Gro. Wok—87B **156**
Woodlawn Rd. SW6—52Za **102**
Woodlea Dri. Brom—71Gc **149**
Woodlea Gro. N'wd—23T **36**
Woodlea Rd. N16—34Ub **63**
Woodleigh Av. N12—23Gb **41**
Woodleigh Gdns. SW16—62Nb **126**
Woodley Clo. SW17—66Hb **125**
Woodley Rd. Orp—75Yc **151**
Wood Lodge Gdns. Brom
—66Nc **130**
Wood Lodge La. W Wick
—76Ec **148**
Woodmancote Gdns. Wey
—85J **157**
Woodman La. E4—15Gc **27**
Woodman Path. Ilf—23Uc **46**
Woodman Rd. Brtwd—22Yd **50**
Woodman Rd. Coul—87Lb **164**
Woodman's M. W10—43Xa **80**
Woodmansterne La. Bans
—87Eb **163**
Woodmansterne La. Cars & Wall
—84Jb **164**
Woodmansterne Rd. SW16
—67Mb **126**
Woodmansterne Rd. Cars
—84Hb **163**
Woodmansterne Rd. Coul
—87Lb **164**
Woodmansterne St. Bans
—87Gb **163**
Woodman St. E16—46Qc **86**
Woodman's Yd. Wat—14Z **19**
Wood Meads. Epp—1Wc **15**
Woodmere. SE9—60Pc **108**
Woodmere Av. Croy—73Zb **148**
Woodmere Av. Wat—10Z **5**
Woodmere Clo. Croy—73Zb **148**
Woodmere Gdns. Croy—73Zb **148**
Woodmere Way. Beck—71Fc **149**
Woodmount. Swan—73Fd **152**
Woodnook Rd. SW16—64Kb **126**
Woodpecker Clo. N9—16Xb **25**
Woodpecker Clo. Bush, Wat
—18Ea **20**
Woodpecker Clo. Cob—84Aa **159**
Woodpecker Mt. Croy—81Ac **166**
Woodpecker Rd. SE14—51Ac **106**
Woodpecker Rd. SE28—45Yc **87**
Woodpecker Way. Wok—96A **172**
Woodplace Clo. Coul—91Lb **180**
Woodplace La. Coul—91Lb **180**
Woodquest Av. SE24—57Sb **105**
Woodridden Hill. Wal A—7Lc **13**
Wood Ride. Barn—11Fb **23**
Wood Ride. Orp—70Tc **130**
Woodridge Clo. NW2—34Xa **60**
Woodridge Way. N'wd—23U **36**
Woodridings Av. Pinn—25Ba **37**
Woodridings Clo. Pinn—24Da **37**
Woodriffe Rd. E11—31Fc **65**
Wood Rise. Pinn—29W **36**
Wood Rd. Shep—70Q **120**
Wood Rd. West—90Lc **167**
Woodrow. SE18—49Pc **86**
Woodrow Av. Hay—43V **76**
Woodrow Clo. Gnfd—38Ka **58**
Woodrow Ct. N17—24Xb **43**
Woodrush Way. Romf—28Zc **47**
Woods Dri. Slou—6D **52**
Woodseer St. E1—43Vb **83**
Woodsford Sq. W14—47Ab **80**
Woodshire Rd. Dag—34Dd **68**
Wood Side. NW11—29Cb **41**
Woodside. SW19—64Bb **125**
Woodside. Borwd—14Pa **21**
Woodside. Buck H—19Lc **27**
Woodside. Lea—94Da **175**
Woodside. Lea—98S **174**
(West Horsley)
Woodside. Orp—78Xc **151**
Woodside. Tad—100Bb **179**
Woodside. Wal X—3Wb **11**
Woodside. Wat—8W **4**
Woodside Av.—29Hb **41**
N6 1-37 & 2-68
N10 remainder
Woodside Av. N12—21Db **41**
Woodside Av. SE25—72Xb **147**
Woodside Av. Chst—64Sc **130**
Woodside Av. Esh—73Ga **142**
Woodside Av. W on T—77X **141**
Woodside Av. Wemb—39Na **59**
Woodside Clo. Bexh—56Fd **110**
Woodside Clo. Brtwd—15Fe **33**
Woodside Clo. Cat—96Ub **181**
Woodside Clo. Ger X—26A **34**
Woodside Clo. Rain—42Ld **89**
Woodside Clo. Stan—22Ka **38**
Woodside Clo. Surb—73Sa **143**
Woodside Clo. Wemb—39Na **59**
Woodside Clo. Wok—5A **188**
Woodside Ct. Rd. Croy—73Wb **147**
Woodside Cres. Sidc—62Uc **130**
Woodside Dri. Dart—63Gd **132**
Woodside End. Wemb—39Na **59**
Woodside Gdns. E4—23Dc **44**
Woodside Gdns. N17—26Vb **43**
Woodside Grange Rd. N12
—21Db **41**
Woodside Grn. SE25—72Wb **147**
Woodside Gro. N12—20Eb **23**
Woodside Hill. Ger X—26A **34**
Woodside La. N12—20Eb **23**
Woodside La. Bex—58Zc **109**
Woodside La. Wind—4A **116**
Woodside Pk. SE25—72Xb **147**
Woodside Pk. Av. E17—28Fc **45**
Woodside Pk. Rd. N12—21Db **41**
Woodside Pl. Wemb—39Na **59**
Woodside Rd. E13—42Lc **85**
Woodside Rd. N22—24Pb **42**
Woodside Rd. SE25—72Xb **147**
Woodside Rd. Bexh—56Fd **110**
Woodside Rd. Brom—71Nc **150**
Woodside Rd. Cob—85Ca **159**
Woodside Rd. King—66Na **123**
Woodside Rd. N Mald—68Ta **123**
Woodside Rd. N'wd—24V **36**
Woodside Rd. Purl—85Mb **164**
Woodside Rd. St Alb—2Ba **5**
Woodside Rd. Sev—95Jd **188**
Woodside Rd. Sev—96Ad **185**
(Sundridge)
Woodside Rd. Sidc—62Uc **130**
Woodside Rd. Sutt—76Eb **145**
Woodside Rd. Wat—3W **4**
Woodside Rd. Wind—5A **116**
Woodside Rd. Wfd G—21Jc **45**
Woodside View. Sev—82Dd **170**
Woodside Way. Croy—72Yb **148**
Woodside Way. Mitc—67Lb **126**
Woodside Way. Vir W—9M **117**
Woods M. W1—45Jb **82** (4G **197**)
Woodsome Lodge. Wey—79S **140**
Woodsome Rd. NW5—34Kb **62**
Wood's Pl. SE1—48Ub **83** (4J **207**)
Woodspring Rd. SW19—61Ab **124**
Woods Rd. SE15—53Xb **105**
Woodstead Gro. Edgw—23Na **39**
Woods, The. N'wd—22W **36**
Woods, The. Uxb—35R **56**
Woodstock. Guild—100K **173**
Woodstock Av. NW11—31Ab **60**
Woodstock Av. W13—48Ja **78**
Woodstock Av. Iswth—57Ja **100**
Woodstock Av. N'holt—41Ba **77**
Woodstock Av. Romf—23Rd **49**
Woodstock Av. Slou—9P **73**
Woodstock Av. Sutt—73Bb **145**
Woodstock Clo. Bex—60Bd **109**
Woodstock Clo. Stan—26Na **39**
Woodstock Ct. SE12—58Jc **107**
Woodstock Cres. N9—16Xb **25**
Woodstock Dri. Uxb—35N **55**
Woodstock Gdns. Beck—67Dc **128**
Woodstock Gdns. Hay—43V **76**
Woodstock Gdns. Ilf—33Wc **67**
Woodstock Gro. W12—47Za **80**
Woodstock La. N. Surb—75La **142**
Woodstock La. S. Esh & Chess
—78Ka **142**
Woodstock M. W1—(1J 197)
Woodstock Rise. Sutt—73Bb **145**
Woodstock Rd. E7—38Lc **65**
Woodstock Rd. E17—26Fc **45**
Woodstock Rd. N4—32Qb **62**
Woodstock Rd. NW11—31Bb **61**
Woodstock Rd. W4—48Ua **80**
Woodstock Rd. Bush, Wat
—17Ga **20**
Woodstock Rd. Cars—78Jb **146**
Woodstock Rd. Coul—88Kb **164**
Woodstock Rd. Croy—76Tb **147**
Woodstock Rd. Wemb—39Pa **59**
Woodstock St. E16—44Hc **85**
Woodstock St. W1
—44Kb **82** (3K **197**)
Woodstock Ter. E14—45Dc **84**
Woodstock Way. Mitc—68Kb **126**
Woodstone Av. Eps—78Wa **144**
Wood St. E16—45Kc **85**
Wood St. E17—27Ec **44**
Wood St. EC2—44Sb **83** (2E **200**)
Wood St. W4—50Ua **80**
Wood St. Barn—14Ya **22**
Wood St. Grays—51Ee **113**
Wood St. King—68Ma **123**
Wood St. Mitc—73Jb **146**
Wood St. Red—100Lb **180**
Wood St. Swan—68Ld **133**
Woodsway. Lea—86Ga **160**
Woodsyre. SE26—63Vb **127**
Woodthorpe Rd. SW15—56Xa **102**
Woodthorpe Rd. Ashf—64M **119**
Wood Vale. N10—29Lb **42**
Wood Vale. SE23—60Xb **105**
Woodvale Av. SE25—69Vb **127**
Wood Vale Est. SE23—58Yb **106**
Woodvale Wlk. SE27—64Sb **127**
Woodview. Chess—83La **160**
Wood View. Grays—48Fe **91**
Woodview Av. E4—21Ec **44**
Wood View Clo. Sev—79Ud **154**
Woodview Clo. S Croy—86Xb **165**
Woodview Rd. Swan—68Ed **132**
Woodville Clo. SE12—57Jc **107**
Woodville Clo. Tedd—63Ja **122**
Woodville Ct. Wat—12W **18**
Woodville Gdns. NW11—31Za **60**
Woodville Gdns. W5—44Na **79**
Woodville Gdns. Ilf—28Rc **46**
Woodville Gdns. Ruis—31S **56**
Woodville Pl. Cat—93Sb **181**
Woodville Rd. E11—32Hc **65**
Woodville Rd. E17—28Bc **44**
Woodville Rd. E18—26Kc **45**
Woodville Rd. N16—36Ub **63**
Woodville Rd. NW6—40Bb **61**
Woodville Rd. NW11—31Za **60**
Woodville Rd. W5—44Ma **79**
Woodville Rd. Barn—13Db **23**
Woodville Rd. Lea—92Ka **176**
Woodville Rd. Mord—70Cb **125**
Woodville Rd. Rich—62Ka **122**
Woodville Rd. T Hth—70Sb **127**
Woodville St. SE18—49Nc **86**
Wood Wlk. Rick—12G **16**
Woodward Av. NW4—29Wa **40**
Woodward Clo. Grays—49De **91**
Woodwarde Rd. SE22—58Ub **105**
Woodward Gdns. Dag—38Yc **67**
Woodward Heights. Grays
—49De **91**
Woodward Rd. Dag—38Xc **67**
Woodward's Footpath. Twic
—58Fa **100**
Woodward Ter. Grnh—58Ud **112**
Woodway. Brtwd—18Ce **33**
Wood Way. Orp—75Qc **150**
Woodway Cres. Harr—30Ja **38**
Woodwaye. Wat—17Y **19**
Woodwell St. SW18—57Eb **103**
Woodwicks. Rick—22F **34**
Woodyard Clo. NW5—36Jb **62**
Woodyard La. SE21—59Ub **105**
Woodyates Rd. SE12—58Jc **107**
Woolacombe Rd. SE3—54Lc **107**
Woolacombe Way. Hay—49U **76**
Wooler St. SE17—50Tb **83** (7F **207**)
Woolf Clo. SE28—46Xc **87**
Woolf Wlk. Til—4E **114**
Woolhampton Way. Chig
—20Xc **29**
Woollard St. Wal A—6Ec **12**
Woollaston Rd. N4—30Rb **43**
Woolmead Av. NW9—31Wa **60**
Woolmer Gdns. N18—22Wb **43**
Woolmer Rd. N18—22Wb **43**
Woolmongers La. Ing—4Wd **11**
Woolmore St. E14—45Ec **84**
Woolneigh St. SW6—55Db **103**
Wool Rd. SW20—65Xa **124**
Woolstaplers Way. SE16
—49Wb **83**
Woolston Clo. E17—26Zb **44**
Woolstone Rd. SE23—61Ac **128**
Woolwich Chu. St. SE18—48Nc **86**
Woolwich Comn. SE18—51Qc **108**
Woolwich Dockyard Industrial Est.
SE18—48Nc **86**
Woolwich Industrial Est. SE28
—48Uc **86**
Woolwich Mnr. Way. E16
—45Rc **86**
Woolwich New Rd. SE18—50Qc **86**
Woolwich Rd.—51Zc **109**
SE2 75-303 & 120-324
Belv remainder
Woolwich Rd.—50Hc **85**
SE10 1-265 & 2-160
SE7 remainder
Woolwich Rd. Bexh—56Cd **110**
Wooster Gdns. E14—44Fc **85**
Woosters M. Harr—27Ea **38**
Wootton Clo. Horn—29Md **49**
Wootton Gro. N3—25Cb **41**
Wootton St. SE1—46Qb **82** (7A **200**)
Worbeck Rd. SE20—68Yb **128**
Worcester Av. N17—24Wb **43**
Worcester Av. Upm—33Vd **70**
Worcester Clo. Croy—75Cc **148**
Worcester Clo. Grav—6B **136**
Worcester Clo. Grnh—56Xd **112**
Worcester Clo. Mitc—69Kb **126**
Worcester Cres. NW7—20Ua **22**
Worcester Cres. Wfd G—21Lc **45**
Worcester Gdns. Gnfd—37Fa **58**
Worcester Gdns. Ilf—31Nc **66**
Worcester Gdns. Wor Pk
—76Ua **144**
Worcester M. NW6—37Db **61**
Worcester Pk. Rd. Wor Pk
—76Ta **143**
Worcester Pl. EC4
—45Sb **83** (4E **200**)
Worcester Rd. E12—35Pc **66**
Worcester Rd. E17—26Zb **44**
Worcester Rd. SW19—64Bb **125**
Worcester Rd. Sutt—80Cb **145**
Worcester Rd. Uxb—43L **75**
Worcesters Av. Enf—10Wb **11**
Wordsworth Av. E12—38Nc **66**
Wordsworth Av. E18—27Hc **45**
Wordsworth Av. Gnfd—41Fa **78**
Wordsworth Av. Kenl—87Tb **165**
Wordsworth Clo. Romf—25Ld **49**
Wordsworth Clo. Til—4E **114**
Wordsworth Ct. Harr—31Fa **58**
Wordsworth Dri. Sutt—77Ya **144**
Wordsworth Pde. N8—28Rb **43**
Wordsworth Rd. N16—35Ub **63**
Wordsworth Rd. SE20—66Zb **128**
Wordsworth Rd. Hmptn
—63Ba **121**
Wordsworth Rd. Slou—2B **72**
Wordsworth Rd. Wall—79Lb **146**
Wordsworth Rd. Well—53Uc **108**
Wordsworth Rd. Wey—77M **139**
Wordsworth Wlk. NW11—28Cb **41**
Wordsworth Way. Dart—56Qd **111**
Wordsworth Way. W Dray
—49N **75**
Worfield St. SW11—52Gb **103**
Worgan St. SE11
—50Pb **82** (7H **205**)
Worland Rd. E15—38Gc **65**
World's End. Cob—86W **158**
World's End La. N21 & Enf
—15Pb **24**
Worlds End La. Orp—79Vc **151**
World's End Pas. SW10—52Fb **103**
Worlidge St. W6—50Ya **80**
Worlingham Rd. SE22—56Vb **105**
Wormholt Rd. W12—45Wa **80**
Wormley Ct. Wal A—5Jc **13**
Wormwood St. EC2
—44Ub **83** (2H **201**)
Wormyngford Ct. Wal A—5Jc **13**
Wornington Rd. W10—42Ab **80**
Woronzow Rd. NW8
—39Fb **61** (1D **190**)
Worple Av. SW19—66Za **124**
Worple Av. Iswth—57Ja **100**
Worple Av. Stai—65K **119**
Worple Clo. Harr—32Ba **57**
Worple M. SW19—65Bb **125**
Worple Rd.—67Za **124**
SW19 1-95 & 2-140
SW20 remainder
Worple Rd. Eps—87Ta **161**
Worple Rd. Iswth—56Ja **100**
Worple Rd. Lea—95Ka **176**
Worple Rd. Stai—65K **119**
Worplesdon Hill. Wok—10A **188**
Worple St. SW14—55Ta **101**
Worple, The. Wray, Stai—58B **96**
Worple Way. Harr—32Ba **57**
Worple Way. Rich—57Na **101**
Worrin Clo. Brtwd—18Be **33**
Worrin Rd. Brtwd—19Be **33**
Worships Hill. Sev—95Gd **186**
Worship St. EC2—42Tb **83** (6G **195**)
Worslade Rd. SW17—63Fb **125**
Worsley Bri. Rd. SE26 & Beck
—63Bc **128**
Worsley Rd. E11—35Gc **65**
Worsopp Dri. SW4—57Lb **104**
Worsted Grn. Red—100Lb **180**
Worth Clo. Orp—77Uc **150**
Worthfield Clo. Eps—80Ta **143**
Worth Gro. SE17—(7F 207)
Worthing Clo. E15—39Gc **65**
Worthing Rd. Houn—51Ba **99**
Worthington Rd. Surb—74Pa **143**
Wortley Rd. E6—38Mc **65**
Wortley Rd. Croy—73Qb **146**
Worton Gdns. Iswth—54Fa **100**
Worton Hall Est. Iswth—56Ga **100**
Worton Rd. Iswth—56Fa **100**
Worton Way. Iswth—54Fa **100**
Wotton Grn. Orp—70Zc **131**
Wotton Rd. NW2—34Ya **60**
Wotton Rd. SE8—51Bc **106**
Wotton Way. Sutt—82Ya **162**
Wouldham Rd. E16—44Hc **85**
Wrabness Way. Stai—67K **119**
Wragby Rd. E11—34Gc **65**
Wrampling Pl. N9—18Wb **25**
Wrangley Ct. Wal A—5Jc **13**
Wray Av. Ilf—27Qc **46**
Wray Clo. Horn—31Ld **69**
Wray Cres. N4—33Pb **62**
Wrayfield Rd. Sutt—76Za **144**
Wray Rd. Sutt—81Bb **163**
Wraysbury Rd. Stai—61D **118**
Wrays Way. Hay—42U **76**
Wrekin Rd. SE18—52Sc **108**
Wren Av. NW2—36Ya **60**
Wren Av. S'hall—49Ba **77**
Wren Clo. S Croy—81Zb **166**
Wren Ct. Slou—48C **74**
Wren Cres. Bush, Wat—18Ea **20**
Wren Cres. Wey—78M **139**
Wren Gdns. Dag—36Zc **67**
Wren Gdns. Horn—32Hd **68**
Wren Path. SE28—48Tc **86**
Wren Pl. Brtwd—20Zd **33**
Wren Rd. SE5—53Tb **105**
Wren Rd. Dag—36Zc **67**
Wren Rd. Sidc—63Yc **131**
Wren's Av. Ashf—63S **120**
Wrens Hill. Lea—87Ea **160**
Wrens Pk. Rd. E5—33Xb **63**
Wren St. WC1—42Pb **82** (5J **193**)
Wrentham Av. NW10—40Za **60**
Wrenthorpe Rd. Brom—63Gc **129**
Wrenwood Way. Pinn—28X **37**
Wrestlers Ct. EC3—(2H 201)
Wrexham Rd. E3—40Cc **64**
Wrexham Rd. Romf—20Md **31**
Wricklemarsh Rd. SE3—53Lc **107**
Wrigglesworth St. SE14
—52Zb **106**
Wright. Wind—5A **94**
Wright Clo. Swans—58Zd **113**
Wright Rd. N1—37Ub **63**
Wright Rd. Houn—52Y **99**
Wrights All. SW19—65Ya **124**
Wrights Clo. SE13—56Fc **107**
Wrights Grn. SW4—56Mb **104**
Wright's La. W8—48Db **81**
★Wrights La. Brtwd—8Zd
Wrights Pl. NW10—37Sa **59**
Wright's Rd. E3—40Bc **64**
Wrights Rd. SE25—69Ub **127**
Wrights Row. Wall—77Kb **146**
Wright's Wlk. SW14—55Ta **101**
Wright Way. Wind—5A **94**
Wrigley Clo. E4—22Fc **45**
Writtle Wlk. Rain—39Qd **88**
★Wrotham By-Pass. Sev—89Ce
★Wrotham Hill Rd. Sev—85Be
Wrotham Rd. NW1—38Lb **62**
Wrotham Rd. W13—46La **78**
Wrotham Rd. Barn—12Ab **22**
Wrotham Rd. Grav—9B **136**
★Wrotham Rd. Sev—91Ce
Wrotham Rd. Well—53Yc **109**
★Wrotham Water Rd. Sev—86Fe
Wroths Path. Lou—11Pc **28**
Wrottesley Rd. NW10—40Wa **60**
Wrottesley Rd. SE18—51Sc **108**
Wroughton Rd. SW11—58Hb **103**
Wroughton Ter. NW4—28Xa **40**
Wroxall Rd. Dag—37Yc **67**
Wroxham Gdns. N11—24Mb **42**
Wroxham Gdns. Enf—7Rb **11**

AREAS COVERED BY THIS ATLAS
with their map square reference

ABBOTS LANGLEY—3T 4
ABRIDGE—14Xc 29
ACTON—46Qa 79
ADDISCOMBE—74Wb 147
ADDLESTONE—78L 139
ALPERTON—39Na 59
ASHFORD—64P 119
ASHTEAD—90Na 161
AVELEY—45Sd 90

BADGER'S MOUNT—82Dd 170
BALHAM—60Jb 104
BANSTEAD—88Db 163
BARKING—38Rc 66
BARKINGSIDE—27Rc 46
BARNES—53Xa 102
BARNET—13Ab 22
BATTERSEA—53Hb 103
BECKENHAM—67Dc 128
BECONTREE—35Ad 67
BEDDINGTON—76Nb 146
BELVEDERE—49Bd 87
BERMONDSEY—47Wb 83
BETHNAL GREEN—42Xb 83
BEXLEY—59Ad 109
BEXLEYHEATH—55Bd 109
BIGGIN HILL—87Lc 167
BLACKFEN—58Vc 109
BLACKHEATH—55Fc 107
BOREHAMWOOD—12Sa 21
BOVINGDON—1D 2
BRASTED—96Yc 185
BRENTFORD—51La 100
BRENTWOOD—19Xd 32
BRICKET WOOD—2Ba 5
BRIXTON—56Pb 104
BROMLEY—68Jc 129
BUCKHURST HILL—20Lc 27
BURNT OAK—24Ra 39
BUSHEY—16Ea 20
BUSH HILL PARK—16Ub 25
BYFLEET—84N 157

CAMBERWELL—54Sb 105
CAMDEN TOWN—38Mb 62
CANNING TOWN—45Gc 85
CARSHALTON—78Gb 145
CATERHAM—96Vb 181
CATFORD—60Ec 106
CHADWELL HEATH—30Zc 47
CHADWELL SAINT MARY—9C 92
CHALFONT COMMON—22A 34
CHALFONT SAINT PETER—24C 34
CHEAM—80Bd 145
CHELSEA—50Fb 81
CHELSFIELD—78Yc 151
CHENIES—10D 2
CHERTSEY—74J 139
CHESHUNT—2Ac 12
CHESSINGTON—81La 160
CHIGWELL—19Tc 28
CHINGFORD—18Dc 26
CHIPSTEAD (KENT)—94Ed 186
CHIPSTEAD (SURREY)—91Jb 180
CHISLEHURST—66Rc 130
CHISWICK—50Ta 79
CHORLEYWOOD—15F 16
CITY OF LONDON—45Tb 83
CLAPHAM—55Kb 104
CLAPTON—33Xb 63
CLAYGATE—80Ja 142

CLAY HILL—9Sb 11
CLERKENWELL—42Pb 82
COBHAM—86W 158
COCKFOSTERS—15Gb 23
COLNBROOK—52E 96
COULSDON—88Mb 164
COWLEY—42L 75
CRANBOURNE—1A 116
CRANFORD—52W 98
CRAYFORD—57Gd 110
CRICKLEWOOD—35Bb 61
CROCKENHILL—72Fd 152
CROXLEY GREEN—15G 18
CROYDON—76Rb 147
CUDHAM—87Tc 168
CUFFLEY—1Nb 10

DAGENHAM—37Cd 68
DALSTON—38Vb 63
DARENTH—64Sd 134
DARTFORD—59Ld 111
DATCHET—3N 95
DENHAM—33J 55
DEPTFORD—56Ac 106
DOWNE—83Qc 168
DULWICH—61Vb 127
DUNTON GREEN—91Gd 186

EALING—45Ma 79
EARLS COURT—50Cb 81
EAST BARNET—17Gb 23
EAST BEDFONT—60T 98
EAST HAM—40Nc 66
EAST MOLESEY—70Fa 122
EAST SHEEN—56Ta 101
EDGWARE—23Ra 39
EDMONTON—21Vb 43
EGHAM—63B 118
ELMERS END—69Zb 128
ELSTREE—16Na 21
ELTHAM—58Nc 108
ENFIELD TOWN—13Tb 25
ENGLEFIELD GREEN—4M 117
EPPING—2Wc 15
EPSOM—86Sa 161
ERITH—50Gd 88
ESHER—77Ea 142
ETON—1G 94
ETON WICK—9C 72
EWELL—82Va 162
EYNSFORD—76Md 153

FARNBOROUGH—78Rc 150
FARNHAM COMMON—6H 53
FARNHAM ROYAL—10G 52
FARNINGHAM—73Pd 153
FELTHAM—61X 121
FETCHAM—95Fa 176
FINCHLEY—25Db 41
FINSBURY—41Qb 82
FINSBURY PARK—33Qb 62
FLAUNDEN—4C 2
FOREST GATE—36Jc 65
FOREST HILL—61Zb 128
FRIERN BARNET—21Hb 41
FULHAM—53Za 102

GERRARDS CROSS—30A 34
GIDEA PARK—26Jd 48

GOLDERS GREEN—32Cb 61
GRAVESEND—7D 114
GRAYS—48De 91
GREAT WARLEY—25Wd 50
GREENFORD—41Da 77
GREENHITHE—57Xd 112
GREENWICH—51Fc 107

HACKNEY—38Xb 63
HADLEY WOOD—10Fb 9
HAINAULT—23Uc 46
HALSTEAD—84Bd 169
HAMMERSMITH—50Ya 80
HAMPSTEAD—34Gb 61
HAMPTON—67Da 121
HANWELL—46Ha 78
HAREFIELD—26K 35
HARLESDEN—39Va 60
HARLINGTON—51S 98
HARMONDSWORTH—51N 97
HAROLD HILL—22Pd 49
HAROLD WOOD—26Nd 49
HARRINGAY—30Qb 42
HARROW—31Ha 58
HATCH END—24Ca 37
HAVERING-ATTE-BOWER—20Fd 30
HAWLEY—630d 133
HAYES (KENT)—72Jc 149
HAYES (MIDDX)—45U 76
HENDON—29Xa 40
HERNE HILL—57Sb 105
HERONGATE—24Fe 51
HERSHAM—79Z 141
HESTON—52Ba 99
HEXTABLE—66Jd 132
HIGHBURY—35Qb 62
HIGHGATE—31Jb 62
HILLINGDON—41S 76
HOLBORN—44Pb 82
HOLLOWAY—34Nb 62
HOMERTON—36Ac 64
HOOLEY—93Jb 180
HORNCHURCH—33Nd 69
HORNSEY—29Pb 42
HORSELL—88B 156
HORTON—55C 96
HORTON KIRBY—70Sd 134
HOUNSLOW—56Ea 100
HUTTON—16Fe 33

ILFORD—34Sc 66
INGRAVE—22De 51
ISLEWORTH—55Ha 100
ISLINGTON—39Rb 63
ISTEAD RISE—6A 136
IVER—45H 75

KENLEY—88Tb 165
KENNINGTON—51Rb 105
KENSINGTON—47Bb 81
KENTISH TOWN—36Kb 62
KENTON—29Ka 38
KESTON—77Mc 149
KEW—52Pa 101
KILBURN—40Cb 61
KINGSBURY—28Ra 39
KINGS LANGLEY—1P 3
KINGSTON-UPON-THAMES
    —68La 122

KINGSWOOD—93Bb 179
KNOCKHOLT—89Xc 169

LALEHAM—69L 119
LAMBETH—43Qb 82
LANGLEY—48C 74
LATIMER—9A 2
LEATHERHEAD—94Ja 176
LEE—58Hc 107
LEWISHAM—56Ec 106
LEYTON—34Fc 65
LEYTONSTONE—32Hc 65
LIMPSFIELD—100Jc 183
LITTLETON—69R 120
LONDON (CITY OF)—45Tb 83
LOUGHTON—15Pc 28
LYNCH HILL—1C 72

MAIDA VALE—42Db 81
MANOR PARK—35Nc 66
MARYLEBONE—42Hb 81
MEOPHAM STATION—10D 136
MERSTHAM—100Kb 180
MERTON—67Db 125
MILL HILL—22Wa 40
MITCHAM—69Jb 126
MORDEN—70Db 125
MORTLAKE—54Sa 101
MOTTINGHAM—61Mc 129
MUSWELL HILL—27Lb 42

NEASDEN—34Ua 60
NEW ADDINGTON—80Fc 149
NEW ASH GREEN—75Be 155
NEW CROSS—53Ac 106
NEW MALDEN—71Ua 144
NEW SOUTHGATE—21Lb 42
NORTHFLEET—57Fe 113
NORTHAW—2Jb 10
NORTHOLT—38Z 57
NORTHWOOD—23U 36
NOTTING HILL—45Bd 81

OAKLEY GREEN—4A 94
OCKHAM—93R 174
OLD WINDSOR—8L 95
ORPINGTON—74Uc 150
ORSETT—3D 92
OTFORD—86Ld 171
OTTERSHAW—78E 138
OXSHOTT—86Fa 160

PADDINGTON—44Fb 81
PALMERS GREEN—20Qb 24
PECKHAM—52Vb 105
PENGE—67Yb 128
PETTS WOOD—71Tc 150
PILGRIM'S HATCH—15Xd 32
PINNER—28Aa 37
PLAISTOW—41Kc 85
PLUMSTEAD—50Tc 86
PONDERS END—15Yb 26
POPLAR—45Cc 84
POTTERS BAR—6Db 9
PRATT'S BOTTOM—82Xc 169
PURFLEET—51Qd 111
PURLEY—83Qb 164
PUTNEY—57Za 102

RADLETT—6Ka 6
RAINHAM—42Jd 88
RICHINGS PARK—48G 74
RICHMOND—57Ma 101
RICKMANSWORTH—17N 17
RIPLEY—93L 173
RIVERHEAD—94Gd 186
ROEHAMPTON—57Va 102
ROMFORD—29Hd 48
ROTHERHITHE—47Yb 84
RUISLIP—31T 56

SAINT JOHN'S WOOD—41Eb 81
SAINT MARY CRAY—72Wc 151
SAINT PANCRAS—42Pb 82
SANDERSTEAD—84Wb 165
SARRATT—7J 3
SEAL—92Pd 187
SELSDON—82Ac 166
SEND—96F 172
SEVEN KINGS—31Uc 66
SEVENOAKS—97Ld 187
SHADWELL—45Yb 84
SHEERWATER—85F 156
SHENFIELD—17Ce 33
SHENLEY—6Pa 7
SHEPHERD'S BUSH—45Xa 80
SHEPPERTON—72R 140
SHOREDITCH—40Tb 63
SHOREHAM—83Gd 170
SHORNE—4N 137
SIDCUP—63Vc 131
SLOUGH—6N 73
SNARESBROOK—29Jc 45
SOUTHALL—46Aa 77
SOUTH DARENTH—67Td 134
SOUTHGATE—18Nb 24
SOUTH MIMMS—5Va 8
SOUTH NORWOOD—69Vb 127
SOUTH OCKENDON—41Zd 91
SOUTH OXHEY—21Z 37
SOUTHWARK—46Sb 83
STAINES—64J 119
STANFORD-LE-HOPE—2M 93
STANMORE—23Ka 38
STANWELL—59N 97
STAPLEFORD ABBOTTS—16Ed 30
STEPNEY—43Yb 84
STOKE D'ABERNON—88Ba 159
STOKE NEWINGTON—33Ub 63
STOKE POGES—9K 53
STONE—57Ud 112
STRATFORD—38Ec 64
STREATHAM—63Pb 126
SUNBURY—69X 121
SUNDRIDGE—96Bd 185
SUNNINGHILL—10A 116
SURBITON—73Na 143
SUTTON—78Cb 145
SUTTON-AT-HONE—66Qd 133
SWANLEY—70Hd 132
SWANSCOMBE—58Be 113
SYDENHAM—63Yb 128

TADWORTH—94Ya 178
TATSFIELD—91Mc 183
TEDDINGTON—66Ha 122
THAMES DITTON—72Ha 142
THEYDON BOIS—8Uc 14
THORNTON HEATH—70Rb 127
THORPE—69E 118

TILBURY—5D 114
TOLWORTH—75Qa 143
TOOTING—65Gb 125
TOTTENHAM—24Ub 43
TOTTERIDGE—18Ab 22
TULSE HILL—60Qb 104
TWICKENHAM—60Ja 100

UPMINSTER—32Rd 69
UPPER NORWOOD—67Tb 127
UPSHIRE—4Mc 13
UPTON—38Kc 65
UPTON PARK—39Mc 65
UXBRIDGE—39M 55

VAUXHALL—51Pb 104

WADDON—76Qb 146
WALLINGTON—78Lb 146
WALTHAM ABBEY—6Dc 12
WALTHAM CROSS—6Ac 12
WALTHAMSTOW—26Dc 44
WALTON-ON-THAMES—75V 140
WALTON ON THE HILL—97Wa 178
WALWORTH—51Ub 105
WANDSWORTH—57Cb 103
WANSTEAD—31Kc 65
WARLEY—21Zd 51
WARLINGHAM—90Zb 166
WATFORD—13W 18
WEALDSTONE—27Ha 38
WELLING—54Xc 109
WEMBLEY—36La 58
WEST BROMPTON—51Db 103
WEST BYFLEET—85K 157
WEST DRAYTON—48N 75
WESTERHAM—99Tc 184
WEST HAM—39Jc 65
WEST HORNDON—30Ee 51
WESTMINSTER—49Mb 82
WEST MOLESEY—70Ca 121
WEST NORWOOD—64Sb 127
WEST THURROCK—50Wd 90
WEST WICKHAM—75Fc 149
WEYBRIDGE—77P 139
WHETSTONE—19Eb 23
WHITTON—59Da 99
WHYTELEAFE—90Vb 165
WILLESDEN—38Wa 60
WILMINGTON—63Ld 133
WIMBLEDON—65Ab 124
WINCHMORE HILL—17Rb 25
WINDSOR—3J 95
WOKING—90A 156
WOLDINGHAM—95Cc 182
WOODFORD—23Kc 45
WOODFORD GREEN—22Jc 45
WOOD GREEN—26Nb 42
WOODHAM—82H 157
WOODMANSTERNE—88Hb 163
WOOLWICH—49Pc 86
WORCESTER PARK—75Wa 144
WRAYSBURY—58B 96

YIEWSLEY—45Q 76

311

HOSPITALS AND CLINICS

**Where the Publishers have been unable to actually indicate the hospital or clinic
on the atlas map pages the reference given is to the road in which it is situated.**

ABBOTS LANGLEY HOSPITAL—4W **4**
College Rd., Abbots Langley, Watford, Herts. WD5 0NT
Tel: Kings Langley 74211/4

ACTON HOSPITAL—47Ra **79**
Gunnersbury La., London. W3 8EG
Tel: 01-992 2277

ALBERT DOCK HOSPITAL—44Mc **85**
Alnwick Rd., London. E16 3EZ
Tel: 01-476 2234

ALL SAINTS HOSPITAL—49Rb **83**
Austral St., London. SE11 4SL
Tel: 01-828 9811

ANGAS HOME—86Tc **168**
Church App., Cudham, Sevenoaks, Kent. TN14 7QF
Tel: Biggin Hill 72033

ASHFORD HOSPITAL—61N **119**
London Rd., Ashford, Middx. TW15 3AA
Tel: Ashford (Middx) 51188

ASHFORD CHEST CLINIC—61N **119**
Ashford Hospital, London Rd., Ashford, Middx. TW15 3AA
Tel: Ashford (Middx) 51188

ASHTEAD HOSPITAL, THE.—92Na **177**
Leatherhead Rd., Ashtead, Surrey. KT21 2SN
Tel: Ashtead 76161

ATKINSON MORLEY'S HOSPITAL—66Xa **124**
Copse Hill, Wimbledon, London. SW20 0NE
Tel: 01-946 7711

ATHLONE HOUSE—32Hb **61**
60 Hampstead La., London. N6 4RX
Tel: 01-348 5231

AVENUE CLINIC—38Fb **61**
12 Avenue Rd., London. NW8 6BP
Tel: 01-722 7131

BALHAM CHEST CLINIC—60Hb **103**
St James' Hospital, Sarsfield Rd., London. SW12 8HW
Tel: 01-672 1222

BANSTEAD HOSPITAL—84Eb **163**
Sutton La., Sutton, Surrey. SM2 5PA
Tel: 01-642 6611

BARKING HOSPITAL—38Vc **67**
Upney La., Barking, Essex. IG11 9LX
Tel: 01-594 3898

BARNES DAY HOSPITAL—55Ua **102**
South Worple Way, London. SW14 8SU
Tel: 01-878 4981

BARNET CHEST CLINIC—14Za **22**
Wellhouse La., Barnet, Herts. EN5 3DJ
Tel: 01-440 5111

BARNET GENERAL HOSPITAL—14Za **22**
Wellhouse La., Barnet, Herts. EN5 3DJ
Tel: 01-440 5111

BATTERSEA CHEST CLINIC—56Fb **103**
St John's Hospital, St John's Hill, Battersea, London. SW11 1SP
Tel: 01-874 1022

BECKENHAM GENERAL HOSPITAL—68Bc **128**
379 Croydon Rd., Beckenham, Kent. BR3 3QL
Tel: 01-650 0125

BECKENHAM MATERNITY HOSPITAL—70Cc **128**
Stone Pk. Av., Beckenham, Kent. BR3 3LY
Tel: 01-650 2213

BECONTREE DAY HOSPITAL—35Xc **67**
Becontree Av., Dagenham, Essex. RM8 3HS
Tel: 01-593 7111

BEECHCROFT HOSPITAL—90B **156**
Heathside Rd., Woking, Surrey. GU22 7HS
Tel: Woking 5911

BELGRAVE HOSPITAL FOR CHILDREN—52Qb **104**
1 Clapham Rd., London. SW9 0JF
Tel: 01-274 6222

BETHLEM ROYAL HOSPITAL, THE.—73Cc **148**
Monks Orchard Rd., Eden Pk., Beckenham, Kent. BR3 3BX
Tel: 01-777 6611

BETHNAL GREEN HOSPITAL—40Yb **64**
Cambridge Heath Rd., London. E2 9NP
Tel: 01-980 3413

BEXLEY HOSPITAL—61Gd **132**
Old Bexley La., Bexley, Kent. DA5 2BW
Tel: Crayford 526282

BOLINGBROKE HOSPITAL—57Gb **103**
Wandsworth Comn., London. SW11 6HN
Tel: 01-223 7411

BOTLEY'S PARK HOSPITAL—76E **138**
Guildford Rd., Chertsey, Surrey. KT16 0QA
Tel: Ottershaw 2000

BOW ARROW HOSPITAL—58Rd **111**
Bow Arrow La., Dartford, Kent. DA2 6PQ
Tel: Dartford 23223

BOWDEN HOUSE CLINIC—33Ga **58**
London Rd., Harrow-on-the-Hill, Middx. HA1 3JL
Tel: 01-864 0221

BRENTFORD HOSPITAL—51La **100**
Boston Manor Rd., Brentford, Middx. TW8 8DR
Tel: 01-560 39390

BRENTWOOD CHEST CLINIC—18Yd **32**
High Wood Hospital, Ongar Rd., Brentwood, Essex. CM15 9DY
Tel: Brentwood 219262

BRENTWOOD DISTRICT HOSPITAL—18Ae **33**
Crescent Dri., Brentwood, Essex. CM15 8DR
Tel: Brentwood 212244

BRITISH HOME & HOSPITAL FOR INCURABLES—64Rb **127**
Crown La., Streatham, London. SW16 3JB
Tel: 01-670 8261

BRITISH HOSPITAL FOR MOTHERS & BABIES—49Nc **86**
Samuel St., Woolwich, London. SE18 5LL
Tel: 01-854 8016

BROMLEY CHEST CLINIC—70Kc **129**
Tiger La., Bromley, Kent. BR2 9JL
Tel: 01-460 2686

BROMLEY HOSPITAL—70Kc **129**
Cromwell Av., Bromley, Kent. BR2 9AJ
Tel: 01-460 9933

BROMPTON HOSPITAL—50Fb **81**
Fulham Rd., London. SW3 6HP
Tel: 01-352 8121

BROOK GENERAL HOSPITAL—53Nc **108**
Shooters Hill Rd., Woolwich, London. SE18 4LW
Tel: 01-856 5555

BROOK HOUSE—76J **139**
Addlestone, Surrey. KT15 2TE
Tel: Weybridge 47602

BROOKSIDE YOUNG PEOPLE'S UNIT—31Wc **67**
Barley La., Goodmayes, Essex. IG3 8XJ
Tel: 01-599 5188

BROOKWOOD HOSPTIAL—7A **188**
Knaphill, Woking, Surrey. GU21 2RQ
Tel: Woking 4545

BUPA HOSPTIAL BUSHEY—18Ha **20**
Heathbourne Rd., Bushey, Watford. WD2 1RD
Tel: 01-950 9090

BUSHEY & DISTRICT HOSPITAL—18Ga **20**
Windmill St., Bushey Heath, Herts. WD2 1NA
Tel: 01-950 1281

CANE HILL HOSPITAL—89Lb **164**
Cane Hill, Coulsdon, Surrey. CR3 3YL
Tel: Downland 52221

CARSHALTON, BEDDINGTON & WALLINGTON
                   WAR MEMORIAL HOSPITAL—79Hb **145**
The Park, Carshalton, Surrey. SM5 3DB
Tel: 01-647 5534

CASSEL HOSPITAL—63Ma **123**
Ham Comn., Richmond, Surrey. TW10 7JF
Tel: 01-940 8181

CASTLEWOOD DAY HOSPITAL—53Qc **108**
25 Shooter's Hill, London. SE18 4LG
Tel: 01-856 4970

CATERHAM & DISTRICT HOSPITAL—95Vb **181**
Church Rd., Caterham, Surrey. CR3 5RA
Tel: Caterham 47522

CAVENDISH MEDICAL CENTRE—43Jb **82**
99 New Cavendish St., London. W1M 7FQ
Tel: 01-637 8941

CENTRAL CLINIC—38Sc **66**
Vicarage Dri., Barking, Essex. IG11 7NR
Tel: 01-594 2412

CENTRAL MIDDLESEX HOSPITAL—41Sa **79**
Acton La., London. NW10 7NS
Tel: 01-965 5733

CHADWELL HEATH HOSPITAL—29Xc **47**
Grove Rd., Chadwell Heath, Romford, Essex. RM6 4XH
Tel: 01-599 3007

CHALFONT CENTRE FOR EPILEPSY—22B **34**
Penn Gaskell La., Chalfont St Peter, Gerrards Cross, Bucks. SL9 0RJ
Tel: Chalfont St Giles 3991

CHALFONTS & GERRARDS CROSS HOSPITAL, THE.—25A **34**
Hampden Rd., Chalfont St Peter, Gerrards Cross, Bucks. SL9 9DR
Tel: Gerrards Cross 883821

CHARING CROSS HOSPITAL—50Za **80**
Fulham Palace Rd., London. W6 8RF
Tel: 01-748 2040

CHARTER CLINIC—50Gb **81**
1-5 Radnor Wlk., London. SW3 4PB
Tel: 01-351 1272

CHASE FARM HOSPITAL—10Qb **10**
The Ridgeway, Enfield, Middx. EN2 8JL
Tel: 01-366 6600

CHEAM HOSPITAL—75Ya **144**
132 London Rd., North Cheam, Surrey. SM3 9DG
Tel: 01-337 4488

CHELSEA HOSPITAL FOR WOMEN—50Gb **81**
Dovehouse St., London. SW3 6LJ
Tel 01-352 6446

CHEPSTOW LODGE—45Cb **81**
Chepstow Pl., London. W2 4TR
Tel: 01-727 3531

CHEST CLINIC—29Sb **43**
St Ann's Hospital, St Ann's Rd., S. Tottenham, London. N15 3TH
Tel: 01-800 0121

CHEST CLINIC—48Yb **84**
St Olave's Hospital, Lower Rd., Rotherhithe, London. SE16 2TS
Tel: 01-237 6622

CHESHUNT COTTAGE HOSPITAL—1Zb **12**
Church La., Cheshunt, Herts. EN8 0EA
Tel: Waltham Cross 22157

CHEYNE—77Dc **148**
Woodland Way, West Wickham, Kent. BR4 9LT
Tel: 01-777 9426

CHEYNE CENTRE FOR SPASTIC CHILDREN—51Gb **103**
61 Cheyne Wlk., London. SW3 5HG
Tel: 01-352 8434

CHILD GUIDANCE TRAINING CENTRE—37Fb **61**
120 Belsize La., London. NW3 5BA
Tel: 01-435 7111

CHILD GUIDANCE TRAINING CENTRE DAY UNIT, THE.—36Fb **61**
33 Daleham Gdns., London. NW3 5BU
Tel: 01-794 3353

CHILD HEALTH CLINIC—39Pc **66**
Town Hall Annexe, East Ham, London. E6 2RP
Tel: 01-472 1430

CHILD PSYCHIATRIC UNIT—77Sb **147**
Victoria Ho., Southbridge Rd., Croydon, Surrey. CRO 4HA
Tel: 01-686 0393

CHILDREN'S HOSPITAL—63Ac **128**
321 Sydenham Rd., London. SE26 6ER
Tel: 01-778 7031

CHINGFORD HOSPITAL—20Ec **26**
Larkshall Rd., Chingford, London. E4 6NL
Tel: 01-529 7141

CHURCHILL CLINIC—48Pb **82**
80 Lambeth Rd., London. SE1 7PW
Tel: 01-928 5633

CITY OF LONDON MATERNITY—33Kb **62**
St Mary's Wing, Whittington Hospital, Highgate Hill, London. N19 5NF
Tel: 01-272 3070

CLAYBURY HOSPITAL—24Qc **46**
Woodford Bridge, Woodford Green, Essex. IG8 8BY
Tel: 01-504 7171

CLAYPONDS HOSPITAL—49Ma **79**
Occupation La., Ealing, London. W5 4RN
Tel: 01-560 4011

CLEMENTINE CHURCHILL HOSPITAL—34Ha **58**
Sudbury Hill, Harrow, Middx. HA1 3RX
Tel: 01-422 3464

CLERKENWELL & ISLINGTON MEDICAL MISSION EYE CLINIC—42Rb **83**
Woodbridge Chapel, Woodbridge St., London. EC1R 0EX
Tel: 01-253 7347

COBHAM & DISTRICT COTTAGE HOSPITAL—85X **159**
Portsmouth Rd., Cobham, Surrey. KT11 1HT
Tel: Cobham 2751

COLINDALE HOSPITAL—26Ta **39**
Colindale Av., London. NW9 5HG
Tel: 01-200 1555

CONVENT OF SAINT PETER—89D **156**
Maybury Hill, Woking, Surrey. GU22 8AE
Tel: Woking 61137

COPPETTS WOOD HOSPITAL—25Hb **41**
Coppetts Rd., Muswell Hill, London. N10 1JN
Tel: 01-883 9792

CROMWELL HOSPTIAL, THE.—49Db **81**
Cromwell Rd., London. SW5 0TU
Tel: 01-370 4233

CROYDON GENERAL HOSPITAL—74Sb **147**
London Rd., Croydon, Surrey. CR9 2RH
Tel: 01-684 6999

CUDDINGTON HOSPITAL—85Bb **163**
Banstead Rd., Banstead, Surrey. SM7 1RF
Tel: 01-642 0047

CUMBERLAND HOSPITAL—69Hb **125**
Whitford Gdns., Mitcham, Surrey. CR4 4YA
Tel: 01-648 1144

DAGENHAM HOSPITAL—39Ed **68**
Rainham Rd. S., Dagenham, Essex. RM10 9YL
Tel: 01-592 0034

DARENTH PARK HOSPITAL—60Td **112**
Gore Rd., Dartford, Kent. DA2 6LZ
Tel: Dartford 22381

DENTAL HOSPITAL & SCHOOL—55Sb **105**
King's College Hospital, Denmark Hill, London. SE5 9RS
Tel: 01-274 6222

DENTAL HOSPITAL—42Lb **82**
Mortimer Mkt., London. WC1E 6AU
Tel: 01-387 0351

DEVONSHIRE HOSPITAL—43Jb **82**
29-31 Devonshire St., London. WIN 1RF
Tel: 01-486 7131

DISPENSAIRE FRANCAIS—42Kb **82**
6-12 Osnaburgh St., London. NW1 3DH
Tel: 01-387 5132

DONALD WINNICOTT PAEDIATRIC ASSESSMENT CENTRE—41Vb **83**
Hackney Rd., London. E2 8PS
Tel: 01-729 2333

DOWNVIEW HOSPITAL—83Eb **163**
Banstead Hospital, Sutton La., Sutton, Surrey. SM2 5PA
Tel: 01-642 6611

DREADNOUGHT SEAMAN'S HOSPITAL—51Ec **106**
King William Wlk., Greenwich, London. SE10 9LE
Tel: 01-858 8111

DULWICH HOSPITAL—56Ub **105**
E. Dulwich Gro., London. SE22 3PT
Tel: 01-693 3377

DUNORAN HOME—67Mc **129**
4 Park Farm Rd., Bromley, Kent. BR1 2PS
Tel: 01-467 3701

DUVALS HOSTEL—49Be **91**
Meesons La., Grays, Essex. RM17 5HR
Tel: Grays Thurrock 73860

EALING HOSPITAL—47Ea **78**
Uxbridge Rd., Southall, Middx. UB1 3HW
Tel: 01-574 2444

EASTERN HOSPITAL—36Zb **64**
Homerton Gro., London. E9 6BY
Tel: 01-985 1193

EASTMAN DENTAL HOSPITAL—41Pb **82**
Gray's Inn Rd., London. WC1X 8LD
Tel: 01-837 3646

EDENHALL—36Fb **61**
(Marie Curie Memorial Foundation)
11 Lyndhurst Gdns., London. NW3 5N3
Tel: 01-794 0066

EDGWARE CHEST CLINIC—24Ra **39**
Edgware General Hospital,
Edgware, Middx. HA8 0AD
Tel: 01-952 2381

EDGWARE GENERAL HOSPITAL—24Ra **39**
Edgware, Middx. HA8 0AD
Tel: 01-952 2381

EDMONTON CHEST CLINIC—22Ub **43**
North Middlesex Hospital, Sterling Way, Edmonton, London. N18 1QX
Tel: 01-807 3071

EGHAM HOSPITAL—5N **117**
98 St Jude's Rd., Englefield Green, Egham, Surrey. TW20 0DG
Tel: Egham 2132

ELIZABETH GARRETT ANDERSON HOSPITAL—41Mb **82**
144 Euston Rd., London. NW1 1YA
Tel: 01-387 2501

ELLESMERE HOSPITAL—78U **140**
Queens Rd., Walton-on-Thames, Surrey. KT12 5AA
Tel: Egham 2132

ELM PARK CLINIC—34Ld **69**
Abbs Cross La., Hornchurch, Essex. RM12 4YG
Tel: Hornchurch 43681

ELTHAM & MOTTINGHAM HOSPITAL—58Pc **108**
Passey Pl., Eltham, London. SE9 5DH
Tel: 01-850 2611

EMILY JACKSON WING—96Kd **187**
Eardley Rd., Sevenoaks, Kent. TN13 1XT
Tel: Sevenoaks 452559

ENFIELD WAR MEMORIAL HOSPITAL—11Sb **25**
Chase Side, Enfield, Middx. EN2 0QY
Tel: 01-363 8234

EPSOM & EWELL COTTAGE HOSPITAL—85Va **162**
Alexandra Rd., Epsom, Surrey. KT17 4BL
Tel: Epsom 26100

EPSOM CHEST CLINIC—87Sa **161**
Epsom District Hospital, Dorking Rd., Epsom, Surrey. KT18 7EG
Tel: Epsom 26100

EPSOM DISTRICT HOSPITAL—87Sa **161**
Dorking Rd., Epsom, Surrey. KT18 7EG
Tel: Epsom 26100

ERITH & DISTRICT HOSPITAL—51Fd **110**
Park Cres., Erith, Kent. DA5 2BW
Tel: Erith 30161

ESSEX NUFFIELD HOSPITAL—19Zd **33**
Shenfield Rd., Brentwood, Essex. CM15 8EH
Tel: Brentwood 224644

FARNBOROUGH HOSPITAL—77Qc **150**
Farnborough Comn., Orpington, Kent. BR6 8ND
Tel: Farnborough 53333

FARNHAM PARK REHABILITATION CENTRE—9G **52**
Farnham Pk. La., Farnham Royal, Slough, Berks. SL2 3LR
Tel: Farnham Common 2271

FINCHLEY MEMORIAL HOSPITAL—24Eb **41**
Granville Rd., N. Finchley, London. N12 0JE
Tel: 01-349 3121

FINSBURY HEALTH CENTRE & PHYSIOTHERAPY CLINIC—42Qb **82**
Pine St., London. EC1R 0JH
Tel: 01-837 0031

FITZROY HOSPITAL—44Hb **81**
(Nuffield Nursing Homes Trust)
10-12 Bryanston Sq., London. W1H 8BB
Tel: 01-723 1288

FOREST HOSPITAL—18Mc **27**
Roebuck La., Buckhurst Hill, Essex. IG9 5PA
Tel: 01-504 2285/6

FOREST HOUSE HOSPITAL—24Qc **46**
Claybury Hospital, Woodford Green, Essex. IG8 8BY
Tel: 01-504 7171

FREEDOWN HOSPITAL—84Eb **163**
Banstead Hospital, Sutton La., Sutton, Surrey. SM2 5PA
Tel: 01-642 6611

FRIERN HOSPITAL—23Jb **42**
Friern Barnet Rd., New Southgate, London. N11 3BP
Tel: 01-368 1288

GABLES, THE.—55Hc **107**
MH Hostel, Blackheath Pk., Blackheath, London. SE3 9RR
Tel: 01-852 7910

GALSWORTHY HOUSE—67Qa **123**
Kingston Hill, Kingston-upon-Thames, Surrey. KT2 7LX
Tel: 01-549 9861

GARDEN HOSPITAL, THE.—26Xa **40**
46-50 Sunny Gardens Rd., Hendon, London. NW4 1RX
Tel: 01-203 0111

GARDINER HILL—62Eb **125**
Burntwood La., London. SW17 7DJ
Tel: 01-767 4626

GARSTON MANOR MEDICAL REHABILITATION CENTRE—3Y **5**
High Elms La., Garston, Nr. Watford, Herts. WD2 7JX
Tel: Garston 7306

GERMAN HOSPITAL—37Wb **63**
Ritson Rd., Dalston, London. E8 1DF
Tel: 01-254 5202

GOLDIE LEIGH HOSPITAL—51Yc **109**
Lodge Hill, Abbey Wood, London. SE2 0AY
Tel: 01-311 9161

GOLDSMITHS NURSING HOME—30Hb **41**
Denewood Rd., London. N6 4AL
Tel: 01-348 4611

GOODMAYES HOSPITAL—29Wc **47**
Barley La., Goodmayes, Ilford, Essex. IG3 8XJ
Tel: 01-590 6060

GORDON HOSPITAL—49Mb **82**
126 Vauxhall Bri. Rd., London. SW1V 2RM
Tel: 01-828 9811

GRANLEIGH ROAD CLINIC—33Gc **65**
Granleigh Rd., London. E11 4RQ
Tel: 01-539 8565

GRAVESEND & NORTH KENT HOSPITAL—8C **114**
Bath St., Gravesend, Kent. DA11 0DG
Tel: Gravesend 64333

GREAT WEST HATCH HOSPITAL—21Qc **46**
High Rd., Chigwell, Essex. IG7 5BS
Tel: 01-504 2855

GREENTREES HOSPITAL—23Rb **43**
Tottenhall Rd., London. N13 6DN
Tel: 01-889 1041

GREENWICH DISTRICT HOSPITAL—50Hc **85**
Vanbrugh Hill, Greenwich, London. SE10 9JH
Tel: 01-858 8141

GROUP PATHOLOGICAL LABORATORY—51Eb **103**
St Stephen's Hospital, Fulham Rd., London. SW10 9TH
Tel: 01-352 8161

GROUP PATHOLOGICAL LABORATORY—15X **19**
Shrodells Hospital, Vicarage Rd., Watford, Herts. WD1 8DE
Tel: Watford 44366

GROVE PARK HOSPITAL—61Lc **129**
Marvels La., London. SE12 0PG
Tel: 01-857 1191

GUY'S HOSPITAL—46Tb **83**
St Thomas St., London. SE1 9RT
Tel: 01-407 7600

HACKNEY HOSPITAL—36Ac **64**
Homerton High St., London. E9 6BY
Tel: 01-985 5555

HAMMERSMITH HOSPITAL—44Wa **80**
Du Cane Rd., London. W12 0HS
Tel: 01-743 2030

HAREFIELD HOSPITAL—25K **35**
Harefield, Uxbridge, Middx. UB8 6JH
Tel: Harefield 3737

HARESTONE—97Vb **181**
Harestone Dri., Caterham, Surrey. CR3 6YQ
Tel: Caterham 42226

HARLEY STREET CLINIC—43Jb **82**
35 Weymouth St., London. WIN 4BJ
Tel: 01-935 7700

HAROLD WOOD HOSPITAL—25Nd **49**
Gubbins La., Harold Wood, Essex. RM3 0BE
Tel: Ingrebourne 45533

HARPERBURY HOSPITAL—3La **6**
Harper La., Shenley, Radlett, Herts. WD7 9HQ
Tel: Radlett 4861/6

HARROW CHEST CLINIC—29Ha **38**
199 Station Rd., Harrow, Middx. HA1 2TU
Tel: 01-427 1075

HARROW HOSPITAL—33Ga **58**
Roxeth Hill, Harrow, Middx. HA2 0JX
Tel: 01-864 5432

HATCH LANE CLINIC—21Fc **45**
2a Hatch La., Chingford, London. E4 6NG
Tel: 01-529 3706

HAYES COTTAGE HOSPITAL—44U **76**
Grange Rd., Hayes, Middx. UB3 2RR
Tel: 01-573 2052

HAYES GROVE PRIORY HOSPITAL—75Jc **149**
Prestons Rd., Hayes, Kent. BR2 7AS
Tel: 01-462 7722

HEALTH SERVICE CLINIC—30Jc **45**
35 Wanstead Pl., London. E11 2SW
Tel: 01-989 0031

HENDERSON HOSPITAL—81Cb **163**
2 Homeland Dri., Sutton, Surrey. SM2 5LY
Tel: 01-661 1611

HENDON DISTRICT HOSPITAL—30Xa **40**
357 Hendon Way, London. NW4 3NA
Tel: 01-202 7637

HRH PRINCESS CHRISTIAN'S HOSPITAL—3E **94**
12 Clarence Rd., Windsor, Berks. SL4 5AG
Tel: Windsor 53121

HIGHLANDS HOSPITAL—15Nb **24**
Worlds End La., London. N21 1PN
Tel: 01-360 8151

HIGH WOOD HOSPITAL—18Yd **32**
Ongar Rd., Brentwood, Essex. CM15 9DY
Tel: Brentwood 219262

HILLCREST HOSPITAL—94Mb **180**
Coulsdon, Surrey. CR3 1YE
Tel: Downland 56121

HILLINGDON HOSPITAL—43P **75**
Uxbridge, Middx. UB8 3NN
Tel: Uxbridge 38282

HITHER GREEN HOSPITAL—58Fc **107**
Hither Grn. La., London. SE13 6RU
Tel: 01-698 4611

HOLLY HOUSE PRIVATE HOSPITAL—19Kc **27**
High Rd., Buckhurst Hill, Essex. IG9 5HX
Tel: 01-505 3311

HOLLYWOOD LODGE—83Qa **161**
Manor Hospital, Horton La, Epsom, Surrey. KT19 8NN
Tel: Epsom 26291

HONEY LANE HOSPITAL—6Jc **13**
Honey La., Waltham Abbey, Essex. EN9 3AZ
Tel: Waltham Cross 711555

HORNSEY CENTRAL HOSPITAL—29Mb **42**
Park Rd., Crouch End, London. N8 8JL
Tel: 01-340 6244

HORTON HOSPITAL—83Ra **161**
Long Gro. Rd., Epsom, Surrey. KT19 8PZ
Tel: Epsom 29696

HOSPITAL FOR SICK CHILDREN, THE.—43Nb **82**
Great Ormond St., London. WC1N 3JH
Tel: 01-405 9200

HOSPITAL FOR SICK CHILDREN, THE.—93Za **178**
(County Branch)
Tadworth Ct., Tadworth, Surrey. KT20 5RR
Tel: Tadworth 57171

HOSPITAL FOR TROPICAL DISEASES—39Mb **62**
4 St Pancras Way, London. NW1 0PE
Tel: 01-387 4411

HOSPITAL FOR WOMEN—44Mb **82**
Soho Sq., London. W1N 6JB
Tel: 01-580 7928

HOSPITAL OF SAINT JOHN AND SAINT ELIZABETH—40Fb **61**
60 Grove End Rd., St John's Wood, London. NW8 9NH
Tel: 01-286 5126

HUMANA HOSPITAL WELLINGTON—41Fb **81**
Wellington Pl., London. NW8 9LE
Tel: 01-586 5959

ILFORD CHEST CLINIC—31Qc **66**
287-289 Cranbrook Rd., Ilford, Essex. IG1 4UA
Tel: 01-554 8811

ILFORD MATERNITY—30Kc **45**
Eastern Av., Ilford, Essex. IG2 7RJ
Tel: 01-554 8811

INVERFORTH HOUSE HOSPITAL—32Db **61**
N. End Way, Hampstead, London. NW3 7EU
Tel: 01-455 6601

313

Hospitals and Clinics

ISLINGTON CHEST CLINIC—33Kb **62**
Whittington Hospital, Highgate Hill, London. N19 5NF
Tel: 01-272 3070

ITALIAN HOSPITAL—42Nb **82**
Queen Sq., London. WC1N 3AN
Tel: 01-831 6961

IVER, DENHAM & LANGLEY COTTAGE HOSPITAL—44G **74**
Iver, Bucks. SL1 2BJ
Tel: Iver 653339

JEWISH HOME & HOSPITAL AT TOTTENHAM, THE.—28Vb **43**
295 High Rd., S. Tottenham, London. N15 4RT
Tel: 01-800 5138

JOYCE GREEN HOSPITAL—54Pd **111**
Joyce Grn. La., Dartford, Kent. DA1 5PL
Tel: Dartford 27242

JUBILEE HOSPITAL—24Jc **45**
Woodford Green, Essex. IG8 9HG
Tel: 01-504 8891

KENWOOD GARDENS CLINIC—31Qc **66**
Cranbrook Rd., Ilford, Essex. IG2 6YG
Tel: 01-550 4541

KING EDWARD VII HOSPITAL—5G **94**
Windsor, Berks. SL4 1DT
Tel: Windsor 60441

KING EDWARD VII'S HOSPITAL FOR OFFICERS(SISTER AGNES)—43Jb **82**
Beaumont Ho., Beaumont St., London. W1N 2AA
Tel: 01-486 4411

KING GEORGE HOSPITAL—30Tc **46**
Eastern Av., Newbury Pk., Ilford, Essex. IG2 7RL
Tel: 01-554 8811

KINGSBURY HOSPITAL—28Qa **39**
Honeypot La., Kingsbury, London. NW9 9QY
Tel: 01-204 2292

KING'S COLLEGE HOSPITAL—55Sb **105**
Denmark Hill, London. SE5 9RS
Tel: 01-274 6222

KINGSTON HOSPITAL—67Qa **123**
Galsworthy Rd., Kingston, Surrey. KT2 7QB
Tel: 01-546 7711

KINGSTON HOSPITAL CHEST CLINIC—67Qa **123**
Kingston Hospital, Galsworthy Rd., Kingston, Surrey. KT2 7QB
Tel: 01-546 7711

LANGTHORNE HOSPITAL—35Fc **65**
Leytonstone, London. E11 4HJ
Tel: 01-539 5511

LEATHERHEAD HOSPITAL—94La **176**
Poplar Rd., Leatherhead, Surrey. KT22 8SD
Tel: Leatherhead 373466

LEAVESDEN HOSPITAL—3W **4**
College Rd., Abbots Langley, Nr. Watford, Herts. WD5 0NU
Tel: Kings Langley 74090

LENNARD HOSPITAL—74Qc **150**
Lennard Rd., Bromley, Kent. BR2 8LW
Tel: 01-462 1254

LEOPOLD STREET TREATMENT CLINIC—43Bc **84**
Leopold St., London. E3 4LA
Tel: 01-987 3252

LEWISHAM CHEST CLINIC—58Dc **106**
1 Blagdon Rd., Lewisham, London. SE13 7HL
Tel: 01-690 1424

LEWISHAM GROUP LABORATORY—57Dc **106**
Lewisham Hospital, High St., London. SE13 6LH
Tel: 01-690 4311

LEWISHAM HOSPITAL—57Dc **106**
High St., London. SE13 6LH
Tel: 01-690 4311

LEYS CLINIC—39Dd **68**
Ballards Rd., Dagenham, Essex. RM10 9AD
Tel: 01-592 0607

LEYTON GREEN HEALTH CLINIC—30Ec **44**
36 Leyton Grn. Rd., London. E10 6BL
Tel: 01-539 8646

LEYTONSTONE HOUSE HOSPITAL—31Hc **65**
High Rd., Leytonstone, London. E11 1HS
Tel: 01-989 7701

LISTER HOSPITAL—50Kb **82**
Chelsea Bri. Rd., London. SW1W 8RH
Tel:

LITTLE HIGH WOOD—18Xd **32**
Ongar Rd., Brentwood, Essex. CM14 5HQ
Tel: Brentwood 219262

LITTLE WARLEY LODGE—25Ae **51**
Little Warley, Brentwood, Essex. CM13 3DT
Tel: Brentwood 211400

LIVINGSTONE HOSPITAL—59Pd **111**
East Hill, Dartford, Kent. DA1 1SA
Tel: Dartford 92233

LOCKE-KING CLINIC—77Q **140**
Balfour Rd., Weybridge, Surrey. KT13 8H
Tel: Weybridge 42523

LONDON CHEST HOSPITAL—40Yb **64**
Bonner Rd., London. E2 9JX
Tel: 01-980 4433

LONDON CLINIC, THE.—42Jb **82**
20 Devonshire Pl., London. W1N 2DH
Tel: 01-935 4444

LONDON CLINIC OF PSYCHO-ANALYSIS—43Jb **82**
63 New Cavendish St., London. W1M 7RD
Tel: 01-580 4952

LONDON FOOT HOSPITAL & SCHOOL OF CHIROPODY—42Lb **82**
33 & 44 Fitzroy Square, London. W1P 6AY
Tel: 01-636 0602

LONDON HOSPITAL (MILE END), THE.—41Zb **84**
275 Bancroft Rd., London. E1 4DG
Tel: 01-980 4855

LONDON HOSPITAL (ST CLEMENTS), THE.—41Bc **84**
Bow Rd., London. E3 4LL
Tel: 01-980 4899

LONDON HOSPITAL (WHITECHAPEL), THE.—43Xb **83**
Whitechapel, London. E1 1BB
Tel: 01-247 5454

LONDON GROVE HOSPITAL—81Qa **161**
Horton La., Epsom, Surrey. KT19 8PU
Tel: Epsom 26200

MAIDA VALE HOSPITAL FOR NERVOUS DISEASES—42Eb **81**
4 Maida Vale, London. W9 1TL
Tel: 01-286 5172

MANOR HOSPITAL, THE.—83Qa **161**
Horton La., Epsom, Surrey. KT19 8NN
Tel: Epsom 26291

MANOR HOUSE HOSPITAL—32Db **61**
N. End Rd., Golders Green, London. NW11 7HX
Tel: 01-455 6601

MARILLAC, THE.—23Zd **51**
Eagle Way, Warley, Brentwood, Essex. CM13 3BL
Tel: Brentwood 220276

MARLBOROUGH DAY HOSPITAL—40Eb **61**
38 Marlborough Pl., London. NW8 0PJ
Tel: 01-624 8605

MAUDSLEY HOSPITAL, THE.—54Tb **105**
Denmark Hill, London. SE5 8AZ
Tel: 01-703 6333

MAYDAY HOSPITAL—72Rb **147**
Mayday Rd., Thornton Heath, Surrey. CR4 7YE
Tel: 01-684 6999

MAYESBROOK CLINIC—34Wc **67**
Goodmayes La., Ilford, Essex. IG3 6PX
Tel: 01-590 0790

MEDICAL REHABILITATION CENTRE—38Lb **62**
152-154 Camden Rd., London. NW1 9HL
Tel: 01-485 1124

MEMORIAL HOSPITAL—54Qc **108**
Shooters Hill, Woolwich, London. SE18 3RZ
Tel: 01-856 5511

METROPOLITAN EAR, NOSE & THROAT HOSPITAL—48Db **81**
Marloes Rd., London. W8 5LQ
Tel: 01-937 8207

MIDDLESEX HOSPITAL—43Lb **82**
Mortimer St., London. W1N 8AA
Tel: 01-636 8333

MILDMAY MISSION HOSPITAL—41Vb **83**
Hackney Rd., London. E2 7NA
Tel: 01-739 2331

MOLESEY HOSPITAL—71Ca **141**
High St., East Molesey, Surrey. KT8 0LU
Tel: 01-979 5060

MOORFIELDS EYE HOSPITAL—41Tb **83**
City Rd., London. EC1V 2PD
Tel: 01-253 3411

MOORFIELDS EYE HOSPITAL—44Nb **82**
High Holborn Branch, London. WC1V 7AN
Tel: 01-836 6611

MORRIS MARKOWE UNIT—69Ra **123**
Kingston Rd., New Malden, Surrey. KT3 3RL
Tel: 01-942 0779

MOTHER'S HOSPITAL (SALVATION ARMY)—35Xb **63**
143-153 Lwr. Clapton Rd., London. E5 8EN
Tel: 01-985 6661

MOUNT PLEASANT HOSPITAL—44Ca **77**
North Rd., Southall, Middx. UB1 2SH
Tel: 01-574 1394

MOUNT VERNON HOSPITAL & THE RADIUM INSTITUTE—23R **36**
Northwood, Middx. HA6 2RN
Tel: Northwood 26111

MURRAY HOUSE—79E **138**
Ottershaw, Surrey. KT16 0HW
Tel: Ottershaw 2000

NATIONAL HEART HOSPITAL, THE.—43Jb **82**
Westmoreland St., London. W1M 8BA
Tel: 01-486 4433

NATIONAL HOSPITALS COLLEGE OF SPEECH SCIENCES—43Kb **82**
59 Portland Pl., London. W1N 3AJ
Tel: 01-636 1433

NATIONAL TEMPERANCE HOSPITAL—41Lb **82**
Hampstead Rd., London. NW1 2LT
Tel: 01-387 9300

NATIONAL HOSPITAL, THE.—42Nb **82**
Queen Square, London. WC1N 3BG
Tel: 01-837 3611

NATIONAL HOSPITALS FINCHLEY, THE.—29Gb **41**
Gt. North Rd., East Finchley, London. N2 0NW
Tel: 01-883 8335

NEASDEN HOSPITAL—37Ta **59**
Brentfield Rd., London. NW10 8EY
Tel: 01-459 2251

NELSON HOSPITAL—68Bb **125**
Kingston Rd., Merton, London. SW20 8DB
Tel: 01-540 7261

NETHERNE HOSPITAL—94Mb **180**
Coulsdon, Surrey. CR3 1YE
Tel: Coulsdon 56700

NEUROSURGICAL UNIT OF GUY'S, MAUDSLEY & KING'S COLLEGE
HOSPITALS—54Tb **105**
The Maudsley Hospital, De Crespigny Pk., London SE5 8AZ
Tel: 01-703 6333

NEW CROSS HOSPITAL—52Yb **106**
Avonley Rd., London. SE14 5ER
Tel: 01-639 4380

NEW END HOSPITAL—35Eb **61**
Hamstead, London. NW3 1JB
Tel: 01-435 7131

NEWHAM HOSPITAL—42Lc **85**
Glen Rd., Plaistow, London. E13 8SL
Tel: 01-476 1400

NEWHAM MATERNITY HOSPITAL—36Hc **65**
Forest La., London. E7 9BD
Tel: 01-555 3262

NEW VICTORIA HOSPITAL, THE.—67Ra **123**
184 Coombe La. W., Kingston-upon-Thames, Surrey. KT2 7EG
Tel: 01-949 1661

NIGHTINGALE BUPA HOSPITAL—42Fb **81**
19 Lisson Gro., London. NW1 6SJ
Tel: 01-723 1288

NORMANSFIELD—66La **122**
Kingston Rd., Teddington, Middx. TW11 9JH
Tel: 01-977 7583

NORTHGATE CLINIC—29Ua **40**
Goldsmith Av., London. NW9 7HR
Tel: 01-205 8012

NORTH LONDON NUFFIELD HOSPITAL—12Qb **24**
Cavell Dri., Uplands Pk. Rd., Enfield, London. EN2 7PR
Tel: 01-366 2122

NORTH MIDDLESEX HOSPITAL—22Ub **43**
Sterling Way, Edmonton, London. N18 1QX
Tel: 01-807 3071

NORTHWICK PARK HOSPITAL—31Ja **58**
Watford Rd., Harrow, Middx. HA1 3UJ
Tel: 01-864 5311

NORTHWOOD, PINNER & DISTRICT HOSPITAL—25W **36**
Pinner Rd., Northwood, Middx. HA6 1DE
Tel: Northwood 24182

NORWOOD & DISTRICT HOSPITAL—65Tb **127**
Hermitage Rd., London. SE19 3JX
Tel: 01-653 1171

NUFFIELD HOUSE—46Tb **83**
Guy's Hospital, St Thomas St., London. SE1 9RT
Tel: 01-407 7600

OLDCHURCH HOSPITAL—30Fd **48**
Oldchurch Rd., Romford, Essex. RM7 0BE
Tel: Romford 46090

OLD COURT HOSPITAL—43Ma **79**
19 Montpelier Rd., Ealing, London. W5 2QT
Tel: 01-998 2848

OLD WINDSOR HOSPITAL—9K **95**
Old Windsor, Berks. SL4 2HN
Tel: Windsor 62121

OPHTHALMIC CLINIC FOR SCHOOLCHILDREN—25Pd **49**
Harold Wood Clinic, Gubbins La., Harold Wood, Romford, Essex.
RM3 0QA
Tel: Ingrebourne 40022

OPHTHALMIC CLINIC FOR SCHOOLCHILDREN—22Nd **49**
Health Centre, Gooshays Dri., Harold Hill, Romford, Essex. RM3 9LB
Tel: Ingrebourne 43991

ORCHARD HOUSE—24Qc **46**
Claybury Hospital, Woodford Green, Essex. IG8 8BY
Tel: 01-504 7171

ORPINGTON HOSPITAL—77Wc **151**
Sevenoaks Rd., Orpington, Kent. BR6 9UJ
Tel: Orpington 27050

ORSETT HOSPITAL—3C **92**
Rowley Rd., Orsett, Grays, Essex. RM16 3EU
Tel: Grays Thurrock 891100

OTTERSHAW HOSPITAL—79F **138**
Ottershaw, Chertsey, Surrey. KT16 0HW
Tel: Ottershaw 2000

OXTED & LIMPSFIELD HOSPITAL—99Fc **183**
Eastlands Way, Oxted, Surrey. RH8 0LR
Tel: Oxted 4344

PADDINGTON & KENSINGTON CHEST CLINIC—44Db **81**
14-18 Newton Rd., Westbourne Gro., London. W2 5LT
Tel: 01-229 8821

PADDINGTON CENTRE FOR PSYCHOTHERAPY—44Ab **80**
63-65 Lancaster Rd., London. W11 1QG
Tel: 01-221 4656

PADDINGTON GREEN CHILDREN'S HOSPITAL—43Fb **81**
Paddington Green, London. W2 1LQ
Tel: 01-723 1081

PERIVALE MATERNITY HOSPITAL—41Ha **78**
Stockdove Way, Greenford, Middx. UB6 8EL
Tel: 01-997 5661

PHYSIOTHERAPY CLINIC FOR SCHOOLCHILDREN—22Nd **49**
Health Centre, Gooshays Dri., Harold Hill, Romford, Essex. RM3 9LB
Tel: Ingrebourne 43991

PLAISTOW HOSPITAL—40Lc **65**
Samson St., Plaistow, London. E13 9EH
Tel: 01-472 7001

PORTERS AVENUE CLINIC—36Yc **67**
Porters Av., Dagenham, Essex. RM8 2AW
Tel: 01-592 8223

PORTMAN CLINIC—35Eb **61**
8 Fitzjohn's Av., London. NW3 5NA
Tel: 01-794 8262

POTTERS BAR HOSPITAL—4Db **9**
Mutton La., Potters Bar, Herts. EN6 2PB
Tel: Potters Bar 53286

PRINCE OF WALES'S HOSPITAL, THE—28Vb **43**
The Green, Tottenham, London. N15 4AW
Tel: 01-808 1081

PRINCESS GRACE HOSPITAL, THE—43Jb **82**
42-52 Nottingham Pl., London. W1M 3FD
Tel: 01-486 1234

PRINCESS LOUISE HOSPITAL—43Za **80**
St Quintin Avenue, London. W10 6DL
Tel: 01-969 0133

PRINCESS MARGARET HOSPITAL, THE—4G **94**
Osborne Rd., Windsor, Berks. SL4 5EJ
Tel: Windsor 68292

PRIORY HOSPITAL, THE—58Ua **102**
Priory La., Roehampton, London. SW15 5JJ
Tel: 01-876 8261

PUBLIC HEALTH CENTRE (CLINIC)—49Vb **83**
108 Grange Rd., London. SE1 3BW
Tel: 01-237 2826

PURLEY & DISTRICT WAR MEMORIAL HOSPITAL—83Qb **164**
Brighton Rd., Purley, Surrey. CR9 2RR
Tel: 01-660 0177

PURLEY DAY HOSPITAL—85Pb **164**
130 Brighton Rd., Purley, Surrey. CR2 4HD
Tel: 01-660 4844

PUTNEY HOSPITAL—55Ya **102**
Lwr. Common, London. SW15 1HW
Tel: 01-789 6633

QUEEN CHARLOTTE'S MATERNITY HOSPITAL—49Wa **80**
Goldhawk Rd., London. W6 0XG
Tel: 01-748 4666

QUEEN ELIZABETH HOSPITAL—90Eb **163**
Holly La., Banstead, Surrey. SM7 2BT
Tel: Burgh Heath 58925

QUEEN ELIZABETH HOSPITAL FOR CHILDREN—40Wb **63**
Hackney Rd., London. E2 8PS
Tel: 01-739 8422

QUEEN ELIZABETH MILITARY HOSPITAL—52Nc **108**
Stadium Rd., Woolwich, London. SE18 6XN
Tel: 01-856 5533

QUEEN MARY'S HOSPITAL—58Wa **102**
Roehampton La., London. SW15 5PN
Tel: 01-789 6633

QUEEN MARY'S HOSPITAL—64Wc **131**
Frognal Av., Sidcup, Kent. DA14 6LT
Tel: 01-302 2678

QUEEN MARY'S HOSPITAL FOR CHILDREN—82Jb **164**
Carshalton, Surrey. SM5 4NR
Tel: 01-643 3300

QUEEN MARY'S HOSPITAL FOR THE EAST END—42Lc **85**
Glen Rd., Plaistow, London. E13 8RU
Tel: 01-476 1400

QUEEN'S HOSPITAL—72Sb **147**
Queen's Rd., Croydon, Surrey. CR9 2PQ
Tel: 01-684 6999

RAINHAM CLINIC—42Jd **88**
Upminster Rd. S., Rainham, Essex. RM13 9AB
Tel: Rainham 52187

RAME HOUSE—64Hb **125**
Church La., London. SW17 9PS
Tel: 01-672 2231

REHABILITATION UNIT FOR THE ELDERLY—55Na **101**
Kew Foot Rd., Richmond, Surrey. TW9 2TE
Tel: 01-940 3331

ROSA MORISON HOUSE (DAY HOSPITAL)—15Db **23**
Gloucester Rd., New Barnet, Herts. EN5 1NA
Tel: 01-449 0712 & 01-441 1240

ROWLEY BRISTOW ORTHOPAEDIC HOSPITAL—88J **157**
Pyrford, Nr. Woking, Surrey. GU22 8GU
Tel: Byfleet 41141

ROXBOURNE HOSPITAL—33Ca **57**
Rayners La., South Harrow, Middx. HA2 0UE
Tel: 01-422 1450

ROYAL DENTAL HOSPITAL—45Mb **82**
32 Leicester Sq., London. WC2H 7LG
Tel: 01-930 8831

ROYAL EAR HOSPITAL—42Lb **82**
Huntley St., London. WC1E 6AU
Tel: 01-387 9300

ROYAL FREE HOSPITAL, THE—36Gb **61**
Pond St., London. NW3 2QG
Tel: 01-794 0500

ROYAL HOMEOPATHIC HOSPITAL—43Nb **82**
Gt. Ormond St., London. WC1N 2LT
Tel: 01-837 8833

ROYAL HOSPITAL—55Na **101**
Kew Foot Rd., Richmond, Surrey. TW9 2TE
Tel: 01-940 3331

ROYAL HOSPITAL & HOME FOR INCURABLES—58Ab **102**
West Hill, Putney, London. SW15 3SW
Tel: 01-788 4511

ROYAL MARSDEN HOSPITAL, THE—50Fb **81**
Fulham Rd., London. SW3 6JJ
Tel: 01-352 8171

ROYAL MARSDEN HOSPITAL, THE—82Eb **163**
Downs Rd., Sutton, Surrey. SM2 5PT
Tel: 01-642 6011

ROYAL MASONIC HOSPITAL—49Wa **80**
Ravenscourt Pk., London. W6 0TN
Tel: 01-748 4611

ROYAL NATIONAL ORTHOPAEDIC HOSPITAL—42Kb **82**
234 Great Portland St., London. W1N 6AD
Tel: 01-387 5070

ROYAL NATIONAL ORTHOPAEDIC HOSPITAL—19Ka **20**
Brockley Hill, Stanmore, Middx. HA7 4LP
Tel: 01-954 2300

ROYAL NATIONAL THROAT, NOSE & EAR HOSPITAL—45Lb **82**
Golden Sq., London. W1R 4EX
Tel: 01-837 8855

ROYAL NATIONAL THROAT, NOSE & EAR HOSPITAL—41Pb **82**
Gray's Inn Rd., London. WC1X 8DA
Tel: 01-837 8855

ROYAL NORTHERN HOSPITAL—34Nb **62**
Holloway Rd., London. N7 6LD
Tel: 01-272 7777

ROYAL STAR & GARTER HOME FOR DISABLED SAILORS, SOLDIERS
& AIRMEN—59Na **101**
Richmond-upon-Thames, Surrey. TW10 5BR
Tel: 01-940 3314

RUSH GREEN HOSPITAL—33Gd **68**
Dagenham Rd., Romford, Essex. RM7 0YA
Tel: Romford 46066

SAINT ANDREWS' HOSPITAL—42Dc **84**
Devons Rd., Bow, London. E3 3NT
Tel: 01-987 2030

SAINT ANDREW'S HOUSE—35Va **60**
Dollis Hill La., Dollis Hill, London. NW2 6HD
Tel: 01-452 5451

SAINT ANN'S HOSPITAL—29Sb **43**
St Ann's Rd., South Tottenham, London. N15 3TH
Tel: 01-800 0121

SAINT ANTHONY'S HOSPITAL—74Za **144**
North Cheam, Surrey. SM3 9DW
Tel: 01-330 3351

SAINT BARTHOLOMEW'S HOSPITAL—43Rb **83**
West Smithfield, London. EC1A 7BE
Tel: 01-600 9000

SAINT BERNARD'S WING—47Ea **78**
Ealing Hospital, Uxbridge Rd., Southall, Middx. UB1 3EU
Tel: 01-574 8141

SAINT CHARLES HOSPITAL—43Za **80**
Exmoor St., London. W10 6DZ
Tel: 01-969 2488

SAINT CHRISTOPHER'S HOSPICE—54Yb **128**
51-53 Lawrie Pk. Rd., Sydenham, London. SE26 6DZ
Tel: 01-778 9252

SAINT CLEMENTS HOSPITAL—41Bc **84**
Bow Rd., London. E3 4LL
Tel: 01-980 4899

SAINT DAVID'S HOME FOR THE DISABLED EX-SERVICEMEN—43La **78**
Castlebar Hill, Ealing, London. W5 1TE
Tel: 01-997 5121

SAINT EBBA'S HOSPITAL—81Sa **161**
Hook Rd., Epsom, Surrey. KT19 8QJ
Tel: Epsom 22212

SAINT FAITH'S HOSPITAL—19Xd **32**
London Rd., Brentwood, Essex. CM14 4QP
Tel: Brentwood 217841

SAINT FRANCIS' HOSPITAL—56Ub **105**
St Francis Rd., London. SE22 8DF
Tel: 01-693 3377

SAINT GEORGE'S HOSPITAL—64Fb **125**
Blackshaw Rd., London. SW17 0QT
Tel: 01-672 1255

SAINT GEORGE'S HOSPITAL—36Nd **69**
Suttons La., Hornchurch, Essex. RM12 6RS
Tel: Hornchurch 43531

SAINT GILES' HOSPITAL—53Ub **105**
St Giles' Rd., London. SE5 7RN
Tel: 01-703 0898

SAINT HELIER HOSPITAL—74Eb **145**
Wrythe La., Carshalton, Surrey. SM5 1AA
Tel: 01-644 4343 (Pathology 01-644 4011)

SAINT JAMES' HOSPTIAL—60Hb **103**
Sarsfield Rd., London. SW12 8HW
Tel: 01-672 1222

SAINT JOHN'S HOSPITAL—59Ja **100**
Amyand Pk. Rd., Twickenham, Middx. TW1 3HQ
Tel: 01-997 2212

SAINT JOHN'S HOSPITAL—41N **75**
Kingston La., Uxbridge, Middx. UB8 3PL
Tel: 01-573 2052

SAINT JOHN'S HOSPITAL—56Fb **103**
St John's Hill, Battersea, London. SW11 1SP
Tel: 01-874 1022

SAINT JOHN'S HOSPITAL FOR DISEASES OF THE SKIN—45Mb **82**
5 Lisle St., Leicester Sq, London. WC2H 7BJ
Tel: 01-437 8383

SAINT JOHN'S HOSPITAL FOR DISEASES OF THE SKIN, IN-PATIENT
DEPARTMENT—36Zb **64**
Homerton Gro. London. E9 6BX
Tel: 01-985 7061

SAINT JOSEPH'S HOSPITAL FOR ELDERLY & HANDICAPPED WOMEN
—51Ua **102**
Burlington La., Chiswick, London. W4 2QF
Tel: 01-994 4641

SAINT JOSEPH'S HOSPICE—39Xb **63**
Mare St., Hackney, London. E8 4SA
Tel: 01-985 0861

SAINT JOSEPH'S NURSING HOME—17Tb **25**
15 Church St., Lwr. Edmonton, London. N9 9DZ
Tel: 01-803 8383/4

SAINT LAWRENCE'S HOSPITAL—95Tb **181**
Caterham, Surrey. CR3 5YA
Tel: Caterham 46411

SAINT LEONARD'S HOSPITAL—40Ub **63**
Nuttall St., London. N1 5LZ
Tel 01-739 8484

SAINT LUKE'S HOSPITAL FOR THE CLERGY—42Lb **82**
14 Fitzroy Sq., London. W1P 6AH
Tel: 01-388 4954

SAINT LUKE'S-WOODSIDE HOSPITAL—28Jb **42**
Woodside Av., London. N10 3HU
Tel: 01-883 8311

SAINT MARGARET'S HOSPITAL—1Xc **15**
The Plain, Epping, Essex. CM16 6TN
Tel: Epping 77322

SAINT MARK'S HOSPITAL FOR DISEASES OF THE RECTUM & COLON
—41Rb **83**
City Rd., London. EC1V 2PS
Tel: 01-253 1050

SAINT MARY ABBOTS HOSPITAL—48Db **81**
Marloes Rd., London. W8 3LQ
Tel: 01-937 8207

SAINT MARY'S COTTAGE HOSPITAL—67Ba **121**
Up. Sunbury Rd., Hampton, Middx. TW12 2DW
Tel: 01-979 4451

SAINT MARY'S HOSPITAL—44Fb **81**
Praed St., London. W2 1NY
Tel: 01-262 1280

SAINT MARY'S HOSPITAL—43Cb **81**
Harrow Rd., London. W9 3RL
Tel: 01-286 4884

SAINT MARY'S MATERNITY HOSPITAL—73Rb **147**
St James' Rd., Croydon, Surrey. CR9 2RR
Tel: 01-684 6999

SAINT MATTHEW'S HOSPITAL—41Sb **83**
Shepherdess Wlk., London. N1 7LH
Tel: 01-253 4218

SAINT MICHAEL'S HOSPITAL—11Tb **25**
Chase Side Cres., Enfield, Middx. EN2 0JB
Tel: 01-363 8234

SAINT MICHAEL'S HOSPITAL—75Ua **144**
(Franciscan Missionaries of Mary)
Cleveland Gdns., Worcester Park, Surrey. KT4 7JJ
Tel: 01-337 1301

SAINT NICHOLAS HOSPITAL—50Uc **86**
Tewson Rd., Plumstead, London. SE18 1BA
Tel: 01-854 2455

SAINT OLAVES HOSPITAL—48Yb **84**
Lower Rd., Rotherhithe, London. SE16 2TS
Tel: 01-237 6622

SAINT PANCRAS HOSPITAL—38Lb **62**
4 St Pancras Way, London. WC1 0PE
Tel: 01-387 4411

SAINT PAUL'S HOSPITAL—44Nb **82**
Endell St., London. WC2H 9AE
Tel: 01-836 9611

Hospitals and Clinics

SAINT PETER'S HOSPITAL—45Nb **82**
Henrietta St., London. WC2E 8NE
Tel: 01-836 9347

SAINT PETER'S HOSPITAL—76F **138**
Chertsey, Surrey. KT16 0PZ
Tel: Ottershaw 2000

SAINT PHILIP'S HOSPITAL—44Pb **82**
Sheffield St., London. WC2A 2EX
Tel: 01-242 9831

SAINT RAPHAEL'S—4Kb **10**
Barvin Pk., Coopers La. Rd., Potters Bar, Herts. EN6 4DH
Tel: Potters Bar 52282

SAINT STEPHEN'S HOSPITAL—51Eb **103**
Fulham Rd., London. SW10 9TH
Tel: 01-352 8161

SAINT STEPHEN'S HOSPITAL—15Za **22**
May's La., Barnet, Herts. EN5 2LU
Tel: 01-440 5111

SAINT TERESA'S HOSPITAL—66Za **124**
The Downs, Wimbledon, London. SW20 8HS
Tel: 01-947 3142

SAINT THOMAS' CHILDRENS PSYCHIATRIC DAY HOSPITAL—49Pb **82**
35 Black Prince Rd., London. SE11 6JJ
Tel: 01-735 1972

SAINT THOMAS' HOSPITAL—47Pb **82**
Lambeth Palace Rd., London. SE1 7EH
Tel: 01-928 9292

SAINT VINCENT'S ORTHOPAEDIC HOSPITAL—27V **36**
Eastcote, Pinner, Middx. HA5 2NB
Tel: 01-866 0151

SAMARITAN HOSPITAL FOR WOMEN—43Hb **81**
Marylebone Rd., London. NW1 5YE
Tel: 01-402 4211

SCHOOL EYE CLINIC—5G **94**
King Edward VII Hospital, Windsor, Berks. SL4 1DT
Tel: Windsor 60441

SEVENOAKS HOSPITAL—93Ld **187**
Hospital Rd., Sevenoaks, Kent. TN13 3PG
Tel: Sevenoaks 455155

SHAFTESBURY HOSPITAL, THE.—44Nb **82**
Shaftesbury Av., London. WC2H 8JE
Tel: 01-836 7211

SHENLEY HOSPITAL—5Na **7**
Shenley, Radlett, Herts. WD7 9HB
Tel: Radlett 5631

SHRODELLS HOSPITAL—15X **19**
60 Vicarage Rd., Watford, Herts. WD1 8DE
Tel: Watford 44366

SLOUGH NUFFIELD HOSPITAL—9N **53**
Wexham St., Slough. SL3 6NH
Tel: Slough 2241

SOUTHALL NORWOOD HOSPITAL—48Ba **77**
The Green, Southall, Middx. UB2 4BH
Tel: 01-574 2616

SOUTH BROMLEY HOSPISCARE—77Wc **151**
Orpington Hospital, Sevenoaks Rd., Orpington, Kent. BR6 9UJ
Tel: Orpington 29010

SOUTH EAST LONDON GENERAL PRACTIONERS' CENTRE—53Yb **106**
St Mary's Rd., London. SE15 2ED
Tel: 01-639 7871

SOUTH MIDDLESEX HOSPITAL—57Ha **100**
Hospital La., Isleworth, Middx. TW7 7LN
Tel: 01-892 2841

SOUTH OCKENDON HOSPITAL—42Zd **91**
South Rd., South Ockendon, Essex. RM15 6SP
Tel: South Ockendon 2335

SOUTH SIDE HOME—65Nb **126**
4 Streatham Comn. S., London. SW16 3BT
Tel: 01-764 8778

SOUTH WESTERN HOSPITAL—55Pb **104**
Landor Rd., London. SW9 9NU
Tel: 01-928 9292

SOUTHWOOD HOSPITAL—31Jb **62**
Southwood La., Highgate, London. N6 5SP
Tel: 01-340 8778

SPRINGFIELD HOSPITAL—61Gb **125**
61 Glenburnie Rd., London. SW17 7DJ
Tel: 01-672 9911

STEPNEY PSYCHOGERIATRIC DAY HOSPITAL—44Yb **84**
Ronald St., (Off Commercial Rd.,) London. E1 0DT
Tel: 01-790 1442

STEPPING STONES UNIT—69Kc **129**
38 Masons Hill, Bromley, Kent. BR2 9JG
Tel: 01-460 1839

STONE HOUSE HOSPITAL—58Sd **112**
Dartford, Kent. DA2 6AH
Tel: Dartford 27211

SUNDRIDGE HOSPITAL—99Ad **185**
Church Rd., Sundridge, Nr. Sevenoaks, Kent. TN14 6AU
Tel: Westerham 62841

SURBITON HOSPITAL—72Na **143**
Ewell Rd., Surbiton, Surrey. KT6 6EZ
Tel: 01-399 7111

SUTTON HOSPITAL—82Eb **163**
Cotswold Rd., Sutton, Surrey. SM2 5NF
Tel: 01-642 6090

TAVISTOCK CLINIC—37Fb **61**
120 Belsize La., London. NW3 5BA
Tel: 01-435 7111

TEDDINGTON MEMORIAL HOSPITAL—65Ga **122**
Hampton Rd., Teddington, Middx. TW11 0JL
Tel: 01-997 2212

THAMES DITTON HOSPITAL—73Ha **142**
Weston Grn. Rd., Thames Ditton, Surrey. KT7 0HY
Tel: 01-398 1130

THORPE COOMBE HOSPITAL—27Ec **44**
714 Forest Rd., Walthamstow, London. E17 3HT
Tel: 01-520 8971

THURROCK HOSPITAL—46Ee **91**
Long La., Grays, Essex. RM16 2PX
Tel: Grays Thurrock 891100

TOLWORTH HOSPITAL—75Qa **143**
Red Lion Rd., Tolworth, Surrey. KT6 7QT
Tel: 01-390 0102

TOOTING BEC HOSPITAL—63Kb **126**
Tooting Bec Rd., London. SW17 8BL
Tel: 01-672 9933

TREES NURSING HOME—31Hb **61**
2 Broadlands Rd., London. N6 4AS
Tel: 01-340 5278

TRINITY HOSPICE—56Jb **104**
30 Clapham Comn. N. Side, London. SW4 0RN
Tel: 01-622 9481

TURRET, THE.—65Nb **126**
16 Streatham Comn. S., London. SW16 3BT
Tel: 01-764 8778

TWYFORD ABBEY NURSING HOME—41Pa **79**
Twyford Abbey Rd., London. NW10 7DP
Tel: 01-965 6312/5461

UNIT FOR DEAF CHILDREN—43La **78**
6 Castlebar Hill, Ealing, London. W5 1TD
Tel: 01-997 8480

UNIT FOR DEAF CHILDREN & PARENTS—43La **78**
8 Castlebar Hill, Ealing, London. W5 1TD
Tel: 01-937 0134

UNIVERSITY COLLEGE HOSPITAL—42Lb **82**
Gower St., London. WC1E 6AU
Tel: 01-387 9300

UNIVERSITY COLLEGE HOSPITAL, PRIVATE PATIENTS' WING—42Ld **82**
Grafton Way, London. WC1E 6DB
Tel: 01-837 9300

UPMINSTER CLINIC—33Rd **69**
St Mary's La., Upminster, Essex. RM14 3PA
Tel: Upminster 26170

UPTON HOSPITAL—7K **73**
Slough, Berks. SL1 2BJ
Tel: Slough 23261

VALE ROAD SPECIAL SCHOOL CENTRE—31Sb **63**
Vale Rd., London. N4 1PJ
Tel: 01-800 4772

VICTORIA HOSPITAL—28Hd **48**
Pettits La., Romford Essex. RM1 4HP
Tel: Romford 42461

VICTORIA MATERNITY HOSPITAL—14Ab **22**
Wood St., Barnet, Herts. EN5 4BH
Tel: 01-440 5111

WADDON HOSPITAL—73Nb **146**
Purley Way, Croydon, Surrey. CR9 4PL
Tel: 01-684 6999

WALLINGTON DAY (PSYCHIATRIC) HOSPITAL—79Kb **146**
77 Woodcote Rd., Wallington, Surrey. SM6 0PU
Tel: 01-647 6321

WALTON HOSPITAL—75X **141**
Sidney Rd., Walton-on-Thames, Surrey. KT12 3LD
Tel: Walton-on-Thames 20060

WANDLE VALLEY HOSPITAL—73Hb **145**
Mitcham Junction, Mitcham, Surrey. CR4 4XL
Tel: 01-648 9441

WANSTEAD HOSPITAL—28Kc **45**
Hermon La., Wanstead, London. E11 1PA
Tel: 01-989 6699

WARLEY HOSPITAL—22Xd **50**
Brentwood, Essex. CM14 5HQ
Tel: Brentwood 213241

WARLINGHAM PARK HOSPITAL—87Dc **166**
Warlingham, Surrey. CR3 9YR
Tel: 01-820 2101

WATFORD CHEST CLINIC—13W **18**
c/o Peace Memorial Wing, Rickmansworth Rd., Watford, Herts.
WD1 7HH
Tel: Watford 29266

WATFORD GENERAL HOSPITAL—13W **18**
Peace Memorial Wing, Rickmansworth Rd., Watford, Herts. WD17HH
Tel: Watford 44366

WATFORD GENERAL HOSPITAL—15X **19**
Shrodells Wing, Vicarage Rd., Watford, Herts. WD1 8HB
Tel: Watford 44366

WELLINGTON HOSPITAL—41Fb **81**
Circus Rd., London. NW8 9SU
Tel: 01-586 5959

WELLINGTON HOSPITAL—41Fb **81**
Wellington Pl., London. NW8 9LE
Tel: 01-586 5959

WEMBLEY HOSPITAL—37Ma **59**
Fairview Av., Wembley, Middx. HA0 4UH
Tel: 01-903 6633

WESTERN OPHTHALMIC HOSPITAL—43Hb **81**
Marylebone Rd., London. NW1 5YE
Tel: 01-402 4211

WEST HENDON HOSPITAL—30Ua **40**
Goldsmith Av., London. NW9 7HR
Tel: 01-205 2367

WEST HILL HOSPITAL—58Md **111**
Dartford, Kent. DA1 2HF
Tel: Dartford 23223

WEST LONDON HOSPITAL—49Za **80**
Hammersmith Rd., London. W6 7DQ
Tel: 01-748 3441

WEST MIDDLESEX UNIVERSITY HOSPITAL—54Ja **100**
Twickenham Rd., Isleworth, Middx. TW7 6AF
Tel: 01-560 2121

WESTMINSTER HOSPITAL—49Nb **82**
Dean Ryle St., London. SW1P 2AP
Tel: 01-828 9811

WESTMINSTER CHILDREN'S HOSPITAL—49Mb **82**
Vincent Sq., London. SW1P 2NS
Tel: 01-828 9811

WEST PARK HOSPITAL—84Na **161**
Horton La., Epsom, Surrey. KT19 8PB
Tel: Epsom 27811

WEXHAM PARK HOSPITAL—2M **73**
Slough, Berks. SL2 4HL
Tel: Slough 34567

WEYBRIDGE HOSPITAL—77Q **140**
Church St., Weybridge, Surrey. KT13 8DY
Tel: Weybridge 47909

WHITTINGTON HOSPITAL—33Kb **62**
Highgate Hill, London. N19 5NF
Tel: 01-272 3070

WHIPPS CROSS HOSPITAL—30Fc **45**
Whipps Cross Rd., Leytonstone, London. E11 1NR
Tel: 01-539 5522

WILLESDEN HOSPITAL—38Wa **60**
Harlesden Rd., London. NW10 3RY
Tel: 01-459 1292

WILSON HOSPITAL—70Hb **125**
Cranmer Rd., Mitcham, Surrey. CR4 4TP
Tel: 01-648 3021

WIMBLEDON DAY HOSPITAL—66Xa **124**
Thurstan Rd., Copse Hill, London. SW20 0EE
Tel: 01-946 1103

WINDSOR GROUP CHEST CLINIC—7K **73**
Upton Hospital, Slough, Berks. SL1 2BJ
Tel: Slough 23261

WINIFRED HOUSE—16Va **22**
Barnet Gate, Arkley, Herts. EN5 3HY
Tel: 01-449 3343

WOKING NUFFIELD HOSPITAL—86A **156**
Shores Rd., Woking. GU21 4BY
Tel: Woking 63511

WOKING VICTORIA HOSPITAL—88B **156**
Chobham Rd., Woking, Surrey. GU21 1JP
Tel: Woking 5911

WOLFSON MEDICAL REHABILITATION CENTRE—66Xa **124**
Copse Hill, Wimbledon, London. SW20 0NQ
Tel: 01-946 7711

WOOD GREEN & SOUTHGATE HOSPITAL—24Mb **42**
Bounds Grn. Rd., London. N11 2EE
Tel: 01-889 1981

YORK CLINIC—46Tb **83**
Guy's Hospital, 117 Borough High St., London. SE1 1NR
Tel: 01-407 7600

BRITISH RAIL AND LONDON UNDERGROUND STATIONS
with their map square reference

ABBEY WOOD, British Rail—49Yc 87
ACTON CENTRAL, British Rail—46Ta 79
ACTON MAIN LINE, British Rail—44Sa 79
ACTON TOWN, District & Piccadilly—47Ra 79
ADDISCOMBE, British Rail—74Vb 147
ADDLESTONE, British Rail—77M 139
ALBANY PARK, British Rail—61Zc 131
ALDGATE, Circle & Metropolitan—44Vb 83
ALDGATE EAST, District & Metropolitan—44Vb 83
ALDWYCH, Piccadilly—45Pb 82
ALPERTON, Piccadilly—39Ma 59
ANERLEY, British Rail—66Xb 127
ANGEL, Northern—40Qb 62
ANGEL ROAD, British Rail—22Yb 44
ARCHWAY, Northern—33Lb 62
ARNOS GROVE, Piccadilly—21Lb 42
ARSENAL, Piccadilly—34Qb 62
ASHFORD, British Rail—63P 119
ASHTEAD, British Rail—89Na 161

BAKER STREET, British Rail, Bakerloo, Circle, Jubilee & Metropolitan
—42Hb 81
BALHAM, British Rail & Northern—60Jb 104
BANK, British Rail, Central & Northern—44Tb 83
BANSTEAD, British Rail—86Ab 162
BARBICAN, British Rail, Circle & Metropolitan—43Sb 83
BARKING, British Rail, District & Metropolitan—38Sc 66
BARKINGSIDE, Central—28Tc 46
BARNEHURST, British Rail—54Ed 110
BARNES, British Rail—55Wa 102
BARNES BRIDGE, British Rail—54Ua 102
BARONS COURT, District & Piccadilly—50Ab 80
BAT & BALL, British Rail—93Ld 187
BATTERSEA PARK, British Rail—52Kb 104
BAYSWATER, Circle & District—45Db 81
BECKENHAM JUNCTION, British Rail—67Cc 128
BECONTREE, District—37Zc 67
BEDDINGTON LANE, British Rail—72Lb 146
BELLINGHAM, British Rail—62Dc 128
BELMONT, British Rail—82Db 163
BELSIZE PARK, Northern—36Gb 61
BELVEDERE, British Rail—48Db 88
BERRYLANDS, British Rail—70Ra 123
BETHNAL GREEN, British Rail—42Xb 83
BETHNAL GREEN, Central—41Yb 84
BEXLEY, British Rail—60Cd 110
BEXLEYHEATH, British Rail—55Ad 109
BICKLEY, British Rail—69Nc 130
BIRKBECK, British Rail—69Yb 128
BLACKFRIARS, British Rail, Circle & District—45Rb 83
BLACKHEATH, British Rail—55Gc 107
BLACKHORSE ROAD, British Rail & Victoria—28Zb 44
BOND STREET, Central & Jubilee—44Jb 82
BOOKHAM, British Rail—95Ba 175
BOROUGH, Northern—47Sb 83
BOSTON MANOR, Piccadilly—49Ja 78
BOUNDS GREEN, Piccadilly—23Mb 42
BOWES PARK, British Rail—24Nb 42
BOW ROAD, District & Metropolitan—41Cc 84
BRENT CROSS, Northern—31Za 60
BRENTFORD, British Rail—51La 100
BRENTWOOD, British Rail—20Yd 32
BRICKET WOOD, British Rail—3Da 5
BRIMSDOWN, British Rail—13Ac 26
BRIXTON, British Rail & Victoria—56Qb 104
BROAD STREET, British Rail—43Ub 83
BROCKLEY, British Rail—55Ac 106
BROMLEY-BY-BOW, District & Metropolitan—41Dc 84
BROMLEY NORTH, British Rail—67Jc 129
BROMLEY SOUTH, British Rail—69Kc 129
BRONDESBURY, British Rail—38Bb 61
BRONDESBURY PARK, British Rail—39Ab 60
BRUCE GROVE, British Rail—26Vb 43
BUCKHURST HILL, Central—19Mc 27
BURNHAM, British Rail—4B 72
BURNT OAK, Northern—25Sa 39
BUSHEY, British Rail—16Z 19
BUSH HILL PARK, British Rail—16Vb 25
BYFLEET & NEW HAW, British Rail—82M 157

CALEDONIAN ROAD, Piccadilly—37Pb 62
CALEDONIAN ROAD & BARNSBURY, British Rail—38Pb 62
CAMBRIDGE HEATH, British Rail—40Xb 63
CAMDEN ROAD, British Rail—38Lb 62
CAMDEN TOWN, Northern—39Kb 62
CANNING TOWN, British Rail—43Gc 85
CANNON STREET, British Rail, Circle & District—45Tb 83
CANONBURY, British Rail—36Sb 63

CANONS PARK, Jubilee—24Na 39
CARPENDERS PARK, British Rail—20Z 19
CARSHALTON, British Rail—77Hb 145
CARSHALTON BEECHES, British Rail—79Hb 145
CASTLE BAR PARK, British Rail—43Ha 78
CATERHAM, British Rail—96Wb 181
CATFORD, British Rail—59Cc 106
CATFORD BRIDGE, British Rail—59Cc 106
CHADWELL HEATH, British Rail—31Zc 67
CHALFONT & LATIMER, British Rail & Metropolitan—11A 16
CHALK FARM, Northern—38Jb 62
CHANCERY LANE, Central—43Qb 82
CHARING CROSS, British Rail, Bakerloo, Jubilee & Northern—46Nb 82
CHARLTON, British Rail—50Lc 85
CHEAM, British Rail—80Ab 144
CHELSFIELD, British Rail—78Xc 151
CHERTSEY, British Rail—74H 139
CHESHUNT, British Rail—2Bc 12
CHESSINGTON NORTH, British Rail—78Na 143
CHESSINGTON SOUTH, British Rail—80Ma 143
CHIGWELL, Central—20Rc 28
CHINGFORD, British Rail—17Gc 27
CHIPSTEAD, British Rail—90Hb 163
CHISLEHURST, British Rail—68Qc 130
CHISWICK, British Rail—52Sa 101
CHISWICK PARK, District—49Sa 79
CHORLEYWOOD, British Rail & Metropolitan—14F 16
CLANDON, British Rail—100K 173
CLAPHAM, British Rail—55Mb 104
CLAPHAM COMMON, Northern—56Lb 104
CLAPHAM JUNCTION, British Rail—55Gb 103
CLAPHAM NORTH, Northern—55Nb 104
CLAPHAM SOUTH, Northern—58Kb 104
CLAPTON, British Rail—33Xb 63
CLAYGATE, British Rail—79Ga 142
CLOCK HOUSE, British Rail—68Ac 128
COBHAM & STOKE D'ABERNON, British Rail—89Aa 159
COCKFOSTERS, Piccadilly—14Jb 24
COLINDALE, Northern—27Ua 40
COLLIERS WOOD, Northern—66Fb 125
COULSDON SOUTH, British Rail—88Mb 164
COVENT GARDEN, Piccadilly—45Nb 82
CRAYFORD, British Rail—58Gd 110
CREWS HILL, British Rail—6Pb 10
CRICKLEWOOD, British Rail—35Za 60
CROFTON PARK, British Rail—57Bc 106
CROUCH HILL, British Rail—31Pb 62
CROXLEY, Metropolitan—16R 18
CROXLEY GREEN, British Rail—15T 18
CRYSTAL PALACE, British Rail—65Wb 127
CUFFLEY, British Rail—1Pb 10
CUSTOM HOUSE, VICTORIA DOCK, British Rail—45Kc 85

DAGENHAM DOCK, British Rail—41Bd 87
DAGENHAM EAST, District—37Ed 68
DAGENHAM HEATHWAY, District—37Bd 67
DALSTON JUNCTION, British Rail—37Vb 63
DALSTON KINGSLAND, British Rail—37Vb 63
DARTFORD, British Rail—58Nd 111
DATCHET, British Rail—3M 95
DEBDEN, Central—14Sc 28
DENHAM, British Rail—31J 55
DENHAM GOLF CLUB, British Rail—31F 54
DENMARK HILL, British Rail—54Tb 105
DEPTFORD, British Rail—52Cc 106
DOLLIS HILL, Jubilee—36Wa 60
DRAYTON GREEN, British Rail—44Ha 78
DRAYTON PARK, British Rail—35Qb 62
DUNTON GREEN, British Rail—91Gd 186

EALING BROADWAY, British Rail, Central & District—45Na 79
EALING COMMON, District & Piccadilly—46Pa 79
EARL'S COURT, District & Piccadilly—49Cb 81
EARLSFIELD, British Rail—60Eb 103
EAST ACTON, Central—44Va 80
EASTCOTE, Metropolitan & Piccadilly—31Y 57
EAST CROYDON, British Rail—75Tb 147
EAST DULWICH, British Rail—56Ub 105
EAST FINCHLEY, Northern—28Gb 41
EAST HAM, District & Metropolitan—38Nc 66
EAST PUTNEY, District—57Ab 102
EAST TILBURY, British Rail—9K 93
EDEN PARK, British Rail—71Cc 148
EDGWARE, Northern—23Ra 39
EDGWARE ROAD, Bakerloo, Circle, District & Metropolitan—43Gb 81
EFFINGHAM JUNCTION, British Rail—95W 174
EGHAM, British Rail—64C 118
ELEPHANT & CASTLE, British Rail, Bakerloo & Northern—48Sb 83

ELMERS END, British Rail—70Zb 128
ELM PARK, District—35Jd 68
ELMSTEAD WOODS, British Rail—65Nc 130
ELSTREE, British Rail—14Qa 21
ELTHAM, British Rail—57Pc 108
EMBANKMENT, Bakerloo, Circle, District & Northern—46Nb 82
EMERSON PARK, British Rail—31Nd 69
ENFIELD CHASE, British Rail—13Sb 25
ENFIELD LOCK, British Rail—9Ac 12
ENFIELD TOWN, British Rail—14Ub 25
EPPING, Central—3Wc 15
EPSOM, British Rail—85Ta 161
EPSOM DOWNS, British Rail—87Xa 162
ERITH, British Rail—50Gd 88
ESHER, British Rail—75Fa 142
ESSEX ROAD, British Rail—38Sb 63
EUSTON, British Rail, Northern & Victoria—41Mb 82
EUSTON SQUARE, Circle & Metropolitan—42Lb 82
EWELL EAST, British Rail—82Xa 162
EWELL WEST, British Rail—81Ua 162
EYNSFORD, British Rail—77Md 153

FAIRLOP, Central—25Tc 46
FALCONWOOD, British Rail—56Tc 108
FARNINGHAM ROAD, British Rail—68Rd 133
FARRINGDON, Circle & Metropolitan—43Rb 83
FELTHAM, British Rail—60X 99
FENCHURCH STREET, British Rail—45Ub 83
FINCHLEY CENTRAL, Northern—25Cb 41
FINCHLEY ROAD, Jubilee & Metropolitan—37Eb 61
FINCHLEY ROAD & FROGNAL, British Rail—36Eb 61
FINSBURY PARK, British Rail & Piccadilly—33Qb 62
FOREST GATE, British Rail—36Jc 65
FOREST HILL, British Rail—61Yb 128
FULHAM BROADWAY, District—52Cb 103
FULWELL, British Rail—63Fa 122

GANTS HILL, Central—30Qc 46
GARSTON, British Rail—7Aa 5
GERRARDS CROSS, British Rail—29A 34
GIDEA PARK, British Rail—28Ld 49
GIPSY HILL, British Rail—64Ub 127
GLOUCESTER ROAD, Circle, District & Piccadilly—49Eb 81
GOLDERS GREEN, Northern—32Cb 61
GOLDHAWK ROAD, Metropolitan—47Ya 80
GOODGE STREET, Northern—43Mb 82
GOODMAYES, British Rail—32Xc 67
GORDON HILL, British Rail—11Rb 25
GOSPEL OAK, British Rail—35Jd 62
GRANGE HILL, Central—21Tc 46
GRANGE PARK, British Rail—15Rb 25
GRAVESEND, British Rail—8D 114
GRAYS, British Rail—51Ce 113
GREAT PORTLAND STREET, Circle & Metropolitan—42Kb 82
GREENFORD, British Rail & Central—38Fa 58
GREENHITHE, British Rail—57Wd 112
GREEN PARK, Jubilee, Piccadilly & Victoria—46Lb 82
GREENWICH, British Rail—52Dc 106
GROVE PARK, British Rail—62Kc 129
GUNNERSBURY, British Rail & District—50Ra 79

HACKBRIDGE, British Rail—75Kb 146
HACKNEY CENTRAL, British Rail—37Xb 63
HACKNEY DOWNS, British Rail—36Wb 63
HACKNEY WICK, British Rail—37Cc 64
HADLEY WOOD, British Rail—10Eb 9
HAINAULT, Central—24Uc 46
HAMMERSMITH, District, Metropolitan & Piccadilly 49Ya 80
HAMPSTEAD, Northern—35Eb 61
HAMPSTEAD HEATH, British Rail—35Gb 61
HAMPTON, British Rail—67Ca 121
HAMPTON COURT, British Rail—70Ga 122
HAMPTON WICK, British Rail—67Ma 123
HANGER LANE, Central—41Na 79
HANWELL, British Rail—45Ga 78
HARLESDEN, British Rail & Bakerloo—40Ta 59
HAROLD WOOD, British Rail—25Pd 49
HARRINGAY, British Rail—30Qb 42
HARRINGAY STADIUM, British Rail—30Rb 43
HARROW & WEALDSTONE, British Rail & Bakerloo—27Ga 38
HARROW-ON-THE-HILL, British Rail & Metropolitan—30Ga 38
HATCH END, British Rail—24Ba 37
HATTON CROSS, Piccadilly—56V 98
HAYDONS ROAD, British Rail—64Eb 125
HAYES, British Rail—74Hc 149
HAYES & HARLINGTON, British Rail—48V 76
HEADSTONE LANE, British Rail—25Da 37

British Rail and London Underground Stations

HEATHROW CENTRAL, Piccadilly—55R **98**
HEATHROW TERMINAL 4, Piccadilly—57S **98**
HENDON, British Rail—30Wa **40**
HENDON CENTRAL, Northern—29Xa **40**
HERNE HILL, British Rail—58Rb **105**
HERSHAM, British Rail—76Aa **141**
HIGHAMS PARK, British Rail—23Fc **45**
HIGH BARNET, Northern—14Cb **23**
HIGHBURY & ISLINGTON, British Rail & Victoria—37Rb **63**
HIGHGATE, Northern—30Kb **42**
HIGH STREET, KENSINGTON, Circle & District—48Db **81**
HILLINGDON, Metropolitan & Piccadilly—36R **56**
HINCHLEY WOOD, British Rail—76Ha **142**
HITHER GREEN, British Rail—58Gc **107**
HOLBORN, Central & Piccadilly—43Pb **82**
HOLBORN VIADUCT, British Rail—44Rb **83**
HOLLAND PARK, Central—46Bb **81**
HOLLOWAY ROAD, Piccadilly—36Pb **62**
HOMERTON, British Rail—37Zb **64**
HONOR OAK PARK, British Rail—58Zb **106**
HORNCHURCH, District—34Md **69**
HORNSEY, British Rail—28Pb **42**
HORSLEY, British Rail—97U **174**
HOUNSLOW, British Rail—56Da **99**
HOUNSLOW CENTRAL, Piccadilly—55Da **99**
HOUNSLOW EAST, Piccadilly—54Ea **100**
HOUNSLOW WEST, Piccadilly—54Aa **99**
HYDE PARK CORNER, Piccadilly—47Jb **82**

ICKENHAM, Metropolitan & Piccadilly—35S **56**
ILFORD, British Rail—34Qc **66**
ISLEWORTH, British Rail—54Ha **100**
IVER, British Rail—47H **75**

KEMPTON PARK, British Rail—66X **121**
KENLEY, British Rail—86Sb **165**
KENNINGTON, Northern—50Rb **83**
KENSAL GREEN, British Rail & Bakerloo—41Ya **80**
KENSAL RISE, British Rail—40Ya **60**
KENSINGTON OLYMPIA, British Rail & District—48Ab **80**
KENT HOUSE, British Rail—67Ac **128**
KENTISH TOWN, British Rail & Northern—36Lb **62**
KENTISH TOWN WEST, British Rail—37Kb **62**
KENTON, British Rail & Bakerloo—30Ka **38**
KEW BRIDGE, British Rail—50Pa **79**
KEW GARDENS, British Rail—53Qa **101**
KIDBROOKE, British Rail—55Kc **107**
KILBURN, Jubilee—37Bb **61**
KILBURN HIGH ROAD, British Rail—39Cb **61**
KILBURN PARK, Bakerloo—40Cb **61**
KINGSBURY, Jubilee—29Qa **39**
KING'S CROSS, British Rail, Circle, Metropolitan, Northern, Piccadilly & Victoria—40Nb **62**
KING'S CROSS MIDLAND CITY, British Rail—41Nb **82**
KINGS LANGLEY, British Rail—2S **4**
KINGSTON, British Rail—67Na **123**
KINGSWOOD, British Rail—93Bb **179**
KNIGHTSBRIDGE, Piccadilly—47Hb **81**
KNOCKHOLT, British Rail—81Ad **169**

LADBROKE GROVE, Metropolitan—44Ab **80**
LADYWELL, British Rail—57Dc **106**
LAMBETH NORTH, Bakerloo—47Qb **82**
LANCASTER GATE, Central—45Fb **81**
LANGLEY, British Rail—47C **74**
LATIMER ROAD, Metropolitan—45Za **80**
LEATHERHEAD, British Rail—93Ja **176**
LEE, British Rail—58Jc **107**
LEICESTER SQUARE, Northern & Piccadilly—45Mb **82**
LEWISHAM, British Rail—54Ec **106**
LEYTON, Central—34Ec **64**
LEYTON MIDLAND ROAD, British Rail—32Ec **64**
LEYTONSTONE, Central—32Gc **65**
LEYTONSTONE HIGH ROAD, British Rail—33Gc **65**
LIVERPOOL STREET, British Rail, Central, Circle & Metropolitan —43Ub **83**
LONDON BRIDGE, British Rail & Northern—46Tb **83**
LONDON FIELDS, British Rail—38Xb **63**
LONGFIELD, British Rail—69Ae **135**
LOUGHBOROUGH JUNCTION, British Rail—55Rb **105**
LOUGHTON, Central—15Nc **28**
LOWER EDMONTON, British Rail—19Wb **25**
LOWER SYDENHAM, British Rail—64Bc **128**

MAIDA VALE, Bakerloo—41Eb **81**
MALDEN MANOR, British Rail—73Ua **144**
MANOR HOUSE, Piccadilly—31Rb **63**
MANOR PARK, British Rail—35Mc **65**
MANSION HOUSE, Circle & District—45Sb **83**
MARBLE ARCH, Central—44Hb **81**
MARYLAND, British Rail—37Gc **65**
MARYLEBONE, British Rail & Bakerloo—42Hb **81**

MAZE HILL, British Rail—51Gc **107**
MEOPHAM, British Rail—10C **136**
MERSTHAM, British Rail—100Lb **180**
MERTON PARK, British Rail—67Cb **125**
MILE END, Central, District & Metropolitan—42Ac **84**
MILL HILL BROADWAY, British Rail—23Ua **40**
MILL HILL EAST, Northern—24Ab **40**
MITCHAM, British Rail—70Gb **125**
MITCHAM JUNCTION, British Rail—71Jb **146**
MONUMENT, Circle & District—45Tb **83**
MOORGATE, British Rail, Circle, Metropolitan & Northern—43Tb **83**
MOOR PARK, British Rail & Metropolitan—20T **18**
MORDEN, Northern—69Db **125**
MORDEN ROAD, British Rail—68Db **125**
MORDEN SOUTH, British Rail—71Cb **145**
MORNINGTON CRESCENT, Northern—40Lb **62**
MORTLAKE, British Rail—55Sa **101**
MOTSPUR PARK, British Rail—71Xa **144**
MOTTINGHAM, British Rail—60Nc **108**

NEASDEN, Jubilee,—36Ua **60**
NEW BARNET, British Rail—15Eb **23**
NEW BECKENHAM, British Rail—65Bc **128**
NEWBURY PARK, Central—30Tc **46**
NEW CROSS, British Rail & Metropolitan—52Bc **106**
NEW CROSS GATE, British Rail & Metropolitan—52Ac **106**
NEW ELTHAM, British Rail—60Sc **108**
NEW MALDEN, British Rail—69Ua **124**
NEW SOUTHGATE, British Rail—22Kb **42**
NORBITON, British Rail—68Ra **123**
NORBURY, British Rail—67Pb **126**
NORTH ACTON, Central—43Ta **79**
NORTH DULWICH, British Rail—57Tb **105**
NORTH EALING, Piccadilly—44Pa **79**
NORTHFIELDS, Piccadilly—48La **78**
NORTHFLEET, British Rail—58De **113**
NORTH HARROW, Metropolitan—29Ca **37**
NORTHOLT, Central—37Ca **57**
NORTHOLT PARK, British Rail—35Da **57**
NORTH SHEEN, British Rail—56Qa **101**
NORTHUMBERLAND PARK, British Rail—25Xb **43**
NORTH WEMBLEY, British Rail & Bakerloo—34Ma **59**
NORTHWICK PARK, Metropolitan—31Ka **58**
NORTHWOOD, Metropolitan—24U **36**
NORTHWOOD HILLS, Metropolitan—26W **36**
NORTH WOOLWICH, British Rail—47Qc **86**
NORWOOD JUNCTION, British Rail—70Wb **127**
NOTTING HILL GATE, Central, Circle & District—46Cb **81**
NUNHEAD, British Rail—55Yb **106**

OAKLEIGH PARK, British Rail—17Fb **23**
OAKWOOD, Piccadilly—15Lb **24**
OCKENDON, British Rail—41Xd **90**
OLD STREET, British Rail & Northern—41Tb **83**
ORPINGTON, British Rail—75Uc **150**
OSTERLEY, Piccadilly—52Ea **100**
OTFORD, British Rail—88Ld **171**
OVAL, Northern—51Qb **104**
OXFORD CIRCUS, Bakerloo, Central & Victoria—44Lb **82**
OXSHOTT, British Rail—85Ea **160**
OXTED, British Rail—100Gc **183**

PADDINGTON, Bakerloo, British Rail, Circle, District & Metropolitan—44Fb **81**
PALMERS GREEN, British Rail—21Pb **42**
PARK ROYAL, Piccadilly—42Qa **79**
PARSONS GREEN, District—53Cb **103**
PECKHAM RYE, British Rail—54Wb **105**
PENGE EAST, British Rail—65Yb **128**
PENGE WEST, British Rail—66Xb **127**
PERIVALE, Central—40Ja **58**
PETTS WOOD, British Rail—72Tc **150**
PICCADILLY CIRCUS, Bakerloo & Piccadilly—45Lb **82**
PIMLICO, Victoria—50Mb **82**
PINNER, Metropolitan—28Aa **37**
PLAISTOW, District & Metropolitan—40Hc **65**
PLUMSTEAD, British Rail—49Tc **86**
PONDERS END, British Rail—15Ac **26**
POTTERS BAR, British Rail—4Bb **9**
PRESTON ROAD, Metropolitan—32Na **59**
PRIMROSE HILL, British Rail—38Jb **62**
PURFLEET, British Rail—50Qd **89**
PURLEY, British Rail—83Rb **165**
PURLEY OAKS, British Rail—81Sb **165**
PUTNEY, British Rail—56Ab **102**
PUTNEY BRIDGE, District—55Ab **102**

QUEENSBURY, Jubilee—27Pa **39**
QUEENS PARK, British Rail & Bakerloo—40Bb **61**
QUEEN'S ROAD (BATTERSEA), British Rail—53Kb **104**
QUEEN'S ROAD (PECKHAM), British Rail—53Yb **106**
QUEENSWAY, Central—45Db **81**

RADLETT, British Rail—7Ja **6**
RAINHAM, British Rail—42Hd **88**
RAVENSBOURNE, British Rail—66Ec **128**
RAVENSCOURT PARK, District—49Xa **80**
RAYNERS LANE, Metropolitan & Piccadilly—31Ba **57**
RAYNES PARK, British Rail—68Ya **124**
RECTORY ROAD, British Rail—34Wb **63**
REDBRIDGE, Central—30Mc **45**
REEDHAM, British Rail—85Pb **164**
REGENT'S PARK, Bakerloo—42Kb **82**
RICHMOND, British Rail & District—56Na **101**
RICKMANSWORTH, British Rail & Metropolitan—17M **17**
RIDDLESDOWN, British Rail—84Tb **165**
RODING VALLEY, Central—21Mc **45**
ROMFORD, British Rail—30Gd **48**
ROTHERHITHE, Metropolitan—47Yb **84**
ROYAL OAK, Metropolitan—43Db **81**
RUISLIP, Metropolitan & Piccadilly—33U **56**
RUISLIP GARDENS, Central—35W **56**
RUISLIP MANOR, Metropolitan & Piccadilly—32W **56**
RUSSELL SQUARE, Piccadilly—42Nb **82**

SAINT HELIER, British Rail—72Cb **145**
SAINT JAMES' PARK, Circle & District—47Lb **82**
SAINT JAMES STREET, WALTHAMSTOW, British Rail—29Bc **44**
SAINT JOHNS, British Rail—54Cc **106**
SAINT JOHN'S WOOD, Jubilee—40Fb **61**
SAINT MARGARETS, British Rail—58Ka **100**
SAINT MARY CRAY, British Rail—70Xc **131**
SAINT PANCRAS, British Rail, Circle, Metropolitan, Northern, Piccadilly & Victoria—41Nb **82**
SAINT PAULS, Central—44Sb **83**
SANDERSTEAD British Rail—81Tb **165**
SELHURST, British Rail—71Tb **147**
SEVEN KINGS, British Rail—32Uc **66**
SEVEN SISTERS, British Rail & Victoria—29Ub **43**
SHADWELL, Metropolitan—45Xb **83**
SHENFIELD, British Rail—17Ce **33**
SHEPHERD'S BUSH, Central—47Za **80**
SHEPHERD'S BUSH, Metropolitan—46Ya **80**
SHEPPERTON, British Rail—71S **140**
SHOREDITCH, Metropolitan—42Vb **83**
SHOREHAM, British Rail—83Jd **170**
SHORTLANDS, British Rail—68Gc **129**
SIDCUP, British Rail—61Wc **131**
SILVER STREET, British Rail—21Vb **43**
SILVERTOWN, British Rail—46Mc **85**
SLADE GREEN, British Rail—53Jd **110**
SLOANE SQUARE, Circle & District—49Jb **82**
SLOUGH, British Rail—6K **73**
SMITHAM, British Rail—87Nb **164**
SNARESBROOK, Central—29Jc **45**
SOUTH ACTON, British Rail—48Sa **79**
SOUTHALL, British Rail—47Ba **77**
SOUTH BERMONDSEY, British Rail—50Yb **84**
SOUTHBURY, British Rail—14Xb **25**
SOUTH CROYDON, British Rail—78Tb **147**
SOUTH EALING, Piccadilly—48Ma **79**
SOUTHFIELDS, District—60Bb **103**
SOUTHGATE, Piccadilly—18Mb **24**
SOUTH GREENFORD, British Rail—41Ga **78**
SOUTH HAMPSTEAD, British Rail—38Fb **61**
SOUTH HARROW, Piccadilly—34Ea **58**
SOUTH KENSINGTON, District & Piccadilly—49Fb **81**
SOUTH KENTON, British Rail & Bakerloo—33La **58**
SOUTH MERTON, British Rail—69Bb **125**
SOUTH RUISLIP, British Rail & Central—36Y **57**
SOUTH TOTTENHAM, British Rail—29Vb **43**
SOUTH WIMBLEDON, Northern—66Db **125**
SOUTH WOODFORD, Central—27Jc **45**
STAINES, British Rail—64J **119**
STAMFORD BROOK, District—49Va **80**
STAMFORD HILL, British Rail—31Ub **63**
STANFORD-LE-HOPE, British Rail—2L **93**
STANMORE, Jubilee—22Ma **39**
STEPNEY EAST, British Rail—44Ac **84**
STEPNEY GREEN, District & Metropolitan—42Zb **84**
STOCKWELL, Northern—54Nb **104**
STOKE NEWINGTON, British Rail—33Vb **63**
STONEBRIDGE PARK, British Rail & Bakerloo—38Ra **59**
STONE CROSSING, British Rail—57Ud **112**
STONELEIGH, British Rail—78Va **144**
STRATFORD, British Rail & Central—38Ec **64**
STRATFORD (LOW LEVEL), British Rail—38Ec **64**
STRAWBERRY HILL, British Rail—61Ha **122**
STREATHAM, British Rail—64Mb **126**
STREATHAM COMMON, British Rail—66Mb **126**
STREATHAM HILL, British Rail—61Nb **126**
SUDBURY & HARROW ROAD, British Rail—36Ka **58**
SUDBURY HILL, Piccadilly—35Ga **58**
SUDBURY HILL, HARROW, British Rail—35Ga **58**
SUDBURY TOWN, Piccadilly—37Ka **58**
SUNBURY, British Rail—67W **120**
SUNDRIDGE PARK, British Rail—66Kc **129**
SUNNYMEADS, British Rail—55A **96**

British Rail and London Underground Stations

SURBITON, British Rail—72Na **143**
SURREY DOCKS, Metropolitan—49Zb **84**
SUTTON, British Rail—79Eb **145**
SUTTON COMMON, British Rail—75Db **145**
SWANLEY, British Rail—70Gd **132**
SWANSCOMBE, British Rail—57Be **113**
SWISS COTTAGE, Jubilee—38Fb **61**
SYDENHAM, British Rail—64Yb **128**
SYDENHAM HILL, British Rail—62Vb **127**
SYON LANE, British Rail—52Ja **100**

TADWORTH, British Rail—94Ya **178**
TATTENHAM CORNER, British Rail—90Xa **162**
TEDDINGTON, British Rail—65Ja **122**
TEMPLE, Circle & District—45Qb **82**
THAMES DITTON, British Rail—73Ha **142**
THEOBALDS GROVE, British Rail—4Zb **12**
THEYDON BOIS, Central—8Vc **15**
THORNTON HEATH, British Rail—70Sb **127**
TILBURY RIVERSIDE, British Rail—6C **114**
TILBURY TOWN, British Rail—4B **114**
TOLWORTH, British Rail—75Ra **143**
TOOTING, British Rail—65Hb **125**
TOOTING BEC, Northern—62Hb **125**
TOOTING BROADWAY, Northern—64Gb **125**
TOTTENHAM COURT ROAD, Central & Northern—44Mb **82**
TOTTENHAM HALE, British Rail & Victoria—27Xb **43**
TOTTERIDGE & WHETSTONE, Northern—18Db **23**
TOWER HILL, Circle & District—45Vb **83**
TUFNELL PARK, Northern—35Lb **62**
TULSE HILL, British Rail—61Rb **127**
TURKEY STREET, British Rail—9Yb **12**
TURNHAM GREEN, District—49Ua **80**
TURNPIKE LANE, Piccadilly—27Qb **42**
TWICKENHAM, British Rail—59Ja **100**

UPMINSTER, British Rail & District—33Sd **70**
UPMINSTER BRIDGE, District—33Qd **69**
UPNEY, District—38Vc **67**
UPPER HALLIFORD, British Rail—68U **120**
UPPER HOLLOWAY, British Rail—33Mb **62**
UPPER WARLINGHAM, British Rail—90Wb **165**

UPTON PARK, District & Metropolitan—39Lc **65**
UXBRIDGE, Metropolitan & Piccadilly—38M **55**

VAUXHALL, British Rail & Victoria—51Nb **104**
VICTORIA, British Rail, Circle, District & Victoria—49Kb **82**
VIRGINIA WATER, British Rail—71A **138**

WADDON, British Rail—77Qb **146**
WADDON MARSH, British Rail—74Qb **146**
WALLINGTON, British Rail—79Kb **146**
WALTHAM CROSS, British Rail—6Bc **12**
WALTHAMSTOW CENTRAL, British Rail & Victoria—28Cc **44**
WALTHAMSTOW QUEENS ROAD, British Rail—29Cc **44**
WALTON-ON-THAMES, British Rail—76X **141**
WANDSWORTH COMMON, British Rail—60Hb **103**
WANDSWORTH ROAD, British Rail—54Lb **104**
WANDSWORTH TOWN, British Rail—56Db **103**
WANSTEAD, Central—30Kc **45**
WANSTEAD PARK, British Rail—35Kc **65**
WAPPING, Metropolitan—46Yb **84**
WARREN STREET, Northern & Victoria—42Lb **82**
WARWICK AVENUE, Bakerloo—42Eb **81**
WATERLOO, British Rail, Bakerloo & Northern—47Qb **82**
WATERLOO (EAST), British Rail—47Qb **82**
WATFORD, Metropolitan—13V **18**
WATFORD HIGH STREET, British Rail—14Y **19**
WATFORD JUNCTION, British Rail & Bakerloo—12Y **19**
WATFORD NORTH, British Rail—9Y **5**
WATFORD WEST, British Rail—15V **18**
WELLING, British Rail—54Wc **109**
WEMBLEY CENTRAL, British Rail & Bakerloo—37Na **59**
WEMBLEY COMPLEX, British Rail—36Qa **59**
WEMBLEY PARK, Jubilee & Metropolitan—34Qa **59**
WEST ACTON, Central—44Qa **79**
WESTBOURNE PARK, British Rail & Metropolitan—43Cb **81**
WEST BROMPTON, District—50Cb **81**
WEST BYFLEET, British Rail—84J **157**
WESTCOMBE PARK, British Rail—50Jc **85**
WEST CROYDON, British Rail—74Sb **147**
WEST DRAYTON, British Rail—46N **75**
WEST DULWICH, British Rail—61Tb **127**
WEST EALING, British Rail—45Ka **78**

WEST FINCHLEY, Northern—23Cb **41**
WEST HAM, British Rail—41Gc **85**
WEST HAM, District & Metropolitan—41Gc **85**
WEST HAMPSTEAD, British Rail—37Cb **61**
WEST HAMPSTEAD, Jubilee—37Db **61**
WEST HAMPSTEAD MIDLAND, British Rail—37Cb **61**
WEST HARROW, Metropolitan—30Ea **38**
WEST HORNDON, British Rail—30Ee **51**
WEST KENSINGTON, District—50Bb **81**
WESTMINSTER, Circle & District—47Nb **82**
WEST NORWOOD, British Rail—62Rb **127**
WEST RUISLIP, British Rail & Central—33S **56**
WEST SUTTON, British Rail—77Cb **145**
WEST WICKHAM, British Rail—73Ec **148**
WEYBRIDGE, British Rail—79Q **140**
WHITECHAPEL, District & Metropolitan—43Xb **83**
WHITE CITY, Central—45Ya **80**
WHITE HART LANE, British Rail—24Vb **43**
WHITTON, British Rail—59Ea **100**
WHYTELEAFE, British Rail—89Vb **165**
WHYTELEAFE SOUTH, British Rail—91Wb **181**
WILLESDEN GREEN, Jubilee—37Ya **60**
WILLESDEN JUNCTION, British Rail & Bakerloo—41Wa **80**
WIMBLEDON, British Rail & District—65Bb **125**
WIMBLEDON CHASE, Brits Rail—68Ab **124**
WIMBLEDON PARK, District—62Cb **125**
WINCHMORE HILL, British Rail—17Rb **25**
WINDSOR & ETON CENTRAL, British Rail—2G **94**
WINDSOR & ETON RIVERSIDE, British Rail—2H **95**
WOKING, British Rail—89B **156**
WOLDINGHAM, British Rail—94Zb **182**
WOODFORD, Central—23Kc **45**
WOODGRANGE PARK, British Rail—36Mc **65**
WOOD GREEN, British Rail—26Nb **42**
WOOD GREEN, Piccadilly—26Qb **42**
WOODMANSTERNE, British Rail—88Kb **164**
WOODSIDE, British Rail—72Xb **147**
WOODSIDE PARK, Northern—21Db **41**
WOOD STREET, WALTHAMSTOW, British Rail—27Fc **45**
WOOLWICH ARSENAL, British Rail—49Rc **86**
WOOLWICH DOCKYARD, British Rail—49Pc **86**
WORCESTER PARK, British Rail—74Wa **144**
WRAYSBURY, British Rail—58C **96**

319

Maps printed in Great Britain by Cripplegate Printing Co. Ltd., Fircroft Way, Edenbridge, Kent.

Index printed and atlas bound in Great Britain by Hazell Watson & Viney Limited,
Member of the BPCC Group, Aylesbury, Bucks.